Television Comedy Series

Television Comedy Series

An Episode Guide to 153 TV Sitcoms in Syndication

by Joel Eisner & David Krinsky

McFarland & Company, Inc., Publishers
Jefferson, N.C., & London

Library of Congress Cataloging in Publication Data

Eisner, Joel, 1959–
  Television comedy series.

  Includes index.
  1. Comedy programs — United States — Plots, themes, etc.
I. Krinsky, David, 1959–   . II. Title.
PN1992.8.C66E37 1984   791.45'09'0917   83-42901

ISBN 0-89950-088-9

Manufactured in the United States of America.

McFarland   Box 611   Jefferson NC 28640

To one of nature's noblest men,
who helped us when we needed him the most —
our friend Murray the Cop

Alan Hale

FOREWORD

In November 1982 I had the pleasure of meeting two dynamic young men, Joel Eisner and David Krinsky, as I was back in New York City for a telecast of "Good Morning America" with all the cast of *Gilligan's Island*. I had just returned to my hotel from viewing the Thanksgiving Day Parade with Ginger Grant, and Tina Louise of course, and had occasion to converse with these bright young fellows, and came to find out that they, literally, are our *Gilligan's Island* historians with dates, facts and figures. With Thanksgiving Day on the threshold of the moment, we "talked turkey" for quite a while on many subjects, and I found them to be most erudite on the subject of comedy and television shows, both past and present. Their keenness for facts is remarkable, as is the information they have gathered.

I consented to do a foreword because, as I was impressed, I wanted to give their readers an up-front insight into these young men's almost incredible penchant for detail in gathering the information they have presented in this book, and in other chronicles they have supervised and published.

Observation, for the actor especially, is the greatest teacher. Retention of those observations are his greatest asset. A person, per se, has two eyes, two ears, and a nose, which relates closely to the sense of taste through smell. Not to retain what one has seen, heard, or scentfully enjoyed is a big loss to the "whole person." These senses relate further to the wondrous amenities that go with observation, such as courtesy, sentimentality and a sense of value (but not in the material vein completely).

Hence, when someone makes a compilation of these senses, amenities and facts he is truly providing a great service, presenting the benefit of his knowledge to those with whom he has made contact and becoming a historian by his efforts.

With warmest personal regards, I remain

Your Friend,

Alan Hale, "The Skipper"

From the ship's log this day
19 May 1983

ACKNOWLEDGMENTS

We would like to thank the following people and organizations for their help in making this book a reality:

Jon Shaps; Jerry Beck, United Artists; Richard J. Concepcion; Howard Frank; Danny Fuchs, ABC; Steven Hirschberg; Don Kimmey, KHTV Houston; Tom Rogers and the staff of WNEW-TV New York.

Also: WUAB-TV; WPGH-TV; WSBK-TV; WPHL-TV; 20th Century Fox-TV; Filmways; MCA-TV; Worldvision; Time-Life TV; Weiss Global Productions; Viacom; Columbia Pictures Television; Tandem; Paramount Pictures TV; MTM Enterprises; and the staff at the Lincoln Center Research Library.

And a special thanks to our friend Alan Hale, Jr.

The quote used in the dedication was adapted from the Odd Couple episode entitled, "I'm Dying of Unger," copyright Paramount Pictures TV.

SOURCES

United States Government Copyright Index; Motion Pictures & Film Strips; TV Film Source Book—Series, Serials and Packages; The New York Times; and *TV Guide.*

PHOTO CREDITS

All photographs are from the collection of the authors (except the Alan Hale photo, courtesy of Alan Hale).

TABLE OF CONTENTS

PREFACE

We remember spending many an hour as children in front of the family TV set watching irrelevant television programs. We remember that our favorite series (then and now), *Lost in Space*, was on every Wednesday night at 7:30 p.n. We were fascinated by the gadgets and loved the comic interludes between Dr. Smith and the Robot.

We believe that is where our first love of comedy began or at least was nurtured into full growth. Up until that time, we were satisfied with juvenile fare like Bozo, Soupy Sales and Gumby, but something happened in the fall of 1965 that changed our viewing habits and our lives. We began to experience prime time comedy programming. We were enjoying television along with the adult world and loving every minute of it.

Our favorite series were *Gilligan's Island, Mr. Ed, F Troop, Captain Nice, Green Acres, I Dream of Jeannie, Mr. Terrific, The Munsters, The Three Stooges* and *Batman* (yes it was a comedy, of sorts). These so-called "escapist" comedy series will always be the guidelines by which we judge all the series that followed. These series had their own atmosphere, which nicely integrated the characters and setting. In contrast, most modern comedies have characters and situations neither as boldly defined nor as outrageously unique. These newer shows have characters based on ordinary people that one might expect to meet every day. We feel that this makes it more difficult for a show to be interesting.

We began refining our skills and understanding of what makes a comedy work: well-defined characters, situations for the characters to act (not just react) in, good plot development, but above all, well-written scripts. We were also enlightened as to the many genres of comedy: slapstick, irony, satire, farce, subtle (not intellectual), social, situational, and a new category: BAD. Oh, we learned about bad comedy, quickly, as the years went on, as all our favorites were cancelled and new so-called hits flourished. We began to wonder why series like *Maude, Rhoda*, and *One Day at a Time* were so amusing to the whole country. We thought these series were poorly written, cheaply produced, used rehashed plots (from past comedy series) and, worst of all, used comedy to get across a political, social or cultural message in a tedious and boring way.

Comedy should not be a tool used as a front for social statement. In the proper context, satire handles this situation. From the Marx Brothers to Woody Allen, comment on the condition of man has been effectively communicated through use of clever statements made at the right time in the right place. They never "pushed" the issue — when Woody Allen in his film *Sleeper* says, "What am I doing here, I'm 198 years old, I should be collecting social security," it is a quick one-line stab. The point is made and the fun continues. True artists know when to use subtlety as opposed to blatant statements. When Maude says that she is pregnant — why is that funny? We understand the circumstances that led up to this and we understand her condition, but we still don't see the humor in it. A producer must decide whether he is producing comedy or drama, not both in a thirty-minute series. If it is both, then he has produced a drama with comedic overtones, not the other way around.

xiii

What harm can come of this? You see the result week after week on current comedy programs. Take *Diff'rent Strokes*, for example: this should have been a comedy about two poor boys who are adopted by a rich liberal. The possibilities are endless for pure comic encounters. Instead of concentrating on the mischievous joy of youth as in *Leave It to Beaver* or *Dennis the Menace*, we see nine-year-old Arnold protesting about busing or 16-year-old Kimberly about to lose her virginity in a ski cabin. Sure, society has changed, and television is a reflection of society, but if these are series intended for children, we wonder what kind of people they will turn out to be. Television banned violence on network shows when they thought it was harmful to children, but did they ever stop to think what mental harm is done when a child believes prostitution, vasectomies, unwed mothers, V.D., etc. are all hilarious subjects?

In retrospect over the history of television comedy, we can say that we believe it has grown from infancy, to full growth to death (what we have now). Television in the 1950s was fresh, alive, vibrant and fun. *The Honeymooners* and *I Love Lucy* are examples of this. How long would Lucy have lasted if Little Ricky thought he got a girl pregnant? Then in the 1960s, television comedy was more mature, refined and still fun. We mentioned our favorite series above, but there were always more domestic series like *Andy Griffith* and *Dick Van Dyke*, which presented family life in a possibly unrealistic but at least amusing way. Then, we had the 1970s and now the 1980s, decades of gradual decline in television social mores, incredibly cheap and unrealistic sets, and comedy used as a front for moral statement. About the only series to stay clear of this trap has been *The Odd Couple*, produced by Garry Marshall. His series may not be the most sophisticated, but at least he makes an attempt at traditional comedy. In fact, we consider *The Odd Couple* the best television series overall (comedy or not) since 1970, but that is all there is to say on current comedy. Frankly, most of it is so boring and unimaginative we still wonder why people enjoy it. We suppose it is because when you lose something you loved (good comedy), you miss it at first, but then you replace it with something not so good and, eventually, you get used to it. All we can say is we still miss it, it can't be replaced, and we will forever love *Gilligan's Island*.

Finally, the purpose of this book: We intended to let the American viewer take a look at where comedy has been and where it is now, in a completely unabridged format. This meant listing every episode of every comedy series from the beginning of television to the present day. Research for this endeavor was time consuming and difficult. Many earlier series were on before accurate records were established. Others have episodes not in syndication which had to be researched. But it was worth it. There is no other reference guide available anywhere on almost all of these series, and since comedy is the most enjoyed genre, we felt this book was necessary. We can only hope you feel this way too.

Joel Eisner and David Krinsky
September 1983

INTRODUCTION

There are only situation comedies contained in this book. Virtually no other form of series is present. There are no soap opera series, such as *Soap, Mary Hartman* and *Fernwood 2 Night*, etc. These may have been amusing but they are a different genre. Variety series are not included, such as *Laugh-In, Milton Berle, Benny Hill, Carol Burnett* and *Saturday Night Live*, etc., because these are not series comedy. It would be virtually impossible to provide an episode listing for these types of shows as each episode contains many short sketches mixed with music (which classifies them as variety shows). Dramatic series with comic overtones have also been eliminated. Series such as *The Thin Man, Mr. & Mrs. North, Julia*, etc., although containing comic relief elements, are basically intended to present dramatic concepts and did so quite effectively.

It would be truly impossible to list every episode of every comedy series which has been on the air, as records are not very complete for the very early years. However, we believe that we have come as close to this as possible. The series that are not included fall into four categories: live shows, shows not in syndication, banned shows, and recent shows.

Live Series: In the early 1950s many series were presented live. They were not filmed or taped and no record of these series exists. Series such as *Mr. Peepers* and some of the *Adventures of Ozzie and Harriet* fall into this category, although it is said that 100 *Mr. Peepers* kinescopes still survive. An absolute complete episode listing remains impossible (at least for us).

Not in Syndication: Short-lived series are basically those in which fewer than 22 episodes were produced. These include: *The Montefuscos, Me & the Chimp*, and *Ball Four* and all the other awful series we might remember. Since these series produced so few episodes, syndication is usually limited to overseas, making United States viewers safe from those shows forever! Certain series which are not in syndication are included because they have retained somewhat of a cult status and, although few episodes were produced, many wish more episodes were available. Series such as *Quark, Captain Nice* and *Mr. Terrific* are all examples of this.

Banned: Because of certain network guidelines or an outraged viewing audience, certain series are not allowed to be broadcast anywhere. Examples of these are *Amos & Andy, Bridget Loves Bernie, Beulah*, and *Life with Luigi*. All of these series offended somebody enough that action was taken to ban them. For this book, however, *Amos & Andy* has been included because it is one of the most popular banned series and is a landmark as far as blacks on TV are concerned.

Recent Series: These include shows which are brand new on the air and have not produced enough episodes to warrant putting them in this book. However, if a new edition of this book is published, sometime in the future, they will be included: such shows as *Facts of Life, Private Benjamin*, and anything that found its way onto the air after the 1979-1980 season.

One may ask, What is included? EVERYTHING ELSE. Every prime time situation comedy series, live or animated, broadcast from 1949 to 1980 and still available for syndication, is in this book. All of the information contained herein we believe to be accurate and complete. Over 150 series and over 11,000 total episodes are contained within. If we were to have included anything other than true sitcoms, we would not have been able to get this book compiled.

How and Why to Use This Book: This book is useful to those doing research on a particular show, or for those just interested in knowing how many episodes of *Gilligan's Island* there are and did I see them all? If you are trying to locate a particular episode of the series, these facts may help. The episodes are almost all listed in order of production, not order of teleplay. If you know the guest star of the episode, try looking for that. If you still can't find it, try to eliminate from the episode descriptions all those you are sure are not it. If you still can't find it, then we volunteer our services to find it for you. (Just write.) You should, however, be able to locate any episode quickly and effectively.

COMEDY PLOTS

There are a number of standard plots used over and over on most sitcoms. We list the most common here.

Lookalikes of one or more characters.

Spies and espionage.

Redecorating the house with disastrous results.

The family car (buying, crashing, etc.).

A pet (dog, goat, chicken, cat, etc.).

Someone gets sick at the wrong time.

A legal story; courtroom scene, fraud, misconduct (some minor offense).

The wedding—some character is thinking of or does get married.

The fight—someone is challenged to a fight.

The fight—characters don't get along with each other.

Someone gets a broken bone.

Character is a witness to a robbery.

Someone is accused of being a crook.

Holiday stories: Christmas, Halloween, Thanksgiving, etc.

Vacation stories: characters go to Hawaii, N.Y., L.A., etc.

A pest of a kid comes for a visit.

The employment caper—character goes through a series of jobs he can't hold.

Someone's new girl/boy friend is using them for some reason.

Flashback to previous episode plot.

Flashback—a character's early youth is established.

The characters get lost or trapped in some silly place.

Jealousy—characters are envious of each other or someone else.

The birthday party (usually a surprise party).

"I think I'm pregnant."

Amnesia (always a bump on the head).

A diet fad.

Someone is due to get a job promotion.

A character saves the life of another, making him eternally grateful.

Grandparents (usually same cast in elderly makeup).

A character appears on a game show.

Someone gets drafted.

An investment in an invention or corporation.

A boat trip.

The move—character thinks about selling his house.

Sports (tennis, baseball, etc.).

The characters go on a picnic with disastrous results.

Someone seems to have run away.

Someone's mother is coming for a visit.

Someone is mistakenly arrested.

The characters babysit for a brat.

A political campaign.

Someone is broke and needs a loan.

Someone tries to sneak out of the house to go somewhere.

A musical story (usually some famous singer as a guest star).

Characters are all excited about entering a big contest (not game show).

A new haircut or dye leads to complications (bald, strange color, etc.).

A character volunteers for some organization (fire patrol, citizen patrol).

A magician or magic.

A horse (racing, stealing, riding, talking, breeding, etc.).

A criminal is hiding out at the character's house.

The anniversary (or some big event that someone usually forgets).

Moonshine, which usually has the characters drunk at the end.

A wild adventure in a department store.

A silly rock and roll group hits town (and usually has a dumb name).

Camping out in the woods.

A haunted house or ghostly tale has everyone frightened.

An ethnic episode (Black, Italian, Chinese, French, etc.).

An old friend comes for a visit and has changed a lot.

A campaign to raise money for something usually involving the characters doing something silly.

The dream—character fantasizes about what they really want to do or feel and it is revealed in dreamlike sequences.

The makeover of an "ugly duckling"

causes the person who made the changeover regret having suggested the change.

The bet—two or more characters are in a big bet over something.

A character is in line for an inheritance (but never gets the amount he expected).

A character mistakenly believes he is dying.

A compliment "goes to the head" of a character.

A trip to the amusement park should be fun but isn't.

Two or more characters are locked together in something and can't get out (usually handcuffs).

A flying saucer episode with everyone seeing little green men.

Rules—an episode involving new rules that make the ruler regret it.

Characters are picked to star in a movie or TV commercial.

A silly relative of a character comes for a visit.

A character finds a lot of money and either finds out that it is counterfeit or that there are gangsters after it.

These above plots are good for any situation comedy, such as *Happy Days*, *The Brady Bunch*, *Gilligan's Island*, etc. These plots usually will not work for contemporary social comedies such as *One Day at a Time*, *M*A*S*H*, and *Barney Miller*. Those and similar series rely on current public mores for plots and the framework of their unique style for continuing stories and episodes. However, the long-term success of such series may be shorter than those of standard comedy formats by the very nature of the series; morals change, political times change, and so do the standards of what each generation considers humorous.

A Brief Explanation: The format of each series is simple and the same for each series. First the show title, when it premiered, when it went off the air, format (film or tape), number of episodes, color or B&W, producer, production company, and/or syndicator. Then the cast, writers, and directors (if known for every episode). Next is a description of the series and then the individual episodes, in order. There are no missing episodes for any series.

Syndication: Syndication is the term given to a show if it is offered to several stations instead of just one single network. An old show in syndication can have its episode played on any station as opposed to the network station that owns it. Some new series are syndicated to local stations rather than go to a network—for various reasons, but mostly for money. A series can be playing on hundreds of stations but do poorly in syndication. The number of stations a relatively new show is on doesn't indicate how popular it is, it just means that a lot of stations bought it.

Symbols Used: A "W" indicates writer credits; a "D," director, and "GS," guest star.

THE ABBOTT & COSTELLO SHOW

On the air 1951, off 1953. Syndicated & CBS. 52 episodes. B&W Film. Broadcast: 1951-1953; exact date varied depending on the station, but CBS stations ran it on Fri. nights 10-10:30. Producer: Pat Costello. Production Company: Revue. Syndicator: Alan Enterprises, Inc.

CAST: Bud Abbott (played by himself), Lou Costello (himself), Hillary Brooke (herself), Sidney Fields (himself), Mike the Cop (Gordon Jones), Stinky (Joe Besser), Mr. Bacciagalupe (Joe Kirk).

WRITERS: Eddie Foreman, Sidney Fields, Clyde Bruckman, Felix Adler, Jack Townley. DIRECTOR: Every episode was directed by Jean Yarbrough.

One of the first syndicated television comedy series. Bud and Lou basically played themselves. They lived at Mr. Fields' apartment/boarding house. They were always unable to pay their room rent, so they were constantly looking for jobs. No matter what they did they always seemed to get into trouble. The series was and still is extremely popular in syndication.

The Drugstore
GS: Joe Besser, Iris Adrian, Elvia Allman. Bud and Lou get jobs working in Fields' drugstore, until they wreck the place.

The Dentist's Office
GS: Virginia Christine, Ray Walker, Vera Marsh, Bobby Barber. Bud takes Lou to a nearsighted dentist when he gets a toothache. Later, Lou prevents a robbery while trying to get arrested.

Jail
GS: Elvia Allman, Stanley Andrews. Lou is arrested and jailed with a man who goes berserk when he hears the words Niagara Falls.

The Vacation
GS: Bobby Barber. Bud and Lou are afraid that Mr. Fields will rent their apartment while they're on vacation in Arizona.

The Birthday Party
GS: Joe Besser, Elvia Allman, Milt Bronson, Glenn Strange, Joyce Jameson. Lou gives food poisoning to every-

one at his birthday party and later orders a giant cake at Bacciagalupe's bakery.

Alaska
GS: Joe Besser. Lou's uncle strikes gold in Alaska, so Bud and Lou plan to help him spend it.

The Vacuum Cleaner Salesman
GS: Dorothy Ford, Bobby Barber, Joe Besser, Robin Raymond. Lou gets a job selling vacuum cleaners door to door.

The Army Story
GS: Joe Besser, James Alexander, Robert Cherry. Bud and Lou join the Army, where they recreate their routines from the feature film "Buck Privates."

Pots and Pans
GS: Anthony Caruso. Lou is now selling pots and pans. He volunteers to cook a demonstration dinner in Mr. Field's apartment.

The Charity Bazaar
GS: Joe Besser, Nicla Di Bruno. Bud

5

Bud Abbott (top) and Lou Costello.

and Lou perform the shell game, only using lemons, at a charity bazaar.

The Western Story
GS: James Alexander, Anthony Caruso, Minerva Urecal, Anthony Hughes. While visiting Hillary's uncle's ranch, Lou enters a shoot out with a gang of outlaws.

The Haunted House
GS: Joan Shawlee, Joe Besser. Bud and Lou help Hillary spend a night in a haunted house in order to inherit a fortune.

Peace and Quiet
GS: Marjorie Reynolds, Eddie Parker, Veda Ann Borg, Murray Leonard. Lou is suffering from insomnia, so he goes to a sanitarium for a rest.

Hungry
GS: Joan Shawlee. Lou gets involved with twin waitresses, a live oyster, and a plate of meatballs.

The Music Lovers
GS: Joe Besser, Raymond Hatton, Minerva Urecal. Lou tries to impress Hillary's father by playing the piano.

The Politician
GS: Joan Shawlee, Selena Walters, Charles Cane, John Shoemaker. Lou runs for office, but causes trouble when he gives a speech in the park.

The Wrestling Match
GS: Joe Besser, Ben Weldon, Ivan the Terrible, Emery Parnell. Lou and Stinky agree to wrestle for a police benefit, but when Stinky becomes ill his kid brother takes his place.

Getting a Job
GS: Vera Marsh, Lucien Littlefield. Bud gets a job as a loafer in a bakery. Lou tries to deliver a box of hats. Later, they both try to get a job from Mr. Fields' employment agency.

Bingo
GS: Joe Besser, Joan Shawlee, Isabel Randolph. Lou causes trouble at the license bureau while trying to get a license for his pet chimp, Bingo.

Hillary's Birthday
GS: Anthony Hughes, Lee Patrick. Lou causes trouble in the supermarket and at Hillary's birthday party when he tries to play the radio.

Television
GS: Bob Hopkins, Ben Weldon, Joan Shawlee, Bobby Barber. Lou becomes a contestant on a TV game show. Later, he becomes the chief witness at Mr. Fields' negligence trial.

Las Vegas
GS: Lucien Littlefield, Joe Devlin, Virginia Christine. Lou buys a used car and drives to Las Vegas where he loses all his money.

Little Old Lady
GS: George Chandler, Benny Rubin, Burt Mustin. Lou tries to win money at a bazaar to help an old lady who was dispossessed.

The Actor's Home
GS: Thurston Hall, Allen Jenkins. Bud is taken away to an old actor's home where he and Lou perform "Who's on First."

Police Rookies
GS: Emory Parnell, Robert Cherry. Bud and Lou attend police rookie school where Lou wrecks the place.

Safari
GS: Bobby Barber, George Barrows. Bud and Lou go to Africa to search for Bingo's parents.

The Paper Hangers
GS: Henry Kulky, Jane Frazee. Bud and Lou wallpaper an apartment to help pay their rent. Later they become waiters in a seafood restaurant.

Uncle Bozzo's Visit
GS: Fortunio Bonanova, Max Wagner. Lou's opera-singing uncle wreaks havoc at the apartment house.

In Society
GS: Jack Rice, Tristram Coffin, Isabel Randolph. Bud and Lou act as British nobles at a high-society party.

Life Insurance
GS: Murray Leonard, Dorothy Granger. After Bud gets Lou insured, Lou thinks Bud wants to kill him for the money.

Pest Exterminators
GS: Creighton Hale, Florence Aver, Helen Millard. Bud and Lou have become exterminators, but are mistaken for famous psychiatrists.

Killer's Wife
GS: Max Baer, Mary Beth Hughes. A boxer moves into the building, believes Lou is fooling around with his wife.

Cheapskates
GS: Paul Fix, Phyllis Coates, Tony Ward. At an auction, Lou buys a crate of rollerskates unaware there are stolen diamonds inside the wheels.

South of Dixie
GS: Glenn Langan, Jean Porter, Bob Hopkins. Bud and Lou become actors in a play about the Civil War.

From Bed to Worse
GS: Dan Weiss, Lucien Littlefield. Bud and Lou try to win a cash prize for having the best garden.

$1000 TV Prize
GS: Ralph Sanford, Milt Bronson, Bob Hopkins. Lou wins a $1000 prize by pretending to be Mr. Fields, then must get Mr. Fields out of the way so he can collect it.

Amnesia
GS: Kathrine Sheldon, Charles Cane, Joel Mulhall. Bud tries to break up Lou's marriage to his lovelorn pen pal by making him think he has amnesia.

Efficiency Experts
GS: Jean Willis, Frank Scanell, Lucille Barkley. As efficiency experts, Bud and Lou must keep two rich girls from spending money.

Car Trouble
GS: Percy Helton, Horace Murphy. Lou wins a car in a baby food contest. The car is a klunker, so he goes to Michigan to buy a new one, where he meets Mike the Cop's twin brother.

Wife Wanted
GS: June Vincent, Frank Jarra. Lou will inherit $10,000 if he gets married, but his old girlfriend is now dating a wrestler.

Uncle from New Jersey
GS: Ralph Gamble, Tim Ryan. Lou disguises himself as his rich uncle in order to convince Mr. Fields Lou will inherit his money when he dies.

Private Eye
GS: Bill Varga, Frank Richards. Lou is now a detective. His first case is to help a girl find some bonds hidden inside a spooky old mansion.

The Tax Return
GS: Thurston Hall, Bennie Bert, Al Hill. Lou gets a tax refund check for a million dollars, and now a gang of crooks are after him. Mr. Fields thinks Lou is a counterfeiter.

Public Enemies
GS: Mike Ross, Joe Sawyer. A gang of crooks move into the building and mistake Lou for another crook.

Bank Holdup
GS: Douglas Fowley. Bud and Lou get involved with bank robbers whom they mistake for business men.

Well-Oiled
GS: Connie Cezan, William Fawcett. Lou poses as a Texas millionaire in order to help Mr. Fields get rid of a gold digger who is suing him.

The Pigeon
GS: Hank Patterson, Gloria Henry, Ted Hecht. A gangster's girlfriend plans to get Lou killed so the police would arrest her boyfriend, then she could run away with another man.

Honeymoon House
GS: Tommy Farrell, Karen Sharpe, George Chandler. Lou buys a prefabricated house for his fiancee, but her former boyfriend wrecks the house.

Fencing Master
GS: Fortunio Bonanova, Byron Foulger. Lou is made indestructible by a scientist, then is involved in a duel.

Beauty Contest Story
GS: James Flavin, Dick Wessel. Bud and Lou are the judges of the Miss Mud Turtle contest. They are pressured to pick Mr. Fields' niece and a gangster's girlfriend as the winner.

Fall Guy
GS: Charlie Hall, Gloria Saunders. Lou tries to sell No Peddlers Allowed signs, then helps put up a TV antenna for a bird watcher.

Barber Lou
W: Sidney Fields and Lou Costello. Lou gives Bud a rubdown, but gives him a paint job instead.

THE ADDAMS FAMILY

On the air 9/18/64, off 9/2/66. ABC. B&W Film. 64 episodes. Broadcast: Sept 1964-Sept 1966 Fri 8:30-9. Producer: David Levy. Prod Co & Synd: Filmways.

CAST: Gomez Addams (played by John Astin), Morticia Frump Addams (Carolyn Jones), Uncle Fester (Jackie Coogan), Lurch (Ted Cassidy), Grandmama Addams (Blossom Rock), Pugsley (Ken Weatherwax), Wednesday (Lisa Loring), Cousin Itt (Felix Silla), Thing (Ted Cassidy).

WRITERS: Hannibal Coons, Sloan Nibley, Preston Wood, Phil Leslie, George Tibbles, Ed James, Seamon Jacobs, Harry Winkler, Carol Henning, Ed Ring, Mitch Person, Paul Tuckahoe. DIRECTORS: Sidney Lanfield, Nat Perrin, Sidney Solkon, Sidney Miller, Jean Yarbrough, Jerry Hopper, Arthur Hiller.

This strange series, based on the cartoons of Charles Addams, was about a family of eccentrics who believed that they were normal and everyone else were the strange ones. The series was extremely popular and still is very successful in syndication. The series spawned a cartoon version for Saturday morning in September 1973 and featured Jackie Coogan and Ted Cassidy reprising their original roles.

The Addams Family Goes to School
GS: Allyn Joslyn, Madge Blake, Rolfe Sedan. Morticia decides to keep the children home from school after she reads the fairy tales the children have to read in school.

Morticia and the Psychiatrist
GS: George Petrie. Morticia takes Pugsley to a psychiatrist when he begins to act strangely.

Fester's Punctured Romance
GS: Merry Anders. Fester thinks a pretty cosmetics saleslady is in love with him.

Gomez the Politician
GS: Allyn Joslyn, Eddie Quillan. Gomez backs a loser in the city council election.

The Addams Family Tree
GS: Frank Nelson, Jonathan Hole, Kim Tyler. Gomez and Morticia trace their heritage to see if their ancestors lacked proper breeding.

Morticia Joins the Ladies League
GS: George Barrows, Dorothy Neumann. Pugsley trains a circus gorilla to do the housework.

Halloween with the Addams Family
GS: Skip Homeier, Don Rickles. Two bank robbers hide out with the Addams Family on Halloween Eve.

Green-Eyed Gomez
GS: Del Moore. Gomez is jealous when Morticia's handsome childhood friend comes for a visit.

New Neighbors Meet the Addams Family
GS: Cynthia Pepper, Peter Brooks. A newlywed couple is frightened out of their wits when they meet the whole Addams Family.

Wednesday Leaves Home
GS: Jesse White, Ray Kellogg. Wednesday runs away from home after being scolded for playing with Fester's dynamite caps instead of her own.

The Addams Family Meets the V.I.P.s
GS: Stanley Adams, Vito Scotti, Frank Wilcox. Visiting dignitaries from an Iron Curtain country think the Addams Family are a typical American family.

Morticia, the Matchmaker
GS: Hazel Shermet. Morticia sets out to find a husband for her cousin, Melancholia.

Lurch Learns to Dance
GS: Jimmy Cross, Penny Parker. The Addamses teach Lurch to dance so he can attend the annual Butler's ball.

The Addams Family: left to right, Lisa Loring, John Astin, Carolyn Jones, Ted Cassidy, Ken Weatherwax.

Art and the Addams Family
GS: Vito Scotti. Gomez sends for Sam Picasso, an unemployed artist, to teach Grandmama Addams to paint abstracts.

The Addams Family Meets a Beatnik
GS: Tom Lowell. The Addams Family befriend a beatnik whose motorcycle broke down in front of their house.

The Addams Family Meets the Undercover Man
GS: Rolfe Sedan, George Neise. A government agent hires the mailman to uncover mysterious radio transmissions coming from the Addams' house.

Mother Lurch Visits the Addams Family
GS: Ellen Corby. Lurch tries to hide the fact that he is a butler from his visiting mother.

Uncle Fester's Illness
GS: Lauren Gilbert. Uncle Fester becomes ill at the same time Morticia and Gomez plan a family outing.

The Addams Family Splurges
GS: Roland Winters, Olan Soule. The Addams Family considers the cost of taking a vacation on the moon.

Cousin Itt Visits the Addams Family
GS: Alan Reed. Cousin Itt gets a job

as a zoo curator, but the zookeeper thinks that Itt belongs in a cage.

The Addams Family Goes to Court
GS: Hal Smith. Grandmama is arrested for operating a fortune-telling business without a license.

Amnesia in the Addams Family
Gomez develops amnesia after getting hit on the head by an Indian club.

Thing Is Missing
GS: Tommy Farrell. Gomez enlists the aid of a detective in tracking down Thing, who has mysteriously vanished.

Crisis in the Addams Family
GS: Eddie Quillan, Parley Baer. Uncle Fester gets a job as an insurance salesman.

Lurch and His Harpsichord
GS: Byron Foulger. Lurch is heartbroken when Gomez donates Lurch's harpsichord to a museum.

Morticia the Breadwinner
GS: Milton Frome. When Morticia learns the stock market has fallen drastically, she assumes that Gomez is broke.

The Addams Family and the Spacemen
GS: Vito Scotti, Tim Herbert. An investigator following up a report on spacemen landing on Earth discovers the Addams Family and mistakes them for the aliens.

My Son, the Chimp
Fester thinks he turned Pugsley into a chimp.

Morticia's Favorite Charity
GS: Parley Baer, Marcia Severn. The Addams Family donates some of their favorite possessions to a charity art auction.

Progress and the Addams Family
GS: Parley Baer, Natalie Masters. The city wants to tear down the Addams mansion to make way for a new freeway.

Uncle Fester's Toupee
GS: Elizabeth Fraser. Fester's pen pal is about to arrive and he is worried that she won't like him.

Cousin Itt and the Vocational Counselor
GS: Richard Deacon. Morticia and Gomez decide Itt should start a career as a marriage counselor.

Lurch, the Teenage Idol
GS: Herbie Styles. Lurch becomes a teenage idol when he records a harpsichord song.

The Winning of Morticia Addams
GS: Lee Bergere. Thinking the only happily married couples are those that argue, Fester plans to get Morticia to fight with Gomez.

My Fair Cousin Itt
GS: Sig Ruman, Douglas Evans. Itt stars in a play and winds up with an inflated ego.

Morticia's Romance [Part 1]
GS: Margaret Hamilton. On their anniversary, Morticia tells the story of how she and Gomez first met.

Morticia's Romance [Part 2]
GS: Margaret Hamilton. Morticia reveals that Gomez originally courted her sister Ophelia before he married her.

Morticia Meets Royalty
GS: Elvia Allman. When Gomez's aunt comes for a visit, Thing falls for Millicent, her "hand" maiden servant.

Gomez the People's Choice
GS: Parley Baer, Eddie Quillan. Gomez decides to run for mayor.

Cousin Itt's Problem
GS: Meg Wyllie, Frankie Darro. The family thinks Itt is losing his hair.

Halloween Addams Style
Morticia tries to prove the existence of witches to the children.

Morticia the Writer
GS: Peter Bonerz. Morticia sets out to write a children's story, while Gomez feels neglected.

Feud in the Addams Family
GS: Fred Clark. Learning that a cousin of Gomez's is socially prominent, their neighbors suddenly become friendly.

Gomez the Reluctant Lover
GS: Jill Andre. Pugsley has a crush on his teacher and uses one of his father's old love letters to prove it.

Morticia the Sculptress
GS: Hugh Sanders, Vito Scotti. Morticia, feeling unfulfilled, takes up sculpting.

Gomez the Cat Burglar
While sleepwalking, Gomez becomes a cat burglar.

Portrait of Gomez
GS: Tom D'Andrea. Gomez tries to get a driver's license so he can have his picture taken.

Morticia's Dilemma
GS: Anthony Caruso, Carlos Rivas. An old girlfriend and her father arrive from Spain, announcing her intentions to marry Gomez.

Christmas with the Addams Family
The Addams Family try to prove the existence of Santa Claus to the children.

Uncle Fester, Tycoon
GS: Roy Roberts. Morticia poses as Fester's future mother-in-law to teach him a lesson in economics.

Morticia and Gomez vs. Fester and Grandmama
GS: Irene Tedrow. Morticia hires a governess for the children, causing Fester and Grandmama to feel useless.

Fester Goes on a Diet
GS: Jack La Lanne. Fester goes on a diet to impress a visiting pen-pal.

The Great Treasure Hunt
GS: Nestor Paiva, Richard Reeves. Finding a treasure map, the Addams Family embark on a secret treasure hunt.

Ophelia Finds Romance
GS: Robert Nichols. Ophelia has fallen madly in love with a wealthy young man.

Pugsley's Allowance
GS: Jack Collins, Parley Baer. Pugsley tries to find a job to supplement his small allowance.

Happy Birthday Grandma Frump
GS: Margaret Hamilton. Morticia and Gomez plan to send Grandma Frump on an all-expense-paid vacation for her birthday, but she thinks they are planning to send her to an old folks home.

Morticia the Decorator
GS: Eddie Quillan, Jeff Donnell. To sell the Addamses an insurance policy, agent Joe Digby lets Morticia redecorate his home.

Ophelia Visits Morticia
GS: George Cisar. Ophelia's boyfriend runs away to join the Peace Corps.

Addams Cum Laude
GS: Allyn Joslyn, Carol Byron, Pat Brown. Morticia enrolls the children in a private school, which they later buy and try to run themselves.

Cat Addams
GS: Marty Ingels. When the Addams' pet lion becomes sick, Gomez sends for the vet.

Lurch's Little Helper
GS: Robby The Robot. Gomez builds a robot to help Lurch with his housework.

The Addams' Policy
GS: Parley Baer, Eddie Quillan. The Addams Family puts in an insurance claim to replace a stuffed bear Uncle Fester burned.

Lurch's Grand Romance
GS: Diane Jergens. Morticia's childhood friend comes for a visit and falls for Lurch.

Ophelia's Career
GS: Ralph Rose, Ben Wright. Ophelia decides to take up a career as an opera singer.

Halloween with the Addams Family
W: George Tibbles. D: Dennis Steinmetz. GS: Elvia Allman, Vito Scotti, Parley Baer, Henry Darrow. A 90-min. 1977 reunion episode: the Addams Family plans their annual Halloween celebration, but are interrupted by a band of burglars who plan on stealing the family valuables. [The episode is not syndicated with the series but as a separate TV movie.]

THE ADVENTURES OF OZZIE AND HARRIET

On the air 10/3/52, off 9/3/66. ABC. 200 syndicated episodes. 435 filmed. Film B&W. Broadcast: Oct 1952-Jun 1956 Fri 8-8:30; Oct 1956-Sept 1958 Wed 9-9:30; Sept 1958-Sept 1961 Wed 8:30-9; Sept 1961-Sept 1963 Thu 7:30-8; Sept 1963-Jan 1966 Wed 7:30-8; Jan 1966-Sept 1966 Sat 7:30-8. Producer: Ozzie Nelson. Prod Co: American International Television. Synd: Filmways Pictures.

CAST: The Nelsons—Ozzie, Harriet, David and Ricky (played by themselves), Thorny Thornberry (Don DeFore), Darby (Parley Baer), Joe Randolph (Lyle Talbot), Clara Randolph (Mary Jane Croft), Doc Williams (Frank Cady), June (June Blair [Nelson]), Kris (Kristin Harmon [Nelson]).

WRITER & DIRECTOR: Ozzie Nelson.

One of the most popular family comedies of all time. It lasted for well over a decade. It was based on the radio series of the same name which went on the air in 1944. In the early 1950s a feature version entitled "Here Come the Nelsons" was released. Although over 400 episodes were filmed, only 200 episodes, mostly the early '60s ones, are in syndication. The episodes relate the problems faced by Ozzie and his family.

The Fall Guy
Ozzie convinces David not to let people take advantage of him.

Rick Goes to a Dance
Ozzie and Harriet are worried that Rick has turned into a "wallflower."

Thorny's Gift
Ozzie doesn't understand why Thorny hasn't thanked him for the birthday present he sent him.

Boys' Christmas Money
David and Rick try to earn extra money to buy Christmas gifts.

Late Christmas Gift
The presents from Grandma Nelson arrive late and confusion starts when they don't know whose gift is whose.

Newspaper Write-Up
Ozzie gets his name in the paper but it is spelled wrong. [Not syndicated]

Basketball Players
Ozzie and Thorny back out when their families are supposed to play basketball together.

The Tuba
Ozzie and Harriet fight over a newspaper article. [Not syndicated]

Separate Rooms
The boys demand separate bedrooms.

The Valentine Show
Thorny agrees to buy Ozzie's gift for Harriet.

The Traffic Signal
The Nelson family try to get a traffic signal installed on their street.

The Speech
Ozzie is asked to speak at a civic club but is replaced by a visiting Army officer.

The Orchid and the Violet
Ozzie orders violets for Harriet but when orchids arrive by mistake, he thinks there is another man.

The Pancake Mix
Rick plans to make a fortune by using the double-your-money-back guarantee on a box of pancake mix.

The Fish Story
Ozzie tells Thorny a story which gives a lot of business to the local fish market.

Night School
Ozzie and Harriet attend night school. [Not syndicated]

The Boxing Matches
Boxing champ Ozzie is knocked out by novice Thorny.

The Traders
Ozzie conducts a trade deal with Rick and David.

Boys' Paper Route
David and Rick try to earn more money by taking paper routes.

Door Key for David
Ozzie and Harriet feel David is old enough to have his own key to the house.

The Play's the Thing
Ozzie and Thorny appear in the women's club play.

New Chairs
Ozzie buys two new chairs for the living room.

The Party
Rick and David plan revenge when they are not invited to their friend Will's birthday party.

Dave's Pipe
Ozzie's friend sends David a pipe, unaware that he is too young to smoke it.

The Window Pane
Harriet gets Ozzie to fix the broken glass in the kitchen door.

David's Birthday
David has an unexpected visitor on his 17th birthday.

The Ladder
Ozzie and Thorny are trapped on the roof when their ladder blows away.

The Suggestion Box
Ozzie builds a suggestion box where the family can write down how each of them feels about the other.

The Insurance Policy
Harriet loses her pin and the whole family goes looking for it.

The Miracle
A flashback episode to when Ozzie was a kid during Christmas.

The Hunter
Ozzie and Thorny go on a hunting trip.

The Camera Show
Ozzie buys some cheap cameras and the whole family starts taking pictures.

Courage
Ozzie has to return a negligee for Harriet.

Old Fashioned Remedy
Ozzie uses his grandmother's remedy to cure a cold.

Father & Son Tournament
Ozzie can't decide whether to enter a ping-pong tournament with David or Rick.

Gentleman David
Ozzie and Harriet worry why David hasn't been invited to the school dance where the girls invite the boys.

Evening with Hamlet
Ozzie helps David learn Hamlet by acting it out at home.

Be on Time
Ozzie tries to teach Rick to be on time, but he can't seem to do that himself.

The Bird's Nest
A robin has built a nest in the Nelson's broken rain gutter.

The Usher
David applies for the job as an usher at the movie theater.

Tuxedo for David
David needs a tuxedo for the senior prom, but they are very expensive. [Not syndicated]

The Dipple Door
Ozzie's neighbor, Wally Dipple, invents an automatic garage door.

Wedding Anniversary
Ozzie and Harriet want to go out and celebrate their anniversary but they have to chaperone Rick's party instead.

A Matter of Inches
Ozzie promises David that he will pay him $50 when he is the same size as he is.

The Fruitcake
Ozzie and Harriet write thank-you notes for all their Christmas presents.

The Bloodhound
Rick tries to train a basset hound while Ozzie and Thorny are trying to watch the fights.

Missing Sandwiches
Harriet and Catherine are assigned to make a basket of sandwiches and potato salad and bring them to the women's club meeting.

Individuality
Harriet thinks David and Rick should be allowed to decorate their rooms any way they want to.

Girl Who Came to Dinner
David invites his new girlfriend to have dinner at his house. [Not syndicated]

Rick's Blind Date
David's date asks him to get someone to take her cousin to the dance, so he gets Rick to take her.

Spring Housecleaning
Ozzie tries to get out of helping Harriet with the housework.

Man Across the Street
Ozzie gets the new neighbor to play football with them.

A Day in Bed
Ozzie decides to stay home in bed for a day to relax.

Invitation to Dinner
Ozzie and Harriet both accept invitations to dinner, now they don't know which one to go to.

David's Engagement
Ozzie and Harriet think David is too young to get married.

Homemade Ice Cream
Ozzie makes homemade ice cream for the family. [Not syndicated]

Football Hero
Harriet tries to talk Rick out of playing football.

Music Appreciation
Rick's rock music is preventing David from studying symphony records.

Ball of Tinfoil
Ozzie rents a trailer to get rid of the junk in his house.

The Honest Face
David must bring a picture of Ozzie to his psychology class to see if he has a face which expresses criminal tendencies.

Harriet's Secret Admirer
Someone is sending Harriet flowers and Ozzie wants to know who it is.

The Car Mix-Up
Harriet takes someone else's car by mistake.

The Volunteer Fireman
Ozzie becomes a volunteer fireman.

The Safe Driver
Ozzie has difficulty with a pretty girl at the license bureau.

Buried Treasure
Rick finds gold coins buried in the back yard.

Captain Salty and the Submarine
Ozzie and his friends like to watch a kiddie TV show.

David Picks Up the Tab
David invites Ozzie and Harriet to be his guests at a nightclub.

The Banjo Player
Ozzie tries to join Rick's rock band with his banjo.

The Kappa Sig Party
David holds a fraternity party at his house.

The Puppy
The puppy that Ozzie and the boys gave Harriet runs away.

Hairstyle for Harriet
Ozzie tries to keep Harriet from changing her hairstyle.

Taking Care of Freddy
Ozzie babysits for the neighbor's cat.

A Doctor in the House
Ozzie's doctor friend moves in with them while his house is being painted.

The Day After Christmas
The Nelsons go ice skating on the day before Christmas.

Hawaiian Party
The Nelsons go to a Hawaiian party.

The Borrowed Tuxedo
Ozzie borrows a neighbor's tuxedo and forgets to return it.

The Reading Room
Ozzie tries to get the family to do more reading.

The Jet Pilot
Ozzie is chosen to be the first civilian to ride in a new jet.

The Editor
Harriet becomes the editor of the women's club newspaper.

Ricky, the Drummer
Rick plays the drums in a big band.

Man Without a Family
Ozzie tries to get Rick to take his rock 'n roll parties to another house.

The Road Race
Ozzie uses his Model T against Rick and David's hot rod in a race.

The 14-Mile Hike
Ozzie promises to take some boys on a hike, but realizes it will prevent him from playing in a golf tournament.

The Treasurer's Report
Ozzie uses Rick's tape recorder to give his report at the men's club.

Free Flowers
Ozzie comes home late and finds that Harriet is mad at him.

Ozzie's Triple Banana Surprise
Ozzie eats too much ice cream and starts seeing things.

Tutti Frutti Ice Cream
Ozzie finds that he has an urge for some tutti frutti ice cream.

The Trophy
The whole family enters the decathlon at the men's club picnic.

The Closed Circuit
Rick builds a do-it-yourself television set.

The Top Gun
Ozzie challenges a cowboy to a shoot-out.

The Bachelor
The Nelsons and their friends try to get a bachelor friend married off.

The Magic of Three
Ozzie and his friends become waiters at the women's club banquet.

A Cruise for Harriet
Harriet cons Ozzie into taking her on a cruise rather than let him go fishing.

The Pony
Ozzie wins a pony in a contest.

David Loses His Poise
David tries to date a coed but everything keeps going wrong.

Ozzie's Daughters
Ozzie becomes a temporary father to two teenage girl houseguests.

Rick's Riding Lessons
GS: Venetia Stevenson. Rick is giving guitar lessons to a beautiful riding instructor in exchange for riding lessons.

The Motorcycle
Ozzie tries to talk David out of motorcycle racing.

The Runaways
Ozzie discovers two young runaways in the back seat of his car.

Rick's Dinner Guest
Rick invites his new girlfriend and her parents over for dinner on the same night of Ozzie's poker game.

Jealous Joe Randolph
Joe Randolph suspects Ozzie of fooling around with his wife.

The Newspaper Interview
Ozzie is selected to appear in the Neighbor of the Week column in the newspaper.

The Exploding Book
GS: Luana Patten. David and Rick plan revenge on Wally who gave David a gag gift to give his girlfriend.

Ricky, the Bullfighter
GS: Joyce Taylor. Rick takes up bullfighting to impress an exchange student.

The Little Black Box
Harriet bets Ozzie he can't keep from opening the box before Saturday.

The Sea Captain
David is offered a job as a crewman on a ship by Ozzie's old friend.

The Law Clerk
David applies for a job as a law clerk.

Nelsons Decide to Move
Ozzie tries to convince his family that they should move to an apartment.

David, the Sleuth
David plays detective in order to follow a strange character.

The Circus
David and Rick perform a trapeze act.

Rick Gets Even
GS: Tuesday Weld. Rick has trouble asking a beautiful girl for a date.

Ozzie Keeps a Secret
Ozzie plans a surprise birthday party for Rick's girlfriend.

Rick's English Literature Class
Ozzie makes a speech at the women's club.

David's Car Payments
David falls behind on his car payments, so he starts to borrow money from everyone.

Dave Goofs Off
David tries to impress the senior partner at the law firm.

His Brother's Girl
David falls for Rick's girlfriend.

The Lost Briefcase
Ozzie helps David who has gotten his briefcase mixed up with someone else's.

A Weekend Vacation
Ozzie wants to spend the weekend alone at the lodge, but Harriet invites the Randolphs to go along.

David Gets a Raise
GS: Joe Flynn. David can't find the right time to ask his boss for a raise.

A Sweater for Rick
Rick's girlfriend plans to knit a sweater for him.

David's Almost In-Laws
Ozzie and Harriet think that David is planning to get married when they are invited to dinner at his girl's house.

A Friend in Need
Ozzie plans to test his friends' loyalty after they decided to play golf instead of helping him fix his plumbing.

The Little House Guest
Ozzie and Harriet babysit with a neighbor's little boy while she goes to the hospital to have a baby.

The Lawnmower
Ozzie breaks into his neighbor's garage to retrieve his borrowed lawnmower.

David Hires a Secretary
GS: Joe Flynn, June Blair. David hires a beautiful girl to be his boss's secretary while the regular one goes on vacation.

Rick Counts the Ballots
Rick is assigned to count the ballots for the Campus Queen Contest.

The Girl Who Loses Things
GS: Roberta Shore. Rick's girlfriend suspects that he is dating another girl at the same time.

Kelley's Important Papers
David's boss wants him to deliver some important papers, but he isn't home so Ozzie and Harriet deliver them instead.

The Dancing Lessons
Ozzie and Joe plan to surprise their wives by taking dancing lessons.

The Newlyweds Get Settled
While David and June are away on their honeymoon, Ozzie and Harriet fix up their apartment.

Dave Goes Back to Work
Dave promises to call June while at work, but other things get in the way.

Rick Comes to Dinner
Rick comes to dinner at David's apartment with one of David's old girlfriends.

The Fraternity Rents Out a Room
GS: Wally Cox. Rick and Wally plan to move into the empty room at the fraternity house.

Ricky, the Milkman
GS: Susan Oliver. Rick meets a beautiful girl while delivering milk for a friend.

Rick Grades a Test
GS: Cheryl Holdridge. Rick keeps his date out too late on the night before a big test; he is then asked to grade the test papers.

The Fraternity Pin
GS: Cheryl Holdridge. A rumor starts that Rick is going to give his fraternity pin to his latest girlfriend.

A Lamp for David and June
David and June want to buy a new lamp but don't have enough money.

The Lonesome Parents
Ozzie and Harriet get lonesome when David and June don't visit them more often.

Making Wally Study
Rick and his friends help Wally pass his test.

The Client's Daughter
Rick breaks his date to go out with the daughter of one of Dave's clients.

Trip to Mexico
Ozzie and Harriet decide to take a trip to Mexico.

Rick and the Maid of Honor
Rick becomes the best man at his friend's wedding, where the maid of honor has eyes for him.

Little Handprints in the Sidewalk
Ozzie and Harriet try to find a place to put the cement block with Rick and David's handprints.

The Tigers Go to a Dance
Harriet is put in charge of the children's dance at the women's club.

Publicity for the Fraternity
D: David Nelson. Rick and his friends try to get some publicity for their fraternity.

Ricky, the Host
GS: Vicki Trickett. Rick tries to find a way to keep his friends from interfering with his dating the new girl in school.

Losing Miss Edwards
GS: Joe Flynn, Connie Harper. David is given the job of reprimanding his boss's secretary.

Rick Sends a Picture
Rick's girlfriend mistakes the autographed picture meant for his grand-

mother as a gift for her.

An Old Friend of June's
GS: Joan Staley. David invites June's old boyfriend to dinner and then gets stuck at the office with his beautiful new secretary.

June and the Great Outdoors
David takes June on her first camping trip.

David and the Teenager
GS: Bernadette Withers. A teenage girl in David's apartment building has a crush on him.

Decorating Dave's Office
June decides to redecorate David's office.

Music Festival
David hosts a program of musical performers.

Dave and the Fraternity Lease
The lease on the fraternity house is expiring and the landlady wants to turn it into a sorority, so Rick goes to David for help.

Ozzie, Joe & the Fashion Models
While on a fishing trip, Ozzie and Joe are joined by two models doing a layout for a magazine.

The Blue Moose
Rick and Wally plan to get another fraternity to paint their house.

The Swami
Ozzie decides to perform a fortune-telling act at the women's club dance.

Wedding Picture
Rick and Kris find that there is a picture missing from their wedding album.

A Wife in the Office
GS: Connie Harper. June becomes David's secretary while his regular one is on vacation.

Rick, the Law Clerk
Rick applies for the job of law clerk at David's office.

A Letter About Harriet
Harriet tries to get Ozzie to enter the Why I Love My Wife contest.

Rick and Kris Go to the Mountains
D: David Nelson. Rick and his friends hold a poker party at Kris's parents' mountain cabin.

A Letter of Recommendation
Wally asks David to write a letter of recommendation to help get him a job.

Rick's Old Printing Press
Ozzie gives Rick's old toy printing press to the neighborhood kids to start their own newspaper.

Rick and the Girl Across the Hall
Kris thinks that Rick and the girl who works in the office opposite the one where Rick works might be fooling around.

The Study System
Rick and his friends try to prevent Wally from bringing the grade average of the fraternity down.

The Ballerina
Rick and Kris perform a ballet for the women's club children's show.

The Big Dog
Rick gives Kris a Great Dane for her birthday.

Ricky Grows a Beard
Rick decides to grow a beard.

The Pennies
Ozzie gambles with the neighborhood kids' valuable coin collection.

The Trunk
Ozzie and Joe buy a trunk full of junk at an auction.

Kris Plays Cupid
D: David Nelson. Kris tries to get Ginger and Wally back together.

Harriet's Quiz
Harriet gives Ozzie a quiz on marital happiness.

Kris Goes to College
Kris goes to college and Rick finds that he cannot spend all of his time with her as she'd like him to.

The Nelsons Revisited
Rick and his friends plan to invite Ozzie and Harriet to their next fraternity party.

The Petition
Dave and Rick investigate a suspicious law client.

A Bedtime Story
The Dean gets Rick and his friends to help him play a practical joke.

The Chess Set
Ozzie buys an extra-large size chess set.

A Helpless Female
Kris thinks that Rick has lost interest in her because she is not feminine enough for him.

Kris's Girlfriend
Kris's old girlfriend moves in with Rick and Kris.

Breakfast for Harriet
Ozzie decides to stay home and take care of Harriet who has a bad cold.

Rick's Raise
Rick tries to get a raise from David.

The Desk Photo
Kris decides that Rick should have her picture on his desk.

A Painting from the Past
Rick brings home a painting he once did for one of his old girlfriends, causing Kris to get mad.

The Tangled Web
Ozzie agrees to go along with the lie that Clara told.

A Rose a Day
Ozzie tries to find out who has been sending Harriet a single rose every day.

Wally's Traffic Ticket
Wally asks David and Rick to help him fight a traffic ticket.

The Equestrians
Rick buys a horse.

Kris and the Queen
Rick and Kris try to get Wally and Ginger back together.

Flying Down to Lunch
Joe and Ozzie fly to Mexico to have lunch.

Helpful June
June decides to be David's private eye and help with the detective work.

David the Worrier
David goes on vacation and leaves Rick in charge.

Ghost Town
Ozzie and Harriet go to an old ghost town in search of antiques.

The Prowler
Ozzie pretends to go on a fishing trip in order to get out of playing bridge with Joe and Clara.

A Message from Kris
Kris is jealous of Rick's interest in a beautiful girl.

David Picks a Pie
June volunteers David for a pie-tasting contest.

An Honor for Oz
Ozzie is given a gift from the Tiger's club.

Ozzie, a Go-Go
Ozzie and Harriet go to a discotheque.

Kris, the Little Helper
Kris resents having to do the laundry for the fraternity.

The Trip Trap
June tries to get David to take on a trip to Hawaii.

Waiting for Joe
Ozzie and Harriet agree to go on a picnic with Clara and Joe providing he is on time for once.

Rick's Assistant
David and Rick show a neighborhood kid how to become a lawyer.

Dave's Other Office
David moves his office into his apartment while the office is being repaired.

Ozzie the Babysitter
Ozzie babysits with a neighbor kid.

The Game Room
Ozzie plans to turn David and Rick's old bedroom into a game room complete with a pool table.

ALICE

On the air 8/31/76; still going in 1983. CBS. Color/video tape. 140 episodes (currently syndicated). Broadcast: Aug 1976 Mon 9:30-10; Sept 1976-Oct 1976 Wed 9:30-10; Nov 1976-Sept 1977 Sat 9:30-10; Oct 1977-Oct 1978 Sun 9:30-10; Oct 1978-Feb 1979 Sun 8:30-9; Mar 1979-Jun 1983 Sun 9-9:30; Jun 1983-present Sun 8-8:30. Producers: William D'Angelo, Ray Allen, Harvey Bullock, Thomas Kuhn. Prod Co/Synd: Warner Bros. TV.

CAST: Alice Hyatt (played by Linda Lavin), Tommy Hyatt (Phillip McKeon), Mel Sharples (Vic Tayback), Florence Jean Castleberry [Flo] (Polly Holliday), Vera Louise Gorman (Beth Howland), Belle Dupree (Diane Ladd), Jolene Hunnicutt (Celia Weston), Henry, the telephone repairman (Marvin Kaplan).

This is the continuing adventures of a widow named Alice Hyatt who, when her truck driver husband was killed in an accident, moved to Arizona with her son, Tommy, where she became a waitress at Mel's diner. Each episode features the crazy events that take place at the diner, which are usually caused by the nutty employees. The series entered syndication in 1983, so the series has had only a short time to test itself in reruns. However, the current rating figures show that this series will probably be successful for many years to come.

Alice [Pilot]
W: Robert Getchell. D: Paul Bogert. GS: Dennis Dugan, Arthur Space. Widow Alice Hyatt and her son Tommy move to Arizona where she gets a job as a waitress at Mel's Diner.

Alice Gets a Pass
W: Martin Donovan. D: Jim Drake. GS: Denny Miller. Alice finds herself attracted to Mel's old college friend, a good looking football player.

Mel's Happy Burger
W: Arnold Kane. D: Burt Brinckerhoff. GS: Ronnie Schell, Burton Gilliam, John Fiedler. Alice gets the opportunity to break into show business when Mel decides to film a TV commercial advertising the diner.

A Call to Arms
W: Lloyd Garver. D: Jim Drake. GS: Geoffrey Lewis, Jack Riley. Mel tries to convince Alice to carry a gun when she is bothered by an obscene phone caller.

Vera's Mortician
W: Bruce Kane. D: Bill Hobin. GS: Tom Poston, Burton Gilliam. Vera surprises everyone when she announces that she is going to marry her mortician boyfriend, unaware that he is already married.

Pay the Fifty Dollars
W: Lloyd Garver. D: Bill Persky. GS: Cliff Norton, Liberty Williams, Caren Kaye, Gordon Jump. Alice is arrested for soliciting when she is caught in a police raid at the nightclub in which she is performing.

The Last Review
W: Harvey Bullock & R.S. Allen. D: James Sheldon. GS: Victor Buono, Noble Willingham. While Mel is away, Alice invites the local food editor to try Mel's chili. She later regrets sending the invitation when the man dies of food poisoning in the diner.

Sex Education
W: Donald Reiker & Patricia Jones. D: Bruce Bilson. GS: Adam West, Lara Parker, Michele Tobin. Alice decides it is time to tell Tommy about the facts of life.

Big Daddy Dawson's Coming
W: Arnold Kane & Bruce Johnson. D: Norman Abbott. GS: Norman Alden, Patrick Cronin. Flo's first husband comes for a visit.

Good Night Sweet Vera
W: Simon Montner. D: Norman Abbott. GS: Darrell Zwerling. Alice and Flo try to prevent a depressed Vera from committing suicide.

The Dilemma
W: Martin Donovan. D: Jim Sheldon. GS: Paul Picerni. Alice's old boyfriend arrives for a visit and winds up proposing to her.

Who Killed Bugs Bunny?
W. Lloyd J. Schwartz. D: Bruce Bilson. GS: Noble Willingham, Peter Zapp. Alice regrets letting Tommy go away on a camping trip when she learns that it is also a hunting trip.

Mother-in-Law [Part 1]
W: Martin Donovan. D: William D'Angelo. GS: Eileen Heckart, Clyde Kusatsu. Alice's mother-in-law moves in when she announces that she is leaving her husband.

Mother-in-Law [Part 2]
W: Arnold Kane, Bruce Johnson & Ray Allen. D: William D'Angelo. GS: Eileen Heckart, Murray Hamilton. Alice sends for her father-in-law in order to get her in-laws back together.

Mel's in Love
W: Gary David Goldberg. D: Alan Rafkin. GS: Susan Lanier, Maureen Arthur. Mel falls in love with Alice's beautiful houseguest.

The Accident
W: Harvey Bullock & Roy Kammerman. D: Alan Rafkin. GS: Hamilton Camp, Leonard Stone. Flo borrows Mel's car and then wrecks it in an accident.

The Failure
W: Ben Joelson & Art Baer. D: William D'Angelo. GS: Henry Polic II, Bernie Kopell, Lupe Ontiveros. The diner is held up by a bumbling would-be bank robber.

The Pain of No Return
W: Rick Mittleman. D: Alan Rafkin. GS: Warren Berlinger, Arlene Golonka, Tom Mahoney. An IRS agent arrives at the diner and tells Alice that she owes the government two thousand dollars.

The Odd Couple
W: Roy Kammerman, Arnold Kane, Harvey Bullock, Ray Allen, Diane Silver & Ellen Sherman. GS: Kenneth Mars. Flo moves in with Alice after her house trailer is stolen.

A Night to Remember
W: Arnold Kane & Ray Allen. D: Alan Rafkin. Flo and Alice fix Vera up with a blind date.

Mel's Cup
W: Harvey Bullock & Roy Kammerman. D: Norman Abbott. GS: Billy Sands. Alice unknowingly donates Mel's treasured silver cup to a charity.

The Bundle
W: Ben Joelson & Art Baer. D: Norman Abbott. GS: Billy Sands, Michael Keenan. Flo finds forty thousand dollars in the diner, causing everyone to think of ways on how to spend it.

A Piece of the Rock
W: Ben Joelson & Art Baer. D: Bill Persky. GS: Lurene Tuttle, Jennifer Billingsley, John Myhers. Alice is shocked when she finds her husband's insurance policy and learns that the beneficiary is another woman.

The Pharmacist
W: Michael Loman & Chris Hayward. D: Noam Pitlik. GS: Bob Dishy. A crazed pharmacist threatens to commit suicide in the diner unless he can speak to the President about the harmful additives being put in the country's food supply.

Earthquake
W: Chris Hayward & Gary Markowitz. D: Noam Pitlik. GS: Edward Binns, J.J. Barry, Ancel Cook, Gordon Hurst. Vera tries to convince everyone that an old Indian's earthquake prediction is about to come true.

The Second Time 'Round
W: Tom Whedon. D: Kim Friedman. GS: Rod McCary, MacIntyre Dixon, Lewis Arquette. Alice has an encounter with a flasher while Flo's third husband pays a visit.

Sixty Minutes Man
W: George Tibbles, Tom Whedon & Warren S. Murray. D: Kim Friedman. GS: Michael V. Gazzo, Bruce Kimmel, Dave Ketchum. Alice discovers that one of their customers is a gangster who is wanted by the FBI.

The Indian Taker
W: Tom Whedon. D: Marc Daniels. GS: Victor Jory, Larry Hovis. Mel and the girls are taken in by a con man who dresses up like an Indian and claims that the diner is built over his ancestral burial grounds.

86 the Waitresses
W: Sybil Adelman. D: Marc Daniels.

GS: Bill Fiore. The girls quit when Mel hires a waiter and pays him more than he pays any of them.

Alice by Moonlight
W: Tom Whedon. D: Kim Friedman. GS: Norman Alden, Morey Amsterdam, Jane Dulo, Gloria LeRoy. Alice gets a job moonlighting at a nightclub.

Single Belles
W: Bruce Howard. D: Kim Friedman. GS: Robert Hogan. The girls unknowingly date the same man.

That Old Back Magic
W: Arthur Marx & Robert Fisher. D: William Asher. GS: Edward Winter. Mel moves in with Alice when he hurts his back.

Love Is Sweeping the Counter
W: Arthur Rabin. D: Kim Friedman. GS: Cliff Pellow. Flo's invitation to Mel to go with her to a football game leads to a blossoming romance.

The Eyes of Texas
W: Arthur Marx & Robert Fisher. D: Kim Friedman. GS: Ron Masak, John Myhers. Alice tries to convince Flo that she needs glasses.

A Semi-Merry Christmas
W: Bob Carroll, Jr., Madelyn Davis, Tom Whedon. D: Marc Daniels. Mel, the girls, and Tommy get stuck in a snowstorm while driving on Christmas Eve.

Oh, George Burns
W: Fred S. Fox & Seamon Jacobs. D: Marc Daniels. GS: George Burns. After George Burns pays a visit to the diner, Vera, who has seen Burns' film "Oh God" three times, is convinced that she has been visited by God himself.

Love Is a Free Throw
W: Robert Fisher & Arthur Marx. D: Marc Daniels. GS: Joe Silver, Brad Gorman. A high school basketball star develops a crush on Alice.

Close Encounters of the Worst Kind
W: Robert Fisher & Arthur Marx. D: William Asher. GS: Boyd Bodwell, Charles Cyphers, Larry Hovis, Barbara Sharma. After a big fight at the diner, Alice invites Mel, Vera and Flo over to her apartment for an encounter session.

Love Me, Love My Horse
W: Tom Whedon. D: William Asher. GS: Burton Gilliam. Flo's brother plans to marry Alice, causing his horse to become very upset.

Mel's Big Five-O
W: Warren Murray. D: William Asher. The girls plan a surprise party for Mel on his 50th birthday.

Florence of Arabia
W: Tom Whedon. D: Kim Friedman. GS: Richard Libertini, George Loros. An Arab oil sheik asks Flo to be his wife.

The Cuban Connection
W: Arthur Marx & Robert Fisher. D: William Asher. GS: Desi Arnaz, Janis Paige. Alice tries to prevent her playboy fashion photographer friend from leaving his wife.

Don't Lock Now
W: Tom Whedon. D: William Asher. GS: Nedra Volz, Bill Lane. Mel and the girls accidentally lock themselves in the storeroom while trying to prevent a thief from breaking in.

Star in the Storeroom
W: Robert Fisher & Arthur Marx. D: Marc Daniels. GS: Jerry Reed, Graham Jarvis. Jerry Reed pays a visit to the diner and finds himself covered with ketchup two hours before he is to perform a concert.

Mel's Recession
W: Arthur Marx, Robert Fisher & Tom Whedon. D: William Asher. In order to save money, Mel decides to fire one of his waitresses, the problem is which one to fire.

Car Wars
W: Arthur Marx & Robert Fisher. D: William Asher. Mel sells his old car to the girls, but then tries to get it back when he gets a higher offer for it.

Better Late Than Never
W: Tom Whedon. D: William Asher. GS: Steve Franken, Jim Varney, Dave Madden. Mel decides to open the diner on Saturday, only to be held up by one of his customers.

Take Him, He's Yours
W: Arthur Marx & Robert Fisher. D: William Asher. Tommy moves in with Mel when he becomes too much for Alice to handle.

Block Those Kicks
W: Arthur Marx & Robert Fisher. D: William Asher. GS: Lou Tiano, Tara Talboy. Mel and the girls all decide to kick their annoying habits.

The Principal of the Thing
W: Arthur Marx & Robert Fisher. D: William Asher. GS: Gary Collins, Lou Frizzell, Miriam Byrd Nethery, Joseph Perry. Alice falls in love with the principal of Tommy's school.

What Happened to the Class of '78?
W: Tom Whedon. D: William Asher. GS: Harvey Goldenberg, Lyman Ward. Flo decides to go to night school in order to get her diploma.

Citizen Mel
W: Charles Isaacs. D: William Asher. GS: William Pierson. Mel becomes afraid for his life after he witnesses a robbery and believes the thief is coming to get him.

Vera's Popcorn Romance
W: Tom Whedon. D: William Asher. GS: Alan Haufrect, Barbara Minkus Barron, Johnnie Decker. Mel and the girls mistake Henry for Vera's new boyfriend.

Mel's in a Family Way
W: Jerry Winnick. D: William Asher.

GS: Michael Pataki, Shirley Mitchell, Dave Shelley. Mel gets the wrong idea when Alice invites him over to her apartment.

Who Ordered the Hot Turkey?
W: Tom Whedon. D: William Asher. GS: Joyce Bulifant, James Cromwell, Peter Leeds, Owen Bush, Nancy McKeon. On Thanksgiving, Mel unknowingly buys some live turkeys which turn out to be stolen.

A Slight Case of ESP
W: Alan Rose & Fred Rubin. D: William Asher. GS: Barbara Minkus Rubin, Tom Williams. Vera tries to prove to everyone that she has ESP.

The Happy Hoofers
W: Arthur Marx & Robert Fisher. D: William Asher. Alice loses her job when she moonlights as a singing messenger.

Sweet Charity
W: Arthur Marx & Robert Fisher. D: William Asher. GS: Cliff Pellow, Alan Haufrect, Michael Ballard, Ron Rifkin, Victoria Carroll. Alice offers Flo and Vera tickets to a charity ball unaware that there won't be enough tickets for all of them.

Vera's Broken Heart
W: Arthur Marx, Robert Fisher & Tom Whedon. D: Lee Lochhead. GS: Dawson Mays, Michael Keenan, Michael Ballard. Vera becomes depressed when her boyfriend dumps her for another woman.

The Fourth Time Around
W: Arthur Marx & Robert Fisher. D: William Asher. GS: Carmine Caridi, Lou Frizzell, Dick Wilson, Roger Bowen. Flo falls in love with Mel's visiting brother.

Tommy's First Love
W: Arthur Marx & Robert Fisher. D: William Asher. GS: Olivia Barash, Bruce Kirby. Tommy and his girlfriend run away from home after

Alice disapproves of the way they have been carrying on.

Alice's Decision
W: Arthur Marx, Robert Fisher & Tom Whedon. D: Lee Lochhead. GS: Karen Morrow, Bobby Ramsen. Alice's old singing partner convinces her to go back into show business.

Mel Grows Up
W: Arthur Marx & Robert Fisher. D: William Asher. GS: Martha Raye, Robert Hogan. Mel's bossy mother comes for a visit and takes over the diner.

What're You Doing New Year's Eve?
W: Marion Freeman & Dawn Aldredge. D: Marc Daniels. GS: Victoria Carroll, Ted Lehman, Randy Doney, Will Hunt. On New Year's Eve, Flo announces on a radio show that she is spending the night alone at the diner and soon finds that she has more company than she can handle.

If the Shoe Fits
W: Charles Isaacs & Tom Whedon. D: Marc Daniels. GS: Fred McCarren, Danny Goldman. Alice falls in love with the 25-year-old theatrical director.

The Last Stow It [Part 1]
W: Arthur Marx & Robert Fisher. D: William Asher. GS: Hans Conried, Bob Hastings. Mel sells the diner to a pushy perfectionist who proceeds to fire the girls.

The Last Stow It [Part 2]
W: Arthur Marx & Robert Fisher. D: William Asher. GS: Hans Conreid, Bob Hastings. Alice tries to frighten the new owner of the diner into selling it back to Mel by disguising herself as a gangster.

My Fair Vera
W: Arthur Marx & Robert Fisher. D: William Asher. GS: Bobby Ramsen, Larry Breeding, Bryan O'Byrne. Vera gets a job as an actress in a TV commercial.

Flo Finds Her Father
W: Marion Freeman & Dawn Aldredge. D: William Asher. GS: Forrest Tucker, Hamilton Camp. Flo receives a visit from her father whom she hasn't seen in 30 years.

The Reporter
W: Michael Loman. D: Dennis Steinmetz. GS: Richard Erdman. A reporter hides out at the diner when he fears that his life is in danger.

The Bus
W: Eric Tarloff & Chris Hayward. D: Noam Pitlik. GS: Michael Alldredge, Rod Browning, Rod Colbin, Gay Rowen, Pat Van Patten. A busload of tourists have lunch at the diner, only to find out later that their bus has disappeared.

Mel Loves Marie
W: Arthur Marx & Robert Fisher. D: Marc Daniels. GS: Victoria Carroll, Ed Carroll. Mel and his girlfriend Marie have a fight after he asks her to sign a premarital agreement.

Mona Lisa Alice
W: Tom Whedon & Charles Isaacs. D: Marc Daniels. GS: Robert Hogan. Mel introduces a new smiling policy at the diner; if a waitress forgets to smile, the customer gets a free dinner.

Vera Robs the Cradle
W: Arthur Marx & Robert Fisher. D: Marc Daniels. GS: Howard Platt, Michael Ballard, Annrae Walterhouse. Tommy develops a crush on Vera after she takes him to the movies.

Flo's Chili Reception
W: Arthur Marx & Robert Fisher. D: Marc Daniels. GS: Richard B. Shull, Med Flory, Ted Gehring, Claude Stroud. Flo's new boyfriend turns out to be Mel's competition and is only using her to get Mel's chili recipe.

Cabin Fever
W: Thad Mumford & Dan Wilcox. D: Marc Daniels. GS: Victoria Carroll, Ed Kenney. The girls plan to spend the

weekend at a mountain cabin unaware that Mel and his girlfriend have the same idea.

Has Anyone Here Seen Telly?
W: Charles Isaacs, Tom Whedon, Arthur Marx & Robert Fisher. D: Marc Daniels. GS: Telly Savalas, George Savalas. Mel and the girls are surprised when Telly and George Savalas pay a visit to the diner.

Little Alice Bluenose
W: Tom Whedon & Charles Isaacs. D: Marc Daniels. GS: Spencer Milligan, Alan Haufrect, Susan Campbell, Terry Wills. Alice is shocked when she learns that her new boyfriend works as a nude model.

Mel's in the Kitchen with Dinah
W: Tom Whedon & Charles Isaacs. D: Norman Abbott. GS: Dinah Shore, Ronnie Schell, Guich Koock, Pamela Myers, Ancel Cook. Mel is invited to appear on the Dinah Shore show, so he can demonstrate how he makes his famous chili.

Alice in TV Land
W: Tom Whedon & Charles Isaacs. D: Norman Abbott. GS: Eve Arden. Alice gets upset when Tommy appears on a TV show and announces that he likes Flo better than her.

Carrie Sharples Strikes Again
W: Arthur Marx & Robert Fisher. D: Lee Lochhead. GS: Martha Raye. When Mel hurts his back, his mother takes over the restaurant and proceeds to double his business.

Carrie's Wedding
W: Mark Egan & Mark Solomon. D: Gary Shimokawa. GS: Martha Raye, Howard Witt, Phil Leeds, Vernon Weddle. Mel gets upset when he learns that his mother is planning to marry a man who is three years younger than he.

My Cousin, Art Carney
W: Charles Isaacs, Tom Whedon, Arthur Marx & Robert Fisher. D: Lee Lochhead. GS: Art Carney, Alan Oppenheimer. Vera tries to get her cousin Art Carney to endorse Mel's chili.

Good Buddy Flo
W: Linda Morris & Vic Rauseo. D: Marc Daniels. GS: Michael MacRae, Sherry Jackson. Flo tries to prove to her new boyfriend that she can drive a truck but only succeeds in wrecking the diner.

Auld Acquaintances Should Be Forgot
W: Arthur Marx & Robert Fisher. D: Marc Daniels. GS: Ed Barth, Reva Rose. Mel's old Navy friend comes for a visit after he breaks up with his wife.

Mel, the Magi
W: Mark Egan & Mark Solomon. D: Marc Daniels. GS: Jack Kruschen. Christmas at the diner is almost ruined when a man dressed as Santa Claus makes off with the presents.

Alice Beats the Clock
W: Katherine Green. D: Marc Daniels. The girls get upset when Mel installs a time clock and then begins to dock them when they come in late.

My Funny Valentine Tux
W: Charles Isaacs & Tom Whedon. D: Marc Daniels. GS: Kelly Parsons, Raleigh Bond, Wayne Storm, Terry Wills. Flo tries to find a tuxedo for Tommy to wear to a school dance.

Flo's Farewell
W: Arthur Marx & Robert Fisher. D: Marc Daniels. Flo prepares to leave her friends at the diner when she gets a new job in another city.

For Whom the Belle Toils
W: Linda Morris & Vic Rauseo. D: Marc Daniels. GS: Victoria Carroll, Hugh Gillin. Belle comes to work at the diner. Diane Ladd joins the cast as Belle.

One Too Many Girls
W: Arthur Marx & Robert Fisher. D: Marc Daniels. GS: Robert Hogan, Kenneth Gilman. Belle decides to steal Vera and Alice's boyfriends.

Vera, the Vamp
W: Linda Morris & Vic Rauseo. D: Linda Lavin & Lee Lochhead. GS: Alan Haufrect, Mickey Morton. Belle tries to turn Vera into a beautiful and seductive woman.

Profit Without Honor
W: Arthur Marx & Robert Fisher. D: Lee Lochhead. In order to pay his income tax, Mel has to decide between cutting the girls' salaries or firing one of them.

Cook's Tour
W: Linda Morris & Vic Rauseo. D: Marc Daniels. GS: Pamela Myers, Reb Brown, Howard Platt. Mel gets into trouble when he dates a beautiful girl with a very jealous muscleman brother.

Here Comes Alice Cottontail
W: Arthur Marx & Robert Fisher. D: Marc Daniels. GS: John Crawford, Hector Elias, John Hawker, Christopher Tayback. While dressed as a rabbit, Alice pays a visit to Tommy who is staying at Mel's apartment.

Mel and the Green Machine
W: Linda Morris & Vic Rauseo. D: Lee Lochhead. GS: George Wyner, John Hawkins. Mel hits the jackpot when an automated bank teller starts spitting out thousands of dollars.

Dog Day Evening
W: George Bloom. D: Marc Daniels. GS: Warren Berlinger. Mel and the girls find themselves trapped inside the diner along with several guard dogs.

Hello Vegas, Goodbye Diner [Part 1]
W: Mark Egan, Mark Solomon, Linda Morris & Vic Rauseo. D: Marc Daniels. GS: Robert Goulet, Lou Criscuolo, Michael Tucci, Nedra Volz. Mel tells the girls that he gambled away the diner.

Too Many Robert Goulets [Part 2]
W: Mark Egan, Mark Solomon, Linda Morris & Vic Rauseo. D: Marc Daniels. GS: Robert Goulet, Lou Criscuolo, Michael Tucci, Nedra Volz. Alice tries to get Robert Goulet to appear at a rundown hotel in order to help Mel get his diner back.

Vera's Aunt Agatha
W: Arthur Marx & Robert Fisher. D: Marc Daniels. GS: Mildred Natwick. Vera's eccentric aunt comes for a visit and tries to convince her niece to come with her to Mexico.

Tommy's T.K.O.
W: Linda Morris & Vic Rauseo. D: Marc Daniels. GS: Susan Tolsky, Richard Balin, Jody Arthur Balsam. Mel teaches Tommy how to fight, so he can stand up to a school bully.

The New Improved Mel
W: Mark Egan, Mark Solomon. D: Marc Daniels. GS: Shavar Ross, Mickey Morton. Mel decides to turn over a new leaf, by being nice to everyone.

Carrie Sings the Blues
W: Mark Egan, Mark Solomon. D: Linda Lavin & Christine Ballard. GS: Martha Raye, Howard Witt. Mel tries to take advantage of his mother's rocky marriage by having her bake pies for the diner.

Henry's Bitter Half
W: Mark Egan, Mark Solomon. D: Lee Lochhead. GS: Ruth Buzzi. Alice comes to the rescue when Henry believes his wife is having an affair.

Alice Locks Belle Out
W: Arthur Marx & Robert Fisher. D: Nick Havings. GS: John Sylvester White. Alice finds that she has to lock Belle out of her apartment when she is made the new manager of the apartment building.

Vera Goes Out on a Limb
W: Linda Morris & Vic Rauseo. D: Marc Daniels. GS: Walter Olkewicz. Vera chains herself to a tree in order to prevent it from being cut down.

Alice's Son the Drop-Out
W: Arthur Marx & Robert Fisher. D: Marc Daniels. Tommy takes a night job to help pay for college, but then finds he is too tired to attend school during the day.

Bye Bye Birdie
W: George Bloom. D: Marc Daniels. GS: William Bogert, Lou Cutell. Vera's new parrot is driving Mel crazy, until it suddenly drops dead, causing Mel to think he killed it.

The Jerry Reed Fish Story
W: Arthur Marx & Robert Fisher. D: Marc Daniels. GS: Jerry Reed. Mel and Jerry Reed are shocked when they learn that the girls chopped up the fish they had just caught.

Carrie Chickens Out
W: Arthur Marx & Robert Fisher. D: Marc Daniels. GS: Martha Raye, Jack Kruschen. Mel has a fight with his mother, causing her to get a job cooking for his competition.

Macho, Macho Mel
W: Mark Egan & Mark Solomon. D: Marc Daniels. GS: Andy Romano, Florence Halop. Mel tries to prove he is a man after he's mugged by a little old lady.

The Great Escape
W: Mark Egan, Mark Solomon, Linda Morris & Vic Rauseo. D: Marc Daniels. GS: Robert Carnegie. A lady truck driver gets a job at the diner. Celia Weston joins the cast as Jolene.

Alice Strikes up the Band
W: Mark Egan & Mark Solomon. D: Marc Daniels. Problems arise when Alice has to decide to go on the road as a band singer or to continue working at the diner.

Who's Kissing the Great Chef of Phoenix?
W: Arthur Marx & Robert Fisher. D: Marc Daniels. GS: Victoria Carroll. After Vera is dumped by her boyfriend and Mel is dumped by his girlfriend, Alice decides to play matchmaker and fixes them up with each other.

Baby Makes Five
W: Tom Whedon & Charles Isaacs. D: Linda Lavin & Christine Ballard. GS: James Murtaugh, Irene Arranga. Vera finds an abandoned baby in a laundromat and decides to keep it.

Vera and the Bouncing Check
W: Bob Brunner & Ken Hecht. D: Marc Daniels. GS: Kip Niven. Problems arise when Vera cashes a check for an old school friend and the check bounces.

Mel's Cousin Wendell
W: Mark Egan, Mark Solomon, Linda Morris & Vic Rauseo. D: Marc Daniels. GS: David Rounds. Mel tries to teach his shy cousin how to handle a woman and almost ruins his chances with Vera.

The Wild One
W: Linda Morris & Vic Rauseo. D: Marc Daniels. GS: Jay Leno, Ron Palillo, Susan Wolf. The leader of a motorcycle gang falls in love with Alice.

Bet a Million Mel
W: Linda Morris & Vic Rauseo. D: Nick Havings. GS: Hamilton Camp. Mel almost loses the diner when he borrows ten thousand dollars and can't pay it back.

Alice's Big Four-Oh!
W: Linda Morris & Vic Rauseo. D: Marc Daniels. GS: Doris Roberts. Alice receives a visit from her bossy mother on her 40th birthday.

Alice's Halloween Surprise
W: Linda Morris & Vic Rauseo. D:

Marc Daniels. GS: Phillip Allen, Nancy McKeon, Evan Cohen. Alice takes her boyfriend's children trick or treating but accidentally loses one of them along the way.

After Mel's Gone
W: Ken Hecht & Bob Brunner. D: Stockton Briggle. GS: Hector Elias, Jerry Potter. Fights break out after Mel reveals the contents of his will.

Comrade Mel
W: Robert Sternin & Prudence Fraser. D: Marc Daniels. GS: Robert Peirce, Allan Rich. A towel boy for a visiting Russian ballet, planning to defect, hides out at the diner.

Guinness on Tap
W: Mark Egan & Mark Solomon. D: Marc Daniels. GS: Donald O'Conner, Byron Webster, Manuel Padilla Jr. Vera tries to break the world's record for non-stop tap dancing.

Monty Falls for Alice
W: Linda Morris, Vic Rauseo, Mark Egan & Mark Solomon. D: Marc Daniels. GS: George Wendt. A busboy threatens to kill himself by jumping off the top of the diner after Alice rejects him.

Alice Calls the Shots
W: Gail Honigberg. D: Marc Daniels. Against his mother's orders, Tommy sneaks out of the house to play in a championship basketball game.

Alice and the Acorns
W: Mark Egan & Mark Solomon. D: Marc Daniels. GS: James Callahan, Marilyn Cooper. Alice tries to convince her shy high school friend to sing at a local dance.

Best Little Waitress in the World
W: Linda Morris & Vic Rauseo. D: Mel Ferber. GS: Arthur Albelson, Richard Andert, Jerry Hausner. Vera almost wrecks the diner after Mel puts her in charge.

Sharples vs. Sharples
W: Mark Egan & Mark Solomon. D: Linda Day. GS: Martha Raye, Edie McClurg, Rose Arrick, Lou Richards. Mel has his mother arrested when she announces that she is going to publish a cookbook that features his secret chili recipe.

Not with My Niece, You Don't
W: Sandy Krinski & Chet Dowling. D: John Pasquin. GS: Kim Richards, Karlene Crockett. Mel begins to worry when Tommy starts dating his visiting niece.

Mel's Christmas Carol
W: Vic Rauseo & Linda Morris. D: Marc Daniels. GS: Jack Gilford. On Christmas Eve, Mel receives a visit from the ghost of his ex-partner.

Vera, Queen of the Soaps
W: Mark Egan & Mark Solomon. D: Marc Daniels. GS: Susan Tolsky, Jerry Hausner. Vera quits her job so she can stay home and watch soap operas.

Jolene Hunnicutt, Dynamite Trucker
W: Chet Dowling & Sandy Krinski. D: Marc Daniels. GS: Robert Carnegie, James Cavan, Ted Gehring. The girls help out Jolene's ex-truckdriving partner by driving a truckload of dynamite over a dangerous canyon road.

Spell Mel's
W: Chet Dowling & Sandy Krinski. D: Marc Daniels. GS: Carl Ballantine, Douglas Robinson. Mel holds a giveaway contest in order to attract more customers.

The Valentine's Day Massacre
W: Mark Egan & Mark Solomon. D: John Pasquin. GS: Victoria Carroll, Phillip Allen. After having a fight with their dates, Mel and the girls find that they will be spending Valentine's Day all by themselves.

Mel Wins by a Nose
W: Vic Rauseo & Linda Morris. D: Marc Daniels. GS: Kenneth Mars,

Susan Tolsky. Mel decides to have a nose job.

My Mother the Landlord
W: Chet Dowling & Sandy Krinski. D: Marc Daniels. GS: Martha Raye, Tom Williams, Susan Davis, Tony Longo. Mel's mother buys the apartment building in which Mel lives. When he refuses to pay the rent increase, she evicts him.

Give My Regards to Broadway
W: Gail Honigberg. D: John Pasquin.

GS: Gail Strickland, Lisa Lindgren. Tommy decides to quit school to become a Broadway actor.

Vera's Reunion Romance
W: Mark Egan, Mark Solomon & Gail Honigberg. D: Linda Lavin & Christine Ballard. GS: Kip Niven, Jane Dulo, Cisse Cameron, Rebecca Clemmons. Vera returns home from her high school reunion engaged to be married.

ALL IN THE FAMILY

On the air 1/12/71, off: as of Sept 1979, series title was changed to "Archie Bunker's Place." CBS. 30 min. Videotape. Color. 204 episodes syndicated. Broadcast: Jan 1971-Jul 1971 Tues 9:30-10; Sept 1971-Sept 1975 Sat 8-8:30; Sept 1975-Sept 1976 Mon 9-9:30; Sept 1976-Oct 1976 Wed 9-9:30; Nov 1976-Sept 1977 Sat 9-9:30; Oct 1977-Oct 1978 Sun 9-9:30; Oct 1978-July 1983 Sun 8-8:30; Jul 1983-Sept 1983 Wed 8-8:30. Producer: Norman Lear. Prod Co: Tandem. Synd: Viacom.

CAST: Archie Bunker (played by Carroll O'Conner), Edith Bunker (Jean Stapleton), Gloria Bunker Stivic (Sally Struthers), Mike Stivic (Rob Reiner), Lionel Jefferson (Mike Evans), Louise Jefferson (Isabel Sanford), George Jefferson (Sherman Hemsley), Henry Jefferson (Mel Stewart), Irene Lorenzo (Berry Garrett), Frank Lorenzo (Vincent Gardenia), Tommy Kelsey (Brendon Dillon 1972-73, Bob Hastings 1973-77), Barney Hefner (Allan Melvin), Stephanie Mills (Danielle Brisbois), Bert Munson (Billy Halop).

The episodes airing under the title "Archie Bunker's Place" are not as yet available for syndication. In the fall of 1982, CBS spun-off Archie's daughter Gloria into her own series entitled "Gloria." Both series were cancelled and left the air in September 1983.

Archibald (Archie) Bunker, residing at 704 Houser St., Queens, NY, is a white middle class American who believes in the American way. His wife Edith is a dim-witted sensitive and honest wife; Gloria, their daughter, is an independent thinker married to Michael Stivic, an unemployed Polish college student. Typical episodes involve Archie and Mike arguing over a socially relevant topic with Archie taking the conservative "normal" viewpoint, and Mike the "Pinko" radical view. Over the years Archie Bunker has become an American institution, a character who has softened and grown with us. He has survived long after his wife's death, and Mike and Gloria's departure, because he represents an idealism, a depth never seen before in any television series, comedy or drama. "All in the Family" changed the face of comedy forever; for good or bad remains to be seen.

Meet the Bunkers [Pilot]
W: Norman Lear. D: John Rich. Gloria and Mike try to hold a party for Archie and Edith's wedding anniversary.

Writing the President
W: Norman Lear, Paul Harrison & Lennie Weinrib. D: John Rich. GS: Helen Page Camp. Archie writes a letter to President Nixon after learning that Mike wrote him a letter.

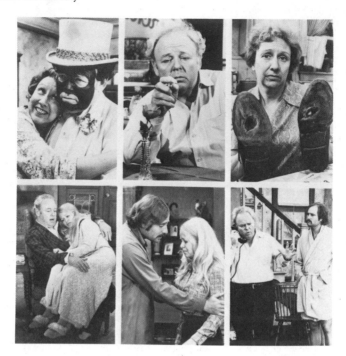

All in the Family: top, Jean Stapleton and Carroll O'Conner; bottom, O'Conner and Sally Struthers and Rob Reiner.

Oh, My Aching Back
W: Stanley Ralph Ross. D: John Rich. GS: George Furth, Salem Ludwig, Richard Stahl. Archie hires a Jewish lawyer to sue for whiplash when he gets into a traffic accident.

Archie Gives Blood
W: Norman Lear. D: John Rich. GS: Jeanie Linero. Archie wants to know who his blood will be going to before he will donate his blood.

Judging Books by Covers
W: Burt Styler. D: John Rich. GS: Phillip Carey. Archie makes fun of Mike's friend, Roger, for being gay, unaware that one of his own friends is also gay.

Gloria's Pregnancy
W: Jerry Mayer. D: John Rich. GS: Holly Near, John Silo. Gloria is pregnant, but she later loses the baby.

Mike's Hippie Friends Come to Visit
W: Phillip Mishkin, Rob Reiner, Bryan Joseph & Don Nicholl. D: John Rich. GS: Jack Bender, Corey Fischer, Jenny Sullivan. Mike's hippie friend and his girl come to spend the night, until Archie learns that they aren't married.

Lionel Moves into the Neighborhood
W: Don Nicholl & Bryan Joseph. D: John Rich. GS: Vincent Gardenia. Archie tries to prevent a black family from moving into the neighborhood, unaware that the family happens to be Lionel's, a friend of the family.

Edith Has Jury Duty
W: Susan Harris, Don Nicholl & Bryan Joseph. D: John Rich. GS: Holly Irving, Doris Singleton. Edith has the whole jury against her when she is the only one who is voting not guilty.

Archie Is Worried About His Job
W: Norman Lear, Don Nicholl & Bryan Joseph. D: John Rich. GS: Holly Irving, Raymond Kark, Burt Austin, Jack Perkins. Archie keeps the whole family up when he begins to worry about losing his job.

Gloria Discovers Woman's Lib
W: Norman Lear. D: John Rich. Gloria moves out of the house when she has a fight with Mike over being treated as an equal.

Success Story
W: Burt Styler, Bryan Joseph & Don Nicholl. D: John Rich. GS: Len Lesser, Herbie Faye, George Savalas, Frank Ford, William Windom. Archie gathers his old army buddies together to welcome their rich friend from California.

The First and Last Supper
W: Jerry Mayer. D: John Rich. GS: Mel Stewart, Billy Benedict. Edith accepts an invitation to dinner at the Jefferson's and Archie is trying to find a way to keep more black families from moving into the neighborhood.

The Sage of Cousin Oscar
W: Burt Styler. D: John Rich. GS: Jack Grimes, Will B. Able, Peggy Rea, Connie Sawyer, Billy Benedict. When deadbeat cousin Oscar dies in Archie's home, Archie finds it is impossible to get any of the relatives to chip in for his funeral.

Gloria Poses in the Nude
W: Norman Lear, Bernie West & Michael Ross. D: John Rich. GS: David Soul. Mike's artist friend asks Gloria to pose for him in the nude.

Archie and the Lock-Up
W: Bernie West, Paul Wayne & Michael Ross. D: John Rich. GS: Allan Melvin, Ken Lynch, Kelly Houser, Corey Fischer. Archie gets arrested while trying to find Mike and Lionel at a student protest.

Edith Writes a Song
W: Lee Kalcheim. D: John Rich. GS:

Cleavon Little, Demond Wilson. Two black burglars break into the Bunker home and keep the Bunkers hostage until the police go away.

Flashback: Mike Meets Archie
W: Phillip Mishkin & Rob Reiner. D: John Rich. While celebrating Mike and Gloria's first anniversary, flashbacks show how and when Archie first met his future son-in-law.

The Election Story
W: Michael Ross & Bernie West. D: John Rich. GS: Barbara Cason. Archie and Mike have a fight over whom to vote for in a local election.

Edith's Accident
W: Michael Ross, Bernie West & Tom and Helen August. D: John Rich. GS: Barnard Hughes. Archie gets mad when Edith leaves a note on an unoccupied car, after she dents it with a can of cling peaches.

The Blockbuster
W: Austin & Irma Kalish, Lee Katcheim, Michael Ross & Bernie West. D: John Rich. GS: Peggy Rea, Jack Crowder. Archie is offered a lot of money to sell his house to a black real estate agent.

Mike's Problem
W: Phillip Mishkin & Alan J. Leavitt. D: John Rich. GS: Brendon Dillon, Mel Stewart. Mike is worried about his upcoming exams, and the pressure is causing him to be impotent.

The Insurance Is Cancelled
W: Bernie West, Lee Katcheim & Michael Ross. D: John Rich. GS: Phillip Proctor, Rafael Campos. Archie has to lay off one of his men and his home insurance has been cancelled.

The Man in the Street
W: Don Nicholl, Len Weinrib & Paul Harrison. D: John Rich. GS: Jack Griffen, Neil J. Schwartz. Archie is interviewed for a man-in-the-street interview, but he can't find a working TV set to watch himself on.

Cousin Maude's Visit
W: Phillip Mishkin, Michael Ross &
Bernie West. D: John Rich. GS: Beatrice Arthur.   Edith's cousin Maude
comes to help out when the entire
family gets the flu.

Christmas Day at the Bunkers
W: Don Nicholl. D: John Rich. GS:
Peggy Doyle, Noam Pitlik, Mel Stewart.
Archie gets depressed when he doesn't
get his Christmas bonus.

The Elevator Story
W: Alan J. Levitt. D: John Rich. GS:
Roscoe Lee Browne, Eileen Brennan,
Hector Elizondo, Edith Diaz. Archie
is trapped in an elevator with a nutty
secretary, a rich black man, and a
Puerto Rican man and his pregnant
wife who is about to give birth.

Edith's Problem
W: Burt Styler & Don Nicholl. D:
John Rich. GS: Jeanie Linero. Edith
is going through menopause and is
driving everyone crazy.

Archie and the FBI
W: Bernie West, Michael Ross & Susan
Harris. D: John Rich. GS: Graham
Jarvis, John Korkes. Archie fears the
worst when a government inspector
investigates his friend and then him.

Mike's Mysterious Son
W: Warren Murray. D: John Rich. GS:
Marcia Rodd, Stephen Manley. One of
Mike's former girlfriends leaves her son
at Archie's door, stating that Mike is
the boy's father.

Archie Sees a Mugging
W: Don Nicholl & Phillip Mishkin. D:
John Rich. GS: Jack Somack, Val Bisoglio, Frank Campanella.   Archie
makes a story about gangsters when he
refuses to be a witness to a mugging.

Archie and Edith Alone
W: Bernie West, Lee Katcheim & Michael Ross. D: John Rich. GS: Connie Sawyer.   While Mike and Gloria
are away, Archie and Edith have the

whole house to themselves, until a
fight breaks out and Archie leaves.

Edith Gets a Mink
W: Ellias Davis, Don Nicholl & Dave
Pollack. D: John Rich. GS: Richard
Dysart, Rae Allen. Archie wants Edith
to return the mink cape her wealthy
cousin gave her.

Sammy's Visit
W: Bill Dana. D: John Rich. GS:
Sammy Davis, Jr., Billy Halop, Fay De
Witt, Keri Shutleton.   Sammy Davis
comes to the Bunker house to retrieve
his briefcase he left in Archie's cab.

Edith, the Judge
W: Lee Katcheim. D: John Rich. GS:
Jack Weston. Edith acts as a judge between Archie and the owner of the
laundromat, where Archie broke one
of the machines.

Archie Is Jealous
W: Rod Parker. D: John Rich. GS:
Brendan Dillon. Archie becomes jeal-
ous when he learns a secret about
Edith and her old boyfriend.

Maude
W: Rod Parker. D: John Rich. GS:
Beatrice Arthur, Marcia Rodd, Bill
Macy, Bob Dishy, Bernie West. Archie
and Edith visit Maude in upstate New
York, on the occasion of her daughter
Carol's wedding. [This was the pilot
for the spinoff series "Maude."]

Archie and the Editorial
W: Don Nicholl. D: Norman Campbell.
GS: Sorrell Booke, Val Bisoglio, Brendan Dillon, Diane Sommerfield, Lyn-
nette Mettey. Archie appears in a television editorial against gun control.
Later he is held up by a robber.

Archie's Fraud
W: Bernie West. D: Michael Ross. GS:
Billy Halop, James McEachin. Archie
tries to bribe an official of the IRS
when he fails to report the money he
took in while driving Munson's cab.

The Threat
W: Michael Elias & Lila Garrett. D:
John Rich. GS: Gloria LeRoy. The
wife of the man who saved Archie's
life during the war pays a visit, making
Edith jealous when she sees just what
she looks like.

Gloria and the Riddle
W: Don Nicholl. D: Bob Livingstone.
GS: Patricia Stich, Brendan Dillon,
Billy Sands. When Edith answers a riddle and Mike can't, he realizes that he
has been narrow minded about the
roles that women play in society.

Lionel Steps Out
W: Michael Ross & Bernie West. D:
Michael Kidd. GS: Diane Hull, Mel
Stewart. Archie tells Lionel to date
his own kind, stay away from his niece.

The Bunkers and the Swingers
W: Lee Katcheim. D: Bob LaHendro.
GS: Vincent Gardenia, Rue McClanahan. Edith answers an ad and unknowingly invites a couple of wife-swapping
swingers to dinner.

Mike's Appendix
W: Michael Ross & Bernie West. D:
Bob LaHendro. GS: John Zaremba,
Ann Summers. When Mike requires an
appendix operation, Archie and Gloria
fight over the use of a female doctor.

Edith Flips Her Wig
W: Sam Locke, Olga Vallance & Don
Nicholl. D: Hal Cooper. GS: Bernard
Hughes, James Gregory. Edith is ar-
rested for shoplifting.

Mike Comes into Money
W: Michael Ross & Bernie West. D:
John Rich & Bob LaHendro. Mike inherits some money, of which he donates $200 to the McGovern campaign
instead of giving it to Archie to pay
for his expenses while in his house.

*Flashback: Mike and Gloria's Wedding
[Part 1]*
W: Rob Reiner & Phillip Mishkin. D:

John Rich & Bob LaHendro. GS: Michael Conrad. Flashbacks show how
Archie and Mike's Uncle Casmir
fought over the plans for the wedding.

*Flashback: Mike and Gloria's Wedding
[Part 2]*
W: Rob Reiner & Phillip Mishkin. D:
John Rich & Bob LaHendro. GS: Mi-
chael Conrad. A new fight breaks out
on who will perform the ceremony.

The Locket
W: Robert Fisher & Arthur Marx. D:
Hal Cooper. GS: Liam Dunn, John
Randolph, Louis Guss, Mario Rocuzzo.
Archie plans to claim that Edith's lost
locket was stolen so he can use the in-
surance money to buy a new color tv.

Edith's Winning Ticket
W: Don Nicholl. D: John Rich & Bob
LaHendro. GS: Mel Stewart. When
Edith finds a winning lottery ticket in
her purse, Archie is thrilled, until she
tells him that the ticket belongs to
Louise Jefferson.

Archie and the Bowling Team
W: Don Nicholl. D: Bob LaHendro.
GS: Brad Logan. Archie learns that
his competition for a spot on a bowling team happens to be black.

Archie Goes to the Hospital
W: Bernie West. D: Bob LaHendro.
GS: Roscoe Lee Browne, Priscilla Morrill, John Heffernan. Archie goes to
the hospital when he suffers a very
painful backache. He is unaware that
his roommate is black.

Archie Is Branded
W: Vincent Bogart. D: Bob LaHendro.
GS: Gregory Sierra, Billy Halop, Michael Gregory, John Putch, Patrick
Campbell. Archie's door is painted
with a swastika when his house is mistaken for that of a Jewish radical.

Oh Say Can You See
W: Michael Ross & Bernie West. D:
Bob LaHendro & John Rich. GS:

Larry Storch, Arlene Golonka. Archie's old friend teaches him how to look and act young.

Archie Goes Too Far
W: Irma & Austin Kalish. D: Bob LaHendro & John Rich. GS: Pamela Murphy, Mary Kay Place, Patty Weaver. Archie searches Mike and Gloria's room, causing a fight.

Class Reunion
W: Don Nicholl. D: John Rich & Bob LaHendro. GS: Harvey Lembeck, Rae Allen, Bernie Hamilton, Priscilla Morrill. Archie takes Edith to her high school reunion to meet her old boyfriend.

Hot Watch
W: Bernie West & Michael Ross. D: Bob LaHendro & John Rich. Archie is worried that the $300 watch he bought for $25 could be stolen property.

Everybody Tells the Truth
W: Don Nicholl. D: John Rich & Bob LaHendro. GS: Ron Glass, Ken Lynch, Maurice Marsac. Three different stories about what happened when the repairman and his assistant came to fix the refrigerator.

Archie Learns His Lesson
W: Michael Ross & Bernie West. D: Bob LaHendro & John Rich. Mike and Gloria are suspicious when Archie sneaks off every night without telling anyone where he is going.

Gloria, the Victim
W: Austin & Irma Kalish & Don Nicholl. D: John Rich & Bob LaHendro. GS: Mel Stewart, Charles Durning. Gloria can't decide whether or not to report the rape attempt on her for fear of the embarrassment.

The Battle of the Month
W: Bernie West & Michael Ross. D: Bob LaHendro & John Rich. Gloria takes offense at the way Archie has been treating Edith.

We're Having a Heat Wave
W: Don Nicholl. D: Bob LaHendro. GS: Mel Stewart, Victor Argo. Archie and Henry Jefferson try to keep other ethnic groups from moving into the house next door to them.

We're Still Having a Heat Wave
W: Michael Ross & Bernie West. D: Bob LaHendro. The Lorenzos move into the house next door.

Edith Finds an Old Man
W: Michael Ross & Bernie West. D: Bob LaHendro. GS: Burt Mustin, Ruth McDevitt. Edith finds a runaway old man and brings him home with her.

Archie and the Kiss
W: John Rappaport. D: Bob LaHendro. A kiss starts a fight between Archie and Gloria.

Archie the Gambler
W: Michael Ross & Bernie West. D: Bob LaHendro. Archie tries to hide the fact that he has been gambling on the horses.

Archie and the Computer
W: Michael Ross & Bernie West. D: Bob LaHendro. GS: Jack Grimes. A computer declares that Archie is dead and Edith receives dozens of quarters from a prune company giveaway.

Henry's Farewell
W: Don Nicholl. D: Bob LaHendro. GS: Mel Stewart. Henry Jefferson is moving away.

The Games Bunkers Play
W: Michael Ross & Bernie West. D: Bob LaHendro. The Bunkers and the Lorenzos play an adult board game.

Edith's Conversion
W: Ray Taylor & Don Nicholl. D: Bob LaHendro. GS: Barnard Hughes, Phyllis Avery. Archie thinks Irene is trying to get Edith to convert to Catholicism.

Archie in the Cellar
W: Don Nicholl. D: Bob LaHendro. GS: Juan DeCarlos. When everyone is away for the weekend, Archie accidentally locks himself in the cellar and can't get out.

Black Is the Color of My True Love's Wig
W: Michael Ross & Bernie West. D: Bob LaHendro. Mike becomes romantic when Gloria wears a black wig.

Second Honeymoon
W: Don Nicholl. D: Bob LaHendro. Archie and Edith go on a second honeymoon to Atlantic City, to celebrate their 25th anniversary.

The Taxi Caper
W: Dennis Klein. D: Bob LaHendro. GS: Michael Pataki, Al Stellone, Robert Mandan. Archie is held up while driving Munson's cab.

Archie Is Cursed
W: John Rappaport, Michael Ross & Bernie West. D: Bob LaHendro. Irene challenges Archie to a game of pool at Kelsey's.

Edith's Christmas Story
W: Austin & Irma Kalish & Don Nicholl. D: John Rich. During the Christmas holiday, Edith tells Gloria that she might have breast cancer.

Mike and Gloria Mix It Up
W: Don Nicholl. D: Bob LaHendro. Mike and Gloria fight over the fact that Gloria seems to be the aggressor in their relationship and Mike resents it.

Archie Feels Left Out
W: Paul Lichtman, Howard Storm & Don Nicholl. D: Bob LaHendro. GS: Burt Mustin, Ruth McDevitt. Archie gets a surprise during his surprise birthday party when he sees his birth certificate.

Et Tu, Archie
W: Bernie West & Michael Ross. D: Bob LaHendro. GS: Vic Tayback. Archie is happy to see his old friend Joe Tucker, until he tells Archie that he is out of a job and that he is taking over Archie's old job.

Gloria's Boyfriend
W: Don Nicholl. D: John Rich. GS: Richard Masur, Joseph Mascolo. Archie causes a retarded boy to lose his job at the grocery store.

Lionel's Engagement
W: Michael Ross & Bernie West. D: John Rich. GS: Charles Aidman, Lynn Moody, Kim Hamilton, Samuel Olden, Jess Bolero, Eddie Carroll, Zara Cully. Archie and Edith go to Lionel's engagement party where Archie starts a fight with George Jefferson's mother.

Archie Eats and Runs
W: Michael Ross & Bernie West. D: John Rich. Archie thinks he may have eaten poisonous mushrooms.

Gloria Sings the Blues
W: Don Nicholl. D: John Rich. Gloria's depression is upsetting the whole family.

Pay the Twenty Dollars
W: Bernie West & Micharl Ross. D: John Rich. Archie unknowingly pays George Jefferson with a phony twenty dollar bill.

Mike's Graduation
W: Don Nicholl. D: John Rich. Archie is happy when Mike's graduation comes. It means he can finally get him out of the house and turn his room into a den.

The Bunkers and Inflation [Part 1]
W: Don Nicholl, Michael Ross & Bernie West. D: H. Wesley Kenney. GS: Billy Halop. Archie's union goes on strike.

The Bunkers and Inflation [Part 2]
W: Don Nicholl, Michael Ross, Bernie West. D: H. Wesley Kenney. Archie's union is still on strike, leaving him

with very little money in the bank and very little food in the refrigerator.

The Bunkers and Inflation [Part 3]
W: Don Nicholl, Michael Ross & Bernie West. D: H. Wesley Kenney. It is three weeks since Archie's last paycheck and the family is suffering.

The Bunkers and Inflation [Part 4]
W: Don Nicholl, Michael Ross & Bernie West. D: H. Wesley Kenney. GS: James Cromwell. Edith goes to work for George Jefferson until Archie goes back to work.

Lionel, the Live-In
W: Woody King. D: H. Wesley Kenney. Lionel moves into the Bunker house after he has a fight with his parents.

Archie's Helping Hand
W: Michael Ross & Bernie West. D: H. Wesley Kenney. Archie tries to get Irene a job at the plant. He is shocked to learn he will now be operating a forklift on his loading platform.

Gloria's Shock
W: Dixie Brown Grossman. D: H. Wesley Kenney. Gloria is shocked when Mike tells her of his plans for their future.

Where's Archie [Part 1]
W: Barry Harman & Harve Brosten. D: H. Wesley Kenney. GS: Hector Elias, Charlotte Rae. Archie is overdue at a lodge convention in Buffalo and Edith prepares to give a Tupperware party.

Archie Is Missing [Part 2]
W: Lloyd Turner & Gordon Mitchell. D: H. Wesley Kenney. GS: James Cromwell, Allan Lurie. Archie has been missing for 24 hours and the family is worried.

The Longest Kiss [Part 3]
W: Lloyd Turner & Gordon Mitchell. D: H. Wesley Kenney. Gloria challenges Mike to hold a kiss until Archie comes home from the airport.

Archie and the Miracle
W: Lloyd Turner & Gordon Mitchell. D: H. Wesley Kenney. GS: James Cromwell. Archie becomes religious when he nearly escapes a fatal accident.

George and Archie Make a Deal
W: David P. Harmon. D: H. Wesley Kenney. George has to be nice to Archie when he finds that he needs his help to run for a political office.

Archie's Contract
W: Ron Friedman. D: H. Wesley Kenney. GS: Dennis Patrick, Mike Wagner, Ed Peck. Archie is conned into buying expensive aluminum siding by a con man.

Mike's Friend
W: Roger Shulman & John Baskin. D: H. Wesley Kenney. GS: Greg Mullavey. Mike makes Gloria feel dumb when he ignores her in favor of his intellectual friend.

The Best of All in the Family [One Hour]
W: Bernie West & Michael Ross. D: H. Wesley Kenney. Henry Fonda shows clips from the past 100 episodes of the series.

Prisoner in the House
W: Bud Wiser, Lou Derman & Bill Davenport. D: H. Wesley Kenney. GS: Cliff Osmond, Sid Clute. Archie becomes afraid when he learns that the plumber working in the house is a convict on a work furlough from prison.

The Jeffersons Move Up
W: Lloyd Turner & Gordon Mitchell. D: H. Wesley Kenney. The Jeffersons move to an apartment in the East Side of Manhattan. [This is the pilot for the spinoff series, "The Jeffersons."]

All's Fair
W: Lloyd Turner & Gordon Mitchell. D: H. Wesley Kenney. Mike and Gloria teach Edith a new way married people can fight fairly.

Amelia's Divorce
W: Lou Derman & Bill Davenport. D:
H. Wesley Kenney. GS: George S. Irv-
ing, Elizabeth Wilson. Edith's cousin
Amelia and her husband visit the
Bunkers.

Everybody Does It
W: Lou Derman & Bill Davenport. D:
H. Wesley Kenney. Archie steals some
nails from the plant.

Archie and the Quiz
W: Michael Morris. D: H. Wesley Kenney. Archie becomes upset when a
magazine's life expectancy test tells
him he will die when he is 57.

Edith's Friend
W: Barry Harmon & Harve Brosten.
D: H. Wesley Kenney. GS: Tim O'Conner, Jane Rose, Ruth Manning. Edith
meets her childhood sweetheart while
attending a wedding in her home town
of Scranton.

No Smoking
W: Lou Derman & Bill Davenport. D:
H. Wesley Kenney. Mike bets Archie
that he can stop eating for 48 hours;
in return, he must try to stop smoking
for 48 hours.

Mike Makes His Move
W: Lou Derman & Bill Davenport. D:
H. Wesley Kenney. GS: Burt Mustin,
Ruth McDevitt, Sherman Hemsley.
Mike finishes school and gets a job and
claims that he will be moved out of
the house by Friday, when he buys the
Jefferson's old house.

The Very Moving Day
W: Hal Kanter. D: Paul Bogart. On
the day that they are moving into their
new house, Gloria announces that she
is pregnant.

Alone at Last
W: Hal Kanter. D: Paul Bogart. Mike
decides to finally let Archie have it,
but realizes he shouldn't have when he
finds that his house is not ready to be
lived in and has to move back with
Archie.

Archie, the Donor
W: Bill Davenport & Larry Rhine. D:
Paul Bogart. GS: J.A. Preston, Don
Randolph, Sorrell Booke. Archie unknowingly becomes an organ donor
when he tries to get on the good side
of his boss, in the hopes of getting a
dispatcher's job.

Archie, the Hero
W: Lou Derman, Bill Davenport &
Larry Rhine. D: Paul Bogart. GS:
Lori Shannon, Sandy Kenyon, Billy
Halop. Archie thinks that he saved a
woman's life when she passed out in
the back of his cab. Actually the wo-
man was a female impersonator.

Mike's Pains
W: Lou Derman & Milt Josefsberg. D:
Paul Bogart. GS: Francine Beers.
Mike is worried what he should be
doing during the birth of his baby.

Chain Letter
W: Lou Derman & Milt Josefsberg. D:
Paul Bogart. GS: Beatrice Colen, Billy
Halop. Robert Guillaume. When
Archie destroys a chain letter, he finds
that accidents begin to happen.

Mike Faces Life
W: Mel Tolkin & Larry Rhine. D: Paul
Bogart. GS: George Furth, Diane
Shalet. Gloria loses her job because
she is pregnant, causing her to fight
back.

Edith Breaks Out
W: Lou Derman & Bill Davenport. D:
Paul Bogart. GS: James Hong. Edith
fights back when Archie orders her to
quit her job at the Sunshine Home for
Senior Citizens.

Grandpa Blues
W: Mel Tolkin & Larry Rhine. D: Paul
Bogart. GS: Sorrell Booke, John Zol-
ler, Greg Mabrey, Tracey Bogart.
Archie is ordered to stay completely
calm in order to keep his blood pressure down for his company physical.

Gloria Suspects Mike
W: Lou Derman & Milt Josefsberg. D:

Paul Bogart. GS: Bernadette Peters.
Gloria thinks Mike is fooling around
when he gives private tutoring lessons
to a beautiful blonde.

The Little Atheist
W: Lou Derman. D: Paul Bogart. During Thanksgiving dinner, Archie and
Mike discuss the religion of his future
child.

Archie's Civil Rights
W: Larry Rhine & Mel Tolkin. D: Paul
Bogart. GS: Frank Campanella, John
Alvin, Charles Siebert, Paulene Myers.
Archie goes on trial instead of the
mugger when it is learned that he was
carrying an illegal weapon when he
was attacked.

Gloria Is Nervous
W: Milt Josefsberg & Ben Starr. D:
Paul Bogart. GS: Robin Wilson, Garn
Stephens, Suzanne Astor, Madeleine
Fisher.   Gloria is nine days overdue
and is worried, so she takes her frus-
trations out on Mike.

Birth of the Baby [Part 1]
W: Larry Rhine & Mel Tolkin. D:
Paul Bogart. GS: Herb Voland, Victor
Rendins. Gloria gets stuck in a phone
booth in an Italian restaurant when
she discovers that she is about to give
birth, while Archie prepares to appear
in a minstrel show for his lodge.

Birth of the Baby [Part 2]
W: Milt Josefsberg & Ben Starr. D:
Paul Bogart. GS: Gene Blakely, John
O'Connell, Barbara Cason, Priscilla
Morrill, Sudie Bond, Sharon Ullrick.
Gloria and Mike race to the hospital,
while Archie, still wearing his black-
face makeup, appears at the hospital
to cause havoc.

New Year's Wedding
W: Lou Derman, Bill Davenport, Milt
Josefsberg & Ben Starr. D: Paul Bo-
gart.   GS: Billy Crystal, Elliot Reid,
Joan Copeland, Elaine Princi, Michael
Mann, Joe Bratcher, Nancy Stephens.
Mike makes decisions without consult-

ing with Gloria and changes ones they
made together, causing a fight.

Archie, the Babysitter
W: Lou Derman & Bill Davenport. D:
Paul Bogart. GS: Jack Somack, Joe
Mantell, Ken Menard, Leslie Acker-
man, Thad Geer.   Archie fires the
babysitter and decides to take care of
Joey, while playing poker with his
friends.

Archie Finds a Friend
W: Mel Tolkin & Larry Rhine. D: Paul
Bogart. GS: Jack Gilford. Archie befriends a Jewish watchmaker who has
an invention Archie feels will make
them both rich.

Mike's Move
W: Milt Josefsberg & Ben Starr. D:
Paul Bogart. GS: Lee Bergere, David
Downing. Mike and a black man are
up for a promotion, and Mike feels he
will lose out because he is white.

Archie's Weighty Problem
W: Mel Tolkin & Larry Rhine. D: Paul
Bogart. GS: Burt Mustin, Billy Halop.
Archie is ordered to go on a diet and
the rest of the family join him.

Love by Appointment
W: Lou Derman & Bill Davenport. D:
Paul Bogart. Mike is feeling neglected
by Gloria who is giving all of her time
to the baby.

Joey's Baptism
W: Milt Josefsberg, Mel Tolkin, Larry
Rhine. D: Paul Bogart. GS: Clyde
Kusatsu. Archie will do anything to
get Joey baptized, despite Mike and
Gloria's refusal.

Mike and Gloria's House Guests
W: Larry Rhine, Mel Tolkin, Milt Josefsberg. D: Paul Bogart. The Bunkers are forced to move in with Mike
and Gloria when their furnace breaks
down.

Edith's Night Out
W: Lou Derman, Douglas Arango &

Phil Doran. D: Paul Bogart. GS: Eleanor Urcan, Scott Brady, Doris Roberts, Ernie Brown. Edith decides she has had enough, so she goes down to Kelsey's to have some fun without Archie.

Archie's Brief Encounter [Part 1]
W: Larry Rhine & Mel Tolkin. D: Paul Bogart. GS: Janis Paige, Scott Brady, Theodore Wilson, Andre Pavon. When Edith goes to the Sunshine Home, Archie, feeling lonely, visits an attractive waitress who makes him feel wanted.

Archie's Brief Encounter [Part 2]
W: Larry Rhine & Mel Tolkin. D: Paul Bogart. GS: Janis Paige, Scott Brady. Edith finds out about Archie and the waitress.

Archie's Brief Encounter [Part 3]
W: Larry Rhine & Mel Tolkin. D: Paul Bogart. GS: Scott Brady, Maxine Elliot, Bella Chronis, Harry Davis. Archie and Edith both try to prove that they are happy without each other, while Mike and Gloria try to get them back together.

The Unemployment Story [Part 1]
W: Ben Starr. D: Paul Bogart. GS: Jinaki, F. Murray Abraham, Raul Mandcada. Archie has been laid off. He now must go to the unemployment office for work.

The Unemployment Story [Part 2]
W: Charles Stewart & Ben Starr. D: Paul Bogart. GS: Gerald Hiken, Neva Patterson, Eliza Garrett, Ellen Travolta, Michael Alldredge, Jeanie Linero. Archie saves a man from jumping off a ledge, while he is on a job interview.

Archie's Operation [Part 1]
W. Milt Josefsberg & Mort Lachman. D: Paul Bogart. GS: Vinnette Carroll, Liz Torres, Milton Selzer. Archie goes in for an operation but he is not prepared for his doctor: a black woman from the Caribbean Islands.

Archie's Operation [Part 2]
W: Mel Tolkin & Larry Rhine. D: Paul Bogart. GS: Vinnette Carroll, Frances Fong. Archie complains when he sees the hospital bill.

Beverly Rides Again
W: Phil Doran & Douglas Arango. D: Paul Bogart. GS: Lori Shannon, Eugene Roche, Phoebe Dorin, Andre Pavon. Archie plans to get even with his practical joker friend by fixing him up with a female impersonator.

Teresa Moves In
W: Michael Loman. D: Paul Bogart. GS: Liz Torres, Alex Colon. Archie rants out Gloria's old room to the nurse who drove him crazy when he was in the hospital.

Mike and Gloria's Will
W: Bill Richmond & Gene Perret. D: Paul Bogart. During Joey's first birthday party, Mike announces that in the event of their death Joey will be raised by their friends, causing Archie and Edith to storm out of the house.

Mr. Edith Bunker
W: Mel Tolkin & Larry Rhine. D: Paul Bogart. GS: Priscilla Morrill, Phil Leeds, Florence Halop, James Greene, Maxine Elliot, Bella Chronis, Bob Duggan. Edith saves a man's life and receives an award on TV, causing Archie to feel left out.

Archie's Secret Passion
W: Michael Loman. D: Paul Bogart. GS: Estelle Parsons, Mike Kellin. Edith invites an old school friend to dinner, causing Archie to be afraid that she will tell Edith about their relationship in the past.

The Baby Contest
W: Larry Rhine & Mel Tolkin. D: Paul Bogart. Archie enters Joey in a beautiful baby contest against Mike and Gloria's wishes.

Gloria's False Alarm
W: Phil Doran & Douglas Arango. D:

Paul Bogart.   GS: Michael Mann, Jeanne Arnole.   When Gloria announces that she might be pregnant again, Mike has a vasectomy to make sure that it doesn't happen again.

The Draft Dodger
W: Jay Moriarty & Mike Milligan. D: Paul Bogart. GS: Eugene Roche, Renny Temple.   Archie gets upset when Mike invites his draft-dodging friend to Christmas dinner at the same time Archie invited his friend, whose son was killed in the war.

The Boarder Patrol
W: Mel Tolkin & Larry Rhine. D: Paul Bogart.   GS: Patrick Cronin.   When Archie and Edith return from their trip early, they find that Teresa has her boyfriend in her room.

Archie's Chair
W: Mel Tolkin & Larry Rhine. D: Paul Bogart. GS: Michael Pataki.   Archie's chair is accidentally given away to an artist by the department store which was repairing it.

Mike Goes Skiing
W: Ben Starr & Charles Stewart. D: Paul Bogart. GS: John Karlen, Rod Loomis, Tom Fitzsimmons, Mark Lenow. Mike gets out of taking Gloria to a party so he can go skiing with his friends.

Stretch Cunningham, Goodbye
W: Phil Doran, Douglas Arango & Milt Josefsberg.   D: Paul Bogart.   GS: Charles Siebert, Jay Gerber. Archie is asked to perform the eulogy at Stretch Cunningham's funeral, unaware that his friend was Jewish.

The Joys of Sex
W: Eric Tarloff. D: Paul Bogart. Gloria asks Mike to give Archie a lesson on the facts of life.

Mike the Pacifist
W: Phil Doran & Douglas Arango. D: Paul Bogart. GS: Wynn Irwin, Nita Talbot, Sudie Bond, Richard Lawson,

William Lanteau. Mike hits a drunken man who attacked Gloria while she was trying to prevent him from hitting his wife.

Fire
W: Michael Loman, Larry Rhine & Mel Tolkin. D: Paul Bogart. GS: Roger C. Carmel.   When the Bunker home is hit by a fire, Archie tries to make the damage worse so he can collect more money on his insurance.

Mike and Gloria Split
W: Mel Tolkin, Larry Rhine, Mort Lachman & Milt Josefsberg. D: Paul Bogart.   A fight breaks out between Mike and Gloria and they split up.

Archie, the Liberal
W: Ben Starr & Charles Stewart. D: Paul Bogart.   GS: James McEachin. Archie tries to liberalize his lodge by adding a Jewish black man to its membership list.

Archie's Dog Day Afternoon
W: Charles Stewart, Ben Starr, Mort Lachman & Milt Josefsberg. D: Paul Bogart.   GS: Bill Hunt, Vanda Barra, Tracey Bogart.   Archie runs over Barney's dog and has to take him to the vet before Barney finds out.

Archie Gets the Business [One Hour]
W: Mel Tolkin & Larry Price. D: Paul Bogart.   GS: Frank Maxwell, Norma Donaldson, Sid Conrad.   Archie forges Edith's signature on an application to mortgage the house so he can buy Kelsey's bar.

Archie's Grand Opening
W: Larry Rhine & Mel Tolkin. D: Paul Bogart.   GS: Sorrell Booke, Joe Petrullo, Paul Larson, Sam Solito, Grace Lee.   Archie's grand opening is in trouble when he has problems with his staff.

Edith's Fiftieth Birthday [One Hour]
W: Bob Weiskopf & Bob Schiller. D: Paul Bogart.   GS: David Dukes, Jane Connell, John Brandon, Ray Colella.

On the night of her surprise birthday party, Edith is attacked by a rapist.

Cousin Liz
W: Bob Weiskopf & Bob Schiller. D: Paul Bogart. GS: K Callan. Archie and Edith attend Cousin Liz's funeral; afterwards they learn she was a lesbian.

Unequal Partners
W: Charles Stewart & Ben Starr. D: Paul Bogart. GS: Ian Wolfe, Merie Earle, Will Mackenzie. Archie's plans for a fishing trip are upset when Edith volunteers to hold the wedding for two of the old people from the Sunshine Home in their house.

Archie's Bitter Pill [Part 1]
W: Mel Tolkin, Larry Rhine & William C. Radar, M.D. D: Paul Bogart. GS: Arny Freeman, A Martinez, Robert Costanzo. Archie is having troubles getting money to pay for his expenses running the bar.

Archie's Bitter Pill [Part 2]
W: Mel Tolkin, Larry Rhine & William C. Radar, M.D. D: Paul Bogart. Archie refuses to ask Harry to become his partner, in order to save the bar from closing, until Edith lends a hand.

Archie and the Ku Klun [Part 1]
W: Bob Weiskopf, Bob Schiller, Mort Lachman & Milt Josefsberg. D: Paul Bogart. GS: Dennis Patrick, Roger Bowen, Owen Bush. Archie considers joining a secret vigilante society, unaware that Mike is their next target.

Archie and the Ku Klun [Part 2]
W: Bob Weiskopf & Bob Schiller. D: Paul Bogart. GS: Dennis Patrick, Roger Bowen. Archie risks his life when he learns that Mike and Gloria's house is the next target for a cross burning by the Kweens Kouncil of Krusaders.

Mike and Gloria Meet
W: Bob Weiskopf & Bob Schiller. D: Paul Bogart. GS: Christopher Guest, Priscilla Lopez. Mike and Gloria recall the day they first met.

Edith's Crisis of Faith [Part 1]
W: Bob Weiskopf, Bob Schiller & Eric Tarloff. D: Paul Bogart. GS: Lori Shannon, Ron Vernan. During Christmas, Edith suffers a tragedy when her friend, female impersonator Beverly LaSalle, is killed when he and Mike are attacked by a street gang.

Edith's Crisis of Faith [Part 2]
W: Mel Tolkin, Larry Rhine & Eric Tarloff. D: Paul Bogart. Archie tries to help Edith, who has given up religion after the death of her friend, just because he was different.

The Commercial
W: Ben Starr & Ron Bloomberg. D: Paul Bogart. GS: Frank Aletter, Darryl Hickman, Alan Hamel, Thomas Middleton. Truthful Edith is asked to act in a television commercial.

Archie and the Super Bowl
W: Bob Weiskopf & Bob Schiller. D: Paul Bogart. GS: Art Metrano, Louis Guss, Gloria LeRoy, J.J. Johnson, Raymond O'Keefe. Two robbers hold up the bar when everyone is watching the Super Bowl.

Aunt Iola's Visit
W: Albert E. Lewin & Michael Loman. D: Paul Bogart. GS: Nedra Volz. Edith's aunt comes for a visit but then has no place to go to.

Love Comes to the Butcher
W: Phil Sharp. D: Paul Bogart. GS: Theodore Bikel, Serena C. Grant. The neighborhood butcher has fallen in love with Edith.

Two's a Crowd
W: Phil Sharp. D: Paul Bogart. Mike and Archie accidentally lock themselves in the storeroom of the bar.

Stale Mates
W: Bob Weiskopf & Bob Schiller. D:

Paul Bogart. GS: Judy Kahan, Terry Kiser. Mike and Gloria go away on a second honeymoon to rekindle their romance.

Archie's Brother
W: Larry Rhine & Mel Tolkin. D: Paul Bogart. GS: Richard McKenzie. Archie and his brother meet after a 29-year silence between them.

Mike's New Job
W: Mel Tolkin & Larry Rhine. D: Paul Bogart. GS: Sherman Hemsley. Mike and Gloria prepare to move to California where Mike has a new job waiting, when George Jefferson shows up.

The Stivics Go West
W: Bob Weiskopf & Bob Schiller. D: Paul Bogart. GS: Clyde Kusatsu. Mike and Gloria find it hard to say goodbye to Archie and Edith.

The Dinner Guest
W: Mel Tolkin & Larry Rhine. D: Paul Bogart. Archie and Edith become upset when Mike and Gloria have other plans, when they prepare a fare-well dinner for them.

Little Miss Bunker
W: Mel Tolkin & Larry Rhine. D: Paul Bogart. GS: Marty Brill, Bhetty Waldron, Santos Morales, Bern Bennett. Edith's cousin Floyd leaves his daughter Stephanie in the charge of Archie and Edith.

Reunion on Hauser Street
W: Milt Josefsberg & Phil Sharp. D: Paul Bogart. GS: Estelle Parsons, Gloria LeRoy. Barney's wife wants to make up and come home to him, but Archie plans to make her jealous by fixing Barney up with Boom Boom.

End in Sight
W: Nate Monaster. D: Paul Bogart. GS: Phil Leeds. Archie becomes lova-ble and Edith wants to know why.

What'll We Do with Stephanie?
W: Larry Rhine & Mel Tolkin. D: Paul

Bogart. GS: Abbey Lincoln. Archie wants to find a new home for Steph-anie but Edith wants to keep her.

Edith's Final Respects
W: Bob Schiller, Bob Weiskopf & Sam Greenbaum. D: Paul Bogart. GS: Howard Morton, Charles Siebert. When an old aunt dies alone and un-wanted, Edith is the only one to come to the funeral.

Weekend in the Country
W: Phil Sharp & Milt Josefsberg. D: Paul Bogart. GS: Estelle Parsons. Archie and Edith get stuck in the mid-dle of a fight between Blanche and Barney Hefner, while spending a week-end in the country.

Archie's Other Wife
W: Bob Schiller & Bob Weiskopf. D: Paul Bogart. GS: Eugene Roche, Har-vey Lembeck, Jonelle Allen, James J. Casino. Archie's practical joker friend makes Archie think he got married to a black woman while drinking it up attending a lodge convention.

Edith vs. the Bank
W: Mel Tolkin & Larry Rhine. D: Paul Bogart. GS: John Harkins. Edith gets mad when she learns that there are dif-ferent rules for men and women when she tries to get a loan.

The Return of the Waitress
W: Milt Josefsberg & Phil Sharp. D: Paul Bogart. GS: Janis Paige. Archie is shocked when he learns that the waitress Harry hired is the same one he had his affair with.

A Night at the PTA
W: Mel Tolkin & Larry Rhine. D: Paul Bogart. Edith loses her voice and can't sing with Stephanie in the school show.

The Bunkers Go West
W: Milt Josefsberg & Phil Sharp. D: Paul Bogart. Mike, Gloria and Joey plan to come to New York to spend Christmas with Archie and Edith.

California, Here We are [One Hour]
W: Milt Josefsberg & Phil Sharp. D: Paul Bogart. When Mike and Gloria can't come to New York, Archie and Edith fly out to California to visit them.

Bogus Bills
W: Bob Schiller & Bob Weiskopf. D: Paul Bogart. GS: Sandy Kenyon, John Finnegan, Charles Hallahan. Edith is arrested as a possible counterfeiter when Archie gets phony money at the bar.

The Appendectomy
W: Phil Sharp & Milt Josefsberg. D: Paul Bogart. GS: George Wyner, Tracy Bogart. Stephanie needs emergency surgery, but the doctor refuses to operate because he was one of Gloria's old playmates.

A Girl Like Edith
W: Bob Schiller & Bob Weiskopf. D: Paul Bogart. GS: Theodore Bikel, Giovanna Pucci. Edith is in the middle of a fight between her friend the butcher and his girlfriend.

Stephanie and the Crime Wave
W: Larry Rhine & Mel Tolkin. D: Paul Bogart. GS: Davis Roberts. Archie finds that several things are missing from the house and Stephanie is the reason.

Barney the Gold Digger
W: Bob Schiller & Bob Weiskopf. D: Paul Bogart. GS: Peggy Rea. Archie and Edith try to get Barney and a rich widow together.

Stephanie's Conversion
W: Patt Shea & Harriet Weiss. D: Paul Bogart. Clyde Kusatsu, Michael Mann. Edith discovers that Stephanie has been trying to hide the fact that she is

Jewish from Archie.

Edith Gets Fired
W: Patt Shea & Harriet Weiss. D: Paul Bogart. GS: Angela Clarke, Dolores Sutton, Michael McGuire, Leonard Stone, Victor Killian, Gerald Castillo. Edith is blamed for negligence when she is the last one to be with an old lady who wants to die at the Sunshine Home.

The 200th Episode of "All in the Family" [90 Minutes]
Norman Lear hosts this episode featuring scenes from past episodes. [This episode is rarely run by most stations, due to its running time.]

The Return of Archie's Brother
W: Mel Tolkin & Larry Rhine. D: Paul Bogart. GS: Richard McKenzie, Elissa Leeds. Archie's brother Fred returns with his new bride who is younger than Gloria.

The Family Next Door
W: Mel Tolkin & Larry Rhine. D: Paul Bogart. GS: Richard Ward, David Byrd, Isabel Sanford, Janet MacLachlan. Edith helps Louise Jefferson rent out their old house.

The Return of Stephanie's Father
W: Larry Rhine & Mel Tolkin. D: Paul Bogart. GS: Ben Stack, Victor Killian. Archie and Edith fight to keep Stephanie when her no-good father tries to blackmail them into giving her back to them.

Too Good Edith
W: Patt Shea & Harriet Weiss. D: Paul Bogart. GS: George Wyner. Edith doesn't tell Archie that she is too sick to do any work. When he finds out he makes sure she never hides anything from him again.

AMOS 'N' ANDY

On the air 6/28/51, off 6/11/53. CBS. 30 min. kinescope. 78 episodes. Broadcast: Jun 1951-Jun 1953 Thu 8:30-9. Producer: James Fonda, Freeman Gosden, Charles Correll. Prod Co: Hal Roach Studios. Removed from syndication in 1966.

CAST: Amos Jones (played by Alvin Childress), Andrew Hogg Brown [Andy] (Spencer Williams), George Stevens [The Kingfish] (Tim Moore), Lawyor A.J. Calhoun (Johnny Lee), Sapphire Stevens (Ernestine Wade), Lightnin' (Horace Stewart), Sapphire's Mama (Amanda Randolph), Madame Queen (Lillian Randolph).

DIRECTOR: Charles T. Barton.

Set in New York City, the show concerns three men: Andy Brown, the naive president of the Fresh Air Taxi Company of America (which consisted of one taxi), Amos Jones, his partner and driver of the taxi, and George Stevens, known as the Kingfish, who was an inept con artist. Stories relate Andy's romantic involvements and efforts to stray from the path of matrimony, and the Kingfish's endless attempts to con money out of everyone, but especially Andy. This series was the first to feature an all-black cast, but it was withdrawn from syndication by CBS in 1966 due to pressure from the NAACP, who felt the show was demeaning to the black society.

Rare Coin [Pilot]
The Kingfish swindles Andy out of a rare coin and Andy swindles it right back by use of a clever trick in a phone booth coin slot.

Andy Goes into Business
Andy goes into business and the Kingfish decides he wants to get in on the deal.

New Neighbors
While trying to get rid of neighbors who borrow everything, the Kingfish uses the crying of a baby and a sound effects record, but the plan backfires as the Kingfish is about to be evicted.

The Lodge Brothers Complain
The Kingfish tries to snatch a bride away from her wedding because he thinks she is his wife.

Viva La France
Andy, Calhoun, and the Kingfish all become engaged to a French girl named Colette Duval who doesn't understand English.

Income Tax Show
Andy and the Kingfish are frightened when they have to appear before the Internal Revenue Service. It turns out all they have to do is fill out new forms.

Vacation Show
The Kingfish tries to swindle Andy by taking him on a trip through Central Park and pretending it is the entire USA.

The Light Blue Car
The Kingfish finds himself accused of robbery when his car is used unknowingly in a holdup.

The Classified Ad
Andy puts a wife-seeking ad in the newspaper and gets a good response, but all the applicants need dental work.

The Society Party
The Kingfish and Andy try to get their ladies to wear the same fur coat at the same time, to the same party.

The Convention
In Chicago, the Kingfish gets a sample of the con game from his wife Sapphire who gets them to turn over their money to her, using a disguise, leaving the boys no money to get home.

Amos 'n' Andy: Tim Moore (The Kingfish), top, Alvin Childress (Amos), left, and Spencer Williams (Andy).

The Girl Upstairs
The Kingfish is convinced that his marriage is headed for disaster when he finds a diary in Sapphire's closet which mentions a rival.

Kingfish Goes to Work
The Kingfish has Andy take over his job as handyman at a university and pays him with a college home study course.

The Engagement Ring
The Kingfish plays matchmaker and arranges a match between Andy and an older woman, in the hope of collecting a services rendered fee.

The Eyeglass
The Kingfish devises a plot to make Andy fail his road test so that he can buy his car cheaply.

Hospitalization
Andy buys hospitalization insurance from the Kingfish and then relaxes in the hospital, turning the Kingfish frantic with bills he can't pay.

Sapphire's Mysterious Admirer
The Kingfish believes that Sapphire is in love with another man and that she and her beau are planning to get rid of him.

The Adoption
The Kingfish falls in love with a baby which is up for adoption, but instead is stuck with Horrible Horace, Sapphire's pesty nephew.

The Broken Clock
Andy and the Kingfish accidentally become involved with a top military secret and the FBI when they mistakenly take a new secret altimeter clock for a replacement for their broken one.

The Ballet Tickets
The Kingfish gives Sapphire some stolen ballet tickets which land her in jail. She ends up in jail a second time when the Kingfish gives her a phony five dollar bill.

The Boarder
Sapphire maintains that her boarder, a singer with a large appetite, is a cultural asset, but to the Kingfish he is a gorging freeloader.

Arabia
The Kingfish sets up a phony raffle that forces him to wind up in Arabia drilling for oil, trying to earn enough money to get home.

The Race Horse
The Kingfish gets conned when Andy sells him a broken down race horse.

Andy Gets Married
Double trouble for Andy, he has gotten engaged to two women.

The Piggy Bank
The Kingfish has been stealing money from Sapphire's piggy bank and wins a quiz show jackpot just in time for his and Sapphire's 25th anniversary.

Superfine Brush
The Kingfish, pushed by Sapphire to get a job, becomes a door-to-door salesman, persuading Andy to take over at no salary.

Mr. Jackson Comes to Town
The Kingfish goes on a self-improvement course because Sapphire goes overboard over an ex-boyfriend and former Mr. America.

Cousin Effie's Will
The Kingfish adopts Andy so that he will become eligible for a $2000 bequest under the terms of Cousin Effie's will.

Restitution
While trying to do a good deed and repay a jeweler for the use of his electricity, the Kingfish becomes a fugitive from justice when he accidentally trips the store's burglar alarm.

The Kingfish Finds His Future
The Kingfish takes an aptitude test and finds he should become a painter, not of pictures but of buildings and walls.

The Antique Shop
The Kingfish outfoxes himself when he sends all his lodge brothers into an antique shop to convince his cousin Leo to buy it, but with all those customers the store owner won't sell.

Kingfish Sells a Lot
The Kingfish decides to dispose of a worthless piece of property to Andy, but it's Andy who gets the last laugh.

Birthday Card
Sapphire gives the Kingfish the third degree and wants to know why he received a birthday card signed Sweetheart.

Andy Falls in Love with an Actress
Andy, jealous over his girlfriend's amorous scenes in a play, decides to become an actor.

Kingfish at the Ball Game
The Kingfish sells Andy a ring he finds in his crackerjack box before he finds out how valuable the ring really is.

Kingfish's Last Friend
The Kingfish has swindled too many people and is losing all of his friends so he goes on a reform kick.

Sapphire's Sister
The Kingfish wangles a marriage between Andy and Sapphire's sister, then learns she has $10,000 in the savings bank.

Seeing is Believing
Sapphire thinks the Kingfish is secretly dating so she decides to make him jealous by having dinner alone with Andy.

Leroy's Suits
The Kingfish stages a clothing sale at the Lodge using a lieutenant's entire wardrobe.

Counterfeiters Rent Basement
Andy is a hero when he overpowers a gang of counterfeiters and collects a fat reward.

Kingfish Has a Baby
The Kingfish decides to reform because he thinks he is about to become a father.

Kingfish's Secretary
The Kingfish mistakenly signs a letter requesting a mail order bride with a letter requesting a wash woman for the building.

Kingfish Gets Drafted
When the Kingfish gets drafted, his wife and his lodge brothers applaud but soon change their tune when his outfit is to go overseas.

The Gun
The Kingfish, trying to pawn a gun, is mistaken for a robber.

Young Girl's Mother
Andy wants to marry a very young girl until he meets her mother, a formidable woman he jilted many years ago.

Fur Coat
Sapphire is so delighted with her surprise from the Kingfish, a fur coat, that he hasn't the heart to tell her that the coat is not for her.

Sapphire Disappears
The Kingfish thinks Sapphire has been murdered when she leaves him in a huff and he can find no trace of her.

Jewelry Store Robbery
Andy and the Kingfish find that a snapshot they took is worth $1000 because it shows a man robbing a store.

The Winslow Woman
The Kingfish wants Andy to marry wealthy Mrs. Winslow, even when the not-so-wealthy woman actually shows up.

Call Lehigh 4-9900
The Kingfish accidentally answers a newspaper ad for a lonely hearts club, and when a girl shows up at his office, Andy poses as the Kingfish.

Leroy Lends a Hand
The Kingfish and Andy go into the parking lot business and wind up in the used car business.

Amos Helps Out
After a domestic fight, the Kingfish writes a fake letter from the license bureau stating that he and Sapphire were never legally married.

Andy Buys a House
The Kingfish takes a job as a real estate agent and must prove himself by selling a house on condemned land—he does, to Andy.

Andy Gets a Telegram
The Kingfish winds up on a cattle boat bound for South America when Sapphire plots to separate him from his worthless friends.

The Christmas Story
Andy is working very hard to earn enough money to buy a doll for his godchild.

The Diner
The Kingfish and Andy buy a diner, which was doing a good business, and run it out of business.

Getting Mama Married [Part 1]
GS: Amanda Randolph. The Kingfish's mother-in-law elopes with a con man and a fleecer of widows.

Getting Mama Married [Part 2]
The Kingfish's mother-in-law is so set on marrying a man that even when his wife shows up she still says he is hers.

The Happy Stevenses
The Kingfish and Sapphire imitate participants in a radio show about a happy marriage, in order to change the pattern of their stormy marriage.

Ready Made Family
When the Kingfish's Uncle Clarence is coming to visit, the Kingfish must put together a phony family quickly, to protect his uncle's gift of $500, he gave the Kingfish by telling him he has a child.

Relatives
Claiming that his mother-in-law disturbs his home, the Kingfish takes his problems to family court. Meanwhile, more relatives show up.

Traffic Violation
The Kingfish and Andy, co-owners of a car, compete with each other in the collection of traffic tickets.

The Turkey Dinner
The Kingfish is conned into buying stolen turkeys from a country bumpkin.

Quo Vadis
The Kingfish goes to a lavish dinner party at which he finds, uncomfortably, that Sapphire is a waitress.

The Chinchilla Business
The Kingfish sells a couple of rabbits to Andy for $50 by telling him they are chinchillas.

The Uranium Mine
Andy shells out money for swampland and invests in the Kingfish's uranium mine scheme.

Madame Queen's Voice
Madame Queen re-enters Andy's life because the Kingfish sees her money-making possibilities as a singer.

Andy, the Godfather
The love of a 12-year-old for Andy's godchild is too much for him to handle.

The Insurance Policy
A heaven-sent opportunity is given the Kingfish, Sapphire thinks he has only three weeks to live, which gives him three weeks to freeload.

The Kingfish Gets Amnesia
The Kingfish gets amnesia when all of his friends come over asking him to repay old debts.

The Girl at the Station
At a party, the Kingfish is in good with the ladies and Sapphire doesn't like it at all.

The Kingfish Teaches Andy to Fly
The Kingfish teaches Andy to fly, so that he can win back his girl from a motor boat enthusiast.

The Kingfish Becomes a Press Agent
The Kingfish takes a job as a press agent in order to make money to pay Andy off and get his mother-in-law's

diamond pin back, but things don't work out.

The Meal Ticket
Sapphire wants intellectuals to break in her new dining room furniture, but the Kingfish wants to sneak paying guests in instead.

Second Honeymoon
Plans for a second honeymoon almost fall apart when the Kingfish and Sapphire argue over how they first met.

Father by Proxy
Driving a pregnant woman to the hospital, Andy is mistaken for the father when a pushy nurse forces him to fill out forms and to sit in the waiting room.

Story of the Invisible Glass
The Kingfish gets into the stock market and sells everyone short, including himself.

The Kingfish Buys a Chair
The Kingfish buys an old chair stuffed with money and then, not knowing the money is in the chair, he gives it away.

ANDY GRIFFITH

On the air 10/3/60, off 9/16/68. CBS. B&W, color. 30 min. film. 249 episodes. Broadcast: Oct 1960-Jul 1963 Mon 9:30-10; Sept 1963-Jun 1965 Mon 8:30-9; Sept 1965-Sept 1968 Mon 9-9:30. Producer: Sheldon Leonard. Prod Co: Danny Thomas Productions. Synd: Viacom.

CAST: Andy Taylor (played by Andy Griffith), Opie Taylor (Ronny Howard), Barney Fife (Don Knotts), Ellie Walker (Elinor Donahue), Aunt Bee Taylor (Frances Bavier), Helen Crump (Anita Corsaut), Floyd Lawson (Howard McNear), Otis Campbell (Hal Smith), Goober Pyle (George Lindsey), Gomer Pyle (Jim Nabors), Clara Edwards (Hope Summers), Warren Ferguson (Jack Burns), Thelma Lou (Betty Lynn), Howard Sprague (Jack Dodson), Emmett Clark (Paul Hartman).

WRITERS AND DIRECTORS: See bracketed notes below, on page 54, and on page 61.

Set in Mayberry, North Carolina, this low-key Southern comedy depicts the relationship between Sheriff Andy Taylor, a widower, and his bachelor cousin Barney Fife. Most episodes involve Andy's attempts to raise his young son Opie while maintaining law and order in their rural community. Also featured in the series were Gomer Pyle, the naive gas station attendant who went on to star in his own series, and Sam Jones, town councilman, who later spun-off into the successful "Mayberry R.F.D." series.

[Every episode from here to the note in the second column of page 54 was written by Jack Ellison & Charles Stewart, except where noted, and directed by Bob Sweeney, except where noted.]

The New Housekeeper
D: Sheldon Leonard. Aunt Bee comes to stay with Andy and Opie.

The Manhunt
D: Don Weis. Andy helps some state troopers capture an escaped convict.

Guitar Player
D: Don Weis. GS: James Best, Henry Slate. A guitar player and his band audition for a show while locked in a jail cell.

Runaway Kid
W: Arthur Stander. D: Don Weis. GS: Pat Rosson. Andy convinces a runaway to return home.

Opie's Charity
W: Arthur Stander. D: Don Weis. GS: Stu Erwin, Lurene Tuttle.   Andy jumps to the wrong conclusion about Opie.

Ellie Comes to Town
D: Don Weis. Ellie Walker comes to town to help her uncle run the local drugstore.

Irresistible Andy
W: David Adler. D: Don Weis. Andy takes Ellie to the church picnic.

A Feud Is a Feud
W: David Adler. D: Don Weis. GS: Arthur Hunnicutt. Andy stops a feud between two families.

Andy the Matchmaker
W: Arthur Stander.   D: Don Weis. Andy tries to get Barney and Rosemary, the dressmaker, together.

Stranger in Town
W: Arthur Stander. D: Don Weis. GS: William Lanteau.   A mysterious stranger comes to town.   He knows who everyone is, but they don't seem to know him.

Christmas Story
W: David Adler.   Andy and Barney hold a Christmas party in the jail for a prisoner and his family.

Ellie for Council
Ellie decides to run for a seat on the town council.

Mayberry Goes Hollywood
W: Benedict Freedman & John Fenton Murray.   A producer decides to film his new project in Mayberry.

The Horse Trader
GS: Casey Adams. Andy tries to trade away the town cannon.

Those Gossipin' Men
GS: Jack Finch.   The town believes that a traveling shoe salesman is a Hollywood talent scout.

Andy Saves Barney's Morale
W: David Adler.   GS: Burt Mustin. Andy tries to help Barney regain his dignity.

Alcohol and Old Lace
Andy and Barney find that a pair of old ladies are actually moonshiners.

Andy, the Marriage Counselor
W: David Adler. D: Gene Reynolds. GS: Jesse White.   Andy tries to get a fighting couple back together again.

Mayberry on Record
W: John Fenton Murray & Benedict Freedman. D: Gene Reynolds. GS: Hugh Marlowe. Andy thinks a traveling record promoter is a con man.

The Beauty Contest
Andy is chosen to be the judge of the local beauty contest.

Andy and the Gentleman Crook
W: Ben Gershman & Leo Solomon. GS: Dan Tobin.   Andy captures a famous gentleman crook.

Cyrano Andy
Barney thinks Andy is after his girlfriend.

Andy and Opie, Housekeepers
W: David Adler.   GS: Rory Stevens. Andy and Opie take over when Aunt Bee has to leave town.

The New Doctor
GS: George Nader. Andy proposes to Ellie in order to beat the new town doctor from marrying her.

A Plaque for Mayberry
W: Leo Solomon & Ben Gershman. GS: Dorothy Neumann, Burt Mustin. Otis, the town drunk, is discovered to be the only living descendant of a Revolutionary War hero.

The Inspector
GS: Willis Bouchey, Tod Andrews. A state inspector comes to see how Andy performs his job.

Ellie Saves a Female
W: David Adler. GS: R.G. Armstrong.
Andy and Ellie help a farmer's daughter to become a woman.

Andy Forecloses
W: Ben Gershman & Leo Solomon.
GS: Ben Wright, Sam Edwards. Andy tries to save a man from being evicted.

Quiet Sam
W: Jim Fritzell & Everett Greenbaum.
GS: William Schallert. Andy delivers a baby when the doctor does not arrive in time.

Barney Gets His Man
W: Leo Solomon & Ben Gershman.
GS: Barney Phillips. Barney captures a dangerous crook.

The Guitar Player Returns
GS: James Best, Tom Browne Henry.
Andy helps the guitar player cope with his new success.

Bringing Up Opie
Andy tries to improve his relationship with Opie.

Barney's Replacement
Barney quits when he thinks Andy plans to replace him.

Opie and the Bully
GS: Terry Dickinson. Andy teaches Opie how to defend himself against a bully.

Andy and the Woman Speeder
GS: Jean Hagen. A woman tries to charm Andy out of giving her a speeding ticket.

Barney on the Rebound
GS: Jackie Coogan. Barney is taken in by a female con artist.

The Perfect Female
GS: Gail Davis. Andy tries to find a girl who fits his standards.

Aunt Bee's Brief Encounter
GS: Edgar Buchanan, Doodles Weaver,

George Cisar. Aunt Bee falls for a traveling handyman.

Mayberry Goes Bankrupt
A man tries to redeem a century-old municipal bond.

Opie's Hobo Friend
W: Harvey Bullock. GS: Buddy Ebsen. Opie befriends a hobo.

Crime-Free Mayberry
W: Paul Henning. A phoney FBI man nearly gets away with all of the town's money.

The Clubmen
W: Fred S. Fox & Iz Elinson. Andy becomes upset when he is invited to join an exclusive club and Barney is not.

The Pickle Story
W: Harvey Pollock. Andy and Opie hate Aunt Bee's homemade pickles but don't have the heart to tell her.

Sheriff Barney
W: Leo Soloman & Ben Gershman.
GS: Dabbs Greer, Ralph Dumke. Barney is offered the job of Sheriff in another town.

The Farmer Takes a Wife
GS: Alan Hale. Andy tries to prevent a farmer from marrying Barney's girlfriend.

The Keeper of the Flame
GS: Everett Sloane. Opie is accused of burning down a barn.

Bailey's Bad Boy
W: Leo Solomon & Ben Gershman.
GS: Bill Bixby. Andy teaches a rich young man how to depend on himself and not on others.

The Manicurist
GS: Barbara Eden. Floyd hires a manicurist, causing the men to go wild and their wives to get mad.

The Jinx
GS: John Qualen. Andy helps a man who thinks he is a jinx.

Jailbreak
W: Harvey Bullock. GS: Ken Lynch, Allan Melvin. Andy helps the state police capture a criminal.

A Medal for Opie
W: David Adler. Opie tries to learn how to lose gracefully.

Barney and the Choir
GS: Olan Soule. Tone-deaf Barney wants to join the choir.

Guest of Honor
GS: Jay Novello. Andy and Barney discover that the town's guest of honor is actually a pickpocket.

The Merchant of Mayberry
W: Leo Solomon & Ben Gershman. GS: Sterling Holloway. Andy helps a struggling salesman make it in Mayberry.

Aunt Bee the Warden
Otis spends his jail term at Andy's house under the strict supervision of Aunt Bee.

The County Nurse
GS: Julie Adams. Andy helps the visiting county nurse with the stubborn townspeople.

Andy and Barney in the Big City
W: Harvey Bullock. Andy and Barney try to catch a jewel thief.

Wedding Bells for Aunt Bee
Andy and Aunt Bee each think the other is planning to get married.

Three's a Crowd
GS: Sue Ane Langdon. Andy and the county nurse fall for each other. Their only problem is how to get rid of Barney long enough to be alone together.

The Bookie Barber
W: Ray Allen Saffian & Harvey Bullock. GS: Herb Vigran. Floyd's new assistant is actually a bookie.

Andy on Trial
GS: Ruta Lee. Andy is accused of malfeasance by a traffic offender who wants to get even with him.

Cousin Virgil
W: Phillip Shukin & Johnny Greene. GS: Michael J. Pollard. Barney's cousin Virgil comes for a visit.

Deputy Otis
W: Iz Elinson & Fred S. Fox. GS: Dorothy Neumann, Stanley Adams. Andy tries to help Otis impress his relatives by making him a deputy.

Opie's Rival
W: Sid Morse. GS: Joanna Moore. Opie's jealous of Andy's new girlfriend.

[Every episode from now on is written by Jim Fritzell & Everett Greenbaum, except where noted. From here to the note in the first column of page 61 every episode is directed by Bob Sweeney, except where noted.]

Andy and Opie—Bachelors
GS: Joanna Moore, Ray Lanier. Andy and Opie have the house to themselves when Aunt Bee leaves on a visit.

Mr. McBeevee
W: Ray Allen Saffian & Harvey Bullock. GS: Karl Swenson. Andy and Aunt Bee believe that Opie has created an invisible friend.

Andy's Rich Girlfriend
GS: Joanna Moore. Andy discovers that his new girlfriend's father is a very rich man.

Barney Mends a Broken Heart
Barney tries to get Andy another date when Peggy breaks her date with him.

Andy and the New Mayor
W: Harvey Bullock & Ray Allen Saffian. GS: Parley Baer. The new mayor is very critical of Andy's work.

The Cow Thief
W: Aaron Rubin. GS: Fred Beir. The mayor orders Andy to send for a crime expert to help him solve the mystery of the missing cows.

Floyd the Gay Deceiver
W: Aaron Rubin. GS: Doris Dowling. Floyd pretends that he is a rich man in order to impress a visiting rich widow.

The Mayberry Band
The Mayberry Band prepares to enter the state band contest.

Lawman Barney
W: Aaron Rubin. GS: Allan Melvin. Barney loses his self-confidence when nobody will listen to him.

Convicts at Large
GS: Reta Shaw, Jane Dulo, Jean Carson. Three escaped female convicts hold Barney and Floyd hostage in a cabin.

The Bed Jacket
W: Ray Allen Saffian & Harvey Bullock. GS: Dabbs Greer. Aunt Bee wanted a bed jacket for her birthday present but nobody gets it for her.

Barney and the Governor
W: Bill Freedman. Barney gives a parking ticket to the governor.

Man in a Hurry
GS: Robert Emhardt. A big businessman's car breaks down in Mayberry.

The Bank Job
Barney tries to prove that the bank vault is not very safe for the town's money.

One Punch Opie
W: Harvey Bullock. GS: Clint Howard, Kim Tyler. Opie learns how to box in order to defend himself against a bully.

High Noon in Mayberry
GS: Dub Taylor, Jim Nabors, Leo Gordon. Barney becomes worried when an ex-convict comes back to town.

The Loaded Goat
W: Harvey Bullock. GS: Bing Russell, Burt Mustin. Andy finds that a goat has eaten a supply of dynamite.

Class Reunion
GS: Peggy McCay, Paul Smith. Andy and Barney attend their high school reunion.

Rafe Hollister Sings
W: Harvey Bullock. GS: Jack Prince, Kay Stewart. Andy and Barney try to help a poor farmer make a good impression when he is chosen to perform at a concert.

Opie and the Spoiled Kid
GS: Ronnie Capo. Opie wants Andy to raise his allowance in order to compete with a rich kid.

The Great Filling Station Robbery
W: Harvey Bullock. GS: Jim Nabors, Pat Colby. Andy and Barney try to catch the crook who has been robbing the gas station.

Andy Discovers America
W: John Whedon. GS: Aneta Corsaut. Andy falls for Opie's new teacher. [This was the first appearance of the character of Helen Crump who would later marry the character Andy Taylor.]

Aunt Bee's Medicine Man
W: John Whedon. GS: John Dehner. Aunt Bee falls for a medicine man who sclls Indian elixir.

The Darlings Are Coming
GS: Denver Pyle. Andy has to deal with a family of hillbilly musicians.

Andy's English Valet
W: Harvey Bullock. GS: Bernard Fox. An Englishman becomes Andy's valet in order to pay off a fine.

Barney's First Car
GS: Jim Nabors, Ellen Corby. Barney buys his first used car.

The Rivals
W: Harvey Bullock. GS: Ronda Jeter. Barney tries to show Opie how to handle a woman.

A Wife for Andy
W: Aaron Rubin. Barney tries to find a wife for Andy.

Dogs, Dogs, Dogs
GS: Robert Cornthwaite. A bunch of hunting dogs upsets Andy's business with a visiting state official.

Mountain Wedding
GS: Howard Morris, Denver Pyle, Dub Taylor, Hoke Howell. Andy has to break up a fight between the hillbilly Darling family and Ernest T. Bass.

The Big House
W: Harvey Bullock. GS: George Kennedy, Lewis Charles, Billy Halop. Barney has to guard two thieves until the rest of the gang is caught.

Briscoe Declares for Aunt Bee
D: Earl Bellamy. GS: Denver Pyle. Hillbilly Briscoe Darling tries to get Aunt Bee to marry him.

Gomer the House Guest
D: Earl Bellamy. GS: Trevor Bardette. Gomer moves in with Andy when he loses his job.

The Haunted House
W: Harvey Bullock. D: Earl Bellamy. GS: Nestor Paiva. Andy, Barney & Gomer visit a haunted house.

Ernest T. Bass Joins the Army
D: Dick Crenna. GS: Howard Morris, Allan Melvin. Hillbilly Ernest T. Bass is rejected by the Army.

The Sermon for Today
W: John Whedon. D: Dick Crenna. GS: David Lewis. A visiting preacher gets the town to relax, leaving most of their work not done.

Opie the Birdman
W: Harvey Bullock. D: Dick Crenna. Opie has to take care of some baby firds when he kills their mother with his slingshot.

A Black Day for Mayberry
W: John Whedon. D: Jeffrey Hayden. GS: Rance Howard, Ken Lynch, Clint Howard. A gold shipment passes through the town on its way to Fort Knox.

Opie's Ill-Gotten Gain
W: John Whedon. D: Jeffrey Hayden. Opie changes his grades on his report card so he can get a bicycle from Andy.

Up in Barney's Room
D: Jeffrey Hayden. GS: J. Pat O'Malley. Barney moves into the sheriff's office when he is evicted for cooking in his room.

A Date for Gomer
D: Dick Crenna. GS: Mary Grace Canfield. Barney fixes Gomer up with his girlfriend's cousin.

Citizen's Arrest
D: Dick Crenna. Barney gives a ticket to Gomer for making a U-turn, then Gomer arrests Barney for making a U-turn himself.

Gomer Pyle USMC
W: Aaron Rubin. GS: Frank Sutton, Alan Reed, Eddie Ryder, Frank Albertson. Gomer joins the Marines. [This is the pilot for the spin-off series "Gomer Pyle, USMC."]

Opie and His Merry Men
W: John Whedon. D: Dick Crenna. GS: Douglas Fowley. Robin Hood, Opie and his friends try to help a hobo.

Barney and the Cave Rescue
W: Harvey Bullock. D: Dick Crenna. GS: Warren Parker. Barney comes to the rescue when Andy and Helen become trapped in a cave.

Andy and Opie's Pal
W: Harvey Bullock. D: Dick Crenna.
GS: David A. Bailey. Opie befreinds
the new kid in town.

Aunt Bee the Crusader
W: John Whedon. D: Coby Ruskin.
Aunt Bee tries to help a chicken farmer whose property is being condemned
to make way for a new road.

Barney's Sidecar
D: Coby Ruskin. Barney buys an old
motorcycle, complete with a sidecar.

My Fair Ernest T. Bass
D: Earl Bellamy. GS: Howard Morris,
Doris Packer. Andy brings Ernest T.
Bass home with him to teach him
some manners.

Prisoner of Love
W: Harvey Bullock. D: Earl Bellamy.
GS: Susan Oliver. Barney and Andy
both fall for a beautiful woman prisoner.

Hot Rod Otis
W: Harvey Bullock. D: Earl Bellamy.
Otis, the town drunk, buys a car and
drives the town crazy.

The Song Festers
D: Earl Bellamy. GS: Barbara Griffith [Andy's wife], Olan Soule. Gomer
beats out Barney for a spot in the
choir.

The Shoplifters
W: Bill Idleson & Sam Bobrick. D:
Coby Ruskin. GS: Tol Avery, Charles
Thompson. Barney pretends to be a
mannequin in order to catch a thief at
a department store.

Andy's Vacation
D: Jeffrey Hayden. While Andy is
away, Gomer and Barney accidentally
let a prisoner escape from the jail.

Andy Saves Gomer
W: Harvey Bullock. D: Jeffrey Hayden. Gomer becomes eternally grateful to Andy who saved him from a
fire.

Bargain Day
W: John Whedon. D: Jeffrey Hayden.
Aunt Bee buys a side of beef in order
to save money.

Divorce, Mountain Style
D: Jeffrey Hayden. GS: Denver Pyle.
Barney interrupts a hillbilly divorce.

A Deal Is a Deal
W: Bill Idelson & Sam Bobrick. D:
Jeffrey Hayden. GS: George Petrie,
Lewis Charles. Barney and Gomer
help Opie who has fallen into the
clutches of a con man.

Fun Girls
W: Aaron Rubin. D: Coby Ruskin.
GS: Joyce Jameson, Jean Carson. Two
beautiful blondes interrupt the lives of
Barney and Andy.

Return of Malcom Merriwether
W: Harvey Bullock. D: Coby Ruskin.
GS: Bernard Fox. Andy's English
valet returns for a visit.

The Rumor
D: Coby Ruskin. Barney thinks Andy
and Helen are getting married.

Barney and Thelma Lou, Phfftt
W: Bill Idleson & Sam Bobrick. D:
Coby Ruskin. Barney becomes jealous
when he sees his girlfriend kiss Gomer.

Back to Nature
W: Harvey Bullock. D: Coby Ruskin.
GS: Willis Bouchey. Andy takes Opie
and his friends on a camping trip
where Barney and Gomer get lost in
the woods.

Barney's Bloodhound
W: Bill Idleson & Sam Bobrick. D:
Howard Morris. GS: Arthur Batanides.
Barney buys a bloodhound.

Family Visit
W: Bob Ross. D: Howard Morris. GS:
James Westerfield. Andy's uncle bor-
rows the squad car to go fishing.

Aunt Bee's Romance
W: Harvey Bullock. D: Howard Mor-

ris. GS: Wallace Ford. Aunt Bee's old practical joker boyfriend comes for a visit.

Opie Loves Helen
W: Bob Ross. D: Aaron Ruben. Opie has a crush on his teacher (and Andy's girlfriend) Helen.

The Education of Ernest T. Bass
D: Alan Rafkin. GS: Howard Morris. Ernest T. Bass goes back to school in order to please his girlfriend.

Man in the Middle
W: Gus Adrian & David Evans. Andy tries to get Barney and his girlfriend back together after they have a fight.

Barney's Uniform
W: Bill Idelson & Sam Bobrick. D: Coby Ruskin. GS: Allan Melvin. Barney refuses to take off his uniform when he is threatened that if he is ever caught without it he will be beat up.

Opie's Fortune
W: Ben Joelson & Art Baer. D: Coby Ruskin. GS: Jon Lormer. Opie finds a change purse containing $50.

Goodbye, Sheriff Taylor
W: Fred Freeman & Lawrence J. Cohen. D: Gene Nelson. When Andy goes looking for another job, Barney takes over as acting sheriff.

The Pageant
W: Harvey Bullock. D: Gene Nelson. GS: Barbara Perry, Olan Soule. Aunt Bee tries to get the starring role in the town centennial pageant.

The Darling Baby
D: Howard Morris. GS: Denver Pyle. Opie is chosen to become the future husband of Charlene Darling's baby girl.

Andy and Helen Have Their Day
W: Bill Idelson & Sam Bobrick. D: Howard Morris. GS: Howard Morris. Andy and Helen go on a picnic together but find that they are constantly being bothered by Barney.

Otis Sues the County
W: Bob Ross. D: Howard Morris. When Otis hurts himself in the jail, he decides to sue the county for damages.

Three Wishes for Opie
W: Richard Powell. D: Howard Morris. Barney plays fortune teller and gives Opie three wishes which seem to be coming true.

Barney Fife, Realtor
W: Bill Idelson & Sam Bobrick. D: Peter Baldwin. Barney tries to get Andy to sell his house.

Goober Takes a Car Apart
W: Bill Idelson & Sam Bobrick. D: Peter Baldwin. GS: Larry Hovis. Goober takes a car apart in Andy's office.

The Rehabilitation of Otis
W: Fred Freeman & Lawrence Cohen. D: Peter Baldwin. Otis comes to town riding a cow, which he thinks is a horse.

The Lucky Letter
W: Richard Powell. D. Ted Flicker. When Barney breaks a chain letter, accidents start to happen.

Goober and the Art of Love
W: Fred Freeman & Lawrence Cohen. D: Alan Rafkin. GS: Josie Lloyd. Andy and Barney try to find a girl for Goober who insists on joining them when they go on a date with their girls.

Barney Runs for Sheriff
W: Richard Powell. D: Alan Rafkin. Barney decides to run for sheriff when Andy decides to take another job.

If I Had a Quarter Million
W: Bob Ross. D: Alan Rafkin. GS: Hank Patterson, Byron Folger, Al Checco. When Barney finds $250,000 which was stolen from a bank, he decides to catch the crooks who stole it.

TV or Not TV
W: Ben Joelson & Art Baer. D: Coby Ruskin.   GS: George Ives, Gavin McCleod.   Andy is asked to star in a television series.

Guest in the House
W: Fred Freeman & Lawrence Cohen. GS: Jan Shutan. Helen becomes jealous of the pretty friend of the family who moves into Andy's house.

The Case of the Punch in the Nose
W: Bill Idelson & Sam Bobrick. D: Coby Ruskin. GS: Frank Ferguson, Larry Hovis. Barney tries to close the case on an assault charge which was never resolved.

Opie's Newspaper
W: Harvey Bullock. D: Coby Ruskin. GS: Dennis Rush. Opie publishes a gossip newspaper and distributes it all over town.

Aunt Bee's Invisible Beau
W: Ben Joelson & Art Baer. D: Ted Flicker.   GS: Woodrow Chambliss. Aunt Bee invents a boyfriend so she can make her friends jealous.

The Arrest of the Fun Girls
W: Richard Powell. D: Ted Flicker. GS: Joyce Jameson, Jean Carson. The two beautiful blondes return to get another speeding ticket and some attention from Andy and Barney.

The Luck of Newton Monroe
W: Bill Idelson & Sam Bobrick. D: Coby Ruskin. GS: Don Rickles. A traveling peddler who is always getting in trouble comes to Mayberry.

Opie Flunks Arithmetic
W: Harvey Bullock. D: Coby Ruskin. Barney helps Opie with his school work.

Opie and the Carnival
W: Fred Freeman & Lawrence J. Cohen. D: Coby Ruskin. GS: Lewis Charles, Richard Keith, Billy Halop.

Opie tries to win a birthday present at a carnival shooting gallery for Andy.

Banjo-Playing Deputy
W: Bob Ross. D: Coby Ruskin. GS: Jerry Van Dyke, Herbie Faye. Andy hires an out of work banjo player to replace Barney, while he is out of town.

Aunt Bee the Swinger
W: Jack Elinson. D: Lawrence Dobkin. Aunt Bee and her new boyfriend stay out late every night.

Opie's Job
W: Art Baer, Ben Joelson. D: Lawrence Dobkin.   GS: Rhonda Jeter, John Bangert. Opie gets a job at the grocery store.

The Bazaar
W: Art Baer & Ben Joelson. D: Sheldon Leonard. Warren, the new deputy, arrests Aunt Bee and her friends for gambling at the charity bazaar.

Andy's Rival
W: Lawrence Marks. D: Peter Baldwin. Andy becomes jealous when another teacher is spending evenings with Helen.

Malcolm at the Crossroads
W: Harvey Bullock. D: Gary Nelson. GS: Bernard Fox, Howard Morris. Andy hires Ernest T. Bass as the new crossing guard, then replaces him with his old English valet Malcolm Merriwether.

Aunt Bee on TV
W: Fred Freeman & Lawrence Cohen. D: Alan Rafkin. Aunt Bee wins a new kitchen on a TV games show.

Off to Hollywood
W: Bill Idelson & Sam Bobrick. D: Alan Rafkin. The whole family goes on a trip to Hollywood.

Taylors in Hollywood
W: Bill Idelson & Sam Bobrick. D: Alan Rafkin. The family visits a movie studio.

The Hollywood Party
W: Fred Freeman & Lawrence Cohen. D: Alan Rafkin. Andy and an actress take a picture together, which later causes Helen to become jealous when it is printed in the town paper.

A Warning from Warren
W: Fred Freeman & Lawrence Cohen. D: Alan Rafkin. Warren tries to prove that he has ESP.

A Man's Best Friend
W: Art Baer & Ben Joelson. D: Alan Rafkin. Goober thinks he can make a fortune in show business with his new talking dog.

Aunt Bee Takes a Job
W: Bill Idelson & Sam Bobrick. D: Alan Rafkin. Aunt Bee gets a job at a print show which is actually a front for a counterfeit operation.

The Cannon
W: Jack Elinson. D: Alan Rafkin. Warren captures two thieves by using the town cannon.

Girl Shy
W: Bill Idelson & Sam Bobrick. D: Lee Phillips. Warren becomes a romantic hero when he sleepwalks.

The Church Organ
W: Paul Wayne. D: Lee Phillips. Andy tries to help the town buy a new organ for the church.

Otis, the Con Artist
W: Fred Freeman & Lawrence Cohen. D: Alan Rafkin. Warren gets Otis to give up drinking and take up painting.

The Return of Barney Fife
W: Bill Idelson & Sam Bobrick. D: Alan Rafkin. Barney returns to attend his high school reunion.

The Legend of Barney Fife
W: Harvey Bullock. D: Alan Rafkin. Barney tries to capture an escaped convict.

Lost and Found
W: John Greene & Paul David. D: Alan Rafkin. Aunt Bee spends the insurance money she got when she lost a valuable pin, only now she found the pin and doesn't know what to do.

Wyatt Earp
W: Jack Elinson. D: Alan Rafkin. An imposter poses as a descendant of Wyatt Earp in order to get special treatment from the townspeople.

Aunt Bee Learns to Drive
W: Jack Elinson. D: Lee Phillips. Aunt Bee buys a used car.

Look, Paw, I'm Dancing
W: Ben Starr. D: Lee Phillips. Opie finds that he likes to dance.

Eat Your Heart Out
W: Art Baer & Ben Joelson. D: Alan Rafkin. Goober falls for a new waitress but she only has eyes for Andy.

The Gypsies
W: Roland MacLane. D: Alan Rafkin. A roving band of gypsies makes camp in the town.

A Baby in the House
W: Bill Idelson & Sam Bobrick. D: Alan Rafkin. Aunt Bee babysits for her niece's baby.

The County Clerk
W: Bill Idelson & Sam Bobrick. D: Alan Rafkin. Andy and Helen try to get Howard and the county nurse together.

Goober's Replacement
W: Howard Merrill & Stan Dreben. D: Alan Rafkin. GS: Alberta Nelson. Goober gets his girlfriend to take over the station for a few days, but she does such a good job his boss decides to fire him and keep her instead.

The Foster Lady
W: Jack & Iz Elinson. D: Alan Rafkin. Aunt Bee is asked to perform in a TV commercial.

The Battle of Mayberry
W: John Greene & Paul David. D: Alan Rafkin. Opie proves that a famous battle never took place.

A Singer in Town
W: Stan Dreben & Howard Merrill. D: Alan Rafkin. Aunt Bee's song about Mayberry becomes a big hit when it is played on a Rock 'n Roll show.

[Every episode from now on is directed by Lee Phillips.]

Opie's Girlfriend
W: Budd Grossman. Opie's new girlfriend is an athlete.

The Barbershop Quartet
W: Fred S. Fox. Andy uses a prisoner as a substitute singer when the barber shop quartet enters a singing contest.

The Lodge
W: Jim Parker & Arnold Margolin. Goober refuses to allow Howard to join the lodge.

The Darling Fortune
W: Jim Parker & Arnold Margolin. GS: Denver Pyle. The hillbilly Darling family inherit three hundred dollars.

Aunt Bee's Crowning Glory
W: Ronald Axe. Aunt Bee buys a blond wig.

The Ball Game
W: Rance Howard & Sid Morse. Andy becomes the umpire for the junior baseball game.

Goober Makes History
W: Paul David & John Greene. GS: Richard Bull. Goober grows a beard and becomes a philosopher.

The Senior Play
W: Bill Idelson & Sam Bobrick. GS: Leon Ames. Helen and her students try to teach the old school principal a lesson.

Big Fish in a Small Town
W: Bill Idelson & Sam Bobrick. GS: Sam Reese. Howard, a novice, is the only one to catch a fish, putting all the other fishermen to shame.

Mind Over Matter
W: Ron Friedman & Pat McCormick. Goober is convinced by his friends, after an accident, that he has whiplash.

Politics Begin at Home
W: Bill Idelson & Sam Bobrick. Both Aunt Bee and Howard decide to run for town councilman.

A New Doctor in Town
W: Ray Brenner & Barry Blitzer. GS: William Christopher. Andy lets the new doctor take out Opie's tonsils to show the town he can be trusted.

Opie Finds a Baby
W: Ray Brenner & Barry Blitzer. GS: Jack Nicholson. Opie and his friend find an abandoned baby.

Only a Rose
W: Jim Parker & Arnold Margolin. GS: John Reilly. Opie ruins Bee's prize rose.

Otis the Deputy
W: Jim Parker & Arnold Margolin. GS: Charles Dierkop, Joe Turkell. Otis and Howard try to rescue Andy from the clutches of two bank robbers.

Don't Miss a Good Bet
W: Fred S. Fox. Andy and his friends are swindled by a con man.

Dinner at Eight
W: Budd Grossman. GS: Emory Parnell, Mabel Albertson. Andy finds that his friends all have made him dinner and he can't hurt their feelings by refusing, so he has to eat it all.

Andy's Old Girlfriend
W: Sid Morse. Andy's old girlfriend moves back, making Helen jealous.

The Statue
W: Fred S. Fox. GS: Dale McKennon. Andy and Aunt Bee discover that their ancestor whom the town is honoring with a statue was a swindler.

Aunt Bee's Restaurant
W: Roland Axe & Lee Roberts. GS: Keye Luke. Aunt Bee becomes the co-owner of a Chinese restaurant.

Floyd's Barbershop
W: Jim Parker & Arnold Margolin. Floyd decides to give up his business when Howard buys his building and raises the rent.

A Visit to Barney Fife
W: Bill Idelson & Sam Bobrick. GS: Richard Chambers. Andy visits Barney who is now a policeman in Raleigh.

Barney Comes to Mayberry
W: Sid Morse. GS: Chet Stratton, Patty Regan. Detective Barney visits Mayberry.

Helen the Authoress
W: Douglas Tibbles. GS: Laurie Main, Keith Andes, Elaine Joyce. Helen writes a children's book which is going to be published.

Goodbye, Dolly
W: Michael Morris & Seaman Jacobs. GS: Tom Tully. Andy and Opie help an old milk wagon horse which has just been retired.

Opie's Piano Lesson
W: Leo & Pauline Townsend. Opie decides he wants to play the piano until it interferes with his football practice.

Howard the Comedian
W: Michael Morris & Seaman Jacobs. Howard goes on a TV amateur show when he decides to be a comedian.

Big Brothers
W: Fred S. Fox. GS: Elizabeth Mac-Rae. Howard volunteers to be a Big Brother to a high school boy.

Opie's Most Unforgettable Character
W. Michael Morris & Seaman Jacobs. GS: Sheldon Golomb. Andy is upset when Opie doesn't choose him for the subject of a school composition.

Goober's Contest
W: Ron Friedman & Pat McCormick. A printing error awards a larger cash prize than he planned to give when he runs a contest.

Opie's First Love
W: Ron Friedman, Pat McCormick. Opie's girlfriend dumps him at the last minute before a party.

Goober the Executive
W: Seaman Jacobs & Michael Morris. Goober buys the gas station.

Howard's Main Event
W. Earl Barret & Robert C. Dennis. Howard is threatened by an old boyfriend when he dates Millie.

Aunt Bee the Juror
W: Kent Wilson. Aunt Bee is the only juror to disagree on the other jurors' decision.

Howard the Bowler
W: Kent Wilson. Howard is chosen as a last-minute substitute for the bowling team.

Opie Steps up in Class
W: Joseph Bonaduce. Andy sends Opie to a fancy boys' camp.

Andy's Trip to Raleigh
W: Joseph Bonaduce. Andy breaks a date with Helen to visit a beautiful lawyer.

A Trip to Mexico
W: Perry Grant & Richard Bensfield. Aunt Bee wins a free trip to Mexico but can't decide whom to take with her.

Tape Recorder
W: Seaman Jacobs & Michael Morris. Opie tape records a bank robber's confession against Andy's orders.

Opie's Group
W: Douglas Tibbles. Opie joins a rock and roll band.

Aunt Bee and the Lecturer
W: Seamon Jacobs & Ed James. Aunt Bee dates a lecturer.

Andy's Investment
W: Michael Morris & Seamon Jacobs. Andy opens a coin laundry to earn some extra money for Opie to go to college.

Suppose Andy Gets Sick
W: Jack Raymond. When Andy gets sick, Goober takes over.

Howard and Millie
W: Joseph Bonaduce. Howard proposes to Millie.

Aunt Bee's Cousin
W: Richard Bensfield & Perry Grant. Aunt Bee thinks her visiting cousin is very rich, only Andy knows better.

Howard's New Life
W: Richard Bensfield & Perry Grant. Howard quits his job to become a beachcomber.

Emmett's Brother-in-Law
W: James L. Brooks. Emmett's wife and her brother convince him to become an insurance man.

The Mayberry Chef
W: James L. Brooks. Aunt Bee is offered a job as a TV chef.

The Church Benefactors
W: Eart Barret & Robert C. Dennis. When someone donates $500 to the church, everyone has an idea how it should be spent.

Opie's Drugstore Job
W: Kent Wilson. Opie breaks an expensive bottle of perfume on the first day of his new job.

Barney Hosts a Summit Meeting
W: Aaron Ruben. Barney gets Andy to let him use his house for an East-West summit meeting.

Mayberry R.F.D.
W: Bob Ross. D: Peter Baldwin. GS: Ken Berry. Sam invites a friend from Italy to help him on the farm. [This was the pilot for the spinoff series "Mayberry R.F.D."]

Goober Goes to the Auto Show
W: Joseph Bonaduce. Goober lies about himself to impress an old mechanic friend.

Aunt Bee's Big Moment
W: Richard Bensfield & Perry Grant. Aunt Bee takes flying lessons.

Helen's Past
W: Douglas Tibbles. Andy learns that Helen has a police record.

Emmett's Anniversary
W: Perry Grant & Richard Bensfield. Emmett tries to keep the mink coat he bought for his wife a secret.

The Wedding
W: Joseph Bonaduce. Howard throws a party when his mother remarries and moves away.

Sam for Town Council
W: Dick Bensfield & Perry Grant. Andy convinces Sam to run for City Council.

Opie and Mike
W: Douglas Tibbles & Bob Ross. Opie tries to help Sam's son Mike solve a problem.

A Girl for Goober
W: Bruce Howard. Sam and Andy enroll in a computer-dating service.

THE ANN SOTHERN SHOW

On the air 10/6/58, off 9/25/61. CBS. 93 episodes. B&W Film. Broadcast: Oct 1958-Jul 1960 Mon 9:30-10; Oct 1960-Dec 1960 Thu 9:30-10; Dec 1960-Mar 1961 Thu 7:30-8; Jul 1961-Sept 1961 Mon 9:30-10. Producer: Desi Arnaz/ Ann Sothern. Prod Co: United Artists. Synd: Metromedia Producers Corp.

CAST: Katy O'Conner (played by Ann Sothern), James Devery (Don Porter), Delbert Gray (Louis Nye), Woody (Ken Berry), Olive Smith (Ann Tyrell), Jason Macauley (Ernest Truex), Johnny Wallace (Jack Mullaney), Flora Macauley (Reta Shaw), Oscar Pudney (Jesse White), Paul Martine (Jacques Scott).

The story of Katy O'Conner, an assistant manager of the Bartley House hotel in New York, and the problems she faced while running the hotel. This series has almost been forgotten, with time and syndication problems. The series is currently running on one station in the entire country. The syndicator does not promote the series.

The Bridal Suite [Pilot]
Katy tries to help a young newlywed couple.

New Lease on Lip
A group of Katy's friends, who fancy themselves amateur psychologists, convince her that she dominates Olive.

Six Wives Plus Two
A guest at the hotel turns out to be a maharajah in disguise.

Love Comes to Olive
Olive falls in love with Paul, the French room clerk.

Governess for a Day
Nine-year-old Donald Carpenter is a permanent guest at the hotel.

It's a Dog's Life
GS: Barry Gordon. Katy gives Donald a puppy and lives to regret it.

Masquerade Ball
GS: Frank Faylon, Alan Carney. A gang of thieves crack the hotel's safe when the Bartley holds a masquerade ball.

Say It with Music
GS: Leo Fuchs. Katy's surprise party turns into a brawl.

The Thanksgiving Story
Katy suspects that young Donald has taken up with a gang of hoodlums.

Countess of Bartley
GS: Alan Marshall, Gladys Cooper. The Duchess of Beldonia and her playboy nephew Count Ferdinand check into the Bartley House.

The Big Gamble
Katy is placed in charge of the Bartley House when Macauley and his wife leave on vacation.

Three Loves Has Katy
GS: Gordon Jones, Phil Reed. Katy is delighted when three of her old boyfriends come to the Bartley House for a college reunion.

East Side Story
GS: Mark Damon. A long-time employee at the Bartley House talks Katy into hiring his near-delinquent son as a bellhop.

Johnny Moves Up
Johnny, the bellhop, comes to Katy for help when he learns his mother is coming for a visit.

Give it Back to the Indians
On a man-in-the-street show, Katy deplores the plight of the American Indian.

The Five-Year Itch
Katy realizes that she has become short tempered and concludes that she is bored with her job.

Ann Sothern.

Hoorah for the Irish
GS: Cecil Kellaway.   After winning a sweepstakes fortune, Sean O'Conner decides to leave Ireland and visit his niece Katy.

The High Cost of Living
Discouraged by the high cost of everything, Katy and Olive become budget conscious.

The O'Conners Stick Together
GS: Cecil Kellaway, Terence DeMarvey. Katy is unhappy to learn that her Uncle Sean, visiting New York after winning the sweepstakes, is still feuding with his brother.

Two on the Aisle, or Happy Days Are Here Again
A press agent sends Katy two tickets to a hit Broadway musical.

Stand-In Heiress
Katy is delighted to learn that her old friend Stella Gordon, a wealthy widow, is engaged to be married.

Katy's Big Surprise
Macauley is being transferred to the Calcutta branch of the hotel chain.

Katy and the New Boss
When it appears that Devery is too hard on the staff, Katy decides to take matters into her own hands.

The Engagement Ring
Devery asks Katy to have the setting of his mother's diamond ring changed.

The Road to Health
Katy is surprised to learn that Devery has fallen in love with a much younger woman.

The Square Peg
Devery decides to make the hotel staff more efficient so he hires a psychologist to give them tests.

Katy's Investment Club
GS: Paul Dubov. Michel, the Bartley House chef, makes spectacular profits from his membership in a stock market club.

Geisha Girl
Tired of doing menial tasks for Devery, Katy considers hiring a houseboy.

The Ugly Bonnet
Katy is surprised when her boss presents her with a gift, a silly hat.

The Raise
At the Bartley House, frantic preparations are made for the visit of Mrs. Thompson.

Springtime for Katy
Katy feels Devery is taking her for granted.

Katy Goes Thru Channels
Katy has decided that military techniques will help him win the Bartley trophy for efficient operation.

The Boss's Son
Tom Bartley, the playboy son of the founder of the hotel chain, drops in at the Bartley House and bothers everyone.

Promotion for Johnny
Overhearing a conversation in which his name is mentioned, Johnny concludes he is about to be fired.

Baby at Bartley House
Katy and Olive promise to watch a neighbor's baby.

Old Buddy Boy
Tom Burke, a manager of the Bartley House in Honolulu, pays a visit to New York.

Katy and Olive's Nervous Breakdown
Katy and Olive decide they no longer wish to share an apartment, then Katy begins looking for a new roommate.

The Sal Mineo Story
GS: Sal Mineo. Musician Nicky Sivero has a girlfriend and Katy is eager for the young couple to get married, but Devery opposes the match.

The Lucy Story
GS: Lucille Ball. Lucy Ricardo checks into the Bartley House loudly denouncing marriage because Ricky has gone skin-diving without her. This is a crossover episode from "I Love Lucy."

Katy and the Cowboy
GS: Guy Madison. The rodeo comes to town and Katy eyes the handsome star, Bill Barker.

Domestic Katy
Katy is envious of a happily married friend and decides to do something about it.

The Pay Off
At the same time that companies are submitting bids on air-conditioning contracts for the hotel, Katy starts sporting a new mink coat.

Queen for a Night
Katy arranges a blind date with Olive for a friend of Devery's.

Katy and the New Girl
GS: Eva Gabor. Olive goes on vacation and a girlfriend named Steffi is hired as a temporary secretary.

Top Executive
GS: Joyce Meadows. An attractive woman named Liza Vincent arrives in town to do an article on Devery for Top Executive magazine.

Katy's Tender Trap
Devery thinks that Katy is out to trap him into marriage.

Katy Mismanages
Devery decides to go on vacation leaving Katy in charge.

Woman Behind the Throne
GS: John Emery. Katy attempts to help Devery become president of the Executive Club.

Slightly Married
Katy gives refuge to a runaway orphan.

Devery's White Elephant
Devery thinks that he has found a tenant for an expensive suite in the hotel.

Katy's New Career
Katy becomes disgusted with her long hours and short pay, so she tries to get new employment.

The Witness
Devery is threatened with a lawsuit because of an accident he caused.

The Dog Who Came to Dinner
A stray puppy appears at Olive and Katy's home and they take it in feeling sorry for it.

Olive's Dream Man
Olive has told all her friends that she has a suave, handsome new boyfriend and must prove it.

A Touch of Larveny
Devery starts looking for a suitable proprietor for the new cigar counter in the hotel lobby.

Common Cents
Olive has a date with a handsome stranger.

The Freeloader
Oscar introduces his parasite cousin as a rich Latin American cattleman.

I Can Get it for You Wholesale
Katy and Olive are in the market for a new piano.

Billy
There is a movie producer staying at the hotel and Katy schemes to get an audition for a talented bellhop.

Katy Meets Danger
GS: John Daly. The Bartley House is hit by a series of robberies.

The Roman Hatter
GS: Nico Minardos. An Italian designer named Giovani Daroda is in town selling wild hats.

Surprise, Surprise
Katy pretends she is sick so she can sneak off and plan a surprise party for Devery.

One for the Books
Two of the oldest residents of the hotel think it is haunted.

Doubting Devery
A fast-talking salesman makes Devery think that his staff is disloyal.

Boy Genius
Katy learns that ten-year-old Richy Gordon gave up music to help support his family.

Wedding March
Katy and Jim go all out to provide Olive with a wedding when she accepts a proposal.

Angels
Singer Johnny Daniels invites prospective backers to the hotel to hear songs from his new show.

Pinch Hitter
Little Richy Gordon wants to be on the baseball team but the other kids don't want him.

Tooth for a Tooth
Olive visits a charming dentist when she has a bad toothache.

The Invitation
The hotel is buzzing as everyone makes plans to attend Olive's wedding.

Vamp Till Ready
When Katy tries to keep Delbert occupied while Olive is away, she finds herself involved in a romantic triangle.

Option Time
It is renewal time on Devery's contract as manager of the hotel and he would like a better deal, so he creates a story about another job offer.

Olive in Love
Olive has a crush on her dentist Dr. Gray.

Setting the Date
Now that Olive has finally coaxed a proposal from her boyfriend Delbert, she is anxious for him to set the wedding date, but Delbert keeps stalling.

The Girls
GS: Janis Page. Katy gets worried that a couple of her old sorority sisters are coming to town. She recalls that neither one was the most popular, so she plans to cover up her own success.

Go-Go Gordon
GS: Jimmy Field, Chick Chandler. Oscar Pudney lures Richy Gordon away from Katy in order that he can practice rock and roll.

Hasta Luego
GS: Cesar Romero. Katy and Olive are awakened by a crashing racket which turns out to be Bernardo Diaz and his Spanish dancers.

The Proposal
GS: Paul Dubov. Olive has tried every trick her romantic mind can think of but she can't get Delbert to propose.

Secret Admirer
Oscar has been insulting customers at his cigar stand, so Devery and Katy decide this is the time to terminate his lease.

The Other Woman
Richy has fallen for a ten-year-old girl.

The Elopement
Katy is convinced that the only way for Olive and Dr. Gray to get married is to elope.

Operation Pudney
There is a watch Katy wants but can't afford, so Pudney decides to start a collection to buy her the watch.

Mr. Big Shot
GS: James Millhollin. Mary Ann Meacham, the girl from back home, comes to the hotel looking for Woody, thinking he is an executive for the hotel.

Just Friends
Devery prepares to take it easy from his nightly routine, but he thinks Katy is lonely so he decides to keep her company.

The Royal Visit
GS: Eva Gabor. A secretary to a princess can't book a hotel room because of the princess's little dog.

Toujours L'Amour
Olive wants a Paris honeymoon but Delbert prefers Camp Winamega, where he spent his summers as a child.

The Widow
Oscar Pudney is shocked when Bertha Schuyler buys an expensive box of chocolates for her pet poodle. Oscar would like a little cash himself, so he decides to date Bertha.

Two's Company
Olive and Delbert find an apartment that is perfect, but Delbert is worried if it is large enough for his mother to move in with them.

Always April
GS: Constance Bennett, Marty Ingels, John Emery. Katy discovers that April Fleming, an aspiring actress staying at the hotel, has run away from home.

Loving Arms
GS: Van Johnson. Terry Tyler, the creator of a TV series which Devery thinks is insulting to hotel operators, comes to the hotel for research.

Pandora
GS: Pat Carroll, Guy Mitchell. Katy goes to Hollywood where she visits Anthony Bardot, an actor. When she arrives at his mansion, he asks her to help find him a secretary.

The Wedding
GS: James Milhollin. It is Olive and Delbert's wedding day and Devery has everything perfectly planned, but he didn't count on Delbert's mother-in-law.

The Beginning
Olive is so happily married to Delbert that she tries to persuade Katy to get married to Devery.

BACHELOR FATHER

On the air 9/15/57, off 9/25/62. CBS, NBC & ABC. 30 min. film. B&W. 153 episodes. Broadcast: Sept 1957-Jun 1959 CBS Sun 7:30-8; June 1959-Sept 1961 NBC Thu 9-9:30; Oct 1961-Sept 1962 ABC Tue 8-8:30. Producer: Harry Ackerman/Everitt Freeman/Robert Sparks. Prod Co/Synd: Universal.

CAST: Bentley Gregg (played by John Forsythe), Kelly Gregg (Noreen Corcoran), Peter Tong (Sammee Tong), Ginger (Bernadette Withers), Howard Meechim (Jimmy Boyd), Cal Mitchell (Del Moore), Cousin Charlie Fong (Victor Sen Yung).

WRITERS: Nate Monaster, Arthur Alsberg, Jay Sommers, Don Nelson, Howard Leeds, Jerry Davis, Tom August, Laurence Marks, Milton Pascal, Ben Starr, Martin Ragaway, Si Rose, Seaman Jacobs, David Schwartz, Bill Raynor, Bob Fisher, Alan Lipscott, Lou Derman, Everett Freeman.

DIRECTORS: Earl Bellamy, John Newland, Stanley Z. Cherry, Sidney Lanfield, Jerry Hopper.

Bentley Gregg, a Beverly Hills attorney, becomes the guardian of his 13-year-old niece Kelly. The youngster upsets the normal household routine of her unmarried uncle, and episodes depict their relationship. Both are cared for by Peter Tong, a wise-cracking Chinese houseboy. The series is hardly (if ever) seen in syndication because in today's society a Chinese servant in a television series is considered derogatory.

Bentley and the PTA
W: Nate Monaster & Arthur Alsberg. D: Jerry Hopper. GS: Madge Blake, Florida Friebus. Bentley is caught in the middle when he has a date with a famous movie star on the same night as his niece's PTA meeting.

Uncle Bentley Keeps His Promise
W: Jay Sommers & Don Nelson. D: Jerry Hopper. Kelly brags that she knows Ronnie Mann, a teen idol, and must produce him for a party she organized.

Bentley vs. the Girl Scouts
W: Jerry David & Howard Leeds. D: Jerry Hopper. GS: June Blair. Bentley is eager to attend his niece's girl scout meeting to impress the beautiful 20-year-old troopleader.

Bentley and the Lady Doctor
W: Nate Monaster & Arthur Alsberg.

D: Jerry Hopper. Bentley seeks the help of a beautiful psychiatrist to help curb Kelly's sloppy habits.

Bentley and the Aunts
W: Nate Monaster & Arthur Alsberg. D: Jerry Hopper. GS: Mabel Albertson. Kelly is barred from a social group because one of the member's relatives hates Bentley.

Bentley and the Revolting Housekeepers
W: Nate Monaster & Arthur Alsberg. D: Jerry Hopper. GS: Barbara Eden. Bentley hires a housekeeper and soon finds his troubles have just begun as his family turns the house into a shambles.

Bentley and the Baby Sitter
W: Nate Monaster & Arthur Alsberg. D: Jerry Hopper. Kelly's babysitting venture ends in disaster when Bentley

is mistaken.

Date with Kelly
W: Jerry David & Howard Leeds. D:
Jerry Hopper. Kelly is all excited
about her first date with a prospective
client of Bentley's.

Uncle Bentley Loans Out Peter
W: Nate Monaster & Arthur Alsberg.
D: Jerry Hopper. To help his girlfriend, Bentley loans out Peter's services and soon finds that he can't live
without his Oriental friend.

Uncle Bentley and the Matchmaker
W: Nate Monaster & Arthur Alsberg.
D: Jerry Hopper. GS: Gavin Gordon,
Jeanne Wood. Bentley is frustrated
when his attractive new neighbor won't
go out with him.

Bentley and the Talent Contest
W: Nate Monaster & Arthur Alsberg.
D: Jerry Hopper. GS: Elvia Allman,
Les Tremayne. Bentley brags to his
friends that Kelly is very talented,
only Kelly wants to know what her
talents are.

Waiting for Kelly
W: Nate Monaster & Arthur Alsberg.
D: Jerry Hopper. GS: Whit Bissell,
Hope Summers. While Kelly is out on
a date, Bentley is so concerned over
his niece that he ignores his own girlfriend.

Bentley and His Junior Image
W: Nate Monaster & Arthur Alsberg.
D: Jerry Hopper. Bentley gets caught
in the middle when Kelly is out on a
double date.

Bentley and the Social Worker
W: Nate Monaster & Arthur Alsberg.
D: Jerry Hopper. Bentley becomes
Kelly's legal guardian and his first task
as father is to control his daughter's
television habits.

Bentley the Homemaker
W: Nate Monaster & Arthur Alsberg.
D: Jerry Hopper. GS: Jack Benny.

Bentley has been spending too much
time away from home and decides to
gather the family for some old-fashioned fun and games.

A Sister for Kelly
W: Nate Monaster & Arthur Alsberg.
D: Jerry Hopper. Kelly tries to marry
off Bentley to her girlfriend's mother
in the hopes of gaining a sister.

Woman of the House
W: Nate Monaster & Arthur Alsberg.
D: Jerry Hopper. To learn the meaning of authority, Bentley lets Kelly
take over the household.

Peter Falls in Love
W: Nate Monaster & Arthur Alsberg.
D: Jerry Hopper. Peter, Kelly and
Bentley all fall in love and then just as
quickly break up.

Bentley's Prospective Son-in-Law
W: Nate Monaster & Arthur Alsberg.
D: Jerry Hopper. Kelly brings home
a shy, bumbling boy, much to Bentley's dismay, who tries his best to
get rid of the boy.

Bentley's Clubhouse
W: Nate Monaster & Arthur Alsberg.
D: Jerry Hopper. Kelly's girlfriends
have all their meetings in her home,
which upsets the girls' mothers so
much they forbid any further meetings.

Parents Night
W: Jerry Davis & Tom August. D:
John Newland. Bentley gets buried in
responsibilities when he volunteers his
services in the school play.

Bentley and the Finishing School
W: Nate Monaster & Arthur Alsberg.
D: John Newland. GS: Jack Albertson. Bentley sends Kelly to charm
school when all his efforts to get her
to keep her room clean fail miserably.

Bentley and the Kleptomaniac
W: Laurence Marks & Milton Pascal.
D: John Newland. To get Bentley off
Kelly's back, Howard convinces his
brother he is a kleptomaniac.

Bentley and Peter's Teacher
W: Laurence Marks & Milton Pascal.
D: John Newland. Peter goes to night
school and soon drives everyone crazy
with his scholarly remarks.

Bentley the Star Maker
W: Nate Monaster & Arthur Alsberg.
D: John Newland. After Bentley
promises a famous teen idol will perform at Kelly's school, he learns the
entertainer will not be able to appear.

Bentley's Big Case
W: Nate Monaster & Arthur Alsberg.
D: John Newland. GS: Olan Soule.
When Peter buys an old car, he pre-
occupies himself with it so much he
neglects Bentley and Kelly.

Decisions Decisions
W: Jerry Davis & Tom August. D:
John Newland. When two boys invite
Kelly to the prom, she is confused as
to which offer to accept.

Bentley's Aunt Caroline
W: Arthur Alsberg & Ben Starr. D:
John Newland. Bentley's Aunt Caroline shows up and transforms Kelly
into a sophisticated, stylishly dressed
young lady.

Bentley Leads a Dog's Life
W: Arthur Alsberg & Ben Starr. D:
John Newland. GS: Gavin Gordon.
The Gregg family is going away for a
weekend and are overly concerned
about what to do about Jasper, the
family dog.

Kelly's Mad Crush
W: Arthur Alsberg & Ben Starr. D:
John Newland. Kelly is in love with a
client of Bentley's and imagines the
boy as a prince who can do no wrong.

Bentley the Hero
W: Arthur Alsberg & Ben Starr. D:
Don Taylor. Bentley saves a young
girl from drowning and soon learns the
girl wants a part in a play being produced by a client of his.

A Phone for Kelly
W: Arthur Alsberg & Ben Starr. D:
Bretaigne Windust. GS: Mabel Forrest.
Kelly is monopolizing the phone and
Bentley tries desperately to get her to
reduce her phone calls, including get-
ting a second phone.

Bentley and the Motorcycle
W: Arthur Alsberg & Ben Starr. D:
Don Taylor. GS: John Hart. Kelly is
going steady with a wild motorcyclist,
sending Bentley into action to break
up the romantic couple.

Bentley the Organizer
W: Arthur Alsberg & Ben Starr. D:
Don Taylor. When Bentley announces
he has business which will take him to
New York for six months, his family
tries to keep the house in order.

Bentley and the Beauty Contest
W: Jerry Davis, Arthur Alsberg & Ben
Starr. D: Bretaigne Windust. Bentley
is a judge in a beauty contest and is
constantly being bothered by prospective beauties who want nothing less
than first prize.

Bentley the Proud Father
W: Arthur Alsberg & Ben Starr. D:
Earl Bellamy. GS: Whit Bissell, Carl
Crow. At a carnival, Bentley is in-
volved in a con game with a little boy.

Bentley Man of Steel
W: Jerry Davis & Tom August. D: Earl
Bellamy. Kelly prompts Bentley to
begin a program of exercise and good
nutrition when he complains of fatigue.

Bentley's New House
W: Arthur Alsberg & Joe Quillan. D:
Bretaigne Windust. Bentley redecorates his home and decides he doesn't
want to part with his old furniture.

Bentley and the Dog Trainer
W: William Raynor & Everett Freeman. D: Bretaigne Windust. GS: Howard McNear. Jasper is sent to a dog
training school after he destroys and
hides all sorts of the family's personal
belongings.

Peter Meets His Match
W: Si Rose & Seamon Jacobs. D: Sidney Lanfield. GS: Mari Aldon. To impress a young lady, Peter takes lessons in courting from Bentley.

Kelly the Politician
W: Henry Sharp. D: Bretaigne Windust. GS: John Eldredge. Kelly is running for President of the Student Council against the daughter of one of Bentley's clients.

Bentley and the Combo
W: Laurence Marks, Jerry Davis & William Raynor. D: Sidney Miller. When Bentley takes over Kelly's high school combo he is pestered by Hughie, an incompetent saxophone player.

Bentley and the Gullible Guitarist
W: Alan Lipscott & Robert Fisher. D: Sidney Lanfield. Bentley and Howard conspire to teach Kelly a lesson after she has been forcing favors out of everybody.

East Meets West
W: Jerry Davis, Dave Schwartz. D: Bretaigne Windust. Peter enlists the aid of his cousin Charlie to convince Bentley to put a TV in the kitchen.

Bentley and the Blood Bank
W: Arthur Alsberg, Joe Quillan & Mel Diamond. D: Earl Bellamy. GS: Joyce Meadows, Sue Ann Langdon. To impress a beautiful nurse, Bentley delivers a phony wartime speech at the annual Red Cross drive.

The Case Against Gisele
W: Si Rose & Seamon Jacobs. D: Sidney Lanfield. GS: Gisele MacKenzie. Peter plans to sue the television station where he injured his back for $10,000.

Bentley and the Brainy Beauty
W: Si Rose & Seamon Jacobs. D: Sidney Lanfield. GS: Barbara English. Bentley is fed up with dumb girls and sets out to find one with intelligence and gets more than he asked for.

Kelly's Secret
W: Martin Ragaway. D: Bretaigne Windust. GS: David Lewis, Whit Bissell. Kelly tries to hide a bridal shower from Bentley when she finds out the groom is being hired by a marriage-hating client of Bentley's.

Kelly's Idol
W: Laurence Marks & William Raynor. D: Bretaigne Windust. GS: Donna Douglas. Kelly tries to turn all her boyfriends into carbon copies of Bentley.

Bentley and Grandpa Ling
W: Cynthia Lindsay & Leo Townsend. D: Sidney Lanfield. GS: Charles Watts. Peter's cunning Grandpa arrives, causing many problems for Bentley.

The Woman's Angle
W: Arthur Alsberg, Joe Quillan & Keith Fowler. D: Earl Bellamy. Kelly feels she is being treated like a child and wants to share in the adult world, so Bentley puts her to work in his office.

A Key for Kelly
W: Robert Fisher & Alan Lipscott. D: Sidney Lanfield. GS: Whit Bissell. Kelly maneuvers Bentley into giving her a key to the house so she can impress her boyfriends.

Bentley and the Majorette
W: Dave Schwartz. D: Sidney Miller. GS: Joan Tompkins. Bentley takes an interest in a very withdrawn schoolmate of Kelly's and prompts her to take up a hobby.

Bentley the Gentleman Farmer
W: Arthur Alsberg & William Raynor. D: Bretaigne Windust. Bentley tries to help Kelly grow vegetables for her botany class and ends up fighting a pesky gopher.

Kelly the Golddigger
W: Mel Diamond & John Kohn. D: Norman Abbott. GS: Jeff Silver. Bentley tries to teach Kelly the value of money after she becomes interested

in a wealthy boy only for his financial success.

Bentley's Double Play
W: Robert Fisher & Alan Lipscott. D: Sidney Lanfield. GS: Linda Wong. Bentley directs Peter's night school play and unwillingly casts Peter in the lead role.

Bentley Plays Cupid
W: Jerry Davis & Howard Leeds. D: Sidney Lanfield. Bentley tries to arrange a match between his overweight secretary and his friend Chuck.

The Fishing Trip
W: Arthur Alsberg & Mel Diamond. D: Richard Kinon. GS: Del Moore, Milton Frome. Bentley and Kelly go on a fishing trip to show Bentley's friends a father and daughter can have as much fun as a father and son.

Bentley Goes to Washington
W: Robert Fisher & Alan Lipscott. D: Bretaigne Windust. GS: William Forrest. Bentley decides to accept a job in Washington despite strong opposition from his family when they learn Jasper will have to be left behind.

Kelly and the College Man
W: Arthur Alsberg & Mel Diamond. D: Ezra Stone. GS: Sally Kellerman. Bentley schemes to break up a romance between Kelly and a 22-year-old college student.

Kelly the Career Woman
W: Si Rose & Seamon Jacobs. D: Earl Bellamy. Kelly decides she wants to start her career as an assistant in her father's office, causing him much grief.

Where There's a Will
W: Robert Fisher & Alan Lipscott. D: Bretaigne Windust. GS: Kip King. Bentley plays detective to figure out who stole the will of a former employee when the lights suddenly go out.

The Very Friendly Witness
W: Si Rose & Seamon Jacobs. D: Earl Bellamy. GS: John Tabor. Bentley interviews a beautiful witness to an accident which makes Elena, his latest girlfriend, extremely jealous.

Bentley and the Bartered Bride
W: Robert Fisher & Alan Lipscott. D: Bretaigne Windust. GS: Whitney Blake. A Chinese matchmaker tries to con Peter out of $200 and into marrying an overweight Chinese girl.

Bentley and the Beach Bum
W: Arthur Alsberg & Mel Diamond. D: Earl Bellamy. GS: Jackie Russell, Lester Parr. Kelly falls for Barry Willis, a beach bum whom Bentley is bent on removing from his and Kelly's life.

The Fortune Cookie Caper
W: Si Rose & Seamon Jacobs. D: Earl Bellamy. GS: Herb Vigran, Olan Soule. When Bentley refuses Peter a raise in pay, Peter decides to go into the fortune cookie business.

The Blonde Issue
W: Robert Fisher & Alan Lipscott. D: Sidney Miller. When Kelly loses the attention of her latest romantic interest Don to a blonde, she decides to dye her hair, sending Bentley into a rage.

Bentley and the Travel Agent
W: Mel Diamond, Arthur Alsberg & Everett Freeman. D: Earl Bellamy. GS: Myrna Fahey, Charles Lane. Bentley's vacation plans backfire when everyone in the family has different ideas on where to spend their holiday.

Bentley the Model Citizen
W: Si Rose & Seamon Jacobs. D: Sidney Miller. Bentley falls for a beautiful member of the city planning committee.

Bentley the Stage Mother
W: Robert Fisher & Alan Lipscott. D: Norman Abbott. GS: George Ives. Kelly enrolls in acting school despite her father's protest.

Bentley Meets the Perfect Woman
W: Robert Fisher & Alan Lipscott. D: Norman Abbott. Bentley's latest girlfriend is an efficiency expert who drives Peter, Kelly and Kitty crazy with her constant cleaning and reorganizing.

A Man of Importance
W: Mel Diamond & Arthur Alsberg. D: Earl Bellamy. GS: Sid Melton, J. Pat O'Malley. Peter is feeling low when Suzie falls for a college student, so Bentley suggests he become a famous inventor.

Bentley's Birthday Gift
W: Everett Freeman & Sam Locke. D: Earl Bellamy. Kelly plans to give Bentley a birthday party but encounters many obstacles she didn't anticipate.

Jasper, the Second
W: Everett Freeman. D: Earl Bellamy. GS: Stanley Adams. After the death of Jasper, Peter and Kelly try and persuade Bentley to adopt another mutt.

Kelly Learns to Drive
W: Si Rose & Seamon Jacobs. D: Earl Bellamy. Kelly is out on her first driving lesson while Bentley is at home worrying himself to death.

Bentley's Mad Friends.
W: Keith Fowler & Everett Freeman. D: Earl Bellamy. GS: Joe Flynn. Bentley tries to patch up a client's marriage and ends up arguing with Peter, Kelly and the client.

A Crush on Bentley
W: Everett Freeman. D: Earl Bellamy. GS: Frank Wilcox. Kelly's friend Liz develops a crush on Bentley and follows him to a mountain resort when he is vacationing.

Kelly the Matchmaker
W: Mel Diamond & Arthur Alsberg. D: Earl Bellamy. GS: Mike Mazurki. Kelly's matchmaking pursuits drive Bentley to come up with a plan to cure her forever.

Hilda the Jewel
W: Lou Derman & Mel Diamond. D: Earl Bellamy. Bentley brings home a helper for Peter at the same time Peter wanted Suzie to act as his assistant.

Trial Separation
W: Robert Fisher & Alan Lipscott. D: Earl Bellamy. GS: Victor Sen Yung. Peter tries a week away from Bentley to release the hostility built up between employer and employee, but Bentley fears Peter has left for good.

Bentley and the Big Board
W: Si Rose & Seamon Jacobs. D: Earl Bellamy. GS: Mary Tyler Moore, Neil Hamilton. Bentley advises Kelly and Peter to invest in the stock market and lives to regret the suggestion when they ruin an important business deal.

It Happens in November
W: Si Rose & Seamon Jacobs. D: Earl Bellamy. Bentley volunteers his home for an upcoming election to get close to the election board's attractive spokeswoman.

Bentley Goes to Europe
W: Keith Fowler & Everett Freeman. D: Earl Bellamy. GS: Beal Wong. Preparing for an unexpected trip to Europe, Peter discovers he can't get a passport because there is no record of his birth.

Bentley and the Lost Chord
W: Danny Simon. D: Earl Bellamy. GS: Alvy Moore. A TV producer wants Peter to record a tune he was humming to use as the theme of his new series, only Peter can't recall the melody.

Dear Bentley
W: Robert Fisher & Alan Lipscott. D: Earl Bellamy. GS: Del Moore, Vito Scotti. Bentley has been interfering in Kelly's school advice column, prompting an angry group of parents to teach Bentley a lesson.

Paris in the Spring
W: Howard Leeds. D: Earl Bellamy.

GS: Fritz Feld. In Paris, Bentley, Peter and Kelly all fall in love, but refuse to admit to each other they have been bitten by the love bug.

Mystery Witness
W: Lou Derman. D: Earl Bellamy. After Kelly is involved in a traffic accident, Bentley tries to persuade a shy witness to appear in court and clear his daughter of any negligence.

Bentley and the Great Debate
W: Charles Marion. D: Earl Bellamy. GS: Ryan O'Neal, Raymond Bailey. Bentley is the negotiator between an incompetent basketball coach and an angry mob which wants him replaced.

How to Catch a Man
W: Mel Diamond & Mel Tolkin. D: Earl Bellamy. GS: Milton Frome. Kelly is chasing Tony Demling, a handsome boy in her class, and is crushed when he rejects her advances.

When in Rome
W: Everett Freeman & Keith Fowler. D: Earl Bellamy. GS: Peter Leeds. On a business trip in Rome, Bentley solves a major setback by enlisting the aid of a feisty tour guide.

Ginger's Big Romance
W: Ralph Goodman & Keith Fowler. D: Earl Bellamy. GS: Billy Gray. Ginger and Kelly are having trouble with their boyfriends Jeff and Dave. To fix things up, the girls end up trading boyfriends.

Bentley's Barbecue
W: Si Rose & Seamon Jacobs. D: Earl Bellamy. Refusing to buy a new barbecue, Howard and Kelly attempt to build a new one using bricks and cement.

The Greggs in London
W: William Raynor & Myles Wilder. D: Earl Bellamy. GS: Laurie Main, Pamela Light. In London, Peter clashes with an English butler over everything from menu selection to table settings.

Kelly's Tangled Web
W: John Elliotte. D: Earl Bellamy. After Bentley scolds Kelly for getting out of appointments, he suddenly finds himself breaking a golf date to spend the weekend with a beautiful woman.

Bentley Cracks the Whip
W: Robert Fisher & Alan Lipscott. D: Earl Bellamy. GS: Sid Melton. Bentley puts the family on a tight budget, causing Grandpa Ling to believe the Greggs are broke.

Bentley and the Woodpecker
W: Si Rose & Seamon Jacobs. D: Earl Bellamy. Bentley is bothered by a noisy woodpecker which prevents him from sleeping, and is frustrated when no one will help him get rid of the pesty bird.

Bentley Builds a Pool
W: Robert Fisher & Alan Lipscott. D: Earl Bellamy. After Kelly tells Bentley her latest boyfriend is a swimmer, Bentley decides to put up a pool in the hopes Kelly will spend more time at home.

Encore in Paris
W: Robert Pirosh. D: Earl Bellamy. GS: Alan Hewitt. In Paris, Kelly falls in love with the brother of one of Bentley's friends, then Bentley falls for Babette, his friend's pretty companion.

No Place Like Home
W: William Raynor & Myles Wilder. D: Earl Bellamy. Back from Europe, Bentley, Kelly and Peter become "Travel Bores" who insist on doing nothing except talk about their trip.

Bentley the Angel
W: Robert Fisher & Alan Lipscott. D: Earl Bellamy. Bentley acts as the producer of a play written by Peter and almost loses his shirt when Cousin Charlie embezzles the funds.

Peter Plays Cupid
W: Si Rose & Seamon Jacobs. D: Earl

Bellamy. GS: Vito Scotti. Peter attempts a match between Bentley and his night school teacher Miss Collins.

Kelly Gets a Job
W: Alan Lipscott. D: Earl Bellamy. To pay for a dress, Kelly takes a chance entering the hectic world of modeling.

A Man Among Men
W: William Raynor & Myles Wilder. D: Earl Bellamy. GS: Joby Baker. Upset that Kelly is impressed by a basketball hero, Howard decides the only way to win his girl is to adopt a rugged he-man personality.

Peter's China Doll
W: Si Rose & Seamon Jacobs. D: Earl Bellamy. Peter brings home a little Chinese girl and wants to adopt her as his daughter.

Bentley Swims Upstream
W: Robert Fisher & Alan Lipscott. D: Earl Bellamy. After a salmon research client of Bentley's wants to use Kelly and Howard in a TV commercial, the kids decide to quit school in favor of show business.

Hilda Rides Again
W: Robert Fisher & Alan Lipscott. D: Earl Bellamy. GS: Gene Roth, Fredd Wayne. Bentley's attempts to help a client with his domestic problem backfires when Hilda, his tidy servant, returns to the Gregg's household.

Bentley and the Nature Girl
W: Si Rose & Seamon Jacobs. D: Earl Bellamy. Bentley becomes involved with Kelly's environment instructor and spends his days birdwatching and communing with nature.

Bentley Slays a Dragon
W: Si Rose & Seamon Jacobs. D: Earl Bellamy. GS: Tommy Farrell. Peter wants to improve his meek nature and Bentley tries to help by getting him elected as an officer in the Purple Dragon Lodge.

Peter Gets Jury Notice
W: Danny Simon & Everett Freeman. D: Earl Bellamy. Peter serves on a jury and discovers he is a witness to the case he has been assigned.

Kelly's Charge Account
W: Robert Fisher & Alan Lipscott. D: Earl Bellamy. Kelly maneuvers a credit card out of Bentley and ends up with a $67 bill she can't afford to pay.

A Favor for Bentley
W: Si Rose & Seamon Jacobs. D: Earl Bellamy. GS: Charles Watts. Kelly wants a movie star client of Bentley's to emcee at her club's charity show.

Drop That Calorie
W: Robert Fisher & Alan Lipscott. D: Earl Bellamy. GS: Lori Nelson. When Ginger tells Kelly she is overweight, she goes on a diet campaign that drives her family nearly insane.

Kelly's Graduation
W: Robert Fisher & Alan Lipscott. D: Earl Bellamy. It's Kelly's graduation day and Bentley is full of his own selfish suggestions that drive her up the wall.

The Law and Kelly Gregg
W: Ray Allen & Jim Allen. D: Stanley Z. Cherry. GS: Bill Bixby. Kelly takes an aptitude test from college and decides she wants to be a newspaper reporter, but Bentley feels she should be a lawyer.

Never Steal an Owl
W: Frank Gill & George Carlton Brown. D: Earl Bellamy. GS: Alan Reed. Kelly and Howard are outraged over the pranks the students of City College have pulled on their college and decide to turn the tables on their rival school.

Bentley and the Time Clock
W: Glenn Wheaton & Elroy Schwartz. D: Earl Bellamy. Peter is conned by Charlie into signing a Chinese houseboy contract that turns the meek servant into a money hungry tyrant.

Peter and the Medicine Man
W: Larry Rhine & Everett Freeman.
D: Earl Bellamy. GS: Parley Baer.
Peter convinces Blossom a hospital is a
good place to be until the doctor discovers that it is Peter himself who
should enter one.

Bentley's Catered Affair
W: Robert Fisher & Alan Lipscott. D:
Earl Bellamy. To earn enough money
to buy a car, Howard and Kelly become food caterers for one of Bentley's clients.

The King's English
W: Dan Beaumont. D: Earl Bellamy.
Everyone tries to help Peter improve
his understanding of Shakespeare, so
he can pass his night school final
exams.

A Party for Peter
W: Unknown. D: Earl Bellamy. GS:
Frankie Laine. Trying to impress a
pretty girl, Peter claims that Frankie
Laine will be appearing at a party
tendered in his honor.

The Twain Shall Meet
W: Robert Fisher & Alan Lipscott. D:
Earl Bellamy. GS: Guy Lee. Bentley
is upset to learn that Kelly is up to her
old matchmaking endeavors, this time
she is trying to unite a Chinese couple.

Star Light, Star Not So Bright
W: Ray Allen & Jim Allen. D: Earl
Bellamy. GS: Vito Scotti. An astrolo-
gist makes some predictions that come
true, prompting Peter to use astrology
to win back his girlfriend Suzie.

Blossom Comes to Visit
W: Si Rose & Seamon Jacobs. D: Earl
Bellamy. A spoiled relative comes for
a visit with Bentley.

Kelly and the Free Thinker
W: Sheridan Gibney. D: John Newland. GS: Charles Robinson. Kelly
and Howard become involved with a
philosophy group and Bentley schemes
to drive them out of this intellectual
phase.

Rush Week
W: Ken Lenard & Jess Carneol. D:
Gregg Garrison. GS: Lisa Gaye. Two
sorority houses try their best to recruit
Kelly, who can't decide which to join.

How to Throw Your Voice
W: Shirley Gordon. D: Earl Bellamy.
Howard's latest venture is as a ventrilo-
quist enlisting the aid of a reluctant
Kelly.

On the Old Camp Ground
W: Si Rose & Seamon Jacobs. D:
Abby Berlin. It's vacation time and no
one can decide where to go. When
everyone finally agrees on a tour of
the United States, no one can decide
whether to camp out or to stay at
hotels.

Summer Romance
W: Sheridan Gibney. D: Earl Bellamy.
Bentley and Peter head to Yellowstone
Park to meet the man Kelly plans to
marry.

A Song Is Born
W: Robert Fisher & Alan Lipscott. D:
Earl Bellamy. GS: Jimmy Boyd.
Howard sings and records an atrocious
song that a client of Bentley's wants to
turn into a pop hit.

Peter's Punctured Wedding
W: Si Rose & Seamon Jacobs. D: Earl
Bellamy. Peter and his cousin Richard
vie for the affection of a beautiful woman, leaving Bentley caught in the
middle.

Bentley Goes to Bat
W: Unknown. D: Earl Bellamy. Bentley helps a tomboy turn from baseball
nut into a cultured young lady.

Kelly the Yes Man
W: Ben Starr & Dan Beaumont. D:
Stanley Z. Cherry. GS: Leslie Parrish.
Kelly and Ginger try to induce votes in
the upcoming school election by
promising a movie star will appear at
the school dance.

The Hong Kong Suit
W: Hannibal Coons & Charles P. Marion. D: Earl Bellamy. Kelly buys a $12 suit from Charlie as a birthday present for her uncle that falls apart the night he attends an elegant dinner party.

Boys Will Be . . .
W: Kay Leonard, Jess Carneol & Larry Rhine. D: Earl Bellamy. Bentley helps organize a group of boys for a play after being tricked into giving up his golf game.

Strictly Business
W: Larry & Maggie Williams & Dan Beaumont. D: Earl Bellamy. Bentley becomes upset when the Internal Revenue investigates his 1958 tax return.

Will Success Spoil Jasper
W: Si Rose & Seamon Jacobs. D: Hollingsworth Morse. GS: George Neise. An actress wants to use Jasper in an upcoming movie, turning their mutt into a pampered pooch.

The House at Smuggler's Cove
W: Calvin Clements, Dick Conway & Roland MacLane. D: Earl Bellamy. Bentley spends the night in a haunted house searching for Peter, Kelly and a missing bedroom.

Bentley and the Homebody
W: Robert Fisher & Alan Lipscott. D: Earl Bellamy. Bentley's latest girlfriend teaches Kelly to cook and plans to marry Bentley and fatten him up.

Gold in Them There Hills
W: Si Rose & Seamon Jacobs. D: Earl Bellamy. GS: Frank Sully. Peter buys land in a ghost town and plans to pan for gold, but all he ends up with is a bag of useless rocks.

A Penny Saved
W: Robert Fisher & Alan Lipscott. D: Earl Bellamy. GS: Eddie "Rochester" Anderson. To teach Peter a lesson in thrift, Bentley hires Rochester which

proves to be more costly than he thought.

Bentley Takes It Easy
W: Si Rose & Seamon Jacobs. D: Earl Bellamy. While trying to take a leisurely vacation at home, Bentley is constantly bothered by Peter and Kelly.

Deck the Halls
W: Ray Allen & Jim Allen. D: Stanley Z. Cherry. GS: Joey Faye. Bentley suggests that the family donate their gifts to charity and enjoy the true spirit of Christmas.

Curfew Shall Not Ring Tonight
W: Robert Fisher & Alan Lipscott. D: Earl Bellamy. Kelly moves into the college dormitory and Peter and Bentley have a hard time adjusting to the loss.

How Howard Won His "C"
W: Si Rose & Seamon Jacobs. D: Earl Bellamy. GS: Fredd Wayne. Howard takes up fencing to compete with a football hero Kelly has fallen for.

Blossom Time at the Greggs
W: Si Rose & Seamon Jacobs. D: Hollingsworth Morse. Peter's niece arrives and is disappointed that her uncle is not president of any organization, prompting Peter to run for president of his lodge.

Kelly the Home Executive
W: Ray Allen & Jim Allen & Mel Diamond. D: Earl Bellamy. After a violent argument with Warren, Kelly vows to learn all about running a house.

A Visit to the Bergens
W: Unknown. D: Earl Bellamy. GS: Edgar Bergen. Bentley and Edgar trade housekeepers and are equally dissatisfied with the results.

Kelly's Engagement
W: William Raynor & Myles Wilder. D: Earl Bellamy. GS: Neil Hamilton. Kelly announces her engagement to Warren which outrages Bentley who

thinks the boy only proposed to maneuver a job offer out of his office.

The Richest Cat
W: Sloan Nibley. D: Earl Bellamy. Bentley and Cal fight each other for possession of a cat believed to be worth one million dollars.

What Men Don't Know
W: Frank Gill & George Carlton Brown. D: Hollingsworth Morse. Kelly takes Peter's advice and tries flattery to win back Warren who has been conned by a clever girl.

House Divided
W: Mel Diamond. D: Earl Bellamy.

Kelly's in-laws decide to go into a competitive business which threatens to disrupt Kelly's marriage, until Bentley finds a solution.

The Rescue of Rufus
W: Cynthia Lindsay & Leo Townsend. D: Sidney Lanfield. Bentley goes to court to save a little boy's dog from certain doom caused by a complaint issued by a notorious animal hater.

Bentley and the Counterspy
W: Robert Fisher & Alan Lipscott. D: Earl Bellamy. Howard is in hot water when he convinces everyone he joined the Army, but he doesn't have the courage to tell them that he failed the physical because he has flat feet.

BARNEY MILLER

On the air 1/23/75, off 9/82. ABC. 125 episodes synd. Video tape color. Broadcast: Jan 1975-Jan 1976 Thu 8-8:30; Jan 1976-Dec 1976 Thu 8:30-9; Dec 1976-Sept 1982 Thu 9-9:30. Producer: Danny Arnold. Prod Co: Four D. Synd: Columbia Pictures TV.

CAST: Capt. Barney Miller (played by Hal Linden), Phillip K. Fish (Abe Vigoda), Chano Amenguale (Gregory Sierra), Stan Wojohowicz (Maxwell Gail), Nick Yemana (Jack Soo), Ron Harris (Ron Glass), Inspector Frank Luger (James Gregory), Arthur Dietrich (Steve Landesberg), Carl Levitt (Ron Carey), Elizabeth Miller (Barbara Barrie), Bernice Fish (Florence Stanley), Janice Wentworth (Linda Lavin).

One of the most successful comedy series in recent years. The adventures of a squad of police detectives who are stationed in New York's Greenwich Village. The average episodes would have the detectives encounter the strangest people in the city. The series left the air in 1982 after a dispute with the network, causing production to be halted. The series still does extremely well in syndication.

The Life and Times of Captain Barney Miller [Pilot] [not in syndication]
The story of a compassionate policeman.

Ramon
W: Danny Arnold & Theodore J. Flicker. D: Bill Davis. GS: Chu Chu Malave, Michael Moore, Buddy Lester. A teenage drug addict holds the squad hostage with Fish's gun.

Experience
W: Steve Gordon. D: John Rich. GS: Jack DeLeon, Rod Perry, Alex Henteloff, Jane Dulo, Ray Sharkey, Noam Pitlik. Barney tries to talk Fish from early retirement and searches for a bomber of public buildings.

Snow Job
W: Danny Arnold & Chris Hawyard. D: Richard Kinon. GS: Ron Feinberg,

Richard Stahl. There is no heat at the station, armored car drivers are on strike, and an exhibitionist in a snowstorm are among the problems at the station.

Graft
W: Danny Arnold & Chris Hayward. D: Noam Pitlik. GS: Dick O'Neill, Buddy Lester. Barney's squad is accused of being on the take by a former squad member.

The Courtesans
W: Jerry Davis, Danny Arnold & Chris Hayward. D: Noam Pitlik. GS: Nancy Dussault, Naomi Stevens. Wojo goes to Barney for advice when he falls for a prostitute.

The Stakeout
W: Danny Arnold. D: John Rich. GS: Lou Jacobi, Ed Barth, Brett Somers, Vic Tayback. The squad stakes out an apartment in an attempt to stop a drug sale.

The Bureaucrat
W: Richard Baer, Danny Arnold & Chris Hayward. D: Bob Finkel. GS: David Wayne, Elliot Reid, Milt Kogan. A drunken government official spends the night in the squad room cell, while Chano's apartment is robbed.

Ms. Cop
W: Danny Arnold, Chris Hayward & Marilyn Miller. D: Noam Pitlik. GS: Linda Lavin, Howard Platt, Wynn Irwin. A new woman cop is assigned to the station, but is not permitted to do anything but typing.

The Vigilante
W: Danny Arnold & Chris Hayward. D: Noam Pitlik. GS: Titos Vandis, Gabe Dell. Chano arrests a man who is beating up muggers.

The Guest
W: Danny Arnold & Chris Hayward. D: Noam Pitlik. GS: Herb Edelman. The squad is ordered to protect a government witness from the syndicate.

The Escape Artist
W: Danny Arnold, Chris Hayward & Howard Leeds. D: Noam Pitlik. GS: Roscoe Lee Browne, Leonard Frey, Danny Dayton. The squad captures a prison escape artist, and has to make sure he doesn't escape before he is transferred to prison. Also, a man tries to fly with a pair of homemade wings.

Hair
W: Danny Arnold, Chris Hayward, Ron Pearlman & Jerry Davis. D: Allen Baron. GS: Charles Fleischer, Michael Lembeck, Henry Beckman. A former narcotics officer is transferred to the 12th, complete with a beard, fatigue jacket and a gold earring.

The Hero
W: Danny Arnold & Chris Hayward. D: Noam Pitlik. GS: Todd Bridges, Cal Gibson. Chano becomes depressed after shooting two bank robbers. Liz arrests an eight-year-old kid who held her up with a wooden stick.

Doomsday
W: Danny Arnold, Chris Hayward & Arne Sultan. D: Noam Pitlik. GS: J.J. Barry, William Windom, Steve Landesberg. A human bomb threatens to blow himself up in the station. Wojo arrests a priest for giving away bibles without a license, and the plumbing breaks down.

The Social Worker
W: Danny Arnold, Chris Hayward & Arne Sultan. D: Noam Pitlik. GS: Art Metrano, Herbie Faye, Alex Henteloff. Liz becomes a social worker in the South Bronx, causing Barney to become a nervous wreck.

The Lay-Off
W: Danny Arnold, Chris Hayward & Arne Sultan. D: Noam Pitlik. GS: Bob Dishy, Oliver Clark, Candy Azzara. Due to the city's financial crisis, Barney has to suspend Wojo, Chano & Harris.

Ambush
W: Danny Arnold, Chris Hayward & Arne Sultan. D: Noam Pitlik. GS: David Doyle, Dick O'Neill. Yemana is shot in the backside and Barney is offered a job as Chief of Police in a small town in Florida.

Heat Wave
W: Danny Arnold, Chris Hayward & Arne Sultan. D: Noam Pitlik. GS: Linda Lavin, Janet Ward, Harold Oblong, Paul Lichtman. The detectives dress up as women to catch a rapist during a summer heat wave.

The Arsonist
W: Tony Sheehan. D: Noam Pitlik. GS: Roger Brown, Jack Somack, Leonard Stone, Steve Franken. Chano arrests a man for shooting a vending machine and Harris believes the reason for a rash of arson fires is a man in need of psychological help.

Grand Hotel
W: Danny Arnold & Chris Hayward. D: Noam Pitlik. GS: Robert Mandan, Adam Arkin, Arnold Soboloff, Queenie Smith. Wojo and Wentworth check into a fancy hotel to trap a robber of the hotel's guests.

Discovery
W: Danny Arnold & Chris Hayward. D: Lee Bernhardi. GS: Jack DeLeon, Ray Stewart, Norman Rice. One of the squad is accused of extorting money from gay people.

You Dirty Rat
W: Tony Sheehan, Danny Arnold & Chris Hayward. D: Noam Pitlik. GS: Ned Glass, J. Pat O'Malley, Franklyn Ajaye, Val Bisoglio. Two kilos of marijuana are missing and Wojo is bitten by a rat.

Horse Thief
W: Tony Sheehan. D: Noam Pitlik. GS: Ron Masak, Jack Dodson, Liam Dunn, Bruce Solomon, Judy Cassmore. During the Bicentennial, the squad investigates a horse thief, a tourist with a black eye, and a lady selling Bicentennial buttons for $60.

Rain
W: Tony Sheehan, Danny Arnold & Chris Hayward. D: Noam Pitlik. GS: Stoney Miller, Phil Leeds. A heavy rainstorm causes the station roof to leak, causing fears that the ceiling will cave in.

Fish
W: Danny Arnold & Chris Hayward. D: Noam Pitlik. GS: Doris Belack, Emily Levine. Fish is put on restricted duty by his doctor and he must also train a new detective, Dietrich.

Hot Dogs
W: Danny Arnold, Chris Hayward & Arne Sultan. D: Lee Bernhardi. GS: Jonelle Allen, Nellie Bellflower, David L. Lander, Howard Honig. Two policewomen want to become detectives, but cause nothing but trouble.

Protection
W: Danny Arnold, Chris Hayward & Tom Reeder. D: Noam Pitlik. GS: Jack Somack, Ralph Manza, Ray Sharkey. A protection racket moves into the neighborhood when it is rumored the station is being closed.

Happy New Year
W: Chris Hayward, Danny Arnold & Arne Sultan. D: Bruce Bilson. GS: Edith Diaz, Johnny Lamotta. On New Year's Eve the squad handles leapers, drunks and pickpockets, plus a Spanish-speaking expectant mother.

The Sniper
W: Tom Reeder, Danny Arnold & Chris Hayward. D: Lee Bernhardi. GS: Charlotte Rae, Jay Robinson, Sully Boyar. Wojo is shot at by a sniper and Fish encounters a travel agent who sells trips to the planet Saturn.

Fear of Flying
W: Reinhold Weege. D: Lee Bernhardi. GS: Jack Riley, Valerie Curtin. Wojo must fly a suspect to Ohio to stand trial, but he is afraid of flying.

Block Party
W: Danny Arnold & Chris Hayward.
D: Noam Pitlik.   GS: Larry Bishop,
George Murdock.   Chano and Went-
worth are assigned to patrol a block
party, which makes Wojo jealous.

Massage Parlor
W: Tony Sheehan.   D: Noam Pitlik.
GS: Florence Halop, Meg Wyllie.
Wentworth arrests a cowboy at a mas-
sage parlor, and an old lady mugs a
man.

The Psychiatrist
W: Tony Sheehan, Danny Arnold &
Chris Hayward.   D: Noam Pitlik.   GS:
Fred Sadoff, Neil J. Schwartz. A psychiatrist decides Wojo is unfit to carry
a gun, then wants to test the rest of
the squad.

The Kid
W: Danny Arnold, Chris Hayward &
Tony Sheehan.   D: Stan Lathan.   GS:
Arny Freeman, Angelina Estrada, Jose
Flores.   Fish falls for a mother of a
pickpocket, then remembers he is
married.

The Mole
W: Danny Arnold, Chris Hayward &
Reinhold Weege. D: Noam Pitlik. GS:
Ron Carey, Severn Darden, Dean Santoro.   Fish must decide whether to
have an operation, while Wojo and Harris track a crook through the sewers.

Evacuation
W: Danny Arnold, Chris Hayward &
Tom Reeder.   D: Noam Pitlik.   GS:
Denise Miller, Paul Lichtman, Kenneth
Mars.   Wojo becomes the public infor-
mation officer and causes impending
disaster rumors, while Fish befriends a
young thief.

Quarantine [Part 1]
W: Tony Sheehan.   D: Lee Bernhardi.
GS: Jack DeLeon, Ray Stewart, Arthur Peterson.   The squad is put in
quarantine when a suspect is believed
to have a contagious disease.

Quarantine [Part 2]
W: Tony Sheehan.   D: Lee Bernhardi.
GS: Jack DeLeon, Ray Stewart, Arthur Peterson.   Confinement releases
hidden feelings among the squad as
they wait for the quarantine to be
lifted.

The Election
W: Tom Reeder, Tony Sheehan &
Danny Arnold.   D: Lee Bernhardi.   GS:
Brett Somers, Richard Venture.   On
election night the squad meets a rich
man who steals lingerie, and a pedestrian is hit by a flying toilet seat.

Werewolf
W: Reinhold Weege, Tony Sheehan &
Danny Arnold.   D: Noam Pitlick.   GS:
Kenneth Tigar, Janet MacLachlan, John
Lormer.   The station's latest prisoner
is a man who thinks he is a werewolf.

Bus Stop
W: Tony Sheehan, Danny Arnold,
Reinhold Weege & Jerry Ross.   D:
Noam Pitlik.   GS: Candy Azzara, Phil
Bruns, Sal Viscuso, Florence Halop.   A
hijacked bus brashes and the driver,
passengers and the hijacker turn up at
the station.

The Recluse
W: Reinhold Weege & Chris Hayward.
D: Bruce Bilson. GS: Arnold Soboloff.
The detectives arrest a 70-year-old
man who evades jury duty by never
leaving his apartment for 35 years.

Non-Involvement
W: Reinhold Weege.   D: Bruce Bilson.
GS: Mike Kellin, Ron Feinberg, June
Gable, Oliver Clark.   Wojo arrests a
man for non-involvement when he re-
fuses to help stop a crook.

Power Failure
W: Tony Sheehan & Danny Arnold.
D: Noam Pitlik.   GS: Susan Brown,
Arny Freeman, Stefan Gierasch.   A
local power failure causes trouble for
the squad, and a woman psychiatrist
falls for Barney.

Christmas Story

W: Tony Sheehan & Reinhold Weege. D: Bruce Bilson. GS: Nobu McCarthy, Jay Gerber, John Morgan Evans. Fish dresses up as Santa Claus to capture a crook, Yemana falls for a Japanese prostitute, and Barney invites Inspector Luger to spend the holidays.

Hash

W: Tom Reeder. D: Noam Pitlik. GS: Walter Janowitz, George Perina, Michael Tocci. Wojo's girlfriend gives him brownies containing hashish, causing strange effects on the squad.

Smog Alert

W: Reinhold Weege & Chris Hayward. D: Bruce Bilson. GS: Lee Kessler, Alan Haufrect. During a first stage smog alert, a suicidal woman and an obscene graffiti writer meet in jail and fall for each other.

Community Relations

W: Tony Sheehan, Dennis Koenig & Larry Balmagia. D: Noam Pitlik. GS: Ralph Manza, Joseph Perry, Judson Morgan. An irate landlord, an old man with a musket, and a blind shoplifter are the latest trouble for the squad.

The Rand Report

W: Reinhold Weege. D: Noam Pitlik. GS: Martin Garner, Anna Berger. A critical report upsets the squad when it says detectives are a waste of money, and Wojo quits rather than walk a beat.

"Fire '77"

W: Tony Sheehan. D: Bruce Bilson. GS: Sal Viscuso, Howard Platt, K Callen. A religious criminal reprimands Wojo for not going to mass, then sets fire to the station.

Abduction

W: Tom Reeder, Tony Sheehan & Reinhold Weege. D: Bruce Bilson. GS: Buddy Lester, Vivi Janiss, Rod Colbin. Parents of a runaway girl kidnap her from a religious cult, leaving Barney to settle the matter. Also, Yemana's bookie is arrested.

Sex Surrogate

W: Tony Sheehan, Dennis Koenig & Larry Balmagia. D: Noam Pitlik. GS: Billy Barty, Marilyn Sokol, Doris Roberts. Barney must decide if a sex clinic is legit or a cover for a house of prostitution.

Moonlighting

W: Reinhold Weege. D: Noam Pitlik. GS: George Pentecost, Cal Gibson. Harris moonlights, while the squad handles a minister who sells stolen goods and a bookie who uses a retarded boy as a numbers runner.

Asylum

W: Roland Kibbee, Tony Sheehan, Reinhold Weege & Danny Arnold. D: Alex March. GS: Ion Teodrescu, Michael Panaleff. Wojo grants political asylum to a defecting Russian musician, which leaves Barney to fight it out with the State Department.

Group Home

W: Tony Sheehan & Danny Arnold. D: Jeremiah Morris. Fish disguises himself as a woman to catch muggers, while the squad tries to capture a man who claims to have planted a bomb at an Army recruiting station.

Strike [Part 1]

W: Reinhold Weege. D: Jeremiah Morris. GS: Peter Hobbs, Peggy Pope. The squad goes on an unauthorized strike leaving Barney to run the station alone.

Strike [Part 2]

W: Reinhold Weege. D: Jeremiah Morris. GS: Peter Hobbs, Peggy Pope. While the squad is still on strike, Barney deals with a man-hungry spinster.

Goodbye Mr. Fish [Part 1]

W: Reinhold Weege & Danny Arnold. D: Danny Arnold. GS: Arny Freeman, Jack Somack, Stanley Brock. Fish does not show up on the last day of work before retiring, and Barney has to deal with neighborhood vigilantes.

Goodbye Mr. Fish [Part 2]
W: Reinhold Weege. D: David Swift.
GS: Larry Gelman, Timothy Jerome.
Fish refuses to accept his retirement,
so he deludes himself into believing
that he is still working.

Bugs
W: Dennis Koenig & Larry Balmagia.
D: David Swift. GS: Sammy Smith,
Mari Gorman. Barney and the squad
become paranoid when hidden microphones are discovered in the squad
room.

Corporation
W: Lee H. Grant, Tony Sheehan &
Danny Arnold. D: Hal Linden. GS:
David Dukes, Fran Ryan, Vernon Weddle. A graffiti artist protests environ-
mental contamination by threatening
to commit suicide in the squad room.

Burial
W: Michael Russnow. D: Danny Ar-
nold. GS: Sy Kramer, Jack Kruschen.
Fish comes out of retirement to help
Barney recover a body stolen from a
mortuary.

Copy Cat
W: Douglas Wyman & Tony Sheehan.
D: Jeremiah Morris. GS: Don Calfa,
Norman Bartold, Don Sherman, John
Dullaghan. The squad arrests a drunk
who tried to rob a store without a
weapon, and a crook who picks his
crimes from watching TV cop shows.

Blizzard
W: Tony Sheehan. D: Danny Arnold.
GS: Alex Henteloff, Lou Cutell, Lewis
Charles. During a blizzard, the squad
are bothered by: a dead body, an irate
lawyer, and a crazy man believing the
new ice age has begun.

Chase
W: Tom Reeder, Reinhold Weege &
Danny Arnold. D: Jeremiah Morris.
GS: Luis Avalos, George Murdock,
Marya Small. Wojo borrows a cab to
chase a liquor store robber and then
wrecks it.

Thanksgiving Story.
W: Reinhold Weege. D: David Swift.
GS: Ian Wolfe, George Skaff, Tom
Lacy. On Thanksgiving, three mental
patients cause havoc at an automat,
and a man stabs his brother-in-law over
a piece of turkey.

The Tunnel
W: Tony Sheehan & Michael Russnow.
D: David Swift. GS: Leonard Stone,
J.J. Barry, Jay Gerber. Wojo is buried
alive, the station's telephone lines are
dead, and Harris can't find an apartment.

Atomic Bomb
W: Tom Reeder & Reinhold Weege.
D: Noam Pitlik. GS: Phil Leeds, Karl
Bruck, Stephen Pearlman. The bomb
squad brings in an atomic bomb cre-
ated by a student, so Barney calls the
FBI.

The Bank
W: Tony Sheehan. D: Noam Pitlik.
GS: Sandy Sprung, Peter Jurasik. Barney handles a dispute between the
owner of a sperm bank and a customer
who says his deposit was destroyed.

The Ghost
W: Reinhold Weege. D: Lee Bernhardi.
GS: Nehemiah Persoff, Titos Vandis,
Kenneth Tigar. Strange things begin
to happen when a man claiming he is
haunted by a poltergeist named Julius
shows up at the station.

Appendicitis
W: Tony Sheehan. D: Noam Pitlik.
GS: Jack Bernardi, Michael Durrell.
Yemana suffers an appendicitis attack
as the squad meets an elderly bounty
hunter and a sugar addict.

Rape
W: Dennis Koenig. D: Noam Pitlik.
GS: Michael Pataki, Joyce Jameson,
William Bogert. Barney sends for a
female District Attorney when a wo-
man charges her husband with rape.

Eviction [Part 1]
W: Tom Reeder & Tony Sheehan. D:

Noam Pitlik. GS: Dave Madden, Rosana Soto. Barney tries to prevent the eviction of a tenement full of poor people, but succeeds in being relieved of command.

Eviction [Part 2]
W: Tom Reeder & Reinhold Weege. D: Noam Pitlik. GS: Dave Madden, Bruce Kirby. Barney is the one the tenants will talk to and by his actions reclaims his command.

Wojo's Problem
W: Tony Sheehan. D: Max Gail. GS: Ray Girarden, Henry Slate, Mari Gorman. Barney encounters a new detective and a shoplifter in a wheelchair, while Wojo suffers from sex problems.

"Quo Vadis?"
W: Tony Sheehan. D: Alex March. GS: Ivy Bethune. Barney and Liz have marital problems, and a woman complains about a nude painting in an art gallery.

Hostage
W: Reinhold Weege. D: Hal Linden. GS: Earle Towne, Oliver Clark, Don Calfa. A gunman forces the squad to spend time in the cell with a crazy ventriloquist and his foul-mouthed dummy.

Evaluation
W: Larry Balmagia & Reinhold Weege. D: Noam Pitlik. GS: Richard Libertini, Kay Medford, Eugene Elman. Barney must write a performance evaluation form for each officer, while dealing with an old couple who own a vandalized porno shop and a crook without a name, only a number.

The Sighting
W: Tony Sheehan. D: Alex March. GS: Doris Roberts, Peter Hobbs, Jack Bannon. A woman complains that her husband is changing everything they own into gold, and Wojo claims he saw a UFO.

Inauguration
W: Reinhold Weege & Carol Gary. D:

Alex March. GS: Phillip Sterling, Basil Hoffman, Florence Halop. Harris is offered a job on the Mayor's staff, the squad rescues a would-be political suicide and reads the Mayor's hate mail.

The Kidnapping [One Hour]
W: Reinhold Weege, Danny Arnold & Tony Sheehan. D: Noam Pitlik. GS: Fred Sadoff, Beverly Sanders, Todd Susman, Barrie Longfellow, Ralph Manza, John O'Connell. A department store owner is kidnapped and the ransom demanded is that he must give away the store's merchandise to the public.

The Search
W: Bob Colleary & Tony Sheehan. D: Noam Pitlik. GS: Jenny O'Hara, Bruce Kirby, Arny Freeman. Barney arrests educational television's Mr. Science and searches for a man who has been missing for 28 years.

Dog Days
W: Reinhold Weege. D: Noam Pitlik. GS: Rosalind Cash, Joseph Perry. Wojo is bitten trying to break up a dog fight. Now, he might have to take rabies shots unless he finds the dog that bit him.

The Baby Broker
W: Tony Sheehan. D: Noam Pitlik. The squad encounters an illegal adoption ring and a man writing a book on obscenity. Also, Levitt gets hooked on pep pills.

The Accusation
W: Wally Dalton & Shelly Zellman. D: Max Gail. GS: George Murdock, Eugene Elman. Dietrich is investigated when a woman accuses him of improper conduct. Also, a rabbi is arrested for running a gambling casino in the temple with an expired permit.

The Prisoner
W: Reinhold Weege, Wally Dalton & Shelley Zellman. D: Noam Pitlik. GS: Jeff Corey, Peggy Pope, Bruce Glover. Barney gets marital counseling from the police chaplain. The detec-

tives arrest an ex-con who wants to return to prison, and a cat burglar's widow who is continuing the family business.

Loan Shark
W: Tony Sheehan.   D: Noam Pitlik. The squad arrests a 14-year-old loan shark and two men fighting over a tattoo.   Yemana rebels after 20 years of being taken for granted.

The Vandal
W: Dennis Koenig & Tony Sheehan. D: Noam Pitlik.   GS: Jay Gerber, Howard Honig, Christopher Lloyd. The squad room is vandalized and a TV executive fights with an upset viewer.

The Harris Incident
W: Wally Dalton, Shelley Zellman & Reinhold Weege.   D: Noam Pitlik. GS: Ed Peck, Michael Lombard. Harris is shot by two cops and Wojo arrests a beggar who happens to be a rich man.

The Radical
W: Tony Sheehan.   D: Noam Pitlik. GS: Corey Fischer, Stuart Pankin. Inspector Luger suffers a possible heart attack during an argument with a famous radical.

Toys
W: Wally Dalton, Shelley Zellman & Tony Sheehan.   D: Noam Pitlik.   A toy store burglar, a claustrophobic holdup man, and Barney has marital problems.

The Indian
W: Reinhold Weege. D: Noam Pitlik. GS: Charles White Eagle, Phil Leeds, Richard Stahl. Wojo befriends an old Indian who wishes to die in Central Park.

Voice Analyzer
W: James Bonnet & Reinhold Weege. D: Noam Pitlik.   GS: George Murdock, Phil Roth, Alan Rich. Barney and the squad must pass a lie-detecting voice test.   Everyone passes except Wojo.

The Spy
W: Tony Sheehan.   D: Noam Pitlik. GS: Phillip Sterling, Estelle Owens, Stanley Brock.   The squad is held hostage by an unemployed CIA spy with a gun.

Wojo's Girl [Part 1]
W: Tony Sheehan & Danny Arnold. D: Noam Pitlik. GS: Michael Conrad, Phil Bruns. Wojo plans to live together with his new girlfriend, who until recently was a prostitute.   The squad discovers a paramilitary group that trains soldiers of fortune.

Wojo's Girl [Part 2]
W: Tony Sheehan & Danny Arnold. D: Noam Pitlik. Wojo learns that he has little in common with his new roommate, and that living together is not what he thought it would be.

Middle Age
W: Tony Sheehan.   D: Noam Pitlik. GS: Nehemiah Persoff, Richard Libertini, Raleigh Bond.   Barney worries about becoming middle-aged and the squad makes matters worse by kidding him about it.

The Counterfeiter
W: Tony Sheehan.   D: Noam Pitlik. GS: Jack Riley, J. Pat O'Malley. The detectives try to catch a counterfeiter and break up a fight between a plastic surgeon and a patient, while Luger seeks advice from Barney.

Open House
W: Wally Dalton & Shelley Zellman. D: Noam Pitlik.   GS: Allan Miller, Christopher Lloyd. An open house at the station attracts only three bums, and a psychiatrist decides whether or not to disclose the name of an arsonist he is treating.

Identity
W: Tom Reeder. D: Noam Pitlik. GS: Jack Somack, Don Calfa. Officer

Levitt becomes a temporary detective and Dietrich saves Harris's life.

Computer Crime
W: Calvin Kelly. D: Max Gail. GS: Mabel King, Barry Gordon. A man steals a half million dollars to buy a stamp collection and a man tries to get a curse removed.

Graveyard Shift
W: Tony Sheehan. D: Noam Pitlik. GS: Paul Smith, Raymond Singer. During the 12-8 a.m. shift: Harris begins a new novel, the station gets a bomb threat from a neighbor, a tourist gets robbed outside her hotel, and a man fights a succubus.

Jack Soo, a Retrospective
W: Danny Arnold. D: Noam Pitlik. The cast remembers Jack Soo with flashbacks of previous episodes.

Inquisition
W: Tony Sheehan. D: Noam Pitlik. GS: George Murdock, Dino Natali, Norman Bartold, Peter Jurasik, David Darlow. A holdup in an adult bookstore, a man destroys a canned music system in a department store, and an officer at the station admits to being gay.

The Photographer
W: Bob Colleary. D: Noam Pitlik. GS: Sal Viscuso, Kenneth Tigar, Phil Leeds, Anita Dangler. A photographer lures women into a park, then robs them. A drug pusher is upset by being arrested by a "short cop," Levitt. A man claims he is Jesus Christ.

Vacation
W: Frank Dungan & Jeff Stein. D: Noam Pitlik. GS: Bruce Kirby, Jack Bernardi, Ben Slack. Barney makes out the annual vacation schedule. A fight over a kidney transplant between two brothers, and a rash of false fire alarms.

The Brother
W: Wally Dalton & Shelley Zellman.

D: Noam Pitlik. GS: Gary Imhoff, John Christy Ewing, Elise Caitlin. A Catholic friar mislays one of his novitiates. Dietrich dresses up as a woman for a mugger detail.

The Slave
W: Frank Dungan & Jeff Stein. D: Noam Pitlik. GS: Manu Tupou, Sumant, Peg Shirley, Stanley Kamel. A minor traffic accident reveals that a man is a slave to a UN delegate.

Strip Joint
W: Jaie Brashar, Frank Dungan & Jeff Stein. D: Noam Pitlik. GS: James Cromwell, Todd Susman, Rosana Soto, Walter Janowitz, Diana Canova. The station is without heat. A man claims he will burst into flames at any minute, and two dancers from a government-owned topless bar arrive at the station.

The Bird
W: Jeff Stein & Frank Dungan. D: Noam Pitlik. GS: Michael Lombard, Martin Garner, Miriam Byrd Nethery. Harris finds a publisher for his book about the station, but must get releases from the reluctant squad. Wojo buys a parrot which suddenly dies.

The Desk
W: Frank Dungan & Jeff Stein. D: Noam Pitlik. GS: Jeff Corey, Alex Henteloff, Fred Sadoff, Don Calfa. Harris deals with an Amish man who was mugged, and a lobotomized bank robber holds up a liquor store.

The Judge
W: Frank Dungan, Jeff Stein & Tony Sheehan. D: Noam Pitlik. GS: Peggy Pope, Phillip Sterling. A crazy judge hits a lawyer on the head with his gavel. A woman accuses her sexy blonde neighbor of running a drug ring.

The DNA Story
W: Rich Reinhart. D: Noam Pitlik. GS: Kay Medford, Jack Kruschen, A Martinez, Stephen Gierasch. A wo-

man claims her husband has been replaced by a robot. A scientist covers up the theft of epidemic-causing cultures.

The Dentist
W: Frank Dungan & Jeff Stein. D: Noam Pitlik. GS: Oliver Clark, Jenny O'Hara, Arthur Malet, Estelle Owens. A lady detective feels rejected when she is unable to trap a lecherous dentist. Wojo has fun making weird noises with his hands.

People's Court
W: Frank Dungan & Jeff Stein. D: Noam Pitlik. GS: Michael Tocci, Howard Honig, Rod Colbin, Ralph Manza. Barney's building becomes a condominium. The detectives arrest a crazy census taker. The neighborhood characters set up their own court.

Vanished [Part 1]
W: Tony Sheehan, Frank Dungan & Jeff Stein. D: Noam Pitlik. GS: Elaine Giftos, John Dullaghan. Harris disappears while working undercover as a bum. Luger is demoted and assigned to Barney.

Vanished [Part 2]
W: Tony Sheehan, Frank Dungan & Jeff Stein. D: Noam Pitlik. GS: Leonard Frey, David Fresco. While everyone searches for Harris, Wojo and Dietrich compete for the attention of a woman who is looking for a volunteer to father her baby.

The Child Stealers
W: Frank Dungan & Jeff Stein. D: Noam Pitlik. GS: Joanna Miles, Ray Stewart, Jack DeLeon, Dino Natali, Richard Libertini. A man claims he is a time traveler from the 21st century. A divorced father tries to kidnap his son.

Guns
W: Rich Reinhart, Tony Sheehan, Frank Dungan & Jeff Stein. D: Noam Pitlik. GS: Jack Dodson, Madison Arnold, Mario Rocuzzo, David Pay-

mer. Wojo believes Luger seems suicidal. Barney must find some stolen heavy artillery from an illegal collection.

Uniform Days
W: Judith Nielson & Richard Beban. D: Noam Pitlik. GS: Leonard Stone, Michael Alaimo, Stuart Pankin. It is mandatory uniform day and Harris refuses to wear his full uniform. Dietrich rushes to finish an old case before the statute of limitations takes effect.

Dietrich's Arrest [Part 1]
W: Tony Sheehan, Frank Dungan & Jeff Stein. D: Noam Pitlik. GS: George Murdock, Candy Azzara, Peter Hobbs. Dietrich attends an anti-nuke demonstration and is arrested. A lottery winner throws the money out of his window.

Dietrich's Arrest [Part 2]
W: Tony Sheehan, Frank Dungan & Jeff Stein. D: Noam Pitlik. GS: George Murdock, Kay Medford, Allan Miller. Dietrich is booked by Barney because of his part in the demonstration. A pro-nuke scientist pours "Atomic Water" on the other prisoners.

The Architect
W: Tony Sheehan, Frank Dungan & Jeff Stein. D: Noam Pitlik. GS: Paul Lieber, Chu Chu Malave, Norman Bartold. Two armed men try to free their friend. Barney deals with a bomb in the building across the street from the station.

The Inventor
W: Frank Dungan, Jeff Stein & Tony Sheehan. D: Noam Pitlik. GS: Ben Piazza, Arny Freeman, Dan Fraser. An inventor steals his own blueprints. Wojo undergoes hypnosis to recall forgotten clues to a crime.

Fog
W: Frank Dungan, Jeff Stein & Tony Sheehan. D: Noam Pitlik. GS: J.J. Barry, Sidney Lassick, Robert Levine, William Dillard. Barney is turned

down for promotion. The detectives arrest a burglar who got lost in the fog.

Homicide [Part 1]

W: Frank Dungan & Jeff Stein. D: Noam Pitlik. GS: Harold J. Stone, Marjorie Bennett, Jack Somack, Allyn Ann McLerie. Luger designates the squad as a specialty squad, which means they will only handle homicide cases. A woman puts out a contract on her husband and then wants to cancel it. An old woman bounces $40,-000 worth of checks.

Homicide [Part 2]

W: Frank Dungan & Jeff Stein. D: Noam Pitlik. GS: Ben Piazza. Barney tries to get his squad's old duties back, while trying to solve a crazy murder case.

The Delegate

W: Jim Tisdale & Tony Sheehan. D: Noam Pitlik. GS: Phil Leeds, Bob Dishy. A robber who plans his crimes, so he can return to jail without getting caught, a mystery cop not on the payroll, and a convention delegate who won't go home are some of the problems the squad has to handle.

Dorsey

W: Tony Sheehan. D: Noam Pitlik. GS: Paul Lieber, Michael Lombard, Darrell Zwerling. A new detective joins the squad. Levitt fears this will prevent him from becoming a permanent detective. He has little to fear. Dorsey thinks he is the only honest cop and he is driving everyone else crazy proving it.

Agent Orange

W: Tony Sheehan. D: Noam Pitlik. GS: Paul Lieber, Peter Hobbs, Doris Roberts. Vietnam Vet Wojo learns he was exposed to dangerous chemicals and begins an all-out investigation.

Call Girl

W: Frank Dungan & Jeff Stein. D: Noam Pitlik. GS: Arthur Malet, Paul Kent, Tasha Zemrus. Dietrich's celibacy is tempted when the squad room is filled with call girls.

Resignation

W: Frank Dungan & Jeff Stein. D: Noam Pitlik. GS: Allan Rich, Steve Franken, Peter Elbling, Mario Rocuzzo. Dietrich plans to resign because he doesn't like the idea of shooting at fleeing suspects. Levitt thinks he can take his place.

Field Associate

W: Jordon Moffet. D: Noam Pitlik. GS: Jeffrey Tambor, Ned Glass, Florence Halop. Someone is informing Internal Affairs about the goings on in the station and Barney knows who it is but won't tell.

Movie [Part 1]

W: Frank Dungan & Jeff Stein. D: Noam Pitlik. GS: Arny Freeman, Dino Natali, George Murdock, Dennis Howard. Lt. Scanlon tracks down a gay cop and Harris investigates the porno movie business by making his own film as a cover.

Movie [Part 2]

W: Frank Dungan & Jeff Stein. D: Noam Pitlik. GS: Jay Gerber, Ralph Manza, J.J. Barry. Harris's porno film finishes $19,000 over budget, and a professional fund raiser threatens a whole office with a letter opener and orders them to turn their money over to charity.

The Psychic

W: Tony Sheehan. D: Noam Pitlik. GS: Kenneth Tigar, Fred Sadoff, Rod Colbin, Larry Hankin. A psychic predicts disaster for Harris, who is out covering an armed robbery.

Stormy Weather

W: Nat Mauldin. D: Noam Pitlik. GS: Phyllis Frelich, Robert Costanza, Seymour Bernstein, Peter Wolf. Levitt's knowledge of sign language helps a deaf woman picked up for soliciting. Wojo swims the icy Hudson River to chase a burglar.

The Librarian
W: Tony Sheehan, Frank Dungan &
Jeff Stein.   D: Noam Pitlik.   GS:
Titos Vandis, Miriam Byrd-Nethery,
Zachery Berger, Allan Miller.   The
owner of a vandalized novelty store
might be a Nazi war criminal. A librarian shoots off a pistol to silence her
reading room.

Rachel
W: Tony Sheehan, Frank Dungan &
Jeff Stein.   D: Homer Powell.   GS:
Anne Wyndham, Stanley Brock, Alex
Henteloff, Chu Chu Malave. Harris is
hit with a lawsuit and Wojo dates
Barney's daughter Rachel.

Contempt [Part 1]
W: Frank Dungan & Jeff Stein.   D:
Noam Pitlik.   GS: Dale Robinette,
Larry Gelman, William Windom. Bar-
ney is jailed for contempt of court
when he refuses to name an informant.

Contempt [Part 2]
W: Frank Dungan & Jeff Stein.   D:
Noam Pitlik.   GS: Jack Murdock, Maggie Brown, J.J. Barry, William Windom.   While Barney's lawyer and the
judge compromise, Barney is accused
by his cellmate of having an affair with
his wife.

The Doll
W: Tony Sheehan, Frank Dungan &
Jeff Stein.   D: Noam Pitlik.   GS: A
Martinez, Phillip Bruns, Oliver Clark,
Dee Croxton. The squad looks for the
kidnaper of an antique doll. A man is
conned out of $500 for a reservation
on a space shuttle. Luger leaves Barney $250,000 in his will.

Lady and the Bomb
W: Lee Grant & Tony Sheehan.   D:
Noam Pitlik.   GS: Abe Vigoda, Peggy
Pope, Howard Mann. A woman with a
pressure cooker bomb threatens to
blow up the squad room. The results
of Harris's lawsuit, and Fish makes a
surprise visit.

Riot
W: Frank Dungan & Jeff Stein.   D:
Noam Pitlik.   GS: Nehemiah Persoff,
Howard Platt, Susan Tolsky, Victor
Brant, Pat McNamara.   Luger tries to
break up a demonstration of Hassidic
Jews, but turns it into a riot.

BATMAN

On the air 1/12/66, off 3/14/68. ABC. Color film. 120 episodes. Broadcast:
Jan 1966-Aug 1967 Wed & Thu 7:30-8; Sept 1967-Mar 1968 Thu 7:30-8. Pro-
ducer: William Dozier. Prod Co: Greenway/20th Century Fox. Synd: 20th Cen-
tury Fox TV.
CAST: Bruce Wayne/Batman (played by Adam West), Dick Grayson/Robin
(Burt Ward), Alfred Pennyworth (Alan Napier), Aunt Harriet Cooper (Madge
Blake), Police Commissioner Gordon (Neil Hamilton), Chief O'Hara (Stafford
Repp), Barbara Gordon/Batgirl (Yvonne Craig). Batman Theme by Neal Hefti.
WRITERS: Lorenzo Semple, Jr., Stanley Ralph Ross, Robert C. Dennis,
Stanford Sherman, Max Hodge, Charles Hoffman, Bill Finger, Robert Dozier.
DIRECTORS: Robert Butler, James Sheldon, Murray Golden, Tom Gries,
Oscar Rudolph, George Waggner, James B. Clark, Sam Strangis.
One of the most popular series of the 1960s. It was one of the few series to
air on two consecutive nights. Based on the comic book characters, *Batman* be-
came the comic rave of its decade. It started a Batman fad across the country.
Although intended as an adventure series, it came off as a bizarre comedy series,
complete with big name actors portraying bizarre villains, often giving hammy
roles to match the plots. Typical stories pitted Batman and Robin against a

Adam West (Batman), Burt Ward (Robin)

super criminal out to cause havoc on Gotham City. The series even spawned a feature film of the same name which was released in 1966. The series was a big hit in the U.S., but it failed in several European countries due to cultural differences in humor and also the strange dialogue did not transfer well into other languages. Towards the end of its run, the character of Batgirl was added to boost the ratings, but it didn't help. It is interesting to note that when ABC decided to cancel the series, NBC considered picking it up, providing the sets were still standing, but it was too late, the sets were dismantled. *Batman* has done well in syndication.

[Every episode following is in two parts except where noted.]

Hi Diddle Riddle . . .
W: Lorenzo Semple Jr. D: Robert Butler. GS: Frank Gorshin, Jill St. John. The Riddler and his Molehill mob kidnap Robin.

. . . Smack in the Middle
Batman and Robin try to prevent the Riddler from stealing a papier-mache elephant filled with rare postage stamps.

Fine Feathered Finks . . .
W: Lorenzo Semple Jr. D: Robert Butler. GS: Burgess Meredith, Walter

Burke, Lewis Charles. The Penguin opens an umbrella shop and tries to feed Bruce Wayne to his furnace.

. . . The Penguin's a Jinx
The Penguin kidnaps a movie star, causing Batman to come to her rescue.

The Joker Is Wild . . .
W: Robert Dozier. D: Don Weis. GS: Cesar Romero, Nancy Kovack. The Joker creates and uses his own utility belt in order to trap Batman. He almost succeeds in exposing Batman's real identity on television.

. . . Batman Gets Riled
The Joker plans to steal an ocean liner

by switching the cork in the champagne bottle used to christen the ship with one that will emit a toxic gas.

Zelda the Great . . .
W: Lorenzo Semple Jr. D: Robert Butler. GS: Anne Baxter, Jack Kruschen. An evil female magician kidnaps Aunt Harriet.

. . . A Death Worse Than Fate
Evil Ekdal plans to use Zelda to trap Batman in his Doom Trap.

Instant Freeze . . .
W: Max Hodge. D: Robert Butler. GS: George Sanders. Mr. Freeze plans to get revenge on Batman by freezing both Batman and Robin.

. . . Rats Like Cheese
Batman and Robin visit Mr. Freeze's hideout and try to capture him.

A Riddle a Day Keeps The Riddler Away . . .
W: Fred De Gorter. D: Tom Gries. GS: Frank Gorshin, Susan Silo, Marvin Miller, Tris Coffin. The Riddler kidnaps a visiting king and straps Batman and Robin to the drive shafts of a giant turbine.

. . . When the Rat's Away, the Mice Will Play
The Riddler plants a bomb inside the Queen of Freedom monument and plans to blackmail the city for one million dollars, in return for deactivating the bomb.

The Thirteenth Hat . . .
W: Charles Hoffman. D: Norman Foster. GS: David Wayne. Jervis Tetch, the Mad Hatter, plans to kidnap the members of the jury that sent him to jail, including Batman.

. . . Batman Stands Pat
The Mad Hatter plans to use the fiendish machines at his hat factory to kill Batman and Robin.

The Joker Goes to School . . .
W: Lorenzo Semple Jr. D: Murray

Golden. GS: Cesar Romero. The Joker tries to get students to drop out of school and become members of his gang.

. . . He Meets His Match, the Grisly Ghoul
The Joker tries to fix a basketball game so he can become the big winner by betting on the opposing team.

True or False Face . . .
W: Stephen Kandel. D: William A. Graham. GS: Malachi Throne, Myrna Fahey, Billy Curtis. False-Face plans to flood Gotham City with counterfeit money.

. . . Super Rat Race
False-Face tries to destroy Batman at his hideout at an abandoned movie studio.

The Purr-Fect Crime . . .
W: Stanley Ralph Ross & Lee Orgel. D: James Sheldon. GS: Julie Newmar, Jock Mahoney, Ralph Manza. The Catwoman plans to steal two valuable golden cat statues which will lead her to a pirate's hidden treasure.

. . . Better Luck Next Time
After trying to feed Batman and Robin to her Tigers, the Catwoman heads to a hidden cave in search of the treasure.

The Penguin Goes Straight . . .
W: Lorenzo Semple Jr. & John Cardwell. D: Leslie H. Martinson. GS: Burgess Meredith, Harvey Lembeck, Al Checco. The Penguin opens his own protective agency.

. . . Not Yet, He Ain't
The Penguin plans to steal the multimillion dollar wedding gifts at his own wedding to a movie star.

The Ring of Wax . . .
W: Jack Paritz & Bob Rodgers. D: James B. Clark. GS: Frank Gorshin, Michael Greene, Linda Gaye Scott, Joey Tata. The Riddler smuggles a universal wax solvent into the country

in order to help him obtain the information which will lead him to the lost treasure of the Incas.

... Give 'em the Axe
The Riddler heads to the museum to steal the treasure contained inside a mummy's sarcophagus.

The Joker Trumps an Ace ...
W: Francis & Marian Cockrell. D: Richard C. Sarafian. GS: Cesar Romero, Dan Seymour, Tol Avery. The Joker kidnaps a visiting Maharajah.

... Batman Sets the Pace
The Joker plans to ransom the Maharajah for $500,000.

The Curse of Tut ...
W: Robert C. Dennis & Earl Barret. D: Charles Rondeau. GS: Victor Buono. King Tut plans to take over Gotham City and claim it as his kingdom.

... The Pharaoh's in a Rut
Alfred and Robin try to rescue Batman who has been captured by King Tut.

The Bookworm Turns ...
W: Rik Vollaerts. D: Larry Peerce. GS: Roddy McDowall, John Crawford, Francine York. The Bookworm captures Robin and ties him to the clapper of a giant bell inside a clock which is about to strike.

... While Gotham City Burns
The Bookworm traps Batman and Robin inside a giant cookbook

Death in Slow Motion ...
W: Dick Carr. D: Charles Rondeau. GS: Frank Gorshin, Sherry Jackson, Francis X. Bushman, Theo Marcuse. The Riddler creates a series of crimes so he can film Batman for his silent movie.

... The Riddler's False Notion
The Riddler tries to steal the valuable silent film collection from a famous collector.

Fine Finny Fiends ...
W: Sheldon Stark. D: Tom Gries. GS: Burgess Meredith, Victor Lundin. The Penguin brainwashes Alfred so he can learn the location of a millionaire's award dinner.

... Batman Makes the Scene
The Penguin and his men try to steal the money from the award banquet.

Shoot a Crooked Arrow ...
W: Stanley Ralph Ross. D: Sherman Marks. GS: Art Carney, Doodles Weaver, Barbara Nichols, Sam Jaffe. The Archer captures Batman and plans to run him through with a lance.

... Walk the Straight and Narrow
The Archer switches the ten million dollars meant for the city's poor people with counterfeit money.

The Minstrel's Shakedown ...
W: Francis & Marion Cockrell. D: Murray Golden. GS: Van Johnson. The Minstrel plans to blackmail every member of the stock exchange.

... Barbecued Batman
The Minstrel plans to destroy the stock exchange building if they do not pay him his ransom.

The Penguin's Nest ...
W: Lorenzo Semple Jr. D: Murray Golden. GS: Burgess Meredith, Vito Scotti. The Penguin opens a restaurant where he collects the signatures of rich people, so when he returns to prison he can get a famous forger to sign phony checks and steal money from the unsuspecting millionaires.

... The Bird's Last Jest
The Penguin kidnaps Chief O'Hara and tries to blackmail Bruce Wayne in an attempt to get himself sent back to prison, where he can carry out his forgery plan.

Hot Off the Griddle ...
W: Stanley Ralph Ross. D: Don Weis. GS: Julie Newmar, Jack Kelly. The

Catwoman tries to fry Batman and Robin with giant magnifying glasses.

... The Cat and the Fiddle
The Catwoman plans to steal two valuable violins and $500,000 in cash.

The Greatest Mother of Them All ...
W: Henry Slesar. D: Oscar Rudolph. GS: Shelley Winters. Ma Parker tries to get herself and her family sent to prison so she can take it over and release all of the criminals contained inside.

... Ma Parker
Ma Parker straps Batman and Robin in a pair of electric chairs and plans to fry them at midnight. Julie Newmar makes a cameo appearance as The Catwoman.

The Spell of Tut ...
W: Robert C. Dennis & Earl Barret. D: Larry Peerce. GS: Victor Buono, Sid Haig. King Tut tries to revive some ancient scarabs which will enable him to create a secret potion which will turn everyone in Gotham City into his slaves.

... Tut's Case Is Shut
Tut takes control of Commissioner Gordon and gets him to lead Batman into a trap.

The Clock King's Crazy Crimes ...
W: Bill Finger & Charles Sinclair. D: James Neilson. GS: Walter Slezak, Michael Pate. The Clock King traps Batman and Robin inside a giant hourglass, where he plans to smother them with sand.

... Clock King Gets Crowned
The Clock King plans to steal a one million dollar cesium clock.

An Egg Grows in Gotham ...
W: Stanley Ralph Ross & Ed Self. D: George Waggner. GS: Vincent Price, Edward Everett Horton, Ben Weldon. Egghead plans to gain control of Gotham City by keeping the city's charter with the Indians from being paid.

... The Yegg Foes in Gotham
Egghead gains control of the city and banishes Batman from the city limits.

The Devil's Fingers ...
W: Lorenzo Semple Jr. D: Larry Peerce. GS: Liberace, Edy Williams. Chandell plans to marry Aunt Harriet and then have his twin brother Harry kill Bruce and Dick so he can inherit their money.

... The Dead Ringers
When Chandell plans to go straight, his brother Harry takes his place and plans to marry Harriet himself.

Hizzoner the Penguin ...
W: Stanford Sherman. D: Oscar Rudolph. GS: Burgess Meredith, Woodrow Parfrey, Paul Revere and the Raiders. The Penguin plans to run for mayor.

... Dizzoner the Penguin
The Penguin plans to kidnap the board of elections in order to keep Batman from winning the election.

Green Ice ...
W: Max Hodge. D: George Waggner. GS: Otto Preminger, Dee Hartford. Mr. Freeze kidnaps Miss Iceland and plans to bring her body temperature down to match his and then marry her.

... Deep Freeze
Mr. Freeze threatens to freeze the entire city unless he is given one billion dollars.

The Impractical Joker ...
W: Jay Thompson & Charles Hoffman. D: James B. Clark. GS: Cesar Romero, Christopher Cary. The Joker kidnaps Batman and Robin and threatens to turn them into giant keys.

... The Joker's Provokers
The Joker plans to take over Gotham City with his time machine.

Marsha Queen of Diamonds ...
W: Stanford Sherman. D: James B.

Clark. GS: Carolyn Jones, Estelle Winwood, Woody Strode. The Queen of Diamonds plans to marry Batman so she can steal the Bat-diamond which powers the Bat-computer.

. . . Marsha's Scheme with Diamonds
Marsha tries to get her Aunt Hilda, the witch, to turn Batman and Robin into toads.

Come Back, Shame . . .
W: Stanley Ralph Ross. D: James B. Clark. GS: Cliff Robertson, Milton Frome, Jack Carter. Cowboy Shame steals the parts from several cars so he can build a super truck which will outrun the Batmobile.

. . . It's the Way You Play the Game
Shame tries to steal four valuable Black Angus bulls.

The Cat's Meow . . .
W: Stanley Ralph Ross. D: James B. Clark. GS: Julie Newmar, Chad & Jeremy. The Catwoman captures Batman and Robin and puts them in an echo chamber where the dripping of a faucet, magnified ten million times, will destroy their brains.

. . . The Bat's Kow Tow
The Catwoman, using her voice eraser, steals Chad and Jeremy's voices and holds them for ransom.

The Puzzles Are Coming . . .
W: Fred De Gorter. D: Jeffrey Hayden. GS: Maurice Evans. The Puzzler sends Batman and Robin aloft in a balloon which, when it reaches 20,000 feet, is rigged to drop the basket in which they are riding.

. . . The Duo Is Slumming
The Puzzler tries to steal a superjet plane.

The Sandman Cometh . . .
W: Ellis St. Joseph & Charles Hoffman. D: George Waggoner. GS: Michael Rennie, Julie Newmar, Spring Byington. The Catwoman teams up with a European criminal known as

the Sandman in order to swindle a rich widow out of her money.

. . . The Catwoman Goeth
The Sandman double crosses the Catwoman and plans to elope with the rich widow and keep the money for himself.

The Contaminated Cowl . . .
W: Charles Hoffman. D: Oscar Rudolph. GS: David Wayne. The Mad Hatter sprays Batman's cowl with radioactive gas in an attempt to gain the cowl for his collection.

. . . The Mad Hatter Runs Afoul
Batman makes the Mad Hatter believe that he killed the Dynamic Duo so he can set a trap for him.

The Zodiac Crimes [Three Parts] . . .
W: Stanford Sherman & Stephen Kandel. D: Oscar Rudolph. GS: Cesar Romero, Burgess Meredith, Terry Moore. The Joker and The Penguin join forces to commit crimes based on the signs of the Zodiac. The Joker captures Batman and Robin and plans to crush them with a giant meteorite.

. . . The Joker's Hard Time
The Joker continues his Zodiac crimes without The Penguin, who was captured in the previous episode. The Joker traps Batman and Robin and plans to feed them, along with his former female assistant, to a giant clam.

. . . The Penguin Declines
The Joker frees The Penguin in order to get his help in turning the Gotham City water supply into Joker-Jelly, and to sneak into the Batcave in order to learn Batman's secret identity.

That Darn Catwoman . . .
W: Stanley Ralph Ross. D: Oscar Rudolph. GS: Julie Newmar, Leslie Gore, Jock Gaynor. The Catwoman turns Robin into a member of her gang by drugging him.

. . . Scat, Darn Catwoman
The Catwoman plans to break into a

Mint and steal all the money contained inside.

Penguin Is a Girl's Best Friend [Three Parts] . . .
W: Stanford Sherman. D: James B. Clark. GS: Burgess Meredith, Carolyn Jones, Estelle Winwood. The Penguin and Marsha, Queen of Diamonds team up to make a movie. The Penguin, using his movie as a cover, steals some bulletproof armor from a museum.

. . . Penguin Sets a Trend
The Penguin uses the stolen armor to steal some old plans from the government. He also traps Batman and Robin in suits of armor and has them carried off to a scrap metal crusher.

. . . Penguin's Disastrous End
The Penguin and Marsha break into a vault at the Sub Treasury where they use the stolen plans to make a solid gold tank.

Batman's Anniversary . . .
W: William P. D'Angelo. D: James B. Clark. GS: John Astin, Deanna Lund, Martin Kosleck. The Riddler plans to rob a bank so he can buy a destructive weapon called a De-Molecularizer. He also traps Batman and Robin on top of a giant cake made of quicksand.

. . . A Riddling Controversy
The Riddler threatens to destroy police headquarters unless the criminal statutes are rescinded.

The Joker's Last Laugh . . .
W: Lorenzo Semple Jr. & Peter Rabe. D: Oscar Rudolph. GS: Cesar Romero, Lawrence Montaigne. The Joker plans to crush Robin in a comic book printing press.

. . . The Joker's Epitaph
The Joker plans to blackmail Bruce Wayne and kill Batman and Robin with his superpowered robots.

Catwoman Goes to College . . .
W: Stanley Ralph Ross. D: Robert Sparr. GS: Julie Newmar, Jacques

Bergerac, Paul Mantee. The Catwoman traps Batman and Robin inside a giant coffee cup which is about to be filled with deadly acid.

. . . Batman Displays His Knowledge
The Catwoman steals some valuable cat's-eye opals.

A Piece of the Action . . .
W: Charles Hoffman. D: Oscar Rudolph. GS: Van Williams, Bruce Lee, Roger C. Carmel. The Green Hornet and Kato, along with Batman and Robin, are captured by the evil Colonel Gumm and are about to be turned into giant postage stamps.

. . . Batman's Satisfaction
The Green Hornet and Kato help Batman and Robin capture Colonel Gumm.

King Tut's Coup . . .
W: Stanley Ralph Ross. D: James B. Clark. GS: Victor Buono, Lee Meriwether, Grace Lee Whitney. King Tut kidnaps a millionaire's daughter and makes her his queen.

. . . Batman's Waterloo
Batman tries to rescue Robin who is about to be thrown into a vat of boiling oil by King Tut.

Black Widow Strikes Again . . .
W: Robert Mintz. D: Oscar Rudolph. GS: Miss Tallulah Bankhead. The Black Widow plans to rob every bank in Gotham City.

. . . Caught in the Spider's Den
The Black Widow puts Batman under her power and gets him to use the Batcomputer to help her find a bank to rob.

Ice Spy . . .
W: Charles Hoffman. D: Oscar Rudolph. GS: Eli Wallach, Leslie Parrish, Elisha Cook, H.M. Wynant. Mr. Freeze plans to vaporize Batman and Robin into part of an ice skating rink.

. . . The Duo Defy
Batman and Robin try to prevent Mr. Freeze from freezing all of Gotham City.

Pop Goes The Joker . . .
W: Stanford Sherman. D: George Waggner. GS: Cesar Romero. The Joker opens an art school so he can hold his millionaire students for ransom.

. . . Flop Goes The Joker
The Joker almost discovers Batman's true identity when he pays a visit to Wayne Manor and accidentally trips the switch and exposes him to the Bat Poles which lead to the Batcave.

[Every episode from now on is in one part except where noted.]

Enter Batgirl, Exit Penguin
W: Stanford Sherman. D: George Waggner. GS: Burgess Meredith. The Penguin kidnaps the Commissioner's daughter Barbara and plans to marry her, unaware that she is Batgirl.

Ring Around The Riddler
W: Charles Hoffman. D: Sam Strangis. GS: Frank Gorshin, Joan Collins. The Riddler plans to take over the fight game in Gotham City with the help of The Siren.

The Wail of The Siren
W: Stanley Ralph Ross. D: George Waggner. GS: Joan Collins, Mike Mazurki, Cliff Osmond. The Siren puts Bruce Wayne under her power and takes control of the Wayne fortune.

The Sport of Penguins [Two Parts] . . .
W: Charles Hoffman. D: Sam Strangis. GS: Burgess Meredith, Ethel Merman. The Penguin teams up with Lola Lasagne in order to fix a horse race.

. . . A Horse of Another Color
The Penguin and Lola try to carry out their evil plan until they are stopped by Batman.

The Unkindest Tut of All
W: Stanley Ralph Ross. D: Sam Strangis. GS: Victor Buono. Tut plans to steal a valuable statue god which will make its possessor the master of the universe.

Louie, The Lilac
W: Dwight Taylor. D: George Waggner. GS: Milton Berle. Louie, The Lilac plans to take over the minds of Gotham City's flower children.

The Ogg Couple
W: Stanford Sherman. D: Oscar Rudolph. GS: Vincent Price, Anne Baxter. Egghead teams up with Olga, queen of the Bessarovian Cossacks to steal the Silver Scimitar of Toras Bulbul and the golden Egg of Ogg.

The Ogg and I [Two Parts] . . .
W: Stanford Sherman. D: Oscar Rudolph. GS: Vincent Price, Anne Baxter. Egghead kidnaps Commissioner Gordon and demands one dime for every egg eaten in Gotham City as a ransom.

. . . How to Hatch a Dinosaur
Egghead plans to hatch a dinosaur's egg with radiation and set it loose on the city.

Surf's Up! Joker's Under!
W: Charles Hoffman. D: Oscar Rudolph. GS: Cesar Romero. The Joker plans to become the surfing champ of the world.

The Londinium Larcenies [Three Parts]
W: Elkan Allan & Charles Hoffman. D: Oscar Rudolph. GS: Rudy Vallee, Glynis Johns. Batman goes to Londinium to solve the crimes being committed by Lord Ffogg and his sister Lady Peasoup.

. . . The Foggiest Notion
Batman tries to rescue Robin who is tied to the winch which opens the Tower Bridge.

... *The Bloody Tower*
Batman captures Lord Ffogg and the other members of his gang.

The Funny Feline Felonies [Two Parts]
W:Stanley Ralph Ross. D: Oscar Rudolph. GS: Cesar Romero, Eartha Kitt. The Joker teams up with The Catwoman in order to find some hidden gunpowder.

... *The Joke's on Catwoman*
The Joker and The Catwoman find the gunpowder which they plan to use to break into the Federal Depository, but are captured and put on trial by Batman.

The Joker's Flying Saucer
W: Charles Hoffman. D: Sam Strangis. GS: Cesar Romero. The Joker builds a flying saucer in an attempt to conquer the world.

Catwoman's Dressed to Kill
W: Stanley Ralph Ross. D: Sam Strangis. GS: Eartha Kitt. The Catwoman tries to steal a solid gold dress and turn Batgirl into a mattress.

Louie's Lethal Lilac Time
W: Charles Hoffman. D: Sam Strangis. GS: Milton Berle, Nobu McCarthy. Louie The Lilac tries to corner the perfume market.

Nora Clavicle and The Ladies' Crime Club
W: Stanford Sherman. D: Oscar Rudolph. GS: Barbara Rush. Batman tries to stop Nora Clavicle from destroying Gotham City, in the hopes of collecting the insurance policy she took out on it.

Penguin's Clean Sweep
W: Stanford Sherman. D: Oscar Rudolph. GS: Burgess Meredith, Monique Van Vooren, Charles Dierkop. The Penguin contaminates the money in Gotham City with sleeping sickness so he can collect all of the money when everyone throws it away.

The Entrancing Dr. Cassandra
W: Stanley Ralph Ross. D: Sam Strangis. GS: Ida Lupino, Howard Duff. Alchemist Dr. Cassandra and her aide Cabala turn themselves invisible in order to free the arch criminals from prison. She also turns Batman, Robin and Batgirl into flat one-dimensional images of themselves with her Alvino-ray gun.

The Great Escape [Two Parts]
W: Stanley Ralph Ross. D: Oscar Rudolph. GS: Cliff Robertson, Dina Merrill, Hermione Baddeley, Victor Lundin. Shame escapes from prison and plans to rob the train which is taking old money back to the Mint to be destroyed.

... *The Great Train Robbery*
Batman and Shame have a showdown at his hideout in a replica of a Mexican town.

I'll Be a Mummy's Uncle
W: Stanley Ralph Ross. D: Sam Strangis. GS: Victor Buono. King Tut discovers Batman's true identity when he accidentally mines under Wayne Manor and finds the Batcave.

Minerva, Mayhem and Millionaires
W: Charles Hoffman. D: Oscar Rudolph. GS: Zsa Zsa Gabor, Jacques Bergerac. Minerva uses her memory extractor to learn where the millionaire customers of her health spa hide their valuables.

THE BEVERLY HILLBILLIES

On the air 9/26/62, off 9/7/71. CBS. B&W/Color film. 30 min. 216 episodes. Broadcast: Sept 1962-Sept 1964 Wed 9-9:30; Sept 1964-Sept 1968 Wed

The Beverly Hillbillies: left to right, top, Buddy Ebsen, Nancy Kulp, Raymond Bailey, bottom, Irene Ryan, Max Baer, Donna Douglas.

8:30-9; Sept 1968-Sept 1969 Wed 9-9:30; Sept 1969-Sept 1970 Wed 8:30-9; Sept 1970-Sept 1971 Tue 7:30-8. Producer: Paul Henning. Prod Co: Filmways. Synd: Viacom.

CAST: Jed Clampett (played by Buddy Ebsen), Daisy Moses [Granny] (Irene Ryan), Elly May Clampett (Donna Douglas), Jethro Bodine (Max Baer, Jr.), Milburn Drysdale (Raymond Bailey), Jane Hathaway (Nancy Kulp), Mrs. Margaret Drysdale (Harriet MacGibbon), John Brewster (Frank Wilcox), Pearl Bodine (Bea Benaderet), Lawrence Chapman (Milton Frome), Elverna Bradshaw (Elvia Allman), Shorty Kellems (George "Shug" Fisher), Homer Cratchit (Percy Helton), Dash Riprock (Larry Pennell), Dr. Roy Clyburn (Fred Clark).

The Ballad of Jed Clampett by Lester Flatt and Earl Scruggs.

The story of the Clampetts, an Ozark family who strike oil on their property and quickly move to a Beverly Hills mansion. The Clampetts consist of Jed, a widowed mountaineer, his unmarried daughter Elly May, his mother-in-law Granny Moses, and his silly nephew Jethro Bodine. Most stories relate their struggles to adjust to the fast, sophisticated modern life of the big city. Conceived by Paul Henning, *The Beverly Hillbillies* was the first and most successful of his three rural comedies. The now-syndicated episodes are popular in many Southern cities but not elsewhere, perhaps because it is felt to be so out of date.

The Clampetts Strike Oil [Pilot]
GS: Frank Wilcox, Bob Osborne, Ron Hagerthy, Bea Benaderet. Jed strikes oil and the whole family moves to California.

Getting Settled
Jed and the family are mistaken for the servants when they move into their mansion.

Meanwhile, Back at the Cabin
GS: Frank Wilcox, Bea Benaderet. The Clampetts miss their mountain cabin.

The Clampetts Meet Mrs. Drysdale
GS: Harriet MacGibbon. Mr. Drysdale introduces his wife to the Clampetts.

Jed Buys Stock
GS: Harriet MacGibbon, Sirry Steffen, Arthur Gould Porter. Drysdale tells Jed to invest in stock, so he buys a whole bunch of animals.

Trick or Treat
GS: Phil Gordon, Teddy Eccles, Frank Wilcox, Shirley Mitchell, Bea Benaderet. The Clampetts decide to visit their neighbors, unaware that it is Halloween eve.

The Servants
GS: Sirry Steffen, Arthur Gould Porter. Drysdale lends the Clampetts his servants.

Jethro Goes to School
GS: Eleanor Audley, Phil Gordon, Lisa Davis, Frank Wilcox, Bea Benaderet. A private teacher comes to tutor Jethro.

Elly's First Date
GS: Louis Nye, Harriet MacGibbon. Elly May dates Drysdale's son.

Pygmalion and Elly
GS: Louis Nye, Harriet MacGibbon. Drysdale's son Sonny tries to turn Elly May into a lady.

Elly Races Jethrine
GS: Louis Nye, Phil Gordon, Bea Benaderet. The Clampetts try to get Elly May to marry Sonny before Cousin Pearl marries off Jethro's sister Jethrine to her boyfriend Jasper.

The Great Feud
GS: Ken Drake, Lyle Talbot, Sirry Steffen, Arthur Gould Porter. A feud starts when Sonny dumps Elly May.

Home for Christmas
GS: Bea Benaderet, Paul Winchell, Frank Wilcox, Jeanne Vaughn, Eilene Janssen. The Clampetts take their first ride on an airplane when they return home for Christmas.

No Place Like Home
GS: Bea Benaderet, Paul Winchell, Frank Wilcox. The Clampetts help Pearl get Mr. Brewster to marry her.

Jed Rescues Pearl
GS: Bea Benaderet, Frank Wilcox, Elvia Allman. Brewster makes a public marriage proposal to Pearl.

Back to Californy
GS: Bea Benaderet, Phil Gordon, Frank Wilcox, Gloria Marshall. Jed invites Pearl and Jethrine to stay at the mansion.

Jed's Dilemma
GS: Bea Benaderet. Jed takes the family on a tour of Beverly Hills.

Jed Saves Drysdale's Marriage
Pearl becomes Drysdale's new housekeeper.

Elly's Animals
GS: Peter Leeds, Eddie Dean, Brian Kelly, Karl Lukas. Pearl gives yodeling lessons, which causes an animal stampede.

Jed Throws a Wingding
GS: Lester Flatt, Earl Scruggs, Joi Lansing, Midge Ware. Two of Pearl's

former boyfriends visit her at Jed's place.

Jed Plays Solomon
GS: Eddie Dean, Brian Kelly, Lucille Starr. Granny calls the police to stop Pearl from Yodeling.

Duke Steals a Wife
GS: Narda Onyx. Duke, the dog, brings Jed and a glamorous Frenchwoman together.

Jed Buys the Freeway
GS: Jesse White, Dick O'Shea. A con man tries to sell Jed some Hollywood landmarks.

Jed Becomes a Banker
GS: Charles Lane, Jack Boyle, Lester Matthews, Laura Shelton. Jed becomes vice president of Drysdale's bank so he can win a bank skeet shooting contest.

The Family Tree
GS: Rosemary De Camp. A historian traces Jed's ancestors to a time before the Pilgrims.

Jed Cuts the Family Tree
GS: Rosemary De Camp. Pearl tries to turn the family into high society people.

Granny's Spring Tonic
GS: Lola Albright. Jed drinks Granny's tonic and falls for a golddigger.

Jed Pays His Income Tax
GS: John Stephenson, Ron Hagerthy, Frank Wilcox. When the IRS comes to collect Jed's income tax, Granny tries to shoot him.

The Clampetts and the Dodgers
GS: Leo Durocher, Skip Ward, Wally Cassell, Norman Leavitt. Leo Durocher tries to sign Jethro to a contract with the Dodgers.

Duke Becomes a Father
GS: Narda Onyx. The Frenchwoman whom Jed fell for returns with Duke's puppies.

The Clampetts Entertain
GS: Jim Backus. The board chairman of Drysdale's bank wants to meet Jed.

The Clampetts in Court
GS: Kathleen Freeman, Murvyn Vye, Roy Roberts, Jess Kirkpatrick, Dean Harens. Jed is sued for $100,000 worth of damages for a traffic accident which never took place.

The Clampetts Get Psychoanalyzed
GS: Dick Wesson, Herbert Rudley, Karen Norris. Granny has a fight with a psychiatrist.

The Psychiatrist Gets Clampetted
GS: Herbert Rudley. Granny's love charm causes the psychiatrist to chase after her and not Pearl.

Elly Becomes a Secretary
GS: John Ashley, Willis Bouchey, Patty Jo Harmon, Bill Baldwin. Jed takes over Drysdale's job for a day and is named Banker of the Year.

Jethro's Friend
GS: Michael Petit, Hayden Rorke. The Clampetts take a spoiled child and show him how to have fun.

Jed Gets the Misery
GS: Fred Clark. Jed pretends to be sick so Granny can practice medicine again.

Hair Raising Holiday
GS: Fred Clark. Granny creates a medicine which grows hair.

Granny's Garden
Granny decides to grow a vegetable garden.

Elly Starts to School
GS: Doris Packer, Sharon Tate, Joanna Barnes, Tom Cound. Elly goes to a finishing school for rich girls.

The Clampett Look
GS: Joanna Barnes, Doris Packer. The Clampetts unknowingly start a new hillbilly fashion craze among the rich folks.

Jethro's First Love
GS: Barbara Nichols, Sharon Tate. Jethro's new girlfriend is a burlesque dancer.

Chickadee Returns
GS: Barbara Nichols, Sharon Tate. Jethro decides to marry his new girl-friend.

The Clampetts Are Overdrawn
GS: King Donovan, Shirley Mitchell, Dick Crockett, Jack Boyle, Gil Perkins, Robert Foulk. A bank error accuses Jed of being overdrawn on his multi-million dollar account.

The Clampetts Go Hollywood
GS: King Donovan, Shirley Mitchell, Sharon Tate. Jed falls under the power of an unemployed actor.

Turkey Day
GS: Benny Rubin, George Sawaya. Elly turns the Thanksgiving dinner turkey into one of her pets.

The Garden Party
GS: Murray Pollack, Curt Massey, Sharon Tate. Mrs. Drysdale's garden party guests leave to go to a party at the Clampetts.

Elly Needs a Maw
GS: Doris Packer, Sharon Tate, Tom Cound. Jed decides Elly needs a mother to turn her from a tomboy into a lady.

The Clampetts Get Culture
GS: Eleanor Audley, Don Orlando, Sharon Tate. The Clampetts try to become as cultured as their neighbors.

Christmas at the Clampetts
Drysdale gives the Clampetts a lot of expensive gifts for Christmas.

A Man for Elly
GS: Henry Gibson, Amedee Chabot. A TV western star comes to the house to date Elly.

The Giant Jackrabbit
GS: Kathy Kersh, Peter Bourne, Sharon Tate. Jed gets a kangaroo as a present and Granny thinks it is a giant jackrabbit.

The Girl from Home
GS: Peter Whitney, Chet Stratton, Muriel Landers, Kathy Kersh. A hillbilly beauty contest winner and her father come to Beverly Hills so she can marry Jethro.

Lafe Lingers On
GS: Peter Whitney. The father from the previous episode moves in and becomes an unwanted guest.

The Race for Queen
GS: Robert Cummings, Kathy Kersh, Susan Hart. Elly almost wins the Miss Beverly Hills beauty contest.

The Critter Doctor
GS: Mark Goddard, Russell Collins. Granny thinks a salesman who sells insecticide is the doctor Elly called to help her sick animals.

Lafe Returns
GS: Peter Whitney, Bobs Watson. The hillbilly freeloader returns to give Granny a tree.

Son of Lafe Returns
GS: Peter Whitney, Bobs Watson, Conlan Carter. Lafe the freeloader sends for his son to court Elly in the hopes of getting his hands on Jed's money.

The Clampetts Go Fishing
GS: Mark Tapscott, Glen Stensel. The Clampetts go fishing at Marineland of the Pacific.

A Bride for Jed
GS: Earl Scruggs, Joi Lansing, Midge Ware, Adele Clair. Miss Jane has an idea on how to find a wife for Jed.

Granny vs. the Weather Bureau
GS: John McGiver, Quinn O'Hara, Helen Kleeb. Granny tries to prove she can predict the weather better than the Weather Bureau.

Another Neighbor
GS: Jean Willes, Susan Hart, Burt Mustin. Granny is giving her tonic to her neighbors in Beverly Hills.

The Bank Raising
Lester Matthews, Bill Baldwin, Addison Richards, Kathy Kersh. The Clampetts go to a ground breaking ceremony for a new bank thinking it is like an old fashioned barn raising.

The Great Crawdad Hunt
GS: Peter Leeds, Addison Richards, Lester Matthews. Two tycoons try to find out the reason why Jed is so good in business.

The Dress Shop
GS: Natalie Schafer, Marjorie Bennett. The Clampetts buy an exclusive dress shop.

The House of Granny
GS: Ray Kellogg, Maurice Marsac, George Cisar, Edna Skinner. The Clampetts turn the dress shop into the House of Granny.

The Continental Touch
GS: Janine Grindel, Maurice Marsac. Mrs. Drysdale mistakes Elly for a European princess.

Jed, Incorporated
Drysdale creates a new company called Clampeo, Inc. and makes Jed the president.

Granny Learns to Drive
GS: Mel Blanc, Harry Lauter. Granny decides to learn how to drive.

Cabin in Beverly Hills
GS: Sheila James, John Stephenson, Jack Bannon. Drysdale has a new cabin built for Granny so she won't be homesick for her old cabin in the hills.

Jed Foils a Home Wrecker
GS: Sheila James, Mike Ross, John Stephenson. Mrs. Drysdale tries to have Granny's cabin torn down.

Jethro's Graduation
GS: Eleanor Audley, Donald Foster, Lisa Davis, Mike Barton, Happy Derman. Elly's pet chimp takes Jethro's place when he misses his graduation from the sixth grade.

Jed Becomes a Movie Mogul
Jed buys controlling interest in the Mammoth Pictures Corporation.

Clampett City
GS: Milton Frome, Sallie James, Russ Conway, John Abbott, Alvy Moore, Ray Kellogg. The Clampetts move into the backlot Old Village set at the studio.

Clampett City General Store
GS: Milton Frome, Theodore Marcuse, Sallie James, Nestor Paiva. The Clampetts get parts in a new movie their studio is making.

Hedda Hopper's Hollywood
GS: Hedda Hopper, Don Hagerty, Bill Baldwin, Ted Fish. Hedda Hopper fights against Drysdale's plan to tear down the movie studio.

Doctor Jed Clampett
GS: Cully Richards, Roy Rogers, Richard St. John, Fabian Dean, Virginia Sale. Jed receives an honorary doctor's degree from a college, making Granny jealous.

Jed the Heartbreaker
Mrs. Drysdale tries to get rid of the Clampetts.

Back to Marineland
GS: Robert Carson, Sharon Tate. Jethro goes to Marineland to join the Marines.

Teenage Idol
GS: Jesse Pearson. The Clampetts are visited by a popular singer from back home.

The Widow Poke Arrives
GS: Jesse Pearson, Alan Reed, Susan Walther, Maria Elena. Granny tries to

get Jed to marry singer Jonny Poke's mother.

The Ballet
GS: Leon Belasco, Barrie Duffus. Mrs. Drysdale asks Jed for money to support a ballet company.

The Boarder
GS: Arthur Treacher. The Clampetts rent a room to the Drysdale's butler.

The Boarder Stays
GS: Arthur Treacher. Drysdale's butler tries to give the Clampetts some culture.

Start the New Year Right
GS: Sue England, Les Tremayne, Jill Jarmyn. The Clampetts visit Mrs. Drysdale in the hospital.

Clampett General Hospital
GS: Willis Bouchey, Jean Howell. The Clampetts try to cure Mrs. Drysdale of her nervous condition.

The Movie Starlet
GS: Sharon Farrell, William Newell, Bernie Kopell, Rodney Bell. Jethro falls for a young movie star.

Elly in the Movies
GS: Larry Pennell, Ann Henry, Bill Quinn, Sally Mills, Diane Bond, Marilee Summers. Movie star Dash Riprock thinks Miss Jane is Elly May, his new leading lady.

Dash Riprock, You Cad
GS: Larry Pennell, Sharon Tate, Jeff Davis, Jack Bannon, Glenn Wilder, Dermot Cronin, Kent Miller, Murray Alper. Elly loses another movie star boyfriend to Miss Jane.

Clampett a Go-Go
GS: Alan Reed, Sylvia Lewis. Drysdale gets a playboy to date Granny.

Jed's Temptation
GS: Don Rickles, Iris Adrian, Sylvia Lewis, Ralph Montgomery. Granny tries to save Jed from gambling.

Double Naught Jethro
GS: Sharon Tate, Joyce Nizzari. Jethro plans on becoming a spy.

Clampett's Millions
GS: Roy Roberts, Joyce Nizzari. Another banker wants Jed's money for his bank.

Drysdale's Dog Days
GS: Grandon Rhodes, John Day, Steve Brodie. Granny demands that she see her share of Jed's money in cash.

Brewster's Honeymoon
GS: Frank Wilcox, Lisa Seagram. The Clampetts let Mr. Brewster use their mountain cabin while he is on his honeymoon.

Flatt, Clampett and Scruggs
GS: Lester Flatt, Earl Scruggs, Frank Scannell. Lester and Earl come to make homesick Granny happy again.

Jed and the Countess
GS: Jean Willes, Burt Mustin. The Countess returns for more of Granny's tonic and another chance at dating Jed.

Big Daddy, Jed
GS: Alan Reed, Marianne Gabs, Diki Lerner, Paul DeRolf, Keva Page. A beatnik comes to Jed for some money.

Cool School Is Out
GS: Alan Reed, Diki Lerner, Marianne Gabs. Granny dresses up as a beatnik to rescue Elly and Jethro from a bunch of beatniks at a coffee house.

The Big Bank Battle
GS: Roy Roberts, Sue Casey. Mr. Cushing offers Jed a job as a vice president if he moves his money to Cushing's bank.

The Clampetts vs. Automation
GS: Byron Foulger, Sharon Tate. The Clampetts befriend one of Drysdale's bookkeepers who has been replaced by a computer.

Luke's Boy
GS: Robert Easton, Pat Winters, Edy Williams, Chanin Hale. Granny tries to get Elly May married to a boy from the hills.

The Brewsters Return
GS: Frank Wilcox, Lisa Seagram, Hal Taggart. The Clampetts welcome Mr. Brewster and his new wife.

Jed, the Bachelor
GS: Peter Leeds, Julie Van Zandt, Ray Kellogg, LaRue Farlow. Granny moves out and heads back home to her little cabin.

The Art Center
GS: Walter Woolf King, Chet Stratton, Gay Gordon. The Clampetts create art work for a new art gallery.

Admiral Jed Clampett
GS: Rick Cooper, Mark Evans, Ray Kellogg, Garrison True, Frank Coghlin. Jed mistakes a Navy destroyer for his new yacht.

That Old Black Magic
GS: Dave Willock, Tristram Coffin, Allison McKay, John Gallaudet. Granny thinks Mrs. Drysdale turned herself into a crow with black magic.

The Sheik
GS: Dan Seymour, Frank Wilcox, Bill Baldwin, Phil Gordon. A sheik gives Jed four dancing girls and then wants to date Elly May.

The Private Eye
GS: Donald Curtis, Eileen O'Neill, James Seay. Jethro unknowingly helps some crooks who want to rob Drysdale's bank.

Possum Day
Drysdale arranges for a Possum Day festival to keep them from going home.

The Possum Day Parade
GS: Barney Elmore, Maurice Kelly, Francisco Ortega, Bill Baldwin. Drysdale promotes the Possum Day parade.

The Clampetts Play the Rams
GS: Nina Shipman, Beecey Carlson. Jethro finds that the next door maid is in love with his color TV and not him.

The Courtship of Elly
GS: Van Williams. Granny creates a love potion in order to get Elly a husband.

A Real Nice Neighbor
GS: Kathleen Freeman, William Bakewell. Drysdale and Granny mistake a maid for a millionaire and try to get her to marry Jed.

The Poor Farmer
GS: Sebastian Cabot, Lester Matthews, Hal Baylor, William Forrest. The Clampetts mistake a billionaire on a diet for a starving farmer.

Hoe Down a Go-Go
GS: Paul DeRolf, The Enemies. Elly and Jethro hire a rock band called The Enemies to play at Jed's old fashioned barn dance.

Mrs. Drysdale's Father
GS: Charles Ruggles. Mrs. Drysdale's father tries to get some money out of the Clampetts.

Mr. Farquhar Stays On
GS: Charles Ruggles. Granny thinks Mrs. Drysdale's father, Mr. Farquhar, is proposing when he asks her to go with him to Las Vegas.

Military School
GS: John Hoyt, Craig Hundley, John Reilly. Jethro goes to a military school.

The Common Cold
GS: Fred Clark, Olan Soule, Tom Browne Henry, Lenore Kingston. Granny opens her own doctor's office.

The Richest Woman
GS: Martha Hyer, Douglas Dumbrille. The richest woman in the world wants to buy the Clampett mansion.

The Trotting Horse
GS: Herb Vigran, Norman Leavitt. Drysdale buys the Clampetts a race horse.

The Buggy
Drysdale convinces his wife to accept Granny's challenge to a horse and buggy race.

The Cat Burglar
GS: John Ashley, Norman Grabowski. A burgler tries to rob the Clampett's home.

The Big Chicken
GS: John Baer. Granny thinks the ostrich that has been eating her tomatoes is a giant chicken.

Sonny Drysdale Returns
GS: Louis Nye. Sonny returns to romance Elly May.

Brewster's Baby
GS: Phyllis Davis, Lisa Seagram, Frank Wilcox. Granny plans to go home to the hills to deliver Mrs. Brewster's baby.

The Great Jethro
GS: John Carradine, Lennie Bremen, Al Eben, Britt Nilsson, Carolyn Williams. A starving magician plans to use Jed to make some fast money.

The Old Folks Home
GS: Edith Leslie, Barney Elmore. Granny thinks Jed and the others plan to send her to an old folks home.

Flatt and Scruggs Return
GS: Lester Flatt, Earl Scruggs, Joi Lansing, Barney Elmore. Lester and Earl return to visit the Clampetts.

The Folk Singers
GS: Tom D'Andrea, Venita Wolf. Jethro tries to become a folk singer.

The Beautiful Maid
GS: Julie Newmar, Milton Frome. A Swedish actress moves in with the Clampetts in order to learn how they speak, so she can play a hillbilly in a movie.

Jethro's Pad
GS: Bettina Brenna, Phyllis Davis. Jethro wants his own bachelor pad.

The Bird Watchers
GS: Wally Cox, Venita Wolf, Larry Pennell. Elly May falls for a birdwatcher.

Jethro Gets Engaged
GS: Larry Pennell, Pat Harrington, Joan Huntington, Dick Winslow, Ray Kellogg. Jethro becomes Dash Riprock's stunt double.

Granny Tonics a Birdwatcher
GS: Wally Cox, Venita Wolf. Prof. Biddle, the birdwatcher, drinks Granny's tonic and turns aggressive.

Jethro Goes to College
GS: Louise Lormer, Gloria Neil, Hope Summers, Shuji Nozawa. Jethro enrolls in a secretarial school.

The Party Line
GS: Vinton Hayworth. Granny wants a party line telephone put in.

The Soup Contest
GS: Gavin Gordon, Steve Pendleton, Steve Dunne. Granny enters one of her recipes in a contest and signs Elly May's name to it, in the hopes she will attract a husband.

Jethro Takes Love Lessons
GS: Larry Pennell, Carol Booth. Jethro falls for a waitress who uses him to get to Dash Riprock.

The Badger Game
GS: Leon Ames, Gayle Hunnicutt. Jed almost falls victim to two blackmailers.

The Gorilla
GS: George Barrows. Jethro buys a gorilla to do his chores around the house.

Come Back, Little Herby
GS: George Barrows. The Clampetts try to get Drysdale to return their gorilla.

Jed in Politics
GS: Paul Reed. Jed runs for the office of Smog Commissioner.

Clampett Cha Cha Cha
GS: Frank Faylen, Iris Adrian. Two out of work dancers try to teach the Clampetts how to dance.

Jed Joins the Board
GS: Frank Wilcox, Tommy Farrell, Owen Cunningham, Jack Grinnage, Barry Kelly. Jed takes a job as a garbage collector in order to keep from being bored.

Granny Lives it Up
GS: Charles Ruggles, Roy Roberts, Jo Ann Pflug. Granny is being chased by two old men, Mr. Cushing and Mrs. Drysdale's father Mr. Farquhar, both of whom are after her money but for different reasons.

The Gloria Swanson Story
GS: Gloria Swanson, Milton Frome, George Neise, Frank Sully, Ray Kellogg. The Clampetts plan a movie comeback for their film idol Gloria Swanson.

The Woodchucks
GS: Nancy Dow, Jerry Rannow, Sandy Berke. Jethro wants to join the bird watcher's club in order to chase a pretty club member.

Foggy Mountain Soap
GS: Lester Flatt, Earl Scruggs, Edward Andrews, Terry Phillips, Bobs Watson. An ad man wants Jed and Granny to appear in a TV commercial to sell soap.

The Christmas Present
GS: James Millhollin, Bruce Hyde, Dee Carroll. The Clampetts take temporary Christmas jobs in a department store.

The Flying Saucer
GS: Frank Delfino, Billy Curtis, Jerry Maren, John Alvin. Drysdale hires three midgets to play spacemen as publicity for the bank.

The Mayor of Bug Tussle
GS: James Westerfield. The Mayor of Bug Tussle, their home town, pays a visit to the Clampetts.

Granny Retires
GS: Fred Clark. Granny plans to take her money out of the bank and go back to the hills.

The Clampett Curse
GS: Sheila James, Toby Kaye, Bernadette Withers, Russ Grieve. Jed gives away his fortune to three college girls.

The Indians Are Coming
GS: John Wayne, Stanley Waxman, Milton Frome, John Considine, Vince St. Cyr. Granny plans for a war when some Indians claim part of the Clampett oil land.

The Marriage Machine
GS: Warrene King, Lurene Tuttle, Richard Collier, Larry Christman, John Ayres. The Clampetts try computer dating.

Elly Comes Out
GS: Robert Strauss, Jenifer Lea. Mrs. Drysdale plans to ruin Elly May's coming out party.

The Matador
GS: Miguel Landa, Milton Frome. Jethro takes up bullfighting.

The Gypsy's Warning
GS: Leon Belasco, Bella Bruck. Mrs. Drysdale tries to scare the Clampetts away with a pair of fortune tellers.

His Royal Highness
GS: Jacques Bergerac, Victoria Carroll, Edward Ashley. The now broke, ex-King of Sabalia tries to marry Elly for her money.

Super Hawg
Granny thinks a hippopotamus is a giant hog and tries to butcher it.

The Doctors
GS: Lorraine Bendix, Fred Clark, Barbara Morrison. Granny has another fight with Dr. Clyburn when she gives away more of her spring tonic.

Delovely and Scruggs
GS: Lester Flatt, Earl Scruggs, Joi Lansing, Bobs Watson. Mrs. Flatt takes a screen test, with Jethro as the director.

The Little Monster
GS: Ted Eccles. Drysdale's nephew tricks the Clampetts out of some valuable art treasures.

The Dahlia Feud
GS: Ted Cassidy. Mrs. Drysdale tries to compete with Granny in a contest to grow some flowers.

Jed Inherits a Castle
GS: Paul Lynde. The Clampetts plan to go to England and live in the castle they just inherited.

The Clampetts in London
GS: Shary Marshall, Larry Blake, Ernest Clarke, Alan Napier, Hugh Dempster. Granny gets into trouble with the customs inspector.

Clampett Castle
GS: John Baron, Richard Caldicot. The Clampetts move into the castle, causing Jethro to act like a knight.

Robin Hood of Griffith Park
GS: Alan Reed, Laurel Goodwin. The Clampetts pay a ten million dollar tax on the castle and leave for home.

Robin Hood and the Sheriff
GS: Alan Reed, Victor French. Jethro plays Robin Hood and attracts a band of hippies in the park.

Greetings from the President
GS: Bea Benaderet, Henry Corden. Jethro gets drafted.

The Army Game
GS: Paul Reed, King Donovan, Joe Conley. Jethro is thrown out of the Army when the psychiatrists think his whole family is crazy.

Mr. Universe Muscles In
GS: Dave Draper, John Ashley, Roy Roberts. Elly May is caught in the middle of a war between Drysdale and Cushing.

A Plot for Granny
GS: Richard Deacon, Jesse White. Two salesmen try to sell Jed a cemetery plot for Granny, whom they think is dead.

The Social Climbers
GS: Mary Wickes, Gail Bonney. The Clampetts get a visit from a hillbilly lady blacksmith.

Jethro's Military Career
Jethro practices to be a Navy frogman in the backyard pool.

The Reserve Program
GS: Lyle Talbot, William Mimms, Ron Stokes, Bob Pickett, Harry Fleer. Granny thinks the Civil War has started again when she sees some movie actors dressed as Union soldiers.

The South Rises Again
GS: Lyle Talbot, Richard O'Shea, Harry Lauter. Granny forms her own army to fight the Union soldiers.

Jethro in the Reserve
GS: Lyle Talbot, William Mimms. Granny thinks she has captured General Grant.

Cimarron Drip
GS: Larry Pennell, Theodore Marcuse, Milton Frome, Jim Hayward. Elly May's chimp gets a starring part in a television series.

Corn Pone Picassos
GS: David Bond, Chet Stratton, Frank Richards. Granny paints a picture to help Mrs. Drysdale win an award.

The Clampetts Play Cupid
GS: Larry Pennell, Valerie Hawkins. Granny tries to get Miss Jane married to Dash Riprock.

The Housekeeper
GS: Fran Ryan. Jed and Drysdale hire a housekeeper to help Granny.

The Diner
GS: Joan Huntington. Jed helps Jethro open up a restaurant.

Topless Anyone
GS: Robert Foulk, Ysabel MacCloskey, James F. Stone, Venita Wolf. Jethro turns the diner into a topless restaurant: the waitresses don't wear caps.

The Great Snow
Drysdale creates a fake blizzard to help Granny get over her homesickness.

The Rass'lin Clampetts
GS: Jerry Randall, Bill Baldwin, Gene Lebell, Gayle Caldwell. Granny believes that a women's wrestling match on television is real, so she goes down to the arena to save the wrestler who is portraying a country girl.

The Great Tag-Team Match
GS: Alan Reed, Gayle Caldwell, Mike Mazurki, Jerry Randall. The Clampetts become tag-team wrestlers.

Jethro Proposes
GS: Lisa Todd, Fritz Feld. Granny forces Jethro to propose to Miss Jane.

The Clampetts Fiddle Around
GS: Hans Conreid, Foster Brooks. Drysdale hires a concert violin player to teach Jethro how to play the violin.

The Soap Opera
GS: John Dehner, Beecey Carlson, Grandon Rhoades. Granny thinks a soap opera is real and plans to rescue a patient who is about to undergo surgery in the series.

Dog Days
GS: Lisa Todd. Granny gets mad when Elly's dog keeps knocking her down every time she announces dinner is ready.

The Crystal Gazers
GS: Connie Sawyer. Granny starts making predictions when she believes she is psychic.

From Rags to Riches
GS: Carolyn Nelson. Granny plans to do the first head transplant on Mr. Drysdale.

Cousin Roy
GS: Roy Clark, Phil Arnold, Peter Leeds. Cousin Roy arrives to sell his mother's medicine, which is the competition to Granny's tonic.

A Bundle for Britain
GS: Richard Caldicott, Ben Wrigley, Alan Mowbray. Jed decides to donate his money to England.

Something for the Queen
GS: Jack Bannon, Richard Caldicott, Dick Wesson. The Clampetts buy Canada so they can give it back to the Queen of England.

War of the Roses
GS: William Kendall, Sydney Arnold, Peter Myers. Drysdale gets Miss Jane to play the part of Queen Elizabeth the First, whom the Clampetts think is the reigning queen.

Coming Through the Rye
GS: Dave Prowse, Richard Caldicott, Ilona Rodgers. Jethro falls for a Scots girl, but the rest of the family think her big brother, who is wearing kilts, is the girl he likes.

Ghost of Clampett Castle
GS: Richard Caldicott. Drysdale tries to scare the Clampetts back home by using the legend of the castle ghost.

Granny Goes to Hooterville
GS: Edgar Buchanan, Frank Cady,

Aron Kincaid. Granny wants to go to Hooterville, but puts it off when she thinks Jed is going to marry Miss Jane.

The Italian Cook
GS: Maria Natonini, Linda Kaye Henning, Mike Minor, Frank Cady. Jethro hires an Italian cook who doesn't speak English.

The Great Cook Out
GS: Maria Mirka. Jethro begins to act and dress like Julius Caesar to get Maria to fall for him.

Bonnie, Flatt & Scruggs
GS: Lester Flatt, Earl Scruggs, Joi Lansing, Percy Helton. The Clampetts play bank robbers in the commercial Drysdale is making for the bank.

The Thanksgiving Story
GS: Lori Saunders, Eddie Albert, Eva Gabor, Tom Lestor, Frank Cady, Mike Minor, June Lockhart, Edgar Buchanan, Meredith MacRae, Linda Kay Henning. The Clampetts go to Hooterville for Thanksgiving with their friends from Petticoat Junction and Green Acres.

The Courtship of Homer Noodleman
GS: Tom Lester, Frank Cady, Larry Pennell. Drysdale gets Dash Riprock to play a farm boy in order to get Elly May to marry him.

The Hot Rod Trick
GS: Lonnie Burr, Georgene Barnes. Jethro trades the family truck for a hot rod.

The Week Before Christmas
GS: Lori Saunders, Frank Cady, Meredith MacRae. The Clampetts go to Hooterville for Christmas, where Granny is planning to marry Sam Drucker.

Christmas in Hooterville
GS: Edgar Buchanan, Tom Lestor, Percy Helton, Frank Cady. Eb dates Elly May while Granny chases after Sam Drucker.

Drysdale and Friend
GS: Percy Helton, Stacy King, J. Pat O'Malley, Mike Ross, Hank Patterson. Drysdale is arrested while on the way to Hooterville for carrying Granny's white lightning and Elly's bear.

Problem Bear
GS: Norma Varden. Granny tries to cure Mr. Drysdale of the flu, using her moonshine.

Jethro the Flesh Peddler
GS: Pamela Rodgers, Roy Clark, Judy Jordan. Jethro opens a talent agency in Drysdale's bank.

Cousin Roy in Movieland
GS: Roy Clark, Judy Jordan, Pamela Rodgers. Jethro refuses to take Roy as one of his clients for his agency.

Jed Clampett Enterprises
GS: Percy Helton, Seamon Glass, Venita Wolf. Drysdale throws Jethro out of the building when Jed moves in.

The Phantom Fifth Floor
GS: Herb Vigran, Seamon Glass. A building inspector looks over the many different services offered by Jed's new company.

The Hired Gun
GS: Charles Lane, Percy Helton. Drysdale hires Homer Bedloe from Petticoat Junction to throw the Clampetts out of the building.

The Happy Bank
GS: Percy Helton, Georgene Barnes. A beautiful secretary goes to Jed for help when she breaks the heel off her shoe.

Sam Drucker's Visit
GS: Frank Cady, Larry Pennell, Lori Saunders. Sam Drucker wins a trip to Hollywood, causing Granny to think he is really coming to marry her.

The Guru
GS: William Mimms. Jethro takes up Yoga and decides to be a guru.

The Jogging Clampetts
GS: Paul Newlan. The Clampetts take up jogging.

Collard Greens an' Fatback
GS: Pat Boone. The Clampetts sell their mansion to Pat Boone, who loves Granny's cooking.

Back to the Hills
GS: Rob Reiner, Bonnie Boland. The Clampetts return home to the hills to find Elly a husband.

The Hills of Home
GS: Chick Allen, Shug Fisher, Elvia Allman, Walter Woolf King, Rob Reiner. Granny starts a feud with her old enemy Elverna Bradshaw.

Silver Dollar City Fair
GS: Chick Allen, Elvia Allman, Lloyd Heller, Shug Fisher. Granny offers Elly May to every man in town.

Jane Finds Elly a Man
GS: Shug Fisher, Robert Torrey, Hope Wainwright. Miss Jane finds a man for Elly to marry.

Wedding Plans
GS: Roger Torrey, Jerry Brutsche. Drysdale tries to stop Elly's wedding from taking place.

Jed Buys Central Park
GS: Phil Silvers. Jed goes to New York to find Elly another man. He meets up with a con man who proceeds to sell him Central Park.

The Clampetts in New York
GS: Phil Silvers. Con man Shifty Shafer sells Jed three other landmarks after he buys Central Park.

Home Again
GS: Brian West, Judy McConnell, John Scott Lindsey. Granny won't admit she needs glasses, even after she mistakes a seal for Elly's new boyfriend.

Shorty Kellems Moves West
GS: Shug Fisher. Shorty Kellems, who owns the hotel in Silver Dollar, sells it and moves in with the Clampetts.

Midnight Shorty
GS: Shug Fisher, Danielle Mardi. Drysdale tries to get Shorty's money for the bank by supplying him with lots of girls.

Shorty Go Home
GS: Shug Fisher. Granny doesn't like Jethro running around with Shorty, living the life of a playboy.

The Hero
GS: Soupy Sales. Mrs. Drysdale gets her Air Force hero nephew a job as a vice president of the bank.

Our Hero the Banker
GS: Soupy Sales. Mrs. Drysdale's nephew, Lance Bradford, takes over her husband's office.

Buss Bodine, Boy General
GS: Mike Minor. The Clampetts go to Hooterville where Jed starts an airplane business with Steve Elliot.

The Clampett-Hewes Empire
Drysdale thinks that farmer Howard Hewes is actually the millionaire Howard Hughes, when he helps Jed start a new airline with him.

What Happened to Shorty?
GS: Shad Heller. Jed and Shad try to fix Shorty up with Granny's enemy, Elverna Bradshaw.

Marry Me Shorty
The Clampetts try to convince Shorty to marry Elverna.

Shorty Spits the Hook
Shorty tries to convince Elverna that he is a gambler so she won't marry him.

Three-Day Reprieve
Jed and Shad have to keep Shorty from running away before the marriage.

The Wedding
Shorty marries one of Drysdale's secretaries to keep from marrying Elverna.

Annul That Marriage
The Clampetts try to show Shorty's new wife what life on a farm will be like.

Hotel for Women
Shorty turns the Clampett mansion into a hotel for single secretaries.

Simon Legree Drysdale
Drysdale tries to collect some of the money the secretaries are paying to stay at the mansion.

Honest John Returns
GS: Phil Silvers. Shifty John Shafer returns to con the Clampetts.

Honesty Is the Best Policy
GS: Phil Silvers. Shafer tries to con Jed into giving him money to drill a channel in the mountains to draw away the smog.

The Pollution Solution
GS: Rich Little, Bill Beckett. The Clampetts go to Washington to see the President so they can give him their millions to fight air pollution.

The Clampetts in Washington
GS: Phil Silvers, Kathleen Freeman, Richard Erdman. The Clampetts arrive in Washington to give the President their money.

Jed Buys the Capitol
GS: Phil Silvers, Kathleen Freeman. Shafer sells Jed several of the city's landmarks.

Mark Templeton Arrives
GS: Roger Torrey, Sherry Miles. Elly's old boyfriend, who is now a frogman in the Navy, pays a visit.

Don't Marry a Frogman
GS: Roger Torrey. Granny tries to cure Mark, whom she thinks is half man and half frog.

Doctor Cure My Frog
GS: Roger Torrey, Richard Deacon. Granny goes to a psychiatrist to ask for advice on how to keep Mark from turning into a real frog.

Do You Elly Take This Frog?
GS: Roger Torrey, Richard Deacon, Vincent Perry. Granny dreams that Elly May marries a giant frog.

The Frog Family
GS: Roger Torrey, Richard Deacon. Granny warns her family to stay out of the swimming pool or they will turn into giant frogs.

Farm in the Ocean
GS: Roger Torrey, Warrene Ott, Richard Deacon. Mark tries to convince Granny that man's future is living on the ocean floor.

Shorty to the Rescue
GS: Shug Fisher, Roger Torrey, Richard Deacon. Granny sends for Shorty to come and break up Elly's romance with Mark.

Welcome to the Family
GS: Shug Fisher, Lori Saunders, Roger Torrey. Granny thinks Shorty has turned into a seal because he swam in the pool.

The Great Revelation
GS: Roger Torrey, Danielle Mardi. Granny finally believes that Mark is a whole man and not part frog.

The Grunion Invasion
GS: Sue Bernard, Danielle Mardi, Jerry Brutsche. The Clampetts believe that grunion are hostile aliens from outer space who are going to attack the mansion.

The Girls from Grun
GS: Danielle Mardi, Sue Bernard, David Moses. The Clampetts get Drysdale to join them in guarding the beach against the attacking grunions.

The Grun Incident
GS: Danielle Mardi, Foster Brooks.

Drysdale's secretaries fight for better money.

Women's Lib
GS: Danielle Mardi, Francisco Ortega. Jed and Jethro are left to do the housework when Elly May and Granny join a women's lib movement.

The Teahouse of Jed Clampett
GS: Fuji, Charles Lane, Lori Saunders. Jed and Jethro hire three Japanese girls to run the house for them.

The Palace of Clampett San
GS: Charles Lane, Miko Mayama, Momo Yashima, Sumi Haru, Kazuka Sakura. Jed and Jethro love having the Japanese girls waiting on them hand and foot.

Lib and Let Lib
GS: Fuji, Miko Mayama, Danielle Mardi. Granny and Elly May return home to the mansion, only to find Jed and the Japanese girls.

Elly the Working Girl
GS: Charles Lane, Danielle Mardi. Elly

gets a job at the bank and moves in with Miss Jane.

Elly the Secretary
GS: Louellen Aden. Jethro moves out when he learns that his former ugly girlfriend from back home is coming to visit him.

Love Finds Jane Hathaway
GS: Mike Minor, Charles Lane. An out of work actor starts dating Elly when he learns about her money.

The Clampetts Meet Robert Audubon Getty
GS: Mike Minor, Charles Lane. The actor from the previous episode plans to marry into the family in order to share their money.

Jethro Returns
GS: Mike Minor. Miss Jane learns that her actor boyfriend has been dating Elly in the hopes of marrying her so he can get his hands on her money.

BEWITCHED

On the air 9/17/64, off 7/1/72. ABC. Color/B&W film. 254 episodes. Broadcast: Sept 1964-Jan 1967 Thu 9-9:30; Jan 1967-Sept 1971 Thu 8-8:30; Sept 1971-Jan 1972 Wed 8-8:30; Jan 1972-Jul 1972 Sat 8-8:30. Producer: Harry Ackerman. Prod Co: Screen Gems. Synd: Columbia Pictures TV.
CAST: Samantha Stephens (played by Elizabeth Montgomery), Darrin Stephens (Dick York, 1964-1969; Dick Sargent, 1969-1972), Endora (Agnes Moorehead), Maurice (Maurice Evans), Larry Tate (David White), Louise Tate (Irene Vernon, 1964-1966; Kasey Rogers, 1966-1972), Tabitha Stephens (Erin Murphy), Abner Kravitz (George Tobias), Gladys Kravitz (Alice Pearce, 1964-1966; Sandra Gould, 1966-1972), Aunt Clara (Marion Lorne), Uncle Arthur (Paul Lynde), Esmeralda (Alice Ghostley), Serena (Pandora Spocks [Elizabeth Montgomery]).
WRITERS: Ed Jurist, Michael Morris, Sol Saks, Danny Arnold, Bernard Slade, Ron Friedman, Howard Morris, John L. Greene, James Henerson, Peggy Chandler Dick, Douglas Tibbles, Lila Garrett, Bernie Kahn, Rick Mittleman, Richard Baer, Phillip and Henry Sharp.
DIRECTORS: William Asher, Richard Michaels, Richard Kinon, R. Robert Rosenbaum, E.W. Swackhamer.

Bewitched was a hit comedy of the sixties lasting eight years on the network. It is still extremely popular in syndication. It is the story of a mortal man who marries a beautiful witch. The average episode depicts the troubles Darrin and his family face from Samantha's magical relatives, especially from his mother-in-law Endora.

I, Darrin, Take This Witch Samantha [Pilot]
GS: Nancy Kovack.   After they are married, Samantha tells Darrin that she is a witch.

Be It Ever So Mortgaged
Samantha tries to prove to her mother that her new house is a nice place to live.

It Shouldn't Happen to a Dog
GS: Jack Warden, Grace Lee Witney. Samantha turns one of Darrin's clients into a dog.

Help, Help, Don't Save Me
GS: Charles Ruggles.   Darrin accuses Samantha of using witchcraft to ruin his ad campaign for a soup company.

Mother, Meet What's His Name
Samantha introduces Darrin to her mother for the first time.

Little Pitchers Have Big Ears
GS: June Lockhart.   Samantha helps a boy with an overprotective mother play baseball.

The Witches Are Out
GS: Shelley Berman, Madge Blake, Reta Shaw.   Samantha and some other witches try to convince Darrin's client to change the trademark on his Halloween candy from an ugly witch to a beautiful witch.

The Girl Reporter
GS: Roger Ewing, Cheryl Holdridge. Darrin is interviewed by a girl reporter who has a jealous boyfriend.

Witch or Wife
GS: Raquel Welch.   Darrin believes that his marriage to Samantha is a mistake, when he finds that she followed him to Paris instead of staying home where she belongs.

Just One Happy Family
Samantha's father comes for a visit, unaware that Samantha has married a mortal.

It Takes One to Know One
GS: Lisa Seagram.   Endora sends a beautiful witch to tempt Darrin away from Samantha.

. . . And Something Makes Three
Larry thinks Samantha is going to have a baby, unaware that it is his own wife that is pregnant.

Love Is Blind
GS: Adam West.   Samantha tries to get her friend and an artist to marry.

Samantha Meets the Folks
Darrin is worried that Samantha's Aunt Clara will ruin his parents' visit.

A Vision of Sugar Plums
GS: Billy Mumy, Cecil Kellaway, Gerry Johnson, Bill Daily, Sara Seegar. Samantha tries to prove to a visiting orphan that Santa Claus really exists.

It's Magic
GS: Walter Burke, Cliff Norton.   Samantha helps a broken down magician regain his confidence.

A Is for Aardvark
When Darrin sprains his ankle and is confined to bed, Samantha gives him the power of witchcraft.

The Cat's Meow
GS: Martha Hyer.   Darrin visits an attractive businesswoman on her yacht and suspects that the cat that he finds there might be Samantha checking up on him.

A Nice Little Dinner Party
Darrin's father falls for Endora.

Your Witch Is Showing
GS: Jonathan Daly. Darrin's new assistant steals his ideas in order to get Darrin's job for himself.

Ling Ling
GS: Jeremy Slate, Greta Chi. Samantha turns their pet cat into an Oriental girl so she can be the model for Darrin's ad campaign.

Eye of the Beholder
GS: Peter Brocco. Endora makes Darrin think that Samantha will remain eternally young, while he grows old.

Red Light, Green Light
GS: Vic Tayback, Dan Tobin. Samantha tries to convince the mayor that a traffic signal is needed on their block.

Which Witch Is Witch?
GS: Ron Randell. Endora transforms herself into an identical copy of Samantha, which causes problems when a young author falls for her.

Pleasure O'Riley
GS: Kipp Hamilton. Darrin and Mr. Kravitz fall for a beautiful model who moves into the neighborhood, unaware that she has a jealous boyfriend.

Driving Is the Only Way to Fly
GS: Paul Lynde. Samantha takes driving lessons from a very nervous instructor.

There's No Witch Like an Old Witch
GS: Reta Shaw, Brian Nash. Aunt Clara becomes a babysitter but causes trouble when she tells the children she looks after that she is a witch.

Open the Door, Witchcraft
The Stephens's new electric garage door opener is affected by passing jets, causing it to open and close constantly.

Abner Kadabra
Samantha makes Mrs. Kravitz think she has ESP and magical powers.

George the Warlock
GS: Christopher George, Beverly Adams. Endora gets a warlock to romance Samantha in order to break up her marriage to Darrin.

That Was My Wife
Larry thinks Darrin is fooling around with another woman, unaware that it was really Samantha wearing a wig.

Illegal Separation
Abner and Gladys Kravitz have a fight and he moves in with the Stephenses.

A Change of Face
Endora changes the features of Darrin's face in order to improve him.

Remember the Main
GS: Byron Morrow. Darrin blames Samantha for getting him involved in politics.

Eat at Mario's
GS: Alan Hewitt, Vito Scotti. Samantha and Endora try to help publicize a restaurant at the expense of one of Darrin's clients.

Cousin Edgar
GS: Arte Johnson. Endora gets Samantha's Cousin Edgar, an elf, to break up her daughter's marriage.

Alias Darrin Stephens
Aunt Clara accidentally turns Darrin into a chimp.

A Very Special Delivery
Samantha tells Darrin that she is pregnant, which makes him very nervous.

We're in for a Bad Spell
GS: William Redfield, Richard X. Slattery. Samantha, Darrin and Clara try to help a man who has fallen under a curse put on one of his ancestors by a witch.

My Grandson, the Warlock
Samantha's father mistakes the Tates's baby for Samantha's, so he tries to teach it to perform witchcraft.

The Joker Is a Card
Samantha, Endora and Darrin try to cure Uncle Arthur of his habit of playing practical jokes.

Take Two Aspirins and Half a Pint of Porpoise Milk
GS: Phillip Coolidge. Samantha loses her powers after she is exposed to a black Peruvian rose.

Trick or Treat
Endora casts a spell on Darrin which will gradually turn Darrin into a werewolf.

The Very Informal Dress
GS: Max Showalter. Clara uses her powers to create new clothes for Darrin and Samantha to wear to a dinner engagement. Unfortunately, the clothes disappear while they are still having dinner.

. . . And Then I Wrote
GS: Chet Stratton. Samantha brings the characters of her Civil War play to life.

Junior Executive
GS: Billy Mumy, Oliver McGowan. Endora turns Darrin into an eight-year-old boy.

Aunt Clara's Old Flame
GS: Charles Ruggles. Aunt Clara's old warlock boyfriend comes for a visit.

A Strange Little Visitor
GS: Craig Hundley, James Doohan. Samantha watches a ten-year-old warlock while his parents are out of town.

My Boss the Teddy Bear
Darrin thinks Endora has turned Larry into a teddy bear.

Speak the Truth
GS: Charles Lane. Endora gives Darrin a statuette which causes anyone who comes near it to tell the absolute truth.

A Vision of Sugar Plums
Samantha recalls the time she took an orphan to see Santa Claus. [This is a recut version of the episode of the same name, only with a new opening.]

The Magic Cabin
GS: Peter Duryea. Samantha uses witchcraft to change Larry's old shack into a beautiful cabin.

Maid to Order
GS: Alice Ghostley. Samantha hires a bumbling maid to do the housework so she can rest until the baby is born.

And Then There Were Three
GS: Eve Arden. Darrin believes that Endora has turned his newly born daughter Tabitha into a grownup when he sees Samantha's lookalike cousin Serena.

My Baby, the Tycoon
The Kravitzes give Tabitha a share of stock as a gift; when the stock goes up in value, Darrin believes Tabitha did it with witchcraft.

Samantha Meets the Folks
Samantha recalls the time she met Darrin's parents for the first time. [This is a recut version with new footage of the previous episode of the same name.]

Fastest Gun on Madison Avenue
GS: Herbie Faye, Rockne Tarkington. Darrin, with Samantha's help, knocks out a boxer and finds himself the number one contender for the boxing title.

The Dancing Bear
Endora creates a dancing teddy bear for Tabitha which Darrin's father tries to sell to a toy manufacturer.

Double Tate
Darrin turns himself into an exact double of Larry when Endora grants him three wishes for his birthday.

Samantha the Dressmaker
GS: Dick Gautier. Samantha helps a

French dress designer break into the American market.

The Horse's Mouth
GS: Patty Regan, Robert Sorrells. Samantha turns a racehorse into a woman who proceeds to help Darrin's friend win at the races.

Baby's First Paragraph
GS: Clete Roberts.   Endora causes trouble when she makes baby Tabitha able to talk.

The Leprechaun
GS: Henry Jones, Parley Baer. Samantha tries to help a leprechaun recover his lost pot of gold.

Double Split
Samantha tries to bring Larry and Darrin back together after they have a fight.

Disappearing Samantha
GS: Bernard Fox, Nina Wayne, Foster Brooks. Samantha falls under the spell of an ancient ring owned by a man who debunks witches.

Follow That Witch [Part 1]
GS: Robert Strauss, Mary Grace Canfield, Steve Franken. A private detective threatens to expose Samantha as a witch if she does not make him a rich man.

Follow That Witch [Part 2]
GS: Robert Strauss, Steve Franken. Samantha teaches the detective never to blackmail a witch.

Divided He Falls
GS: Frank Maxwell, Jerry Catron, Joy Harmon.   Endora splits Darrin into two people. Darrin #1 is a hard worker while Darrin #2 is an irresponsible fun lover.

A Bum Raps
Samantha mistakes a con man for Darrin's eccentric Uncle Albert.

Man's Best Friend
GS: Richard Dreyfuss.   A neurotic

warlock named Rodney tries to break up Samantha's marriage so she can marry him.

The Catnapper
GS: Robert Strauss. Endora turns a beautiful client of Darrin's into a cat which is stolen by the private detective [from a previous episode].   He promises to return the cat in return for a million dollars.

What Every Young Man Should Know
Endora sends Samantha and Darrin back in time to see if Darrin would have married Samantha if he knew she was a witch.

The Girl with the Golden Nose
Darrin is convinced that Samantha used witchcraft to gain a new account, so Samantha tries to show him that he did it all by himself.

Prodigy
GS: Jack Weston.   Samantha tries to help Gladys's brother regain his confidence and play his violin at a benefit.

Nobody's Perfect
GS: David Lewis, Robert Q. Lewis. Samantha tries to find a way to tell Darrin that Tabitha is a witch like her.

The Moment of Truth
Darrin finally learns that Tabitha is a witch. He now has to keep the Tates from finding out when they come for a visit.

Witches and Warlocks Are My Favorite Things
GS: Reta Shaw, Estelle Winwood. Samantha calls for her father when her mother and aunts want to take Tabitha away with them, so she can attend a witches school.

Accidental Twins
While baby sitting, Clara accidentally turns the Tate's baby son into twins.

A Most Unusual Wood Nymph
GS: Michael Ansara, Henry Corden, Kathleen Nolan. A wood nymph re-

veals to Samantha that she has been sent to plague Darrin because his ancestor slew her master, Rufus The Red. So Samantha goes back in time to prevent Darrin the Bold from killing Rufus.

Endora Moves In for a Spell
Endora and Uncle Arthur have a fight, claiming each is a bad influence on Tabitha.

Twitch or Treat
GS: Barry Atwater, Joan Huntington, Willie Mays. Endora holds a wild Halloween party in their house. Uncle Arthur and Samantha try to get rid of her and the party.

Dangerous Diaper Dan
GS: Marty Ingels. A diaper serviceman gives Tabitha a rattle with a microphone in it. He is actually a spy for another advertising agency and wants to listen in on Darrin's conversation so he can steal his ideas.

The Short Happy Circuit of Aunt Clara
GS: Reginald Owen. Aunt Clara, who is depressed because her warlock boyfriend left her for a younger woman, thinks she caused a power blackout all over town.

I'd Rather Twitch Than Fight
GS: Bridget Hanley, Norman Fell, Parley Baer. Endora summons Sigmund Freud to help Samantha and Darrin's marriage problems.

Oedipus Hex
GS: Ned Glass. Endora creates some magic popcorn which will cause anyone who eats it to become lazy and refuse to work.

Sam's Spooky Chair
GS: J. Pat O'Malley, Roger Garrett. Samantha finds that the antique chair she bought is actually her old warlock boyfriend, whom she rejected years earlier.

My Friend Ben [Part 1]
GS: Fredd Wayne, Mike Road, Tim Rooney, Billy Beck. Aunt Clara accidentally summons Benjamin Franklin to help Samantha fix her lamp.

Samantha for the Defense [Part 2]
GS: Fredd Wayne. Samantha defends Benjamin Franklin at his trial when he is accused of stealing a fire engine.

A Gazebo Never Forgets
GS: Paul Reed, Steve Franken. Clara accidentally creates a live baby elephant in the middle of the living room and can't remember how to get rid of it.

Soapbox Derby
GS: Michael Shea, William Bramley. Samantha helps a boy win a race and his father's approval at the same time.

Sam in the Moon
Darrin dreams what might happen if he told the NASA authorities about Samantha and her frequent visits to the moon.

Hoho the Clown
GS: Joey Foreman, Dick Wilson. Endora casts a spell on a TV clown to perform his show only for Tabitha.

Super Car
GS: Dave Madden, Irwin Charone. Endora gives Darrin the prototype of a new car which she stole from its creator, one of Darrin's clients.

The Corn Is as High as a Guernsey's Eye
Samantha thinks Clara turned herself accidentally into a cow and takes it home with her.

Trial and Error of Aunt Clara
GS: Arthur Malet. Samantha defends Clara when the Witches council wants to banish her because of her failing powers.

Three Wishes
GS: Linda Gaye Scott. Endora gives

Darrin three wishes, in order to trap him with another woman.

I Remember You . . . Sometimes
GS: Dan Tobin.   Endora casts a spell on Darrin's watch, so that whenever he wears it he will have a perfect memory.

Art for Sam's Sake
GS: Arthur Julian.   Endora switches a masterpiece for Samantha's painting at a charity exhibit.

Charlie Harper, Winner
GS: Angus Duncan, Joanna Moore. Darrin and Samantha try to compete with Darrin's old college rival who is a bragging millionaire.

Aunt Clara's Victoria Victory
GS: Jane Connell, Robert H. Harris. Aunt Clara accidentally summons Queen Victoria to the Stephens's house.

The Crone of Cawdor
GS: Julie Gregg, Dorothy Neumann. Samantha has to prevent Darrin from kissing a young girl, actually the Crone of Cawdor who has taken over the body of the girl.   If he kisses her, he will age 500 years.

No More, Mr. Nice Guy
GS: Larry D. Mann.   Endora casts a spell on Darrin which makes everyone hate him.

It's Witchcraft
Darrin is afraid that his visiting parents will learn that Tabitha is a witch.

How to Fail in Business with All Kinds of Help
GS: Henry Beckman, Lisa Kirk.   Darrin thinks a domineering businesswoman is really Endora in disguise.

Bewitched, Bothered and Infuriated
Samantha tries to prevent Larry from breaking his leg on his second honeymoon.

Nobody But a Frog Knows How to Live
GS: John Fiedler.   Samantha tries to help a frog, who was transformed into a man, change back into a frog again.

There's Gold in Them Thar Pills
GS: Milton Frome.   Darrin and Larry plan to sell Dr. Bombay's cold pills on the open market, unaware that he is a warlock who treats only witches.

Long Live the Queen
GS: Ruth McDevitt. The queen of the witches decides to abdicate in favor of Samantha.

Toys in Babeland
Tabitha brings all of her toys to life.

Business, Italian Style
GS: Renzo Cesana.   Endora casts a spell on Darrin which causes him to speak only Italian.

Double, Double, Toil and Trouble
Endora summons Serena to take Samantha's place in order to break up her marriage.

Cheap, Cheap!
GS: Parley Baer.   Endora casts a spell which turns Darrin into a miser.

No Zip in My Zap
GS: Mala Powers.   Darrin's old girlfriend comes for a visit, just as Samantha loses her powers.

Birdies, Bogies and Baxter
GS: MacDonald Carey.   Endora puts a spell on Darrin's golf clubs, which will make him make fantastic shots no matter how badly he plays.

The Safe and Sane Halloween
GS: Jerry Maren, Felix Silla, Billy Curtis.   Tabitha causes the characters in a Halloween picture book to come to life.

Out of Sync, Out of Mind
Aunt Clara accidentally casts a spell which causes Samantha to speak out

of sync. She moves her lips and then her voice is heard later.

That Was No Chick, That Was My Wife
GS: Herb Voland, Sara Seegar. Darrin almost loses his job when Samantha appears in New York and Chicago at the same time.

Allergic to Macedonian Dodo Birds
GS: Janos Prohaska. Endora's powers are transferred to Clara, when she comes in contact with a Dodo bird.

Samantha's Thanksgiving to Remember
GS: Jacques Aubuchon, Richard Bull, Laurie Main. Aunt Clara accidentally transfers herself, the Stephenses and Mrs. Kravitz to 17th-century Plymouth on Thanksgiving Day, where Darrin finds himself accused of witchcraft.

My What Big Ears You Have
Endora casts a spell on Darrin which will cause his ears to grow every time he tells a lie.

I Get Your Nannie, You Get My Goat
GS: Reginald Gardiner, Hermione Baddeley. An old warlock puts a spell on Darrin, when he believes Darrin has stolen his servant.

Humbug Not to Be Spoken Here
GS: Charles Lane, Don Beddoe. Samantha tries to teach a lonely old man the meaning of Christmas.

Samantha's Da Vinci Dilemma
GS: John Abbott. Aunt Clara summons Da Vinci to paint Samantha's house.

Once in a Vial
GS: Henry Beckman, Ron Randell, Arch Johnson. Endora drinks a love potion she had intended for Samantha, causing her to fall for one of Darrin's clients.

Snob in the Grass [Part 1]
GS: Nancy Kovack, Frank Wilcox. Darrin's old girlfriend tries to show off and upstage Samantha.

If They Never Met [Part 2]
GS: Nancy Kovack. Endora returns Darrin to a time before he met Samantha to see if he would be happy without her.

Hippie, Hippie, Hippie
GS: Ralph Story. When Serena is arrested at a hippie love-in and gets her picture in the papers, everyone thinks it is Samantha.

A Prince for a Day
GS: William Bassett, Stuart Margolin. Tabitha summons Prince Charming out of her Sleeping Beauty storybook, but can't send him back.

McTavish
GS: Ronald Long, Reginald Owen. Samantha convinces a ghost to stop haunting a castle, but regrets her action when he decides to haunt the Stephens's house instead.

How Green Was My Grass
GS: Richard X. Slattery. A synthetic lawn is accidentally installed at the Stephens's house which causes Darrin to think Samantha created the new lawn with her powers.

To Twitch or Not to Twitch
Darrin and Samantha have a fight when he demands that she should not use her powers.

Playmates
GS: Peggy Pope. Tabitha turns a little bully into a bulldog.

Tabitha's Cranky Spell
A ghost asks Samantha to help him stop his nephew from ruining his company.

I Confess
GS: Woodrow Parfrey. Samantha shows Darrin what would happen to their life together if she were to tell everyone that she is a witch.

A Majority of Two
GS: Richard Haydn. Samantha entertains a Japanese client who falls for

her Aunt Clara.

Samantha's Secret Saucer
GS: Hamilton Camp, Steve Franken.
Aunt Clara accidentally transports a
spaceship with two dog-like aliens into
Samantha's backyard.

The No-Harm Charm
GS: Vaughn Taylor.   Uncle Arthur
plays a joke on Darrin when he gives
him a charm which will protect him
from witchcraft and other disasters.

Man of the Year
GS: Roland Winters.   Endora casts a
magic circle around Darrin.   Anyone
who comes within the circle will be
charmed by him.

Splitsville
GS: Arthur Julian. Gladys has a fight
with Abner and moves in with Samantha and Darrin.

Samantha's Wedding Present
Endora casts a spell which causes Darrin to gradually shrink in size.

Samantha Goes South for a Spell
GS: Isabel Sanford, Jack Cassidy.   A
jealous witch mistakes Samantha for
Serena and sends her back to Old New
Orleans in 1868.

Samantha on the Keyboard
GS: Jonathan Harris, Fritz Feld.   Endora uses witchcraft to turn Tabitha
into a magnificent piano player.

Darrin Gone! And Forgotten?
GS: Steve Franken, Mercedes McCam-
bridge.   A mean witch threatens to destroy Darrin unless Samantha consents
to marry her overprotected son.

*It's So Nice to Have a Spouse Around
the House*
GS: Fifi D'Orsay.   Darrin takes Samantha   on   a   second   honeymoon
unaware that he has really taken
Serena, not Samantha, on their trip.

Mirror, Mirror on the Wall
GS: Herb Voland.   Endora turns Dar-

rin into the most self-centered and
vain man in the world.

Samantha's French Pastry
GS: Henry Gibson. Uncle Arthur accidentally conjures up Napoleon and
finds he can't remember how to send
him back.

Is It Magic or Imagination
Darrin thinks Samantha won a slogan
contest by using witchcraft.

Samantha Fights City Hall
GS: Arch Johnson, Vic Tayback. Samantha fights to keep a new supermarket from taking the place of a neighborhood park.

Samantha Loses Her Voice
Uncle Arthur plays another practical
joke when he switches Darrin's and
Samantha's voices.

Weep No More, My Willow
Dr. Bombay's spell to save a weeping
willow tree backfires when it causes
Samantha to weep uncontrollably.

Instant Courtesy
GS: Mala Powers.   Endora turns Darrin into a perfect gentleman, in order
to teach him a lesson for being rude to
her.

Samantha's Super Maid
GS: Virginia Gregg, Nellie Burt.   Samantha hires a maid who is so devoted
to her job that nothing anyone does
can get her to leave.

Cousin Serena Strikes Again [Part 1]
GS: Nancy Kovack.   Serena turns Darrin's client into a monkey, when she
made a play for Darrin behind Samantha's back.

Cousin Serena Strikes Again [Part 2]
GS: Nancy Kovack, Cliff Norton,
Richard X. Slattery. Samantha has to
try to capture the client turned mon-
key after it escapes from the house, so
Serena can change her back.

One Touch of Midas
GS: Cliff Norton, Meg Wyllie. Darrin falls under the spell of a magical doll called The Fuzz, and anyone who touches it becomes overly generous.

Samantha the Bard
GS: Larry D. Mann. Endora goes to find Dr. Bombay in order to help Samantha, who finds that everything she says comes out in a rhyme.

Samantha the Sculptress
GS: Cliff Norton. Endora causes trouble when she brings Samantha's bust of Darrin to life.

Mrs. Stephens, Where Are You?
GS: Hal England, Ruth McDevitt. Serena turns Darrin's mother into a cat.

Marriage, Witch's Style
GS: John Fiedler, Lloyd Bochner, Peter Brocco. Serena decides she wants to marry a mortal and settle down like Samantha.

Going Ape
GS: Lou Antonio. Samantha turns a chimp into a man for a day.

Tabitha's Weekend
When Endora and Darrin's mother have a fight, Tabitha, believing she is the cause, turns herself into a cookie.

The Battle of Burning Oak
GS: Edward Andrews, Harriet MacGibbon. Endora turns Darrin into a snob when he joins a country club.

Samantha's Power Failure
GS: Ron Masak. Samantha loses her powers when she refuses to obey the witches council and give up Darrin. Arthur and Serena also lose their powers because they sided with her, so they get regular jobs in a candy factory.

Twitching for UNICEF
GS: Bernie Kopell. Samantha uses witchcraft to make a millionaire make good his $10,000 pledge to UNICEF.

Daddy Does His Thing
Maurice turns Darrin into a mule when he refuses the magical lighter he gave him for his birthday.

Samantha's Good News
GS: Murray Matheson. Endora and Maurice have a fight when he starts dating a young secretary. Samantha stops their fighting when she announces that she is going to have another baby.

Samantha's Shopping Spree
GS: Steve Franken, Dave Madden. Samantha's Cousin Henry, a prankster, causes havoc when he goes shopping with Samantha and Tabitha.

Samantha and Darrin in Mexico City
GS: Thomas Gomez. While in Mexico, Endora casts a spell on Darrin which causes him to disappear whenever he speaks in Spanish.

Sam and the Beanstalk
GS: Ronald Long, Johnnie Whitaker, Bobo Lewis. Tabitha brings her storybook of Jack and the Beanstalk to life and changes places with Jack, when she thinks her parents like boys better than girls.

Samantha's Yoo Hoo Maid
GS: J. Edward McKinley. Endora brings a bumbling witch to act as Samantha's new maid.

Samantha's Caesar Salad
GS: Jay Robinson. Esmeralda tries to create a Caesar salad, but conjures up Julius Caesar instead.

Samantha's Curious Cravings
GS: William Schallert. Samantha finds that whatever she craves comes to her magically.

And Something Makes Four
GS: Art Metrano, Pat Priest. Maurice casts a spell over his new grandson, that whoever looks at him immediately like him.

Naming Samantha's New Baby
Maurice puts Darrin inside a mirror when he finds out that the new baby will be named after Darrin's father and not him.

To Trick-or-Treat or Not to Trick-or-Treat
Darrin and Endora have a fight over the value of Halloween.

A Bunny for Tabitha
GS: Bernie Kopell, Carol Wayne. Uncle Arthur performs a magic act for Tabitha's birthday party. He accidentally conjures up a playboy bunny instead of a bunny rabbit, and can't send her back.

Samantha's Secret Spell
GS: Bernie Kopell. Samantha tries to prevent Endora's spell to turn Darrin into a mouse at midnight from taking effect.

Daddy Comes to Visit [Part 1]
GS: John Fiedler. On his birthday, Maurice gives Darrin a watch which will give him magic powers.

Darrin the Warlock [Part 2]
Darrin becomes obsessed with his new powers and refuses to give them up.

Sam's Double Mother Trouble
GS: Jane Connell. Esmeralda, while reading to Tabitha, accidentally conjures up Mother Goose just as Darrin's mother comes for a visit.

You're So Agreeable
GS: Charles Lane. Endora casts a spell that makes Darrin agree with everyone and everything.

Santa Comes to Visit and Stays and Stays
GS: Ronald Long. Esmeralda conjures up Santa Claus.

Samantha's Better Halves
GS: Richard Loo. Endora splits Darrin in two so he can stay home with Samantha as well as go to Japan to entertain a client.

Samantha's Lost Weekend
GS: Bernie Kopell, Pat Priest, Jonathan Hole, Merie Earle. Samantha drinks a glass of milk, on which Esmeralda cast a spell, which causes her to have an insatiable appetite.

The Phrase Is Familiar
GS: Jay Robinson, Cliff Norton, Todd Baron. Endora causes Darrin to speak in cliches whenever he opens his mouth. At the same time, Tabitha's tutor conjures up the Artful Dodger out of Oliver Twist.

Samantha's Secret Is Discovered
GS: Bernie Kopell. Samantha tells Darrin's mother that she is a witch. Thinking she has lost her mind, she goes to a sanitarium where Samantha switches her tranquilizers to hallucinogenics. This way her mother-in-law will think everything that happened was caused by taking the wrong pill. [This episode is not run by many stations, due to the episode's drug-related story.]

Tabitha's Very Own Samantha
GS: Sara Seegar, Parley Baer. Tabitha creates a duplicate Samantha to play with her when the real Samantha has to take care of her little brother Adam.

Super Arthur
When Arthur takes a pill given to him by Doctor Bombar, it causes him to become everything he thinks about, including Superman.

What Makes Darrin Run?
GS: Leon Ames. Endora casts a spell on Darrin which will make him more ambitious.

Serena Stops the Show
GS: Tommy Boyce & Bobby Hart, Art Metrano. Serena tries to get the singing team of Boyce and Hart to sing at an annual dinner dance for witches.

Just a Kid Again
GS: Richard Powell, Ron Masak. Tabitha turns a toy salesman into a nine-

year-old boy.

The Generation Zap
GS: Melodie Johnson, Arch Johnson. Serena turns the daughter of a client into a hippie.

Okay, Who's the Wise Witch
A vapor lock caused by Samantha's non-use of her witchcraft seals the house so no one can get in or out.

A Chance on Love
GS: Jack Cassidy. A playboy client mistakes Samantha for Serena.

If the Shoe Pinches
GS: Henry Gibson. The witches council sends a leprechaun to find the breaking point of the Stephens's marriage.

Mona Sammy
Samantha casts a spell on Darrin that will turn him into a great painter.

Turn on the Old Charm
GS: John Fiedler. Samantha gives Darrin an amulet that causes Endora to be nice to him.

Make Love Not Hate
GS: Charles Lane, Sara Seegar, Cliff Norton. Samantha accidentally pours a love potion into the clam dip she plans to serve to Darrin's client. It causes everyone who eats it to fall in love with the first person they see.

To Go or Not to Go, That Is the Question
GS: Jane Connell. The High Priestess of Witchdom comes to view Samantha and Darrin's marriage, to decide whether or not she should disband their marriage.

Salem Here We Come
GS: Jane Connell. Samantha arranges that the decision to end their marriage be delayed by fixing up the High Priestess with one of Darrin's clients.

The Salem Saga
GS: Joan Hotchkis.   Samantha and Darrin are followed by a bedwarmer which came from the House of Seven Gables.

Samantha's Hot Bedwarmer
GS: Noam Pitlik, Joan Hotchkiss. Darrin is arrested and accused of stealing the bedwarmer. Samantha learns that the bedwarmer is actually a warlock who was transformed by Serena.

Darrin on a Pedestal
GS: Robert Brown.   Serena turns a Seaman's memorial statue to life and puts a petrified Darrin in its place.

Paul Revere Rides Again
GS: Jonathan Harris, Bert Convy. Esmeralda accidentally conjures up Paul Revere.

Samantha's Bad Day in Salem
GS: Hal England. A young warlock, who has a crush on Samantha, creates his own duplicate of her for himself, causing problems for Darrin.

Samantha's Old Salem Trip
GS: Ronald Long, James Westerfield. Esmeralda accidentally sends Samantha back to 17th-century Salem.

Samantha's Pet Warlock
GS: Edward Andrews, Noam Pitlik. An egotistical warlock tries to get Samantha to run away with him.

Samantha's Old Man
GS: Ruth McDevitt.   Endora turns Darrin into a 73-year-old man.

The Corsican Cousins
Endora casts a spell on Samantha and Serena, so that whatever one says the other will say and vice versa.

Samantha's Magic Potion
GS: Charles Lane. Samantha gives Darrin a magic potion which will give him confidence.

Sisters at Heart
GS: Don Marshall, Janee Michelle. Tabitha causes polka dots to appear on herself and her black friend so they

both can be like sisters.

The Mother-in-Law of the Year
GS: John McGiver, Jim Lange, Robert Q. Lewis. Endora becomes the spokeswoman for bon bons when she is named Mother-in-Law of the year.

Mary, the Good Fairy [Part 1]
GS: Imogene Coca. The good fairy comes to collect Tabitha's lost tooth, but gets drunk on brandy when she takes it to cure her cold.

The Good Fairy Strikes Again [Part 2]
GS: Imogene Coca. Samantha tries to get the good fairy to take leave.

The Return of Darrin the Bold
GS: David Huddleston, Richard X. Slattery. Serena goes back in time to the 14th century to visit Darrin's ancestor Darrin the Bold, in order to turn him into a warlock which in turn will cause Darrin to become a warlock also.

The House That Uncle Arthur Built
GS: Barbara Rhoades. Arthur transfers all of his practical jokes to the Stephens house so he will be able to hide his joking nature from a snobby witch he is dating.

Samantha and the Troll
GS: Bob Cummings, Felix Silla. Tabitha brings her dolls to life, including a troll which escapes.

This Little Piggy
GS: Herb Edelman. Endora casts a spell on Darrin by giving him a pig's head.

Mixed Doubles
Samantha and Louise exchange personalities due to a metaphysical molecular disturbance.

Darrin Goes Ape
GS: Herb Vigran, Allen Jenkins, Milton Selzer. Serena turns Darrin into an ape.

Money Happy Returns
GS: Arch Johnson, Karl Lukas, Allen Jenkins. Darrin finds a huge sum of money in the back of a cab.

Out of the Mouth of Babes
GS: David Huddleston. Endora changes Darrin into a ten-year-old boy.

Samantha's Psychic Pslip
Samantha finds that whenever she hiccups something disappears.

Samantha's Magic Mirror
GS: Tom Bosley. Esmeralda asks Samantha to help her with her magic so she can impress her boyfriend into marrying her.

Laugh, Clown, Laugh
GS: Charles Lane. Endora casts a spell on Darrin which causes him to constantly tell bad jokes.

Samantha and the Antique Doll
Samantha tries to convince Darrin's mother that she has magical powers in order to cover up for Adam's witchcraft.

How Not to Lose Your Head to Henry VIII [Part 1]
GS: Ronald Long, Ivor Barry, Arlene Martel, Laurie Main. Samantha is sent back in time to the court of Henry VIII when she helps a nobleman who was transformed into a painting by an evil witch.

How Not to Lose Your Head to Henry VIII [Part 2]
GS: Ronald Long, Arlene Martel. Endora sends Darrin back in time to rescue Samantha.

Samantha and the Loch Ness Monster
GS: Steve Franken, Don Knight, Bernie Kopell. The Loch Ness Monster wants Samantha to get Serena to turn him back into the warlock he was, until Serena changed him.

Samantha's Not So Leaning Tower of Pisa
GS: John Rico, Robert Casper. Esmeralda goes to Italy to straighten the Leaning Tower of Pisa, which she had caused to lean hundreds of years earlier.

Bewitched, Bothered and Baldoni
GS: Francine York, Lou Krugman, Al Molinaro. Endora causes the statue of Venus to come to life in order to cause trouble for Darrin.

Paris Witch's Style
GS: Maurice Marsac. Maurice blames Darrin for not letting Samantha visit him while they were in London, so he sends him to the top of the Eiffel Tower.

The Ghost Who Made a Spectre of Himself
GS: Patrick Horgan, Maurice Dallimore. While staying at a British castle, Darrin is possessed by a ghost who has fallen for Samantha.

A Plague on Maurice and Samantha
GS: Bernie Kopell. Samantha loses her powers, and when Maurice kisses her he too loses his powers.

Hansel and Gretel in Samanthaland
GS: Billie Hayes, Bobo Lewis. Tabitha changes places with Hansel and Gretel in her storybook, which causes Samantha to come after her.

The Warlock in the Gray Flannel Suit
GS: Bernie Kopell, Charles Lane. Endora calls on a warlock to help get Darrin fired so Samantha can attend a wedding.

The Eight-Year-Itch Witch
GS: Julie Newmar. Endora gets Ophelia, a cat, turned into a witch to help her make Samantha jealous.

3 Men and a Witch on a Horse
GS: John Fiedler, Scatman Crothers, Hoke Howell. Endora casts a spell on Darrin, turning him into a gambler.

Adam, Warlock or Washout
GS: Diana Cheshney. Maurice tries to convince the witches council that Adam is a warlock.

Samantha's Magic Sitter
Esmeralda babysits for the son of Darrin's client, which causes problems when the boy tells everyone that she is a witch.

Samantha Is Earthbound
GS: Jack Collins. Samantha is suffering from a disease which makes her very heavy, so as a cure Dr. Bombay makes her lighter than air until he can find a cure for her. Until then, Samantha has to find a way to keep herself from floating away.

Serena's Richcraft
GS: Peter Lawford. Serena loses her powers, so to make up for it she decides to romance a rich bachelor.

Samantha on Thin Ice
GS: Alan Oppenheimer. Endora turns Tabitha into a fantastic ice skater.

Serena's Youth Pill
GS: David Hayward. Serena gives Larry a pill which causes him to grow gradually younger by the minute.

Tabitha's First Day at School
GS: Nita Talbot, Allen Jenkins, Maudie Prickett. Tabitha turns the class bully into a frog.

George Washington Zapped Here [Part 1]
GS: Will Geer, Jane Connell. Esmeralda accidentally zaps George Washington out of a book. When she tries to send him back, she zaps his wife Martha out of the book instead.

George Washington Zapped Here [Part 2]
GS: Will Geer, Jane Connell, Jack Collins. George tries to help Darrin get a new client's account before he and Martha are returned to the book.

School Days, School Daze
GS: Charles Lane, Maudie Prickett. Endora casts a spell which turns Tabitha into a seven-year-old genius.

A Good Turn Never Goes Unpunished
GS: J. Edward McKinley. Darrin and Samantha fight over her use of witchcraft in trying to sell an ad campaign to a client.

Sam's Witchcraft Blows a Fuse
GS: Bernie Kopell, Reta Shaw, Benson

Fong, Janos Prohaska. Samantha becomes affected by a drink in a Chinese restaurant. It causes her face to become covered with red stripes.

The Truth, Nothing But the Truth, So Help Me, Sam
GS: Parley Baer, Sara Seegar. Endora casts a spell on a pin which causes the wearer to tell the absolute truth.

THE BILL COSBY SHOW

On the air 9/14/69, off 8/31/71. NBC. Color film. 30 min. 52 episodes. Broadcast: Sept 1969-May 1971 Sun 8:30-9; Jun 1971-Aug 1971 Tue 7:30-8. Producer: Marvin Miller/Bill Cosby. Prod Co: Gammin Co. Synd: Peter Rogers Organization.

CAST: Chet Kincaid (played by Bill Cosby), Rose Kincaid (Lillian Randolph, 1969-1970; Beah Richards, 1970-1971), Brian Kincaid (Lee Weaver), Verna Kincaid (Olga James), Mr. Langford (Sid McCoy), Mrs. Marsha Peterson (Joyce Bulifant), Max Waltz (Joseph Perry).

The adventures of Chet Kincaid, gym teacher at Richard Allen Holmes High School in Los Angeles. Stories relate Chet's involvement with students who are in the midst of crisis. The series was an obvious inspiration for *The White Shadow*. Although available for syndication, almost no station in the US airs the series.

The Fatal Phone Call
GS: Vic Tayback. Chet answers a pay phone and gets involved in a domestic fight.

The Best Hook Shot in the World
GS: Greg Gordon. A short lad feels he is being discriminated against when Chet won't let him on the basketball team.

A Girl Named Punkin
A little girl from the neighborhood settlement house follows Chet home but refuses to speak.

Growing Growing Grown
GS: Issa Arnal, Bryan O'Byrne. Chet has to chaperone the school dance and escort a new teacher in his brother's garbage truck.

Let X Equal a Lousy Weekend
GS: Hilly Hicks. Chet subs for a sick math teacher and regrets it when he can't answer the math problems.

To Kincaid, with Love
GS: Barbara Parrio. A girl dumps her boyfriend and starts sending Chet gifts.

The Killer Instinct
GS: Nehemiah Persoff, Robert Rockwell. A father tries to force Chet to put his untalented son on the football team.

The Substitute
GS: Sid McCoy, Olga James. Chet teaches a sex education class and babysits for his brother's kids, while trying to get a date with a substitute teacher.

Brotherly Love
GS: Charlene Jones, Fred Pinkard. Chet's brother Brian leaves his wife and moves in with Chet, just when he is about to go on a date.

Going the Route
GS: Donald Livingston. Chet takes over his sick nephew's paper route.

A Word from Our Sponsor
GS: Jon Walmsley, Kathleen Freeman, Alan Oppenheimer. Chet is picked to star in a TV commercial.

A Christmas Ballad
GS: Rex Ingram, Sam Christopher, Richard Collier. Chet helps an old man get a job as Santa Claus at a community center.

Home Remedy
GS: Lillian Randolph, Robert Rockwell. Chet's friends and relatives bring him cures for his cold.

Rules Is Rules
GS: Fran Ryan. Chet has to go through red tape in order to get a valve needle to inflate a basketball.

The Elevator Doesn't Stop Here Anymore
GS: Henry Fonda, Elsa Lanchester. Chet, a stuffy English teacher, and a cleaning lady who speaks very little English get trapped in an elevator between floors.

Lover's Quarrel
GS: Moms Mabley, Mantan Moreland. Chet's aunt and uncle always fight, so Chet decides he should put an end to it.

The Worst Crook That Ever Lived
GS: George Spell, Stuart Nisbet. A businessman buys new baseball uniforms; in return, Chet must counsel a kid shoplifter.

The Gumball Incident
GS: Tom Bosley, John Harmon. Chet goes to court to fight a charge that he broke a gumball machine.

Goodbye Cruel World
GS: Wally Cox, Alice Backes. Chet helps a shy friend get a date with a girl he has a crush on.

Driven to Distraction
GS: Marsha Kramer, James Milhollin. Chet tries to teach a nervous student to drive.

The Blind Date
GS: Cicely Tyson. Chet allows himself to accept a blind date, but is happy when he sees his date.

How to Play the Game
GS: Dave Clark. Chet plays in the city handball finals.

The Return of Big, Bad, Bubba Bronson
GS: Lou Gossett. When his old high school enemy says he is coming for a visit, Chet takes boxing lessons.

This Mouth Is Rated X
GS: Bobo Lewis, Skip Burton. Chet tries to stop a top basketball player from using bad language.

Really Cool
GS: Bob Diamond. A Cosby monologue about an important track meet is the basis of this episode.

Lullaby and Goodnight
GS: Howard Morton, Joseph Perry. Chet is trying to sleep but his neighbor's dog won't let him.

Anytime You're Ready
GS: Gordon Hoban, Eldon Quick, Alberto Isaac. Chet buys a movie camera and has fun making silent movies.

Open House
GS: Richard X. Slattery, Barbara Perry, Paul Comi. Chet helps a friend sell his house when his marriage begins to break up.

Is There a Doctor in the Hospital
GS: Miguel Monsalve, Billy Sands.

Chet injures himself in the gym and is trying to find someone in the hospital to help him.

There Must Be a Pony
GS: Ta-Tanisha, Vonetta McGee. Chet tries to prepare a student who hopes to win a movie contest for a disappointment.

The Old Man of 4-C
GS: Ellen Corby. Chet makes friends with the old man next door, who now won't leave him alone.

The Lincoln Letter
GS: Rupert Crosse. Chet tries to find a valuable letter that President Lincoln wrote to his great aunt.

The Runaways
GS: James Westerfield, Lynn Hamilton. Chet tries to prevent a young boy from running away from home.

The Artist
GS: James Bradley Jr., Michael Ansara. Chet tries to help a talented young artist.

The March of the Antelopes
GS: David Choi. Chet takes a group of boys on a camping trip.

The Deluge [Part 1]
GS: Parley Baer, Gloria Foster. Chet ventures into a rainstorm to help a lady about to give birth.

The Deluge [Part 2]
GS: Jeff Burton. The rain continues and so does Chet's problem of helping a lady deliver her baby at home.

Swan's Way
GS: Don Knotts, John Amos. Chet tries to keep his TV set from being repossessed.

The Poet
GS: Ric Carrott, Mark Hamill. Chet takes credit for a famous love poem in order to encourage a young poet to write.

Teacher of the Year
GS: Jerome Guardino, Marguerite Ray. No one is interested in going to Chet's Teacher of the Year award dinner.

Each According to Appetite
GS: Hilly Hicks, Dick Balduzzi. The students get Chet to help demonstrate for other issues after he wins the fight over the cafeteria menu.

Viva Ortega
GS: Joaquin Martinez, Frank Campanella. Chet helps a Mexican carpenter pass his American history test.

Miraculous Marvin
GS: Dick Van Dyke. Chet tries to help an out of work magician who is about to get married.

The Sesame Street Rumble
GS: Kelvin Cosby, Pedro Gonzales-Gonzales, Lee Weaver. Chet tries to get a TV set away from a five-year-old so he and his friends can watch the football game.

The Generation Gap
GS: Fred Pinkard. Chet tries to spend more time with his father.

Tobacco Road
GS: Herb Edelman. Chet helps a teacher to quit smoking.

A Dirty Business
GS: Darrell Larson, Kip King. Chet tries to get a kid to join the track team.

The Barber Shop
GS: Antonio Fargas. Chet takes his kid cousin to get a haircut, but winds up making a bet with the barber instead.

Power of the Trees
GS: Elsa Lanchester, Byron Morrow, Pat Morita. An old lady gets Chet to help her save the neighborhood trees.

The Green-Eyed Monster
GS: Kim Weston. Chet tells a student to play it cool with women, while his feelings for a pretty teacher are making him jealous.

The Long Road Back
GS: John Marley, Jack Naughton. An old eccentric millionaire wants the community center's kids to act out his childhood on the New York neighborhood he built on his estate.

The Saturday Game
GS: Barry Lee Miller, Milton Selzer. Chet has to face a problem: his home-run hitter is a Chassidic Jew who can't play on Saturday.

THE BOB CUMMINGS SHOW

On the air 1/2/55, off 9/15/59. NBC, CBS. B&W film. 173 episodes. Broadcast: Jan 1955-Sept 1955 Sun 10:30-ll; Jul 1955-Sept 1957 CBS Thu 8-8:30; Sept 1957-Sept 1959 NBC Tue 9:30-10. Producer: Bob Mosher. Prod Co: Revue. Synd: MCA/Universal.

CAST: Bob Collins (played by Bob Cummings), Margaret (Rosemary De-Camp), Schultzy (Ann B. Davis), Chuck (Dwayne Hickman), Pamela (Nancy Kulp), Paul Fonda (Lyle Talbot).

The adventures of a swinging bachelor photographer. This series was originally syndicated under the title *Love That Bob*, but since its last run in the early sixties, it has disappeared from every station. There is a chance that some small UHF stations may still be running it.

Calling Dr. Baxter
Bob tries to fix his widowed sister up with his old college friend who is now a doctor.

Hiring a Receptionist
Bob has to choose between a plain-looking girl who is highly qualified or a beautiful girl who can't even type.

It's Later Than You Think
Bob begins to think that he is getting too old to be fooling around and should get married and settle down.

Boyfriend for Schultzy
Bob fixes up Schultzy with a soda jerk who is afraid of girls.

Chuck Falls for English Teacher
Chuck announces that he has fallen in love with his English teacher.

Bob Becomes a Genius
A glamorous movie star tries to get Bob to photograph her.

A Date for Margaret
Bob Tries to get Margaret a date for the annual Photographer's Ball.

Bob Gives Up Girls
Bob gives up girls to set a good example for Chuck.

The Eyes of Texas
GS: Dick Elliot. Bob tries to tell a Texas advertising executive that his girlfriend is after his money without losing his account.

The Girl from France
Everyone believes that the girl Bob met during the war in France is now coming to marry him.

Ideal Husband
When Bob acts like a perfect gentleman to two middle-aged wives, he causes a great deal of trouble.

The Rival Photographer
Bob discovers that a female photographer is out to steal his accounts.

The Bachelor Apartment
An old high school friend convinces Bob that he should have his own bachelor apartment.

Mrs. Montague's Niece
Mrs. Montague tries to trick Bob into marrying her niece.

Bob to the Rescue
GS: Lyle Talbot.   Bob tries to convince his sister that her airline pilot boyfriend really is a wolf.

Dr. Jekyll and Mr. Cummings
Bob is assigned to photograph Bob Cummings for the cover of a magazine.

Air Corps Marriage
GS: King Donovan.   Bob's two Air Force friends try to trick him into getting married.

Advice to the Lovelorn
GS: Richard Jaeckel.   Bob tries to bring his nephew Chuck and his girlfriend back together again.

Miss Coffee Break
GS: Hal Peary.   Bob is one of the judges of the Miss Coffee Break beauty contest.

Bob Plays Cupid
GS: Hal Peary.   Bob tries to fix his sister up with a man who is running the city council.

Schultzy's Dream World
Schultzy daydreams about falling in love with Bob.

Uncle Bob-Bob
GS: Charles Herbert.   Bob is visited by his Air Force friend and his little boy who turns out to be a little monster.

The Silver-Tongued Orator
GS: Marjorie Bennett.   Bob tries to charm a widow into renting her home so his visiting Air Force friend and his family will have a place to stay.

Bob's Birthday
Bob tells everyone that he does not want a surprise birthday party, even though everyone knows he does.

Return of the Wolf or Absence Makes the Heart Grow Fonda
GS: Lyle Talbot.   Bob tries to discourage Margaret from dating her wolfish boyfriend Paul Fonda by trying to get her to go with him on a fishing trip.

Chuck Goes Hollywood
Chuck gets a swelled head when his picture appears on the cover of a teenage magazine.

El Lobo Strikes Again
Bob once again tries to protect his sister from the advances of her boyfriend who he still thinks is a wolf.

Bob Glamorizes Schultzy
Bob tries to glamorize Schultzy in order to fix her up with the sailor who has come to find the girl whose legs appeared in a magazine photograph.

Bob Meets Fonda's Sister
Margaret and Paul decide to teach overprotective Bob a lesson.

Bob Rescues Mrs. Neemeyer
Bob rescues Mrs. Neemeyer from the clutches of a golddigger, but now finds that she has fallen for him.

Bob Saves the Day
GS: Dick Wesson.   Bob and Margaret have to find a way to keep Schultzy's sailor boyfriend occupied until she returns from her trip.

Too Many Cooks
Bob and Chuck believe they have the whole house to themselves when Margaret goes away on vacation, unaware that she asked dozens of her friends to keep an eye on them.

Bob Falls in Love
Bob's strange behavior can only mean one thing, that he has fallen in love.

Hawaii Calls
GS: Jack Carson.   Bob gets jealous when Jack Carson plans to take his

girlfriend on a trip to Hawaii.

Hawaii Comes Calling
Bob accidentally gets himself engaged to marry a Hawaiian girl.

Hawaii Stays
Schultzy helps Bob get rid of the Hawaiian girl, whom he unknowingly got engaged to, and her family.

Wedding, Wedding, Who's Got the Wedding?
Bob and his girl Kay plan to get Paul and Margaret married off, while Paul and Margaret plot to get Bob and Kay married.

Bob's One Day to Relax
Everyone becomes upset when Chuck begins dating a French exchange student.

Mrs. Neemeyer's Niece
Bob confuses a girl applying for a job as Schultzy's helper with Mrs. Neemeyer's visiting niece.

The Wolf Sitter
Bob learns that Chuck has started a wolf sitting service. He hires out his friends to act as the visiting cousins to models so they can discourage any wolfish men from taking advantage of them.

The Christmas Spirit
Bob brings Chuck and his girl Francine as well as Margaret and Paul back together.

Grandpa's Christmas Vault
Bob's visiting grandfather comes for a visit and proves to be as much of a wolf as his grandson.

The Sheik
Bob is asked to help Pamela out of her romantic dilemma.

The Letter
GS: Tab Hunter. Bob writes a love letter to Kay but decides not to send it after he gets a letter from her.

The School Play
Chuck gets the lead in the school play and asks Bob to help him with the love scenes.

Bob Joins the Drama Group
Bob is offered the lead in a play directed by Chuck's drama teacher.

The Acid Test
GS: Dave Willock. Bob's old friend asks him to try and take his girlfriend away from him. If he fails, it will prove that she loves him.

The Dominant Sex
GS: Marla English. Bob tries to prove to an Italian actress that American men are not dominated by women.

Too Many Women
Bob decides to give up women for a while.

Snowbound
Bob and Paul become trapped in a mountain cabin by a snowstorm for a week.

Long Live the King
Bob pretends to be engaged in order to frighten off a girl he thinks wants to marry him.

The Petticoat Derby
Bob is besieged by girls who want him to take them to the Photographer's Ball.

The Fallen Idol
Bob learns that his hero image to Chuck is weakened when he is too busy to help him build a model plane.

The Wolf Who Came to Dinner
Paul hurts his back and has to stay in Bob's bed until it gets better.

Hail to These, Oh, Alma Mater
GS: Lucien Littlefield. Bob and Margaret fight over which college Chuck is going to attend.

Chuck Visits Grandpa
Bob and Margaret become worried

when Chuck visits with Bob's grandfather.

Masquerade Party
Bob stages a masquerade ball in order
to cover up the fact that he made a
date with several girls for the same
night.

The Con Man
GS: Tristram Coffin. Bob tries to save
Margaret from investing in a phony
uranium mine.

The Trouble with Henry
Bob tries to convince a mother that
her daughter should marry his friend
Henry.

Air Force vs. Navy
Bob and Harvey try to convince Chuck
and his friends to join the Air National
Guard instead of the Navy.

The Boys Join Up
Chuck and his friends join the Air National Guard. Bob tries to help when
one of the boys is too short to be a
pilot.

The Sergeant Wore Skirts
Bob tries to help out when Harvey's
old Air Force girlfriend comes for a
visit.

Scramble for Grandpa
GS: Bea Benaderet, Jerry Paris. Grandpa Collins insists on flying his old
plane over Air Force territory.

Bob the Chaperone
Bob becomes the chaperone for
Chuck's teenage party.

Margaret Becomes Sadie Thompson
Margaret decides to trap Paul into marrying her.

Grandpa Meets Zsa Zsa
GS: Zsa Zsa Gabor. Zsa Zsa mistak-
enly believes that Grandpa Collins is
Bob.

Bob Buys a Plane
Bob tries to buy a plane using the trust

fund Grandpa set up for him, unaware
that he has to be married before he
can collect it.

Bob Batches It
Bob tries to con his models into keeping house for him.

The Beautiful Psychologist
Bob falls for Chuck's student advisor,
a beautiful psychologist.

The Boston Mother Returns
Bob takes Henry's place in order to
impress his visiting mother-in-law.

Miss Joplin Arrives
Bob helps bring a beauty contest
winner and her mother out to Hollywood.

The Double Date
Bob promises Chuck that he will double date with him when he reaches his
18th birthday. Well, the day is here,
but the only problem is Bob's date is a
bubble dancer named Boom Boom.

Schultzy Says No
Schultzy turns down her boyfriend's
proposal.

Chuck Buys a Hot Rod
Bob thinks that Chuck and his girlfriend are going to elope.

Air Force vs. Ruthie
Ruthie gets jealous when she learns
that Bob and her husband Harvey are
escorting five beautiful girls to the Air
Force Reunion.

How to Handle Women
Bob tries to teach Chuck how to handle a woman.

Bob Uncovers Ruthie's Past
Bob tries to convince Ruthie that Harvey's old girlfriend is nothing to be
jealous over, that is, until he meets
her.

Bob Traps a Wolf
Bob tries to trick Paul into marrying
Margaret, but they learn about his plot

and try to get his date to believe that Bob is a married man with three kids.

Beach Bandit
Bob tries to convince the other members of the jury, on which he is serving, that the girl who is on trial is innocent.

Bob Gives Pamela the Bird
GS: Robert Easton. Bob has to find a way of getting out of Pamela's clutches when she asks him to marry her.

The Models Revolt
When his models learn that Bob has made a date with more than one girl for the weekend, they revolt and form a club called the DDT: Don't Date the Two-Timer.

Bob Saves Doctor Chuck
Bob learns that Chuck plans to quit school and become a playboy like Bob.

Bob Becomes Chuck's First Patient
GS: Herbert Rudley. Bob fakes an injury so he can convince Chuck to stay in school and become a doctor.

Bob Tangles with Ruthie
Bob tries to keep Ruthie from dominating Harvey.

Bob Picks a College
GS: John Archer. Bob chooses the college Chuck will be going to attend.

Chuck at College
Bob tries to help Chuck who is ordered by an upper classman to sneak a girl into the men's dormitory.

Bob Clashes with His Landlady
GS: Hope Emerson, El Brendel. Bob tries to convince his landlady not to evict him from his studio.

Bob Meets Schultzy's Cousin
GS: Bonita Granville. Bob tries to date Schultzy's beautiful cousin even though Schultzy warned her not to date him.

Bob Meets the Mortons
GS: Larry Keating, Bea Benaderet, George Burns, Gracie Allen. Gracie and Blanche try to fix Bob up with Schultzy. [This is a crossover episode from the Burns and Allen Show.]

Bob Handles the College Boys
Bob tries to get Chuck away from his "fast" friends who are a bad influence on him.

Bob Escapes Schultzy's Trap
GS: Hans Conreid. Schultzy tries to make Bob jealous by having a Shakespearean actor pretend to be in love with her.

Bob Plays Gigolo
GS: Jay Novello. Bob tries to romance a wealthy woman into donating some money to help his sister with her hospital drive for funds.

Bob's Economy Wave
GS: General Shoop, Maxine Gates. Bob tries to get the whole family to save money.

Bob Meets Miss Sweden
GS: Ingrid Goude, Gordon Scott as Tarzan. Bob causes a great deal of confusion when he gets Margaret, Schultzy, Bertha and Pamela to play chaperone to Miss Sweden.

Bob Enters a Photograph Contest
Due to a mixup, Bob's winning photograph is credited to his rival, Wally Seawell.

Bob Goes Fishing . . . Gets Caught
While preparing to leave on a fishing trip, Bob learns that his former girlfriend Kay has become a big Hollywood actress. This causes him to get mad when he thinks she has forgotten all about him.

Bob Calls Kay's Bluff
Bob thinks the wedding ceremony that he and Kay are taking part in is a fake; he almost learns too late that it is for real.

Bob Ages Margaret
Bob tries to prepare Margaret for old age by having a friend portray a doctor and give her an antidote for aging.

Bob for Mayor
Bob decides to run for mayor when Mrs. Montague tries to use him to get the female vote for her campaign.

Bob Gets Out-Uncled
GS: Elroy Hirsch, Merry Anders. Bob competes against Elroy Hirsch in a series of athletic events to see who is a better athlete.

Air Force Calls Bob—Grandpa Answers
GS: John Hoyt. When Bob is called to Air Force Reserve training, a mixup occurs and Grandpa goes in his place.

Bob Gets Schultzy in Pictures
GS: Alan Ladd. Bob tries to help Schultzy appear as a famous movie star in order to impress her visiting friend.

Bob Gets Neighborly
Bob tries to date the beautiful girl next door.

Bob Hires a Maid
Bob and Paul try to romance the new maid.

Bob Meets Bill Lear
GS: John Archer. Bob tries to fix Margaret up with a bachelor named Bill Lear.

Bob the Body Builder
Bob uses Harvey as the before picture of a weakling in an ad for gym equipment.

Bob Slows Down
Margaret and Bob's doctor conspire to get Bob to slow down by convincing him that he has a fatal disease.

Bob Wins the Olympics
Bob conducts a perfect body contest.

Thanksgiving at Grandpa's
The entire family spend Thanksgiving at Grandpa's. The only problem they face is the fact that Grandpa can't bring himself to kill the turkey he has been fattening up for their dinner.

Bob and the New Receptionist
Bob unknowingly makes a date with his own sister.

Bob, the Gunslinger
GS: Glenn Strange. Chuck and Schultzy daydream that they are back in the old West.

Bob's Christmas Party
Bob plans on getting Miss Sweden all to himself during the office Christmas party, unaware that Schultzy has invited the entire family to come to the party.

Bob Gives Chuck a Psychology Lesson
Bob finds himself taking his date out in Chuck's hot rod because he lent his car to Chuck.

Bob and Harvey Go Hunting
Bob and Harvey try to keep Ruthie from finding out about their planned hunting trip.

Bob and Harvey Get Ambushed
Ruthie gets mad when she learns about the two models Bob and Harvey met on their hunting trip.

Bob the Gorilla Trainer
Bob gets Schultzy to dress up in a gorilla suit in order to frighten Margaret's bridge partners out of going to their out of town tournament. This way he can go out on a date instead of flying them to the tournament.

Bob's Italian Past
Bob is expecting a visit from the Italian girl he met during the war.

Bob Goes Hillbilly
GS: Connie Stevens. Bob and the family pose as hillbillies in order to scare off Chuck's snobbish girlfriend.

Bob's Italian Past Moves Up
Bob tries to prevent Paul from dating

his old Italian girlfriend.

Bob Gives SRO Performance
Bob turns down the chance to play a lover in the play Margaret and her friends are producing, until he learns that he would be starring with a beautiful girl.

Bob Falls for Schultzy???
Through sleepteaching, Bob is tricked into falling for Schultzy.

Bob and Automation
GS: Angie Dickinson. Bob uses a machine to help sort out his many girlfriends.

Bob Gets Harvey a Raise
GS: Jesse White. Bob tries to get Harvey a big business order with an out of town buyer.

Bob Saves Harvey
Once again Bob tries to get a big business order with the same out of town buyer who so far has resisted his sales pitch.

Bob Goes Birdwatching
Bob tries to get Bill to keep Pamela occupied so he can get to know her beautiful bird-watching companion.

Bob's Forgotten Fiancee
Bob is led by his friends to believe that he proposed to a girl and forgot all about it, and that now she is coming to marry him.

Bob Goes to the Moon
Bob tries to convince Miss Sweden that he is going to fly to the moon in a rocket in order to get her interested in him.

Bob Retrenches
Bob tries to get everyone to save money in order to recoup the money taken by the IRS.

Grandpa Attends the Convention
Grandpa goes to Hollywood in search of girls, when he attends the convention of his old San Juan Hill Rough Riders.

Grandpa's Old Buddy
GS: Andy Clyde. Grandpa and his old friend Charley plot to run off with Bob's photographic models.

Bob Digs Rock 'n' Roll
Chuck asks Bob to help him get his girlfriend to forget about the rock and roll singer she has a crush on and return to him.

Bob Sails for Hawaii
Bob tries to find a way to take a cruise with Miss Sweden to Hawaii instead of his rival Wally Seawell.

Bob and Schultzy at Sea
GS: Don Knotts. Bob tries to find a date for Schultzy with one of the passengers on the ship.

Bob Becomes a Stage Uncle
GS: Ozzie Nelson. Bob tries to talk Chuck out of his plan to become a rock and roll singer.

Colonel Goldbrick
Bob creates a fantastic story to impress a lady skindiver.

Bob Frees Schultzy for Romance
GS: Rose Marie. Bob decides to let Schultzy quit her job to take another one at a missile factory so she can find a husband.

Bob and Schultzy Reunite
GS: Steve Marlo, Mike Road. After some bad experiences, Schultzy returns to work for Bob.

Bob Helps Anna Maria
GS: Anna Maria Alberghetti, Alan Reed. Bob tries to get a date with Anna when he doesn't recognize her as the skinny kid he used to know.

Bob and the Ravishing Realtor
GS: Elena Verdugo. Bob falls for the beautiful real estate agent whom Margaret hires to sell the house.

Bob Restores Male Supremacy
Bob tries to turn Harvey from a hen-pecked husband into a man.

Grandpa Moves West
Bob thinks his grandpa has fallen in love with a lady acrobat.

Grandpa Clobbers the Air Force
When Grandpa is rejected by the Air Force, he declares war on them and proceeds to bomb the air base with jugs of apple cider.

Bob Butters Beck . . . Beck Butters Better
GS: George Burns.   George teaches Bob how to be a rock and roll impresario.

Collins the Crooner
Bob becomes a recording star, only to regret it when Pamela falls in love with him.

Bob in Orbit
Bob is taken captive by the Air Force and forced into labor as revenge for Grandpa's bombing of the base.

Bob and the Dumb Blonde
Bob's temporary secretary interferes in his attempts to romance an English model.

Bob Judges a Beauty Contest
Bob is chosen as the judge of the Air Force beauty contest.

Margaret Plays Bob's Game
Bob brings a model home for dinner only to learn that Margaret cleaned out the kitchen before she left on her date.

Bob's Boyhood Love Image
Schultzy uses psychology to get Bob to marry her.

Bob, the Ideal Boss
Schultzy enters Bob in a "What I Think of My Boss" contest.

Bob Clashes with Steve Allen
GS: Steve Allen, Buddy Baer.   Bob

sends a pesty dumb blonde to New York to appear as a billboard girl on the Steve Allen Show, in order to get rid of her.

The King vs. the Chorus
Bob tries to save Chuck from the clutches of a Las Vegas showgirl.

Bob in Surgery
Bob goes to the hospital when he is involved in an auto accident, where he tries to date the nurses.

Bob Creates a New Mamie Van Doren
GS: Mamie Van Doren.   Bob is unaware that the new girl in his office is Mamie Van Doren who has been disguised by Schultzy so she won't be bothered while she prepares for a new movie role.

Bob vs. Linkletter
GS: Art Linkletter.   Bob tries to talk Art into hosting the annual charity dinner given by Margaret's women's club.

Bob Clashes with Ken
GS: Ken Murray.   Ken tries to get Bob married off so he won't keep the showgirls in his show out so late after the show.

Bob Gets Zodiac-Ed
Bob gets interested in astrology in order to impress a beautiful believer.

Bob and the Ballet
Bob becomes interested in ballet when he sees the beautiful ballerinas he has to photograph.

Bob and the Ballerina
Bob's attention to the prima ballerina is upsetting the rehearsals of Margaret's show.

Bob, the Baby Sitter
Bob's evening with a beautiful girl is ruined when he finds that he has to babysit with a six-year-old girl.

Bob Seeks a Wife
Bob spends the day taking a six-year-

old girl to the zoo.

Bob Buys a Dog
Bob buys a dog for his six-year-old houseguest in order to impress her widowed mother.

Bob the Matchmaker
GS: Maxine Gates, Robert Clarke. Bob unknowingly makes himself a blind date with a 250-pound woman who can't stop eating.

Bob Tangles with Engel
Bob claims he is an expert seaman in order to impress a sea-loving widow.

Bob Goes Western
GS: George Montgomery. Bob tries to get George to teach him to be a cowboy so he can impress his six-year-old friend Tammy.

Bob Goes to Sea
Bob is still trying to convince a widow that he is an expert seaman. However, he has a bigger problem, his old Air Force friend Tom has fallen for her too.

Grandpa Strikes Oil
Grandpa plans to celebrate his striking oil by spending the night on the town with a beautiful model.

Grandpa Runs Away
Grandpa runs away when he feels he is no longer wanted in Bob's house.

Bob Helps Martha
GS: Harry Von Zell. Bob tries to fix Schultzy's friend Martha up with Harry Von Zell.

Bob Helps Von Zell
GS: Harry Von Zell, George Burns, Elena Verdugo. Bob and George try to prevent a Latin model from interfering in the romance between Martha and Harry.

Bob and the Pediatrician
GS: Anne Jeffreys. Bob tries to bring his sister and the family doctor together in order to save his own romance with a lady pediatrician.

Bob Gets Hypnotized
GS: Anne Jeffreys. Margaret gets Bob's lady doctor friend to hypnotize him in order to get him to tell the truth about their relationship.

Bob, the Last Bachelor
Bob finds that he is the last of his poker-playing friends that isn't married.

THE BOB NEWHART SHOW

On the air 9/16/72, off 8/26/78. CBS. 120 episodes. Color videotape. Broadcast: Sept 1972-Oct 1976 Sat 9:30-10; Nov 1976-Sept 1977 Sat 8:30-9; Sept 1977-Apr 1978 Sat 8-8:30; Jun 1978-Aug 1978 Sat 8-8:30. Producer: Tom Patchett, Jay Tarses, Mike Zinberg. Prod Co: MTM. Synd: Viacom.

CAST: Robert Hartley (played by Bob Newhart), Emily Hartley (Suzanne Pleshette), Howard Borden (Bill Daily), Jerry Robinson (Peter Bonerz), Carol Kester Bondurant (Marcia Wallace), Ellen Hartley (Pat Finley), Mr. Peterson (John Fiedler), Eliott Carlin (Jack Riley), Mrs. Bakerman (Florida Friebus), Mr. Herd (Oliver Clark), Mr. Gianelli (Noam Pitlik), Michelle Nardo (Renee Lippin), Bernie Tupperman (Larry Gelman).

WRITERS: Gene Thompson, Harvey Miller, Tom Patchett, Jay Tarses, Bill Idelson, Charlotte Brown, Gordon and Lynn Farr, Sy Rosen, Glen and Leo Charles, Earl Pomerantz, Andrew Smith, Lloyd Garver, Jerry Mayer. DIRECTORS: Jay Sandrich, Alan Rafkin, Peter Bonerz, Jerry London, George Tyne, Peter Baldwin, Michael Zinberg, Jim Burrows, Dick Martin.

The story of a Chicago psychologist and his schoolteacher wife. The average episode has Bob facing his nutty patients and kooky friends. The series left the air when the star, Bob Newhart, had had enough. The series was very popular during its original run, but it has been a failure in syndication. It now usually runs during the middle of the night or early afternoon.

Fly the Unfriendly Skies
GS: Penny Marshall. Emily admits to Bob that she has a fear of flying.

Tracy Grammar School, I'll Lick You Yet
Bob feels left out when he is not asked to speak to Emily's class on vocation day.

Tennis, Emily?
GS: Peter Brown, Barbara Barnett, Pat Lysinger. Bob becomes jealous of Emily's new tennis instructor.

Mom, I L-L-Love You
Bob has difficulty telling his mother that he loves her.

Goodnight, Nancy
GS: Penny Fuller, Richard Schaal. Emily becomes jealous when Bob's old girlfriend and her husband come for a visit.

Come Live with Me
Bob and Emily interfere in Carol's love life.

Father Knows Worst
GS: Alice Borden, Moosie Drier. Howard is convinced his son doesn't love him anymore when he spends more time with Jerry than with him.

Don't Go to Bed Mad
Bob and Emily have a fight over his desire to watch football every Monday night instead of spending the night with her.

P-I-L-O-T
GS: Louise Lasser. Bob and Emily decide to adopt a child.

Anything Happen While I Was Gone?
Bob helps Jerry call off his marriage to his domineering assistant.

I Want to Be Alone
GS: Bernie Kopell, Alan Hewitt. Bob takes a hotel room alone in order to be by himself for a while, but Howard thinks Bob and Emily have split up.

Bob and Emily and Howard and Carol and Jerry
Howard and Carol fall for each other, but then she rejects him.

I Owe it All to You . . . But Not That Much
Jerry becomes one of Bob's patients, but finds that it begins to hurt their friendship.

His Busiest Season
Bob invites his therapy group to a Christmas party at their apartment.

Let's Get Away from It Almost
GS: Alan Garfield, Joyce Van Patten, Chuck McCann. Bob and Emily spend the weekend with an annoying couple at a deserted ski resort.

The Crash of 29 Years Old
GS: Dan Barrows. Carol becomes depressed when she becomes 29 and realizes that her life is unfulfilled, so she quits her job.

The Man with the Golden Wrist
GS: Larry Gelman, Mimi Torchin, Michael Lerner. Bob refuses to go to his surprise 40th birthday party and wear the expensive gold watch that Emily bought him.

Not with My Sister You Don't
GS: Heather Menzies, Mel Stewart. Howard becomes upset when his younger sister begins to date Jerry.

The Two Loves of Dr. Hartley
Bob tries to discourage a patient who thinks she is in love with him.

The Bob Newhart Show: Pat Finley (left), Suzanne Pleshette and Bill Daily.

A Home Is Not Necessarily a House
Bob and Emily consider buying a house.

Emily, I'm Home—Emily??
Bob becomes upset when Emily gets a full-time job.

You Can't Win 'em All
GS: Vern Rowe, Larry Gelman. Bob tries to help a has-been baseball player.

Bum Voyage
Emily tries to convince Bob to take a two-month European cruise.

Who's Been Sleeping on My Couch?
Jerry moves in with Bob and Emily after he has a fight with his girlfriend.

Last TV Show
Bob objects when his therapy group wants to accept an invitation to hold one of their sessions on a TV show.

Motel
GS: Zohra Lampert. Bob and Jerry spend the weekend in a motel in Peoria in order to see a football game that is blacked out in Chicago.

Backlash
GS: Michael Conrad. Bob and Emily cancel their trip to Mexico when Bob hurts his back.

Somebody Down Here Likes Me
GS: John McMartin. A minister comes to Bob for advice.

Emily in for Carol
GS: Howard Platt. Emily fills in for Carol when she goes away on vacation.

Have You Met Miss Dietz
GS: Mariette Hartley. Howard and Jerry find that they are dating the same girl.

Old Man Rivers
Carol falls for her doctor despite their age difference.

Mister Emily Hartley
GS: Bill Quinn, Tom Patchett. Bob feels inferior to Emily when he learns that her IQ is higher than his.

Mutiny on the Hartley
Bob tries to tell his therapy group that he is raising his rates.

I'm Okay, You're Okay, So What's Wrong?
GS: Katherine Helmond.   Bob and Emily visit a marriage counselor.

Fit Fat and Forty-One
GS: Bruce Kirby. Bob joins a weight-reducing class to lose some excess weight.

Blues for Mr. Borden
GS: Moosie Drier, Julius Harris. Howard becomes depressed when he learns that his ex-wife has a steady boyfriend.

My Wife Belongs to Daddy
GS: Ann Rutherford, John Randolph. Bob feels inferior to Emily's visiting father.

T.S. Elliot
Mr. Carlin asks Carol for a date.

I'm Dreaming of a Slight Christmas
On Christmas Eve, Bob finds himself trapped in his office because of a power failure.

Oh, Brother
GS: Raul Julia. Jerry's brother moves in with Jerry and proceeds to ruin his life.

The Modernization of Emily
GS: Sharon Gless. Emily decides to buy a new wardrobe to make herself feel younger.

The Jobless Corps
Howard joins Bob's therapy group for the unemployed when he loses his job with the airline.

Clink Shrink
GS: Henry Winkler, Len Lesser. Bob helps a convicted armed robber who is out on parole.

Mind Your Own Business
GS: Ron Rifkin. Bob hires a business manager, but regrets it when he finds that he is given a very small allowance to live on.

A Love Story
Howard falls for Bob's sister who is engaged to be married.

By the Way . . . You're Fired
GS: Richard Schaal, Larry Gelman, Howard Platt.   Carol falls in love, which causes a bad effect on her work so Jerry fires her.

Confessions of an Orthodontist
GS: Roger Perry, Teri Garr. Jerry confesses to Bob that he is in love with Emily.

A Matter of Principal
GS: Milton Selzer. Emily refuses the principal's request to skip a student two grades ahead.

Big Brother Is Watching
Bob is worried that his sister will move in with Howard.

The Battle of the Groups
GS: Howard Hesseman, Daniel J. Travanti.   Bob takes two of his therapy groups to a mountain cabin for a marathon session.

The Separation Story
GS: Bryan O'Byrne. Bob and Emily decide to separate temporarily.

The Great Timpau Medical Arts Co-op Experiment
GS: Merie Earle, Larry Gelman. Jerry tries to get all of the doctors in the building to form a co-op to treat each other for free.

Sorry, Wrong Mother
Howard tries to turn Ellen into the type of mother his son will like.

The Gray Flannel Shrink
GS: John Anderson, Edward Winter, Jerry Fogel.   Bob becomes the staff psychologist with a major insurance company.

Dr. Ryan's Express
Jerry hires a temporary receptionist who is totally incompetent.

Brutally Yours, Bob Hartley
GS: Lawrence Pressman. Bob decides to be honest and open with everyone, which causes several fights.

Ship of Shrinks
GS: David L. Lander, Bobby Ramsen. Bob is reluctant to fly to Hawaii for a convention of psychologists.

Life Is a Hamburger
GS: Richard Schaal. Carol announces she is going to marry the man everyone thinks is a little weird.

An American Family
GS: Barnard Hughes, Martha Scott, John Randolph, Ann Rutherford. Bob and Emily invite their parents to join them for Thanksgiving dinner.

We Love You . . . Goodbye
Emily causes Bob to get kicked out of his own all-women consciousness-raising group.

Jerry Robinson Crusoe
GS: Gail Strickland. Jerry decides to give up his practice and move with his girlfriend to Tahiti.

Serve for Daylight
Bob and Emily are teammates in a doctor's tennis tournament.

Home Is Where the Hurt Is
GS: Bill Quinn. Carol spends Christmas Eve with Bob and Emily when she gets depressed.

Tobin's Back in Town
GS: Fred Willard. Ellen's old boyfriend comes to town to try and get Ellen to come back to him.

Think Smartly—Vote Hartley
GS: George Wyner. Bob runs for the chairmanship of the local school board.

The Way We Weren't
Emily wants to know why Bob refuses to talk to his old girlfriend.

A Pound of Flesh
GS: Merie Earle. Bob refuses to lend Jerry the money for a new motorcycle.

My Business Is Shrinking
Bob goes to see a psychologist when he becomes worried when he starts to lose his patients.

The New Look
GS: Cliff Norton, Marcia Lewis. Emily redecorates the apartment with antiques. Bob has to find a way to tell her that he hates the way she redecorated.

Bob Hits the Ceiling
GS: Mike Henry. Bob agrees to counsel Emily's friends whose marriage is breaking up.

Emily Hits the Ceiling
GS: George Wyner. Bob and Emily agree to help out at a children's summer camp.

The Ceiling Hits Bob
GS: Bill Quinn, Jess Nadelman. Bob has to find another place to conduct his sessions when the ceiling in his office collapses.

The Longest Goodbye
GS: Tom Poston. Bob's old schoolmate Cliff Murdock spends the night at Bob's apartment, but after a week, Bob finds that he can't get rid of him.

Here's Looking at You, Kid
GS: Richard Balin, Vern Rowe. Bob has to propose to Ellen, for Howard, when he chokes up.

Death of a Fruitman
Bob throws one of his patients out of his group sessions only to learn that the man is killed in an accident. This causes the group to blame Bob for his death.

Change Is Gonna Do Me Good
Emily insists that Bob switch the family responsibilities with her.

The Heavyweights
GS: Cliff Osmond, Marcia Lewis. Bob asks Carol to tell his overweight workshop how she lost 100 pounds.

Carol's Wedding
GS: Robert Casper, Howard Hesseman. Carol gets married to a man she met on a blind date.

Shrinks Across the Sea
GS: Rene Auberjonois, Francoise Ruggieri. A French psychologist and his mistress come to visit Bob and Emily as part of a medical exchange program.

What's It All About, Albert?
GS: Keenan Wynn. Bob consults his old college professor when he believes that all his work with his patients is worthless.

Who is Mr. X?
GS: Jennifer Warren. Bob accidentally tells about the public official he once treated, on a talk show.

Seemed Like a Good Idea at the Time
GS: Titos Vandis, Ruth McDevitt. Bob becomes partners with a psychiatrist in order to share the work, but finds that his new partner gives him all the work and runs off to have fun.

Over the River and Through the Woods
Bob stays home with his friends when Emily flies home to spend Thanksgiving with her parents.

Father and Sons and Mothers
GS: William Daniels, Martha Scott. Bob becomes a nervous wreck when his mother comes to stay with them, while his father goes on a fishing trip and their house is being painted.

The Article
GS: Ellen Weston, Bobby Ramsen. Ellen gets a new assignment to interview the doctors in Bob's building.

A Matter of Vice-Principal
GS: Lawrence Pressman. Emily is promoted to the job of Vice Principal, which is making another teacher mad because he thought he was going to get the job.

Bob Has to Have His Tonsils Out, So He Spends Christmas Eve in the Hospital
GS: Graham Jarvis. When Bob has to have an immediate operation to remove his tonsils, it ruins everyone's holiday plans.

No Sale
GS: Malcolm Atterbury. Bob joins Mr. Carlin in a get-rich-quick scheme.

Carol at 6:01
Bob tries to help Carol, whose husband is smothering her with love.

Warden Gordon Borden
GS: William Redfield. Howard's game warden brother comes for a visit and makes a pass at Ellen.

My Boy Guillermo
GS: Gail Strickland, Matthew Laborteaux. Jerry's old girlfriend returns to ask him to marry her.

Duke of Dunk
GS: Anthony Costello. Bob tries to help a basketball player who is suffering from a losing streak.

Guaranteed Not to Shrink
Carol drives everyone crazy when she goes to night school to become a psychologist.

Birth of a Salesman
Bob is sued by a shy patient and Emily fights a parking ticket.

The Boy Next Door
The Hartleys find that they have to take care of Howard's son when his schedule does not permit him the time to stay with him.

Peeper—Two
GS: Tom Poston, Veronica Hamel.

When his wife leaves him, Bob's friend Cliff Murdock moves in with him again.

Enter Mrs. Peeper
GS: Tom Poston, Jean Palmerton. Cliff Murdock returns for another visit, this time bringing his new wife with him.

Caged Fury
Bob and Emily become trapped in the basement storage locker of their building when they were getting some supplies for Howard's 4th of July party.

Some of My Best Friends Are . . .
GS: Howard Hesseman. Bob and his group decide to take in a new member. They are all surprised to learn that the man is a homosexual.

Still Crazy After All These Years
GS: Leonard Stone. Bob sends Howard to a psychologist in order to change his personality, so he won't be too dependent on them anymore.

The Great Rent Strike
Bob stages a sit-in to protest the lack of services in his building.

Et Tu, Carol
GS: Shirley O'Hara. Bob gets depressed when Howard gives him a statue of the Buddha with a clock in his stomach, and because Carol has decided not to work for him anymore.

Send This Boy to Camp
GS: Sorrell Booke. Bob, Jerry and Howard take some orphans on a camping trip.

A Crime Most Foul
Bob suspects everyone when his new expensive tape recorder is stolen.

The Slammer
GS: Tom Poston, Bobby Ramsen, Lucy Lee Flippin. Bob and his friend Cliff Murdock wind up in jail when they are arrested in a bar by two undercover policewomen.

Jerry's Retirement
GS: John Randolph, Howard Morris. Bob finds that he can't get any work done now that Jerry has come into a lot of money and retired from his practice.

Here's to You, Mrs. Robinson
Orphan Jerry decides to go on a world tour to find his parents.

Breaking Up Is Hard to Do
GS: John Holland. Bob is shocked to learn that his parents are separating.

Making Up Is the Thing to Do
GS: Barnard Hughes, Martha Scott. Bob decides to invite his parents for a Christmas dinner in the hopes that he can get them back together.

Love Is the Blindest
GS: Mary Ann Chinn. Mr. Carlin asks for Bob's help in creating a phony life history about himself so he will appear exciting to his new secretary who is in love with him.

The Ironwood Experience
GS: Max Showalter. Bob goes to lecture at a sex seminar unaware that the Redwood Institute is a nudist camp.

Of Mice or Men
Bob invites his group to have a special session at his apartment.

Halls of Hartley
GS: Richard Libertini. Bob applies for a job as a psychology professor at a small rural college, in order to get away from city life.

The Heartbreak Kid
GS: Tovah Feldshuh. Bob thinks his female student trainee has fallen in love with him.

Death of My Destiny
Bob tries to cure his friends and patients of their phobias. However, when he nearly falls into an empty elevator shaft, he develops his own phobia.

Desperate Sessions
GS: Robert Pine. Bob is held hostage by a friendly bank robber.

The Mentor
Carol's husband turns Bob's reception area into a replica of a Polynesian village, and plans to use it as his office when he opens his own travel agency.

Shrinking Violence
GS: Robert Ridgely. Bob tells his patients to always vent their anger and not to let it stay bottled up inside them. He later fails to take his own advice when he gets mad at Emily.

You're Having My Hartley
GS: Tom Poston, Jean Palmerton. Both Carol and Emily announce that they are going to have a baby.

Taxation Without Celebration
GS: Vince Martarano. Bob forgets to pay his taxes, and his seventh wedding anniversary.

Bob's Change of Life
Bob and Emily move to a new apartment.

Ex-Con Job
GS: Bert Rosario, H.B. Haggerty. Bob tries to help five men about to be released from prison.

A Jackie Story
GS: Hope Alexander Willis. Bob tries to help a ventriloquist and his dummy when the dummy decides to break up the act.

Who Was That Masked Man?
Mr. Carlin's encouragement turns Mr. Peterson from a henpecked husband into a fighting tiger.

Carlin's New Suit
GS: Loni Anderson, Mark Lenard, Sparky Marcus. Mr. Carlin comes to Bob for help when he is hit with a paternity suit.

A Day in the Life
GS: Richard Stahl. Bob finds that his patients can't survive without him when he tells them he is planning to visit his friend Cliff for a week.

My Son, the Comedian
GS: Bobby Ramsen. Howard asks for Bob's help when his son decides to quit school to become a comedian.

You're Fired, Mr. Chips
GS: Ralph Bellamy. Bob hires his old professor to take over his sessions while he is out of town.

Shallow Throat
GS: Frank Maxwell, Richard Libertini. One of Bob's patients confides to him that he committed grand larceny. Now Bob is torn between his patient's trust and his responsibility to report the crime.

A Girl in Her Twenties
GS: Mildred Natwick. Emily tries to help a 70-year-old woman whose children want to put her in a home for people who can't cope with reality.

Grand Delusion
GS: Morgan Fairchild. On their 10th anniversary, Bob and Emily daydream about what it would be like if they were married to different people.

'Twas the Pie Before Christmas
Bob finds that his patients refuse to come to his Christmas party when he tells them that he is raising his rates again. One patient even hired a pie-thrower to hit Bob with a pie as his revenge.

Freudian Ship
GS: John Crawford, Jeff Donnell. When on an ocean voyage, Bob tries to help a couple who are having problems with their marriage.

Grizzly Emily
GS: Barnard Hughes. Bob and Emily go on a fishing trip with Bob's father.

Emily Carlin, Emily Carlin
Emily agrees to be Mr. Carlin's wife for one night when he wants to use her to impress his former school friends.

Easy for You to Say
GS: Jerry Fogel, K.C. Martel. A radio personality comes to Bob for help with his stuttering problem.

It Didn't Happen One Night
GS: David Hedison. Emily asks Jerry and Howard to prevent her from having an affair with her old boyfriend who comes for a visit while Bob is away.

Carol Ankles for Indie-Prod
Carol tells Bob that she is quitting to take a job working for Mr. Carlin.

Son of Ex-Con Job
GS: Bert Rosario, Wyatt Johnson.

Once again Bob tries to help a group of ex-cons with their problems.

Group on a Hot Tin Wolf
Bob's patient Mr. Plager gets into trouble when he writes, directs and produces a World War I drama whose characters are identical to the members of his encounter group.

Crisis in Edukation
GS: Edward Andrews, Bill Zuckert. Emily is put in charge of the problem of trying to explain the low reading scores of her school's students to their angry parents.

Happy Trails to You
Bob takes a job as a college professor in Oregon. In flashbacks he explains to his psychology class how difficult it was saying goodbye to his friends and his patients.

THE BRADY BUNCH

On the air 9/26/69, off 8/30/74. ABC. 30 min. Color film. 117 episodes. Broadcast: Sept 1969-Sept 1970 Fri 8-8:30; Sept 1970-Sept 1971 Fri 7:30-8; Sept 1971-Aug 1974 Fri 8-8:30. Producer: Sherwood Schwartz. Prod Co & Synd: Paramount Pictures TV.

CAST: Mike Brady (played by Robert Reed), Carol Brady (Florence Henderson), Alice Nelson (Ann B. Davis), Greg Brady (Barry Williams), Marcia Brady (Maureen McCormick), Peter Brady (Christopher Knight), Jan Brady (Eve Plumb), Bobby Brady (Mike Lookinland), Cindy Brady (Susan Olsen), Oliver (Robbie Rist), Sam (Allan Melvin).

DIRECTORS: Hal Cooper, Jerry London, Leslie H. Martinson, John Rich, Oscar Rudolph, Richard Michaels and Robert Reed.

One of the last innocent comedies produced. *The Brady Bunch* consists of architect Mike Brady, widower, his three sons and Carol Martin, widow, and her three daughters, who marry and establish a home for all eight of them in a Los Angeles suburb. Aided by Alice, their housekeeper, Mike and Carol attempt to cope with the special problems their children encounter as they grow up. The series sported a cartoon spin-off called the *Brady Kids*, a short-lived variety show called the *Brady Bunch Hour* and the recent *Brady Brides* series. *The Brady Bunch* remains one of the most popular reruns of all time.

The Honeymoon [Pilot]
Mike and Carol recall how they first met, got married, and tried to go off on their honeymoon in peace.

Dear Libby
GS: Jo DeWinter. Marcia reads an advice column about a family that is exactly like hers, in which one of the

The Brady Bunch: Left to right, Susan Olsen, Mike Lookinland, Eve Plumb, Christopher Knight, Maureen McCormick, Barry Williams, Ann B. Davis, Florence Henderson and Robert Reed.

parents is extremely unhappy. She concludes that the family in the article is her family.

A Clubhouse Is Not a Home
The girls decide to move into the boys' clubhouse. However, the boys protest, so the girls set out to build their own.

Kitty Karry-All Is Missing
Cindy's favorite doll is missing and the family thinks Bobby has hidden it.

Katchoo
Jan is allergic to something and everyone thinks it is the family dog Tiger.

Eenie, Meenie, Mommy, Daddy
Cindy has only one ticket to the school play and her problem is deciding which parent to give it to.

Alice Doesn't Live Here anymore
Alice decides that the Bradys no longer

need her and prepares to leave.

Father of the Year
GS: Oliver McGowan, Lee Corrigan. Marcia enters her father in a newspaper contest for Father of the Year.

The Grass Is Always Greener
Mike and Carol decide to switch roles when they think each has the easier job.

Sorry Right Number
Mike installs a pay phone in the house when the phone bill skyrockets. He then gets frustrated when he runs out of change while making an important call.

Is There a Doctor in the House?
The kids have the measles and Mike and Carol have to decide whether to call Mike's male or Carol's female doctor.

54-40 and Fight
The Bradys can't decide whether to get a boat or a sewing machine with their trading stamps, causing a violent argument.

A-Camping We Will Go
Mike plans a camping trip and the boys don't want the girls to go along.

Vote for Brady
GS: Martin Ashe. Both Greg and Marcia are running for student body president and begin campaigning against each other.

Every Boy Does It Once
GS: Michael Lerner. Bobby is convinced that nobody loves him anymore so he runs away from home.

The Voice of Christmas
GS: Hal Smith. Carol gets laryngitis and may not be able to sing at the Christmas services.

Mike's Horror-Scope
GS: Abbe Lane. Carol reads Mike's horoscope and feels Mike is going to meet a strange new woman.

The Undergraduate
GS: Wes Parker. Greg gets some baseball tips from Los Angeles Dodger Wes Parker, but what he really needs is girl advice.

To Move or Not to Move
GS: Fran Ryan. The kids decide the house is too small and they decide they want to move, until they think about it some more. They then try to make the house seem haunted in order to scare away potential buyers.

Tiger, Tiger
GS: Maggie Malooly. Tiger runs away, sending the family on a wild searching expedition.

Brace Yourself
GS: Molly Dodd, Brian Naish. Marcia refuses to face anyone when she gets braces.

Big Sprain
The Bradys are in trouble. Alice sprains her ankle as Carol leaves to visit a sick aunt, leaving Mike and the kids in charge of the household chores.

The Hero
GS: Pitt Herbert, Melanie Baker. Peter gets a big head when he saves a little girl's life and his friends praise him for the act.

Lost Locket Found Locket
GS: Jack Griffin. Jan receives a locket from an unknown admirer, sending her on a search to find out who the locket comes from.

The Possible Dream
GS: Desi Arnaz Jr., Gordon Jump. Marcia's diary is accidentally given away by Cindy, which sends everyone to local bookshops to find it.

Going, Going . . . Steady
Marcia is in love with a 13-year-old boy who collects bugs.

The Dropout
GS: Don Drysdale. Greg gets a compliment from Don Drysdale which gives him a big head.

The Babysitters
Marcia and Greg become mad with power when they babysit for the younger kids.

The Treasure of Sierra Avenue
Bobby finds a wallet containing over $1000 in cash.

The Underground Movie
Greg decides to use the whole family in a film about the Pilgrims.

The Slumber Caper
GS: E.G. Marshall. Marcia almost loses out on her slumber party when she is accused of making fun of her teacher and is suspended.

Confessions, Confessions
Peter breaks Carol's vase and tries to

find a way to fix it before she finds out.

The Tattletale
Cindy becomes a pest by tattling on the other kids.

Call Me Irresponsible
GS: Annette Ferra. Greg gets his first job.

The Impractical Joker
GS: Lennie Bremen. Jan learns a lesson after she plays one too many practical jokes.

Fistful of Reasons
Peter has a fight with a bully.

What Goes Up . . .
The Bradys try to help Bobby overcome his fear of high places.

Coming Out Party
GS: John Howard. Tonsillitis hits the Brady family.

Not So Ugly Duckling
Jan becomes love sick.

Tell It Like It Is
GS: Richard Simmons. Carol writes a story about her life in the Brady family.

The Drummer Boy
GS: Deacon Jones. Musical problems strike the family.

Where There's Smoke
GS: Marie Denn. Carol joins an anti-smoking group and then finds cigarettes in Greg's jacket.

Will the Real Jan Brady
GS: Marcia Wallace. Jan becomes a saleswoman and causes problems for the family.

Our Son, the Man
Greg learns that there is more to being a man than he thought.

The Liberation of Marcia Brady
GS: Ken Sansom. Marcia begins to start her own women's lib campaign. [This episode is not run by many stations due to its stereotyping of women.]

Lights Out
GS: Snag Werris. Cindy is bothered by nightmares and wants to sleep with the lights on.

The Winner
Bobby is feeling sorry for himself when he thinks he is a loser in a family of winners.

Double Parked
GS: Jack Collins. Carol goes on a campaign to save a neighborhood park from demolition.

Alice's September Song
Alice's old boyfriend comes for a visit.

Ghost Town USA [Part 1]
The Bradys leave on a trip to the Grand Canyon.

Grand Canyon or Bust! [Part 2]
GS: Jim Backus. An old prospector locks the Bradys in a jail cell in a ghost town.

The Brady Braves [Part 3]
GS: Jay Silverheels, Michael Campo. Bobby and Cindy encounter an Indian boy and later the entire family are made honorary Indians.

Juliet Is the Sun
GS: Lois Newman, Randy Case. Marcia gets an inflated ego when she gets the lead in the school play.

The Wheeler-Dealer
Greg buys a lemon of a used car.

The Personality Kid
GS: Sheri Cowart, Margie DeMayer. Peter is told that he has no personality.

Her Sister's Shadow
GS: Gwen Van Dam. Jan becomes jealous of Marcia.

The Teeter Totter Caper
GS: Dick Winslow. Bobby and Cindy set out to break the record for riding a teeter totter.

My Sister Benedict Arnold
A lesson in the danger of playing with people's feelings.

The Private Ear
Peter uses his tape recorder to listen in on the other kids' conversations.

And Now a Word From Our Sponsor
GS: Paul Winchell. The Brady family is chosen to do a TV commercial for a detergent.

Click
GS: Bart LaRue. Greg wants to join the football team, but Carol is afraid he will get hurt.

The Not So Rose Colored Glasses
Jan is ashamed to admit she needs glasses.

Big Little Man
Bobby resents being little, so he tries to stretch himself.

Getting Davy Jones
GS: Davy Jones. Marcia promises to get Davy Jones to sing at the school prom.

Dough-Re-Mi
Peter's voice begins to change, right in the middle of a musical recording session.

The Big Bet
Greg loses a bet to Bobby, who proceeds to take advantage of the situation.

Jan's Aunt Jenny
GS: Imogene Coca. Eccentric Aunt Jenny teaches Jan about the meaning of beauty.

Cindy Brady Lady
Cindy gets a secret admirer.

Power of the Press
GS: Jennifer Reilly, Milton Parsons. Peter uses his column in the school newspaper to further his own gains.

Sergeant Emma
Alice's lookalike strict Cousin Emma visits the family.

The Fender Benders
GS: Jackie Coogan. Carol gets into a traffic accident in a parking lot with a man who plans to fake an injury so he can collect the insurance money.

My Fair Opponent
Marcia turns a plain-looking girlfriend into a real beauty.

Hawaii Bound [Part 1]
The Bradys take a trip to Hawaii, where Bobby finds a bad-luck Tiki.

Pass the Tabu [Part 2]
GS: Don Ho. Bad luck seems to follow whoever wears Bobby's Tiki.

The Tiki Caves [Part 3]
GS: Vincent Price. An eccentric archeologist holds the boys prisoner until they show him where they found that Tiki.

Today I Am a Freshman
Marcia tries to be popular in her new school by joining every club in the school.

Cyrano De Brady
Peter asks for Greg's help in trying to get a date with a girl he has a crush on.

Fright Night
The boys try to frighten their sisters with homemade ghosts.

Career Fever
Greg decides that he doesn't want to be an architect like his father.

Law and Disorder
Bobby becomes power-crazed when he is appointed school safety monitor.

Jan the Only Child
Jan wants to be left alone, but with a big family it seems impossible.

The Show Must Go On
The Bradys prepare to perform at the high school talent show.

You Can't Win Them All
Bobby and Cindy enter a competition where the winners will appear on a TV quiz program.

Goodbye, Alice Hello
Alice leaves home when the kids give her the cold shoulder treatment.

Love and the Older Man
Marcia has a crush on the family dentist.

Everybody Can't Be George Washington
Peter gets the part of Benedict Arnold in the school play, and everyone now calls him a traitor.

Greg's Triangle
Greg has to decide between his girlfriend and his sister when he has to choose the new school cheerleader.

Boby's Hero
GS: Burt Mustin. Carol and Mike try to discourage Bobby from thinking that his hero, Jesse James, was a great man.

Great Earring Caper
The family tries to find Carol's favorite earrings.

Greg Gets Grounded
Greg gets grounded for staying out too late.

The Subject Was Noses
Marcia breaks a date to go out with her high school sweetheart, but then she gets hit in the face and suffers a swollen nose.

How to Succeed in Business
Peter gets his first job and then proceeds to lose it.

Amateur Nite
The Brady kids appear on a local TV show so that they could use the prize money to pay for their parent's anniversary present.

You're Never Too Old
The family tries to get Alice a boyfriend.

Room at the Top
A fight breaks out after both Greg and Marcia decide to move into the attic.

Snow White and the Seven Bradys
The Bradys put on a benefit show to raise money for a teacher's retirement gift.

Mail Order Hero
GS: Joe Namath. Bobby claims that he knows Joe Namath and now all of his friends want him to prove it.

The Elopement
The Bradys are convinced that Alice and Sam are going to elope.

Adios Johnny Bravo
Greg is selected to become a new singing star by a talent scout.

Never Too Young
Bobby's girlfriend tells him that she might have the mumps, which makes him regret his kissing her.

Peter and the Wolf
Greg helps Peter prepare for his date with an older woman.

Getting Greg's Goat
Greg tries to hide a rival school's mascot, a goat, in his room.

The Cincinnati Kids
Jan loses her father's blueprints in an amusement park in Cincinnati.

Quarterback Sneak
GS: Denny Miller. A football player from the rival team dates unsuspecting Marcia so he can get a chance to steal Greg's football playbook.

Marcia Gets Creamed
GS: Henry Corden, Michael Gray. Marcia gets Peter a job working with her at the local ice cream parlor, but when he takes advantage of her she fires him.

My Brother's Keeper
Bobby saves Peter's life and turns him into his slave when Peter pledges eternal loyalty.

Try, Try Again
Jan is trying to find something she is good at, but she finds that there is nothing she hasn't tried at which she is a success.

Kelly's Kids
GS: Ken Berry, Brooke Bundy. The Brady's friends set out to adopt one little boy, but wind up with three of all different races. [This was a pilot for a series that didn't sell.]

The Driver's Seat
Marcia bets Greg that she will beat his score on the driver's license test.

Miss Popularity
Jan is trying to win a school popularity contest.

Out of This World
GS: Frank and Sadie Delfino. Peter and Bobby sight a UFO in their backyard.

Two Petes in a Pod
Peter finds that his new classmate is his exact double, which he plans to use to his advantage.

Welcome Aboard
GS: Robbie Rist. Carol's nephew Oliver comes to stay with the family, but finds that he doesn't seem to fit in with the other kids.

The Snooper-Star
Marcia tries to teach Cindy a lesson when she reads Marcia's diary.

The Hustler
GS: Jim Backus. Bobby gives up all his other activities to play with their new pool table.

Top Secret
When the FBI visits Mike, Bobby is convinced his father is a spy.

The Hairbrained Scheme
Bobby sells Greg a bottle of hair tonic that turns his hair orange.

BRINGING UP BUDDY

On the air 10/10/60, off 9/25/61. CBS. 34 episodes. B&W film. Broadcast: Oct 1960-Sept 1961 Mon 8:30-9. Producer: Joe Connelly and Bob Mosher. Prod Co: Revue. Synd: MCA/Universal TV.
   CAST: Aunt Violet Flower (played by Enid Markey), Aunt Iris Flower (Doro Merande), Buddy Flower (Frank Aletter).
   The story of a single investment broker who lives with his two maiden aunts. The aunts are a bit nutty and are always trying to find Buddy a wife. The series hasn't been seen since the early 1960s, but is still available for syndication. The series was based on the comic strip of the same name.

The Girl Next Door
GS: Diane Foster, John Holland. Aunt Violet and Aunt Iris think it would be nice for Buddy to marry his childhood sweetheart Gloria Monahan.

Girls in Court
GS: George Neise, Bill Giorgio. Violet and Iris go shopping, but they come back with a lawsuit. A passenger on the bus mistook their mop handle for the handrail.

Cesare Comes Calling
GS: Robert Weede, Robert Curtis. An Italian baritone named Cesare looks up his old friends the Flower sisters in order to con them into giving him money so he can revive his failing career.

The Blind Date
GS: Joanne Linville. Buddy agrees to date Angela Brent, the daughter of an important client.

Nephew for Sale
GS: Christin White, Valerie Allen. Buddy's aunts put an ad in the newspaper offering him as a good husband. Buddy objects, until he sees who answers the ad.

Gentlemen Callers
GS: Percy Helton, Harry Shannon. Violet and Iris decide to set an example for Buddy by dating swingers.

Buddy's Birthday
GS: George Neise, Yvonne Lime. Buddy's friend Jay Fuller plans a surprise party for him.

Poppa's Eagle
GS: Paul Smith, Yvonne Lime, George Neise. Buddy redecorates his office in Swedish Modern. Everyone but Buddy hates it.

The Exchange Student
GS: Danielle De Metz, Douglas Dumbrille. Violet and Iris take a French exchange student into their home.

Repair of Robespierre
GS: Helen Spring. Buddy tries to get Violet and Iris to give their old car, Robespierre, an overhaul.

Call Me Charlie
GS: Bill Lechner, Dennis Holmes. Buddy tries to brighten up a young orphan's life.

Buddy's Transfer
GS: Joanna Barnes. Buddy is offered a job in a New York investment firm.

The Singer
GS: Joan O'Brien, Irene Ryan. Buddy is trapped in an elevator with a night club singer.

Cousin Jordan
GS: Reginald Denny, Sally Hughes. Cousin Jordan tries to talk Buddy into helping him create the Bottle of the Month Club.

The Girls Rent a House
GS: Eduardo Ciannelli, Dee Carroll. Violet and Iris try to rent their grandfather's old house.

The Education of Nicky Marlo
GS: Portland Mason, Jimmy Hawkins, Frank Albertson, Francine York. A 12-year-old girl beatnik comes for a visit.

The Painting
GS: Joe Devlin, Dick Reeves. Buddy sells the junk in the garage, including Cousin Margo's portrait.

Selling Shingles
GS: John Hoyt, Tommy Farrell. Violet and Iris try to earn money to help a needy sick man and his wife.

Buddy Hires a Maid
GS: Bettylou Gerson, Laurie Mitchell. Buddy hires a maid to help his aunts with the housework.

Cynthia's Boyfriend
GS: Irene Ryan, George Chandler. Cynthia says she is getting married to a man she met on a bus.

Buddy's Wife
GS: Gloria Talbott, Jackie Russell, Rory Stevens. The aunts get a call from a girl who claims to be Buddy's wife.

Poppa's Memoirs
GS: Adele Mara, Frank Albertson, Henry Hunter. A writer arrives to write a book about the aunts' famous father.

Buddy and Fennimore
GS: Jimmy Hawkins. The aunts arrange a date for visiting Fennimore Cooper.

Buddy and the Amazon
GS: Lee Merriwether. The aunts try to fix Buddy up with a nurse.

Poppa's Picture
GS: Patrick Houston, John Holland, Burt Mustin. Buddy's grandfather left his portrait to the local museum, which is now a museum of modern art.

Auntie's Cake
GS: Joyce Meadows, Phillip Ober, Arte Johnson. The aunts are asked to endorse a frozen cake mix.

The Aunts Have a Baby
GS: Nancy Rennick, Joan Staley. A baby is found in the back seat of the aunts' car.

Cynthia's Concert Tour
GS: Irene Ryan, Marcel Dalio. Cynthia's voice teacher signs her for a concert tour.

Buddy's Re-Enlistment
GS: Harry Carey Jr., Robert Foulk. Violet and Iris think Buddy is rejoining the Army.

Big Game Hunter
GS: Edgar Buchanan. The aunts hire a phony hunter to entertain at the Women's League show.

Buddy and Janis
GS: Sherry Jackson, Charles Watts. A teenage orphan who is staying with the aunts falls for Buddy.

Room for Rent
GS: Audrey Dalton, Burt Mustin. The aunts rent a room to a pair of twins.

Buddy and the Teenager
GS: Cheryl Holdridge, Frank and Grace Albertson. Buddy agrees to teach night classes at an all-girl college.

Behind Bars
The aunts try to prune an old tree with disastrous results.

Couple Next Door
GS: Leslie Parrish, Joe Flynn. Buddy tries to help the woman next door who has a jealous husband.

Working Girls
[This episode was never aired. No story exists.]

THE BURNS AND ALLEN SHOW

On the air 10/12/50, off 9/22/58. CBS. B&W film. 130 syndicated episodes. 239 episodes made. Broadcast: Oct 1950-Mar 1953 Thu 8-8:30; Mar 1953-Sept 1958 Mon 8-8:30. Producer: Fred DeCordova. Prod Co: Screen Gems. Synd: Columbia Pictures TV.

CAST: George Burns, Gracie Allen, Ronnie Burns, Harry Von Zell (played by themselves), Blanche Morton (Bea Benaderet), Harry Morton (Larry Keating), Mr. Beasley (Rolfe Sedan), Bonnie Sue McAfee (Judi Meredith).

The adventures of George Burns, his nutty wife Gracie, and their neighbors, the Mortons. The average episode would always have Gracie causing trouble for everyone when she confuses every situation she encounters. The series was a big hit in the 1950s until Gracie retired. George tried to continue the series without her and with the same cast under the title *The George Burns Show*, but it didn't even last one season on the air. The series was a big hit in syndication, but it has become dated due to the age of the series.

George Burns and Gracie Allen

[Every episode was written by Harvey Helm, Keith Fowler, Norman Paul and William Burns.]

Wardrobe Woman Wins Free Trip to Hawaii
Gracie tries to make a match between Harry Von Zell and a wardrobe woman, unaware that she is already married.

Gracie Giving Party for Atomic Scientist
Gracie plans a dinner for a French physicist.

George Sneezing—Gracie Thinks He's Insane
George practices sneezing for a TV show and Gracie picks up his sneezing habit.

Gracie Buying Boat for George
Gracie gets Harry Von Zell to buy a boat for George.

Gracie Having George's Portrait Painted
Gracie plans to have George's portrait painted for his birthday present.

Gracie and Blanche Hire Two Gigolos to Take Them Out
The girls hire gigolos to take them to a nightclub.

Sampter Clayton Ballet—Selling Tickets
Gracie tries to get George to sponsor a ballet.

Skating Pearsons Come to Visit
George and Gracie's old vaudeville friends ask them to help keep their son out of show business.

Gracie Selling Swamp So Harry Will Buy TV Set
Gracie helps the Mortons sell their swamp.

Silky Thompson—Gracie Writes—My Life with George Burns
Gracie makes up a story about George once being a gangster.

Gracie Thinks George Is Going to Commit Suicide
Gracie thinks George is going to kill himself.

Von Zell Dates Married Woman—Jealous Husband
Everyone thinks Harry Von Zell is fooling around with a married woman.

Uncle Clyde Comes to Visit—Renting Room
Gracie's mooching uncle plans to move in with them.

Gracie Thinks Harry Morton Is in Love With Her
Gracie gets the idea that Harry has fallen for her.

Gracie Trying to Keep Mortons from Moving Away
Gracie learns that Harry is planning to move to a house a mile away from where they now are living.

Gracie Thinks She's Not Married to George
GS: Jack Benny. Jack tries to convince Gracie that her marriage to George is legal.

Tax Refund
Gracie wants to use her canary as a dependent on her income tax form.

Cigarette Girl—Georgie Jessel—Teddy Bear
Gracie is suspicious of a man named George who gave a fifty dollar tip to the girl who sold him a teddy bear at a restaurant.

Gracie on Train—Murder
Gracie thinks that there has been a murder committed on the train she is riding.

Blanche Wants New Car—Gracie Gets Von Zell a Wife
Gracie tries to get Harry Von Zell a wife so he can save money on his income taxes.

Gracie Gives a Swamp Party
Gracie throws an auction party to help sell the Morton's swamp.

George and Gracie Hear a Burglar—Up All Night
Gracie hears footsteps and suspects a burglar is on the loose.

Gracie Buying a Ranch for George
Gracie buys a ranch for George and he tries to get her to believe that he isn't well enough to enjoy the outdoor life on a ranch.

Gracie Gets George in the Army
Gracie tries to get George drafted into the Army.

Gracie Reports Car Stolen
Gracie has the police look for her stolen car.

Gracie Pretends to Be College Boy's Mother
Gracie pretends to be a boy's mother so he can invite his girlfriend and her parents to her home for tea.

Misunderstanding Over Buying Mountain Cabin
Gracie thinks George is buying a cabin without using Harry as his real estate agent.

Blanche Secretly Buys a Fur Stole
Blanche buys a mink and hides it from Harry at Gracie's house.

Gracie Takes Spanish Lessons
Gracie takes Spanish lessons to improve her IQ.

Gracie and Cleaning Woman—Vanderlips
Gracie tries to help her new cleaning woman.

Von Zell's Girlfriend Between Trains
Harry Von Zell gets into trouble with his new girlfriend.

George Lectures at UCLA
George is the guest speaker at UCLA.

Gracie and Harry Morton—Missing Persons Bureau
When Harry misses his lunch with Gracie, she thinks he was kidnapped.

Surprise Party for Mortons—Sanitarium Routine
Gracie mistakes Harry's surprise party for George's party.

Perry and Pete—Gracie's Cousins—Sneak Thieves
Gracie believes the story two thieves told her when they broke in.

Gracie Doing a Picture Without George
Gracie leaves George out of their next film when she thinks she can do it alone.

Gracie Trying to Get George to Go on Trip East
Gracie wants to take the Mortons with them on their trip to New York.

Gracie Sees a Hold-Up—Johnny Velvet
Gracie goes to court to be a witness to a bank robbery.

Gracie and George Locked Out of Their Home
George and Gracie locked themselves out of the house and can't get back in.

Gracie at Department Store
Gracie trips and falls in a department store.

Morton Buys Iron Deer—Gracie Thinks George Needs Glasses
Harry buys an iron deer to give class to his front lawn.

Gracie Helps Morton Get CPA Account
Gracie tries to make Harry into a playboy in order to get an important account.

Gracie Gets a Jury Summons
George tries to get Gracie out of jury duty.

George Teaches Gracie Not to Be Careless
George tries to teach Gracie about safety.

George and Harry Morton Mad at Each Other
Gracie gets George to become mad at the Mortons.

Gracie Getting a Business Manager—Roger
George accuses Gracie of spending too much money.

Raccoon Coat Story
Gracie gets Harry Von Zell into trouble with a widow and a raccoon coat.

Gracie Thinks Harry Von Zell Is Broke
Gracie thinks that Harry Von Zell hasn't any money when she sees him borrow some money from George.

Gracie Trades Home for Mountain Cabin
Gracie trades their house for an old cabin when she thinks George plans to retire.

George and Gracie Going to Rose Marie Premiere
Gracie gets ready to leave for a movie premiere and then realizes she gave away the tickets.

Jane (Wardrobe Woman) and Her Problem
Gracie tries to help the wardrobe woman solve her problem.

Gracie's Anniversary Present
Gracie thinks that George is planning on buying her a plane for an anniversary gift.

Uncle Harvey's Invention
Gracie's uncle invents a chemical which will cause plants to become giants.

George Reading Play to Be Done in London
Gracie starts packing when she thinks that they are going to London.

Gracie Helps Mechanic with Girlfriend
Gracie tries to show her mechanic's

actor-loving girlfriend that living with George is not all that easy.

Gracie Discovers George's Secret Weakness
Gracie tries to discover George's secret vice.

Gracie Has to Sell George's Car by Five O'Clock
Gracie tries to sell her car.

Gracie Wins a Television Set
Gracie tries to claim the television set she would have won if she answered the quiz question that the radio show host asked her before he hung up.

No Fan Mail for George
Gracie gets Blanche to write George a fan letter using another name, in order to get George out of his depression about not getting any fan letters.

George and Gracie Going to Opera "Carmen"
George and Gracie go to the opera.

Harry Morton Is Missing
Gracie, George and Blanche try to find Harry when he turns up missing.

Gracie Goes to Psychiatrist for Blanche's Dream
Gracie consults a psychiatrist in order to help Blanche understand her dream.

Gracie's Old Boyfriend, Dan Conroy, Comes to Town
Gracie's old boyfriend and the basketball team that he coaches come for a visit.

Gracie Tries to Get George in College
Gracie tries to get George enrolled at UCLA.

Columbia Pictures Doing Burns and Allen Story
When it is announced that their life story will become a movie, all of their friends try to be in it.

An Elephant Sits on Gracie's Fender
An elephant sits on her car while she was watching the circus tents go up and now she has to explain it to the insurance company.

George Gets Black Eye from Open Door
George finds that he has to explain how he got his black eye to just about everyone.

Dolores De Marco, George's Ex-Vaudeville Partner
Gracie becomes jealous of George's ex-partner.

Vanderlip Buys Black Negligee for His Wife
Gracie thinks her banker is fooling around so she tells him that his wife is also fooling around.

Gracie and George Have a Mystery Anniversary
Gracie mistakes the gift that Harry Von Zell left at the house as a gift from George for an anniversary she has forgotten about.

George Resting for Insurance Examination
George tries to rest up for a medical examination.

Harry Morton Has Only One Week to Live
Gracie thinks Harry Morton is dying.

Gracie Buys Old Movies to Sell to Television
Gracie buys some old movies for George to distribute when a fortune teller informs her it is a good day for him to do business.

Emily Vanderlip's Elopement
Gracie tries to get her banker's daughter to elope with her boyfriend.

Gracie Runs for City Council
Gracie decides to run for political office.

Burnses and Mortons Choosing Movie to Attend
George, Gracie and the Mortons try to find a movie none of them has seen.

Gracie Buys a Toaster Wholesale
Gracie creates her own financial plan to save money when George tells her he can get her a toaster wholesale.

Mortons Exchange Houses with the Gibsons From New York
Gracie arranges for her friends to move into the Mortons' house and the Mortons to move into her friend's house in New York.

George Teaches Gracie Not to Start Rumors
Gracie makes up a story about how much George won gambling.

George Invites Critics to Watch First Show of Season
George invites reporters to the house to watch the first episode of their TV show.

Gracie Goes to the Do It Yourself Show
Gracie makes a mess of the Do It Yourself Show.

Gracie Gives Wedding in Payment of a Favor
Gracie wishes to give a wedding party for a friend's daughter as payment for the favor her friend did for her.

Gracie Gives a Baby Shower for Virginia Measely
Gracie gives a baby shower for the mailman's daughter.

Auto License Bureau—George Becomes an Author
Gracie goes to apply for a driver's license

George Trying to Keep Doctor's Appointment
GS: Rolfe Sedan. George starts his car and then goes back to the house for his coat, causing both Harrys and the mailman to wonder what happened to him.

Gracie Thinks She and George Moving to New York
Gracie thinks they are moving to New York.

Shoplifter and the Missing Ruby Clip
Gracie sees a shoplifter put a piece of jewelry in Mrs. Vanderlip's purse, causing her to think she is helping the shoplifter.

Gracie Saves Blanche's Marriage
Gracie thinks Blanche is trying to hide the fact that she is going to meet another man who is in love with her.

Burnses and Mortons Going to Hear Antonelli Concert
George tries to get Gracie interested in a puzzle so she will forget about the concert she wants them to go to.

George Gets Call from Unknown Visitor About Him.
Gracie forgets part of an important telephone message for George, and now he is trying to figure out just who called.

Harry Morton's Alumni Banquet
Gracie goes to an all-men's lounge club, uninvited.

Gracie Thinks Bob Cummings Is in Love With Her
GS: Robert Cummings. Gracie thinks that Bob Cummings has fallen for her.

George's Mother-in-Law Trouble
George invites Gracie's mother to visit them when he thinks Gracie is upset.

George and the Glendale Eagle Publicity Stunt
George pretends to hurt his ankle so he won't have to appear in Gracie's publicity stunt.

No Seats for Friar's Club Dinner
Gracie tries to get seats for her friends at the Friar's dinner.

Blanche and Clara Bagley Leave Their Husbands
Blanche and Clara move in with Gracie

when they leave their husbands.

Gracie Gets a Valet for George
Gracie gets George a valet to help him dress right.

Vanderlip Leaves His Parakeet with George
George agrees to watch Mr. Vanderlip's bird, but regrets it when Gracie sets it free.

Blanche's Brother, Roger the Moocher, Visits
Gracie tries to get a job at an aircraft company.

George and the Missing Five Dollars, and Missing Baby Pictures
George has problems with a baldheaded lawyer, disappearing baby pictures, and a missing five dollar bill.

Gracie Becomes a Portrait Artist After Museum Visit
Gracie thinks she can paint abstracts just as good as the ones in the museum.

George and the Fourteen Karat Gold Trombone
George gives a trombine player fifty dollars after he hears his sad story.

The Romance of Harry Morton and Countess Braganni
Gracie saves Harry from a man-hungry countess.

The Mistaken Marriage of Emily Vanderlip and Roger
Gracie tries to get Emily and Roger married off.

Gracie Adopts Great Dane Dog
Gracie hides a Great Dane puppy for little Joey Bagley in her guest room.

Gracie Tries to Select George's Next Wife
Gracie goes to a matrimonial agency to find George another wife to replace her when she is gone.

Gracie Gets a Ticket Fixed by the Judge
Gracie gets into a fight with a judge who won't fix her parking ticket.

Gracie Hires a Safe Cracker for Her Wall Safe
Gracie buys George a wall safe and locks the combination inside it for safe keeping.

Gracie Consults Dr. Kirby's Problem Clinic
Gracie consults a marriage counselor about her friend's problem of unintended bigamy.

Gracie Wants the House Painted
George refuses to paint the house so Gracie divides the house in half and has her half painted.

Gracie Plays Talent Scout for Imitator
Gracie invites a talented grocery delivery boy to perform his impressions on a benefit show with her and George.

Gracie and George Try for a Day at the Beach
George has an appointment with a man who lives in a beach house and Gracie invites her friends to go along to use the beach while they are there.

The Uranium Caper
Gracie plans to help George dig uranium at the biggest uranium mine on the West Coast.

Blanche and Brother Roger Move in With the Burnses
Gracie thinks Blanche is going to divorce Harry.

Gracie Believes George Has a Criminal Record
Gracie finds a picture of George in a prison uniform and thinks he was in jail.

Gracie Gets an Extension Visa for Jeannette Duval
Gracie tries to help her French friend extend her visa.

Gracie Tries to Cure Roger of Amnesia
Gracie fakes a case of amnesia.

Lucille Vanderlip Gives a Barbecue Party
Gracie gives George the wrong directions to the location of the party.

Burnses and Mortons Going to Hawaii
George, Gracie, and the Mortons sail to Hawaii when they learn that Blanche's brother wants to spend the summer with them.

Burnses Going to New York
On the way to New York, Gracie plays cards with the professor George planned to use for publicity, while George finds he has been talking to a salesman and not the professor as he thought.

Ronnie Arrives
George and Gracie are surprised when their son Ronnie visits them in New York.

Ronnie Meets Sabrina
George and Gracie try to talk Ronnie out of dating an older woman.

Changing Names
Ronnie plans to change his name when he becomes an actor.

Harry Morton's Cocktail Party
Gracie takes a job in a book store in order to push George's book.

The Musical Version
George and the cast sing and dance to popular musical hits.

Gracie Helps Lola
Gracie helps a waitress who has had a fight with her boyfriend.

Anniversary Party
Gracie ruins her anniversary dinner by trying to help an artist and his wife get back together.

George Becomes a Dictator
George helps Ronnie get a job on a comedy show, but later gets him out of it so he can perform in a dramatic show instead.

Ronnie's Elopement
Gracie thinks Ronnie is planning to elope with a salesgirl.

Company for Christmas
Gracie poses as a maid in order to get the pest in the hotel to move out so an old couple can use it for their second honeymoon.

Gracie Pawns Her Ring
Gracie pawns her diamond ring to raise money to back Ronnie's friend's play.

Appearances Are Deceiving
Gracie tries to cool off an overprotective father who caught Ronnie kissing his daughter.

Let's Dance
Gracie sells tickets to every man in the hotel by promising them that they will be the one who takes the beautiful cigarette girl to the dance.

George Goes Skiing
George takes up skiing in order to share his son's interest.

Ronnie Gets an Agent
GS: Jack Benny. Gracie gives a high society dinner party, Ronnie has trouble with his agent, and George finds four acrobats in his living room.

Politeness Never Pays
Gracie hires a gigolo to show George how she would like to be treated.

Alice Gets Married
Harry Von Zell asks Gracie to save him from his girlfriend who he thinks is coming to New York to marry him.

George Needs Glasses
Gracie thinks George needs glasses, but she sends Harry Von Zell for the eye test so she can surprise George with his new glasses.

The Indian Potentate
Gracie dresses up as a harem girl to meet an Indian Maharajah.

The Ladies Club
Gracie is considered for membership in a fancy ladies club.

Cyrano De Bergerac
GS: Jose Ferrer. Ronnie studies Jose Ferrer's readings of Cyrano for his drama class.

The Stolen Plants
Gracie goes to jail when she takes flowers from Central Park to put in her hotel room.

The English Playwright
Gracie claims she is a widow to get Ronnie a part in a British playwright's new play.

A Week-End on Long Island
Gracie arranges a surprise party, but doesn't invite George.

The Newlyweds
Gracie helps a chaperone to a newlywed couple who has a sweetheart in the same hotel get some time off.

Night of Vaudeville
George puts on a vaudeville show to raise money for Ronnie's acting school.

Burlesque
Gracie enters burlesque to keep an eye on Ronnie who has also entered burlesque in search of more experience on the stage.

The Right People
Gracie thinks that Ronnie and his girl-friend are planning to get married.

The Magic Act
Gracie joins a magic act and confuses the magician.

A Paris Creation
George and Gracie go to Paris. She tells George that she plans to alter an expensive dress, and George wants her to have the designer do it.

Back from Paris
Gracie buys dozens of dresses as souvenirs of her trip to Paris.

The 24 Dresses
Gracie plans to open a dress shop with the dresses she bought in Paris.

Ronnie Is Lovesick
Gracie tries to cure Ronnie's lovesickness by getting him interested in another girl.

The Night Out
A hatcheck girl returns George's coat. Unaware that Harry Von Zell borrowed it, Gracie thinks George is fooling around.

The Triple Surprise Party
George tries to keep a secret from Gracie that Blanche is planning to give a surprise party for Harry, in George's apartment, by telling her the party is for Ronnie.

Questions and Answers
Gracie prepares to answer a literary quiz which will allow her to qualify for admission to a ladies' club.

Mrs. Sohmers Needs a Psychologist
A psychiatrist tries to psychoanalyze Gracie and almost loses his mind.

The Switchboard Operator
Blanche and Gracie take over the switchboard for the afternoon in order to stop a call from coming through.

Return to California
Ronnie lets his friends from USC use the house while George and Gracie are in New York, however they have returned two weeks earlier than they were supposed to.

The Shakespeare Paper
GS: Dr. Frank C. Baxter. A noted authority on Shakespeare comes to the Burns's home.

The Woman in the Car
Gracie is being labeled as the other woman in a love triangle.

The Interview
GS: Dan Jenkins. A reporter from TV Guide comes to do a story on Geroge and Gracie.

Ronnie's Initiation
Ronnie joins a fraternity.

Ronnie's Bashful
Gracie thinks Ronnie is staying home because he is too bashful to ask for a date.

The Missing Stamp
Gracie uses one of Harry's valuable stamps to mail a letter.

George's Blue Tweed Suit
Gracie makes up a story to explain George's missing suit.

Von Zell's Raises
Harry Von Zell makes up a story about getting married in order to get a raise from George, only Gracie believes the story and prepares for the wedding.

The Refrigerator Salesman
Ronnie gets a job selling electric razors in a department store during Christmas. Gracie tries to help him by buying a few razors.

The Girl Behind the Perfume Counter
Gracie tries to fix the girl who works behind the perfume counter up with a date.

Ronnie Quits College Because His Father Is Broke
Gracie tries to convince Ronnie that going to college is necessary.

Christmas in Jail
George is identified as a swindler and may have to spend Christmas in jail.

The Costume Party
George unknowingly throws out the guests of honor at a costume party.

Gracie and the Bullfighter
Gracie and George try to share Ronnie's hobbies. They regret their decision when Ronnie takes up bullfighting.

The Ugly Duckling
Gracie tries to help an unattractive girl become beautiful.

The Aptitude Test
George takes an aptitude test when Gracie feels he isn't cut out for show business.

Going to Palm Springs
Gracie tries to trick George into taking her to Palm Springs by getting a fake doctor to tell him it will be good for his health.

The Matrimonial Bureau
Gracie goes to a matrimonial agency to find Ronnie a wife.

The Fortune Teller
Gracie goes on a buying trip when a fortune teller informs her that George is about to come into a lot of money.

Fighting for Happiness
Gracie tries to start a fight with George to save her marriage.

The Termites
Gracie invents a story about termites so she can get George out of the house long enough to redecorate.

$15,000 Error
Gracie's error might cost George $15,000.

The Ring
Gracie tells George that she lost her ring down the sink.

The Plumber's Friend
Blanche finds herself having a phone conversation with Miss Livingstone for no apparent reason.

Going to Houston
The Burns family goes to Texas to keep one of Ronnie's classmates in college.

The Stray Dog
Gracie finds a stray poodle and tries to bring it back to her hotel room where dogs are not allowed.

Ronnie Gets a Movie Role
Ronnie has to attend classes in the afternoon while shooting a movie in the morning.

The Plumber's Union
Gracie tries to fix up her plumber, a widower with four daughters, with a girl.

Harry Returns Early (Harry's Homecoming)
George and Harry plan to teach their wives a lesson they will never forget.

The Publicity Tour
Ronnie's fiancee won't believe that his love affair with an Italian actress is a publicity stunt.

The Texan Lady MacBeth
One of Ronnie's friends asks Gracie to convince his sister that show business is not for her.

Ronnie's Boat
Gracie tries to help Ronnie explain his new expensive boat.

A Trip to Tahiti
GS: Bob Ellis. Ronnie and his friend plan to sail to Tahiti on his new boat.

The Home Graduation
A friend of Ronnie's asks Gracie for help.

Blanche's Mother Arrives
Gracie helps out when Blanche's mother pays a visit.

A Marital Mix-Up
Gracie once again tries to help her plumber find a wife.

Wading Pool at Acapulco
George and Gracie take a trip to Mexico.

A Pain in the Back
George suffers from back trouble.

Ronnie's Twenty-One
Ronnie celebrates his 21st birthday.

The General
Gracie tries to keep a young couple's marriage a secret from the boy's military father.

Too Much Pot Roast
Four Miss Universe contestants make an appearance on George and Gracie's show.

The Texan Italian
Gracie plans to turn a girl from Texas into an Italian actress.

An English Tea
Gracie tries to impress the British mother of Ronnie's girlfriend.

September and May
GS: Howard McNear. Gracie's plumber is accused of dating a very young girl.

The Starmaker
Gracie helps a college student pass a test.

The African Hunter
Ronnie wants to bring his girl home to meet George and Gracie at the same time that George has an African witch doctor in the house.

One Little Fight
Ronnie and his friend Ralph accuse each other of stealing each other's girlfriend.

With or Without Glasses
Gracie tries to help a failing college student.

Box of Cigars
Ronnie and his friends campaign for the Homecoming Queen. Gracie gives him the idea of giving away cigars to get votes.

Misery Loves Company
Gracie gets everyone to pretend they are as miserable as Ralph, who just lost his girl, in order to cheer him up.

The Hole in the Carpet
Gracie sues a department store over a damage in her new carpet.

The Old Mink Coat
Gracie and Blanche try to find the Christmas presents George and Harry have bought for them.

Invitation to the Party
Gracie invites the Mortons to go with them to a society party on New Year's Eve.

The Stolen Car
Gracie tries to get Ronnie a job on the school paper by creating a story about her car getting stolen.

Ronnie Finds a Friend an Apartment
Ronnie tries to find an apartment for one of his friends.

McAffee and the Manicurist
Harry Von Zell helps Gracie bring two people together.

Too Many Fathers
Gracie and George pose as the parents of one of Ronnie's friends.

The Accident
Gracie and Harry get into a traffic accident.

The Japanese Texan
Gracie tries to help a girl from Texas get the part of a Japanese girl in a movie.

Hypnotizing Gracie
Gracie winds up with a different personality after she sees a hypnotist.

Gracie Is Brilliant
Gracie is now a mental giant, thanks to that hypnotist.

Ronnie's Fan Club
Ronnie has a date with a member of his fan club.

Frozen Passion
Ronnie and his fiancee read in the paper that Ronnie is married.

High Blood Pressure
Gracie schedules George for a medical examination, just when he wants to play golf.

Softening the Professor
Ronnie's teacher gets married.

The Publicity Marriage
GS: Judi Meredith.   Ronnie reads about his marriage in the newspapers.

Blanche Gets a Jury Notice
Harry wants to make sure that he is free of Blanche for a month, so he calls the judge to make sure she is accepted on the jury.

Gracie and the Jury
Gracie ruins the trial of a counterfeiter,

Ronnie Makes a Record
Gracie tries to help Ronnie when he is about to make his first record.

Ronnie's Royalty Check
When Ronnie gets his first royalty check for $160, Gracie is worried about his ability to manage money.

A Visit from Charles Vidor
GS: Charles Vidor. Gracie and Blanche plan to get Ronnie's girlfriend from Texas a part in Vidor's new film.

Ronnie Goes Into the Army
Gracie tries to prevent Ronnie from being drafted.

Locked Out
Gracie loses the house key on the eve of a big dinner party.

A Week in New York
Gracie and Blanche plan to trick

George and Harry into taking them back to New York.

June Wedding
George and Gracie invite a newlywed couple to spend their honeymoon at their house in Beverly Hills.

Summer School
George ruins Ronnie's vacation when he makes him go to summer school in order to raise his grades.

Grammar School Dance
Gracie is asked to help another college student pass an exam.

The Exchange Student
A foreign student comes to live at the Burns's house.

CAMP RUNAMUCK

On the air 9/17/65, off 9/2/66. NBC. 26 episodes. Color film. Broadcast: Sept 1965-Sept 1966 Fri 7:30-8. Producer: David Swift. Prod Co: Screen Gems. Synd: Columbia Pictures TV.

CAST: Spiffy (played by Dave Ketchum), Wivenhoe (Arch Johnson), Mahala May Gruenecker (Alice Nunn), Pruett (Dave Madden), Doc (Leonard Stone), Caprice (Nina Wayne), Eulalia Divine (Hermione Baddeley), Malden (Mike Wagner), Sheriff (George Dunn).

The adventures of the campers and counselors of two summer camps, Camp Runamuck for boys and Camp Divine for girls, each one in constant competition with the other. The episodes depict the rivalry between the two camps and the trouble the kids cause to the staff. The series has not been rerun since it went off the air, but it is still available.

Camp Runamuck [Pilot]
W: David Swift. D: David Swift. GS: Hermione Baddeley. The girls at Camp Divine want Commander Wivenhoe's bathtub, so they bribe the camp's staff with an endless supply of food in return for the tub.

Rabbits of the World, Unite
W: David Swift. D: David Swift. GS: Forest Lewis. In order to join a country club, Wivenhoe must agree to appear along with Doc, Spiffy and Pruett in Camp Divine's version of Alice in Wonderland.

Fraternize
W: David Swift. D: Robert Rosenbaum. GS: Frederic Downs, Frances Rey. Wivenhoe forbids all contact between Camp Runamuck and Camp Divine, but Doc disobeys the order in order to help a patient.

I'm in Luv with Your Beautiful Limpid Eyes But I Can't Marry You Be- *cause You're a Cow*
W: David Swift. D: David Swift. GS: Maidie Norman, Ralph Roberts, Lindy Davis. The staff buys a cow so they can have meat for dinner, but can't bring themselves to slaughter it.

"Say, You're a Bleeder, Aren't You?" Tom Asked Cuttingly
W: David Swift. D: Hal March. Wivenhoe's in bed with a cold; Doc tries to help, but all he causes is trouble so he leaves the camp.

They're Not Making Hurricanes Like They Used To!
W: David Swift. D: Howard Duff. GS: Charles Seel. The camp prepares for an impending hurricane. Little does the staff know the hurricane is in India.

Turtle???
W: Sid Mandel & Bob Rodgers. D: Robert Rosenbaum. GS: Jeanne Arnold, Robert Q. Lewis, Eddie Rosson,

Michael St. Clair. The camp's pet turtle dies, much to the dismay of Wivenhoe who hired an expensive photographer to take photos of happy campers for his new brochure.

Slaughter
W: David Swift. D: David Swift. A rainy day confines the staff to their tents to read, where they daydream about the books they were reading.

Parent's Day
W: David Swift. D: David Swift. GS: Virginia Gregg. Rain washes out Parent's Day, so Wivenhoe sends the kids to the movies and tries to prevent the staff from playing poker.

Masquerade
W: Bob Rodgers & Sid Mandel. D: Howard Duff. In order to pass inspection, the counselors of both camps dress up as the opposite sex to fulfill the necessary quota of counselors.

Spiffy Quits [Part 1]
W: Bob Rodgers & Sid Mandel. D: David Swift; GS: Edward Everett Horton, Reginald Owen. Spiffy, tired of taking abuse from the rest of the staff, packs his bags and leaves.

Spiffy Quits [Part 2]
W: David Swift. D: David Swift. GS: Edward Everett Horton, Reginald Owen. Spiffy, realizing he had an exciting life and not wanting to spend his life in an office, returns to the camp.

Soapsuds
W: Bob Rodgers & Sid Mandel. D: Robert Rosenbaum. GS: George Dunn, Hollis Morrison, Carol Anderson. The staff of Camp Divine trick the staff of Camp Runamuck into cleaning up their camp. When the boys find out the truth, they proceed to wreck the camp.

The New Swimming Pool
W: Bob Rodgers & Sid Mandel. D: Robert Rosenbaum. GS: Beverly Adams, George Dunn. The staff builds a new swimming pool, but because of a local water shortage they must find another way to fill the pool.

Wivenhoe's New Car
W: Bob Rodgers & Sid Mandel. D: Howard Duff. GS: William Benedict, Mason Curry, Sarah Selby, Chet Stratton, Eddie Rosson. Wivenhoe reluctantly agrees to take accident-prone Norton home while on the way to get his new car.

Tomboy
W: Ann Marcus. D: Hal March. GS: Maureen McCormick, Laurence Haddon, Lindsey Workman, Anne Bellamy. Tomboy Maureen Sullivan would rather stay at the boys' camp, until Spiffy finds a way to discourage her.

Look Out Here Comes Arnie
W: Bob Rodgers & Sid Mandel. D: Howard Duff. GS: Michael Jackson. Wivenhoe hires America's top camper to make the counselors the best in the country. Much to the dismay of the counselors, Arnie turns out to be a tyrant.

Diet
W: Bob Rodgers & Sid Mandel. D: Robert Rosenbaum. In order to get into shape, the staff goes on a diet but they soon wish they hadn't.

Air Conditioner
W: Bob Rodgers & Sid Mandel. D; Robert Rosenbaum. GS: Gil Lamb. During a heat wave, Pruett's mother sends him an air conditioner, causing fights among the staff.

Food Poisoning
W: Bob Rodgers & Sid Mandel. D: Howard Duff. GS: Joe Yore. Practical jokes on the Camp Divine staff backfire when Spiffy believes he has eaten toadstools and asks the girls for help.

Building
W: David Swift. D: Robert Rosenbaum. The girls once again trick the

boys into doing work for them. This time to build them a cottage.

Termites
W: Bob Rodgers & Sid Mandel. D: Charles T. Barton. GS: Ned Glass. The camp is infested with termites, so Spiffy and Caprice proceed to get rid of them.

Peace
W: Bob Rodgers & Sid Mandel. D: Howard Duff. GS: Henry Corden, Hollis Morrison. Spiffy has a vision of peace so he convinces the staff to offer tokens of friendship to the girls.

Malden Falls in Love
W: William Freedman & Ben Gershman. D: David Butler. GS: Joanie Larson, Monty Margetts. Malden falls in love with a fortune-hunting woman,

so he passes himself off as the commander of the camp.

Senior Citizens
W: Bob Rodgers & Sid Mandel. D: Howard Duff. GS: Peter Leeds, Whit Bissell, Dick Balduzzi, Burt Mustin, Lillian Bronson, Thomas Jackson. Wivenhoe opens up the camp to senior citizens for three weeks, only to learn a freeway is to be built through the camp.

Commander for a Day
W: William Freedman & Ben Gershman. D: Bruce Bilson. GS: Michael Shea, Jackie Jones, Bobby Moran. Wivenhoe makes a camper the commander for a day, but regrets it when he and the staff are locked in a cage.

CAPTAIN NICE

On the air 1/9/67, off 8/28/67. NBC. 30 minutes. Color film. 15 episodes. Broadcast: Jan 1967-Aug 1967 Mon 8:30-9. Producer: Buck Henry. Prod. Co: Talent Artists. Synd: National Telefilm.

CAST: Carter Nash [Captain Nice] (played by William Daniels), Mrs. Nash (Alice Ghostley), Sgt. Candy Kane (Ann Prentiss), Mayor Finney (Liam Dunn), Chief Segal (William Zuckert), Mr. Nash (Byron Foulger).

WRITERS: Arne Sultan, Bruce Shelly, Dave Ketchum, Buck Henry, Treva Silverman, Peter Meyerson. DIRECTORS: Jud Taylor, Richard Kinon, Gene Reynolds.

Slapstick comedy involving the exploits of Carter Nash, a mild-mannered police chemist who discovers Super-Juice, a liquid that transforms him into crime fighter Captain Nice. Along for the ride is Carter's mother who is constantly nagging her superhero son into rescuing victims and fighting criminals. *Captain Nice* is not in syndication in the United States but is regarded as a cult series by many science fiction and comedy enthusiasts.

The Man Who Flies Like a Pigeon [Pilot]
GS: Arthur Malet, Kelton Garwood. While working in the lab, police chemist Carter Nash invents a liquid that gives him super powers, so he then decides to dedicate his life to fighting evil.

How Sheik Can You Get
GS: Larry D. Mann. A visiting sheik

plans to add Candy Kane to his harem.

That Thing
GS: Johnny Haymer, Frank Maxwell. A caterpillar accidentally drinks Carter's secret formula turning it into a monster, which even defeats Carter until he decides to give the secret formula to his parakeet Sheldon.

William Daniels as Captain Nice

That Was the Bridge That Was
GS: Edward Binns, Phil Roth, Sabrina Scharf. A phony bridge builder kidnaps the mayor, sending Carter to the rescue.

The Man with Three Blue Eyes
GS: John Dehner, Florence Halop. A crook dies before revealing where he hid two million dollars, so the mayor hires a psychic to contact the deceased and locate the money.

Is Big Town Burning?
GS: Vic Tayback, Gene Reynolds. Carter witnesses a landlord set fire to his own building. Before he can testify, the man threatens to reveal his identity if he talks.

Don't Take Any Wooden Indians
GS: Joe Flynn, Joseph Perry. Anthropologist returning from an expedition plans to kill the man who financed his trip.

That's What Mothers Are For
GS: Felice Orlandi. After Carter and most of the police department are fired, Carter's mother decides to steal a diamond to show that the police are needed.

Whatever Lola Wants
GS: Barbara Stuart, Jack Perkins. Carter discovers that the music from a bar across the street from the city jail is a front to cover up the digging sounds made by some prisoners tunneling their way out.

Who's Afraid of Amanda Woolf
GS: John Fiedler, Madlyn Rhue. The wife of a syndicate boss volunteers to testify against her husband, but really intends to retrieve the book of syndicate names which Carter is holding.

The Week They Stole Payday
GS: Pat Harrington, Victor French. A gang hijacks an armored car and steals the city's payroll and kidnaps Candy and Carter's mother.

It Tastes OK But Something's Missing
GS: Simon Oakland, Dick Curtis. Carter is missing one ingredient in his formula but can't get it. So he tries to find a substitute.

May I Have the Last Dance
GS: Marlyn Mason. Candy portrays a dance instructor in order to catch some fur thieves.

One Rotten Apple
GS: Bob Newhart. When the owner of a nightclub chain feels someone is out to get him, he asks for protection. So Candy poses as a waitress.

Beware of Hidden Prophets
GS: John Dehner, Joseph Campanella. Carter finds a tablecloth which is covered with the escape plans of an art thief. Carter now plans to trap the thief when he returns to recover the plans.

CAR 54 WHERE ARE YOU?

On the air 9/17/61, off 9/8/63. NBC. 30 minutes. B&W film. 60 episodes. Broadcast: Sept 1961-Sept 1963 Sun 8:30-9. Producer: Nat Hiken. Prod Co: NBC Films. Synd: National Telefilm.

CAST: Officer Gunther Toody (played by Joe E. Ross), Officer Francis Muldoon (Fred Gwynne), Lucille Toody (Bea Pons), Captain Martin Black (Paul Reed), Officer Leo Schnauser (Al Lewis), Officer Anderson (Nipsey Russell), Sylvia Schnauser (Charlotte Rae).

DIRECTORS: Nat Hiken, Stanley Prager.

This situation comedy was set in the 53rd police precinct on Tremont Avenue in the Bronx, New York. It was concerned with the escapades of two bumbling policemen named Gunther Toody and Francis Muldoon in police car Number 54. Star Fred Gwynne and co-star Al Lewis later went on to star together in the popular series *The Munsters* a few years later.

Who's For Swordfish
GS: Al Henderson, Sybil Lamb. Toody and Muldoon have to decide between writing traffic tickets or going fishing on a yacht.

Something Nice for Sol
GS: Gerald Hiken. Sgt. Abrams has been on the force for 25 years, so Toody and Muldoon decide to get him a good gift for a man with flat feet: orthopedic shoes.

Home Sweet Sing Sing
GS: Gene Baylos. Toody and Muldoon try to help an ex-con go straight.

Change Your Partner
After the press praises Gunther and Francis' harmonious relationship, the two men have a fight.

I Won't Go
GS: Molly Picon, Matt Crowley. A woman refuses to leave a condemned building, leaving Toody and Muldoon to find her a new place to live.

Muldoon's Star
GS: Nancy Donohue, Lisa Loughlin. Toody and Muldoon are assigned to protect a movie star from her fans, including Francis.

Paint Job
GS: Al Nelson. While getting their patrol car repaired, Toody and Muldoon uncover a stolen car-painting ring.

Love Finds Muldoon
GS: Alice Ghostley. Lucille fixes Francis up with a woman who ignores him because he reminds her of her old boyfriend.

The Gypsy Curse
GS: Maureen Stapleton. A gypsy puts a curse on Toody, which he believes in, causing him to drive the other officers crazy with his superstitions.

Thirty Days' Notice
GS: Henry Lascoe, Michael Vale, Ralph Stantley. Toody wants to move out of his rundown building.

Catch Me on the Paar Show
GS: Hugh Downs, Mickey Deems, Larry Storch. Toody convinces his friend Charlie to appear on Jack Paar's show, but Toody is the one who becomes the hit of the show.

The Taming of Lucille
GS: Martha Greenhouse, Carl Ballantine. Gunther and his wife decide to act out the play Taming of the Shrew

in real life.

Put It in the Bank
GS: James Dukas, Gilbert Mack. Toody invests Precinct Brotherhood Club's funds in the stock market.

Get Well, Officer Schnauser
Leo hurts his foot and has to go to the hospital. Muldoon is mistaken for a holdup man when he goes to the bank to withdraw some money to help Leo.

Christmas at the 53rd
GS: Alice Ghostley, Carl Ballantine. The police hold their annual Christmas party where everyone sings and toasts each other.

The Sacrifice
Toody feels that Muldoon has sacrificed a promotion to detective in order to be able to stay with him, so he decides to help build up Muldoon's confidence.

Boom, Boom, Boom
GS: Jan Murray. Toody and Muldoon practice their introduction song for the barbershop quartet contest where Jan Murray will be the judge.

Toody and Muldoon Crack Down
GS: Jake LaMotta, Laurence Fletcher. An inspector finds Toody and Muldoon's beat has gross violations.

Toody's Paradise
GS: Elizabeth Fraser, Paul O'Keefe. Toody is assigned to catch a purse snatcher in Brooklyn Park. He is joined by a policewoman and a little boy, causing his friends to think he is leading a secret life.

How High Is Up?
GS: Shari Lewis. Muldoon is worried that he is too tall for police requirements.

Toody and the Art World
GS: Severn Darden, Sheppard Strudwick. Toody and Muldoon must evict an artist in a loft, but in the process become impressed with his paintings.

What Happened to Thursday?
GS: Martha Greenhouse. Leo has a fight with his wife every Thursday night, so Toody and Muldoon convince him that it is actually Friday and not Thursday, causing everyone at the station to become confused.

How Smart Can You Get
GS: Bobby Morse. A rookie graduate from Harvard joins Toody and Muldoon on patrol.

Today I Am a Man
GS: Bob Hastings. Muldoon goes to a nightclub and spends the evening with a girl in order to prove he isn't shy.

No More Pickpockets
GS: Wally Cox, Billy Sands. Toody arrests a pickpocket who steals his wallet and starts arresting other pickpockets, pretending he is a cop.

The Beast Who Walked The Bronx
While their regular captain goes on vacation, a timid captain takes over. The men, however, mistakenly believe the new captain is a tyrant.

The Courtship of Sylvia Schnauser
After plans are made to hold a real wedding ceremony for Leo and his wife of 15 years, they once again run off to City Hall to get married.

The Auction
GS: Jack Healy, Louise Kirtland. The officers at the precinct buy a rare old chair for Captain Block's 25th anniversary at an auction, only to learn that it was the chair the Captain's wife threw away.

Quiet! We're Thinking
GS: Paul O'Keefe, Frank Campanella. A little boy knowingly helps Toody and Muldoon solve a string of robberies.

I Love Lucille
GS: Phil Leeds, Florence Henderson. Lucille becomes a blonde to attract Gunther's attention.

Hail to the Chief
GS: Simon Oakland. Toody and Muldoon are chosen to drive President Kennedy to the United Nations.

One Sleepy People
Gunther and Lucille are convinced that Gunther is having an affair.

A Man Is Not an Ox
GS: Ned Wertimer. A police psychologist decides to examine Toody and Muldoon to figure out why they do everything alike.

Schnauser's Last Ride
GS: Dan Morgan. Leo's old horse Sally has taken up a life of crime, visiting crap games and bookie joints.

Toody and Muldoon Sing Along with Mitch
GS: Mitch Miller, George S. Irving. A quartet made up of Gunther, Francis, Leo and Officer Wallace is scheduled to appear on Mitch Miller's TV show.

Occupancy August First
GS: Charles Nelson Reilly, Molly Picon. Mrs. Bronson moves into an unfinished building claiming her lease is good.

Remember St. Petersburg
GS: Larry Storch, Fay De Witt. A crooked medium mistakes Sylvia Schnauser for the wife of a count.

That's Show Business
GS: Larry Storch, David Hurst. A play written about police brutality causes violent reactions at the station.

Toody Undercover
GS: Bruce Gordon, Barnard Hughes. Toody goes undercover to capture a famous gangster.

I Hate Captain Block
GS: Patricia Bright, Heywood Broun, Barbara Long. Captain Block leaves his pet bird with Toody. When he returns from his vacation he finds the bird repeating the words, I Hate Captain Block.

A Star Is Born in the Bronx
GS: David Doyle, Kenny Delmar. Sylvia goes on a diet so she can get the leading role in Muldoon's play for the Police Brotherhood club.

Pretzel Mary
GS: Larry Storch, Bernie Allen. Toody and Muldoon, feeling sorry for an old pretzel vendor, sell her old furniture to replace it with new furniture. They were unaware that the old lady had stashed a lot of money in the furniture for safekeeping.

142 Tickets on the Aisle
GS: Bernie West, Parker McCormick. After seeing Toody and Muldoon leaving a theater, people assume the play is going to be closed for obscenity, causing a rush to buy tickets.

Stop Thief
GS: Alan Manson. Toody and Muldoon suspect Captain Block of being a kleptomaniac when they see him hiding Christmas presents.

Je T'Adore Muldoon
GS: Jean Stapleton. Muldoon is turned into a Don Juan by Toody and the Captain.

The White Elephant
GS: Arlene Golonka, Jake LaMotta, Eugene Troobnick. The three owners of a new restaurant are actually crooks drilling into the bank next door.

Benny the Bookie's Last Chance
GS: Margaret Hamilton, Gene Baylos. Benny the Bookie opens a store, but gets in debt over his head.

The Presidential Itch
Gunther runs against Francis for the head of the Brotherhood.

Toody and Muldoon Meet the Russians
Toody and Muldoon are ordered to guard two Russians who are out to stop capitalism.

Here We Go Again
GS: Conrad Nagel. Crooks pull off a crime by using the information they found in Muldoon's father's diary.

The Star Boarder
GS: Tom Bosley, Dana Elcar. Gunther takes in a boarder to help pay for a piano, unaware that he is a counterfeiter.

The Biggest Day of the Year
GS: Jimmy Little. Toody and Muldoon celebrate ten years together at a ballroom party.

Here Comes Charlie
GS: Larry Storch, Margaret Hamilton, Ossie Davis. Toody and Muldoon try to help the town drunk.

See You at the Bar Mitzvah
GS: B.S. Pully, Gerald Hiken, Claude Gersene. A young boy becomes depressed when no one wishes to attend his Bar Mitzvah.

I've Been Here Before
GS: Jake LaMotta, Dort Clark. Toody has to solve the crimes committed by a gang of crooks who are imitating the TV show Crimebusters.

Joan Crawford Didn't Say No
GS: Molly Picon, Jacob Kalish. Mrs. Bronson begins matchmaking by using Hollywood stars as her matches.

Lucille is 40
GS: Jimmy Little, Elizabeth Eustis. A blonde wig causes a mixup that threatens Gunther's marriage.

The Loves of Sylvia Schnauser
GS: Charles Nelson Reilly, David Doyle, Joe De Santis. Sylvia is taken in by a con artist who promises to make her rich.

Puncher and Judy
GS: Rocky Graziano, Sugar Ray Robinson, Shari Lewis. A timid hairdresser wants to become a prizefighter.

The Curse of the Snitkins
GS: Jack Gilford, Bruce Kirby, Phil Carter. Muldoon and Toody are assigned a new partner, a genuine jinx.

CARTER COUNTRY

On the air 9/15/77, off 8/23/79. ABC. 44 episodes. Color videotape. Broadcast: Sept 1977-Mar 1978 Thu 9:30-10; May 1978-Aug 1978 Tue 9:30-10; Sept 1978 Sat 8-8:30; Oct 1978-Jan 1979 Sat 8:30-9; Mar 1979-Aug 1979 Thu 9:30-10. Producer: Bud Yorkin. Prod Co: Toy Productions. Synd: Columbia Pictures TV.

CAST: Chief Roy Mobey (played by Victor French), Curtis Baker (Kene Holliday), Mayor Teddy Burnside (Richard Paul), Jasper (Harvey Vernon), Harley (Guich Koock), Cloris (Barbara Cason), Lucille (Vernee Watson).

The adventures of a Southern sheriff and his New York-born black deputy in a small Georgia town. The series was created to cash in on the presidency of Jimmy Carter. The series didn't last more than two seasons on the air, probably due to the limited viewing audience in all but the South. Despite its small number of episodes, the series does turn up on some rural stations.

[Every episode was directed by Peter Baldwin (except where noted).]

Hail to the Chief
W: Douglas Arango & Phil Doran. D: Bud Yorkin. Mayor Teddy wants a token black on the platform when Jimmy Carter comes to town.

Beating the Pounds
W: Al Gordon & Jack Mendelsohn. Roy is in a bad mood when the man he arrested for wife beating is out and he finds himself on suspension, charged with brutality, and helplessly overweight.

Out of the Closet
W: Phil Doran & Douglas Arango. GS: Richard Jaeckel. Roy is shocked when his old friend Bill admits that he is gay.

Fireside Burnside Budget Chat
W: George Bloom. The mayor's announcement that he'll cut the budget means that Roy has to find a way to cut his budget even further.

Baker Buys a House [Part 1]
W: Al Gordon & Jack Mendelsohn. Roy talks Baker into buying a house with his insurance money, but his white neighbors are giving him a rough time.

Baker Buys a House [Part 2]
W: Al Gordon & Jack Mendelsohn.

Jasper is suspected when someone defaces Baker's front door.

Bye, Bye, Baker
W: Kevin Hartigan & David Garber. Baker applies for a better job then finds himself up against Roy for the same job.

Senior Citizen Siege
W: Kevin Hartigan & David Garber. Two desperate old people hold the mayor hostage in his office while Roy handles the negotiating.

Chicks and Turkeys
W: David Pollock & Elias Davis. Baker decides to cook his own turkey when Lucille cancels their Thanksgiving date at the last moment.

Chief to Chief
W: Sheldon Bull. The annual softball game between the fire and police departments causes big rivalry with Roy who is dreaming of winning this year.

Union vs. the Confederacy
W: Sheldon Bull. Teddy hires a professional to protect him from Roy's bullying for pay raises for his staff.

A-Hunting We Will Go
W: Guy Thomas. When Roy is shot in a hunting accident, the mayor becomes the chief suspect.

By the Light of the Moonlight
W: Al Gordon & Jack Mendelsohn. The chief moonlights only to find himself working for Baker.

The Physical
W: Bruce Kalish & Phillip Taylor. An insurance physical indicates that Baker might have a lung disease.

Roy's Separation
W: David Pollock & Elias Davis. Roy leaves his wife and moves into a swinging singles apartment.

Red Armstrong, Goodbye
W: Douglas Arango & Phil Doran. Roy turns the annual police show into a benefit for a dying police chief and Baker refuses to take part.

Ballots for Burnside
W: Tom Moore & Jeremy Stevens. The discovery of an unopened ballot box threatens to replace Teddy with a black mayor.

Chief's Dressing Down
W: Mort Scharfman & Harvey Weitzman. The mayor's mother picks Roy to play a chorus girl in the ladies auxiliary show.

All About Floyd
W: Ann Gibbs & Joel Kimmel. Baker urges Roy to hire another black cop.

Roy Pays His Taxes
W: Phil Doran & Douglas Arango. Roy is upset with Baker when the IRS decides to audit his return which Baker helped him prepare.

Roy's Encounter
W: Alan Eisenstock & Larry Mintz. Roy believes that he saw a flying saucer.

Baker Saves a Life
W: Harvey Weitzman & Mort Scharfman. Thinking that Baker saved his life, Jasper reforms his redneck ways.

One of Our Chiefs Is Missing
W: Austin & Irma Kalish. Roy, enroute to Atlanta with a prisoner, disappears.

The Tracy Report
W: Harvey Weitzman & Mort Scharfman. GS: Melanie Griffith. A cub reporter is following Roy who finds himself interrogating a dead suspect.

The Selling of the Mayor [Part 1]
W: Phil Doran & Douglas Arango. Mayor Teddy is up for re-election and everybody in City Hall is expected to help him win, but when he pushes Roy too far his campaign hits a snag.

The Selling of the Mayor [Part 2]
W: Phil Doran & Douglas Arango. When Teddy is caught in a vice raid, it looks as though Roy will be the new mayor.

Poor Butterfly
W: Marty Brill & Barry Meadow. GS: Nedra Volz, William Lanteau. An endangered butterfly brings an intruder into Baker's love life.

Gamblers Unanimous
W: Mark Fink. Roy and Baker have a big all-or-nothing bet on a local football game, but the mayor assigns them to official duty on the day of the game.

Roy Makes the Grade
W: Huskell Barkin. Roy is picked as alumnus of the year by the local high school, but it could cost him his job because Teddy wanted the honor for himself.

Hurricane Jasper
W: Martin Rips & Joseph Staretski. Weekend soldier Jasper takes charge when a hurricane moves into the town.

Owed to Billy Joe
W: Mike Baser & Kim Weiskopf. Roy finds that a cop who accepts gifts can easily be a cop on the take.

The Russians Are Coming
W: David Braff & Nick Thiel. Cloris arrests a Russian ballet troupe with a prima ballerina who wants to defect only to Roy.

Happy Anniversary, Roy
W: Bruce Kalish & Phil Taylor. The Clinton Corners police department has a surprise for Roy who has a group encounter session planned for them.

Teddy the Tiger
W: Phil Doran & Douglas Arango. Sick of being bullied, Teddy decks Roy with one punch but Roy refuses to fight back.

New Kid in Town
W: Austin & Irma Kalish. GS: Kyle Richards. A runaway girl blames Roy for the death of her father in prison.

Baker's First Day
W: Mort Scharfman & Harvey Weitzman. GS: Jack Carter, John Brandon. Baker tries to run Chief Roy's department with New York methods.

The Last Dinosaur
W: David Balkan. GS: Patrick Campbell, Hugh Gillin. When a burglar outruns him, Roy thinks he is over the hill and plans to retire.

The Big Move [Part 1]
W: Mark Fink. Lucille has marital expectations when she moves in with Baker, but he doesn't agree.

The Big Move [Part 2]
W: Mark Fink. GS: June Christopher. Roy asks wild Wanda to give Baker a bachelor party he will never forget, but Lucille shows up by surprise.

The Big Move [Part 3]
W: Mark Fink. GS: Candy Mobley. On their wedding day, Lucille and Baker start having second thoughts after he locks himself in the bank's vault by accident.

Teddy's Folly
W: Phil Doran & Douglas Arango. GS: Marla Adams. In order to impress his golddigging fiancee, Teddy invests in an amusement park which sinks into a swamp.

The Prisoner of Clinton Corners
W: Mort Scharfman & Harvey Weitzman. GS: Kyle Richards, Danny Wells. Roy goes to jail when he refuses to pay alimony to his ex-wife because she's living with a guy.

The Firing of a Harley
W: Saul Turtletaub & Bernie Orenstein. Roy becomes an outcast for firing the popular Harley Puckett.

The Abominable Showman
W: Mort Scharfman & Harvey Weitzman. GS: Sid Gould, Amzie Strickland. It is the annual pension show; Roy wants to do a burlesque skit but Teddy wants to do an old Civil War play instead.

CHICO AND THE MAN

On the air 9/13/74, off 7/21/78. NBC. Color videotape. 88 episodes. Broadcast: Sept 1974-Jan 1976 Fri 8:30-9; Jan 1976-Mar 1976 Wed 9-9:30; Apr 1976-Aug 1976 Wed 9:30-10; Aug 1976-Feb 1978 Fri 8:30-9; Jun 1978-Jul 1978 Fri 8:30-9. Producer: James Komack. Prod Co & Synd: Warner Bros. TV.
CAST: Ed Brown (played by Jack Albertson), Chico Rodriguez (Freddie Prinze), Louie Wilson (Scatman Crothers), Rev. Bemis (Ronny Graham), Della Rogers (Della Reese), Raul Garcia (Gabriel Melgar), Aunt Charo (Charo).
Theme: Chico and the Man by Jose Feliciano.

Freddie Prinze (left) and Jack Albertson as Chico and the Man.

The story of a grouchy old man who runs a garage and the young Chicano who comes to work for him. The series was a big success during its original run on the networks. However, the series has all but died in syndication even though it is still run all over the country. This is due to the death of Freddie Prinze during the series. What makes matters worse is now that Jack Albertson has also died, the series is in worse trouble. Within a few years, the show will probably disappear from the air completely.

Pilot Episode
Chico tries to persuade Ed to give him a job in the garage.

Borrowed Trouble
Chico tries to persuade Ed to take out a loan and improve the garage.

The Manuel Who Came to Dinner
GS: Danny Nunez. The irate Chicano owner of a car towed into the garage turns out to be a former friend of Ed's.

No Room in the Garage
When a Spanish-speaking pregnant girl arrives at the garage, Ed assumes that Chico is the father of her child.

Natural Causes
GS: Shirley O'Hara. After he hears about the death of an old acquaintance, Ed becomes convinced that his own days are numbered.

Second Thoughts
Ed is trying desperately to get rid of Chico.

Old Dog
Ed becomes convinced that he has lost his touch as a mechanic.

New Suit
Ed refuses to attend his old army reunion.

E. Pluribus Used Car
Chico dreams of going into the used car business when Louie gives him and Ed his car to sell for him.

Life Style
Ed gets the wrong idea about what Chico and his girlfriend were doing in the back of Chico's van.

The Veterans
Veterans Chico and Ed try to get financial aid from the government.

The Letter
GS: Bonnie Boland. Chico decides to go into business with his cousin in New York.

Garage Sale
Ed holds a garage sale after the new inspector says he must clean up the place or get a fine.

Ed Steps Out
GS: Shelley Winters. A widow buys a bakery down the street from the garage and soon finds herself sweet on Ed.

Out of Sight
Ed insists on testifying in court as a witness to a car accident, despite his failing eyesight.

The Beard
GS: Jim Backus. A philandering husband depends on Ed to cover for him on his nights out.

If I Were a Rich Man
Chico has fallen head over heels in love and Ed is trying to turn him right side up.

Sammy Stops In
GS: Sammy Davis, Jr. Sammy awes everyone but Ed when he brings his car to the garage to be serviced.

Long Live the Man
Ed is depressed. Everyone thought he had died and he is convinced that nobody mourned for him.

The Doctor Story
Ed's shoulder hurts, but he would rather use a homemade remedy than see a doctor.

The Giveaway
Chico is suddenly keeping strange hours and is carrying a large amount of cash.

Louie's Retirement
Louie plans to spend his retirement hanging around the garage.

The Hallowed Garage
City officials plan to tear down the garage to make way for a power station.

Chico and the Van
A city official claims Chico's van is illegal, so he moves in with Ed.

Play Gypsy
GS: Avery Schreiber. A gypsy wants Ed to teach him to be a mechanic.

Auntie Connie
Ed falls in love with Chico's Aunt Connie.

The Paint Job
Ed and Chico have a fight over the alley wall Ed contributed to an art contest.

The Juror
GS: Jack Bernardi. Chico finds that the defendant in the case he is a juror on is a friend of Ed's.

The Misfortune Teller
GS: Avery Schreiber, Ronny Graham. Ed tries to find a way of saving the garage from foreclosure by seeing a fortune teller.

The Strike
Chico joins the mechanic's union and is forced to picket the garage.

The Disappearance
Chico is afraid that Ed is spending too much time remembering the past.

Mister Butterfly
GS: George Takei. A Japanese man claims to be Ed's son.

Ms. Liz
Chico falls in love. He now plans to get married and leave the garage.

Bird in a Gilded Cage
GS: Carmel Myers. Ed is upset when his favorite silent screen actress becomes a waitress.

The Big Brush-Off
GS: Irene DeBari, Tony Orlando. Chico falls in love with a girl who won't go out with him because he looks like her ex-fiance.

The Invention
Ed and Chico are cheated out of $500 when they try to patent Ed's invention: motorcycle training wheels.

The Dream
GS: Shirley Kirkes. Chico tries to convince Ed into retiring and going to a senior-citizen home.

The Hypnotist
GS: Carole Cook. Chico hypnotizes Ed into marrying Flora.

Reverend Bemis's Altar Ego
After Chico makes a guest sermon at Bemis's church, the parishioners find that they want Chico and not Bemis to lead them.

The Accident
After Chico's accident, Ed borrows money on his insurance to send him to school.

Chico's Cousin Pepe
GS: Jose Feliciano. Chico's blind, women-chasing, singing cousin visits. [The title song is sung in this episode.]

Return of Aunt Connie
GS: Cesare Danova. Chico and Ed decide that Connie's new boyfriend is a con artist.

Too Many Crooks
GS: Joey Bishop. Ed gives a handout to a bumbling crook, then every crook in the neighborhood comes to Ed for money.

The Face Job
Ed is offered a free face lift, which almost destroys his social life.

Chico Packs His Bags
GS: Dee Dee Sescher. Chico decides to leave the garage rather than give in to Ed's demands.

Della Moves In [Part 1]
Ed is threatened with eviction by his new landlady.

Second Coming of Della [Part 2]
When Ed gives up the fight and becomes a recluse, Della gives in and renews his lease.

Ed Brown vs. the IRS
Ed refuses to pay his taxes, so Chico and Louie forge his name to the form.

Chico's Problem
Chico's girlfriend decides to give up nursing, but after saving Ed's life Chico changes her mind.

Ed's Recuperation
The nurse that Ed hired is only interested in marriage, so it is up to Chico and Della to discourage her.

In Your Hat
Ed refuses to have necessary surgery unless he finds his lucky hat which was stolen.

Old Is Old
GS: Jim Jordan, Charles Lane. Ed hires a senior citizen to work in the garage.

Mucho Macho Ed
GS: Maria O'Brien. Ed plans to marry the woman who claims Ed is the father of her unborn child.

The Dress
GS: Charles Pierce. Ed is upset when

he donates his late wife's dress to a charity auction and it is bought by a female impersonator.

Minority of One
GS: Nono Arsu. Ed is elected President of the Better Barrio Business Bureau.

Morgan and the Man
GS: Rose Portillo, Jill Wood. When Chico proposes to an old high school classmate, she refuses.

Champs Ain't Chumps
GS: Milton Frome, Chuck Bergansky. Ed worries when Chico considers becoming a professional fighter.

Chico's Padre
GS: Cesar Romero. Chico's long-lost rich father, Gilberto, returns to give him a better life.

Ready When You Are, CB
Ed spends New Year's Eve on the CB with a CBer named Kissy Face.

Black Tie Blues
GS: Rosey Grier. Ed, Chico and Louie all find ways out of taking Della to a formal dance.

Matchmaker, Matchmaker
When Ed finds out that his meeting with his new girlfriend was set up by Della, he breaks off the relationship.

Ed Talks to God
GS: Edward Andrews. Chico tries to change Ed's mind about not attending his own birthday party by having Ed's old friend impersonate God.

Louie's Can Can
GS: George Gobel. Louie is forced to retire, so he opens his own garbage business and hires Ed as a driver.

Gregory Peck Is a Rooster
GS: Pat Buttram. Ed tries to get his pet rooster back from a cockfighting promoter he sold it to.

Uncle Sonny
GS: Lisa Mordente. While Ed's away his wild Uncle Sonny throws an all-girl party.

Who's Been Sleeping in My Car?
Ed returns from Mexico with an 11-year-old boy who is determined to stay with him.

Su Casa, Mi Casa?
Ed waits for word from Raul's parents, only to learn he is an orphan.

Take Me, I'm Yours
GS: Barbara Sharma. A social worker comes to take Raul away, so Ed adopts him.

The Third Letter
GS: Rodolfo Hoyos. Ed needs a third letter of reference in order to adopt Raul.

The Bed
Raul trades Ed's bed for a new one, unaware that he had $700 stuffed in the mattress.

Della and Son
Della convinces her son Tony to stay and join her in the catering business.

A Matter of Privacy
Ed tries to teach Raul the meaning of privacy, but the lesson backfires when Ed opens a package belonging to Raul.

Ed the Hero
In a class composition, Raul writes that Ed fixes poor people's cars for free. Ed is then besieged by the poor people in the neighborhood.

The Hot Rock
Ed is trying to collect money from the insurance company in order to invest in Louie's new invention: a solar barbecue.

Ed's Team
Ed sponsors a basketball team so Raul can play on it.

The Proposal
Ed and Della get drunk at a holiday dinner and Ed proposes to her.

Aunt Charo
GS: Charo. Raul's aunt comes to take him back to Spain with her.

Raul Runs Away [Part 1]
When Raul finds out about the first Chico, he runs away back to Mexico.

Raul Runs Away [Part 2]
GS: Robert Hegyes. Ed goes to Mexico to bring Raul back.

The Americanization of Charo
GS: Charo. Aunt Charo becomes an American citizen.

Charo and the Matador
Charo's fiance Antonio, a matador, comes to America to marry her.

A New Girl in Town
Monica comes to live in the garage.

Waiting for Chongo
A motorcycle gang comes to the garage.

Help Wanted
Monica gets a job at a low-class restaurant, causing Ed to become upset.

Buenas Dias, Mr. President
The President is coming to visit Ed's garage and it is making him a nervous wreck.

Ed Brown's Car Wash
Monica opens an all-girl car wash in the garage.

The Peeping Tom
Ed is accused of being a Peeping Tom.

COLONEL FLACK

On the air 1958, off 1959. 38 episodes. B&W film. Synd. Broadcast: Varied depending on the station running the show. Producer: Unknown. Prod. Co: Jody Pam Prod. Synd: Viacom.

CAST: Col. Humphrey Flack (played by Alan Mowbray), Uthas P. Garvey (Frank Jenks).

The story of two men, Humphrey Flack, a retired colonel and his sidekick, Uthas P. Garvey. The two travel throughout the world searching out the truly needy citizens and offer to help them acquire possessions or other items. The two act as modern day Robin Hoods in their actions. Although available for syndication since 1958, no one has run the old series for over a decade. The series was originally aired live in 1953-1954 over the Dumont network. Then in 1958 this film version was syndicated across the country.

Back to the Coal Mines
The lure of mining stock and a need for cash draws Col. Flack into the fight for a controlling interest in a mine.

Big Wheels
Col. Flack and Garvey are stranded in a French village with no means of returning to the US.

The Blackmailer
A curator of a museum is being black-mailed by an employee, so Col. Flack searches for the missing party.

Colonel Cupid
Col. Flack and Garvey pose as two wealthy business tycoons in order to obtain some money.

Col. Flack and the Gangster
Col. Flack and Garvey pose as big-time gangsters.

Col. Flack to the Rescue
A beautiful blonde on the run from foreign spies seeks refuge in the Colonel's hotel room.

The Diamond Ring
When Col. Flack sees a beautiful girl switch diamonds in a jewelry shop, he sets out to catch her.

The Emperor's Snuff Box
The Colonel and Garvey meet a pretty museum directress who has been selling Aztec relics to tourists.

Flack and the Maharajah
The Colonel uncovers trouble in an electric fan factory.

The Friendship Club
Flack attempts to get information on a phony lonely hearts agency.

The Hypnotist
A crooked fight manager is floored by the Colonel's hypnotic gaze.

In Flack We Trust
Col. Flack attempts to help a political dandidate.

The Producers
Col. Flack disguises himself as a Hollywood producer to help some new young actors get a break.

The Star Maker
A young singer falls prey to a phony agent, causing the Colonel to come to her rescue.

The Tycoon
Col. Flack and Garvey pose as two different people.

The Bank Teller
Col. Flack goes out on a ledge to prevent an embezzling bank teller from committing suicide.

Col. Flack Gets Kilt
Col. Flack poses Garvey as a missing Scotsman in order to solve a case.

Col. Flack's Big Deal
Col. Flack and Garvey find that they cannot pay their Las Vegas hotel bill.

The Formula
Col. Flack tries to prevent a scientist's formula from falling into the wrong hands.

The Real Estate Caper
Col. Flack tangles with two real estate swindlers.

Saddle Sore
Col. Flack and Garvey rent a suite at a dude ranch. They soon discover that the groom assigned to them is being held a prisoner at the ranch. Their decision to help him puts them in great danger.

Something for the Birds
A rich old birdwatcher witnesses a crime. The accused man's fiancee gets Col. Flack to investigate the validity of the charges.

[The stories for the remaining episodes were unavailable.]

Lady Bluebeard
The Treasure Hunt
Up From the Apes
West of the Weirdos
Surplus
Spaceship Ahoy
Pearls of Wisdom
Lo, the Etruscans
Follow the Bouncing Meatball
Garviola the Matador
The Happy Medium
A Horse of Another Color
Col. Flack's New Muffler
Col. Flack and the Little Leaguers
Col. Flack and the Counterfeiter
Col. Flack and the Dragon.

THE COURTSHIP OF EDDIE'S FATHER

On the air 9/11/69, off 6/14/72. ABC. Color. 30 min. 73 episodes. Broadcast: Sept 1969-Sept 1970 Wed 8-8:30; Sept 1970-Sept 1971 Wed 7:30-8; Sept 1971-Jan 1972 Wed 8:30-9; Jan 1972-Jun 1972 Wed 8-8:30. Producer: James Komack. Prod Co & Synd: MGM TV.

CAST: Tom Corbett (played by Bill Bixby), Eddie Corbett (Brandon Cruz), Mrs. Livingston (Miyoshi Umeki), Norman Tinker (James Komack), Tina Rickles (Kristina Holland).

Theme: "Best Friend" by Harry Nilsson.

The series revolved around widower Tom Corbett, the editor of a magazine, and his six-year-old son Eddie. Tom and Eddie have a unique relationship built on trust, who seek each other's help whenever either has a problem. Most episodes depict Eddie's attempts to find his father a wife, or the pain of growing up. The series is seen on relatively few stations because it is more of an adult drama than a children's comedy.

Mrs. Livingston, I Presume
Mrs. Livingston quits because she is afraid that if she stays she will be destroying Tom's chances of remarrying.

Teacher's Pet
GS: Ruth McDevitt. A retired school teacher unknowingly alienates Eddie from his father.

And Eddie Makes Three
GS: Diana Muldaur. Tom's new girlfriend wonders if she can be a good mother to Eddie.

The Computer
GS: Sabrina Scharf. Tom tries computer dating.

Pain
GS: Ann Richards, Ron Ely. It is Eddie's first day at school and he doesn't want to go.

Guess Who's Coming for Lunch
GS: Cicely Tyson, James Cole. A blind date for Tom teaches him a lesson in human relations.

Bully for You
GS: Jody Foster, Dave Ketchum. Eddie is having trouble with a bully.

Gentleman Friend
Eddie and Tom try to find out who is the new man in Mrs. Livingston's life.

Any Friend of Dad's
Tom teaches Eddie about the responsibilities of friendship.

An F for Mrs. Livingston
Mrs. Livingston failed her Englist test, causing Eddie to think she will commit hara kiri to save face.

Member of the Wedding
Tina proposes to Norman.

A Night Out for the Boys
GS: Teddy Quinn. An overnight camping trip leads to a Corbett-Lockwood quarrel.

Who Pulled the Blues Right Out of the Horn
GS: Francine York. Eddie's flamboyant Aunt Kate comes for a visit.

The Library Card
Eddie loses the very first library book he takes out.

How Do You Know If It's Really Love
GS: Lori Specter, Gabie Grammer. Eddie is suffering from a case of puppy love.

The Road to You Know Where Is Paved with You Know What
GS: Ann Prentiss. Eddie gets burned by his dad's romance with his teacher.

They're Either Too Young or Too Old
Eddie has a crush on his babysitter, who has a crush on Tom.

The Mod Couple
Mrs. Livingston departs, leaving Eddie and Tom alone.

Guardian for Eddie
GS: Martha Scott. Tom tries to find a future guardian for Eddie.

The Promise
Tom tries to prevent Mrs. Livingston from being deported.

A Five-Pound Monkey on His Stomach
Norman has to lose five pounds in two days.

Free Is a Four Letter Word
GS: Tippi Hedren. Tom has been ordered by his boss to fire his best friend.

The Littlest Kidnapper
GS: Pat Morita. Eddie finds a Japanese son for Mrs. Livingston.

Money Is a Five Letter Word
Eddie finds ten thousand dollars.

Mother of the Year
GS: James Cole, Gwynne Gilforo, Tani Phelps. Tom tries to take Eddie's mother's place at a school party.

The Unbirthday Present
A spoof about the problems of making home movies.

A Loaf of Bread, a Bar of Soap and a Jug of Peanut Butter
GS: Jody Foster, Dave Ketchum. A story about a little girl whose widowed father is about to remarry.

The Important Word Is And . . .
GS: Jonathan Daly. Tom learns a lesson in what not to do when Eddie joins a boys' club.

I Thought, You Thought
GS: Victoria Vetri. Eddie tries to get his dad to marry an aspiring actress.

The Business Trip
Tom has to tell Eddie that he has to work on the night of the school play.

Eddie's Will
A lesson for Eddie about the pain of growing up.

Hello, Mrs. Bessinger
GS: Suzanne Pleshette. A free-spirited girl enters Tom's life.

Love Is for Sharing
GS: Lee Joseph Casey. An Indian orphan teaches Eddie and Tom about sharing.

Who Wants to Sail Down the Amazon, Anyway
GS: Will Geer. Eddie's grandfather visits.

When the Shoe Is on the Other Foot, It Doesn't Fit
GS: Lori Saunders. A liberated woman has Tom delighted but not in love.

The Secret Box
GS: Gabie Grammer. Eddie begins to think that he was adopted.

Fear Is for Understanding
Tom tries to exorcise a ghost.

Gifts Are for Giving
A story about Norman's highly treasured gift.

Don't Look Now, But Your Scorpio's Rising
Tom's nutty secretary has become interested in astrology and quits her job.

A Little Get Together for Cissy
Tom's sophisticated boss Cissy falls for him.

The Ghetto Girl
Tom tries to help a girl from the ghetto with a chip on her shoulder.

The Hospital
GS: Andrew Prine. Eddie gets scared

when Tom goes to the hospital for a routine physical.

The Rift
Tom refuses to buy a horse for Eddie.

The Encounter Group
Tina expresses her feelings about Tom and Norman in a group encounter meeting.

Eddie Meets an Astronaut or Dear Mrs. Cooper
Eddie meets Apollo 13 astronaut L. Gordon Cooper in a story about privacy.

The Magic Mrs. Rickles
GS: Lisa Kirk. Tina's mother's belief in magic leaves an impression on Eddie,

To Catch a Thief
Eddie joins a gang which demands that its members practice shoplifting.

Everybody Needs a Brother
Eddie wants a brother and will do anything to see that he gets one.

Discipline Is a Four Letter Word Spelled Love
Tom worries if he is being too permissive with Eddie.

The Lonely Weekend
GS: Brenda Benet.   While Eddie's away, Tom plans to spend the weekend with his girlfriend.

The Candidate
GS: Kirk Mee, Joseph Allen, Virginia Hawkin. Tom might be the next member of the school board.

Getting Back on the Horse
GS: Richard X. Slattery. Eddie learns to cope with fear.

Tell It Like I'm Telling You It Is
GS: Lou Jacobi, Alan Oppenheimer, Frank Corsentino. A small accident causes big legal problems.

A Very Different Drummer
GS: Ned York. Tom and Eddie try to

convince Norman it is okay to be a kook.

The Bicycle Theft
GS: Bruce Kirby. A lesson in responsibility for Eddie gets out of hand.

Two's Company
GS: Madlyn Rhue, Ronny Graham. A divorced couple makes Tom's life miserable.

Happy Birthday to You
Norman doesn't want the surprise birthday party Tom and Eddie are planning for him.

Or Else
Tina asks Tom for a raise.

Thy Neighbor Loves Thee
GS: Jerry Stiller and Anne Meara. Tom's new neighbors are driving him crazy with kindness.

My Son, the Artist
GS: Angus Duncan, Patti Cohoon. Nude models are the subject in this story about the trials of parenthood.

A Little Red
GS: Carol Lawrence. A Soviet editor encounters a conflict of values.

A Brave at Natchanoony
Eddie's first camping trip is a trauma to mother hen Norman.

The Blarney Stone Girl
GS: Sally Struthers.   Tom meets a charming klutz with an inferiority complex.

The Investors
GS: Hal Cooper. Tom and Norman invest in an oil well.

Prince Charming
GS: Aldine King, Geoffrey Thorpe. Eddie's part in the school play requires him to kiss a girl on the lips, which he finds he can't do.

The Choice
GS: Trisha Noble.   Tom's romance

with a lady doctor depends on her choice to either get married or continue her studies abroad.

The Karate Story
GS: Ed Parker, Willie Aames. Eddie takes karate lessons so he can defeat the school bully.

Very Young Man with a Horn
GS: Ivor Barry, Alan Oppenheimer. Eddie's saxophone playing is disturbing the bagpiper upstairs.

It's All Write with Me
GS: Pat Harrington. Tom feels his creative writing is causing him to neglect Eddie.

A Little Help from My Friend
GS: Sammy Davis, Jr. An insurance man proves to be a disastrous house guest.

In the Eye of the Beholder
GS: Lou Cutell, Willie Aames, William Lanteau. A sixteen dollar gift of friendship becomes a $50,000 headache.

Time for a Change
GS: Michael Link, Barbara Cason. Tom considers buying a charming but rundown house.

We Love Annie
GS: Jerry Stiller and Anne Meara. A story about an answering service with Jerry as Anne's boss.

DECEMBER BRIDE

On the air 10/4/54, off 9/24/59. CBS. B&W film. 157 episodes. Broadcast: Oct 1954-Jun 1958 Mon 9:30-10; Oct 1958-Sept 1959 Thu 8-8:30. Producer: Parke Levy/Fred DeCordova. Prod Co: Desilu. Synd: Viacom.

CAST: Lily Ruskin (played by Spring Byington), Ruth Henshaw (Frances Rafferty), Matt Henshaw (Dean Miller), Hilda Crocker (Verna Felton), Pete Porter (Harry Morgan).

The story of a lovely old widow who comes to live with her daughter and her husband. Each week Lily would either go looking for a boyfriend, or help her daughter with her marriage, or run off somewhere with her friend Hilda on some adventure. A very popular series during the fifties, which even had a spin-off called *Pete and Gladys*, which spun-off the character of Pete Porter and his never seen wife. The series is quite dated now and is rarely seen.

Lily Ruskin Arrives [Pilot]
Lily moves in with her daughter and son-in-law.

The Accident
Lily asks Matt to testify for her at a hearing for her auto accident.

Chicken Salad
The doctor advises the Henshaws that Lily is bored and they had better liven up her life.

Chinese Dinner
Ruth and Lily prepare a complete Chinese dinner to honor a visiting

Chinese businessman.

The Veterinarian
GS: Raymond Greenleaf. In order to cheer Lily up, Matt invites a doctor to the house for dinner.

My Soldier
GS: Herb Vigran. Lily has to find a young girl to take her place when her soldier pen pal arrives from Korea.

Lily Is Bored
Lily refuses to leave the house or answer her phone calls, causing her son to worry.

Grunion Hunting
Lily and Hilda plan a grunion hunt to keep themselves out of Ruth and Matt's way.

Lily's Mother-in-Law
GS: Grandon Rhodes. The family thinks Lily is getting serious about her new boyfriend.

Lily Hires a Maid
GS: Lyle Talbot, Nancy Kulp. Lily hires a maid in order to repay Matt and Ruth's kindness, but she quits when they really need her.

The Luau
Lily and Hilda recreate Hawaii for Matt and Ruth when they have to cancel their Hawaiian vacation.

The Gigolo
GS: Fortunio Bonanova. Lily tries to prove Hilda's boyfriend, a mambo teacher, is a gigolo.

Christmas Show
Lily looks for a Christmas gift for Matt and Ruth.

The Rich Man
GS: Walter Woolf King, Paul Cavanagh. Lily bangs her car into a man's car, but he is so attracted to her he asks her out for a date.

Lily Wants to Pay Her Way
Lily wants to pay for her room and board, but Matt and Ruth say no so she moves out.

Lily, the Artist
GS: Sig Arno. Lily takes up oil painting as a hobby.

The Grandfather Clock
Lily's clock sounds off at all hours of the night, causing Matt and Ruth to fight.

The Sentimentalist
GS: Ludwig Stossel. Lily wants to recapture her past when an old boyfriend pays a visit.

Uranium Show
Lily and Hilda go uranium hunting in the desert.

Insurance Show
Lily bumps her head on an awning and Peter tries to get her to sue.

Jealousy
Lily is jealous of her boyfriend's beautiful secretary and plans to do something about it.

Surprise Party
Lily is curious about the contents of some packages in the house, especially since her birthday is almost here.

Wedding Preparations
Ruth and Lily make out the guest list to Lily and Tom Anderson's wedding.

The Breakup
Tom's daughter's disapproval causes their marriage plans to break up.

Mexico
Lily and Hilda go to Mexico on a vacation but wind up in jail.

Lily's Niece
Lily's niece runs away from home to go to Hollywood and Lily tries to get her to return home.

Matt Cooks
Matt and Pete are left to run the house when Ruth and Gladys leave for Palm Springs because they are not getting enough attention.

Theater Tickets
Lily promises to buy theater tickets for Ruth's anniversary, but Hilda and Lily get mixed up with a theater scalper.

Psychiatrist
Lily is convinced that Hilda needs to see a psychiatrist.

Gossip
When Matt and Ruth plan to go to the mountains for the weekend, Hilda

plans to move in with Lily but they have a fight.

Matt's Mustache
Matt and Lily have a fight over his mustache.

The Lineup
Lily gets into trouble when she calls an upholsterer in order to surprise Matt and Ruth.

The Other Couple
Lily invites a newlywed couple to the house to show them how a house can function with a mother-in-law living there.

Lily's Song
Lily and Hilda write a song for their club's bazaar, but it winds up on TV.

The Pizza Show
Lily becomes a waitress in a restaurant turned pizza parlor.

The Boxing Show
Lily arranges a charity boxing match to raise money for a summer camp.

Ruth Neglects Matt
Ruth becomes chairwoman of the club's charity bazaar and neglects her family and her friends.

Let Yourself Go
GS: Rolfe Sedan.   Everybody takes Lily's newspaper article too seriously.

The Laundromat Show
GS: Herbert Marshall.   Lily gets her laundry mixed up with actor Herbert Marshall's.

Lily and the Wolf
GS: Charles Coburn. Lily gets a job as a secretary to a dirty old businessman.

The Shoplifter
GS: Fritz Feld. Lily is a witness to a crime but the paper mistakenly lists her as the crook.

Skid Row
GS: Percy Helton, Joe Besser. Lily's

newspaper article gets her involved with skid row characters.

Big Game Hunter
Lily must find a boyfriend to bring to dinner or her friends won't leave her alone.

Family Quarrel
Lily believes she is no longer welcome in the house.

High Sierras
GS: Dan Duryea, Douglas Fowley. Hilda and Lily go to the mountains to get material for her column but the car breaks down.

Rate Your Mate
Lily and her boyfriend take a compatibility test.

Operation Cole Slaw
Lily tries to prevent a grouchy man from moving in next door.

Trailer Show
GS: Robert Foulk, Robert Burton. Lily invites a family whose trailer broke down into the house, but one of their kids has the mumps.

Matt's Movie Career
Lily puts Matt in her club play. Matt gets good reviews, so he thinks he will become a movie star.

Rudy Vallee Show
GS: Rudy Vallee, Benny Rubin. At an auction, Lily buys one of Rudy Vallee's old records which was sold by mistake.

Texas Show [Part 1]
GS: Lyle Talbot, Howard McNear. Matt thinks Lily was swindled when she invests in an oil well.

Texas Show [Part 2]
GS: Lyle Talbot.   Lily tries to fix Hilda up with her Texas boyfriend's foreman.

Texas Show [Part 3]
GS: Lyle Talbot, Lou Krugman, Dick Wessel. Hilda and the foreman are in

love and Bill plans to ask Lily to marry him.

Sunken Den
GS: Desi Arnaz, Joseph Kearns, Richard Deacon. Lily doesn't deliver some plans for Matt, so the rumpus room in Desi Arnaz's house collapses.

The Wrestler
GS: Sandor Szabo, Sandra Gould, Jules Strongbow. A singing wrestler asks Lily to be his manager.

Lily in a Gas Station
GS: Frank Cady. Lily invests in a gas station when Matt moves to New York.

Ruth Gets a Job
Ruth gets a job to get enough money to buy a new refrigerator.

Handcuffs
GS: Dick Elliot, Irving Bacon. Hilda's boyfriend handcuffs Hilda and Lily together and then loses the key.

Ruth's Haircut
GS: Mabel Albertson. Against Matt's orders, Ruth gets an Italian haircut before she meets Matt's mother.

Jaywalker
GS: King Donovan, Arte Johnson, Howard McNear. Lily fights a jaywalking ticket causing Matt to fear losing entrance to a country club.

Pete's Brother-in-Law
GS: Arnold Stang, Pierre Watkin, Dick Wessel. Matt and Lily try to get Pete's brother-in-law out of the house and into the marines.

Lily and the Sailor
GS: Nestor Paiva. Lily invents a romance between herself and a sailor in order to stop a fight between Matt and Ruth.

Lily the Matchmaker
GS: Nancy Kulp, Richard Deacon, Robert Foulk. Lily tries to fix a shy homely girl with a date.

Swimming Pool
GS: Frank Jenks, Damian O'Flynn. Lily acts as mediator in a fight. Matt wants a pool and Ruth wants new carpeting.

Beauty Pageant
Lily and Matt arrange a beauty contest to raise money for her club.

Rory Calhoun Show
GS: Rory Calhoun. No available story.

House on Blocks
Lily and Hilda buy a house that must be moved away from a new freeway.

The Prize Fighter
GS: Arnold Stang, Stanley Clements. A boxer helps Pete's brother-in-law Marvin who challenged his girlfriend's suitors to a fight.

Ritzy Neighborhood
GS: Peter Leeds. Matt and Ruth want to return to their old neighborhood despite having sold their home.

Lily and the Prowler
Pete and Martha fight over whether they should do the dishes or not.

The Jockey
GS: Arnold Stang. Hilda and Lily win a horse in a drawing and Marvin wants to be the jockey.

Redecorating Show
GS: Howard McNear. Lily gets Matt to hire a decorator to redo the house.

Indian Show
GS: Joseph Kearns, Rodd Redwing. Matt, Lily, Pete and Hilda stop in a New Mexican town en route to Chicago.

Marjorie Main Show
GS: Marjorie Main. No available story.

Man Town/Man Hunt
They all visit Matt's uncle in a town where the men outnumber the women.

Football Hero
Everyone wants to go to the college football game at Matt's college except Matt.

New Year's Party
Pete only gets three reservations for a party, so Lily and Hilda pretend they have other plans.

Royalty
GS: John Qualen, Iphigenie Castiglioni. Hilds falls for a count at a friend's party.

Chicken Farm Show
Matt and Ruth celebrate their anniversary, at Hilda's uncle's chicken farm.

Homecoming Show
GS: Elvia Allman. The Henshaws come home to the redecorated house, but Ruth's attitude drives the men to the garage.

Budget Show
Ruth upsets the budget by buying a new dress.

Study Group
No available story.

Mother-in-Law Club
GS: Ruth Warren. Lily forms a club to help solve problems faced by mothers-in-law.

Piano Show
GS: Chick Chandler, Arlene Harris, Maxine Gates. Lily and Hilda try to win a piano for Ruth on a quiz show.

Duck Hunting
Matt and Pete take Lily duck hunting in order to make her forget her fallen romance.

Engagement Show
GS: Raymond Greenleaf. Lily announces her engagement to her boyfriend Paul.

Masquerade Party
Paul's housekeeper won't let Lily announce her engagement to Paul.

Kissing Booth
GS: Elvia Allman, Robert Fortier. Lily and Hilda run the kissing booth at the charity bazaar.

The Hobo Show
GS: Dick Wessel, Sid Melton, Parley Baer. Lily and Hilda try to save hobo jungle from becoming the city dump.

The Englishman
GS: Paul Cavanagh. Matt grows a beard to show a British lecturer he is not henpecked.

Do It Yourself
Lily tries to fix the broken TV set herself.

The Old Man
Lily helps out when Hilda's boyfriend's father doesn't approve of them going together.

Song Plugging
GS: Sandor Szabo, Sandra Gould, Sid Melton, Fuzzy Knight. Lily and Hilda try to get a wrestler to give up wrestling and stick to singing.

Lily-Hilda Fight
Lily takes up with a new friend leaving Hilda rejected, so she goes to Canada.

Mountain Climbing
GS: Morey Amsterdam. Ruth doesn't want Matt going on a camping trip with Pete and a beautiful guide.

Photography Show
Lily accidentally destroys a photograph Matt entered in a contest.

Vallee's Protege
GS: Rudy Vallee, Joel Grey. Lily's nephew visits. She introduces him to Rudy Vallee in order to help him be become a movie star.

Mean Grandfather
Lily's nephew is having problems with his girlfriend's grandfather who wants her home very early.

The Golf Lesson
Ruth wants Matt to take up golf.

Sports Car
Matt buys a sports car and plans to enter it in a race.

Microphone Show
Lily uses a tape recorder to prevent a swindler from taking Hilda's money.

Matt's Gray Hair
Ruth dyes Matt's hair gray while he is asleep.

Butler Show
GS: Edward Everett Horton. Matt's boss lends him his butler who falls in love with Lily.

Airplane Show
Lily tries to help Pete lose his fear of flying.

Hot Meal
Matt wants Ruth to stay home and cook instead of going to her social club.

The Parrot Show
GS: Mel Blanc provides the voice of the parrot. Hilda's landlord wants her to get rid of her parrot.

Antique Show
Ruth is disappointed by Matt's anniversary gift so she brags to her friends that he got her an expensive watch.

The Other Woman
GS: Barbara Eden, Hillary Brooke. Ruth thinks Matt is seeing another woman, an explorer who just returned from the jungle.

Ruth Goes Home to Mother
Ruth, Pete and Hilda desert Matt when he complains about his torn newspaper.

Housemother
Lily is appointed as housemother for a college sorority.

Muscleman Show
Matt takes up weightlifting to impress Ruth.

Contour Chair
Matt buys a vibrating chair that suddenly disappears.

Baby Rehearsal
Lily prepares Pete for the birth of his child by holding a rehearsal.

Army Buddy
Matt gets a letter from the government asking payment for a plane lost during his days in the Army.

Bouncer Show
GS: Sandor Szabo. Lily tries to get her singing wrestler friends a job in a nightclub.

Sleep Teaching
Ruth plans to use Lily's sleep teaching equipment to get Matt to ask his boss for a raise.

Fred MacMurray Show
GS: Fred MacMurray. Lily decides to choose Fred as her newspaper's honorary candidate for mayor.

Ed Wynn Show
GS: Ed Wynn. Ed tells Lily that he would like to play Abraham Lincoln in an upcoming play, but they tell him that he is too short.

Gilbert Roland Show
GS: Gilbert Roland. Lily helps a young man win the hand of his girlfriend, but he decides he doesn't want to marry her. However, Spanish tradition demands it, so Lily tries to break up the engagement.

Aunt Emily
GS: Isabel Randolph. Lily and Pete try to show Hilda's cousin how to have fun.

Mickey Rooney Show
Lily helps Mickey Rooney with his new film.

Matt-Pete Fight
Lily and Hilda try to bring Matt and Pete back together, after a fight about an unpaid golf debt.

Wedding Float
Matt and Ruth are scheduled to appear on the wedding float for Lily's club, but they have a fight before the parade.

Lily's Birthday
Lily borrows the dress Matt and Ruth were going to give her for her birthday so she can go on a blind date.

Edgar Bergen Show
GS: Edgar and Frances Bergen. Lily helps Edgar get his brother-in-law to propose to his girl.

Alaska Show
Matt is assigned to Alaska when his Air Force reserve unit is called into action.

Fenwick Arms
Lily tries to save her friend's job as an apartment building manager.

Bride's Father-in-Law
Matt and Ruth have trouble with their father-in-law.

Chimp Show
Lily watches a chimp when her friends go on a honeymoon.

Hilda Gets Engaged
Hilda tells her friends that her boyfriend proposed to her in order to make them jealous.

Zsa Zsa Gabor Show
GS: Zsa Zsa Gabor. Lily asks Zsa Zsa to be the guest speaker at a safety award dinner.

Horse Phobia
Pete claims to be an expert rider in order to impress a client.

Tough Mother-in-Law
Pete's mother-in-law's boyfriend falls in love with Lily.

Power Saw
Ruth feels neglected when Matt spends all his time with the power tools Lily gave him for his birthday.

Post Office Show
Matt writes a letter of resignation to his boss and takes another job.

Car for Christmas
Ruth tries to get Matt to buy a new car for Christmas.

Child of Nature
Matt goes to the movies with Pete rather than take Ruth to the ballet, which makes her mad.

Beatnik Show
Hilda's nephew plans to drop out of school to become a beatnik.

Nurse Show
Lily tries to help Pete hire a nurse for his expected baby.

Pete Has a Baby
GS: Terry Becker, Sid Melton. Lily gets her friend to perform his magic act to keep Pete's mind off the baby.

Nurse is Fired
Pete's new baby is in the care of an overzealous nurse.

Lily's Blind Date
Ruth and Matt arrange a blind date for Lily with a friend of Matt's boss.

Lily's Advice Column
Lily takes over the advice column for the newspaper.

Hi-Fi Show
Ruth tries to convince Matt to buy her a new stereo.

The Scotch Show
Lily advises a Scottish exchange student to move in with an American family to learn our way of life, so he moves in with Matt and Ruth.

The Martian Show
GS: Roger Perry. Lily advises a young man to pursue his singing career instead of going into business with his father.

Lily Babysits
Lily and Hilda, babysitting for Pete's baby, take it to a drive-in movie, but on the way the car breaks down in a deep fog.

Ruth the Brain
Matt takes an IQ test to see if he is smarter than Ruth.

Stan Loses His Nerve
GS: Jim Davis, Linda Gaye. Lily tries to help Hilda's boyfriend regain his confidence.

The Texan, Rory Calhoun
GS: Rory Calhoun. A teenage boy, after meeting Rory at Lily's home, decides to become a cowboy instead of going to college.

Lily Goes Fishing
Lily cooks the fish Matt wanted to

have stuffed and mounted.

Lily Helps Twilly
Lily tries to help Miss Twilly, the nurse for Pete's baby, find romance.

Linda on TV
GS; Hayden Rorke, Peter Leeds. Lily gets a RV role for Pete's baby girl Linda.

Lily, the Example
GS: Jesse White, Allen Jenkins. Matt tells Ruth that she should start doing things like Lily does.

Bald Baby
Pete worries that his baby has inherited his tendency toward baldness.

Capistrano Show
The Henshaws invite the niece of Matt's boss to be their house guest.

Lily on Boat
Lily misunderstands when Matt and Ruth want to send her on an ocean cruise; she thinks they want her out of the way.

DENNIS THE MENACE

On the air 10/4/59, off 9/22/63. CBS. 30 min. film. B&W. 146 episodes. Broadcast: Oct 1959-Sept 1963 Sun 7:30-8. Producer: Harry Ackerman. Prod Co & Synd: Screen Gems/Columbia Pictures TV.

CAST: Dennis Mitchell (played by Jay North), Henry Mitchell (Herbert Anderson), Alice Mitchell (Gloria Henry), George Wilson (Joseph Kearns, 1959-1962), John Wilson (Gale Gordon, 1962-1963), Martha Wilson (Sylvia Field, 1961-1962), Eloise Wilson (Sara Seegar, 1962-1963), Esther Cathcart (Mary Wickes), Tommy Anderson (Billy Booth), Joey McDonald (Gil Smith), Margaret Wade (Jeannie Russell).

627 Elm Street, Hillsdale, USA, the residence of the Mitchell family: Henry, an engineer, his housewife Alice, and their son Dennis. The series concentrated on Dennis's mischievous escapades which usually spell trouble for Mr. Wilson, Dennis's nervous neighbor. The series success relied on the disorder of the adult world compared to the innocent kid world of Dennis. The series is not run in many cities as it is in black and white, a fact that most stations feel hurts ratings.

Herb Anderson, and Jay North as Dennis the Menace.

Dennis Goes to the Movies
GS: Madge Blake. Dennis outwits a babysitter, sneaks off to the movies, gets Mr. Wilson in trouble, and returns undetected.

Dennis and the Signpost
Dennis accidentally turns a signpost the wrong way, causing construction crews to go to the wrong houses.

The Fishing Trip
GS: Ronny Howard. Dennis, his father, and Mr. Wilson go on a fishing trip together.

Grandpa and Miss Cathcart
Dennis tries to fix his visiting grandfather up with Miss Cathcart.

Innocents in Space
GS: Parley Baer. Dennis and his friends play spaceman.

Dennis's Garden
Dennis wrecks Mr. Wilson's chances of winning a gardening contest.

The New Neighbors
GS: Ralph Dumke, Lewis Martin. Mr. Wilson's plan to keep Dennis and his friends away from his real estate deal backfires when they throw a party for him.

Tenting Tonight
GS: Dave Willock, Jenna McMahon. Dennis and his friend Tommy camp out in the backyard.

Dennis Sells Bottles
GS: Irene Tedrow, Hope Summers. When Dennis collects pop bottles to earn some money, his neighbors think his family is broke.

Mr. Wilson's Award
Henry and Alice try to convince Mr. Wilson that they are moving to New

York in order to get him to attend a surprise party.

Dennis and Christmas
The Mitchells hide Dennis's Christmas present in Mr. Wilson's house, but Dennis still finds it.

Dennis and the Cowboy
Dennis wants a part in the yearly pageant so he can meet TV's leading cowboy, Whip Crawford.

Dennis Haunts a House
GS: Ronny Howard.   Mr. Wilson thinks his house is haunted by the ghost of his ancestor, when he hears strange noises coming from the basement.

Dennis's Tree House
GS: Byron Foulger.   Dennis's new treehouse disrupts Mr. Wilson's plans to start a bird sanctuary.

Dennis and the Rare Coin
GS: Michael Fox, George Cisar. Dennis throws Mr. Wilson's rare penny into a wishing well.

Dennis and the Bike
When Dennis's scooter is smashed, he enters a contest to guess the number of beans in a fish bowl in an attempt to replace it with a brand new bicycle.

Dennis and the Open House
GS: Dub Taylor, Grandon Rhodes. Dennis puts a "For Sale" sign in front of his house at the same time his father is planning on entertaining an important client.

Dennis and the Duck
Dennis sends a trail of snails followed by a duck into Mr. Wilson's yard.

Dennis and the Swing
Dennis, upon seeing a picture of an old fashioned swing, starts a campaign to have one built in his backyard.

Dennis and the Dog
When Dennis gets a dog, the shaggy mongrel destroys a valuable painting Mr. Wilson had started working on.

Mr. Wilson's Sister
After hearing the story "Treasure Island," Dennis and his friends dig for buried treasure in Mr. Wilson's back yard.

Dennis and the TV Set
Dennis causes havoc with Mr. Wilson's television set when he borrows his friend's remote control unit.

Dennis Creates a Hero
Dennis tries to prove his father is a hero and ends up embarrassing him with a newspaper photo of him in a bathing suit.

Dennis's Paper Drive
Dennis collects enough old newspapers to wind up winning top prize in the charity paper drive, an 1895 coin worth $600.

Dennis and the Bees
Dennis begins breeding bees in Mr. Wilson's flower garden.

Alice's Birthday
Dennis's attempts to buy his mother a birthday present end in disaster when he inflates a life raft inside a drugstore.

Dennis Becomes a Baby Sitter
Dennis takes up babysitting to earn extra money to buy a pair of white mice.

Dennis and the Starlings
While Mr. Wilson has been attempting to remove some starlings from his yard, Dennis has accidentally been attracting them.

The Party Line
Dennis causes confusion on the telephone party line when he interrupts a call between Henry and a client.

Dennis by Proxy
GS: Ronny Howard. Dennis attempts to build a new bench and winds up

using the lumber from Mr. Wilson's yard.

Dennis Runs Away
GS: James Callahan. When his parents and his friends are too busy to play with him, Dennis runs away from home.

Miss Cathcart's Sunsuit
Dennis causes a mixup between Mr. Carlson and Miss Cathcart when he peddles valentines.

Out of Retirement
GS: Vinton Hayworth. Dennis thinks he is responsible for Mr. Wilson's decision to move away.

Dennis and the Wedding
GS: Jonathan Hole. When Dennis is the ring bearer at the wedding of Mr. Wilson's niece, he loses the ring through a vent and into the cellar.

Dennis and the Radio Set
GS: Ellen Corby, Ronald Long. Dennis finds $1650 in an old radio and sets out to find the rightful owner.

Dennis and the Ham-Pher
Dennis's pet hamster turns out to be a gopher who has found a permanent home in Mr. Wilson's backyard.

The Stock Certificate
GS: Chet Stratton. When Mr. Wilson puts a stock certificate worth $500 in a phone book, Dennis mistakenly gives the book to the phone company.

Man of the House
GS: Alan Hewitt. After listening to a caterer plan a party for eight people, Dennis invites eight of his friends over to the Mitchell home.

The Rock Collection
Mr. Wilson sends Dennis out on a rock expedition where he finds rocks containing gold ore.

Henry and Togetherness
Dennis's fish tank has sprung a leak, so he uses pots, pans and even Margaret's bubble gum to stop the stream of water pouring out of the tank.

Paint Up Clean Up Week
After Mr. Wilson paints his backyard furniture, Dennis sends a pile of dust from his treehouse down onto the freshly painted furniture.

Dennis Learns to Whistle
GS: Willard Waterman. Dennis and Mr. Wilson both cannot whistle and are depressed, but after they get a loose tooth they miraculously develop the ability to whistle.

The Raffle Ticket
Dennis sells a raffle ticket that Mr. Wilson was saving, which turns out to be the winning ticket.

The Christmas Horse
GS: Ernest Truex. All Dennis wants for Christmas is a pony, but he only gets a record player, sending him off on a search for his pony.

Dennis's Allowance
Dennis and Tommy attempt to earn money by collecting junk for a garage sale.

Dennis's Penny Collection
Dennis is on a search for a missing coin to complete his penny collection.

Dennis the Campaign Manager
Dennis and Mr. Wilson campaign on television to keep the playgrounds open during the weekdays, instead of only on weekends.

Miss Cathcart's Friend
GS: John Zaremba, Mel Blanc. When Alice says it would be nice if Miss Cathcart had a best friend, Dennis sets out to find her a large dog.

Pythias Was a Piker
Dennis writes a composition on his very best friend, Mr. Wilson.

Dennis and the Saxophone
Mr. Wilson's plan to prevent Dennis

from buying a noisy saxophone back-fires when the Mitchells agree to buy anything the boy desires after a talk from Mr. Wilson.

Wilson Sleeps Over
When the Wilsons sleep over at the Mitchell's, Dennis must find a quiet, peaceful place to put his pet bullfrog.

Dennis's Birthday
GS: Vaughn Taylor, Elvia Allman, Spring Byington. Dennis is able to convince Spring Byington to come to his birthday party, complete with magic tricks.

Dennis Goes to Camp
When Mr. Wilson drives Dennis to camp, he is almost forced to become a permanent camper himself.

Dennis's Tool Chest
Dennis's cat jumps into the trunk of Mr. Wilson's car, fooling him into believing he has engine trouble.

The Going Away Gift
Dennis buys a pair of earrings for his mother and hides them in Mr. Wilson's house.

Dennis and the Fishing Rod
GS: Stanley Adams, Charles Lane. Dennis finds a rare $50 bill in an old coat and is offered $400 for it by Mr. Wilson, enabling Dennis to buy the fishing rod he wanted for his father.

Dennis and the Good Example
GS: Alan Hewitt. Dennis tries to improve his grades in the hope of receiving a mynah bird as a reward.

Dennis's Obligation
Dennis starts breeding baby chicks and then brings them all over to Mr. Wilson's house.

The Dog Trainer
Dennis attempts to teach Mr. Wilson's dog Fremont to obey his commands.

Woodman, Spare That Tree
Mr. Wilson starts a campaign to stop the city from cutting down an ancient tree.

The Boy Wonder
Mr. Wilson and a teenage friend build a brick barbecue that ends up with the fire department destroying the newly built disaster.

The Soapbox Derby
Dennis enters the soapbox derby to prove to another boy his homemade car is as fast as a fancy department store version.

Dennis and the Camera
Dennis wants to become a cub scout and involves Mr. Wilson in his plans.

Dennis and the Miracle Plant Food
After Dennis destroys one of Mr. Wilson's plants, he replaces it with a taller one, fooling Mr. Wilson into believing his new plant food caused the plant's rapid growth.

Dennis's Newspaper
Dennis decides to publish his own newspaper and uses Mr. Wilson as the subject of all the news.

Mr. Wilson's Paradise
Mr. and Mrs. Wilson are planning to spend a year in Mexico, but change their minds when they discover that if they leave they'll miss the birth of their first grandchild.

The Fortune Cookie
Dennis helps Mr. Wilson recover his coin collection from a con man.

The Pioneers
Mr. Wilson and Henry set out to prove that men are just as rugged and resourceful as the pioneers who founded their town.

Father's Day for Mr. Wilson
Dennis tries to make Father's Day a happy occasion for Mr. Wilson and even helps him win a lawsuit.

Dennis and the Picnic
Henry finds a suitcase filled with

stolen money, and Dennis sells autographs of his heroic father.

Trouble from Mars
Dennis and his friends are on an outer space kick and, wearing helmets and spacesuits, scare a barber into ruining Mr. Wilson's haircut.

Best Neighbor
While trying to win the award for best citizen, Mr. Wilson helps Dennis become a member of the Junior Pathfinders by spending a night in the forest.

Keep Off the Grass
After Dennis tramples on some protected grass, a policeman gives Henry a fine.

Mr. Wilson's Safe
After Mr. Wilson forgets the combination to his safe, he is hypnotized into revealing the forgotten numbers.

The Haunted House
GS: Harold Gould.   Mr. Wilson and Henry buy an old house which is believed to be haunted, sending Dennis and Tommy out to scare Mr. Wilson.

The School Play
On the night of the school play, Mr. Wilson accidentally gets handcuffed to Tommy.

The Fifty Thousandth Customer
GS: Charles Lane.   Mr. Wilson competes in a contest to win five minutes of free shopping and ends up losing to Dennis.

Dennis and the Pee Wee League
Dennis volunteers Mr. Wilson as the new league president of their baseball team.

Mr. Wilson's Inheritance
Mr. Wilson's aunt dies, leaving him a valuable art collection and an undetermined amount of money. Upon hearing this, Mr. Wilson envisions living a new life of luxury.

Dennis Is a Genius
A school grading error convinces the Mitchells that Dennis is a boy genius.

The Lucky Piece
When Mr. Wilson cheats Dennis out of fifty cents, Alice and Mrs. Wilson set out to teach him a good lesson.

The 15-Foot Christmas Tree
Henry, Dennis and Mr. Wilson set out to cut down their own Christmas tree, instead of relying on one bought in a department store.

Dennis's Bank Account
When Mr. Wilson is given the job of new accounts manager at the local bank, Dennis and all of his piggy bank carrying friends are all eager to open savings accounts.

Through Thick and Thin
Dennis tricks Mr. Wilson into filling in the back half of a lion's suit for the upcoming cub scout circus.

Calling All Bird Lovers
While trying to be elected state delegate to the National Bird Lovers convention, Mr. Wilson is bothered by Henry, Dennis and a group of jazz musicians.

Silence Is Golden
After Dennis bothers Mr. Wilson, he tells Dennis he will give him a magnifying glass if he doesn't talk for the rest of the day.

Dennis Has a Fling
GS: Emory Parnell.   When Mr. Wilson learns an automobile will be awarded to the person putting on the best show at a school pageant, he puts on kilts and dresses as a Scotsman.

The Frog Jumping Contest
GS: Alan Hewitt.   Dennis and Mr. Wilson become partners in a frog jumping contest and are shocked to learn that Sam, Dennis's frog, has fallen in love with Mr. Wilson's female frog.

Where There's a Will
After Mr. Wilson makes out his will, he begins to feel he is over the hill and dying.

Mr. Wilson's Uncle
GS: Edward Everett Horton. Mr. Wilson's physical fitness-loving uncle comes for a visit and drives Henry and Wilson up a tree.

A Quiet Evening
GS: Kirk Alyn.   Seymour, a small friend of Dennis's, takes a rare dime of Mr. Wilson's and puts it in a candy machine.

The Private Eye
GS: Bob Hastings. Dennis plays detective and helps recover Mr. Wilson's stolen wallet.

Mr. Wilson's Housekeeper
GS: Jean Stapleton. Mr. Wilson hires a housekeeper who immediately takes over the Wilson home, regulating all of Mr. Wilson's daily activities.

A Dog's Life
Mr. Wilson is followed home by a big shaggy dog and embarks on a fruitless campaign to find the rightful owner.

Dennis's Documentary Film
When Dennis films a documentary about all the people in his town, it turns out to be a surprise comedy hit.

The Horseless Carriage Club
GS: Robert Burton. Mr. Wilson promises to take Dennis and his friends on a picnic the same day he plans to enter his 1912 car in the first vintage auto race.

Junior Pathfinders Ride Again
GS: Lloyd Corrigan.   Mr. Wilson's attempts to join the Pioneer Club end in disaster as he almost burns down a building attempting to start a fire Indian style.

The Treasure Chest
GS: Edward Everett Horton. Mr. Wilson buys an old treasure chest which only contains a map and an old coat.

Wilson Goes to the Dentist
GS: Arthur Malet.   Dennis receives a basketball from Mr. Wilson after he finds a cure for his ailing tooth.

The Man Next Door
Dennis mistakes Mr. Wilson for a burglar, unaware the real burglar is their neighbor, Mr. Sweetzer.

Dennis and the Dodger
GS: Sandy Koufax. Mr. Quigley, hoping to keep the boys coming to his store with their parents' orders, volunteers to become the new coach for their Pee Wee baseball team.

Dennis's Lovesick Friend
Dennis plays guidance counselor in an attempt to help his friend Jerry win Helen, the girl of his dreams.

John Wilson's Cushion
Mr. Wilson's brother John, a feature story writer, finds it difficult to write without an old cushion he has been sitting on for twenty years, so Dennis sets off to find him a new one.

John Wilson Wins a Chicken
Dennis is outraged to learn Mr. Wilson plans to eat a baby chick he won in the school raffle.

The Bully
GS: Richard Reeves.   Dennis has a fight with the school bully whose father turns out to be a client of Henry's.

The Club Initiation
Dennis must pass a tough initiation to gain entrance to a new social club.

Community Picnic
Mr. Wilson and Henry compete in an athletic contest against two other men at the community picnic.

Dennis and the Witch Doctor
When Mr. Wilson writes an article on

witchcraft, Dennis believes he can control people's lives by the use of voodoo.

The Chinese Girl
GS: Cherylene Lee, Arthur Wong. Dennis fears he will be forced into marrying a young Chinese girl.

You Go Your Way
GS: Alice Pearce. Two old ladies mistakenly believe the Wilsons are breaking up.

Dennis's Circular Circumstances
Dennis is falsely accused of disposing of campaign circulars he was paid to hand out.

The Little Judge
Dennis is assigned the job of town judge on Children's Day and his first act is to oversee a case involving Mr. Wilson.

Poor Mr. Wilson
When Mr. Wilson loses some money in a supermarket, Dennis mistakenly believes that he is broke.

Dennis in Gypsyland
While trying to get an in-depth look into the lives of gypsies, Mr. Wilson accidentally accepts a marriage proposal from a young gypsy girl.

The New Principal
Dennis almost loses the chance to pitch in the school baseball game when a jealous boy blackmails him into admitting he drew an embarrassing picture of the principal.

San Diego Safari
The Wilsons and the Mitchells travel to San Diego to bring home a chimpanzee to put in their their own zoo.

Dennis at Boot Camp
GS: Allan Hunt. Dennis and Mr. Wilson try their best to escape from a naval base before a series of demolitions are set off.

Henry's New Job
When Henry's boss offers him an exciting job in a foreign country, Dennis doesn't want to move.

Wilson's Second Childhood
Mr. Wilson gets a magazine assignment for a story on modern children and decides to spend the day with Dennis and his friends.

Jane Butterfield Says
Mr. Wilson, posing as an advice columnist named Jane Butterfield, supplies some strange advice to two old ladies trying to marry off Sgt. Mooney.

Dennis and the Hermit
GS: Edgar Buchanan. Dennis befriends an old recluse and Mr. Wilson is determined to interview the man believed to be a Civil War veteran.

My Uncle Ned
GS: Alvy Moore, Edward Everett Horton. Uncle Ned returns and Mr. Wilson writes a biography of his life which outrages Ned who doesn't want any publicity.

The Junior Astronaut
Dennis tries to save up enough stamps to win a contest Mr. Wilson is running to meet a real astronaut.

Wilson's Little White Lie
When Mr. Wilson decides to play sick to get a day off from work, Dennis spreads word all over town that Mr. Wilson is gravely ill.

Dennis the Rainmaker
Mr. Wilson wants to purchase an ancient-looking Indian pot that Dennis discovers was made in Japan.

The Creature with the Big Feet
Dennis uses trick plastic feet to fool Mr. Wilson into believing monsters have invaded his backyard.

Dennis, the Confused Cupid
Dennis sets out to find the meaning of

love by writing love notes to a young girl using Mr. Wilson's old love letters as inspiration.

Dennis Goes to Washington
Dennis and Mr. Wilson venture to Washington on a campaign to insure that local Hickory Mountain be made a national forest.

The Big Basketball Game
Dennis winds up being the star of the school basketball game when one of the regular players has to be replaced.

Wilson's Allergy
GS: Brendon Dillon. Dennis, fearing that Mr. Wilson's allergy is a result of his presence, decides to run away to prevent Mr. Wilson from any further suffering.

Baby Booties
GS: Alan Hewitt. Dennis spreads the word all over town that Mrs. Wilson is pregnant, but in reality what Dennis thought were baby socks were golf club covers for Mr. Wilson.

My Four Boys
Mr. Wilson must prove that he has a family, to collect a prize he won in a writing contest. He enlists the aid of Dennis and his friends to solve the problem.

Dennis and the Homing Pigeons
Dennis trains his pigeons with a piece of paper Mr. Wilson and his father needed in order to invest in a profitable stock.

A Tax on Cats
Mr. Wilson is appointed City Cat Catcher, but his every effort fails when Dennis releases every cat he collects.

The Uninvited Guest
GS: James Millhollin, Stafford Repp. Dennis uses a water pistol to help capture a notorious burglar.

Dennis Plays Robin Hood
Mr. Wilson lands in jail as a result of Dennis's campaign to steal from the rich and give to the poor.

The Three F's
Mr. Wilson spends the day in school to see for himself where all his tax money goes.

Never Say Dye
Mr. Wilson dyes his hair in an attempt to prove to a famous screenwriter he is a young author.

The Lost Dog
Mr. Wilson takes in a stray dog he believes to be worth a $100 reward.

Tuxedo Trouble
On the evening Mr. Wilson is to appear at a Civic Improvement League Dinner, Dennis ruins his tuxedo when he attempts to wash the dirty suit all by himself.

Hawaiian Love Song
The Wilsons and the Mitchells plan a trip to Hawaii that somehow never gets off the ground.

The Lucky Rabbit's Foot
Mr. Wilson buys a rabbit's foot after Dennis tells him he has been having a streak of good luck ever since he bought one.

Listen to the Mockingbird
Dennis disrupts Mr. Wilson's bird-watching efforts.

First Editions
GS: Ronald Long. Mr. Wilson loses an important telephone number written inside a pile of comic books owned by Dennis and purchases every one to try to locate the missing number.

A Man Among Men
Dennis settles a dispute between Mr. Wilson and Mr. Jessup, the owner of the local bookstore.

Aunt Emma Visits the Wilsons
GS: Verna Felton. When Mr. Wilson's Aunt Emma pays a visit she takes an instant liking to Dennis, causing Mr. Wilson to fear she will make Dennis her heir.

THE DICK VAN DYKE SHOW

On the air 10/3/61, off 9/7/66. CBS. B&W film. 158 episodes. Broadcast: Oct 1961-Dec 1961 Tue 8-8:30; Jan 1962-Sept 1964 Wed 9:30-10; Sept 1964-Sept 1965 Wed 9-9:30; Sept 1965-Sept 1966 Wed 9:30-10. Producer: Carl Reiner/Sheldon Leonard. Prod Co: Paramount/Danny Thomas. Synd: Viacom.
   CAST: Rob Petrie (played by Dick Van Dyke), Laura Petrie (Mary Tyler Moore), Richie Petrie (Larry Mathews), Sally Rogers (Rose Marie), Buddy Sorrell (Morey Amsterdam), Mel Cooley (Richard Deacon), Jerry Helper (Jerry Paris), Millie Helper (Ann Morgan Guilbert), Alan Brady (Carl Reiner).
   This is considered one of the classic television comedies. It is the story of a comedy writer, his family and friends. Each week Rob would find himself in all sorts of trouble whether it would be at the office or at home. The series ended when the cast decided to move on to other things. The show was a big hit during the first years of its syndication. However, it has died out in popularity because of its dated look—caused by the black and white film and fashions of that time.

The Sick Boy and the Sitter
GS: Mary Lee Dearing, Stacey Keach, Barbara Eiler. Rob tries to talk Laura into leaving Richie with a babysitter while they go to a party.

The Meershatz Pipe
GS: John Silo. Rob feels useless when Buddy and Sally write a show without his help.

Jealousy!
GS: Joan Staley. Laura becomes jealous of a beautiful TV star that Rob is working with at night.

Sally and the Lab Technician
GS: Eddie Firestone, Jamie Farr. Laura plays matchmaker when she fixes Sally up with her pharmacist cousin.

Washington vs. the Bunny
GS: Jesse White, Jamie Farr. Laura wants Rob to see Richie star in the school play, but Rob has other plans.

Oh How We Met the Night That We Danced
GS: Marty Ingels, Nancy James, Glen Turnbull. Rob and Laura reminisce about how they first met and how he broke her foot.

The Unwelcome House Guest
Rob agrees to take care of Buddy's dog for the weekend.

Harrison B. Harding of Camp Crowder, MO
GS: Allan Melvin, June Dayton, Peter Leeds. Rob invites an old Army buddy for dinner, then begins to think his friend is a jewel thief.

My Blonde-Haired Brunette
GS: Benny Rubin. Laura dresses up as a blonde in order to save her marriage.

Forty-Four Tickets
GS: Joe Devlin, Paul Bryar, Eleanor Audley. Rob invites 44 PTA members to his TV show and then forgets about getting the tickets.

To Tell or Not to Tell
GS: Jamie Farr. Rob and Richie feel left out when Laura resumes her dancing career.

Dick Van Dyke

Sally Is a Girl
GS: Jamie Farr, Barbara Perry, Paul Tripp.   Rob stops treating Sally as one of the boys, and is accused of trying to take advantage of her.

Empress Carlotta's Necklace
GS: Gavin McLeod, Will Wright, Carol Veasie.   Rob gives Laura a necklace and Laura can't tell him that she hates it.

Buddy, Can You Spare a Job?
GS: Len Weinrib.   Sally and Rob plan to get Buddy his job back when he quits to take another job.

Who Owes Who What?
Rob turns a forgotten loan into script material.

Sol and the Sponsor
GS: Marty Ingels, Isabel Randolph, Patty Regan.   Rob's old Army buddy brightens up a dinner party for a sponsor.

The Curious Thing About Women
GS: Frank Adamo.   Rob writes a script about Laura's habit of opening his mail.

Punch Thy Neighbor
GS: Jerry Hausner, Frank Adamo, Peter Oliphant.   Jerry knocks Rob's show in public, causing Rob to become upset.

Where Did I Come From?
GS: Bill Braver, Herbie Faye, Jerry Hausner.   Richie confronts Rob and Laura with the question "Where Did I Come From?"

The Boarder Incident
Buddy moves in with Rob and Laura when his wife is away.

A Word a Day
GS: William Schallert, Lisa Waggoner.   Richie's vocabulary is expanding in unexpected ways.

The Talented Neighborhood
GS: Barry Van Dyke, Christian Van Dyke. Rob is pestered by parents of talented kids when his show holds a talent contest.

Father of the Week
GS: Patrick Thompson, Allen Fielder. Rob is upset when he learns Richie is ashamed of him.

The Twizzle
GS: Jack Albertson, Freddie Blassie. Sally takes the staff to a bowling alley to see a new dance.

One Angry Man
GS: Sue Ane Langdon, Dabbs Greer, Lee Bergere, Doodles Weaver, Patsy Kelly, Herb Vigran, Herbie Faye. Rob is called for jury duty.

Where You Been, Fassbinder?
GS: George Neise, Barbara Perry. Sally falls for Leo Fassbinder, an insurance salesman.

The Bad Old Days
Buddy convinces Rob he is dominated by Laura.

I Am My Brother's Keeper [Part 1]
GS: Jerry Van Dyke. Rob's sleepwalking brother comes for a visit.

The Sleeping Brother [Part 2]
GS: Jerry Van Dyke, Carl Reiner. Rob's brother auditions for the Alan Brady Show.

The Return of Harry Spangler
GS: J.C. Flippen. Rob tries to help an old radio comedy writer make a comeback.

Never Name a Duck
GS: Jane Dulo, Jerry Hausner. One of Richie's pet ducks dies and the family is heartbroken.

The Two Faces of Rob
Rob tries to prove Laura can't recognize his voice on the telephone by disguising his voice.

Bank Book 6565696
Rob is surprised when he learns Laura has her own bank account.

The Attempted Marriage
GS: Dabbs Greer, Ray Kellogg, Sandy Kenyon. Rob is two hours late for his own wedding.

Hustling the Hustler
GS: Phil Leeds. Rob knowingly plays pool with a pool shark.

What's in a Middle Name
GS: Cyril Delevanti, J. Pat O'Malley. Rob has to explain to Richie why his middle name is Rosebud.

My Husband Is Not a Drunk
GS: Roy Roberts, Charles Aidman. While under hypnosis Rob is conditioned to act drunk when he hears a bell.

Like a Sister
GS: Vic Damone. Sally falls for a ballad singer.

The Night the Roof Fell In
Rob leaves home after fighting with Laura.

The Secret Life of Buddy and Sally
GS: Phil Arnold. Rob thinks Buddy and Sally are fooling around.

A Bird in the Head Hurts
GS: Cliff Norton. Richie is pecked on the head by a giant woodpecker.

Gesundheit Darling
GS: Sandy Kenyon. Rob is allergic to Laura and Richie.

A Man's Teeth Are Not His Own
Rob feels he betrayed Jerry by going to another dentist.

Somebody Has to Play Cleopatra
GS: Bob Crane, Eleanor Audley, Shirley Mitchell. Rob directs an amateur play, but problems arise over the casting.

The Cat Burglar
GS: Barney Phillips, Johnny Silver. A phanton burglar robs the Petrie home.

The Foul Weather Girl
GS: Joan O'Brien. Laura is jealous of the new singing weather girl.

Will You Two Be My Wife?
GS: Barbara Bain, Allan Melvin, Ray Kellogg, Elizabeth Harrower. Rob is attacked by the girl he left behind when he entered the Army.

Ray Murdock's X-Ray
GS: Gene Lyons. During a TV interview Rob describes Laura as a nut.

I Was a Teenage Headwriter
Rob reminisces about his early days as a comedy writer.

My Husband Is a Check-Grabber
GS: Joan Shawlee, Phil Arnold. Laura tries to stop Rob's habit of picking up the check.

It May Look Like a Walnut
GS: Danny Thomas. After watching a science fiction movie, Rob dreams that an imported walnut will steal his thumbs and his imagination.

Don't Trip Over That Mountain
GS: Jean Allison, Ray Kellogg. Laura warns novice Rob not to ski on the big slopes.

Give Me Your Walls!
GS: Vito Scotti. Rob hires a famous painter to paint the living room.

The Sam Pomerantz Scandals
GS: Henry Calvin, Len Weinrib, Joan Shawlee. Rob, Laura and the office staff put on a variety show to help an old friend.

I'm No Henry Walden!
GS: Everett Sloane, Carl Reiner. Comedy writer Rob feels out of place at a party for several famous writers.

The Square Triangle
GS: Jacques Bergerac. A French sing-ing idol out of Rob and Laura's past comes for a visit.

Racy Tracy Rattigan
GS: Richard Dawson. Rob is jealous of a British film star's attention to Laura.

Divorce
GS: Joan Shawlee, Charles Cantor. Buddy is planning to divorce Pickles.

It's a Shame She Married Me
GS: Robert Vaughn. Rob is jealous of Laura's old boyfriend.

A Surprise Surprise Is a Surprise
Rob learns about Laura's plan to throw a surprise party for him.

Jilting the Jilter
GS: Guy Marks. A comic proposes marriage to Sally in order to get her to write his material.

When a Bowling Pin Talks, Listen
GS: John Silo, Herbie Faye, Carl Reiner. Rob unknowingly steals comedy material from another show.

All About Eavesdropping
Rob and Laura listen in on Jerry and Millie's conversation and risk losing their friendship.

That's My Boy
GS: Greg Morris. Rob remembers the day Richie was born, when he thought the hospital gave him the wrong baby.

The Masterpiece
GS: Alan Reed, Howard Morris. Rob and Laura buy two mysterious art objects at an auction.

Laura's Little Lie
GS: Charles Aidman. Laura tells Rob she lied about her age on their marriage license.

Very Old Shoes, Very Old Rice
GS: Burt Mustin, Madge Blake, Russell Collins. Rob and Laura learn they are not legally married.

Uncle George
GS: Denver Pyle, Elvia Allman. Rob's visiting uncle asks Rob to find him a wife.

Too Many Stars
GS: Sylvia Lewis, Eddie Ryder. Rob directs the parent's council annual show.

Who and Where Was Antonio Stradivarius?
GS: Betty Lou Gerson, Hal Peary, Chet Stratten. Rob attends a party in a strange town with a woman who adores him.

Big Max Calvada
GS: Sheldon Leonard, Arthur Batanides, Jack Larsen. A gangster gets Buddy, Sally and Rob to write for him.

The Ballad of The Betty Lou
GS: Danny Scholl. Rob and Jerry buy a sailboat.

Turtles, Ties and Toreadors
GS: Miriam Colon, Alan Dexter. Rob hires a maid to help Laura.

The Sound of the Trumpets of Conscience Falls Deafly on a Brain That Holds Its Ears . . . or Something Like That!
GS: Bernie Hamilton, Ken Lynch. Rob gets involved when he thinks he saw two crooks making a getaway.

The Third One from the Left
GS: Cheryl Holdridge, Jimmy Murphy. A young chorus girl has a crush on Rob.

The Alan Brady Show Presents
GS: Carl Reiner, Brendan Freeman, Cornell Chulay. The entire staff puts on a Christmas show.

My Husband Is the Best One
GS: Carl Reiner, Valerie York. Rob gets in trouble when Laura butts in to his interview with Alan Brady.

Happy Brithday and Too Many More
GS: Johnny Silver, Tony Paris. Rob and Laura give a birthday party for Richie and 63 friends.

The Lady and the Tiger and the Lawyer
GS: Anthony Eisley, Lyla Graham. Rob and Laura play matchmaker when a bachelor moves in next door.

The Life and Love of Joe Coogan
GS: Michael Forest, Johnny Silver. Laura's old boyfriend is now a priest.

A Nice Friendly Game of Cards
GS: Ed Platt, Shirley Mitchell. Rob uses a marked deck of cards and almost loses his friends.

The Brave and the Backache
GS: Ken Berry, Ross Elliott. Rob visits a psychiatrist.

The Pen Is Mightier Than the Mouth
GS: Dick Patterson, Herb Vigran, Johnny Silver. Sally becomes a TV personality, leaving Rob and Buddy to do her work.

My Part-Time Wife
GS: Jackie Joseph. Laura drives Rob crazy while helping out in the office.

Honeymoons Are for the Lucky
GS: Peter Hobbs, Allan Melvin, Kathleen Freeman. Rob recalls his marriage to Laura while still in the Army.

How to Spank a Star
GS: Lola Albright. Rob takes over as producer in order to please a temperamental star.

The Plot Thickens
GS: J. Pat O'Malley, Carl Benton Reid. Rob's and Laura's parents try to get the couple cemetery plots in their respective family burial grounds.

Scratch My Car and Die
Rob goes crazy when he finds a scratch on his new car.

The Return of Edwin Carp
GS: Richard Haydn, Arlene Harris, Bert Gordon. Rob gets three old-time radio stars to appear on the show.

October Eve
GS: Carl Reiner, Howard Wendell. A nude painting of Laura returns to haunt her.

Dear Mrs. Petrie, Your Husband Is in Jail
GS: Barbara Stuart, Arthur Batanides, Jackie Joseph. While visiting an army buddy in a night club, Rob is arrested.

My Neighbor's Husband's Other Life
GS: Johnny Silver. Rob and Laura suspect Jerry is fooling around with another woman.

I'd Rather Be Bald Than Have No Head at All
GS: Ned Glass. Rob thinks he is losing his hair.

Teacher's Petrie
GS: Bernard Fox, Cherrio Meredith. Rob can't believe Laura's writing teacher said she has talent.

My Two Showoffs and Me
GS: Doris Singleton. Rob, Buddy and Sally let their egos go wild when they are selected to be featured in a national magazine.

My Mother Can Beat Up My Father
Laura is better than Rob when it comes to self defense.

The Ghost of a Chantz
GS: Milton Parsons, Maurice Brenner. Rob, Laura, Buddy and Sally spend the night in a haunted mountain cabin.

The Lady and the Babysitter
GS: Eddie Hodges. Richie's babysitter has a crush on Laura.

The Vigilante Ripped My Sportscoat
Rob has a fight with Jerry over a lawn of crab grass.

The Man from Emperor
GS: Tracy Butler, Gloria Neil, Lee Phillips. Laura objects when Rob gets a job writing for a men's magazine.

Romance, Roses and Rye Bread
GS: Sid Melton. Sally is dating her secret admirer, a delicatessen owner.

4½
GS: Don Rickles. Rob and Laura are trapped in an elevator with a holdup man.

The Alan Brady Show Goes to Jail
GS: Don Rickles, Robert Strauss, Arthur Batanides, Allan Melvin, Ken Lynch. While entertaining at a prison, Rob is mistaken for an inmate.

Three Letters from One Wife
GS: Carl Reiner, Valerie Yerke. Rob's job is on the line when he gets Alan Brady to do a cultural documentary.

It Wouldn't Hurt Them to Give Us a Raise
GS: Roger C. Carmel. Rob, Buddy and Sally try to get raises.

Pink Pills for Purple Parents
GS: Tom Tully. Laura takes a couple of pills and suffers side effects.

The Death of the Party
GS: Pitt Herbert, Jane Dulo, Patty Regan. Rob goes to a party for Laura's relatives with a bad cold.

Stretch Petrie vs. Kid Schenk
GS: Jack Carter, Peter Hobbs, Lynn Borden. Rob has to stop his old friend from taking advantage of him.

The Impractical Joke
GS: Lennie Weinrib, Alvy Moore, Johnny Silver. Rob tries psychology to fight a practical joker.

Brother, Can You Spare $2500?
GS: Herbie Faye, Brian Nash. Rob receives a ransom demand for his lost script.

Stacey [Part 1]
GS: Jerry Van Dyke, Howard Wendell. Rob's brother is romantically involved with Sally.

Stacey Petrie [Part 2]
GS: Jerry Van Dyke, Jane Wald, Herbie Faye, Carl Reiner. Stacey tries to save his coffee house from closing and his romance from ending.

The Redcoats Are Coming
GS: Chad Stuart and Jeremy Clyde. Rob and Laura entertain two British rock stars.

Boy #1 vs. Boy #2
GS: Colin Male. Laura and Millie become typical stage mothers when their sons star in a TV commercial.

The Case of the Pillow
GS: Ed Begley, Alvy Moore, Joel Fluellen. Rob becomes a lawyer in order to defend a crooked salesman.

Young Man with a Shoehorn
GS: Lou Jacobi, Milton Frome, Jane Dulo. Rob invests in a shoe store.

Girls Will Be Boys
GS: Bernard Fox, Tracy Stratford, Doris Singleton. Richie is beaten up by a little girl.

Bupkiss
GS: Greg Morris, Tim Herbert, Robert Ball. Rob and an old Army buddy fight over the rights to a song they wrote while in the service.

Your Home Sweet Home Is My Home
GS: Eddie Ryder, Stanley Adams. Rob remembers when he and his friend tried to buy the same house.

Not Now Anthony Stone
GS: Richard Angarola, Frank Adamo. Sally's new boyfriend is mysterious about his profession.

Never Bathe on Saturday
GS: Bernard Fox, Arthur Malet, Kathleen Freeman. Laura gets her toe stuck in the bathtub waterfaucet.

100 Terrible Hours
GS: Dabbs Greer, Fred Clark, Harry Stanton, Johnny Silver. Rob recalls the day he went on his job interview with Alan Brady.

A Show of Hands
GS: Joel Fluellen, Henry Scott, Herkie Styles. Rob and Laura accidentally dye their hands black.

Baby Fat
GS: Sandy Kenyon, Strother Martin, Carl Reiner, Richard Erdman. Rob rewrites a play to help his boss.

Br-Room, Br-Room
GS: Sandy Kenyon, Johnny Silver. Rob buys a motorcycle and then gets arrested for joyriding.

There's No Sale Like Wholesale
GS: Lou Krugman, Peter Brocco, Jane Dulo. Rob and Laura buy a hot fur coat from Buddy's friend.

A Farewell to Writing
GS: Guy Raymond. Rob tries to write a book with great difficulty.

Coast to Coast Big Mouth
GS: Dick Curtis, Carl Reiner. Laura appears on a quiz show and blabs Alan Brady's secret: He wears a toupee.

Uhny Uftz
GS: Karl Lukas, Madge Blake, Ross Elliott. Rob follows a flying saucer to an upstairs office.

The Ugliest Dog in the World
GS: George Tyne, Michael Conrad, Florence Halop. Rob and Laura try to find a home for an ugly dog.

No Rice at My Wedding
GS: Van Williams, Bert Remsen, Allan Melvin. Rob and Laura recall the early days when they were first dating.

Draw Me a Pear
GS: Ina Balin, Jackie Joseph, Dorothy Neumann. Rob and Laura's art class teacher has a crush on Rob.

The Great Petrie Fortune
GS: Herb Vigran, Elvia Allman, Dan Tobin. Rob dreams of inheriting a fortune when he finds a valuable old photograph.

Odd But True
GS: Hope Summers, James Millhollin. Rob's freckles might win him $500.

Viva Petrie
GS: Joby Baker, Jack Bernardi. Rob and Laura's new house guest is a bullfighter turned handyman.

Go Tell the Birds and the Bees
GS: Peter Hobbs, Alberta Nelson. Richie's wild stories cause Rob and Laura to go see the school psychologist.

Body and Sol
GS: Garry Marshall, Michael Conrad, Paul Stader, Allan Melvin. Rob recalls the days when he was the boxing champ of the Army.

See Rob Write, Write, Rob, Write
GS: John McGiver. Rob and Laura both write a children's story.

You're Under Arrest
GS: Bella Bruck, Phillip Pine, Ed McCready. After fighting with Laura, Rob gets in trouble with the law.

Fifty-Two Forty-Five or Work
GS: Reta Shaw, Dabbs Greer, Al Ward. Rob recalls when he was out of work and Laura was pregnant.

Who Stole My Watch?
GS: Milton Frome. Rob suspects his friends when his watch disappears.

Bad Reception in Albany
GS: Tom D'Andrea, John Haymer, Robert Nichols. Rob tries to find a TV set while attending a cousin's wedding.

I Do Not Choose to Run [Part 1]
GS: Peter Brocco, Arte Johnson. Rob is asked to run for city council.

The Making of a Councilman [Part 2]
GS: Wally Cox, Arte Johnson, George Tyne. Rob agrees to run, but would rather see his opponent win.

The Curse of the Petrie People
GS: Tom Tully, Leon Belasco, Isabel Randolph. Laura accidentally drops a family heirloom down the garbage disposal.

The Bottom of Mel Cooley's Heart
GS: Carl Reiner. Mel takes Rob's advice and gets fired.

Remember the Alimony
GS: Allan Melvin, Don Diamond, Bernie Kopell. Rob and Laura recall the time they filled in an application for a divorce.

Dear Sally Rogers
GS: Richard Stahl, Bert Remsen. Sally advertises for a husband on a TV show and gets hundreds of answers.

Buddy Sorrell—Man and Boy
GS: Pippa Scott, Ed Peck. Buddy is suspected of having an affair or visiting a psychiatrist.

Long Night's Journey Into Day
GS: Ogden Talbot. Laura is frightened to spend the night alone in the house.

Talk to the Snail
GS: Paul Winchell, Henry Gibson. Rob applies for a job with a ventriloquist.

A Day in the Life of Alan Brady
GS: Joyce Jameson, Lou Willis. Rob and Laura's party for the Helpers becomes a TV documentary for Alan Brady.

Obnoxious, Offensive, Egomaniac, Etc.
GS: Forrest Lewis, Carl Reiner. Rob and his staff are in trouble when they write insults about their boss into a script.

The Man from My Uncle
GS: Godfrey Cambridge, Biff Elliott. Government agents move in with the Petries in order to watch a neighbor's home.

You Ought to Be in Pictures
GS: Michael Constantine, Jayne Massey. Rob is cast with a beautiful Italian actress in a low-budget film.

Love Thy Other Neighbor
GS: Joby Baker, Sue Taylor. Millie is jealous of the new neighbors.

The Last Chapter
GS: Carl Reiner. Rob's autobiography is seen in flashbacks.

The Gunslinger
GS: Allan Melvin. Rob dreams he is a sheriff in the Old West.

DIFF'RENT STROKES

On the air 11/3/78, off: Still continuing. NBC. Color videotape. Currently 40 episodes in reruns. Broadcast: Nov 1978-Oct 1979 Fri 8-8:30; Oct 1979-Sept 1982 Wed 9-9:30; Sept 1982-Cont. Sat 8-8:30. Producer: Norman Lear. Prod: Tandem. Synd: Embassy Pictures.

CAST: Philip Drummond (played by Conrad Bain), Arnold Jackson (Gary Coleman), Willis Jackson (Todd Bridges), Kimberly Drummond (Dana Plato), Mrs. Edna Garrett (Charlotte Rae), Mrs. Adelaide Brubaker (Nedra Volz).

The series is about two black orphans who are adopted by a white millionaire when their mother, his former housekeeper, died. Together with his own daughter and their housekeeper they live in a Park Avenue penthouse, where the boys cause all kinds of trouble. This series is primarily built around Gary Coleman. The series is still going strong on the network, but its reruns are shown during the morning network lineup.

[All episodes are directed by Herbert Kenwith.]

Movin' In [Pilot]
Arnold and Willis move in with Mr. Drummond.

The Social Worker
Arnold and Willis ask the social worker to find a black family who will have them, when they think Mr. Drummond doesn't want them.

Mother's Visit
Drummond's prejudiced mother comes for a visit, unaware that he has adopted two black kids.

The Spanking
When Drummond plans to spank Arnold, Willis objects because he feels he should be the one to discipline his brother.

Prep School
Drummond wants to send the kids to his old prep school, only to learn they won't accept blacks.

Goodbye Dolly
GS: Jack Riley. Arnold's doll is given away and he finds that he has been unable to sleep for days without it.

The Trial
Willis demands that Arnold be given a trial when Drummond accuses him of doing something wrong.

The Fight
Arnold is afraid to fight the school bully.

The Club Meeting
Willis's old club from Harlem rejects him when they think he believes he is now better than they are.

Gary Coleman (left), and Todd Bridges in the "Return of the Gooch" episode of Diff'rent Strokes.

The Woman
Arnold, Willis and Kimberly try to break up Drummond's marriage plans when they learn that his future wife plans to send them to school out of the country.

No Time for Arnold
Arnold pretends that he is a bedwetter in order to get attention from the family.

The Relative
Arnold and Willis's cousin fake an accident so she can also have a good life.

The Tutor
Drummond hires a tutor to help Willis with his work.

The New Landlord
GS: Jack Riley. The new landlord tries to throw the Drummond family out because children are not allowed in the building.

Willis's Privacy
Willis moves out when he feels he needs a room of his own, but Drummond won't give him one.

Hour Retrospective [One Hour]
At the end of the year, the family reminisces about the boys' first few months in the family.

Mrs. Garrett's Crisis
Mrs. Garrett feels she wants to do something with her life and plans to leave.

Willis's Job
Willis takes a job to pay for some skates, but gets fired on the first day.

The Trip
GS: McLean Stevenson, Kim Richards. Drummond goes to Seattle to see the new radio station he bought and to visit his old friend. [This is a crossover episode to the series "Hello Larry."]

Getting Involved
Arnold witnesses a mugging of a UN delegate, but when he plans to testify he is threatened.

Willis's Birthday
Willis wants to have his birthday party in Harlem, but Drummond is afraid to let his family go there on Saturday night.

The Girls' School/Garrett's Girls
Mrs. Garrett decides whether or not to become the housemother at Kimberly's school. [This was the first pilot for the spinoff series "Facts of Life."]

Arnold's Hero
GS: Muhammad Ali. Arnold pretends he is dying so he can get Muhammad Ali to visit him.

Arnold's Girlfriend [Part 1]
Arnold goes to the hospital where he befriends a white girl who will share a room with him, until her bigoted father forbids it.

Arnold's Girlfriend [Part 2]
Arnold comes home from the hospital. He later returns to visit the white girl who shared his room.

Feudin' and Fussin'
GS: McLean Stevenson, Kim Richards. The cast of "Hello Larry" come to New York to pay a visit to the Drummond family.

Garrett's Romance
Mrs. Garrett falls for a younger man.

The Adoption [Part 1]
Drummond is about to adopt Willis and Arnold when a man who claims he is their legal guardian shows up to claim them.

The Adoption [Part 2]
The man who shows up to claim Arnold and Willis turns out to be a phony.

Birds and Bees
Willis and Drummond explain the facts of life to Arnold.

Father and Son Day
GS: Reggie Jackson. Arnold asks an athlete to be his father for a contest at the YMCA so he can beat another boy.

The Rivals
A girl uses Arnold to make Willis jealous.

Thanksgiving Crossover
GS: McLean Stevenson, Kim Richards. The cast of "Hello Larry" visit again. Larry wants Drummond to buy a TV station so he can run it for him.

The Hot Watch
Willis and Arnold are accused of stealing a watch.

The Dog Story
Arnold is bitten by a dog that might have rabies.

The Election
Drummond is asked to run for a political office.

Friendly-Mate
Arnold and Willis fix Drummond up with a computer date, who happens to be a black lady.

Big Business
The boys go into the cookie business.

Poor Drummond
The boys try to get welfare when it seems that Drummond is broke.

Return of the Gooch
Arnold is bothered by the school bully, but Arnold thinks he is unstoppable when he learns he has a killer foot.

Valentine's Day Retrospective
The boys remember past episodes while they are locked in the basement storage room.

Teacher's Pet
Arnold is called the teacher's pet when

Drummond starts dating his teacher.

Guess Who?
Kimberly plans to teach her new boy-friend a lesson when she finds out he is a bigot.

Slumber Party
Kimberly wants to have a slumber party, at the same time Willis wants to have his friends spend the night.

Drummond's Will
Arnold thinks that Drummond is dy-ing when he rewrites his will.

The Squealer
When Willis joins a gang, Arnold can't decide whether to keep it a secret or to tell Drummond about it.

It's Magic
Arnold's disappearing trick leaves him stuck out on the window ledge thirty stories up.

DOBIE GILLIS

On the air 9/29/59, off 9/18/63. CBS.   B&W film. 30 min.   147 episodes.
Broadcast: Sept 1959-Sept 1962 Tue 8:30-9; Sept 1962-Sept 1963 Wed 8:30-9.
Producer: Martin Manulis. Prod Co & Synd: 20th Century Fox TV.
CAST: Dobie Gillis (played by Dwayne Hickman), Maynard G. Krebs (Bob Denver), Herbert T. Gillis (Frank Faylen), Winifred Gillis (Florida Friebus), Zelda Gilroy (Sheila James), Thalia Menninger (Tuesday Weld), Milton Armitage (Warren Beatty), Davey Gillis (Darryl Hickman), Chatsworth Osborne, Jr. (Steve Franken), Duncan [Dunky] Gillis (Bobby Diamond), Mr. Pomfritt (William Schallert).
The adventures of Dobie Gillis, a young dreamer who is always thinking about life, the pursuit of happiness and most of all girls. If Dobie isn't asking for money from his tightwad father, who owns a grocery, he is contemplating life with his best friend, Maynard Krebs, a true beatnik. *Dobie Gillis* is not a typical comedy; it represents the youth of America in a period of our society that shunned young people and their ideas. Dobie and Maynard lived through high school, the Army and college before this series was cancelled. *Dobie Gillis* is rarely seen in syndication because it really is a timepiece that today's young peo-ple cannot identify with, and remains a pleasant memory for most of us.
On May 10, 1977, a reunion episode was aired on CBS, starring most of the original cast, in the hopes that it would reactivate the series again. However, nothing ever came of it.
The original title of the series was *The Many Loves of Dobie Gillis*, but it is just called *Dobie Gillis* in syndication.
DIRECTORS: David Davis, Thomas Montgomery, Ralph Murphy, Stanley Z. Cherry, Rod Amateau, Guy Scarpitta.

The Best Dressed Man
GS: Mel Blanc.   Dobie and Milton compete for a date with Thalia.

The Big Sandwich
GS: Gordon Jones.   Dobie's plan to sell sandwiches at the school picnic backfires when a rainstorm causes the picnic to be cancelled.

Caper at the Bijou.
GS: Herbert Anderson, Stanley Adams. Dobie plans to fix the weekly jackpot at the local movie theater so he can use the prize money to take Thalia on a date.

The Chicken from Outer Space
Dobie and Maynard carry out a biol-

Bob Denver (right) as Maynard G. Krebs, and Jim Backus, in (The Many Loves of) Dobie Gillis.

ogy experiment on a couple of chickens. The experiment backfires when the chickens grow to become eight feet tall.

Competition Is the Life of Trade
GS: Jack Albertson. Dobie and Chatsworth compete for the attentions of a girl whose father runs a rival grocery store.

Couchville, USA
Herbert tries amateur psychiatry to find out what is bothering Dobie.

Deck the Halls
GS: Jack Albertson, Milton Frome, Alan Carney. Herbert revolts against the impossible demands made upon him by his family at Christmas time.

Dobie's Birthday Party
GS: Ronny Howard. Dobie almost misses his own surprise birthday party.

Dobie Gillis—Boy Actor
Dobie sabotages the school play in order to replace the lead player.

Dobie's Navy Blues
GS: Harry Von Zell, Yvonne Craig. Dobie falls for the daughter of a retired Chief Petty Officer.

Dobie Spreads a Rumor
GS: Dabbs Greer. Dobie spreads a rumor that Zelda has come into a lot of money to get her off his back for a while.

The Fist Fighter
Dobie becomes a fighter when he tries to impress Thalia.

The Flying Millicans
GS: Francis X. Bushman, Yvonne Craig. Dobie dates a girl athlete.

The French They Are a Funny Race
GS: Joey Faye. Maynard cleans himself up and shaves off his beard in order to impress the French girl who has fallen for him.

The Gaucho
GS: Alberto Morin. Dobie tries to get rid of the Argentinian boy who is interfering in his love life.

Greater Love Hath No Man
Dobie helps his friend Maynard court his new girlfriend.

Here Comes the Groom
GS: Dabbs Greer, Burt Mustin. Dobie decides to marry Zelda.

Hunger Strike
GS: Ryan O'Neal. Dobie goes on a hunger strike in order to get Thalia interested in him.

It Takes Two
Dobie tries to prove his father isn't as mean as he seems when Thalia refuses to date him, because she is afraid that if they got married their children might be as mean as Dobie's father.

Live Alone and Like It
Dobie and Maynard decide to leave home and share an apartment together.

The Long Arm of the Law
GS: Richard Reeves. Dobie gets in trouble when the father of his new girlfriend is a fat cop who doesn't like him.

Love Is a Fallacy
GS: Jason Wingreen. Dobie finds himself between his two girlfriends, when each of them tries to make him into her own version of the perfect man.

Maynard's Farewell to the Troops
Maynard joins the Army when he feels rejected by his friends.

The Old Goat
Dobie steals the mascot of the school's rival football team.

The Power of Positive Thinking
GS: John Abbott. Dobie studies philosophy in order to impress his girlfriend Thalia.

The Prettiest Collateral in Town
GS: Sherry Jackson, Rose Marie. Dobie finds that he must devote his attentions to the banker's daughter in order to soften up her father to give his dad a needed loan.

Put Your Feet in Our Hands
Dobie tries to prove himself to his new girlfriend by working in her father's shoe store.

The Right Triangle
Dobie tries to trick his new girlfriend into giving him her sympathy by convincing her that he is involved with a married woman. This causes her to think he is involved with the new math teacher.

Rock-a-Bye Dobie
Dobie's parents jump to the wrong conclusions when Dobie becomes engaged to his latest girlfriend and then they see him taking care of a baby.

Room at the Bottom
GS: Ronny Howard. Thalia talks Dobie's parents into sending him to a fancy Eastern prep school.

The Smoke-Filled Room
Dobie enters and wins the election for class president.

Soup and Fish
Dobie and Maynard are invited to a high society party.

The Sweet Singer of Central High
GS: Michael J. Pollard, Joey Faye. Dobie becomes a singing idol after a case of tonsilitis.

Taken to the Cleaners
GS: Alan Carney, Ben Welden. Dobie and Maynard accidentally capture some crooked dry cleaners.

A Taste for Lobster
Dobie tries to outdo a rival for Thalia.

That's Show Biz
GS: Reta Shaw, Richard Deacon, Burt Mustin. Herbert is conned into helping out at a parents' amateur charity show.

The Unregistered Nurse
GS: John Stephenson, Herb Vigran.
Dobie pretends to have a contagious
disease in order to attract the attention of a pretty nurse.

Where There's a Will
Herbert complains about signing his
will right before he and Wini are
about to leave on a delayed honeymoon.

Aah! Yer Fadder Wears Army Shoes
GS: Fuji. Dobie claims his father was
a war hero in order to impress a pretty
WAC.

Around My Room in 80 Days
GS: Steve Harris. Dobie tries to keep
a talented student from dropping out
of school.

Baby Shoes
Herbert decides to have Dobie's baby
shoes bronzed as cherished memories
when Dobie and Maynard prepare to
join the Army.

Baby Talk
Maynard finds an abandoned baby in
the park.

The Battle of Maynard's Beard
GS: Richard Bakalyan, Barlett Robinson. Dobie fights against the Army in
order to allow Maynard to keep his
beard.

*The Bitter Feud of Dobie and May-
nard*
Maynard tries to start a fight between
Dobie and himself in order to allow
Dobie to move on to better things
without being held back by him.

The Day the Teachers Disappeared
All of the teachers come down with
the flu at the same time.

The Chicken Corporal
GS: Jack Mullaney. Dobie is put in
charge of his squad.

The Big Question
Dobie and Maynard are required to

write an essay on the subject "Whither
Are We Drifting?" in order to graduate from school.

Be It Ever So Humble
GS: Norman Fell, Jonathan Hole. Do-
bie thinks Maynard has deserted the
Army because he was homesick.

Dobie Plays Cupid
Dobie tries to boost Maynard's confidence with girls.

Dobie vs. the Machine
Herbert tries to get Dobie to let a
psychometrician help him decide what
to do with the rest of his life. When
Dobie learns that a machine will make
the final decision, he decides to join
the Army.

Drag Strip Dobie
Dobie decides to build a hot rod in
order to impress his car-crazy girlfriend.

Everything But the Truth
Zelda invents a secret engagement to
Dobie in order to put a snooty girl in
her place.

The Face That Stopped the Clock
GS: Richard Reeves, Joey Faye.
Dobie talks Maynard into selling for an
Army surplus store in order to help
him overcome his anti-work complex.

*Goodbye, Mr. Pomfritt—Hello, Mr.
Chips*
GS: Jo Anne Worley. Dobie and his
friends try to convince their old school
teacher not to quit.

*Have You Stopped Beating Your
Wife?*
GS: Jack Albertson, Milton Frome.
Dobie tries to get his father to spend
more time at home with his mother
and less time at his lodge meetings.

*I Didn't Raise My Boy to Be a Soldier,
Sailor or Marine*
GS: John Fiedler, Frank Wilcox. Maynard misses the bus on the first day in
the Army and finds that his stand-in,

Chatsworth, has made him eligible for
Officers Candidate School.

I Was a High School Scrooge
GS: Douglas Dumbrille, James Millhollin. Dobie believes that an old grad is
broke so he tries to raise money to
help him out, unaware that he is a
wealthy miser.

Jingle Bells
Dobie becomes haunted by the Ghost
of Maynard when he decides to attend
a high society Christmas party with
Zelda rather than attend his friend's
party.

Like Father, Like Son, Like Trouble
Dobie and Maynard accidentally convince a colonel's daughter that they
are a war hero and his trusty aide.

*Like Mother, Like Daughter, Like
Wow*
GS: Jane Dulo, Yvonne Craig. Wini
becomes jealous when she learns that
the mother of Dobie's latest girl is an
attractive widow who was also Herbert's old girlfriend.

Maynard G. Krebs—Boy Millionaire
GS: Jack Albertson, Joey Faye, Milton
Frome. Dobie tries to prevent Maynard from losing the large sum of
money he found to a tricky con man.

Mystic Powers of Maynard G. Krebs
GS: John Banner, Dan Frazer. Maynard becomes a famous celebrity when
his powers of ESP land him on a TV
show.

Parlez-Vous English?
GS: Marcel Hillaire. Wini tries to get
Dobie to date the daughter of a
French artist.

*The Second Childhood of Herbert T.
Gillis*
GS: Marvin Kaplan, Robert Foulk.
Herbert decides to go to night school
to get his high school diploma.

The Solid Gold Dog-Tag
Chatsworth decides to join Dobie and
Maynard in the Army.

Spaceville
GS: Willis Bouchey, Bea Benaderet.
Maynard is accidentally launched with
a chimp in a space capsule to a deserted island which Maynard thinks is
the moon.

Take Me to Your Leader
GS: Ronny Howard, Peter Brocco,
Alan Carney. Maynard convinces
Dobie that Martians have taken over
the town disguised as familiar people,
causing him to lock his parents, Zelda,
the police chief and members of a
movie company in a freezer.

This Ain't the Way We Used to Do It
GS: Jack Grinnage. Herbert puts his
son's squad through some pre-graduation training when he feels that the
new soldiers are too soft.

What's My Lion?
GS: Henry Corden, James Millhollin.
Maynard finds that the lion which
escaped from the zoo has become
attached to him.

Who Needs Elvis?
Zelda helps Dobie win a school jazz
contest.

Will Success Spoil Dobie's Mother?
GS: Joyce Jameson. Wini enters a
contest in Dobie's name. When he
wins, he winds up with a date with a
beautiful movie star.

You Ain't Nothin' But a Houn' Dog
Dobie wins a newspaper contest with
an essay on Why My Father Is My
Pal.

Zelda, Get Off My Back
Dobie is glad to get rid of Zelda for a
while when she tutors Chatsworth
with his homework.

An American Strategy
Dobie gets a job at a lumber company

and begins to date the boss's daughter.

Bachelor Father . . . and Son
GS: Reta Shaw. Dobie and his father spend a week like real bachelors when Wini goes to visit her sister.

Back-to-Nature Boy
Chatsworth's Cousin Edwina meets Maynard at a party and decides to become a beatnik like him.

The Big Blunder and Egg Man
Dobie enters the stock market to impress his girlfriend.

Birth of a Salesman
Thalia convinces Dobie to quit college and become a salesman like her.

The Blue-Tail Fly
GS: Tom Reese. Dobie becomes a candidate in the race for student council.

Crazy Legs Gillis
GS: Joyce Van Patten, Michele Lee. Dobie and his friends decide to help a football player support his family.

Dig, Dig, Dig
Dobie goes with his Egyptology class on a field trip to Egypt because he has a crush on his professor.

Dobie, Dobie, Who's Got the Dobie?
Zelda becomes jealous when the most beautiful girl in school becomes interested in Dobie.

Dobie Gillis, Wanted Dead or Alive
GS: Joyce Van Patten, Stafford Repp, Hal England. Dobie tries to find a way to pass his poetry class in order to obtain the grades needed to transfer to Harvard so he can be near his girlfriend who has decided to attend Radcliffe.

Eat, Drink and Be Merry—For Tomorrow Ker-Boom
Maynard refuses to join his history class in deciding the contents of the time capsule which is going to be placed beneath a statue, because he thinks the world is going to end.

The Fast White Mouse
Dobie uses the heredity factor to discourage Zelda's interest in him.

For Whom the Wedding Bell Toils
Dobie and Maynard stow away on a boat headed for South America in order to escape from Zelda who is trying to get Dobie to marry her.

The Frat's in the Fire
Dobie's father bribes the members of a fraternity in order to get Dobie to be accepted as a member.

The Gigolo
GS: Bill Bixby. When Bernadine's fiance attends an out of town college, she pays Maynard to date her so she won't be tempted to date other boys.

Girls Will Be Boys
Maynard is unaware that his tomboy friend is really a girl until the night of the school dance.

Happiness Can't Buy Money
Chatsworth wants Herbert to teach him how to be a man.

Have Reindeer Will Travel
GS: James Millhollin. Maynard goes to work to pay back the class Christmas fund which he gave to a poor Mexican family as a present.

How to Cheat an Honest Man
Dobie tries to impress a girl who believes in complete honesty.

I Do Not Choose to Run
GS: John Fiedler. Herbert decides to run for office on the City Planning Commission.

I Remember Muu-Muu
Maynard decides to write an article about a beautiful anthropology professor for the school newspaper.

I Was a Boy Sorority Girl
Dobie and Maynard get jobs serving at a sorority party in order to earn enough money to take a society girl on a date. When the girl shows up at the party, Dobie and Maynard have to dress up like girls so they won't be recognized.

It Takes a Heap o' Livin' to Make a Cave a Home
GS: Douglas Dumbrille, Tom Reese. Dobie gets scared when his old enemy is returning home after becoming the heavyweight boxing champ of the Army. Dobie now believes he is coming to get him.

Like, Oh, Brother!
GS: Richard Reeves, Gary Walberg. Dobie and Maynard are forced to help their professor establish a settlement house in a rough neighborhood in order to pass their sociology class.

The Magnificent Failure
GS: James Dobson. Herbert decides to sell his store and use the money on gifts for his family.

The Marriage Counselor
Once again, Dobie decides to marry Zelda, and once again Maynard comes to the rescue.

Move Over, Perry Mason
GS: Charles Lane. Maynard decides to sue Herbert's insurance company when he gets his hand stuck in the gumball machine at the store.

Names My Mother Called Me
GS: Casey Adams, Russell Collins. Dobie decides to have his name changed until he meets the famous scientist he is named after.

The Richest Squirrel in Town
Dobie believes Maynard stole some money from a teacher's desk, even though he says he got it from a squirrel.

The Ruptured Duck
GS: John Fiedler. Dobie and Maynard enroll in college after the Army refuses to let them re-enlist.

The Second Most Beautiful Girl in the World
The parents of Dobie's new girlfriend refuse to allow her to go on a date with one boy at a time. She must take two on a date so she will not be tempted to marry a boy until she is sure that she is in love.

Sweet Success of Smell
GS: Yvonne Craig. Dobie and Maynard open up a Private Nose agency when it is discovered that Maynard can find missing items just by using his sense of smell.

This Town Ain't Big Enough for Me and Robert Browning
Dobie decides to follow the advice given in one of Robert Browning's poems and find that it costs him his new girlfriend and Zelda as well.

The Truth Session
Maynard embarks on a policy of always telling the truth, until he gets himself into all kinds of trouble.

When Other Friendships Have Been Forgot
Dobie becomes heartbroken when Maynard moves away with his parents to another town, until Maynard comes to live with him.

All Right, Dobie, Drop the Gun
A gangster and his girlfriend hold the Gillises hostage until their friend can pick them up.

And Now a Word from Our Sponsor
Dobie becomes the school disc jockey and finds that he is being bribed by a gangster to play his girlfriend's record over the air.

The Beast with Twenty Fingers
Maynard accidentally gets himself

handcuffed to Herbert, who is forced to dress him up as a woman, so he can attend a grocer's convention.

Beauty Is Only Skin Deep
Dobie's parents try to get the older sister of Dobie's girlfriend married off so he can marry the younger sister.

Beethoven, Presley and Me
Maynard becomes a zombie when the powers of a machine which can predict if a song will be a hit or a flop are transferred to him by accident.

The Call of the Life Wild
GS: Howard Caine, Sally Kellerman. Maynard accidentally uses a bottle containing a formula duplicating the odor of musk ox as hair oil. This makes him irresistible to any woman he comes in contact with.

The Devil and Dobie Gillis
Dobie and Chatsworth arrange to fix a raffle in order to split the first prize of five thousand dollars.

Dr. Jekyll and Mr. Gillis
GS: Paul Tripp, Howard McNear. Maynard drinks a chemical potion which turns him into a monster.

Flow Gentley, Sweet Money
GS: Yvonne Craig. Dobie tries to turn his Cousin Dunky into a tycoon.

A Funny Thing Happened to Me on the Way to a Funny Thing
GS: James Millhollin. Maynard tries to save a man from jumping off a window ledge. He saves the man but accidentally loses his balance and falls into the net below. He is then taken to the hospital when he is believed to be the jumper.

The General Cried at Dawn
While vacationing in a Latin American country, Dobie and Maynard are asked to help the President of the country sign a peace treaty by having Maynard take the place of a lookalike general, as a decoy, in case the wicked dictator of an adjoining country tries to interfere in the ceremony.

I Was a Spy for the F.O.B.
While in Washington, Maynard is mistaken by some foreign spies for a famous scientist who has developed a new rocket fuel.

The Iceman Goeth
Maynard and Dunky accidentally lock Herbert in the meat freezer. When they return hours later they discover his parka and a pool of water. They think he melted, so they run away to hide thinking they killed him.

Lassie, Get Lost
Dobie and Herbert try to find a movie star's missing dog in order to collect a reward.

Like Hi, Explosives
Maynard unknowingly drives around in a truck loaded with a can of nitorglycerin.

The Little Chimp That Couldn't
GS: Paul Tripp. Maynard tries to prove that a chimp named Seymour is not dumb, takes him home and tries to teach him a few tricks.

The Moon and No Pence
Dobie tries to impress a Russian ballerina by dancing outside her window on the grounds of her private estate.

Northern Comfort
Herbert's country cousin Virgil tries to con the family out of some money so he can become a singing star.

Now I Lay Me Down to Steal
Maynard is accused of stealing the jewels of the rich mother of Dobie's new girlfriend when he walks in his sleep.

Requiem for an Underweight Heavyweight
Maynard becomes a boxing champion when he takes some pills which give him superstrength.

The Rice-and-Old-Shoes Caper
Zelda gets Maynard to marry her, hoping Dobie will come to the rescue and agree to take his place.

A Splinter Off the Old Block
Dobie's Cousin Dunky tells his girl-friend that Dobie has a drinking prob-lem, which causes her to call a social worker to help him.

Strictly for the Birds
GS: Julie Parrish. Dobie and Maynard teach a mynah bird the answers to a history test, so it will give them the needed answers when they take the test.

Thanks for the Memory
Zelda tries to train Dobie's memory so he won't be a dope, in order to dis-courage the attentions of a girl who feels secure with him because he is a dope.

There's a Broken Light for Every Heart on Broadway
GS: Linden Chiles, Sid Gould. May-nard becomes the manager of a girl who wants to be a pop singer. When a big agent decides to take over her ca-reer, Maynard decides to stand aside and let her make it to the top without him.

There's Always Room for One Less
Herbert lets Chatsworth move in with him when his mother throws him out, in order to collect a reward for taking care of him when he returns home.

Three Million Coins in the Fountain
Chatsworth tricks Maynard into col-lecting money to help a needy family. What he doesn't tell him is that the money is to help his own family who have gone broke.

Too Many Kooks Spoil the Broth
Cousin Virgil decides to move in on Dobie's new girlfriend in the hopes of getting her and a job working for her father's company, at Dobie's expense of course.

Two for the Whipsaw
Chatsworth pays Dobie to take his place at a dinner engagement with an old friend of the family and his daugh-ter, while he goes on a date.

What's a Little Murder Between Friends?
GS: Dennis Patrick, Mousie Garner. Dobie thinks Thalia and Maynard are trying to kill him so she can collect the ten thousand dollars from his life in-surance.

What Makes the Varsity Drag?
GS: Bert Freed, Mickey Morton. Dobie joins the football team in order to impress the girlfriends of another player who is very big and equally very jealous.

Where Is Thy Sting?
GS: Howard McNear, Burt Mustin. Dobie confuses everyone when he claims to have six months to live, in order to impress a medical student.

Who Did William Tell?
Dobie tries to convince his Cousin Dunky to marry the young opera star he has a crush on, unaware that she has a jealous boyfriend.

Will the Real Santa Claus Please Come Down the Chimney?
Herbert tries to convince Maynard that there is no Santa Claus by climbing down the chimney, and then revealing it is only him. The only problem is that he gets stuck in the chimney com-ing down.

THE DONNA REED SHOW

On the air 9/24/58, off 9/3/66. ABC. B&W film. 274 episodes. Broadcast: Sept 1958-Sept 1959 Wed 9-9:30; Oct 1959-Sept 1966 Thu 8-8:30; Jan 1966-

Sept 1966 Sat 8-8:30. Producer: Bill Robert/Tony Owen. Prod Co: Screen Gems. Synd: Columbia Pictures TV.

CAST: Donna Stone (played by Donna Reed), Dr. Alex Stone (Carl Betz), Mary Stone (Shelley Fabares), Jeff Stone (Paul Peterson), Trisha Stone (Patty Peterson), Dr. Dave Kelsey (Bob Crane), Midge Kelsey (Ann McCrea).

WRITERS: Seymour Freedman, Tom and Helen August, John Elliotte, Phil Sharp, John Whedon. DIRECTORS: Andrew McCullough, Robert Ellis Miller, Jeffrey Hayden, Norman Tokar.

Theme: "Happy Days" by William Loose and John Seely.

The adventures of Donna Stone, her doctor husband and their children. Each week a typical family problem would pop up and they would try to solve it. The series was extremely popular during its original run of eight seasons, but it has since disappeared from every station.

Weekend Trip
GS: Jack Kelk. Donna and Alex plan to take the kids away for the weekend, but find that it is not so easy to get away as they thought.

Pardon My Gloves
Jeff gets beat up when he defends his mother against the nasty remarks made by a neighbor's kid about her acting ability.

The Hike
Donna takes Jeff and his friends on a camping trip when Alex is unable.

The Male Ego
GS: Sid Tomack, Alvy Moore, Lawrence Dobkin. Alex feels threatened when he feels that Donna has taken over his job as head of the house.

The Football Uniform
Jeff tries to earn enough money to buy a football uniform.

The Foundling
GS: Paul Picerni. Donna finds a baby on their doorstep and sets out to find to whom it belongs.

The Three Part Mother
GS: Ross Elliott. Donna finds that she must attend different functions on the same night.

Change Partners and Dance
Donna volunteers to teach Mary's date for the prom how to dance. The only problem now is that the boy has a crush on Donna.

Dough Re Mi
GS: Roger Til. Donna tries to get a concert pianist to perform at a benefit and Jeff tries to raise money to buy a tackling dummy for his football team.

Guest in the House
GS: Charles Herbert. A boy who ran away from a military school hides out with the Stones.

The Baby Contest
GS: Virginia Christine. Alex is named as the judge of a beautiful baby contest run by Donna's club.

The Beaded Bag
Donna tricks Alex into buying her an expensive beaded handbag.

The Busy Body
GS: Rhys Williams, Ann Doran, Irving Bacon. Donna's Uncle Fred pays a visit and almost wrecks everyone's life when he butts into their business.

A Very Merry Christmas
GS: Buster Keaton. Donna helps the janitor at the hospital put on a Christmas party for all the children.

Mary's Double Date
Mary tries to figure out which football player to take to the school prom.

Jeff's Double Life
GS: Peter Adams, Kathleen Freeman. Jeff hurts his arm when he and his friend Tommy take a joyride in Tommy's father's car. Jeff decides to use a different name when he goes to see the doctor, this way he won't hurt his father's practice.

Nothing But the Truth
GS: Charles Herbert. David, the runaway boy from a past episode, returns to celebrate his birthday with the Stones.

It's the Principle of the Thing
GS: Hans Conreid, Richard Deacon. Donna helps a poor man earn enough money to pay for his son's medical treatment.

Jeff vs. Mary
Jeff thinks his parents love his sister more than they love him.

Have Fun
GS: George Hamilton. Donna tells Mary about her first date with Alex.

Donna Plays Cupid
GS: Joanna Lee, Hal Baylor. Donna tries to find a suitable wife for Dr. Boland.

Love Thy Neighbor
GS: Howard McNear, Kathleen Freeman, Maudie Prickett. Donna tries to bring a fighting married couple back together again.

Report Card
Donna becomes concerned when Jeff brings home an all-"C" report card. She believes he can do better.

Boys Will Be Boys
GS: Charles Herbert, John Harmon. David Barker returns again, this time his father brings him to Dr. Stone when he thinks he might get rabies from the bite he got.

The Ideal Wife
GS: Sid Tomack, Keith Richards.

Donna becomes a tyrant when everyone thinks she is the perfect wife and will never become upset or mad at anyone.

Mary's Campaign
GS: Gigi Perreau. Mary runs for the office of class secretary with the help of a pushy campaign manager.

The Flowered Print Dress
GS: Addison Richards. Donna thinks the life has gone out of her marriage.

April Fool
GS: James Darren, Melinda Plowman, Ted Knight, Jesse White. A singing idol moves in with the Stones when he comes down with the measles.

The Parting of the Ways
Mary's friend thinks her parents are breaking up so she runs to Mary for advice.

The Hero
Alex's college roommate and football hero comes for a visit.

Do You Trust Your Child?
GS: Richard Tyler, Florida Friebus. Donna gives a speech at the PTA on how to handle children then finds that she is asked to solve more problems than she can handle.

The Grateful Patient
GS: Howard McNear, Kathleen Freeman. A patient gives Alex some business advice in return for helping his wife, but the advice turns out to be bad when the deal falls through.

The Testimonial
GS: James Bell. Donna gets the townspeople to give a retiring doctor a farewell dinner.

Miss Lovelace Comes to Tea
GS: Estelle Winwood, Margaret Dumont. Alex and the kids hire a housekeeper to help Donna with the housework.

Tomorrow Comes Too Soon
Donna and Alex complain that they never have time for themselves because they are always doing things for the children.

Advice to Young Lovers
Mary tries to win her boyfriend back after he is stolen away by another girl.

Operation Deadbeat
GS: Alan Reed. Alex tries to get Jeff to pay off his debts, while Donna tries to collect some of the bills Alex's patients owe him.

That's Show Business
Mary and a very shy boy are selected for the leading roles in the school play.

Sleep No More My Lady
Donna takes some sleeping pills and falls asleep during the middle of Alex's speech to a medical convention.

A Penny Earned
GS: Raymond Bailey. Donna is the only member of the family who is not getting a new outfit for an upcoming wedding.

A Friend Indeed
Jeff takes the blame for some pranks pulled by one of his friends, but he refuses to tell who he is protecting.

The First Child
GS: Dave Willock, Alice Backes. Alex and Donna are constantly being interrupted by a nervous couple who have just had their first baby.

Going Steady
GS: Sherry Alberoni. Mary wants Jeff to accept an invitation to a party from a girl so she can have a chance to meet the girl's older brother.

The Neighborly Gesture
GS: Robert Nichols. Alex becomes jealous when Jeff spends more time with the new neighbors than with him.

Nothing Like a Good Book
GS: Frank Wilcox, J. Edward McKinley. Donna and Alex try to interest their kids in reading books when they feel that they spend too much time watching TV.

Flowers for the Teacher
GS: Marion Ross. Jeff and the other students feel that the new teacher is out to get them.

All Mothers Worry
GS: William Schallert. A mother makes her son resign from the football team when she feels he will be hurt. Alex tries to teach her a lesson.

Jeff Joins a Club
Jeff tries to join his friend's club, but is rejected thanks to the help of his boastful friend.

The Punishment
Jeff and Mary are punished by Donna and not allowed to leave the house the next weekend, which upsets their plans.

A Difference of Opinion
GS: Hal Smith, Chet Stratton. Donna and Alex try to hide their arguments from the children when they learn that they become embarrassed by the manner in which their friends' parents fight.

The Homecoming Dinner
GS: Jay Strong. Alex and Donna are worried about Mary's date with a college boy who makes a play for every girl he sees.

Lucky Girl
Donna begins to resent the fact that Alex is considered a wonderful guy by all the women in the neighborhood.

The Broken Spirit
GS: Raymond Hatton. Jeff thinks he is responsible when an old man slips and breaks his leg.

The Secret
Mary hides an engagement ring given to her by a friend for safekeeping. When Donna finds the ring, she thinks that Mary is planning to elope.

The New Mother
GS: Charles Herbert.   David Barker runs away from the military school again and Jeff hides him in the basement.   David thought he would have a permanent home now that his father was planning to get married, but his father wants him to stay at the school.

Just a Housewife
GS: Constance Moore, Jerry Hausner. Donna takes offense at the way a radio show host treats the women he interviews on his program.

The Free Soul
GS: Myron McCormick.   Jeff quits school after he is influennced by an old man who tells him to do what he really wants to do.

The First Quarrel
Donna and Alex try to bring a fighting doctor and his wife back together again.

A Place to Go
GS: Stafford Repp.   Donna and her women's club try to find a place where Jeff and his friends can play.

A Night to Howl
GS: Richard Reeves.   Alex and Donna spend the night on the town when they feel that they are falling into a rut.

The Editorial
Jeff is thrown off the school paper for writing an editorial against homework. He stages a homework revolt in his class.

The Gentle Dew
Alex and Donna become worried when Mary doesn't return home after being on a date.

The Fatal Leap
GS: Jack Albertson.   Alex plans to attend a bachelor party for one of his friends.

Perfect Pitch
GS: Harry James.   Donna asks Harry James to see if Jeff has any musical talent.

Pickles for Charity
Donna decides to sell her homemade pickles to raise money for a charity.

Mary's Growing Pains
GS: Jack Hilton.   Mary falls for a young intern.

Alex Runs the House
Alex and Mary find that they have to take care of themselves when Donna and Jeff go away on a vacation.

The Career Woman
GS: Esther Williams, Richard Garland. A famous fashion designer comes to town to see if she would be happy being married to a doctor.

Jeff, the Financial Genius
GS: Herb Vigran.   Alex tries to teach Jeff a lesson in the act of swapping.

Mary's Crusade
Mary tries to make an unattractive girlfriend beautiful in time for the school dance.

The First Time We Met
GS: Bob Hastings.   Donna and Alex discuss the circumstances under which they first met.

The Gossip
Donna and Alex are rumored to be having problems with their marriage.

Love's Sweet Awakening
GS: Dan Tobin.   The son of their next door neighbor returns home from military school and falls in love with Mary.

The Wedding Present
GS: Tommy Farrell, Harriet MacGib-

bon. When Donna expects a visit from her aunt, she desperately tries to find the wedding present her aunt gave her.

Cool Cat
Donna and the family try to find a home for the kittens of Jeff's new cat.

Weekend
The Stones vacation at a rundown mountain resort.

The Mystery Woman
GS: Andrea King, Madge Blake. Donna finds that she cannot remember the name of the woman who claims she is an old friend.

Donna Decorates
GS: Jay North, Joseph Kearns. Donna redecorates the house with the help of Dennis the Menace.

The Love Letter
GS: Jay Novello. Donna mistakes the love letters Jeff wrote for their Greek handyman for his own love letters to his girlfriend.

How the Other Half Lives
Mary invites her friend to spend the weekend and goes all out to impress her.

Alex's Twin
GS: Jack Albertson. Mary is dating a boy who looks just like Alex did when he was the boy's age.

Worried Anyone?
Donna and Alex become worried when Mary goes on a date with a boy in an old car.

Higher Learning
GS: Richard Deacon. Jeff gets a high grade on an IQ test and is thought to be a genius.

Never Marry a Doctor
GS: Eddie Firestone. Donna thinks their new handyman stole the twenty dollars left on the kitchen counter.

It Only Hurts When I Laugh
Donna tries to prove that doctors make the worst patients when Alex has his appendix removed.

The Model Daughter
GS: Henry Beckman. Mary tries to become a fashion model.

Decisions, Decisions, Decisions
GS: Harvey Korman, Dick Wilson. Donna decides to let Mary make her own decisions from now on.

Donna Goes to a Reunion
Alex goes with Donna to her class reunion in the hopes of seeing her old boyfriend.

Someone Is Watching
Jeff's friend fakes an injury so he can have all the attention for himself.

Lean and Hungry Look
Alex and Donna go on a diet to lose some weight.

Character Building
Donna tries to prove that parents are responsible people to her children.

The World's Greatest Entertainer
Jeff tries out for the PTA amateur show with his impersonation act.

Variations on a Theme
GS: Harvey Lembeck. Mary invites a visiting rock 'n' roll pianist to play at her party.

The Stones Go to Hollywood
GS: George Sidney, Lassie. The Stones go on a trip to a Hollywood movie studio where they meet Lassie.

Donna Directs a Play
When the actor scheduled to direct a play cancels out, Donna is asked to direct the play instead.

Trip to Nowhere
Donna promises to take Jeff and Mary on a camping trip while Alex is away.

The Geisha Girl
GS: Miyoshi Umeki. Donna and Alex invite a visiting doctor and his Japanese wife over for dinner.

The Busy People
Donna and her friends decide that their husbands need a new interest in their lives, so Alex takes up painting.

Tony Martin Visits
GS: Tony Martin, Herb Vigran. Tony Martin and Donna fight traffic citations in court.

Aunt Belle's Earnings
GS: Gladys Hurlbut. Donna's aunt comes for a visit and convinces her old boyfriend to sell his land to the hospital for a new clinic.

The Poodle Parlor
GS: Frank Wilcox. Donna and her friend decide to open a poodle shop in town.

Mary's Heart Throb
GS: Claude Johnson, Sara Seegar. Mary is tricked into babysitting by her girlfriend who is now taking Mary's place with her boyfriend at a dance.

Merry Month of April
Donna surprises Alex by having his income tax prepared for him, instead of letting him do it himself.

Donna's Helping Hand
GS: Robert Shayne, Vladimir Sokoloff. Donna tries to get Alex to accept the job as director of the hospital.

Music Hath Charms
Donna gives Alex a music box which plays "their song."

Let's Look at Love
GS: Robert Singer. Mary decides to give up boys after she breaks up with her current boyfriend.

For Better or Worse
GS: Dort Clark. Alex is surprised when his friends have to ask their wives' permission to go on a fishing trip.

Jeff, the Treasurer
GS: Doodles Weaver. Jeff becomes the treasurer for the class but he proceeds to lose the money.

The Good Guys and the Bad Guys.
GS: Leonard Stone. Jeff is reluctant to join the church choir.

Military School
GS: Chris Robinson. Mary dumps her boyfriend Herbie when she sees his friend Ken who is visiting from military school.

Mary's Driving Lesson
Mary decides to take driving lessons from her friend Scotty instead of going to a driving school.

The Mustache
GS: Doodles Weaver. Donna becomes upset when Alex decides to grow a mustache.

Mary's Little Lambs
Mary's boyfriend Mark gets her to help him babysit with several children.

One Starry Night
GS: James Darren. Mary has a date with a singer but is unaware just who he really is.

A Rose Is a Rose
GS: John Zaremba. Jeff is unable to attend a baseball game with Alex because he has to rewrite his English composition.

The Close Shave
Jeff believes he is growing a beard and asks permission to buy a shaving kit.

The Mouse at Play
GS: John Astin, Cloris Leachman. Donna tries to learn if Alex has lost interest in her by getting her hair dyed.

The Monster
A huge dog turns up on the Stones' doorstep and Jeff decides to keep him.

New Girl in Town
GS: Candy Moore. Donna tries to fix Jeff up with the new girl in town.

One of Those Days
Alex and Donna prepare to spend a day in the country, but find everything seems to go wrong on the way there.

All Is Forgiven
GS: William Windom. Alex and Donna try to bring a fighting couple back together by trying to get them to adopt a baby.

The Electrical Storm
GS: Richard Deacon. Jeff is expelled from school when he refuses to turn in his friends who have been playing around with the school's bell system.

The Paper Tycoon
Jeff decides to buy three paper routes and hire three kids to work for him.

Private Tutor
Donna hires a boy in Mary's class to tutor her in French, unaware that he is the boy that Mary has a secret crush on.

Alex, the Professor
Alex decides to use psychology on his children but finds it doesn't work the way he planned.

The Fabulous O'Hara
GS: Cecil Kellaway. Jeff decides to help an orphan and his grandfather find a permanent home.

Way of a Woman
Alex promises to take Mary with him on a trip to Chicago when her boyfriend breaks a date with her to go skiing.

A Very Bright Boy
GS: Johnny Crawford. The lazy but bright son of one of Donna's friends comes for a visit.

The Toughest Kid in School
GS: Kirk Alyn. A new kid tries to impress Jeff by making it seem like he is a delinquent.

Dr. Stone and His Horseless Carriage
GS: Oliver McGowan, Gale Gordon. Alex gets an old 1911 horseless buggy as payment for his services.

For Angie with Love
GS: Candy Moore. Jeff tries to impress his girlfriend by buying her an expensive present.

Aloha, Kimi
GS: Miyoshi Umeki. Alex goes to Hawaii to help a girl who was hurt in a surfboard accident.

Donna's Primadonna
GS: James Stacy. Donna becomes upset when Mary decides to become a singer rather than go to college.

Explorers Ten
Jeff and his friends try to earn enough money to buy a telescope for their club.

The New Office
GS: Alan Hewitt. Alex plans to move his office from the house to a new medical office building.

The Golden Trap
Mary convinces her parents that she can take care of the house and Jeff while they go away on a trip.

Free Flight
GS: William Lanteau. Donna writes to the head of an airline to complain and gets a free flight in return.

Wide Open Spaces
GS: William Windom. Donna and Alex visit their friend's farm, only to find them unhappy about farm life and wanting to return to the city.

The Fire Ball
GS: Candy Moore. Jeff and his girl-friend are chosen to play the leads in the school play.

Once Upon a Timepiece
Donna buys Alex a watch in a pawn shop and tries to help the former owner of the watch.

Hilldale 500
GS: Candy Moore. Alex helps Jeff build a racing cart to enter in a race.

Winner Take All
GS: Ken Lynch, Allan Hunt. Alex tries to help a father who is disap-pointed in his son's pitching at a base-ball game.

Skin Deep
Mary is reluctant to date a boy be-cause he has big ears.

The Fortune Teller
Donna finds the predictions she made while playing fortune teller at a bazaar start coming true.

Man of Action
Alex finds himself babysitting for a little boy when everyone else find they have other things to do.

Donna Meets Roberta
GS: Roberta Sherwood, Gale Gordon, Robert Lansing. Alex buys the house of a poor widow when he learns a shopping center is going to open which will increase the value of the prop-erty.

The Caravan
GS: Al Checco. Donna decides to rent a house on wheels and have the family spend their summer vacation on the road.

The Swingin' Set
Jeff tries to help his friend get a date for the prom.

On to Fairview
GS: Paul Tripp. Jeff tries to earn enough money riding a bicycle for a publicity stunt in order to pay for a crystal pendant for his mother.

The Man in the Mask
GS: Don Drysdale. Don Drysdale coaches Jeff when he has been chosen to umpire a girls' baseball game.

The Father Image
Alex tries to help his family with their problems while worrying about one of his patients on whom he just per-formed surgery.

Dear Wife
Donna and Alex think Mary is plan-ning to elope with the man she met at a friend's wedding.

Mister Nice Guy
Jeff suddenly becomes considerate to Mary who is planning to leave for col-lege, so she thinks he must want some-thing from her but she doesn't know what.

Mrs. Stone and Dr. Hyde
GS: Dick Wilson. Donna substitutes for Alex's nurse who has left to get married. She learns that working for Alex is not all the fun she thought it would be.

To Be a Boy
GS: Brooke Bundy. Jeff and his friend Smitty promise not to date an-other girl in order to save enough money to build a boat and sail the Caribbean.

Who Needs Glasses?
GS: Harvey Korman. Jeff tries to prove that he needs glasses so he can wear them to impress his girlfriend.

Mary, Mary, Quite Contrary
Mary decides to move out and rent a room at college.

My Dad
Alex and Jeff's plans to do things to-gether are constantly being interrupt-ed by his father's emergency calls.

Fine Feathers
Jeff finds a bird which he believes to be worth a few hundred dollars.

Rebel with a Cause
GS: Harvey Korman, Harold Gould, William Zuckert, Dick Wilson. Donna is selected to take part in a survey of housewives to determine how long they spend doing each household chore.

Big Star
GS: Arthur Malet. Mary tries to help a gardener's assistant become a singing star.

Man to Man
Jeff tricks his father into taking him and his friends on a camping trip.

The Make-Over Man
GS: James Stacy, Bob Rodgers. Mary tries to remodel her boyfriend into the man she wants him to be.

The Winning Ticket
Jeff finds a raffle ticket and is surprised when he wins a car.

The Soft Touch
Jeff sets out to collect the money his friends owe and Alex tries to collect payment from some of his patients.

Jeff Stands Alone
GS: James Stacy. Jeff goes to the city to try and make it on his own.

Just a Little Wedding
GS: Brenda Scott, Robert Hogan, Binnie Barnes. Alex and Donna regret lending their home for their friend's wedding when the bride's mother redecorates the house and invites hundreds of guests.

A Woman's Place
Donna runs for a position on the Town Council.

The Chinese Horse
GS: Paul Winchell, Jerry Douglas. Donna is asked by a strange woman to buy a Chinese horse statue for her.

The New Look
GS: Allan Hunt. Mary tries to change her personality.

A Way of Her Own
An eight-year-old orphan girl comes to live with the Stone family.

Three Is a Family
Mary becomes jealous of all the attention Trisha is getting.

Big Sixteen
GS: Brooke Bundy. Jeff falls in love with an older woman after he has a fight with his girlfriend on his 16th birthday.

Pioneer Woman
GS: Jim Davis. Alex and Jeff spend the weekend at the cabin of Alex's friend Red. Donna and Mary follow them in order to show them that they are capable of roughing it like the men.

The House on the Hill
Donna visits the home of an old recluse and finds she is not allowed to leave.

Where the Stones Are
Alex and Donna follow Mary to a resort for the weekend in order to check up on her.

The Two Doctor Stones
GS: Bob Crane. Alex and Donna prepare to go away for the weekend, but Donna changes her mind when she thinks Trisha is going to be sick.

Everywhere That Mary Goes
Mary's new boyfriend follows her around to protect her from other boys.

The Handy Man
GS: Doodles Weaver. Donna hires a bumbling handyman to fix the house.

Friends and Neighbors
Alex's friend and his wife buy the house next door. Donna offers to turn the wife, Midge, into a good housekeeper.

Boys and Girls
GS: Cheryl Miller. Jeff takes his girl to a college dance where she runs off with Mary's date.

All Those Dreams
GS: Don Drysdale, Ginger Drysdale, Kelly Drysdale, Paul Winchell. The family goes on a trip to Chicago where Jeff tries to get an interview with his friend Don Drysdale.

All Women Are Dangerous
Jeff finds that two girls want to go to a party with him but he can't make up his mind whom to take.

The Big Wheel
Jeff buys an old bus at an auction.

Day of the Hero
Jeff makes a date with a girl to take her to the prom, but when he believes he is going to be voted class president he asks another girl to go. He now finds himself stuck with two dates.

What Are Friends For?
Jeff gets his friend Smitty to take his place when his father asks him to take a friend's daughter on a date.

Brighten the Corner
GS: Oliver McGowan. Trisha messes up the house right before Alex is expecting company for dinner.

Whatever You Wish
GS: Whit Bissell, Dort Clark. Jeff saves the life of a rich lady's daughter and in return she says he can have anything he wants.

House Divided
The Stones and the Kelseys plan to share a cabin for the summer.

The Boys in 309
Jeff becomes a football hero but is badly hurt during the game.

The Bigger They Are
GS: Jacques Aubuchon, Peter Leeds. Donna tries to convince an Armenian farmer to allow a freeway to be built on his land, otherwise the freeway will be built on her land.

It Grows on Trees
GS: Henry Kulky. Jeff and Smitty try to sell some trees in order to earn some money so they can go on a skiing trip.

Mary Comes Home
Mary comes home for a visit, so Donna plans a surprise party.

Post Time
GS: George Chandler. Jeff and his friends borrow a race horse in order to try and win enough money to pay for the band's new uniforms.

Sweet Mystery of Life
Alex gets a telegram but forgets to read it, causing Donna to become curious over its contents.

A Touch of Glamour
GS: Alice Pearce. Alex buys Donna an expensive gown but she thinks it is too expensive and returns it.

Air Date
Jeff gets a CB and makes a date with a mystery girl.

Moon-Shot
GS: John Banner. Jeff and Smitty try to make some money by selling tickets to a dance.

Nice Work
Jeff gets a job escorting a girl around town.

First Addition
GS: Sam Jaffe, Walter Janowitz, Mary Wickes. Donna relates to her friend Midge the story of what her life was like when Mary was born.

The Combo
Jeff tries to get his musical group a job playing at a girls' club.

Who's Rockin' the Partnership?
Alex and Donna recall the time Jeff and Smitty tried to make some money operating a gas station while the owner was away for the summer.

Something Funny Happened on the Way to the Altar
Dave tells the Stones how he met his wife on a blind date.

Today I Am a Girl
Donna tries to turn tomboy Trisha into a lady.

Will the Real Chicken Please Stand Up?
GS: William Lanteau. Donna teaches Midge how to drive a car so she can get her license.

Guest in the Nursery
Trisha decides to keep the baby fawn that Dave Kelsey found.

Home Sweet Homemaker
Dave moves in with the Stones when he has a fight with Midge over her cooking.

Teamwork
GS: Peter Robbins. Trisha and her friends help Donna around the house.

Neither a Borrower Nor a Lender Be
Donna tries to get Midge to repay all of the money she borrowed from her.

Pandemonium in the Condominium
GS: Fritz Feld. Donna and Alex and the Kelseys decide it would be cheaper if they were to buy one washer and one set of golf clubs and share them.

Day for Remembering
As Jeff prepares for his graduation, the family remembers via flashback some previous happenings in their lives.

One Little Word
Donna tries to figure out the meaning of the word Alex says in his sleep.

Love Letters Are for Burning
GS: Kathleen Crowley. Dave is worried that his former girlfriend will use his love letters to her as the subject matter for her next book.

Four's a Crowd
The Stones and the Kelseys try to find a way to keep from spending all of their time together.

My Son the Catcher
GS: Don Drysdale, Leo Durocher, Willie Mays, William Bramley. Donna becomes worried when Jeff decides that playing baseball is more important than his education.

The Pros and the Cons
Donna and Midge try to learn how to play golf in order to teach their husbands a lesson.

Operation Anniversary
Jeff tries to earn some money to take his parents to a restaurant to celebrate their anniversary.

Dad Drops By
Alex's father causes trouble when he pays a visit to his son's family.

Play Ball
GS: Leo Durocher, Don Drysdale, Willie Mays. Leo, Willie and Don join a charity baseball game when the hospital staff takes on the college freshmen.

Who's Who on 202?
GS: Richard Conte, Byron Morrow. Donna thinks the man who helped her when her car broke down is an escaped convict.

The Daughter Complex
Mary becomes so interested in psychology that she starts to analyze everyone in the family.

The Tycoons
Alex and Dave invest in the stock market and plan to use their profits to buy color TV sets.

Instant Family
Dave and Midge take care of the kids when Alex and Donna leave town.

Royal Flush
GS: Vito Scotti, Maxie Rosenbloom. Two con men pose as visiting royalty.

Circumstantial Evidence
Alex gets jealous when he finds a picture of Donna's boyfriend in the house.

Anyone Can Drive
Jeff tries to teach his girlfriend Karen how to drive.

Surprise Surprise
Alex and Dave plan a surprise birthday party for Midge.

Quads of Trouble
GS: Dr. Edward R. Annis. Alex delivers quadruplets in his house when a pregnant woman couldn't make it to the hospital in time, only now his house has become a nursery.

Donna's Bank Account
Donna writes a check and gives it to Midge, only to find that she has overdrawn her account. She now has to get the check back before it bounces.

It's All in the Cards
Midge takes up fortune telling and begins to believe she has mystic powers when the predictions come true.

Old Faithful
Mary becomes depressed when she learns that her boyfriend Scotty is dating another girl.

Overture in A-Flat
Jeff and Smitty move into an apartment but wish they hadn't when all of their school friends come over to freeload.

Thy Name Is Woman
Midge becomes jealous when a strange man takes an interest in Donna.

Joe College
Alex's father returns, this time he enrolls at Jeff's college when he is retired from his old job.

Painter Go Home
GS: John Fiedler, Nora Marlowe. Donna hires a painter to paint the living room, but soon finds she hired a busybody who makes himself right at home.

Home Wreckonomics
Midge offers her home to Karen who must run the finances of a home for her economics class.

The Windfall
GS: Oliver McGowan. Jeff buys a suitcase at an auction and discovers that it contains over five hundred dollars.

Now You See It Now You Don't
GS: Buster Keaton. Donna tries to get the car fixed before her husband sees the damage caused by the truck that hit her.

The Gift Shop
GS: Ellen Corby, Peter Hobbs. Jeff gets a job at a gift shop but gets bored when there is no business.

The Stamp Collector
GS: John Hiestand. Donna and Alex go to cash in her trading stamps for a pressure cooker, but Alex decides he would rather have a new putter.

Peacocks on the Roof
Alex claims he has seen several animals in their yard, but when anyone comes to look they disappear, causing Alex to think he is seeing things.

Guests, Guests, Who Wants Them?
Donna prepares a dinner for Dave's god-daughter who is visiting from college.

The Unheroic Hero
GS: Frank Gerstle, Allan Hunt. Jeff's friend saves a dog that ran into an abandoned mine.

That Mysterious Smile
GS: Barry Atwater, Michael Fox, Kim Darby, Cheryl Miller, Robert Fortier. Jeff writes a note to the girl he wants to take with him on a skiing weekend, but it unfortunately is given to the wrong girl and now Jeff has to try to get out of the date.

The Rolling Stones
GS: Aron Kincaid.   The Stones and the Kelseys run into all kinds of trouble while on the way to spend a weekend on a boat.

Indoor Outing
GS: Jim Davis, Al Checco, James Stacy. Donna stays home with Trisha when she gets sick. Since they can't go on their scheduled fishing trip, she relates to Trisha via flashbacks what happened on past camping and fishing trips.

Pop Goes Theresa!
GS: Tisha Sterling. Jeff dates a wild girl named Theresa who causes Jeff and herself to get arrested.

With This Ring
Donna loses her wedding ring and tries to replace it with a cheap lookalike so Alex won't realize it is missing until after she finds the ring.

The Boy Meets Girl Machine
Jeff decides to use the school computer to pick the dates for the Freshman-Sophomore party.

Think Mink
Donna and Midge fight over the mink coat which one of them won, but don't know who because they shared the cost of the raffle tickets.

Four on the Floor
Jeff buys a car from Karen's uncle but regrets it when the car stops running.

Charge!
GS: Arch Johnson.   Donna's credit application at a department store is rejected, but Trisha finds that she has been able to get her pet monkey a charge account at the store.

Do Me a Favor—Don't Do Me Any Favors
GS: Lloyd Corrigan. Jeff tries to prevent one of his professors from being retired, unaware that that is just what he wants to do.

Author! Author!
Donna tries to write a story about her family without them finding out.

Trees
GS: Paul Reed, Karl Lukas. Donna tries to prevent the town from replacing the carob tree in front of their house with an elm tree.

The Big League Shock
GS: Mark Slade, Charles Lane. A student, the son of Donna's friend, forges Alex's name on a prescription to get some pep pills to help him pass his test.

The Gladiators
GS: Lee Patrick.   Alex's father and Midge's mother both come for a visit at the same time and find that they have fallen for each other.

Rallye Round the Girls, Boys
GS: Dabney Coleman. Jeff and Smitty agree to race against their girlfriends in an auto race.

Slipped Disc
GS: Janis Hansen. Jeff and his friends form a corporation to earn enough money to have their songs recorded on a record.

Uncle Jeff Needs You
GS: DeForest Kelley. Jeff tries to get two kids to sign up for summer camp before he can get a job as a counselor.

Never Look a Gift Horse in the Mouth
Jeff and his friends agree to fix up a cabin in return for permission to hold his fraternity parties at the cabin.

How to Handle Women
GS: Linda Gaye Scott. Jeff tries to prove that he knows how to handle a woman.

My Son, the Councilman
GS: Paul Reed, Buddy Lewis, John Qualen. Jeff runs for city councilman in order to keep the city parks open.

Do It Yourself Donna
GS: Sandy Kenyon. Donna and Alex attempt to put together a stereo from a do-it-yourself kit in time to give to Jeff for his birthday.

When I Was Your Age
GS: John Stephenson. Alex and Donna try to discourage Jeff from wanting to marry his girlfriend.

Calling Willie Mays
GS: Willie Mays. Willie reserves two seats for Alex and his client, but finds that Jeff has beaten them to the tickets.

All This and Voltaire Too?
GS: Stanley Adams, Barbara Shelley. Donna and Midge join a French class given by the owner of a French restaurant.

The Return of Mark
GS: Warren Stevens. Donna's old boyfriend who is now a millionaire comes for a visit.

Is There a Small Hotel?
GS: Arte Johnson, James Hong. The Stones try to find a place to stay while on vacation in California.

No More Parties—Almost
GS: Kirk Alyn. Donna tries to get out of a dinner party because she and Alex have become exhausted from attending several functions week after week.

So You Really Think You're Young at Heart
Dave and Alex think they are getting old, so Midge and Donna set out to prove they are wrong.

What Price Home?
GS: Sarah Marshall. Alex sells his house to the couple who used to live in it before they did. When the time comes to move, Alex changes his mind about selling.

By-Line—Jeffrey Stone
GS: Leslie Gore, Binnie Barnes. Jeff and Smitty try to get Leslie Gore to sing their song.

THE DORIS DAY SHOW

On the air 9/24/68, off 9/10/73. CBS. Color film. 128 episodes. Broadcast: Sept 1968-Sept 1969 Tue 9:30-10; Sept 1969-Sept 1973 Mon 9:30-10. Producer: Terry Melcher. Prod Co: Arwin Hilltop Company. Synd: Worldvision.

CAST: Doris Martin (played by Doris Day), Buck Webb (Denver Pyle), Leroy (James Hampton), Billy Martin (Phillip Brown), Toby Martin (Todd Starke) Juanita (Naomi Stevens), Myrna Gibbons (Rose Marie), Michael Nicholson (McLean Stevenson), Ron Harvey (Paul Smith), Angie Palucci (Kaye Ballard), Louis Palucci (Bernie Kopell), Cy Bennett (John Dehner), Jackie Parker (Jackie Joseph).

The story of Doris Martin, a widow, who goes to work for a national magazine as a reporter. The series went through several cast and format changes during its five-year run, which is one reason it is rarely if ever run. The show is somewhat dated and no longer fits in with today's audiences.

The Job
Doris's former employer tries to get her to come back to her old job.

Let Them Out of the Nest
When the boys get an egg route, Doris helps out so much that the boys decide to pretend they are sick, leaving Doris to deliver the eggs herself.

Love a Duck
Doris tries to prevent a poacher from killing ducks on her farm.

Buck's Girl
Buck and a veterinarian both fall in love with a manicurist.

The Songwriter
Doris tries to convince Leroy that he is the victim of a phony music publisher.

The Matchmakers
The boys try to fix their mother up with the deputy sheriff.

The Camping Trip
Buck invites the boys to go with him and his old Indian friend on a camping trip.

The Uniform
Toby becomes jealous when his brother joins the little league and his mother raves about his uniform.

The Librarian
Leroy falls for the local librarian and in order to impress her he cons her into believing he is an expert on 19th century poetry.

The Friend
In return for donation of milk for the school kids, Doris and her family agree to pose for a milk ad. In order to complete the family picture they need two girls, so she asks each of the boys to invite home a girl in their class they would like to have as a sister. So Toby chooses a black girl.

Dinner for Mom
The boys take their mother out to dinner with the money they earned; the only problem is they don't have enough to pay the bill and Doris didn't bring her wallet.

Leroy B. Simpson
Buck accuses Leroy of stealing Doris's jewelry.

The Antique
Two old ladies conned the kids out of a valuable antique. Doris has to try to get it back.

The Black Eye
Billy gets hit in the eye by a little girl.

The Relatives
Leroy's bumbling relatives help Doris and Juanita repaint the house.

The Tiger
A tiger escapes from a circus van and Doris unknowingly takes it home with her in the back of her truck.

The Still
Doris tries to help her two elderly neighbors from being arrested by federal agents for running an illegal whiskey still.

The Gift
Leroy believes that he is going to be fired when he sees the family doing his chores, unaware they are just practicing for when they send him on a trip to visit his grandma as a gift for his first anniversary with the family.

The Baby Sitter
Doris volunteers to babysit with the neighbor's kids when their mother goes to the hospital to have a baby.

Love Thy Neighbor
A crafty neighbor keeps Doris prisoner until she can get her son to marry her (the neighbor), so her son won't have to pay for the horse Doris sold him.

The Musical
Buck volunteers Doris to direct the grammar school musical.

The Con Man
Doris is put in charge of raising money for the new convention center, and falls prey to an architect who is really a con man out to steal the money she raised.

The Flyboy
An Air Force officer bets his friends that he will get Doris to fall in love with him after their first date. Doris finds out about the bet and plans to ruin his plans.

The Five Dollar Bill
When Billy returns a wallet he found, the owner accuses him of stealing five dollars from it.

The Buddy
A woman Marine puts the household on a strict schedule when Doris is out of town.

The Tournament
Buck tries to get Leroy to be his partner in the horseshoe throwing contest.

The Clock
Leroy gives Doris a clock as a gift, but the clock chimes so loudly that she can't fall asleep.

The Date
Doris plays matchmaker between Juanita and the owner of a sporting goods store.

Doris Gets a Job
Doris gets a job working on a magazine in San Francisco as the secretary to the managing editor.

The Woman Hater
Doris tries to convince a woman hater to change his views about women.

A Frog Called Harold
Toby's frog escapes from Doris's purse

and ruins Nicholson's chances of getting a needed bank loan.

The Chocolate Bar War
Doris helps Billy beat out another boy and his aggressive mother to win a candy selling contest, only to learn that the woman is the wife of an important client of the magazine.

Married for a Day
Doris poses as her boss's wife in order to scare away a husband-hunting female.

Buck's Portrait
Buck is reluctant to have his portrait painted by a woman artist until he learns that it is going to appear on the cover of the magazine Doris works for.

The Health King
Doris tries to get the publishing rights to a health fanatic's book.

The Gas Station
Doris and Myrna take over Leroy's gas station while he is visiting his wife who is in the hospital having a baby.

Doris Strikes Out
GS: Jacques Bergerac. Doris has to umpire the boys' basketball game and go on a date with a French movie star at the same time.

Doris vs. the Computer
Doris gets into a fight with Mr. Jarvis and the electric computer when she claims she paid her electric bill and the computer says she didn't.

Doris, the Model
Doris finds that she has to model all of the new clothes for a fashion show when the other models fail to show up for work.

The Prizefighter and the Lady
GS: Larry Storch. Doris finds herself interviewing a boxer who has developed a crush on her.

A Two-Family Christmas
Doris invites her boss and her friends at the office to spend Christmas at the ranch with her family.

Hot Dogs
Doris rescues six poodles from a locked car and is accused of stealing them.

Togetherness
Doris plans to spend the weekend with the kids, unaware that they have made other plans.

Singles Only
Doris tries to help Myrna break her lease when she finds out that her new apartment at a swinging singles apartment house is not what she expected it to be.

You're as Old as You Feel
Doris tries to make Buck believe that he is not getting too old.

Doris Hires a Millionaire [Part 1]
GS: Lew Ayres. Doris mistakes an eccentric millionaire for a bum and gives him a job at the ranch.

Doris Hires a Millionaire [Part 2]
GS: Lew Ayres. Doris decides to get the magazine to do a story on her new farmhand, unaware that the reason he accepted the job on her farm was to avoid any publicity.

Today's World Catches the Measles
GS: Edward Andrews. Doris invites her boss and reporter Ron Harvey to spend the weekend at her ranch, where they are quarantined when they are exposed to the measles.

Kidnapped
GS: Kaye Ballard. Doris and the writer she was visiting are kidnaped by a gangster.

A Woman's Intuition
Doris's intuition causes her boss and herself to be hijacked to Cuba, where they get an interview with a very elusive man.

The Duke Returns
GS: Larry Storch. Doris volunteers to help out her boxer friend who has now opened a dance studio, when his staff is lured away by a competitor.

Doris Meets a Prince
GS: Cesare Danova. A visiting prince asks Doris to marry him and become his princess.

Colonel Fairburn Takes Over
GS: Edward Andrews. The publisher of the magazine takes over the office and Doris finds him falling for her.

The Office Troubleshooter
Doris has to find a way to get rid of Mr. Jarvis who is now an efficiency expert hired by Colonel Fairburn to work for the magazine.

Doris Finds an Apartment
Doris finds an apartment above an Italian restaurant.

The Forward Pass
GS: Dick Gautier. Paul tries to get Doris to date a football player so he can get an interview for the magazine.

Dinner for One
GS: Stubby Kaye. Doris arranges for a food columnist to review Angie's restaurant, but she unfortunately mistakes a bum for the columnist and gives the full treatment to the wrong man.

Doris the Spy
GS: John McGiver. Doris accidentally exchanges attache cases with a government agent and is mistakenly believed to be a foreign spy.

Doris vs. Pollution
GS: Edward Andrews. Doris writes an article against a factory which is causing air pollution, unaware that the factory is owned by the same man who owns the magazine, Colonel Fairburn.

Doris Leaves Today's World [Part 1]
GS: Lew Ayres. Doris quits the magazine when she becomes the assistant to

her millionaire friend.

Doris Leaves Today's World [Part 2]
GS: Lew Ayres. Doris decides to quit her new job when her son Toby disappears while she is in Greece and she has to fly home to look for him.

Duke the Performer
GS: Larry Storch. Doris tries to turn her boxer friend Duke into a nightclub entertainer.

The Feminist
GS: Elvia Allman. Doris is assigned to get the publishing rights to a book written by a militant feminist.

How Can I Ignore the Man Next Door?
Doris tries to be friends when a new man moves into the next apartment.

The Fashion Show
Doris once again becomes a model in order to help a fashion designer. This time, however, a rival designer has hired an agent to ruin the show.

Tony Bennett Is Eating Here
GS: Tony Bennett. Doris invites Tony Bennett to eat at Angie's restaurant.

Lost and Found
Doris and Myrna go to a nightclub to retrieve a manuscript Doris left there by accident the night before, only to be mistaken for auditioning go-go dancers.

Cousin Charlie
GS: Van Johnson. Doris gets her Cousin Charlie a job as an advertising salesman for the magazine.

Love Makes the Pizza Go Round
Doris fixes Angie over in order to help her bring the romance back to her marriage.

Lassoin' Leroy
Doris tries to keep Leroy from spending the prize money he won at a rodeo on anything but the ranch he wants to buy for his family.

Buck Visits the Big City
Doris has to try to keep Buck from getting bored when he visits her and the kids.

Jarvis' Uncle
Jarvis' lookalike old uncle comes for a visit and Doris finds that he is nothing like his nephew. In fact, he spends more time with her than with his nephew, making Jarvis think Doris wants to marry his uncle.

Doris Goes to Hollywood
GS: Henry Fonda. Doris wins a Doris Day lookalike contest.

It's Christmas Time in the City
Mr. Jarvis tries to stop Doris's Christmas party when he feels it has gotten too noisy.

Duke's Girlfriend
GS: Larry Storch. Doris tries to save Duke from the clutches of a golddigger.

Billy's First Date
GS: Ricardo Montalban. When Billy has his first date, Doris has a fight with the father of his girlfriend over who is going to chaperone their children's date.

Colonel Fairburn, Jr.
GS: Edward Andrews. The Colonel's hippie son takes over the magazine when his father and Mr. Nicholson go to a convention.

Skiing Anyone?
GS: John Gavin. Doris falls for a doctor at a ski resort.

The Father-Son Weekend
GS: John Astin. Doris takes Toby on the YMCA's father-son campout.

Young Love
Doris tries to help bring her young niece and her college student husband back together after they have a fight.

Whodunnit, Doris
GS: Charles Nelson Reilly. Doris tries to solve a murder committed by a man dressed as Santa Claus.

A Fine Romance
GS: Robert Lansing. Doris joins a computer dating service in order to write an article for the magazine.

Happiness Is Not Being Fired
Doris tries to get a story about an exhibition in order to sell it to another magazine when her boss Cy Bennett fires her.

There's a Horse Thief in Every Family Tree
Doris writes an article about a horse thief ancestor of a now prominent family, which causes her to almost lose her job when the family gets upset.

Mr. and Mrs. Raffles
When Doris and Mr. Jarvis investigate an open door at a jewelry store at night, they are arrested and believed to be burglars.

And Here's . . . Doris
GS: Bob Crane. Doris is assigned to interview a late-night talk show host.

The Crapshooter Who Would Be King
GS: John Banner. The butler of a reclusive prince cons Doris into believing he is the prince in order to have some fun with her.

Chairty Begins at the Office
GS: Joey Foreman, Will B. Able. Doris finds that a charity benefit organizer is a crook.

When in Rome, Don't
GS: Cesare Danova. Doris unknowingly falls in love with a famous Italian artist.

The People's Choice
GS: Hal Peary. Doris convinces Mr. Jarvis to run for the office of city councilman.

The Wings of an Angel
Doris goes to the state pen to get the deathbed confession of a famous gangster.

The Sorrow of Sangapur
Doris becomes the unwitting accomplice in the theft of a famous diamond while on a French train.

A Weighty Problem
Doris and Angie go to a health spa to watch the wife of a soon-to-be released convict, in the hopes she will lead them to their hidden loot.

The Sheik of Araby
GS: Dick Gautier. Doris is captured by a band of rebels and used as a hostage when they plan to get a Middle Eastern king to abdicate.

Doris and the Doctor
GS: Peter Lawford. Doris falls in love with the doctor she is sent to investigate.

The Albatross
GS: Van Johnson. Doris becomes mixed up with spies when her Cousin Charlie brings some secret microfilm into the country for the government.

Have I Got a Fellow for You
Angie tries to fix Doris up with a man.

The Blessed Event
Doris plans a baby shower for Angie, unaware that the baby she is expecting is her dog's.

To England with Doris
Doris goes to England to get a British author to give her the rights to publish his book in the magazine.

Doris at Sea
GS: Peter Lawford. Doris acts as a nurse when her boyfriend Peter has to perform emergency surgery on the Greek billionaire Doris was sent to interview on his yacht.

Cover Girl
GS: Cesare Danova, Rory Calhoun. Doris hires her Italian artist friend to paint the cover illustration for the magazine.

Doris's House Guest
GS: Barbara Hale. Doris brings Cy's sister-in-law and Mr. Jarvis together.

Who's Got the Trenchcoat?
GS: Regis Toomey. Jackie donates Cy's old trenchcoat to a thrift shop, which causes him to order her to retrieve it.

Gowns by Louie
GS: Werner Klemperer. Doris tries to get her tailor's new designs in a fashion show run by a French designer.

Peeping Tom
Cy is mistakenly arrested as a peeping tom.

Forgive and Forget
GS: Peter Lawford. Doris becomes jealous when Peter dates another woman.

The Press Secretary
GS: Patrick O'Neal. Doris goes to work as the press secretary to her old boyfriend who is running for Congress.

The New Boss
GS: Edward Andrews. Colonel Fairburn gives Cy's job to Doris and Doris's job to Cy in an attempt to give the magazine a fresh new look.

No More Advice . . . Please
GS: Peter Lawford. Peter thinks Doris has fallen in love with an author.

Detective Story
Doris tries to interview a defecting Russian general.

Debt of Honor
Doris tries to collect on a large debt in order to pay back a defaulted loan on which she was a co-signer.

The Great Talent Raid
Doris tries to get out of a contract she signed with a rival magazine.

Family Magazine
Doris tries to con her British author friend into selling the rights to his latest book to the magazine.

The Last Huzzah
GS: Henry Jones. Doris tries to save an old employee from being forced to retire now that he has reached 65.

Just a Miss Understanding
GS: Peter Lawford. Doris moonlights as an all-night radio show host.

Follow That Dog
GS: Bruce Gordon. Doris babysits for a gangster's dog for two weeks in order to collect ten thousand dollars.

Jimmy the Gent
GS: Peter Lawford. Doris fakes an accident so she can enter the hospital in order to interview an injured safecracker.

The Co-Op
Doris becomes shocked when she learns that Mr. Jarvis has bought her apartment building and now plans to raise the rent.

The Magnificent Fraud
Doris tries to prevent her Cousin August, an art forger, from getting caught.

The Music Man
Doris interviews a famous rock star and is rumored to be his new girlfriend.

Hospital Benefit
GS: Peter Lawford, Lee Meriwether. Doris believes that a member of the hospital arrangements committee cancelled a charity fashion show she organized for the hospital because she is in love with Peter and did it out of jealousy.

It's a Dog's Life
Doris adopts two stray dogs, much to the dismay of her complaining landlord Mr. Jarvis.

Anniversary Gift
GS: Peter Lawford. Peter gives Doris an antique car as an anniversary gift.

Welcome to Big Sur
GS: Patrick O'Neal. Doris's weekend with Jonathan is interrupted by Jackie and her boyfriend Sid who plan to join them on their trip.

Byline . . . Alias Doris
GS: Joey Foreman. A reporter gets Doris to write his articles for him, but he takes all the credit.

The Hoax
GS: Andy Griffith. Doris joins a phony talent agency in order to expose the owner as a fraud.

Meant for Each Other
GS: Patrick O'Neal. Doris accepts Jonathan's proposal and the two plan to get married.

A Small Cure for Big Alimony
Cy tries to keep Doris from stealing his ex-wife's boyfriend, so he can get them married and save him from paying alimony to her.

THE DUMPLINGS

On the air 1/28/76, off 3/24/76. NBC. Color video tape. 11 episodes. Broadcast: Jan 1976-Mar 1976 Wed 9:30-10. Producer: Don Nicholl/Mike Ross/Bernie West. Prod Co: Tandem. Synd: Tandem Comm.

CAST: Joe Dumpling (played by James Coco), Angela Dumpling (Geraldine Brooks), Charles Sweetzer (George S. Irving), Frederic Steele (George Furth), Stephanie (Marcia Rodd), Cully (Mort Marshall), Bridget (Jane Connell).

The story of a fat couple who own a lunch counter in a busy office building. A funny series that was not given a chance and cancelled after three months. It has not turned up since 1976.

The Dumplings [Pilot]
The Dumplings try to convince a businessman that their anniversary of the day they first met is more important than getting his large catering job.

Joe Gets Jugged
Joe is fired and is ashamed to look for another job.

Cully's Sister
Cully's sister moves in and brings her problems along with her.

The Parting
Stephanie convinces Angela to go with her to Florida for the weekend. This would be the first time the Dumplings were apart since they were married 15 years ago.

Sweetzer's Image
Sweetzer has a fight with his wife, so he moves in with the Dumplings.

The Other Woman
GS: John Steadman. The Dumplings try to help Stephanie who saw her boyfriend with another woman.

Gourmet's Delight
GS: Beeson Carroll. When Angela's mushroom and barley soup gets a good review by a newspaper, they now find that they have more business than they can handle.

The Ultimatum
When Joe calls their landlord a thief, he orders them out of the apartment.

Joe Takes a Fall
Joe considers suing when he falls on a broken step outside his apartment.

The Foundling
Angela invites the Puerto Rican immigrant who she found on the roof trying to break in, to stay with them.

To Drink or Not to Drink
The Dumplings inherit a 900-year-old bottle of wine. They now find that dozens of potential buyers show up to purchase it from them.

ENSIGN O'TOOLE

On the Air 9/23/62, off 9/15/63. NBC. B&W film. 32 episodes. Broadcast: Sept 1962-Sept 1963 Sun 7-7:30. Producer: Unknown. Prod Co: Revue. Synd: MCA/Universal.

CAST: Ensign O'Toole (played by Dean Jones), Homer Nelson (Jay C. Flippen), Rex St. John (Jack Mullaney), Gabby Di Julio (Harvey Lembeck), Virgil Stoner (Jack Albertson), Howard Spicer (Beau Bridges), Claude White (Robert Sorrells).

The story of a junior officer assigned to the destroyer Appleby during peacetime. Each week the nutty crew would cause all kinds of trouble for O'Toole. The series was rerun the following year in prime time on ABC and has since disappeared, but it is still available.

Operation Kowana
The ship docks in Japan and the crew is warned to stay out of trouble.

Operation Model T
GS: Harvey Lembeck, Robert Sorrells. The crew buy an old car and have to smuggle it on board one piece at a time.

Operation Daddy
GS: Molly Dodd, Merle Pertile. O'Toole tries to get leave papers for a seaman whose wife is having a baby.

Operation Benefit
GS: Dick Powell. The crew stages a show to raise money for some Korean orphans.

Operation Jinx
GS: Soupy Sales. A seaman who is considered bad luck is assigned to the ship.

Operation Holdout
GS: Tige Andrews, Eddie Ryder. Two GIs send an SOS to the ship. They claim they are being held captive by Japanese soldiers.

Operation Birthday
GS: Charles Tannen. The crew wants to buy Nelson a present, but doesn't have any money.

Operation Mess
GS: Harry Morgan. Charlie the cook's great food seems to be getting worse by the day.

Operation Impersonation
GS: Edgar Barrier, Stuart Margolin, Pamela Searle. Stoner gets drunk and ruins a Malayan general's garden.

Operation Hypnosis
O'Toole masters hypnosis and begins to put some of the crew under his power.

Operation Potomac
O'Toole has been getting gifts from a secret admirer.

Operation Gaslight
GS: Steve Franken. O'Toole tries to convince a strict sailor he has a strange disease.

Operation Brooklyn
GS: Romo Vincent, Penny Stanton. Gabby wants to leave the Navy to take over his parents' restaurant.

Operation Swindle
GS: Rosemary De Camp, Charles Watts. Nelson loses his money to a golddigging Southern girl.

Operation Treasure
The crew finds a treasure map in a bottle.

Operation Intrigue
GS: Robert Emhardt, Howard Morris, Phillip Ahn. O'Toole helps a Scotland Yard detective find some jewel thieves in Hong Kong.

Operation Psychology
Stoner's brother-in-law, a psychologist, says the crew is depressed.

Operation Royalty
GS: Lou Krugman, Michael Davis, Dennis Cross. A 12-year-old prince visits the ship and bosses everyone around.

Operation Whodunit
The crew tries to find the last reel of an English mystery film.

Operation Casanova
O'Toole boosts St. John's ego by surrounding him with girls.

Operation Souvenir
While in Japan, St. John takes a cannon as a souvenir for his girl.

Operation Arrivederci
GS: Doris Packer, Sharon Huguery.

O'Toole lets an artist use the ship for an exhibition site.

Operation Re-Enlist
GS: Cathy Lewis. O'Toole must improve Stoner's image with the crew.

Operation Boxer
GS: Gary Crosby, Cal Boulder. O'Toole bets on a boxing match.

Operation Stowaway
GS: Nita Talbot. O'Toole finds a girl hiding on the ship.

Operation Arctic
GS: Andrew Golman. The crew goes on a trip to the Arctic.

Operation Physical
O'Toole gets Stoner's old friends to come to his 45th birthday party.

Operation Tubby
GS: Stubby Kaye. O'Toole tries to keep a seaman from overeating.

Operation Sabotage
GS: George Petrie. Stoner bets the ship can't be sabotaged during war games.

Operation Contest
The crew enters a jingle contest.

Operation Geisha
GS: Eddie Ryder, Jack Carter. The crew opens a geisha house to make extra money.

Operation Dinner Party
No story available.

F TROOP

On the air 9/14/65, off 8/31/67. ABC. 65 episodes. 31 color/34 B&W. 30 min. Film. Broadcast: Sept 1965-Aug 1966 Tue 9-9:30; Sept 1966-Aug 1967 Thu 8-8:30. Producer: William T. Orr and Hy Averback. Prod Co/Synd: Warner Bros. TV.

The F Troop: Larry Storch (left), Melody Patterson, and Forrest
Tucker in the "That's Show Biz!" episode.

CAST: Capt. Wilton Parmenter (played by Ken Berry), Sgt. Morgan O'Rourke
(Forrest Tucker), Cpl. Randolph Agarn (Larry Storch), Wrangler Jane (Melody
Patterson), Chief Wild Eagle (Frank DeKova), Crazy Cat (Don Diamond), Hanni-
bal Dobbs (James Hampton), Duffy (Bob Steele), Vanderbilt (Joe Brooks), Hof-
fenmeuller (John Mitchum), Roaring Chicken (Edward Everett Horton), Papa
Bear (Ben Frommer), Pete (Benny Baker), Dudleson (Irving Bell).
WRITERS: Arthur Julian, Ed James, Stan Dreban, Seaman Jacobs, Howard
Merrill. DIRECTORS: Charles Rondeau, Leslie Goodwins.
The misadventures of a troop of cavalry men in Fort Courage, located in Kansas. Episodes depict Captain Wilton Parmenter, a bumbling buffoon constantly
being outwitted by Sergeant Morgan O'Rourke, the head of the illegal O'Rourke
Enterprises, a business dealing in Indian souvenirs made by the friendly Hekawi
Indian tribe. His long-time friend, Corporal Randolph Agarn, often assists him
in his scheme to expand their business. Other stories deal with efforts of the
beautiful general store owner, "Wrangler" Jane Angelica Thrift, to convince Captain Parmenter to marry her. F Troop remains popular, even though only two
seasons were produced, because of the comedic talents of Larry Storch and his
pal Forrest Tucker. They later starred together on a Saturday morning series
called the Ghost Busters.

Scourge of the West [Pilot]
Captain Parmenter takes command of
Fort Courage.

Dirge for the Scourge
GS: Jack Elam. Outlaw Sam Erp
comes for a showdown with Captain
Parmenter.

The Girl from Philadelphia
GS: Linda Marshall. Jane and an East-
erner vie for the affection of Captain
Parmenter.

The 86 Proof Spring
GS: Parley Baer. Parmenter launches
a search for the Indian whiskey supply.

Corporal Agarn's Farewell to the Troops
Agarn believes his days are numbered after overhearing that someone is dying.

A Gift from the Chief
Captain Parmenter saves the Chief's life and receives a baby in return.

Iron Horse Go Home
The Hekawis sell their land and move into the fort in order to make room for the railroad.

She's Only Built in a Girdled Cage
GS: Patrice Wymore. Laura Lee, a famous dancehall singer, comes to the fort to entertain the men.

The Phantom Major
GS: Bernard Fox. A British major teaches the troop new ways to fight Indians by using camouflage.

O'Rourke vs. O'Reilly
GS: Lee Meriwether. Lilly O'Reilly almost drives O'Rourke out of business.

Our Hero—What's His Name
GS: Mike Mazurki. It is rumored that Agarn killed Geronimo, which sends Geronimo after Agarn.

Honest Injun
GS: John Dehner. A con man muscles in on O'Rourke's enterprises.

The Return of Bald Eagle
GS: Don Rickles. A renegade Indian tries to go straight but just can't.

Old Iron Pants
O'Rourke's newest venture is mail order brides.

Go for Broke
GS: George Gobel, Del Moore. Jane's inventor cousin helps Parmenter win a poker game.

El Diablo
GS: Hal England. Agarn's lookalike Mexican bandit cousin pays a visit to the Fort.

Will the Real Captain Try to Stand Up
GS: Frank McHugh. The town drunk poses as the Commander of F Troop, in order to impress his only daughter.

The New I.G.
GS: Andrew Duggan. Major Winchester plots to wipe out the peaceloving Hewakis.

Spy, Counterspy, Counter Counterspy
GS: Abbe Lane, Pat Harrington. Agarn is chosen to test a bulletproof vest. Before he can test it, it is stolen.

Too Many Cooks Spoil the Troop
O'Rourke tries to fatten his wallet by adding to the cook's food list.

Reunion for O'Rourke
GS: Dick Reeves. Agarn arranges a This Is Your Life Sgt. O'Rourke type party in his honor.

The Courtship of Wrangler Jane
O'Rourke decides to play cupid for Jane and Parmenter.

Captain Parmenter—One-Man Army
The F Troop men learn that they are not legally enlisted so they leave.

Heap Big Injun
Agarn leaves the Army to become an Indian brave.

Don't Ever Speak to Me Again
A fight erupts just as the troop is being cited for high morale.

Johnny Eagle Eye
GS: Paul Peterson. A young scout is entered in the cavalry sharpshooting contest.

The Day the Indians Won
The peaceloving Hewakis are ordered on the warpath.

Indian Fever
GS: Victor Jory. Agarn thinks he is going crazy when he sees an Indian and no one else does.

A Fort's Best Friend Is Not a Mother
GS: Jeanette Nolan.   Parmenter's bossy mother comes to town.

Lieutenant O'Rourke, Front and Center
GS: James Gregory. O'Rourke faces a promotion, which will mean the end of O'Rourke Enterprises.

Wrongo Starr and the Lady in Black
GS: Henry Gibson, Sarah Marshall. Wrongo Starr, a famous jinx, comes to town and meets up with the Black Widow who marries her husbands and then kills them for their money.

Play, Gypsy, Play
GS: Zsa Zsa Gabor. Wandering gypsies invade Fort Courage.

Don't Look Now But One of Our Cannon Is Missing
O'Rourke plots to reclaim the cannon which he loaned to the Hewakis.

Here Comes the Tribe
F Troop comes to the rescue when the Chief's daughter is kidnapped.

From Karate with Love
GS: Mako, Miko Mayana. A samurai warrior is looking for a Japanese girl.

The West Goes Ghost
O'Rourke and Agarn take over an old ghost town which still might be haunted.

Reach for the Sky Pardner
GS: Charles Lane, Paul Sorenson. The town banker wants to repossess the saloon, sending Agarn and O'Rourke aboard a train to guard the payroll.

The Great Troop Robbery
GS: Milton Berle. A phony medicine man has been stealing from the troop and tries to blame it on Agarn.

The Singing Mountie
GS: Paul Lynde. A singing mountie is after the burglar of Banff. Also, Agarn's French-Canadian fur trapping cousin arrives at the Fort.

Yellow Bird
GS: Julie Newmar. An Indian girl takes a liking to Parmenter.

How to Be F Troop Without Really Trying
GS: George Tyne, Les Brown, Jr. Everyone is being transferred except Agarn; he has to train G Troop, which is worse than F Troop.

The Loco Brothers
GS: Med Flory. Two wild Indians kidnap Parmenter and hold him hostage.

Bring on the Dancing Girls
GS: Peter Leeds. A blackmailer takes over the saloon so O'Rourke tries to get even.

Bye, Bye, Balloon
GS: Harvey Korman. A Prussian balloonist arrives at Fort Courage.

Miss Parmenter
GS: Patty Regan. Parmenter's husband-hunting sister goes after Dobbs, and assists in Chief Wild Eagle's appendectomy.

Did Your Father Come from Ireland?
O'Rourke's father comes to town just as O'Rourke leaves town. While waiting for his return, he tries to turn the town into another version of Ireland.

For Whom the Bugle Tolls
GS: Richard X. Slattery. A no-nonsense colonel enjoys bugle calls. The trouble is no one can play the bugle.

La Dolce Courage
GS: Letitia Roma, Jay Novello, Joby Baker. An Italian suitor is challenged by the Black Foot.

Milton, the Kid
GS: Sterling Holloway. A lookalike for Captain Parmenter has been robbing banks.

The Return of Wrongo Starr
GS: Henry Gibson. Wrongo Starr the jinx returns to Fort Courage, where he gets mixed up with a goat and some dynamite.

Survival of the Fittest
Parmenter and Agarn are alone on a Wilderness Survival Test.

Our Brave in F Troop
GS: Cliff Arquette, Hal England. Wild Eagle has a toothache, so O'Rourke tries to sneak him into the Fort to see a visiting dentist.

That's Show Biz
GS: Factory Rock Quartet. Agarn leaves the Army to manage a singing group called the Bedbugs.

The Sergeant and the Kid
GS: Peter Robbins, Pippa Scott. A ten-year-old boy wants to join the troop.

Where Were You at the Last Massacre?
GS: Phil Harris. A 147-year-old Indian warrior returns to take over all of America.

A Horse of Another Color
Jane and O'Rourke both try to capture a wild stallion.

V Is for Vampire
GS: Vincent Price. A Dracula-like Count is believed responsible for the disappearance of Wrangler Jane.

Only One Russian Is Coming! Only One Russian Is Coming!
Agarn's lookalike Russian Cossack cousin falls for Wrangler Jane, which makes Parmenter very jealous.

The Day They Shot Agarn
GS: Victor French, Fred Clark. Agarn faces a firing squad because he is believed to have killed Sgt. O'Rourke.

Guns, Guns, Who's Got the Guns?
GS: Arch Johnson. Parmenter goes undercover to try and capture the man who has been selling guns to the Apaches.

Marriage, Fort Courage Style
GS: Mary Wickes. Agarn and O'Rourke try to rescue Parmenter from a marriage broker.

Is This Fort Really Necessary?
GS: Charles Drake, Patrice Wymore, Amzie Strickland. An efficiency expert puts the bite on all of F Troop.

Carpetbagging, Anyone?
GS: James Gregory. F Troop faces eviction when a rich carpetbagger takes over the town.

Majority of Wilton
Parmenter takes a promotion test with disastrous results.

The Ballot of Corporal Agarn
GS: Tol Avery, Lew Parker. Agarn casts the deciding vote in a Passaic, New Jersey election.

FAMILY AFFAIR

On the air 9/12/66, off 9/9/71. CBS. Color film. 138 episodes. Broadcast: Sept 1966-Sept 1969 Mon 9:30-10; Sept 1969-Sept 1971 Thu 7:30-8. Producer & Prod Co: Don Fedderson Productions. Synd: Viacom.

CAST: Bill Davis (played by Brian Keith), Mr. Giles French (Sebastian Cabot), Buffy (Anissa Jones), Jody (Johnnie Whitaker), Cissy (Kathy Garver), Emily Turner (Nancy Walker), Niles French (John Williams).

The story of a bachelor who becomes the guardian for his brother's children, when he and his wife are killed in an accident. Together with his butler/valet Mr. French, they find themselves involved in various domestic problems while trying to raise the three kids. The series is still run occasionally but has become too dated for many people and has begun to disappear from many stations.

Buffy [Pilot]
GS: Louise Latham, Heather Angel, Phillip Ober, Nora Marlowe. Buffy, Jody and Cissy come to live with their Uncle Bill Davis.

Jody and Cissy
GS: Noel Drayton, Betty Lyn. Bill decides to send Cissy away.

The Gift Horse
GS: Paul Hartman. The twins buy Bill a broken down horse as a present.

The Matter of School
GS: John Hubbard. Bill wants to send Cissy to boarding school, causing her to think he wants to get rid of her.

Marmalade
GS: Woodrow Parfrey, Mary Murphy, Richard Peel. French is asked to endorse a brand of marmalade.

Room with a Viewpoint
Buffy gets jealous when Cissy gets her own telephone.

Mrs. Beasley, Where Are You?
GS: Frank Maxwell, Pamelyn Ferdin. French accidentally knocks Buffy's doll off the terrace, causing everyone to go on a hunt for the missing doll.

Who's Afraid of Nural Shipeni?
GS: Magda Harout, Henry Corden, Peter Mamakos, Abraham Sofaer, Vic Tayback. French unknowingly gets engaged to a Lebanese girl.

A Matter for Experts
GS: Jean Engstrom. A child psychologist recommends that the twins be separated.

Beware the Other Woman
GS: Rita Gam. Cissy's friend tells her that Bill's girlfriend is trying to trap him into marrying her.

Take Two Aspirin
GS: Norman Alden. Bill worries about the kids while he is away from home.

Love Me, Love Me Not
GS: Romo Vincent. Jody tries to get Bill to punish him, thus showing how much he really loves him.

The Thursday Man
GS: Eugene Martin, Richard Peel. Cissy finds more than she expected when she writes a composition about French.

Think Deep
GS: Robert Reed, Diane Mountford. Cissy has a crush on her psychology teacher.

Hard Hat Jody
GS: Brian Donlevy, Dale Ishimoto. Bill tries to find an elusive millionaire. He doesn't know that Jody is friends with him.

That Was the Dinner That Wasn't
GS: Jacqueline Bertrand. Bill can't seem to understand what has been bothering Cissy.

All Around the Town
GS: Vic Tayback, Harold Fong, Tommy Lee, Rodolfo Hoyos. Buffy and Jody find twenty dollars and search the entire city to find who it belongs to.

One for the Little Boy
GS: John Williams. French leaves town for a while, so he asks his brother Nigel French to take over for him until he returns.

Fancy Free
GS: John Williams, Sterling Holloway, Roy Roberts. Buffy and Jody ask a friendly window washer to help them with their math.

A Helping Hand
GS: John Williams, Myrna Loy, June Vincent. A former rich lady, who is now broke, asks Nigel to help her to become a good housekeeper.

Once in Love with Buffy
GS: John Williams, Louise Latham,

Bill Zuckert. Bill lets Aunt Fran take care of the twins.

Ballerina, Buffy
GS: Judith Landon [Mrs. Brian Keith], John Williams, Frank Maxwell. Buffy deliberately messes up her dance recital when she thinks she will be sent away to study dancing.

The Mother Tongue
GS: John Williams, Richard Loo, Lisa Fong, May Lee, Noel Troy. Nigel tries to show off by trying to speak Chinese, but he unknowingly insults the daughter of a Chinese diplomat.

Everybody Needs Somebody
GS: John Williams, Pitt Herbert, Richard Peel, Heather Angel. Nigel thinks the twins want to get rid of him.

The Way It Was
GS: John Williams, Lynn Borden, Julie Parrish. Bill sends the twins to camp.

All Nephews Are Created Equal
GS: John Williams, Martin Horsey. Nigel gets a visit and a shock from his nephew: he doesn't want to be a butler.

The Prize
GS: John Williams, Olan Soule, Annette Cabot. The twins are heartbroken when they win a lamb in a contest and find that they can't keep it.

What Did You Do in the West, Uncle?
GS: John Agar. Buffy and Jody want to live with a visiting rodeo cowboy.

The Award
GS: Oliver McGowan, Templeton Fox. The twins suffer from an allergic itch.

The Butler Method
GS: Christopher Dark. Bill gets a movie star friend to take Cissy to a dance.

Birds, Bees and Buffy
GS: Pamelyn Ferdin, Randy Whipple. Bill and French have to explain the birds and the bees to Buffy.

First Love
GS: Lee Meriwether. Bill falls for a lady geologist and Buffy has a crush on a boy.

Go Home, Mr. French
GS: Patric Knowles, Cathleen Cordell. French is asked to return to work for his former boss, the Duke of Glenmore.

Arthur, the Invisible Bear
GS: John Alvin, Adrienne Marden, Mitzi Hoag. Jody invents an invisible bear to play with.

The Other Cheek
GS: Sean McClory, Kellie Flanagan. Jody is bothered by a female bully at school.

The Candy Striper
GS: Audrey Dalton, Sherry Alberoni. Cissy becomes a hospital candy striper, while Buffy joins the Brownies.

Fat, Fat, the Water Rat
GS: Jackie Coogan, Marcia Mae Jones. A workman thinks Bill is broke when he sees Buffy wearing rags.

The Toy Box
Bill complains about the twins leaving their toys all over the apartment.

Take Me Out of the Ball Game
GS: David Brandon. Buffy joins the neighborhood baseball team.

You Like Buffy Better
GS: Del Moore, Gregg Fedderson. Buffy and Jody fight for Bill's attention.

Freddie
Freddie comes to visit Bill and finds she wants her own children.

Our Friend Stanley
GS: Michael Freeman, John Lupton. The twins befriend a crippled boy.

Somebody Upstairs
GS: Joan Blondell. A Broadway musical star moves in upstairs.

Star Dust
GS: Martha Hyer. A movie star wants to marry Bill.

Best of Breed
GS: Richard Bull, Kym Karath. The twins bring home a stray dog.

Family Reunion
GS: Louise Latham, Bill Zuckert. Bill takes the kids to Indiana for a family reunion.

A Man's Place
GS: Ann Sothern, Laurie Main, Ralph Manza. French decides to quit his job and open up a restaurant.

The Great Kow-Tow
GS: Keye Luke, Beulah Quo, Benson Fong, Lisa Lu. An old Chinese man adopts Buffy and Jody as his new grandchildren.

The Fish Watchers
Bill finds that someone on his construction site is a thief.

The Day Nothing Happened
Bill has to watch the kids when French is out of town.

A House in the Country
Bill tries to buy a house in the country.

A Matter of Tonsils
GS: Oliver McGowan, Carol Nugent. Buffy has to have her tonsils removed.

Member of the Family
GS: Richard Peel, Eddie Rosson. French is upset when he thinks Cissy left his picture out of the school art exhibit.

His and Hers
Bill meets a widow with three kids.

The New Cissy
GS: Charles Herbert. Cissy gets beauty advice from some fashion models.

The Family Outing
Bill takes the family camping.

Mr. French's Holiday
French takes the children with him on his vacation to a western town.

The Beasley Story
GS: Ivan Bonar. Buffy's doll is broken.

The Baby Sitters
GS: Doris Singleton, James Hong. When their babysitter is sick, the girl's father takes her place.

Family Portrait
GS: Pippa Scott, John Milford. Bill tries to spend more time with the kids.

The Latch Key Kid
GS: Susan Benjamin, Eve Brent. Buffy wants her own house key.

By a Whisker
GS: Butch Patrick. Jody must get a piece of French's beard so he can join a gang of older boys.

A Waltz from Vienna
GS: Mark De Vries, Jan Arvan. Cissy wants to get married to a boy from Vienna.

Your Friend, Jody
GS: Archie Moore. Bill sends Jody away to a boys' camp.

The Substitute Teacher
GS: June Lockhart. Jody has a crush on the new substitute teacher.

Oliver
GS: Eric Shea, Vince Howard, Richard Bull. The twins bring home a big dog which hates Bill.

Christmas Came a Little Early
GS: Eve Plumb, Paul Sorensen. Bill arranges for a Christmas party for a sick girl in Buffy's class.

The Unsound of Music
GS: Kaye Stevens. A nightclub singer tries to teach Buffy to sing.

Albertine
GS: Alycia Gardner. The twins meet a strange little girl.

A Matter of Choice
GS: Susan Abbott, Jane Webb. Bill tries to make his family have a little more class.

Ciao, Uncle Bill
GS: Brioni Farrell, Ralph Manza. Bill plans to marry an Italian girl in Rome.

A Nanny for All Seasons
French plans to marry in order to show his valet friends that he is not a nanny.

Family Plan
GS: Nancy Kovack. The family tries to help Bill who has a broken leg.

To Love with Buffy
GS: Kenneth Tobey, Sue Casey. Bill takes Buffy on a trip to Puerto Rico.

A Family Group
GS: Liam Sullivan, Kathleen Crowley. The daughter of a theatrical family wants to spend all her time with Cissy and her family.

A Lesson for Grownups
GS: Horace McMahon, David Roberts. The children try to raise money when it looks like Bill is going broke.

Oh To Be in England
GS: Alan Napier, Barbara Babcock. French looks forward to returning to England.

A Matter of Privacy
GS: Russ Caldwell, Larry Thor. Buffy and Jody use a tape recorder to listen to other people's conversations.

Lost in Spain [Part 1]
GS: Jay Novello, Valentin De Vargas. Bill takes the family on a trip to Spain.

Lost in Spain [Part 2]
GS: Jay Novello, John Aladdin. French loses the children on a sightseeing trip.

Lost in Spain [Part 3]
GS: John Aladdin, Anna Navarro. French and Bill search for Buffy and Jody.

A Diller, A Dollar
GS: Lisa Gerritsen. Buffy tries to act dumb in order to attract a boy.

The Young Man from Bolivia
GS: Carlos Romero, Miguel Monsalve. Jody's pen-pal from Bolivia comes for a visit.

Speak for Yourself, Mr. French
GS: Leslie Parrish. French and a young girl fall for each other.

The Flip Side
GS: Eddie Hodges, Warren Berlinger. Cissy dates a singing idol.

The Matter of Dignity
GS: Irene Tedrow, Gary Tigerman. French is accused of being involved in a scandal with a young girl.

Flower Power
GS: Veronica Cartwright, Jamie Farr, Corey Fischer. Cissy wants to become a hippie.

My Man, the Star
GS: Joe Flynn, Dick Patterson, Jerry Hausner, Del Moore. French plays Henry VIII in a cheap movie.

No Uncle Is an Island
GS: Peter Leeds, Pamelyn Ferdin. Bill wants to spend a quiet evening alone, but that seems to be impossible.

The Wings of an Angel
GS: Dana Andrews. An ex-con asks Bill for a job.

Uncle Prince Charming
GS: Gregg Fedderson, Darlene Carr. Cissy's friend has a crush on Bill.

Cissy's Apartment
Cissy moves into her own apartment.

The Jody Affair
GS: Pitt Herbert, Teddy Quinn. Jody

is accused of breaking a window in the school cafeteria.

With This Ring
Cissy and boyfriend Gregg become engaged.

What's Funny About a Broken Leg?
GS: Laurie Main, Richard Bull, Oliver McGowan. Buffy breaks her leg and can't go to the circus.

The Birthday Boy
The kids plan a birthday party for French.

The Stowaway
GS: Michael James Wixted. Buffy and Jody hide a runaway orphan boy in their room.

Number One Boy
GS: Benson Fong, Frances Fong, James Hong. French quits when Bill's houseboy in Hong Kong comes to take over the operation of the household.

A Tale of Two Travels
The family goes to Boston on a vacation, except Cissy who visits a friend in Long Island.

Maudie
GS: Ida Lupino. A rich English widow asks French to marry her.

Goodbye Harold
Buffy's pet hamster runs away in the park.

The Girl Graduate
Cissy plans to stay out all night to celebrate graduating from high school.

Grandpa, Sir
GS: Paul Fix. The children's grandfather pays a visit.

Marooned
French and the kids are trapped in a blizzard while on their way to Vermont.

Mr. Osaki's Tree
GS: Teru Shimada. Jody thinks that when the miniature tree he got from a Japanese man dies so will the man who gave it to him.

The Language of Love
GS: Audree Norton, Diane Holly. Bill asks a doctor to help Buffy's deaf friend.

The Inheritance
GS: Booth Coleman. Buffy and Jody inherit a small amount of money.

There Goes New York
GS: Erin Moran, Byron Morrow. Buffy and Jody believe a TV psychic's prediction that New York will be destroyed by a tidal wave.

Wouldn't It Be Lovely
Buffy and Jody want Bill to do away with the house rules.

The Boys Against the Girls
GS: Francine York. Buffy is thrown off a stickball team by the new girl-hating captain.

The Old Cowhand
GS: Bob Steele. Bill asks a one-time western star to teach a lesson to Jody.

Angel in the Family
GS: Jill Townsend, Del Moore. French asks Bill to get a producer to get one of his English friends a part in a play.

Family in Paradise [Part 1]
GS: Maurice Marsac. French and the kids visit Bill in Tahiti.

Family in Paradise [Part 2]
GS: Napua, Bernie Grozier, Maurice Marsac, Danielle Aubrey. Bill plans to marry a French girl and move his family to the island for good.

The Good Neighbors
Buffy and Jody find that the people in the building aren't very friendly towards each other.

Desert Isle-Manhattan Style
GS: Ronne Troup.   French leaves

Cissy in charge when he wants to visit his cousin in Washington.

Eastward Ho
GS: Benson Fong, Irene Tsu, Brian Fong, Anita May Wong. Bill invites the intended bride of a Chinese restaurant owner to stay with him at the apartment until the wedding.

Meet Emily
GS: Nancy Walker. Bill lets the office cleaning lady help out at the house.

The Return of Maudie
GS: Ida Lupino, Laurie Main. The rich widow comes to New York to watch her horse run in a race and to spend some time with French.

It Can't Be Five Years
GS: Nancy Walker, J. Edward McKinley. Bill doesn't come home to celebrate the fifth anniversary of the kids coming to live with him.

Travels with Cissy
GS: Walter Brooke. Bill takes the whole family on a trip to Hollywood.

Stamp of Approval
GS: Lisa Gerritsen. Jody dates a girl so he can get a valuable stamp from her collection.

And Baby Makes Eight
GS: Linda Kaye Henning, Nancy Walker. Cissy brings home a pregnant friend.

Say Uncle
GS: Clint Howard, John Lawrence. Jody gets Bill into a fight with the father of one of his friends.

Class Clown
GS: Joyce Van Patten. Bill dates a comedienne.

Unsinkable Mr. French
GS: Marj Dusay. French blows his top when everything seems to go wrong.

Wish You Were Here
GS: Scott Garrett. Jody is worried that Bill isn't allowed to come to father and son night.

Feat of Clay
GS: Julie Parrish. The kids take a valuable piece of sculpture to school for show and tell.

Heroes Are Born
Leif Garrett, Larry Pennell. Jody meets the nephew of a famous football player.

Nobody Here But Us Uncles
GS: Joan Freeman. The kids try to fix Bill up with their teacher.

Too Late, Too Soon
GS: Peter Duryea, Nancy Walker. Emily tries to fix French up with Miss Faversham, the nanny.

The Littlest Exile
GS: Radames Pera. Jody plays with a boy whose mother won't let him play.

Put Your Dreams Away
GS: David Ladd. Cissy meets an old boyfriend who has joined the Peace Corps.

The Joiners
Buffy is the only one who is not a member of a club.

Cinder-Emily
GS: Nancy Walker, Peter Duryea. Buffy and Jody try to get an escort for Emily so she can go to her son's medical school graduation ball.

Goodbye, Mrs. Beasley
GS: Kym Karath, Lori Nelson. Buffy is convinced she is too old for dolls.

Buffy's Fair Lady
Jody is being followed by a little girl who is in love with him.

You Can Fight City Hall
GS: Carlos Romero, John Carter. Buffy and Jody help a poor Mexican boy.

FARMER'S DAUGHTER

On the air 9/20/63, off 9/2/66. ABC. B&W film. 30 min. 101 episodes. Broadcast: Sept 1963-Nov 1963 Fri 9:30-10; Dec 1963-Sept 1964 Wed 8:30-9; Sept 1964-Jun 1965 Fri 8-8:30; Jun 1965-Oct 1965 Mon 9:30-10; Nov 1965-Sept 1966 Fri 9:30-10. Producer: Harry Ackerman/Peter Kortner. Prod Co/ Synd: Screen Gems/Columbia Pictures TV.

CAST: Katrin "Katy" Holstrum (played by Inger Stevens), Glen Morley (William Windom), Agatha Morley (Cathleen Nesbitt), Steve Morley (Mickey Sholder), Danny Morley (Rory O'Brien), Cooper, the Butler (Phillip Coolidge), Lars Holstrum (Walter Sande), Mama Holstrum (Alice Frost).

WRITERS: John McGreevey, Jerry Davis, Lee Loeb, Steve Gethers, Peggy Chandler Dick, Meyer Dolinsky, Stan Cutler, Richard Powell, Martin Donovan, Winston Cutler, Janet Carlson, Warner Law, Don Richman, Stanley Silverman.

DIRECTORS: Ralph Nelson, Don Taylor, Mel Ferrer, Gene Nelson, William D. Russell, Gene Reynolds, Fred De Cordova, Bob Claver, Herb Wallerstein, Richard Kinon, Seymour Robbie, Sam Freedle.

The story of Glen Morley, congressman and widower, his children, and Katy Holstrum, a beautiful Minnesota farmgirl who is the family governess. Episodes depict the hectic life of a Washington-based politician and the attempts of a simple Swedish girl to adjust to city life. Later in the series Glen marries Katy, adding a new dimension to the series. The series is not seen in syndication although it is available because it is a dated series whose ideas and cultural styles do not fit in with our contemporary society.

The Speechmaker [Part 1]
W: John McGreevey. D: Ralph Nelson. GS: Woodrow Parfrey. Katy quits her job after Morley feels that the speech she and Steve approved cost him an important government position.

The Speechmaker [Part 2]
W: Steve Gethers. D: Don Taylor. Katy, now living at the YWCA, must find a way to get her job back and insure Morley the chairmanship he so badly desires.

Where's Katy?
W: Charles Woolf. D: Don Taylor. GS: Jeremy Slate. Feeling that Morley takes her for granted, Katy tries to make him jealous by dating a handsome young Swede.

An Enterprising Young Man
W: Steve Gethers. D: William D. Russell. GS: Bob Denver. After a visit from an old military friend, Morley becomes a man who rules his family and his friends with an iron fist.

An Affair of State
W: Jerry Davis & Lee Loeb. D: Don Taylor. GS: Charles Nelson Reilly. A visiting Arab oil tycoon asks Katy to be his wife in exchange for signing an oil agreement.

The Washington Spotlight
W: Budd Grossman. D: William D. Russell. GS: Harry Townes. Chaos reigns on the day Morley is to appear on a television program.

The Stand-In
W: Steve Gethers. D: Gene Nelson. GS: Russell Johnson. The birth of her first child does not deter a congresswoman from her plans to attend a political convention.

Comes the Revolution
W: John McGreevey. D: Mel Ferrer. GS: Michael Ansara. Three delegates from behind the Iron Curtain are given a lesson in American history from Glen, Katy and Agatha.

Miss Cheese
W: Jerry Davis. D: William D. Russell. GS: Sherry Alberoni. A 12-year-old girl interferes with Glen's love life.

The Editorial Whee
W: Jerry Davis. D: Paul Nickell. Mr. Cooper winds up dating a woman who opposes all of Glen's legislative efforts.

I Am the Most Beautiful
W: Steve Gethers. D: Mel Ferrer. Katy turns a boxer into a lover of peace.

One Rainy Night
W: Jerry Davis. D: Paul Nickell. GS: Ernest Truex, Arch Johnson. Glen's car breaks down in front of a justice of the peace who thinks Glen and Katy have come to get married.

The Simple Life
W: Steve Gethers. D: William D. Russell. GS: George Kennedy. After Glen refuses to take a stand on an important issue, Katy quits and flies home.

Gypsy Love Song
W: Steve Gethers. D: Mel Ferrer. A 12-year-old traveler stays at the Morley home while his father tours the country.

Mrs. Golden's Opportunity
W: Jerry Davis & Lee Loeb. D: Paul Nickell. GS: Naomi Stevens. Two old women try to unite Glen and Katy.

Nobody's Perfect
W: William Cowley. D: Paul Nickell. Cooper goes out in search of a new secretary after he has a fight with Katy.

Mr. Smith and the Birds
W: Jerry Davis & Lee Loeb. D: Paul Nickell. GS: John Abbott. Katy becomes involved in the plight of a poor old pigeon lover named Mr. Smith.

Cousin Helga Came to Dinner
W: Meyer Dolinsky. D: Paul Nickell.

Katy's Cousin Helga comes for a visit and stirs up trouble with her women's liberation ideas.

Marriage Is for Real People
W: Steve Gethers. D: Don Taylor. Agatha sets out to convince Katy the way to a man's heart is to cater to him.

Katy and the Imagemaker
W: Peggy Chandler Dick. D: Paul Nickell. GS: George Furth. Rex Tinkerton, running in the Minnesota election, promises Katy she could win a seat in the assembly.

Playboy of Capitol Hill
W: William Cowley. D: Gene Reynolds. GS: Peter Graves. An attractive congressman makes a play for Katy.

Bless Our Happy Home
W: Jerry Davis & Lee Loeb. D: Gene Reynolds. GS: John Astin. Glen invites a newlywed couple to stay in his home until they can find an available hotel room.

Katy and the Prince
W: Walter D.F. Black. D: Paul Nickell. GS: Edward Mulhare. A visiting prince vows to marry Katy and take her back to his country.

The Swinger
W: Steve Gethers. D: Gene Reynolds. GS: John Fiedler. Papa Holstrum has become a mod swinger in an attempt to recapture his youth.

Katy Gets Arrested
W: Jerry Davis & Lee Loeb. D: Gene Reynolds. GS: Rodolfo Acosta. Katy becomes involved in the plight of a group of Latin Americans picketing dictator Pedro Perez.

Turkish Delight
W: Jerry Davis & Lee Loeb. D: Don Taylor. Glen tries to break the news to a fellow congressman that Sally, his 18-year-old daughter, is married.

Christopher Columbus Who?
W: Arnold Hewitt. D: Don Taylor.
GS: Gregory Morton. An Italian actress is convinced that Christopher Columbus discovered America while Katy insists that it was Leif Ericsson.

The One-Eyed Sloth
W: Steve Gethers. D: Peter Kortner.
GS: William Demarest. Glen's brother takes a sudden interest in Katy, much to Glen's dismay.

Young and in Love
W: Peggy Chandler Dick. D: William D. Russell. Steve falls in love with Katy and is taunted by his friends.

The Morley Report
W: Meyer Dolinsky. D: Jerry Paris.
GS: Peter Hobbs. Steve causes chaos in school when he writes an essay advocating free love.

The Octopus
W: John McGreevey. D: William D. Russell. A 16-year-old con artist sets Steve up in business and runs away when it is time to deliver payment.

Rendezvous for Two
W: Steve Gethers. D: William D. Russell. GS: Fritz Feld, Patricia Barry.
Glen and Katy are alone for the weekend and turn a quiet evening into a wild feud.

Mismatch Maker
W: Steve Gethers. D: Don Taylor.
GS: Vito Scotti. Two feuding congressmen's son and daughter fall in love, leaving Katy to patch things up between the two men.

My Son, the Athlete
W: Mike Adams & Peggy Chandler Dick. D: William D. Russell. A general is convinced his son is a great athlete, but in reality he is a timid book scholar.

The Next Mrs. Morley
W: Charles Woolf. D: Paul Nickell.
GS: Phillip Coolidge. Katy and Agatha feel a socialite divorcee is trying to snare Glen for her next husband.

A Locket for Agatha
W: Lee Loeb. D: William D. Russell.
GS: David White. Agatha is dating a man who publicly denounces Congressman Morley.

The Waiting Game
W: Steve Gethers. D: Don Taylor.
GS: Jeremy Slate. Acting as hostess at a reception in the Morley home, Katy faints when Glen introduces Gunnar Gustafson, Katy's first love.

The Mink Machine
W: Stan Cutler. D: Don Taylor. GS: David Hedison. Katy is dating a man who has an interest in computers just as Glen's office buys him a computer to help with his work.

A Real Live Congressman
W: Steve Gethers. D: Don Taylor.
Katy falls for a handsome young congressman.

Past Perfect
W: Steve Gethers. D: Don Taylor.
Katy finds the diary of Glen's dead wife Ann which reveals the story of how they met and fell in love.

Scandal in Washington
W: Jerry Seelen & Jack Raymond. D: William D. Russell. Katy's chances of being accepted as a member of the Washington Mothers' Club is affected when Danny reads a scandalous essay in class.

Love On the Picket Line
W: Richard Powell. D: William D. Russell. GS: Barry Atwater, Oliver McGowan. An 18-year-old political activist pickets in front of the Morley home to get the vote for all 18-year-olds.

The Name of the Game
W: Richard Powell. D: William D. Russell. The Morleys return to Minnesota where Glen is to campaign for re-

election using a beautiful woman as campaign manager.

Help Not Wanted
W: Mae Day & Peggy Chandler Dick. D: Don Taylor. Katy hires a housekeeper to help her and discovers the new employee takes over the Morley home.

Big Sultan, Little Sultan
W: Peggy Chandler Dick. D: William D. Russell. GS: Victor Jory. An oil sultan proposes marriage to Agatha.

Katy's 76th Birthday
W: Jerry Davis. D: Don Taylor. GS: Celia Lovsky, Anthony Eisley. Katy considers marriage after dreaming of a future without a husband.

The Neutral
W: Stan Cutler. D: Don Taylor. Katy is delighted and Glen becomes upset when her parents decide to visit Washington, announcing their drive to detour the new federal highway.

Speak for Yourself, John Katy
W: Peggy Chandler Dick. D: William D. Russell. GS: Peter Robbins. Katy is worried that Glen's involvement with a widow and her three children will end in marriage.

Matter of Honor
W: Stan Cutler & Martin Donovan. D: Fred De Cordova. Papa decides to campaign to speed up Glen and Katy's romantic involvement.

The Helping Hand
W: Stan Cutler. D: Leonard Horn. GS: Fritz Feld. Glen tries to unite a couple in the hopes of winning political favor.

Like Father, Like Son
W: Peggy Chandler Dick. D: Bob Claver. GS: Heather Menzies. Steve speaks out for political honesty in government.

Another Country Heard From
W: Stan Cutler & Martin Donovan. D:

Gene Nelson. GS: Ron Randell. A visiting author proposes to Katy.

Follow the Leader
W: Stan Cutler & Martin Donovan. D: Gene Nelson. GS: Phil Ober. Steve starts to rebel against Katy and Glen's control when he makes friends with a shady youth.

The Oscar Hummingbird Story
W: Stan Cutler & Martin Donovan. D: Gene Nelson. GS: Harold Gould, Albert Paulsen. A pompous film director decides to use the Morley home as the setting for a scene in his latest motion picture.

The Nesting Instinct
W: Peggy Chandler Dick. D: Gene Nelson. Nancy Beth's mother maneuvers Steve into dating her daughter.

A Plague on Both Their Houses
W: Stan Cutler & Martin Donovan. D: Alan Rafkin. GS: Emil Sitka. Katy has her horoscope read and believes that her house is about to come into a violent collision with Senator Ames's house.

Katy By Moonlight
W: Phil Leslie & Keith Fowler. D: Gene Nelson. GS: Bill Daily, Gerald Hiken. Feeling that Glen no longer needs her full-time assistance, Katy gets a job as a night clerk in a book store.

Exit Katy
W: Peggy Chandler Dick. D: William Colleran. GS: Jane Dulo. Katy plans to leave the Morley home and take over her friend Eve's apartment so she can meet some new young men.

Rich Man Poor Man
W: Stan Cutler & Martin Donovan. D: Gene Nelson. GS: Paul Lynde. A millionaire visits the Morley home convinced that Katy wants to marry him.

Crime of Passion
W: Stan Cutler & Martin Donovan. D:

Fred De Cordova. GS: Barbara Shelley, Bernard Fox. Katy is jealous when an English beauty takes up with the congressman.

Why Don't They Ever Pick Me?
W: Stan Cutler & Martin Donovan. D: Bob Claver. GS: Maureen McCormick. Katy tries to comfort an eight-year-old orphan who believes she will never be adopted because she is not pretty enough.

Katy's New Job
W: Peggy Chandler Dick. D: Herb Wallerstein. GS: David Opatoshu. Katy becomes secretary to a sly business tycoon.

Katy's Campaign
W: Stan Cutler & Martin Donovan. D: Bob Claver. Katy runs for president of the Washington women's club.

The Woman Behind the Man
W: Joanna Lee & Howard Merrill. D: Fred De Cordova. GS: Tom Tully, Ellen Corby. Glen becomes the butt of Washington gossip when Katy is portrayed as the source of most of his legislative thinking.

Katy the Diplomat
W: James Allardice & Tom Adair. D: Edmond Levy. GS: Arch Johnson. Katy tries to make amends between an ultraconservative publisher and a visiting Russian Ambassador.

Katy's Castle
W: Warner Law. D: William D. Russell. GS: Parley Baer. Katy inherits a castle and plans to turn it into a tourist hotel.

Never Listen to Rumors
W: Phil Leslie. D: William D. Russell. GS: Julie Gregg. Glen promises to take Steve on a fishing trip and finds he has to cancel the trip due to pressing business.

Ja, Ja, a Thousand Times, Ja
W: Stan Cutler & Martin Donovan. D:

William D. Russell. Glen buys an engagement ring he hopes to present to Katy, but is constantly interrupted by Danny and his cub scout troop.

Nej, Nej, a Thousand Times, Nej
W: Peggy Chandler Dick. D: William D. Russell. GS: Ann Elder. Papa refuses to give permission to Katy's marriage, causing his daughter to vow to marry Glen with or without consent.

The Hottest Ticket in Town
W & D: Unknown. Glen tries to keep Katy out of the house to prepare for a bridal shower.

Why Wait Till November
W & D: Unknown. Katy and Glen are pressured by their friends and family to move up their November wedding date.

Here Comes the Bride's Father
W: Stan Cutler & Martin Donovan. D: Richard Kinon. GS: Molly Dodd. Papa interferes with Katy and Glen's wedding plans.

Babe in the Woods
W: Stan Cutler & Martin Donovan. D: Richard Kinon. GS: Cliff Arquette as Charlie Weaver. Katy and Glen spend a weekend in the woods and find themselves lost.

Stag At Bay
W: Stan Cutler & Martin Donovan. D: Bob Claver. GS: Paul Lynde. To ease the tension before their wedding, Katy organizes a bachelor party for a worried Glen.

Sleeping Beauty Revisited
W: Peggy Chandler Dick. D: Bob Claver. GS: Woodrow Parfrey. While Katy prepares for the wedding, Glen begins to have second thoughts.

Forever Is a Cast Iron Mess
W: Phil Leslie. D: Richard Kinon. GS: Bill Daily, Harold Gould. Katy and Glen receive a huge abstract statue as a wedding present.

Powder Puff Invasion
W: Peggy Chandler Dick.   D: Herb Wallerstein.   Senator Ames tells Glen that when he is married he won't have a place to put any of his treasured belongings.

To Have and to Hold
W: Stan Cutler & Martin Donovan.   D: Bob Claver.   GS: Regis Toomey.   Katy and Glen finally get married, with Steve acting as best man and Papa as bridesmaid.

Crisis at Crystal Springs
W: Stan Cutler & Martin Donovan.   D: Bob Claver.   GS: Frank DeVol.   On their wedding night, Katy and Glen spend a restless time in an overcrowded hotel.

A Sonny Honeymoon
W: Stan Cutler & Martin Donovan.   D: Bob Claver.   GS: Bernard Fox, Judy Carne.   In a New York hotel the Morleys are disturbed by loud music coming from the adjoining suite of a rock and roll star.

High Fashion
W: Joseph Cavella.   D: Richard Kinon.   GS: Bernie Kopell, Vito Scotti.   Katy is chosen to head a committee for a charity fashion show.

The Platinum Swizzle Stick
W: Warner Law.   D: Richard Kinon.   GS: Booth Coleman.   Cousin Stella comes for a visit, leaving lavish wedding gifts for all.

Steve, Boy Lovelorn
W: Peggy Chandler Dick.   D: Bob Claver.   Steve receives his driver's license and asks his girlfriend to go steady.

Jewel Beyond Compare
W: Stanley H. Silverman.   D: Richard Kinon.   GS: Mary Grace Canfield, Tom D'Andrea.   Katy hires a housekeeper who can't cook for beans.

Glen a Gogh-Gogh
W: Stanley H. Silverman.   D: Seymour

Robbie.   GS: Harvey Lembeck, Barbara Stuart.   Katy decides she and Glen must develop independent interests to realize their full potential as individuals.

Simple Joys of Nature
W: Warner Law.   D: Richard Kinon.   GS: Emmaline Henry, Hans Conreid.   When Glen complains about the gardening bills, Katy enrolls in gardening school to learn how to take care of the yard by herself.

Moe Hill and the Mountains
W: Joseph & Carol Cavella.   D: Richard Kinon.   GS: Davy Jones.   Steve and his friends form a rock and roll group with Katy as their manager.

Oh Boy, Is the Honeymoon Over
W: Peggy Chandler Dick.   D: Sam Freedle.   GS: Hoagy Carmichael.   Glen and Katy's discussion of each other's faults erupts into a violent argument.

The Fall and Rise of Steven Morley
W: Warner Law.   D: Bob Claver.   GS: Barbara Hershey.   Steve is running for class president against a boy believed to be a thief.

Have You Ever Thought of Building?
W: Stan Cutler & Martin Donovan.   D: Sam Freedle   An interior decorator tries to con Katy and Glen into remodeling their whole house.

Katy in a Capsule
W & D: Unknown.   GS: Richard Deacon, Gary Crosby.   Katy believes her life needs broadening.

Lo, the Smart Indian
W: Stanley H. Silverman.   D: Herb Wallerstein.   GS: Paul Fix.   An Indian Chief claims a large portion of Minnesota is still owned by his tribe and demands its return.

Steve, Boy Bohemian
W: Peggy Chandler Dick.   D: Richard Kinon.   GS: Leslie Nielson.   Steve decides to quit school and take up writing a book.

Alias Katy Morley
W: Janet Carlson & Don Richman. D: Sam Freedle. GS: Del Moore. Before an important television interview, Katy is arrested for shoplifting.

Anyone for Spindling?
W: Stan Cutler & Martin Donovan. D: Bob Claver. GS: Bernie Kopell, Karen Steele, Bernard Fox. Katy tries desperately to cut off service from a book club which constantly sends her unwanted books, bills and punch cards.

Twelve Angry Women
W: Janet Carlson & Don Richman. D: Richard Kinon. GS: J. Pat O'Malley. Katy is called for jury duty while Glen suffers at home with a bad cold.

The Last to Know
W: Janet Carlson & Don Richman. D: Richard Kinon. GS: Sabrina Scharf. Glen mistakenly believes Katy is expecting a baby.

My Papa the Politician
W: Peggy Chandler Dick. D: Sam Freedle. Papa Holstrum announces he has decided to run for public office and seeks Glen's backing.

The Wife of Your Friend May Not Be a Friend of Your Wife
W: Stan Cutler & Martin Donovan. D: Bob Claver. GS: John McGiver. Katy is involved in a fight with the wife of a senator.

Is He or Isn't He
W: Peggy Chandler Dick. D: Jerry Bernstein. GS: Emmaline Henry. Glen enrolls in a gym class to lose weight but doesn't tell Katy, who fears he is cheating.

Half an Anniversary
W & D: Unknown. Katy buys Glen an anniversary gift that she can't afford.

FATHER KNOWS BEST

On the air 10/3/54, off 4/5/63. CBS, NBC, ABC. 30 min. film B&W. 191 episodes. Broadcast: Oct 1954-Mar 1955 CBS Sun 10-10:30; Aug 1955-Sept 1958 NBC Wed 8:30-9; Sept 1958-Sept 1960 CBS Mon 8:30-9; Oct 1960-Sept 1961 CBS Tue 8-8:30; Oct 1961-Feb 1962 CBS Wed 8-8:30; Feb 1962-Sept 1962 CBS Mon 8:30-9; Sept 1962-Dec 1962 ABC Sun 7-7:30; Dec 1962-Apr 1963 ABC Fri 8-8:30. Producer: Eugene P. Rodney. Prod Co /Synd: Screen Gems/Columbia Pictures TV.

CAST: Jim Anderson (played by Robert Young), Margaret Anderson (Jane Wyatt), Betty Anderson (Elinor Donahue), James Anderson Jr. [Bud] (Billy Gray), Kathy Anderson (Lauren Chapin), Kippy Watkins (Paul Wallace), Ed Davis (Robert Foulk), Myrtle Davis (Vivi Jannis), Claud Messner (Jimmy Bates).

WRITERS: Roswell Rogers, Phil Davis, Paul West, Dorothy Cooper, Sumner Long, John Elliotte. DIRECTORS: William D. Russell, Peter Tewksbury, James Neilson.

The trials and tribulations of the Anderson family, residing in Springfield, USA. Jim Anderson, father of three children, runs an insurance company, and typical episodes concern his involvement in the problems faced by his wife and children. The series is still seen in syndication. It is hailed as one of the best domestic comedies available. On May 17, 1977, NBC aired a 90-minute reunion episode which reunited all the members of the cast.

Bud Takes Up the Dance
W: Dorothy Cooper. D: James Neilson. Bud anxiously prepares to attend his first dance and needs all the family support he can get.

Lesson in Citizenship
W: Roswell Rogers. D: William D. Russell. After Jim tells his family to help others, he winds up fighting bums, the courts and a social club.

The Motor Scooter
W: Harry Clark & Sumner Long. D: William D. Russell. Bud wants a motor scooter but Margaret is dead set against it.

Football Tickets
W: Phil Davis. D: William D. Russell. Jim has only two tickets to a football game and must decide whom to take with him.

Live My Own Life
W: Roswell Rogers. D: William D. Russell. Bud moves out and finds he can't cook, clean or take care of himself.

Grandpa Jim's Rejuvenation
W: Phil Davis. D: William D. Russell. GS: Burt Mustin. After a series of mishaps, Jim feels he is over the hill and ready for an old folks' home.

Bud's Encounter with the Law
W: Roswell Rogers. D: William D. Russell. Jim receives a summons to appear at the police station, but he can't read the charge because the document was accidentally tossed into the washing machine.

Thanksgiving Story
W: Dorothy Cooper. D: William D. Russell. Jim plans to take his family out for a Thanksgiving dinner, but his family has other plans.

Second Honeymoon
W: Paul West. D: William D. Russell. When Jim decides to take Margaret on a second honeymoon, he is constantly worrying about the kids.

Typical Father
W: Dorothy Cooper. D: William D. Russell. Jim thinks Betty plans on eloping with her current boyfriend.

Margaret Goes Dancing
W: Roswell Rogers. D: William D. Russell. Margaret and Jim both join social clubs which they find are boring.

Christmas Story
W: Paul West & Roswell Rogers. D: William D. Russell. GS: Wallace Ford. Jim, appalled by his family's Christmas attitude, decides to recapture the Christmas spirit by cutting down his own tree.

Sparrow in the Window
W: Harry Clark & Sumner Long. D: William D. Russell. An injured sparrow serves to reunite the family after a violent argument.

Boy's Week
W: Paul West. D: William D. Russell. Jim receives a traffic ticket and must face his son Bud who has been appointed Judge of the Day marking the beginning of Boy's Week.

A Friend of Old George's
W: Dorothy Cooper. D: William D. Russell. GS: Parley Baer. A pesty old friend of Jim's arrives at the Anderson home and spoils a birthday party for Kathy.

Bud, the Snob
W: Roswell Rogers. D: William D. Russell. Jim helps Bud overcome his shyness toward women.

The Promised Playhouse
W: Roswell Rogers. D: William D. Russell. GS: Robert Foulk. Jim promises to help Kathy build a playhouse, and then spends an uncomfortable night in the child's new abode.

Jim, the Farmer
W: Roswell Rogers. D: William D. Russell. Jim, fed up with the city, embarks on a search for a quiet farm on which to settle.

Father of the Year
W: Dorothy Cooper. D: William D.

Russell. Bud and Betty write an essay they believe will nominate their dad as Father of the Year in a contest run by a local paper.

The Mink Coat
W: Roswell Rogers.   D: William D. Russell.   A bargain mink coat causes havoc for Jim who is suddenly hit with more bills than he can handle.

The Matchmaker
W: Dorothy Cooper.   D: William D. Russell.   Margaret plays matchmaker in a scheme to unite her Cousin Louise and her sometimes boyfriend Tom.

Bud, the Bridesmaid
W: Dorothy Cooper & Barbara Hammer.   D: William D. Russell. Bud acts as bridesmaid in a plan to enable Tom and Margaret's Cousin Louise to be married.

Proud Father
W: Dorothy Cooper.   D: William D. Russell.   Jim solves his children's problems in school by accepting an invitation to be the emcee of the next PTA meeting.

Father Delivers the Papers
W: Roswell Rogers & Dane Lussier. D: William D. Russell.   GS: Dabbs Greer.   When Bud injures his back, Jim reluctantly takes over his paper route.

No Partiality
W: Roswell Rogers, Alan Woods & John Kohn.   D: William D. Russell. Kathy and Betty both vie for the attention of the same man.

Close Decision
W: Roswell Rogers.   D: William D; Russell.   Bud admits he didn't tag a runner in their church baseball game, prompting Reverend Swain to praise the boy for his honesty.

Art of Salesmanship
W: Roswell Rogers.   D: William D. Russell.   Jim, upset over Bud's inability to sell, decides to teach the boy the

proper way to conduct door-to-door sales.

Father's Private Life
W: Roswell Rogers.   D: William D. Russell.   Jim tells his family to solve their own problems.

Lessons in Civics
W: Dorothy Cooper.   D: William D. Russell.   The Anderson family embarks on a venture to save the old meeting hall from being torn down to make room for a highway.

First Disillusionment
W: Roswell Rogers.   D: William D. Russell.   When Bud is rejected for a job in favor of a boy who faked an impressive employment record, he believes dishonesty is the key to success in business.

Woman in the House
W: Roswell Rogers.   D: William D. Russell.   GS: Harry Hickox.   Jill, an old friend of Jim's, reveals she is unhappy because she cannot make friends, prompting Margaret to invite the girl to remain at their home.

New Girl at School
W: Roswell Rogers.   D: William D. Russell.   GS: Susan George.   Bud falls in love with April, the new girl in school, and is crushed when he learns that she is dating his rival.

Kathy Makes Magic
W: Roswell Rogers.   D: William D. Russell.   Kathy takes up magic and believes a spell she has cast on Bud will cause him to die.

Advantage to Betty
W: Roswell Rogers.   D: William D. Russell.   Betty is named queen of the school sports banquet causing a fight between her and Eula Craig, the former queen.

The Big Test
W: Roswell Rogers.   D: William D. Russell.   Bud is falsely accused of cheating on an important exam.

Father Is a Dope
W: Roswell Rogers. D: William D. Russell. GS: Robert Foulk. Jim thinks his family is trying to trick him into skipping his hunting trip, only to discover that their excuses for keeping him home are all valid.

Spirit of Youth
W: Roswell Rogers. D: William D. Russell. Margaret and Jim go off to their college reunion to prove to their children they are still young at heart.

Bud, the Ladykiller
W: Sumner Long & Dorothy Cooper. D: William D. Russell. After Bud helps a young girl break out of her shell, she drops him for another man.

Margaret's Premonition
W: Roswell Rogers. D: William D. Russell. The family is convinced that Margaret has psychic powers.

Stage to Yuma
W: D.D. Beauchamp. D: William D. Russell. In a flashback sequence, Tate Ibsen saves six passengers riding in a stagecoach from doom by defeating savage Indians.

Bad Influence
W: Roswell Rogers. D: William D. Russell. Bud takes up with a kleptomaniac to teach him there is more to life than material goods.

Betty Hates Carter
W: Roswell Rogers. D: William D. Russell. After Betty sets up a date between Carter Mawson and her girlfriend Janie, she decides that she wants Carter for herself.

Jim, the Tyrant
W: Roswell Rogers & Herman J. Epstein. D: William D. Russell. Jim has a bad day at the office so he takes his frustrations out on the family.

Betty's Brother
W: Paul West. D: William D. Russell. After Betty is chosen to appear on a TV youth program, Bud starts failing his subjects and causing trouble.

Betty Earns a Formal
W: Paul West. D: William D. Russell. Betty takes a part-time job to earn enough money to buy a dress for the high school dance.

The House Painter
W: Roswell Rogers. D: William D. Russell. A house painter rekindles Jim's belief that integrity and pride are basic human drives.

The Grass Is Greener
W: Dorothy Cooper. D: William D. Russell. GS: Paul Harvey, Frank Wilcox. After a business tycoon arrives in town, Jim feels his life has not been as successful as he hoped.

The Bus to Nowhere
W: Roswell Rogers. D: William D. Russell. GS: John Qualen. Betty feels life is devoid of significance and sets out on a journey to find the true meaning of life.

Kathy, the Indian Giver
W: Kay Leonard. D: William D. Russell. Jim tries in vain to show Kathy the importance of keeping a bargain.

The Historical Andersons
W: Roswell Rogers. D: William D. Russell. Bud is surprised to discover that Major Nathan Anderson, his revolutionary ancestor, was a traitor.

Bud, the Wallflower
W: Paul West. D: William D. Russell. Bud decides to go camping with Jim when he is not invited to the Sadie Hawkins dance.

The Persistent Guest
W: Paul West. D: William D. Russell. Fred, a shabbily dressed schoolmate of Bud's, takes up permanent residence with the Andersons after being deserted by his divorced parents.

Family Reunion
W: Roswell Rogers.   D: William D. Russell.   Margaret is frantic when her family conceive a series of excuses for not attending her family reunion.

Family Dines Out
W: Dorothy Cooper.   D: William D. Russell.   Bud needs his family's support at the same time Jim and Margaret have accepted a dinner invitation at a country club.

Bud, the Boxer
W: Paul West.   D: William D. Russell. Jim decides to teach Bud how to fight in order to defend himself against the school bully.

Betty, Girl Engineer
W: Roswell Rogers.   D: William D. Russell.   GS: Roger Smith.   Betty decides to become an engineer, but on her first assignment she is harrassed by a man who believes that a woman's place is in the home.

The Martins and the Coys
W: Paul West.   D: William D. Russell. GS: Tristram Coffin.   Jim and his neighbor Frank start a feud that leaves Betty and Frank's son Bob caught in the middle.

Dilemma for Margaret
W: Kay Leonard.   D: William D. Russell.   Margaret accepts an invitation to speak to a PTA seminar and reluctantly admits she is unable to control her own children.

Hero Father
W: Dorothy Cooper.   D: William D. Russell.   GS: Duke Snider.   Jim arranges for baseball great Duke Snider and his touring All-Stars to play a game in their town.

Father, the Naturalist
W: Roswell Rogers.   D: William D. Russell.   Jim spends a harrowing night in the woods to help Kathy complete her nature folder to become a Tribal Princess in the Little Squirrels.

The Ten Dollar Question
W: Barbara Hammer & Dorothy Cooper.   D: William D. Russell.   GS: Frank Sully.   Jim decides to offer a ten-dollar prize to the member of his family who refrains from tattling for a whole week.

Adopted Daughter
W: Roswell Rogers.   D: William D. Russell.   Kathy feels she is an adopted child when her birth record shows her parents paid $25 to the children's society.

Betty's Graduation
W: Roswell Rogers.   D: William D. Russell.   Betty refuses to attend her high school graduation because she fears the best days of her life are behind her and can never be recaptured.

No Apron Strings
W: Roswell Rogers.   D: Peter Tewksbury.   A demanding girl asks Bud to take her out the same night as he is supposed to attend a birthday party for his mother.

Never the Twain
W: Paul West.   D: Peter Tewksbury. On a dude ranch, Betty falls in love with a cowboy only to discover the relationship won't last.

Betty Goes to College
W: Roswell Rogers & Dorothy Cooper. D: Peter Tewksbury.   Betty enters state college and is angered that her parents are making all of her decisions without consulting her first.

Man About Town
W: Dorothy Cooper.   D: Peter Tewksbury.   Bud prepares for a date with a taller and older woman by putting lifts in his shoes and powder in his hair.

The Homing Pigeon
W: Paul West.   D: Peter Tewksbury. Betty and Bud's homing pigeons both leave home only to return sooner than they expected.

Spaghetti for Margaret
W: Roswell Rogers. D: Peter Tewksbury. Margaret campaigns to help an old retired author receive some recognition for his work.

Betty's Birthday
W: Dorothy Cooper. D: Peter Tewksbury. GS: Eleanor Audley. Betty shocks her family when she tells them that she doesn't want a birthday party or any presents.

Bud, the Millionaire
W: Paul West. D: Peter Tewksbury. Bud talks Jim into giving him a ten dollar a week allowance.

The Old Days
W: Dorothy Cooper. D: Peter Tewksbury. Betty and Bud become upset when they have to wear 1920s style clothing in order to attend a costume dance.

Whistle Bait
W: Paul West. D: Peter Tewksbury. A striking beauty causes Betty to feel a lack of esteem.

The Great Guy
W: Roswell Rogers. D: Peter Tewksbury. GS: Whit Bissell. Bud takes a job on the local newspaper.

The Family Goes to New York
W: Dorothy Cooper. D: Peter Tewksbury. Betty falls in love when she goes to New York to attend her friend's wedding.

Betty Goes Steady
W: Roswell Rogers. D: Peter Tewksbury. Betty becomes a member of the "In-Crowd" at college.

The Good Prospect
W: Roswell Rogers. D: Peter Tewksbuty. GS: Don Beddoe. Aldus Lydom lives in a dream world and feels he is a worldly success, only to cause Kathy great anguish when he reluctantly backs out of buying six dozen doughnuts he ordered from her.

The Angel's Sweater
W: Roswell Rogers. D: Peter Tewksbury. Aunt Neva, Jim's spinster sister, arrives to spend Christmas with the family.

The Promising Young Man
W: Paul West. D: Peter Tewksbury. GS: Richard Crenna. Jim teaches the boss's son the fine merits of the insurance business.

Margaret Hires a Gardner
W: Roswell Rogers. D: Peter Tewksbury. GS: Natividad Vacio. A Spanish gardener turns their yard into a beautiful flower bed at a price Jim can't afford.

Swiss Family Anderson
W: Paul West. D: Peter Tewksbury. Jim and the family become marooned on a deserted island.

Brief Holiday
W: Roswell Rogers. D: Peter Tewksbury. GS: John Banner. Jim believes that Margaret is bored, so he decides to take her out for a night on the town.

The Lawn Party
W: Roswell Rogers. D: Peter Tewskbury. Bud volunteers his backyard as the site for a party.

Short Wave
W: Paul West. D: Peter Tewksbury. Bud uses his short-wave set to help rescue a small boat from a violent storm.

Carnival
W: Paul West. D: Peter Tewksbury. GS: Dick Foran. Bud goes to work for a crooked carnival owner.

Betty and Jet Pilot
W: Paul West. D: Peter Tewksbury. Betty falls for an Army jet pilot, but becomes heartbroken when he is transferred to Alaska.

Trip to Hillsborough
W: Roswell Rogers. D: Peter Tewksbury. Bud ventures out into the world to find material for the book he plans to write.

An Evening to Remember
W: Roswell Rogers. D: Peter Tewksbury. GS: Cornel Wilde. Cornel Wilde asks Jim to help him stop a man from suing him after a car accident.

Bud Buys a Car
W: Paul West. D: Peter Tewksbury. Bud buys his first car to impress a young lady.

Safety First
W: Paul West. D: Peter Tewksbury. Bud is forced to become a school crossing guard after he receives a traffic ticket.

Bud, the Hero
W: Roswell Rogers. D: Peter Tewksbury. Bud brags about catching some bank robbers, but then is asked to give a speech at the church explaining how he captured the bank robbers, that never existed.

Betty Track Star
W: Paul West. D: Peter Tewksbury. Betty wins a track meet and is crowned flower queen of her school.

The Spelling Bee
W: Roswell Rogers. D: Peter Tewksbury. Kathy loses her lucky penny on the day she is to take part in the school spelling bee.

Bud, the Philanthropist
W: Roswell Rogers. D: Peter Tewksbury. Bud gets upset when Kippy takes the credit for a church donation that he really made.

Baby in the House
W: Paul West. D: Peter Tewksbury. After her parents give Betty permission to babysit, they end up taking care of the baby.

Class Prophecy
W: Roswell Rogers. D: Peter Tewksbury. Jim's old friend is ashamed to admit that he is a salesman instead of the doctor he planned to be while they were still in college.

Art of Romance
W: Paul West. D: Peter Tewksbury. While Jim gives Bud advice to win over his girl Judy, she is getting advice from Margaret on how to win over Bud.

Margaret Disowns Her Family
W: Roswell Rogers. D: Peter Tewksbury. Margaret helps a young girl overcome her fear of getting married and starting a family.

Grandpa Retires
W: Roswell Rogers. D: Peter Tewksbury. GS: Ernest Truex. After Grandpa retires, he realizes that he would rather go back to work instead of sitting around doing nothing.

Shoot for the Moon
W: Roswell Rogers. D: Peter Tewksbury. GS: Royal Dano. An old workman named Sageman helps the Andersons recapture their belief in themselves.

Follow the Leader
W: Paul West. D: Peter Tewksbury. Bud has to choose to either stand up for his new teacher or join his classmates in a revolt.

The Awkward Hero
W: Paul West. D: Peter Tewksbury. Betty tutors a football star who offers to take her to the school dance as payment.

The Good Neighbor
W: Andy White. D: Peter Tewksbury. Margaret's parents give her a small home, which she decides to rent out.

Bud, the Executive
W: Paul West. D: Peter Tewksbury. Bud is appointed chairman of his high school picnic committee.

Sentenced to Happiness
W: Roswell Rogers. D: Peter Tewksbury. GS: Natividad Vacio. Frank, their former gardner, is forced to take a regular job and winds up fighting in court.

Mother Goes to School
W: Roswell Rogers. D: Peter Tewksbury. Margaret and Betty become classmates when Margaret takes a course in English literature at Betty's college.

The Indispensable Man
W: John Elliotte. D: Peter Tewksbury. When Bud breaks the coach's rule to go to bed early before the big football game, he is told to sit out the game.

Kathy's Big Chance
W: Roswell Rogers. D: Peter Tewksbury. GS: Greer Garson. Kathy enters a writing contest in the hopes of being the guest of Greer Garson at the opening of her latest film.

Margaret Learns to Drive
W: Paul West. D: Peter Tewksbury. Jim tries to teach Margaret how to drive.

Way of a Dictator
W: Roswell Rogers. D: Peter Tewksbury. Bud takes over the job of raising Kathy when he tells his parents they are not bringing her up correctly.

Mr. Beal Meets His Match
W: Roswell Rogers. D: Peter Tewksbury. GS: John Williams. Betty writes a story for class using the Faust legend and casting the members of her family in the various roles.

Kathy Makes a Wish
W: Paul West. D: Peter Tewksbury. Kathy feeds jelly beans to a pony, causing the animal to follow her home.

Man with a Plan
W: Andy White. D: Peter Tewksbury. Bud's new girl plans a going away party when she thinks he joined the Army.

Big Sister
W: Paul West. D: Peter Tewksbury. GS: Stanley Adams, Florida Friebus. At summer camp, Betty becomes a tyrant counselor pushing her sister Kathy to rebellion.

Calypso Bud
W: Roswell Rogers. D: Peter Tewksbury. Bud takes up drumming to impress a beautiful young lady.

Father's Biography
W: Roswell Rogers. D: Peter Tewksbury. Jim must decide between attending his daughter's PTA meeting or his important Chamber of Commerce meeting.

The Rivals
W: Paul West. D: Peter Tewksbury. GS: Barbara Eden. Betty makes a date with two boys for the same night.

Bud, the Mind Reader
W: Roswell Rogers. D: Peter Tewksbury. Bud takes up mindreading while Betty tries to make the school debate team.

Margaret's Other Family
W: Roswell Rogers. D: Peter Tewksbury. GS: Henry Jones. Jim feels that Margaret is neglecting her family when she spends all her time helping out an old furniture maker and his family.

The Trial
W: Roswell Rogers. D: Peter Tewksbury. Bud is falsely accused of causing one hundred dollars in damage to a neighbor's property.

Revenge Is Sweet
W: Paul West. D: Peter Tewksbury. Betty ridicules Bud for being sloppy after being overwhelmed by the social prestige of her latest boyfriend.

Country Cousin
W: Paul West. D: Peter Tewksbury.
GS: Susan Oliver. The Anderson's
country cousin Milly arrives for a
visit.

Poor Old Dad
W: Roswell Rogers. D: Peter Tewksbury. Bud thinks his father is henpecked.

Betty's Crusade
W: Roswell Rogers. D: Peter Tewksbury. GS: Harold Lloyd, Jr. Betty
tries to help another student improve
his home in order to prevent him
from being evicted.

Young Love
W: Paul West. D: Peter Tewksbury.
Bud falls in love with a married wo-
man.

Tell It to Mom
W: Roswell Rogers. D: Peter Tewksbury. Bud accidentally sells the pair
of rollerskates that Betty was hiding
for a friend.

A Friend in Need
W: Dorothy Cooper. D: Peter Tewksbury. The Andersons become unwilling owners of a shaggy dog.

A Medal for Margaret
W: Roswell Rogers. D: Peter Tewksbury. Margaret becomes upset when
she realizes that she doesn't have any
trophies to place in the family show-
case.

The Weaker Sex
W: Paul West. D: Peter Tewksbury.
Betty tricks a neighbor's son into tak-
ing her to the community picnic.

Jim the Answer Man
W: Paul West. D: Peter Tewksbury.
Jim's plan to finish his work before
leaving on a business trip, but finds
that his family won't leave him alone.

Bud Quits School
W: Paul West. D: Peter Tewksbury.
Bud quits school after a self-made
businessman tells him that he never
went to high school.

A Matter of Pride
W: Roswell Rogers. D: Peter Tewksbury. Bud is chosen as the most popular boy in his class.

Betty Finds a Cause
W: Paul West. D: Peter Tewksbury.
Betty tries to get a neighbor to remove
a dangerously high hedge which is
interfering with traffic.

Vine Covered Cottage
W: June de Roche. D: Peter Tewksbury. Betty's boyfriend Ralph asks
Jim for his daughter's hand in marriage.

Be Kind to Bud Week
W: Roswell Rogers. D: Peter Tewksbury. GS: Henry Kulky. When Betty
becomes more friendly to Bud, he
assumes that she must have an ulterior
motive.

Kathy's Romance
W: Roswell Rogers. D: Peter Tewksbury. GS: Richard Eyer. Kathy's
new boyfriend is more fascinated by
Jim than by her.

Voice from the Past
W: Dorothy Cooper. D: Peter Tewksbury. Bud prepares for the arrival of
the homecoming queen.

Frank's Family Tree
W: Roswell Rogers. D: Peter Tewksbury. Frank, the gardener, claims his
relatives are famous Spanish entertainers.

Always Plan Ahead
W: Roswell Rogers. D: Peter Tewksbury. Jim realizes that his family
never plans ahead, so he sets out to
teach them a lesson.

Second Wedding
W: Paul West. D: Peter Tewksbury.
On their wedding anniversary, Jim and
Margaret decide to remarry.

Bud, the Carpenter
W: Roswell Rogers. D: Peter Tewksbury. GS: John McIntyre. Bud accidentally dents his vacationing neighbor's car.

Betty, the Pioneer Woman
W: Ben Gershman. D: Peter Tewksbury. GS: William Schallert. Betty stages a play depicting the founding of Springfield.

Fair Exchange
W: Roswell Rogers. D: Peter Tewksbury. GS: Rita Moreno. Betty brings an Indian exchange student home for the weekend.

Margaret Wins a Car
W: John Elliotte. D: Peter Tewksbury. Margaret wins a car in a raffle.

The Great Experiment
W: Dorothy Cooper. D: Peter Tewksbury. Jim wants his family to learn all about the modern world and persuades them each to do something different on Saturday afternoons.

The Basketball Coach
W: Roswell Rogers. D: Peter Tewksbury. Jim becomes the new basketball coach when the old one moves away.

Kathy, Girl Executive
W: Roswell Rogers. D: Peter Tewksbury. Bud decides a power lawnmower will let him make more money and persuades the family to invest in his venture.

The Good Samaritan
W: Dorothy Cooper. D: Peter Tewksbury. Bud tries to do good deeds for a report he is writing in English literature.

The Ideal Father
W: Paul West. D: Peter Tewksbury. Uncle Charlie is convinced that Jim's children are spoiled when they ignore him on his birthday.

Big Shot Bud
W: Ben Gershman. D: Peter Tewks-

bury. Bud decides to buy his mother an expensive bottle of perfume, but finds that he doesn't have enough money.

Hard Luck Leo
W: Roswell Rogers. D: Peter Tewksbury. GS: Arthur O'Connell. Jim's cousin Leo visits the Andersons, stating that he has never been given a break by his past employers or fellow employees.

Bud, the Campus Romeo
W: John Elliotte. D: Peter Tewksbury. Bud's overinflated ego causes the girls in his class to start an anti-Bud campaign.

Crisis Over a Kiss
W: John Elliotte. D: Peter Tewksbury. GS: Ron Ely. Bud gets a crush on a new girl and takes her to lover's lane where he finds Betty in a nearby car.

Kathy Grows Up
W: Roswell Rogers. D: Peter Tewksbury. Kathy wants to be treated like an adult.

A Man of Merit
W: Roswell Rogers. D: Peter Tewksbury. GS: Oliver McGowan. Jim is involved in a race to be named the outstanding citizen in community affairs.

Betty Makes a Choice
W & D: Peter Tewksbury. Betty has a hard decision to make regarding her future career.

It's a Small World
W: Dorothy Cooper. D: Peter Tewksbury. Margaret must decide between attending the women's club luncheon or joining Jim on an important trip.

Two Loves Has Bud
W: Roswell Rogers. D: Peter Tewksbury. Bud must decide which of his two girlfriends he will take to the school prom.

An Extraordinary Woman
W: Roswell Rogers. D: Peter Tewks-

bury. Jim and Margaret are visited by a famous author on African culture.

Formula for Happiness
W: Roswell Rogers. D: Peter Tewksbury. Jim dreams that he appears on television and reveals the secret for happiness in life.

Bud, the Debutante
W: Roswell Rogers. D: Peter Tewksbury. Bud gets in over his head when he dates a wealthy girl.

The Meanest Professor
W: Roswell Rogers. D: Peter Tewksbury. Bud regrets writing a demeaning article about one of his professors.

Bud Has a Problem
W: Roswell Rogers. D: Peter Tewksbury. Bud blames his teacher instead of himself when he gets a poor grade in physics.

The Great Anderson Mystery
W: Roswell Rogers. D: Peter Tewksbury. GS: Hillary Brooke. When the TV set breaks down during a mystery program, the Andersons play detective to solve the crime.

The Gold Turnip
W: Roswell Rogers. D: Peter Tewksbury. Bud believes that he is too mature to participate in the traditional high school graduation activities.

A Day in the Country
W: Roswell Rogers. D: Peter Tewksbury. GS: Olin Howlin. While on the way to visit Margaret's parents, the car breaks down leaving the family stranded on a deserted road.

Bud Branches Out
W: Roswell Rogers. D: Peter Tewksbury. Bud falls in love with his college French professor.

The Gardener's Big Day
W: Roswell Rogers. D: Peter Tewksbury. GS: David White. Frank is chosen to represent the town at the opening of a new park.

The Imposter
W: Roswell Rogers. D: Peter Tewksbury. GS: Robert Reed. Betty becomes involved with a young lawyer pretending to be the owner of a radio store.

Bud Plays It Safe
W: Roswell Rogers. D: Peter Tewksbury. Bud decides to date the coach's daughter in order to make sure he gets on the football team.

Bicycle Trip for Two
W: Roswell Rogers. D: Peter Tewksbury. Jim's plans for a quiet bicycle trip end up with the whole family fixing and repairing their badly abused bikes.

First Disillusionment
W: Roswell Rogers. D: Peter Tewksbury. Bud tells Kathy about the job he didn't get when another boy faked his credentials. [This is a recut version of a previous episode.]

Margaret's Old Flame
W: Dorothy Cooper. D: Peter Tewksbury. Jim and Margaret both look forward to their college reunion.

Kathy Becomes a Girl
W: John Elliotte. D: Peter Tewksbury. The family change Kathy from a tomboy into a beautiful girl.

Bud, the Willing Worker
W: Paul West. D: Peter Tewksbury. GS: James Franciscus. Bud looks for a part-time job in order to get enough money to buy a boat.

Turn the Other Cheek
W: Dorothy Cooper. D: Peter Tewksbury. Both Jim and Kathy are double-crossed by their friends.

Good Joke on Mom
W: Roswell Rogers. D: Peter Tewksbury. Margaret tricks the family into believing that she has been elected

chairwoman of the children's clinic building program.

Betty's Double
W: Dorothy Cooper. D: Peter Tewksbury. Betty wins a trip to Hollywood and appears on a television talk show.

Bud Hides Behind a Skirt
W: Roswell Rogers. D: Peter Tewksbury. Betty is campaigning for safe driving, while Bus is accused of reckless driving.

Togetherness
W: Roswell Rogers. D: Peter Tewksbury. A reporter visits the family in order to do an article on family togetherness.

Second Best
W: Roswell Rogers. D: Peter Tewksbury. Betty competes in the college fencing tournament.

Kathy's Big Deception
W: Paul West. D: Peter Tewksbury. Bud tries to get Kathy a date for the community picnic.

Cupid Knows Best
W: Roswell Rogers. D: Peter Tewksbury. Betty arranges a match between Frank and Mama Berta, the owner of a flower shop.

Jim's Big Surprise
W: Dorothy Cooper. D: Peter Tewksbury. GS: Marion Ross. Jim is surprised by his family's lack of interest when he is named Father of the Year.

Time to Retire
W: John Elliotte. D: Peter Tewksbury. GS: Charles Ruggles. When Bud reaffirms an old man's belief in life, he decides to open his own insurance company and hire Bud as his assistant.

Bud, the Speculator
W: Paul West. D: Peter Tewksbury. GS: Eddie Foy. Bud invests money in a phony stock and winds up losing

fifty dollars, which his mother secretly replaces.

The $500 Letter
W: Roswell Rogers. D: Peter Tewksbury. The Andersons get a check for from an admirer and must find out which member of the family the check was meant for.

Family Contest
W: John Elliotte. D: Peter Tewksbury. GS: Stu Erwin. Kathy destroys a picture of a family competing against hers in a photo contest.

Love and Learn
W: Roswell Rogers. D: Peter Tewksbury. Bud falls in love with his English tutor.

Blind Date
W: Paul West. D: Peter Tewksbury. Betty dates a boy everyone regards as a loser.

Betty's Career Problem
W: John Elliotte. D: Peter Tewksbury. GS: Jim Hutton. Betty becomes frustrated when every college contest she enters, she loses to Cliff Bowman, who may even steal her job, too.

Bud Lives It Up
W: Tom & Helen August. D: Peter Tewksbury. Bed spends more money than he has in order to impress a girl in Chicago.

Not His Type
W: John Elliotte & Roswell Rogers. D: Peter Tewksbury. Betty is caught in the middle of an argument between two of her friends who are planning to marry.

Betty's Graduation
W: Roswell Rogers. D: Peter Tewksbury. When Kathy refuses to graduate from high school, the family tells her about Betty's reluctance to graduate from high school, too. [This is a recut version of a previous episode.]

FISH

On the air 2/5/77, off 6/8/78. ABC. Color video tape. 34 episodes. Broadcast: Feb 1977-May 1977 Sat 8:30-9; Jun 1977-Aug 1977 Thu 9:30-10; Aug 1977-Nov 1977 Sat 8-8:30; Jan 1978-Apr 1978 Thu 8:30-9; May 1978-Jun 1978 Thu 9:30-10. Producer: Danny Arnold. Prod Co: Four D. Synd: Columbia Pictures TV.

CAST: Phil Fish (played by Abe Vigoda), Bernice (Florence Stanley), Loomis (Todd Bridges), Victor (John Cassisi), Jilly (Denise Miller), Diane (Sarah Natoli), Mike (Lenny Bari), Charlie (Barry Gordon).

A spin-off from *Barney Miller*. Detective Phil Fish and his wife Bernice decide to take in five foster children. Each week the kids cause trouble for Fish. Fish was a popular character on *Barney Miller*, but he couldn't make it on his own. The series turns up once in a while on a local station.

The Really Longest Day
Fish and Bernice meet the five kids who will be part of their group home.

The Car
Mike spends the night in jail after joyriding in Fish's car.

Cold Cash
Fish finds that Victor is involved in a numbers game.

Power Play
The furnace isn't working, the house is freezing, and Diane says she wants to have Charlie's baby.

Bernice's Problem
Bernice can't cope with the kids, so she seeks professional help.

The Neighbors
GS: Howard Honig, K Callan, Queenie Smith. Bernice throws a party for the neighbors so they can meet the kids.

Fire
GS: Steve Landesberg. Everyone thinks Victor burned down a house in the neighborhood.

The Social Worker
GS: Vicky Huxtable. A social worker threatens to replace Fish and Bernice when she sees how the house is run.

Fish and Roots
GS: Herbert Jefferson, Jr. Charlie asks

an African student to talk to Loomis, who has become a racist after watching "Roots."

Anniversary
GS: Dennis Maury. Diane sneaks off with her boyfriend on a date, when Fish and Bernice celebrate their 36th wedding anniversary at a hotel.

Fish's Job
Bored and restless, Fish takes a job as a security guard.

The Adoption
Everyone misses Victor, who is away with his prospective foster parents.

The New Kid
GS: David Yanez. A young Puerto Rican thief invades Fish's house.

The Missing Fish
Fish starts out for his last day at the station but never arrives. [The story concludes with the two-part episode "Goodbye Mr. Fish," on "Barney Miller."]

Retirement Blues
GS: Ralph Manza. Fish gets drunk with a neighbor, who is also a retired person.

Fish Behind Bars [Part 1]
GS: Alvin Childress, Ivor Francis. Fish refuses to join a senior citizens group.

Fish Behind Bars [Part 2]
GS: Vicky Huxtable, Peter Hobbs. Charlie tries to charm the social worker who wants to replace Fish because he is in jail.

Fish and the Rock Star
GS: John Lansing, Judith Baldwin. Fish considers taking a job as chief of security to a rock star.

Fish's Daughter
GS: Phillip Sterling, Adrien Royce. Fish refuses to give his okay when his daughter plans to marry a man 25 years older than she.

Jilly's Job
Jilly gets a modeling job but she doesn't know that she will have to pose in the nude.

A Fish Christmas
Fish is putting a downer on the kids' first Christmas together.

Mike's Career
GS: Dorothy Green. Mike's patron for his singing career is a rich divorcee.

Close Encounters of a Fishy Kind
GS: Sean McClory. A neighbor claims he was inside a UFO.

The Million Dollar Misunderstanding
A computer sends Fish an enormous pension check.

A Fine Kettle of Fish
GS: Erica Yohn.   While Bernice is away, Fish visits with an attractive widow.

Charlie Resigns
GS: Vicky Huxtable. Charlie resigns after being treated like a child.

Love in Bloom
Fish gives Diane's boyfriend macho lessons.

It Shouldn't Happen to a Dog
GS: Ned Glass. Fish finds his name in the obituaries and the kids bring home a dog.

Sweet Sixteen
Jilly wants birth control pills for her 16th birthday.

Love Thy Neighbor
GS: Erica Yohn. Fish's secret admirer helps out when Bernice sprains her ankle.

A Pinch of Class
Diane gets appendicitis and the house gets redecorated.

For the Love of Mike
GS: Stacey Nelkin. Mike's new girlfriend is a rich girl who likes expensive things.

The Chief Fish
Fish plans to take a job as Chief of Police in a Southern town.

Fire and Ice
Fish and Bernice fight over reupholstering the couch.

Separation
Fish and Bernice have a fight and decide to separate.

THE FLYING NUN

On the air 9/17/67, off 9/18/70. ABC. Color. 30 min. film. 82 episodes. Broadcast: Sept 1967 Thu 8-8:30; Feb 1969-Sept 1969 Thu 7:30-8; Sept 1969-Jan 1970 Wed 7:30-8; Jan 1970-Sept 1970 Fri 7:30-8. Producer: Harry Ackerman. Prod Co/Synd: Screen Gems/Columbia Pictures TV.
CAST: Sister Bertrille (played by Sally Field), Sister Jacqueline (Marge Redmond), Mother Superior (Madeleine Sherwood), Carlos Ramirez (Alejandro Rey), Sister Sixto (Shelley Morrison), Police Capt. Gaspar Formento (Vito Scotti),

Sally Field and friends in The Flying Nun.

Marcello (Manuel Padilla, Jr.), Chief Galindo (Don Diamond, Rodolfo Hoyos), Salazar (Michael Pataki), Sister Teresa (Naomi Stevens).

WRITERS: Bernard Slade, Richard DeRoy, Irma & Austin Kalish, John Mc-Greevey, Searle Kramer, Ed Jurist, Michael Morris, Harlan Ellison, Stanley Adams, John L. Greene, George Slavin, Arnold Horwitt, Roy Kammerman, Burt Styler. DIRECTORS: E.W. Swackhamer, Jerry Bernstein, John Erman, Murray Golden, Oscar Rudolph, Jerome Cortland, Marc Daniels, Lou Antonio, Harry Falk, Ezra Stone, Jon Anderson, Richard Kinon.

A woman named Elsie Ethrington decides to devote herself to helping the less fortunate and joins a convent. Renamed Sister Bertrille, she is assigned to the convent San Tanco in San Juan, Puerto Rico. Sister Bertrille possesses the ability to fly while wearing her coronet, but doesn't have much control over her destinations, leading to the premise of most of the episodes. The series is seen frequently throughout the U.S.

The Flying Nun [Pilot]
W: Bernard Slade.   D: E.W. Swackhamer. GS: Henry Beckman. Sister Bertrille takes advantage of the fact that she can fly by convincing Carlos to part with a valuable piece of property.

The Convent
W: Bernard Slade. D: E.W. Swackhamer. GS: Arlene Golonka. Sister

Bertrille helps Carlos collect on a gambling debt to insure his land donation.

Old Cars for New
W: Searle Kramer. D: Jerry Bernstein. GS: Gino Conforti. Sister Bertrille and Carlos turn the tables on a used car dealer.

A Bell for San Tanco
W: Max Wylie & Harry Ackerman. D:

E.W. Swackhamer. GS: Louise Sorel. Sister Bertrille and Carlos recover a sunken bell to replace the broken convent bell.

Fatal Hibiscus
W: Max Wylie & Harry Ackerman. D: E.W. Swackhamer. The nuns learn that Sister Bertrille is leaving and mistakenly believe she is dying.

Flight of the Dodo Bird
W: Bernard Slade. D: E.W. Swackhamer. GS: John Astin. Despite training in psychology, a young priest can't cope with the problems of convent San Tanco.

Polly Wants a Crack in the Head
W: Richard DeRoy. D: Jerry Bernstein. GS: Jonathan Hole. Sister Bertrille tries to find a home for a talkative parrot.

Ah Love, Could You and I Conspire
W: Richard DeRoy. D: Jerry Bernstein. GS: Herb Edelman, Maureen Arthur. A gangster's girlfriend takes refuge in the convent.

Days of Nuns and Roses
W: Austin & Irma Kalish. D: E.W. Swackhamer. To raise money, the sisters try their luck at bottling grape juice.

With Love from Irving
W: Dorothy Cooper Foote. D: E.W. Swackhamer. GS: Harold Gould. A pelican falls in love with Sister Bertrille and causes difficulty for her with the Mother Superior.

It's an Ill Wind
W: John McGreevey. D: Jerry Bernstein. GS: Noam Pitlik. Flying important papers to Mother Superior, Sister Bertrille interrupts a mobster's meeting.

A Young Man with a Coronet
W: Bernard Slade. D: E.W. Swackhamer. GS: Foster Brooks, Brian Nash. A little orphan feels he can fly if he wears Sister Bertrille's coronet.

The Patron of Santa Thomasina
W: James Henerson. D: Jerry Bernstein. Sister Bertrille, caught between rival villages, is mistaken for a patron saint.

If You Want to Fly, Keep Your Coronet Dry
W: Seymour Freedman. D: Jerry Bernstein. Sister Bertrille and her school children get lost in a storm while on a picnic.

The Dig In
W: Dorothy Cooper Foote. D: Jerry Bernstein. While searching for rare stones, Sister Bertrille is trapped in a mine with an escaped prisoner.

Walking in a Winter Wonderland
W: Richard DeRoy. D: Jerry Bernstein. GS: Celia Lovsky, Woodrow Parfrey. An old nun tells Sister Bertrille all she wants is a white Christmas and Sister Bertrille is determined to help her.

With a Friend Like Him
W: Phyllis & Robert White. D: Russ Mayberry. GS: Rich Little. Sister Bertrille helps bumbling Brother Paul fix up the convent library.

Tonio's Mother
W: Albert Mannheimer, John McGreevey & Krishna Shah. D: Don Taylor. A little boy believes that Sister Bertrille is his mother returning from heaven.

A Fish Story
W: John McGreevey. D: Richard Kinon. GS: David Hurst. Sister Bertrille helps an old fisherman spot fish from the sky.

The Hot Spell
W: James Henerson. D: Matt Bing. GS: Micharl Pataki, Peter Leeds. To save his casino from gangsters, Carlos turns it over to the convent.

Sister Lucky
W: Gene Thompson. D: John Erman.

GS: Michael Constantine. Sister Bertrille is followed by a gambler who feels she brings him good luck.

The Sister and the Old Salt
W: Bernard Slade. D: Richard Kinon. GS: J. Pat O'Malley, Jonathan Daly. Sister Bertrille saves an old sea captain when he sets out on a 1000-mile voyage.

Cyrano De Bertrille
W: Paul Wayne. D: Stan Schwimmer. GS: Albert Paulsen. Sister Bertrille helps an old grocer learn to read so he can impress his girlfriend with a love letter.

Reconversion of Sister Shapiro
W: Austin & Irma Kalish. D: Jerry Bernstein. GS: Pamelyn Ferdin. A little Jewish girl's decision to become a nun thoroughly upsets her parents.

My Sister, the Sister
W: Bernard Slade. D: John Erman. GS: Elinor Donahue. Carlos falls in love with Sister Bertrille's visiting sister.

Where There's a Will
W: Searle Kramer. D: Stan Schwimmer. GS: Ron Masak. The convent inherits a prizefighter who hates to fight.

The Puce Albert
W: Bernard Slade. D: John Erman. Facing court-martial for frivolous living during Marine Reserve maneuvers, Carlos is saved by Sister Bertrille.

May the Wind Be Always at Your Back
W: Al Beich. D: Jerry Bernstein. A homely teenager develops a crush on Carlos.

Love Me, Love My Dog
W: Ted Sherdeman & Jane Klove. D: Russ Mayberry. The convent children adopt a dog which has acquired the knack of pickpocketing.

You Can't Get There From Here
W: Cordwainer Bird [Harlan Ellison]. D: Bruce Kessler. GS: Bridget Hanley. Sister Bertrille is stranded on an island with Carlos and a girl who threw him off his yacht.

Song of Bertrille
W: Michael Morris. D: Murray Golden. GS: Paul Peterson, The Sundowners. To raise money for the convent, Sister Bertrille writes a song.

The Crooked Convet
W: Arthur Julian. D: Hal Cooper. A police captain is sure the nuns are running an illegal gambling operation.

The Rabbi and the Nun
W: Michael Morris. D: Jerry Bernstein. GS: Harold Gould. Sister Bertrille helps a Jewish couple solve their differences and then prompt them to marry in the convent garden.

The Return of Father Lundigan
W: Lee Irwin & Stan Dreben. D: Jerry Bernstein. GS: Sid Haig, Paul Lynde, Bernie Kopell. Under hypnosis, Sister Bertrille and the Reverend Mother switch personalities.

This Convent Is Condemned
W: Arthur Julian. D: Murray Golden. To keep Carlos in San Tanco, Sister Bertrille tricks the police captain into condemning the convent building.

The Organ Transplant
W: Larry Markes. D: Jerome Courtland. GS: Abbe Lane. Sister Bertrille gets an ancient organ for the convent.

Two Bad Eggs
W: Bruce Howard. D: E.W. Swackhamer. GS: Del Moore. A tourist thinks Sister Bertrille is an invader from outer space when he happens to see her flying.

All Alone by the Convent Phone
W: Michael Morris. D: Jerry Bernstein. GS: Cliff Osmond. A robber terrorizes Sister Bertrille, alone in the

convent with a sick little boy.

It's an Ill Windfall
W: Searle Kramer. D: Jerry Bernstein. GS: Larry Gelman. Sister Bertrille discovers a shady politician after searching for the donor of a check.

Slightly Hot Parking Meters
W: Elroy Schwartz. D: Claudio Guzman. Chaos erupts when Captain Fomento installs parking meters that end up with marked coins.

To Fly or Not to Fly
W: John McGreevey. D: John Erman. GS: Spring Byington. Sister Bertrille tries to keep from flying during a rededication ceremony.

How to Be a Spanish Grandmother
W: Ed Jurist & Michael Morris. D: Jerry Bernstein. GS: Lillian Adams, Elinor Donahue. Carlos must find a wife and children before his visiting mother arrives.

The Landlord Cometh
W: Frank Crow & Searle Kramer. D: Oscar Rudolph. GS: Jay Novello, Ivor Francis. The owners of the land on which the convent is built decide to sell it.

Sisters Socko in San Tanco
W: Bernard Slade. D: Robert Rosenbaum. GS: Victor Buono. Sister Bertrille turns an old magician's farewell appearance into his greatest triumph.

A Star Is Reborn
W: Ed Jurist. D: Murray Golden. GS: Gavin MacLeod. Rescued from drowning by Sister Bertrille, a movie star feels that she had a religious experience.

Great Casino Robbery [Part 1]
W: Michael Morris. D: Jerome Courtland. GS: Alan Hale, Dick Gautier, Ruta Lee. The nuns are used as pawns in a scheme to rob the casino.

Great Casino Robbery [Part 2]
W: Michael Morris. D: Jerome Courtland. Sister Bertrille sets out to trap the casino thieves.

The Boyfriend
W: Michael Morris. D: Jerome Courtland. GS: Dwayne Hickman, Bob Hastings. An old boyfriend feels Sister Bertrille became a nun because he jilted her.

The Kleptomonkeyac
W: Sam Locke & Joel Rapp. D: Ezra Stone. Soon after a monkey arrives at the convent, Sister Bertrille is suspected of kleptomania.

The Moo Is Blue
W: Frank Crow & Leo Rifkin. D: Murray Golden. Sister Bertrille buys a cow for the convent that only gives milk when it hears music.

The Breakaway Monk
W: Arthur Julian. D: Murray Golden. GS: Rich Little, Charles Lane. Accident-prone Brother Paul works on Carlos's income tax.

Happy Birthday Dear Gasper
W: Arthur Alsberg. D: Ezra Stone. Captain Gasper mistakes a surprise party for one of the convent children for a birthday party for himself.

Cast Your Bread Upon the Waters
W: William Raynor & Myles Wilder. D: Murray Golden. GS: Jamie Farr. In another attempt to raise money, the sisters go into the bakery business.

The Convent Gets the Business
W: Paul Richards. D: Jon G. Anderson. The convent inherits a dry goods store and hires Carlos's Cousin Luis to run it.

Cousins By the Dozens
W: Frank Crow & Leo Rifkin. D: Jerome Courtland. GS: Henry Corden, Lisa Gaye. Sister Bertrille unwisely invites a horde of Carlos's relatives to San Tanco.

The Lottery
W: Laurence Marks. D: Oscar Ru-

dolph. A poor farmer donates a lottery ticket to the convent that turns out to be the big winner.

The Big Game
W: Clifford Goldsmith. D: Jerome Courtland. GS: Don Drysdale, Willie Davis. Sister Bertrille manages the baseball team to a 43-1 loss that she calls a great moral victory.

My Sister the Star
W: Dorothy Cooper Foote. D: Marc Daniels. GS: Paul Winchell. Sister Bertrille almost becomes an overnight sensation in show business after appearing on a children's television program.

Speak the Speech, I Pray You
W: Milt Rosen. D: Marc Daniels. GS: Gary Crosby, Bob Cummings. Sister Bertrille helps a shy priest overcome his shyness and gain confidence in himself.

The Paolo Story
W: Michael Morris. W: Jerry Bernstein. GS: Naomi Stevens. Sister Bertrille sets out to find the owner of a baby left on her doorstep.

Marcello's Idol
W: John L. Greene. D: Jerome Courtland. GS: Farrah Fawcett, Michael Pataki, Manuel Padilla, Jr. A little boy advertises for a wife so Carlos can adopt him.

Guess Who's Coming to Picket
W: Milt Rosen. D: Harry Falk. The nuns become involved in a strike at Carlos's casino.

The Not So Great Imposter
W: Dorothy Cooper Foote. D: Harry Falk. GS: Larry Storch. A journalist disguised as a priest photographs Sister Bertrille in flight.

A Convent Full of Miracles
W: Michael Morris. D: Jerry Bernstein. GS: Nehemiah Persoff. Miraculous gifts appear after the convent hires an old handyman.

Hector and the Brass Bed
W: Stanley Adams & George Slavin. D: Lou Antonio. GS: Titos Vandis. The sisters get caught caring for a donkey named Hector.

The New Habit
W: Burt Styler. D: Jerry Bernstein. Sister Bertrille tries out a new coronet; it prevents her from flying.

Bertrille and the Flicks
W: Michael Morris. D: Harry Falk. The convent arranges a benefit show and personal appearance of Gloria Davenport, a silent film star, who is now Sister Adelaide.

A Ticket for Bertrille
W: Ron Kammerman. D: Jerry Bernstein. GS: Lisa Gaye. Sister Bertrille tries to prove that nuns aren't immune to the law and goes to jail to prove it.

The New Carlos
W: Michael Morris. D: Oscar Rudolph. GS: Sandra Smith. Carlos changes his clothes and personality in an attempt to impress a young woman.

Dear Aggie
W: Leo Rifkin. D: Joseph Bernard. GS: Henry Corden. Carlos and Sister Bertrille both give advice to an unhappy couple and end up fighting each other.

My Sister the Doctor
W: Milt Rosen & Michael Morris. D: Richard Kinon. GS: Elinor Donahue. Sister Bertrille's sister Jenny, tired of playing doctor, arrives for her vacation.

Armando and the Pool Table
W: Michael Morris. D: Lou Antonio. GS: John Hoyt, Farrah Fawcett. The convent gets a pool table and Armando gets a challenge as Sister Bertrille gets in trouble with Mother Superior.

Hello Columbus
W: Arnold Horwitt. D: Ezra Stone. Sister Bertrille stages a play and dis-

covers she has trouble casting the role of Columbus.

The Dumbest Kid in School
W: Roy Kammerman.   D: Jerome Courtland. GS: Robert Lansing, Eric Shea, Vincent Perry.   The convent loses its biggest prankster, but the child finds a father and a new home.

Man's Best Friend Isn't
W: Milt Rosen. D: Jerry Bernstein. GS: Gino Conforti. Sister Bertrille befriends a dog and a plumber, getting Carlos into hot water.

The Somnaviatrix
W: John L. Greene. D: Jerry Bernstein. Instead of sleepwalking, Sister Bertrille begins flying in her sleep.

Papa Carlos
W: Stanley Adams & George Slavin. D: Jerome Courtland.   GS: Gregory Sierra. Kim and Ramon make Carlos happy when they announce they are married, but Carlos is stunned at the thought of being a grandfather.

The Candid Commercial
W: John L. Greene. D: Harry Falk.

GS: Pat Harrington.   Sister Bertrille sells laundry detergent to keep the convent clothes on the line.

A Gift for El Charro
W: Stanley Adams & George Slavin. D: Lou Antonio.   GS: Corinne Camacho, Ben Archibek.   El Charro, world famous matador, finds out that being a handyman isn't the best way to learn English.

When Generations Gap
W: Burt Styler. D: Leon Benson. GS: Tommy Boyce and Bobby Hart.   A famous singing duo get their reputation scorned by unfair publicity.

Operation Population
W: Arnold Horwitt. D: Jerome Courtland.   GS: Hilarie Thompson, Pedro Gonzales-Gonzales. A business tycoon loses an office site, but helps to save a park from closing.

No Tears for Thomas
W: Stanley Adams & George Slavin. D: Jon G. Anderson. GS: Larry Gelman, Booth Coleman. Sister Bertrille talks a 70-year-old man into remarrying for the fifth time.

GET SMART

On 9/18/65, off 9/11/70. NBC, CBS. Color film. 138 episodes. 117 currently airing. Broadcast: Sept 1965-Sept 1968 NBC Sat 8:30-9; Sept 1968-Sept 1969 NBC Sat 8-8:30; Sept 1969-Feb 1970 CBS Fri 7:30-8; Apr 1970-Sept 1970 CBS Fri 7:30-8. Producer: Arne Sultan/Mel Brooks. Prod Co: Talent Artists. Synd: National Telefilm.

CAST: Maxwell Smart (played by Don Adams), Susan Hilton [99] (Barbara Feldon), Thaddeus, The Chief (Ed Platt), Larrabee (Robert Karvelas), Hymie the Robot (Dick Gautier), Conrad Siegfried (Bernie Kopell), Starker (King Moody), Agent 13 (Dave Ketchum), 99's Mother (Jane Dulo).

One of the funniest and most original comedy series ever made. The episodes centered around a bumbling secret agent and his fight with bizarre villains who worked for the evil spy agency, Kaos. Maxwell Smart, Agent 86, and his girlfriend, Agent 99, eventually got married on the show and later had twins. Don Adams returned in 1980 to play Maxwell Smart in the film called "The Nude Bomb a.k.a. The Return of Maxwell Smart." He was no longer working for Control, but instead he was working for Pits. The format was similar but without Barbara Feldon as 99 and the Chief [Ed Platt died years earlier], it did rather

Don Adams and Barbara Feldon in Get Smart.

poorly at the box office. The series is run constantly all over the country; however 21 episodes are not run by most stations [these episodes are marked with a *]. They consist of an original black and white pilot film and 20 episodes from its last season. Due to residual fees problems, they are only allowed to appear three times during a run on a particular station. So, many stations decide not to run these episodes because of the enormous amount of paperwork involved in keeping track of the number of times each segment was run. An interesting note: King Moody, who portrayed Siegfried's assistant Starker, went on to become Ronald McDonald in the McDonalds' TV commercials.

*Mr. Big [Pilot]
GS: Michael Dunn, Vito Scotti. Mr. Big, an evil dwarf, plans to use a doomsday machine created by Professor Dante, called Dante's Inthermo, to destroy major cities of the world unless he gets 100 million dollars. [This episode was filmed in black and white.]

Our Man in Toyland
GS: John Hoyt. Smart tries to put a Kaos kingpin, who has been using a department store as a cover for his operations, out of operation.

Kaos in Control
Smart is put in charge of security for a meeting of six top scientists. When a new secret weapon, the retrogressor gun, is stolen, he suspects that one of the Control staff is a spy.

School Days
Smart joins the Control Espionage training school to find a Kaos agent.

Diplomat's Daughter
GS: Leonard Strong, Inger Stratton. Smart must protect a visiting Scandinavian princess from being captured by the head of the Chinese branch of Kaos, The Claw.

Now You See Him—Now You Don't
GS: Joseph Ruskin, Gregory Morton. Smart must protect a scientist from being captured by an invisible Kaos spy.

Washington 4, Indians 3
GS: Anthony Caruso.   Smart must prevent a tribe of Indians from launching their new secret weapon in an attempt to take back the land taken by the white man, namely the whole country.

Our Man in Leotards
GS: Michael Pate.   Smart and 99 attempt to recover Immobilo, a new drug which causes momentary paralysis, from Emilio Naharana, a Latin American ballet dancer and Kaos agent.

The Day Smart Turned Chicken
GS: Simon Oakland.   A dying cowboy tells Smart about an assassination attempt on an ambassador's life, but when he reports this to Control, no one believes him.

Satan Place
GS: Joseph Sirola.   Smart must rescue the Chief from Kaos agent, Harvey Satan.

Too Many Chiefs
GS: Susanne Cramer.   Smart must protect a Control witness against Kaos from Alexi Sebastian, a master of disguise, who has been sent to kill her.

My Nephew the Spy
GS: Conrad Janis, Maudie Prickett, Charles Lane.   Smart must hide the fact that he is a spy from his visiting aunt and uncle.

Weekend Vampire
GS: Ford Rainey, Martin Kosleck. Smart and 99 search for a vampire in the house of former Control scientist, Dr. Drago.

Aboard the Orient Express
GS: Johnny Carson.   Smart must carry a $500,000 payroll to their agents behind the Iron Curtain, in a briefcase chained to his wrist.

Double Agent
Smart pretends to be a bum in order to trick Kaos into hiring him as an agent.

Survival of the Fattest
GS: Karen Steele, Tania Lemoni, Patti Gilbert.   Smart must try to rescue a captive prince from the strongest female spy in the world.

Kisses for Kaos
GS: Michael Dante.   Smart must stop Kaos agent and art dealer Rex Savage from planting exploding paintings in foreign consulates.

The Dead Spy Scrawls
GS: Leonard Nimoy.   Smart must find an electronic brain hidden in a pool hall.

Back to the Old Drawing Board
GS: Patrick O'Moore.   Kaos sends Hymie, a human-looking robot, to kidnap a famous scientist.   Hymie is later reprogrammed and is put to work for Control.

All in the Mind
GS: Torin Thatcher.   Smart tries to find out how a psychiatrist has been obtaining top secret information for Kaos.

Smart, the Assassin
Kaos brainwashes Smart into killing the Chief.

Dear Diary
GS: Burt Mustin, Ellen Corby, Byron Foulger.   Smart must try to find the diary of a retired Control agent at the Spy City home for old spies.

I'm Only Human
Smart sends dog agent Fang and Agent B-17, the parrot with the computer mind, to a Kaos kennel to find out how they are getting dogs to kill their scientist owners.

Stakeout on Blue Mist Mountain
Smart sneaks into a Kaos hideout in the mountains where he must attempt to disarm a bomb with a dime.

The Amazing Harry Hoo
GS: Joey Foreman, Leonard Strong, Lee Kolima. Oriental detective Harry Hoo joins Smart in his fight against the evil Claw, who leads them into a trap at a Chinese laundry.

Hubert's Unfinished Symphony
GS: Bert Freed, John Myhers. Smart must find the new head of Kaos whose name is spelled out in the last six notes of an unfinished symphony written by a Control agent who was killed.

Ship of Spies [Part 1]
Smart tries to find the person who stole the plans to a nuclear amphibian battleship.

Ship of Spies [Part 2]
Smart and 99 board a freighter in his search for the thief, where he is almost killed by a falling ship's mast.

Shipment to Beirut
GS: Judy Lang, Lee Bergere. Smart tries to find a set of secret plans sewn into a dress at a dress shop owned by a Kaos agent.

The Last One in Is a Rotten Spy
GS: Alice Ghostley, Jane Massey, Elisa Ingram, Barbara Stanek, Victoria Carroll. Smart must try to get a list of Kaos agents from a defecting spy at a swim

A Spy for a Spy
Siegfried kidnaps the Chief and offers to return him in exchange for the new laser-powered missile detector.

The Only Way to Die
GS: Edmund Hashim, Dave Ketchum. Smart plays dead in order to find an agent called the Blaster, who returns every year to destroy a national monument.

Strike While the Agent Is Hot
GS: Lisa Pera, Dino Natali, Alan Dexter. Smart and the other agents go on strike during an investigation into a counterfeit money operation.

Maxwell Smart, Alias Jimmy Ballantine
GS: Tim Herbert, Dave Ketchum. Smart impersonates a famous safecracker in order to trap a band of Kaos agents planning to rob the biggest bank vault in the country.

Anatomy of a Lover
GS: King Moody, Laurel Goodwin, Larry Gallery. Smart tries to find the spy who reprogrammed Hymie the Robot into working for Kaos again, while the Chief's niece falls in love with Hymie.

Kiss of Death
GS: Geraldine Brooks, Dave Ketchum. A rich heiress plans to kill Smart by using poisoned lipstick.

Casablanca
GS: Morton Jacobs, Louis Wills, Stacy Keach, Dave Ketchum, Gordon Jump. A takeoff on the movie "Casablanca." Smart follows 99 to a cafe which is believed to be the headquarters of The Choker.

The Greatest Spy on Earth
GS: Harry Varteresian, Victor Lundin, Mickey Manners, Paul Dooley. Smart and 99 pose as reporters so they can spy on the members of a Kaos circus.

Hoo Done It
GS: Joey Foreman. Smart and detective Harry Hoo investigate strange happenings on a deserted Pacific island inhabited by people who look like TV heroes.

Rub-a-Dub-Dub . . . Three Spies in a Sub
Smart and 99 are sent to destroy a computer used to guide Siegfried's submarine in acts of piracy.

The Decoy
GS: Dave Ketchum. Smart is sent on a decoy mission, aboard an airplane, when Kaos breaks the Control code.

Bronzefinger
GS: Joseph Sirola, Robert Patten, Dave Ketchum. Smart and 99 try to find an agent named Bronzefinger, who has been stealing famous paintings and replacing them with fakes.

The Whole Tooth and . . .
GS: Robert Strauss, John Alvin, Joseph Mell, Howard Wendell, Stuart Nisbet. Smart hides the plans for an exploding reactor in the teeth of a convict headed for prison and then has to get himself sent to prison to retrieve it.

Island of the Darned
GS: Harold Gould, Kai Hernandez, Fabian Dean, Stacy Keach, Julius Johnson. Smart and 99 go to an island to find a Kaos killer who now plans to hunt them down for sport.

Perils in a Pet Shop
GS: Donald Murphy, Dave Ketchum. Smart, 99 and Fang try to find out how Kaos is sending top secret information from their pet shop headquarters.

It Takes One to Know One
GS: Gayle Hunnicutt, Woodrow Parfrey, Martin Kelley, Paul Hahn. Hymie falls in love with a notorious Kaos female killer, who also happens to be a robot.

Someone Down Here Hates Me
GS: Craig Heubing. Smart suspects everyone of being a Kaos agent when he is named number one on the Kaos hit list.

Cutback at Control
Smart accepts Siegfried's offer of a job with Kaos when he is laid off from Control.

The Mummy
GS: Laurie Main, Lisa Gaye, Marc London. Smart finds that Kaos agents are arriving into the country dressed as mummies, and that captured Control agents leave the country the same way.

The Girls from Kaos
GS: Tisha Sterling, Virginia Lee, Valerie Hawkins, Sidney Clute. Smart becomes a judge at a beauty contest so he can guard Miss USA from Kaos kidnappers who want to use her as hostage to gain secrets from her scientist father.

The Man from Yenta
GS: Walker Edmiston, Paul Comi, Alan Oppenheimer. Smart pretends to be a visiting prince to find a Kaos agent, unaware that an Israeli spy has been sent to kill the prince.

Smart Fit the Battle of Jericho
GS: Steve Gravers, William Chapman. Smart tries to find out how Kaos is blowing up buildings built for the American space agencies.

Where-What-How-Who Am I?
Smart is on his way to give the Chief some vital information when his car crashes and he gets amnesia.

How to Succeed in the Spy Business Without Really Trying
GS: Marc London, Alex Rocco. Siegfried manages to pull off a giant kidnapping caper by tricking the Chief into diverting all of his agents elsewhere, leaving him free to carry out his fiendish plot.

The Expendable Agent
GS: Irwin Charone, Dick Patterson. Smart teams up with a British spy named Cain to protect a British scientist who plans to give a secret rocket fuel formula to the American scientists.

Appointment in Sahara
Smart and 99 try to prevent Kaos from firing a missile which will destroy the world unless a Kaos agent is made a member of each country's government.

Pussycats Galore
GS: Angelique, Ted Knight, H.M. Wynant. The Chief gets an agent who is a

master of disguise to become a woman who will act as Smart's contact when he spies on a Kaos nightclub.

A Man Called Smart [Part 1]
GS: Howard Caine. Smart takes the part of a wounded Kaos informer in order to find the Kaos headquarters.

A Man Called Smart [Part 2]
GS: Howard Caine, William Schallert. Kaos demands one billion dollars or it will dry up the country's water supply.

A Man Called Smart [Part 3]
GS: John Myhers, William Schallert. Smart goes to Hollywood when he suspects that Otto Hurrah, the head of a large movie studio, is behind the plot to dry up all the water.

Viva Smart
GS: Joey Bishop, Monty Landis. Max and 99 try to depose a Latin American dictator.

Witness for the Persecution
Trouble begins when Smart moves in with a scientist.

The Spy Who Met Himself
Problems arise between Control and Kaos: nobody can tell the good guys from the bad guys.

The Spirit Is Willing
Smart poses as a magician to prove that a theatrical agent is also a Kaos agent.

Maxwell Smart, Private Eye
All of Control is put on part-time status. So he can make extra money, Smart becomes a private eye in this takeoff of the "Maltese Falcon."

Supersonic Boom
GS: Farley Granger, Bill Dana. Smart and 99 try to find the Kaos sonic boom machine before it destroys all of New York.

One of Our Olives Is Missing
GS: Carol Burnett. Smart and Sieg-fried fight to get a miniaturized radio receiver which was concealed inside an olive and accidentally swallowed by a nutty western singer.

When Good Fellows Get Together
GS: H.B. Haggerty. Kaos challenges Hymie the Robot to fight their new super robot Gropo. However, Hymie would rather make friends with Gropo than fight with him.

Dr. Yes
GS: Donald Davis, Todd Martin, Andre Phillippe, Wally Cox. Smart and 99 pose as campers while they try to find the secret laboratory of Kaos agent Dr. Yes.

That Old Gang of Mine
GS: Iggie Wolfington, Raoul Franck, Diahn Williams, Sid Haig, Larry Duran. Smart is ordered to capture the head of a gang of thieves by disguising himself as a safecracker.

The Mild Ones
GS: Susan Albert, Steve Allen, Michael Bell. Smart and 99 are ordered to join a hippie gang to find the foreign minister they kidnapped for Kaos.

Classification: Dead
GS: Eileen Weston, John Fiedler. Smart has swallowed a poison, for which the only known antidote is in the hands of the Kaos agent who created the poison.

The Mysterious Dr. T
GS: Craddock Munro, Peter Robbins. Smart and Siegfried try to find a 12-year-old genius named Dr. T.

The King Lives?
GS: Michael Forest, Richard Angarola, John Doucette, Judith McConnell, Johnny Carson. Smart takes the place of his lookalike, a foreign king, in order to prevent the king's half brother and his Kaos assistants from killing the king.

The Groovy Guru
GS: Larry Storch, Barry Newman, Eileen Weston. Smart and 99 try to prevent the evil Guru from taking over the minds of teenagers and having them commit vast destruction for Kaos.

The Little Black Book [Part 1]
GS: Don Rickles, Ann Prentiss, Arlene Golonka. Smart's old friend Sid Krimm pays him a visit and unknowingly gets hold of the book of Kaos agents. He thinks it's Smart's little black book and arranges a date with two Kaos spies.

The Little Black Book [Part 2]
GS: Don Rickles, Arlene Golonka, Eddie Ryder, James Komack, Robert Easton, Ann Prentiss, Alan Drake, Ernest Borgnine, Corbett Monica, Joey Forman. Sid finally believes that Smart is a spy and agrees to help him get the book back from the Kaos agent called the Maestro.

Don't Look Back
GS: Bruce Gordon, Stuart Nisbet, Allen Jaffe, Larry Anthony, Milton Berle. A takeoff on "The Fugitive" as Smart looks for the one-handed man who was a witness to the crime that he was framed for, by a spy wearing a Maxwell Smart mask.

99 Loses Control
GS: Jacques Bergerac, Bob Hope. 99 agrees to marry casino owner Victor Royale, until Smart finds out he is a Kaos agent.

The Wax Max
GS: Richard Devon, Robert Ridgely. Smart is captured by the owner of the wax museum who plans to turn him into wax.

Operation Ridiculous
GS: George Macready, Eileen Weston, Patti Gilbert. The Chief tries to prove to a magazine writer that Control is very efficient.

Spy, Spy, Birdie
GS: Percy Helton, King Moody. Smart, 99 and Siegfried team up to find an inventor who can't stand noise, so he created a silent explosive and now threatens to destroy cities in the East and the West.

Run, Robot, Run
GS: John Orchard, Lyn Peters. A pair of Kaos agents named Mr. Snead and Mrs. Neal try to prevent U.S. athletes from participating in a track meet. Hymie the Robot joins the team to make sure nothing interferes with the event.

The Hot Line
GS: Richard Yarmy, John Byner, Robert Doqui, Regis Philbin, Helen Boll. A Kaos agent imitates the President's voice and orders Smart to become the new Chief and to open Control's files to a Kaos agent.

The Reluctant Redhead
GS: Cesar Romero, Alan Baxter, Julie Sommars, Noam Pitlik. Smart trains a lookalike girl to pose as an informer's missing wife so he can obtain a list of enemy agents from him.

Die, Spy
GS: Stu Gilliam, Poupee Bocar, Robert Culp. A takeoff on "I Spy." Smart and 99 are given an assistant in an attempt to find a spy.

The Impossible Mission
GS: Aron Kincaid, Eddie Rice, Ann Elder, Jamie Farr. When 99 and Smart are trapped in a TV studio together, Max proposes to her.

Snoopy Smart vs. the Red Baron
GS: King Moody, Jane Dulo, Pat Houtchens. While visiting 99's mother, Smart tries to prevent Siegfried from destroying the country's potato crop.

Closely Watched Planes
GS: Pete Barbutti, Maurine Dawson. Smart and 99 go aboard an airplane in

an attempt to find out why government couriers are disappearing while in the air.

The Secret of Sam Vittorio
GS: J. Carrol Naish. Smart and 99 pose as lookalike gangsters to learn an old bank robber's secret.

Diamonds Are a Spy's Best Friend
Smart tries to prevent a group of bald-headed spies from stealing a valuable diamond.

The Worst Best Man
GS: Bernard E. Barrow, Avery Schreiber. Hymie is chosen to be Smart's best man at his wedding. However, Kaos plants a bomb inside Hymie which, when it explodes, will kill all of the agents attending Max's bachelor party.

A Tale of Two Tails
GS: Fred Willard, Victor Sen Yung, Vico Grecco. Smart takes his two student spies on a practice mission: to follow 99, unaware that she is on a real mission, causing her to think that they are enemy agents trying to kill her.

The Return of the Ancient Mariner
GS: Jack Cassidy, William Schallert. Smart has to guard the old Chief of Control and search for a Kaos agent called the Chameleon.

With Love and Twitches
GS: William Schallert, Alan Oppenheimer, Jay Lawrence, Sharon Cintron, Larry Vincent, Ned Wever, Jane Dulo, Dorothy Adams [Mrs. Don Adams]. On the day of his wedding, Smart swallows a liquid which will cause him to break out in a rash, actually a detailed map, which Kaos is very anxious to get their hands on.

The Laser Blazer
GS: Julie Newmar, Leonard Strong. Smart is given a new blazer jacket with a laser built in, which his new maid is very interested in obtaining for Kaos.

The Frakas Fracas
GS: Alice Ghostley, Tom Bosley. When the Chief comes to dinner, 99 serves him a poisoned dessert given to her by a couple of Kaos agents next door who plan to steal the list of Kaos agents who plan to defect to Control.

Temporarily Out of Control
Smart and the Chief are ordered to report for Naval duty when Kaos forges their orders. This way they are out of the way long enough for Kaos to pass an agent off as a visiting dignitary.

Schwartz's Island
GS: King Moody. Smart and 99 are shipwrecked on Siegfried's homemade island, where he plans to use a giant magnet to attract the entire Navy and destroy them when the island is blown up.

One Nation Invisible
GS: Lyn Peters. Smart tries to convince a beautiful female scientist, who has invented a spray to turn herself invisible, to join Control.

Hurray for Hollywood
GS: Ivor Francis, Terence Kilburn, Claude Woolman, Don Ross. Smart and 99 join an acting troupe who are actually a group of Kaos agents using a theater as a cover.

The Day They Raided the Knights
GS: John Harding, Nancy Kovack. 99 gets a job at a trading stamp redemption center, unaware that it is a Kaos weapons supply center.

Tequila Mockingbird
GS: Oscar Beregi, Lewis Charles, Poupee Bocar. Smart and 99 try to find a hidden gem in a small town in Mexico by passing themselves off as entertainers.

I Shot 86 Today
GS: Charles Bateman, Irwin Charone. Smart and the Chief wind up at a golf course where nuclear golf balls are destroying government buildings.

Absorb the Greek
GS: Alizia Gur, Jack DeLeon, Jane Dulo, Joseph Mell. The Chief is dating a pretty Greek girl so he can learn a secret formula from her without anyone suspecting.

To Sire, with Love [Part 1]
GS: John Doucette. Smart hides the lookalike foreign king at his house, causing a mixup for 99 when she mistakes Max for the king and vice versa.

To Sire, with Love [Part 2]
GS: John Doucette, Don Rickles, Pat Henry, Pat McCormick. Kaos finds out about King Charles of Caronia staying with the Smarts, so they plan to kill him. But they have trouble telling who is the king and who is Smart so they plan to kill them both.

Shock It to Me
GS: Tom Poston. Dr. Eric Zharko, a mad Kaos scientist, plans to put Smart to sleep using electricity.

Leadside
GS: Ronald Long, Paul Carr, Annazette Chase. Smart is in danger when Leadside, a Kaos killer in a wheelchair, is out to kill him.

Greer Window
GS: Lynn Borden, Barney Phillips. Smart finds that looking with his binoculars at a pretty secretary in the window of the research firm across from his apartment building was all that he expected to see, except he finds that he has discovered a Kaos headquarters as well.

The Not-So-Great Escape [Part 1]
GS: Kathie Brown, King Moody, Johnny Haymer, John S. Ragin. Smart finds himself, along with all the rest of the Control agents, in Siegfried's prisoner of war camp.

The Not-So-Great Escape [Part 2]
GS: King Moody. The Chief believes that there is an informer among the agents, while Smart tries to tunnel his way out of the camp.

Pheasant Under Glass
GS: Virginia Jaeger, Ned Wertimer, Peter Canon, Peter Brocco, Henry Brandon, Paul Hahn. Smart must use an opera singer to shatter the glass dome which holds Professor Pheasant prisoner. 99 tells Max that she is pregnant.

Ironhand
GS: Paul Richards, Billy Barty, Edward G. Robinson, Jr., Al Molinaro, Judy Farrell, Tom Castronova, Diana Hale, Barbara Fuller. Smart tries to prevent the new head of Kaos, Ironhand, from obtaining the Anti-Anti-Anti-Missile-Missile plans.

Valerie of the Dolls
GS: Antoinette Bower, Danny Dayton, Henry Corden, Caroline Adams. Smart tries to find the missing pieces of a deadly formula which is being smuggled into the country by little girls.

Widow Often Annie
GS: Dana Wynter, Raoul Franck. Smart romances a beautiful widow to get proof that she killed her 12 husbands for the insurance money which she donates to Kaos.

The Treasure of C. Errol Madre
GS: Broderick Crawford, Don Diamond, Alberto Monte, Natividad Vacio, Andy Albin, Richard Yarmy, Al Travis. When Kaos steals all of Control's money, Smart is sent disguised as Froggsy Debs, an old prospector, to find Debs' old partner C. Errol Madre in order to get the other half of the map which will lead Control to a gold mine where they can get all the money they need. The only thing is that Madre is working for Kaos.

Smart Fell on Alabama
GS: John Dehner, Don Megowan, Victor Bozeman, Diahn Williams, Stanley Clements, Larry Vincent. Smart must

try to exchange a fake code-key document for the real thing when it is stolen by Colonel Kyle Kirby, who distributed Kaos information through his chain of Tennessee-Fricassee Frog Legs Restaurants.

*And Baby Makes Four [Part 1]
GS: Dana Elcar, Sid Grossfeld, Judy Dan, Ralph Manza, Roy Dean. Smart is ordered to trail a spy who is about to steal some plans when 99 informs him that the baby is on the way, so he grabs the wrong map and drives her to Kaos's headquarters instead of the hospital.

*And Baby Makes Four [Part 2]
GS: Dana Elcar, Sid Grossfeld, Ralph Manza, Jane Dulo, Judy Dan. Smart escapes from Kaos with 99 to reach the hospital in time. Kaos however, follows him and starts a chase through the hospital. Later, 99 gives birth to twins: a boy and a girl.

*Physician Impossible
GS: Henry Corden, B.S. Pully, Than Wyenn, Ella Edwards. Smart is mistaken for a doctor by a gangster and is ordered to remove a bullet from the shoulder of a Kaos boss.

The Apes of Rath
GS: Maury Wills, Charles Bateman, Bob Carroll, Reuben Singer, John Barbour. Kaos has turned an ape into a human, so that he can pass for a Control agent, but when he hears a bell he turns into an ape again and kills several Control agents.

*Age Before Duty
GS: John Fiedler, John Dennis, Raymond O'Keefe, Sandra Kent, Ralph Moody, Hary Bash, Chuck Harrod, Lennie Bremen. A Kaos agent has developed a paint called Dorian Gray, which when painted on a photograph of a Control agent makes him die of old age.

*Is This Trip Necessary?
GS: Vincent Price, Billy Barty, Andre

Phillippe, Dodd Denney. A mad pharmacist plans to drug the water supply of Washington with his new hallucination-causing drug unless he gets $50,-000. When the Smarts try to stop him he puts them in a giant airtight gelatin capsule.

*Ice Station Siegfried
GS: Bill Dana, King Moody, Regis Cordic, Al Molinaro, Cliff Norton, Del Moore, Owen Bush. 99 and CIA agent Quigley set out to the North Pole to find a crazy professor who has covered the United States with snow in August. Along the way they meet Siegfried and Starker, who leave them stranded in the frozen wilderness.

*Moonlighting Becomes You
GS: Victor Buono, Maudie Prickett, Sid Haig, Ron Husmann, Allen Joseph, Billy Bletcher. The Smarts join the staff of Hannibal Day, a vain radio actor who has been transmitting information to Kaos concealed in the dialogue of his scripts.

*House of Max [Part 1]
GS: Hedley Mattingly, Kurt Kreuger, Terence Pushman, Bill Oberlin, E.J. Schuster, Marcel Hillaire, Ian Abercrombie, George Sawaya, Jim Mac-George. In London, Max and Inspector Sparrow track down a killer who appears to be Jack the Ripper. The trail leads them to a wax museum where the statue of the Ripper is missing and the owner is a former scientist who chose to make wax statues instead of pursuing a career in research.

*House of Max [Part 2]
GS: Marcel Hillaire, Hedley Mattingly, Kurt Kreuger, George Sawaya, Jim MacGeorge, Ian Abercrombie, Bill Oberlin, E.J. Schuster. When Smart is recognized as a Control agent, Duval sends his wax dummies after him, including Laurel and Hardy and W.C. Fields.

*Rebecca of Funny-Folk Farm
GS: Gale Sondergaard, Bryan O'Byrne,

Paul Wexler, Judith McConnell. The Smarts pay a visit to a crazy old lady to recover a package dropped on her roof. She mistakes 99 for her dead sister and tries to poison them.

The Mess of Adrian Listenger
GS: Pat Paulsen, Tommy Farrell. The members of the Control baseball team are being murdered one by one. When the only suspect is found dead, the Chief and Max suspect each other as they are the only members of the team still alive.

*Witness for the Execution
GS: William Schallert, Jim Connell, Fabian Dean, Joe Bernard. Kaos hires an agent known as the Exterminator to kill the Kaos defector who is hiding out at Smart's house as their babysitter.

*How Green Was My Valet
GS: Jonathan Harris, Diana Webster, Julie Bennett, John Trayne. Smart poses as the new valet to the ambassador of Bulmania in order to recover a new type of liquid rocket fuel the ambassador had stolen. There is only one thing standing in his way. The fuel is hidden in the wine cellar and the only key is around the ambassador's neck.

And Only Two Ninety-Nine
GS: Nicholas Georgiade, H.M. Wynant. A phony 99 is planted in the Smarts home where Max is supposed to believe she is the real one. Her mission is to poison him. However, the real 99 escapes from the enemy agents and warns the Chief who lets Max know in time.

*Smartacus
GS: Ronald Long, Michael Long, John Zaremba. Max is sent to guard a senator while he is at the Roman Baths, a health spa run by a Kaos agent who obtains military secrets by putting truth serum vapor into the steam room, which would cause the senator to tell what he knows.

What's It All About, Algie?
GS: John Van Dreelen, Eddie Ryder, Loree Frazier, Walter Seifert. Smart takes a job in a nursery to learn how the owner, Algernon DeGrasse, is getting top secret information. When he discovers Smart is an agent, he tries to feed him to his man-eating plant.

*Hello Columbus, Goodbye America
GS: Vito Scotti, Billy Barty, Jerry Maren, Ralph Manza, Oscar Beregi, Buddy Lewis. A man who is a direct descendant of Christopher Columbus comes to America to claim it for himself, and with the deed that the original Columbus had written he can indeed claim ownership to the entire country. Kaos kidnaps him and Smart in the hopes that they can get him to sign over the deed to them.

Do I Hear a Vaults?
GS: Ned Glass, Ann Summers, George Sawaya, Herb Voland. While on a case, Max accidentally locks the Chief inside a vault and can't get him out. So they call for a safecracker to set him free.

*I Am Curiously Yellow
GS: Robert Middleton, Victor Sen Yung. Max is hypnotized by a special Chinese gong, created by a dangerous Chinese Kaos agent called The Whip because he whips people with his very long mustache. He orders Max to steal the only existing model of the new weapon, the Narko 512.

THE GHOST AND MRS. MUIR

On the air 9/21/68, off 9/18/70. NBC, ABC. Color film. 50 episodes. Broadcast: Sept 1968-Sept 1969 NBC Sat 8:30-9; Sept 1969-Jan 1970 ABC Tue 7:30-

Hope Lange in The Ghost and Mrs. Muir.

8; Jan 1970-Sept 1970 ABC Fri 8:30-9.   Producer: David Gerber.   Prod Co/
Synd: 20th Century Fox TV.

CAST: Mrs. Carolyn Muir (played by Hope Lange), Captain Daniel Gregg
(Edward Mulhare), Martha Grant (Reta Shaw), Candice Muir (Kellie Flanagan),
Jonathan Muir (Harlen Carrather), Claymore Gregg (Charles Nelson Riley).

The story of a widow and her two children who move, along with their housekeeper, into a New England home which is still inhabited by the ghost of its former owner, a sea captain. The Captain at first tries to scare them away, but he
soon grows to like them. Each week the Captain or his bumbling descendant
Claymore would cause some trouble for the family. This series has done better
in reruns than it did during its original run, although it is slowly disappearing
from some stations due to its small number of episodes. It does surface as a
summer replacement series on local stations across the country.

The Ghost and Mrs. Muir [Pilot]
W: Jean Holloway. D: Gene Reynolds.
Mrs. Muir discovers the ghost of Cap-
tain Gregg when she moves into Gull
Cottage.

Haunted Honeymoon
W: Bill Idleson & Harvey Miller. D:
Gene Reynolds. GS: Yvonne Craig,
Jonathan Daly.   An eloping couple
spend the night at Gull Cottage when
their car breaks down.

Treasure Hunt
W: Howard Leeds. D: Hollingsworth
Morse. Mrs. Muir and Captain Gregg
trick Claymore into cleaning up the
house by telling him there is treasure
hidden in it.

The Ghost Hunter
W: Joseph Bonaduce. D: Gary Nelson.
GS: Bill Bixby. Captain Gregg tries to
scare a ghost hunter out of the house.

Here Today, Gone Tomorrow
W: Peggy Elliot & Ed Scharlach. D: Gary Nelson. GS: Mabel Albertson. Captain Gregg tries to prove that the sea captain the town wants to honor was a coward.

Vanessa
W: Joseph Bonaduce. D: Lee Phillips. Mrs. Muir becomes jealous when a beautiful girl becomes interested in the Captain.

The Real James Gatley
W: Albert E. Lewin. D: Gene Reynolds. GS: Stafford Repp. Claymore tries to sell the Captain's barometer without him finding out.

Uncle Arnold the Magnificent
W: Paul Wayne. D: Sherman Marks. GS: Jack Gilford. Mrs. Muir's uncle, a third-rate magician, comes for a visit.

Way Off Broadway
W: Albert E. Lewin. D: Lee Phillips. Mrs. Muir becomes the lead actress in the town's amateur production.

The Monkey Puzzle Tree
W: Jean Holloway. D: Lee Phillips. Mrs. Muir plans to redecorate the house against the Captain's wishes.

Captain Gregg's Whiz Bang
W: Peggy Elliot & Ed Scharlach. D: John Erman. GS: Kenneth Mars. The Captain changes Mrs. Muir's article such that it makes her seem like a swinger.

Madeira My Dear
W: Nate Monaster. D: Ida Lupino. The Captain tries to get Mrs. Muir to become romantically interested in him.

Love Is a Toothache
W: Howard Leeds. D: Lee Phillips. Mrs. Muir interferes in Martha's love life.

Mr. Perfect
W: John McGreevey. D: Gene Reynolds. GS: William Daniels. Mrs. Muir's old boyfriend returns to ask her to marry him.

Dear Delusion
W: Jean Holloway. D: Gary Nelson. A psychiatrist claims that there is no ghost in the house; it only exists in Mrs. Muir's mind.

Dog Gone
W: Tom & Helen August. D: Oscar Rudolph. GS: Larry Hovis. Scruffy, the dog, leaves home after fighting with the Captain.

A Pain in the Neck
W: Joseph Bonaduce. D: Lee Phillips. Claymore hurts his back and drives everyone crazy when he moves into Gull Cottage to recover.

Strictly Relative
W: Albert E. Lewin. D: Hollingsworth Morse. Mrs. Muir's inlaws are coming for a visit.

Chowderhead
W: Joseph Bonaduce & Edwin Waite. D: Hollingsworth Morse. GS: Cecil Kellaway. A picture of the Captain turns up on the label of a can of clam chowder.

It's a Gift
W: Peggy Elliot & Ed Scharlach. D. Lee Phillips. GS: J. Pat O'Malley. The Captain and Jonathan try to buy a gift for Mrs. Muir.

Buried on Page One
W: Peggy Elliot & Ed Scharlach. D: John Erman. GS: Richard Dreyfuss. Mrs. Muir has trouble with her boss and the Captain.

Make Me a Match
W: Howard Leeds. D: Gary Nelson. The Captain helsp Claymore court Mrs. Muir.

Jonathan Tells It Like It Was
W: Joseph Bonaduce. D: Gary Nelson. Jonathan is threatening to change his prizewinning essay.

The Medicine Ball
W: Albert E. Lewin. D: Gary Nelson.
Mrs. Muir drinks a little too much and
dreams she goes back in time, where
she falls for the Captain, who at that
point in time was alive.

Son of the Curse
W: Albert E. Lewin. D: John Erman.
Claymore makes plans for his funeral
when he thinks he is going to die.

The Music Maker
W: Paul Wayne. D: George Tyne. GS:
Harry Nilsson. A bunch of wandering
minstrels visit Gull Cottage, much to
the dismay of the Captain.

The Great Power Failure
W: Dan Beaumont & Joel Kane. D:
Jay Sandrich. A mysterious ghost ship
causes trouble for the Captain.

Centennial
W: Ron Friedman. D: Jay Sandrich.
Claymore gives away the Captain's
silver tea set, causing the Captain
to get very angry.

There's a Seal in My Bathtub
W: Miles Wilder & William Raynor. D:
John Erman. A runaway seal finds its
way into Gull Cottage.

Double Trouble
W: Jean Holloway. D: John Erman.
A ghostly friend of the Captain's
named Sean Callahan makes a play for
Mrs. Muir.

Today I Am a Ghost
W: Si Rose. D: Lee Phillips. GS: Dom
DeLuise. The bumbling ghost of one
of the Captain's crewmen appears to
cause trouble.

Madam Candidate
W: Ben Goodman & Sam Locke. D:
Bruce Bilson. GS: Ed Begley. Clay-
more plans to run for a political office.

Not So Desperate Hours
W: Arthur Ailsberg & Don Nelson. D:
Gary Nelson. GS: Guy Marks, Elisha

Cook. Escaped convicts hold Mrs.
Muir and her family hostage.

Medium Well Done
W: Gerald Gardner & Dee Caruso. D:
Jay Sandrich. GS: Shirley Booth. A
spiritualist tries to contact Captain
Gregg.

Surprise Party
W: Peggy Elliot & Ed Scharlach. D:
Gary Nelson. The Captain gets a les-
son in loneliness.

The Firehouse Five Plus Ghost
W: Tom and Frank Waldman. D: Gary
Nelson. GS: Avery Schreiber. Mrs.
Muir tries to get a new fire engine for
the town.

Spirit of the Law
W: Joseph Bonaduce. D: John Erman.
GS: Mark Lester. Candy falls in love
with an English boy.

Host Is a Ghost
W: Ron Friedman. D: Bruce Bilson.
Everyone thinks Gull Cottage is
haunted so the Captain leaves.

The Ghost of Christmas Past
W: Jean Holloway. D: Jay Sandrich.
Mrs. Muir gets an unusual Christmas
present from Captain Gregg, an abandoned baby.

Ladies Man
W: Howard Leeds. D: John Erman.
Mrs. Muir and the Captain try to make
Claymore into a swinging bachelor.

Not So Faust
W: Arthur Ailsberg & Don Nelson. D:
Lee Phillips. GS: Joe Flynn. The Cap-
tain arranges for Claymore to have a
nightmare: he has died and gone to
Hades.

Tourist Go Home
W: Dan Beaumont & Joel Kane. D:
Lee Phillips. GS: Kenneth Mars. The
Captain tries to prevent a tourist mu-
seum from opening in Schooner Bay.

No Hits No Runs No Oysters
W: John Fenton Murray, Elon Park-ard. D: David Alexander. Captain Gregg helps Jonathan regain his confidence after he loses the baseball game.

Dig for the Truth
W: Ruth Flippen. D: Lee Phillips. Captain Gregg is rewriting Mrs. Muir's articles without her knowledge.

Pardon My Ghost
W: Jean Holloway. D: Jay Sandrich. Claymore steals the Captain's rarest antiques.

Martha Meets the Captain
W: Arthur Ailsberg & Don Nelson. D: Lee Phillips. Martha begins to think

that nobody cares about her.

Amateur Night
W: Arthur Ailsberg & Don Nelson. D: Jay Sandrich. The local charity show allows the townspeople to show off.

Curious Cousin
W: Dan Beaumont & Joel Kane. D: Lee Phillips. Mrs. Muir's visiting cousin detects the presence of Captain Gregg's ghost.

Wedding Day????
W: Jean Holloway & Carl Shain. D: John Erman. GS: Jane Wyatt, Leon Ames. Mrs. Muir's parents arrive, to find her a husband.

GIDGET

On the air 9/15/65, off 9/1/66. ABC. Color film. 32 episodes. Broadcast: Sept 1965-Jan 1966 Wed 8:30-9; Jan 1966-Sept 1966 Thu 8-8:30. Producer: Harry Ackerman. Prod Co: Screen Gems. Synd: Columbia Pictures TV.

CAST: Francine Lawrence [Gidget] (played by Sally Field), Prof. Russ Lawrence (Don Porter), Anne Cooper (Betty Conner), John Cooper (Peter Deuel), Larue (Lynette Winter), Siddo (Mike Nader).

The adventures of a 15-year-old girl who lives with her widower father. Gidget is the constant cause of trouble when she and her surfing friends get into a variety of messes. The series is dated, but is still available.

Dear Diary—Et Al.
W: Ruth Brooks Flippen. D: William Asher. GS: Stephen Mines, Pamela Colbert. Anne reads Gidget's diary and jumps to the wrong conclusion.

In God, and Nobody Else, We Trust
W: Ruth Brooke Flippen. D: William Asher. GS: Beverly Adams, Heather North. John takes Gidget to a Luau, leaving Anne to worry.

The Great Kahuna
W: Albert Mannheimer. D: William Asher. GS: Martin Milner, Julie Parrish. Gidget falls for a Hawaiian surfer who uses her to make his girlfriend jealous.

Daddy Come Home
W: Ruth Brooke Flippen. D: William

Asher. GS: Marian Collier, Joseph Perry, Harvey Korman. Gidget worries when her father dates a golddigger.

Gidget Gadget
W: Stephen Kandel. D: E.W. Swackhamer. GS: Janis Hansen. Gidget schemes to bring Ann and John Back together again.

A Hearse, A Hearse, My Kingdom for a Hearse
W: John McGreevey. D: William Asher. GS: James Davidson, Richard Sinatra, Herb Ellis. Gidget buys a hearse in order to become independent.

Gidget Is a Proper Noun
W: Austin & Irma Kalish. D: E.W. Swackhamer. GS: Noam Pitlik. Gidget

believes her English teacher, a former student of her father, is prejudiced against her.

Image Scrimmage
W: Barbara Avedon. D: E.W. Swackhamer. GS: Jan Crawford, Melissa Murphy. Gidget falls for Larue's Cousin Roger.

Is It Love or Symbiosis?
W: A.J. Mady & Frederick Kohner. D: E.W. Swackhamer. GS: Roy Stuart, Judy Carne, Kevin O'Neal. Anne and John arrange for Gidget to attend school in Paris.

All the Best Diseases Are Taken
W: Tony Wilson. D: E.W. Swackhamer. GS: Henry Jaglom, Dick Wilson, Noah Keen, Dick Balduzzi. Gidget stages a demonstration to keep theater prices down.

My Ever Faithful Friend
W: Ruth Brooke Flippen. D: Gene Reynolds. GS: Stephanie Hill, Russ Bender. Gidget plans to improve the appearance of her friend Larue.

Chivalry Isn't Dead
W: John McGreevey. D: E.W. Swackhamer. GS: Bob Random, Barbara Hershey, Bonnie Franklin. Gidget and her friends scheme to get the boys to stop taking them for granted.

The War Between Men, Women and Gidget
W: Pauline & Leo Townsend. D: E.W. Swackhamer. GS: Mako, Linda Gaye Scott, Randy Kirby. Gidget and the girls battle against the boys for possession of an isolated cove at the beach.

Gidget's Foreign Policy
W: Stephen Kandel. D: Jerry Bernstein. GS: Walter Koenig, Brooke Bundy. Gidget tries to bring a bride-to-be into the modern world, but almost wrecks the marriage.

Now There's a Face
W: Dorothy Cooper Foote. D: E.W.

Swackhamer. GS: Daniel J. Travanti, Sabrina Scarf, Lillian Adams. Gidget falls for a photographer who happens to be engaged.

Too Many Cooks
W: Albert Mannheimer. D: Oscar Rudolph. GS: Peter Brooks, Larry Merrill, Bonnie Franklin. Gidget unwittingly makes a date with the Cook Brothers on the same night.

I Love You, I Love You, I Love You, I Think
W: Ruth Brooke Flippen. D: William Asher. GS: Tom Gilleran, Maida Severn, Lennie Bremen. Gidget falls for a surfer only to find out he is her new math teacher.

Like Voodoo
W: Albert Mannheimer. D: E.W. Swackhamer. GS: Jeanne Gerson, Peggy Rea, Arthur Adams. Gidget believes that a curse put on her by a gypsy is coming true when accidents begin to happen.

Gidget's Career
W: Joanna Lee. D: E.W. Swackhamer. GS: Sandy Kenyon, Murray McLeod, Dennis Joel. Gidget and Larue join a singing group and appear on a TV show.

Ego a Go Go
W: Barbara Avedon. D: Jerry Bernstein. GS: Richard Dreyfuss, Ed Griffith. Gidget tries to build up the confidence of a teenage nervous wreck.

In and Out with the In-Laws
W: Ruth Brooke Flippen. D: Bruce Bilson. GS: Hal March, Hazel Court, Janis Hansen. Misunderstandings occur when Gidget visits with Jeff's parents.

We Got Each Other
W: John McGreevey. D: Bruce Bilson. GS: Michael York, Ann Bellamy. Gidget tries to prove she is not jealous of her father's dates.

Operation Shaggy Dog
W: Dorothy Cooper Foote. D: Hal Cooper. GS: Lee Parker, Tim Rooney, Burt Douglas. Gidget tries to save a hamburger shack from being torn down.

Ringa-Ding-Dingbat
W: Barbara Avedon. D: Hal Cooper. GS: Greg Mullavey, Jeff Burton, Irwin Charone. Gidget helps a singing star avoid his fans so he can get married.

Love and the Single Gidget
W: John McGreevey & Stephen Kandel. D: Hal Cooper. GS: David Macklin, Barbara Hershey, Ron Rifkin. While her Dad is away, Gidget stays with Anne and John, causing them to hire a chaperone for her.

Take a Lesson
W: Ruth Brooke Flippen. D: Jerry Bernstein. GS: Paul Lynde, Jeff Donnell. Russ thinks Gidget was kidnapped when Shirley's parents take her to find a new car in her pajamas.

Independence—Gidget Style
W: Joanna Lee. D: Bruce Bilson. GS: Richard Bull, Celeste Yarnell, Viola Harris. Gidget tries to find a job in order to buy her father a birthday present.

One More for the Road
W: Austin & Irma Kalish. D: Jerry Bernstein. GS: John McGiver. Gidget's job at the florist shop requires her to drive the delivery truck, but she can't drive.

Ask Helpful Hannah
W: Don Richman. D: Lee Phillips. GS: Jim Connell, Candace Howard. Gidget takes over as the writer of the school advice column.

A Hard Night's Night
W: Barbara Avedon. D: Don Porter. GS: Frank DeVol, Bill Zuckert, Vince Howard. Russ's friend moves into the Lawrence home, while he is away, causing Gidget to think the house is haunted.

I Have This Friend Who—
W: Gary Flavin. D: Chris Cary. GS: Herb Voland, Bob Beach. Gidget's boyfriend's father insists on joining them on their dates.

Don't Defrost the Alligator
W: Ruth Brooke Flippen. D: E.W. Swackhamer. GS: Marvin Kaplan, Jack Fletcher, Robert Cornthwaite, Frankie Abbott. Gidget tries to comfort Davey Seldon who is upset over the death and impending burial of his pet alligator.

GILLIGAN'S ISLAND

On the air 9/26/64, off 9/4/67. CBS. 30 min. Film. 98 episodes (36 B&W, 62 Color). Broadcast: Sept 1964-Sept 1965 Sat 8:30-9; Sept 1965-Sept 1966 Thu 8-8:30; Sept 1966-Sept 1967 Mon 7:30-8. Producer: Sherwood Schwartz. Prod Co: Gladasya-UATV. Synd: United Artists.

CAST: Gilligan (played by Bob Denver), Jonas Grumby, the Skipper (Alan Hale, Jr.), Thurston Howell III (Jim Backus), Lovey Wentworth Howell (Natalie Schafer), Ginger Grant (Tina Louise), Roy Hinkley, the Professor (Russell Johnson), Mary Ann Summers (Dawn Wells).

Theme "The Ballad of Gilligan's Island," by Sherwood Schwartz and George Wyle.

The passengers and crew aboard the S.S. Minnow, a small sightseeing vessel, were marooned on an uncharted island about 200 miles southeast of Hawaii, for fifteen years. Each week the castaways found themselves in the most unusual

Bob Denver (left), Dawn Wells and Alan Hale, Jr., castaways on Gilligan's Island.

situations in which Gilligan, the lovable but bumbling first mate, somehow managed to ruin their chances of being rescued. Despite contemptuous reviews by critics, who claimed the series would quickly be cancelled, *Gilligan's Island* has remained one of the most successful syndicated comedy series of all time. Even though there were only 98 produced episodes, the show has retained its freshness and originality. It is so popular that three Gilligan's Island TV movies were produced between 1978 and 1981 (*Rescue from Gilligan's Island, The Castaways on Gilligan's Island* and *The Harlem Globetrotters on Gilligan's Island*). Plans for a continuing weekly series have been temporarily suspended. In September 1974, ABC aired an animated version of the series entitled *The New Adventures of Gilligan*, which featured many of the original cast members providing the voices of their individual characters. In September 1982, CBS began airing another animated version entitled *Gilligan's Planet*, where the castaways are marooned on another planet. Many of the cast members again provided the voices. It seems *Gilligan's Island* will never be forgotten, which is as it should be.

Two on a Raft
W: Lawrence J. Cohen & Fred Freeman. D: John Rich. After being shipwrecked, the Skipper and Gilligan set sail on a raft to find help. They land on what seems to be an island full of cannibals.

Home Sweet Hut
W: Bill Davenport & Charles Tannen. D: Richard Donner. A storm is approaching so the Castaways attempt to build a community hut with disastrous results.

Voodoo Something to Me
W: Austin Kalish & Elroy Schwartz.
D: John Rich. The Skipper thinks Gilligan has been turned into a monkey by a voodoo curse.

Goodnight Sweet Skipper
W: Dick Conway & Roland MacLane.
D: Ida Lupino. The radio transmitter is broken and only the Skipper can fix it, but only when he is asleep.

Wrongway Feldman
W: Lawrence J. Cohen & Fred Freeman. D: Ida Lupino. GS: Hans Conreid. The Castaways discover the incompetent pilot Wrongway Feldman living on the island. They try to get him to rescue them.

President Gilligan
W: Roland Wolpert. D: Richard Donner. Gilligan is elected President of the island.

Sound of Quacking
W: Lawrence J. Cohen & Fred Freeman. D: Ray Montgomery. There is no sign of food so the Castaways plan to eat Gilligan's pet duck.

Goodbye Island
W: Albert E. Lewin & Burt Styler. D: John Rich. The Castaways try to repair the Minnow using Gilligan's new glue made from tree sap.

The Big Gold Strike
W: Roland Wolpert. D: Stanley Z. Cherry. Mr. Howell discovers a gold mine on the island but refuses to share it with the others.

Waiting for Watubi
W: Lawrence J. Cohen & Fred Freeman. D: Jack Arnold. The Skipper finds a Tiki and believes he has fallen under the curse of Kona, when accidents begin to happen.

Angel on the Island
W: Herbert Finn & Alan Dinehart. D: Jack Arnold. Mr. Howell plans to back a Broadway version of "Cleopatra" starring Ginger.

Birds Gotta Fly, Fish Gotta Talk
W: Sherwood & Elroy Schwartz. D: Rod Amateau. On Christmas Eve, the Castaways remember the day that they were shipwrecked.

3 Million Dollars More or Less
W: Bill Davenport & Charles Tannen. D: Ray Montgomery. Mr. Howell gambles and loses an oil well to Gilligan then schemes to win it back.

Water, Water Everywhere
W: Tom & Frank Waldman. D: Stanley Z. Cherry. Water is scarce, so each of the Castaways tries to steal the remaining water supply for himself.

So Sorry, My Island Now
W: David P. Harmon. D: Alan Crossland. GS: Vito Scotti. The Castaways are taken captive by a Japanese sailor who is still fighting World War II.

Plant You Now, Dig You Later
W: Elroy Schwartz & Oliver Crawford. D: Lawrence Dobkin. Gilligan finds a treasure chest, so the Castaways hold a trial to determine who owns it.

Little Island, Big Gun
W: Charles Tannen & George O'Hanlon. D: Thomas Montgomery. GS: Larry Storch, Jack Sheldon, K.L. Smith, Louis Quinn. Gangster Jackson Farrell hides out on the island.

X Marks the Spot
W: Sherwood & Elroy Schwartz. D: Jack Arnold. GS: Harry Lauter. The Air Force plans to use the island as the test site for a new missile.

Gilligan Meets Jungle Boy
W: Al Schwartz & Howard Harris. D: Lawrence Dobkin. GS: Kurt Russell. Gilligan discovers a jungle boy living on the island.

St. Gilligan and the Dragon
W: Lawrence J. Cohen & Fred Freeman. D: Ray Montgomery. Gilligan and Skipper try to scare the girls back to camp, when they leave to set up their own camp.

Big Man on a Little Stick
W: Charles Tannen & Lou Huston. D: Tony Leader. GS: Denny Scott Miller. A Hawaiian surfer lands on the island and doesn't want to leave.

Diamonds Are an Ape's Best Friend
W: Elroy Schwartz. D: Jack Arnold. GS: Janos Prohaska. A gorilla steals Mrs. Howell's brooch and later Mrs. Howell.

How to Be a Hero
W: Herbert Finn & Alan Dinehart. D: Tony Leader. Gilligan is upset when the Skipper saves Mary Ann and he couldn't.

The Return of Wrongway Feldman
W: Lawrence J. Cohen & Fred Freeman. D: Ida Lupino. GS: Hans Conreid. Fed up with civilization, pilot Wrongway Feldman returns to the island.

The Matchmaker
W: Lawrence J. Cohen & Fred Freeman. D: John Rich. Mrs. Howell plans to get Gilligan and Mary Ann married.

Music Hath Charm
W: Al Schwartz & Howard Harris. D: Jack Arnold. GS: Paul Daniel, Russ Grieve, Frank Corsentino. The Castaways form a musical band causing the natives on a nearby island to attack.

New Neighbor Sam
W: Charles Tannen & George O'Hanlon. D: Ray Montgomery. The Castaways believe a gang of criminals have invaded the island.

They're Off and Running
W: Walter D.F. Black. D: Jack Arnold. Mr. Howell wins everything the Skipper owns turtle racing, including Gilligan.

Three to Get Ready
W: David P. Harmon. D: Christian Nyby. Gilligan finds a stone the Skipper claims will bring the owner three wishes.

Forget Me Not
W: Herbert Margolis. D: Jack Arnold. The Skipper loses his memory when he gets hit on the head and believes he is still fighting World War II.

Diogenes, Won't You Please Go Home?
W: David P. Harmon. D: Christian Nyby. GS: Vito Scotti. Everybody wants to know what Gilligan has been writing in his diary. The Castaways recall their adventure with the Japanese soldier.

Physical Fatness
W: Herbert Finn & Alan Dinehart. D: Gene Nelson. The Skipper goes on a diet in order to be able to rejoin the Navy.

It's Magic.
W: Elroy Schwartz & Oliver Crawford. D: Lawrence Dobkin. The Castaways use a crate of magician's props to frighten away some visiting headhunters.

Goodbye, Old Paint
W: David P. Harmon. D: Jack Arnold. GS: Harold J. Stone. The Castaways have another visitor—a Famous Painter who ran away from civilization.

My Fair Gilligan
W: Al Schwartz. D: Jack Arnold. When Gilligan saves Mrs. Howell's life, Mr. Howell adopts him.

A Nose by Any Other Name
W: Elroy Schwartz. D: Hal Cooper. Gilligan gets a swollen nose in a fall, causing the others to be scared of him.

Gilligan's Mother-in-Law
W: Budd Grossman. D: Jack Arnold. GS: Russ Grieve, Henny Backus, Mary Foran, Eddie Little Sky. A native family comes to the island to find a husband for their fat daughter.

Beauty Is as Beauty Does
W: Joanna Lee. D: Jack Arnold. GS: Janos Prohaska. The Castaways hold a beauty contest with Gilligan as the judge.

The Little Dictator
W: Bob Rodgers & Sid Mandel. D: Jack Arnold. GS: Nehemiah Persoff. An exiled dictator of a Latin American country takes over the island.

Smile, You're on Mars Camera
W: Al Schwartz & Bruce Howard. D: Jack Arnold. GS: Booth Coleman, Larry Thor, Arthur Peterson. A camera intended for Mars lands on the island, causing scientists to think the Castaways are Martians.

The Sweepstakes
W: Walter D.F. Black. D: Jack Arnold. Gilligan wins one million dollars in a South American sweepstakes, but finds he has lost the ticket.

Quick Before It Sinks
W: Stan Burns & Mike Marmer. D: George Cahan. The Professor discovers that the island is sinking, so they begin to build an ark.

Castaways Pictures Presents
W: Herbert Finn & Alan Dinehart. D: Jack Arnold. The Castaways find some silent movie equipment and make a movie showing how they were shipwrecked hoping someone will find it and rescue them.

Agonized Labor
W: Roland MacLane. D: Jack Arnold. While listening to the radio, the Skipper and Gilligan learn that Mr. Howell is broke.

Nyet, Nyet—Not Yet
W: Adele T. Strassfield & Bob Riordan. D: Jack Arnold. GS: Vincent Beck, Danny Klega. A space capsule with two Russian Cosmonauts accidentally lands on the island.

Hi-Fi Gilligan
W: Mary C. McCall. D: Jack Arnold. The Skipper accidentally hits Gilligan in the mouth, causing him to become a radio receiver.

The Chain of Command
W: Arnold & Lois Peyser. D: Leslie Goodwins. The Skipper is afraid something might happen to him, so he prepares Gilligan to replace him.

Don't Bug the Mosquitoes
W: Brad Radnitz. D: Steve Binder. GS: Les Brown, Jr. & The Wellingtons (Ed Wade, George Patterson, Kirby Johnson). A rock and roll group called The Mosquitoes come to the island for a rest.

Gilligan Gets Bugged
W: Jack Gross, Jr. & Mike Stein. D: Gary Nelson. Gilligan is bitten by a deadly bug, causing everyone to think he is going to die in 24 hours.

Mine Hero
W: David Braverman & Bob Marcus. D: Wilbur D'Arcy. While fishing, Gilligan hooks a World War II mine, then accidentally activates it.

Erika Tiffany Smith to the Rescue
W: David P. Harmon. D: Jack Arnold. GS: Zsa Zsa Gabor, Michael Whitney. A rich socialite comes to the island looking to build a hotel resort for very rich people.

Not Guilty
W: Roland MacLane. D: Stanley Z. Cherry. A recent newspaper informs the Castaways that one of them could be a murderer.

You've Been Disconnected
W: Elroy Schwartz. D: Jack Arnold. A telephone cable washes up on the island. The Castaways plan to tap into the cable and call for help.

The Postman Cometh
W: Herbert Finn & Alan Dinehart. D: Leslie Goodwins. The men learn that Mary Ann's boyfriend married another girl, so they plan to make her forget him by making a play for her.

Seer Gilligan
W: Elroy Schwartz. D: Leslie Goodwins. Gilligan is able to read the others' minds by eating the seeds of an island bush.

Love Me, Love My Skipper
W: Herbert Finn & Alan Dinehart. D: Tony Leader.   The Skipper doesn't get an invitation to the Howell's party, so the others hold a party of their own in the Skipper's honor.

Gilligan's Living Doll
W: Bob Stevens. D: Leslie Goodwins. GS: Bob D'Arcy. A robot crash lands on the island which the Castaways use to do the housework.

Forward March
W: Jack Raymond. D: Jerry Hopper. GS: Janos Prohaska.   A gorilla is throwing hand grenades and firing a machine gun at the Castaways.

Ship Ahoax
W: Charles Tannen & George O'Hanlon. D: Leslie Goodwins. In a seance, Ginger predicts a ship is coming in order to prevent the others from suffering from island madness.

Feed the Kitty
W: J.E. Selby & Dick Sanville. D: Leslie Goodwins. GS: Janos Prohaska. A lion washes ashore and Gilligan makes him his pet.

Operation: Steam Heat
W: Terence & Joan Maples. D: Stanley Z. Cherry. The Professor tries to prevent a volcano from destroying the island.

Will the Real Mr. Howell Please Stand Up
W: Budd Grossman. D: Stanley Z. Cherry.   A Mr. Howell lookalike is spending all of the real Mr. Howell's money.

Ghost a Go Go
W: Roland MacLane. D: Leslie Goodwins. GS: Richard Kiel, Charles Maxwell. A spy disguised as a ghost tries to scare the Castaways off the island.

Allergy Time
W: Budd Grossman. D: Jack Arnold. The Castaways find that they are allergic to Gilligan.

The Friendly Physician
W: Elroy Schwartz. D: Jack Arnold. GS: Vito Scotti, Mike Mazurki. The Castaways visit the island of mad doctor Boris Balinkoff, who proceeds to transfer their personalities into each others' bodies.

"V" For Vitamins
W: Barney Slater. D: Jack Arnold. The Castaways, suffering from vitamin deficiency, are all after Gilligan's orange.

Mr. and Mrs. ???
W: Jack Gross, Jr. & Michael Stein. D: Gary Nelson. The Howells learn that the minister who married them was a phony.

Meet the Meteor
W: Elroy Schwartz. D: Jack Arnold. A meteor crashes on the island and is giving off cosmic rays which will cause the Castaways to die of old age within a week.

Up At Bat
W: Ron Friedman. D: Jerry Hopper. Gilligan is bitten by a bat, causing him to think he is turning into a vampire.

Gilligan vs. Gilligan
W: Joanna Lee. D: Jerry Hopper. A foreign spy who looks like Gilligan invades the island.

Pass the Vegetables Please
W: Elroy Schwartz. D: Leslie Goodwins. Gilligan finds a crate of radioactive seeds which grow some very strange vegetables.

The Producer
W: Gerald Gardner & Dee Caruso. D: Jack Arnold. GS: Phil Silvers. Movie producer Harold Hecuba crash lands on the island and proceeds to direct a musical version of "Hamlet."

Voodoo
W: Herbert Finn & Alan Dinehart. D:

Jack Arnold.   GS: Eddie Little Sky. The Castaways fall under the spell of a native witch doctor.

Where There's a Will
W: Sid Mandel & Roy Kammerman. D: Charles Norton.   Mr. Howell includes the Castaways in his will and then believes they plan to kill him for his money.

Man with a Net
W: Budd Grossman. D: Leslie Goodwins. GS: John McGiver. A famous butterfly collector arrives on the island looking for a rare butterfly.

Hair Today, Gone Tomorrow
W: Brad Radnitz. D: Tony Leader. Gilligan finds his hair has turned white and later, while trying to dye it back, he goes bald.

Ring Around Gilligan
W: John Fenton Murray. D: George Cahan.   GS: Vito Scotti.   Doctor Boris Balinkoff returns to put the Castaways under his power with his magic rings.

Topsy Turvy
W: Elroy Schwartz. D: Gary Nelson. GS: Eddie Little Sky, Allen Jaffe, Roman Gabriel.   Gilligan bumps his head and now he sees everything upside down.

The Invasion
W: Sam Locke & Joel Rapp. D: Leslie Goodwins. Gilligan finds a government attache case and dreams he is a secret agent.

The Kidnapper
W: Ray Singer. D: Jerry Hopper. GS: Don Rickles.   Norbert Wiley, a compulsive kidnapper, proceeds to kidnap the Castaways.

And Then There Were None
W: Ron Friedman. D: Jerry Hopper. The Castaways fall one by one into a pit, causing Gilligan to think he turned into Mr. Hyde and killed them.

All About Eva
W: Joanna Lee. D: Jerry Hopper. GS: Vernon Scott. Eva Grubb, a lookalike for Ginger, lands on the island.

Gilligan Goes Gung Ho
W: Bruce Howard. D: Robert Scheerer. When Gilligan is made a deputy, he proceeds to arrest the other Castaways, including the Skipper who happens to be the sheriff.

Take a Dare
W: Roland MacLane. D: Stanley Z. Cherry. GS: Strother Martin. A game show contestant arrives to spend a week on a deserted island.

Court Martial
W: Roland MacLane. D: Gary Nelson. The Maritime Board relieves the Skipper of his command when they decide the shipwreck was his fault.

The Hunter
W: Ben Greshman & William Freedman. D: Leslie Goodwins. GS: Rory Calhoun, Harold "OddJob" Sakata. A big game hunter arrives to hunt a human—Gilligan.

Lovey's Secret Admirer
W: Herbert Finn & Alan Dinehart. D: David McDearmon. GS: Billy Curtis. Mrs. Howell has been receiving secret love notes—from Mr. Howell.   She later dreams she is Cinderella.

Our Vines Have Tender Apes
W: Sid Mandel & Roy Kammerman. D: David McDearmon.   GS: Denny Scott Miller, Janos Prohaska.   The Castaways are attacked by an ape man who turns out to be an actor practicing for a role.

Gilligan's Personal Magnetism
W: Bruce Howard. D: Hal Cooper. Gilligan gets a rock bowling ball stuck on his hand when he gets struck by lightning.

Splashdown
W: John Fenton Murray. D: Jerry

Hopper. GS: Jim Spencer, Scott Graham, George Neise, Chick Hern. The Castaways try to find a way of contacting an orbiting spacecraft.

High Man on the Totem Pole
W: Brad Radnitz.   D: Herbert Coleman. GS: Jim Lefebra, Al Ferrar, Pete Sotoge.   Gilligan believes he is a head hunter when he finds the head on the totem pole looks like him.

The Second Ginger Grant
W: Ron Friedman.   D: Steve Binder. Mary Ann hits her head, causing her to believe she is Ginger Grant.

The Secret of Gilligan's Island
W: Bruce Howard & Arne Sultan.   D: Gary Nelson. Gilligan discovers a prehistoric stone tablet which tells how to get off the island, or does it?

Slave Girl
W: Michael Fessier. D: Wilbur D'Arcy. GS: Michael Forest, Midori, Mike Reece, Bill Hart. Gilligan saves the life of a native girl, then regrets it when she becomes his slave.

It's a Bird, It's a Plane, It's Gilligan!
W: Sam Locke & Joel Rapp. D: Gary Nelson.   A jet pack washes up on the island and the Professor believes it can get them rescued.

The Pigeon
W: Jack Raymond, Joel Hammil & Brad Radnitz.   D: Michael J. Kane. GS: Sterling Holloway, Harry Swoger. The Professor finds a homing pigeon and plans to use it to send a message for help.

Band! Bang! Bang!
W: Leonard Goldstein.   D: Charles Norton. GS: Rudy Larusso, Bartlett Robinson, Kirk Duncan. Gilligan finds a supply of molding plastic, unaware that it is also plastic explosive.

Gilligan, the Goddess
W: Jack Paritz & Bob Rodgers.   D: Gary Nelson.   GS: Stanley Adams, Mickey Morton, Robert Swimmer. A native king comes to the island to find a white goddess to marry a volcano.

THE GIRL WITH SOMETHING EXTRA

On the air 9/14/73, off 5/24/74. NBC. Color film. 22 episodes. Broadcast: Sept 1973-Dec 1973 Fri 8:30-9; Jan 1974-May 1974 Fri 9-9:30. Producer: Mel Swope/Larry Rosen. Prod Co/Synd: Columbia Pictures TV.
CAST: John Burton (played by John Davidson), Sally Burton (Sally Field), Anne (Zohra Lampert), Jerry Burton (Jack Sheldon), Owen Metcalf (Henry Jones), Stuart Kline (William Windom), Angela (Stephanie Edwards), Amber (Teri Garr).
A short-lived series about a woman who tells her husband on their wedding night that she has ESP and can read his mind and everyone else's. The episodes show the trouble she gets into because of her mind-reading ability. It has not been rerun since it went off in 1974 because of the small number of episodes, but still is available.

Sally on My Mind
W: Bernard Slade.   D: Bob Claver. John becomes upset when he learns his new bride can read his mind.

Everything You Wanted to Hide and Couldn't

W: Bernard Slade.   D: Bob Claver. GS: Pat Delany, Dennis Robertson. Sally and John have several mishaps causing them to realize they must make adjustments to Sally's powers.

A Gift for the Gifted
W: Warren S. Murray.   D: Richard Kinon.   GS: Liam Dunn.   John can't buy Sally a surprise birthday present so he asks Anne to buy it, but not to tell him what it is.

How Green Was Las Vegas
W: Bernard Slade.   D: Richard Kinon. GS: Mark Lenard, Eddie Ryder, Farrah Fawcett.   Sally uses her powers in Las Vegas to win enough money for Jerry to start his own musical group, but John tries to stop her.

All the Nude That's Fit to Print
W: Bernard Slade.   D: Richard Kinon. GS: Merv Griffin, Hope Summers, Corinne Camacho.   John is asked to do a nude centerfold for a women's magazine.

John & Sally & Fred & Linda
W: Earl Barret.   D: Charles Rondeau. GS: Pat Harrington, Diane Ewing, Carol Wayne.   Sally and John try to break off a friendship with a couple of boring acquaintances.

One of Our Hens Is Missing
W: Bernard Slade.   D: Bob Claver. GS: Teri Garr.   Sally and John have their first fight over a missing chocolate hen.

No Benefit of Doubt
W: Dick Bensfield & Perry Grant.   D: E.W. Swackhamer.   GS: William Schallert, Peggy McCay.   John's first case is defending a woman shoplifter, causing Sally to become upset when she reads her mind and finds that she is guilty.

And Baby Makes Two
W: Stan Cutler.   D: Leo Penn.   GS: John Gabriel, Ysabel MacCloskey, Patricia Stevens.   Anne surprises her friends when she wants to have her baby without getting married.

It's So Peaceful in the Country
W: Steven Zacharias.   D: Robert Scheerer.   GS: Yvonne Wilder, Michael Bell, Richard Hurst, Ken Swofford, Patti Deutsch.   John, Sally, Jerry, and Anne spend a weekend in a cabin where they encounter a bank robber.

Sugar and Spice and a Quarterback Sneak
W: Dale McRaven.   D: Bob Claver. GS: Patti Cohoon, Victoria Carroll, Allison McCay.   Sally's 12-year-old niece causes problems for John.

Mind-Ing Mama
W: Stan Cutler.   D: Robert Duchowny. GS: Jeff Donnell, Teri Garr.   Sally is nervous about meeting John's mother for the first time, especially when she reads her mind and learns that she hates her.

A Meeting of Minds
W: Stan Cutler.   D: William Wiard. GS: Jack Riley, Rod Gist, Judy Cassmore.   To prove he isn't predictable, Sally and John go to a sensitivity session.

Guess Who's Feeding the Pigeons
W: William Davenport & Lou Derman. D: Roger Duchowny.   GS: Keenan Wynn, Gary Crosby, Gordon Jump, Ray Young.   Sally invites a lonely man to dinner only to learn he is a gangster.

The Greening of Aunt Fran
W: Stan Cutler.   D: Richard Kinon. GS: Eve Arden, William Windom, Lloyd Kino.   Sally and John try to fix her visiting aunt up with John's boss.

The Cost of Giving
W: Lloyd Turner & Gordon Mitchell. D: William Wiard.   GS: Jayne Meadows, Nell Bellflower.   Sally sells an antique brooch to get John a gift, but he tries to get it back.

A Zircon in the Rough
W: Jim Fritzell & Everett Greenbaum. D: Alan Rafkin.   GS: Joan Van Ark, Teri Garr.   Sally and John try to culturize Jerry when they fix him up with a sophisticated lady.

The Sour Grapevine
W: Stan Cutler.   D: Richard Kinon.

GS: William Windom, Charlie Brill, Mitzi McCall. John resigns his job when he is accused of having an affair with his secretary Angela.

Irreconcilable Sameness
W: Bill Davenport & Lou Derman. D: John Erman. GS: Donald O'Conner, Audra Lindley. Sally and John try to prevent Sally's parents from separating.

Three for the Road
W: Stan Cutler. D: Richard Kinon. GS: Woodrow Parfrey, Susan Silo, Len Lesser. John nearly loses his job while away on a disaster-filled weekend in San Diego.

The Not-So-Good Samaritan
W: Stan Cutler. D: Bob Claver. GS: Don Knotts, Arlene Golonka. An insecure mailman saves Sally's life. In return, she tries to help him gain his confidence.

The New Broom
W: Stan Cutler. D: Richard Kinon. GS: Dick Van Patten, Arch Johnson, David Lewis. John is considered as a possible candidate for a council seat, but Sally's power warns him of political difficulties.

THE GOLDBERGS

On the air 9/55, off 9/56. Synd. B&W film. 39 episodes. Producer: Gertrude Berg. Synd: Prime TV Films Inc.

CAST: Molly Goldberg (played by Gertrude Berg), Jake Goldberg (Robert H. Harris), Sammy Goldberg (Tom Taylor), Rosalie "Rosie" Goldberg (Arlene McQuade), Uncle David (Eli Mintz).

The adventures of a middle-class Jewish family who reside in the Bronx. *The Goldbergs* originally began on radio and then moved to networks for six years of live shows. In 1955, a series of filmed episodes were syndicated on local stations. Until recently, the filmed episodes had not been repeated for over 20 years.

Moving Day
After 25 years in the same apartment, the family plans to move to a house in Haverville. Molly wants to buy a particular house, but she may not be able to get it.

Social Butterfly
Molly finds that it is difficult to make friends with the new neighbors in Haverville.

Picnic
The ladies of Haverville refuse to attend a picnic given by a very beautiful widow. So Molly asks Jake to keep her company.

Fledermaus
Molly produces a production of "Fledermaus" to help her ladies' auxiliary.

Rosie's Nose
Molly tries to prevent Rosie from having plastic surgery performed on her nose.

Desperate Men
GS: Frank Sutton. Two escaped criminals invade the Goldberg home. Molly, thinking they are college boys performing an initiation stunt, welcomes them.

Dreams
Molly takes up the piano when her dreams show that she has been supressing her artistic talents.

Brief Encounter
Molly feels old and tired, but she soon changes her mind when she falls for her dentist.

Reach for the Moon
Molly appears on a TV quiz show where she chooses cooking as her category.

Molly's Pocketbook
Molly mistakenly takes the wrong pocketbook when she leaves a restaurant.

The Inheritance
Molly's cousin Harold, who has an inferiority complex, goes to work at Jake's dress factory but soon changes when he learns he has inherited a lot of money.

Treasury Book
The family buys coupon books for free merchandise, but spends so much money on additional purchases that Jake decides to teach them a lesson in saving money.

The Poet
While on her way to the dentist in New York, Molly meets a man on the train who recites poetry to her. She then believes that the romance has gone out of her marriage.

Insurance
When Jake and Mendel decide to rest before they take an insurance physical, Molly and Mrs. Mendel think they are sick.

Rosie the Actress
Rosie is offered a one-line speaking part in a professional play.

The Boyfriends
When several boyfriends ask Rosalie to go out with them, she can't make up her mind whom to go out with.

The Engagement Ring
Sammy and Dora decide to become engaged, but they don't think an engagement ring is necessary.

Sammy Gets Married
Sammy's wedding is two weeks away when Molly learns that all of the relatives have refused to attend because of a misplaced invitation.

Wedding Plans
Sammy wants to have a small wedding, but the guest list is still growing.

Girl Scouts
Molly volunteers to become a troop mother for a girl scout brownie troop.

The Partners
Jake accuses his business partner of giving him an inferiority complex.

Bad Companions
Trouble begins when Uncle David buys a pool table and then lets the table sit in the basement unused.

Is There a Doctor in the House?
Uncle David and a visiting uncle have a fight and refuse to live in the same house together.

Marriage Broker
Molly plays matchmaker in a story of unfriendly encounters.

The Hobby
Molly and the family try to convince Jake that he is working too hard at the factory and that he should take up a hobby.

The Milk Farm
Molly goes to a milk [fat] farm to reduce but gets thrown out when she sneaks some food into her room and all the ladies gain weight.

Ultima Thule
Sammy and Dora try to find a place to live where they won't have any trouble from their mothers-in-law.

Nurses Aid
Molly becomes a nurses aid, and is soon bringing the patients home with her.

Silence Is Not Golden
An old friend of Molly's arrives with desperate news.

The Singer
Rosalie rehearses a song for the school play. Molly decides that her voice is beautiful and she should have the correct musical training.

Seymour Story
Molly convinces Jake to rehire his former clerk who wants to escape his domineering mother.

Beauty Parlor Story
Molly wants to help a beautician who wants to spend more time with her family.

David's Cousin
Uncle David receives word that his second cousin Boojie is coming for a visit.

Members of the Jury
Molly loses her wristwatch.

Boojie Comes Back
When his Irish cousin leaves a broken-hearted widow to return to Ireland, Uncle David is left to console her.

David's Obituary
The members of Uncle David's lodge mistakenly believe he is dead.

Molly's Fish
A food packager tastes Molly's homemade gefilte fish at a charity bazaar and offers to sell it commercially to his chain of supermarkets.

Simon's Maid and Butler
Molly's rich uncle offers to let the Goldbergs have his two servants while he is away.

The Car
When the family car breaks down on a lonely road in a blinding rainstorm, Molly accuses Jake of car-neglect.

GOMER PYLE

On the air 9/25/64, off 9/19/69. CBS. 30 min. Film. B&W/Color. 150 episodes. Broadcast: Sept 1964-Jun 1965 Fri 9:30-10; Sept 1965-Sept 1966 Fri 9-9:30; Sept 1966-Aug 1967 Wed 9:30-10; Sept 1967-Sept 1969 Fri 8:30-9. Producer: Sheldon Leonard, Aaron Ruben. Prod Co: Ashland Prods./Paramount Studios. Synd: Viacom.

CAST: Gomer Pyle (played by Jim Nabors), Sgt. Vince Carter (Frank Sutton), Duke Slater (Ronnie Schell), Bunny Harper (Barbara Stuart), Sgt. Hacker (Allen Melvin), Lou Ann Poovie (Elizabeth MacRae), Colonel Gray (Forrest Compton).

Gomer Pyle, the gas station attendant on *The Andy Griffith Show*, enlists in the Marines. Stationed at Camp Henderson in Los Angeles, the series deals with the chaos that develops when the simple-minded private decides to do things his own way, thoroughly upsetting his neurotic sergeant, Vince Carter. Still a popular series today, *Gomer Pyle*'s main audience is in rural areas of the U.S.

Gomer Overcomes the Obstacle Course
Gomer tries to pass the obstacle course to please Sgt. Carter.

Guest in the Barracks
GS: Joey Tata, Robert Hogan. Gomer sneaks a recruit's girlfriend into the barracks.

Pay Day
Gomer refuses to accept his paycheck when he believes he has done nothing to deserve it.

Captain Ironpants
GS: Pippa Scott, Yvonne Lime. Gomer tries to turn a strict female officer into a lady.

Frank Sutton (left), and Jim Nabors as Gomer Pyle.

Gomer Learns a Bully
A trouble-making recruit decides to use Gomer as his fall guy.

Private Ralph Skunk
Gomer adopts a pet skunk.

Nobody Loves a Sergeant
GS: Liam Sullivan. Carter is bothered by the fact that no matter what he does to Gomer, Gomer still likes him.

Gomer and the Dragon Lady
GS: Barbara Stuart. Carter sets Gomer up with a beautiful but unkissable Dragon Lady.

Survival of the Fattest
Gomer and Carter go on a five-day survival test.

A Date for the Colonel's Daughter
GS: Joan Tompkins, Karl Swensen, Suzanne Benoit. Gomer escorts the colonel's daughter to the enlisted men's dance.

They Shall Not Pass
GS: Tommy Leonetti. Gomer creates his own rules when his platoon participates in war games.

Sergeant Carter, Marine Baby Sitter
GS: Greg Mullavey, Betty Conner, Richard Sinatra. Carter gives Gomer a lift in his jeep and finds himself helping Gomer babysit.

The Case of the Marine Bandit
GS: Kathie Browne, Ellen Corby. Gomer and Carter unknowingly help two bank robbers pull a heist.

Sergeant of the Week
Carter thinks Gomer is dying, so he tries to be nice to him.

Grandpa Pyle's Good Luck Charm
GS: Norris Goff. Grandpa Pyle gives Gomer a good luck charm to help him gain self-confidence.

Dance, Marine, Dance
GS: Gavin MacLeod, Frank Maxwell, Sylvia Lewis. Gomer and Carter are taken in by a phony dance studio when they both sign lifetime contracts to take dancing lessons.

Sergeant Carter's Farewell to His Troops
GS: Larry Hovis. The men try to change Carter's mind when he decides to leave the Marine Corps.

The Feuding Pyles
GS: James Hampton. Gomer befriends a country boy from a neighboring hometown, until he learns that their two families have been feuding with each other.

Sergeant Carter Gets a Dear John Letter
GS: Sherry Jackson, Tommy Leonetti. Carter discovers that his girlfriend dumped him for Gomer.

Love Letters to the Sarge
GS: Larry Hovis, Jean Carson, Jackie Joseph. Gomer writes secret love letters to Carter in order to cheer him up.

Daughter of the Sarge
GS: Sue Linn. Carter thinks that his adopted Korean daughter is going to marry Gomer.

Officer Candidate Gomer Pyle
GS: Tom Hatten. Gomer and Carter take the exam for the officer's training program.

Old Man Carter
GS: Alvy Moore. When the platoon celebrates Carter's birthday, he begins to think he is getting old.

Gomer Makes the Honor Guard
Carter tries to keep Gomer from becoming one of the honor guard.

My Buddy—War Hero
GS: Don Rickles. Gomer tries to prevent Carter and his old friend from becoming enemies.

Double Date with the Sarge
GS: Jeanine Burnier, Patty Regan. Carter and Gomer go on a double date.

The Jet Set
GS: Byron Morrow, Karen Sharpe. Gomer accidentally goes on a round trip jet flight to Rome.

Sergeant of the Guard
GS: Stanley Clements, Arthur Batanides, Ken Lynch. Gomer tries to capture a gang of thieves who have been robbing the Marine warehouse.

Gomer Dates a Movie Star
GS: Ruta Lee. Gomer is asked to escort a movie star and the colonel's daughter to a dance.

Gomer the MP
GS: Robert Emhardt, John Lupton. MP Gomer arrests a government investigator.

PFC Gomer Pyle
GS: Jack Larson. Gomer is the only one to fail his PFC test.

Third Finger, Left Loaf
GS: Ted Bessell, Al Checco. Gomer is asked to be the best man at his friend's wedding, but he loses the ring.

Gomer Un-Trains a Dog
GS: Paul Trinka, Fred Holiday, Sandy Kenyon. Gomer turns a guard dog into a pet.

Home on the Range
GS: Dabbs Greer. Gomer unknowingly finds shelter for a family of hillbillies in a shack which will be the target of war games.

Supply Sergeants Never Die
GS: Jeff Corey, William Christopher. Gomer gets the job as Supply Sergeant.

The Blind Date
Carter sets Gomer up with a blind date who thinks he is an oil millionaire.

Cat Overboard
The platoon goes on sea duty, and Gomer sneaks a cat on board the ship.

Gomer Captures a Submarine
Gomer ruins a reconnaissance mission.

The Grudge Fight
Carter challenges the fleet's retired boxing champion to a fight.

Gomer the Star Witness
GS: Willis Bouchey, Michael Forrest. Gomer is the only witness to Carter's auto accident.

A Visit from Cousin Goober
GS: George Lindsey, John S. Ragin, Charles Aidman. Goober pays Gomer a visit.

A Groom for Sergeant Carter's Sister
GS: Marlyn Mason. Gomer tries to help convince Carter that his sister's fiance is a nice guy.

Gomer Minds His Sergeant's Car
GS: Tol Avery, Ken Lynch. Gomer takes care of Carter's car, but it gets stolen and then wrecked.

Gomer Pyle, POW
GS: Jamie Farr. Carter sends Gomer into the enemy camp to be captured when they go on maneuvers.

Gomer the Peacekeeper
GS: David Lewis. Gomer tries to bring Carter and his girlfriend back together again.

Gomer Pyle, Civilian
Gomer becomes a civilian employee at the base.

Arrivederci, Gomer
GS: Gigi Perreau. Gomer sings an Italian love song to his friend's sister and her mother thinks he is proposing to her.

Grandma Pyle, Fortune Teller
GS: Enid Markey. Gomer's fortune-telling Grandma pays a visit.

Gomer and the Beast
GS: Michael Conrad. Gomer dates the girlfriend of a tough Marine sergeant.

Sergeant Carter Dates a Pyle
GS: Bobo Lewis. Gomer arranges a date between Carter and his cousin Bridey Pyle.

Little Girl Blue
Gomer befriends the little daughter of a visiting colonel.

A Star Is Born
GS: Jerome Cowan, Herb Vigran. Carter becomes the star of a documentary about the Marine Corps.

Gomer and the Phone Company
GS: Parley Baer, Dort Clark. Gomer tries to return some money to the phone company, but gets arrested instead.

Vacation in Las Vegas
GS: Joyce Jameson, Tristram Coffin, Felix Walking Wolf. Gomer and Carter win a fortune in Las Vegas.

Duke Slater, Night Club Comic
GS: Milton Frome. Duke wins an amateur talent contest.

Opie Joins the Marines
GS: Andy Griffith, Ronny Howard. Opie runs away from Mayberry to join Gomer in the Marines. [This is a crossover episode from the "Andy Griffith Show."]

A Date with Miss Camp Henderson
GS: Susan Oliver. Carter bets Gomer that he can't get a date with Miss Camp Henderson.

Gomer and the Father Figure
GS: Douglas Fowley. Gomer and Carter are taken by a con man.

A Desk Job for Sergeant Carter
GS: David Frankham, William Christopher. Carter decides to resign when he feels his platoon can get along without him.

Gomer, the Would-Be Hero
GS: Ralph Manza, Ted Knight, Peter Hobbs. Carter prevents a holdup but gives the credit to Gomer.

Lies, Lies, Lies
GS: Deborah Walley. Gomer tries to convince his friends that a movie star has invited them all to a barbecue at her house.

Crazy Legs Gomer
Carter plans to use Gomer to win the inter-squad competition.

Caution: Low Overhead
GS: Sid Melton, Roger Til. Carter tries to prove to Gomer that the man who sold him a cheap watch is a fraud.

Gomer, the Carrier
Gomer and Carter are the only ones who don't come down with the German measles.

Show Me the Way to Go Home
GS: Pert Kelton. Gomer is accused by a drunk's wife of turning her husband into a drunk.

Gomer and the Little Men from Outer Space
GS: Johnny Silver, Richard Bull. Carter sends Gomer to the psychiatrist when he claims he has seen men from outer space.

How to Succeed in Farming Without Really Trying
Carter sabotages Gomer's garden by putting vodka in his prize watermelon.

The Borrowed Car
GS: Herbie Faye. Gomer borrows Carter's car and is arrested as a car thief.

Gomer Pyle, Super Chef
Carter bets Sgt. Hacker that he can't teach Gomer to cook a meal.

Marry Me, Marry Me
GS: Francine York, Anthony Eisley. Gomer finds a girl with his same interests. After one date together he finds that they are engaged.

Cold Nose, Warm Heart
Carter gives his girlfriend a puppy.

It Takes Two to Tangle
GS: Grant Sullivan. Carter tries to get revenge when he learns that his girlfriend Bunny has been seeing other men.

Love's Old Sweet Song
Carter becomes jealous when a nightclub singer gives Gomer a kiss for singing a song.

Follow That Car
GS: Alan Hewitt, William Bramley. Gomer and Carter are captured by smugglers.

Whither the Weather
Gomer predicts the weather better than the weather bureau.

Gomer the Recruiter
GS: Arthur Batanides, Rob Reiner. Gomer unknowingly signs up a fugitive bank robber as a new recruit.

The Secret Life of Gomer Pyle
GS: Hope Summers, Dave Willock, George Tyne. Carter believes that Gomer has been spending his Sundays at the beach, so he goes along with him to find out for sure.

Go Blow Your Horn
GS: Richard Erdman. Carter tries to transfer Gomer to the marine band.

You Bet Your Won Ton
GS: James Hong, Victor Sen Yung. Gomer holds a farewell dinner in a Chinese restaurant which, unknown to him, is a front for a gambling operation.

Gomer and the Card Shark
GS: Buddy Lester. Carter and Duke are taken by a card shark.

Sue the Pants Off 'Em
GS: Jay Novello, John Stephenson, Danny Dayton. Two shyster lawyers try to get Gomer and Carter to file a false damage suit.

To Re-Enlist or Not to Re-Enlist
Carter tries to prevent Gomer from re-enlisting.

Lou-Ann Poovie Sings Again
GS: Elizabeth MacRae. A nightclub singer returns to town.

Gomer the Welsh Rarebit Fiend
GS: Richard Bull. Every time Gomer eats Welsh Rarebit, it causes him to sleepwalk and tell Sgt. Carter what he really thinks about him.

Sing a Song of Papa
GS: Anthony Caruso, Milton Frome. A nightclub owner tries to get Gomer to sing at his club.

Where There's a Will
Gomer names Carter as the beneficiary of his insurance policy.

Lost, the Colonel's Daughter
GS: Bella Bruck, Rob Reiner. Gomer loses the colonel's daughter at a Go-Go club.

The Crow Ganef
Gomer befriends a crow who is a sneak thief.

One of Our Shells Is Missing
GS: Jesse White. Gomer loses a live mortar shell.

Lou-Ann Poovie Sings No More
Gomer gets singer Lou Ann Poovie a job as a salesgirl when she loses her job.

A Visit from Aunt Bee
GS: Frances Bavier, Tommy Noonan. Aunt Bee comes to tell off Carter when she objects to his attitude towards Gomer during a radio interview. [This is a crossover from the "Andy Griffith Show."]

Corporal Carol
GS: Carol Burnett. Gomer is chased by a man-hungry Marine.

The Recruiting Poster
GS: Pat Morita. Gomer learns that his face will appear on the new recruiting poster and not Sgt. Carter's.

Gomer the Beautiful Dreamer
Gomer believes that if you dream about something three times in a row it will come true, so he dreams that Carter will marry his girlfriend Bunny.

A Leader of Men
GS: Jeff Morrow. A visiting congressman asks that Gomer be promoted to corporal.

The Great Talent Hunt
GS: Jack Riley. Carter enters Gomer in the base talent contest.

Gomer Says "Hey" to the President
Gomer finds himself in the President's office when he gets separated from a sightseeing tour.

A Child Shall Lead Them
GS: Helen Funai, Allison Hayes, Lucas Shimatsu. Carter and Gomer are taken in by a little Japanese boy who pretends he is lost.

The Show Must Go On
GS: Roland Winters. Gomer gets stage fright when he is scheduled to appear in the Navy relief show in Washington, D.C.

The Better Man
GS: Tol Avery, Med Flory. Gomer's romance with Lou Ann is disturbed when her father and ex-boyfriend come for a visit.

To Watch a Thief
GS: Doris Singleton, Jane Dulo, Whit Bissell, Maudie Prickett. Gomer thinks Carter stole a watch from the base PX.

Friendly Freddy Strikes Again
GS: Sid Melton, Chet Stratton. Con artist Friendly Freddy returns to sell Gomer a pearl ring for his girlfriend Lou Ann.

The Prize Boat
GS: Frank Gerstle, Dabbs Greer, Charles Lane. Gomer wins a boat in a

jingle contest.

Change Partners
Carter and Bunny have a fight.

Wild Bull of the Pampas
GS: Larry Storch. A Latin American military man plots the overthrow of Sgt. Carter.

Gomer, the Good Samaritan
GS: Madge Blake, Don Haggerty. Gomer is assigned to pick up a general but becomes sidetracked on the way.

Gomer the Privileged Character
GS: Fred Beir. Gomer gets excused from his regular duties because of his singing rehearsals.

Gomer Goes Home
GS: Burt Mustin, Arthur Batanides, Lewis Charles. Gomer goes home to Mayberry where he gets involved in the search for a bank robber.

A Dog Is a Dog Is a Dog
GS: Leonard Stone, Billy Halop. Carter and Gomer are assigned to watch the colonel's dog, but Gomer loses it.

Luv Finds Gomer Pyle
A 15-year-old girl has a crush on Gomer and begins to follow him around every place he goes.

Chef for a Day
Gomer's cooking skill might get him assigned to the kitchen permanently.

Gomer and the Queen of Burlesque
GS: Fay Spain.   Sgt. Hacker gets Gomer a date with an exotic dancer.

The Carriage Waits
GS: Marvin Kaplan, Jackie Joseph. A department store accidentally sends Gomer a baby carriage.

Sergeant Iago
Gomer tries to make Lou Ann jealous.

Goodbye Dolly
GS: Trevor Bardette, Vaughn Taylor.

Gomer saves an old horse from the glue factory and tries to hide her at the base.

The Price of Tomatoes
GS: Denver Pyle. Gomer discovers a tomato farmer living on military land.

Friendly Freddy, the Gentleman's Tailor
GS: Sid Melton.   Gomer and Carter buy Hong Kong suits from con man Friendly Freddy.

Love and Goulash
GS: Oscar Beregi. Gomer becomes involved in a family feud when he spends the weekend with one of his friends.

Gomer and the Night Club Comic
GS: Jerry Van Dyke, Anthony Caruso. Gomer tries to help a night club comic who is going to be fired.

And Baby Makes Three
GS: Yvonne Lime, Chris Robinson. Gomer sneaks a baby onto the base when he babysits for a friend.

Car for Sale
Hacker plans to get even, when Carter sells his car to Gomer instead of selling it to him.

Corporal Duke
Duke is promoted to corporal, but finds that his old reputation is getting in his way.

The Booty Prize
Gomer and Carter are the victims of the lead boot, the battalion's booby prize.

The Return of Monroe
GS: Med Flory, Joyce Jameson. Lou Ann's old boyfriend returns for a visit.

A Marriage of Convenience
GS: Nita Talbot, Jesse White. A movie star tries to get Carter to marry her, but only after Gomer refuses.

All You Need Is One Good Break
GS: George Fenneman. Gomer and Carter are given credit when a stunt girl captures a pair of robbers.

A Star Is Not Born
GS: Hamilton Camp, Sheldon Leonard, Tommy Farrell, Jamie Farr. Carter appears in a Hollywood movie, but finds acting is harder than he thought it would be.

Just Move Your Lips, Sergeant
Carter insists on joining the platoon chorus even though he can't sing.

Come Blow Your Top
Hacker bets Carter that he can't go 24 hours without losing his temper.

Gomer the Perfect MP
When Gomer becomes the guard at the back gate, he refuses to let Carter pass through.

The Wild Bull Returns
GS: Larry Storch. The Latin American general returns to date Carter's girl Bunny.

A Little Chicken Soup Wouldn't Hurt
GS: Molly Picon, Dave Ketchum. Gomer and his friends befriend a lonely widow who loves to cook for them.

Hit and Write
GS: Al Lewis, Kathleen Freeman. When Carter scratches a fender on a parked car, the owner tries to sue him for heavy damages.

A Tattoo for Gomer
GS: Ned Glass. Gomer gets a fake tattoo as a practical joke on Lou Ann.

Win-A-Date
GS: Leonard Stone, John Considine, Dick Patterson, Jeannine Riley. Gomer and Carter become contestants on the Win-A-Date program.

Marriage Sgt. Carter Style
GS: Don Diamond, Bobo Lewis. Carter tries to get Gomer married so he won't re-enlist.

Two on the Bench
GS: Glenn Ash. Carter doesn't believe that Gomer knows a football star.

Dynamite Diner
GS: Noam Pitlik, Lewis Charles. Gomer and Lou Ann help the owners of a new diner, unaware that they are planning to rob the bank next door.

To Save a Life
Carter saves Gomer's life and lives to regret it when Gomer pledges to give him eternal gratitude.

Freddy's Friendly Computer
GS: Sid Melton. Gomer and Carter join Friendly Freddy's computer dating service.

Here Today, Gone Tomorrow
GS: Hal Smith. Carter unknowingly lets the General's son's pet rabbit escape.

Gomer Tends a Sick Kat
Gomer thinks Carter is critically ill.

Gomer Maneuvers
GS: Mabel Albertson. Gomer unknowingly reveals the location of his platoon to the enemy during camp maneuvers.

I'm Always Chasing Gomers
Carter tries to get away from Gomer in order to avoid a nervous breakdown.

The Short Voyage Home
GS: Jay Novello, Ellen Corby. A little old lady picks Carter's pocket and steals Gomer's life savings.

Proxy Poppas
GS: Warren Berlinger, Jackie Joseph. Carter and Gomer take a pregnant woman to the hospital when her husband breaks his leg.

Flower Power
GS: Leigh French, Rob Reiner. Three hippies help Gomer paint a truck for maneuvers.

Showtime with Sgt. Carol
GS: Carol Burnett. Sgt. Carol wants
Gomer to sing in her Marine camp
show.

My Fair Sister
GS: Reva Rose, Jane Dulo. Gomer

escorts Carter's sister to the dance.

*Goodbye Camp Henderson, Hello Sgt.
Carter*
Gomer is transferred to another base.

GOOD TIMES

On the air 2/1/74, off 8/1/79. CBS. Color Videotape. 133 episodes. Broadcast: Feb 1974-Sept 1974 Fri 8:30-9; Sept 1974-Mar 1976 Tue 8-8:30; Mar
1976-Aug 1976 Tue 8:30-9; Sept 1976-Jan 1978 Wed 8-8:30; Jan 1978-May
1978 Mon 8-8:30; Jun 1978-Sept 1978 Mon 8:30-9; Sept 1978-Dec 1978 Sat
8:30-9; May 1979-Aug 1979 Wed 8:30-9. Producer: Norman Lear. Prod Co:
Tandem. Synd: PITS.
CAST: Florida Evans (played by Esther Rolle), James Evans (John Amos),
J.J. (Jimmie Walker), Thelma (Bernadette Stanis), Michael (Ralph Carter), Willona Woods (Janet DuBois), Bookman (Johnny Brown), Penny (Janet Jackson),
Keith Anderson (Ben Powers).
WRITERS: Eric Monte, Larry Siegel, Lou Derman, Bill Davenport, Jack Eli-
son, Norman Paul, Michael Morris, Eric Cohen, Robert Shayne, Richard Bensfield, Perry Grant, Roger Shulman, John Baskin, Bob Peete, Jay Sommers, Aus-
tin and Irma Kalish. DIRECTOR: Herbert Kenwith.
The story of a poor black family trying to make ends meet while living in a
ghetto in Chicago. The character of Florida was originally the maid on the series
Maude; her husband James was introduced later into the series and they later left
the series to star in this one. The series was a big hit on the network, but when
the viewing audience had enough of Jimmie Walker the series started to die out.
It is seen on dozens of stations across the country.

Getting Up the Rent
The entire family try to raise enough
money to pay the rent so they won't
get evicted.

Black Jesus
When J.J. paints a picture of a Black
Jesus, the family find that they start
having a run of good luck.

Too Old Blues
The family plans to celebrate James's
new job, only to find that he didn't
get it.

God's Business Is Good Business
GS: Roscoe Lee Browne. James's old
Army friend is now a TV minister who
offers James a job for one hundred
dollars a day.

Michael Gets Suspended
Michael gets suspended from school
when he calls George Washington a
racist because he owned slaves.

Junior Gets a Patron
J.J.'s art patron turns out to be one of
James's old enemies.

Sex and the Evans Family
Florida finds a sex book in the house
and is shocked to find that it belongs
to Thelma.

Junior the Senior
Florida and James become upset when
J.J. is passed from one grade to another without having to earn passing
marks.

The Visitor
A letter written by Michael brings an unexpected visitor to the apartment.

Springtime in the Ghetto
Florida stands to lose the award for the best apartment because Michael brings home Ned the Wino.

The TV Commercial
Florida is chosen to appear in a TV commercial.

The Checkup
The family make James take a physical when they think he has hypertension.

My Son the Lover
J.J. falls for a girl who is using him just so she can have her portrait painted.

Florida Flips
Florida appears to have a nervous breakdown.

Crosstown Buses Run All Day, Doo-dah, Doodah
Michael has been selected to be bused to a better school across town.

J.J. Becomes a Man [Part 1]
On his 18th birthday J.J. is arrested for holding up a liquor store.

J.J. Becomes a Man [Part 2]
Although J.J. is falsely accused, he learns that his arrest will always be on his record.

The Man I Most Admire
Michael choses his mother for the subject of his school composition.

The Encyclopedia Hustle
GS: Ron Glass. The family gets taken by a blind con man to buy a set of black history encyclopedias.

The IQ Test
Michael deliberately fails his IQ test when he feels it is unfair to black people.

Thelma's Young Man
Thelma becomes engaged to an older man.

Florida the Matchmaker
Florida tries to get Willona married off, whether she wants to or not.

The Windfall
James finds a large sum of money, but considers keeping part of it when he decides to turn it in.

The Gang [Part 1]
The family try to prevent J.J. from taking part in a gang fight, which causes the gang leader to shoot J.J.

The Gang [Part 2]
James goes to court to testify against the boy who shot J.J.

Sometimes There's No Bottom in the Bottle
Florida's visiting teenage relative turns out to be an alcoholic.

Florida's Big Gig
GS: Dick O'Neil, Charlotte Rae. Florida is offered the job James was supposed to get at a department store, which makes him very mad.

Florida Goes to School
Florida goes to night school to get her high school diploma.

The Nude
J.J. receives a commission to paint a portrait of a nude woman, in their apartment.

The Family Business
James tries to run a small appliance repair business in his apartment.

The Debutante Ball
The parents of J.J.'s new girlfriend don't want her dating him because he comes from a poor family.

The Dinner Party
The Evans family try to help an old

woman who eats pet food because she can't afford people food.

The House Guest
James's old childhood friend, a compulsive gambler, comes for a visit.

My Girl Henrietta
Florida and James think J.J. got his girlfriend Henrietta pregnant.

The Enlistment
J.J. decides to help the family by joining the Army.

Thelma's Scholarship
Thelma gets a scholarship to an upper class college because they need a token black.

The Lunch Money Rip-Off
Michael invites the tough kid who has been stealing his lunch money every day to spend the weekend with his family.

The Family Gun
James brings home a gun to protect his family.

A Real Cool Job
James is offered a good job in Alaska.

Operation Florida
James tries to find a way to pay for Florida's gall bladder operation.

Florida's Rich Cousin
GS: Percy Rodrigues. Florida plans to ask her rich cousin for a loan to pay her bills, unaware that he lost his job.

The Politicians
James and Florida back opposing candidates in a local election.

Love in the Ghetto
Florida and James object to Thelma's engagement to her boyfriend.

The Weekend
James and Florida spend the weekend in a mountain cabin in order to celebrate their 20th anniversary, alone.

Michael's Big Fall
Michael falls in love and it is affecting his school work.

Willona's Dilemma
Willona is dating a deaf man, but she doesn't know how to tell him she doesn't love him.

Florida's Protest
Florida holds a protest against a supermarket when the kids get food poisoning from eating meat that was bought at the market.

The Mural
J.J. is commissioned to paint a mural of ghetto life on the wall of a local bank.

A Loss of Confidence
J.J. loses his confidence when Thelma's girlfriend rejects him.

Cousin Cleatus
Florida's bankrobbing cousin pays them a visit when he is chased by the FBI.

The Family Tree
GS: Richard Ward. Thelma discovers that James's father is still alive; when she invites him home James refuses to see him.

A Place to Die
An old man comes to stay with the Evans family for the holidays. He wants to be with a loving family when he dies.

J.J.'s Fiancee [Part 1]
J.J. and his girlfriend announce that they are getting married.

J.J.'s Fiancee [Part 2]
J.J. and his girlfriend elope. She later runs off when he discovers that she is a junkie.

Sweet Daddy Williams
GS: Theodore Wilson. J.J. is hired by a local gangster to paint his girlfriend's portrait, in return for a one-man exhibition.

The Investigation
The family is investigated by the FBI when Michael writes a letter to a Communist country for research materials for his term paper.

J.J. in Trouble
J.J.'s girlfriend tells him that he gave her VD. Now he has to get himself cured before his parents come back from their weekend trip.

Florida the Woman
Florida accepts a lunch date with another man because she feels that her family takes her for granted.

The Breakup
Thelma has to decide whether to marry her boyfriend and move to California or to stay home and break off their relationship.

The Rent Party
The Evanses throw a party and charge admission in order to help a neighbor pay her back rent.

The Big Move [Part 1]
Willona throws a big party for the Evans family when James get a job in Mississippi and the family plans to move. Then they hear that James has been killed in an auto accident.

The Big Move [Part 2]
The kids become worried when Florida shows no sign of grief.

J.J. and the Older Woman
J.J. falls for Thelma's teacher who asks him to live with her.

Michael the Warlord
Michael joins a school gang but finds out that the only way out of the gang is to fight your way out.

J.J.'s New Career [Part 1]
J.J. takes an offer to be a numbers runner in order to pay the family's expenses.

J.J.'s New Career [Part 2]
Florida throws J.J. out until he learns that a life of crime is not for him.

Rich Is Better Than Poor . . . Maybe
GS: Shirley Hemphill. The student whom Thelma tutors tries to rob them of the $2500 J.J. won in the lottery.

Michael's Great Romance
Michael hits J.J. when he steals his girl away from him.

Florida's Night Out
Florida and Willona go to a nightclub where she meets a nice widower.

Evans vs. Davis
J.J. is invited to speak at a function on behalf of Alderman Davis.

The Judith Cohen Story
GS: Judith Cohen. J.J. becomes the manager of a comedian who has very little confidence in herself.

Grandpa's Visit
GS: Richard Ward. Grandpa Evans comes for Thanksgiving dinner with his live-in girlfriend.

The Comedian and the Loan Sharks
J.J. borrows money from a loan shark to back his new talented comedian.

Willona's Surprise
Willona's ex-husband makes a surprise visit at her birthday party. She throws him out when he makes a pass at Thelma.

Thelma's African Romance [Part 1]
Thelma falls for an African exchange student.

Thelma's African Romance [Part 2]
Thelma's boyfriend asks her to marry him and move to Africa. [This was originally a one-hour episode.]

The Hustle
The kids sell underwear to raise enough money to send Florida on a vacation.

A Friend in Need
During a wild party at the apartment, J.J. saves the life of one of the guests who has overdosed on pills.

A Stormy Relationship
Florida gets mad when Michael's new boss converts him into an atheist.

Florida and Carl
Florida is reluctant to go out on a date with Michael's boss.

My Son, the Father
Michael and Carl try to put J.J. in his place after being the head of the house gives him a swelled head.

Love Has a Spot on His Lung [Part 1]
Carl tells the kids that he is going to propose to Florida.

Love Has a Spot on His Lung [Part 2]
Carl tells everyone that he has cancer and that he is selling his shop and moving to Arizona for his health.

J.J. in Business
J.J. opens his own greeting card business, but when he finds that he can't handle large orders he goes out of business.

Breaker Breaker
Michael learns that the girl he has been talking to on his CB is confined to a wheelchair.

The Evanses Get Involved [Part 1]
Penny, a ten-year-old abused child, follows J.J. home.

The Evanses Get Involved [Part 2]
A social worker is called in when Penny and her mother disappear.

The Evanses Get Involved [Part 3]
Penny's mother admits her problem and abandons Penny with the Evans family.

The Evanses Get Involved [Part 4]
Willona becomes Penny's foster mother.

Thelma Moves Out
Thelma moves into an apartment with some strange roommates.

Willona the Fuzz
Willona catches a shoplifter and gets promoted to store detective.

Wheels
J.J. and his friends buy a used car.

Bye Bye Bookman
The Evans's petition causes Bookman to be fired.

Thelma's Brief Encounter
Thelma unknowingly falls for a man who is a bigamist.

Requiem for a Wino
Fishbone the Wino fakes his own death so he can attend his own wake.

I Had a Dream
J.J. dreams that he wins a promotion at the office because he is white.

Willona's Mr. Right
Willona's old boyfriend asks her to marry him.   She must now decide whether to marry him or to stay where she is with Penny.

No More Mr. Nice Guy
J.J. has to discipline Michael when he doesn't do his school work.

Penny's Christmas
Penny is arrested for shoplifting.

J.J. and the Boss's Daughter
J.J. falls for the boss's daughter.

Where There's Smoke
Four different stories about how the couch caught fire are told.

The Boarder
The Evanses take in a boarder to earn some extra money.

Something Old Something New
GS: Richard Ward. The Evanses convince Grandpa to marry his girlfriend.

J.J.'s Condition
J.J. gets an ulcer after having an affair with a married woman.

Willona the Other Woman
Mrs. Bookman thinks her husband is fooling around with Willona.

Write on, Thelma
Thelma disagrees with the director of her new play when she wants too many changes.

Willona's New Job
Willona gets a promotion but her old boyfriend tries to get her to quit. When that doesn't work, he buys the company where she works.

That's Entertainment—Evans Style
The Evanses and their friends stage a benefit show to raise money for a day-care center.

Florida's Homecoming [Part 1]
Thelma becomes engaged to a football player.

Florida's Homecoming [Part 2]
Florida returns from Arizona to attend Thelma's wedding.   [The first two parts of this story were originally a one-hour show.]

Florida's Homecoming [Part 3]
Thelma's wedding takes place. However, J.J. accidentally breaks Keith's leg during the ceremony.

Florida's Homecoming [Part 4]
Keith learns that if he plays football again he will be crippled for life.

Stomach Mumps
Willona makes up a story to protect Penny when she sees a 13-year-old pregnant girl.

Florida Gets a Job
Florida gets a job as a school bus driver.

The Teacher
J.J.'s prize art class pupil acts very strangely.

Michael's Decision
Michael shock his family when he plans to move out

The Witness
J.J. is a witness to an auto accident and will get himself in trouble if he testifies.

J.J. and the Plumber's Helper
J.J. tries to hide the fact that he is broke from his girlfriend who likes expensive things.

Househunting
The Evans family apply for a loan to buy a house.

Florida's Favorite Passenger [Part 1]
Florida interferes in the family life of one of the children on her school bus when she thinks the child's life is in danger.

Florida's Favorite Passenger [Part 2]
Florida's concern for a child convinces the child that his own mother doesn't care about him.

The Snowstorm
Florida and her bus load of children become trapped in an empty tenement building during a snowstorm.

The Traveling Christmas
The entire family performs a Christmas show.

The Evans's Dilemma
Keith's depression is causing the entire family to become concerned.

The Art Contest
J.J. accidentally enters someone else's painting in an art contest.

Blood Will Tell
GS: Theodore Wilson. J.J. has to decide whether or not to save Sweet Daddy's life by donating his blood to him.

The Physical
Florida finds that her chances of passing a necessary physical for her job are

almost ruined when Michael lands in jail.

A Matter of Mothers
Willona has to fight for Penny when her real mother returns to take her back.

Where Have All the Doctors Gone?
Florida visits a doctor who plans to move out of the ghetto and into a better neighborhood, despite the fact that he is needed where he is.

Cousin Raymond
Florida discovers that her rich cousin is a gambler.

The End of the Rainbow
Good fortune makes this the happiest day in Florida's life.

J.J. and T.C.
A tomboy tries to get J.J. to take her to a dance and to stop taking her for granted.

THE GREAT GILDERSLEEVE

On the air 9/55, off 9/56. NBC. B&W film, 30 min. 39 episodes. Producer: Unknown. Broadcast: Day and time varied. Prod Co: Robert S. Finkel & Matthew Rupf. Synd: National Telefilm.

CAST: Throckmorton P. Gildersleeve [Gildy] (played by Willard Waterman), Marjorie Forrestor (Stephanie Griffin), Leroy Forrestor (Ronald Keith), Leila Ransom (Shirley Mitchell), Lois (Doris Singleton), Birdie Lee Coggins (Lillian Randolph), Peavey (Forrest Lewis), Judge Hooker (Earle Ross).

The story of Throckmorton P. Gildersleeve, water commissioner, and his orphaned niece and nephew, Marjorie and Leroy Forrester. Episodes involved the adventures of a bachelor caring for two young children. The television series is based on the radio program of the same name which starred Hal Peary in the title role. Believed to be syndicated, but has not been seen in the United States since the early 1960s.

Practice What You Preach
Gildy's girlfriend Lois starts seeing other men and he realizes that something must be done to get her back.

The Whistling Bandit
Gildy is appointed acting Police Commissioner at the height of a crime wave.

Circumstantial Evidence
Gildy is unjustly accused of taking a bribe.

Gildy Goes Diving
Gildy buys a Navy surplus diving suit and dives into the reservoir in order to impress a girl and a TV panel.

One Too Many Secretaries
Gildy gets in trouble when he tries to

pass off his latest girlfriend as his secretary.

Orange Blossoms in Summerfield
Gildy tries to break off his engagement by trying to get the girl's family mad at him.

Gildy Goes Broke
Gildy tries to stop a romance between his nephew and a pretty girl.

Gildy Tangles with Leroy's Teacher
Gildy decides to talk to Leroy's teacher when Leroy tells him he is being overworked.

Gildy Stews About a Cook
Gildy is forced to find himself a fiancee in order to prevent his housekeeper from sacrificing her own mar-

riage plans for the sake of the Gildersleeve household.

Gildy, the Private Eye
Gildy wants to solve the robbery of Sally Fuller's jewels, but Police Sgt. Rogers stands in his way.

Gildy and the Con Men
Two con men try to put the pinch on Gildy.

Gildy King of Hearts
Gildy finds himself engaged to two women within 24 hours.

The Nightmare
Gildy finds that he recreates the plots of the mystery books he has been reading in his dreams. They soon become so real he can't tell fact from fiction anymore.

Gildy's Juvenile Delinquent
Gildy punishes Leroy for pulling a prant. Leroy tries to convince Gildy that it was someone else who did it and not him.

Gildy Pulls the Switch
When $50,000 is stolen from City Hall the mayor blames Gildy and threatens to take the money out of his salary.

Gildy Goes to Hollywood
Gildy dreams of becoming a movie star when a movie company comes to town to film a picture.

Golf Ball Incident
Gildy starts a feud when he accidentally hits a congressman on the head with a golf ball.

Prisoner of Love
Gildy sacrifices himself for the city's aqueduct project.

Gildy's Command Performance
Gildy has to take Leroy's place on a TV show when he gets too scared to go on.

The Political Plum
Gildy discovers that his bachelor status is of greater interest to the Governor than his clean record as Water Commissioner.

The Quiet One
Gildy must remain silent for 24 hours as part of an initiation to a club.

Gildy Bard of Summerfield
Gildy is accused of plagiarism when he writes some poetry to impress a lady.

Gildy's Dancing Lessons
Gildy becomes attracted to Leroy's dancing teacher.

Water Commissioner's Water Color
Gildy checks into the background of his niece's boyfriend.

Two Girls, One Birthday
Gildy plans to celebrate his birthday with his two girlfriends at two different times so the girls will never meet.

The Raffle
Gildy tries to impress a society lady with his own wealth.

Gildy's Efficiency Kick
Gildy tries to get a job as the head of a committee to investigate the efficiency of City Hall.

Gildy's All-American Boy
Gildy gets Leroy to build a raft, like Huck Finn, in order to keep him out of trouble.

The Good Scout
A meddling aunt interrupts Gildy's relationship with his new girlfriend.

Calling Dr. Bergstrom
Gildy falls for a lady doctor who mistakes his interest in her for an illness and sends him to the hospital.

Birdie's Golden Dreams
Gildy regrets ignoring the psychic dreams of his housekeeper.

Gildy Hires an Eager Beaver
When Gildy hires an unnecessary

assistant to impress his girlfriend, the mayor decides that Gildy is the unnecessary employee.

The Deed
Gildy is deceived by a phony deed to the reservoir, causing him to think that he now has to find a way to move the water.

Gildy and the Expectant Father
Gildy organizes a club called the Jolly Boys which almost wrecks the hospital maternity ward and ruins his romance with a pretty nurse.

Protective Parent
Gildy thinks his niece is planning to elope, so he tries to stop her.

Gildy Loves Well, But Unwisely
Gildy almost gets himself married when he tries to save the judge from a blonde.

Marjorie's Apartment
Marjorie moves into her own apartment to escape the madness of Gildy's house.

Gildy the Go-Between
Gildy invites one of his employees to stay at his house when he has a fight with his wife.

Beauties and the Beast
While Gildy is talking to one girlfriend, a beauty shop owner, another girlfriend's hair is ruined in the back of the shop. Gildy finds that he is now a witness for both sides.

GREEN ACRES

On the air 9/15/65, off 9/2/71. CBS. 30 min. Film. 170 episodes. Color. Broadcast: Sept 1965-Sept 1968 Wed 9-9:30; Sept 1968-Sept 1969 Wed 9:30-10; Sept 1969-Sept 1970 Sat 9-9:30; Sept 1970-Sept 1971 Tue 8-8:30. Producer: Paul Henning, Jay Sommers, Dick Chevillat. Prod Co: Filmways. Synd: Orion Pictures TV.

CAST: Oliver Wendell Douglas (played by Eddie Albert), Lisa Douglas (Eva Gabor), Mr. Haney (Pat Buttram), Eb Dawson (Tom Lester), Hank Kimball (Alvy Moore), Fred Ziffel (Hank Patterson), Doris Ziffel (Barbara Pepper, 1965-69, Fran Ryan, 1969-70), Sam Drucker (Frank Cady), Alf Monroe (Sid Melton), Ralph Monroe (Mary Grace Canfield).

Green Acres gave producer Paul Henning his third successful television series. The show was set in Hooterville, Illinois, only a short ride away from Pixley where Henning enjoyed the success of his *Petticoat Junction* series. The show concentrated on the exploits of city slickers Oliver and Lisa Douglas who moved from their New York penthouse to a small, rundown farmhouse. During the series' run, Oliver was constantly bothered by the looney Hooterville residents who included Mr. Haney, a con man, Mr. Ziffel, a pig farmer, Mr. Kimball, an absentminded county agent, and Eb Dawson, his pesty farmhand. The series was played strictly for laughs and offered such gimmicks as the writer/director credits often showing up in Lisa's hotcake batter, and a pig named Arnold who upstaged the entire cast. *Green Acres* remains one of the most popular syndicated series.

[All episodes are written by Jay Sommers and Dick Chevillat except where noted. Every episode was directed by Richard L. Bare except the pilot which was directed by Ralph Levy.]

Oliver Buys a Farm [Pilot]
GS: John Daly. Oliver and Lisa Douglas move from New York to a farm in Hooterville, Illinois.

Eddie Albert and Eva Gabor in Green Acres.

Lisa's First Day on the Farm
Oliver and Lisa plan on moving into their new farm but find that the old owner, Mr. Haney, has removed everything from the house.

The Decorator
Oliver and Lisa hire a decorator to fix over the farm.

The Best Laid Plans
GS: Eleanor Audley.   It is rumored that Lisa has left Oliver and moved back to New York.

My Husband the Rooster Renter
Oliver rents a rooster from Mr. Haney.

Furniture, Furniture, Who's Got the Furniture?
The Douglas's furniture is accidentally sent to Mr. Haney who tries to sell it to them.

Neighborliness
Oliver gets help from the other farmers when he finds he will not be able to get his field plowed in time for planting.

Lisa the Helpmate
Oliver has his soil tested by the State Scientific College and finds it is full of strange ingredients.

You Can't Plug in a 2 with a 6
Lisa burns out the generator, just when Oliver has to hear the farm report.

Don't Call Us, We'll Call You
The phone company installs the Douglas's phone on top of a telephone pole.

Parity Begins at Home
Oliver learns that he is not allowed to plant his fields with just wheat, if he does he will be fined.

Lisa Has a Calf
Oliver tries to hide the fact that the cow Mr. Haney sold Oliver was pregnant.

The Wedding Anniversary
Oliver remembers his anniversary but doesn't remember just how long he has been married.

What Happened in Scranton
Lisa opens a beauty parlor in the town, causing trouble because the women now refuse to work on their farms for fear of messing up their hairstyles.

How to Enlarge a Bedroom
Oliver begins work on the enlargement of his bedroom when a building inspector suddenly condemns the house.

Give Me Land, Lots of Land
Oliver buys the land adjacent to his property while Lisa begins to fix up the house on the property, unaware that the house was not included in the sale.

I Didn't Raise My Husband to Be a Fireman
Oliver is asked to join the Hooterville fire department, but only if he can play a musical instrument.

Lisa Bakes a Cake
Oliver gets annoyed when Lisa puts a listing in the phone book claiming he is still practicing law, which he said he gave up when he became a farmer.

Sprained Ankle Country Style
Oliver sprains his ankle putting up a TV antenna.

The Price of Apples
Oliver plans to market his apples himself, but he finds he runs into difficulty trying to get them to the market to sell them.

What's in a Name
Ralph falls in love with Mr. Kimble, but he refuses to go out with her because her name is Ralph.

The Day of Decision
This is the day that Lisa decides whether she and Oliver stay or return to New York.

A Pig in a Poke
Lisa and Oliver unknowingly take Arnold the pig to his Harvard reunion.

The Ballad of Molly Turgiss
Oliver writes a folk song about an old hag who put a curse on the valley.

The Deputy
Mr. Drucker makes Oliver the deputy sheriff while he goes on vacation. Oliver wants to show Lisa how his new handcuffs work, so he handcuffs himself to Lisa and then can't find the key.

Double Drick
Oliver's faulty wiring is blamed as the cause of the power blackout in New York City.

Send a Boy to College
Oliver plans to send Eb to college to become a veterinarian.

Never Look a Gift Tractor in the Mouth
Lisa buys the biggest tractor she can find as Oliver's birthday present.

Horse? What Horse?
A horse follows Oliver home, but disappears every time he wants to show it to Lisa.

Culture
Lisa tries to get a famous conductor to perform in Hooterville.

The Rains Came
Haney is suing Oliver because he did not pay him for the services of the Indian he rented to him to perform a rain dance.

Uncle Ollie
W: Elon Packard & Dick Chevillat. Oliver's beatnik nephew comes for a visit.

Wings Over Hooterville
The deadly bing bug threatens to destroy the entire corn crop of Hooterville.

The Ugly Duckling
W: Al Schwartz & Lou Houston. Lisa performs a two-day beauty treatment on Ralph.

Water, Water Everywhere
Mr. Haney's new well drains off the Douglas's water supply.

How to See South America by Bus
Lisa thinks Oliver has fallen for a lady farmer.

I Didn't Raise My Pig to Be a Soldier
Arnold the pig gets drafted into the Army.

One of Our Assemblymen Is Missing
Oliver contacts his assemblyman when he receives a tax bill for a strange tax.

The Good Old Days
Oliver tells Lisa a story on how to be a better farm wife.

Eb Discovers the Birds and the Bees
Oliver tells Eb the facts of life.

The Hooterville Image
The other farmers think Oliver is giving them a bad name by wearing a suit and tie to do his farming chores.

You Ought to Be in Pictures
The Department of Agriculture plans to make a documentary about Oliver.

A Home Isn't Built in a Day
Oliver fires Alf and Ralph and hires an architect when Lisa demands that the house be renovated.

A Square Is Not Round
One of Oliver's chickens is laying square eggs.

It's So Peaceful in the Country
Oliver invites his mother to visit them on the farm.

An Old Fashioned Christmas
W: Buddy Atkinson & Jay Sommers. Oliver finds that he can't chop down a spruce tree on his own property.

His Honor
W: Dick Chevillat & Al Schwartz. Oliver thinks he has been appointed as the new circuit court judge.

School Days
Oliver has Lisa go to high school to learn homemaking.

Exodus to Bleedswell
W: David Braverman & Bob Marcus. When another town offers defense plant jobs to the people of Hooterville, Oliver has the town council reactivate a defense contract from WW I.

It's Human to Be Humane
W: Joel Rapp & Sam Locke. Lisa turns the house into an animal shelter when she becomes the humane officer.

Never Take Your Wife to a Convention
Lisa and Oliver meet an ex-gangster who has turned farmer at a farm convention.

Never Start Talking Unless Your Voice Comes Out
Oliver's neighbors become suspicious when he gets a letter from Washington and won't tell them what it is about.

The Beverly Hillbillies
The Hooterville players give a charity show performance of the "Beverly Hillbillies" in which Oliver plays Jethro, Lisa plays Granny and Mr. Kimble plays Jed.

Lisa's Vegetable Garden
Lisa decides to plant her own vegetables.

The Saucer Season
Eb claims to have seen a flying saucer with little green men.

The Vulgar Ring Story
Lisa tells the story of why every fourth generation of her family had to marry an American man.

Getting Even with Haney
Oliver represents the Ziffels in court when the washing machine Haney sold them goes berserk and nearly wrecks their farm.

Kimball Gets Fired
GS: Dave Ketchum. Mr. Kimble is replaced just when he was saving up enough money to marry Ralph.

Who's Lisa?
Lisa gets hit on the head and loses her memory.

My Mother the Countess
Lisa's mother, a countess, is going to come for a visit.

Music to Milk By
Oliver buys Eb a radio which is later eaten by Eleanor the cow.

The Man for the Job
Oliver is selected as a possible candidate for the office of State Senator.

Love Comes to Arnold Ziffel
Arnold the pig falls in love with Haney's basset hound Cynthia.

Lisa's Jam Session
Lisa tries to put up her own jam preserves.

Oliver vs. the Phone Company
Oliver plans to take the phone company to court.

Oliver Takes Over the Phone Company
Oliver and Lisa take over control of the phone company and make a mess of things.

Don't Count Your Tomatoes Before They're Picked
Oliver plans to pick his own tomato crop.

A Kind Word for the President
As president of the phone company, Oliver plans to have his phone moved inside the house and to raise the rates to balance the budget.

Not Guilty
Eb is accused of stealing $300 from Mr. Drucker's safe to buy a car.

Eb Elopes
GS: Guy Raymond. Oliver hires another farm hand to replace Eb who has eloped.

The Thing
Oliver finds that he has been paying storage charges for an eight foot high thing made of water pipes.

Das Lumpen
Lisa tells the story of how Oliver and she first met during WW II.

Won't You Come Home, Arnold Ziffel
When Arnold turns up missing, Lisa thinks he has been pig-napped.

Jealousy, English Style
Lisa thinks the farm symposium Oliver is planning to go to is really a stag party.

Haney's New Image
W: Bobby Bell & Bill Lee. Haney plans to buy back the farm when he learns that a new highway might be going through the property.

No Trespassing
Oliver claims to have been talking to a man everyone said died twenty years earlier.

Alf and Ralph Break Up
Ralph has a fight with her brother Alf and moves in with Oliver and Lisa.

Eb Returns
Lisa plans a big celebration when Eb returns from his honeymoon. The only thing is he isn't married.

Home Is Where You Run Away From
A boy claiming to be from outer space shows up on the Douglas's doorstep.

Flight to Nowhere
Oliver and the other farmers are offered a free trip to Europe as part of a government agricultural exchange program.

How to Succeed in Television Without Really Trying
A ten-year-old boy automates the entire Douglas farmhouse.

Arnold, Boy Hero
Oliver and Lisa are held hostage by two bank robbers.

The Spring Festival
Lisa prepares to create a Spring Festival celebration.

Our Son, the Barber
Eb gets Oliver to put him through a mail order course on how to become a barber.

Oliver's Jaded Past
Lisa and Oliver go to New York on their vacation.

The Hungarian Curse
A Hungarian who saved Lisa's uncle's life moves into the house so she can repay him for his heroics.

The Rutabaga Story
Oliver and the other farmers set out to promote the rutabaga.

Instant Family
GS: Pamelyn Ferdin, Chris Shea, Bobby Ritta. While a pregnant mother is in the hospital, Oliver and Lisa take care of her seven children.

A Star Named Arnold Is Born [Part 1]
Lisa gets her old producer friend to turn Arnold into a movie star.

A Star Named Arnold [Part 2]
GS: Oscar Beregi, Peter Leeds. Arnold gets the starring role in a movie.

Guess Who's Not Going to the Luau
Lisa, Oliver, Arnold and the entire town enter a contest to win a free trip to Hawaii.

The Rummage Sale
GS: John Van Dreelen, Charles Lane. Oliver and Lisa reminisce about their pasts when they go through some old clothes they plan to give to the town rummage sale.

Eb's Romance
GS: Melody Patterson. Eb plans to get married, so in order to impress the girl's father he tells him that Mr. Douglas is his father.

Hail to the Fire Chief
GS: Edgar Buchanan. Joe Carson tries to get Oliver to pay for his trip to the fire chiefs' convention in Miami by making him the assistant fire chief.

The Candidate
GS: J. Pat O'Malley. Oliver runs for the office of State District Representative.

Handy Lessons
Lisa plans to become a lady carpenter to surprise Oliver.

A Husband of Eleanor
Oliver tries to get a bull to make Eleanor the cow happy so she can start giving milk again.

Old Mail Day
Sam Drucker announces that he will be delivering any old mail he finds lying around his store.

The Agricultural Student
GS: Francine York. A beautiful girl is sent to Hooterville to observe Mr. Kimble's work.

How Hooterville Was Floundered
GS: Edgar Buchanan. Oliver is chosen to be the head of the Centennial pageant.

The Blue Feather
Lisa gets a blue feather in the mail and says it means she has been put under a curse.

The Birthday Gift
Lisa gives Oliver a list of presents she wants for her birthday.

Everywhere a Chick Chick
Oliver buys 1000 baby chickens when he plans to become a chicken farmer.

How to Get from Hooterville to Pixley Without Moving
Oliver learns that his farm is actually zoned for Pixley and not Hooterville.

The Marital Vacation
When Lisa goes on a vacation by herself, the townspeople think she and Oliver are splitting up.

A Prize in Each and Every Package
GS: Alan Hale. Oliver and the townspeople find expensive jewelry in their boxes of cereal.

Law Partners
Oliver decides to take a young law graduate in as a law partner in a Hooterville law practice.

A Day in the Life of Oliver Wendell Holmes
Lisa becomes the new secretary to Oliver and his new partner.

Economy Flight to Washington
GS: Dave Willock. Lisa and Oliver go to Washington, D.C.

Retreat from Washington
While the Douglases are still in Washington, Haney turns their farm into a tourist inn.

A Hunting We Won't Go
GS: Roy Roberts. Lisa starts a petition to put an end to hunting.

Oh, Promise Me
GS: Henry Oliver. Lisa and Oliver discover that their Hungarian marriage license is actually a license to practice dentistry.

Eb Uses His Ingenuity
Eb turns the farm into a baby nursery in order to get some extra money.

The Old Trunk
Oliver and Lisa read about a 19th-century romance while going through the contents of an old trunk.

The Milk Maker
A crazy inventor creates a milk-making machine, causing Haney to ask Oliver for money to invest in it.

The Reincarnation of Eb
When Eb disappears, Lisa thinks he died and came back as a dog.

Where There's a Will
Oliver becomes Arnold's lawyer when it seems Arnold may be the sole heir to a 20 million dollar estate left by an eccentric meat-packing tycoon.

A Tale of a Tail
Oliver has to prove that Arnold is the pig mentioned in the will.

You and Your Big Shrunken Head
Lisa and Oliver return with Arnold who is now a millionaire.

Lisa's Mudder Comes for a Visit
Lisa's mother moves in with them for three weeks.

Everybody Tries to Love a Countess
GS: Edgar Buchanan. Mr. Haney and Joe Carson both try to get the Countess to marry them.

Oliver and the Cornstalk
A giant cornstalk, complete with the Jolly Green Giant, grows in Oliver's cornfield.

Beauty Is Skin Deep
Lisa turns Sam Drucker's store into a beauty parlor and plans to make all the women in town beautiful.

Oliver's School Girl Crush
When Oliver addresses a class at the high school, one of the students develops a crush on him.

The Four of Spades
Lisa tells Oliver's fortune and predicts the visit of Eb's friend.

The Road
Oliver and Lisa try to get the state to pave the roads in Hooterville.

The Youth Center
The town turns Oliver's barn into the new town youth center.

The Ex-Con
GS: John Dualin.   Oliver's new hired hand is an ex-con.

The Wishbook
Oliver and Lisa find an old mail order catalog in the wall of the house.

The Special Delivery Letter
Oliver tries to find the special delivery letter which was never delivered but has gotten the whole town interested in knowing its contents.

Ralph's Nuptials
Lisa plans an outdoor wedding for Ralph and Mr. Kimball.

Bundle of Joy
While Oliver is in New York, Lisa winds up with a baby puppy which was left on her doorstep.

Rest and Relaxation
GS: Bob Cummings.   Oliver's old friend comes for a visit; he plans to have a nice rest in the country, or so he thinks.

Trapped
Oliver and Lisa get trapped in the cave under their house.

The Cow Killer
Lisa calls Oliver a cow killer when he gets rid of the cow that has been ruining his crops.

The Confrontation
Oliver becomes the school board president and must face a protest movement to get Arnold the pig un-expelled from school.

The Case of the Hooterville Refund Fraud
Oliver is the cause of the trouble when the government sends over $500,000 to the townspeople in tax refunds.

The Picnic
Oliver and Lisa plan to have a quiet picnic alone, but the entire town decides to join them.

The Beeping Rock
A crazy kid shows up with a strange rock which he said he found while on the moon.

The Wealthy Landowner
Eb claims that he is a rich landowner when he advertises for a wife but, when his bride-to-be arrives, he has to prove it.

Uncle Fedor
GS: Leo Fuchs. Lisa's uncle comes for a visit with a crazy story about being chased by spies.

Happy Birthday
Oliver thinks that the surprise birthday party for Arnold is his party.

Jealousy
GS: Victoria Meyer.   When a little house guest named Lori comes to stay with Oliver and Lisa, Eb becomes jealous of their attention to her.

The City Kids
Lisa and Oliver take in four city kids in order to show them what life on a farm is like.

The Coming Out Party
Lisa wants to hold a coming out party for Lori.

Eb's Double Trouble
GS: Judy McConnell, Kate Nelson. Eb falls in love with the new school teacher, despite the fact he has a girlfriend, and Arnold falls for two cows.

A Royal Love Story
Lisa tells Lori a story about her courtship with Oliver.

Oliver Goes Broke
GS: Victoria Meyer. The townspeople

pitch in when they think Oliver has gone broke.

Apple Picking Time
GS: Joe Higgins, John Wheeler. Oliver has to find someone to pick his apple crop and has to teach Lisa how to drive.

Enterprising Eb
Eb introduces Oliver and Lisa as his parents when he plans to marry his girlfriend Darlene.

Oliver's Double
W: Dan Beaumont. GS: Charin Hale. Oliver's lookalike causes problems with him and the townspeople.

The High Cost of Loving
GS: Judy McConnell. Eb takes a mail order course on how to become an actor.

The Liberation Movement
W: Dan Beaumont & Dick Chevillat. Lisa takes over the farm and makes Oliver do the housework when she discovers Women's Lib.

The Great Mayoralty Campaign
Oliver and Lisa both run for the office of Mayor.

Charlie, Homer and Natasha
GS: Bob Hastings. Eb and Lisa believe there are little invisible people in the house.

The Engagement Ring
W: Dan Beaumont & Dick Chevillat. Lisa gives her engagement ring to Eb so he can give it to Darlene.

The Free Paint Job
GS: Tom Lowell. Lisa and Oliver get their house painted for free as part of a paint company's advertising campaign.

Son of Drobney
W: Dan Beaumont. GS: Gordon Connell. Lisa's house guest is the son of a famous war hero who happens to be a duck.

Lisa, the Psychologist
GS: William Sylvester. Lisa goes to college to study psychology.

The Carpenter's Ball
Oliver refuses to take Lisa to the Carpenter's Ball.

Star Witness
W: Dan Beaumont & Dick Chevillat. GS: Milton Selzer, Al Lewis. Arnold is the witness to a robbery.

The Wedding Deal
Eb plans to be married in a car wash or a department store so he can collect lots of gifts.

Hawaiian Honeymoon
GS: Pamela Franklin, Don Porter. Lisa gets Oliver to take her to the Moana Rexford Hotel in Hawaii for a fifth honeymoon visit. [This was a pilot for a possible series about the hotel run by Don Porter and Pamela Franklin (playing his daughter).]

The Spot Remover
GS: George Ives. Lisa plans to sell her uncle's cabbage soup as a spot remover.

A Girl for Drobney
Drobney the duck is starting to get homesick.

The Hole in the Porch
Mr. Kimball falls through the porch and hurts his leg, so he moves in till he recovers.

The Ex-Secretary
GS: Richard Deacon, Elaine Joyce, Emmaline Henry. Oliver asks his ex-secretary to find him the only jeweler capable of fixing his antique watch. [This was also a pilot for a possible series about Oliver's ex-secretary.]

King Oliver I
Hooterville secedes from the state when taxes are increased and name Oliver their king.

GUESTWARD HO!

On the air 9/29/60, off 9/21/61. ABC. 30 min. Film. B&W. 38 episodes. Broadcast: Sept 1960-Sept 1961 Thu 7:30-8. Producer: Jerry Thorpe. Prod Co/ Synd: Paramount TV.

CAST: Hawkeye (played by J. Carrol Naish), Bill Hooten (Mark Miller), Babs Hooten (Joanne Dru), Brook Hooten (Flip Mark), Lonesome (Earle Hodgins), Pink Cloud (Jolene Brand), Rocky (Tony Montenaro, Jr.).

Bill Hooten, an unhappy New York advertising executive, purchases Guestward Ho, a dude ranch in New Mexico. Stories relate the attempts of a city dweller and his wife Babs, and son Brook, to adjust to new responsibilities and acquire paying customers. Opposing them is Chief Hawkeye, the owner of the local trading post, who is on the warpath to win America back for the Indians. Although available, it is not seen in the United States.

The Hootens Buy a Ranch
A sophisticated New York family moves west to operate a dude ranch in New Mexico. However, the ranch is not what they expected.

The Social Director
The Hootens are expecting some company but no one wants to play host to them.

Babs and the Cow
Mrs. Hooten wants to buy some garden chairs for the ranch, but her husband says the cow comes first.

Babs's Mother
GS: Natalie Schafer, Stafford Repp. Mrs. Crawford visits the Hootens. She attempts to run the ranch for them, but almost succeeds in wrecking it.

The Lost Tribe
Babs and Bill invite a famous magazine writer on a camping trip, hoping he will write something about the ranch. Unfortunately, Hawkeye is their guide.

You Can't Go Home Again
GS: Robert Strauss, Connie Sawyer. Babs doesn't like having to do all of the work involved in fixing up the ranch and wants to return to New York instead.

Babs Meets Phyllis Brady
GS: Michael Hinn, Carole Mathews.

Babs becomes jealous when Bill's old girlfriend comes for a visit.

Babs and the Lion
GS: Ann Morrison, James Waters. Bill sends Babs to stay at another ranch in the hopes that she will not learn about the mountain lion which is on the loose.

The Thanksgiving Story
Bill and Brook have a hard time trapping a turkey for their holiday dinner. Hawkeye offers to sell them one at a nominal price.

Model Mother
When Babs takes a job as a model, Bill and Brook get Hawkeye to find a way to get her to return home.

The Hootens Fire Lonesome
The Hootens fire Lonesome when he loses a valuable horse.

Babs's Vanity
GS: Constance Moore, Frances Robinson. Babs refuses to perform any of the heavy chores around the ranch.

The Matchmakers
GS: Jackie Coogan, Alan Reed, Jr. The Hootens hire a young Indian wrangler in order to make their lovesick cook happy. Hawkeye, however, does not believe in inter-tribe dating, so he plans to break up their relationship.

Spirit of Christmas
GS: Howard Wendell, Harry Chesire.
Brook announces that he thinks that
Christmas is silly except for the pres-
ents, so the family returns all of the
presents they got him.

Injun Bill
Hawkeye tries to get the Hootens to
rent him their ranch so he can use it as
the site of the Corn Festival celebration.

Frontier Week
GS: Adam Williams.   When the town
decides to have a centennial parade,
both Bill and Jim Gates want to lead
it, so Hawkeye decides they should
have a race.

Dimples Goes to Hollywood
Babs wants to take a trip to Hollywood, but Bill says they don't have
the money. However, a movie director
is looking for new talent, so she decides to audition.

Too Many Cooks
GS: Richard Deacon, Sara Seegar.
Babs finds that she has to cook a Mexican dinner in order to complete a big
deal which will attract visiting tourists.

No Vacancy
GS: Addison Richards, Madge Blake.
Bill and Babs's quiet evening is disturbed by a couple from Pittsburgh
who show up claiming they have a reservation.

Manhattan Merry-Go-Round
Bill and Brook want to go fishing but
don't know how to tell Babs, so Hawkeye asks her to go along with them.

Bill the Candidate
GS: Whit Bissell, Iron Eyes Cody.
When a candidate for presidency of
the Chamber of Commerce refuses
Hawkeye's help, he decides to back
Bill as an opposing candidate.

Babs the Guest
When business becomes slow, Babs de-

cides that everyone should take a vacation.

Hawkeye's First Love
GS: Jeanette Nolan.   Hawkeye's old
girlfriend is coming for a visit.

Hawkeye the Mother
GS: Melody Gail, Karen Norris.   The
Mother's League is planning an open
house and Hawkeye wants to join the
club.

Hawkeye's Stadium
GS: Eileen O'Neill.   The Chamber of
Commerce installs a bus stop right in
front of Hawkeye's store, but the
local children would rather have a new
baseball field instead.

The Honorary Indian
GS: Milton Frome, Bella Bruck.   Bill
is named Great White Eagle and is
accepted as the first immigrant member of the local Indian council.

The Hootens Build a Barbecue
GS: Charles Lane, Louis Nicoletti.
Bill wants to install a new barbecue,
but Babs thinks it will cost too much.

The Hooten's Statue
GS: Frank Cady, Alan Dexter.   Hawkeye becomes upset when the town
votes to erect a statue of Bill's pioneer
grandfather instead of a statue of himself.

Two Guests from the East
GS: Ned Glass, Henry Corden.   Hawkeye suggests to two men that the Hooten ranch would be a perfect place to
set up their bookmaking operation.

Bill the Fireman
GS: Adam West.   Babs's playboy brother comes to town.   He causes trouble
when Brook would rather ride in his
sports car than go on a fishing trip
with Bill.

Babs the Manager
GS: Art Passarella.   Brook wants to
have his birthday present three months

in advance: new uniforms for his little league team.   Bill says they can't afford it, but Hawkeye agrees to sponsor the team.

Lonesome's Gal
GS: Zasu Pitts. Bill teaches shy Lonesome how to court his girlfriend.

The Hootens vs. Hawkeye
GS: Hanley Stafford. The Hootens sue Hawkeye when he sells them a defective floor waxer.

The Wrestler
GS: Jody McCrea, Frank Cady, Diane Cannon.   Hawkeye arranges a wrestling match between Bill and a savage Indian.

The Hooten's Second Car
Hawkeye promises to give Bill a new car in return for Bill becoming his advertising manager of his new car business.

The Wild West Show
GS: Charles Maxwell, Clem Bevans. Hawkeye decides to make Babs the queen of the rodeo when the Hootens allow him to hold an annual rodeo at the ranch.

The Beatniks
Hawkeye opens an espresso coffee house, but regrets it when he sees Pink Cloud's new beatnik boyfriend King Cool.

No Place Like Home
GS: Virginia Vincent. Bill's old boss comes for a visit and offers him a job as vice president if he will return to the company and New York.

HAPPY DAYS

On the air 1/15/74, off: still continuing. ABC. 166 synd. episodes. Color Film.   Broadcast: Jan 1974- Tue 8-8:30. Producer: Garry Marshall. Prod Co/ Synd: Paramount TV.

CAST: Richie Cunningham (played by Ron Howard), Fonzie (Henry Winkler), Howard Cunningham (Tom Bosley), Marion (Marion Ross), Warren Weber [Potsie] (Anson Williams), Joanie (Erin Moran), Ralph Malph (Donny Most), Arnold (Pat Morita), Alfred (Al Molinaro), Chachi (Scott Baio).

The series is based around the adventures of Richie Cunningham and his friends and family during the 1950s. Extremely popular on the network and is still going strong.   However, the reruns have not done very well at all. Syndicated under the title *Happy Days Again*, it has been a big disappointment to the local stations which run the show.

All the Way
Richie has a date with a bombshell who goes all the way.

Richie's Cup Runneth Over
GS: Louisa Moritz. Richie attends his first bachelor party where he meets an exotic dancer who drives him home.

The Lemon
GS: Cindy Eilbacher, Tita Bell. Richie and Potsie buy their first car and prepare to take it to the Saturday night sock hop, only the car refuses to go.

The Skin Game
GS: Barbara Rhoades. Richie and Potsie attend their first burlesque show and get a surprise when they find Richie's father there.

Fonzie Drops In
GS: Tita Bell, Jessica Guest. Fonzie decides to re-enroll in high school and then wants Richie to do his homework for him.

Guess Who's Coming to Visit
Richie and Potsie can't resist the temp-

Donny Most (left), Henry Winkler, Anson Williams, and Ron Howard in Happy Days.

tation to attend a midnight drag race that Fonzie is racing in.

Hardware Jungle
GS: George Ives, Peter Brocco. Passing up a rock concert, Richie volunteers to take care of his father's hardware store.

The Deadly Dares
GS: Ed Begley, Jr. Potsie convinces Richie that in order to get girls they should join a club called the Demons.

Breaking Up Is Hard to Do
GS: Laurette Spang. Richie and his girlfriend Arlene split up two weeks before the prom and then discover they can't get dates.

Because She's There
GS: Diana Canova. Richie, in order to satisfy Potsie's wishes, agrees to go on a blind date and then discovers that his date is much too tall.

Give the Band a Hand
In order to make some extra money, Richie, Potsie and Ralph decide to form a band. At their first gig, a fraternity party, they gamble their wages at a poker game.

In the Name of Love
Potsie and Ralph are in love with the new girl in school. She likes Richie but only as a friend.

Great Expectations
GS: Udana Power, Danny Goldman. Richie brings a girl beatnik home and Howard doesn't like the idea. Richie thinks things are fine until she tells him she is pregnant.

Knock Around the Clock
GS: Darrell Fetty. Richie thinks the Dukes, the neighborhood gang, isn't that bad, until they steal his bicycle.

Best Man
GS: Bill Henderson, Gail Bryant. The

Cunninghams invite a black couple to be married in their home, causing the neighbors to get upset.

Be the First on Your Block
GS: Ronnie Schell. A salesman talks the Cunninghams into building a bomb shelter. They get more than they bargained for when all of their friends and neighbors want to use it.

Open House
GS: Joan Prather, Patricia Wilson, Nancy Bell. Three beauty pageant contestants spend the night at the Cunningham house when their car breaks down.

Richie's Car
GS: Karl Swenson, Joshua Shelley. Richie buys a $200 hot rod from Fonzie which turns out to be a stolen vehicle.

Not with My Sister, You Don't
GS: Danny Butch, Misty Rowe. Richie is upset that Joanie's first date is with Fonzie's nephew Spike.

Richie Moves Out
GS: Linda Purl, Randolph Roberts. Fed up with no privacy, Richie leaves home and moves in with his brother, only to find bachelor life is tougher than he thought.

You Go to My Head
GS: Ivor Francis, Christina Hart. Richie reads a book on abnormal psychology which drives him to seek psychiatric help.

Wish Upon a Star
GS: Cheryl Ladd, Linda Purl. Richie wins a date with a Hollywood starlet to the school dance and must find a way to tell his current girlfriend Gloria she is not invited.

Richie's Flip Side
GS: Jesse White, Warren Berlinger, Beatrice Colen. Richie gets his own radio show as a Dee Jay and seems to abandon his friends for his new image.

The Not Making of the President
GS: Stephanie Steele. It is election time and the Cunninghams are all for Ike, except Richie who is campaigning for Stevenson in order to get a date with a cute blonde.

A Star Is Bored
GS: Ronnie Schell, Britt Leach. Richie tries to drum up baseball uniforms for his losing team by putting on a fund raising performance of "Hamlet."

Who's Sorry Now?
GS: Tanis Montgomery. When Richie is apprehensive about a date with an old girlfriend he hasn't seen in three years, he discovers the girl likes him so much that she wants to go steady.

Fish and Fins
GS: Sam McFadin, Kris Moe, Jeff Stewart, Linn Phillips. When the rock group Fish and Fins comes to town, everyone wants free tickets from Richie who says he once knew the band's drummer.

Big Money
GS: Dave Madden. Richie has a chance to win $3200 on a game show called Big Money. He discovers the show is fixed when he is given the answers to all the questions.

R.O.T.C.
GS: Dave Ketchum, Richard Kuller. During R.O.T.C. training Richie is chosen to be squad leader, leaving him the decision of being a hated great leader or a soft leader his men will love.

Haunted
Ralph holds his annual Halloween party at an old haunted house where Richie thinks he saw a headless ghost.

Kiss Me Sickly
GS: Misty Rowe, Laurette Spang, Didi Conn. When Fonzie has to go out of town for a week, he asks Richie to watch his girlfriend for him but soon regrets it when she falls for Richie.

Fonzie Joins the Band
GS: Adam Arkin, Susan Richardson. Fonzie takes up the bongos to play with Richie's band at an important club dance.

Goin' to Chicago
GS: George Furth, Phil Leeds, Pamela Myers. Richie, Potsie and Ralph head to Chicago with the school chorus. They sneak out of their hotel room to sample the night life, but trouble follows when they discover they forgot to bring money.

Guess Who's Coming to Christmas
The Cunningham family plan a quiet Christmas all by themselves, until they learn that Fonzie has no place to go for the holiday.

The Cunningham Caper
GS: Herb Edelman. Richie is home sick in bed when he hears noises downstairs. He assumes it is Potsie and Ralph, but it turns out to be a burglar.

Get a Job
GS: Leslie Charleson, Beatrice Colen. Richie, Potsie and Ralph are hired by a young divorcee for a repair job. Everything is fine until Richie becomes romantically involved with her.

The Howdy Doody Show
GS: Bob Smith, Robert Brunner. Richie, working for the school newspaper, decides to interview Buffalo Bob Smith and Howdy Doody in order to get a picture of Clarabell the clown without his makeup on.

Cruisin'
GS: Maureen McCormick, Michael Lembeck. Richie, Potsie and Ralph go searching for girls across town but run into trouble when the girls' boyfriends arrive.

Fonzie's Getting Married
GS: Nellie Bellflower. When Fonzie stuns everyone with his decision to get married, Howard remembers the girl of Fonzie's dreams as a stripper he saw in Chicago.

Fonzie Moves On
GS: Lillian Bronson. Fonzie's grandmother takes over his old apartment when he moves out.

The Motorcycle [Part 1]
Fonzie's motorcycle is totaled.

The Other Richie Cunningham [Part 2]
Fonzie winds up in the hospital.

Fearless Fonzie
Fonzie takes a daring motorcycle leap over 14 garbage cans.

Fonzie the Flatfoot
GS: Ed Peck. The police ask Fonzie to stop a gang fight.

Jail House Rock
GS: Ed Peck. The boys plan to challenge a curfew that may land them in jail.

Fonzie Came to Dinner
Fonzie can't stand it when the new owner of the garage wants him to get a haircut.

Richie
GS: Jeff Conaway. Richie decides to take ju-jitsu lessons.

A Date with the Fonz
Richie is sure that he has lost his touch with the girls, so he asks Fonzie for help.

Howard's 45th Fiasco
Howard's 45th birthday makes him realize that he hasn't done anything important.

Fonzie's New Friend
Fonzie's new black friend is causing hidden feelings to surface in many people.

Three on a Porch
GS: Ned Wertimer. Howard asks Richie to entertain a visiting businessman's daughter.

Fonzie the Salesman
The boys can't rent a cabin because of

a lack of money.

They Call it Potsie Love
Joanie has a crush on Potsie.

Tell It to the Marines
GS: Amy Irving.   Ralph threatens to
join the Foreign Legion.

Beauty Contest
The boys stage a beauty contest and
rig it so nobody wins.

Arnold's Wedding
GS: Nobu McCarthy.   Arnold wants
Fonzie to be his best man at his wed-
ding.

Dance Contest
Marion is practicing for a dance contest.

Football Frolic
The boys babysit to raise money for
a football game.

Two Angry Men
GS: June Lockhart.   Fonzie's birds
cause Howard's roof to cave in.

Fonzie the Superstar
GS: Cindy Williams and Penny Mar-
chall.   The boys teach Fonzie so he
can sing at the school dance.

Bringing Up Spike
GS: Danny Butch.   Fonzie has to
spend a week looking after Spike.

A Sight for Sore Eyes
GS: Jack Dodson.   Fonzie needs
glasses but doesn't want to wear them.

Second Anniversary Special
Flashbacks of previous episodes are
shown.

A Mind of Their Own
GS: Bill Idelson.   Fonzie goes to see a
psychiatrist.

Fonzie Loves Pinky [Part 1]
GS: Roz Kelly.   Pinky, an ace cyclist,
is   Fonzie's   partner   in   an   all-male
demolition derby.

Fonzie Loves Pinky [Part 2]
Fonzie falls in love with Pinky.

Fonzie Loves Pinky [Part 3]
Fonzie asks Pinky to marry him.

Fonzie the Father
A pregnant girl comes looking for
Fonzie.

A Place of His Own
GS: Conrad Janis.   Richie brings his
date to Fonzie's apartment.

The Muckrakers
School reporter Richie looks into a
scandal at the high school cafeteria.

A.K.A. The Fonz
GS: Ed Peck.   A new sheriff wants to
run Fonzie out of town.

They Shoot Fonzies
GS: Charlene Tilton, Gary Epp. Joanie
teams up with Fonzie in a dance marathon.

Marion Rebels
Marion becomes a waitress at Arnold's.

Fonzie's Hero
Potsie saves Fonzie's life and he becomes eternally grateful.

The Time Capsule
The boys become locked in Howard's
vault after putting away a time capsule.

Richie Branches Out
Richie devises a scheme to meet the
poster girl of his dreams.

The Book of Records
GS: Charles Gallioto.   Fonzie's clumsy
cousin comes to work for Arnold.

Fonzie's "Old" Lady
GS: Diana Hyland.   Fonzie is dating an
older woman.

The Last of the Bigtime Malphs
GS: Jack Dodson.   Ralph becomes a
bigtime gambler in the football pool
racket.

The Physical
GS: Warren Berlinger, Linda Kaye Henning. The boys receive orders to report for their Army physicals.

Graduation [Part 1]
GS: Dick Van Patten, Laurette Spang. The boys graduate from high school and Fonzie wants to graduate from night school.

Graduation Party [Part 2]
Fonzie learns he can only get his diploma by mail, but he eventually does join the graduating class.

A Shot in the Head
GS: Dave Ketchum. Richie sinks the winning basket in the state-wide basketball game.

Joanie's Weird Boyfriend
Joanie joins a motorcycle gang called the Red Devils.

Fonz-How, Inc.
Fonzie and Howard invent a trash compactor called the Garbage Gulper.

Fonzie's Baptism
After a motorcycle accident, Fonzie prepares for the hereafter.

Spunky Come Home
Potsie and Ralph lose Fonzie's dog.

Anniversary Wrap Around
Howard's surprise anniversary party brings flashbacks to previous episodes.

The Apartment
Ralph, Fonzie and Richie move into a rundown apartment.

Hard Cover
GS: Marcia Lewis and Linda Goodfriend. Richie goes to college and learns that coeds don't date freshmen, so the Fonz takes him to the library to meet some nice girls. [This was the first appearance of Lori Beth who would later become Richie's wife.]

Hollywood [Part 1]
GS: Lorne Greene. The Fonz is offered a screen test.

Hollywood [Part 2]
Fonzie and his friends go to Hollywood.

Hollywood [Part 3]
Fonzie is challenged to jump over a shark tank with his motorcycle.

Fonsilectomy
GS: Kathi & Scott Marshall. Tonsilitis has Fonzie hospitalized on the night he wanted to attend a Halloween party.

My Cousin the Cheat
Chachi cheats on an exam so he can qualify for a job in the garage.

Fonz—Rock Entrepreneur [Part 1]
Leather Tuscadero gets an audition for her rock group at Arnold's.

Fonz—Rock Entrepreneur [Part 2]
Joanie wants to go on the tour with the group.

Nose News
GS: Henry Beckman. Richie gets a "D" in investigative reporting, so he decides to look for a big story.

My Fair Fonzie
GS: Morgan Fairchild. Fonzie is invited to a yacht club party by a socialite.

Bye Bye Black Ball
As fraternity pledges, the boys are going through all sorts of initiations.

Requiem for a Malph
GS: Red Browne, Audrey Landers. Ralph dates the girlfriend of a football player who challenges him to a boxing match.

Joanie's First Kiss
GS: Tim Dial. Joanie is asked out by a senior who owns a car.

Grandpa's Visit
GS: Danny Thomas. Howard's father, a retired police detective, comes for a visit.

Potsie Gets Pinned
Potsie gets ready to propose to his new girlfriend.

Marion's Misgivings
When a friend leaves his wife for a younger woman, Marion wonders if Howard will do the same thing.

Richie Almost Dies
Richie cracks up his new motorcycle and lies comatose in the hospital, where the Fonz becomes emotionally upset.

Rules to Date By
Richie gets angry when Lori Beth is nice to other guys.

Spunkless Spunky
GS: Dr. Joyce Brothers. Fonzie's dog has no energy left in him.

Our Gang
Flashbacks show how Richie first met the Fonz.

My Favorite Orkan
GS: Robin Williams. Richie is selected to go to the planet Ork to be the subject of an experiment. [This is the first appearance of Mork.]

Be My Valentine
GS: Christopher Knight. Joanie dreams about love songs that would befit her friend.

Do You Have to Dance?
GS: Leslie Browne. Fonzie falls for a ballerina who has the chance to become a superstar.

Fonzie for the Defense
GS: Barney Martin, Ralph Wilcox. Fonzie is the only juror who believes a biker is innocent of purse snatching.

Anniversary Special '78
Lori Beth uses a college report to look back on past adventures.

Sweet Sixteen
GS: Ray Underwood, Dan Spector. Joanie's date for the upcoming Sweet Sixteen party is an amorous quarterback who doesn't take no for an answer.

Fearless Malph
GS: Leon Askin. Richie wants to use Ralph as a subject in his college paper about fear.

Smokin' Ain't Cool
Fonzie tries to prove to Joanie that she should not smoke.

Westward Ho! [Part 1]
GS: Ruth Cox, Jason Evers. The gang goes out West to help Marion's uncle whose ranch is about to be closed down.

Westward Ho! [Part 2]
Further adventures in the West for Fonzie and the Cunninghams.

Westward Ho! [Part 3]
Fonzie rides a killer bull.

Fonzie's Blindness
Fonzie loses his sight after getting hit on the head.

Casanova Cunningham
GS: Mary Margret. Richie must escort a baton twirler to his frat dance, but he tells Lori Beth that he will be out with the police on a journalism case.

Kid Stuff
GS: John Waldron. Fonzie is touched by his girlfriend's son whose father, like his, walked out on him.

Fonzie Is Allergic to Girls
Fonzie finds that he has an allergy to girls.

Claw Meets Fonz
GS: Arthur Batanides, Phillip Pine. A gangster wants to take over Al's restaurant.

Richie Gets Framed
GS: Steve Richmond. Richie finds that his opposition for the office of class president is offering free beer and shorter classes.

The Evil Eye
A little old lady puts a curse on Al.

The Kissing Bandit
Richie is accused and arrested for suspicion of being the kissing bandit.

The First Thanksgivings
Marion tells a story about the meaning of Thanksgiving.

Magic Show
GS: The Amazing Randi. A magician drinks a glass of vodka instead of water, leaving Richie to perform his magic act.

Christmas Time
GS: Eddie Fontaine. Fonzie has bitter Christmas memories about his father.

Stolen Melodies
GS: Fred S. Fox. Leather and the boys audition for a musical talent show, only to have their songs stolen from them.

Marion Plays Pygmalion
GS: Terry McGovern. Marion stars in a play opposite an actor who thinks he is the romantic lover type.

Ralph vs. Potsie
Ralph and Potsie write to the Aunt Fanny advice column in the paper for roommate advice, unaware that Richie is Aunt Fanny.

Potsie Quits School
GS: Allan Rich. Potsie thinks he flunked his anatomy course.

Married Strangers
GS: Vito Scotti. Howard and Marion go on a second honeymoon.

Fonzie's Funeral [Part 1]
GS: Cliff Emmich. The Fonz discovers counterfeit bills in a coffin, while fixing a hearse. When he takes the hearse back to the owner, he disappears.

Fonzie's Funeral [Part 2]
Fonz is thought to be dead and a fun-

eral is held.

The Duel
GS: Patrick Gorman. Fonzie fights a duel with a bigoted Frenchman.

Chachi's Wonder Wax
Chachi's new wax destroys whatever it shines.

Mork Returns
GS: Robin Williams. Mork returns to Earth to learn about relationships in the 1960s.

Richie's Job
GS: Ted Gehring. Richie starts his journalism career by loading newspapers on a truck.

Joanie's Dilemma
Marion has a long talk with Joanie when she accepts a senior's ring.

Shotgun Wedding [Part 1]
Richie and Fonzie chase after a farmer's daughter, which makes her gun-toting father very angry. [This concludes on an episode of "Laverne and Shirley."]

Chachi Sells His Soul
Chachi sells his soul to the Devil's nephew to become warm and wonderful.

Fonzie Meets Kat
GS: Debbie Pratt. When a merchant ship docks in Milwaukee, a mysterious woman and an old enemy get off.

Mechanic
GS: Jim Knaub. Fonzie hires a crippled mechanic with a chip on his shoulder.

Inspiration Point
The gang tries to stop construction on a new highway which would destroy Inspiration Point.

Marion Goes to Jail
Marion hits Arnold's Restaurant with her car.

Richie in Love
GS: Jenny Sullivan. Richie falls for a lady photographer.

Ralph's Problem
GS: Jack Dodson.   Ralph's parents want a divorce.

Fonzie's a Thespian
Fonzie takes up acting.

Burlesque
Howard's burlesque show is in trouble when his troupe is stuck in Buffalo when a snowstorm hits.

Richard's Big Knight
Richie is crowned king of the Delta Gammas.

Joanie Busts Out
Joanie applies for a modeling job.

Here Comes the Bride Again
Marion wants a real wedding for her 25th anniversary.

The She Devils
GS: Karen Jensen. Richie, Potsie and Ralph attend a nerd party.

Hot Stuff
Chachi sets fire to Arnold's Restaurant and must pay for his actions.

Ah, Wilderness
To prove he is a good leader, Richie takes the gang on a camping trip.

The New Arnold
Fonzie and Al rebuild Arnold's Restaurant; can't decide what to name it.

The Hucksters
GS: Hank Aaron. Howard tries to get Hank Aaron to advertise his hardware store on TV.

Roaring '20s
GS: Pat O'Brien. The family remembers Richie's great Uncle Cecil who was the Assistant DA who closed down the speakeasies.

Allison
GS: Linda Bove. Fonzie falls for a young deaf woman.

Father and Son
GS: Dave Ketchum.   Howard takes Richie to his lodge convention in Chicago.

Fools Rush In
Chachi tries to get Joanie to take him seriously after all these years.

The Potsie Show
GS: Arthur Batanides, Pat Crowley. Potsie is offered a job singing at a supper club.

THE HATHAWAYS

On the air 10/6/61, off 8/31/62. ABC. 26 episodes. B&W Film. 30 min. Broadcast: Oct 1961-Aug 1962 Fri 8-8:30. Producer: Ezra Stone. Prod Co/ Synd: Screen Gems/Columbia Pictures TV.
CAST: Elinor Hathaway (played by Peggy Cass), Walter Hathaway (Jack Weston), Jerry Roper (Harvey Lembeck), Thelma Brockwood (Barbara Perry), Amanda Allison (Mary Grace Canfield), Mrs. Harrison (Belle Montrose [Steve Allen's mother]), The Marquis Chimps.
DIRECTOR: Ezra Stone.
Set in Los Angeles, the show concerns the trials and tribulations of Walter Hathaway, real estate agent, and his wife Elinor. The couple also happen to be the owners of three chimps who have their own rewarding career in show business. *The Hathaways* is available for syndication but is never seen due to the small number of episodes produced.

Love Thy Neighbor
GS: George Ives, Barbara Perry. A couple wants to buy the house next door, until they learn about the chimps.

Elinor Buys a Hat
GS: King Calder. Charlie Chimp hides Elinor's parking ticket in his pocket.

Walter Takes a Partner
GS: Joe Flynn, Carol Seffinger. Walter invents a new soda pop.

Elinor's Guilt
Elinor does not want to leave the chimps to go on a vacation.

Income Tax Returns
GS: William Lanteau. Elinor and Walter get a large refund check by mistake.

Candy's Tonsils
GS: Vaughn Taylor. Candy refuses to take her medicine when she gets tonsillitis.

Trash Day
GS: George Ives, Barbara Perry, Mary Grace Canfield. Walter trains Charlie to get the newspaper from the front porch. However, Charlie returns with every paper in the neighborhood.

TV or Not TV
GS: Robert Q. Lewis. Walter owes free food and transportation to prospective real estate buyers.

The Kids Go to School
GS: Barbara Eiler, Frances Robinson. Elinor enrolls the chimps in a day nursery.

The Practical Joker
GS: Norman Leavitt. Charlie loses Elinor's purse when he plays a practical joke.

Double Birthday Party
GS: Frank Wilcox. Walter thinks Candy's birthday party is actually his birthday party.

The Hathaways Sleep Out
GS: Robert Foulk, Bert Remsen. Elinor takes the chimps away so their room can be painted.

The Jingle Contest
GS: Bob Jellison, Max Mellinger. Walter and Bert enter Charlie's tune in a jingle contest.

Waltzing with Walter
GS: Peter Leeds, Louise DeCarlo, Valentin De Vargas. Elinor wins free dancing lessons.

Foxy Chimp
GS: Marjorie Bennett. Charlie, Candy and Enoch are jealous of Peppy, a sick chimp from the zoo that Elinor is taking care of.

It's in the Cards
GS: Barbara Perry. Elinor is jealous of Walter's interest in photographer Charlene Gray.

The Headliners
GS: Harvey Lembeck. Elinor and the chimps get a job at a night club in Hawaii, but Walter can't go along with them.

The Paint Job
GS: Alan Carney. The chimps help Elinor by painting the car.

Grandma's Lamp
GS: David Lipp. When Elinor brings home her grandma's old lamp, Walter and the chimps plan to get rid of it.

Help Wanted
GS: Charles Irving, George Taylor, Joe Greene. Elinor plans to collect the chimps' unemployment checks in order to buy Walter a present.

Swami Chimp
GS: Leonard Stone, Charles Reade. When a mindreading chimp appears at the club, Elinor is afraid her chimps will be forced out of the show.

A Man for Amanda
GS: Doodles Weaver. Walter tries to

get a boyfriend for Amanda, the house-keeper, who wants to quit work in order to find romance.

Pop Goes the Budget
GS: Alan Carney, Raymond Mayo. Walter puts Elinor and the chimps on a strict budget.

Charlie Goes to the Races
GS: Frankie Darro, Caroline Richter. Charlie makes friends with a racehorse

named Beanstalk.

Shrewd Trader
GS: Bob Williams and his dog Hula. Elinor trades a handbag for an original Paris hat.

Elinor's Best Friend
GS: Marge Redmond, Robert Shayne. Walter is jealous of Elinor's school friend's rich husband.

HAZEL

On the air 9/28/61, off 9/5/66. NBC, CBS. B&W/Color film. 154 episodes. Broadcast: Sept 1961-Jul 1964 NBC Thu 9:30-10; Sept 1964-Sept 1965 NBC Thu 9:30-10; Sept 1965-Sept 1966 CBS Mon 9:30-10. Producer: Harry Acker-man. Prod Co: Screen Gems. Synd: Columbia Pictures.
CAST: Hazel Burke (played by Shirley Booth), George Baxter (Don DeFore), Dorothy Baxter (Whitney Blake), Harold Baxter (Bobby Buntrock), Rosie (Maudie Prickett), Harvey Griffin (Howard Smith), Steve Baxter (Ray Fulmer), Barbara Baxter (Lynn Borden), Susie Baxter (Julia Benjamin), Mona Williams (Mala Powers), Millie Ballard (Ann Jillian), Enzio (Gregory Morton).
WRITERS: William Cowley, Peggy Chandler, Robert Crutcher, Ted Sherde-man, Jane Klove, Louella MacFarlane, John McGreevey. DIRECTORS: William D. Russell, Charles T. Barton, E.W. Swackhamer.
The story of the Baxter family and their lovable know-it-all housekeeper/maid Hazel Burke. Hazel would cause all kinds of trouble for the Baxters while trying to help them any way she could. Later, when the series changed networks, Hazel went to work for her boss's brother's family. *Hazel* was very well received during the early sixties, but the age of the films and the poor quality of the early color film has caused this series to disappear from all but a few stations.

Hazel and the Playground
GS: Maurice Mason. Hazel tries to get a playground built in the neighbor-hood botanic gardens.

Hazel Makes a Will
George thinks Hazel plans to sue him when she calls in a lawyer after she falls over the loose brick he forgot to fix.

Hazel Plays Nurse
Hazel tries to keep George in bed when he comes down with a cold, de-spite the fact that he has to meet with an important client.

A Matter of Principle
George defends Hazel when she fights her ticket for overtime parking.

Dorothy's New Client
Hazel tries to get Dorothy a job redec-orating the home of their new neigh-bor.

What'll We Watch Tonight?
George buys Hazel a color TV set for her room so she won't interfere with the family's TV watching.

A Dog for Harold
Hazel tries to convince George to let Harold keep the dog he found.

George's Niece
GS: Davey Davidson, Cathy Lewis. Hazel gets George's niece a date with her nephew Eddy.

Everybody's Thankful but Us Turkeys
Hazel spends Thanksgiving dinner with the Baxters.

Winter Wonderland
Hazel tries to delay the family's trip to the Snowman's Lodge.

Hazel's Winning Personality
Hazel attends a class in personality improvement.

Hazel's Christmas Shopping
GS: Byron Foulger. Hazel works at a department store in order to earn the extra money needed to buy Dorothy a Christmas present.

Dorothy's Obsession
Dorothy tries to make her friend buy an antique desk at an auction.

Hazel's Dog Days
Harold is heartbroken when the owner of the dog he found comes to claim him.

A Replacement for Phoebe
Hazel tries to find a new maid for their neighbors.

Hazel's Famous Recipes
Hazel tries to sell her cookbook of her mother's recipes to a publisher.

Hazel's Tough Customer
Hazel tries to get Mr. Griffin to buy a house in their neighborhood so he won't be lonely.

Hazel's Secret Wish
Hazel goes to a rich resort for two weeks and proceeds to turn it upside down.

Hazel, the Tryst-Buster
GS: Kathie Browne. Hazel thinks George's old girlfriend, who has left her husband, wants to break up the

Baxter's marriage so she can have George for herself.

The Investment Club
A phony investment company tries to trick Hazel and her friends into buying some worthless stock.

Hazel's Mona Lisa Grin
George learns that the painting Hazel sold was very valuable.

Hazel and the Gardener
GS: O.Z. Whitehead. Hazel tries to prevent George from firing their old gardener.

Dorothy's Birthday
Hazel plans a surprise birthday dinner for Dorothy, unaware that George planned to take her out to dinner.

Number Please
GS: Vinton Hayworth. George orders an unlisted phone number.

Them New Neighbors Is Nice
The son of their new neighbor develops a crush on Dorothy.

Hazel's Pajama Party
Hazel tries to get George to give his permission for their 14-year-old neighbor to have her pajama party at their house.

Three Little Cubs
Hazel tries to get the snobbish son of a doctor to join the cub scouts.

Bringing Out the Johnsons
Hazel and the family try to get everyone out to vote.

Hazel Quits
Hazel quits her job in order to protect George's practice, when his client requests that he fire her.

Hazel the Matchmaker
GS: Doris Singleton, John Newton. Hazel tries to get Harold's teacher and their neighbor Mr. Blake together.

Rock-a-Bye Baby
Hazel takes care of a neighbor's baby until they can get a nurse.

The Burglar in Mr. B's PJs
GS: Alan Hale. Hazel helps a burglar who tried to break into the house.

Heat Wave
GS: Virginia Gregg. Hazel tries to get George to air condition the house.

George's Assistant
Hazel tries to get her friend's son a job as George's new assistant.

Hazel's Day
GS: Walter Woolf King. The family decides that they are going to celebrate Hazel Day, so they make plans to take her out for the evening.

Hazel's Cousin
When Hazel's niece plans to get married, her snobbish secretary tries to keep Hazel away from the wedding.

Rosie's Contract
GS: Richard St. John. George tries to keep Hazel from learning about Rosie's contract with her boss because he is afraid that Hazel will want one too.

We've Been So Happy Till Now
GS: Jonathan Hale. Hazel learns that the Baxters had a fight over her, so she tries to being them back together again.

How to Lure an Epicure
GS: Alan Hewitt, Peter Mamakos. Hazel tries to get her friend's restaurant some publicity to keep it in business.

Barney Hatfield, Where Are You?
Hazel thinks something bad has happened to their mailman when it appears that he disappeared.

. . . A Four-Bit Word to Chew On
Hazel causes Mr. Griffin to feel inferior, because of his lack of education, when Hazel starts using big words and George feels obligated to tell him what they mean.

Hazel's Tax Deduction
Hazel tries to help George get the tax refund he deserves when the tax investigator questions George's deductions.

Mr. B. on the Bench
GS: Willis Bouchey. George is offered the opportunity to become a judge when the appointed judge becomes ill and has to retire.

License to Wed
Hazel tries to discourage her nephew and George's niece from rushing into marriage.

Genie with the Light Brown Lamp
Harold believes an old gravy boat is a magic lamp which contains a genie who will return Harold's lost dog to him.

The Natural Athlete
GS: Bill Zuckert. George practices his bowling in order to beat Hazel in an upcoming tournament.

New Man in Town
GS: Robert Lowery. Hazel and Rosie both try to date the chauffeur of their new neighbors.

Herbert for Hire
Hazel tries to get George to get their neighbor Herbert a job with Mr. Griffin.

Hazel and the Love Birds
GS: Susan Silo. George's sister tries to break up her daughter's romance with Hazel's nephew.

Top Secret
GS: Larry Gates. Hazel takes a little girl to meet a visiting senator and accidentally leaves with some of his important papers.

The Sunshine Girls Quartette
Hazel and her friends plan to audition for a talent scout on the same night as the surprise party for Mr. Griffin.

A Good Example for Harold
GS: Phil Ober. Hazel makes everyone tell the truth in order to set a good example for Harold.

Hazel's Highland Fling
GS: James Doohan, Katherine Henryk. Mr. Griffin tries to get George to break the contract he signed when he hired a Scottish cook because she is a rotten cook.

Ain't Walter Nice?
GS: Frank Aletter. Hazel tries to get George to invest in her visiting nephew's get-rich-quick scheme.

Mr. Griffin Throws a Wedding
GS: Dick Sargent. Hazel helps Mr. Griffin arrange the wedding of his nephew and George's secretary.

Hazel and the Stockholders Meeting
GS: Max Showalter, Byron Foulger. When George buys a defective vacuum cleaner, Hazel, who owns stock in the company that made it, goes to the stockholders meeting to show them the defects in the machine.

Hazel's Day Off
GS: James Westerfield, William Schallert, Percy Helton. Hazel tries to get one of George's clients to relax and take it easy.

I Been Singing All My life
GS: Max Showalter. George's sister tries to keep Hazel from singing at a benefit show she is arranging.

The Fire's Never Dead While the Ashes Are Red
GS: Vaughn Taylor. Hazel tries to bring an author and his old girlfriend back together.

Hazel's Navy Blue Tug-Boats
GS: Ronald Long. Hazel finds that getting to an annual shoe sale is harder than she thought when she finds herself making some side trips along the way to the store.

The Hazel Walk
Hazel organizes a hike in order to pro-against the new highway ruining the beautiful Pocono Trail.

Hazel Digs a Hole for Herself
GS: Vinton Hayworth. Hazel sets George's mother up in the gardening and landscaping business when she finds that she needs an interest to be happy.

Hazel Sounds Her "A"
GS: Torin Thatcher. Hazel tries to prevent the daughter of Harold's music teacher from being fired by the new conductor of the local symphony.

Hazel's Luck
Hazel breaks a chain letter and bad things begin to happen.

Oh, My Aching Back
George tries to hide the fact he hurt his back from Hazel.

Maid of the Month
Hazel is selected as maid of the month by a national magazine.

So Long Brown Eyes
GS: Patrick McVey. Hazel's old boyfriend returns to ask Hazel to marry him.

Potluck ala Mode
GS: Phil Ober, Russell Collins. George tries to get Hazel out of the way so he can entertain a potential client without her interference.

An Example for Hazel
GS: Herb Vigran, Jack Bernardi. Hazel tries to get George's cousin to become independent.

Dorothy Takes a Trip
When Dorothy visits her sister, Hazel tries to keep George from fooling around behind her back.

You Ain't Fully Dressed Without a Smile
GS: Ellen Corby.   George is given a desk which might have belonged to Abraham Lincoln as a gift.

Cheerin' Up Mr. B.
Hazel tries to cheer up George while Dorothy is away visiting her sister.

Piccolo Mondo
Hazel's Italian boyfriend helps George speak to a non-English speaking Italian businessman whom he is helping close a business deal.

Hazel Scores a Touchdown
GS: Alan Hale, Willis Bouchey, John Archer.   Hazel tries to bring the two fighting owners of a football team together.

George's 32nd Cousin
GS: Diane Ladd.   Hazel tries to help George get rid of his distant cousin who has moved into the house.

The Baby Came C.O.D.
GS: Oliver McGowan, James Stacy. Hazel and George help a young law student whose wife is having a baby.

All Hazel Is Divided into Three Parts
GS: Douglas Dick. Hazel holds a charity auction to help some poor children in an Italian village.

The Vanishing Hero
GS: Leif Erickson.   George tries to help his old classmate get a job as an athletic coordinator for Mr. Griffin's company.

Call Me Harve
Hazel tries to get George and Mr. Griffin back together again, after she caused their break up.

The Retiring Milkman
GS: Sterling Holloway. Hazel tries to prevent an incompetent milkman from losing his job.

Hazel's Nest Egg
GS: Charles Herbert.   Hazel tries to

help Harold's friend pass his tests for membership in the boy scouts.

Hazel and the Halfback
GS: Frank Gifford. Hazel tries to get Frank Gifford to watch her put on a trick bowling exhibition at the bowling alley.

Hazel and the Model T
Hazel buys the Johnsons' old Model T car, which she later sells, to help George close a deal with a client.

Hot Potato ala Hazel
GS: Alice Pearce. Hazel tries to help the owner of a china shop and her friend get married.

Scheherazade and Her Frying Pan [Part 1]
GS: Roland Winters, Linda Watkins, Lou Krugman, Bobby Remsen. Hazel and her friend Gracie are held prisoner in the home of her gangster employer, where a meeting of top gangsters is being held.

Scheherazade and Her Frying Pan [Part 2]
GS: Roland Winters, Linda Watkins, Lou Krugman, Bobby Remsen. Hazel puts tranquilizers in the scrambled eggs that she serves to the gangsters. When they are all drugged, Hazel calls in the police.

The Fashion Show
GS: Reginald Gardiner. Hazel accidentally becomes a model in a fashion show when Dorothy sprains her ankle and is unable to appear.

George's Ordeal
Hazel puts George on a diet so he can lose ten pounds.

The Reluctant Witness
GS: John Archer.   Dorothy is being sued by a woman whose house she redecorated.

Democracy at Work
Hazel tries to convince George to give her a raise.

The Countess
Hazel learns that she might be an heir to the estate of a countess.

Hazel's Midas Touch
GS: Leo G. Carroll. George tries to get a rich man to donate his art collection to the art museum.

Everybody's a Comedian
George tries to convince Hazel that she needs glasses.

All Mixed Up
GS: Alan Hewitt, Jan Arvan. Hazel is selected to appear in a TV commercial as the spokeswoman for a cake mix.

Arrivederci, Mister B.
GS: Luciana Paluzzi. Hazel tries to help a non-English speaking Italian girl keep her baby when her husband goes into the Army and her rich mother-in-law tries to have the baby taken away from her.

Such a Nice Little Man
GS: Byron Foulger. George believes the Johnson's new handyman is a thief.

Campaign Manager
GS: Harold Gould, Phil Ober. Hazel convinces George to run for city councilman.

Let's Get Away from It All
GS: Jamie Farr, Bill Zuckert. Hazel and the family help the owner of an Italian restaurant, when his wife is going to have a baby, by working in the restaurant.

Maid for a Day
GS: Harvey Korman. Hazel coaches George's sister to be a maid in a play.

Never Trouble Trouble
GS: Robert Shayne, Harold Gould. George's cousin is suspected of robbing the Baxter house.

Luncheon with the Governor
GS: Oliver McGowan. The Governor comes to the Baxter house for lunch, where he is met by a student protest.

Ain't That a Knee Slapper
Hazel helps George arrange a business merger for Mr. Griffin.

The Marriage Trap
GS: Ken Berry. Hazel tries to bring George's secretary and her boyfriend back together after they have a fight.

The Flagpole
GS: Frank Cady. Hazel tries to get George to buy a flagpole to fly his gift flag from the Defense Department.

Welcome Back, Kevin
GS: Michael Callan, Jerry Dexter. Hazel tries to reconcile George's nephew and his wife accused of fooling around.

Mind Your Own Business
GS: Francine York. Hazel and George promise to keep out of each other's private business.

High Finance Hits a New Low
Hazel convinces George to help the Johnsons with financial problems.

Just Me, Harold and the Unisphere
GS: Woodrow Parfrey, Sue England. Hazel is contest finalist; winner gets a trip for two to the world's fair.

Mixup on Marshall Road
GS: Karen Steele, Ross Elliot. Hazel arranges to sell their neighbor's house to George's partner and his new bride.

Lesson in Diplomacy
GS: Oscar Homolka. The Baxter family are unaware that the Russian dignitary who is a guest in their home is really a phony sent to test them, to see if they are the right family to host the real Russian when he arrives.

To Build or Not to Build
Hazel tries to trick George into having the kitchen remodeled.

Better to Have Loved and Lost
Hazel unknowingly causes a fight between George's partner Harry and his wife.

Hazel Squares the Triangle
Hazel tries to get George's sister and her husband back together after they have a fight.

Just 86 Shopping Minutes to Christmas
Harry asks George to keep the mink coat he bought as a Christmas present for his wife in his house so his wife won't find it. Problems arise when Dorothy finds it and thinks it's for her.

Champagne Tony
GS: Tony Lema, Kathie Browne. Hazel causes problems when she goes to meet a famous golfer at the airport.

It's a Dog's World
Hazel tries to help the Baxters get rid of their unwanted guests and their untrained dog.

Love 'Em and Leave 'Em
Hazel escorts Harold and his date to the school dance.

Temper! Temper!
GS: Barbara Shelley. Hazel's boyfriend Enzio helps pacify a temperamental opera singer.

Bonnie Boy
GS: Willis Bouchey. Hazel buys a sweepstakes ticket to give to George as a present, unaware that he has been chosen by the mayor to join the committee investigating the sale of sweepstakes tickets.

Stop Rocking Our Reception
GS: Reginald Gardiner, William Bramley. George accuses his neighbor's short-wave radio of ruining his television reception.

What's Bugging Hazel?
GS: Jonathan Hole, Parley Baer. Hazel's friend Gus is accused of being a spy for a rival department store when he is caught with a bugging device by the store owner.

Hazel's Day in Court
GS: Hugh Marlowe, Charles Macaulay. Hazel finds herself in court when she paints a crosswalk in the street in front of their house.

Hazel's Inquisitive Mind
GS: Aki Aleong. Hazel tries to get the maid of their new neighbor to join her club, unaware that the maid is actually a Japanese houseboy.

George's Man Friday
GS: Paul Hartman, Harold Gould. Hazel gets a bumbling horse player a job as George's assistant.

The Investor
GS: John Banner. Hazel invests in a bakery in order to help the baker, whose wife has left him, when he refuses to sell the store.

Who's in Charge Here?
GS: Ernest Truex. While the Baxters are out of the country, Hazel goes to work for George's brother Steve. As soon as she moves in, she takes over the house.

Hazel's Second Week.
GS: Mala Powers. Hazel thinks Barbara is unhappy with her work so she decides to leave.

How to Lose 30 Pounds in 30 Minutes
Hazel signs up with a health spa to lose 30 pounds.

Do Not Disturb Occupants
GS: Oliver McGowan, Edith Atwater. Hazel tries to convince Steve not to sell his house.

The Hold Out
GS: Ellen Corby, James Westerfield. Hazel tries to get her old friend Minnie to sell her house and move into another house so an office building can be built on her property.

A-Haunting We Will Go
GS: Vaughn Taylor, Dabney Coleman. Hazel investigates a haunted house when its new owner threatens to sue Steve for selling them the house.

Hazel Needs a Car
GS: Mala Powers, James Westerfield. Hazel tries to con Steve into giving her the money she needs as a down payment on a car.

Hazel Sits It Out
GS: Mabel Albertson, Malcolm Atterbury. Hazel helps sell a house when Steve goes on a family picnic.

A "Lot" to Remember
GS: Anne Seymour. Hazel buys an unseen lot at a real estate auction.

A Bullseye for Cupid
GS: Mala Powers. Hazel tries to bring Barbara's friend Mona and her husband back together again.

The Crush
Steve's secretary Millie has a crush on him.

Kindly Advise
Steve's sister tries to get Barbara to send their daughter to an elocution school.

Noblesse Oblige
GS: Lee Patrick. Hazel mistakes a millionaire for a chauffeur and asks him to help her convince a rich woman to sponsor a historical pageant, unaware that the woman is his wife.

Hazel's Endearing Young Charms
Hazel tries to win Steve's acceptance by praising his brother George.

A Car Named Chrysanthemum
GS: Alvy Moore, Peter Brocco. Hazel buys a car from Millie and attempts to fix it up. When she fails to improve its looks, she tries to sell it.

Once an Actor
GS: Pat O'Brien. Barbara's uncle, a former actor, comes to stay with the Baxters.

$285 by Saturday
GS: Mala Powers. Hazel tries to raise enough money to buy an organ for the children of a missionary school.

Boom or Bust!
Steve puts the entire family on a budget to save money.

But Is It Art?
GS: Claude Akins. Hazel mistakes a famous artist for a house painter and gets him to paint her room.

Please Don't Shout
GS: Emil Sitka. Steve tries to sell a friend's house because it is too close to the highway and the noise is keeping him and his wife awake.

My Son the Sheepdog
Harold and his friends form a rock and roll band.

How to Find Work Without Really Trying
GS: Victor Jory. Hazel befriends an old man who lost interest in working after his wife died.

Harold's Gift Horses
GS: James Westerfield, Anne Seymour. Mr. Turner and Miss Kirkland both try to get Harold to spend some time with them.

Who Can Afford a Bargain?
Hazel tries to prevent Fred and Mona from buying a house that is too expensive for them.

Hazel's Free Enterprise
Hazel and Barbara try to sell Hazel's chili sauce in order to earn enough money to pay for the pool table Barbara ordered for Steve's birthday present.

Bee in Her Bonnet
GS: Guy Raymond. Steve helps a man who was forced off the road by an at-

tacking bee. When he learns that Steve is about to collect a lot of money from a business deal, the man tries to blame Steve for the accident and threatens to sue him for damages.

The Perfect Boss
Hazel enters Steve in the perfect boss contest.

A Little Bit of Genius
When Harold's friend Jeff is transferred to a class for bright students, Harold becomes depressed so Steve tries to get him interested in a hobby.

A Question of Ethics
GS: John Qualen. Steve is accused of using unfair tactics to steal a client away from another real estate agent, when Hazel tells a couple that they aren't getting enough money for their farm and that Steve can get them a better offer.

HE & SHE

On the air 9/6/67, off 9/18/68. CBS. 26 episodes. Color Film. Broadcast: Sept 1967-Sept 1968 Wed 9:30-10. Producer: Leonard Stern/Arnold Margolin. Prod Co: Talent Associates. Synd: Viacom-export only. Not syndicated in the United States.

CAST: Paula Hollister (played by Paula Prentiss), Dick Hollister (Richard Benjamin), Oscar North (Jack Cassidy), Harry Zarakardos (Kenneth Mars), Andrew Hummel (Hamilton Camp), Norman Nugent (Harold Gould).

The story of a successful cartoonist who draws the "Jetman" comic strip, his social worker wife and their nutty friends including Oscar North, an egotistical actor who portrays Jetman on television. The series is not syndicated in this country but it is still a unique and different series that should be remembered.

The Old Man and the She
GS: Charles Lane. Paula forces Dick into helping an old Greek gentleman from being deported.

The 2nd Time Around
The Hollisters plan a second wedding with all the fuss and formality they didn't have at the first one.

How to Fail in Business
GS: Herb Ellis, Dodo Denny. Dick and Paula buy their apartment building but regret it when the tenants complain constantly.

Phantom of 84th St.
GS: Jack Kruschen. Oscar's $65,000 Picasso is stolen from Dick and Paula's apartment.

One of Our Firemen Is Missing
Harry is fined for helping Dick and Paula when he should have been on duty.

Before You Bury Me Can I Say Something?
When Dick writes his will, Paula thinks Dick is dying.

Dick's Van Dyke
Dick plans to spend his vacation time painting, but he is constantly being interrupted.

The Background Man
GS: Julie Sommars, Tol Avery. Dick hires a girl to help him draw the Jetman comic strip. Unfortunately, all she can do is spill paint all over him.

Vote Yes or No
Paula pickets Dick's office because he is against a pay raise for firemen and she is for it.

He and She vs. Him
GS: Jane Dulo. Dick has run out of ideas for the comic strip and is about to be sued for plagiarism.

The Coming Out Party
GS: John Astin. Paula throws a party so she can match her friend up with a doctor. However, the doctor has plans to take out Dick's tonsils.

Deep in the Heart of Taxes
Dick is about to be audited by the IRS and Paula hasn't told him about all the money she won on the horses.

Don't Call Us
The Hollisters are having a problem getting an invitation to a party because they have just gotten an unlisted phone number.

North Goes West
Oscar insists that Dick and Paula move out to California with him and the Jetman series. So, they pack up and prepare to move out.

The Midgets from Broadway
The Jetman show is made into a musical comedy.

Poster Boy
A wanted poster of the neighborhood robber looks just like Andrew, the building handyman.

A Rock by Any Other Name
The Hollisters exchange birthday gifts: She gets a fur coat and He gets a rock, which he proceeds to lose.

Goodman, Spare That Tree
GS: Dick Curtis. Paula helps her cousin smuggle an Italian olive tree past customs. The big problem now is keeping the tree alive.

The White Collar Worker
The Hollisters prepare to confront the driver who hit Paula's car.

Along Came Kim
The Hollisters' Korean War orphan and foster son comes for a visit.

What Do You Get for the Man Who Has Nothing?
The Hollisters try to keep Harry out of his apartment for three days so they can redecorate it for a surprise birthday party.

Dog's Best Friend
GS: Larry Storch, Bonnie Scott. Dick and Paula watch as their close friends Bart and Myra split up.

It's Not Whether You Win or Lose, It's How You Watch the Game
Dick has to get 30 tickets to a football game in two days. He had promised his classmates they would hold the reunion at the game but he had forgotten to reserve the seats.

Knock, Knock. Who's There? Fernando. Fernando Who?
GS: Fernando Lamas. Harry jumps to the wrong conclusion when he finds Fernando Lamas massaging Paula's leg while Dick is out of town.

What's in the Kitty?
GS: Alice Ghostley, Harold Gould. The Hollisters' dinner party for Dick's boss is marred by a mouse, a sick cat and a poison scare.

HENNESEY

On the air 9/28/59, off 9/17/62. CBS. B&W Film. 96 episodes. Broadcast: Sept 1959-Sept 1962 Mon 10-10:30. Producer: Jackie Cooper. Prod Co: Jackie Cooper Prod. Synd: National Telefilm.
CAST: Chick Hennesey (played by Jackie Cooper), Martha (Abby Dalton), Capt. Shafer (Roscoe Karns), Max Bronski (Henry Kulky), Harvey Spencer Blair

(James Komack), Seaman Shotz (Arte Johnson), Dan Wagner (Herb Ellis), Owen King (Robert Gist), Pulaski (Norman Alden), Mrs. Shafer (Meg Wyllie).

The adventures of a Navy medical officer who found himself in the strangest situations. Popular for a while, but never has been repeated since the early 1960s.

Hennesey [Pilot]
Hennesey is assigned to report to the Navy base in San Diego.

Hennesey and Peyton Place
GS: Ruta Lee, Alan Dexter. An authoress joins the WAVES in order to write a book about the Navy.

Hennesey Meets Honeyboy
GS: Bobby Darin, Frank Gorshin, Norman Alden. A young singer is unhappy with the Navy and faces a dishonorable discharge for his bad behavior.

Hennesey Meets Harvey Spencer Blair III
GS: Raymond Bailey, Ross Ford. Harvey, the girl-chasing dentist, arrives at the base.

Hennesey Goes Home
Chick goes home on leave where he hears bad news about old Doc Hardy.

The Baby Sitter
No available story.

Shore Patrol
GS: Larry Storch, Stafford Repp. Chick is assigned to the shore patrol where he expects a quiet time until he learns that the fleet has landed.

Pork Chops and Applesauce
GS: Dick Wessel. Chick assigns a diet for all of the officers including the heavy-eating admiral.

Hennesey and the Lady Doctor
GS: Phyllis Coates. Chick helps a lady psychologist in a research project.

Hennesey Joins the Marines
GS: Ken Lynch, William Fawcett. Chick fills in for a doctor in a Marine unit.

Hennesey Meets Mrs. Horatio Grief
Chick is assigned to help an old dowager raise money for the Navy relief fund.

Harvey Blair Returns
Harvey goes wild causing the commander to take drastic action by sending him to Guam.

Hennesey Meets Fuji
GS: Fuji. Chick gets a Japanese wrestler to teach Seaman Peabody judo.

The Christmas Show
GS: Bartlett Robinson, Joseph Corey. Chick plans to organize a singing group to entertain the hospital patients, but the commander objects.

The Annapolis Man
GS: James Franciscus. Chick is ordered to find the brightest man to take a test for Annapolis.

Angel Face
GS: Doug McClure. A seaman recovering from bad burns has a bad attitude despite plastic surgery.

The Matchmaker
GS: Sue Randall, Meg Wyllie. Captain Shafer tries to get Chick and his daughter together.

Space Man
GS: Bob Hastings. Chick and Lt. Bolt are chosen to test applicants for the space program.

More of Harvey Spencer Blair
Harvey is flirting with the captain's wife.

Dr. Blair Again
Blair promises the admiral's wife he can get big stars to appear at a PTA fund raiser.

Hennesey and the Ancient Vehicle
Chick wins a replica of an early car in a contest.

Hello Cobra Leader
Chick is ordered to treat a young girl in a desolate area. He must get there in a broken-down helicopter with a nearsighted pilot.

Scarlet Woman in White
GS: Yvonne Craig. A beautiful nurse is disrupting the hospital.

Senior Nurse
Chick and the captain try to find out why the head nurse is so rough on the other nurses.

Hennesey Meets Mr. Wilkins
GS: Raymond Greenleaf, Rudi Solari. Chick and Martha visit an old corpsman in order to cover for the captain.

Which One Is Wagner?
GS: Lonie Blackman. Captain Shafer does not know who Wagner is, although he has been on his staff for two years.

Calling Dr. King
GS: Alan Reed, Kasey Rogers. Dr. King plans to give up medicine for art.

What Is Dr. Blair?
GS: King Calder. Harvey is against a transfer to field duty with the Marines.

We're Glad It's You
GS: John Stephenson, Ellen Corby. A TV producer wants to do Captain Shafer's life story.

Big Brother
Chick tries to break up a feud between two doctors who happen to be brothers.

Bonjour Mr. Hennesey
Chick and a Marine doctor are to represent the State Department at a medical convention in Paris.

Goodbye, Dr. Blair
Blair invents a jet-propelled dental drill.

Hennesey at La Gunn
GS: Charles Bronson. Chick helps an intelligence man look for stolen goods.

Tell It to the Chaplain
GS: Cecil Kellaway. Chick has been ordered to examine the ailing chaplain.

Hail to the Chief
Everybody expects Max to apply for the job of pharmacist's mate.

The Captain's Dilemma
When he makes a wrong diagnosis, the captain feels he is washed up as a doctor.

The Marriage of Dr. Blair
GS: Joan Marshall. Harvey is in trouble when a girl named Consuelo Maddox claims to be his wife.

Miss San Diego Navy
Chick and Max are called to judge a beauty contest.

Hennesey and the Submarine
No available story.

The Hat
GS: Chris Robinson, Howard McNear. Two young punks steal Chick's hat in a theater.

The Stutterer
GS: Richard Evans. Max and his friend Rocco try to keep two seamen from tormenting a seaman who stutters.

The Underfed Fullback
The Navy's star fullback refuses to show up for practice because he doesn't like the coach or the Navy.

Come Home Dr. Rogers
Chick tries to get a former Navy doctor back into the service.

Harvey's Horse
GS: Jack Grimes. Harvey buys an old race horse.

The Reunion
Chick chooses to meet his old service

friends instead of going to the New Year's Eve party at the base.

The Promotion
GS: Bob Hastings. Chick tries to get a promotion for Captain Shafer.

Join the Navy, Please
Chick goes to a medical school to recruit more Navy doctors.

The Specialist
GS: Robert Culp, Marty Ingels. Chick is jealous of a handsome orthopedic surgeon.

Hennesey vs. Crandall
GS: Jean Allison. Chick doesn't get along with a visiting female pediatrician.

Max Remembers Papa
GS: Vladimir Sokoloff. Max's visiting father tries to find his son a wife.

The Apartment
GS: Ellen Corby, Joey Faye. Chick moves to an apartment but it has a nosy landlady.

Harvey's Doll
Harvey's voodoo doll of the captain is causing the captain real pains.

The Novelist
GS: Milton Frome. Chick decides to write a novel and Wagner wants to sell it to the movies.

Harvey and His Electric Money Machine
GS: Olan Soule. Harvey invents a machine which causes a counterfeit Treasury Agent to come to the base.

Admiral and Son
GS: William Schallert. The admiral's son is being transferred to Japan just as his wife is going to have a baby.

The Wedding
GS: Alan Reed, Arte Johnson, Marge Redmond. Chief Rocco and WAVE Eva Jackson are engaged, then she breaks off the engagement, ruining the captain's plans to give them a party.

The Green-Eyed Monster
Chick planned to spend the weekend with Martha, but she is going skiing with her friend Gloris who is bringing a man along for her.

Harvey's Pad
GS: Arte Johnson, George Takei. Harvey lets Chick rest up at his beachhouse.

His Honor, Dr. Blair
GS: Donna Douglas. Harvey plans to run for Mayor of San Diego.

The Nogoodnick
GS: Charles Bronson, Alan Reed. Seaman Pierce is wounded escaping from the brig.

The Patient Vanishes
GS: Marty Ingels, Karl Lukas. Chick's patient disappears from the hospital and he has until nightfall to find him or else.

Shore Patrol Revisited
GS: Mickey Rooney, Stafford Repp, Ken Berry. Chick is assigned to shore duty again. This time a sailor carrying a saxophone arrives to disturb Chick's peace.

The Sign Over
GS: Norman Fell. Chick's tour of duty is ending and he wants out of the Navy despite his freinds asking him to stay.

A Star Is Born
GS: Jean Byron. Chick is ordered to help a movie star who accidentally injures herself.

Aloha Dr. Hennesey
Martha lets Chick go to Hawaii, but changes her mind at the last minute.

Aunt Sarah
GS: Gertrude Berg, Arte Johnson. Mrs. Green comes to the base worried about her nephew Seymour's hay

fever. [This is a crossover episode from "Mrs. G. Goes to College."]

The Best Man
It is rumored that the captain is getting a promotion to the Surgeon General's office in Washington.

The Bicep Caper
GS: Gordon Jones. Chick decides to take up boxing again but forgot he put on weight since he last fought.

Big Bertha
Corpsman Bertha Bartosik is breaking everything in sight.

Buttons and Bones
GS: Jack Carter. Chick enrolls in a speech class to get more confidence and poise.

Calling Dr. Good-Deed
The admiral tells Chick to stop meddling in other people's affairs.

Close Enough for Jazz
GS: Les Brown and his band, Bill Peterson, Eddie Quillan. Chick finds an old friend is playing with Les Brown's band.

The Cohen Mutiny
GS: Mark Todd, Milton Frome. Chick is assigned as defense counselor for Seaman Herbert Cohen.

Get Me Clyde Dingle
Chick plays the stock market against Martha's wishes.

Going Home
GS: Ed Nelson, Grace Lee Whitney. Chick and Martha visit the ejection seat training area at the air base before going home.

The Gossip-Go-Round
Everybody thinks Chick is writing a Broadway show, but he is only doing a medical paper.

Harvey and the Ring
GS: William Schallert. Harvey offers to help Chick get an engagement ring for Martha.

Harvey's Pills
Harvey invents a pill that makes movie stars appear before your eyes.

Hennessey Meets Soupy Sales
GS: Soupy Sales. Chick gets a pie in the face when he goes to pick up Soupy Sales, who is going to appear at the base hospital.

The Hobby
Chick takes up painting as a hobby.

The Holdout
GS: Arch Johnson. A young patient refuses to take part in a birthday party at the hospital.

Hystersis Synchronous Can Be Fun
GS: James Lydon. Chick buys an elaborate hi-fi for the admiral, but can he figure out how to work it?

I Thee Wed
GS: Jack Cassidy. Chick and Martha get married.

Little Girl
GS: Karen Balkin, Jane Dulo. A little girl finds her way on to the base.

The Man in the Crow's Nest
GS: Richard Evans, Stafford Repp. Chick, suffering a hangover, is called to help a sailor on board a destroyer.

Martha
Martha suffers from lapses of memory.

My Daughter the Nurse
GS: Rosemary La Planche. Chick's father-in-law comes for a visit.

No Down Payment
GS: Henry Corden. Chick and Martha plan and buy a house.

The Old Pro
GS: Bill Zuckert, Vivi Janiss. Chick's old high school football coach is a patient at the hospital.

Patti's Tune
GS: Jaye P. Morgan. Lt. Alexander takes Chick to a party where he meets a jazz singer.

Professional Sailor
GS: Don Rickles. Chief Petty Officer Schmidt plans to re-enlist after 24 years in the Navy.

Remember Pearl Harbor?
GS: Roy Barcroft, John Astin. Chick and Martha are invited aboard the fleet commander's ship on Pearl Harbor Day.

Santa Hits Harvey
GS: Hoke Howell. Captain Shafer is picked to play Santa at the staff Christmas party.

The Sightseers
GS: Bella Bruck, Sid Clute. Chick and Martha plan a list of what they are going to see in Hawaii, including a restaurant recommended by Bronski.

Tight Quarters
GS: Sammy Davis, Jr., Buck Kartalian. Chick is assigned to a submarine where he meets frogman Cannonball Pipper.

Welcome Home, Dr. Blair
GS: Steven Marlo, Freeman Lusk. Dr. Blair signs on for another hitch because his inheritance won't arrive for a few years yet.

HERE'S LUCY

On the air 9/23/68, off 9/2/74. CBS. Color Film. 144 episodes. Broadcast: Sept 1968-Sept 1971 Mon 8:30-9; Sept 1971-Sept 1974 Mon 9-9:30. Producer: Garry Morton. Prod Co: Universal/Lucille Ball Prod. Synd: Telepictures Corp.

CAST: Lucy Carter (played by Lucille Ball), Kim Carter (Lucy Arnaz), Craig Carter (Desi Arnaz, Jr.), Harrison Carter (Gale Gordon), Mary Jane Lewis (Mary Jane Croft).

The crazy adventures of Lucy Carter and her two kids and her brother-in-law boss. A big hit when on the network but it has proven to be the weakest of Lucille Ball's three series. It has not done very well in syndication and it is often run in the middle of the night or in mid-afternoon.

Mod Mod Lucy
Lucy gets Kim and Craig's rock band a playdate, but when Kim loses her voice, Lucy takes her place as the band's singer.

Lucy Visits Jack Benny
GS: Jack Benny, Jackie Gleason [as Ralph Kramden]. Lucy rents a room from Jack Benny and has to pay for everything else.

Lucy, the Process Server
GS: Reta Shaw, Jonathan Hole. While in a department store, Lucy tries to serve a summons and loses Harry's money instead.

Lucy and Miss Shelley Winters.
GS: Shelley Winters. Lucy is hired to stop a famous actress from overeating.

Lucy the Conclusion Jumper
GS: Jack Donahue, Don Crichton. Lucy thinks Kim is going to run off and elope.

Lucy's Impossible Mission
GS: Joseph Ruskin, Jack Collins, Richard Derr. The Carters impersonate Middle Eastern royalty in order to get a roll of microfilm from the shoe of an Eastern ambassador.

Lucille Ball and Ricardo Montalban in the "Lucy and Her Prince Charming" episode of Here's Lucy.

Lucy and Eva Gabor
GS: Eva Gabor. A famous writer, Eva von Gronnitz, stays with Lucy in order to get peace and quiet so she can finish writing her new book.

Lucy's Birthday
Kim and Craig try to find a gift to give Lucy on her birthday.

Lucy Sells Craig to Wayne Newton
GS: Wayne Newton. Lucy pushes Wayne Newton to use Craig as a drummer in his show.

Lucy's Working Daughter
GS: Barbara Morrison, Karen Norris. Lucy tries to help out Kim when she gets a job as a salesgirl.

Guess Who Owes Lucy $23.50
GS: Van Johnson. Lucy gets Van Johnson to sing to a cow for one of Harry's rich clients.

Lucy, the Matchmaker
GS: Vivian Vance, Rhodes Reason. Lucy's old friend Vivian turns up as Harry's computer date.

Lucy and the Gold Rush
Kim and Craig bring home a rock containing gold, causing Harry and Lucy to get gold fever.

Lucy the Fixer
Lucy wrecks Harry's house when she tries to repair a light switch.

Lucy and the Ex-Con
GS: Wally Cox, Bruce Gordon. Lucy and a reformed safecracker try to catch the crooks who just framed him for a robbery.

Lucy Goes on Strike
GS: Mary Wickes, Whit Bissell. Lucy organizes a strike with her secretary friends when Harry won't give her a raise.

Lucy and Carol Burnett
GS: Carol Burnett. Carol Burnett is trapped into doing a benefit show for the high school.

Lucy and the Great Airport Chase
GS: Sid Haig, Larry Duran, Walter Janowitz, Albert Reed. Lucy is chased by two spies when she is given a secret formula from a dying scientist.

A Date for Lucy
GS: Cesar Romero. Lucy's high society date is also a jewel thief.

Lucy the Shopping Expert
Lucy wrecks the supermarket where Craig is working when she tries to show Kim how to shop.

Lucy Gets Her Man
GS: Victor Buono. Lucy goes undercover to get evidence on a foreign spy.

Lucy's Safari Man
GS: Howard Keel, Janos Prohaska. Lucy, her family, and a professional hunter search for an escaped Gorbonna which is half gorilla and half baboon.

Lucy and Tennessee Ernie Ford
GS: Tennessee Ernie Ford. Lucy puts on a TV musical to help Ernie get some farmhands.

Lucy Helps Craig Get a Driver's License
GS: Jack Gilford. Lucy is driving Craig and everyone at the bureau, including the nervous inspector, crazy.

Lucy Goes to the Air Force Academy [Part 1]
GS: Roy Roberts, Frank Marth. Lucy wants Craig to look over the academy, but she proceeds to wreck the place.

Lucy Goes to the Air Force Academy [Part 2]
GS: Roy Roberts. Lucy is caught on a runaway floor polisher.

Lucy and the Indian Chief
GS: Paul Fix, Mickey Manners. Lucy unknowingly marries an Indican Chief.

Lucy Runs the Rapids
In Arizona, Lucy and the family get trapped on a life raft going down the rapids.

Lucy and Harry's Tonsils
GS: Mary Wickes. Harry is a nervous wreck between a tonsil operation and Lucy's efforts to make him comfortable.

Lucy and the Andrews Sisters
GS: Patty Andrews. Lucy and Kim join Patty in recreating the act.

Lucy's Burglar Alarm
GS: Guy Marks, Elliott Reid. Craig invents a burglar alarm after a crook steals their TV set.

Lucy at the Drive-In Movie
GS: Jackie Joseph. Lucy and Harry dress up as hippies in order to spy on Kim and her date at the drive-in.

Lucy and the Used Car Dealer
GS: Milton Berle. A used car dealer sells a lemon to the kids and it is up to Lucy to get their money back.

Lucy the Cement Worker
GS: Paul Winchell. Lucy loses a valuable heirloom in a batch of wet cement.

Lucy and Johnny Carson
GS: Johnny Carson, Ed McMahon. Lucy goes to the Johnny Carson Show.

Lucy and the Generation Gap
GS: Victor Sen Yung. Harry and Lucy help Kim and Craig put on a show about the generation gap through the ages.

Lucy and the Bogie Affair
GS: Jack La Lanne. The kids bring home a sheep dog who gives birth to nine puppies.

Lucy Protects Her Job
GS: Robert Carson. Lucy thinks she will lose her job, so she gets Kim to stop Harry from replacing her.

Lucy the Helpful Mother
Lucy helps Craig and Kim build model airplanes, and watch a zoo full of animals, so they can afford another phone.

Lucy and Liberace
GS: Liberace. Lee lends Craig a candelabra and Lucy thinks it's stolen and tries to put it back.

Lucy the Laundress
GS: James Hong, Heather Lee. Lucy is working in a Chinese laundry to pay for the damage she did to the owner's truck.

Lucy and Lawrence Welk
GS: Lawrence Welk, Vivian Vance. Lucy promises Viv she will meet Lawrence Welk, but Lucy doesn't know him.

Lucy and Viv Visit Tijuana
GS: Vivian Vance, Don Diamond, Don Megowan. A shop owner gets Viv, Lucy and Harry to unknowingly smuggle diamonds across the border.

Lucy and Ann Margret
GS: Ann Margret. Ann helps Craig by letting him appear and sing his song on her TV special.

Lucy and Wally Cox
GS: Wally Cox, Alan Hale. Lucy arranges for a timid man to become a

hero when he joins her on warehouse guard duty.

Lucy and Wayne Newton
GS: Wayne Newton. Lucy and the family visit Wayne at his ranch.

Lucy Takes Over
Lucy finds an IOU from Harry's ancestor to her ancestor, which means Harry owes her $138,000.

Lucy and Carol Burnett
GS: Carol Burnett, Robert Alda. Lucy and Carol enter the Miss Secretary Beautiful contest.

Lucy Meets the Burtons
GS: Elizabeth Taylor, Richard Burton. Lucy gets Liz's ring stuck on her finger and can't get it off.

Lucy the Sky Diver
GS: Rhodes Reason. Lucy takes up sky diving.

Lucy and Sammy Davis, Jr.
GS: Sammy Davis, Jr., Elliot Reid. Sammy regrets letting Lucy visit him on the set of his new movie.

Lucy and the Drum Contest
GS: Buddy Rich, Richard Yniguez. Lucy tries to get Buddy Rich to coach Craig in order to win a drum contest.

Lucy's Vacuum
GS: Charles Nelson Reilly, Jerome Cowan. Lucy crusades against the company that won't replace her defective vacuum cleaner.

Lucy the Coed
GS: Robert Alda, Marilyn Maxwell. Lucy and the kids help Harry put on a 1920s show for his class reunion.

Lucy the American Mother
Craig makes a documentary about a day in the life of an average mother, starring Lucy in the title role.

Lucy's Wedding Party
GS: Bruce Gordon, Paul Picerni. Lucy

lets a friend use the vacationing Harry's house for a Greek wedding reception.

Lucy Cuts Vincent's Price
GS: Vincent Price. Lucy buys a painting at an auction and takes it to Vincent Price to get it appraised, only to be mistaken for an actress in his new horror film.

Lucy and the Diamond Cutter
GS: Wally Cox, Ruth McDevitt. Harry hires a diamond cutter to cut a famous stone, but he needs peace and quiet to work so he moves in with Lucy.

Lucy and Jack Benny's Biography
GS: Jack Benny, George Burns. Jack Benny tells his life story with Lucy playing all the female parts.

Lucy and Rudy Vallee
GS: Rudy Vallee. Lucy tries to turn Rudy into a rock singer.

Lucy, Part-Time Wife
Harry asks Lucy to act as his pregnant wife to get rid of an old girlfriend.

Lucy and Ma Parker
GS: Carole Cook, Billy Curtis, Jerry Maren, Stafford Repp. Lucy gets mixed up with a dangerous woman counterfeiter and her two midget assistants when they move in next door.

Lucy Stops a Marriage
GS: Jayne Meadows. Lucy tries to keep Harry from marrying a wealthy widow for her money.

Lucy Loses Her Cool
GS: Parley Baer. Lucy tries to get herself fired in order to get some time off.

Lucy and the 20-20 Vision
Lucy tries to trick Harry into getting glasses.

Lucy and the Raffle
GS: Hayden Rorke. The Carters stage a raffle to pay the taxes on the car Kim won in a raffle.

Lucy's House Guest Harry
Harry moves in with Lucy while his house is being redecorated and his habits are driving Lucy wild.

Lucy the Crusader
GS: Carol Burnett, Jack Benny, Richard Deacon. Lucy and Carol stage a show starring unemployed actors to raise money for themselves.

Lucy and Aladdin's Lamp
GS: Robert Foulk, George Neise. Lucy's brass cigarette lighter is granting her every request.

Lucy Goes Hawaiian [Part 1]
GS: Vivian Vance, Robert Alda, Jean Byron. Lucy works her way to Hawaii on an ocean liner as a social director.

Lucy Goes Hawaiian [Part 2]
GS: Vivian Vance, Robert Alda. Lucy gives hula lessons and prepares a big show on board the ship.

Lucy and Flip Go Legit
GS: Flip Wilson. Lucy gets Flip to appear as Prissy in a theater group's version of "Gone With the Wind."

Lucy the Mountain Climber
GS: Tony Randall, Janos Prohaska. Lucy goes up against a health fanatic in a mountain-climbing contest.

Lucy and Harry's Italian Bombshell
GS: Kaye Ballard. Harry is waiting to see his Italian girlfriend he met during the war.

Lucy and Mannix Are Held Hostage
GS: Mike Conners, Marc Lawrence, John Doucette. Lucy is being chased by two bank robbers whom she saw leaving the bank.

Lucy and the Astronauts
GS: Roy Roberts, Robert Hogan. Lucy is put into quarantine with the returning Astronauts.

Lucy Makes a Few Extra Dollars
GS: Gary Morton. Lucy gets several

jobs in order to earn more money.

Someone's on the Ski Lift with Dinah
GS: Dinah Shore. Dinah is stuck at the same ski resort with Lucy.

Lucy and Her All-Nun Band
GS: Freddy Martin, Mary Wickes, Lew Parker. Lucy tries to book a band for a hospital benefit.

Ginger Rogers Comes to Tea
GS: Ginger Rogers. Lucy invites Ginger over for tea. [This episode was rehearsed and filmed in one day, instead of the usual four days, due to a possible actors' strike.]

Lucy and the Celebrities
GS: Rich Little, Jack Benny. Rich does some famous voices for an endorsement of the employment agency.

Won't You Calm Down Dan Dailey
GS: Dan Dailey. Lucy goes to work as Dan Dailey's secretary.

Lucy Helps David Frost Go Night Night
GS: David Frost, Ivor Barry. Lucy is hired to keep passengers from disturbing David's nap while flying to London.

Lucy in the Jungle
Lucy and Harry go to the African jungle on a vacation when she agrees to swap houses with the African homeowner.

Lucy and Candid Camera
GS: Allen Funt. Lucy and Harry appear as musical bankrobbers on "Candid Camera," or so they think.

Lucy's Lucky Day
Lucy has to train a chimp as a stunt on a TV giveaway show.

Lucy's Bonus Bounces
GS: Parley Baer. Harry gives Lucy an unexpected $50 bonus.

Lucy and the Little Old Lady
GS: Helen Hayes. An Irish little old

lady pulls a con game on Lucy.

Lucy and the Chinese Curse
GS: Keye Luke. Lucy saves the life of a laundryman, which makes her eternally responsible for him.

Lucy's Replacement
GS: R.G. Brown. Harry is trying to replace Lucy with a computer.

Kim Moves Out
GS: Tim Matheson. Kim moves to her own place but Lucy is still doing the cleaning and the cooking.

Lucy Sublets the Office
GS: Wally Cox, Richard Deacon. Lucy sublets the office to a toy distributor who has turned the office into a playroom.

Lucy's Punctured Romance
GS: Bob Cummings. Kim tries to break up Lucy's romance by trying to convince her suitor that the whole family is nuts.

With Viv as a Friend Who Needs an Enemy?
GS: Vivian Vance. Viv replaces Lucy in the office.

Kim Finally Cuts You Know Who's Apron Strings
GS: Alan Oppenheimer, Susan Tolsky. Kim moves into her own apartment where the landlord is uncle. [This was a pilot for a series that didn't sell.]

Lucy's Big Break
GS: Lloyd Bridges. Lucy breaks her leg while skiing and winds up in the hospital with a handsome doctor.

Lucy and Eva Gabor Are Hospital Roommates
GS: Eva Gabor, R.G. Brown, Mary Wickes. Lucy and her friends are driving her roommate Eva Gabor crazy.

Harrison Carter, Male Nurse
Harry plays nurse to the bedridden Lucy when she goes home from the hospital.

A Home Is Not an Office
GS: Susan Tolsky. Lucy tries to get rid of Harry who turns her home into a temporary office.

Lucy and Joe Namath
GS: Joe Namath. Joe helps Craig play football.

The Case of the Reckless Wheelchair
GS: Jesse White, Harry Hickox. Lucy is charged with reckless wheelchair driving by a shyster lawyer.

Lucy the Other Woman
GS: Totie Fields, Herbie Faye. The milkman's wife thinks Lucy is playing around with her husband.

Lucy and Petula Clark
GS: Petula Clark, Claude Wolfe, Tommy Farrell. Lucy becomes an over-protective secretary to pregnant Petula Clark.

Lucy and Jim Bailey
GS: Jim Bailey, Mayor Sam Yorty. Female impersonator Jim Bailey steps in when Phyllis Diller can't appear at a benefit show.

Dirtie Gertie
GS: Craig Stevens, Bruce Gordon, Hal Smith. Lucy plays an old drinking apple peddler in order to help capture a gangster.

Lucy and Donny Osmond
GS: Donny Osmond, Eve Plumb. Donny falls for an older woman: Kim.

Lucy and Her Prince Charming
GS: Ricardo Montalban. A foreign prince wants to marry Lucy.

My Fair Buzzi
GS: Ruth Buzzi. Lucy tries to make a shy, unattractive girl beautiful.

Lucy and the Group Encounter
GS: Kurt Kasznar. Lucy and Harry take group encounter therapy in order to release their hostile feelings.

Goodbye Mrs. Hips
Lucy and her friends go on a diet, but can't resist the gourmet meal in her freezer.

Lucy Is Really in a Pickle
GS: Dick Patterson. Lucy and Kim appear as pickles in a TV commercial.

Lucy Goes on Her Last Blind Date
GS: Don Knotts. Lucy's blind date is a visiting country boy who tries to become a Hollywood swinger.

Lucy and Her Genuine Twimby
GS: Bob Cummings. Bob tries to recover an antique chair Lucy bought from him by accident.

Lucy Goes to Prison
GS: Elsa Lanchester. Lucy becomes the roommate to a dizzy old bankrobber in order to find out where she hid her loot.

Lucy and the Professor
GS: John Davidson, Murray Matheson. Lucy mistakes an old man for Kim's young music teacher whom she has a crush on.

Lucy and the Franchise Fiasco
Lucy and Harry buy an ice cream stand and Lucy wears a penguin suit as a publicity stunt.

Lucy and Uncle Harry's Pot
Lucy tries to replace a valuable vase she accidentally broke.

The Not-So-Popular Mechanics
GS: Robert Rockwell. Lucy wrecks Harry's antique car while trying to give it a tuneup.

Lucy and Harry's Memoirs
Flashbacks of previous episodes are used when Lucy and Harry get drunk after he sells the business.

The Big Game
GS: O.J. Simpson, Tom Kelly. Harry is involved in ticket scalping to a sold-out USC game.

Lucy the Peacemaker
GS: Steve Lawrence and Edie Gorme. Lucy helps bring fighting Steve and Edie back together again.

Lucy and Danny Thomas
GS: Danny Thomas, Hans Conreid. Lucy helps a frustrated artist sell his work by helping him die.

Lucy the Wealthy Widow
GS: Ed McMahon, Henry Beckman. Harry needs Lucy's help in order to get a business loan from the bank.

The Bow Wow Boutique
GS: Bob Williams and his dogs. Lucy helps out at a dog beauty parlor.

Lucy Gives Eddie Albert the Old Song and Dance
GS: Eddie Albert. Eddie agrees to do Lucy's show because he mistook her for a crazy lunatic.

Lucy's Tenant
GS: Jackie Coogan, Rhodes Reason. Lucy tries to get an obnoxious tenant to move out of her house.

Lucy and Andy Griffith
GS: Andy Griffith. Lucy and Kim help a charity worker raise money for a youth camp.

Lucy and Joan Rivers Do Jury Duty
GS: Joan Rivers. Lucy is the only juror who is delaying the verdict.

Tipsy Through the Tulips
GS: Foster Brooks. Lucy is a secretary to a famous writer who also likes to drink.

The Carters Meet Frankie Avalon
GS: Frankie Avalon. Lucy gets Frankie to appear with Kim as Sonny and Cher in a contest.

Lucy Plays Cops and Robbers
GS: Gary Crosby, Dick Sargent, Al Lewis, Mary Wickes. Lucy gets to play a cop when she joins the neighborhood burglar watch.

Harry Catches Gold Fever
GS: J. Pat O'Malley, Janos Prohaska. Harry tries to keep all of the gold for himself when he and Lucy strike gold.

Lucy and Chuck Conners Have a Surprise Slumber Party
GS: Chuck Conners, Ryan McDonald. Chuck rents Lucy's house to shoot a movie.

Lucy Is a Bird Sitter
GS: Arte Johnson. Lucy birdsits for a valuable ruby-throated Weehawk for a famous ornithologist.

Meanwhile Back at the Office
GS: Don Porter, George Chandler. Harry sells the business, but gets the new owner, himself and Lucy mixed up in a bookie joint.

Lucy is N.G. as R.N.
GS: Roy Roberts, Al Checco. Lucy plays nurse to Harry's sprained knee, Mary Jane's broken fingers, and a cat who is going to have kittens.

Lucy the Sheriff
GS: Cliff Osmond, Mary Wickes, Ross Elliot. In a western town, Lucy is made sheriff for a day and encounters two robbers.

Milton Berle Is the Life of the Party
GS: Milton Berle, Elliot Reid. Lucy wins Milton Berle in a TV charity auction to entertain at her party.

Mary Jane's Boyfriend
GS: Cliff Norton, John Gabriel. Mary Jane's boyfriend has the hots for Lucy.

Lucy and Phil Harris Strike Up the Band
GS: Phil Harris. Lucy and Phil Harris put together a big band concert made up of ethnic musicians.

Lucy Carter Meets Lucille Ball
GS: Garry Morton, Tom Kelly. Lucy and Kim enter a Lucille Ball Lookalike Contest with Lucille as the judge.

THE HERO

On the air 9/8/66, off 1/5/67. NBC. 30 min. film. Color. 16 episodes. Broadcast: Sept 1966-Jan 1967 Thu 9:30-10. Producer: Leonard Stern. Prod Co: Talent Artists. Not syndicated.

CAST: Sam Garret (played by Richard Mulligan), Ruth Garret (Mariette Hartley), Paul Garret (Bobby Horan), Fred Gilman (Victor French), Burton Gilman (Joey Baio), Dewey (Marc London).

The misadventures of Sam Garret, a bumbling fool who portrays a heroic law enforcer on the fictitious television series "Jed Clayton, US Marshal." Episodes revolve around his attempts to conceal his real life from his fans. Not seen anywhere because only 16 episodes were produced.

A Night to Remember to Forget
GS: Chuck Conners. Sam has to find a way to attend his son's play and the TV Guide Awards banquet at the same time.

The Big Return of Little Eddie
GS: Harvey Korman. Sam's old friend, an actor turned insurance salesman, comes to town in order to get back into show business.

Pardon Me, But Your Party's Showing
GS: Joseph Perry. Sam forgets to invite Fred to his party, so he tries to hide it from him.

Curiosity Killed a Key
GS: Ned Glass. Sam and Fred try to find out where the key Ruth found while redecorating fits. They find it is the house key of a beautiful blonde.

Rumble without a Cause
GS: Allen Jaffe, Paul Smith. Sam is appointed the chairman of the anti-violence on TV committee.

The Kid's Revenge
GS: Paul Brinegar. An 84-year-old gunslinger challenges Sam to a shoot-out when he dislikes the way Sam had him portrayed on his show.

The Matchbreaker
GS: Ron Husmann, Laurel Goodwins. Sam lets an actor use his apartment to rehearse. Ruth arranges a date for him with Sam's niece.

The Day They Shot Sam Garretta
GS: Phil Leeds, Charles Aidman. A journalist comes to visit Sam in order to see how much of a hero he is off the set.

If You Loved Me, You'd Hate Me
GS: Charles Holt. Ruth is jealous of Sam's old girlfriend who has a kissing part in Sam's show. Matters get worse when they are handcuffed together and can't get apart.

The Universal Language
GS: Kurt Kasznar. Sam gives a part to a famous Mexican actor—who can't speak a word of English.

I Wouldn't Wish It on a Dog
Fred becomes a pest when his dog wins an audition at Sam's studio.

The Truth Never Hurts . . . Much
GS: Shelley Berman, Dick Wilson. Sam takes a pain reliever prior to a talk show appearance. When he falls asleep, his friends give him pep pills to

wake him up, causing strange results when he goes on the show.

Who Needs a Friend in Need?
GS: Maureen Arthur. Fred gets Sam mixed up in a scheme to sell ladies' hair dryers.

I Have a Friend
GS: Bernie Kopell. Sam helps out his friend who owns a nightclub which is in financial trouble by helping him

prepare a show which will raise some money.

My Favorite Father
Fred gets upset when his kids find Sam more interesting than he is when they all go on a camping trip together.

The Terribly Talented Trayton Tyler Taylor
GS: Joel Fabiani, Mickey Manners. Sam tries to help a pinball-addicted writer finish a script for his show.

HEY LANDLORD

On the air 9/11/66, off 5/14/67. NBC. Color film. 31 episodes. Broadcast: Sept 1966-May 1967 Sun 8:30-9. Producer: Garry Marshall. Prod Co/Synd: United Artists TV.

CAST: Woody Banner (played by Will Hutchins), Chuck Hookstratten (Sandy Baron), Timothy Morgan (Pamela Rodgers), Kyoko Mitsui (Miko Mayama), Jack Ellenhorn (Michael Constantine).

The story of a naive young bachelor from Ohio who comes to New York to manage an old brownstone left to him by his uncle. He shares his apartment with a streetwise rising comic and, together with the usual help from his crazy tenants, gets into all kinds of trouble. The series was run for a while on local stations but it has since disappeared.

If She Catches the Bouquet, I'll Die
GS: Marian Hailey. Chuck's girlfriend is becoming possessive and overprotective of him.

Pursuit of a Dream
GS: Eileen O'Neil. Woody decides he must meet the girl he saw in a poster.

From Out of the Past Come the Thundering Hoofbeats
GS: Rob Reiner, Bobby Byles, Robert Liep. Woody is overcome by nostalgia when he finds his old childhood radio in the basement. He now insists on restoring the old relic.

The Daring Duo vs. the Incredible Captain Kill
GS: Dave Ketchum, Richard Stahl, Paul Reed. Woody and Chuck's script for a talking toy crow could get Woody a job for a toy company.

Instant Family
GS: Jeanne Bal, Ann Doran, Peter Whitney. Woody makes a date with a divorcee with two children.

The Shapes of Wrath
GS: Sid Melton, Henry Corden, Monroe Arnold, Bella Bruck. Jack tells Woody that he may have hired someone to kill Chuck.

Chuck Nobody
GS: Naomi Stevens, Jane Dulo. Chuck's old babysitter tells him that he was adopted.

The Long Hot Bus
GS: Jack Albertson, Herb Edelman, Stuart Margolin. Woody's bus-driving uncle drives his bus from Miami to New York for a visit.

Safari
GS: Larry Hankin, Leigh French, Jes-

sica Myerson. Chuck and Woody look for girls while on a swinging night in New York City.

When You Need a Hidden Room You Can Never Find One
GS: Hamilton Camp. Woody and Chuck search for a hidden room containing treasures belonging to Woody's uncle.

Divorce Bachelor Style
GS: Naomi Stevens, Dave Ketchum. Chuck goes home to mother while Woody looks for a new roommate.

Sizzling Sidney
GS: Hal March, Kay Reynolds, Arnold Margolin. Woody is trying to date a pretty secretary, but her playboy boyfriend doesn't like it.

The Big Fumble
GS: Peter Bonerz, Ron Husmann. Woody recalls his college days when he was nearly expelled for a hazing stunt.

By the Sea or at Least Rent It
GS: Sammy Shore. Woody and Chuck try to find a way to pay the rent for their beach house.

Roommate, Stay Away from My Door
GS: Edward Andrews. Woody and Chuck stay away from the apartment; each thinks the other has a date.

A Legend Dies
GS: Garry Marshall, Kathleen Freeman, Larry Bishop. Chuck, a former gang member, tries to stop a gang fight.

Same Time, Same Station, Same Girl
GS: Marlyn Mason. Jack moves in with Woody and Chuck when he gives his room to a homeless girl who gives all of them a different sob story.

How Do You Follow Hi-Lites from Hamlet?
GS: Elizabeth Fraser. A women's club has chosen to perform Woody's dramatic play, but Chuck and the director are turning it into a comedy.

Woody Can You Spare a Sister?
GS: Sally Field, Tom Tully, Ann Doran. Woody's sister Bonnie stops her wedding to come to New York for a good time.

Sharin' Sharon
GS: Ann Elder, Sally Field. Chuck plans to test his girlfriend's loyalty, but Bonnie warns her.

Big Brother Is Watching You
GS: Larry Hankin, Richard Dreyfuss. Bonnie tries to get back at her nosy brother by dating a hippie named Beast.

A Little Off the Top
GS: Paul Lynde. Chuck and Woody check up on Bonnie when she goes to work at a men's hairstylist shop run by an egotist.

Testing, One, Two
GS: Richard Dreyfuss, Dave Ketchum, Rob Reiner, Larry D. Mann. Woody and Chuck become human guinea pigs in order to earn extra money. Woody has to eat dirt while Chuck sleeps for very short periods.

Swingle City, East
GS: Noam Pitlik, Aron Kincaid. Woody and Chuck turn the apartment house into a house for swingers.

Czech Your Wife, Sir?
GS: John Astin, Leigh French. Woody and Chuck help a non-English speaking tenant deliver a baby.

The Dinner Who Came to Man
GS: Linda Gaye Scott, Connie Hunter. Woody and Chuck prepare a live lobster for a dinner with two college coeds.

Aunt Harriet Wants You
GS: Rose Marie, Noam Pitlik, Henry Gibson. Jack spends two nights on the town with Woody's Navy aunt.

[The following episodes have no available story.]

Go Directly to Jail
How You Gonna Keep 'Em Down On
the Farm After They've Seen the
Rug?
Oh, How We Danced
Stranger in the Night Than in the
Morning

HOGAN'S HEROES

On the air 9/17/65, off 7/4/71. CBS. Color film. 168 episodes. Broadcast: Sept 1965-Sept 1967 Fri 8:30-9; Sept 1967-Sept 1969 Sat 9-9:30; Sept 1969-Sept 1970 Fri 8:30-9; Sept 1970-Jul 1971 Sun 7:30-8. Producer: Bernard Fein/ Bill Calihan. Prod Co: Bing Crosby Prods. Synd: Viacom.

CAST: Col. Robert Hogan (played by Bob Crane), Col. Klink (Werner Klemperer), Sgt. Schultz (John Banner), LeBeau (Robert Clary), Newkirk (Richard Dawson), Kinchloe (Ivan Dixon), Carter (Larry Hovis), Hilda (Sigrid Valdis), Baker (Kenneth Washington), Gen. Burkhalter (Leon Askin), Maj. Hockstedder (Howard Caine), Col. Crittendon (Bernard Fox).

The adventures of a band of prisoners of war in a German prison camp run by a bumbling German officer and his inept head guard. Very popular during its run and in reruns as well. The series has become a bit dated for many, but it still is seen on late night lineups across the country.

The Informer [Pilot]
Hogan discovers a spy among his men. [This episode was filmed in black and white.]

Hold the Tiger
GS: Arlene Martel. Hogan and his men smuggle a new German tank into the camp.

Kommandant of the Year
Stalag 13 is named one of the top ten prison camps in Germany.

The Late Inspector General
A visiting Inspector General upsets Hogan's plan to dynamite a train.

The Flight of the Valkyrie
Hogan is replaced as POW officer-in-charge by another officer.

The Prisoner's Prisoner
GS: Roger C. Carmel. Hogan captures a German general.

German Bridge Is Falling Down
Hogan and his men plan to blow up a bridge near the camp.

Movies Are Your Best Escape
Hogan fakes a radio broadcast in order to smuggle photos out of the camp.

Go Light on the Heavy Water
Hogan plans to destroy a heavy water supply by having Klink drink it.

Top Hat, White Tie and Bomb Sight
Hogan uses Klink to make contact with an Allied spy.

Happiness Is a Warm Sergeant
Klink replaces Schultz with a tough sergeant.

The Scientist
LeBeau pretends to be a famous French scientist while Hogan smuggles the real scientist out of the camp.

Hogan's Hofbrau
A German army division camps out near the camp causing problems for Hogan.

Oil for the Lamps of Hogan
Hogan convinces two German officers that there is an oil supply under the camp.

John Banner (left), Bob Crane, and Werner Klemperer in Hogan's Heroes.

Reservations Are Required
Hogan tries to arrange for the escape of 20 men.

Anchors Aweigh, Men of Stalag 13
Hogan creates an officers' club in the shape of a ship.

Happy Birthday, Adolf
Hogan and his men plan to destroy a gun emplacement, allowing the Allies to attack on Hitler's birthday.

The Gold Rush
Hogan and his men plan to steal the gold the Germans took from the Bank of France.

Hello, Zolle
Hogan tries to detain a German general at the camp for 24 hours.

It Takes a Thief . . . Sometimes
Hogan is unaware that the members of the underground he is working with are actually Germans planning to trap him.

The Great Impersonation
Hogan gets Schultz to protray Klink in order to free three prisoners.

The Pizza Parlor
GS: Hans Conreid. Hogan bribes an Italian officer with pizza to fight for the Allies.

The 43rd, a Moving Story
Hogan's plans to destroy an anti-aircraft battery are upset by a visiting major.

How to Cook a German Goose by Radar
An American corporal tells Hogan he is actually a general in disguise.

Psychic Kommandant
Hogan convinces Klink that he has ESP in order to get the designs to a new German airplane engine.

The Prince from the Phone Company
A prisoner dresses up as an African prince in order to ask the Germans for money to open a submarine base.

The Safecracker Suite
Klink agrees to help Hogan steal the evidence to the assassination plot against Hitler.

I Look Better in Basic Black
Hogan tries to find out why three American girls were brought to the camp.

The Assassin
Hogan tries to help a German scientist escape from Germany.

Cupid Comes to Stalag 13
Hogan helps Klink when he falls in love.

The Flame Grows Higher
Hogan looks for a stool pigeon who has been telling the Germans about the underground escape route.

Request Permission to Escape
A prisoner asks Hogan to let him escape from the camp to rejoin his girlfriend back home.

Hogan Gives a Birthday Party
Hogan plans to hijack a German bomber and use it to destroy an oil refinery.

The Schultz Brigade
Klink is arrested for conspiring against the commanding general.

Diamonds in the Rough
A German officer threatens to expose Hogan's operation unless he pays him off.

Operation Briefcase
Hogan is ordered to give a time bomb to a German general to aid him in an assassination plot.

The Battle of Stalag 13
Two German officers interfere with Hogan's sabotage plan.

The Rise and Fall of Sergeant Schultz
Schultz becomes a hero and wins a medal, thanks to Hogan.

Hogan Springs
Hogan uses a broken water main to get captured Resistance fighters out of the camp.

A Klink, a Bomb and a Short Fuse
General Burkhalter wants Hogan to defuse a bomb which landed in the camp.

Tanks for the Memory
Hogan is ordered to photograph and destroy a model for a radio-controlled tank.

The Tiger Hunt [Part 1]
Hogan and Klink go to Paris to free a lady spy.

The Tiger Hunt [Part 2]
Hogan continues his efforts to free a lady spy.

Will the Real Adolf Please Stand Up
Hogan plans to use a phony Hitler as part of a hoax.

Don't Forget to Write
Klink has been chosen for combat duty.

The General Swap
Hogan captures a German officer to use in trade for a captive American officer.

Information Please
The Germans replace Klink with another officer.

Art for Hogan's Sake
Hogan tries to keep a painting stolen from France from ending up in Goering's art collection.

Klink's Rocket
Hogan plans to detour German bombers from going to London.

The Great Brinksmeyer Robbery
Hogan robs a bank to pay for information needed to help the Allies.

Praise the Fuehrer and Pass the Ammunition
Hogan switches real bullets for the fake ones to be used in the German war games.

Hogan and the Lady Doctor
Hogan resents having a woman scientist as the leader of a mission to destroy a research lab.

The Swing Swift
Newkirk gets drafted into the German Army, as part of Hogan's plan to destroy a gun factory.

Heil Klink
Hogan tells Klink that the defecting German officer he is hiding in the camp is really Hitler in disguise.

Everyone Has a Brother-in-Law
Hogan plans to destroy an ammunition train.

Reverend Kommandant Klink
Hogan sneaks a pilot's girl into camp and gets Klink to marry them.

The Most Escape-Proof Camp I've Ever Escaped From
A British escape artist escapes from the camp against Hogan's orders.

The Tower
Hogan blackmails a general in order to keep Klink from being transferred.

Colonel Klink's Secret Weapon
Klink suffers at the hands of a tough sergeant sent to discipline the prisoners.

The Top Secret Top Coat
Hogan steals a top secret document from Klink's coat, saving him from being arrested.

The Reluctant Target
Hogan gets Klink to let him play camp commander so he can learn secret information.

The Crittendon Plan
GS: Bernard Fox. Hogan's plan to destroy a Nazi convoy are disrupted by a bumbling British officer.

Some of Their Planes Are Missing
The Germans plan to send their pilots in captured British planes in order to sneak into England.

D-Day at Stalag 13
Hogan gets Klink promoted to German Chief of Staff.

Sergeant Schultz Meets Mata Hari
The Gestapo gets a female spy to pry information out of Schultz.

Funny Thing Happened on the Way to London
Hogan discovers a plot to kill Churchill.

Casanova Klink
General Burkhalter plans to get Klink to marry his widowed sister.

How to Win Friends and Influence Nazis
Hogan tries to get a Swedish scientist to work for the Allies.

Nights in Shining Armor
Hogan has to get a French courier and some bullet-proof vests out of the camp.

Hot Money
Hogan plans to destroy the Nazis' counterfeiting operation.

Drums Along the Dusseldorf
Hogan mines a bridge and then learns a truck of American prisoners will be the first to cross it.

Is General Hammerschlag Burning?
GS: Barbara McNair. Hogan uses a French entertainer's friendship with a German general as part of a spy plot.

One in Every Crowd
Hogan has to capture a renegade American POW.

A Russian Is Coming
Hogan tries to get a Russian pilot back to Russia.

Evening of the Generals
Hogan plans to destroy a roomful of Nazi generals.

Everybody Loves a Snowman
Hogan and his men build a hollow snowman to smuggle a pilot out of the camp.

The Hostage
Hogan may become the unknowing victim of a female Russian spy's time bombs.

Carter Turns Traitor
Carter pretends to be a defector so he can learn the location of a chemical factory.

Two Nazis for the Price of One
Hogan learns that a Gestapo agent knows about the Manhattan bomb project.

Is There a Doctor in the House?
Klink gets sick just when Hogan needs him to complete one of his missions.

Hogan, Go Home
GS: Bernard Fox. Hogan is ordered home when Colonel Crittendon comes to replace him.

Sticky Wicket Newkirk
Newkirk unknowingly sneaks a beautiful German informer into the camp.

War Takes a Holiday
Hogan plans a hoax to trick Klink and Hochstetter into thinking the war is over.

Duel of Honor
Hogan helps Klink get ready to leave for Argentina when he is challenged to a duel by a general.

Axis Annie
Hogan plans to use a propaganda radio announcer to get a message to the underground.

What Time Does the Balloon Go Up?
Hogan transports an agent to England in a balloon.

LeBeau and the Little Old Lady
LeBeau tells the others that the underground agent he has been taking messages to is an old woman, when she is really a beautiful girl.

How to Escape from a Prison Camp Without Really Trying
Hogan hides 30 prisoners in order to keep an army of S.S. men busy while the Allies get more men.

The Collector General
Hogan tries to keep a fortune in paintings from winding up in the collection of a German general.

The Ultimate Weapon
Hogan plans to trick German planes into going to the wrong location so that the Allies can destroy an important target.

Monkey Business
Hogan uses a German chimp to deliver a radio part to the underground.

Clearance Sale at the Black Market
Schultz has been ordered to the Russian front.

Klink vs. the Gonculator
Klink mistakes a rabbit trap for a secret electronic device.

How to Catch a Papa Bear
GS: Fay Spain. Hogan unknowingly sends Newkirk into a trap set by the Germans.

Hogan's Trucking Service . . . We Deliver the Factory to You
GS: Bernard Fox. Colonel Crittendon ruins Hogan's plans to destroy a ball-bearing plant.

To the Gestapo with Love
The Gestapo gets three girls to pry secrets out of Hogan and his men.

Man's Best Friend Is Not His Dog
A dog buries a bone containing valuable microfilm scheduled to be smuggled out of the camp immediately.

Never Play Cards with Strangers
Hogan tries to blow up a rocket fuel factory.

Color the Luftwaffe Red
Hogan and his men paint the headquarters of the Luftwaffe.

Guess Who Came to Dinner
Hogan thinks his pretty underground contact is a double agent.

No Names Please
An American paper tells about Hogan's operation at the camp.

Bad Day at Berlin
Hogan and his men go to Berlin to capture a defector.

Will the Blue Baron Strike Again?
Hogan is ordered to find the headquarters of the Blue Baron.

Will the Real Colonel Klink Please Stand Up Against the Wall?
Hogan's plan to destroy a train carrying airplane engines gets Klink into trouble.

Man in Box
Hogan is ordered to capture LeBeau, but not before he lets him complete the mission he is on.

The Missing Klink
Hogan plans to kidnap a general and trade him for an underground agent fail when Klink is kidnapped and not the general.

Who Stole My Copy of Mein Kampf?
Hogan plans to eliminate a beautiful defector.

Operation Hannibal
Hogan and the daughter of a German general try to photograph secret plans which were created to prolong the war.

My Favorite Prisoner
A baroness is asked by Klink to try and get some secrets out of Hogan.

Watch the Trains Go By
While General Burkhalter's sister is keeping Klink occupied, Hogan uses the time to blow up a train.

Klink's Old Flame
Hogan uses Klink's old girlfriend to deliver radios to the French Underground.

Up in Klink's Room
Hogan gets himself sent to the hospital so he can get information from a wounded British agent.

The Witness
The Germans plan to show Hogan their new secret weapon which will get the Allies to surrender.

The Purchasing Plan
Hogan and his men are ordered to collect air-dropped ammunition and give it to the underground.

The Big Dish
A beautiful English woman defects to the Germans and designs an aircraft defense system for them.

The Return of Major Bonacelli
GS: Vito Scotti.   An Italian agent helps Hogan photograph a Nazi anti-aircraft base.

Happy Birthday, Dear Hogan
Hogan's men plan to surprise him on his birthday by blowing up an ammunitions dump.

Hogan Goes Hollywood
Klink plans to use an American actor POW in a German propaganda film.

The Well
Hogan steals a Luftwaffe code book but can't use the radio to send it to London.

The Klink Commandos
Hogan and the female Russian spy try to prevent the Germans from finding a secret transmitter.

The Gasoline War
Hogan and his men plan to destroy a Nazi gasoline station installed in the camp.

Unfair Exchange
Hogan plans to trade General Burkhalter's sister in exchange for a female agent.

The Kommandant Dies at Dawn
When Klink gives away a military secret, he is ordered shot by a firing squad.

Bombsight
Hogan plans to interfere with the test of a new weapon at the camp.

The Big Picture
Hogan plans to steal the picture which the Gestapo is using to blackmail Klink.

The Big Gamble
Hogan must prevent the Germans from finding the secret equipment which was in a plane shot down near the camp.

The Defector
Hogan must get a defecting German Field Marshal to England.

The Empty Parachute
Hogan once again tries to stop the Germans from making counterfeit money.

The Antique
Hogan gets Klink to open an antique business in an attempt to smuggle out secret information.

Is There a Traitor in the House?
Hogan plans to send vital information to London by using a Nazi propaganda program.

At Last—Schultz Knows Something
Hogan uses Schultz to discover and destroy a secret atomic installation.

How's the Weather?
Hogan makes an anniversary party for Klink so he can hear the weather broadcast which will enable him to tell the Allied bombers when to attack.

Gowns by Yvette
Hogan plans to use the wedding of Burkhalter's niece as an opportunity to contact an underground agent.

Get Fit or Go Fight
Klink is ordered to get back in shape or he will be sent to the Russian front.

Fat Herman, Go Home
Hogan and the female Russian spy plan to get a trainload of stolen paintings back to London.

The Softer They Fall
Kinchloe fights a German boxing champ.

One Army at a Time
Carter convinces the Germans he is one of them when he is caught in a German uniform.

Standing Room Only
Hogan tries to save Klink from an offi-

cer who plans to turn him in for borrowing money from the camp's treasury.

Six Lessons from Madame LaGrange
Hogan and a singer plan to stop the Gestapo from arresting all of the Allied agents in the area.

The Sergeant's Analyst
Schultz is going to be sent to the Russian front because Burkhalter found him goofing off.

The Merry Widow
Hogan sets Klink up with a female agent so he can get information about a new land mine.

Crittendon's Commandos
GS: Bernard Fox. Bumbling Crittendon parachutes into the camp on a mission to capture an enemy officer.

Klink's Escape
Hogan gets Klink to believe he is about to capture a POW escape ring.

Cuisine a la Stalag 13
LeBeau decides to escape, leaving the camp without a chef.

The Experts
Hogan saves a German officer whom the Nazis want to kill.

Klink's Masterpiece
Hogan gets Klink to believe he is a great painter.

Lady Chitterly's Lover [Part 1]
GS: Anne Rogers. An English traitor parachutes into the camp with information for Hitler.

Lady Chitterly's Lover [Part 2]
GS: Anne Rogers. Lady Chitterly arrives at the camp to tell them that her husband is a traitor.

The Gestapo Takeover
The Gestapo moves into the camp and sends Schultz and Klink to the Russian front.

Kommandant Schultz
Schultz is put in temporary command of the camp.

Eight O'Clock and All Is Well
Hogan finds that the new prisoner is a German spy.

The Big Record
Klink gives the prisoners a recorder so they can send home messages of their life in the camp.

It's Dynamite
Hogan tries to find under which bridges the Nazis have planted dynamite.

Operation Tiger
Hogan and his men try to rescue a French underground leader captured by the Gestapo.

The Big Broadcast
Hogan installs their transmitter in Klink's car, to avoid detection.

The Gypsy
LeBeau tries to convince Klink that he can tell his fortune.

The Dropouts
Hogan helps three German scientists escape to England.

Easy Come, Easy Go
Hogan and Klink go to England to steal an American airplane.

The Meister Spy
Hogan discredits a Nazi spy posing as an American officer.

That's No Lady, That's My Spy
GS: Alice Ghostley. Newkirk poses as a general's wife to escape from camp.

To Russia with Love
GS: Ruta Lee. Klink falls in love with a Russian spy and decides that life on the Russian front won't be too bad after all.

Klink for the Defense
Klink is chosen to defend a German

officer who is accused of treason.

The Kamikazes Are Coming
Hogan and his men fire a new German rocket towards England so the Allies can capture and study it.

Kommandant Gertrude
General Burkhalter's sister becomes the new head of the camp.

Look at the Pretty Snowflakes
Hogan and his men cause an avalanche in order to stop a German panzer division.

Hogan's Double Life
Hogan dresses up as a German officer in order to discredit a witness's testimony.

Rockets or Romance
Hogan and his men destroy a guided missile battery.

THE HONEYMOONERS

On the air 10/1/55, off 9/22/56. CBS. B&W film. 39 episodes; 10 hour episodes (Trip to Europe), (color, film). Broadcast: Oct 1955-Feb 1956 Sat 8:30-9; Feb 1956-Sept 1956 Sat 8-8:30. The hour episodes aired during the late 1960s and were first rerun as a series in 1971 (Jan 1971-May 1971). Producer: Jackie Gleason. Prod Co: DuMont (original B&W only). Prod Co: Gleason Productions (hour episodes). Synd: Viacom (both versions).

CAST: Ralph Kramden (played by Jackie Gleason), Ed Norton (Art Carney), Alice Kramden (Audrey Meadows), Trixie Norton (Joyce Randolph). The cast was the same for the later episodes except: Alice (Sheila MacRae), Trixie (Jane Kean).

Considered to be one of the most favored and remembered of all comedy reruns. It has now become a comedy cult classic. The adventures of a bigmouth bus driver and his wife and their friends, a not very bright sewer worker and his wife. This series is run constantly across the country. The hour version created from an assortment of shows from Jackie Gleason's later variety hour have not been as successful as the old shows. Aside from there being only ten, they are not as funny as the originals.

TV or Not TV
Ralph cons Norton into sharing the cost of a new television set.

Funny Money
Ralph spends the money he found on the bus unaware it is counterfeit.

The Golfer
Ralph tries to get a promotion by bragging he is an expert golfer.

A Woman's Work Is Never Done
Alice hires a maid who quits after working for Ralph. Ralph and Norton do the household chores until he can get a new maid or con Alice into quitting her job.

A Matter of Life and Death
Ralph mistakes a report about a sick dog for his own doctor's report, causing him to believe he is dying.

The Sleepwalker
Norton's sleepwalking is causing Ralph not to get any sleep.

Better Living Through TV
Ralph and Norton go on TV to sell Handy Housewife Helpers.

Pal O' Mine
GS: Ned Glass. Ralph gets a ring meant for Norton's boss stuck on his finger and can't get it off.

Jackie Gleason, Audrey Meadows, Art Carney, and Jane Kean in The Honeymooners.

Brother Ralph
Alice passes off Ralph as her brother when she gets a job.

Hello, Mom
A fight starts when Ralph learns Alice's mother is coming for a visit.

The Deciding Vote
Ralph regrets fighting with Norton when he learns Norton has the deciding vote in the Raccoon election.

Something's Fishy
Ralph and Norton try to find a way to keep their wives from going on the lodge fishing trip.

'Twas the Night Before Christmas
Ralph buys a Christmas gift for Alice then regrets it when he realizes he bought a piece of junk.

The Man from Space
Ralph schemes to get ten dollars to rent a costume for the Raccoon party.

A Matter of Record
Ralph records an apology to Alice, but Norton makes matters worse when he gives her the wrong record.

Oh My Aching Back
Ralph hurts his back bowling on the night before a Bus Company physical exam.

The Baby Sitter
Alice takes a job babysitting to pay for a telephone, only Ralph thinks she is fooling around.

The $99,000 Answer
Ralph appears on a quiz show hoping to win money by answering questions about popular songs.

Ralph Kramden, Inc.
Ralph believes he is rich when he finds he has been mentioned in an old lady's will.

Young at Heart
GS: Ronnie Burns. Alice cons Ralph into going rollerskating in order to make them feel young again.

A Dog's Life
Ralph tries to get his boss to back him in a venture to sell Alice's appetizer, unaware that it is really dog food.

Here Comes the Bride
Ralph interferes in the marriage of Alice's sister and his lodge brother.

Mama Loves Mambo
GS: Charles Korvin. A dancing instructor moves in, upsetting the men in the building when he teaches their wives how to dance.

Please Leave the Premises
Ralph refuses to pay a rent increase so his landlord tries to throw him out.

Pardon My Glove
Alice tries to surprise Ralph when she wins the services of an interior decorator.

Young Man with a Horn
Ralph tries to make himself a success by taking an exam to get a better job.

Head of the House
Ralph tries to prove he is the head of the house after his answer to the Questioning Photographer is printed in the paper.

The Worry Wart
Ralph is upset when the Internal Revenue Service calls him down for a visit.

Trapped
Ralph witnesses a robbery, and the robbers are after him.

The Loudspeaker
Ralph thinks he is being named Raccoon of the Year.

On Stage
Ralph appears in a play for the lodge, but lets it go to his head.

Opportunity Knocks But
Ralph and Norton try to show Ralph's boss how to play pool, but only succeed in getting Norton a job as Ralph's superior.

Unconventional Behavior
Ralph and Norton are accidentally handcuffed together while on a train going to the Raccoon Convention.

The Safety Award
Ralph has a car accident with the judge who is going to present him with a safety award.

Mind Your Own Business
Ralph gets Norton fired and then tries to find him another job.

Alice and the Blonde
Alice is jealous of the wife of a bus company executive whom Ralph is trying to impress.

The Bensonhurst Bomber
GS: George Matthews. Ralph plans a fight with a tough guy which he later regrets when he realizes he will be killed.

Dial J for Janitor
In order to collect two salaries and live rent free, Ralph becomes the janitor of his building.

A Man's Pride
Ralph boasts about his status at the bus company to impress an old friend.

[The Honeymooners' Trip to Europe]

In Twenty-Five Words or Less
Ralph wins a trip to Europe for four in the Flakey Wakey Cereal Contest.

Ship of Fools
While on board a ship bound for Europe, Ralph and Norton get themselves lost in a lifeboat.

The Poor People of Paris
While in France, Ralph and Norton are mistaken for counterfeiters.

Confusion Italian Style
In Rome, Ralph believes Alice is fooling around with another man and tries to prove it.

The Curse of the Kramdens
In Ireland, Ralph and Norton spend the night in a haunted castle.

The Honeymooners in England
In London, Ralph writes, directs, produces and stars in a TV commercial for the Flakey Wakey Cereal Company.

You're in the Picture
In Madrid, Ralph is the victim of a blackmailer and his girlfriend.

We Spy
In Germany, Ralph and Norton are mistaken for Russian Commissars.

Petticoat Jungle
In Africa, Ralph and Norton go on a safari, where they encounter a gorilla, before returning home.

King of the Castle
Ralph moves in with Norton and Trixie moves in with Alice when Ralph butts into the Nortons' private lives.

HOUSE CALLS

On the air 12/17/79, off 9/82. CBS. Color/Video Tape. 56 episodes. Broadcast: Dec 1979-Mar 1980 Mon 9:30-10; May 1980-Sept 1982 Mon 9:30-10. Producer: Jerry Davis. Prod Co/Synd: Universal TV (MCA-TV).

CAST: Dr. Charley Michaels (played by Wayne Rogers), Ann Anderson (Lynn Redgrave), Dr. Norman Solomon (Ray Buktenica), Dr. Amos Weatherby (David Wayne), Mrs. Phipps (Deedy Peters), Conrad Peckler (Mark L. Taylor), Head Nurse Bradley (Aneta Corsaut), Jane Jeffreys (Sharon Gless).

This short-lived series featured the comic misadventures of the staff of Kensington General Hospital. The staff consists of Dr. Michaels, a competent surgeon who is always chasing after women, especially the assistant administrator Ann Anderson. The head surgeon is an eccentric old doctor named Amos Weatherby, who is thought by many to be senile. Then there is Dr. Norman Solomon, a young doctor who has an overprotective mother. Of course, there is the bubbleheaded Mrs. Phipps, the hospital volunteer, and Conrad Peckler, the prudish chief administrator. During the last season, Ann Anderson was replaced by Jane Jeffreys who turned out to be one of Dr. Michaels's old girlfriends. The most unfortunate thing about this entire series is that it was not cancelled because of low ratings but for contract problems. First, Lynn Redgrave tried to force the producers into giving her more money, but instead of getting more money she was replaced by Sharon Gless. Then, during the middle of the last season, Wayne Rogers held out for more money. This time the producers had a different problem: after all, they couldn't replace the star of the series, so instead they shut down the show and ended production. Less than six months later the existing episodes were pushed into syndication.

Paging Dr. Michaels
W: Max Shulman & Julius Epstein. D: Alex March. GS: Candy Azzara, Vivi Janess, Margaret Nesbitt. Ann joins the staff as the new assistant administrator and discovers that the staff is made up of crazy people.

Side to Side
W: Kathy & Bill Greer. D: Mel Ferber. GS: John Van Dreelen, Roger Bowen. Charley finds that he has to entertain two dates at the same time and at the same restaurant.

Final Exams
W: Kathy & Bill Greer. D: Nick Havings. GS: Irene Tedrow. Charley is accused of being shy when he refuses to treat his old high school teacher.

Crisis of Confidence
W: Sheldon Keller & Bryan Blackburn. D: Mel Ferber. GS: Teri Wagner Otis, Sylvia Walden, Mickey Deems, Hank Brandt, Sid Gould. Both Charley and Norman find that they have lost confidence in themselves.

Defeat of Clay
W: Kathy & Bill Greer. D: Bob Claver. GS: Fernando Lamas, Charles Lampkin. Charley becomes jealous when Ann finds herself attracted to a famous doctor who is visiting the hospital.

I'll Be Suing You
W: Mark Egan & Mark Solomon. D: Mel Ferber. GS: June Allyson, George Dickerson, Billy Beck, Frank Corsentino. A con woman tries to extort money from the hospital by faking an accident.

Beast of Kensington
W: Sheldon Keller, Bryan Blackburn & Jeffrey Davis. D: Bob Claver. GS: Kay Medford, Conrad Janis, Richard Stahl, Allen Joseph. Charley causes unrest among the nurses when he is hospitalized for a bad back.

A Slight Case of Quarantine
W: Lee Aronsohn. D: Bob Claver. GS: David Hollander, Markie Post. Charley, Ann, Norman, Amos and Mrs. Phipps become trapped in the cafeteria when a seven-year-old boy exposes them to a smallpox vial he stole from the lab.

Mobster Tale
W: Kathy & Bill Greer. D: Mel Ferber. GS: Stuart Lancaster, Raymond St. Jacques. Charley is chosen to perform surgery on a convicted mobster.

Old Is Beautiful
W: Sheldon Keller & Bryan Blackburn.

D: Mel Ferber. GS: John O'Leary, Sandy Balsom. Amos is fired when he is thought to be too old by the new hospital administrator.

Take My Granddaughter, Please
W: Kathy & Bill Greer, Jeffrey Davis & Mort Greene. D: Nick Havings. GS: Antoinette Stella. Amos's clumsy granddaughter tries to prove that she is capable of carrying on the Weatherby tradition by becoming a doctor.

Phantom of Kensington
W: Kathy & Bill Greer. D: Bob Claver. GS: Richard Lewis, Sarah Rush. The staff tries to find out who has been stealing from the hospital and the identity of an unidentifiable doctor.

Sex and the Single Surgeon
W: Kathy & Bill Greer, Lou & Dianne Messina. D: Ray Austin. GS: John Edwards, Rachel Thorne, Juanin Clay. A new female doctor causes trouble for everyone at the hospital.

Tenants, Anyone?
W: Kathy & Bill Greer. D: Jeremiah Morris. GS: James A. Watson, Jr., Elizabeth Kerr, Jessamine Milner. Ann learns that Charley is her landlord when he plans to turn her building into a condominium.

All About Adam
W: Kathy & Bill Greer, Lou & Dianne Messina. D: Allen Baron. GS: Dack Rambo, Martin Speer. Charley becomes jealous when Ann falls for the new doctor at the hospital.

In Case of Emergency
W: Kathy & Bill Greer. D: Allen Baron. GS: Beth Jacobs, Diane Markoff. Charley finds that he has to handle the emergency room on the same night as his date with Ann.

The Six O'Clock Noose
W: Kathy & Bill Greer. D: Mel Ferber. GS: Marlyn Mason, Will Gill, Jr., Norman Klar. A television news team wants to film the everyday operations at the hospital.

No Balls, One Strike
W: Kathy & Bill Greer, Tom Chehak.
D: Bruce Bilson. GS: David Paymer.
The doctors find themselves doing all
the work when the nurses and order-
lies go out on strike.

Bombing Out
W: Ken Rothrock. D: Allen Baron.
GS: Richard Stahl, Mark Tapscott,
Stuart Pankin. A crazy man plants a
bomb in the hospital.

Adieu, Kind Friend
W: Donald Ross. D: John Clarke. GS:
Robert Hogan, Ray Baumann, Shelley
Price, Teri Landrum. Ann tries to
make Charley jealous after he con-
stantly breaks their dates.

The Dead Beat
W: Kathy & Bill Greer. D: Allen
Baron. GS: Jerry Van Dyke, James
Gallery. Charley's practical-joking
doctor friend comes for a visit.

Jailhouse Doc
W: Kathy & Bill Greer. D: Mel Ferber.
GS: Greg Mullavey, Freeman King,
Dean Santoro, John Clavin. Charley
goes to jail when he refuses to divulge
a patient's medical history to a senator.

The Nude Girl in Town
W: Kathy & Bill Greer. D: Bruce Bilson. GS: Jeannie Wilson, Shauna Sullivan, Adrienne Moore. Ann comes to
the defense of a nurse who is about to
be fired for posing nude in a men's
magazine.

Muggers and Other Strangers
W: Laurie Gelman. D: Ray Austin.
GS: Edd Byrnes, Diane Lander. The
nurses become upset when a mugger
runs loose in the hospital.

Officer Needs Assistance
W: Kathy & Bill Greer. D: Wayne
Rogers. GS: Howard Witt, George
Petrie, Joe Terry. Charley fakes an
operation in order to keep Mr. Peckler from interfering with operation
room procedures.

Kensington Follies
W: Kathy & Bill Greer. D: Ray Austin. GS: Shavor Ross, Jonathan Ian.
The staff of the hospital puts on a
show in order to entertain the patients on Christmas Eve.

My Son the Anarchist
W: Laurie Gelman. D: Ray Austin.
GS: Jerry Douglas, Martin Garner,
Stanley Kamel. Ann and Charley help
a wanted man sneak past the police in
order for him to be able to visit his
dying father.

Bye, Bye, American Spy
W: Wayne Rogers. D: Fernando
Lamas. GS: Willian Bogert, Ken Kim-
mons. A government spy sneaks into
the hospital in order to talk to a seriously ill patient.

Have Peckler, Will Travel
W: Richard Lewis & Richard Dimitri.
D: Fernando Lamas. GS: Judi Dur-
land, Karen Salkin, Frank Farmer.
Charley, Norman, Ann & Amos find
themselves trapped in a mountain
cabin in the middle of a forest fire.

The Magnificent Weatherbys
W: Kathy & Bill Greer. D: Bruce Bilson. David Wayne not only portrays
his character of Amos Weatherby in
this episode, but also his three visiting
relatives, Travis, Lyndon and Lucretia,
who pay a visit to the hospital when
they learn that Amos is dying, in order
to collect his estate.

The Hostage Situation
W: Donald Ross. D: Dick Martin. GS:
Roger Bowen, Jeff Maxwell, Tony
Acvarenga. A crazy man holds Ann
and Peckler hostage with a gun.

Lust Weekend
W: Erik Tarloff. D: Alan Bergman.
GS: Roger Bowen, Wendy Fulton,
Glen Vernon. Charley proposes to
Ann and she accepts, but then begins
to have second thoughts.

Kleptos and Other Maniacs
W: Kathy & Bill Greer. D: Alan Bergman. GS: Jed Mills, Robin Haynes, Tony Plana. Charley tries to capture the kleptomaniac who has been running loose in the hospital.

The Yes Man
W: Bob Baublitz. D: Bruce Bilson. GS: Bill Cort, Frank Biro, John Steadman. Amos tricks Ann into letting him stay at her apartment while his house is being painted.

The Kensington Connection
W: Kathy & Bill Greer. D: Wayne Rogers. GS: Phillip Sterling, John Elerick, Dana Gladstone. Trouble begins when Amos's marijuana plant winds up on Mrs. Phipps's hospital cart.

The Sex Police
W: Walter Dishell, M.D., & Bob Baublitz. D: Fernando Lamas. GS: Dean Santoro, Donna Wilkes. Charley disobeys the law when he refuses to reveal the name of a pregnant teenager.

Uncle Digby
W: Kathy & Bill Greer. D: Fernando Lamas. GS: Patrick MacNee, Mary Ann Gibson. Ann's womanizing uncle comes for a visit and proceeds to turn the hospital upside down.

Alien Food
W: Wayne Rogers. D: Robert Douglas. GS: Bill Shilling, Bert Rosario, Ralph Strait. Norman gets in trouble when he puts the hospital chef on a strict diet which causes him to have a heart attack.

The Rising Cost of Poverty
W: Debra Frank & Scott Rubenstein. D: Robert Douglas. GS: Justin Dana, Hank Brandt, Jay MacIntosh, Connie Hill. Charley tries to help a family get the needed money to help pay for their son's operation.

Son of Emergency
W: Richard Lewis & Richard Dimitri.

D: Bruce Bilson. GS: Lewis Arquette, Graham Jarvis, Allan Rich. Peckler puts the entire staff on emergency night duty when he learns that a hospital inspector is coming for a visit.

Doctor Solomon, Mr. Hide
W: Laurie Gelman. D: Allen Baron. GS: Victoria Carroll, Denny Miller. Norman leaves the hospital when he believes it is interfering with his love life.

Bradley's Brat
W: Kathy & Bill Greer. D: Dick Martin. GS: Stephen Sachs. Ann tries to help Nurse Bradley who is worried about her son's problems at school.

Losers Weepers
W: Kathy & Bill Greer. D: Fernando Lamas. GS: Scott McGinnis, Tracy Morgan. Ann returns to England leaving Charley heartbroken.

Fun with Doc and Jane
W: Kathy & Bill Greer. D: Allen Baron. GS: Heather Hewitt, Connie Hill. Charley is shocked when he learns that Ann's replacement is one of his former girlfriends. [Sharon Gless joins the cast with this episode.]

Conventional Warfare
W: Kathy & Bill Greer. D: Wayne Rogers. GS: Ray Stewart, Jere Lea Rae, Faith Minton. Ann, Charley, Jane and Norman attend the doctors' convention in Las Vegas.

Con-Con
W: Laurie Gelman. D: Alan Cook. GS: Carl Strano, Barbara Horan. Norman tries to help Mrs. Phipps who has been taken by a con man staying at the hospital.

A Man for All Surgeons
W: Bruce Ferber & David Lerner. D: Fernando Lamas. GS: Jon Cypher, George Petrie, Claude Earl Jones, K Callan. Charley loses his confidence when a patient refuses to believe him and hires a staff of specialists.

It Ain't Necessary to Sew
W: Jewel Jaffe & Martin Ross. D: Alan Bergman. GS: Stephen Brooks, Jim Weston. Charley tries to prove that a doctor is performing unnecessary operations.

Campaign in the Neck
W: Erik Tarloff. D: Philip Minor. GS: Michael Durrell, George Petrarca. Charley tries to convince a senator to have a needed operation, despite his insistence that it will interfere with his campaigning.

The Gays of Our Lives
W: Kathy & Bill Greer, Sam Greenbaum. D: Alan Bergman. GS: Dennis Howard, Lew Brown. Peckler plans to fire a new doctor when he learns that he is gay.

Bone of My Bone, Flesh of My Flesh
W: Howard Ostroff. D: Fernando Lamas. GS: Roy London. Norman tries to prove to his mother that he is an adult, and a neurotic patient adopts Charley as his substitute father.

Deafenwolf
W: Joel Tappis, Jackie McKane, Kathy & Bill Greer. D: Bruce Bilson. GS: Ray Baumann, Billie Bird, Sandy Helberg. The hospital is plagued by a patient who thinks he is a werewolf.

Hook, Line & Sinker
W: Bruce Ferber & David Lerner. D: Allen Baron. GS: Ruth Cox. Charley believes that Amos's young girlfriend is a golddigger out for his money.

In Norman We Trust
W: Bruce Ferber & David Lerner. D: Alan Cook. GS: Melanie Vincz, Bob Delegall. While Charley suffers from insomnia, Norman believes he is a superhuman doctor.

The Ducks of Hazard
W: Bob Baublitz, Bruce Ferber & David Lerner. D: Fernando Lamas. GS: James Hong, Pat Corley, Kate Williamson. Charley and Jane try to prevent ducks from being poisoned by exposure to pesticides.

The Weatherbys Ride Again
W & D: Unknown. GS: Herbert Rudley. David Wayne once again portrays his nutty relatives as they pay him a visit to his surprise anniversary party.

HOW TO MARRY A MILLIONAIRE

On the air 10/57, off 8/59. 30 min. B&W film. 51 episodes. Broadcast: Oct 1957-Aug 1959, date and time varied on each station. Producer: Nat Perrin. Production Co: Talent Artists. Synd: National Telefilm.
CAST: Mike McCall (played by Merry Anders), Loco Jones (Barbara Eden), Greta (Lori Nelson), Gwen Kirby (Lisa Gaye).
The story of three beautiful career girls, a model and two secretaries, who live in New York searching for a millionaire to marry. Episodes depict their individual attempts to meet the man of their dreams. The series is based on the movie of the same name. Available for syndication, but there is no known station currently running the show. The character of Greta was married off and replaced by Gwen during the middle of the second season.

The Penthouse
GS: Dabbs Greer. The girls mistake three bums for millionaires and when real millionaires show up they kick them out.

Subletting the Apartment
GS: Peter Leeds, Alan De Witt. The girls take in male boarders to earn enough money to send Greta to Florida to stay with a millionaire.

Barbara Eden in How to Marry a Millionaire.

The Three Pretenders
GS: Morey Amsterdam. The girls disguise themselves at a party in the hopes of meeting a millionaire.

To Hock or Not to Hock
GS: Joseph Kearns. Greta has met a millionaire who loves her, the only problem is that he is married.

It's a Dog's Life
GS: Larry White, Jimmy West. Loco brings home a Great Dane which they can't afford to keep.

The Cruise
Greta and Loco become accidental stowaways when they see Mike off on a cruise.

The Brat
GS: Brad Dexter. The girls use a millionaire's seven-year-old son to get revenge on the guy who got them fired.

Loco, the Heiress
Loco inherits three million dollars, only to have it taken away from her.

Alias the Secretary
No available story.

The Sea Island Story
Loco goes on a quiz show to win tickets to a millionaire's resort.

Society Mother
GS: Eleanor Audley. Mike finds a membership card to a yacht club. The girls use the card in the hopes that they will find a millionaire at the club.

Tom, Dick, and Harry
The girls discover that they are all dating the same millionaire who is using three different names.

Good Time Charlie
The girls date the son of a rich construction company executive, unaware

that he has given up all claims to his father's money.

The Bird Man
GS: William Swan, Joseph Kearns. Loco studies ornithology to impress a rich bird watcher.

The Fourth Girl
The girls take their plain girlfriend with them to a party, but they regret it when she winds up with the millionaire.

For the Love of Art
GS: Werner Klemperer. The girls try to impress a millionaire art lover.

The Playwright
GS: Burt Metcalfe. The girls take a poor playwright and promote him so well that he is offered a Hollywood contract and ends up marrying a movie star.

Youth for the Asking
Loco mistakes a 20-year-old model for her 56-year-old mother.

Loco Leaves Home
Loco ruins Greta's chances of meeting a wealthy bachelor so she leaves home.

The Maid
The girls hire a maid, unaware that she is actually a bookie.

Prince Kaudim Story
GS: Anthony George. A visiting prince asks the girls to marry him.

The Yachting Party
GS: Bob Hopkins. Loco becomes the smuggler of a diamond brooch when she asks two crooks for directions at a waterfront cafe.

The Utterly Perfect Man
Loco thinks that Mike's latest boyfriend is a Bluebeard.

Loco and the Cowboy
GS: George O'Hanlon. Loco becomes queen of the rodeo and falls for an oil tycoon.

Loco vs. Wall Street
GS: Gavin Gordon. Loco has to find a way to get Mike's Wall Street job after she gets her fired.

A Call to Arms
GS: Ted Knight, Jimmy Cross. The girls believe that Loco has joined the WACs.

For the Love of Mink
GS: Lloyd Corrigan. Loco has ten days to pay for a mink stole she bought and now has to find the money.

Operation Greta
The girls plan to fake an illness in order to attract a doctor's interest in them.

Loco Goes to Night School
GS: Richard Deacon. Loco goes to night school to learn about culture.

A Job for Jesse
The girls attempt to get the elevator boy his job back after he was fired by an efficiency expert.

Day in Court
GS: John Hoyt, Dan Tobin. Loco spends a day in court after being in a car accident.

A Man for Mike
GS: Charles Gray. Loco ruins Mike's chances for romance with a hunter when she gets the mumps and the measles at the same time.

The Truthivac
GS: Charles Lane, Stafford Repp. Loco gets a computer date.

The New Lease
GS: Stacy Keach. The landlord throws the girls out when their lease expires.

Situation Wanted
Loco pawns the silver to buy a dress,

causing the other girls to call the police when they think it has been stolen.

Loco and the Gambler
GS: Vito Scotti, William Cassidy. A gambler dates Loco because she is his good luck charm; when his luck changes for the worse, he dumps her.

The Big Order
The girls help a mining executive impress a visiting South American client.

The Shortstop
Loco dates the owner of the Chicago White Sox who is more interested in the team than in her.

Greta's Big Chance
GS: Booth Coleman. Greta loses her job when she tries to impress a Hollywood producer.

Cherchez La Roommate
Greta gets married to a gas station attendant and moves out; the girls must now find a new roommate.

What's Cookin' with Loco?
Agnes is giving cooking tips to Loco, in return she cooks dinner for Agnes's boss.

Guest with a Gun
GS: Gerald Mohr, Milton Frome. Loco and her boyfriend try to capture a jewel thief without getting killed.

Hit and Run
GS: Robert Foulk. The girls must prove that they are innocent of causing $1800 worth of damage to a car by producing an Army private as a witness before they are jailed.

The Three Stacked Stockholders
The girls go to a stockholders meeting where they cause trouble.

Gwen's Secret
GS: Werner Klemperer. Gwen is in charge of guarding a secret celebrity in the empty apartment next door, but Loco thinks he is a burglar.

Loco the Teenager
GS: John Stephenson. Loco, posing as a teenager, is asked to be the subject of a story about the typical teenager.

The Seal Who Came to Dinner
GS: Willard Waterman. The girls have to hide from their landlord the seal they got as a gift.

The Method
GS: Ron Ely. A millionaire practices his acting abilities on Loco by claiming he is a poor boy.

The Golf Tournament
GS: Gavin Gordon. The girls become caddies at a country club in the hope of finding rich men.

[The stories for the next few episodes are unavailable.]

The Comic
A Husband
Love on Approval

I DREAM OF JEANNIE

On the air 9/18/65, off 9/1/70. NBC. 30 min. Film. 139 episodes, 109 color, 30 B&W. Broadcast: Sept 1965-Sept 1966 Sat 8-8:30; Sept 1966-Aug 1967 Mon 8-8:30; Sept 1967-Aug 1968 Tue 7:30-8; Sept 1968-Sept 1969 Mon 7:30-8; Sept 1969-Sept 1970 Tue 7:30-8. Producer: Sidney Sheldon. Prod Co/Synd: Screen Gems/Columbia Pictures TV.
CAST: Jeannie (played by Barbara Eden), Tony Nelson (Larry Hagman), Roger Healey (Bill Daily), Dr. Alfred Bellows (Hayden Rorke), General Peterson

Barbara Eden and Larry Hagman in "The Fastest Gun in the East" episode of I Dream of Jeannie.

(Barton MacLane), Amanda Bellows (Emmaline Henry), General Schaeffer (Vinton Hayworth), General Stone (Phil Ober), Melissa Stone (Karen Sharpe), Jeannie's mother and sister were played by Barbara Eden.

WRITERS: Sidney Sheldon, Tom & Frank Waldman, Arnold Horwitt, Bob Fisher, Arthur Alsberg, Ron Friedman, Marty Roth, James Henerson, Christopher Golato, Perry Grant, Dick Bensfield, Bill Daily. DIRECTORS: Gene Nelson, Hal Cooper, Alan Rafkin, Claudio Guzman, E.W. Swackhamer, Larry Hagman, Jerry Bernstein, Michael Ansara.

Captain Anthony Nelson, an astronaut on a flight from the NASA space center, Cape Kennedy, Florida, crash lands on a desert island in the South Pacific. He finds an old green bottle, out of which pops a beautiful genie named Jeannie who forms an immediate attachment to the dazed Captain. Episodes depict the inexplicable situations that result from Jeannie's tricks which fascinate Tony's superior officer, Dr. Alfred Bellows, the NASA psychiatrist, who is constantly observing the nervous astronaut. Throughout the series Jeannie's identity is known only to Tony and his best friend Roger Healey, who only wishes he had a genie of his own. Later in the series Tony and Jeannie are married. *I Dream of Jeannie* is one of the more popular reruns, although it seems to be disappearing from stations as time goes on. An *I Dream of Jeannie* reunion special was planned right before Larry Hagman landed the starring role on *Dallas*; since then, plans for the reunion have been suspended.

The Lady in the Bottle
W: Sidney Sheldon. D: Gene Nelson. Astronaut Tony Nelson is stranded on a desert island where he finds a 2000-year-old genie named Jeannie in a bottle.

My Hero
W: Sidney Sheldon. D: Gene Nelson. GS: Richard Kiel. Tony ventures to ancient Persia to avenge an insult rendered on Jeannie by Ali, an enormous brute.

Guess What Happened on the Way to the Moon
W: Tom & Frank Waldman. D: Alan Rafkin. Jeannie sneaks along on a desert survival mission that Tony and Roger are engaged in . . . only Tony doesn't want Jeannie's help.

Jeannie and the Marine Corps
W: Tom & Frank Waldman. D: Alan Rafkin. GS: Karen Sharpe. When Melissa, Tony's fiancee, wants to speed up their marriage plans, Tony begins to have second thoughts.

GI Jeannie
W: William Davenport. D: Alan Rafkin. GS: Jane Dulo. Jeannie joins the WAAFs in the hopes of becoming Tony's new secretary.

The Yacht Murder Case
W: David Braverman & Bob Marcus. D: Gene Nelson. On a yacht, everyone is convinced that Tony has killed Jeannie.

Anybody Here Seen Jeannie?
W: Arnold Horwitt. D: Gene Nelson. Worried about Tony's safety, Jeannie causes Tony to fail a physical before an important space launching.

Americanization of Jeannie
W: Arnold Horwitt. D: Gene Nelson. Jeannie takes lessons in how to be the perfect American woman.

The Moving Finger
W: Harry Essex & Jerry Seelen. D:

Gene Nelson. GS: Nancy Kovack. Jeannie tries her luck at becoming a Hollywood star, only to discover that genies can't be photographed.

Djinn and Water
W: Mary McCall. D: Gene Nelson. GS: J. Carrol Naish. Tony's latest problem is how to get fresh water from salt water.

Whatever Happened to Baby Custer?
W: Austin & Irma Kalish. D: Gene Nelson. GS: Billy Mumy. An eight-year-old boy is certain that Jeannie is a genie, prompting Dr. Bellows to psychoanalyze the child.

Where'd You Go-Go?
W: Robert Fisher & Arthur Alsberg. D: E.W. Swackhamer. Roger has a date with Jeannie while Tony is dating an old friend.

Russian Roulette
W: Robert Fisher & Arthur Alsberg. D: E.W. Swackhamer. GS: Arlene Martel. Tony is designated to escort a pretty Russian cosmonaut around town, but Jeannie won't hear of it.

What House Across the Street?
W: Robert Fisher & Arthur Alsberg. D: Theodore Flicker. GS: Oliver McGowan. Jeannie blinks up a phony house and phony parents in her latest attempts at marrying Tony.

Too Many Tonys
W: Arnold Horwitt. D: E.W. Swackhamer. In her latest scheme, Jeannie invents a phony Tony, in order to show the real Tony how much fun a real wedding will be.

Get Me to Mecca on Time
W: James Alladice & Tom Adair. D: E.W. Swackhamer. GS: Jamie Farr. Jeannie must make a trip to Mecca to perform an ancient ceremony or disappear forever.

Richest Astronaut in the World
W: William Davenport. D: E.W.

Swackhamer. Roger finally discovers the secret of Jeannie's existence and then steals her for his own greedy purposes.

Is There an Extra Jeannie in the House?
W: Charles Tannen. D: Hal Cooper. GS: Bernard Fox, Judy Carne. Trying to help Roger on a date, Jeannie gives him a genie of his own—her Cousin Myrt.

Never Try to Outsmart a Jeannie
W: Martin Ragaway. D: Herb Wallerstein. GS: Peter Brocco. Jeannie tries to convince Tony that an ocean voyage will be too dangerous . . . unless she comes along.

My Master, the Doctor
W: Sidney Sheldon. D: Hal Cooper. GS: Peter Leeds, Maureen McCormick, Jane Dulo. Jeannie fulfills Tony's secret wish of becoming a doctor, only to find his first patient is Roger.

Jeannie and the Kidnap Caper
W: Sidney Sheldon. D: Hal Cooper. GS: Richard Loo, James Hong. Tony is captured by Red Chinese spies, leaving Jeannie to rescue her master from certain death.

How Lucky Can You Get?
W: Sidney Sheldon. D: Claudio Guzman. GS: Ted DeCorsia. In Reno, Jeannie changes the gambling odds so Roger wins big, only to have it all taken away when Tony finds out.

Watch the Birdie
W: Sidney Sheldon. D: Hal Cooper. GS: Herbert Anderson. To impress the general, Jeannie helps improve Tony's golf game.

Permanent House Guest
W: Sidney Sheldon. D: Hal Cooper. Tony must find a way of explaining to Dr. Bellows how an elephant got in his bedroom.

Bigger Than a Bread Box
W: Sidney Sheldon. D: Claudio Guzman. Roger is fooled by a phony fortune teller and it's up to Tony and Jeannie to save him.

My Master, the Great Rembrandt
W: Sidney Sheldon. D: Claudio Guzman. GS: Booth Coleman, Jonathan Hole. Jeannie turns a duplicate Rembrandt painting into an original, causing Dr. Bellows to start an investigation.

My Master, the Thief
W: Robert Kaufman & Sidney Sheldon. D: Claudio Guzman. Jeannie sees a pair of slippers in a museum and takes them home, claiming they belonged to her 2000 years ago.

This Is Murder
W: Sidney Sheldon. D: Hal Cooper. GS: Gila Golan. Jeannie tries to kill a visiting princess because her family insulted Jeannie's 3000 years ago.

My Master, the Magician
W: Sidney Sheldon. D: Hal Cooper. GS: Chet Stratton. Tony must convince Dr. Bellows that he is a great magician when he catches him floating in mid-air.

I'll Never Forget What's Her Name
W: Sidney Sheldon. D: Hal Cooper. Tony gets amnesia and then falls in love with the first girl he sees, Jeannie.

Happy Anniversary
W: Sidney Sheldon. D: Claudio Guzman. GS: Michael Ansara. Celebrating their first anniversary on the same island where they met, Jeannie and Tony rescue the evil Blue Djinn who vows to kill his rescuer.

Always on Sunday
W: Sidney Sheldon. D: Hal Cooper. Jeannie stops the days of the week and turns every day into Sunday.

My Master, the Rich Tycoon
W: Sidney Sheldon. D: Claudio Guzman. GS: Paul Lynde. Tony must explain to the Internal Revenue how he acquired a house full of famous art,

a safe full of money, and a staff of servants.

My Master, the Rainmaker
W: Sidney Sheldon. D: Claudio Guzman. GS: Steve Ihnat. Dr. Bellows believes Tony knows how to control the weather when snow falls on his house, in July, in Florida.

My Wild-Eyed Master
W: Sidney Sheldon. D: Hal Cooper. Jeannie plays havoc with Tony's vision on an important eye test.

What's New, Poodle Dog?
W: Sidney Sheldon. D: Hal Cooper. GS: Dick Wilson, Norman Burton. When Roger tells Jeannie he's arranged a double date for Tony and himself, she turns Roger into a French poodle.

Fastest Gun in the East
W: Sidney Sheldon. D: Hal Cooper. GS: Stephanie Hill, Hoyt Axton. Jeannie sends Tony back to the Old West where he must defend a town singlehandedly against rustlers, murderers and thieves.

How to Be a Jeannie in 10 Easy Lessons
W: Sidney Sheldon. D: Hal Cooper. Feeling that Jeannie causes him too much trouble, Tony mistakenly gives her a guide book of tortures to use on him.

Who Needs a Green-Eyed Jeannie?
W: Sidney Sheldon. D: Hal Cooper. While Tony is on a date, a jealous Jeannie turns his companion into a chimp.

The Girl Who Never Had a Birthday [Part 1]
W: Sidney Sheldon. D: Claudio Guzman. Tony must find out the exact date Jeannie was born before she disappears forever.

The Girl Who Never Had a Birthday [Part 2]
W: Sidney Sheldon. D: Claudio Guzman. Tony tries to keep Dr. Bellows busy while Roger uses a government computer to determine Jeannie's birthday.

How Do You Beat Superman?
W: Sidney Sheldon. D: Claudio Guzman. GS: Mike Road. To make Tony jealous, Jeannie conjures up a phony suitor.

My Master, the Great Caruso
W: Sidney Sheldon. D: Hal Cooper. GS: Frank De Vol. Through Jeannie's magic, Tony is transformed into one of the greatest singers of all time.

My Master, the Author
W: Sidney Sheldon. D: Richard Goode. GS: Butch Patrick, Kimberly Beck. Tony has supposedly written a book on motherhood and Dr. Bellows doesn't believe it, so he decides to put Tony to the test.

Jeannie Breaks the Bank
W: Sidney Sheldon. D: Hal Cooper. GS: John McGiver. Jeannie blinks six million dollars into Tony's bank account, leaving him the task of explaining the large sum to Dr. Bellows.

The World's Greatest Lover
W: Sidney Sheldon. D: Hal Cooper. Feeling sorry for Roger's inability to get a date, Jeannie puts a spell on him making him irresistible to women.

Greatest Invention in the World
W: Sidney Sheldon. D: Hal Cooper. GS: Groucho Marx. Jeannie's new spot remover almost lands Dr. Bellows in Iceland when he decides to test out the product on General Peterson.

My Master, the Spy
W: Sidney Sheldon. D: Claudio Guzman. In Paris, Jeannie blinks up a duplicate Tony, setting Dr. Bellows off on a hunt for spies.

You Can't Arrest Me . . . I Don't Have a Driver's License
W: Sidney Sheldon. D: Hal Cooper. GS: Alan Hewitt. Jeannie tries to

drive Tony's car without a driver's license, which lands them both in court.

One of Our Bottles Is Missing
W: Sidney Sheldon. D: Claudio Guzman. Mrs. Bellows walks off with Jeannie's bottle . . . with Jeannie still inside.

My Master, the Civilian
W: Sidney Sheldon. D: Hal Cooper. Jeannie shows Tony what his future would be like if he left NASA for a desk job in Ohio.

There Goes the Best Genie I Ever Had
W: Sidney Sheldon. D: Hal Cooper. When Tony decides to send Jeannie away forever, he suddenly realizes he can't live without her.

The Greatest Entertainer in the World
W: Sidney Sheldon. D: Claudio Guzman. GS: Sammy Davis, Jr. To help Tony stage a celebration for General Peterson, Jeannie produces a duplicate of Sammy Davis, Jr.

The Incredible Shrinking Master
W: Sidney Sheldon. D: Claudio Guzman. Jeannie accidentally blinks Tony to the size of a mouse, causing him to be menaced by a cat.

My Master, the Pirate
W: Sidney Sheldon. D: Claudio Guzman. Jeannie blinks Tony back to the days of the pirates, where he tries to rescue a woman believed to be his great-great-great grandmother.

A Secretary Is Not a Toy
W: Sidney Sheldon. D: Claudio Guzman. GS: Eileen O'Neill. When Jeannie decides Tony should be a general, she almost gets him kicked out of the space program.

There Goes the Bride
W: Sidney Sheldon. D: Larry Hagman. GS: Abraham Sofaer. Jeannie tricks Tony into proposing to her, which causes trouble with Haji, King of all the genies.

My Master Napoleon's Buddy
W: Sidney Sheldon. D: Claudio Guzman. GS: Aram Katcher. Tony can't change the course of history when Jeannie takes him to visit Napoleon.

The Birds and the Bees Bit
W: Alan Devon. D: Larry Hagman. GS: Abraham Sofaer. Tony proposes to Jeannie thinking she will lose her powers once they are married, but changes his mind when he learns their children will be genies.

My Master, the Swinging Bachelor
W: Sidney Sheldon. D: Hal Cooper. GS: Bridget Hanley. At a dinner party, Jeannie bakes a cake that, when eaten, turns you back into a child.

The Mod Party
W: Ed Jurist. D: William Asher. GS: Hilarie Thompson. Dr. Bellows schedules an outdoor exercise for Tony and Roger on the same night of Roger's Mod party.

Fly Me to the Moon
W: Robert Marcus. D: Hal Cooper. GS: Larry Storch. Tony is almost sent to the moon as a chimp, when Jeannie's blink goes wrong.

Jeannie or the Tiger
W: James Henerson. D: Hal Cooper. Jeannie's sister tries to steal Tony away from her by blinking him all over the world, including the jungles of Africa.

Second Greatest Con Artist in the World
GS: Milton Berle. In Honolulu, a con man tries to acquire a rare scarab of Jeannie's but it's Jeannie who gets the last laugh.

My Turned-On Master
W: Dennis Whitcomb. D: Hal Cooper. GS: Pedro Gonzales-Gonzales. Jeannie switches her powers to Tony, who unknowingly gives them to Dr. Bellows.

My Master, the Weakling
W: Cristopher Golato. D: Hal Cooper.

GS: Don Rickles. Jeannie tries to save Tony and Roger from the wrath of a new tough physical fitness instructor.

Everybody's a Movie Star
W: Mark Rowane. D: Claudio Guzman. GS: Paul Lynde. Roger thinks he has been chosen for stardom by a famous movie director.

Jeannie, the Hip Hippie
W: Ron Friedman. D: Claudio Guzman. GS: Boyce and Hart. Jeannie assembles a rock group, needed for Mrs. Bellows, so Tony and she can go on vacation.

Who Are You Calling a Jeannie?
W: Marty Roth. D: Hal Cooper. GS: Richard Deacon. Dr. Bellows is sent into space as a mouse after Jeannie loses her memory.

Meet My Master's Mother
W & D: Claudio Guzman. GS: Spring Byington. Jeannie gets upset when Tony's mother visits declaring her son needs someone to take care of him.

Here Comes Bootsie Nightingale
W: Paul West. D: Hal Cooper. GS: Carol Wayne. Jeannie is jealous when Tony is ordered to escort a glamorous movie star.

Tony's Wife
W: Christopher Golato. D: Claudio Guzman. Jeannie's evil sister convinces Jeannie she is bad luck to Tony and must leave him.

Jeannie and the Great Bank Robbery
W: Seamon Jacobs & Fred Fox. D: Larry Hagman. GS: Mike Mazurki, Severn Darden. When Tony tells Jeannie to help someone other than himself, she helps two crooks rob a bank.

My Son, the Genie
W: Bill Richard. D: Claudio Guzman. GS: Bob Denver. The president is coming to Tony's house at the same time as a bumbling new genie who is in training.

Jeannie Goes to Honolulu
W: Mark Rowane. D: Claudio Guzman. GS: Brenda Benet, Don Ho. After Tony tells Jeannie he is off to the North Pole, she finds him on the beach at Waikiki.

The Battle of Waikiki
W: Marty Roth. D: Hal Cooper. GS: Michael Ansara. Jeannie blinks up King Kamehameha, an ancient Hawaiian king, who plans to retake Hawaii.

Genie, Genie, Who's Got the Genie? [Part 1]
W: James Henerson. D: Claudio Guzman. GS: Edward Andrews, Lou Antonio. Jeannie is accidentally locked inside a safe destined for the moon.

Genie, Genie, Who's Got the Genie? [Part 2]
W: James Henerson. D: Claudio Guzman. Still locked in the safe, Jeannie is sold to a junk dealer who plans to crush the safe in a scrap compressing machine.

Genie, Genie, Who's Got the Genie? [Part 3]
W: James Henerson. D: Claudio Guzman. Knowing that Jeannie is still locked inside the safe, her wicked sister tries once again to nab Tony for herself.

Genie, Genie, Who's Got the Genie? [Part 4]
W: James Henerson. D: Hal Cooper. GS: Ron Masak, Benny Rubin. Tony panics when he learns that Jeannie becomes the property of the one who frees her from the safe.

Please Don't Feed the Astronauts
W: Ron Friedman. D: Hal Cooper. GS: Paul Lynde, Ted Cassidy. Jeannie helps Tony and Roger pass a wilderness survival test complete with giant chickens and harem girls.

My Master, the Ghost Breaker
W: Christopher Golato. D: Hal Cooper. GS: Jack Carter. Tony in-

herits a castle in England, only to discover that it is haunted by thieves who want to get rid of him.

Divorce, Jeannie Style
W: James Henerson. D: Hal Cooper. GS: Woodrow Parfrey, Abraham Sofaer. Mrs. Bellows thinks Tony is a rotten husband and tries to arrange a divorce for Jeannie.

My Doublecrossing Master
W: Mark Rowane. D: Hal Cooper. Tony poses as a dashing Britisher named Geoffrey to prove that Jeannie is faithful to him.

Have You Ever Had a Jeannie Hate You?
W: Unknown. D: Claudio Guzman. Jeannie's wicked sister tricks her into hating Tony and Roger.

Operation: First Couple on the Moon
W: Arthur Julian. D: Claudio Guzman. GS: Kay Reynolds, Bill Smith. Jeannie's sister offers to keep Tony from getting to the moon with a pretty woman scientist.

Haven't I Seen Me Someplace Before?
W: Marty Roth. D: Claudio Guzman. GS: Pat Delany. When Jeannie gives Roger one birthday wish, Roger mistakenly wishes that he could be Tony.

U-F-Oh Jeannie
W: Marty Roth. D: Hal Cooper. GS: J. Pat O'Malley, Lisa Gaye, William Bassett. A family of hillbillies mistake Tony and Roger for Martians.

Jeannie and the Wild Pipchicks
W: James Henerson. D: Claudio Guzman. GS: Reta Shaw. Candy sent by Jeannie's mother brings out hidden desires in anyone who eats it.

Tomorrow Is Not Another Day
W: Bruce Howard. D: Hal Cooper. Jeannie accidentally blinks up a copy of the next day's newspaper, delighting Roger who plans a get-rich-quick scheme.

Abdullah
W: Marty Roth. D: Claudio Guzman. GS: Jane Dulo. Jeannie's baby nephew lands Tony in a maternity ward.

The Used Car Salesman
W: James Henerson. D: Hal Cooper. GS: Carl Ballantine, Bob Hastings. A crooked car salesman swindles Jeannie when she sells Tony's car, sending her off to get revenge.

Djinn, Djinn, Go Home
W: James Henerson. D: Hal Cooper. Jeannie's uniform-hating dog shows up and attacks everyone in sight.

Strongest Man in the World
W: Ray Singer. D: Claudio Guzman. GS: Jerry Quarry, Richard X. Slattery. Tony enters the armed forces boxing tournament unaware that the power in his boxing abilities came from Jeannie.

Indispensable Jeannie
W: Janes Henerson. D: Claudio Guzman. While Jeannie is away, she blinks the house to fulfill all of Tony's wishes . . . only Tony doesn't know it.

Jeannie and the Top Secret
W: Searle Kramer. D: Hal Cooper. GS: Sabrina Scharf. On his way to Washington with a top secret film, Tony is constantly bothered by a jealous Jeannie.

How to Marry an Astronaut
W: James Henerson. D: Hal Cooper. Jeannie's sister almost tricks Tony into marrying her.

Dr. Bellows Goes Sane
W: James Henerson. D: Richard Kinon. GS: Joe Flynn. Dr. Bellows's wild report on Tony prompts General Peterson to hire another psychiatrist to analyze Dr. Bellows.

Jeannie My Guru
W: James Henerson. D: Claudio Guzman. GS: Hilarie Thompson. A general's hippie daughter uses Jeannie's secret to blackmail Tony into letting her boyfriend hide out in his house.

The Case of My Vanishing Master [Part 1]
W: Sidney Sheldon. D: Hal Cooper. Jeannie is unaware that Dr. Bellows has planted a double in Tony's house while he is away on a secret mission.

The Case of My Vanishing Master [Part 2]
W: Sidney Sheldon. D: Hal Cooper. Tony's double proves to be an enemy agent.

Ride 'Em Astronaut
W: James Henerson. D: Hal Cooper. GS: Mark Miller, John Myhers. When Jeannie becomes Queen of the Rodeo, Tony accidentally enters a bucking bronco contest.

Invisible House for Sale
W: James Henerson. D: Hal Cooper. GS: Ed Peck, Joan Tompkins, Harold Gould. Feeling Tony would spend more time with her, Jeannie puts his house up for sale.

Jeannie, the Governor's Wife
W: Christopher Golato. D: Hal Cooper. Jeannie and Roger insist Tony run for governor of Florida.

Is There a Doctor in the House?
W: Christopher Golato. D: Oscar Rudolph. When Jeannie's mother pays a visit, she immediately falls in love with Dr. Bellows.

The Biggest Star in Hollywood
W: James Henerson. D: Claudio Guzman. GS: Judy Carne, Arte Johnson, Gary Owens, George Schlatter. Jeannie appears on the "Laugh-In" show, making her an instant celebrity.

The Case of the Porcelain Puppy
W: James Henerson. D: Claudio Guzman. GS: Woodrow Parfrey. Jeannie's recipe for turning things into porcelain backfires when she accidentally turns her dog Djinn Djinn into a porcelain statue.

Jeannie for the Defense
W: Bruce Howard. D: Hal Cooper.

GS: Dick Sargent, J. Pat O'Malley. In a small town, Tony is arrested for hit and run driving.

Nobody Loves a Fat Astronaut
W: Christopher Golato. D: Claudio Guzman. Jeannic's sister fouls up Tony's chances of flying to the moon by increasing his weight to 300 pounds.

Around the Moon in 80 Blinks
W: James Henerson. D: Claudio Guzman. GS: Richard Mulligan. On a moon mission, Jeannie blinks Tony home fearing for his safety.

Jeannie-Go-Round
W: James Henerson. D: Claudio Guzman. While Tony is out on a date, Jeannie's sister tries to steal him.

Jeannie and the Secret Weapon
W: Larry Markes. D: Leo Garen. GS: Ron Masak. Jeannie's working toy model of a spacecraft almost gets Tony court martialed when an enterprising manufacturer tries to market the toy.

Blackmail Order Bride
W: James Henerson. D: Claudio Guzman. GS: George Furth. A reporter tries blackmail to get an in-depth interview with Major Nelson.

Jeannie at the Piano
W: James Henerson. D: Hal Cooper. After Jeannie blinks a piano, Tony winds up playing it like a master musician.

Djinn Djinn, the Pied Piper
W: James Henerson. D: Claudio Guzman. Djinn Djinn, Jeannie's dog, reappears, this time causing havoc with General Schaeffer's dog Jupiter.

Guess Who's Going to Be a Bride [Part 1]
W: James Henerson. D: Hal Cooper. Tony refuses the wish of Jeannie to be his bride, causing her to leave him forever.

Guess Who's Going to Be a Bride [Part 2]
W: James Henerson. D: Hal Cooper. GS: Jackie Coogan, Mickey Morton, Frank DeVol. Tony risks everything to find Jeannie and asks for her hand in marriage.

Jeannie's Beauty Cream
W: Joanna Lee. D: Hal Cooper. Jeannie's face cream turns Mrs. Bellows into a beautiful teenager.

Jeannie and the Bachelor Party
W: Richard Bensfield & Perry Grant. D: Hal Cooper. GS: Francine York, Judith Baldwin. A bachelor party for Tony surprises everyone, including Tony.

The Blood of a Jeannie
W: John L. Greene. D: Claudio Guzman. GS: Ned Glass, Ruth McDevitt. Jeannie's blood test for marriage causes problems when it turns out she has green corpuscles.

See You in C-U-B-A
W: John McGreevey. D: Hal Cooper. GS: Farrah Fawcett, Pedro Gonzales-Gonzales. Jeannie accidentally blinks Tony's plane to Cuba where he is taken prisoner.

The Mad Home Wrecker
W: Howard Ostroff. D: Hal Cooper. GS: Michael Lipton.   An interior decorator turns Tony's house into a shambles.

Uncles a Go-Go
W: Ron Friedman. D: Russ Mayberry. GS: Ronald Long, Arthur Malet. Before Jeannie may marry, her uncles will have final approval.

The Wedding
W: James Henerson. D: Claudio Guzman. GS: Cliff Norton. On the day of their wedding, Jeannie reveals that she cannot be photographed.

My Sister, the Homemaker
W: James Henerson. D: Claudio Guz-

man.   GS: Farrah Fawcett, Michael Ansara.   Jeannie's sister masquerades as Tony's wife until Jeannie figures out her disguise.

Jeannie, the Matchmaker
W: Don Richman & Bill Daily. GS: Janis Hanson. Jeannie tries to find Roger a perfect mate at the same time Roger is supposed to escort a general's niece.

Never Put a Genie on a Budget
W: Sidney Sheldon.   D: Oscar Rudolph. Tony puts Jeannie on a tight budget after she misuses his credit cards.

Please Don't Give My Jeannie No More Wine
W: James Henerson. D: John G. Anderson.   GS: Alan Oppenheimer. Jeannie's special wine causes the Bellowses to disappear.

One of Our Hotels Is Growing
W: Bob Rodgers. D: Jerry Bernstein. GS: Marvin Kaplan, Fran Ryan, Ned Wertimer. When there is no room at a hotel, Jeannie blinks on an extra floor.

The Solid Gold Jeannie
W: Joanna Lee. D: Jerry Bernstein. GS: Robert Hogan. In isolation after a moon trip, Jeannie blinks in on Tony and is mistaken for a creature from outer space by a fellow astronaut.

Mrs. Djinn Djinn
W: Richard Bensfield & Perry Grant. D: Russ Mayberry.   When Roger spreads the news that Jeannie is expecting, he doesn't know that Mrs. Djinn Djinn is the only one about to become a mother.

Jeannie and the Curious Kid
W: Richard Bensfield & Perry Grant. D: Claudio Guzman.   Dr. Bellows's nephew sees Jeannie come out of the bottle, prompting him to tell his uncle of the strange happenings.

Jeannie, the Recording Secretary
W: James Henerson. D: Claudio Guzman. GS: Joan Tompkins, Norma Connolly. Jeannie tries to get Tony the Best Husband award at the same time he is expected on an important moon mission.

Help, Help a Shark
W: James Henerson. D: Claudio Guzman. GS: Jim Backus. Tony tries to outwit a pool hustler.

Eternally Yours, Jeannie
W: James Henerson. D: Joseph Goodson. GS: Denny Miller, Damian Brodie. Tony has an unexpected reunion with his high school sweetheart and her jealous husband.

An Astronaut in Sheep's Clothing
W: James Henerson. D: Bruce Kessler.

Jeannie tries to give Tony a hand-knit sweater for their anniversary, using a live goat for material.

Hurricane Jeannie
W: James Henerson. D: Claudio Guzman. Tony dreams Dr. Bellows discovers that Jeannie is a real genie.

One Jeannie Beats Four of a Kind
W: Richard Bensfield & Perry Grant. D: Michael Ansara. To capture a card shark, Tony and Roger play poker with disastrous results.

My Master, the Chili King
W: James Henerson. D: Claudio Guzman. GS: Gabriel Dell. Tony's conniving cousin Arvel makes him the unauthorized chili king of Cocoa Beach.

I LOVE LUCY/THE LUCY-DESI COMEDY HOUR

On the air 10/15/51, off 6/24/57. CBS. B&W Film. 179 episodes. Broadcast: Oct 1951-Jun 1957 Mon 9-9:30. 10 hour episodes of the Comedy Hour. B&W Film. Producer: Desi Arnaz. Prod. Co: Desilu. Synd: Viacom (both versions).

CAST: Lucy Ricardo (played by Lucille Ball), Ricky Ricardo (Desi Arnaz), Ethel Mertz (Vivian Vance), Fred Mertz (William Frawley), Little Ricky (Richard Keith).

Theme: "I Love Lucy" by Harold Adamson and Eliot Daniel.

The adventures of a screwball redhead, her Cuban bandleader husband, and their landlord friends. This is the most classic of all comedy shows. It was a great success when it first aired and it is still a success after thirty years. After the series went off the air, the cast continued to make ten specials, which are now syndicated as a separate series that does not get played very often.

The Girls Want to Go to a Night Club
Lucy and Ethel want to celebrate the Mertzes' 18th wedding anniversary by going to a nightclub, but Ricky and Fred want to go to the fights.

Be a Pal
GS: Dick Reeves, Tony Michaels. Lucy, thinking Ricky is no longer interested in her, follows the advice of a book on how to save your marriage.

The Diet
GS: Marco Rizo. Lucy goes on a diet in order to get a job as a singer at Ricky's club.

Lucy Thinks Ricky Is Trying to Do Away with Her
GS: Jerry Hausner. After reading a murder mystery, Lucy convinces herself that Ricky wants to kill her.

The Quiz Show
GS: Frank Nelson, John Emery, Phil

Lucille Ball (center) and William Frawley with Tallulah Bankhead in "The Celebrity Next Door" episode of the Lucy-Desi Comedy Hour (a continuation of I Love Lucy).

Ober. Lucy will win $1000 if she convinces Ricky that she had a first husband.

The Audition
GS: Jess Oppenheimer, Harry Ackerman. Lucy tries to get into Ricky's act when she learns a TV network talent scout is going to be in the audience.

The Seance
GS: Jay Novello. Lucy and Ethel hold a seance in order to convince a theatrical producer to hire Ricky.

Men Are Messy
GS: Kenny Morgan. Sloppy Ricky and neat Lucy divide the apartment in half.

The Fur Coat
GS: Ben Weldon. Lucy believes the mink coat Ricky brought home is her anniversary present.

The Adagio
GS: Shep Menken. In order to appear in a show at Ricky's club, Lucy hires an amorous Frenchman to teach her to dance.

Drafted
Lucy and Ethel believe that Ricky and Fred have been drafted, while they believe the girls are pregnant.

Jealous of Girl Singer
GS: Helen Silver. Lucy believes Ricky is fooling around with Rosemary, a singer at the club.

The Benefit
Lucy tries to get Ricky to appear in a benefit show for Ethel's women's club.

The Amateur Hour
GS: David Stollery. Lucy babysits for twins in order to get enough money to pay for a new dress.

Lucy Plays Cupid
GS: Bea Benaderet, Edward Everett Horton. Lucy tries to get her spinster neighbor and the local grocer together.

Lucy's Fake Illness
GS: Hal March. Lucy fakes an illness to trick Ricky into hiring her for a new act at the club.

Lucy Writes a Play
Lucy writes a play and tries to get Ricky to appear in it.

Break the Lease
GS: Barbara Pepper. Lucy and Ricky try to break their lease when they have a fight with Fred and Ethel.

The Ballet
GS: Mary Wickes, Frank DeMille. Lucy takes ballet lessons so she can appear at Ricky's club.

The Young Fans
GS: Janet Waldo, Richard Crenna. A teenager falls for Ricky, causing Lucy to find a way to get her and her boyfriend back together.

New Neighbors
GS: Hayden Rorke, K.T. Stevens, Allen Jenkins. Lucy and Ethel suspect the new neighbors of being spies.

Fred and Ethel Fight
Lucy and Ricky try to stop the Mertzes from fighting, but wind up fighting themselves.

The Mustache
When Ricky grows a mustache, Lucy gets even by wearing a fake beard.

The Gossip
GS: Bobby Jellison, Dick Reeves. The boys bet they can keep from gossiping longer than the girls.

Pioneer Women
GS: Ruth Stern, Florence Bates. The boys bet that they can survive longer without modern conveniences than the girls.

The Marriage License
GS: Irving Bacon, Elizabeth Patterson. Lucy wants to recreate her courtship when she learns her marriage license is invalid.

The Kleptomaniac
GS: Joseph Kearns. When Ricky finds the items Lucy was collecting for a charity bazaar, he thinks she is a kleptomaniac.

Cuban Pals
GS: Robert Morin, Lita Baron, Rita Convy. Lucy becomes jealous when a beautiful girl who used to dance with Ricky in Cuba comes for a visit.

The Freezer
GS: Frank Sully. Lucy and Ethel buy a meat freezer and then unknowingly buy 700 pounds of meat.

Lucy Does a TV Commercial
GS: Ross Elliott, Jerry Hausner, Maurice Thompson. Lucy gets drunk while doing a live TV commercial.

The Publicity Agent
GS: Peter Leeds, Bennett Green, Gil Herman, Dick Reeves. Lucy dresses up as a Maharincess in order to get publicity for Ricky.

Lucy Gets Ricky on the Radio
GS: Bobby Ellis, Roy Rowan, Frank Nelson. Lucy and Ricky appear on a radio quiz show.

Lucy's Schedule
GS: Gale Gordon. Ricky puts Lucy on a time schedule in order to impress the new owner of the club.

Lucy Thinks Ricky's Getting Bald
GS: Milton Parsons. Lucy, thinking Ricky is afraid of going bald, tries to find a way of convincing him that he is not.

Ricky Asks for a Raise
GS: Gale Gordon, Maurice Marsac. Lucy tries to save Ricky's job when he is fired after asking for a raise.

Job Switching
GS: Alan DeWitt, Elvia Allman. The girls go to work in a candy factory while the boys stay home and do the housework.

The Saxophone
GS: Herb Vigran. When Ricky won't let Lucy play the saxophone in his band, she plots to make him jealous.

The Anniversary Present
GS: Gloria Blondell. Lucy believes Ricky is fooling around with their beautiful neighbor.

The Handcuffs
GS: Will Wright. Lucy accidentally locks Ricky and herself together in a pair of handcuffs.

The Operetta
Lucy, Ricky, Fred and Ethel appear in a gypsy operetta.

Vacation from Marriage
The boys separate from the girls for a week in order to save their marriages.

The Courtroom
GS: Moroni Olsen. The Ricardos and the Mertzes go to court for breaking each other's television sets.

Redecorating
GS: Hans Conreid. Lucy sells all of their old furniture when she thinks she won new furniture in a contest.

Ricky Loses His Voice
GS: Barbara Pepper. Lucy takes over when Ricky loses his voice and can't stage the show for the club's new owner.

Lucy Is Enceinte
GS: Dick Reeves, William Hamil. Lucy tries to tell Ricky she is pregnant.

Pregnant Women
Lucy believes Ricky is only interested in the baby and not her.

Lucy's Show Biz Swan Song
GS: Jerry Hausner, Pepito the Spanish Clown. Lucy tries to get into Ricky's Gay Nineties revue at the Club.

Lucy Hires an English Tutor
GS: Hans Conreid. Lucy hires an English tutor when she fears Ricky's bad English could affect the baby.

Ricky Has Labor Pains
GS: Lou Merrill, Jerry Hausner. Ricky is jealous of all the attention Lucy and the expected baby are getting.

Lucy Becomes a Sculptress
GS: Shep Menken, Paul Harvey. Lucy buys fifty pounds of clay and sets out to create a masterpiece.

Lucy Goes to the Hospital
GS: Barbara Pepper, Peggy Rea, Charles Lane, Bennett Green, Ralph Montgomery. Ricky becomes a nervous wreck when Lucy is about to have the baby.

Sales Resistance
GS: Sheldon Leonard, Verna Felton. Ricky recalls the day when Lucy couldn't say no to a pushy salesman.

The Inferiority Complex
GS: Gerald Mohr. Ricky hires a psychiatrist to cure Lucy of her feelings of inferiority.

The Club Election
GS: Ida Moore, Doris Singleton. Ethel recalls the time she and Lucy ran for president of their ladies club.

The Black Eye
GS: Bennett Green. The Mertzes believe Ricky hit Lucy when she suffers a black eye.

Lucy Changes Her Mind
GS: Johnny Hart, Phil Arnold, Frank Nelson. Lucy tries to make Ricky jealous by visiting her old boyfriend who is now in the fur business.

No Children Allowed
GS: Peggy Rea, June Whitley, Elizabeth Patterson, Janet Lawrence, Kay Wiley. Little Ricky's crying is disturbing their crabby neighbor Mrs. Trumbull.

Lucy Hires a Maid
GS: Verna Felton. Lucy hires a bossy maid, but is now afraid to fire her.

The Indian Show
GS: Dick Reeves, Jerry Hausner. Ricky is staging an Indian show at the club and Lucy wants to be in it.

Lucy's Last Birthday
GS: Byron Foulger, William Hamil, Ransom Sherman, Elizabeth Patterson. When Lucy believes everyone has forgotten her birthday, she joins the Friends of the Friendless. [This was the only time the theme song was sung.]

The Ricardos Change Apartments
GS: Norma Varden. Lucy tries to trick Ricky into moving into the larger apartment in the building.

Lucy the Matchmaker
GS: Hal March. Lucy plots to fix up the Mertzes' single friend with her girlfriend.

Lucy Wants New Furniture
Lucy buys new living room furniture and tries to hide it from Ricky.

The Camping Trip
In order to share their husbands' interests, Lucy and Ethel join them on a camping trip.

Ricky and Fred Are TV Fans
GS: Lawrence Dobkin, Allen Jenkins, Frank Nelson. While Ricky and Fred are glued to their TV set watching the fights, Lucy and Ethel are arrested.

Never Do Business with Friends
GS: Elizabeth Patterson, Herb Vigran. Lucy and Ricky sell their old washing machine to the Mertzes, then it breaks down.

Ricky's Life Story
Lucy still wants to get into show business, so Ricky tries to show her just how hard show business really is.

The Girls Go Into Business
GS: Mabel Paige, Kay Wiley, Barbara Pepper. Lucy and Ethel try to strike it rich by buying a dress shop.

Lucy and Ethel Buy the Same Dress
GS: Doris Singleton, Shirley Mitchell. Lucy and Ethel appear on a TV show wearing the same dress.

Equal Rights
The girls want to be treated equal, so the boys try to teach them a lesson.

Baby Pictures
GS: Hy Averback, Doris Singleton. Lucy and Ricky and Caroline and Charlie Appleby each try to outdo each other by bragging over their children.

Lucy Tells the Truth
GS: Doris Singleton, Shirley Mitchell, Charles Lane, Mario Siletti. Ricky and the Mertzes bet Lucy can't tell the absolute truth for 24 hours.

The French Revue
GS: Dick Reeves, Louis Nicoletti. Lucy hires a French waiter to teach Ethel and herself to speak French so they could appear in a French show at Ricky's club.

Redecorating the Mertzes' Apartment
Lucy ruins the Mertzes' furniture, while helping to redecorate their apartment.

Too Many Crooks
GS: Elizabeth Patterson, Allen Jenkins. Lucy and Ethel suspect each other of being Madame X, the neighborhood robber.

Changing the Boys' Wardrobe
GS: Jerry Hausner. Lucy and Ethel sell the boys' old clothes against their wishes.

Lucy Has Her Eyes Examined
GS: Dayton Lummis. Lucy auditions for a dance number after taking eye drops which blur her vision.

Ricky's Old Girlfriend
GS: Jerry Hausner. Ricky invents an old girlfriend to make Lucy jealous, then learns that the girl really exists.

The Million Dollar Idea
GS: Frank Nelson. Ethel and Lucy sell Homemade salad dressing on TV.

Ricky Minds the Baby
Ricky takes care of Little Ricky with disastrous results when he disappears.

The Charm School
GS: Natalie Schafer. Lucy and Ethel join a charm school when Fred and Ricky fall for a beautiful woman.

Sentimental Anniversary
GS: Barbara Pepper, Bennett Green. Lucy and Ricky want to spend their 13th anniversary alone, but the Mertzes plan a surprise party for them.

Fan Magazine Interview
GS: Elvia Allman, Jerry Hausner, Joan Banks. Lucy becomes upset when a publicity stunt backfires on her.

Oil Wells
GS: Harry Cheshire, Sara Jane Gould. The Ricardos and the Mertzes buy oil stock which might be phony.

Ricky Loses His Temper
GS: Madge Blake. Lucy bets Ricky that he will lose his temper before she buys another new hat.

Home Movies
Lucy and the Mertzes make their own pilot film when they hear a TV producer is coming to see Ricky's pilot film.

Bonus Bucks
Lucy and Ethel fight over who owns the dollar bill worth $300.

Ricky's Hawaiian Vacation
GS: Frank Nelson. Lucy tries to win a trip to Hawaii on a game show.

Lucy Is Envious
GS: Mary Jane Croft, Herb Vigran. In order to earn money to cover a pledge to charity, Lucy and Ethel appear as Martians in a publicity stunt.

Lucy Writes a Novel
GS: Dayton Lummis. Lucy writes a novel which includes Ricky and the Mertzes as its characters.

The Club Dance
GS: Shirley Mitchell, Doris Singleton. Lucy puts together an all-girl band to play at her club dance.

The Black Wig
GS: Louis Nicoletti. Lucy dons a black wig in order to test Ricky's fidelity.

The Diner
GS: Marco Rizo, James Burke, Joe Miller, Nick Escalante, Alberto Calderone. The Ricardos and the Mertzes invest in a local diner.

Tennessee Ernie Visits
GS: Tennessee Ernie Ford. A hillbilly relative moves in with the Ricardos.

Tennessee Ernie Hangs On
GS: Dick Reeves, Tennessee Ernie Ford. The Ricardos try to get rid of Ernie.

The Golf Game
GS: Jimmy Demaret, Louis Nicoletti. Ricky and Fred try to discourage Lucy and Ethel from playing golf.

The Sublease
GS: Jay Novello. The Ricardos sublet their apartment when they plan to spend the summer in Maine.

The Business Manager
GS: Charles Lane. Ricky hires a business manager and Lucy schemes to get rid of him.

Mertz and Kurtz
GS: Charles Winninger. Fred tries to impress his old vaudeville partner.

Lucy Cries Wolf
Lucy tests Ricky's loyalty when she pretends to be kidnapped.

The Watchmaker
GS: Sarah Selby, Milton Frome. Lucy tries to get two friends married by showing them how happy her marriage to Ricky is.

Mr. and Mrs. TV Show
Lucy and Ricky do a husband and wife TV show for a local department store.

Ricky's Movie Offer
GS: Frank Nelson, Elizabeth Patterson. Everybody tries to audition for a visiting movie talent scout.

Ricky's Screen Test
GS: Clinton Sundberg. Lucy tries to be the star in Ricky's screen test.

Lucy's Mother-in-Law
GS: Mary Emery. Lucy has to entertain Ricky's Spanish-speaking mother all by herself.

Ethel's Birthday
GS: John Emery. A fight breaks out between Lucy and Ethel while trying to celebrate Ethel's birthday.

Ricky's Contract
Ricky is glued to the phone waiting to hear if he got his Hollywood contract.

Getting Ready
The Ricardos and the Mertzes prepare to leave for Hollywood.

Lucy Learns to Drive
Ricky tries to teach Lucy how to drive their brand new car.

California, Here We Come
GS: Kathryn Kard, Elizabeth Patterson. Lucy's mother plans to join them on their trip to California.

First Stop
GS: Olin Howlin. The Ricardos and the Mertzes spend the night in a run-down cabin in Ohio.

Tennessee Bound
GS: Tennessee Ernie Ford, Will Wright, Border Twins. Ernie helps the Ricardos and the Mertzes escape from jail.

Ethel's Home Town
GS: Irving Bacon, Chick Chander. While visiting Ethel's father in New Mexico, Ethel is believed to be a future movie star and not Ricky.

L.A. at Last
GS: William Holden, Eve Arden, Bob Jellison, Harry Bartell, Dayton Lummis. In a restaurant, Lucy dumps a tray of food on William Holden.

Don Juan and Starlets
GS: Maggie McGuiness, Ross Elliott, Jesslyn Fax. Lucy believes Ricky is fooling around when he doesn't come home after a Hollywood premiere.

Lucy Gets in Pictures
GS: Louis Nicoletti, Bob Jellison, Lou Krugman. Lucy gets the part of a show girl in a Hollywood musical.

The Fashion Show
GS: Sheila MacRae, Don Loper. Lucy joins the wives of movie stars as a model in a fashion show.

The Hedda Hopper Story
GS: Kathryn Kard, Hy Averback, Bob Jellison, Hedda Hopper. Ricky's agent plans a publicity stunt to get Hedda Hopper to do a story on Ricky.

Don Juan Is Shelved
GS: Phil Ober. Lucy tries to get Ricky another film contract when his film is cancelled.

Bullfight Dance
GS: Marco Rizo. Lucy blackmails Ricky in order to appear in a TV benefit show.

Hollywood Anniversary
GS: Bob Jellison. Ricky forgets his anniversary and Lucy won't let him forget it.

The Star Upstairs
GS: Cornel Wilde. Lucy gets trapped

on Cornel Wilde's terrace while trying to sneak a look at him.

In Palm Springs
GS: Rock Hudson, Kathryn Kard. Rock Hudson helps Ricky to get even with Lucy.

The Dancing Star
GS: Van Johnson, Wilbur Hatch, Doris Singleton. Lucy tries to impress her friend by trying to get Van Johnson to make her his dancing partner.

Harpo Marx
GS: Harpo Marx, Doris Singleton. Lucy encounters Harpo Marx when he comes to help Lucy impress her friend.

Ricky Needs an Agent
GS: Parley Baer, Helen Kleeb. Lucy pretends to be Ricky's agent in order to get the studio to put him in another film.

The Tour
GS: Richard Widmark, Benny Rubin, Barbara Pepper. Lucy tries to steal a grapefruit from Richard Widmark's backyard.

Lucy Visits Grauman's
Lucy steals John Wayne's footprints from Grauman's Theatre for a souvenir.

Lucy and John Wayne
GS: John Wayne, Louis Nicoletti. Ricky gets John Wayne to make another set of footprints to replace the ones that Lucy stole and broke.

Lucy and the Dummy
Lucy dances with a stuffed dummy when Ricky refuses to perform at a studio party.

Ricky Sells the Car
Ricky sells the car and buys train tickets, but forgets to buy tickets for the Mertzes.

The Great Train Robbery
GS: Frank Nelson, Sam McDaniel, Louis Nicoletti, Harry Bartell, Lou Krugman. While on the train, Lucy has a run-in with a jewel thief.

Homecoming
GS: Bennett Green, Elvia Allman, Elizabeth Patterson. When they return home, Ricky is called a star so Lucy treats him like one, but Ricky hates it.

The Ricardos Are Interviewed
GS: Elliott Reid, John Gallaudet. The Ricardos prepare to appear on a TV interview show, causing a fight between the Ricardos and the Mertzes.

Lucy Goes to a Rodeo
GS: John Gallaudet, Dub Taylor. Fred tries to get Ricky to appear at his lodge's western show.

Nursery School
GS: Jesslyn Fax, Olan Soule. Ricky wants to send Little Ricky to nursery school against Lucy's wishes.

Ricky's European Booking
GS: Barney Phillips, Harry Antrim, Hazel Pierce. Lucy and Ethel try to raise money to go to Europe by holding a raffle.

The Passports
GS: Sheila Bromley. Lucy can't find her birth certificate, meaning she can't get her passport, so she plans to stowaway by locking herself in a trunk.

Staten Island Ferry
GS: Charles Lane. Lucy takes a handful of seasickness pills and nearly misses her chance of getting her passport when she falls asleep on the ferry.

Bon Voyage
GS: Jack Albertson, Frank Gerstle, Ken Christy. Lucy misses the boat, so she takes a helicopter to the boat.

Second Honeymoon
GS: Marco Rizo, Harvey Grant. Lucy plans to kidnap Ricky in order for her to spend more time with him.

Lucy Meets the Queen
GS: Nancy Kulp. In England, Lucy tries to get into Ricky's show in order to meet the Queen.

The Fox Hunt
GS: Trevor Ward, Walter Kingsford, Hillary Brooke. The Ricardos spend the weekend at a British movie producer's estate.

Lucy Goes to Scotland
Lucy dreams she is in the village of her Scottish ancestors and is about to be fed to a dragon.

Paris at Last
GS: Fritz Feld, Lawrence Dobkin, Rolfe Sedan, Shep Menken, Maurice Marsac. Lucy is arrested for passing counterfeit money.

Lucy Meets Charles Boyer
GS: Charles Boyer. Lucy hires what she thinks is a Charles Boyer look-alike in order to trick Ricky.

Lucy Gets a Paris Gown
Lucy goes on a hunger strike in order to force Ricky into buying her a Jacques Marcel dress.

Lucy in the Swiss Alps
The Ricardos and the Mertzes are trapped in a cabin by an avalanche.

Lucy Gets Homesick
GS: Brad Bradley. In Italy, Lucy holds a birthday party for Little Ricky, even though he is still in New York.

Lucy's Italian Movie
GS: Franco Consaro, Teresa Tirelli. Lucy practices grape stomping in order to get a part in a movie.

Lucy's Bicycle Trip
Lucy can't cross the border to the French Riviera without her passport which is locked in her suitcase that was sent to the hotel in Nice.

Lucy Goes to Monte Carlo
Lucy wins a fortune at a casino, then has to tell Ricky who told her not to go to the casino.

Return Home from Europe
GS: Mary Jane Croft, Frank Nelson. Lucy tries to smuggle a 25-pound piece of cheese aboard the plane disguised as a baby.

Lucy and Bob Hope
GS: Phil Leeds, Lou Krugman, Henry Kulky, Dick Elliot, Bennett Green. Lucy tries to get Bob Hope to appear at Ricky's club.

Little Ricky Learns to Play the Drums
GS: Elizabeth Patterson. Little Ricky's drum playing is driving everyone crazy.

Lucy Meets Orson Welles
GS: Orson Welles, Ellen Corby. Lucy tries to appear with Orson Welles at Ricky's club, unaware he is doing his magic act and not Shakespeare.

Little Ricky Gets Stage Fright
GS: Howard McNear. Little Ricky gets stage fright and refuses to play his drums in public.

Visitor from Italy
GS: Jay Novello, Eduardo Ciannelli, Peter Brocco, James Flavin. A gondolier from Venice visits the Ricardos who help him raise money so he can visit his brother in San Francisco.

Off to Florida
GS: Elsa Lanchester, Strother Martin. Lucy and Ethel share a ride to Florida with a strange woman who may be a hatchet murderess.

Deep Sea Fishing
It is the men versus the women in a contest to see who can catch the biggest fish.

Desert Island
GS: Claude Akins, Joi Lansing, Jil Jarmyn. The Ricardos and the Mertzes are stranded on a deserted island when their boat runs out of gas.

The Ricardos Visit Cuba
GS: Mary Emery, George Trevino. Lucy insults Ricky's Uncle Alberto when the Ricardos visit Cuba.

Little Ricky's School Pageant
GS: Candy Rogers. The Ricardos and the Mertzes appear in Little Ricky's school play.

Lucy and the Loving Cup
GS: Phillips Tead, Robert Foulk, Johnny Longden. Lucy gets a loving cup stuck on her head and then gets lost on the subway.

Lucy and Superman
GS: George Reeves, Madge Blake, Ralph Dumke. Lucy promises to get TV's Superman, George Reeves, to appear at Little Ricky's birthday party.

Little Ricky Gets a Dog
GS: John Emery. Little Ricky's pet dog is annoying the new neighbor.

Lucy Wants to Move to the Country
GS: Eleanor Audley, Frank Wilcox. The Ricardos buy a house in Connecticut, then Lucy and the Mertzes try to get the owner to buy it back.

Lucy Hates to Leave
The Ricardos move in with the Mertzes when Fred wants to rent the apartment before they move out.

Lucy Misses the Mertzes
The Ricardos go to New York to visit the Mertzes while the Mertzes are on their way to visit them in Connecticut.

Lucy Gets Chummy with the Neighbors
GS: Parley Baer, Mary Jane Croft. Lucy and neighbor Betty Ramsey go shopping for new furniture although Lucy can't afford it.

Lucy Raises Chickens
The Ricardos and the Mertzes go into the egg business with 500 baby chickens.

Lucy Does the Tango
After exchanging the chicks for hens, Ricky wants to get rid of them when they don't lay eggs. Lucy and Ethel try to help by buying eggs to put under the hens.

Ragtime Band
Lucy, Fred, Ethel and Little Ricky plan to perform at a benefit when Ricky refuses to bring his band.

Lucy's Night in Town
GS: Joseph Kearns. The Ricardos and the Mertzes go to the theater to see a play, but Lucy gets the wrong tickets.

Housewarming
GS: Frank Nelson. Ethel and Betty Ramsey become friends, leaving Lucy out in the cold.

Building a Bar-B-Q
Lucy thinks she lost her wedding ring in the cement Ricky used to build their new Bar-B-Q.

Country Club Dance
GS: Barbara Eden. Fred, Ricky and Ralph fall for a beautiful girl, causing the girls to become jealous.

Lucy Raises Tulips
Lucy tries to win a prize for the best looking garden.

The Ricardos Dedicate a Statue
GS: Lucie Arnaz and Desi Arnaz, Jr. Lucy wrecks the statue which Ricky has been chosen to dedicate.

[The Lucy-Desi Comedy Hour.]

Lucy Takes a Cruise to Havana
GS: Ann Sothern, Hedda Hopper, Cesar Romero, Rudy Vallee. Lucy recalls how she, Ricky and the Mertzes first met on a ship bound for Cuba. [This was also a crossover episode from the "Ann Sothern Show."]

The Celebrity Next Door
GS: Tallulah Bankhead. Lucy tries to get neighbor Tallulah Bankhead to appear at the PTA Benefit show.

Lucy Hunts Uranium
GS: Fred MacMurray, June Havoc. Lucy goes to Las Vegas and hunts uranium with Fred MacMurray.

Lucy Wins a Racehorse
GS: Betty Grable, Harry James. Lucy wins a racehorse in a cereal contest.

Lucy Goes to Sun Valley
GS: Fernando Lamas. Lucy goes skiing in Sun Valley.

Lucy Goes to Mexico
GS: Maurice Chevalier. Lucy gets into trouble with U.S. Customs in Tijuana, while Ricky and Maurice Chevalier rehearse for their show aboard the U.S.S. Yorktown.

Lucy Makes Room for Danny
GS: Danny Thomas. The Ricardos rent their house to Danny Thomas. [This is a crossover episode from "Make Room for Daddy."]

Lucy Goes to Alaska
GS: Red Skelton. Lucy looks for gold in Alaska and helps Red Skelton put on a show.

Lucy Wants a Career
GS: Paul Douglas. Lucy gets a job assisting actor Paul Douglas.

Lucy's Summer Vacation
GS: Howard Duff, Ida Lupino. The Ricardos unknowingly share a cabin with Howard Duff and Ida Lupino.

Milton Berle Hides Out at the Ricardos
GS: Milton Berle. Milton Berle moves in with the Ricardos.

The Ricardos Go to Japan
GS: Bob Cummings. The Ricardos take a trip to Japan.

The Redhead Meets the Moustache
GS: Ernie Kovacs, Edie Adams. Lucy tries to meet Ernie Kovacs.

I'M DICKENS, HE'S FENSTER

On the air 9/28/62, off 9/13/63. ABC. 30 min. Film. B&W. 32 episodes. Broadcast: Sept 1962-Sept 1963 Fri 9-9:30. Producer: Leonard Stern. Synd: Worldvision.

CAST: Arch Fenster (played by Marty Ingels), Harry Dickens (John Astin), Kate Dickens (Emmaline Henry), Mel Warshaw (Dave Ketchum), Mulligan (Henry Beckman), Myron Bannister (Frank DeVol).

The adventures of carpenters Harry Dickens, a henpecked husband, and Arch Fenster, a swinging young bachelor. Typical episodes concern Harry's desire to go places with Arch while Kate, Harry's wife, strongly objects. Available for syndication but not seen because of small number of episodes.

A Small Matter of Being Fired
Mr. Bannister needs a foreman for a construction job. So Arch guarantees Harry that he has got the job.

Nurse Dickens
GS: Peter Lupus, Jacques Foti. Harry is afraid his wife will meet a handsome doctor while working as a part-time nurse.

The Double Life of Mel Warshaw
While at the Post Office, Arch and Harry find a Wanted poster that looks just like their friend Mel.

Harry, the Father Image
GS: Ellen [Burstyn] McRae, Danica D'Handt. Arch is engaged to his latest girlfriend, but Harry doesn't think it is a good idea.

Part-Time Friend
Harry is saying bad things about Arch in his sleep.

The Acting Game
GS: Jack Perkins, Harvey Korman, Sue Randall. Harry has been chosen to do a TV commercial for a tool company.

The Toupee Story
GS: Hank Ladd. Mr. Bannister's indecisiveness is causing Arch and Harry to work overtime.

A Wolf in Friend's Clothing
A friend's daughter is staying with Harry. So "wolf" Arch moves in for the kill.

Party, Party, Who's Got the Party?
Arch throws a big party at Harry's house, without asking him.

The Yellow Badge of Courage
Bannister fires Arch when he spends more time with his girlfriends than on the job.

The Joke
GS: James Milhollin, Rory O'Brien, Robert Ball. Harry tries to find a joke to tell at the Safety Award Dinner.

Love Me, Love My Dog
GS: Tracy Morgan, Chickie Lind. Harry and Kate get lonely Arch a dog.

Here's to the Three of Us
GS: Don Briggs.   Harry and Kate throw a party for their married friends causing Arch to feel left out.

Get Off My Back
GS: Francine York. Harry can't keep Arch away from him long enough to buy him a present.

How Not to Succeed in Business
GS: Buddy Lester, Jan Arvan. Harry and Arch plan to quit their jobs in order to go into business together.

The Godfathers
GS: Jack Perkins, Jacqueline Malouf. Harry and Arch are named godfathers to Mel's kids.

The Carpenters Four
GS: Henry Beckman.   Harry is in charge of the entertainment for the Carpenter's annual show.

The Great Valenciaga
Mulligan's sister comes for a visit. So he tries to protect her from Arch.

Mr. Takeover
Harry finds out if the crew can work without him or not when an accident puts him in the hospital.

Have Car, Will Quarrel
Harry, Arch and Mulligan split the cost of a used car.

Say It with Pictures
Arch and Harry plan to write a new Carpenter's Manual complete with pictures.

Senior Citizen Charlie
GS: Dabbs Greer. A retiring carpenter isn't happy about the idea of a retirement party.

The Bet
GS: Jericho Brown, Sally Kellerman. The carpenters bet that Arch can get a date with a beautiful girl.

The Syndicate
GS: Dan Frazer. Harry and Arch find a strongbox in an old gangster's house.

Is There a Doctor in the House?
GS: Dorothy Brown, Michael Fox. Arch's new girl thinks he is a doctor.

Harry, the Contractor
Kate can't get Harry to fix up the house, so she hires a carpenter, Arch.

Table Tennis, Anyone?
GS: Alan Hewitt. Harry is chosen captain of the company ping pong team.

Kick Me, Kate
Harry thinks Kate doesn't love him anymore because she is never jealous.

Number One, Son
GS: Roger Mobley. Mel takes his son camping.

Big Opening at the Hospital
GS: Jesse White. Kate is going to sing at a benefit show, but Harry is afraid a talent scout will see her.

King Archibald, the First
GS: John Abbott, Brenda Scott. Arch is dating a real princess.

Hotel Fenster
After fighting with their wives, Mel, Harry and Mulligan move in with Arch.

IT'S ABOUT TIME

On the air 9/11/66, off 8/27/67. CBS. Color Film. 27 episodes. Broadcast: Sept 1966-Aug 1967 Sun 7:30-8. Producer: Sherwood Schwartz. Prod Co/ Synd: United Artists TV.

CAST: Hector (played by Jack Mullaney), Mac (Frank Aletter), Shad (Imogene Coca), Gronk (Joe E. Ross), Boss (Cliff Norton), Clon (Mike Mazurki), Mrs. Boss (Kathleen Freeman), Mlor (Mary Grace), Breer (Pat Cardi).

Two astronauts accidentally break through the time barrier and wind up in a prehistoric world where they befriend a family of cave people and try to fix their ship so they can return. Halfway through the season, they fixed their ship and unknowingly brought the cave family back to the future with them. This series can best be described as the prehistoric version of *Gilligan's Island*, which is not surprising as they were created by the same producer, Sherwood Schwartz. This series is not running on any station due to the small number of episodes.

And Then I Wrote Happy Birthday to You [Pilot]
W: Sherwood & Elroy Schwartz & David P. Harmon. D: Richard Donner. Two astronauts, Mac and Hector, break through the time barrier and land on Earth in the year 1 Million B.C. There they befriend a family of cave people.

The Copper Caper
W: Joel Kane. D: George Cahan. In order to repair their spaceship the astronauts need copper, but they have to get it from Boss who won't give it up.

The Initiation
W: Bruce Howard. D: Jack Arnold. The cave people issue an ultimatum to Mac and Hector, either leave or become members of the tribe.

Tailor-Made Hero
W: Herbert Finn & Alan Dinehart. D: Jack Arnold. When Mac and Hector rescue Breer from a cave, he loses faith in his father, sending his father off on a search for a way to regain his son's admiration.

The Rain Makers
W & D: Unavailable. [This episode is not in syndication.] The cave people believe that Mac and Hector are the cause of a drought, so they offer them a choice: either end the drought or die at noon as sacrifices to the water god.

The Courtship of Miles Gronk
W: Budd Grossman. D: Jack Arnold. Hector tells Shad and Gronk about how couples act, in the future, causing domestic rivalry everywhere because the women approve of the new ways and the men don't.

The Champ
W: Herbert Finn & Alan Dinehart. D: Jerry Hopper. GS: Ron Feinberg. A fight is held to settle the differences between two villages.

Mark Your Ballots
W: Roland MacLane. D: Jerry Hopper. GS: Blossom Rock. The boys convince the cave people to hold an election to pick a new boss.

Have I Got a Girl for You
W: Jerry Adelman. D: Leslie Goodwins. GS: Mary Foran. When Shad tries to fix the boys up with wives, they run into the jungle where they meet a dinosaur.

Cave Movies
W: Bruce Howard. D: Jerry Hopper. The boys prepare to go home by filming the cave people to prove where they have been. However, Boss thinks the camera is an evil spirit so he tries to smash it.

Androcles and Clon
W: Roland MacLane. D: Jerry Hopper. GS: Janos Prohaska. Hec and Mac make a model airplane for Breer which Boss thinks is an evil spirit, so he sends Clon to capture it.

Love Me, Love My Gnook
W: Herbert Finn and Alan Dinehart. D: George Cahan. Hec and Mac give a dog to Breer for a pet. However, Boss plans to punish the boys because dogs (gnooks) bring bad luck.

The Broken Idol
W: Brad Radnitz. D: Leslie Goodwins. The boys deface a local fire god idol while looking for aluminum for their spaceship. The Boss now thinks that the volcano will erupt.

The Sacrifice
W: Bill Freedman & Marty Roth. D: George Cahan. Mac and Hec plan to stop the cave people from sacrificing Mlor to the dinosaurs.

King Hec
W: Arthur Weingarten. D: George Cahan. When Hec uses a barometer to predict an approaching storm, the cave people make him their king.

The Mother-in-Law
W: Jerry Adelman. D: George Cahan. GS: Janos Prohaska, Andy Albin. Shad's mother comes for a visit and interferes with Mlor and Breer's activities.

Which Doctor's Witch?
W: Albert E. Lewin. D: Leslie Goodwins. GS: Kathleen Freeman. Gronk becomes sick, so Boss and Shad both play witch doctor. Shad puts a curse on Boss, threatening to turn him into a monkey; later that day, a monkey is seen wearing Boss's clothes.

To Catch a Thief
W: Budd Grossman. D: Jerry Hopper. Hec and Mac are accused of stealing, so they set out to discover who the real thief is or suffer the consequences.

The Stowaway
W: Burt Styler. D: George Cahan. The boys find Mlor hiding on their ship so she won't have to be forced into marrying the Boss's son.

20th Century Here We Come
The astronauts are finally able to repair their ship and return home, but they realize too late that Shad, Gronk and their kids have stowed away on the ship.

Shad Rack and Other Tortures
W: David P. Harmon. D: Jerry Hopper. GS: Frank Wilcox, Alan DeWitt. Mac and Hec have a difficult time convincing the General about where they have been, so they invite him home to meet the cave people.

The Cave Family Swingers
W: Joel Rapp & Sam Locke. D: Steve Binder. GS: Karen Valentine, Evelyn King. A talent scout wants to promote the cave family's song "Dinosaur Stew" as a pop single.

The Stone Age Diplomats
W: Joel Kane. D: Leslie Goodwins. GS: Herb Edelman, Leon Askin. Mac

and Hec have to convince their building super that the cave people are visiting diplomats from Nordania or else he will have them thrown out.

To Sign or Not to Sign
W: Joel Kane. D: David McDearmon. GS: Henry Corden, Susan Brown. The boys teach the cave people how to sign their names. Now they are signing everything, including applications to join the Army.

School Days, School Days
W: Michael Morris. D: Jack Shea. GS: Joe Conley, Jackie Russell. Breer tries to convince his teacher that the world is flat.

Our Brother's Keeper
W: Bill Freedman & Ben Gershman. D: David McDearmon. GS: Brad Trumbull, Alan Davis. Hec and Mac bring the cave people down to the air base to prove a trip to the past is possible.

THE JACK BENNY SHOW

On the air 10/28/50, off 9/10/65. CBS, NBC. 30 min. B&W Film. 104 episodes. Although 343 episodes were made, only 104 are syndicated as most of the shows were done live. Only the episodes from the 1960s are rerun. Broadcast: Oct 1950-Jan 1959 CBS Sun 7:30-8; Oct 1959-Jan 1960 CBS Sun 10-10:30; Oct 1960-Jun 1962 CBS Sun 9:30-10; Sept 1962-Jun 1963 CBS Tue 9:30-10; Sept 1963-Sept 1964 CBS Tue 9:30-10; Sept 1964-Sept 1965 NBC Fri 9:30-10. Producer: Fred De Cordova (filmed episodes only). Prod Co/Synd: Universal TV.

CAST: Cast members portrayed themselves: Jack Benny, Eddie "Rochester" Anderson, Don Wilson, Dennis Day, Mary Livingstone (Mrs. Jack Benny), Frank Nelson, and Mel Blanc as Prof. LeBlanc.

Jack Benny plays himself in this situation comedy focusing on his home and working life. Episodes revolve around Jack, his faithful servant Rochester, and Mary Livingstone, who played his girlfriend but in real life was his wife. *The Jack Benny Show* is frequently seen on late-night television and is considered one of television's classic comedies.

How Jack Found Mary
Rochester and Roy dry dishes. The knives have "Hilton" written on them. Jack tells how he first met Mary.

Bedroom Burglar Show
Burglars enter Jack's bedroom, he calls the police and finds out the Beverly Hills police have an unlisted number.

Carnival Story
Jack goes to a carnival and gets into a lion's cage, thinking it is really Mr. Kitzel in a lion's suit.

4 O'Clock in the Morning Show
A disc jockey wakes Jack up with a silly question.

Rochester Falls Asleep, Misses Program
Roy invites Rochester up to his cabin for the weekend. He turns on Jack's show, falls asleep and misses it.

Jack Dives into Empty Swimming Pool in Palm Springs
In Palm Springs, Jack jumps into an empty swimming pool and has to stay in bed for a whole week.

Massage and Date with Gertrude
Jack gets massage with chicken fat and then takes Gertrude to a restaurant.

Jack Hunts for Uranium
Don talks Jack into hunting for uran-

ium and then Jack asks Mary to go along.

Mary Has May Company Reunion
Mary invites Jack to a reunion she is giving for the May Company girls who used to work with her.

Don Invites Gang to Dinner
Don thanks everyone for some anniversary presents and invites the gang over for dinner.

Isaac Stern Show
GS: Isaac Stern.   Jack threatens to jump out of the window because he is not a good violinist, so Isaac Stern plays for him.

Jack in Paris
GS: Maurice Chevalier. In Paris, Mary and Jack go up to the top of the Eiffel Tower, and Jack finds Maurice Chevalier in a local shop.

Jack Locked in Tower of London
Jack takes a lesson in English money

and then goes on a sightseeing tour of Trafalgar Square and the Tower of London.

Jack Falls into Canal in Venice
Waiting for a gondola, Jack falls into a canal, twice.

Jack Hires an Opera Singer in Rome
A crowd at the Rome airport wants an opera singer's autograph.

Ginger Rogers Show
GS: Ginger Rogers. A producer tells Jack they have to find a new script for the next show, so he asks Ginger Rogers and Fred Astaire for their help.

Hillbilly Act
Jack says he hasn't changed since he was young so he takes off his shirt and acts like a hillbilly.

Jack Goes to the Races
Dennis gives a long routine on how to pick horses.   Meanwhile, Jack bets on the sponsor's horse and wins.

Jack's Life Story
GS: Van Johnson. Jack's ego has gone to his head when he hears they are going to film his life story.

Jack Takes Beavers to Dentist
The mother of one of Jack's Beavers asks Jack to take the boy to the dentist, who then pulls Jack's tooth by mistake.

Railroad Station Program
At the railway station the ticket Jack was supposed to get went to a fat girl, and it turns out the girl is Jack's daughter.

The Bergen Show
GS: Edgar Bergen. Jack tells jokes about ventriloquists and then goes over to see Edgar Bergen at his house, and finds Charlie McCarthy and Mortimer Snerd are real children.

Pasadena Fan Club
Two old ladies ask Jack to come to

their Jack Benny Fan Club meeting in Pasadena.

Jack Arrested for Disturbing the Peace
Jack goes to bed, can't fall asleep, gets up to play the violin and gets arrested for disturbing the peace.

Jack Goes to Doctor
GS: Oscar Levant. Jack is irritable and unreasonable at rehearsal, so Oscar Levant persuades him to go to his doctor.

Jack Goes to Nightclub
GS: Danny Thomas. Jack takes his sponsor and wife to a nightclub, one with no comedians, but the regular entertainer is sick so Danny Thomas takes over.

Jimmy Stewart Show
GS: Jimmy Stewart. Barbara Nichols and Jack join the Stewarts at a nightclub to celebrate the Stewarts' wedding anniversary.

Musicale
A look into Jack's past reveals: Sunday musicales at his house.

Jack at Supermarket
Rochester beats Jack at cards so Jack has to do the housework, including the dreaded chore of going supermarket shopping.

Jack Casting for TV Special
Jack wrote his life story and is casting it for TV. He casts a child agent to play him as a boy and the child is as cheap as he.

Lunch Counter Murder
Jack is running a lunch counter when two tough guys come in to rob him, so Jack shoots them both.

Hong Kong Suit
Jack goes to the barber shop but no one will cut his hair because he is wearing a suit he got in Hong Kong for $12.00.

Jack Goes to Vault
Two men from the Treasury visit Jack to see all the devices he has worked up over the years to protect his money.

Don's Anniversary
It's Don's anniversary and Jack tells the story of how he found Don.

Jack Goes to Concert
GS: Jimmy Stewart. Jack and Barbara Nichols go to the same concert as Mr. and Mrs. Stewart. Jack mistakenly goes to their house after the concert because of fog.

Death Row Sketch
GS: Mamie Van Doren. Jack's wife is playing around with the boarder, so Jack ends up in jail condemned for murder.

Jack Becomes a Surgeon
Jack applies to medical school. In a sketch, Jack is a crazy doctor operating on a patient.

Jack Goes to Las Vegas
Jack hires only two Mills Brothers and tricks the other into joining them to sing.

Variety Show
George Burns comes on to introduce Ann Margret, his latest discovery.

Main Street Shelter
Rochester gives Jack's jacket to a mission, unaware that there is $200 in the lining. Jack goes down to get it back and is mistaken for a bum.

English Sketch
Jack is in love with Diana Dors, Peter Lawford's wife. However, Jack trades Diana for a stamp collection in order to get his picture in the papers.

How Jack Found Rochester
Jack is on the train coming East, Rochester is the porter on the train. Jack gets Rochester fired, so he hires him as his butler.

Jack Gets a Passport
Jack is planning a trip to Australia and is having trouble getting a passport.

Tennessee Ernie Ford Show
Jack visits Tennessee Ernie Ford on his farm in Northern California.

Modern Prison Sketch
GS: Mickey Rooney. Mickey explores what might happen to prisons if they continue to be easier and easier on prisoners.

Jack Goes to Cafeteria
Jack has difficulties taking Jane Morgan to lunch as everything is too expensive.

Dennis's Surprise Party
Jack decides to give Dennis a surprise party for his birthday.

Jack on Trial for Murder
GS: Raymond Burr. Jack is being sued for having a chicken which disturbs the peace, and dreams Raymond Burr is his lawyer and he loses.

Jack Followed Home
Jack is followed home after having Bobby Rydell on his show. It turns out to be Dennis who is out to kill him for having Bobby on the show.

Golf Show
Jack goes out to play golf and no one will play against him.

Jack Writes Song
Jack finds a song he wrote years ago and he tries to get Dimitri Tiomkin to write an arrangement of it.

Jack Does Opera
Jack sings an excerpt from an opera with Roberta Peters and Don Wilson.

Ghost Town Western Sketch
GS: Gisele MacKenzie. Jack imagines he is a western hero with a gun that shoots backwards.

Jack Going Back into Pictures
Billy Wilder wants Jack for a part in a picture, but it is a very small part.

Alexander Hamilton Story
Jack dreams that he is Alexander Hamilton, first Secretary of the Treasury of the U.S.

Julie London Show
Jack sings songs with Julie London.

Jack Is Violin Teacher
Jack takes a look at what would happen if he had been a violin teacher.

Jack and the Cab Driver
After a plane is airborne, Jack discovers an emotional cab driver unable to say goodbye has come along on the trip.

The Story of My Gang Comedy
Members of "Our Gang" pay a visit and Jack, Rochester, Spanky McFarland and Darla Hood perform a sketch.

Air Force Sketch
Jack tries to teach Raymond Burr how to become a comedian. Then Raymond asks Jack to turn a WWII battle scene into a comedy.

The Phil Silvers Show
While Phil Silvers borrows Jack's pants for his appearance, Jack borrows Don's pants. Later, Don arrives wearing the pants Phil returned.

Jack Meets Japanese Agent
Jack introduces guest Romi Yamada, who does a song. Jack wants him to appear again on the show so he deals with his Japanese agent.

The Lawrence Welk Show
Jack has written a torch song and wants Lawrence Welk to perform it; he does, as a polka.

Jack Meets Max Bygraves
Jack tells the story of how he met Max Bygraves, one of England's top performers.

The Story of the New Talent Show
It is the new talent show and Mel

Blanc shows up as Mr. Fingue, whose specialty is imitating dogs and horses, and then he impersonates an organ.

The Story of Jack Refereeing Wrestling Match
Jack is insulted when he has not been asked to appear at a charity fair, then he gets his chance when one of the guests cancels out.

Bob Hope Show
Bob and Jack reminisce over their old days at the office of the Weber Theatrical Agency.

Jack Plays Tarzan
GS: Carol Burnett. In a Tarzan sketch, Jack drives three gorillas crazy with his violin playing, while Jane decides to leave home.

Jack Fires Don
Jack is about to replace Don when they have a dispute over a famous naval saying and neither would back down.

The Peter Lorre-Joanie Sommers Show
Jack goes to a doctor to treat his cold, but the doctor is a plastic surgeon. Meanwhile, an escaped criminal causes havoc in the studio.

Jack Does the USO Show
Jack answers letters and tells his listeners about the USO show. At the end of the show, two Japanese soldiers arrive claiming they'll surrender if Jack will stop playing his violin.

The Spanish Sketch
Jack introduces Rita Moreno who acts out a movie scene with Jack in a Spanish cafe.

The Frankie Avalon Show
Frankie discusses how he became a guest star on Jack's show.

The Connie Francis Show
Jack introduces Connie Francis who does a sketch about Stephen Foster.

Jack Answers Request Letters
Jack answers request letters from his fans.

Riverboat Sketch
Carol Burnett plays a Southern belle along with Jack's riverboat gambler routine.

Jack Takes Boat to Hawaii
Jack goes to Hawaii when he meets Jayne Mansfield and Schlepperman.

Johnny Carson Guests
Johnny Carson sings, dances, plays the drums and converses with Jack.

The Tall Cowboy Sketch
Guest Clint Walker makes his singing debut and leads Jack into the world of the western star.

The Robert Goulet Show
Robert and Jack both vie for affection from the same girl.

The Ed Sullivan Show
Ed and Jack play opposing attorneys in the trial of a beautiful Parisienne accused of slaying her husband.

Don Breaks Leg
An ecdysiast performs her specialty to Jack's chagrin, Don Wilson fakes a broken leg, and his son Harlow takes over Don's job.

Jack Directs Film
Jack crashes the set where Jimmy Stewart is making a film and gives his advice on how movies should be made.

Amateur Show
GS: George Jessel. Jack holds his annual amateur show which ends in pandemonium when all the contestants feel they have won.

Harlow Gets a Date
Jack does all he can to please a sponsor, including getting his daughter an escort for sightseeing, only Don's son Harlow has no interest in girls.

How Jack Found Dennis
Jack takes a look back in time at how he discovered Dennis Day. Jack tells how his quest for a singer for his old radio show led him to many faces.

Jack Takes a Violin Lesson
Professor LeBlanc gives Jack music lessons.

Peter, Paul and Mary
Peter, Paul and Mary show Jack how folklore can be adapted to songs. Jack then succeeds in getting the three to record a song he wrote.

How Jack Met George Burns
George and Jack demonstrate what and who killed vaudeville.

Bobby Darin Guests
Jack thinks Bobby would be the perfect man to play him in a movie based on his life.

Nat King Cole Guests
A musical show has Nat singing and playing piano in a musical group that has Jack on the violin.

Jack Goes to Allergy Doctor
Jack goes to two doctors to determine why his arm itches, and doesn't like either method of dealing with his problem.

The Lettermen Guest
Jack plays an enterprising college dormitory student rooming with the Lettermen.

Hillbilly Sketch
Jack and guest Connie Francis play hillbillies concerned over their 28-year-old son who they think doesn't know the facts of life.

Andy Williams Guests
Andy accompanies Jack to a big opening, which turns out to be the opening of a meat market.

Jack Makes Comedy Record
Jack urges guest Bob Hope to join forces with him in recording a comedy record.

The Kingston Trio Guests
Jack is arrested and thrown into the Tijuana jail for being double parked, while the Kingston Trio sing "Tijuana Jail."

The Smothers Brothers Show
The Smothers Brothers relive a London bombing raid when Jack entertained servicemen at the Palladium.

The Income Tax Show
Jack has his income tax return investigated for a $3.90 dinner deduction, an amount the IRS can't believe is so small.

The Lucille Ball Show
Jack and Lucille give their version of the story behind Paul Revere's famous midnight ride.

Jack Adopts a Son
GS: Milton Berle. Jack plays a man who has everything in life except a son, so he tries to adopt a lad named Marvin.

Wayne Newton Show
Jack, Wayne, and Louis Nye donate their talents to help underprivileged Beverly Hills children jet to camp on the French Riviera.

Jack Jones Show
Jack and Jack Jones spoof ways of coping with problems that confront the teaching profession.

Jack Goes to Gym
It is Rochester's day off and he won't lift a finger, so Jack takes up body building to impress his girl.

THE JEFFERSONS

On the air 1/18/75, still going in 1983. CBS. Color Videotape. 159 currently syndicated episodes. Broadcast: Jan 1975-Aug 1975 Sat 8:30-9; Sept 1975-Oct 1976 Sat 8-8:30; Nov 1976-Jan 1977 Wed 8-8:30; Jan 1977-Aug 1977 Mon 8-8:30; Sept 1977-Mar 1978 Sat 9-9:30; Apr 1978-May 1978 Sat 8-8:30; Jun 1978-Sept 1978 Sat 8-8:30; Sept 1978-Jan 1979 Wed 8-8:30; Jan 1979-Mar 1979 Wed 9:30-10; Mar 1979-Jun 1979 Wed 8-8:30; Jun 1979-present Sun 9:30-10. Producer: Norman Lear. Prod Co: Tandem. Synd: Embassy Pictures.

CAST: George Jefferson (played by Sherman Hemsley), Louise (Isabel Sanford), Lionel (Mike Evans, 1975, 1979-present; Damon Evans, 1975-78), Helen Willis (Roxie Roker), Tom Willis (Franklin Cover), Jenny (Belinda Tolbert), Harry Bentley (Paul Benedict), Mother Olivia Jefferson (Zara Cully), Ralph (Ned Wertimer), Florence (Marla Gibbs), Charlie (Danny Wells).

The comic adventures of the Jefferson family and their neighbors the Willises. This spinoff of *All in the Family* has been very popular on the network, but like many popular series they do not do as well in syndication; *The Jeffersons* is no exception. The series is not doing as well as it was expected to do.

A Friend in Need
W: Barry Harman & Harve Brosten. George wants Louise to hire a maid.

Louise Feels Useless
W: Lloyd Turner & Gordon Mitchell. Louise decides to get a job but not to tell George about it.

George's Family Tree
W: Perry Grant & Dick Bensfield. George finds out he is a descendant of a royal African tribe.

Lionel the Playboy
W: Roger Shulman & John Baskin. Lionel decides to quit college and spend his father's money instead.

Mr. Piano Man
W: Lloyd Turner, Gordon Mitchell & Don Nicholl. George buys a piano to impress his landlord when he holds a tenants' meeting in his apartment.

George's Skeleton
W: Lloyd Turner, Gordon Mitchell & Eric Tarloff. George's childhood friend threatens to tell his family a secret from the past unless George pays him not to.

Lionel Cries Uncle
W: Jim Carlson. GS: Albert Reed. George and Lionel believe Louise's visiting uncle is an Uncle Tom.

Mother Jefferson's Boyfriend
W: Gordon Farr & Arnold Kane. Mother Jefferson plans to move to Florida with her new boyfriend.

Meet the Press
W: Dixie Grossman. George invites an interviewer to the apartment to gain publicity for his cleaning business.

Rich Man's Disease
W: Bruce Howard. George has an ulcer, causing Louise to protect him from any kind of stress.

Former Neighbors
W: Ben Joelson & Art Baer. Louise invites their old Harlem neighbors on the same night George has invited some rich business people.

Like Father, Like Son?
W: Frank Tarloff. Tom and George find they are backing the same political candidate.

Jenny's Low
W: John Ashby. Jenny's white brother returns after two years, causing resentment by Jenny.

The Jeffersons: left to right, top, Franklin Cover, Roxie Roker, Belinda Tolbert, and Damon Evans; bottom, Paul Benedict, Isabel Sanford, Sherman Hemsley, and Zara Cully.

A Dinner for Harry
W: Don Nicholl, Michael Ross, Bernie West. Louise's birthday party for Mr. Bentley is interrupted when Helen gets mugged, causing Tom to think about moving away.

George's First Vacation
W: Frank Tarloff. George decides to take Louise on a cruise.

Louise's Daughter
W: Jay Moriarty & Mike Mulligan. The Jeffersons have a visit from a girl who claims that Louise is her mother.

Harry and Daphne
W: Lloyd Turner & Gordon Mitchell. Harry tries to avoid a marriage proposal from his girlfriend.

Jefferson vs. Jefferson
W: Robert Fisher & Arthur Marx. Louise objects when George gets into a bicycle accident and wants her to lie about what she saw.

Mother Jefferson's Fall
W: Eric Tarloff. Mother Jefferson fakes a back injury in order to gain some attention from the rest of the family.

Movin' on Down
W: Ken Levine & David Isaacs. George becomes depressed when his businesses aren't doing very well.

Uncle Bertram
W: Nicholl, Ross, West, Turner & Mitchell. GS: Victor Killian. George becomes upset when his mother begins dating Tom's white uncle.

George Won't Talk
W: John Ashby. George is invited to speak at a ghetto college.

George's Best Friend
W: Calvin Kelly. George's old Navy friend comes for a visit and makes a pass at Louise.

Jenny's Grandparents
W: James Ritz. GS: Leon Ames, Victor Killian. The Jeffersons and the Willises try to bring Tom and Helen's fathers together.

George's Alibi
W: Sandy Krinski. George thinks he caused the damage to the fender of his delivery van when it was actually Lionel who caused it.

George and the Manager
W: Don Boyle. George is reluctant to hire one of his employees as the new store manager because she is a woman.

Lunch with Mama
W: Nicholl, Ross, West, Turner & Mitchell. Louise wants George to go with her to a funeral at the same time he is to take his mother to lunch.

George vs. Wall Street
W: George Burditt. Lionel turns down a high-paying job.

The Break-Up [Part 1]
W: Dixie Grossman. Jenny breaks off her engagement to Lionel when he plans to use the term paper George bought for him.

The Break-Up [Part 2]
W: Lloyd Turner & Gordon Mitchell. George unknowingly brings home a prostitute to meet Lionel.

Florence's Problem
W: Jay Moriarty & Mike Milligan. Florence plans to commit suicide.

Mother Jefferson's Birthday
W: Fred S. Fox & Seaman Jacobs. George and Louise invite Mama's sister Emma to her surprise birthday party, even though they haven't spoken to each other for 25 years.

Louise's Cookbook
W: Ann Gibbs & Joel Kimmel. Louise is asked to publish her collection of her grandmother's recipes.

George Meets Whittendale
W: Lloyd Turner & Gordon Mitchell. George and the Willises accidentally get locked in the bathroom, causing George to miss out on meeting Mr. Whittendale.

Lionel's Problem
W: Mea Abbott & James Ritz. Lionel gets drunk when he believes he will not live up to George's expectations of him.

Tennis, Anyone?
W: Sandy Veith. George learns that he is to be the token black at a tennis club.

The Wedding
W: Lloyd Turner, Gordon Mitchell & John Donley. George and Louise have a fight on the day they plan to renew their wedding vows.

Louise Suspects
W: Lloyd Turner & Gordon Mitchell. Louise thinks George is fooling around with another woman.

George and the President
W: Howard Albrecht & Sol Weinstein. An advertising man tries to pass George off as a descendant of Thomas Jefferson in order to improve George's business

Louise Gets Her Way
W: Lloyd Turner & Gordon Mitchell. Louise decides to hire Florence as a live-in maid, but now she has to convince George that it is a good idea.

The Lie Detector
W: Tedd Anasti & David Talisman. Lionel turns down a good paying job because the company requires him to take a lie detector test.

The Retirement Party
W: Dixie Grossman. George plans to sell his stores to a conglomerate until he learns that all employees must retire when they are 60, including him.

Lionel's Pad
W: Booker Bradshaw & Kurt Taylor. Lionel and Jenny decide to rent an apartment and live together.

George's Diploma
W: Lloyd Turner & Gordon Mitchell. George plans to get a High School Equivalency Diploma.

The Agreement
W: Lloyd Turner & Gordon Mitchell. Jenny and Lionel have a fight over the prenuptial agreement George wants them to sign.

Tom the Hero
W: Jay Moriarty & Mike Milligan. Tom saves George's life and no one will let him forget it.

Jenny's Discovery
W: Bob Baublitz. Jenny has doubts about her love for Lionel, until she thinks he was killed in a bus crash with George and Tom.

Florence in Love
W: Paul Belous, Robert Wolterstorff. Florence quits when the Jeffersons object to her boyfriend spending the night at their apartment.

Louise Forgets
W: Bill Davenport. Louise forgets to give George a message from her stockbroker, causing him to lose out on a lot of money.

The Christmas Wedding
W: Jay Moriarty & Mike Milligan. GS: Robert Sampson. Louise has a minister perform Jenny and Lionel's wedding ceremony at the apartment.

George's Guilt
W: Jay Moriarty & Mike Milligan. George invites his childhood friends over to the house for a reunion.

Bentley's Problem
W: Lloyd Turner & Gordon Mitchell. George helps Bentley with a nasty neighbor, but only succeeds in getting Bentley arrested.

Jefferson Airplane
W: Dixie Grossman & Brian Levant. George takes up flying as a hobby.

A Case of Black and White
W: Fred S. Fox, Seaman Jacobs, Lloyd Turner & Gordon Mitchell. GS: J.A. Preston, Barbara Cason. George tries to impress an interracial couple by using the Willises as examples.

Louise vs. Jenny
W: John Ashby. Louise and Jenny fight over who will take care of Lionel who is down with a bad cold.

Louise's Friend
W: Richard Freiman & Stephen Young. George objects when Louise is escorted to her French class by an attractive man.

The Marriage Counselors
W: John Hanrahan. The Willises try to teach the Jeffersons how to improve their marriage.

The Old Flame
W: Jay Moriarty & Mike Milligan. George's first girlfriend comes for a visit and makes a play for George.

Jenny's Opportunity
W: Paul Belous & Robert Wolterstorff. Jenny wins a scholarship to Oxford, causing problems for everyone.

George the Philanthropist
W: Dennis Koenig & Larry Balmagia. George tries to win the Black Businessman's Association award by donating money for a Harlem youth center.

Louise's Physical
W: Lloyd Turner, Gordon Mitchell, Jay Moriarty & Mike Milligan. Louise becomes depressed when she feels she is wasting her life, while George plans to throw a surprise birthday party for her.

The Grand Opening [Part 1]
W: Roger Shulman & John Baskin. Louise is kidnapped by two men when

George Brags about all of the money he has.

The Grand Opening [Part 2]
W: Jay Moriarty & Mike Milligan. George learns that the kidnappers captured Florence and not Louise. [This episode was originally aired as a one-hour special.]

Once a Friend
W: Michael Baser & Kim Weiskopf. George's old friend from the Navy returns with a surprise: he is now a woman.

George's Help
W: Patt Shea & Jack Shea. George believes the boy he hired from the Neighborhood Help Center is stealing from his store.

Good News, Bad News
W: Jay Moriarty & Mike Milligan. Louise becomes upset when Helen gets the job of editor of the Help Center newsletter and not she.

George's Legacy
W: Don Segall. George has a bust made of himself so he can leave it behind as a legacy to his family.

Louise's New Interest
W: Olga Vallance. Louise almost has an affair with the man she works with at the museum.

The Visitors
W: Roger Shulman & John Baskin. Florence's fighting parents come for a visit.

The Camp Out
W: Jay Moriarty & Mike Milligan. George takes Marcus on a camping trip.

The Costume Party
W: Martin Donovan. George holds a costume party so he can impress a client.

The Last Leaf
W: Laura Levine. Louise loses her wedding corsage, causing her to think her marriage is over.

Florence Gets Lucky
W: Bob DeVinney. One of George's clients takes Florence with him on a business trip, because he feels that she brings him luck.

George Needs Help
W: Roger Shulman & John Baskin. Louise and Florence try to get George to hire a general manager to run his businesses for him.

The Jefferson Curve
W: Paul Belous & Robert Wolterstorff. Marcus tells his girl that the Jeffersons are his parents.

984 W. 124th St., Apt. 5C
W: Roger Shulman & John Baskin. Louise finds that George has been giving presents and money to the family living in the old apartment where he grew up.

George and Whitty
W: Howard Albrecht & Sol Weinstein. George tries to convince Whittendale not to throw them out of their apartment, unaware that he was not talking to the right Whittendale.

Lionel Gets the Business
W: Nancy Vince & Ted Dale. Lionel goes to work for George and almost wrecks his business.

Florence Union
W: Patt & Jack Shea. Florence and the other maids in the building decide to form a union.

The Blackout
W: Richard Eckhaus. During a blackout, George and Marcus go to the Bronx to check on one of his stores and are arrested as looters.

George and Jimmy
W: Richard Freiman. George makes a threatening call to the White House, causing him to be visited by the FBI.

George and Louise in a Bind
W: Jim Rogers. GS: Carroll O'Conner, Jean Stapleton. [Flashback sequence.] George and Louise remember [via flashbacks] past events. [This episode was originally a 90-minute special, but is now shown in two parts.]

Thomas H. Willis & Co.
W: Jay Moriarty & Mike Milligan. George cosigns a loan which will allow Tom to open his own publishing business.

Uncle George and Aunt Louise
W: Shulman & Baskin.   George's nephew visits, causing everyone to become upset.

Jenny's Thesis
W: Paul Belous & Robert Wonterstorff. Jenny chooses a ghetto gang as the subject of her thesis.

Louise's Painting
W: Nancy Vince & Ted Dale. Louise joins an art class where she has to paint a nude male model.

George's Dream
W: Bob Baublitz.   George falls asleep and dreams what life will be like twenty years from now.

Homecoming [Part 1]
W: Jay Moriarty & Mike Milligan. George and Louise try to get Tom's son Allan to sell them the warehouse he inherited from his grandfather.

Homecoming [Part 2]
W: Jay Moriarty & Mike Milligan. Allan decides to sell the warehouse to the Help Center and move in with the Jeffersons.

How Slowly They Forget
W: Erwin Washington. George asks his old friend to get the Help Center a health permit.

Louise's Convention
W: Paul Belous & Robert Wolterstorff. Louise wants to attend the Help Center Convention in L.A., but George wants her to stay home and celebrate their anniversary.

Harry's House Guest
W: Fred S. Fox & Seaman Jacobs. George helps Bentley get rid of his British house guest, who expects Harry to marry her.

Louise's Reunion
W: Howard Albrecht & Sol Weinstein. Louise and George go to her high school reunion.

George's New Stockbroker
W: Jim Rogers. GS: Willie Tyler & Lester.   George learns that his new stockbroker is a ventriloquist who is a former mental patient.

Half a Brother
W: Bob Baublitz. George believes he will lose his chance to become a board member of a bank when Allan begins dating the daughter of one of the board members.

Me and Billy Dee
W: Jay Moriarty & Mike Milligan. GS: Billy Dee Williams. Florence doesn't believe that the visiting Billy Dee Williams is the real one. She thinks he is a lookalike George hired to fool her.

What Are Friends For?
W: Skip Usen. George has to decide whether or not to donate one of his kidneys to his cousin.

George Who?
W: Christine Houston. Louise is suffering from amnesia.

Louise's Sister
W: Bob Baublitz. Louise gets a visit from her sister and her son.

Louise's Award
W: H. Martez Thomas. George makes a large donation in the hopes it will win Louise an award at the Help Center.

George Finds a Father
W: Kurt Taylor & John Donley. At Christmas, George learns some family secrets from his Uncle Buddy.

The Ones You Love
W: Stephen Neigher. Florence takes Louise's place when an interviewer comes to write a story about the Jeffersons.

The Hold Out
W: Bernard Mack. George refuses to sell one of his stores in order to get more money from the conglomerate that wants to buy it.

Florence Meets Mr. Right
W: Peter Casey & David Lee. Florence decides to marry the man she has known for less than a month.

A Bedtime Story
W: Stephen Neigher. George goes to a psychiatrist when he becomes worried about his sex life.

The Other Woman
W: Jack Shea. Tom escorts his boss's mistress to a convention in Mexico.

Three Faces of Florence
W: Bernard Mack. The psychiatrist at the Help Center believes that Florence has a split personality.

Every Night Fever
W: Bryan Joseph. Louise can't stop George from going dancing every night.

The Freeze-In
W: Jay Moriarty & Mike Milligan. The Willises and Mr. Bentley join the Jeffersons when the heat goes out in their apartments, ruining George and Louise's anniversary of their first date together.

The Announcement
W: Jay Moriarty & Mike Milligan. Lionel and Jenny try to keep her pregnancy a secret from George.

Louise's Old Boyfriend
W: Jerry Perzigian & Donald Siegel. Florence takes over when Louise refuses to have dinner with her old boyfriend.

A Short Story
W: Neil Lebowitz. George receives an award from an association of short businessmen.

The Expectant Father
W: Michael C. Moya. George tries to help Lionel who is nervous about becoming a father.

Where's Papa?
W: Peter Casey & David Lee. George decides to have his father's grave moved next to his mother's grave.

Now You See It, Now You Don't [Part 1]
W: Susan Harris. Louise thinks she sees a man dressed as a rabbit murder someone in the next building.

Now You See It, Now You Don't [Part 2]
W: Susan Harris. The Rabbit learns that Louise is a witness, so he plans to kill her.

Joltin' George
W: Jerry Perzigian & Donald Siegel. George finds himself preparing to fight a boxer, after Marcus brags about George's fighting abilities.

Me and Mr. G
George almost ruins Louise's foster home project when he teaches an orphan how to gamble.

Baby Love
W: Joanne Pagliaro. Florence tries a video dating service to find a husband.

Louise vs. Florence
W: Paul Belous & Robert Wolterstorff. Florence and Louise have a fight during the middle of George's party for some rich people.

Louise's Setback
W: Robert Wolterstorff. Louise blames herself when the girl she tried to help tries to kill herself.

One Flew into the Cuckoo's Nest
W: Peter Casey & David Lee. George is mistaken for a mental patient when he makes a delivery to a mental hospital.

Brother Tom
W: Jerry Perzigian & Donald Siegel. Tom asks George to teach him how to be black.

The Arrival [Part 1]
W: Neil Lebowitz. George has to help Jenny, while Lionel is out of town, when she goes into labor.

The Arrival [Part 2]
W: Michael C. Moya. Jenny gives birth to a girl.

The Shower
W: Anthony & Celia Bonaduce. Lionel goes to work on the day of his daughter Jessica's baby shower.

The Longest Day
W: Bob Baublitz.   Tom and George babysit for Jessica.

George's Birthday
W: Jerry Perzigian & Donald Siegel. George thinks no one remembers that it is his 50th birthday, unaware that Louise has planned a surprise party for him.

The Loan
W: Anthony & Celia Bonaduce. The Jeffersons and the Willises try to get a loan for Lionel and Jenny.

The First Store
W: Jay Moriarty & Mike Milligan. George and Louise remember the day they opened their first store on the day of Martin Luther King's assassination.

A Night to Remember
W: Stephen Miller.   Louise accuses George of having an affair with his secretary, while trying to celebrate their 30th annviersary.

Louise Takes a Stand
W: Bryan Joseph, Perzigian & Siegel. Louise refuses to give George permission to take over Charlie's bar in order to expand the store downstairs.

Once Upon a Time
W: Michael C. Moya. George tells a fairy tale to Jessica about inflation which is acted out by the cast as he tells it.

THE JIM BACKUS SHOW

On the air 9/60, off 9/61. B&W Film. 30 min. 39 episodes. Broadcast: 9/60 time and date varied for each station. Producer: Ray Singer, Dick Chevillat. Synd: National Telefilm.

CAST: John Michael O'Toole (played by Jim Backus), Dora (Nita Talbot), Sidney (Bobs Watson).

Comedy about John Michael O'Toole, editor/reporter of the Headline Press Service, a newspaper in financial trouble. Segments depict his efforts to avoid creditors, acquire major stories, and improve circulation to obtain more money. The series is not aired on any station since it went off the air in 1961. The series was also known as *Hot Off the Wire*.

The Mad Bomber
A man heads for the city room of the newspaper with a homemade bomb.

Marriage-Go-Round
O'Toole goes to great lengths to get the story on a rich old man.

No Help Wanted
O'Toole and Dora mistake actress Catherine Lyden for a poverty stricken housekeeper.

Mike O'Toole, Angler
O'Toole is asked to write some articles

that will raise funds for an orphanage.

The Nephew
An old lady dies and leaves her fortune to her cat.

Frame-Up
A beloved neighborhood cop is accused of beating up a young boy.

The Three Sisters
Three little old ladies come to keep house for O'Toole.

Baby Come Home
No available story.

The Patriots
When a subscriber to the paper wants to cancel, O'Toole makes up a journalistic story.

Uncle Chester
O'Toole's uncle comes for a visit, unfortunately he is a freeloader who gets himself and his nephew accused of bribery.

South Hampton Story
O'Toole goes to get a story on an heiress.

Crime a la Carte
In order to get a scoop, O'Toole poses as a stool pigeon with information about a fictitious crime.

Painting Caper
O'Toole poses as an art expert in order to impress a potential subscriber.

Piano Prodigy
The paper jumps at the opportunity to do publicity for a child piano prodigy.

Mike Cheats a Cheater
O'Toole wants to expose a phony drama teacher, so he poses as a millionaire's son and enters the acting class.

Meet Melvin
O'Toole isn't too receptive to Dora's request for a raise.

The Woman's Touch
Dora takes over for a week and hires a new sales manager.

Sidney's Scoop
Mike's office boy writes a story that might put the paper out of business.

Once Upon a Moose
Mike and Dora try to prove that a man accused of murder is really innocent.

Pinkmalion
Mike is refused an interview with a famous actress, so he decides to create a movie star of his own.

When a Body Meets a Body
Mike gets a scoop: There is a dead man lying in the back room of a barbershop and the police have not been notified.

Arabian Night
O'Toole uses Dora as bait to get an interview with an Arabian prince.

Old Army Game
Private Dillingham asks Mike to help him break up a gang that specializes in mugging soldiers.

The Fix
Mike gets Sidney to pose as a boxer in order to get the goods on a crook who has been fixing fights.

Sad Sack Santa
GS: J. Pat O'Malley. Mike finds a man sitting on a stoop who is dressed like Santa Claus in the middle of summer and who has been out of a job since last Christmas.

The Plant
Members of Mike's staff demand a raise; all Mike is offering them is retirement benefits at age 96.

The Temporary Scoundrel
Mike makes a deal to change places for a day with a millionaire playboy.

Floundered in Florida
Mike and Sidney go to Florida to par-

ticipate in a convention for bathing suit manufacturers.

Advice Column
GS: Zasu Pitts. Minnie Morgan writes a lonely-hearts column but she can't follow her own advice.

In the Rough
GS: Henny Backus. Wealthy Henrietta Updyke goes on an African safari and discovers a golfer.

Dora's Vacation
GS: Yvonne Craig. Dora insists upon taking her long overdue vacation, so Mike hires a giddy teenager to take her place.

The Birthday Boy
A party isn't the only surprise that Mike gets on his birthday. He gets a pair of black eyes as one of his gifts.

Farewell to Dora
Dora has decided to accept a better job. Mike plots to see that she stays put.

Texas Millionaire
GS: Alan Hale, Nita Talbot. Mike wants to bag a Texas millionaire as a financial backer.

Gift for Grandma
Mike and Sidney buy a present for grandma, a hot necklace.

O'Toole and Son
Mike tries to adopt a son in order to qualify as heir to his uncle's fortune.

THE JOEY BISHOP SHOW

On the air 9/20/61, off 9/7/65. NBC, CBS. B&W Film. 124 episodes. Broadcast: Sept 1961-Jun 1962 NBC Wed 8:30-9; Sept 1962-Sept 1964 NBC Sat 8:30-9; Sept 1964-Dec 1964 CBS Sun 9:30-10; Dec 1964-Sept 1965 CBS Tue 8-8:30. Producer & Prod Co: Danny Thomas Prods. Synd: William Morris Agency.

CAST: Joey Barnes (played by Joey Bishop), Ellie Barnes (Abby Dalton), Mr. Jillson (Joe Besser), Hilda (Mary Treen), Larry Corbett (Corbett Monica), Freddie (Guy Marks), Dr. Sam Nolan (Joey Foreman), Frank (Joe Flynn), Mrs. Barnes (Madge Blake), J.P. Whiloughby (John Griggs), Barbara Simpson (Nancy Hadley), Betty (Virginia Vincent), Larry Barnes (Warren Berlinger), Stella Barnes (Marlo Thomas).

The adventures of Joey Barnes. During the first season he worked as an assistant to a press agent. During the remaining seasons he was the host of a late-night talk show. After the first season most of the cast was dropped and the format changed. The series actually served as a pilot for Joey Bishop's talk show a couple of years later. Although in black and white, the series would prove interesting provided it was run soon. The show is available but no one has picked it up since it went off in 1965. The reason is that nobody remembers Joey Bishop's having a sitcom, they only remember his talk show.

The Bachelor
GS: Dennis O'Keefe, Sue Ann Langdon. Joey moves into a swinging actor's apartment complete with girls.

On the Spot
GS: Joey Foreman, Mel Bishop. Joey badmouths his boss on a hidden camera TV show.

A Windfall for Mom
GS: Barbara Stanwyck, Leonid Kinsky. Joey's mother goes to work in a supermarket.

Joey Meets Jack Paar
GS: Jack Paar, Randy Paar, Hollis Irving. Joey tries to get a trained chimp on Jack Paar's show.

This Is Your Life
GS: Danny Thomas, Marjorie Lord, Sid Melton. Joey arranges to get Danny Williams on "This Is Your Life." [A crossover episode from "Make Room for Daddy."]

The Contest Winner
No available story.

Five Brides for Joey
Everyone tries to find lonely Joey a girlfriend.

Back in Your Own Backyard
GS: Peter Leeds, Chet Stratton. Frank discovers oil on Joey's property while digging a hole.

Help Wanted
GS: Joe Flynn. Joey gets his brother-in-law a job with his public relations firm.

Ring-a-Ding-Ding
GS: Henry Silva. Joey has to put up with an egotistical movie star who thinks he is a great lover.

Charity Begins at Home
GS: Howard McNear. Johnny Silver. Mrs. Barnes unknowingly rents a room to a bookie.

The Ham in the Family
GS: Marlo Thomas, Herbie Faye, Jack Albertson. Larry is such a success in a school show that he wants to turn pro.

Follow That Mink
GS: Eleanor Audley. Joey agrees to hold a mink stole so his boss can surprise his wife, but Joey's wife thinks it's for her.

Barney the Bloodhound
GS: Joan Benny, Raymond Bailey, Sig Rumann, Jack Mullaney. The cartoon dog in a dog food commercial that Joey is promoting looks like him.

The Taming of the Brat
Joey has to hide a bratty child star for a publicity stunt.

Home Sweet Home
GS: Jean Carson, Bob Hopkins, Bill Bixby. Joey sells the house when he plans to move to New York but then changes his mind.

A Letter from Stella
GS: Leonid Kinsky, Roxanne Bernard. Joey and Larry think their sister is in love with her ballet teacher.

Jury Duty
GS: Jonathan Hale, William Keene. Joey is called to jury duty during his vacation.

Double Exposure
GS: Neville Brand, Lee Van Cleef. Lookalike Joey is kidnapped when he is mistaken for Joey Bishop.

The Income Tax Caper
GS: Roy Roberts, Alvy Moore, Herbie Faye. Joey is being audited, but he didn't keep the receipts.

A Man's Best Friend
GS: Bill Bixby, Nancy Kulp. Larry comes home with a Great Dane which proceeds to eat them out of house and home.

Very Warm for Christmas
GS: Fuzzy Knight, Willard Waterman. Mrs. Barnes buys a stuffed Santa and four reindeer for a lawn display in the middle of spring.

The Big Date
GS: Nick Adams, Trevor Bardette, Jenny Maxwell. Joey holds a contest and the prize is a date with a rock and roll star.

Joey Hires a Maid
GS: Nora Marlowe, Jack Albertson. Joey hires a maid to help Mrs. Barnes.

That's Show Biz
GS: Jaye P. Morgan. Joey hires a new secretary who can't type.

A Young Man's Fancy
GS: Dawn Wells. Stella is expecting an

actress friend, but Joey and Larry refuse to dress up for her.

Surprise, Surprise
Joey doesn't want the surprise party his mother is planning for him.

Must the Show Go On?
Mrs. Barnes hires several acts for her show.

Once a Bachelor
GS: Marty Ingels, Christine Nelson. Joey throws a bachelor party for his friend Freddie.

Route 78
GS: John Gallaudet, Chick Chandler Reeves. The city plans to build a freeway through Joey's house.

A Show of His Own
GS: Milton Berle, Jackie Coogan. Joey gets his own TV show.

The Image
GS: Peter Leeds, Patricia Blair. Joey's image is being built up to publicize his new show.

The Honeymoon
Joey is scheduled to play at a nightclub while on his honeymoon.

Door to Door Salesman
GS: Fuzzy Knight, Buddy Lewis. Joey tries to teach Ellie how to resist door-to-door salesmen.

Three's a Crowd
Joey and Ellie want to celebrate their third month of marriage alone, but Freddie won't take no for an answer.

Penguins Three
Joey refuses to appear at Jillson's Penguin lodge show.

Joey's Replacement
GS: Corbett Monica. Joey is afraid to go on his vacation because his replacement may get his job.

The Fashion Show
GS: Eleanor Audley. Ellie gets a mod-

eling job in order to get extra money to buy Joey a present.

The Breakup
Joey would rather play his mandolin than talk to Freddie.

Baby It's Cold Inside
No available story.

Wife vs. Secretary
GS: Carol Byron. Ellis is jealous of Joey's new secretary.

A Woman's Place
GS: Eleanor Audley. Ellie plans to run for the office of assemblywoman.

Joey Takes a Physical
Joey refuses to take his physical, so Ellie tries to trick him into it.

Deep in the Heart of Texas
Ellie is lonesome for her home in Texas.

The Honeymoon Is Over
When Joey stays out with the boys, Ellie thinks their marriage is over.

Chance of a Lifetime
GS: Peter Lupus, Herbie Faye. Freddie and Joey invest in a boxer.

Joey's Lucky Cuff Links
GS: Jane Dulo, Muriel Landers. On the night of the governor's dinner, Joey can't find his lucky cuff links.

Kiss and Make Up
Ellie picks a fight with Joey, so they can kiss and make up afterwards.

Double Time
GS: Johnny Silver, Sheldon Leonard. While doing a prison show, Joey is knocked out by a lookalike who takes his place.

Jillson and the Cimmaron Buns
Jillson goes on a diet, but finds that he has a yearning for Ellie's cinnamon buns.

Freddie Goes Highbrow
GS: Merry Anders.   Freddie falls for a British society lady.

Joey Leaves Ellie
GS: Joi Lansing. Ellie accuses Joey of kissing a girl on his show.

A Crush on Joey
GS: Michael Petit, Katie Swees. A little girl has a crush on Joey and her boyfriend doesn't like it.

Joey's House Guest
GS: Isabel Randolph, Benny Rubin. Joey tries to keep Aunt Celia from moving in with them.

We're Going to Have a Baby
GS: Henry Gibson, William Keene. Joey announces on his show that he is going to have a baby.

The Baby Formula
GS: Henry Gibson, Mary Grace Canfield. Joey minds a neighbor's baby.

Joey's Dramatic Debut
GS: Leonid Kinsky, Buddy Lewis, Peter Leeds. Joey tries his hand at doing a dramatic show.

Joey and the Laundry Bags
GS: Jane Dulo, Muriel Landers. Two laundresses want to appear on Joey's show.

The Masquerade Party
Joey, Ellie, Larry and Jillson go to a masquerade party as Robin Hood and his friends.

Joey, the Good Samaritan
Joey has a 16-year-old opera star on his show.

My Son, the Doctor
Ellie dreams that Joey, Jr. will become a doctor when he grows up.

The Expectant Father's School
GS: Gordon Jones. Joey demonstrates his skills to the class.

The Baby Nurse
GS: Yvonne Lime. Joey is afraid that Hilda will be as bad a nurse as she is a housekeeper.

My Buddy, My Buddy
GS: Buddy Hackett, Milton Frome. Buddy Hackett brings a live baby elephant as a gift for the baby.

The Baby Cometh
GS: Frank Wilcox. Joey is calm when it's time for the baby to be born. After the baby is born he falls apart.

Danny Gives Joey Advice
GS: Danny Thomas. Danny and Joey play their own teenage sons when they both look ahead to see how they will react to discipline.

Joey and the Andrews Sisters
GS: The Andrews Sisters. Joey plans to sing along with the Andrews Sisters, but they don't want him to.

The Baby's First Day
GS: Sandra Gould.   Everyone must wear a mask when going near the baby.

Joey and Milton and Baby Makes Three
GS: Milton Berle. Milton would rather help take Joey, Jr. home from the hospital than rehearse for Joey's show.

Joey's Mustache
GS: Vito Scotti, Judi Sherwin. Joey is going to wear his mustache on the show.

The Babysitter
Joey and Ellie have to give up their evening out when they can't get a babysitter.

Joey Plugs the Laundry
GS: Herbert Rudley. Joey talks about the laundry he uses on the show, causing the laundry to demand equal time.

Joey's Lost What-Cha-Ma-Call-It
GS: Sterling Holloway.   Joey lost

something valuable at a hotel, but can't remember what it is he lost.

Joey Meets Edgar Bergen
GS: Edgar Bergen, Charlie McCarthy and Mortimer Snerd. Edgar agrees to teach Joey how to be a ventriloquist.

Joey's Surprise for Ellie
GS: Cindy O'Hara, Beverly Adams. Joey buys Ellie a wig.

Ellie Gives Joey First Aid
GS: Joan Staley. Ellie practices first aid and gets Joey's arm stuck in a plaster cast.

Joey, Jr.'s TV Debut
GS: Charles Cantor. Joey and family will appear on a TV interview show.

Two Little Maids Are We
While Ellie takes Joey, Jr. to Grandma, Larry watches Joey, Sr.

The Baby's First Christmas
Joey and Jillson both want to play Santa Claus for Joey, Jr.

Vic Damone Brainwashes Joey
GS: Vic Damone, Mickey Manners. Joey is subconsciously learning Russian from hearing Vic's language records.

Jack Carter Helps Joey Propose
GS: Jack Carter, Merry Anders, Paula Stewart. In a flashback, Jack and his wife double date with Joey and Ellie.

Bobby Rydell Plugs Ellie's Song
GS: Bobby Rydell, Charles Cantor. Joey is embarrassed to ask Bobby to sing Ellie's rotten song.

Joey's Hideaway Cabin
Joey rents a cabin without seeing it first.

Zsa Zsa Redecorates the Nursery
GS: Zsa Zsa Gabor. Zsa Zsa redecorates the nursery while visiting Joey's house.

Double Play from Foster to Durocher to Joey
GS: Leo Durocher, Phil Foster. Joey tries to break up a feud between Leo Durocher and Phil Foster.

Ellie the Talent Scout
GS: Henry Gibson. Ellie holds auditions for new talent in their living room.

Weekend in the Mountains
GS: Milton Frome, Al Fisher. Joey recalls the day he started in show biz while in the Catskills for a weekend.

Joey Insults Jack E. Leonard
GS: Jack E. Leonard, Dave Ketchum. Joey thinks there is something wrong with Jack E. Leonard when he doesn't fight back when Joey insults him.

Joey the Comedian vs. Larry the Writer
When Larry is named comedy writer of the year, Joey becomes jealous when he doesn't make comedian of the year.

Joey and Roberta Sherwood Play a Benefit
GS: Roberta Sherwood. Larry's date and Ellie are wearing the same dress, so Ellie won't go to the benefit show.

Joey and Buddy Hackett Have a Luau
GS: Buddy Hackett. Buddy plays a practical joke on Joey and Ellie by removing all of their furniture right before a big dinner party.

Hilda the Maid Quits
Joey and Ellie overhear a telephone call and assume that Hilda is quitting.

Every Dog Should Have a Boy
GS: Ivan Henry and his dogs. Joey announces he is going to buy a dog on the show and fans send him dozens of them.

Joey and the Los Angeles Dodgers
GS: Don Drysdale, Vin Scully. The Dodgers are scheduled to appear on his

show but got tied up in an extra inning game, leaving Joey without a guest.

Joey, Jack Jones and the Genie
GS: Jack Jones, Ed McMahon, The Crocodiles. Joey dreams about becoming a famous singer.

Joey Introduces Shecky Greene
GS: Shecky Greene. Ellie's butcher wants to be a comedian.

Andy Williams Visits Joey
GS: Andy Williams, Robert Goulet, Danny Thomas. For the fifth year, Andy and Joey are the surprise guests at the ladies club and they are sick of it.

Joey Goes to CBS
GS: George Tobias, Peter Hobbs. Joey hears that his show has been cancelled.

Joey, the Patient
GS: Joey Foreman, Richard Keith, Dave Ketchum. Joey goes to the hospital for a tonsillectomy.

Joey vs. Oscar Levant
GS: Oscar Levant and his wife June Levant. Eccentric Oscar and his wife become Joey's house guests.

Joey and Larry Split
Joey forgets to announce a birthday greeting to Larry's girl on the show.

In This Corner Jan Murray
GS: Jan Murray, Barbara Stuart. Joey and Jan put on a comic boxing match for a boys club.

The Nielson Box
No available story

You're What? Again?
Ellie doesn't know how to tell Joey that she is pregnant again.

Joey Goes to a Poker Party
In order to prove he is not a henpecked husband, Joey decides to play poker.

The Perfect Girl
GS: Shirley Bonne. Larry thinks Joey's beautiful house guest is going to trap him into marriage.

Joey's Courtship
Ellie feels deprived because she didn't get a courtship.

Ellie Goes to Court
GS: Parley Baer. Ellie fights a traffic ticket in court.

Jillson's Toupee
GS: Robert S. Carson. Joey buys Jillson a toupee for his birthday.

A Hobby for Ellie
Joey agrees to do all of the housework.

Rusty Arrives
GS: Rusty Hamer. College student Rusty Williams is a house guest at the home of his Dad's old friend Joey Barnes.

The Weed City Story
GS: Cliff Arquette, Burt Mustin. Joey is held in a small town in order to officiate at a ground breaking ceremony.

Rusty's Education
GS: Rusty Hamer. Rusty plans to drop out of school until Ellie tells him that Joey went to college.

The Sultan's Gift
GS: Frank Wilcox, Pat Winters. Joey is given two harem girls as a present from a Sultan.

Joey Entertains Rusty's Fraternity
GS: Rusty Hamer, Cliff Norton. Rusty has to bring a boy dressed as a girl to a frat dance.

The Do-It-Yourself Nursery
GS: Herbie Faye. House painter Krupnick agrees to turn the spare room into a nursery if Joey is kept out of the way.

The Sergeant's Testimonial
GS: Allan Melvin, Cliff Norton. Joey goes to his Army reunion.

Joey Changes Larry's Luck
GS: Allan Melvin, Cliff Norton. Joey and his friends plan to fix their card game in order to let Larry win.

Never Put It in Writing
GS: Bobs Watson. Larry thinks he is losing his job when Joey hires another writer.

Larry's Habit
GS: Frank Wilcox, Allan Melvin. Larry's knuckle cracking is driving Joey crazy.

Joey the Star Maker
GS: Barbara Stuart, Allan Melvin. Joey's neighbor wants him to get his wife into show business.

What'll You Have?
GS: Carol Byron. Ellis is jealous of Joey's new secretary.

Joey Discovers Jackie Clark
No available story.

LAUREL & HARDY

The films of Laurel and Hardy have been running on television since the early 1960s, perhaps even earlier. They are a collection of two-and three-reel shorts made during the 1930s. The films are in constant syndication all over the United States and around the world in several different languages. Producer: Hal Roach. Synd: Janus Films. Laurel and Hardy portray themselves in these films, which are usually run late at night or during the early afternoon.

Berth Marks
Stan and Ollie are musicians who create havoc aboard a train.

Men O' War
Stan and Ollie are sailors who take two girls to a park and cause nothing but trouble.

Perfect Day
Stan and Ollie and their families plan to spend a day in the country but somehow never manage to get there.

They Go Boom
Stan tries to cure Ollie's cold.

The Hoose-Gow
Stan and Ollie play prisoners who create havoc in a prison camp.

Night Owls
A cop wants Stan and Ollie to break into a house so he can arrest them.

Blotto
Stan sneaks out of the house to go to a nightclub with Ollie.

Brats
Stan and Ollie babysit for their look-alike sons.

Below Zero
Stan and Ollie play street musicians who find a policeman's wallet and treat the cop to dinner with his own money.

Hog Wild
Stan helps Ollie put a radio antenna on his roof.

The Laurel-Hardy Murder Case
Stan and Ollie go to a haunted house to collect an inheritance.

Another Fine Mess
Stan and Ollie hide out in a mansion

Oliver Hardy (top) and Stan Laurel.

in order to escape a cop. Stan plays the butler and Ollie poses as the owner of the house in order to confuse the cop even more.

Be Big
Stan and Ollie send their wives on a vacation so they can go to a lodge meeting.

Chickens Come Home
Ollie plans to run for mayor but is blackmailed by his old girlfriend.

Laughing Gravy
Stan and Ollie try to hide their pet dog from their landlord.

Our Wife
Stan helps Ollie elope with his girl-friend.

Come Clean
Stan and Ollie prevent a woman from committing suicide, but then find that they can't get rid of her.

One Good Turn
Stan and Ollie help an old lady who is going to be evicted.

Helpmates
Ollie and Stan try to clean up the house after a big party, before Ollie's wife comes home.

Any Old Port
Ollie volunteers Stan as a fighter in a boxing match against Ollie's old enemy.

The Music Box
Stan and Ollie have to deliver a piano to a house on the top of a hill.

The Chimp
When the circus for which Stan and Ollie work goes out of business, Stan is given a flea circus and Ollie winds up with a chimp.

County Hospital
Stan tries to keep Ollie from getting bored while he is in the hospital.

Scram
A drunk takes Stan and Ollie to his house, but goes to the wrong house.

Their First Mistake
Stan convinces Ollie to adopt a child to soften up his relationship with his wife.

Towed in a Hole
Ollie and Stan buy a boat to catch fish to sell.

Twice Two
Stan and Ollie and their wives have a dinner party.

Me and My Pal
Stan's working on a jigsaw puzzle is upsetting Ollie who is about to get married.

The Midnight Patrol
Stan and Ollie play cops who walk a night beat.

Busy Buddies
Stan and Ollie work in a lumber yard and make a mess of it.

Dirty Work
Stan and Ollie are chimney sweeps who get mixed up with a mad scientist who is trying to discover a fountain of youth formula.

Oliver the Eighth
Ollie meets his future wife through the classifieds, unaware that she is a black widow who wants to make him her eighth husband.

Going Bye Bye
Stan and Ollie testify against a crook and then decide it would be safer if they left town.

Them Thar Hills
Stan and Ollie go to the mountains for Ollie's health, where they drink from a well filled with homemade liquor.

The Live Ghost
Stan and Ollie are hired to shanghai men for a ship, but wind up on the ship themselves.

Tit for Tat
Stan and Ollie open an electrical store only to find their old enemy (from Them Thar Hills) owns the store next door.

The Fixer Uppers
Stan and Ollie sell greeting cards and help a woman try to make her husband jealous.

Thicker Than Water
Stan and Ollie buy a grandfather clock at an auction.

LAVERNE & SHIRLEY

On the air 1/27/76, off September 1983. ABC. Color film. 112 currently syndicated episodes. Broadcast: Jan 1976-Jul 1979 Tue 8:30-9; Aug 1979-Dec 1979 Thu 8-8:30; Dec 1979-Feb 1980 Mon 8-8:30; Feb 1980-Sept 1983 Tue 8:30-9. Producer: Garry Marshall. Prod Co/Synd: Paramount TV.

CAST: Laverne De Fazio (played by Penny Marshall), Shirley Feeney (Cindy Williams), Carmine Ragusa (Eddie Mekka), Frank De Fazio (Phil Foster), Squiggy (David L. Lander), Lenny (Michael McKean), Edna Babish (Betty Garrett).

A spinoff of *Happy Days*, this concerns the adventures of two crazy girls during the 1950s. They work in the bottle cap division of a brewery. The series is still doing well on the network, but it is a complete failure in reruns despite the fact that it is running all over the country. The syndicated title of the series is *Laverne & Shirley & Company*.

The Society Party [Pilot]
GS: Henry Winkler, Kathrine Ish Stahl. Laverne and Shirley move into their Milwaukee home.

The Bachelor Party
GS: Henry Winkler. Laverne rents out her father's pizza parlor for a bachelor party.

Bowling for Razzberries
Laverne has a cold and can't bowl in the tournament.

Faulter at the Altar
Laverne suddenly decides to marry her next boyfriend.

A Nun Story
Laverne and Shirley expect one of their wild friends to turn their class reunion into a success, unaware that she is now a nun.

One Flew Over Milwaukee
Shirley is driving everyone crazy worrying about her bird.

Dog Date Blind Dates
GS: Fred Willard, Guich Kooch. Laverne and Shirley meet two strange guys on a blind date.

Did She or Didn't She?
Lenny ruins Laverne's reputation when he jumps to the wrong conclusion about Squiggy and her.

It's the Water
Laverne is promoted to the job of beer taster.

Dating Slump
Shirley's boyfriend dumps her for another girl.

Fake Out at the Stake Out
GS: Bo Kaprall. Laverne becomes a decoy to help catch a thief.

Hi-Neighbor
Lenny and Squiggy move into Laverne and Shirley's apartment.

How Do You Say . . . in German?
GS: Brenda Verrett, Harold Oblong. The German delivery man faints in Laverne and Shirley's house.

Suds to Stardom
After losing four talent contests, Laverne and Shirley decide to do something about it.

Mother Knows Worst
GS: Pat Carroll. Shirley's mother comes for a visit.

Drive She Said
GS: Bo Kaprall. Laverne offers Shirley free driving lessons in exchange for some money to buy a new car.

Angels of Mercy
Laverne and Shirley become hospital volunteers.

Penny Marshall (left) and Cindy Williams as Laverne & Shirley.

Two Weirdos
Lenny and Squiggy disappear after Laverne and Shirley decide not to go to the circus.

Goodtime Girls
Laverne and Shirley babysit as a favor to Fonzie.

Bachelor Mothers
Laverne has morning sickness after a party, causing her to think she is pregnant.

Bridal Shower
Laverne and Shirley get an invitation to a bridal shower.

Steppin' Out
The girls have big dates, now if only they can get themselves together in time.

Excuse Me, May I Cut In?
The girls convince two high school students into taking them to a dance contest to win a TV.

Look Before You Leap
GS: Severn Darden. A famous impresario claims he can make stars out of anyone, including Laverne and Shirley.

Dear Future Model
GS: Billy Sands. Laverne and Shirley decide to become high fashion models.

Christmas Eve at the Booby Hatch
GS: Howard Hesseman. Laverne and Shirley perform a Christmas show at a hospital.

Guilty until Proven Not
GS: Louis Nye. Laverne is arrested for shoplifting.

Playing Hookey
The girls play hookey from work, but everything goes wrong.

Guinea Pig
GS: Robert Cornthwaite, Kenneth Gilman. The girls become guinea pigs in order to raise some money to go to a cocktail party. Laverne is allowed to sleep for a few minutes at a time and Shirley has to eat dirt.

Tough in the Middle
GS: Maureen Arthur. Laverne asks Lennie, Squiggy and Carmine to dress up as gangsters in order to scare away a golddigger who wants to marry her father.

Call Me a Taxi
The girls take jobs as taxi dancers when they get laid off.

Buddy Can U Spare Father
GS: Scott Brady. Shirley goes to a sleazy bar to look for her father.

Honeymoon Hotel
GS: Geoffrey Lewis. Shirley wins a vacation at a newlywed hotel.

Hi-Neighbors Book 2
Laverne and Shirley come to the rescue when Lenny and Squiggy get stood up.

Frank's Fling
GS: Kirk Duncan. Edna's ex-husband drops in for a visit, causing Frank to look for another girl.

Haunted House
The girls want new furniture and go looking for a used couch, in a haunted house.

Citizen Krane
GS: Pat McCormick. Shirley is promoted to supervisor and has the other workers hating her for it.

Anniversary Wrap-Around
Flashbacks of scenes from previous episodes.

Take My Plants—Please
GS: Ralph James. The girls get laid off so they go to work in a flower shop.

Cruise [Part 1]
The girls take a job dressed as Jack and Jill to sell children's shoes to earn extra money for their vacation.

Cruise [Part 2]
GS: Phillip Clarke. Laverne and Shirley go on a Great Lakes cruise and Shirley falls for one of the ship's crew.

Airport 1959
Laverne and Shirley go on their first plane and end up flying it.

Tag Team Wrestling
Laverne teams up to enter a charity wrestling match.

The Pact
Laverne tries to find out if she was really adopted.

Robot Lawsuit
A giant robot attacks Laverne in a toy store.

Laverne and Shirley Meet Fabian
GS: Fabian. Fabian's concert is sold out, but the girls still want to see him.

Laverne's Arranged Marriage
Laverne's father arranges a marriage for her to a wealthy cheese manufacturer.

Shirley's Operation
Shirley panics in the hospital and has her friends who are dressed in Alice in Wonderland costumes looking for her.

The Stakeout
Carmine is suspected of being a counterfeiter.

The Mortician
Laverne has a crush on a mortician who is more interested in her dead than alive.

The Slow Child
GS: Linda Gillian. Edna's retarded daughter is left with Laverne and Shirley, but later disappears with Lenny.

New Year's Eve 1960
GS: Craig Littler. It is New Year's Eve and Laverne is dumped by her date and Shirley has a cold.

The Horse Show
GS: Robert Casper. Shirley rescues a horse from a glue factory and puts it in her bedroom.

The Dentist
GS: Bob McClurg.   Laverne has a chipped tooth and goes to Shirley's dentist.

Shotz Talent Show
GS: Francis Williams, Margery Marshall. Mr. Shotz wants the girls to find a spot in the talent show for his no-talent son.

Bus Stop
GS: Tom Leopold. The girls take a bus to a distant city to visit two medical students who leave them stranded.

Driving Test
Unless Squiggy passes his driving test, he will lose his job.

Obstacle Course
GS: Bo Kaprall. Shirley takes an obstacle course for a volunteer policewoman's job.

Debutante Ball
Laverne and Lenny go to a debutante ball where Lenny learns he is 89th in line for the Polish throne.

2001: A Comedy Odyssey
Laverne dreams she and Shirley are in their 80s, still living together and still single.

Breaking Up and Making Up
GS: Dale Robinette. A spoiled playboy makes out with both Laverne and Shirley.

Eraserhead Date
GS: Paul Wilson. Shirley has a blind date with Eraserhead and it isn't quite what she had in mind.

Festival [Part 1]
The girls to to New York to visit all of Laverne's relatives and to attend the Italian festival.

Festival [Part 2]
Frank tries to win the climbing the greased pole contest so he can win a trip to Italy for his mother.

The Quiz Show
Laverne and Shirley appear on a game show called Be Silly For Dollars.

The Robbery
GS: Larry Bishop. Out for kicks, Laverne teams up with a tough guy who commits a crime.

Playing the Roxy
GS: Tim Jerome. Shirley gets amnesia and thinks she is a stripper named Roxy.

Laverne and Shirley Go to Night School
GS: Hans Conreid. Shirley wants to become a medical assistant, and wants reluctant Laverne to go to night school with her.

The Bully Show
Lenny and Squiggy are forced to make a date between Laverne and their foreman.

Chorus Line
Laverne dreams of going to Broadway when she auditions for "West Side Story" in Chicago.

Move In
Shirley recalls how she and Laverne first moved in together.

Visit to a Cemetery
Laverne comes to accept the death of her mother and visits her grave.

Dinner for Four
GS: Denny Evans, Jeff Kramer. The girls inadvertently cook dinner for their dates' girlfriends.

It's a Dog's Life
GS: Jack Somack, Murphy Dunne. Laverne handcuffs herself to a homeless dog at the pound to protest the scheduled death of the dog.

O Come All Ye Bums
Laverne and Shirley turn into street performers to raise cash for Frank's annual holiday hobo dinner.

Supermarket Sweep
Laverne wins five minutes of free shopping and everyone wants something.

Who's Poppa?
GS: Kirk Duncan. Frank looks once again for another girl when Edna's ex-husband comes to visit her again.

Lennie's Crush
Lenny falls in love with Laverne after misunderstanding what she told him.

Talent Show
In the third annual Shotz talent show, Laverne and Shirley perform as human puppets.

Fire Show
GS: Larry Driscoll. One of the firemen who come to put out the fire in their apartment falls for Laverne.

Feminine Mistake
GS: Jay Leno. Shirley tries to make Laverne beautiful in order to impress a guy.

Squiggy in Luv
GS: Cynthia Harrison. Squiggy's girlfriend is just using him.

Tenants Are Revolting
GS: Rose Michton. The girls believe they are doing a good deed by calling in a building inspector to make repairs, until Mrs. Babish is given a deadline to fix it or pay a fine.

Shirley and the Old Man
GS: Robert Alda. Shirley's friendship with a rich older man is resented by Carmine, who is jealous, and the man's daughter is suspicious of Laverne's intentions.

Industrial Espionage
GS: Dick Yarmy. No one believes Laverne saw an industrial spy in the brewery.

Upstairs Downstairs
GS: Dick Shawn. A fight over returning a wrongly issued check sets the girls to dreaming about Shirley in heaven and Laverne in hell.

Fat City Holiday
GS: Susan Kellerman. The girls get jobs at a weight loss camp.

Shotgun Wedding [Part 2]
The girls get engaged to Richie and Fonzie to avoid a shotgun wedding. [The first part of this episode was aired as part of "Happy Days."]

One Heckuva Note
Shirley finds an old love note written to Laverne by Carmine.

Bad Girls
GS: Michele Greene. The girls arrange for Edna's niece to join their old club, only to learn that their old club has now become a street gang of thieves.

A Drunken Sailor
GS: Ed Begley, Jr. Shirley's brother returns home from the Navy, an alcoholic.

The Wedding
Edna accepts a marriage proposal from Frank, who waited to the last minute to ask her.

Pushed Me Too Far
Lenny refuses to have anything to do with Squiggy after he pushes him into a garbage can.

Testing-Testing
Shotz hires a psychiatrist to evaluate job aptitudes.

Shotz Talent Show IV
A patriotic theme is in store for the fourth annual talent show.

In the Army [Part 1]
Laverne and Shirley enlist in the WACs to get even for a missed promotion.

In the Army [Part 2]
Laverne and Shirley regret joining the Army.

Take Two They're Small
GS: Tommy Madden, Jimmy Briscoe. Lenny and Squiggy fix Laverne and Shirley up with computer dates, who turn out to be two midgets.

Not Quite South of the Border
GS: Neil Thompson, Lu Leonard. The girls can't wait to go on a vacation to Mexico.

You Ought to Be in Pictures
The girls are recruited for an Army film about prostitution.

Beatnik Show
GS: Art Garfunkel. The girls' coffee house performance attracts a band of beatniks.

Why Did Fireman . . .
GS: Ted Danson. Laverne falls for a fireman who is always being called to duty.

Aunt Mary-Margret
Laverne's aunt comes for a visit.

Murder on the Moose Jaw Express [Part 1]
GS: Roger C. Carmel, Charlene Tilton, Scatman Crothers, Wilfred Hyde-White. The girls are riding the Moose Jaw Express when a murder victim enters their compartment.

Murder on the Moose Jaw Express [Part 2]
GS: Roger C. Carmel. Laverne and Shirley try to find out who the murderer is.

The Collector
GS: Richard Stahl. To protest a false bill, the girls chain themselves inside the gas company building.

The Duke of Squigman
GS: Charles Murphy. Squiggy sleepwalks thinking he is a rich duke.

The Survival Test
GS: Vicki Lawrence. A mean Army sergeant takes the girls on a survival test against the men.

Dante the Daring
GS: Ed Marinaro. Laverne's Italian cousin arrives from Italy looking for a job.

Separate Tables
GS: Julius La Rosa, Pat Morita. To overcome her fear of being alone, Laverne eats in a Chinese restaurant by herself.

The Diner
Lenny inherits a greasy spoon diner.

LEAVE IT TO BEAVER

On the air 10/4/57, off 9/12/63. CBS, ABC. B&W Film, 30 min. 234 episodes. Broadcast: Oct 1957-Mar 1958 CBS Fri 7:30-8; Mar 1958-Sept 1958 CBS Wed 8-8:30; Oct 1958-Jun 1959 ABC Thu 7:30-8; Jul 1959-Sept 1959 ABC Thu 9-9:30; Oct 1959-Sept 1962 ABC Sat 8:30-9; Sept 1962-Sept 1963 ABC Thu 8:30-9. Producer: Joe Connelly & Bob Mosher. Prod Co/Synd: Universal TV.

CAST: Theodore "Beaver" Cleaver (played by Jerry Mathers), Wally Cleaver (Tony Dow), Ward Cleaver (Hugh Beaumont), June Cleaver (Barbara Billingsley), Eddie Haskell (Ken Osmond), Larry Mondello (Rusty Stevens), Whitey Whitney (Stanley Fatara), Clarence "Lumpy" Rutherford (Frank Bank), Fred Rutherford (Richard Deacon).

WRITERS: Dick Conway, Roland MacLane, Joe Connelly, Bob Mosher. DIRECTOR: Norman Tokar.

The adventures of the all-American Cleaver family residing in Mayfield USA. Ward Cleaver, an accountant, his wife June and their children Wally and Theodore (The Beaver). Typical episodes depict the trials and tribulations of the Beaver learning to experience new ideas and solving problems with the help of his brother and understanding parents. *Leave It to Beaver* is one of the most popular reruns in America, enjoying cult status in most cities. In the fall of 1982, CBS aired a *Leave It to Beaver* reunion episode entitled "Still the Beaver" and it starred almost all of the original cast.

Captain Jack
GS: Edgar Buchanan, Irving Bacon. The boys buy a baby alligator.

The Black Eye
Beaver gets a black eye when he gets into a fight with a girl.

Beaver Gets 'Spelled
GS: Diana Brewster, Doris Packer. Beaver gets a note from his teacher causing him to think he is getting expelled from school.

Water, Anyone?
Beaver decides to sell water to his friends during a summer heat wave.

Wally's Girl Trouble
GS: Susan Seaforth, Eric Nelson. Beaver feels neglected because Wally spends most of his time with his girlfriend and not with him.

Part-Time Genius
When Beaver gets a high grade on a test, everyone thinks he is a genius.

New Neighbors
GS: Charles Gray, Phyllis Coates. Beaver thinks the lady next door is in love with him.

The Haircut
GS: Benny Baker. Beaver gives himself a haircut, in order to hide the fact that he lost the money his parents gave him to get a haircut.

Brotherly Love
GS: Herb Vigran. The boys decide that they will never do anything without the other, no matter what the consequences.

The Perfume Salesmen
GS: Ann Dore. The boys decide to sell perfume in order to get a movie projector as a prize.

The Clubhouse
GS: Johnny Silver, James Gleason, Raymond Hatton. Beaver tries to get three dollars so he can join his brother's club.

Beaver's Short Pants
GS: William Schallert, Madge Kennedy. Beaver's visiting Aunt Martha buys him a new suit complete with short pants, which he is expected to wear to school.

Beaver's Crush
The other children in his class accuse Beaver of being the teacher's pet.

Voodoo Magic
After seeing a film called "Voodoo Curse," Beaver decides to put a curse on Eddie.

The Paper Route
GS: Bill Idleson. Wally and Beaver decide to take a paper route in order to earn extra money to buy new bicycles for themselves.

Party Invitation
GS: Lyle Talbot. Beaver gets an invitation to go to a birthday party, the only problem is that he is the only boy invited.

Lumpy Rutherford
GS: Richard Deacon, Helen Parrish. The boys plan to get even with the new bully on the block.

Child Care
GS: Ray Montgomery. Wally and Beaver babysit with a four-year-old girl.

The Bank Account
Wally and Beaver decide to use their money they saved to surprise their father with a new hunting jacket.

Lonesome Beaver
Beaver finds that he has to have fun by himself when Wally joins the Boy Scouts.

Perfect Father
GS: Lyle Talbot, Richard Smiley. Ward becomes jealous when the boys spend their time with their neighbor rather than with him.

Cleaning Up Beaver
Ward and June try to get Beaver to keep himself clean and not get dirty so much.

The State vs. Beaver
GS: Frank Wilcox. Beaver gets a ticket when he recklessly drives his home-made racer down the street.

Beaver and Pancho
GS: Maudie Prickett. Beaver brings home a Mexican Chihuahua, and then tries to find its rightful owner.

The Broken Window
Wally and Beaver break the window in their father's car and try to have it repaired before he finds out.

Train Trip
GS: Karl Swenson, Madge Kennedy. Wally and Beaver find that they spent most of the money they were given to buy train tickets home, after visiting with their aunt.

My Brother's Girl
Wally is reluctant to ask a girl to go with him to a school dance.

Next Door Indians
Eddie tricks Beaver into thinking that there are old Indian relics buried in the lot across the street from his house.

Music Lesson
Beaver takes clarinet lessons so he can join the school band.

Tenting Tonight
The boys camp out in the backyard.

Beaver's Old Friend
Beaver finds that he can't give up his old teddy bear so easily.

Wally's Job
Wally promises Ward that he will paint the garbage cans but then tries to get out of doing it.

New Doctor
GS: Stuart Wade. Beaver becomes jealous of all the attention Wally gets when he gets sick, so Beaver decides to get sick himself.

Boarding School
Wally decides that he wants to attend a military school.

Beaver's Bad Day
Beaver gets into trouble when he rips his suit and then lies about how it happened.

Beaver's Poem
Ward helps Beaver write a poem for the school paper.

Beaver and Henry
Beaver learns that his pet rabbit, Henry, is going to be a mother.

Beaver's Guest
GS: Madge Blake, Frank Sully. Beaver invites Larry to spend the night at his house.

Cat Out of the Bag
GS: Charles Gray. Wally and Beaver take care of the neighbor's valuable cat, and find they wish they hadn't when it runs away.

Ward's Problem
GS: Sue Randall. Ward promises to take Wally fishing on the same day he is supposed to go on a school picnic with Beaver.

Beaver Runs Away
Beaver plans to run away after Ward punishes him for misusing his tools.

Beaver and Chuey
GS: Allen Robert. Beaver's new friend can't speak a word of English, only Spanish.

The Lost Watch
GS: Jonathan Hale. Lumpy accuses Beaver of losing his watch, which he asked him to hold for him while he played baseball.

The Pipe
Beaver and Larry decide to smoke Ward's new pipe.

Wally's Present
Beaver decides to buy himself a present instead of getting one for Wally, when Wally refuses to take him to the movies.

Her Idol
Beaver spends the day with Linda, despite the ribbing he expects to get from his friends.

The Grass Is Always Greener
GS: Don Lyon, Billy Chapin. Beaver visits the garbageman and his family in order to see how poor people live.

Beaver's Hero
Beaver brags about Ward being a hero in the war, but now finds that he has to prove it.

Wally's New Suit
GS: John Hoyt. Wally buys a new suit for the dance, but his parents don't like his taste in clothes.

The Shave
Wally decides to take up shaving when he thinks he is starting to grow a beard.

The Visiting Aunts
GS: Madge Kennedy, Irene Tedrow. Wally and Beaver's plans to go to the carnival are upset when Aunt Martha comes for a visit.

The Tooth
Beaver is scared to go to the dentist.

Beaver's Ring
GS: Anne Loos. Beaver gets a ring stuck on his finger and can't get it off.

Beaver Gets Adopted
GS: Lurene Tuttle, Lee Torrance. Beaver tries to get himself adopted by another family when he thinks his parents don't love him anymore.

Eddie's Girl
Eddie's girlfriend finds that she would rather date Wally instead.

Price of Fame
GS: Bill Erwin. Beaver gets locked in the principal's office and gets his head stuck in between the bars of a park fence.

School Play
GS: Dorothy Adams. Beaver is given the lead role in the school play, but then develops a case of stage fright.

The Boat Builders
Beaver tries to hide the fact that he tried out Wally's homemade boat and almost drowned, when it turned over, from his parents.

The Happy Weekend
GS: Harry Tyler. Ward takes the family to a mountaincabin for the weekend.

Beaver Plays Hookey
GS: John Hart. Beaver and Larry decide to play hooky when they think their teacher will get mad at them because they are late for class.

The Garage Painters
GS: Sara Anderson. The boys volunteer to paint the garage, but trick their friends into doing it for them.

Beaver's Pigeons
Beaver buys two pigeons, but when he gets sick the rest of the family find that they have to take care of them for him.

Wally's Pug Nose
GS: Sheryl Holdridge, Ralph Brooks. Wally tries to change the shape of his nose when he thinks his new girlfriend doesn't like it.

The Haunted House
GS: Lillian Bronson. Beaver thinks the old lady who asked him to walk her dog is a witch because she lives in the house everyone thinks is haunted.

Wally's Haircomb
GS: Howard Wendell. Wally gets a new hairstyle which nobody likes but him.

Beaver and Gilbert
GS: Steve Talbot. Beaver's new friend likes to make up wild stories instead of telling the truth.

The Bus Ride
GS: Yvonne White, Bill Idleson, Frank Sully. Wally loses Beaver on a bus trip to visit one of his old friends.

A Horse Named Nick
GS: Bill Baldwin, Mike Ross. Beaver and Wally get a tired old horse as their payment for working at a carnival.

Beaver Says Goodbye
GS: Rodney Bell. Beaver's class gives him a farewell party when it seems he will be moving away.

Beaver's Newspapers
Beaver finds Wally's old typewriter and uses it to create his own newspaper.

Beaver's Sweater
Beaver tries to get his parents to let him spend his money on a new sweater.

Friendship
Beaver and Larry promise to be friends forever, like Damon and Pythias.

Dance Contest
Wally's old girlfriend enters them in a dance contest, the only problem is Wally can't dance.

The Cookie Fund
GS: John Eldredge. Beaver and Larry are put in charge of the class Cookie fund.

Forgotten Party
GS: Johnny Collier, Mary Lawrence, Bill Baldwin. Beaver is invited to his friend's party, but forgets to show up.

Beaver the Athlete
Beaver practices for the annual school baseball game between the boys and the girls.

Found Money
Beaver finds some money in Larry's backyard and spends it at the carnival.

Most Interesting Character
Beaver writes a composition about the most interesting character he has known, his father.

School Bus
GS: James Parnell.   Beaver gets suspended from riding on the school bus.

Beaver's Tree
Beaver goes back to their old house to dig up his tree and take it home with him.

Wally's Play
Wally gets the part of a dancehall girl in the school play.

Blind Date Committee
GS: Beverly Washburn. Wally is chosen to find a blind date for the new girl in school.

Beaver's Fortune
GS: Callen Thomas, Jr. Beaver believes this is his lucky day after reading his fortune on a weighing machine.

Beaver Takes a Walk
Beaver bets Larry that he can walk twenty miles in one day.

Beaver Finds a Wallet
Beaver finds a wallet and eagerly awaits the arrival of the present the owner said she would send him as a reward.

Beaver Takes a Bath
Wally babysits with Beaver who leaves the water running in the bathtub until it floods the bathroom and the kitchen ceiling.

Beaver's Prize
Beaver wins a bicycle at a movie theater, but can't bring it home because he disobeyed his father's order forbidding him to leave the house.

Borrowed Boat
Beaver and Larry are accused of breaking into a boathouse and stealing a ride in a rowboat.

Beaver's Library Book
Beaver takes a book out of the library but then loses it.

Baby Picture
Beaver has to bring in one of his baby pictures to enter in a class beautiful baby contest.

Teacher Comes to Dinner
Larry charges his friends to watch their teacher eat dinner at Beaver's house.

June's Birthday
Beaver buys a gaudy blouse for his mother's birthday.

Pet Fair
Beaver claims he owns the talking parrot he saw in a pet shop window so he wouldn't be the only one in school without a pet.

Wally's Election
Wally and Lumpy are both nominated for the office of sophomore class president.

School Sweater
GS: Ann Barnes.   Wally lends his sweater to one of his girlfriends, but finds that she won't give it back.

Beaver the Magician
GS: Madge Kennedy, Joey Scott. Larry tricks Benjie into believing that he turned Beaver into a rock.

Beaver Makes a Loan
Beaver lends Larry some money, but he refuses to pay it back.

Tire Trouble
Beaver decides to go into the chinchilla business and proceeds to build a house for the animals.

Larry Hides Out
Larry hides in Beaver's closet after running away from home because he was caught reading his sister's diary to Beaver.

Wally's Test
Eddie blames Wally for the disappearance of his crib sheets from the bathroom towel dispenser.

Beaver and Andy
GS: Wendall Holmes. Ward and June try to hide the fact that Andy, the man they hired to paint the house, drinks too much.

Beaver's Dance
Beaver and Larry disobey their parents and play hooky from dancing school.

The Hypnotist
Eddie tricks Beaver into believing that he hypnotized him.

Larry's Club
Larry creates his own club in order to make Beaver jealous when he isn't allowed to join Beaver's club.

Wally and Alma
Wally tries to palm off his new girl to his friends when her mother turns into a matchmaker.

Ward's Baseball
Beaver and Larry take Ward's autographed baseball to play catch. They later try to replace it when it gets run over by a truck.

Beaver's Monkey
Beaver brings home a monkey to keep as a pet.

Wally's Orchid
Wally tries to get an orchid to give to his new girlfriend on their date.

Beaver's Bike
Beaver rides his new bicycle to school where it is stolen.

Mother's Day Composition
Beaver is asked to write a composition about what his mother did before she was married.

Beaver and Violet
Beaver thinks Violet is in love with him.

The Spot Removers
Beaver accidentally spills some oil on Wally's suit and tries to get the stain out before anyone notices.

Beaver the Model
Beaver disobeys his father and signs with a modeling agency which now demands he pay them $30.

Wally the Businessman
Wally takes an after-school job selling ice cream.

Beaver and Ivanhoe
After reading the book "Ivanhoe," Beaver decides to become a knight.

Beaver's Team
Beaver tells his team's secret football play to the sister of one of his teammates who then blabs it to the other team.

Last Day of School
Beaver unknowingly takes the wrong box to school as a gift for his teacher.

Beaver's House Guest
Beaver's new friend comes from a broken home, which Beaver finds fascinating.

Beaver Becomes a Hero
GS: Larry Thor. Beaver creates a story about himself being a hero, but regrets it when it is printed in the newspaper.

Beaver's Freckles
GS: Stephen Wootton. Beaver hates his freckles and tries to get rid of them.

Beaver Won't Eat
June becomes upset when Beaver won't eat his Brussels sprouts.

Beaver's Big Contest
Beaver wins a sports car in a raffle, which Ward wants to sell and put the money towards Beaver's college fund.

Wally the Lifeguard
Wally gets a job as a lifeguard but loses it when it turns out he is too young for the job.

Beaver's IQ
Beaver worries about passing his IQ test.

Beaver Goes into Business
Beaver goes into the lawn-cutting business but can't find any customers.

Wally's Glamour Girl
Wally is reluctant to take a wealthy girl to a dance because he lied to her about his background in order to impress her, and he is afraid she will learn the truth.

Eddie's Double-Cross
Wally tells Eddie that his new girlfriend is just using him, but he refuses to believe it.

Miss Lander's Fiance
Beaver becomes depressed when his teacher becomes engaged.

Chuckie's New Shoes
Beaver takes a little kid to get a pair of new shoes, but loses him in the store.

Ward's Millions
Beaver buys his father a book on how to become a millionaire.

Teacher's Daughter
Wally is dating his teacher's daughter and he is sure it will affect his grades so he plans to do something about it.

Beaver and Kenneth
The new boy in class gives Beaver several gifts in order to get him to be his friend.

Beaver's Accordion
Beaver sends for an expensive accordion against his father's wishes.

The Dramatic Club
Beaver gets the lead part in the dramatic club's play, only to learn that the role requires him to kiss a girl.

Uncle Billy
Beaver believes the wild stories and empty promises told to him by his visiting Uncle Billy.

Beaver's Secret Life
GS: Keith Taylor. Beaver performs some dangerous acts so he could write something exciting about himself in his diary.

Wally's Track Meet
Wally is suspended from the track team when he is accused of horsing around in the locker room.

Beaver's Old Buddy
Beaver's old friend comes for a visit, but they soon find they are bored with each other's company.

Beaver's Tonsils
GS: John Gallaudet. Beaver becomes worried when the doctor says that he might have to have his tonsils removed.

The Big Fish Count
Beaver tries to win a dog in a fish counting contest at the pet shop.

Mother's Helper
Wally falls for the teenage girl who is helping his mother with the housework.

Beaver's Poster
Beaver tries to get his father to help him win the school poster contest.

Wally and Dudley
Wally is given the task of showing the son of one of his mother's friends around and introduce him to his friends.

Beaver's Report Card
Eddie changes Beaver's arithmetic grade on his report card, causing everyone to think Beaver is improving.

Eddie Spends the Night
Eddie spends the night with the Cleavers while his parents are out of town.

Wally's Dream Girl
Wally learns that his dream girl is not all that he thought she was.

Mistaken Identity
Beaver's friend Richard is caught by the police breaking a window, but he gives them Beaver's name and address so they won't blame him.

The School Picture
Beaver ruins the class picture by making a horrible face.

Beaver's Frogs
Beaver decides to collect some frogs in order to sell them to make extra money to buy a canoe.

Community Chest
Beaver helps his mother by collecting money for the community chest, but he loses the money on the way home.

Beaver's Rat
Beaver buys a pet rat but his mother doesn't want it in the house.

Kite Day
Beaver and his father build a kite to enter in a contest, but Beaver takes it for a trial run and wrecks it.

In the Soup
GS: Jack Mann, Jimmy Gaines, Harry Holcombe. Beaver climbs on top of a billboard which has a giant-size soup bowl and a steam-producing mechanism in it in order to see what is inside the bowl. He falls in and can't get out.

Junior Fire Chief
Beaver is elected Junior Fire Chief, but lets the job go to his head.

Beaver's Doll Buggy
Beaver plans to use the wheels off a doll buggy for his new coaster, the only problem is how to wheel the buggy home without anyone seeing him.

Substitute Father
Beaver gets into trouble at school and has to bring one of his parents with him the next day, but he brings Wally instead.

Wally's Summer Job
When Wally gets a job at the drugstore, Eddie and Lumpy plan to play a trick on him.

Wally's Car
GS: George Spicer, Dick Porter. Wally buys an old car but his parents refuse to let him keep it.

One of the Boys
GS: Stephanie Hill. Wally is asked to join an exclusive club at school, but he is not sure if he wants to belong.

Beaver's First Date
GS: Pam Smith. Beaver asks a girl in his dancing class if she will be his date for an upcoming dance party.

Wally's Big Date
Eddie tricks Wally into swapping dates with him for the school dance.

No Time for Baby Sitters
GS: Barbara Parkins. Beaver tries to convince his friends that he is allowed to stay home by himself without a babysitter.

Going Steady
GS: Ryan O'Neal. Ward is afraid that Wally is planning to marry his current girlfriend after listening to the girl's bragging father.

Beaver's Birthday
GS: William Newell. Beaver buys a model car with some of his birthday money but hides the car from his parents, thinking they wouldn't approve.

Beaver Takes a Drive
GS: Maurice Manson. Beaver accidentally releases the brake on his father's car, causing it to roll into the street, which gets Wally in trouble when he drives it back to the house without having a driver's license.

Beaver's Cat Problem
Beaver finds a neighbor's runaway cat causes him a lot of trouble when it keeps returning to him.

Weekend Invitation
GS: David Scott. Wally is asked to spend the weekend at a friend's cabin without adult supervision.

Beaver's Ice Skates
GS: Stanley Clements. Beaver buys a pair of ice skates three sizes too large for him.

Beaver's English Test
Beaver studies one of Wally's old English tests, only to find that he is given the exact test by his teacher the next day.

Wally's Chauffeur
Wally is reluctant to have his girlfriend drive them to the dance for fear that his friends will laugh at him for letting a girl drive.

Farewell to Penny
Beaver finds that he has been invited to a farewell party for Penny, a girl in his class whom he hates.

Ward's Golf Clubs
GS: Henry Hunter. Beaver thinks he broke one of his father's golf clubs.

Beaver's Electric Trains
Beaver decides that he wants to keep his train set after his mother promised to give it to a neighbor's boy.

Beaver the Bunny
Beaver finds that he must walk to school in his bunny costume in order to get there in time to appear in the school pageant.

Nobody Likes Me
Beaver thinks that his parents no longer like him and don't want him anymore.

Beaver's Laundry
Beaver and Richard create a flood while trying to do the laundry.

Beaver's Jacket
Beaver shares his new jacket with a friend who has lost his own jacket.

Beaver's Fear
Beaver plans to join Wally and his friends on their trip to the amusement park, but he finds that he is scared to go on the roller coaster.

Eddie Quits School
GS: Bert Remsen, Frank Wilcox. Eddie quits school to take a job, but then wishes he were back in school.

Three Boys and a Burro
GS: Jane Dulo. Beaver and his friends buy a burro but none of their parents will allow them to keep it on their property.

Wally Stays at Lumpy's
Wally plans to stay all night at Lumpy's house for a party.

The Younger Brother
Beaver is afraid to tell his parents that he was thrown off the basketball team.

Lumpy's Car Trouble
Wally and his friends disobey his father when, returning home from a track meet, they take a shortcut and damage the car.

Beaver the Babysitter
GS: Marjorie Reynolds. Beaver babysits for a ten-year-old girl.

Brother vs. Brother
Beaver falls for the new girl in his class, but she has a crush on Wally.

Beaver's Typewriter
GS: Ed Prentiss. Beaver takes the credit when Eddie types Beaver's school assignment.

The Merchant Marine
Ward thinks Wally plans to join the Merchant Marine when he receives an application in the mail.

Yard Birds
GS: Bartlett Robinson. Ward makes Beaver and Wally clean up the backyard.

Tennis Anyone?
GS: Jim Drake, Cindy Robbins. Wally thinks he has fallen in love with his new tennis partner, unaware that she is just using him to make her boyfriend jealous.

Sweatshirt Monsters
Beaver buys a sweatshirt with the picture of a monster on it and plans to wear it to school despite the school dress code.

A Night in the Woods
GS: John Hart. Wally is forced to take Beaver and his friends on a camping trip.

Stocks and Bonds
Wally and Beaver invest in the stockmarket, with their parents' help.

Long Distance Call
GS: Don Drysdale.   Beaver and his friends make a long distance call to baseball player Don Drysdale.

Un-Togetherness
GS: Brenda Scott. Wally asks not to go with the family on their annual vacation, but then feels left out.

Wally's License
GS: Larry Blake.   Wally passes his driving test and gets a license, but his parents are afraid to let him drive the family car.

Wally Buys a Car
GS: Ed Peck. Wally and Ward disagree over the type of car Wally should buy.

Wally's Dinner Date
GS: Than Wyenn. Wally takes his date to a fancy restaurant but forgets his wallet.

The Clothing Drive
GS: Tim Matheson.   Beaver accident-

ally takes three of his father's new suits for the clothing drive at school.

Beaver's Autobiography
Beaver gets one of his classmates to write his autobiography for English class.

The Late Edition
Beaver has a fight with the new paper boy, who is actually a girl.

Eddie, the Businessman
GS: Howard Caine.   Eddie and Wally get jobs at an ice cream factory.

Beaver's Football Award
Beaver wears his school clothes while the rest of his friends wear a suit to the father-son dinner.

Double Date
Beaver agrees to go with Wally on a double date, but his girl backs out at the last moment.

Beaver Joins a Record Club
GS: George Cisar.   Beaver joins a record club without reading the contract, now he must pay the bill or be sued.

Tell It to Ella
Beaver writes an anonymous letter to an advice column, claiming that his parents are too strict.

Bachelor at Large
Eddie moves into his own apartment, but after seeing what a mess it is Wally tries to get him to move home again.

Beaver the Sheep Dog
Beaver tries to change his hairstyle when a girl tells him he looks like a sheep dog.

Wally's Car Accident
Wally gets into an accident with his father's car and doesn't know how to tell him about it.

Beaver the Hero
GS: John McKee, Jan Stine.   Beaver

gets a swelled head when he thinks he is a football hero just because he catches the winning pass.

The Party Spoiler
GS: Cheryl Miller. Beaver decides to destroy his brother's party when he refuses to invite him.

The Mustache
Wally decides to grow a mustache to impress his girlfriend.

The Parking Attendants
GS: Richard Simmons, Kim Hamilton. Eddie and Wally get jobs as parking attendants at a wedding.

More Blessed to Give?
GS: Buddy Lewis. Beaver wins a gold locket at carnival and gives it to his girlfriend.

Beaver's Good Deed
GS: Frank Ferguson. Beaver decides to perform a good deed by inviting a tramp to come home with him.

The Credit Card
GS: George Petrie. Wally decides that he wants a gasoline credit card because Eddie has one.

Uncle Billy's Visit
GS: Edgar Buchanan. Beaver and Gilbert sneak into the movie theater. Beaver thinks he can talk his uncle, who is taking care of him while his parents are away, out of punishing him.

Beaver on TV
Beaver claims that he is going to appear on a TV show.

Box-Office Attraction
Wally asks Eddie to get him a date with the ticket seller at the theater.

Beaver the Caddy
GS: John Gallaudet. Beaver finds that the man he is caddying for cheats, in order to win a bet.

Lumpy's Scholarship
Wally throws a party for Lumpy when he wins a scholarship to the State College.

The Silent Treatment
Beaver decides to give his mother the silent treatment when she asks him to go to the market at an inopportune moment.

Eddie's Sweater
Eddie becomes upset when he thinks Wally is dating his girlfriend, unaware that she is only using him as a model for a sweater she is making for Eddie.

Beaver's Prep School
Beaver decides to go to a prep school, but changes his mind when he realizes that he will miss all of his friends.

Wally and the Fraternity
Wally and Eddie consider joining Wally's father's old fraternity when they attend college.

The Book Report
Beaver decides to watch a movie version of the book "The Three Musketeers" instead of reading the book for a book report, unaware that it is a comical version.

The Poor Loser
Beaver becomes upset when his father gets two seats to a baseball game, but takes Wally instead of him.

Summer in Alaska
GS: Harry Harvey, Sr. Eddie brags about spending his summer vacation on a fishing boat going to Alaska.

Don Juan Beaver
GS: Veronica Cartwright. Beaver makes a date with a girl to take her to the dance, but finds himself in trouble when he makes a date with another girl to take her to the same dance.

Beaver's Graduation
Beaver thinks he is not going to graduate because he cut a class.

Wally's Practical Joke
GS: Kathleen O'Malley. Eddie and Wally play a practical joke on Lumpy in order to get even with the ones he played on them. Only this time the jokes backfire on them.

The All-Night Party
GS: Marjorie Reynolds, Frank Sully, Herbert Rudley. The father of Wally's date accuses him of taking her to a wild party when she is accidentally knocked into a fountain by a drunk.

Beaver Sees America
GS: Lori Martin. Beaver doesn't want to join his parents on a trip across the country because he is afraid that he will lose his new girlfriend to one of his friends.

Family Scrapbook
The entire family looks through their old scrapbook and reminisce about all of their past adventures (seen in flashbacks).

THE LIFE OF RILEY

On the air 10/4/49, off 3/28/50. NBC. B&W Film. 26 episodes. Prod & Synd: Unknown.

CAST: Chester A. Riley (played by Jackie Gleason), Peg (Rosemary DeCamp), Junior (Lanny Rees), Babs (Gloria Winters), Gillis (Sid Tomack), Digger (John Brown).

On the air 1/2/53, off 8/22/58. NBC. B&W Film. 212 episodes. Producer: Tom McKnight, Irving Brecher. Prod Co: Dumont. Synd: Unknown.

CAST: Riley (played by William Bendix), Peg (Marjorie Reynolds), Junior (Wesley Morgan), Babs (Lugene Sanders), Gillis (Tom D'Andrea), Honeybee (Gloria Blondell), Egbert (Gregory Marshall), Cunningham (Douglas Dumbrille), Otto (Henry Kulky), Waldo Binny (Sterling Holloway).

The adventures of Chester A. Riley and his family. Based on the radio show starring William Bendix. When Bendix was unable to appear in the series because of movie commitments, the role went to a young and much thinner Jackie Gleason. However, the series bombed. Three years later, Bendix returned and the series ran for five years. He also starred in the feature version of the same name. The series has a syndication problem; it has gone from one company to the next. Information about the current syndicator is unavailable; no one knows who currently has the rights to the series. Besides, the series is quite dated. The few stations that still run it use it to fill in time.

[The following episodes of the Jackie Gleason version of the series did not have episode titles, only production numbers which are unavailable.]

After Gillis brags about Egbert, Riley refuses to attend the father/son banquet with untalented Junior.

Riley plans to return the silver fox scarf he found on a street car, until Peg mistakes it for her birthday present.

Babs's French teacher charms the family, but not jealous Riley.

Riley learns not to judge a book by its cover when Babs reads a book banned in Boston.

Everyone knows Riley wants a bathrobe for his birthday, except Junior who doesn't seem to know it is Riley's birthday.

An enormous valentine leads Riley to believe that Peg has a suitor.

Riley's tonsils have to come out, but Riley loses his nerve.

Riley falls for Junior's teacher. GS: Marie Dwyer.

Riley inadvertently turns a job opportunity into a fiasco.

While trying to discourage Junior from gambling, Riley has a winning streak.

The Rileys suspect their new janitor is a jailbird. GS: Alan Reed.

Riley's family rebels when he tries to enforce the idea of domestic tranquillity.

Riley tries to prove he loves Junior by throwing a surprise party for him.

Riley's job on the assistant manager's desk isn't what he expected. GS: Emory Parnell.

Peg's missing five dollars, and Riley thinks Junior stole it.

A phony theater operator has Babs aspiring to be a star.

The Gillises' fight has drastic results on the Rileys.

Riley gets expelled from the night school that he and Tony were attending. GS: Tito Vuolo.

Riley objects to Babs's boyfriend: a greeting card salesman named Simon. GS: James Lydon.

Riley thinks he has solved Babs's problem when he gets her a date for the college dance.

Riley thinks Junior is a coward when the boy runs from a fight.

Riley and Peg each think the other is having a nervous breakdown.

Riley thinks he is not long for this world when he confuses the butcher's message with his doctor's.

Flashbacks recreate the events surrounding the birth of the Rileys' first baby.

Riley and Gillis want to go into business with accounting student Simon. GS: James Lydon.

Junior infuriates his father by quitting school to go to work.

[The following episodes all starred William Bendix.]

Junior Wins the Soapbox Derby
Riley offers to help build Junior's soapbox racer.

Peg's Birthday Present
Riley finds a silver fox fur while riding on the bus. He brings it home with him and has every intention of returning it, until Peg finds it.

Riley's Surprise Package
Riley becomes jealous when he thinks that Gillis has won an award.

Riley's Old Flame
Riley thinks an old friend he knew in Brooklyn is still in love with him.

Riley's Stomach Ache
Riley makes a midnight raid on the icebox and winds up with an upset stomach.

Riley, the Animal Lover
Riley buys a junkman's broken-down horse to save it from the glue factory, but can't find a place to keep it.

Riley Faces Fatherhood
Riley thinks he's about to be a father again when Gillis plays a trick on him.

Riley's Surprise Party
Riley plans a surprise party for Babs, but the party holds more surprises for him than her.

Junior's Vacation
Riley and Gillis worry about their sons who are off on a trip.

Riley's Burning Ambition
When the plant foreman is sent out of town on a special job, Riley takes his place.

Riley's Haunted House
Riley and Peg are bored with their new ranch house.

Riley's Separation
Riley insists that Peg go to a wedding she doesn't want to attend.

Riley Gets Engaged
In an attempt to hold off the immigration bureau, a beautiful French girl tricks Riley into becoming engaged despite his marital state.

Riley the Worrier
Riley fixes Babs up with a blind date.

Riley's Second Honeymoon
Riley is advised to take a vacation.

Riley Teaches Junior Boxing
Riley teaches Junior to box.

Riley Balances the Budget
Riley takes a job in a department store to earn extra money.

Riley's Love Letters
Riley finds a love letter to his wife while going through some old papers.

Junior's Double Date
Riley gives Junior advice when he learns Junior is about to go on his first date.

Riley's Uranium Mine
Riley thinks he has discovered uranium in the backyard of his friend Gillis. He finds himself in trouble when he tries to get the rights to the alleged uranium deposits.

Riley Brightens the Corner
In a weak moment, Riley donates the family's beds to the Darkest Hour Mission.

Babs's Used Car
Riley buys a used car, but it turns out to be a stolen vehicle.

Riley and the Boss's Niece
Riley's boss asks Riley to find a date to escort his niece to a dance.

Riley and the Cop
Riley rents his attic in an attempt to solve his budget problems.

The Circus Comes to Town
Riley fears Junior has run off to join the circus.

Riley in a Rut
Trying to get a new job, Riley does some research in the local library.

Riley, Surprise Witness
Waldo sprains his thumb on a lawn-mower he borrowed from Gillis.

Riley Outwits Cupid
Riley discovers that Babs is going steady.

Riley and the Beaux Arts Ball
Riley learns that Babs is going to the Beaux Arts Ball.

Riley Holds the Bag
When involved in an automobile accident, Riley demands that he and the other driver exchange licenses.

Riley Takes Up Art
Riley has decided to become a painter.

Riley's Good Deed
Riley is determined to do a good deed every day.

Riley Takes Out Insurance
Babs's boyfriend sells Riley an insurance policy covering all types of accidents.

Riley Faces Mother's Day
Riley has a special surprise for Peg on Mother's Day.

Riley the Newsboy
Riley volunteers to take over Junior's paper route.

Riley, the Heir
Riley is notified that he has inherited a fortune.

Riley Meets the Press
Riley arranges to have the newspapers cover his wife's club meeting.

Riley and the Foreman's Gift
Riley and his co-workers take up a collection to buy a farewell gift for their shop foreman.

Riley Takes a Roomer
Junior's teacher, Miss Jessup, decides to become a boarder in Riley's house.

Riley and the Suggestion Contest
There's a brand new suggestion box installed at the plant.

Junior's Secret
Riley gets involved in a family mix-up.

Riley in the Wild Blue Yonder
Riley and his friend Gillis decide to take flying lessons.

Destination Brooklyn
Riley and his family return to Riley's old neighborhood in Brooklyn.

The Dog Watch
Riley becomes temporary custodian of the boss's dog.

Babs and Junior Try Home Economics
Babs and Junior convince Riley that their finances can be stretched through scientific buying.

The Duck Hunting Trip
Riley and Gillis go duck hunting at a nearby mountain lake.

Junior the Chief Magistrate
It's boys day and the kids take over the town.

Riley Buys a Statue
Riley buys a genuine Indian statue.

Riley vs. Numerology
Riley consults his pal Waldo, an expert on numerology, and finds that he starts believing in it too.

Riley the Friendly Neighbor
Gillis starts filling his garage with various household appliances.

Riley's Wild Oats
Riley comes home from a bachelor party and tells Peg he wants to sow some wild oats.

Puppy Love
When Riley learns Junior has a girlfriend, he has a heart-to-heart talk with him about the unhappiness of marriage.

The Car Pool
Riley's latest money-making scheme is car pooling.

Job Open
Riley and his pal Gillis are both interested in the same out-of-town job.

Brotherly Love
The Rileys soon learn that a little brotherly love is better than a lot all at once.

The Unwelcome Guests
Riley agrees to take care of the Gillis home while the family is away on vacation.

Come Back, Little Junior
Riley wants Junior to go out and get a job.

Riley Buys a Wrestler
Riley must find a professional wrestler to fight the plant champ for an annual charity event.

Light-Fingered Babs
Riley thinks Babs has become a kleptomaniac when she starts wearing a whole new wardrobe.

A Bride for Otto
Riley and Gillis decide to get a mail order bride for their friend Otto.

The Auction
Riley buys a suitcase at an auction.

Sister Cissy Returns
Riley is told that Peg has broken her heel. He is convinced it's her foot, but actually it is the heel of her shoe.

Night Shift
Riley and Gillis have another argument.

Chicken Ranch
Riley is determined to prolong his parent's visit.

Up to the Jury
Riley is proud that Peg has been chosen for jury duty.

The Gymnasium
When a friend of his is fired at the plant, Riley helps him start a gymnasium.

Singing Cowboy
Riley objects to Babs's new boyfriend, a cowboy singer.

Look Peg, I'm Dancing
A reluctant Riley and Gillis are enrolled by their wives in a dancing class.

Meet the Neighbor
Riley can't resist boasting to his new neighbor.

Babs Gets Engaged
Riley is upset over his daughter's romantic escapades.

Brotherhood of the B.P.L.A.
Learning that his father is going back to Brooklyn, Riley tries to interest him in other activities.

The Blockade
A tree is blown across Riley's driveway.

The Diet
Riley and Gillis diet in an effort to fit into last year's bowling jackets.

Out to Pasture
Riley is told to show a new man the ropes of his trade.

Top Secret
Riley and Gillis are assigned to work on a top secret project.

Riley Unites the Family
Riley has come to the conclusion that his family has lost interest in him.

School Board Critic
Riley schemes to get an all-expense paid trip to Chicago.

Letter of Introduction
Terrible developments occur which change Riley's mind about an old friend.

The Big Sacrifice
Riley wants to be invited to the formal dinner of the department heads.

The Marines Have Landed
Babs is depressed because she hasn't heard from her Marine fiance since he's been at camp.

Love Comes to Waldo Binny
Riley's confirmed bachelor friend Waldo finally falls in love.

Darling, I Am Growing Old
Riley believes that you are as young as you feel and he is feeling pretty old.

Do It Yourself
Riley is unable to rent a boat for a fishing trip with his boss.

Wedding Plans for Babs
Riley goes all out in his plans for Bab's wedding.

Dudley, the Burglar
Neighbor Calvin Dudley puts Riley's watch in a vase for safekeeping, only no one knows it.

Pay the Penalty
As a gift for his family, Riley tries to win a free vacation by entering a TV contest.

Ghost Town
Riley gets a week off by telling his boss he's suffering from a severe backache.

The Famous Chester A. Riley, Junior
Junior lets his football fame go to his head.

Riley the Tycoon
Riley gets a day off from the plant and decides to spend it in the park.

Repeat Performance
Riley and Peg plan surprise parties for each other on the same night.

Middle Age Blues
Riley thinks a job will cheer up Peg and get her out of the dumps.

Waldo's Mother
Riley helps a friend out of the frying pan and into the fire.

Shower for Babs
A surprise bridal shower is planned for Babs, and Riley is asked to take care of Don, the groom-to-be.

Head of the Family
Riley's Uncle Chester doesn't approve of Babs's engagement to Don.

Riley and the Widow
A charming Southern widow talks Riley into helping her with her new dress shop.

Babs's Wedding
Babs seems destined to be late for her wedding when her excited father leaves without her.

Riley's Raffle
Riley decides that the family needs a second car.

Junior Quits School
Junior decides that having a job is more profitable than finishing high school.

The Tree That Grew in Brooklyn
Riley is appointed custodian of a sickly tree by the Brooklyn Patriots of Los Angeles.

Babs's School Election/Babs's New Job
Riley tries to insure his daughter's election as freshman class president.

The Train Trip
Riley unknowingly helps a convict escape from police custody.

The Contestant
Riley enters a newspaper contest.

The Song Writer
Junior enters a high school song writing contest.

His Brother-in-Law's Keeper
Riley has in-law trouble when his sister and her husband move in with them.

Partnership
Riley and Dudley decide to go into business together.

Riley's Allergy
Riley's mother-in-law thinks he is in love with another woman.

Stage Door Riley
Riley wants Peg to drop out of the dramatics club she just joined.

Riley's Club for Service Wives
Riley's concern over Babs's lack of outside interests leads Otto to suggest that she join the B.M.C.

Waterfront
Riley and Otto are on the waterfront to repair the wing of a plane.

Expectantly Yours
When Riley stumbles onto Babs's instruction list from the doctor, he thinks Babs's mother-in-law is going to have a baby.

Junior Gets a Car
Riley discovers that his driver's license has expired.

From Rags to Riches
A pair of con men sell Riley some phony uranium stock.

House for Sale
The honeymoon cottage Riley bought as a surprise for Babs and her new Marine husband is right in the path of the new freeway.

Babs Moves Out
Riley doesn't like the idea of Babs and her husband moving into their own place.

Riley Trades His House
The Riley-Dudley good neighbor policy has reached the breaking point, so Riley decides to sell the house.

When Women Were Women
Dudley and Riley remark that women have it too easy in this modern age, unaware that their wives are listening.

A Wire for Gillis
Riley believes that Gillis has come into a lot of money when he gets a telegram.

The First Quarrel
Babs quarrels with Don when he wants to go fishing.

Buttering Up a Millionaire
Riley goes overboard on his welcome home party for the Gillises.

The New Job
In an attempt to get Gillis a job, Riley manages to confuse the personnel office at the plant.

Destination Del Mar Vista
Riley and Gillis have acquired new jobs.

Uncle Bixby Takes Over
Riley is shocked to learn that Peg's eccentric uncle has arrived at the house.

Friends Are Where You Find Them
Riley and Gillis decide they see too much of each other and decide to find new friends.

Juvenile Delinquent
Junior says he wants to get a hot-rod, causing Riley to worry.

Riley's Lonely Night
Riley's feelings are hurt because Peg and Junior leave him alone on a Saturday night.

A Man's Pride
Junior fights with his girlfriend and refuses to make up with her.

Riley Hires a Nurse
Babs hires the only available baby nurse in town.

Blessed Event
Riley is resting in bed with a cold when the phone call comes announcing that Babs has gone to the hospital to have the baby.

Benefit for Egbert
Riley throws a benefit barbecue in the backyard for Gillis's old friends.

Honeybee's Mother
A visitor creates much havoc until Riley forces her to go home.

World's Greatest Grandson
In order to get pictures of his new grandson for boasting purposes, Riley has to avoid the baby's nurse.

Double Double Date
Riley mistakes a couple of gun molls for the girls he is supposed to pick up for his son's double date.

Riley Wins a Trip
Riley gets himself entered in a teenager's dance contest to win a free trip to Hawaii.

Aloha, Riley, Goodbye
Riley thinks he has killed a man and goes to the police with a confession.

Change in Command
Riley and Gillis scheme to get rid of foreman Hawkins and replace him with their friend Otto.

Strolling Through the Park
Riley takes his new grandchild for a stroll in the park, and comes home with the wrong baby.

Deep in the Heart of . . .
Riley and his friends startle the whole town with a midnight horse ride that gets out of hand.

Candid Camera
While trying out his new camera at the scene of an auto accident, Riley turns up some damaging evidence.

Foreign Intrigue
In order to help a friend out of a jam, Riley brings home a lovely French maid.

All-American Brain
A handsome young football coach proves to be a disrupting influence in the Riley home.

Riley the Executive Type
Riley is convinced he deserves better pay, but his boss accepts his resignation instead.

Riley Engages an Escort
Riley overhears Babs trying to arrange a date for Sadie Hawkins Day and decides to help her along.

Riley's Operation
Riley accidentally swallows a fishbone and the company doctor insists that he have his tonsils removed.

The Rileys Step Out
When Riley finds two banquet tickets discarded by his boss, he decides to surprise Peg.

A Young Man's Fancy
Riley confuses his son's love interest with an older woman who has a boyfriend named Junior.

Babs's Dream House
Riley is sure he can save on an architect's fee for Babs's dream house.

A Match for Gillis
The purchase of an inexpensive watch as a gift for Gillis proves to be no bargain for Riley.

Getting Riley's Goat
Junior brings home a goat to keep for a ten-day 4-H Club assignment.

A Day at the Beach
The Rileys and the Gillises plan to spend a quiet weekend at the beach.

A House Divided
When a new owner buys the duplex which the Rileys and Gillises share, trouble starts which almost gets both families evicted from the house.

Return to Blue View
Riley breaks into his old house in order to retrieve the $3000 he left behind when they moved to their new house.

The High Cost of Riley
Riley and Gillis are convinced that they can buy food for much less than their wives can.

Babs Comes Home
Riley volunteers as a substitute when Babs's husband must go away.

Father-in-Law vs. Father-in-Law
Riley tries to break up Junior's romance with his new girlfriend.

Annie's Radio Romance
Annie has a crush on a crooner and enters a contest where the winner will get a date with the star. Riley and Gillis decide that she needs a little help.

The Stray Dog
Hoping for a large reward, Riley provides overnight shelter for a noisy dog.

Vacation Plans
The Rileys and the Gillises plan a camping trip together.

Homeless Otto
Otto demands a raise and loses his job.

Summer Job for Junior
Riley has to pay out $50 on a busboy job in the event that his son doesn't make it.

Gossip
Riley explains to Junior how gossip spreads, but the lesson backfires.

Riley's Ups and Downs
Riley takes a downstairs apartment and agrees to switch with Gillis and move upstairs at the end of the year.

The New Den
Peg tries to convert an unused room into a den for Riley.

Gillis's Childhood Friend
An old friend of Gillis spends so much time with him that Riley feels neglected.

Dudley Comes to Town
Riley's old friend Dudley comes for a visit and talks Riley and Gillis into going into business with him.

Down for the Count
In the hopes of winning a contest, Riley hits on a scientific method of determining the number of beans in a glass jar.

Gruesome Twosome
Peg and Honeybee suggest golf lessons as a diversion for their tired husbands.

Happy Birthday Little Chester
As baby Chester's birthday approaches, Riley decides a surprise party is in order.

Babs and the Latin
Riley and Gillis can't understand why Babs is acting so strange lately.

Anchors Away
Riley and Gillis join a team from their factory and enter a fishing contest.

Framed
The factory foreman names Riley and Gillis as the organizers of a charity play.

Nobody Down Here Likes Me
Riley organizes a fishing party.

Live Modern
While Peg is away visiting Babs, Riley decides to surprise her by redecorating the house with modern furniture.

Mrs. Aircraft Industries
Riley tries to convince his boss that Babs should be entered in an aircraft industry beauty contest, representing his company.

Baby Chester's First Words
Babysitters Riley and Gillis hear baby Chester talking, so Riley calls Don in South America and forgets to watch the baby.

A Trip for Peg
Riley writes a letter to his relatives informing them that Peg is going to visit, but the letter isn't clear, so the relatives misunderstand and a niece arrives at Riley's house for a visit.

Going Steady
Riley has great plans for father-son activities during Junior's school vacation, but the plans are upset when Junior starts to go steady.

A Guest from England
A young English student comes to spend two weeks at the Riley household, but Riley has trouble understanding his Cockney way of speaking.

The Letter
Riley and Gillis persuade an unhappy friend to quit his job.

Little Awful Annie
Annie becomes infatuated with Junior's friend Moose.

Music Hath Charm
Riley decides to bone up on a field he knows little about: music.

Movie Struck
A cowboy movie idol sets out to destroy the illusions of lovesick girls who have a crush on him, by using Riley and Gillis as his agents.

Bowling Beauties
An efficiency expert at the factory invites Riley and Gillis to teach bowling to the girls at the plant, but Peg and Honeybee protest.

After You're Gone
Riley brings a friend home from the plant for dinner who brings flowers and candy to Peg. Riley later realizes he hasn't been spending enough time with Peg lately.

Riley's Burst Bubble
Riley believes that his niece Annie, who has been visiting with him, is reluctant to go home because she hates her father.

Teenage Troubles
Junior and his girlfriend Bobby decide not to see each other for two weeks so that he can study, but he has to keep others from dating Bobby so Riley helps out.

Otis Yonder Story
A hillbilly from Oklahoma comes to work at the plant, so Riley and Gillis decide that his singing voice has a great female appeal and plan to capitalize on it.

Barracks Bag
Riley collects a duffel bag that the Army is belatedly returning to Gillis.

Price of Fame
Riley becomes a neighborhood hero when he accidentally captures a robber.

Riley's Gift from the Boss
Riley has been with the plant for ten years. When he sees the initials C.A.R. after his name on a memo, he now thinks that he will be given the car as a reward for his good work.

Riley's New Suit
Riley tears his suit on the way to work. The children plan to buy him a new one for his birthday and borrow the torn one to get his measurements.

Riley Proves His Manhood
Riley tells a reporter that all housewives should work.

Ten O'Clock Scholar
The men at the plant are told that all employees holding high school diplomas will be considered for promotion, so Riley goes to night school to get his diploma.

Riley's Kiss in the Dark
Riley reluctantly accompanies Peg to a fancy dress party. When the lights go off suddenly, an unknown woman kisses him.

The Cake Contest
Riley persuades Peg to enter a baking contest. Her entry is perfect until Riley accidentally crushes it, so she heads to the nearest bakery.

Riley's Sister Cissy/Stupid Cupid
Riley finally succeeds in getting his sister Cissy married off.

Riley and the Bean Contest
Dejected over his failure to provide the family with a car, Riley sees hope when he discovers a bean counting contest in a local store in which the first prize is a brand new car.

Riley the Scoutmaster
Scoutmaster Riley is boasting again, this time he informs his wife that he could do her housework in half the time it takes her to do it.

Riley Invades the Fight Game
GS: Lou Nova. Killer Cooper, a boxer,

is scheduled to take on Chester Riley in an exhibition bout.

Help for Honeybee
When Riley overhears an argument between Honeybee and Gillis, he thinks they are breaking up so he gets Honeybee a date with a man from the plant.

Riley's Lost Weekend
Riley decides to take the family on a trip to the country to spend a three-day weekend.

Riley's Family Reunion
A radio program plans a surprise party for Riley.

Riley's Business Venture
Riley and Dudley decide to go into business for themselves.

Riley Camps Out/Oily Birds
Riley and Gillis decide to go on a camping trip to get away from their daily boredom.

Riley Cultivates Babs
Riley decides to become better acquainted with his daughter.

Riley's Uncle Baxter
Peg's Uncle Baxter comes for a visit.

Riley Punishes Junior/Junior's Future
Riley is named Father of the Month by his lodge, but he finds the honor gets in the way when he has to punish his son.

A Test for Gillis
Riley has decided that Gillis, his best friend, has turned against him, so he decides to put Gillis to the test.

Riley Meets a Rival
Peg, tired of hearing Riley complain about his lot in life, decides to teach him a lesson.

Riley, the Typical Worker
Riley learns that an award for the most typical worker is to be given at the plant and he feels confident that he is going to get it.

Here Comes Constance
Peg and Honeybee invite a guest to visit with them, and now Riley and Gillis are miserable because they must attend the symphony and the ballet with her.

Riley's Anniversary
Riley and Peg plan surprise parties for each other.

THE LITTLE RASCALS

The Little Rascals is a collection of old *Our Gang* shorts from the 1930s. They have now been cut down to about seven minutes each from their original 20-minute versions. They have been cut for reasons mainly to do with complaints that they embody offensive stereotypes of blacks, Chinese, etc. Several films are considered so racist that they have been removed from syndication completely. B&W film. 79 episodes. Producer: Hal Roach. Syndicator: King World Features.

Boxing Gloves
Chubby and Joe have a boxing match.

Shivering Shakespeare
The gang appears in an unintentionally funny stage version of "Quo Vadis."

The First Seven Years
Jackie and Speck fight a duel to see who takes possession of Mary Ann.

When the Wind Blows
Jackie tries to get back into his house

The Little Rascals (of Our Gang): from the left, Alfalfa, Porky, Buck-wheat, Darla, Spanky, and Pete the Dog.

after he gets himself locked out and is mistaken for a burglar.

Bear Shooters
The gang goes on a camping trip and unknowingly get mixed up with a gang of bootleggers.

Pups Is Pups
The gang tries to enter their pets in the city pet show.

Teacher's Pet
Jackie and his friends plan to play several tricks on their new teacher.

School Is Out
The gang mistakes Miss Crabtree's bro-

ther for her boyfriend and try to keep him from marrying her.

Helping Grandma
The gang helps out an old lady who runs a grocery store.

Love Business
Jackie, who is in love with Miss Crabtree, gets a big surprise when she becomes a boarder in his house.

Fly My Kite
The gang tries to help an old lady who is being forced to move to the old folks' home by an evil son-in-law.

Shiver My Timbers
Miss Crabtree and an old sea captain plan to teach the gang a lesson when they play hookey from school.

Dogs Is Dogs
Wheezer is the scapegoat for his mean stepmother and her bratty son.

Readin' and Writin'
Brisbane tries to get himself kicked out of school.

Free Eats
The gang unknowingly helps a gang of crooks rob the home of a rich woman who is throwing a party for some poor children.

Spanky
Spanky goes bug hunting in his home and accidentally discovers the hidden panel where his miser father has hidden all his money.

Choo-Choo!
The gang is mistaken for some orphans and are put aboard a train where they cause trouble for their guardian and the other passengers.

The Pooch
Stymie has to find five dollars in order to get his dog out of the dog pound.

Hook and Ladder
The gang become volunteer firemen and help put out a fire in a warehouse full of explosives.

Free Wheeling
Stymie takes Dickie on a wild ride in a runaway taxi in order to help him cure his stiff neck.

Birthday Blues
Dickie charges admission to a party so he can use the money to buy his mother a birthday present.

Fish Hooky
The gang get involved with the truant officer when they decide to play hooky from school.

Forgotten Babies
Spanky is left to watch the gang's baby brothers and sisters when they go swimming.

Mush and Milk
The gang has to put up with a grouchy old lady, cold bedrooms and mush for breakfast when they attend a prison-like boarding school.

Bedtime Worries
Spanky is scared to sleep by himself for the first time.

Wild Poses
Spanky's parents take him to have his picture taken by a nutty photographer.

Hi-Neighbor!
The gang build a homemade fire engine.

For Pete's Sake
Wally has to find a way to raise enough money to buy a new doll for a little girl.

The First Round Up
The gang decides to go camping for a week, but never make it past the first night.

Honky Donkey
A rich kid invites the gang and their pet donkey over to his house to play.

Mike Fright
The gang appear on a radio show when they form a band.

Washee Ironee
The gang help a rich kid clean his clothes so his mother won't know that he was playing football with them instead of practicing his violin.

Mama's Little Pirate
Spanky falls asleep and dreams that he and the gang become trapped in a giant's cave when they go exploring for treasure.

Shrimps for a Day
Two adults find a magic lamp and change themselves into children.

Anniversary Trouble
Spanky is accused of stealing the money his father left as an anniversary present to his wife.

Beginner's Luck
Spanky appears in a talent show dressed as a Roman warrior.

Teacher's Beau
The gang decides to sabotage the dinner prepared by their teacher in order to break up her upcoming marriage.

Sprucin' Up
Spanky and Alfalfa compete for the attentions of the little girl who just moved into the neighborhood.

The Lucky Corner
The gang helps Scotty and his grandfather with their lemonade stand.

Little Papa
Spanky, with Alfalfa's help, tries to get his little sister to go to sleep so he can go out and play football.

Our Gang Follies of 1936
The gang stages a musical show in order to entertain the other kids in the neighborhood.

Divot Diggers
The gang and their pet chimp become caddies at a golf course.

The Pinch Singer
Alfalfa accidentally takes Darla's place on a radio station amateur contest when she doesn't arrive in time.

Second Childhood
The gang teaches an old lady how to be young again.

Arbor Day
A pair of singing midgets are mistaken for children by the truant officer and sent to school where they help the gang put on a show for Arbor Day.

Bored of Education
Spanky tries to make it appear that Alfalfa has a toothache so the two of them can be excused from going to school.

Two Too Young
Spanky and Alfalfa try to trick Porky and Buckwheat into giving them their firecrackers.

Pay As You Exit
The gang puts on their version of "Romeo and Juliet."

Spooky Hooky
Spanky, Alfalfa, Buckwheat and Porky sneak into the schoolroom at night, during a rainstorm, in order to retrieve the letter they wrote excusing themselves from school so they could sneak off to the circus.

Reunion in Rhythm
The gang puts on a musical show as part of the entertainment for their class reunion.

Glove Taps
Butch and Alfalfa have a boxing match.

Hearts Are Thumps
Spanky and Buckwheat try to break up Alfalfa's relationship with Darla on Valentine's Day.

Three Smart Boys
Alfalfa, Spanky and Buckwheat try to make it look like they are sick, so the superintendent will close the school, thus allowing their teacher to attend her sister's wedding.

Rushin' Ballet
Spanky and Alfalfa hide out in a ballet school when they are chased by two bullies.

Roamin' Holiday
Spanky, Porky, Buckwheat and Alfalfa run away from home to escape their responsibilities, and wind up in a little town where they are taught a good lesson by a nice old couple.

Night 'n' Gales
Spanky and his friends spend the night at Darla's house when, after singing for her family, they find themselves trapped by a heavy rainstorm.

Fishy Tales
Alfalfa fakes an accident so he won't have to fight Butch.

The Pigskin Palooka
Alfalfa tells Darla that he was a football hero at school, but now finds that he has to prove it when the gang plays an important game.

Mail and Female
Alfalfa tries to retrieve a love letter he sent to Darla, before the other members of the women haters club find out.

Our Gang Follies of 1938
Alfalfa dreams that he is an unsuccessful opera singer who is forced to sing in the streets by his cruel manager.

Canned Fishing
Spanky, Alfalfa, Buckwheat and Porky plan to play hooky from school in order to go fishing.

Bear Facts
Alfalfa tries to get himself and his friends jobs as animal trainers when he learns that Darla's father owns a circus.

Three Men in a Tub
Alfalfa and his homemade boat challenge Waldo and his motorboat to a race.

Came the Brawn
Alfalfa plans to wrestle Waldo in order to impress Darla, unaware that Butch has taken his place.

Feed 'Em and Weep
Alfalfa and his friends go to Darla's house to visit her father on his birthday.

The Awful Tooth
Alfalfa and his friends visit a dentist in order to have their teeth removed, so they can have them changed into dimes by the Tooth Fairy.

Hide and Shriek
Alfalfa, Porky and Buckwheat play detectives and go on a wild chase that leads them to a haunted house ride at an amusement park.

[The following episodes are syndicated with the above, but are not run by most stations.]

Small Talk
When Wheezer is adopted by a rich lady, Mary, who is unhappy about being separated from her brother, runs away from the orphanage to join him. The gang also decides to run away from the orphanage in order to visit Wheezer.

Bouncing Babies
Wheezer is jealous of his new baby brother, so he takes it back to the hospital to have it sent back to heaven.

Bargain Day
Wheezer and Stymie go from door to door trying to sell the stuff they stole from the gang.

[The following episodes are no longer available for syndication.]

Railroad
The gang spend the day down at the railroad yard. [This episode is not syndicated because of soundtrack problems.]

Lazy Days
Farina spends the day cleaning up her brother to enter him in a baby contest.

Moan & Groan, Inc.
The gang encounter a madman in a haunted house. [This episode also suffers from a bad soundtrack.]

A Tough Winter
The gang helps Stepin Fetchit read a love letter and then he helps them clean up after they wrecked the house

making taffy.

Little Daddy
Farina and the gang try to prevent Stymie from being sent to an orphanage.

Big Ears
Wheezer tries to make himself sick in the hopes that his fighting parents would become so concerned about him that they won't get a divorce.

A Lad and a Lamp
After reading about Aladdin's lamp, Spanky thinks he turned Stymie's brother Cotton into a monkey after he rubbed a magic lamp.

The Kid from Borneo
Dickie and the gang mistake an African wild man for his uncle when they visit his sideshow.

Little Sinner
Spanky plays hooky from Sunday school in order to go fishing.

LOVE AMERICAN STYLE

On the air 9/29/69, off 1/11/74. ABC. Color Film. Broadcast: Sept 1969-Jan 1970 Mon 10-11; Jan 1970-Sept 1970 Fri 10-11; Sept 1970-Jan 1971 Fri 9:30-10; Jan 1971-Jan 1974 Fri 10-11. Producer: Arnold Margolin/Jim Parker. Prod Co/Synd: Paramount TV.

The format of this series is an anthology one. There were no regular cast members as the stories were constantly different. Although originally an hour series, the individual stories were split up into half-hour segments. There was also an attempt to spin off a black version of *Barefoot in the Park* from this show, but it failed. However, the pilots for *Happy Days* and *Wait Till Your Father Gets Home* were also aired on this show.

Love and the Good Samaritan
W: Dale McRaven. D: Alan Rafkin. GS: Sandy Baron, Kenneth Mars. A man named Freddy gets caught without his pants by the husband of the woman he tried to help with her plumbing problem.

Love and the King
W: Harvey Bullock & R.S. Allen. D: Alan Rafkin. GS: Herb Edelman, Kathie Browne. Bob Curtis receives an unwelcome visit from his old Army friend.

Love and the Other Love
W: Bud Freeman. D: Charles Rondeau. GS: David Hedison, Mary Ann Mobley. Rob buys a sports car causing his wife Pat to think he is in love with his new car and not her.

Love and the Nutsy Girl
W: Carl Kleinschmitt. D: Alan Rafkin. GS: Jerry Van Dyke, Ross Martin. A model tries to get an artist interested in her so she can get a job.

Love and the Heist
W: Susan Harris. D: Charles Rondeau. GS: Phyllis Diller, Nanette Fabray, Hermione Gingold, Ruth McDevitt, Walter Burke. Four women plan to rob a jewelry story in order to prove that they are as good as men.

Love and the Young Unmarrieds
W: Carl Kleinschmitt. D: Alan Rafkin. GS: Mary Ann Mobley, Jane Actman, John McMartin. A minister tries to talk a young couple who are planning to live together into getting married.

Love and the Young Executive
W: Bill Idelson & Harvey Miller. D: Charles Rondeau. GS: John Davidson, Brenda Benet, James Millhollin, Tony Young, Robert F. Simon. A mail clerk poses as an executive in order to date the daughter of the vice president of the company where he works.

Love and the Phone Booth
W: Dale McRaven. D: Charles Rondeau. GS: Peter Kastner, Dwayne Hickman. A country boy takes his city friend's advice and calls a girl whose phone number was written on the wall of the phone booth for a date.

Love and the Legal Agreement
W: George Kirgo. D: Jeff Hayden. GS: Bill Bixby, Connie Stevens, Denny Miller. A married couple decides to share the same house but lead separate social lives when they plan to separate.

Love and the Proposal
W: Dave Evans. D: Richard Michaels. GS: Joan Van Ark, Warren Berlinger, Joan Hackett, Joe Besser, Ron Harper. A man hires an actress to play his long-lost wife in order to get out of marrying his new girlfriend.

Love and the Watchdog
W: Bill Idelson & Harvey Miller. D: Bruce Bilson. GS: Michael Callan. A couple can't decide whether to move from their apartment to a safer neighborhood or to buy a watchdog.

Love and the Other Guy
W: Terry Ryan. D: Charles Rondeau. GS: Donna Douglas, Gary Collins. A man and his girlfriend's date is interrupted by a visit from a notorious swinger.

Love and Grandma
W: Oliver Crawford. D: Bruce Bilson. GS: Paul Ford, Patrick Wayne, Meredith MacRae, Ruth McDevitt. A girl visits her grandmother in a retirement home, only to find that she is living with a man.

Love and the Roommate
W: Allan Burns. D: Charles Rondeau. GS: Ted Bessell, Anjanette Comer. A man falls for his girlfriend's roommate, but he doesn't know how to tell his girlfriend.

Love and the Divorce Sale
W: Lila Garrett & Bernie Kahn. D: Oscar Rudolph. GS: Jesse White, Andrew Prine, Lesley Warren. A young couple sell off their furniture before they divorce.

Love and the Modern Wife
W: Allan Burns. D: Alan Rafkin. GS: Bob Crane, Patricia Crowley, Allan Melvin. When his wife says it is all right for her husband to fool around after being married for seven years, Howard does just that.

Love and the Great Catch
W: Bud Freeman. D: Gary Nelson. GS: Adam West, George Lindsey, Pat Carroll. When actor Adam West plans to visit Harry Clurman in order to buy some stamps from him for his collection, Harry's family goes movie star crazy.

Love and the Big Night
W: Harvey Bullock & Ray Allen. D: Seymour Robbie. GS: Tony Randall, Julie Newmar. A secretary won't let her boss leave her apartment because she is afraid of burglars.

Love and the Teacher
W: Dale McRaven. D: Harry Falk. GS: Orson Bean, Bridget Hanley, Clint Howard. An artist who paints nudes goes to have a talk with his son's sex education teacher when she flunks him.

Love and the Tattoo
W: Roy Kammerman. D: Charles Rondeau. GS: Gary Collins, Stephanie Powers. A man refuses to take his shirt off in front of his girl because he has the name of his former girlfriend tattooed on his chest.

Love and the Living Doll
W: Larry Markes. D: Bruce Bilson.
GS: Arte Johnson, Marlyn Mason. A
man tries to make the girl who lives
across the street from him jealous by
using an inflatable girl.

Love and the Bed
W: Roy Kammerman. D: Jerry Bernstein. GS: Roger Perry, Sue Lyon,
George Tobias. Peter and Barbara,
tenants in the same building, both try
to buy a bed from their landlord.

Love and the Neighbor
W: Roy Kammerman. D: Charles
Rondeau. GS: James Farentino, Michelle Lee. A young couple are bothered by a nosey neighbor.

Love and the Doorknob
W: Frank & Doris Hursley. D: Bruce
Bilson. GS: Gary Lockwood, Stephanie Powers. A man gets a doorknob
stuck in his mouth when he tries to
prove to his wife that he doesn't have
a small mouth.

Love and Mother
W: Roland Wolpert. D: Bruce Bilson.
GS: Chris Connelly, Shelley Fabares.
A young couple's wedding night is
upset when her mother moves in with
them when she has a fight with her
husband.

Love and the Pulitzer Prize Baby
W: Roy Kammerman. D: Charles
Rondeau. GS: Will Geer, Roger Perry,
Leslie Parrish. A movie star tries to
get a Pulitzer Prize writer to father
her baby.

Love and the Singles Apartment
W: Robin Carson. D: Gary Nelson.
GS: Mel Torme, Joyce Van Patten,
Mort Sahl. A man who moves into a
singles apartment while away on business is surprised by a visit from his
wife.

Love and the Safely Married Man
W: George Kirgo. D: Coby Ruskin.
GS: Ronnie Schell, Beth Brickell. A

bachelor invents a family in order to
date a girl who will only date married
men.

Love and the Optimist
W: Bob Rodgers. D: Seymour Robbie.
GS: Jo Anne Worley, Dave Ketchum,
Don Diamond. A man tries to save a
woman from committing suicide.

Love and the Medium
W: Arnold & Lois Peyser. D: Charles
Rondeau. GS: George Gobel, Vivian
Vance. A psychic tries to break up the
upcoming marriage of one of her cli-
ents because she is in love with him.

Love and the Marriage Counselor
W: Norman Lessing. D: Gary Nelson.
GS: Jim Backus, Bernie Kopell. A
couple of business partners visit a marriage counselor in order to decide how
to choose a new secretary for their
office.

Love and Those Poor Crusaders' Wives
W: Gene Fawcett. D: Leslie Martinson. GS: Monte Markham, Dorothy
Provine. A newlywed couple's honeymoon is upset when he accidentally
gets himself locked in an ancient chas-
tity belt and can't get it off.

Love and the Phonies
W: Arnold & Lois Peyser. D: Bruce
Bilson. GS: Phyllis Diller, Richard
Deacon. A couple return home from a
dinner party complaining about how
everyone there was a real phony, including them.

Love and the Eskimo
W: Susan Harris. D: Bruce Bilson.
GS: Bill Bixby, Anthony Caruso. A
man makes a deal with an Eskimo for
the oil rights to his property, but in
return he must let the Eskimo have his
wife for the evening.

Love and the Unlikely Couple
W: Bob Rodgers. D: Bruce Bilson.
GS: Alice Ghostley, Lou Jacobi, Barbara Rhoades. A young man's parents
can't understand why a beautiful girl
wants to marry their plain-looking son.

Love and the Letter
W: Bill Idelson & Harvey Miller. D: Alan Rafkin. GS: Reni Santoni, Robert Clary. An Italian immigrant falls in love with his night-school teacher.

Love and the Serious Wedding
W: Peggy Elliot & Ed Scharlach. D: Leslie Martinson. GS: Paul Winchell, E.J. Peaker. Two practical jokers plan to have a serious wedding, but it doesn't turn out that way.

Love and the Pill
W: Norman Lessing. D: Jud Taylor. GS: Bob Cummings, Jane Wyatt. The parents of a young girl become worried when she tells them that she is going on a swinger's tour with her boyfriend.

Love and the Good Deal
W: Garry Marshall & Jerry Belson. D: Jerry Paris. GS: Jane Wyatt, Hans Conreid, Norman Fell, Skye Aubrey. A young couple try to get a custommade bed to fit into their small bedroom.

Love and the Geisha
W: Harry Winkler & Harry Dolan. D: Bruce Bilson. GS: Red Buttons, Carolyn Jones, Nobu McCarthy. A man receives a visit from his old Japanese girlfriend, making his wife jealous.

Love and the Comedy Team
W: Ed Scharlach & Doug Tibbles. D: Alan Rafkin. GS: Ruta Lee, Jack Carter. A comedy writer finds that her wedding date will prevent her and her partner from finishing a script on time.

Love and the Cake
W: Dennis Klein. D: Charles Rondeau. GS: Julie Newmar, Bob Denver. A man prevents his girlfriend from taking a job as the girl who will pop out of a giant cake at a convention.

Love and the Minister
W: Bob Brunner. D: Gary Nelson. GS: Richard Long, Van Williams, Claudine Longet. When a minister is reject-

ed by his girlfriend, she then asks him to marry her to another man.

Love and the Shower
W: Bruce Howard. D: Jud Taylor. GS: Henry Gibson, Joe Flynn, Carl Ballantine. When his wife leaves him, Lenny Grainger's friends give him a divorce shower complete with two young girls.

Love and Operation Model
W: Terry Ryan. D: Charles Rondeau. GS: Karen Jensen, Albert Brooks. Two guys try to pick up girls at the airport by claiming that they are looking for photographic models.

Love and the High School Flop-Out
W: Larry Siegel. D: Richard Michaels. GS: Barry Gordon, Melodie Johnson. A shy high school student is convinced by his friends to ask a waitress for a date.

Love and the Nuisance
W: Arnie Kogen. D: Bruce Bilson. GS: Fred Willard, Joyce Van Patten, Jan Arvan. A man's proposal to a baroness is interrupted by his high school girlfriend.

Love and Double Trouble
W: Arnold Margolin & Jim Parker. D: Harry Falk. GS: Malachi Throne, Sean Garrison, Pamela Mason. A man tries to explain to his fiancee about the slave and the two harem girls he got for his birthday from his father, an Arab king.

Love and the Vampire
W: Jim Parker & Arnold Margolin. D: Charles Rondeau. GS: Robert Reed, Judy Carne, Tiny Tim. A young couple spend their wedding night in a house owned by a vampire.

Love and the Advice Givers
W: Bruce Howard. D: Bruce Bilson, GS: Tina Louise, Avery Schreiber, Aldo Ray. When a couple feel that their marriage is getting stale, they seek advice from their friends.

Love and the Love Potion
W: Susan Harris. D: Leslie Martinson. GS: Tammy Grimes, Dick Sargent, Pat Morita. A woman uses a Chinese love potion on her boyfriend in order to get him to marry her.

Love and the Motel
W: Susan Silver & Iris Rainer. D: Leslie Martinson. GS: Harry Morgan, Barbara Rush. A man and a woman, who are married to other people, go to a motel to have an affair.

Love and the Kidnapper
W: Arnold & Lois Peyser. D: George Tyne. GS: Tommy Smothers, Jessica Walter. A bumbling kidnapper finds himself in big trouble when his victim's husband refuses to pay the ransom.

Love and the Only Child
W: Roy Kammerman. D: Terry Becker. GS: Ozzie & Harriet Nelson, Tony Dow. A girl leaves her husband and returns home to find that her parents are also leaving each other.

Love and the Wig
W: Larry Markes. D: Bruce Bilson. GS: Mimi Hines, Phil Ford, Guy Raymond. A neglected wife finds that her husband becomes interested in her when she buys a blonde wig.

Love and the Big Game
W: Jack Winter. D: Charles Rondeau. GS: Jack Klugman, Yvonne Craig, Jack Cassidy. Two couples get together to play cards, only to find that one of them is cheating.

Love and the Second Time
W: William Bickley. D: Leslie Martinson. GS: Jack Albertson, Bob Cummings, Joan Bennett. The children of a widow and widower become worried when their parents go out on a date.

Love and the Dating Computer
W: Michael Elias & Frank Shaw. D: Gary Nelson. GS: Broderick Craw-

ford, Herb Edelman, Dorothy Neumann, Melinda Fee. A computer foul-up matches a man named Marion with another man named Francis.

Love and the Happy Couple
W: Bob Rodgers. D: Terry Becker. GS: Sue Ane Langdon, Allan Melvin, Jan Murray. A man tries to get his ex-wife to pose as his wife again in order to fool a millionaire they met on their honeymoon, the only thing is that her new husband won't let her.

Love and the Baker's Half Dozen
W: David Evans. D: Richard Michaels. GS: Alan Sues, Susan Oliver. A baker tries to solve the problems of three couples, while trying to sell them a wedding cake.

Love and the Boss
W: Ray Brenner. D: Allen Baron. GS: Alice Ghostley, Lou Jacobi, Fritz Feld. A man and his wife spot his boss out with a young girl, causing them to fear for his job if he spots them.

Love and the Nervous Executive
W: Terry Ryan. D: Harry Falk. GS: Paul Lynde, Carol Wayne, Herb Voland. A man is promoted to an executive position where he falls for his new secretary.

Love and the Bachelor
W: Lila Garrett & Bernie Kahn. D: Bruce Bilson. GS: Ann Sothern, Brandon DeWilde. A young man brings his future wife to meet his mother.

Love and Murphy's Bed
W: Gene Thompson. D: Leslie Martinson. GS: Jim Hutton, Jo Ann Pflug. A married couple try to hide each of their lovers from each other.

Love and the Lost Dog
W: Bill O'Hallaren. D: Coby Ruskin. GS: Irene Ryan, Alvy Moore, Edward Andrews. A lonely widow advertises for her lost dog, which she never had, in the hopes it will attract some nice men.

Love and the Elopement
W: William Bickley. D: Charles Rondeau. GS: Davy Jones, Karen Valentine. A man climbs into the wrong girl's room when he plans to elope with his girl.

Love and the Pen Pals
W: David Davis & Lorenzo Music. D: Herbert Kenwith. GS: Monte Markham, Diane Keaton. Two pen pals plan to meet after many years.

Love and the Understanding
W: Bud Freeman. D: George Tyne. GS: Jim Backus, Virginia Graham, Pamela Mason. Two divorcees try to convince their friend that her husband has been fooling around.

Love and the Pregnancy
W: Don Boyle. D: Charles Rondeau. GS: Paul Lynde, Jo Anne Worley. A man prepares for any emergency when his wife tells him she is going to have a baby.

Love and the Gangster
W: Bob Rodgers. D: Murray Golden. GS: Jerry Van Dyke, Nehemiah Persoff, Mike Mazurki, Steve Franken, Marianna Hill, Lewis Charles. An interior decorator dates a gangster's daughter.

Love and the V.I.P. Restaurant
W: Bob Weiskopf & Bob Schiller. D: Gary Nelson. GS: Shelley Berman, Kaye Ballard. A man finds that his favorite restaurant has gone topless, but his wife has just become the head of a committee against nudity in public.

Love and the Hitchhiker
W: Peter Myerson. D: Harry Falk. GS: Bob Denver, Joey Heatherton. A conservative man picks up a hippie girl and takes her home to his apartment.

Love and the Banned Book
W: Alan Dinehart & Sidney Resnick. D: Charles Rondeau. GS: Elizabeth Ashley, Burt Reynolds. A GI returns home to find that his wife wrote a sexy novel.

Love and the Boss's Ex
W: John Fenton Murray. D: Leslie Martinson. GS: Ray Walston, Pat Harrington. An executive bribes one of his employees to marry his ex-wife, when he learns that they have been dating.

Love and the Sack
W: Roy Kammerman. D: Leslie Martinson. GS: Sonny & Cher Bono. A girl receives a moaning sack just when her boyfriend is about to ask her to marry him.

Love and the Trip
W: David Davis & Lorenzo Music. D: Bruce Bilson. GS: Ann B. Davis, John McGiver. A couple find what they think is "grass' in the suitcase of their son's fiancee so they decide to smoke it.

Love and the Mountain Cabin
W: Skip Webster. D: Oscar Rudolph. GS: Andy Devine, Leslie Parrish, Peter Marshall. A honeymoon couple learn that their cabin might contain money left by a robber.

Love and the Fighting Couple
W: Rubin Carson. D: Bruce Bilson. GS: Dick Sargent, Mariette Hartley, Shecky Greene, Imogene Coca. A couple are told by a marriage counselor that the only happily married couples are the ones that constantly fight.

Love and the Duel
W: Jack Winter. D: Alan Rafkin. GS: George Lindsey, Tina Louise, Bob Hastings, Jay Novello, Cesar Romero. A press agent for a beautiful movie star is challenged to a duel when he tries to keep a Spanish Captain from bothering his client.

Love and the Note
W: Gene Thompson. D: James Parker. GS: James Brolin, Henry Gibson. A man brags to his friend about his way

with women and about the notes he is getting from a secret admirer.

Love and the Burglar
W: Bill Idelson & Harvey Miller. D: Charles Rondeau. GS: Noel Harrison, Judy Carne. An out-of-work writer unknowingly breaks into another out-of-work writer's apartment when he decides to try burglary to make some money.

Love and the Many-Married Couple
W: Bill Brown. D: Alan Rafkin. GS: Steve Allen, Jayne Meadows, Jack Cassidy. A secretly married movie star couple reveal many shocking things to an interviewer.

Love and Las Vegas
W: Rick Richards. D: Harry Falk. GS: Bill Dana, Edward Everett Horton. Two teachers at a convention in Las Vegas decide to get married.

Love and the Teddy Bear
W: Arnold & Lois Peyser. D: Richard Michaels. GS: Arlene Dahl, Don Porter. A couple find their college son sleeping with a girl.

Love and the Triangle
W: Samuro Mitsubi. D: Herbert Kenwith. GS: Peter Kastner, Sally Struthers. A ventriloquist upsets his new bride when he takes his dummy along with them on their honeymoon.

Love and the Fly
W: George Kirgo. D: Charles Rondeau. GS: Darren McGavin, Suzanne Pleshette. A woman tries to get her husband to take his mind off his work and get a pet fly.

Love and the Arctic Station
W: Dick Bensfield & Perry Grant. D: Charles Rondeau. GS: Larry Storch, Forrest Tucker, James Hampton. The men await the arrival of Miss August in an isolated weather station.

Love and the Co-Ed Dorm
W: Phil Mishkin. D: Gary Nelson.

GS: Karen Valentine, Don Grady. A college freshman finds that his new roommate is a girl.

Love and the First Nighters
W: Terry Ryan. D: Charles Rondeau. GS: Kurt Russell, Jackie Coogan, Debbie Watson. Two teenagers spend the night in a motel because they think it is the mature thing to do.

Love and the Big Date
W: Jack Winter. D: Bruce Bilson. GS: Jeanine Riley, Angus Duncan. Two roommates compete on a TV dating show for a date with a movie star.

Love and the Logical Explanation
W: R.S. Allen. D: Richard Michaels. GS: Bob Crane, Gayle Hunnicutt. A woman finds a pair of black panties in her husband's car and asks him to explain how they got there.

Love and the Groupie
W: Shari Evans & Erwin Goldman. D: Charles Rondeau. GS: Richard Dawson, Angel Tompkins. A rock singer's manager pretends to be his client for one night.

Love and the Housekeeper
W: Arnold Margolin & Jim Parker. D: Ross Bowman. GS: Harry Guardino, Valerie Harper. A woman changes from a slob into a perfect maid when she develops amnesia.

Love and the Joker
W: Bill Box. D: Bruce Bilson. GS: Larry Storch, E.J. Peaker. A man's practical jokes are upsetting his girlfriend.

Love and the Nurse
W: Terry Ryan. D: Leslie Martinson. GS: Julie Sommars, Arte Johnson. A man gets himself admitted to a hospital so he can be with the nurse he has a crush on.

Love and the Hypnotist
W: Roy Kammerman. D: Bruce Bilson. GS: Rich Little, Burgess Mere-

dith.   Hypnotized, a man acts like a kid when he hears a bell, and acts very strange at his wedding.

Love and the Fuzz
W: George Kirgo.   D: Charles Rondeau.   GS: Michael Anderson, Shelley Fabares.   A cop arrests a young couple and finds himself interested in the girl.

Love and the Champ
W: Stan Dreban.   D: Bruce Bilson.   GS: Godfrey Cambridge, Sonny Liston.   A man planning to defend his wife's honor finds the other guy is a boxing champion.

Love and the Big Leap
W: Dale McRaven.   D: Bruce Bilson.   GS: Rich Little, Jessica Walter, Dennis Day.   A man has second thoughts about having a mid-air wedding, right before he has to jump out of a plane.

Love and the Rug
W: Paul Wayne.   D: Jim Parker.   GS: Bill Bixby, Nancy Kovack Mehta.   A man tells his fiancee that he is bald, right before he is about to get married.

Love and Who?
W: David Davis & Jerry Music.   D: Dick Michaels.   GS: Sid Caesar, Maureen Arthur.   On New Year's Day a man finds himself in a motel room with a woman it seems he married.

Love and the Fur Coat
W: Tom Wade.   D: Herbert Kenwith.   GS: Stu Gilliam, Mantan Moreland.   A man tries to impress his girlfriend with a fur coat.

Love and the Intruder
W: Susan Harris, Lorna Sloan, Peggy Elliot.   D: Herbert Kenwith.   GS: John Astin, Abby Dalton, George Furth.   A couple find that the burglar they find in their house is her ex-husband.

Love and the Millionaires
W: David Davis & Jerry Music.   D: Gary Nelson.   GS: Forrest Tucker, Jane Kean, Jonathan Harris.   A poor couple cause confusion for everyone

when they pretend to be millionaires.

Love and the Haunted House
W: Woody Kling.   D: Allen Baron.   GS: Vincent Price, Frank Sutton, Ruth Buzzi.   An engaged couple spend the night in an old house where strange things begin to happen.

Love and the Athlete
W: Alan Mandel & Lloyd Schwartz.   D: Alan Rafkin.   GS: Marty Allen, Eddie Mayehoff, Pamela Curran.   A man is sent to disqualify an East German female athlete because chromosome tests prove she is a man.

Love and the Dummies
W: Deborah Haber & Aubrey Goodman.   D: Charles Rondeau.   GS: Shari Lewis, Paul Winchell, Cliff Norton, Scatman Crothers, George O'Hanlon.   Two shy ventriloquists use dummies to express their feelings for each other.

Love and the Busy Husband
W: Terry Ryan.   D: Coby Ruskin.   GS: Bill Patterson, Emmaline Henry, Dave Willock.   A man busy with his work doesn't realize that his wife left him.

Love and the Hustler
W: Robert Goodwin.   D: Bruce Bilson.   GS: Flip Wilson, Gail Fisher, Eddie "Rochester" Anderson, Mantan Moreland.   A pool shark teaches a girl how to play pool while waiting for a pool hustler to arrive for a match.

Love and the Old Boyfriend
W: Barry Trivers.   D: Allen Baron.   GS: Milton Berle, Strother Martin, Connie Hines, Phyllis Davis.   A man brings his wife's old boyfriend, who is now a bum, home with him to show his wife what she could have married.

Love and the Jury
W: Stanley Hart.   D: Charles Rondeau.   GS: Joan Hackett, Richard Mulligan.   Two people fall in love while serving on a jury.

Love and the Decision
W: Dave Evans.   D: Coby Ruskin.   GS:

Pat Paulsen, Jo Morrow. A married man finds himself in a bridal shop with the two girls he promised to marry.

Love and the Psychiatrist
W: Paul Friedman & Howard Morganstern. D: Coby Ruskin. GS: Larry Hagman, Corinne Camacho, Jerry Paris. A psychiatrist falls in love with the wife of his friend, who is also a psychiatrist.

Love and the Visitor
W: Valerie Harper & Richard Schaal. D: Bruce Bilson. GS: Anne Francis, William Windom, Janos Prohaska. A man returns from a safari to his wife with a gorilla.

Love and the Pickup
W: Carl Kleinschmitt. D: Charles Rondeau. GS: Dorothy Lamour, Edd Byrnes, Patricia Harty, Penny Marshall. A couple restage their first meeting at a singles bar, in order to put more romance back into their marriage.

Love and the Father
W: Dave Ketchum & Bruce Shelly. D: Charles Rondeau. GS: Keenan Wynn, Wes Stern, Judy Strangis, James Millhollin. A man visits his girlfriend's father in prison to ask his permission to marry his daughter. The father later turns up at the wedding.

Love and Women's Lib
W: Roy Kammerman. D: Charles Rondeau. GS: Michael Callan, Dick Gautier. A reporter dresses himself up as a woman in order to do a story on women's lib.

Love and the New Roommate
W: Peggy Elliot & Ed Scharlach. D: Allen Baron. GS: Eve Arden, Chris Connelly. Two married college students pretend to be single so that their parents will continue to support them.

Love and Take Me Along
W: George Slavin & Stanley Adams. D: Oscar Rudolph. GS: Ozzie & Harriet Nelson. A clergyman allows a young singer to pretend to be his wife in order to be able to fly to New York.

Love and the Longest Night
W: Tawasaki Kwai. D: Leslie H. Martinson. GS: Maureen Arthur, Pat Buttram, Roger Miller, Leonard Barr. A couple on their way to Las Vegas to get married wind up in a desert town.

Love and Mr. Nice Guy
W & D: Not available. GS: Wally Cox, Alexandra Hay, Ray Danton. A shy man asks his playboy friend how to get girls interested in him.

Love and the Former Marriage
W: Bill Idelson & Harvey Miller. D: Coby Ruskin. GS: Carl Betz, Dana Wynter, Harrison Ford, Elliott Reid, Jenny Sullivan. A woman's ex-husband tries to help his ex-wife calm down when their daughter is late coming home from a date.

Love and the Positive Man
W: Louis Bryant. D: Charles Rondeau. GS: Ann Rutherford, Hamilton Camp. A short man falls in love with a tall girl.

[The next ten episodes were an attempt to create a spinoff series "Barefoot in the Park," using an all-black cast.]

Barefoot in the Park [Pilot]
W: Bill Idelson & Harvey Miller. D: Bruce Bilson. Starring: Scoey Mitchlll, Tracy Reed, Nipsey Russell & Thelma Carpenter. GS: Agnes Moorehead, Herbert Rudley, Patsy Kelly. Paul and Corey help his friend Honey out by serving at a party for Mabel's boss. He later regrets it when his own boss arrives at the party.

Down with the Landlord
W: Stanley Ralph Ross. D: Charles Rondeau. GS: Sugar Ray Robinson. Paul learns that Sugar Ray Robinson is the owner of his apartment building.

In Sickness and Health
W: William Bickley. D: Jerry Paris. GS: Penny Marshall, Arthur Batanides. Paul helps a pregnant neighbor to the hospital and is mistaken for a patient.

Nothin' but the Truth
W: Alan Mandel & Charles Shyer. D: Charles Rondeau. Corie decides that she and Paul must always be honest with each other, even when his boss comes to dinner.

The Bed
W: Jerry Belson & Garry Marshall. D: Jerry Paris. GS: Charles Lampkin, Gino Conforti. Paul and Corie buy a bed from Honey's friend which collapses as soon as they get it home.

You'll Never Walk Alone
W: Susan Harris. D: Jerry Paris. GS: Stanley Adams, Bryan O'Byrne, Jonathan Hole. Paul gets himself into trouble when he attends a charity auction party where Corie will be modeling an expensive dress.

Corie's Rear Window
W: Jack Winter. D: Charles Rondeau. GS: Avery Schreiber, Richard X. Slattery. Corie thinks she saw a man killed in the apartment across the street, and tries to prove it to Paul.

Disorder in the Court
W: Dave Ketchum & Bruce Shelly. GS: Huntz Hall, Jackie Coogan, Vito Scotti. Paul is reluctant to help Mabel who is being sued by a crooked taxi driver.

You Gotta Have Soul
W: Charles Shyer & Alan Mandel. D: Charles Rondeau. GS: Allison Mills. Paul hires an incompetent secretary who redecorates his office with Mod-Afro decor.

Somethin' Fishy
W: Richard DeRoy. D: Bruce Bilson. GS: Scatman Crothers, Lillian Hyman. Paul and Honey go fishing when Corie's aunt comes for a visit, only to

get themselves arrested.

Love and the Sweet Sixteen
W: Lloyd Turner & Gordon Mitchell. D: Bruce Bilson. GS: Henry Gibson, Susan Howard, Lee Meriwether, Barbara Luna. A man with three wives goes on trial and finds himself stuck with a strict female judge.

Love and the Hotel Caper
W: Hugh Wedlock, Jr. D: E.W. Swackhamer. GS: Tony Roberts, Edie Adams. A Navy lieutenant is accidentally framed by a photographer and a model when he is loaned a hotel suite.

Love and the Well-Groomed Bride
W: Gene Thompson. D: Richard Michaels. GS: The Lennon Sisters, George Furth. A man attaches himself to his former girlfriend on the day of her wedding.

Love and the Lovesick Sailor
W: Burt Styler. D: E.W. Swackhamer. GS: Peter Kastner, Joan Blondell. A sailor misses out on a date with a beautiful girl because his mother fixed him up with a librarian.

Love and the Test of Manhood
W: Lee Karson. D: Charles Rondeau. GS: Jay Silverheels, Tom Nardini, Brenda Benet. A man has to take several tests before he can marry an Indian girl.

Love and the Guru
W: Roy Kammerman. D: Coby Ruskin. GS: Frank Sutton, Jerry Fogel, Melodie Johnson. A guru upsets the marriage of a happily married couple.

Love and the Physical
W: Bruce Howard. D: Oscar Rudolph. GS: Gary Vinson, Phyllis Davis. A girl asks two doctors to dinner in order to find out why her boyfriend never wants to make love to her.

Love and the Detective
W: Bruce Howard. D: William Wiard. GS: Charles Nelson Reilly, Noam Pit-

lik.   The detective a man hires to spy on his girlfriend falls in love with her.

Love and the Advice Column

W: Peggy Elliot.   D: Charles Rondeau. GS: Herb Edelman, Judy Carne, Al Molinaro.   An advice column upsets the future marriage of two people.

Love and the Single Sister

W: Harvey Bullock & R.S. Allen.   GS: Judy Carne, Bill Daily. A girl who has been dumped by her boyfriend visits her sister and brother-in-law.

Love and the Monsters

W: Jim Fritzell & Everett Greenbaum. D: Hy Averback.   GS: James Darren, Maud Adams, Jack Mullaney, George Chandler.   An actor and actress make a date with each other while dressed as monsters.

Love and Formula 26B

W: Perry Grant & Dick Bensfield.   D: Charles Rondeau.   GS: Christopher George, Stephanie Powers, Edward Andrews, Steve Franken.   A pharmaceutical executive gives his wife a stimulant which causes her to become overly romantic.

Love and the Intruder

W: Arnold Horwitt.   D: Gary Nelson. GS: Alan Sues, Valorie Armstrong. A man borrows a company-owned apartment to entertain his girlfriend, only to be interrupted by a burglar.

Love and the Bashful Groom

W: Dave Ketchum & Bruce Shelly.   D: Charles Rondeau.   GS: Paul Peterson, Meredith MacRae.   A man reluctantly marries his girlfriend in a nudist colony.

Love and the Neglected Wife

W: Harvey Bullock & R.S. Allen.   D: Jack Arnold.   GS: Michele Lee, Roger Perry.   A girl pretends that her old boyfriend is still interested in her in order to make her husband jealous.

Love and the Contact Lens

W: Lila Garrett & Stan Dreben.   D: Peter Baldwin.   GS: Eve Arden, Michele Lee.   A girl's mother refuses to let her tell her boyfriend that she wears contact lenses.

Love and the Unhappy Couple

W: Lila Garrett.   D: Coby Ruskin. GS: Louis Nye, Robert Q. Lewis, Jo Anne Worley.   A married couple takes the advice of a psychiatrist cousin and soon find that they no longer get along.

Love and the Lady Athlete

W: Woody Kling.   D: Howard Morris. GS: Tina Louise, Bernard Fox, Michael Callan.   An American athlete falls for an athlete from a socialist country.

Love and the Ledge

W: Bill Box.   D: Charles Rondeau. GS: Robert Morse, Arlene Golonka, Shelley Berman.   A man prepares to jump off a ledge when he is saved by the girl next door.

Love and the Wake-Up Girl

W: George Slavin.   D: Gary Nelson. GS: E.J. Peaker, Dick Patterson.   An answering service girl makes a blind date with one of her clients.

Love and Lover's Lane

W: R.S. Allen & Harvey Bullock.   D: Charles Rondeau.   GS: Dick Sargent, Paul Winchell, Janis Hansen, Jamie Farr.   A couple decides to celebrate their anniversary by going to Lover's Lane.

Love and the Plumber

W: Ralph Goodman.   D: Richard Morris.   GS: Howard Morris, Louise Lasser.   A woman tries to get a plumber interested in her.

Love and the New Size 8

W: Skip Webster.   D: Jack Arnold. GS: Shelley Fabares, Alex Henteloff.

When a fat woman returns much thinner from a health spa, her romance with her fat boyfriend suffers.

Love and the Boomerang
W: Stan Dreban. D: Coby Ruskin. GS: Arte Johnson, Dick Patterson, Anita Gillette. A man takes his friend's advice and dates other women, despite his long-term relationship with his current girlfriend.

Love and the Old Cowboy
W: Jim Fritzell & Everett Greenbaum. D: Hy Averback. GS: Regis Philbin, Jeanette Nolan, John McIntyre. Two old movie stars have a reunion on a TV talk show.

Love and the Awakening
W: Sam Locke & Milton Pascal. D: Charles Rondeau. GS: Bernie Kopell, Elaine Giftos. A film director finds that he has to give love lessons to his star and her boyfriend.

Love and the Small Wedding
W: Ray Singer & Phil Shukin. D: George Tyne. GS: Diane Baker, Jim Hutton. A couple regret lending their apartment to a friend for a small wedding when the guest list becomes too large.

Love and the Tuba
W: Samuro Mitsubi & Robert Brunner. D: Garry Marshall. GS: Frankie Avalon, Annette Funicello, Hans Conreid, Gary Crosby. A man regrets bringing his tuba along on his honeymoon when he and his wife get stuck in it.

Love and the Dream Burglar
W: David Evans. D: Charles Rondeau. GS: Kaye Ballard, Stubby Kaye, Larry Storch. A woman wakes her husband up in the middle of the night because she dreamed a burglar will be breaking into their house at any minute.

Love and the Vacation
W: Arnold Hewitt. D: Charles Rondeau. GS: Milton Berle, Phyllis Diller.

A man wears a disguise so he can spy on his wife when she goes to a resort.

Love and the Naked Stranger
W: Gene Thompson. D: Charles Rondeau. GS: Ronnie Schell, Joyce Van Patten, Frank Aletter, Dana Elcar. A man enters the wrong hotel room and gets in bed with someone else's wife.

Love and the Loud-Mouth
W: David P. Harmon. D: Charles Rondeau. GS: Yvonne Craig, Michael Callan. A couple's honeymoon is interrupted when her mouth gives off radio reports.

Love and the Split-Up
W: Alan Dinehart & Toni Van Horen. D: Coby Ruskin. GS: Denise Nicholas, John Amos, Hans Conreid. A couple getting a divorce fight over who gets possession of their dog.

Love and the Anxious Mama
W: Harvey Bullock & R.S. Allen. D: Coby Ruskin. GS: Dick Curtis, Deborah Walley. A mother tries to get a man to propose to her daughter while they are all having dinner.

Love and the Reincarnation
W: George Kirgo. D: E.W. Swackhamer. GS: Robert Reed, Marianne McAndrew. An archaeologist falls for his beautiful assistant only when he notices that she resembles an Egyptian princess.

Love and the Motel Mixup
W: Harvey Bullock & R.S. Allen. D. Bruce Bilson. GS: Desi Arnaz, Jr., Heather Menzies. A couple go to a motel but can't decide if they want a room or not.

Love and the Alibi
W: R.S. Allen & Harvey Bullock. D: Charles Rondeau. GS: James Stacy, Shari Lewis, John Wheeler, Louisa Moritz. A man tries to cover up his friend's affair with a model from the friend's wife.

Love and the Plane Truth
W: Harvey Bullock & R.S. Allen. D: Hal Cooper. GS: Rich Little, Joyce Van Patten. A couple go on a trip to Paris and, thinking the plane is going to crash, relate their private secrets to each other.

Love and the Anniversary Crisis
W: Harvey Bullock & R.S. Allen. D: Bruce Bilson. GS: Kay Medford, Lou Jacobi, Susan Oliver, Martin E. Brooks. A couple who are celebrating their 48th anniversary announce to their children that they are getting a divorce.

Love and the Married Bachelor
W: David P. Harmon. D: Charles Rondeau. GS: Monte Markham, Marlyn Mason. A man pretends that he is married to keep his girlfriends from wanting to marry him.

Love and the Mixed Marriage
W: Dave Ketchum & Bruce Shelly. D: Gary Nelson. GS: Alice Ghostley, Joe Flynn. Confusion starts between a young couple and her parents over just who is the pregnant one.

Love and the Eskimo's Wife
W: Dave Ketchum & Bruce Shelly. D: Jerry London. GS: Joe Flynn, Frank De Kova, Alex Karras. A successful oil deal depends on an Eskimo custom of Napoola.

Love and the Instant Father
W: Larry Markes. D: Harry Harris. GS: Corbett Monica, Paul Smith, Pamelyn Ferdin. A man must produce a 10-year-old daughter in order to continue his relationship with a divorcee he met at a single parents' club.

Love and the Big Mother
W: Joseph Hoffman. D: Jack Arnold. GS: Milt Kamen, Jo Anne Worley. A man's overprotective mother causes her son to bring home a roller derby skater for dinner.

Love and the Baby
W: Joseph Hoffman. D: Jack Arnold.

GS: Ivan Dixon, Gail Fisher. A man divorces his wife but decides to return to her when he thinks she is pregnant.

Love and the Waitress
W: Gerald Gardner & Dee Caruso. D: Charles Rondeau. GS: Bob Crane, Sherry Jackson, Abby Dalton. A man's date with an actress is upset when he learns that the waitress serving them at a restaurant is his ex-wife.

Love and the Lady Killers
W: Skip Webster. D: Harry Harris. GS: Jack Burns, Carol Wayne. Two partners have fun with their new secretary until she starts dating one of their clients.

Love and the Guilty Conscience
W: David Evans. D: Charles Rondeau. GS: Jo Anne Worley, Sandy Baron. A woman accuses her friend of trying to seduce her husband.

Love and the Big Surprise
W: Stan Dreban. D: Harry Harris. GS: Soupy Sales, Stephanie Powers, Bob Hastings. A man gives his wife a surprise for her birthday which almost destroys their marriage.

Love and the Liberated Lady Boss
W: Sidney Resnick. D: Charles Rondeau. GS: Nanette Fabray, Stephanie Edwards, Bernard Fox. A man discovers that his lady boss likes to fool around after work.

Love and the Fullback
W: Joe Mooney. D: Howard Morris. GS: Ray Walston, Max Baer, Jr. A football player gets married without telling his strict coach.

Love and the Black Limousine
W: Joseph Cavella. D: Peter Baldwin. GS: Pippa Scott, Ned Glass, Jane Dulo, Richard Schaal, Gary Walberg. When a girl brings her mortician boyfriend home to meet her parents, they think he is a gangster.

Love and the Hiccups
W: Madelyn Davis & Bob Carroll, Jr.

D: Oscar Rudolph. GS: Richard Dawson, John Amos, Anjanette Comer, Richard Bakalyan. Hiccups and a burglar interfere in a newlywed couple's honeymoon.

Love and the Mistress
W: Joe Terry. D: Charles Rondeau. GS: Kenneth Mars, Jaye P. Morgan. A man tries to impress his friend by pretending that his wife is really his mistress.

Love and Accidental Passion
W: Joe Terry. D: Charles Rondeau. GS: E.J. Peaker, Jack Kruschen, Alan Hewitt. A man's fiancee becomes a nymphomaniac after being injured in an auto accident.

Love and the Sex Survey
W: Coslough Johnson. D: Charles Rondeau. GS: Gary Collins, Mary Ann Mobley. An interviewer for a sex survey has to interview his ex-wife.

Love and the Particular Girl
W: Bernie Kahn. D: Oscar Rudolph. GS: Stephanie Powers, Agnes Moorehead. Mrs. Cooper worries about her daughter because she always seems to use judo and karate on her boyfriends, thus preventing her from ever finding a husband.

Love and the Jealous Husband
W: Gene Thompson. D: George Tyne. GS: Jerry Van Dyke, Jessica Walter. A man asks his friend to take his wife out to lunch to test her fidelity.

Love and the Free Weekend
W: Ruth Flippen. D: Charles Rondeau. GS: Don Grady, Pat Carroll, Hilarie Thompson. A man asks his girlfriend to spend the weekend in a plush apartment.

Love and the Bachelor Party
W: Stan Dreban. D: Richard Kinon. GS: Jack Carter, Fannie Flagg. Sally's sister is getting married, but Sally's husband ruins the wedding by throwing a bachelor party for the groom.

Love and the Fountain of Youth
W: Laurence Marks. D: Gary Nelson. GS: Richard Deacon, Anne Archer. A man in his 40's dresses like a teenager in order to attract younger girls.

Love and the Check
W: Roy Kammerman. D: Charles Rondeau. GS: Jonathan Harris, Nina Wayne, Dave Ketchum, Bryan O'Byrne, Cliff Norton. A girl tries to cash a check for one million dollars which was written on her stomach with berry juice by a millionaire.

Love and the See-Through Man
W: Samuro Mitsubi. D: Garry Marshall. GS: Nancy Walker, Nancy Dussault. A newlywed has to explain to her mother that she is married to an invisible man.

Love and the Eyewitness
W: Skip Webster. D: Peter Baldwin. GS: Michael Anderson, Jack Burns, Joanna Cameron, Charles Dierkop. A newlywed couple are constantly being interrupted by a deputy searching for a bank robber.

Love and the Security Building
W: Lester Colodny. D: Charles Rondeau. GS: Pat Paulsen, Dick Gautier. A man agrees to give his friend his blind date when he trusts his closed circuit TV system to view his date.

Love and the Conjugal Visit
W: Jack Lloyd & Joel Kane. D: Bruce Bilson. GS: Jerry Stiller & Anne Meara. A prisoner is allowed to visit with his wife for two days.

Love and the Lovely Evening
W: Gene Thompson. D: Charles Rondeau. GS: Jack Mullaney, Roger Perry, Francine York, Herbie Faye, James Hampton. A burglar interrupts the lives of three married couples.

Love and the Bathtub
W: Gene Thompson. D: Howard Morris. GS: Julie Newmar, Charlie Callas,

Jed Allen, Richard Stahl. A movie star gets her toe stuck in a bathtub faucet just before she is about to have a live TV wedding.

Love and the Latin Lover
W: Skip Webster. D: Charles Rondeau. GS: Reva Rose, Leonard Stone, Marvin Kaplan. A movie producer gets a Latin film star to romance his sister after her boyfriend dumped her.

Love and Traveling Salesman
W: Harvey Bullock & R.S. Allen. D: Jack Arnold. GS: Dick Gautier, Jeannine Riley. A traveling salesman spends the night at a farmhouse with the farmer's daughter.

Love and the Topless Policy
W: Roy Kammerman. D: Charles Rondeau. GS: Dave Madden, Dwayne Hickman. Two partners decide to turn their cocktail lounge into a topless lounge.

Love and the Water Bed
W: John Christopher Strong III & Michael Stern. D: Oscar Rudolph. GS: Anita Gillette, Bernie Kopell. A woman orders a water bed when she learns her GI husband is coming for a visit.

Love and the Lady Barber
W: Martin Cohan. D: William Wiard. GS: Frank Sutton, Joe Besser, Ann Prentiss. A man tries to impress his lady barber by buying a toupee to cover his balding head.

Love and the College Professor
W: Madelyn Davis & Bob Carroll, Jr. D: Charles Rondeau. GS: Shelley Berman, Ivor Francis, Angel Tompkins. A professor tries to discourage the amorous advances of one of his students.

Love and the House Bachelor
W: Stan Dreban. D: Gary Nelson. GS: Van Johnson, Paul Lynde, Sue Ane Langdon. A couple try to keep his best friend from showing up for

dinner every night.

Love and the Newscasters
W: Garry Marshall. D: Gary Nelson. GS: Kenneth Mars, Sid Melton, Ruta Lee, Harold Gould, Jackie Coogan. Two newscasters try to get a visiting producer to choose one of them for a job on her new show.

Love and the Scroungers
W: Jim Fritzell & Everett Greenbaum. D: Hy Averback. GS: John Davidson, Karen Valentine. Two young men hide out in a movie studio to see how the stars work.

Love and the Artful Codger
W: Harvey Bullock & R.S. Allen. D: Hal Cooper. GS: Burgess Meredith, Tom Bosley, Sandra Gould. A college professor arranges for three women to take care of him.

Love and the Old-Fashioned Father
W: Harvey Bullock & R.S. Allen. D: William Hanna & Joseph Barbera. A girl asks permission from her parents to spend the weekend with her hippie boyfriend. [This animated story was the pilot for the series "Wait Till Your Father Gets Home."]

Love and the Doctor's Honeymoon
W: Harvey Bullock & R.S. Allen. D: Hal Cooper. GS: Jo Ann Pflug, Don Galloway. A man finds that marrying a lady doctor can lead to a lot of disappointments.

Love and the Penal Code
W: Skip Webster. D: Charles Rondeau. GS: Ken Berry, Marj Dusay, Carol Wayne. A man claims he was attacked by two love-starved women.

Love and the Four-Sided Triangle
W: Harvey Bullock & R.S. Allen. D: Jack Arnold. GS: Dick Gautier, Ruta Lee, Karen Valentine. A secretary is in love with her boss, whose wife doesn't mind.

Love and the Bowling Ball
W: Madelyn Davis & Bob Carroll, Jr. D: Jerry London. GS: Sid Caesar, Allan Melvin, Kathleen Nolan, Gordon Jump. A man has to explain to his fiancee how he got his toe stuck in a bowling ball.

Love and the TV Weekend
W: Donald Boyle. D: Oscar Rudolph. GS: William Windom, Bert Convy. A man decides to have a wild weekend while his wife is away.

Love and the Happy Days
W: Garry Marshall. D: Gary Nelson. GS: Ronny Howard, Harold Gould, Jackie Coogan. Richie falls in love, while his family are the first ones to get a TV set. [This was the pilot for the series "Happy Days."]

Love and the Private Eye
W: Harvey Bullock & R.S. Allen. D: William Hanna & Joseph Barbera. The animated adventures of private eye Melvin Danger. [This was a pilot for a series which never sold.]

Love and the Hairy Excuse
W: Ron Friedman. D: Charles Rondeau. GS: Ann Prentiss, Dick Shawn. A man pretends to be a werewolf in order to explain his fooling around with another woman to his wife.

Love and the Little Black Book
W: Gene Thompson. D: Charles Rondeau. GS: Dick Clair, Jenna McMahon. A newlywed couple discover a little black book of girls' addresses while they are entertaining some friends.

Love and the Perfect Wife
W: Dave Ketchum & Bruce Shelly. D: Charles Rondeau. GS: Jack Burns, Avery Schreiber, Phyllis Davis. A man uses a checklist to find his perfect girl.

Love and the Wee He
W: Jerry Rannow & Greg Strangis. D: Alan Rafkin. GS: Sarah Kennedy, Billy Barty, Marvin Miller. A man gives his wife a mechanical elf for Christmas which seems to have a mind of its own.

Love and the Ghost
W: Steve Zacharias & Michael Leeson. D: Gordon Wiles. GS: Betsy Palmer, Anthony Holland, Pat Delany. A man's late wife returns to criticize his new bride.

Love and the Happy Family
W: Susan Harris. D: Ross Bowman. GS: Sian Barbara Allen, Ed Begley, Jr., Kim Hunter, Murray Hamilton. Two divorced people discover they are in trouble when their children fall in love, thus preventing their own marriage.

Love and the Mail Room
W: Peggy Elliott. D: James Sheldon. GS: Michael Burns, Susan Sennett. A postal clerk finds a girl who is mailing herself across the country.

Love and the Old Swingers
W: Charlotte Brown. D: Leslie H. Martinson. GS: Lou Jacobi, Irene Ryan. Two senior citizens decide to live together.

Love and the Triple Threat
W: Doug Tibbles & Ed Scharlach. D: Charles Rondeau. GS: Warren Berlinger, Chris Connelly, Joan Van Ark. A man gets his friend to portray some weird members of his family in order to discourage his girlfriend's desire to marry him.

Love and the Girlish Groom
W: Lloyd Garver & Ken Hecht. D: Leslie Martinson. GS: Vincent Gardenia, Peter Kastner. A law student who works as a female impersonator has to meet his future in-laws dressed as a woman.

Love and the Crisis Line
W: Lloyd Garver & Ken Hecht. D: Jim Parker. GS: Gary Burghoff, Fabian. Two bachelors call a crisis hot line in order to have a visit with a beautiful psychiatrist.

Love and the Soap Opera
W: Susan Silver.   D: Ken Johnson.
GS: Kaye Ballard, Sarah Kennedy. A
girl who can't tell reality from fantasy
becomes more confused when her
actor boyfriend gets a part on a soap
opera.

Love and the Mind Reader
W: Michael Leeson & Steve Zacharias.
D: James Sheldon. GS: Danny Goldman, Michael Lembeck, Judy Strangis.
A man tries to convince his friend that
he has psychic powers and he has
learned that the girl sitting next to
them at a restaurant is mad about him.

Love and the Unbearable Fiancee
W: Ron Friedman. D: Charles Rondeau. GS: Werner Klemperer, Peggy
Cass, Beverly Sanders, Janos Prohaska.
A girl brings home a bear and introduces him to her parents as her future
husband.

Love and the Oldy Weds
W: Lynn Roth. D: Charles Rondeau.
GS: Richard Deacon, Nancy Walker,
Cheryl Miller, Cyril Delevanti. A cou-
ple try to convince their daughter not
to marry an old man.

Love and the Christmas Punch
W: Gene Thompson. D: Charles Rondeau. GS: Henry Gibson, John Mc-
Giver, Ann Miller, E.J. Peaker. A
delivery man gets drunk at a Christmas
party and tells everyone off.

Love and Dear Old Mom and Dad
W: Frank Buxton. D: James Sheldon.
GS: Roger Bowen, Audrey Meadows,
Hal England. A married couple solves
their problems with the help of her
son and his mother.

Love and the Playwright
W: Lee Erwin. D: Stuart Margolin.
GS: Dick Sargent, Joyce Van Patten.
The wife of a playwright tries to teach
her husband a lesson after he constantly uses her to test reactions to the situations in his plays.

Love and the Confession
W: Joseph Hoffman. D: Charles Rondeau. GS: James Callahan, Yvonne
Craig, Robert Webber, Cher Fontaine.
A man tells his wife about a past affair
when they think their cruise ship is
going to sink.

Love and the New You
W: Ron Friedman. D: Charles Rondeau. GS: Cass Elliott, Shecky Greene.
Two unattractive people visit a new
company called New You which transforms them into beautiful people.

[All episodes hereafter directed by
Charles Rondeau (except as noted).]

Love and the High School Sweetheart
W: Stanley Ralph Ross. GS: Michael
Constantine, Alice Ghostley. A married couple have a fight when she invites one of her old boyfriends to
dinner.

Love and the Amateur Night
W: Jerry Rannow & Greg Strangis.
GS: Peter Marshall, Alvy Moore, Barbara Rhoades. The honeymoon of a
TV amateur show host is interrupted
by people who want to audition for
his show.

Love and the Legend
W: Lloyd Garver & Ken Hecht. GS:
Joanna Barnes, David White, Joe Besser. When a married couple moves
into an old mansion, a spirit takes over
the wife.

Love and the Perfect Setup
W: Peggy Elliott. D: Leslie H. Martinson. GS: Victoria Principal. A girl
moves in with a man who is tired of
having sloppy male roommates.

Love and the Favorite Family
W: Jerry Rannow & Greg Strangis.
D: Allen Baron. GS: June Lockhart,
William Schallert, James Millhollin.
A TV family show their true feelings
for everyone when they learn that
their show is going to be cancelled.

Love and the Cheaters
W: Arthur Marx & Robert Fisher. D: Sam Strangis. GS: Jack Klugman, Brett Somers, Robert Karvelas. A man insists that his wife fool around when she discovers that he has been fooling around.

Love and the Laughing Lover
W: Lloyd Garver & Ken Hecht. GS: Charles Nelson Reilly, Sandra Gould, Kelly Jean Peters. A new bride finds that she can't stop laughing while on her honeymoon.

Love and the Overnight Guests
W: Jerry Rannow & Greg Strangis. D: Gary Nelson. GS: Bill Bixby, Susan Stafford. A man invites a stripper to help him watch his sister's house while she is away.

Love and the Country Girl
W: Joe Glauberg. GS: Pat Buttram, Bill Daily, Bridget Hanley. A man wins a farmer's daughter while playing poker, the only problem is he is already engaged to be married.

Love and Lady Luck
W: Dick Bensfield & Perry Grant. GS: Catherine Burns, Todd Susman, Pat Morita. A young couple spend their honeymoon in Las Vegas where the groom finds out that his new bride is a compulsive gambler.

Love and the Cryptic Gift
W: Hannibal Coons & Joe Terry. GS: Jack Carter, Bert Convy, Liz Torres. A man buys some cemetery plots for his wife.

Love and the Unmarriage
W: Nate Monaster. D: Alan Rafkin. GS: Ozzie & Harriet Nelson. When a girl decides to live with her boyfriend, her parents have a fight and decide to divorce.

Love and the Super Lover
W: Ed Scharlach & Doug Tibbles. D: Bob Birnbaum. GS: Frank Converse, Hamilton Camp, Francine York, Gary Walberg, Jonathan Hole. A man rents a superhero costume and finds that he has super powers.

Love and the Impossible Gift
W: Jerry Rannow & Greg Strangis. D: Sam Strangis. GS: Richard Haydn, William Dozier, Ann Rutherford. A woman tries to find a birthday present for her rich husband.

Love and the Old Lover
W: Don Appel. D: Jerry London. GS: William Daniels, Sissy Spacek. A middle-aged divorced man becomes a swinging single.

Love and the Lucky Couple
W: Milt Rosen. GS: Harvey Lembeck, Eileen Brennan. A married man takes a girl to a motel and finds that he is their one millionth guest, which means he will have his picture in the papers.

Love and the Family Hour
W: Norman Lessing & Joe Terry. D: Richard Michaels. GS: Edgar Buchanan, Walter Burke, James Hampton, Rick Hurst. An Army corporal gets stuck in an elevator with a strange assortment of people.

Love and the New Act
W: William L. Stuart. GS: Paul Winchell, Gwen Verdon, Stanley Adams. A married show biz couple find that they have a new act when he makes music when he is hit on the head.

Love and the Secret Life
W: Paul Harrison & Lennie Weinrib. D: Richard Michaels. GS: Frank Sutton, Al Molinaro, Barbara Heller. The surprise a man plans for his anniversary nearly wrecks his marriage.

Love and the Perfect Wedding
W: Frank Buxton. D: Jerry London. GS: Mike Evans, Isabel Sanford, Scatman Crothers, Brenda Sykes. The hidden thoughts of everyone attending a wedding are heard out loud.

Love and the Pick-Up Fantasy
W: Bob Rodgers.   D: Allen Baron.
GS: Herb Edelman, Loretta Swit, Robert Hogan.   A man tries to act out his
fantasy by having his wife pose as a
stranger in a singles bar so he can pick
her up.

Love and the Caller
W: Dennis Klein. D: Norman Abbott.
GS: Austin Pendleton, Fredricka
Weber. A lonely girl invites an anonymous caller over for a visit.

Love and the Hot Spell
W: Dick Bensfield & Perry Grant. GS:
Mike Farrell, Gary Walberg, Virginia
Grey. A young bride has herself hypnotized so she won't be nervous when
she meets her new in-laws.

Love and the Return of Raymond
W: Jerry Rannow & Greg Strangis. D:
Jerry London.   GS: Charles Nelson
Reilly, Estelle Parsons, Burt Mustin,
Hank Patterson. A honeymoon couple
are visited by a dog whom the bride
thinks is her late husband reincarnated.

Love and the Postal Master
W: Gene Thompson. GS: Ben Murphy,
Celeste Yarnell, Barbara Minkus. A
weak man sends his pen pal a picture
of his well-built roommate in order
to impress her.

Love and the Jinx
W: Peggy Elliott. D: Richard Michaels.
GS: Ken Berry, Zohra Lampert. A girl
who believes she is a jinx finds that she
causes nothing but trouble for her new
boyfriend.

Love and the First Kiss
W: Lloyd Garver & Ken Hecht. D:
Leslie H. Martinson.   GS: Claude
Akins, Deanna Lund. A caveman discovers the kiss.

Love and the Spaced-Out Chick
W: Maurice Richlin. D: Arnold Margolin. GS: Rene Auberjonois, Michele
Lee. A writer is visited by a woman
who claims she is from the planet
Venus.

Love and the Missing Mister
W: Ron & Al Friedman. GS: Ruth
Buzzi, Kenneth Mars, Paul Smith. A
woman cannot forget her first husband
who disappeared during the war, only
now she is remarried and he reappears.

Love and the Old Flames
W: Joyce Eliason & Helen Winer. D:
James Parker. GS: Paul Ford, Estelle
Winwood. An old actor and actress
fall for each other while watching one
of their old films on TV.

Love and the Growing Romance
W: Lynn Roth. GS: Rick Lenz, E.J.
Peaker. A girl gives her house plant
to her new boyfriend which proceeds
to die in his care, giving her second
thoughts about him.

Love and the Know-It-All
W: Peggy Elliott. GS: Jack Cassidy,
Anita Gillette. A woman plans to
prove to her husband that he doesn't
know everything.

Love and the Swinging Philosophy
W: Terry Ryan. D: Norman Abbott.
GS: Craig Stevens, Roger Perry, Lynn
Carlin. A married couple pretend to
be swingers so he can get a job with a
singles magazine.

Love and the Clinic
W: Lloyd Garver & Ken Hecht. GS:
Norman Fell, Charlotte Rae. A couple
visit a marriage clinic to help them
with their failing marriage.

Love and the Trampled Passion
W: Roy Kammerman. D: Allen Baron.
GS: Susan Tolsky. A girl tries to meet
the flamenco dancer who has moved
into her apartment building.

Love and the Woman in White
W: Ron Friedman. D: Jerry London.
GS: Art Metrano, Larry Storch, Pat
Morita, Linda Scott, Peter Brocco.
Two bachelors try to meet the young
woman who is taking care of an old
man.

Love and the Burglar Joke
W: Lou Shaw.   GS: Christopher George, Marlyn Mason. A woman mistakes a burglar for the practical-joking brother of her roommate.

Love and the President
W: Susan Harris.   D: Gary Nelson. GS: Robert Sterling, Anne Jeffreys, John Schuck, Jan Shutan, Eric Olsen. A boy wanders off a White House tour and finds himself in the President's bedroom, taking a picture of the President and his wife having a fight.

Love and the Mystic
W: Jerry Rannow & Greg Strangis. GS: George Kirby, Lou Gossett. A man has a mystic tell his girlfriend terrible things about him so he can get rid of her.

Love and the Wishing Star
W: Calvin Clements, Jr.   D: James Sheldon. GS: Sam Jaffe, Soupy Sales. A bumbling fairy godfather visits an old woodcarver in order to turn a statue of his late wife into a real person.

Love and the Vertical Romance
W: Frank Buxton. D: Jerry London. GS: Karen Morrow, Albert Salmi, Dave Ketchum. A newlywed discovers that her new husband cannot sleep in a bed.

Love and the Face Bow
W: Perry Grant & Dick Bensfield. D: Leslie H. Martinson. GS: Wendell Burton, Sterling Holloway, Cindy Williams. A newlywed couple find that they both wear orthodontic face bows to bed.

Love and the Happy Medium
W: Stanley Ralph Ross. D: Leslie H. Martinson. GS: John Astin, Gino Conforti. A lonely man goes to a medium to arrange for someone to keep him company in the hereafter.

Love and the Sexpert
W: David Evans. D: Jerry London.

GS: Dick Gautier, Misty Rowe, Joe E. Ross. A shy man is constantly attacked by girls who think he wrote a famous sex book.

Love and the Sensuous Twin
W: Roy Kammerman.   D: Leslie H. Martinson. GS: Sandra Dee, Roddy McDowall. A girl with a split personality causes trouble for the boyfriends of each personality.

Love and the Love Nest
W: Ed Scharlach & Doug Tibbles. GS: Bob Dishy, Al Lewis, Ruth McDevitt. A man gets arrested for being a Peeping Tom when he was only out looking for his pet chicken.

Love and the Tycoon
W: Jerry Rannow & Greg Strangis. D: Richard Michaels. GS: Jackie Coogan, Susan Tolsky, Dick Van Patten, Howard Platt. A plain girl becomes involved with the head of her company, who she doesn't know is a computer.

Love and the Baby Derby
W: Roy Kammerman. D: Richard Michaels. GS: John Davidson, Jim Boles, Wes Stern. A rich man plans to leave his money to the first of his two nephews who produces an heir.

Love and the Out-of-Town Client
W: Dick Gautier. GS: Imogene Coca, Richard Schaal, Joe Silver. A man plans to surprise his wife with an anniversary party recreating their wedding party at the same time he has to meet an important client.

Love and the Hand Maiden
W: Mimi Greenberg & Harold Clein. D: Alan Rafkin. GS: Michele Lee, Jed Allen. A man dates a nude model who always wears gloves.

Love and the Twanger Tutor
W: Ron Friedman. D: Jerry London. GS: Roy Clark, Florence Marley, Jessica Walter, Larry D. Mann. An illiterate country singer falls in love with his English tutor.

Love and the Impressionist
W: Jerry Rannow. D: Frank Buxton.
GS: Rich Little, Michele Carey. An
impressionist hides his real self behind
his impressions, causing his girlfriend
to demand that he show her his real
self.

Love and the Secret Habit
W: Charlotte Brown. D: Arnold Margolin. GS: Michael Brandon, Michael
Callan. A man unknowingly fixes his
best friend up with an ex-nun.

Love and the End of the Line
W: Jerry Rannow & Greg Strangis. D:
Leslie H. Martinson. GS: Howard Da
Silva, Robert Klein. A son creates
problems for his father when he plans
to have a vasectomy, thus denying him
grandchildren.

Love and Mr. and Mrs.
W: Charlotte Brown. D: Leslie H. Martinson. GS: Peter Kastner, Victoria
Principal, Shelley Duvall. A man joins
his wife in the public defender's office,
where he almost ruins his marriage
when he takes a more than passing interest in a young shoplifter.

Love and the Love Kit
W: Dave Ketchum & Bruce Shelly.
D: James Parker. GS: Donna Douglas,
Stuart Margolin, Dub Taylor, Lori
Saunders. A man uses a love kit to
win the hand of his girlfriend.

Love and the Singing Suitor
W: Ed Scharlach. GS: Bridget Hanley,
Dave Madden, Warren Berlinger. A
musical episode about an executive
who thinks he will experience love just
like in the movies.

Love and the Anniversary
W: Charlotte Brown. D: Alan Rafkin.
GS: John Carradine, Keith Carradine,
Rosemary De Camp, Valerie De Camp,
Milton Frome, Michael Frome. An old
couple return to the hotel where they
spent their honeymoon and reminisce
about their first night together.

Love and the Big Top
W: Howard Rayfiel. D: Bill Hobin.
GS: Beverly Garland, Robert Pine.
Four trapeze artists find that they are
in love with one another.

Love and the Golden Memory
W: Ron Friedman. D: William Wiard.
GS: David Doyle, J. Pat O'Malley, Bernard Fox. A man and his wife return
to London where they first met, to
reminisce about the past.

Love and the Hoodwinked Honey
W: William Keenan. D: Herbert Kenwith. GS: Jerry Orbach, Bernadette
Peters. A girl meets up with a gangster
in a motel only to have it surrounded
by the police.

Love and the Cozy Comrades
W: Lloyd Garver & Ken Hecht. D:
James Sheldon. GS: Kurt Kasznar,
Gloria LeRoy, Chuck Woolery, Martin
Kosleck. A chambermaid and a visit-
ing Russian find that they have a lot in
common.

Love and the Blue Plate Special
W: Joe Terry. D: Ezra Stone. GS:
Lorna Luft, Ivor Barry. A young millionaire tries to get his girlfriend from
her job as a waitress and join him at
his mansion.

Love and the See-Thru Mind
W: Perry Grant & Dick Bensfield. D:
Lee Phillips. GS: Morey Amsterdam,
Tina Louise, Fred Grandy. A waiter at
an ESP convention becomes worried
when he gets wild thoughts about another man's wife.

Love and Other Mistakes
W: Jerry Davis. D: George Tyne. GS:
Herb Edelman, Pat Harrington, Abbe
Lane. A man plans to get even with
his ex-wife.

Love and the Lie
W: Eric Bercovici. D: Lee Phillips.
GS: Stuart Whitman, Dennis Dugan,
Suzanne Zenor. A man uses his bro-

ther's reputation to propose to a girl.

Love and the Pretty Secretary
W: Tom & Helen August. D: George Tyne. GS: Don Galloway, Robin Millan. A man falls in love with his bumbling secretary.

Love and the Fortunate Cookie
W: Skip Webster. D: Oscar Rudolph. GS: Mako, Robert Ito, Dale Ishimoto, Linda Bush. Two fortune cookie dealers hire a fortune-hunting secretary.

Love and the Wierdo
W: Norman Mark. D: Peter Baldwin. GS: Peter Marshall, Jessica Walter. A woman consults every known fortune-telling device to see if her new boyfriend is compatible with her.

Love and the Awkward Age
W: Nate Monaster. D: Norman Abbott. GS: Art Metrano, Joyce Bulifant. A husband and wife confess to each other that they lied about their ages.

Love and the Hidden Meaning
W: Saul Turtletaub & Bernie Orenstein. D: Jerry Davis. GS: Jacqueline Susann, Martha Raye, Joyce Haber. A plumber's wife accuses authoress Jacqueline Susann of having based the male character of her book on her husband.

Love and the Model Apartment
W: George O'Hanlon. D: Jerry London. GS: Davy Jones, Kathleen Cody. A young couple move into a model apartment in a department store.

Love and the Spendthrift
W: Lan O'Kun. D: Jerry London. GS: Henry Gibson, Gary Walberg, E.J. Peaker. A man is challenged by his girlfriend to win her love, using imagination and wit.

Love and the Competitors
W: Saul Turtletaub & Bernie Orenstein. D: William Wiard. GS: Bobby Riggs, Rosemary Casals, Pat Buttram, Tom Lester. A couple spend a jail sentence in constant competition with each other.

Love and the Footlight Fiancee
W: Ron Friedman. D: Herbert Kenwith. GS: Hans Conreid. A famous actor has to direct a summer stock show with an actress with a Brooklyn accent.

Love and the Generation Gap
W: George Tibbles. D: Jerry London. GS: John Williams, Nehemiah Persoff, Stewart Moss, Chip Zien, Oliver Clark. When an old millionaire marries a young girl and has some more kids, his sons begin to worry over just who will get his fortune.

Love and Carmen Lopez
W: Doug Tibbles & Ed Scharlach. D: Hollingsworth Morse. GS: Carmen Zapata, William Schallert. A housekeeper and a gardener have a big wedding thanks to their employer.

Love and the Patrol Person
W: Joseph Bonaduce & Charles Stewart. D: Danny Simon. GS: Kenneth Mars, Al Molinaro. A patrolman is upset when he learns his new partner is a woman.

Love and the Forever Tree
W: Leonard & Arlene Stadd. D: Jerry London. GS: Bobby Morse, Elaine Joyce. A couple reminisce about their lives and how they promised to marry each other when they got older.

Love and the Last Joke
W: Ed Scharlach & Doug Tibbles. D: Norman Abbott. GS: Rich Little, Judy Carne. A comedy-writing couple find that they have to write a comedy script while on their honeymoon.

Love and the Odd Couples
W: Roger Shulman & John Baskin. D: Danny Simon. GS: Marty Brill, Ron Masak. Two couples go before a judge in order to exchange their mates.

Love and the Games People Play
W: Walter Dalton & Brooke Harris. D: Ezra Stone. GS: Max Baer, Jr., Jo Anne Worley. The wife of a football player wants a church wedding, even though she got married during a football game in front of 75,000 people.

Love and the Three-Timer
W: Lynn Farr. D: Jerry London. GS: Dennis Cole, Colleen Camp, Jonathan Hole. Three girls meet at a junkyard while buying the same present for the same boyfriend.

Love and the Clinical Problem
W: Tony Webster. D: Krishna Shah. GS: Anne Meara, Jerry Stiller, Dr. Joyce Brothers. A fighting couple seek out professional help to solve their problems.

Love and the Parent's Sake
W: Warren Murray. D: James Sheldon. GS: Dick Van Patten, Nanette Fabray, Burt Mustin, Queenie Smith. A couple living with the husband's parents find that they are always fighting.

Love and the Time Machine
W: John G. Bonaduce. D: Krishna Shah. GS: Cindy Williams, Cyril Delevanti. A scientist's assistant uses a time machine to get his girl to love him.

Love and the Cover
W: Jerry Rannow & Greg Strangis. D: Joshua Shelley. GS: Doc Severinsen, Beth Howland. A man tells his wife that their marriage was a cover for his spying on the next-door neighbors and that he is a spy.

Love and the Weighty Problem
W: Skip Webster. D: Norman Abbott. GS: Warren Berlinger, Pat Finley. When his girlfriend returns from a fat farm with a new figure and several new boyfriends, a man finds that his romance with her might be over.

Love and the Novel Love
W: Walter Dalton & Brooke Harris. D:

Oscar Rudolph. GS: Jim Hutton, Jo Ann Pflug. A film writing couple put their romantic feelings for each other in their script and then act them out.

Love and the Swinging Surgeon
W: Bill Persky. D: Lee Phillips. GS: Martin Sheen, Phyllis Davis. A man tries to cure his girlfriend's fear of entering a man's apartment.

Love and the Golden Worm
W: Christine Tibbles. D: Peter Baldwin. GS: Keye Luke, Phillip Ahn. Two Chinese fathers consult an ancient book which tells them that their children are to marry each other.

Love and the Man of the Year
W: Marilyn Hall. D: Norman Abbott. GS: Monty Hall, Natalie Schafer, Marlyn Mason. A wife tries to get her emcee husband to spend more time with her.

Love and the Extra Job
W: Alex Barris. D: Danny Simon. GS: Sue Lyon, Joey Foreman, Frank Bonner. A girl informs her roommate that she has taken an extra job as a girl who jumps out of cakes at stag parties.

Love and Mr. Bunny
W: Jerry Rannow. D: Jerry London. GS: Larry Storch, Joyce Van Patten. A couple move to a hotel while their house is being painted but they forget to take along their Mr. Bunny alarm clock; without it, they can't fall asleep.

Love and the Single Husband
W: Arnold Hewitt. D: William Claxton. GS: Michael Callan, Elaine Giftos. A man, separated from his wife, is shocked when she announces she is marrying another man.

Love and the Flunky
W: Winston Moss. D: George Tyne. GS: Bill Russell, Gloria Hendry. The girlfriend of a basketball player falls for his roommate.

Love and the Flying Finletters
W: Peggy Elliott & Ed Scharlach. D: William Wiard. GS: Steve Forrest, Abby Dalton, David Spielberg, Skye Aubrey. A pilot learns that his daughter, a stewardess, is fooling around with other pilots.

Love and the Teller's Tale
W: Lynn Farr. D: William Wiard. GS: Penny Fuller, Ken Berry. A teller and a bank president accidentally lock themselves in the bank vault.

Love and the Memento
W: George Yanok & Bob Garland. D: William Claxton. GS: Edward Andrews, Dick Shawn, Bridget Hanley. A playboy won't inherit his father's fortune until his father's secretary decides what she wants from the estate.

Love and the Fractured Fibula
W: Dick Gautier. D: James Sheldon. GS: Nancy Dussault, Dick Gautier, Billy De Wolfe. A man spends his honeymoon in a hospital bed when he breaks his leg.

Love and the Heavy Set
W: George Tibbles. D: William Wiard. GS: Kay Medford, Neil Schwartz. A mother arranges a date for her fat daughter.

Love and the Unsteady Steady
W: Jerry Rannow & Greg Strangis. D: Ross Martin. GS: Bert Convy, Joanie Sommers, Brandon Cruz, Kristie McNichol. A boy imagines what it would be like to be married to his girlfriend.

Love and the Cryin' Cowboy
W: Peggy Elliott. D: James Sheldon. GS: Mel Tillis, Joe Sirola, Lonnie Shore. A singing cowboy's career is upset when he gets married and no longer wants to sing sad songs.

Love and the Opera Singer
W: Joseph Bonaduce. D: Bill Hobin. GS: Jack Burns, Avery Schreiber. A young doctor tells his girlfriend about the adventures of his opera-singing uncle.

Love and the Comedienne
W: Gene Perret. D: Jack Donahue. GS: Phyllis Diller, Tom Bosley. The husband of a comedienne objects to his wife's jokes about him in her act.

Love and the Locksmith
W: Jack Turley. D: Peter Baldwin. GS: Richard B. Shull, Loretta Swit. A locksmith falls for a woman for whom he is installing a lock.

Love and the Lifter
W: Jerry Rannow & Greg Strangis. D: Oscar Rudolph. GS: John Byner, Sarah Kennedy. A woman falls for a thief.

Love and the Suspicious Husband
W: Mickey Rose. D: William Wiard. GS: Lou Jacobi, Gordon Jump, Jane Connell. A man hires a detective to follow his wife.

Love and the Image Makers
W: Roger Shulman & John Baskin. D: Jerry London. GS: Gavin McLeod, James Hampton. A debate between two candidates for mayor backfires when they fall for each other.

Love and the Seven-Year Wait
W: Roy Kammerman. D: Jerry London. GS: Gary Collins, Mary Ann Mobley. A woman has waited seven years until her missing husband can be declared dead. On the very last day, her missing husband turns up.

Love and the Secret Spouse
W: Ed Scharlach & Peggy Elliott. D: Hugh Robertson. GS: Bob Cummings, John Dehner, Bruce Davidson, Renne Jarrett, Maggie Roswell. A couple try to hide their marriage from their fathers so they won't stop sending them money.

LOVE ON A ROOFTOP

On the air 9/6/66, off 8/?/67. ABC. Color film. 30 episodes. Broadcast: Sept 1966-Jan 1967 Tue 9:30-10; Jan 1967-Apr 1967 Thu 9-9:30; Apr 1967-Aug 1967 Thu 9:30-10. Producer: E.W. Swackhamer. Prod Co: Screen Gems. Synd: Columbia Pictures TV.

CAST: David Willis (played by Peter Deuel), Julie Willis (Judy Carne), Stan Parker (Rich Little), Carol Parker (Barbara Bostock), Phyllis Hammond (Edith Atwater), Fred Hammond (Herb Voland), Jim Lucas (Sandy Kenyon).

The story of a rich girl and a poor struggling architect who marry and move into a windowless top floor apartment. The series was rerun during the summer of 1971 but hasn't been seen since.

Pilot
W: E.W. Swackhamer. D: Albert Mannheimer. GS: Lillian Adams. David and Julie try to hide their windowless apartment from her parents.

117 Ways to Cook Hamburger
W: Bernard Slade. D: E.W. Swackhamer. GS: Noam Pitlik, Norm Burton, Majel Barrett, Vince Howard. Julie spends all of their food money on 50 pounds of chopped meat.

My Husband, the Knight
W: Bernard Slade. D: E.W. Swackhamer. GS: Charles Lane, Hope Summers, Joseph Perry, Sandy Kenyon. In order to pay for a new chair, Dave takes an extra job requiring him to wear a suit of armor.

The Big Brass Bed
W: Bernard Slade. D: E.W. Swackhamer. GS: Vic Tayback, Milton Frome, Len Lesser, Howard Morton. David and Julie go hunting for a bed. They find an old brass one which breaks loose on top of a hill and crashes into a cop.

The Six Dollar Surprise
W: Bernard Slade. D: E.W. Swackhamer. GS: Sandy Kenyon, Digby Wolfe, Paul Micale. Dave hates birthday parties, but agrees to let Julie give him one as long as she doesn't spend more than six dollars.

The Chocolate Hen
W: Bernard Slade. D: E.W. Swackhamer. GS: Peter Robbins. Julie gives Dave's chocolate hen to a six-year-old kid. Dave gets upset and walks out.

Homecoming
W: Bernard Slade. D: E.W. Swackhamer. GS: Frank Wilcox, Bridget Hanley, Dick Anders, Rollin Moriyama. Dave and Julie spend the weekend at her parents' estate, where Dave learns just how well she used to live before they were married.

One Picture Is Worth...
W: Bernard Slade. D: E.W. Swackhamer. GS: Daniel Travanti. Julie's former artist boyfriend turns up only to cause Dave to be jealous.

Chinchilla Rag
W: James Henerson. D: Robert Rosenbaum. GS: Harold Gould. Stan convinces Julie to keep his chinchillas, even though they could be evicted for keeping them.

Who Is Sylvia?
W: Richard Baer. D: Claudio Guzman. GS: Bridget Hanley. Dave and Julie are both confused when a real Sylvia calls after they both fight about the one they dreamed about.

War on a Rooftop
W: Bernard Slade. D: E.W. Swackhamer. GS: Jill Foster. Stan's new pigeon Homer causes trouble between David and Julie and Stan and Carol.

Dave's Night Out
W: John McGreevey. D: Claudio Guzman. GS: Reta Shaw, Virginia Sale. Taking a friend's advice, Dave takes one night a week to play poker only to wind up at a laundromat helping two old ladies with their wash.

There's Got to Be Something Wrong with Her
W: John McGreevey. D: Jerry Bernstein. GS: Gayle Hunnicutt, Arlene Charles. After meeting Dave's old girlfriend, Julie can't understand why he didn't marry her instead.

But Is It Really You?
W: Bernard Slade. D: E.W. Swackhamer. GS: Anne Seymour, Benny Baker, Corinne Conley. David and Julie receive an expensive Chinese vase as a gift, causing their friend Sheila to redecorate their apartment.

The Fifty Dollar Misunderstanding
W: James Henerson. D: Alex Grasshoff. GS: Paul Mazursky, Larry Tucker. Stan spends Dave's $50 bonus on art materials for Julie's one-woman show.

Frocks of Trouble
W: Barbara Avedon. D: Claudio Guzman. Both David and Mr. Hammond buy dresses for Julie to wear at a banquet.

Going Home to Daughter
W: James Henerson. D: Robert Ellenstein. GS: David Brian. Julie's mother leaves her father on their 25th wedding anniversary.

Let It Rain
W: Dorothy Cooper Foote. D: E.W. Swackhamer. Julie and her parents switch apartments; each learning how the other half lives.

King of the Castle
W: Bernard Slade. D: Jerry Bernstein. GS: Oliver McGowan, Sidney Clute, Owen Bush. Dave takes on extra jobs when he learns Julie is making more

money than he.

My Father, the TV Star
W: Bernard Slade. D: Richard Kinon. GS: Don Keefer, Yau Shan Tung. Julie's father does a TV commercial and unknowingly becomes a comic smash.

Who Was That Husband I Saw You With?
W: Marty Roth. D: Gene Reynolds. GS: Dick Gautier, David Lewis. Julie's relatives want copies of their wedding photo, so Stan sends them a shocking photo.

Shotgun Honeymoon
W: Dorothy Cooper Foote. D: Mack Bing. GS: Howard Morton, Byron Foulger, Hoke Howell. Mr. Hammond thinks David and Julie just got married after living together for eight months.

Musical Apartments
W: James Henerson. D: Jerry Bernstein. GS: Robert Ellenstein, Connie Sawyer. Stan's ant colony forces David and Julie to move into a shabby hotel.

Low Calorie Love
W: Tom & Helen August. D: Russell Mayberry. GS: Charles Lane, Hal Baylor, Jan Arvan. Julie tries to gain weight, while Dave tries to lose weight.

The Sellout
W: Ron Friedman. D: Lee Phillips. GS: Ned Glass, Maxine Stuart. Dave must redesign a house against his better judgment in order to put Julie through art school.

The Letter Bug
W: James Henerson. D: Russell Mayberry. GS: John S. Ragin. Dave's old friend gives Julie a letter which Dave wrote before they were married which causes trouble.

Debt of Gratitude
W: John McGreevey. D: Russell Mayberry. GS: David Winters, Ivor Barry.

Dave's old Army buddy and his weird friends move into a tent on the roof.

Murder in Apartment D
W: Bernard Slade.   D: Jerry Bernstein.   GS: Ian Wolfe, Wesley Addy. After new tenants move in, everyone believes they murdered a rich old man.

One Too Many Cooks
W: James Henerson.   D: Mack Bing.

GS: Chick Chandler, Jill Foster, Irene Harvey, Vince Howard. Dave does not want to tell Julie he is an expert chef for fear of upsetting her.

Stork on a Rooftop
W: Bernard Slade.   D: E.W. Swackhamer.   GS: Marjorie Bennett, John Newton, Ivan Bonar. Carol's strange diet causes everyone to think she is pregnant.

THE LUCY SHOW

On the air 10/1/62, off 9/16/68. CBS. Color Film. 157 episodes. Broadcast: Oct 1962-Jun 1964 Mon 8:30-9; Sept 1964-Sept 1965 Mon 9-9:30; Sept 1965-Jun 1967 Mon 8:30-9; Sept 1967-Sept 1968 Mon 8:30-9. Producer: Gary Morton. Prod Co/Synd: Paramount.

CAST: Lucy Carmichael (played by Lucille Ball), Vivian Bagley (Vivian Vance), Theodore J. Mooney (Gale Gordon), Harry Conners (Dick Martin), Mr. Barnsdahl (Charles Lane), Chris Carmichael (Candy Moore), Jerry Carmichael (Jimmy Garrett), Sherman Bagley (Ralph Hart), Harrison Cheever (Roy Roberts).

The adventures of Lucy and Viv as they try to raise their kids in the same house while trying to find themselves boyfriends. This series is far funnier than *Here's Lucy*, but the only problem is unlike *I Love Lucy*, *The Lucy Show* has become more outdated in appearance than the rest. It is still syndicated around the country but it doesn't appear on the lineups of too many stations.

Lucy Waits Up for Chris
Chris goes on a date and the rest of the house waits up for her return.

Lucy Digs Up a Date
GS: William Windom, Don Briggs. Lucy and Viv look for someone to escort them to a Saturday night dance, so they settle for Jerry's math teacher.

Lucy Is a Referee
GS: Dennis Rush, Roy Rowan. Lucy volunteers to referee Jerry and Sherman's football game.

Lucy Misplaces Two Thousand Dollars
GS: Charles Lane, Reta Shaw. Lucy gets a check for two thousand dollars instead of twenty, when she closes out her Christmas Club account at the bank.

Lucy Buys a Sheep
Lucy buys a sheep when she can't get anyone to mow her lawn.

Lucy Becomes an Astronaut
GS: Nancy Kulp. Lucy and Viv accidentally volunteer for a two-woman simulated space flight at a WAVE reunion.

Lucy Is a Kangaroo for a Day
GS: John McGiver, Charles Lane, Majel Barrett. Lucy gets a temporary job, but she soon breaks the water cooler and floods the office.

Lucy the Music Lover
GS: Frank Aletter. When Lucy sees the blind date she passed on to Viv, she tries to get him back by using his interest in classical music.

Lucy Puts Up a TV Antenna
GS: Del Moore, Lloyd Corrigan. Lucy and Viv install the new TV antenna on the roof by themselves.

Vivian Sues Lucy
Viv trips over Jerry's toy and tries to get sympathy from Lucy by exaggerating the injuries.

Lucy Builds a Rumpus Room
GS: Chris Warfield, Don Blake. Lucy and Viv both want to give their dates home-cooked meals, but they don't want to share the kitchen.

Lucy and Her Electric Mattress
Lucy buys Viv a mattress with a built-in vibrator.

Together for Christmas
GS: Joseph Mell, Tom Lowell, Mitchell's Boys Choir. Lucy and Viv look forward to Christmas together until Lucy buys a green tree and Viv buys a white one.

Chris's New Year's Eve Party
Lucy and Viv plan activities for Chris's party, only Chris doesn't want the two of them at the party.

Lucy's Sister Pays a Visit
GS: Janet Waldo, Peter Marshall. Lucy's newlywed sister is having trouble with her marriage, so Lucy lends a hand.

Lucy and Viv Are Volunteer Firemen
GS: Carole Cook, Patrick McVey. When the firehouse is rezoned to another area, Lucy forms her own volunteer fire department.

Lucy Becomes a Reporter
GS: John Vivyan. Lucy becomes a society columnist in order to earn extra money.

Lucy and Viv Put in a Shower
GS: Stafford Repp, Don Briggs. Lucy and Viv decide to finish the job that neighbor Harry started when he put in a stall shower for them.

Lucy's Barbershop Quartet
GS: Hans Conreid. Lucy will become a member of the women's volunteer fire department singing quartet provided that she takes voice lessons first.

Lucy and Viv Become Tycoons
GS: Don Briggs, Bern Hoffman. Lucy and Viv decide to put Viv's carmel corn on the market, so they set up the factory in Lucy's kitchen.

No More Double Dates
GS: Don Briggs. Lucy and Harry don't want to share their Saturday night dates with Viv and Eddie anymore, so Lucy tries not to hurt Viv's feelings.

Lucy and Viv Learn Judo
GS: James Seay, Ed Parker, Louis Coppola. Lucy and Viv take judo lessons to protect themselves from the neighborhood prowler.

Lucy Is a Soda Jerk
GS: Paul Hartman, Lucie Arnaz. Chris and her friend Cynthia get jobs to earn extra money at Wilbur's Ice Cream store.

Lucy Drives a Dump Truck
GS: Carole Cook, Dorothy Konrad. Lucy collects paper for a fund-raising drive to help the volunteer fire department.

Lucy Visits the White House
GS: Elliot Reid, Frank Nelson. Lucy and Viv plan to go to Washington as Den Mothers to their sons' Cub Scout pack with a sugar cube model of the White House.

Lucy and Viv Take Up Chemistry
GS: Lou Krugman. At night school, Lucy plans to create the fountain of youth when she studies chemistry.

Lucy Is a Chaperone
GS: Hanley Stafford, Lucie Arnaz, Charlotte Lawrence. Lucy and Viv join the kids in doing the limbo at the school party.

Lucy and the Little League
GS: Herb Vigran, William Schallert. Lucy and Viv try to sneak back into the ball park after they were thrown out.

Lucy and the Runaway Butterfly
GS: Jack Donahue, Benton Reid. When out on a date, Lucy chases a butterfly for Jerry's collection.

Lucy Buys a Boat
Lucy and Viv are adrift in their new boat which begins to spring a few leaks.

Lucy Plays Cleopatra
GS: Hans Conreid. Lucy wants to play Cleopatra in the volunteer fire department's play.

Kiddie Parties, Inc.
GS: Lyle Talbot. Lucy and Viv plan to give birthday parties for children in order to earn extra money.

Lucy and Viv Play Softball
GS: William Schallert. Lucy and Viv play softball for the volunteer fire department team.

Lucy Gets Locked in the Vault [Part 1]
Mr. Mooney is becoming the new bank president, only he is even cheaper than the last president.

Lucy and the Safe Cracker [Part 2]
GS: William Woodson, Jay Novello. Lucy and Mr. Mooney are locked in the bank vault for 18 hours.

Lucy Goes Duck Hunting
GS: Keith Andes. Lucy and Viv try to share their dates' interests.

Lucy and the Bank Scandal
Lucy assumes Mr. Mooney has been embezzling the bank's money.

Lucy Decides to Redecorate
Lucy tries to con some money out of Mr. Mooney to redecorate the house.

The Loophole in the Lease
Lucy and Viv try to plaster a hole in the kitchen ceiling.

Lucy Puts Out the Fire at the Bank
Lucy decides to have the volunteer fire department trained by real firemen.

Lucy and the Military Academy
GS: Leon Ames, Jackie Coogan, Stephen Talbot. Lucy tries to visit Jerry at the military academy even though she is not allowed.

Lucy's College Reunion
GS: Roland Winters. Lucy and Viv steal the statue of the college's founder as a stunt for the college reunion.

Lucy Conducts the Symphony
GS: Wally Cox. Lucy tries to cure Viv's cousin of his stage fright with hypnosis.

Lucy Plays Florence Nightingale
GS: Kathleen Freeman, Paula Winslowe. Lucy goes to play nurse to Mr. Mooney who is in the hospital.

Lucy Goes to Art Class
GS: John Carradine, Howard Caine, Robert Alda. Lucy goes to art class to meet a man she saw in an art store.

Chris Goes Steady
GS: Michael J. Pollard. Chris goes steady with Mr. Mooney's son and Lucy and Mooney don't like it.

Lucy Takes Up Golf
GS: Gary Morton, Jimmy Demaret, Bo Wininger. Lucy takes up golf in order to share her boyfriend Gary's interests.

Lucy Teaches Ethel Merman to Sing [Part 1]
GS: Ethel Merman. Lucy gets mad when Ethel Merman lookalike Agnes Schmidlapp will host the boy scout show and not she.

Ethel Merman and the Boy Scout Show [Part 2]
GS: Ethel Merman. Lucy and Viv are hurt when their kids don't put them in

the show.

Lucy and Viv Open a Restaurant
GS: Jack Albertson, Kathleen Freeman. Lucy and Viv open a restaurant, but their only customers are bill collectors and the mailman.

Lucy Takes a Job at the Bank
Lucy turns the bank into a wreck when she starts to work there.

Viv Moves Out
GS: Roberta Sherwood, Robert Lanning. Viv has a fight with Lucy and moves out, especially since Lucy took in a singing tenant.

Lucy Is Her Own Lawyer
GS: John McGiver, James Westerfield. Lucy goes to court to fight Mr. Mooney and his howling sheepdog.

Lucy Meets a Millionaire
GS: Cesare Danova. Lucy meets an Italian millionaire who speaks very little English.

Lucy Goes into Politics
GS: J. Pat O'Malley. Lucy and Viv help Mr. Mooney run for City Controller.

Lucy and the Scout Trip
GS: Desi Arnaz, Jr. Lucy and Viv help Mr. Mooney take the Cub Scouts on a camping trip.

Lucy Is a Process Server
GS: Richard Keith, Lee Millar. Lucy has to deliver a summons to Mr. Mooney.

Lucy Enters the Baking Contest
GS: Carole Cook. Lucy tries to prove that she is a good cook after Viv insults her cooking.

Lucy the Good Skate
GS: Charles Drake. Lucy buys a pair of skates and can't get them off.

Lucy and the Plumber
GS: Jack Benny, Bob Hope. Lucy tries to get her butcher on a TV show in order to win enough money to afford the plumber.

Lucy and the Winter Sports
GS: Keith Andes. Lucy's boyfriend is athletic and she isn't, so she claims she does well in sports that happen to be out of season.

Lucy Gets the Bird
GS: Max Showalter. Lucy's old boyfriend subs for Mr. Mooney, so she tries to get him to give her money.

Lucy and the Great Bank Robbery.
GS: John Williams, Lloyd Corrigan. Lucy rents a room to two gentlemen who claim they are visiting the World's Fair but are really bank robbers.

Lucy the Camp Cook
GS: Harvey Korman, Madge Blake. Lucy and Viv become the cooks at a summer camp in order to finance their sons' stay there.

Lucy and the Monsters
GS: George Barrows, Sid Haig, Bob Burns. Lucy and Viv check out the effect of horror movies on kids and wind up with nightmares.

Lucy Becomes a Father
GS: Hal Smith, George Neise, Cliff Norton. Lucy wants to go on the father and son camping trip, so the men treat her like a man.

Lucy and Arthur Godfrey
GS: Arthur Godfrey. Lucy and Viv get Arthur Godfrey to appear in a musical with the community players.

Lucy and the Beauty Doctor
GS: Dick Patterson, Tommy Farrell. Lucy asks Mooney to give her some money for treatments, the only thing she doesn't tell him is that they are beauty treatments.

My Fair Lucy
GS: Ann Sothern, Bob Jellison, Reta Shaw, Byron Foulger. Lucy and the

Countess try to raise money to open a charm school.

Lucy and the Countess Lose Weight
GS: Ann Sothern. Mooney uses the bank's money to finance a health farm and wants Lucy and the Countess to publicize it.

Lucy and the Old Mansion
GS: Ann Sothern, Lester Matthews, Maida Severn. The Countess is expecting visiting royalty, but has no place for them to stay.

Lucy and the Missing Stamp
GS: Mabel Albertson, Herb Vigran, Nestor Paiva. A valuable stamp disappears after saleswoman Lucy demonstrates a vacuum cleaner.

Lucy and the Ceramic Cat
GS: Larry Dean. Lucy wants to know what Mooney bought for his wife's birthday.

Lucy Makes a Pinch
GS: Jack Kelly. Lucy is a police school rookie who goes on a stakeout for the Lover's Lane bandit.

Lucy's Contact Lenses
GS: Teddy Eccles. Lucy loses a contact lens while icing a cake for a benefit sale, so she goes to the sale to find it.

Lucy Meets Danny Kaye
GS: Danny Kaye, Leon Belasco, Ray Kellogg, Sue Casey. Lucy goes to Danny Kaye to get tickets for his show but winds up in it.

Lucy and the Countess
GS: Ann Sothern, Carole Cook. Mooney invites the Countess and Lucy to the local wine tasting society.

Lucy the Stockholder
GS: Harvey Korman, Elliott Reid. Lucy vests her money in the bank by buying stock. Now a part owner, she plans to help Mooney out at the bank.

Lucy the Disc Jockey
GS: Pat Harrington. Lucy is trying to win a mystery sound contest.

Lucy at Marineland
GS: Jimmy Piersall, Harvey Korman. Lucy and Mooney move to California and Lucy takes Jerry to Marineland.

Lucy Dates a Lifeguard
GS: Howard Morris, Robert Fortier. Lucy gets a date with a playboy lifeguard.

Lucy and the Music World
GS: Mel Torme, Lou Krugman. Lucy becomes the secretary to the president of a record company.

Lucy and Clint Walker
GS: Clint Walker, Mary Wickes. Lucy dates a rugged building contractor who wants to show Lucy his building from the 39th floor.

Lucy and the Golden Greek
GS: Joan Blondell, Keith Andes, Queenie Smith. Lucy tries to get an escort to a fancy ball.

Lucy the Stunt Man
GS: Joan Blondell, Don Megowan, Eddie Quillan, Lou Krugman. Lucy becomes a stuntman named Iron Man Carmichael in order to earn extra money for a leopard jacket.

Lucy and the Countess Have a Horse Guest
GS: William Frawley, Ann Sothern. Lucy and the Countess plan to race her late husband's racehorse.

Lucy Helps Danny Thomas
GS: Danny Thomas, Mickey Manners. Lucy wrecks the rehearsal of Danny Thomas's TV show.

Lucy Helps the Countess
GS: Ann Sothern, Karen Norris. Lucy helps the Countess, who is now a real estate agent, rent Mooney a new apartment.

Lucy the Undercover Agent
GS: Ann Sothern, Jack Cassidy, Jack Dodson, Parley Baer. Lucy and the Countess go undercover to capture what they think is a spy.

Lucy and the Return of Iron Man
GS: Saul Gorss. Lucy goes to work as a stuntman again to earn more money.

Lucy Saves Milton Berle
GS: Milton Berle, Milton Frome. Milton, doing research for a movie role as a drunken bum, is taken home by Lucy to help him give up drinking.

Lucy the Choirmaster
GS: Lloyd Corrigan, Teddy Eccles, St. Charles Catholic Boys Choir. Lucy shops for a Christmas tree.

Lucy Discovers Wayne Newton
GS: Wayne Newton, Gary Morton. Lucy introduces her discovery to the owner of a record company.

Lucy the Rain Goddess
GS: Willard Waterman, Douglas Fowley. Lucy gets involved with Indians while looking for Mooney at a dude ranch.

Lucy and Art Linkletter
GS: Art Linkletter, Jerome Cowan, Doris Singleton, Roy Rowan. Lucy appears on Art Linkletter's TV show and is given $200 if she doesn't speak for 24 hours.

Lucy Bags a Bargain
Lucy gets a bargain at a department store sale, but finds that she can't pay for it.

Lucy Meets Mickey Rooney
GS: Mickey Rooney, Steven Marlo. Mickey Rooney asks Mooney to loan him money to open an acting school. Lucy and Mooney immediately sign up.

Lucy and the Soap Opera
GS: Jan Murray, John Howard, John Alvin. Lucy tracks down a soap opera writer when she learns that her actor neighbor is going to be killed off.

Lucy Goes to a Hollywood Premiere
GS: Kirk Douglas, Edward G. Robinson, Jimmy Durante, Vince Edwards, Reta Shaw. Lucy becomes a doorman at a theater in order to see some big stars.

Lucy Dates Dean Martin
GS: Dean Martin, Tommy Farrell. Dean Martin's lookalike stand-in Ed Feldman asks Lucy to go to a ball and the real Dean Martin comes in his place.

Lucy and Bob Crane
GS: Bob Crane, Oscar Beregi, and John Banner as Sgt. Schultz. Bob Crane dates Lucy, unaware that she is also stuntman Iron Man Carmichael.

Lucy and the Robot
GS: Jay North, Vito Scotti, Larry Dean. Lucy's inventor friend creates a robot for Mooney's nephew.

Lucy and the Sleeping Beauty
GS: Clint Walker. Lucy tries to get the measurements of her construction worker boyfriend in order to knit him a sweater.

Lucy the Gun Moll
GS: Robert Stack, Bruce Gordon. Lucy helps the FBI to capture a gangster by posing as his girlfriend who has been released from jail.

Lucy the Superwoman
GS: Robert F. Simon, Parley Baer, Joel Marston. Lucy becomes a superwoman when her adrenal glands malfunction.

Lucy Goes to Vegas
Lucy goes to Las Vegas.

Lucy Gets Her Maid
Lucy tries to get a maid to help with the housework.

Lucy the Coin Collector
Lucy loses a valuable penny down a storm drain, so she goes in after it to get it back.

Lucy Gets Amnesia
Mooney tries to help Lucy who has lost her memory, or so he thinks she did.

Lucy the Meter Maid
Lucy gets a job as a meter maid.

Lucy and George Burns
GS: George Burns. George uses Lucy as a partner in his act.

Lucy and the Submarine
GS: Robert Carson, Steven Marlo. Lucy has to contact Mooney, who is on reserve submarine duty, in order to get him to sign some important papers.

Lucy and the Bean Queen
GS: Ed Begley. Lucy tries to make money on a bean company's double-your-money-back offer.

Lucy and Paul Winchell
GS: Paul Winchell. Lucy tries to get Paul to appear at a bank benefit show.

Lucy and the Ring-a-Ding Ring
GS: Don Beddoe, Ray Kellogg. Lucy gets Mrs. Mooney's diamond ring stuck on her finger and can't get it off.

Lucy Flies to London
GS: Pat Priest, James Wellman. Lucy wins a trip to London in a dog food contest.

Lucy Gets a Roommate [Part 1]
GS: Carol Burnett. A quiet librarian answers Lucy's ad for a roomate.

Lucy and Carol in Palm Springs [Part 2]
GS: Carol Burnett, Dan Rowan. Lucy joins Carol's musical act for a weekend in Palm Springs.

Lucy Gets Caught in the Draft
GS: Harry Hickox and Jim Nabors as

Gomer Pyle. Lucy accidentally gets drafted into the Marines.

Lucy and John Wayne
GS: John Wayne, Morgan Woodward, Joseph Ruskin, Milton Berle. Lucy disrupts John Wayne while he films a new movie.

Lucy and Pat Collins
GS: Pat Collins. A nightclub hypnotist puts Lucy and Mooney under her power.

Mooney the Monkey
GS: Lew Parker, Hal March, Janos Prohaska. Lucy goes to a psychiatrist when she thinks Mooney keeps changing into a monkey.

Lucy's Substitute Secretary
GS: Ruta Lee, Barbara Morrison. Lucy dresses up as some strange characters in order to watch her temporary replacement who wants her job.

Viv Visits Lucy
Lucy and Viv dress up as hippies to prowl the sunset strip.

Lucy the Baby Sitter
GS: Mary Wickes, The Marquis Chimps, Lucy babysits with three chimps.

Mainstreet USA [Part 1]
GS: Mel Torme, John Bubbles, Paul Winchell. Lucy holds a protest against a freeway destroying a small town.

Lucy Puts Main Street on the Map [Part 2]
GS: Dan Rowan. Lucy fakes a shootout in order to get a TV reporter's attention.

Lucy Meets the Law
GS: Claude Akins, Iris Adrian. Lucy is mistaken for a shoplifter named Red Flash.

Lucy the Fight Manager
GS: Don Rickles. Lucy trains an ex-fighter for a comeback when Mooney

won't lend him the money to open a flower shop.

Lucy Meets Tennessee Ernie Ford
GS: Tennessee Ernie Ford, Robert Easton, Carole Cook, William O'Connell. Lucy stages a country hoedown in order to get a country singer's money for the bank.

Lucy Meets Sheldon Leonard
GS: Sheldon Leonard. Lucy thinks producer Sheldon Leonard is a crook planning to rob the bank.

Lucy and the Efficiency Expert
GS: Phil Silvers. An efficiency expert working at the bank hires Lucy as his assistant.

Lucy Meets the Berles
GS: Milton Berle, Ruta Lee. While working as a secretary for Milton Berle, Lucy thinks Milton and Ruta Lee are having an affair so she tries to stop it.

Lucy Gets Trapped
Lucy calls in sick but goes to a sale, only she gets her picture in the papers as the store's 10 millionth customer.

Lucy and the French Movie Star
GS: Jacques Bergerac. Lucy falls for a French movie star playboy.

Lucy the Star Maker
GS: Frankie Avalon, Lew Parker. Lucy tries to help Mr. Cheever's singing nephew break into show business.

Lucy Gets Her Diploma
GS: Robert Pine, Lucie Arnaz. Lucy returns to high school to get her diploma and graduates as valedictorian.

Lucy Gets Jack Benny's Account
GS: Jack Benny, George Barrows. Lucy tries to get Jack Benny's money for the bank, so she creates a burglar-proof vault for him.

Little Old Lady
GS: Dennis Day. Lucy dresses up as an old lady to be a date for the swinging but old president of the bank.

Lucy and Robert Goulet
GS: Robert Goulet, Mary Wickes, Lucie Arnaz. When a trucker is turned down for a loan, Lucy persuades him to enter a Robert Goulet lookalike contest.

Lucy Gets Mooney Fired
Mooney is fired because of Lucy's bookkeeping, so she sets out to "Gaslight" Mr. Cheever into getting Mooney back.

Lucy's Mystery Guest
GS: Mary Wickes. Lucy's health fiend aunt arrives to put her back in shape.

Lucy the Philanthropist
GS: Frank McHugh. Mooney thinks a bum asking for a job is really an eccentric millionaire in disguise.

Lucy Sues Mooney
GS: Jack Carter. A low-class lawyer wants Lucy to sue Mooney for injuries she got while working overtime.

Lucy and Carol Burnett [Part 1]
GS: Carol Burnett, Rhodes Reason. Lucy and Carol become airline stewardess trainees.

Lucy and Carol Burnett [Part 2]
GS: Carol Burnett, Richard Arlen, Buddy Rogers. Lucy and Carol do a musical salute to aviation.

Lucy and the Pool Hustler
GS: Dick Shawn, Stanley Adams, Herbie Faye. A pool hustler dresses up like a woman in order to join a ladies pool tournament, but has to play against Lucy.

Lucy Gets Involved
GS: Jackie Coogan. Lucy moonlights as a waitress at a drive-in and wrecks the place.

Mooney's Other Wife
GS: Edie Adams. Lucy plays Moon-

ey's wife in order to scare off a young woman out for Mooney's money.

Lucy and the Stolen Stole
GS: Buddy Hackett. Lucy and Mooney unknowingly buy a stolen fur from a fence and wind up in jail.

Lucy and Phil Harris
GS: Phil Harris, Lew Parker. Lucy tries to help a drunken hasbeen songwriter make a comeback.

Lucy and Ken Berry
GS: Ken Berry, Ralph Story, Stanley Adams. Lucy tries to help a dance teacher open a dance school.

Lucy and the Lost Star/Lucy Meets Joan
GS: Joan Crawford, Lew Parker. Lucy and Viv, thinking that she is broke, get Joan Crawford a job in a 1920s revue.

Lucy and Sid Caesar
GS: Sid Caesar. Lucy tries to help capture Sid Caesar's lookalike forger.

Lucy and the Boss of the Year
Lucy enters Mr. Mooney and Mooney enters Mr. Cheever in the Boss of the Year contest.

MAKE ROOM FOR DADDY

On the air 9/29/53, off 9/14/64. ABC, CBS. B&W Film. 30 min. 195 syndicated episodes. 336 episodes made. Broadcast: Sept 1953-Jun 1956 ABC Tue 9-9:30; Oct 1956-Feb 1957 ABC Mon 8-8:30; Feb 1957-Jul 1957 ABC 9-9:30; Oct 1957-Sept 1964 CBS Mon 9-9:30. Producer: Sheldon Leonard. Synd: Weiss-Global.

CAST: Danny Williams (played by Danny Thomas), Kathy Williams (Marjorie Lord), Rusty Williams (Rusty Hamer), Linda Williams (Angela Cartwright), Terry Williams (Sherry Jackson; Penney Parker, 1959-60), Uncle Tonoose (Hans Conreid), Pat Hannigan (Pat Harrington), Charley Halper (Sid Melton), Bunny Halper (Pat Carroll), Gina (Annette Funicello), Louise (Amanda Randolph).

The adventures of the Williams family: Danny, a nightclub entertainer, his wife and children, residing in New York. Episodes involve the home and working life of Danny, a man whose career often leaves him with little time to spend with his family. The series was revived in two specials: *Make More Room for Daddy* on NBC in 1967 and *Make Room for Granddaddy* on CBS in 1969, which served as the pilot for the one season show of the same name on ABC in 1970-1971. *Make Room for Daddy* is rarely seen today even though it survived many years on the networks. The syndicated episodes are the ones filmed in the late 1950s and early 1960s. The earlier episodes are not syndicated.

Lose Me in Las Vegas
GS: Jack Benny, Peter Lind Hayes, Mary Healy. Danny's popularity almost ruins his honeymoon in Las Vegas.

The Honeymoon Flashback
Danny tells Schultz, the waiter, about what happened to him on his honeymoon.

Terry vs. Kathy
Problems arise when daughter Terry

fights with Kathy.

The Non-Orgs
Terry's high school social life interferes with family life.

Parents Are Pigeons
Danny and Kathy are the victims of a plan created by Linda and Rusty.

Two Sleepy People
Danny and Kathy try to prove that each has more energy than the other.

Marjorie Lord, Rusty Hamer, Danny Thomas, and Angela Cartwright in Make Room for Daddy.

Terry the Breadwinner
Terry gets a job in a dress shop, so Danny tries to make her look good.

Kathy Is Approved
Uncle Tonoose arrives to check out Kathy.

Honesty Is the Best Policy
Danny tries to show Rusty that honesty is the best policy.

Danny Meets His Father-in-Law
GS: William Demarest. Danny prepares himself to meet Kathy's father.

Man's Best Friend
Danny regrets letting the kids have a pet.

The Dinah Shore Show
GS: Dinah Shore. Danny tries to get Dinah Shore to appear at Terry's school dance.

The Chess Game
GS: Tom Tully. Kathy's Irish uncle comes for a visit.

Evil Eye Schultz
Danny is given the "evil eye" on the night of an important night club opening.

The Raffle Tickets
Danny tries to boost Rusty's spirit by getting him to enter a ticket-selling contest.

Soap Box Derby
GS: William Demarest. Danny and Kathy's father both try to help Rusty build a soap box racer.

Rusty the Bully
Danny tries to get Rusty to stand up to the school bully.

Make Room for Father-in-Law
GS: William Demarest. Danny helps Kathy's father get a job.

Pardon My Accent
Rusty wins a neatness award at school and Danny is asked to accept it, causing him to think the award is for him.

The Bob Hope Show
GS: Bob Hope. Danny is chosen to be the MC at a benefit show where Bob Hope is scheduled to appear.

Family Ties
Danny tries to get the family to do things together.

St. Vincent Frolics
Danny produces a lot of problems for himself when he agrees to produce a benefit show.

Rock 'n' Roll Show
Danny tries to help the school principal overcome his being prejudiced.

Terry's Crush
GS: Dean Martin. Terry has a crush on Dean Martin and Danny tries to break it up.

Uncle Tonoose Met Mr. Daly
GS: William Demarest. A fight breaks out when Uncle Tonoose meets Kathy's father.

You've Got to Be Miserable to Be Happy
Kathy is jealous of the beautiful new dancer at the club.

Danny Roars Again
Danny shocks his family when he tries to be calm and quiet instead of his excitable self.

The Country Girl
GS: Judy Canova. Danny discovers a country singer and books her in a high-class club.

Terry's Girlfriend
One of Terry's girlfriends spends the weekend.

Terry's Coach
GS: Hans Conreid. Terry asks an out of work Shakespearean actor to help her learn her part in the school play.

Danny the Performer
Danny gets into trouble when he brings Rusty's friends to the club.

Too Good for Words
Danny changes his personality after a female columnist does a story on him.

Rusty the Man
Danny refuses to let 10-year-old Rusty get a job.

The First Anniversary
GS: William Demarest. While celebrating their first anniversary, Danny and Kathy fight over who proposed to whom.

Rusty, the Ward-Heeler
Danny helps Rusty run for class president.

Jack Benny Takes Danny's Job
Danny is upset when Rusty's scout troop asks Jack Benny to perform at its benefit show and not him.

Terry Goes Steady
Danny becomes a nervous wreck when Terry announces she is going steady.

Take a Message
Kathy forgets to give Danny his telephone messages, causing problems for Danny.

A Locket for Linda
Linda gets an unusual locket as a present.

The Reunion
After a reunion with some old friends, Danny dreams about what he could have become if he had not gone into show business.

Uncle Tonoose's Fling
Uncle Tonoose asks Danny to help him to become a professional playboy.

Dinah Shore and Danny Are Rivals
GS: Dinah Shore, Missy Montgomery. A fight develops between Danny and Dinah Shore.

Linda's Tonsils
Linda is afraid to have her tonsils taken out.

Lucille Ball Upsets the Williams Household
GS: Lucille Ball, Desi Arnaz. Lucy and Ricky Ricardo move into the Williams's house. [This was a crossover episode from "I Love Lucy."]

Kathy's Career
GS: Kathy Lewis. Kathy takes a job in the fashion industry.

The Saints Come Marching In
Danny finds that Rusty has joined a gang.

Tony Bennett Gets Danny's Help
GS: Tony Bennett. Danny's singing Cousin Stephen doesn't want to take over the family dry goods business, leaving Danny to be the peacemaker.

Tennessee Ernie Stays for Dinner
GS: Tennessee Ernie Ford. Rusty and Linda befriend a country singer called Kentucky Cal.

Bob Hope and Danny Become Directors
GS: Bob Hope. Bob and Danny help produce a production of Alice in Wonderland.

Red Tape
Danny takes offense when he is told that show business people are not "representative" Americans.

Shirley Jones Makes Good
GS: Shirley Jones, Lauritz Melchior. Lauritz and Shirley appear as father and daughter singers at Danny's club.

Gina from Italy
GS: Annette Funicello. Gina, an exchange student from Italy, moves in with the Williams family.

Frankie Laine Sings for Gina
GS: Annette Funicello, Frankie Laine. Gina asks Frankie Laine to sing at the school dance.

Gina's First Date
GS: Annette Funicello. Danny teaches Gina about dating American boys.

Growing Pains
Rusty has a crush on one of his classmates.

Kathy Leaves Danny
Kathy moves out when they have a fight over who is the boss of the house.

The Latin Lover
GS: Annette Funicello. Gina's friend from Italy tries to use Danny to better her career.

Loser's Weepers
Danny gets upset when Kathy and his agent lose the script for his new routine.

Grandpa's Diet
GS: Charles Coburn. Grandpa is on a strict diet so it is up to Danny and the others to make sure he doesn't sneak food into the house.

The Double Dinner
GS: Jack Albertson. Danny is named the Abbot of the Friars Club.

Danny's Big Fan
GS: Salvatori Baccaloni. A rich fan wants to buy Danny's friendship.

The Surprise Party
Danny is upset when he thinks everyone forgot his birthday.

Gina for President
GS: Annette Funicello. Gina runs against her boyfriend for class president.

The Practical Joke
Danny finds himself on the receiving end of a string of practical jokes.

Linda's Giant
GS: Buck Maffei. Danny and Kathy don't believe Linda's stories about her nine-foot-tall friend.

Terry Comes Home
GS: Robert Reed. Terry comes home from college.

Rusty's Day in Court
GS: Francis X. Bushman. Danny argues a traffic case in court.

The Chinese Doll
GS: Marvin Miller, Ginny Tiu. A Chinese gentleman gets a lesson in child psychology.

Cupid's Little Helper
Terry tries to improve her parents' image.

Terry Meets Him
GS: Pat Harrington, Elliott Reid. Terry falls for a man named Pat Hannegan.

Terry Goes Bohemian
GS: Pat Harrington. Terry decides to become a beatnik.

Danny and Milton Berle Quit Show Biz
GS: Milton Berle. Milton talks Danny into quitting show business.

Tonoose, The Matchmaker
GS: Pat Harrington, Hans Conreid. Tonoose tries to get Terry married.

Rusty, the Weight-lifter
Danny tries to use psychology to get Rusty to stand up to a bully.

Jealousy
Danny wears different disguises to stop Kathy's jealousy.

A Dog's Life
GS: Gale Gordon. A Saint Bernard chooses the Williams's apartment to give birth, causing the landlord to try and throw Danny out.

Kathy Crashes TV
GS: Joe Flynn. Kathy finds that appearing on TV is not all that she thought it would be.

Danny and the Little Men
GS: Pat Harrington. Danny's home is invaded by a bunch of dwarfs.

Nightclub Owners
GS: Beatrice Kay, Pat Harrington, The Guardsman Quartet. A woman buys the nightclub.

How to Be Head of the House
GS: Pat Harrington. Danny tries to show Pat how to handle his future wife.

That Old Devil, Jack Benny
GS: Jack Benny. Jack sells his soul to the devil.

Tonoose Makes the Wedding Plans
GS: Pat Harrington, Hans Conreid. Tonoose plans an old-fashioned Lebanese wedding for Terry.

Danny, the Housewife
Danny takes over the household chores when Kathy serves on a jury.

The Apple Polishers
Danny goes over his agent's head to get a job on a TV show.

Danny Meets Andy Griffith
GS: Andy Griffith, Ronny Howard. Danny winds up in Mayberry. [This was the pilot for "The Andy Griffith Show."]

Battle of the In-Laws
GS: Pat Harrington, Jack Haley. Danny gets into trouble over the invitation list to the wedding.

Eulogy for Tonoose
GS: Hans Conreid. Uncle Tonoose wants to hear his eulogy before he dies.

Linda Wants to Be a Boy
Danny has a big problem: Linda wants

to be a boy.

Bachelor Party
GS: Pat Harrington.   Scared Pat decides to call off the marriage.

Danny the Handyman
Danny and Rusty work together to build a dog house.

The Wedding
As the family prepares for the wedding, Danny feels left out.

Three on a Honeymoon
GS: Pat Harrington. Danny interferes in Terry and Pat's honeymoon.

The Deerfield Story
GS: Jim Backus. Danny's fast-talking friend pays a visit.

The Singing Delinquent
GS: Bobby Rydell. Danny helps a young singer who thinks he is a tough guy.

Rusty and the Tomboy
Danny tries to get Rusty a date with a girl on his baseball team.

Family Portrait
GS: Gale Gordon. A fussy painter tries to capture the Williams family in a portrait.

Rusty Meets Little Lord Fauntleroy
Rusty has to put up with a military school trained house guest.

Rusty's Advice to Linda
Linda plans to run away after she loses her skates and Danny won't buy her another pair.

Kathy & the Glamour Girl
GS: Zsa Zsa Gabor. Kathy is jealous of beautiful Zsa Zsa Gabor.

Danny and the Actor's School
Danny gives up comedy to pursue a career in dramatic acting.

Kathy Delivers the Mail
Linda tries to help the mailman and

almost gets Danny arrested.

The Report Card
Danny thinks Rusty is a genius when he gets all A's on his report card.

Danny Proposes to His Wife
Danny courts Kathy again after he reminds her that she was the one who proposed to him.

Kathy, the Matchmaker
Kathy tries to be a matchmaker only to learn that one of the two she tried to bring together has other plans.

Tonoose the Liar
GS: Hans Conreid. Danny and Kathy don't believe any of Tonoose's tall stories until he convinces them that they are the truth.

Linda the Performer
Danny prepares Linda for her debut on TV.

The Scrubwoman
Danny and Kathy become the temporary adopted children of their cleaning lady who wants to impress her boyfriend into marrying her.

The Singing Sisters
Kathy and her sister audition for Danny's club.

Fugitive Father
GS: Buddy Hackett. Danny's vacation replacement is being followed by a welfare worker who wants to take his daughter away.

Rusty the Rat
Rusty breaks Danny's golf clubs and tries to blame it on Linda.

Danny and the Dentist
GS: Richard Deacon. Danny gets his boss to go to the dentist for him.

Democracy at Work
Danny learns that majority vote is not always a good thing.

The Plant
GS: Gale Gordon. Danny gets a plant from a fan and the landlord thinks it deserves special treatment because it is a very rare plant.

You Can Fight City Hall
Danny tries to fight a parking ticket.

The Rum Cake
GS: Gale Gordon. The landlord gets drunk on Danny's rum cake.

The Whoopee Show
Danny gets an idea for a new act from Kathy's hair curlers.

Tonoose the Boss
GS: Hans Conreid. Tonoose tries to take over the operation of Danny's club.

Good Old Neighbors
Danny tries to help an old burlesque comedian make a comeback.

Rusty, the Millionaire
Danny tries to teach Rusty the value of money.

The Four Angels
Danny tries to book an act on the Ed Sullivan show, but finds that Rusty is their manager.

The Dog Walkers
GS: Bill Dana. Jose the elevator operator and Danny become dog walkers.

The Old Man Danny
GS: Paul Anka. Danny feels old when a young singer is hired to sing rock 'n' roll at the club.

Everything Happens to Me
Danny tries to put on a television show from Hollywood.

Danny and the Hoodlums
Another comic is bothered by gangsters who claim he is stealing his material from Danny.

Rusty's Punishment
Danny refuses to let Rusty play in a big basketball game because of bad grades.

The Scoutmaster
GS: Gale Gordon. Danny and the landlord both try to be the new scoutmaster.

The Magician
Magic ruins Danny's speech to the UN.

The Woman Behind the Man
Kathy tries to prove she is the driving force behind Danny.

Teenage Thrush
GS: Brenda Lee. Danny tries to promote a young singer while the girl's mother wants her to continue her education.

The Party Wrecker
GS: Gale Gordon. Danny is upset when he isn't invited to the landlord's party.

The Trumpet Player
GS: Harry James. Danny gets upset when the band director at the YMCA refuses to let Rusty join the band.

Love Letters
Linda once again delivers the mail, only now she is delivering her parents' old love letters.

Linda Runs Away
Linda plans to run away again, this time because she gets yelled at for not cleaning her room.

For Every Man There's a Woman
GS: Bill Dana. Danny tries to get Jose and his girlfriend married.

Tonoose vs. Daly
GS: Hans Conreid, William Demarest. Tonoose and Kathy's father face each other in an athletic competition.

Danny Weaves a Web
GS: Jack Albertson, Bill Bixby. Danny tries to get away with telling a little white lie but gets caught.

Henpecked Charley
GS: Pat Carroll. Danny interferes in someone else's marriage.

Danny and Durante
GS: Jimmy Durante, Bill Bixby. Danny helps Jimmy regain his confidence; it seems he was ashamed to associate with his niece's educated friends.

Tonoose's Plot
GS: Hans Conreid. Uncle Tonoose moves out of Toledo because of something to do with the family burial plot.

Keeping Up with the Joneses
GS: Pat Carroll. The Williamses and the Halpers each try to keep up with each other.

Danny and the Brownies
Danny takes eight members of the Brownies on a picnic but winds up in court.

A Baby for Charley
GS: Pat Carroll. Child-hater Charley changes his ways when he learns he is going to be a father.

Teacher for a Day
Danny takes over for the teacher when he claims it looks too easy, but soon changes his mind.

Useless Charley
GS: Pat Carroll. Danny tries to convince Charley that he isn't useless.

Linda the Tomboy
Danny tries to turn tomboy Linda into a young lady.

The Big Fight
Danny has a fight with Charley and goes to work in a rival nightclub.

Casanova Tonoose
GS: Hans Conreid. Uncle Tonoose comes to New York to find a wife.

Charley Does It Himself
GS: Pat Carroll. Danny helps Charley redecorate the house.

The PTA Bash
Danny tries to make a routine about the PTA meetings.

A Nose by Any Other Name
Danny goes to a plastic surgeon to have his nose shortened.

Casanova Junior
Danny teaches Rusty how to be popular with the girls.

The Hunger Strike
Rusty goes on a hunger strike because Danny won't let him go on an overnight saddle trip.

Temper, Temper
Danny loses his temper, which means he will have to buy Kathy an expensive present in order to make up with her.

Bunny Cooks a Meal
GS: Pat Carroll, Louis Nye. Rotten cook Bunny Halper cooks a dinner for a gourmet.

Jose's Protege
GS: Bill Dana. Jose tries to get his nephew on Danny's TV show.

Danny and Bob Hope Get Away from It All
GS: Bob Hope. Danny and Bob go to a small town to avoid autograph collectors, only they soon realize that they miss giving autographs.

Extrasensory Charley
GS: Pat Carroll. Bunny gets Danny and Kathy to help play a trick on Charley.

Kathy the Pro
GS: Pat Carroll. Danny has difficulty getting Kathy to return to housework after she works as a nightclub performer.

A Promise Is a Promise
GS: Art Linkletter. Danny is afraid of what Linda will say about him on a children's TV show, especially since he just yelled at her.

The Smart Aleck
Danny doesn't like the fact that his Cousin Don is coming to New York to enter show business

The Baby
GS: Pat Carroll. Charley is a bundle of nerves as he waits for Bunny to have the baby.

MANY HAPPY RETURNS

On the air 9/21/64, off 4/12/65. CBS. B&W Film. 26 episodes. Broadcast: Sept 1964-Apr 1965 Mon 9:30-10. Producer: Unknown. Prod Co/Synd: MGM TV.

CAST: Walter Burnley (played by John McGiver), Harry Price (Richard Collier), Joan Randall (Elinor Donahue), Wilma Fritter (Jesslyn Fax), Bob Randall (Mark Goddard), Joe Foley (Mickey Manners), Laurie Randall (Andrea Sacino), Lynn Hall (Elena Verdugo), Owen Sharp (Russell Collins).

The adventures of Walter Burnley, manager of the complaint department at Krockmeyer's department store. The series had an interesting premise, but failed to attract an audience. It has never been repeated.

Pilot Program
Walter tries to talk customers out of demanding refunds.

Walter Meets the Machine
GS: Russell Collins. The store manager plans to replace Walter's complaint department with a computer.

It Shouldn't Happen to a Dog
GS: Don Briggs, Elinor Donahue, Regina Gleason. Walter gives a puppy, which was returned to the store, to his granddaughter as a present.

Bye, Bye Cupid
GS: Majel Barrett, William O'Connell, Joan Tompkins. Sharp invites Walter to spend the weekend on his boat with his unmarried sister.

Burnley at the Bridge
Walter and Wilma try to keep the housewreckers from destroying his house until her cat gives birth.

The Best Seller
GS: Elena Verdugo, Willard Waterman. Walter promotes an unsuccessful fraternity brother's books at the store.

Mother Burnley's Chickens
GS: Richard Price, Rickey Allen. Walter babysits with Harry's eight kids.

Krockmeyer on Avon
GS: Arte Johnson. Walter takes over the store's drama group after the regular director is fired.

The Surprise Visit
Walter thinks the staff needs a raise and Mr. Sharp wants to fire someone.

Taming of the Beast
GS: Arte Johnson, Richard Collier. Walter's plans to throw a surprise party for Sharp are halted by Sharp's nephew the efficiency expert.

The Diamond
GS: Tommy Rettig, Gigi Perreau, George Cisar, Portia Nelson. Walter steps in when the father of Eddie Benson's fiancee returns his ring saying he is unworthy to marry his daughter.

Foster Father of the Bride
Walter comes to the rescue when Lynn becomes engaged to a soldier she has known for only a month.

Three on a Honeymoon
GS: Sharla Doherty, Clive Clerk. Walter mistakes two honeymooners for prowlers.

Pop Goes the Easel
GS: Elvia Allman. Walter unknowingly gives Mrs. Sharp a valuable painting to use as scrap to practice her painting on.

The Krockmeyer Caper
GS: Robert Donner, Harvey Lembeck. Two crooks are after Walter who has their stolen loot in his golf bag.

Big White Lie
GS: Don Beddoe, Ilka Windish. Walter pretends to be Mr. Sharp in order to get a woman to merge her company with the store.

Idol Threats
GS: Chet Stratton, Fay De Witt. A customer returns an ivory statue because he thinks there is a curse on it.

A Date for Walter
GS: Alice Pearce, Shirley Bonne. Walter learns the reason why Joe is always late and sleepy. It is his girl's mother.

The Woodsman
GS: Brian Nash, Mike Banton, Jimmy Lydon. Walter volunteers to take two kids on a camping trip.

It's a Gift
GS: Ina Victor, Bobby Buntrock, Martin Braddock. Walter tries to stop a fight between Ralph and Ellie so he orders an inexpensive bracelet, but the store sends a $300 dress instead.

[The remaining episodes have no available story.]

East Is West
The Fashion Show
The House Divided
Joe's Place
No Nose Is Good Nose
The Shoplifter

THE MARY TYLER MOORE SHOW

On the air 9/19/70, off 9/3/77. CBS. Color Videotape. 168 episodes. Broadcast: Sept 1970-Dec 1971 Sat 9:30-10; Dec 1971-Sept 1972 Sat 8:30-9; Sept 1972-Oct 1976 Sat 9-9:30; Nov 1976-Sept 1977 Sat 8-8:30. Producer: James L. Brooks/Alan Burns. Prod Co: MTM. Synd: Viacom.

CAST: Mary Richards (played by Mary Tyler Moore), Lou Grant (Ed Asner), Ted Baxter (Ted Knight), Murray Slaughter (Gavin MacLeod), Rhoda (Valerie Harper), Phyllis (Cloris Leachman), Bess (Lisa Gerritsen), Gordy (John Amos), Georgette (Georgia Engel), Sue Ann Nivens (Betty White), Marie Slaughter (Joyce Bulifant), David Baxter (Robbie Rist), Edie Grant (Priscilla Morrill).

The adventures of Mary Richards, a producer of the news for a TV station in Minnesota. The series dealt with the problems presented to her by friends and co-workers ranging from an egotistical anchorman to neurotic neighbors. The show was praised for its intelligent approach and humanistic qualities. This was a very popular series during its run, but has suffered in syndication. This is also a more sophisticated series which fails to attract the attention of children.

[Every episode is directed by Jay Sandrich (except where noted).]

Love Is All Around [Pilot]
W: James L. Brooks & Allan Burns. GS: Angus Duncan. Mary comes to Minneapolis, starts work at WJM-TV.

Today I Am a Ma'am
W: Treva Silverman. GS: Richard Schaal, Jack De Mave, Sheila Wells. Mary's old boyfriend and the man that Rhoda hit with her car (and his wife) come to dinner at Mary's apartment.

Bess, You Is My Daughter Now
W: John D.F. Black. Mary finds her-self taking care of Bess for a few days.

Divorce Isn't Everything
W: Treva Silverman. D: Alan Rafkin. GS: Gino Conforti, Shelley Berman. Mary and Rhoda join a club for divorced people, in order to get a group rate on a trip to Paris.

Keep Your Guard Up
W: Steve Pritzker. D: Alan Rafkin. GS: John Schuck, Tim Brown. Mary finds that an ex-football player will not leave her alone until she gets him an audition for a sports announcer's job.

Support Your Local Mother
W: James L. Brooks & Alan Burns. D: Alan Rafkin. GS: Nancy Walker. Rhoda's mother comes for a visit, but Rhoda refuses to see her so she moves in with Mary.

Toulouse Lautrec Is One of My Favorite Artists
W: Lloyd Turner & Gordon Mitchell. GS: Hamilton Camp. Mary falls for a professional writer who is shorter than she.

The Snow Must Go On
W: Lorenzo Music. GS: Richard Schaal, Ivor Francis. Mary produces an election night program during a snowstorm.

Bob & Rhoda & Teddy & Mary
W: Bob Rodgers. D: Peter Baldwin. GS: Henry Corden, Dick Patterson, Greg Mullavey. Rhoda's new boyfriend falls for Mary, while Ted hopes to win a Teddy award.

Assistant Wanted, Female
W: Treva Silverman. D: Peter Baldwin. Mary hires Phyllis as her new assistant, but later regrets it when she disrupts the whole office.

1040 or Fight
W: David Davis & Lorenzo Music. GS:

Paul Sand. Mary finds herself dating the man who is auditing her tax return.

Anchorman Overboard
W: Lorenzo Music. GS: Bill Fiore. Ted loses his confidence when he is asked to speak at a ladies club.

He's All Yours
W: Bob Rodgers. GS: Wes Stern. A young cameraman finds that he has a crush on Mary.

Christmas and the Hard Luck Kid-II
W: Jim Brooks & Allan Burns. GS: Ned Wertimer. Mary finds that she has to work on Christmas day, causing her to become depressed.

Howard's Girl
W: Treva Silverman. GS: Richard Schaal, Henry Jones, Mary Jackson. Mary dates the brother of her former boyfriend, which upsets his parents.

Party Is Such Sweet Sorrow
W: Martin Cohan. GS: Dick Clair. Mary agrees to take a producing job at another station.

Just a Lunch
W: Jim Brooks & Allan Burns. D: Bruce Bilson. GS: Monte Markham. Mary finds herself dating a married newsman.

Second Story Story
W: Steve Pritzker. GS: Bob Dishy, Vic Tayback. Mary's apartment is robbed twice, in two days.

We Closed in Minneapolis
W: Kenny Solms & Gail Parent. GS: Elliot Street. The newsroom staff all take part in a play written by Murray about a newsroom.

Hi!
W: Treva Silverman. GS: Pat Carroll, Bruce Kirby, Robert Casper. Mary goes to the hospital to have her tonsils removed. She is also stuck with a grouchy roommate.

The Boss Isn't Coming to Dinner
W: David Davis & Lorenzo Music. Mary tries to help out when she learns that Mr. Grant and his wife are planning to separate.

A Friend in Deed
W: Susan Silver. GS: Patte Finley. Mary's childhood friend comes for a visit and annoys everyone at the station.

Smokey the Bear Wants You
W: Steve Pritzker. GS: Michael Callan. Rhoda falls for a man who plans to be a forest ranger.

The 45-Year-Old Old Man
W: George Kirgo. D: Herbert Kenwith. GS: Slim Pickens, Richard Libertini. Mary goes to see the cowboy owner of the station, in order to get Mr. Grant his job back when he is fired.

The Birds . . . and . . . um . . . Bees
W: Treva Silverman. Phyllis asks Mary to teach Bess the facts of life.

I Am Curious Cooper
W: David Davis & Lorenzo Music. GS: Michael Constantine. Lou fixes Mary up with one of his bachelor friends.

He's No Heavy—He's My Brother
W: Allan Burns. D: Jerry Paris. GS: Frank Ramirez. Mary and Rhoda plan to take a trip to Mexico with the help of the owner of a Mexican restaurant.

Room 223
W: Susan Silver. GS: Michael Tolan, Florida Friebus. Mary falls for her night-school professor.

A Girl's Best Mother Is Not Her Friend
W: David Davis & Lorenzo Music. GS: Nancy Walker. Rhoda's mother comes for a visit and tries to act like her friend and not her mother.

Cover Boy
W: Treva Silverman. GS: Jack Cassidy. Ted gets Mary to pretend she is his girlfriend in order to impress his brother.

Didn't You Used to Be . . . Wait . . . Don't Tell Me
W: Allan Burns. GS: Richard Schaal, Kermit Murdock, Pippa Scott. Mary goes to her high school reunion where she meets her old boyfriend Howard.

Thoroughly Unmilitant Mary
W: Martin Cohan. Mary and Lou have to run the entire news program by themselves when the staff goes on strike.

And Now, Sitting In for Ted Baxter
W: Steve Pritzker. D: Jerry Paris. GS: Jed Allan. Ted is afraid that his temporary replacement will become permanent when he is forced to take a vacation.

Don't Break the Chain
W: David Davis & Lorenzo Music. D: Jerry Paris. GS: Jack de Mave, Gino Conforti. Mary gets a chain letter from Lou and decides to break the chain, despite warnings from Lou.

The Six-and-a-Half-Year Itch
W: Treva Silverman. GS: Lawrence Pressman, Elizabeth Berger. Lou finds his son-in-law in a movie theater with another woman.

. . . Is a Friend in Need
W: Susan Silver. GS: Beverly Sanders. Mary tries to find Rhoda another job when she is fired.

The Square-Shaped Room
W: Susan Silver. Mary gets Rhoda to redecorate Lou's house.

Ted Over Heels
W: David Davis & Lorenzo Music. D: Peter Baldwin. GS: Arlene Golonka. Ted falls in love with the daughter of Chuckles the Clown.

The Five-Minute Dress
W: Pat Narde & Gloria Banta. Mary's new boyfriend, the governor's aide,

keeps breaking their dates.

Feeb
W: Dick Clair & Jenna McMahon. D: Peter Baldwin. GS: Barbara Sharma. Mary hires an incompetent waitress to work in the newsroom because she feels guilty over getting her fired from her job at a restaurant.

The Slaughter Affair
W: Rick Mittleman. D: Peter Baldwin. Murray moonlights to buy Marie a present, but she thinks he is having an affair with Mary.

Baby-Sit-Com
W: Treva Silverman. GS: Leslie Graves, Joshua Bryant. Mary regrets having to babysit Bess when an old boyfriend calls for a date.

More Than Neighbors
W: Steve Pritzker. GS: Yvonne Wilder, Jack Bender. Ted plans to move into the vacant apartment next to Mary.

The Care and Feeding of Parents
W: Dick Clair & Jenna McMahon. GS: Jon Locke, Brad Trumball. Phyllis wants Mary to get Bess's composition published as a book.

Where There's Smoke, There's Rhoda
W: Martin Cohan. GS: Michael Bell. Rhoda moves in with Mary when a fire destroys her apartment.

You Certainly Are a Big Boy
W: Martin Cohan. GS: Bradford Dillman, John Rubinstein. Mary falls for an architect who is afraid of getting involved.

Some of My Best Friends Are Rhoda
W: Steve Pritzker. D: Peter Baldwin. GS: Mary Frann. Mary's new friend turns out to be prejudiced.

His Two Right Arms
W: Allan Burns. GS: Bill Daily. Mary tries to make an incompetent politician look intelligent when he is scheduled to appear on a news talk show.

The Good Time News
W: Allan Burns & James L. Brooks. D: Hal Cooper. GS: Robert Hogan. Mary is chosen to make the news show become more entertaining.

What Is Mary Richards Really Like?
W: Susan Silver. D: Jerry Belson. GS: Peter Haskell. Mary dates the newspaper columnist who is writing an article about her.

Who's in Charge?
W: Martin Cohan. Lou is promoted to station manager.

Enter Rhoda's Parents
W: Martin Cohan. GS: Nancy Walker, Harold Gould. Rhoda's parents come for a visit.

It's Whether You Win or Lose
W: Martin Donovan. Mary gets the staff together for a poker game, unaware that Murray is a compulsive gambler.

Rhoda the Beautiful
W: Treva Silverman. Rhoda is chosen as a candidate for the beauty contest her store is holding.

Just Around the Corner
W: Martin Cohan. GS: Bill Quinn, Nanette Fabray. Mary's parents move to town to be near her.

Farmer Ted and the News
W: Allan Burns. Ted appears in some local TV commercials to earn extra money.

But Seriously, Folks
W: Phil Mishkin. D: Peter Baldwin. GS: Jerry Van Dyke. Mary tries to help a comedy writer get a job in the newsroom.

Have I Found a Guy for You
W: Charlotte Brown. D: Hal Cooper. GS: Bert Convy, Beth Howland. Mary becomes involved when her married friends separate and he finds he is in love with Mary.

You've Got a Friend
W: Steve Pritzker.   D: Jerry Belson.
GS: Nanette Fabray, Bill Quinn. Mary
tries to find her father a friend, so she
picks Lou.

It Was Fascination, I Know
W: Ed Weinberger. GS: Gerald Miche-
naud. Bess's boyfriend dumps her for
Mary.

Operation: Lou
W: Martin Cohan. GS: Florida Friebus. Ted drives Lou crazy when he
visits him in the hospital.

*Rhoda Morgenstern: Minneapolis to
New York*
W: Treva Silverman. GS: Robert Cas-
per. Rhoda plans to move back to
New York so Mary plans a surprise
party for her.

*The Courtship of Mary's Father's
Daughter*
W: Treva Silverman.   GS: Gordon
Jump, Michael Tolan, Steve Franken.
Mary's old boyfriend Dan invites her
to his engagement party, which causes
the end of his future marriage.

Lou's Place
W: Martin Cohan. GS: Dick Balduzzi.
Lou and Ted buy a bar but almost lose
their shirts.

My Brother's Keeper
W: Dick Clair & Jenna McMahon. GS:
Robert Morse. Phyllis tries to get her
brother interested in Mary, unaware
that he is gay.

The Georgette Story
W: Ed Weinberger. D: Peter Baldwin.
Mary tries to convince Georgette that
Ted is taking her for granted.

Romeo and Mary
W: Ed Weinberger. GS: Arnold Margolin. Mary dates a crazy man who
tries to get her to marry him.

*What Do You Say When the Boss Says,
I Love You?*
W: Elias Davis & David Pollock. GS:

Lois Nettleton. Lou thinks the new
woman station manager is in love with
him.

Murray Faces Life
W: Martin Cohan.   Murray gets depressed because he thinks he hasn't
done anything worthy in his life.

Remembrance of Things Past
W: Dick Clair & Jenna McMahon. GS:
Joseph Campanella. Mary's old boy-
friend returns for a visit.

Put On a Happy Face
W: Marilyn S. Miller & Monica Mc-
Gowan.   GS: Art Gilmore, Steve
Franken. Mary finds that everything
she does turns out wrong, right when
she is about to win an award for the
show she produced.

*Mary Richards and the Incredible
Plant Lady*
W: Martin Cohan. D: John Chulau.
GS: Louise Lasser, Henry Corden,
Robert Karvelas, Craig Nelson. Rhoda
borrows some money from Mary to go
into the plant business.

The Lars Affair
W: Ed Weinberger. Phyllis's husband
Lars is having an affair with Sue Ann.

Angels in the Snow
W: Monica McGowan & Marilyn S.
Miller. GS: Peter Strauss. Mary dates
a younger man which causes her to
feel old.

Rhoda's Sister Gets Married
W: Ed Weinberger. GS: Nancy Walker,
Harold Gould, Brett Somers. Rhoda
and Mary go to New York to attend
Rhoda's sister's wedding.

The Lou and Edie Story
W: Treva Silverman.   GS: Darrell
Zwerling. Lou and his wife Edie
visit a marriage counselor.

Hi There, Sports Fans
W: Jerry Mayer. DS: Dick Gautier.
Lou gives Mary the job of firing the
old sports announcer and hiring a new
one.

Father's Day
W: Ed Weinberger. GS: Liam Dunn, John Holland. Ted's father, who left home many years ago, comes for a visit.

Son of But Seriously, Folks
W: Phil Mishkin. GS: Jerry Van Dyke, Mark Gordon. Mary's comedy writing boyfriend gets a job in the newsroom.

Lou's First Date
W: Ed Weinberger & Stan Daniels. Mary tries to find Lou a date for an important banquet.

Love Blooms at Hemples
W: Sybil Adelman & Barbara Gallagher. GS: William Burns. Rhoda falls in love with the owner of the store she works in.

The Dinner Party
W: Ed Weinberger. GS: Henry Winkler, Irene Tedrow. Mary invites a congresswoman over to her apartment for a dinner party.

Just Friends
W: William Wood. D. Nancy Walker. Mary tries to get Lou and Edie back together.

We Want Baxter
W: David Lloyd. Phyllis gets Ted to run for City Council.

I Gave at the Office
W: Don Reo & Allan Katz. GS: Bruce Boxleitner, Tammi Bula. Mary hires Murray's daughter to help out in the office.

Almost a Nun's Story
W: Ed Weinberger & Stan Daniels. GS: Gail Strickland. Georgette plans to become a nun when she sees Ted kissing another woman.

Happy Birthday Lou
W: David Lloyd. D: Buddy Tyne. Mary plans to give Lou a surprise party for his birthday, even though he says he doesn't want one.

WJM Tries Harder
W: Karyl Geld. GS: Anthony Eisley, Ned Wertimer, Regis Cordic. Mary spies on the competition when she dates the anchorman from a competing station.

Cottage for Sale
W: George Atkins. Phyllis tries to get Lou to sell his house.

The Co-Producers
W: David Pollock & Elias Davis. Mary finds that she is the producer on a show starring Ted and Sue Ann.

Best of Enemies
W: Marilyn Miller & Monica McGowan (Johnson). Rhoda and Mary have a fight, which might end their friendship.

Better Late . . . That's a Pun . . . Than Never
W: Treva Silverman. D: John Chulay. Mary is almost fired when Ted reads one of her joke obituaries, instead of a real one on the air.

Ted Baxter Meets Walter Cronkite
W: Ed Weinberger. GS: Walter Cronkite. Ted finally gets to meet Walter Cronkite, but not the way he would have liked.

Lou's Second Date
W: Ed Weinberger. D: Jerry London. Lou and Rhoda go out on a date.

Two Wrongs Don't Make a Writer
W: David Lloyd. D: Nancy Walker. GS: Shirley O'Hara. Ted decides he wants to join the same creative writing class that Mary is attending.

I Was Single for WJM
W: Treva Silverman. D: Mel Ferber. GS: Penny Marshall, Arlene Golonka. Mary decides to produce a show from a singles bar.

Will Mary Richards Go to Jail?
W: Ed Weinberger & Stan Daniels. GS: Jimmy Randolph, Barbara Colby. Mary goes to jail when she refuses to reveal a news source.

Not Just Another Pretty Face
W: Ed Weinberger & Stan Daniels.
GS: Robert Wolders. Mary dates a
man just for his looks.

You Sometimes Hurt the One You Hate
W: David Lloyd. D: Jackie Cooper.
Lou almost kills Ted when he throws
him out of the office, causing him to
be extra nice to Ted.

Lou and That Woman
W: David Lloyd. GS: Sheree North.
Lou falls for a lounge singer.

The Outsider
W: Jack Winter. D: Peter Bonerz. GS:
Richard Masur. The staff becomes upset when Lou hires a consultant who
tells them how they should be doing
their jobs.

What Are Friends For?
W: Treva Silverman. GS: Barbara Barrie. Murray considers having an affair
with a woman he met at Mary's party.

A New Sue Ann
W: David Lloyd. GS: Linda Kelsey,
Ron Rifkin. Sue Ann tries to get rid
of the beautiful girl who has taken
over her show.

Not a Christmas Story
W: Ed Weinberger & Stan Daniels. D:
John Chulay. The staff are invited to
Sue Ann's Christmas party, in Novem-
ber.

I Love a Piano
W: Treva Silverman. GS: Barbara Barrie. Murray once again is tempted to
have an affair with the same woman
as before.

A Boy's Best Friend
W: David Lloyd. D: Mary Tyler
Moore. Ted becomes upset when his
mother decides to live with her boyfriend rather than marry him.

Menage-a-Phyllis
W: Treva Silverman. GS: John Saxon.
Mary and Phyllis date the same man,
but for different reasons.

A Son for Murray
W: Ed Weinberger & Stan Daniels.
Murray wants to have a son, but Marie
refuses to have another child.

Neighbors
W: Ziggy Steinberg. D: Jim Burrows.
GS: Clifford David. Lou moves into
Rhoda's old apartment.

A Girl Like Mary
W: Ann Gibbs & Joel Kimmel. GS:
Rosalind Cash. Lou decides to hire a
woman newscaster, prompting Mary
and Sue Ann to apply for the job.

An Affair to Forget
W: Ed Weinberger & Stan Daniels.
Ted starts a rumor that he and Mary
are dating.

Mary Richards: Producer
W: David Lloyd. D: Norman Campbell. GS: Anthony Holland. Mary
convinces Lou to make her the producer of the news.

The System
W: Ed Weinberger & Stan Daniels.
Ted invents a system for betting on
football games.

Phyllis Whips Inflation
W: Ed Weinberger & Stan Daniels.
GS: Doris Roberts. Phyllis tries to
find a job when her husband takes
away her credit cards.

The Shame of the Cities
W: Michael Elias. GS: Sheree North,
Robert Emhardt. Lou tries to find a
scandal in a politician's office.

Marriage Minneapolis Style
W: Pamela Russell. GS: Eileen Mc-
Donough. Ted announces his engage-
ment to Georgette while on the air.

You Try to Be a Nice Guy
W: David Lloyd. D: Marge Mullen.
GS: Fred Grandy. Lou refuses to ac-
cept an award because it means he is

over the hill.

You Can't Lose Them All
GS: Barbara Colby. Mary helps the hooker she met while in jail go straight.

Ted Baxter's Famous Broadcasters School
W: Michael Zinberg. GS: Bernie Kopell, Leonard Frey, Norman Bartold. Ted is tricked by a con man to invest in a broadcasting school.

Anybody Who Hates Kids and Dogs
W: Jerry Mayer. GS: Lawrence Luckinbill, Lee H. Montgomery, Mabel Albertson. Mary finds that she hates her new boyfriend's obnoxious son.

Edie Gets Married
W: Bob Ellison. GS: Brad Trumbull, Nora Heflin. Lou finds that he is invited to Edie's wedding when she remarries.

Mary Moves Out
W: David Lloyd. GS: Jim Curry, Claude Stroud. Mary moves into an apartment building when she feels she is getting into a rut.

Mary's Father
W: Earl Pomerantz. GS: Ed Flanders. Mary thinks a priest is planning to leave the church, for her.

Murray in Love
GS: Penny Marshall, Peter Hobbs, Mary Kay Place. Murray tries to tell Mary that he is in love with her.

Ted's Moment of Glory
W: Charles Lee & Gig Henry. GS: Richard Balin. Ted auditions and wins a job as the host of a game show.

Mary's Aunt
W: David Lloyd. GS: Eileen Heckart. Lou finds himself falling for Mary's newspaper journalist aunt.

Chuckles Bites the Dust
W: David Lloyd. D: Joan Darling. GS: John Harkins. A dark satire about

death. Chuckles the Clown dies and everyone finds that they can't stop making jokes.

Mary's Delinquent
W: Mary Kay Place & Valerie Curtin. GS: Mackenzie Phillips, Tamu. Mary and Sue Ann volunteer to help two delinquent girls.

Ted's Wedding
W: David Lloyd. GS: John Ritter. Ted and Georgette get married in Mary's apartment.

Lou Douses an Old Flame
W: David Lloyd. GS: Beverly Garland. Lou's old girlfriend, the one who dumped him during the war, makes a date to see him.

Mary Richards Falls in Love
W: Ed Weinberger & Stan Daniels. GS: David Groh, Ted Bessell. Mary calls Rhoda to tell her that she has finally found the right man at last.

Ted's Tax Return
W: Bob Ellison. D: Marge Mullen. GS: Paul Lichtman. Ted is being audited for making too many deductions.

The Happy Homemaker Takes Lou Home
W: David Lloyd. D: Jim Burrows. GS: Titos Vandis, Wynn Irwin. Lou is tricked into having dinner at Sue Ann's house.

One Boyfriend Too Many
W: David Lloyd. GS: Ted Bessell, Michael Tolan. Mary is torn between her current boyfriend Joe , or her old boyfriend Dan when he returns to continue their relationship.

What Do You Want to Do When You Produce?
W: Shelley Nelbert & Craig Alan Hafner. Murray becomes the producer of Sue Ann's show.

Not with My Wife I Don't
W: Bob Ellison. GS: Alan Manson.

Georgette and Ted plan to split up when she thinks that he doesn't love her any more.

Lou Proposes
W: David Lloyd. GS: Eileen Heckart. Lou asks Mary's Aunt Flo to marry him.

Murray Can't Lose
W: David Lloyd. Murray is depressed because he has never won a Teddy award.

Ted's Temptation
W: Bob Ellison. D: Harry Mastogeorge. GS: Trisha Noble. While at a convention in Hollywood, a beautiful reporter tries to seduce Ted.

Look at Us, We're Walking
W: David Lloyd. GS: David Ogden Stiers. Mary and Lou quit when they don't get their raises.

The Critic
W: David Lloyd. D: Martin Cohan. GS: Eric Braeden. The station manager hires a famous critic to boost the ratings.

Lou's Army Reunion
W: Bob Ellison. GS: Alex Rocco, Dort Clark. Lou's Army buddy tries to get Mary to spend the night with him.

The Ted and Georgette Show
W: David Lloyd. GS: Alex Henteloff, David Ogden Stiers. Ted and Georgette host their own television talk show, until Georgette decides she wants to quit.

Sue Ann Gets the Axe
W: Bob Ellison. GS: Linden Chiles.

Sue Ann's show is cancelled, but she refuses to give in when the station tries to get her to break her contract.

Hail the Conquering Gordy
W: Earl Pomerantz. GS: David White. Gordy returns to the station. He is now the host of a talk show in New York. Ted tries to get Gordy to hire him as a co-host.

Mary and the Sexagenarian
W: David Lloyd. GS: Lew Ayres. Mary dates Murray's father.

Murray Ghosts for Ted
W: David Lloyd. GS: Helen Hunt. Murray writes an article for Ted in return for $200. When the article is considered by another magazine for publication, Ted plans to keep all of the credit and the $2500 they are paying for himself.

Mary's Three Husbands
W: Bob Ellison. Murray, Ted & Lou each daydream about what it would be like being married to Mary.

Mary's Big Party
W: Bob Ellinson. GS: Johnny Carson, Irene Tedrow. Mary gives a party with Johnny Carson as her special guest, when suddenly there is a blackout and everyone is in the dark.

Lou Dates Mary
W: David Lloyd. Lou and Mary decide to date each other.

The Last Show
W: James L. Brooks & Allan Burns. GS: Vincent Gardenia. The new station manager fires everyone but Ted in order to boost the ratings.

M*A*S*H

On the air 9/17/72, off 9/19/83. CBS. Color Film. 251 episodes. Broadcast: Sept 1972-Sept 1973 Sun 8-8:30; Sept 1973-Sept 1974 Sat 8:30-9; Sept 1974-Sept 1975 Tue 8:30-9; Sept 1975-Nov 1975 Fri 8:30-9; Dec 1975-Jan 1978 Tue

Gary Burghoff (left) and Harry Morgan in M*A*S*H.

9-9:30; Jan 1978-Sept 1983 Mon 9-9:30. Producer: Burt Metcalfe. Prod Co/ Synd: 20th Century Fox TV.

CAST: Hawkeye (played by Alan Alda), Trapper John (Wayne Rogers), Hot Lips (Loretta Swit), Frank Burns (Larry Linville), Radar (Gary Burghoff), Henry Blake (McLean Stevenson), Klinger (Jamie Farr), Col. Potter (Harry Morgan), BJ (Mike Farrell), Major Winchester (David Ogden Stiers), Dr. Freedman (Allan Arbus), Col. Flagg (Edward Winter).

WRITERS: Larry Gelbart, Larry Marks, Burt Styler, Bob Klane, Hal Dresner, Bruce Shelly, Dave Ketchum, Jerry Mayer, Alan Alda, Carl Kleinschmitt, Jim Fritzell, Everett Greenbaum, Sid Dorfman. DIRECTORS: Hy Averback, F. W. Swackhamer, Alan Alda, Jackie Cooper, William Wiard, Don Weis, Gene Reynolds, Burt Metcalfe, Charles S. Dubin.

The crazy adventures of a group of Army doctors in Korea during the 1950s. The series featured a wide range of personalities ranging from the sarcastic Hawkeye to the timid Radar, all working as medics during the Korean War. A very popular series on the network and one of the biggest hits in syndication for the past few years. The series is based on the 1970 movie of the same name.

Pilot Episode
W: Larry Gelbart. D: Gene Reynolds. The story of some Army doctors in Korea who alternate between surgery and making each other laugh away their fears.

Henry Please Come Home
W: Laurence Marks. D: William Wiard. When Henry is transferred to Tokyo, Hawkeye and the others try to find a way of getting him back.

To Market, to Market
W: Burt Styler. D: Michael O'Herlihy. GS: Robert Ito, Jack Soo. Hawkeye trades Henry's antique desk to a black-marketer for a shipment of hydrocortisone.

Germ Warfare
W: Larry Gelbart. D: Terry Becker. Hawkeye suspects that Frank has hepatitis.

The Moose
W: Laurence Marks. D: Hy Averback. The doctors try to save a Korean girl who was sold to a soldier as a slave.

I Hate a Mystery
W: Hal Dresner. D: Hy Averback. Hawkeye tries to discover which one of the camp personnel is a thief.

Chief Surgeon Who?
W: Larry Gelbart. D: E.W. Swackhamer. GS: Sorrell Booke. Frank complains when Hawkeye is appointed chief surgeon and not he.

Requiem for a Lightweight
W: Bob Klane. D: Hy Averback. GS: Marcia Strassman. Trapper enters the inter-camp boxing tournament in order to save a beautiful nurse from being transferred.

Cowboy
W: Bob Klane. D: Don Weis. Henry refuses to let a wounded helicopter pilot named Cowboy go home.

Yankee Doodle Doctor
W: Laurence Marks. D: Lee Phillips. GS: Ed Flanders. The doctors make their own film in protest to the film that was made about them by a general.

Bananas, Crackers and Nuts [After Me the Deluge]
W: Burt Styler. D: Bruce Bilson. Hawkeye pretends that he is nuts when he doesn't get an R&R pass.

Edwina
W: Hal Dresner. D: James Sheldon. GS: Arlene Golonka. The nurses try to find a boyfriend for a depressed nurse.

Dear Dad
W: Larry Gelbart. D: Gene Reynolds. Hawkeye writes to his father and tells him what happened to him during Christmas.

Love Story
W: Laurence Marks. D: Earl Bellamy. The doctors try to help Radar when he gets a Dear John letter.

Tuttle
W: Bruce Shelly & Dave Ketchum. D: William Wiard. Hawkeye, Trapper and Radar create a phony captain so they can donate his salary to an orphanage.

The Ringbanger
W: Jerry Mayer. D: Jackie Cooper. GS: Leslie Nielsen. Hawkeye and his friends try to get a general who always loses too many men in battle retired.

Dear Dad . . . Again
W: Sheldon Keller & Larry Gelbart. D: Jackie Cooper. Hawkeye writes another letter to his father to tell him about the crazy things that have happened to him.

Sometimes You Hear the Bullet
W: Carl Kleinschmitt. D: William Wiard. GS: James Callahan, Ronny Howard. Hawkeye sends an underaged kid back home, and mourns for his dead friend.

The Longjohn Flap
W: Alan Alda. D: William Wiard. During a cold spell, Hawkeye gets a pair of longjohns in the mail causing everyone else to become jealous.

Major Fred C. Dobbs
W: Sid Dorfman. D: Don Weis. Hawkeye and Trapper try to prevent Frank from leaving.

Sticky Wicket
W: Richard Baer, Laurence Marks & Larry Gelbart. D: Don Weis. Hawkeye has a fight with Frank about his failures and then learns that one of his own patients is dying.

The Army-Navy Game
W: Sid Dorfman & McLean Stevenson. D: Gene Reynolds. An unexploded bomb upsets the doctors' chances of listening to the Army-Navy game.

Ceasefire
W: Laurence Marks & Larry Gelbart. D: Earl Bellamy. The doctors prepare to go home when a ceasefire is declared.

Showtime
W: Robert Klane & Larry Gelbart. D: Jackie Cooper. GS: Joey Foreman. An entertainer performs a show in the compound while doctors perform surgery.

Divided We Stand
W: Larry Gelbart. D: Jackie Cooper. The doctors try to prevent themselves from being reassigned to other units.

Radar's Report
W: Sheldon Keller & Laurence Marks. D: Jackie Cooper. GS: Joan Van Ark. Radar describes what goes on in a typical week at the camp.

Five O'Clock Charlie
W: Keith Walker, Larry Gelbart & Laurence Marks. The camp is constantly attacked by a bumbling Korean pilot.

For the Good of the Outfit
W: Jerry Mayer. D: Jackie Cooper. GS: Frank Aletter. Hawkeye and Trapper become upset when a village full of people is shelled by accident.

Dr. Pierce and Mr. Hyde
W: Alan Alda & Robert Klane. D: Jackie Cooper. Hawkeye goes berserk after working for three days straight.

L.I.P. (Local Indigenous Personnel)
W: Carl Kleinschmitt. D: William Wiard. Hawkeye tries to help a soldier who wants to marry a Korean girl.

Kim
W: Marc Mandel, Larry Gelbart & Laurence Marks. D: William Wiard. Trapper and the others fall in love with a small Korean boy.

The Trial of Henry Blake
W: McLean Stevenson, Larry Gelbart & Laurence Marks. D: Don Weis. Margaret and Frank challenge Henry's ability to command and report him to headquarters.

Dear Dad Three
W: Larry Gelbart & Laurence Marks. D: Don Weis. Hawkeye writes to his father again about the funny things that have happened to him.

The Sniper
W: Richard M. Powell. D: Jackie Cooper. GS: Teri Garr. The camp is attacked by a young sniper who thinks the camp is Army Headquarters.

Carry on, Hawkeye
W: Bernard Dilbert. D: Jackie Cooper. When the camp comes down with the flu, Hawkeye is the only one who is still able to work.

The Incubator
W: Larry Gelbart & Laurence Marks. D: Jackie Cooper. GS: Vic Tayback. Hawkeye and Trapper go all the way to headquarters in order to get an incubator for the camp.

Deal Me Out
W: Larry Gelbart & Laurence Marks. D: Jackie Cooper. GS: Pat Morita, John Ritter. The doctors' poker game is constantly being interrupted by emergencies.

Hot Lips and Empty Arms
W: Linda Bloodworth & Mary Kay

Place. D: Jackie Cooper. Margaret decides to get herself transferred.

Officers Only
W: Ed Jurist, D: Jackie Cooper. The camp gets an officers' club when Hawkeye and Trapper save a general's son.

Henry in Love
W: Larry Gelbart & Laurence Marks. D: Don Weis. While in Tokyo, Henry falls in love with a young American girl.

For Want of a Boot
W: Sheldon Keller. D: Don Weis. GS: Michael Lerner. Hawkeye tries to get himself a new pair of boots.

Operation Noselift
W: Erik Tarloff & Paul Richards. D: Hy Averback. Hawkeye and Trapper try to help a soldier who wants a nosejob.

The Chosan People
W: Laurence Marks, Sheldon Keller, Larry Gelbart, Gerry Renert & Jeff Wilhelm. D: Jackie Cooper. The doctors try to help a dispossessed Korean family and a girl who is carrying an American soldier's baby.

As You Were
W: Larry Gelbart, Gene Reynolds & Laurence Marks. D: Hy Averback. After a few days with no wounded, the camp is once again jumping with hurt soldiers.

Crisis
W: Larry Gelbart & Laurence Marks. D: Don Weis. The camp is in trouble when their supplies are running out and they have no way of replacing them.

George
W: John Regier & Gary Markowitz. D: Gene Reynolds. Hawkeye tries to prevent Frank from having a gay soldier thrown out of the Army.

Mail Call
W: Larry Gelbart & Laurence Marks. D: Alan Alda. When the mail arrives, everyone goes into a frenzy.

A Smattering of Intelligence
W: Larry Gelbart & Laurence Marks. D: Larry Gelbart. GS: Edward Winter. The camp is caught in the middle when two spies begin to investigate each other.

Rainbow Bridge
W: Larry Gelbart & Laurence Marks. D: Hy Averback. Hawkeye and Trapper's R&R is interrupted by more wounded.

Life with Father
W: Everett Greenbaum & Jim Fritzell. D: Hy Averback. Henry believes his wife may be fooling around, and the Father finds that he has to perform a circumcision.

Springtime
W: Linda Bloodworth & Mary Kay Place. D: Don Weis. Radar falls in love, and Klinger gets married to his girlfriend by short-wave radio.

Iron Guts Kelly
W: Larry Gelbart & Sid Dorfman. D: Don Weis. GS: James Gregory, Keene Curtis. When a general dies while in bed with Margaret, his aide tries to make it look as if he died in battle.

Payday
W: John Regier & Gary Markowitz. D: Hy Averback. When payday arrives, the camp decides how they are going to spend their money.

O.R.
W: Larry Gelbart & Laurence Marks. D: Gene Reynolds. The operating room is kept busy all day with more wounded than the doctors know what to do with.

Officer of the Day
W: Laurence Marks. D: Hy Averback. Frank and Margaret are in charge of

the camp while Henry is on vacation in Seoul.

The General Flipped at Dawn
W: Everett Greenbaum & Jim Fritzell. D: Larry Gelbart. A new area commander visits the camp and the doctors believe that he is crazy.

There Is Nothing Like a Nurse
W: Larry Gelbart. D: Hy Averback. The nurses are evacuated, leaving Hawkeye and Trapper to entertain the camp.

Private Charles Lamb
W: Larry Gelbart & Sid Dorfman. D: Hy Averback. GS: Titos Vandis. Radar has a baby lamb shipped home so he won't become the main course at a Greek festival.

A Full Rich Day
W: John D. Hess. D: Gene Reynolds. Hawkeye tape records a letter to his father telling him what crazy things happened to him in O.R.

Checkup
W: Laurence Marks. D: Don Weis. Trapper believes that his ulcer will enable him to be transferred home.

Big Mac
W: Laurence Marks. D: Don Weis. GS: Graham Jarvis. The camp prepares for a visit from General MacArthur.

Alcoholics Unanimous
W: Everett Greenbaum & Jim Fritzell. D: Hy Averback. While Henry is away, Frank declares prohibition and orders all liquor to be destroyed.

House Arrest
W: Everett Greenbaum & Jim Fritzell. D: Hy Averback. Margaret is a witness when Hawkeye hits Frank.

Adam's Ribs
W: Laurence Marks. D: Gene Reynolds. Hawkeye calls Chicago to order some spare ribs when he gets fed up with the Army food.

Mad Dogs and Servicemen
W: Linda Bloodworth & Mary Kay Place. D: Hy Averback. The doctors search for the dog that bit Radar.

The Consultant
W: Larry Gelbart & Robert Klane. D: Gene Reynolds. GS: Robert Alda. An alcoholic doctor visits the camp and prepares to perform a new type of surgery, but gets too drunk to operate.

White Gold
W: Larry Gelbart & Simon Muntner. D: Hy Averback. Colonel Flagg drives the doctors crazy, so in return they perform an appendectomy on him.

Bombed
W: Everett Greenbaum & Jim Fritzell. D: Hy Averback. Frank proposes to Margaret when Trapper tries to make him jealous.

Love and Marriage
W: Arthur Julian. D: Lee Phillips. Hawkeye and Trapper prevent a soldier from marrying a prostitute and help another soldier rejoin his pregnant wife.

Aid Station
W: Larry Gelbart & Simon Muntner. D: William Jurgenson. Hawkeye and Margaret work at an aid station which is under constant fire.

Bulletin Board
W: Larry Gelbart. D: Alan Alda. The camp bulletin board lists the camp activities which take place in this episode, which include a movie and a picnic.

Abyssinia, Henry
W: Everett Greenbaum & Jim Fritzell. D: Larry Gelbart. Henry is killed while on his way back home.

Change of Command
W: Everett Greenbaum & Jim Fritzell. D: Gene Reynolds. Colonel Potter takes over command of the camp.

It Happened One Night
W: Larry Gelbart, Gene Reynolds & Simon Muntner. D: Gene Reynolds. A chain of bad events takes place all in one night.

Of Moose and Men
W: Jay Folb. D: John Erman. GS: Tim O'Conner. Hawkeye fights with a strict Army colonel and Frank looks for Korean saboteurs.

Welcome to Korea
W: Larry Gelbart, Everett Greenbaum & Jim Fritzell. D: Gene Reynolds. Hawkeye jumps camp to say goodbye to Trapper, and the camp welcomes BJ to the staff. [This was originally an hour episode, but it is now shown in two parts.]

Dear Mildred
W: Everett Greenbaum & Jim Fritzell. D: Alan Alda. Radar saves a horse and presents it to the colonel as a present.

The Late Captain Pierce
W: Glen & Les Charles. D: Alan Alda. GS: Richard Masur. Hawkeye has to try to call home to tell his father he is still alive, when he learns that the Army has declared him dead.

Smilin' Jack
W: Larry Gelbart & Simon Muntner. D: Charles S. Dubin. GS: Robert Hogan. The doctors meet a chopper pilot who loves his job so much he doesn't want to leave.

Dear Peggy
W: Everett Greenbaum & Jim Fritzell. D: Burt Metcalfe. BJ writes a letter to his wife to tell her of the crazy things that go on in the camp.

Hey, Doc
W: Rick Mittleman. D: William Jurgenson. The camp gets a tank to frighten away snipers.

The Kids
W: Everett Greenbaum & Jim Fritzell. D: Alan Alda. The doctors entertain a group of orphans who were bombed out of their home.

The Bus
W: John D. Hess. D: Gene Reynolds. GS: Soon Teck Oh. The doctors become stuck in the wilderness when Radar gets lost and stalls the bus.

Quo Vadis, Captain Chandler?
W: Burt Prelutsky. D: Larry Gelbart. GS: Edward Winter, Allan Arbus, Alan Fudge. A soldier claims he is Jesus; the doctors try to get him some help before Colonel Flagg can arrest him.

Soldier of the Month
W: Linda Bloodworth. D: Gene Reynolds. Frank makes out his will when he believes he is going to die.

Dear Ma
W: Everett Greenbaum & Jim Fritzell. D: Alan Alda. Radar writes home to his mother about what happened that day in the camp.

Deluge
W: Larry Gelbart & Simon Muntner. D: William Jurgenson. The camp is flooded with wounded, a fire starts in the camp, and a sudden rainstorm ruins the whole day.

The Gun
W: Larry Gelbart & Gene Reynolds. D: Burt Metcalfe. Hawkeye and BJ try to trick Frank into returning a gun he stole from a patient.

Mail Call Again
W: Everett Greenbaum & Jim Fritzell. D: George Tyne. The delivery of some more mail tells Potter that he is going to be a grandfather, and that Frank's wife is planning to get a divorce.

The Price of Tomato Juice
W: Larry Gelbart & Gene Reynolds. D: Gene Reynolds. Radar tries to get some tomato juice for Colonel Potter.

Hawkeye
W: Larry Gelbart & Simon Muntner.

D: Larry Gelbart.   GS: Phillip Ahn. Hawkeye takes refuge with a Korean family when he is hurt in a jeep accident and finds that he has to keep himself awake when he believes he has a concussion.

Some 38th Parallels
W: John Regier & Gary Markowitz. D: Burt Metcalfe.   Frank tries to sell the camp's garbage.

Der Tag
W: Everett Greenbaum & Jim Fritzell. D: Gene Reynolds.   Potter tries to get the other doctors to be more friendly towards Frank.

The Novocaine Mutiny
W: Burt Prelutsky. D: Harry Morgan. Frank piles a whole list of charges against Hawkeye while Potter is away and he is left in charge.

The More I See You
W: Larry Gelbart & Gene Reynolds. D: Gene Reynolds. GS: Blythe Danner.   Hawkeye is reunited with his old girlfriend.

The Interview
W & D: Larry Gelbart. GS: Clete Roberts.   The doctors are interviewed by a reporter.

Bug Out
W: Everett Greenbaum & Jim Fritzell. D: Gene Reynolds.   The doctors prepare to move to a new location after the enemy starts moving closer to the camp.   [This was originally an hour episode which is now shown in two parts.]

Margaret's Engagement
W: Gary Markowitz.   D: Alan Alda. Margaret announces that she has just become engaged to be married.

Hawkeye's Nightmare
W: Burt Prelutsky. D: Burt Metcalfe. Hawkeye has a visit from a psychiatrist when he starts sleepwalking and having bad dreams.

Lt. Radar O'Reilly
W: Everett Greenbaum & Jim Fritzell. D: Alan Rafkin.   Radar is promoted to lieutenant, but finds he liked it better when he was a corporal.

Out of Sight, Out of Mind
W: Ken Levine & David Isaacs.   D: Gene Reynolds. GS: Tom Sullivan. Hawkeye is nearly blinded when a stove blows up in his face.

The General's Practitioner
W: Burt Prelutsky. D: Alan Rafkin. GS: Leonard Stone, Edward Binns. Hawkeye is being considered for the job of personal doctor to a general.

The Abduction of Margaret Houlihan
W: Allan Katz, Don Reo & Gene Reynolds. D: Gene Reynolds. Everyone fears that Margaret was captured by the enemy.

The Nurses
W: Linda Bloodworth. D: Joan Darling. GS: Linda Kelsey. Hawkeye and BJ sneak one of the nurses and her visiting husband into Margaret's tent so they can be alone.

Dear Sigmund
W & D: Alan Alda. GS: Allan Arbus. Dr. Freedman, feeling depressed, comes to the camp to cheer himself up.

The Colonel's Horse
W: Everett Greenbaum & Jim Fritzell. D: Burt Metcalfe.   When the colonel leaves on vacation to Tokyo, his horse gets sick, and Hot Lips has her appendix removed.

Mulcahy's War
W: Richard Cogan.   D George Tyne. Mulcahy and Radar visit an aid station where he performs an emergency operation.

Hawkeye Get Your Gun
W: Gene Reynolds & Jay Folb. D: William Jurgenson. Hawkeye and Potter are ambushed on their way back from visiting a hospital.

The Korean Surgeon
W: Bill Idelson. D: Gene Reynolds.
BJ and Hawkeye try to pass off a North Korean surgeon who arrives with some wounded as a South Korean so they won't have any trouble from Frank.

Exorcism
W: Gene Reynolds & Jay Folb. D: Alan Alda. When a Korean spirit post is removed, bad things begin to happen until a Korean version of a witch doctor performs an exorcism. At least, this is what an old Korean man who refused surgery until the ceremony was performed believes.

End Run
W: John D. Hess. D: Harry Morgan. Radar tries to help a black football player who lost his leg want to live.

Ping Pong
W: Sid Dorfman. D: William Jurgenson. The doctors help a wounded ping pong player marry his girlfriend.

The Most Unforgettable Characters
W: Ken Levine & David Isaacs. D: Burt Metcalfe. Radar writes a story about his impressions of the camp and its staff.

Souvenirs
W: Burt Prelutsky & Reinhold Weege. D: Joshua Shelley. The doctors try to stop a soldier who pays children to venture into mine fields to collect war souvenirs which he sells to the soldiers.

Margaret's Marriage
W: Everett Greenbaum & Jim Fritzell. D: Gene Reynolds. Margaret gets married and goes off to Tokyo on her honeymoon.

38 Across
W: Everett Greenbaum & Jim Fritzell. D: Burt Metcalfe. GS: Oliver Clark, Dick O'Neil. Hawkeye calls his old Army friend up to ask him for an answer to a crossword puzzle.

Hanky Panky
W & D: Gene Reynolds. BJ spends the night with a nurse who was dumped by her boyfriend, in order to console her.

Hepatitis
W & D: Alan Alda. Father Mulcahy comes down with hepatitis and Hawkeye suffers a backache.

Movie Tonight
W: Gene Reynolds, Don Reo, Allan Katz & Jay Folb. D: Burt Metcalfe. The camp spend the night watching a movie, but when the movie keeps breaking they begin to entertain each other.

Post Op
W: Ken Levine, David Isaacs, Gene Reynolds & Jay Folb. D: Gene Reynolds. Everyone in camp has to donate blood when the camp supply runs dry.

Fade Out, Fade In
W: Everett Greenbaum & Jim Fritzell. D: Hy Averback. When Frank goes berserk in Tokyo, Potter requests a replacement surgeon, which brings Major Winchester to the camp under protest. [This was originally an hour episode which is now run as two parts.]

Last Laugh
W: Everett Greenbaum & Jim Fritzell. D: Don Weis. GS: James Cromwell. BJ and his old friend named Bardonaro play an endless supply of practical jokes on each other.

Fallen Idol
W & D: Alan Alda. Radar loses his respect for Hawkeye after he performs an emergency operation on him.

Images
W: Burt Prelutsky. D: Burt Metcalfe. Radar decides to get a tattoo in order to make himself more attractive to women.

War of Nerves
W & D: Alan Alda. The camp build a bonfire to release all of their pent up emotions.

The Winchester Tapes
W: Everett Greenbaum & Jim Fritzell. D: Burt Metcalfe. Winchester tape records a letter to his parents back home, asking them to get him transferred out of Korea.

The Light That Failed
W: Burt Prelutsky. D: Charles S. Dubin. BJ gets a mystery book which everyone wants to read, but the only problem is the last page of the book is missing so nobody can figure out just how it ends.

Tea and Empathy
W: Bill Idelson. D: Don Weis. Klinger and Mulcahy go out in search of some needed penicillin.

The Grim Reaper
W: Burt Prelutsky. D: George Tyne. GS: Charles Aidman. Hawkeye finds himself in trouble when he roughs up a colonel who loves to predict the number of wounded before each battle takes place.

*The M*A*S*H Olympics*
W: Ken Levine & David Isaacs. D: Don Weis. GS: Mike Henry. Potter decides to hold an olympics in order to get everyone back in shape.

In Love and War
W & D: Alan Alda. Hawkeye falls in love with a Korean girl.

Change Day
W: Laurence Marks. D: Don Weis. Winchester plans to get rich when he learns that the Army is changing the color of its money.

Patent 4077
W: Ken Levine & David Isaacs. D: Harry Morgan. Hawkeye and BJ get a local jeweler to create a surgical clamp needed for a special operation.

The Smell of Music
W: Everett Greenbaum & Jim Fritzell. D: Stuart Miller. Hawkeye and BJ refuse to bathe until Winchester stops playing his annoying French horn.

Comrades in Arms [Part 1]
W: Alan Alda. D: Burt Metcalfe. Hawkeye and Hot Lips spend the night with each other when they are trapped in an old farmhouse when the shooting starts.

Comrades in Arms [Part 2]
W & D: Alan Alda. Hawkeye and Hot Lips return to camp when the shooting finally stops.

The Merchant of Korea
W: Ken Levine & David Isaacs. D: William Jurgenson. Winchester cleans out everyone when they let him join their poker game.

What's Up Doc?
W: Larry Balmagia. D: George Tyne. Hawkeye wants to use Radar's rabbit in order to see if Hot Lips is pregnant.

Potter's Retirement
W: Laurence Marks. D: William Jurgenson. Potter decides to retire when he is informed that headquarters has been receiving complaints about him.

Mail Call Three
W: Everett Greenbaum & Jim Fritzell. D: Charles S. Dubin. Hawkeye gets love letters which were meant for another Benjamin Pierce, and Radar learns that his mother has a boyfriend.

Dr. Winchester and Mr. Hyde
W: Ronny Graham, Ken Levine & David Isaacs. D: Charles S. Dubin. Winchester gets hooked on pep pills.

Major Topper
W: Allyn Freeman. D: Charles S. Dubin. When the morphine runs out, the doctors use some placebos.

Your Hit Parade
W: Ronny Graham. D: George Tyne.

GS: Ronny Graham. Radar plays disc jockey when a supply of records arrive at the camp.

Temporary Duty
W: Larry Balmagia. D: Burt Metcalfe. GS: George Lindsey. Hawkeye changes places with another doctor during a temporary reassignment of personnel.

Peace on Us
W: Ken Levine & David Isaacs. D: George Tyne. GS: Kevin Hagen. Hawkeye visits the Peace Conference in order to help them come to a conclusion.

BJ Papa San
W: Larry Balmagia. D: James Sheldon. BJ becomes a foster father to a Korean family.

Baby, It's Cold Outside
W: Gary David Goldberg. D: George Tyne. Winchester becomes the envy of everyone when the cold weather sets in, because he has received a polar suit from home.

Commander Pierce
W: Ronny Graham. D: Burt Metcalfe. Hawkeye becomes the temporary commander of the camp.

The Billfold Syndrome
W: Ken Levine & David Isaacs. D: Alan Alda. Charles refuses to talk to anyone when he is turned down for a medical position back home.

Lil
W: Sheldon Bull. D: Burt Metcalfe. GS: Carmen Mathews. Potter falls for a nurse who has the same interests and age as he. Radar tries to see that the relationship doesn't get too far.

They Call the Wind Korea
W: Ken Levine & David Isaacs. D: Charles S. Dubin. The camp prepares for a terrible windstorm.

Our Finest Hour [One Hour]
W: Ronny Graham, Larry Balmagia,

Ken Levine & David Isaacs. D: Burt Metcalfe. GS: Clete Roberts. The doctors and staff are interviewed by a reporter about their life in the camp. [This episode is in black and white.]

None Like It Hot
W: Ken Levine, David Isaacs & Johnny Bonaduce. D: Tony Mordente. The staff all have strange reactions to the sudden heat wave that hits the area.

Out of Gas
W: Tom Reeder. D: Mel Damski. Mulcahy and Charles deal with some blackmarketeers for some needed pentothal.

Major Ego
W: Larry Balmagia. D: Alan Alda. GS: Greg Mullavey. Charles suffers a swelled head when he saves a dying patient and begins to consider himself a hero.

Dear Comrade
W: Tom Reeder. D: Charles S. Dubin. Hawkeye and BJ discover that Winchester has a Korean servant who performs his every command.

An Eye for a Tooth
W: Ronny Graham. D: Charles S. Dubin. Mulcahy becomes upset when he is passed over for a promotion.

Point of View
W: Ken Levine & David Isaacs. D: Charles S. Dubin. In this episode the viewer sees everything from the point of view of a wounded soldier.

Preventive Medicine
W: Tom Reeder. D: Tony Mordente. GS: James Wainwright. Hawkeye tries to prevent a careless colonel from killing any more men in combat.

Dear Sis
W & D: Alan Alda. Mulcahy writes a letter to his sister the nun, explaining the depression that everyone gets right before the Christmas holiday.

The Price
W: Erik Tarloff. D: Charles S. Dubin.
The colonel's horse disappears and
Hawkeye tries to prevent a Korean
boy from being drafted into the Army.

Hot Lips Is Back in Town
W: Larry Balmagia & Bernard Dilbert.
D: Charles S. Dubin. Hot Lips celebrates her divorce, and Radar falls in
love with a nurse.

Inga
W & D: Alan Alda. GS: Mariette Hartley. Hawkeye falls for a visiting Swedish doctor.

The Young and the Restless
W: Mitch Markowitz. D: William Jurgenson. The doctors learn that they
are out of touch with all of the new
medical discoveries and procedures.

Ain't Love Grand
W: Ken Levine & David Isaacs. D:
Mike Farrell. Charles falls for a Korean
girl, and a nurse falls for Klinger.

C-A-V-E
W: Larry Balmagia & Ronny Graham.
D: William Jurgenson. The camp is
evacuated to a nearby cave, where
Hawkeye has to face up to his claus-
trophobia.

The Party
W: Alan Alda & Burt Metcalfe. D:
Burt Metcalfe. BJ plans a big party for
the staff's relatives back in the states.

Rally Round the Flagg, Boys
W: Mitch Markowitz. D: Harry Morgan. GS: Edward Winter. The nutty
Colonel Flagg accuses Hawkeye of
being a Communist sympathizer.

A Night at Rosie's
W: Ken Levine & David Isaacs. D:
Burt Metcalfe. GS: Keye Luke. The
staff spends the night getting drunk at
Rosie's bar.

Too Many Cooks
W: Dennis Koenig. D: Charles S. Dubin. GS: Ed Begley, Jr. The doctors
try to prevent a gourmet chef from returning to his combat unit when they
learn about his wonderful cooking.

Are You Now, Margaret?
W: Thad Mumford & Dan Wilcox. D:
Charles S. Dubin. GS: Lawrence Pressman. A congressional aide touring the
camp falls for Hot Lips.

Guerrilla My Dreams
W: Bob Colleary. D: Alan Alda.
Hawkeye tries to treat a wounded Korean woman while she is being inter-
rogated by an ROK officer who wants
to learn about guerrilla activities.

Period of Adjustment
W: Jim Mulligan & John Rappaport.
D: Charles S. Dubin. Klinger finds
that it is very difficult taking over
Radar's Job.

Private Finance
W: Dennis Koenig. D: Charles S.
Dubin. Klinger tries to help a Korean woman with money, and Hawkeye is bothered by the promise he
made to a dying soldier.

Mr. & Mrs. Who?
W: Ronny Graham. D: Burt Metcalfe.
Winchester returns from Tokyo believing that he got drunk and then got
married.

The Yalu Brick Road
W: Mike Farrell. D: Charles S. Dubin.
BJ and Hawkeye get lost while returning to the camp with some needed
medicine.

Nurse Doctor
W: Sy Rosen, Thad Mumford & Dan
Wilcox. D: Charles S. Rubin. The
camp runs out of water, and a nurse
falls for Mulcahy.

Life Time
W: Alan Alda & Walter D. Dishell,
M.D. D: Alan Alda. The staff tries to
save a severely wounded patient within twenty minutes.

Goodbye Radar [Part 1]

W: Ken Levine & David Isaacs. D: Burt Metcalfe. Radar is needed back at the camp but is unavoidably delayed in Tokyo. Meanwhile, Klinger tries to find a needed generator.

Goodbye Radar [Part 2]

W: Ken Levine & David Isaacs. D: Burt Metcalfe. Radar prepares to go home, but finds that he can't leave when everybody needs him.

Dreams

W: Alan Alda & James Jay Rubinfier. D: Alan Alda. GS: Ford Rainey, Fred Stuthman. The staff daydream about their worst fears.

Dear Uncle Abdul

W: John Rappaport & Jim Mulligan. D: William Jurgenson. Klinger tries to write a letter to his uncle but finds that his new job of camp clerk is keeping him very busy.

Captain's Outrageous

W: Thad Mumford & Dan Wilcox. D: Burt Metcalfe. The doctors take over the bar when Rosie gets hurt.

Stars and Stripe

W: Dennis Koenig. D: Harry Morgan. BJ and Winchester must write an article on how they saved a soldier's life.

Heal Thyself

W: Dennis Koenig & Gene Reynolds. D: Mike Farrell. GS: Edward Herrmann. When Potter and Winchester come down with the mumps, the replacement surgeon who comes to help out suffers a nervous breakdown.

Yessir, That's Our Baby

W: Jim Mulligan. D: Alan Alda. GS: William Bogert, Howard Platt. The doctors try to get a baby of mixed parentage sent back to the states.

Bottle Fatigue

W: Thad Mumford & Dan Wilcox. D: Burt Metcalfe. GS: Shelly Long. Hawkeye promises to give up drinking for a week.

Morale Victory

W: John Rappaport. D: Charles S. Dubin. GS: James Stephens. Hawkeye and BJ try to find a way to boost the camp's morale.

Old Soldiers

W: Dennis Koenig. D: Charles S. Dubin. Hawkeye is put in command when Potter goes to Tokyo on a secret mission.

Lend a Hand

W & D: Alan Alda. GS: Robert Alda, Anthony Alda. Hawkeye runs out on his own surprise birthday party to help a wounded soldier at the front.

Goodbye, Cruel World

W: Thad Mumford & Dan Wilcox. D: Charles S. Dubin. GS: Clyde Kusatsu. The doctors are surprised by the reactions of an Oriental war hero who is told he is being sent home.

April Fools

W: Dennis Koenig. D: Charles S. Dubin. GS: Pat Hingle. Potter tries to keep the doctors from fooling around when a strict Army colonel comes for a visit.

War Co-Respondent

W & D: Mike Farrell. GS: Susan Saint James. BJ falls for a beautiful war correspondent.

Back Pay

W: Thad Mumford, Dan Wilcox & Dennis Koenig. GS: Richard Herd. D: Burt Metcalfe. Hawkeye sends the Army a bill for his services when he learns how much money he could be getting for his services back home.

Cementing Relationships

W: David Pollack & Elias Davis. D: Charles S. Dubin. Hot Lips is being chased by an Italian soldier who was dumped by his girlfriend.

No Sweat

W: John Rappaport. D: Burt Metcalfe. The staff have to suffer through a very uncomfortable heat wave.

Letters
W: Dennis Koenig. D: Charles S. Rubin. GS: Richard Paul. The staff reply to letters sent to them by a class of fourth graders.

The Best of Enemies
W: Sheldon Bull. D: Charles S. Dubin. GS: Mako. Hawkeye is captured by a North Korean soldier while on his way to Seoul for a two-day vacation.

Father's Day
W: Karen L. Hall. D: Alan Alda. GS: Andrew Duggan. Hot Lips gets a visit from her father.

Your Retention, Please
W: Erik Tarloff. D: Charles S. Dubin. Klinger is dumped by his ex-wife.

Taking the Fifth
W: Elias Davis & David Pollack. D: Charles S. Dubin. Hawkeye gets a bottle of vintage French wine and tries to get a nurse to share it with him.

Death Takes a Holiday
W & D: Mike Farrell. GS: Keye Luke. During a Christmas cease fire, the doctors hold a party for some Korean orphans.

A War for All Seasons
W: Thad Mumford & Dan Wilcox. D: Alan Alda. On New Year's, everyone looks back on the year 1951.

Tell It to the Marines
W: Hank Bradford. D: Harry Morgan. Major Winchester takes over command of the camp while Colonel Potter is away.

Depressing News
W: Thad Mumford & Dan Wilcox. D: Alan Alda. Klinger starts his own newspaper, and Hawkeye builds a tower out of tongue depressors.

Operation Friendship
W: Dennis Koenig. D: Rena Down. GS: Tim O'Conner. Klinger saves Winchester's life, which makes him eternally grateful.

No Laughing Matter
W: Elias Davis & David Pollack. D: Burt Metcalfe. GS: Robert Symonds. Hawkeye bets BJ that he can give up jokes for 24 hours, and Charles prepares to meet the doctor who sent him to Korea.

Oh, How We Danced
W: John Rappaport. D: Burt Metcalfe. GS: Yuki Shimoda. The doctors prepare a surprise wedding anniversary for BJ, and Charles makes an inspection tour to the front lines.

Bottoms Up
W: Dennis Koenig. D: Alan Alda. Hawkeye becomes the villain when his practical joke on Winchester backfires, and Hot Lips tries to stop one of her nurses from drinking.

The Red/White Blues
W: Elias Davis & David Pollack. D: Gabriel Beaumont. Everyone tries to keep Potter's blood pressure down so he can pass his physical.

Bless You, Hawkeye
W: Thad Mumford & Dan Wilcox. D: Neil Cox. GS: Barry Schwartz. Hawkeye can't stop sneezing.

The Life You Save
W: John Rappaport & Alan Alda. D: Alan Alda. Charles becomes obsessed with death after he is nearly killed by a sniper.

Blood Brothers
W: Elias Davis & David Pollack. D: Harry Morgan. GS: Ray Middleton, Patrick Swayze. Mulcahy prepares for a visit from a Cardinal, and a soldier learns that he has leukemia when he offers to be the donor for a transfusion.

The Foresight Saga
W: Elias Davis & David Pollack. D: Charles S. Dubin. GS: Rummel Mor, Phillip Sterling. The doctors receive some fresh vegetables from a grateful Korean boy.

That's Show Biz [Part 1]
W: Elias Davis & David Pollock. D: Charles S. Dubin. GS: Gwen Verdon, Gail Edwards, Danny Dayton. A touring USO troupe pays a visit to the camp when their lead singer becomes ill.

That's Show Biz [Part 2]
W: Elias Davis & David Pollock. D: Charles S. Dubin. GS: Gwen Verdon, Gail Edwards, Danny Dayton. The USO troupe find themselves stuck at the camp when a battle breaks out very close to the camp.

Identity Crisis
W: Dan Wilcox & Thad Mumford. D: David Ogden Stiers. GS: Dirk Blocker, Squire Fridell. Camp life is interrupted by the arrival of three wounded soldiers.

Rumor at the Top
W: Elias Davis & David Pollock. D: Charles S. Dubin. GS: Nicholas Pryor. A rumor that they might be split up into other M*A*S*H's has the staff on edge.

Give 'Em Hell, Hawkeye
W: Dennis Koenig. D: Charles S. Dubin. GS: Stefan Gierasch. Hawkeye decides to write a letter to President Truman, asking him to stop the war.

Wheelers and Dealers
W: Thad Mumford & Dan Wilcox. D: Charles S. Dubin. GS: Anthony Charnota. Colonel Potter asks Klinger to tutor him when he is ordered to attend driving school.

Communication Breakdown
W: Karen L. Hall. D: Alan Alda. GS: James Saito, Byron Chung. Charles tries to hide the newspapers he received from home from everyone in camp.

Snap Judgment [Part 1]
W: Paul Perlove. D: Hy Averback. GS: Peter Jurasik, Nathan Jung. Klinger is accused of stealing Hawkeye's camera.

Snappier Judgment [Part 2]
W: Paul Perlove. D: Hy Averback. GS: Peter Jurasik, Nathan Jung. Klinger asks Charles to defend him when he is put on trial for stealing Hawkeye's camera.

'Twas the Day After Christmas
W: Elias Davis & David Pollock. D: Burt Metcalfe. GS: Michael Ensign, Val Bisoglio. The camp helps some wounded British soldiers celebrate an old tradition by having the officers trade places with the enlisted men for a day.

Follies of the Living—Concerns of the Dead
W & D: Alan Alda. GS: Kario Salem, Randall Patrick, Jeff Tyler. While suffering from a high fever, Klinger finds that he can talk to the ghost of a dead soldier who is still wandering around the camp.

The Birthday Girls
W: Karen L. Hall. D: Charles S. Dubin. GS: Jerry Fujikawa. While on the way to the airport so she can celebrate her birthday in Japan, Margaret and Klinger become lost when their jeep breaks down.

Blood and Guts
W: Lee H. Grant. D: Charles S. Dubin. GS: Gene Evans. Hawkeye gets mad when a war correspondent fictionalizes stories about the soldiers who received blood transfusions from the blood donated by his readers.

A Holy Mess
W: Elias Davis & David Pollock. D: Burt Metcalfe. GS: Cyril O'Reilly, David Graf. An AWOL soldier seeks out Father Mulcahy in order to escape punichment by demanding sanctuary.

The Tooth Shall Set You Free
W: Elias Davis & David Pollock. D: Burt Metcalfe. GS: Tom Atkins, John Fujioka. Cowardly Charles refuses to have a tooth removed.

Pressure Points
W: David Pollock. D: Charles S. Dubin. GS: Allan Arbus, John O'Connell. Potter loses his self-confidence, and Charles gets tired of living with his sloppy tentmates Hawkeye and BJ.

Where There's a Will There's a War
W: Elias Davis & David Pollock. D: Alan Alda. GS: Dennis Howard, Larry Ward. The staff becomes concerned when Hawkeye is sent to the front lines.

Promotion Commotion
W: Dennis Koenig. D: Charles S. Dubin. GS: John Matuszak. Hawkeye, BJ and Charles find themselves on the receiving end of trouble when they are put in charge of promotions for the enlisted men.

Heroes
W: Thad Mumford & Dan Wilcox. D: Neil Cox. GS: Earl Boen, Jay Gerber. A visiting champion boxer suffers a stroke while visiting the camp.

Sons and Bowlers
W: Elias Davis & David Pollock. D: Hy Averback. GS: Dick O'Neill. Potter challenges the Marines to a bowling tournament but then finds that there aren't enough good bowlers in the camp to form a team.

Picture This
W: Karen L. Hall. D: Burt Metcalfe. GS: John Fujioka. Potter decides to paint a picture of the staff as a present for his wife.

That Darn Kid
W: Karen L. Hall. D: David Ogden Stiers. GS: John P. Ryan. Hawkeye tries to prove that a goat ate the camp's payroll.

Hey Look Me Over
W: Alan Alda. D: Susan Oliver. GS: Peggy Feury, Perry Lang. Margaret becomes frantic when she has to prepare for an inspection.

Trick or Treatment
W: Dennis Koenig. D: Charles S. Dubin. GS: George Wendt, Andrew Clay. The camp's Halloween festivities are upset by a large inflow of wounded.

Foreign Affairs
W: Elias Davis & David Pollock. D: Charles S. Dubin. GS: Jeffrey Tambor, Soon Teck Oh, Melinda Mullins. Charles falls in love with a Frenchwoman who is visiting the camp as a member of the Red Cross.

The Joker Is Wild
W: John Rappaport & Dennis Koenig. D: Burt Metcalfe. GS: Clyde Kusatsu, David Haid. Hawkeye tries to avoid becoming a victim when BJ goes on a practical joke rampage.

Who Knew?
W: Elias Davis & David Pollock. D: Harry Morgan. Hawkeye finds that he has to write the eulogy for a nurse nobody really knew.

Bombshells
W: Thad Mumford & Dan Wilcox. D: Charles S. Dubin. GS: Gerald S. O'Loughlin. Charles and Hawkeye start a rumor that Marilyn Monroe is going to pay a visit to the camp.

Settling Debts
W: Thad Mumford & Dan Wilcox. D: Mike Switzer. GS: Guy Boyd, Jeff East. Mrs. Potter asks Hawkeye to hold a surprise mortgage burning party for her husband after she pays off the house six months early.

The Moon Is Not Blue
W: Larry Balmagia. D: Charles S. Dubin. GS: Hamilton Camp. Hawkeye tries to get a copy of the film "The Moon Is Blue" because it was banned in certain parts of the States causing him to believe that it is a real racy movie.

Run for the Money
W: Mike Farrell, David Pollock & Elias Davis. D: Neil Cox. GS: Robert Alan

Browne, William Schilling. The camp bets a week's salary on a long-distance race between Father Mulcahy and an Olympic athlete.

Friends and Enemies
W: Karen L. Hall. D: Jamie Farr. GS: John McLiam. Potter receives a visit from an old Army friend who could be headed for a great deal of trouble.

UN the Night and the Music
W: Elias Davis & David Pollock. D: Harry Morgan. GS: George Innes, Kavi Raz, Dennis Holahan. The camp is visited by three members of the United Nations.

Strange Bedfellows
W: Mike Farrell. D: Karen L. Hall. GS: Dennis Dugan. Potter becomes upset when he learns that his visiting son-in-law had an affair while in Tokyo.

Say No More
W: John Rappaport. D: Charles S. Dubin. GS: John Anderson, Michael Horton. A general visits his wounded son at the camp and learns the meaning of war when the boy dies.

Give and Take
W: Dennis Koenig. D: Charles S. Dubin. GS: Craig Wasson. Charles is given the position of Charity Collections Officer and soon finds it more than he bargained for.

As Time Goes By
W: Thad Mumford & Dan Wilcox. D: Burt Metcalfe. GS: Rosalind Chao. The staff tries to decide what should be buried in a time capsule so there will always be a record of their existence.

Goodbye Farewell and Amen
W: Alan Alda, Burt Metcalfe, John Rappaport, Thad Mumford, Dan Wilcox, David Pollock, Elias Davis & Karen Hall. D: Alan Alda. GS: Allan Arbus. Hawkeye suffers a nervous breakdown, Father Mulcahy loses some of his hearing during an explosion, and Klinger marries a Korean girl. All of this leads up to a final cease fire which ends the war and the need for the M*A*S*H unit. So, the staff say their goodbyes and prepare to leave for home. [This episode originally ran two-and-a-half hours, but has been cut into single episodes for syndication.]

MAUDE

On the air 9/12/72, off 4/29/78. CBS. Color. Videotape. 142 episodes. Broadcast: Sept 1972-Sept 1974 Tue 8-8:30; Sept 1974-Sept 1975 Mon 9-9:30; Sept 1975-Sept 1976 Mon 9:30-10; Sept 1976-Sept 1977 Mon 9-9:30; Sept 1977-Nov 1977 Mon 9:30-10; Dec 1977-Jan 1978 Mon 9-9:30; Jan 1978-Apr 1978 Sat 9:30-10. Producer: Norman Lear. Prod Co: Tandem. Synd: Viacom.
CAST: Maude (played by Bea Arthur), Walter (Bill Macy), Carol (Adrienne Barbeau), Phillip (Brian Morrison, Kraig Metzinger 1977-78), Arthur (Conrad Bain), Vivian (Rue McClanahan), Florida (Esther Rolle), Mrs. Naugatuck (Hermione Baddeley), Bert Beasley (J. Pat O'Malley), Chris (Fred Grandy), Victoria Butterfield (Marlene Warfield), Henry Evans (John Amos).
The story of Edith Bunker's cousin Maude and her family and her friends. *Maude* was a very popular show that dealt with many subjects never covered on a TV show before. Unfortunately, the series is dated by the subject matter which once made it so popular. It has done very poorly in syndication.

Maude Meets Florida
Maude hires a black maid.

Maude and the Psychiatrist
Maude tries to find out why Carol is going to see a psychiatrist.

Doctor, Doctor
Phillip and Arthur's granddaughter play doctor, causing problems for Arthur and Maude.

Like Mother, Like Daughter
Carol is dating one of Maude's old boyfriends.

Maude and the Radical
Maude gives a party for a black militant leader.

Maude's Dilemma
Maude is pregnant.

Love and Marriage
Maude tries to break up Carol's wedding plans.

The Ticket
Maude fights a speeding ticket.

Flashback
A flashback to 1968 shows Maude and Walter courting during the presidential election.

The Slumlord
Walter unknowingly buys a tenement.

Maude's Reunion
Maude's old school friend comes for a visit.

The Grass Story
Maude and her friends protest harsh marijuana laws by trying to get arrested.

Walter's Dilemma
Maude decides to have an abortion, while Walter decides to have a vasectomy.

The Convention
Walter and Maude have a fight while attending a convention.

The Double Standard
Carol plans to sleep with her boyfriend in Maude's house.

Walter's Fiftieth Birthday
Walter is worried about getting old when he reaches his 50th birthday.

The Medical Profession
Maude tries to sue a doctor for malpractice.

Arthur Moves In
Arthur moves in with Maude and Walter while his house is being repaired.

Florida's Problem
Florida's husband doesn't want her to work for white people anymore.

Walter's Secret
Maude thinks Walter is fooling around.

Maude's Good Deed
Maude steps in to stop a fight between her friend and her friend's daughter.

The Perfect Marriage
Maude fears her marriage is falling apart.

Maude's Night Out
A married man makes a pass at Maude.

Maude Takes a Job
Maude takes a job selling real estate.

Walter's Holiday
Vivian's divorce is ruining Walter's I Love You Day.

Life of the Party [Part 1]
Maude realizes that Walter is an alcoholic.

Life of the Party [Part 2]
Walter goes for professional help in order to stop his drinking.

Florida's Affair
The furnace repairman makes a pass at Florida, just when her husband enters the room.

Stitch in Time [Part 1]
Vivian has a facelift, making Maude jealous.

Stitch in Time [Part 2]
Maude has a facelift, but Walter doesn't notice the difference.

Vivian's Problem
Vivian is dating an old man.

Maude's Musical
Maude produces a burlesque benefit show to raise money for the school library.

The Will
Walter refuses to let Maude manage his estate after he dies.

Music Hath Charms
After Walter has an accident, Maude decides that they will never fight with each other again.

The Wallet
Maude finds a man's wallet, but Walter refuses to let her search it.

The Office Party
Walter's employees come to his annual Christmas party to tell him they are going to join a union.

Carol's Problem
Carol accuses Maude of interfering in her life when she chooses a house for her as a wedding present.

Florida's Goodbye
Florida retires, leaving Maude without a maid.

The Lovebirds
After a fight, Arthur and Vivian become engaged.

Maude's Guest
Maude invites a black girl to spend her vacation with a white family.

The Commuter Station
Arthur and Vivian get married in a train station when they get stuck in a blizzard.

Maude's Revolt
Maude starts a fight at her birthday party.

The Tax Audit
The man who is performing Walter's tax audit is a former sailor who tried to rape Maude many years ago.

Phillip's Problem
Phillip becomes jealous of Carol and Chris when they go away for the weekend.

The Investment
Walter loses a lot of money on the stock Arthur told him to buy.

The Kiss
Walter and Vivian are caught kissing by Arthur and Maude.

The New Housekeeper
Maude hires a British housekeeper, Mrs. Naugatuck.

Vivian's Party
Maude offers to help Vivian prepare for a party, until she learns that she is not invited.

Maude's New Friend
Maude helps a gay writer promote his book.

Walter's Heart Attack
Walter has a heart attack in a girl's apartment.

Maude Meets the Duke
GS: John Wayne. John Wayne is coming to visit his number one fan, Arthur.

A Love in Common
Maude and Vivian prepare for a visit from a man they both had an affair with many years ago.

Speed Trap
Walter and Arthur are arrested for speeding while they are going fishing.

A Night to Remember
Maude worries about the hysterectomy she is going to have.

Maude the Boss
Maude becomes the branch manager of the real estate agency she works for.

Last Tango in Tuckahoe
Maude finds that Mrs. Naugatuck has a man hiding in her room.

Walter's Ex
Walter's ex-wife and Maude's uncle are getting married to each other.

All Psyched Out
A psychic predicts Maude will get married a fifth time, so to play it safe she marries Walter another time.

Nostalgia Party
Maude tells everyone to celebrate his favorite year at her New Year's Eve party.

The Wife Swappers
Arthur introduces Maude and Walter to the wife swapping head psychiatrist at the hospital.

The Telethon (Musical)
Maude produces a telethon for the Gall Bladder foundation.

Then There Were None
Carol moves out when Maude interferes in her life again.

The Emergence of Vivian
Vivian has a fight with Arthur who wants her to stay home and do the housework.

Naugatuck in Love
Mrs. Naugatuck is in love and plans to get married.

Walter's Pride
Walter refuses to allow Maude to mortgage the house to save his business.

Walter Gets Religion
Walter goes to church in order to sell appliances for the new social hall.

The Cabin
The Findlays and the Harmons spend the weekend in a broken-down cabin in the woods.

Maude's Mother
Maude's mother comes for a visit.

Viv's Dog
Vivian's dog, which she left with Maude, dies.

The Split
Walter leaves when Maude plans to run for the state senate.

Consenting Adults
Maude and Walter decide to get divorced.

Rumpus in the Rumpus Room
Walter and Maude show up at the Harmons's anniversary party with dates.

Maude's Big Decision
Walter gives in and allows Maude to run for office.

The Election
Maude loses the election.

The Fling
Vivian's ex-husband makes a pass at Maude.

For the Love of Bert
Mrs. Naugatuck is playing the horses to win enough money to get a place of her own.

The Analyst
Maude goes to an analyst when she reaches her 50th birthday.

Arthur's Medical Convention
Arthur and his friends play a practical joke on Walter who went with Arthur to a medical convention.

Walter's Ethics
A client would rather have a date with Carol than with Walter's secretary.

Arthur Gets a Partner
Vivian wants Arthur to share his problems with her.

Maude's Moods [Part 1]
Maude is suffering from manic depression, causing her to promote Henry Fonda as a candidate for president.

Maude's Moods [Part 2]
GS: Henry Fonda. Maude goes for professional help when she realizes she is sick.

The Christmas Party
Maude's old Women's Lib friend pays a visit during Christmas.

Poor Albert
Maude's third husband dies and wills that she dispose of his ashes.

The Case of the Broken Bowl
Three different stories of how Maude's punch bowl was broken.

Walter's Stigma
Walter is arrested for being a flasher.

Tuckahoe Bicentennial
Maude puts on a women's lib bicentennial show.

Mrs. Naugatuck's Citizenship
Mrs. Naugatuck suffers a stroke right before she is to take her citizenship test.

Maude's Nephew
Maude's nephew and his pregnant girlfriend come for a visit.

Carol's Promotion
Carol finds that she must go to bed with her boss in order to get a promotion.

Maude's Rejection
A famous poet comes to visit Vivian but refuses to see Maude.

Maude's Ex-Convict
Maude hires an ex-con to fill in for Mrs. Naugatuck, who is in England.

Vivian's First Funeral
Maude has to get back the brooch she loaned a woman; the only thing is, the woman is dead and Maude has to remove the brooch from the body before she is buried.

Walter's Crisis [Part 1]
Walter is named businessman of the year, just as he is about to declare bankruptcy.

Walter's Crisis [Part 2]
Walter gets drunk and then takes a handful of pills when he can't find a job.

Walter's Crisis [Part 3]
Walter is in the hospital and Maude is very nervous about his homecoming.

Bert Moves In
Bert moves in with Mrs. Naugatuck when they plan to get married.

Maude and Chester
Maude and one of her ex-husbands get trapped together in a Xerox room in an empty office building.

The Election
Maude is upset when Carol is dating a man 11 years younger than she.

Arthur's Worry
Arthur worries about Walter's dream in which he kisses Arthur, when the two of them go away on a fishing trip.

The Game Show
Maude and Vivian appear on the game show Beat the Devil.

The Rip-Off
Arthur plans to form an armed neighborhood patrol when the Findlays' house is robbed.

Arthur's Crisis
An old friend of Arthur's comes to him to perform an operation.

Mrs. Naugatuck's Wedding
Bert and Mrs. Naugatuck have a fight right before the wedding.

Maude's New Friends
Maude entertains another doctor and his wife who are into wife swapping.

Walter's Christmas Gift
Arthur and his friends buy out an appliance store, so they ask Walter to run it for them.

Captain Hero
Maude's cousin thinks he is a super-hero.

Maude's Adult Relationship
Maude thinks she can date another man without it getting serious and affecting her marriage.

Maude's Desperate Hours
Maude thinks that the man who painted the house is planning to kill her.

Maude's Aunt
GS: Eve Arden. Maude's aunt pays a visit and spends the evening with Bert.

Maude's Reunion
GS: Nanette Fabray. Maude goes to a school reunion where she discovers that her old friend has suffered a stroke.

Feminine Fulfillment
Vivian joins a group of women who like catering to their men's every wish.

Vivian's Surprise
GS: Bonar Bain. Arthur's twin brother, an escapee from a mental hospital, shows up and Maude mistakes him for Arthur.

Arthur's New Friend
GS: Larry Gelman. Walter is jealous of Arthur's new friend.

The Household Feud
Maude has a fight with Mrs. Naugatuck, while Bert tells her that they are leaving for Ireland to take care of his old mother.

The New Maid
Maude hires a new maid, a Jamaican girl, whom Maude accuses of stealing her wallet.

Maude's Guilt Trip
GS: Bella Bruck, Maude convinces her old aunt to fly down for a visit, only her plane crashes en route to New York.

The Doctor's Strike
Arthur refuses to treat Walter because of a doctors' strike.

Phillip and Sam
Phillip invites his girlfriend to spend the night with him.

The Flying Saucer
Maude sees a UFO and plans to go on TV to talk about it.

Victoria's Boyfriend
GS: Roscoe Lee Browne. Victoria's father comes for a visit but gets mad when she wants to marry an American black man instead of one from the Islands.

The Ecologist
Walter is jealous of an ecologist who has been spending time with Maude.

Walter's Temptation
Walter is tempted to have an affair with one of his employees who is also a friend of Maude's.

My Husband the Hero
Walter saves a man's life during a fire.

Phillip's Birthday Party
Phillip's party is crashed by his entire class at school.

Maude's New Client
Maude tries to sell a house to a man who is a gangster.

The Gay Bar
Maude and Arthur fight about the new gay bar which is opening around the corner.

Businessperson of the Year
Walter and Maude are in the running for the businessperson of the year award.

The Obscene Phone Call
Maude thinks the man who has been making obscene phone calls to her is a friend of Walter's.

Maude's Christmas Surprise
Maude finds a baby on her doorstep.

Carol's Dilemma
Carol's ex-husband wants to take Phillip away with him.

Arthur's Grandson
Arthur is expecting a visit from his five-year-old grandson. He has never seen the boy before, as his son ran to Canada to evade the draft.

Musical '78
Maude puts on a telethon to help a little girl walk again.

Maude's Foster Child
Maude's foster son in Ethiopia comes for a visit.

Vivian's Decision
Vivian decides to leave Arthur and have a life of her own.

Phillip's Mature Romance
Phillip is dating a 19-year-old college girl.

Mr. Butterfield's Return
GS: Roscoe Lee Browne. Victoria's father wants her to return with him to the Islands.

Maude's Big Move: The Chinese Dinner [Part 1]
Maude becomes a congresswoman's assistant, only to have the congresswoman die in her house.

Maude's Big Move: The Wake [Part 2]
Maude is appointed by the governor to take over the congresswoman's job.

Maude's Big Move: Washington [Part 3]
Maude and Walter move to Washington where they meet their new staff.

MAYBERRY R.F.D.

On the air 9/23/68, off 9/6/71. CBS. Color Film. 30 min. 78 episodes. Broadcast: Sept 1968-Sept 1971 Mon 9-9:30. Producer: Andy Griffith. Prod. Co: R.F.D. Mayberry Co. Synd: Metromedia.

CAST: Sam Jones (played by Ken Berry), Aunt Bee (Frances Bavier), Goober Pyle (George Lindsey), Howard Sprague (Jack Dodson), Emmett Clark (Paul Hartman), Millie Swanson (Arlene Golonka), Mike Jones (Buddy Foster), Alice (Alice Ghostley).

Mayberry, North Carolina, is the setting for this series, a spinoff of *The Andy Griffith Show.* The show concentrates on the plight of Sam Jones, full-time farmer and part-time councilman. *Mayberry R.F.D.* is much like *Andy Griffith* in that most of the cast is the same, the slow-moving atmosphere continues, and the town looks familiar. The series infrequently turns up on some stations as a summer replacement.

Andy and Helen Get Married
W: John McGreevey. Andy and Helen get married and Aunt Bee moves in as Sam's new housekeeper.

The Harvest Ball
W: Bob Mosher. Sam writes a letter for Goober to Millie to invite her to the ball.

Mike's Losing Streak
W: Dick Bensfield & Perry Grant. Mike wants to go to the baseball game but Sam thinks he's irresponsible so he punishes him, until the townspeople start making Sam feel like a heel.

Help on the Farm
W: Dick Bensfield & Perry Grant.

Ken Berry (left), Arlene Golonka, and Buddy Foster in Mayberry R.F.D.

Andy convinces Sam to hire two ex-convicts. Later they disappear and so does the money from the cookie jar.

Sam Gets a Ticket
W: Elroy Schwartz. Sam plans to fight a traffic ticket he got in Mount Pilot.

Sam and the Teenager
W: Dick Bensfield & Perry Grant. GS: Darlene Carr. A teenager has a crush on Sam and he doesn't know what to do about it.

Driver Education
W: John McGreevey. Goober gets a job as the high school driving teacher, until he collides with the principal's car.

Howard's Hobby
W: Dick Bensfield & Perry Grant. Howard collects coins. He meets a girl who loves to skydive, so he begins to take lessons in skydiving.

The Church Play
W: John McGreevey. Millie updates the church play when she is selected to direct it.

The Race Horse
W: Henry Garson & Edward Bellon.
Aunt Bee enters her horse Ginger Snap
in a horse race.

The Copy Machine
W: Burt Styles. GS: Carl Ballantine.
Mike gets a copying machine and the
problems begin to multiply.

The Panel Show
W: Joseph Bonaduce. GS: Pamela
Mason. Howard and Emmett appear
on a TV talk show.

Emmett's 50th Birthday
W: Dick Bensfield & Perry Grant.
Emmett becomes depressed when he
reaches his 50th birthday.

Sister Cities Birthday
W: Albert E. Lewin. Sam prepares to
welcome Mexican officials from its
sister city to the south.

Youth Takes Over
The kids take over the adults' jobs on
Civic Youth Day.

Miss Farmerette
W: Joseph Bonaduce. Millie wins the
title of Miss Farmerette in the county
fair and an old agent friend wants her
to go to Hollywood with him.

New Couple in Town
W: Dan Beaumont. A writer and his
wife move to Mayberry for inspiration,
which prompts Goober to help.

Aunt Bee's Cruise [Part 1]
W: Dick Bensfield & Perry Grant. GS:
Will Geer. Aunt Bee goes on a Caribbean cruise and falls for the Captain of
the ship.

Aunt Bee and the Captain [Part 2]
W: Dick Bensfield & Perry Grant. GS:
Will Geer. Aunt Bee and the Captain
plan to get married, but then she gets
second thoughts.

Sam the Expert Farmer
W: Elroy Schwartz. Sam feels em-

barrassed when his bean crop fails and
Millie's is successful.

The Camper
W: Dick Bensfield & Perry Grant.
Mike and Harold have a fight and
claim that their friendship is over, but
still go on the annual fishing trip.

An Efficient Service Station
W: Joel Swanson & John McGreevey.
Goober has been ordered to clean up
the station or lose it.

The Pet Shop
W: Paul West. Mike gets a job in the
pet shop.

Emmett's Retirement
W: Dick Bensfield & Perry Grant.
When Emmett retires he finds he has
nothing to do, so he begins to hang
out with his friends until he drives
them crazy.

The Church Bell
W: Joel Swanson & Paul West. The
townspeople plan on buying a church
bell that they can afford.

Millie's Girlfriend
W: Dick Bensfield & Perry Grant. Millie's girlfriend breaks up with her boyfriend and moves in with Millie.

Goober's Brother
W: John McGreevey. Goober tries to
become as well known as his brother,
an engineer.

Howard the Poet
W: Roswell Rogers. Howard's poem is
scheduled to be published, now if only
his friends would allow him to finish
it.

Millie the Model
W: Burt Styles. When Millie goes to
New York, Sam becomes jealous and
plans to follow her.

Goober and the Telephone Girl
W: Dick Bensfield & Perry Grant. GS:
Luana Anders. The gossiping tele-

phone operator is causing trouble for Goober.

Andy's Baby
W: Roswell Rogers. Emmett, Howard and Goober want to be the godfather of Andy and Helen's new baby.

Mike's Birthday Party
W: Dick Bensfield & Perry Grant. Mike plans on having a "No Girls Allowed" birthday party.

Saving Morelli's
W: Bob Reiss & Paul West. Sam turns entertainer to save Morelli's restaurant.

Millie the Secretary
W: Roswell Rogers. Millie doesn't know that her new employers are actually bookies.

The Farmer Exchange Project
W: Dennis Whitcomb & Paul West. A Russian agricultural expert comes to visit the farmers.

The New Farmhand
W: Bob Mosher. GS: Glenn Ash. Sam learns how to handle hero-worshipping Mike.

The Caper
W: Roswell Rogers. Howard robs the bank to prove that Goober is not a good deputy.

Palm Springs Here We Come
W: Dick Bensfield & Perry Grant. Sam promises Mike that he can go on a trip to Palm Springs if he passes his math course in school.

Palm Springs Here We Are
W: Dick Bensfield & Perry Grant. The trip to Palm Springs is almost ruined by a fight.

Millie and the Palm Springs Golf Pro
W: Dick Bensfield & Perry Grant. Millie plans to make Sam jealous.

Palm Springs Cowboy
W: Dick Bensfield & Perry Grant.

Howard tries to help a hasbeen cowboy star make a comeback.

Emmett Takes a Fall
W: Bob Mosher. GS: Elliot Street. Emmett hires a talented teenager to help out in the store when he has an accident.

Goober's Niece
W: Dick Bensfield & Perry Grant. GS: Erica Chandler. Goober's 15-year-old niece pays him a visit.

The Mynah Bird
W: Dick Bensfield & Perry Grant. Mike loses Howard's valuable mynah bird.

The Mayberry Road
W: Bob Mosher. Aunt Bee and her friends try to save some trees which will be destroyed when a new road is put down.

Emmett and the Ring
W: John McGreevey. Emmett pawns his wife's ring to invest in the stock market.

The Mayberry Float
W: Paul West. GS: Hope Summers. Millie and Clara compete for the honor of appearing as a pioneer woman on a parade float.

The New Well
W: Dick Bensfield & Perry Grant. GS: Douglas V. Fowley. Aunt Bee hires a dowser to find water using his divining rod, while Sam tries his scientific methods.

The Health Fund
W: Bob Mosher & Joel Swanson. When Howard has an operation, his lodge gets upset when they are afraid that his medical costs will bankrupt their health fund.

The Sculptor
W: Bob Mosher. A New York sculptor creates an abstract statue for the town, and nobody can figure out just what it is supposed to be.

Aloha Goober
W: Dick Bensfield & Perry Grant.
Everybody thinks Goober is going to
Hawaii.

Millie and the Great Outdoors
W: Dick Bensfield & Perry Grant.
Millie joins Howard and Sam on a
camping trip.

Sensitivity Training
W: Dick Bensfield & Perry Grant. GS:
Fred Sadoff, Roy Applegate. An en-
counter group comes to Mayberry.

Hair
W: Bob Mosher. Emmett tries to look
young by buying a toupee.

Howard's Nephew
W: Dick Bensfield & Perry Grant. GS:
Brad David. Howard's hippie nephew
visits.

Emmett's Domestic Problem
W: Dick Bensfield & Perry Grant. GS:
Ruta Lee, Mary Lansing. Emmett's
wife joins a women's lib group.

The New Housekeeper
W: Gene Thompson. Sam gets a new
housekeeper, a former Army officer.

Millie's Dream
W: Bob Mosher. Millie is worried
when she dreams that something bad
will happen to Sam.

All for Charity
W: Bob Mosher. Sam and Emmett
help put on a show for the church.

Goober the Housekeeper
W: Bob Mosher. Goober passes himself off as the owner of the big estate
he is housewatching in order to impress his new girlfriend.

Goober's New Gas Station
W: David Evans & Bob Ross. A dinosaur bone is discovered under Goober's
station, and any attempts to uncover

the rest of the skeleton would mean
wrecking the station.

The Harp
W: Dick Bensfield & Perry Grant. GS:
Leonid Kinskey, Lavina Dawson. Cousin Alice, the housekeeper, takes harp
lessons.

Millie the Best-Dressed Woman
W: Bob Mosher. The mini-skirt hits
Mayberry.

Mike's Project
W: Dick Bensfield & Perry Grant.
Mike's school project turns into a com-
petition between fathers.

The Bicycle Club
W: Walter D.F. Black. Middle-aged
Emmett wants to join a young men's
bicycle riding club.

Goober the Elder
W: Dick Bensfield & Perry Grant.
Goober is sent to jail in a gambling
raid, just after Sam nominated him for
church elder.

Community Spirit
W: Bob Mosher. Goober, Howard and
Emmett decide to paint Sam's house
as a surprise.

Millie's Egg Farm
W: Dick Bensfield & Perry Grant.
Millie starts her own egg farm.

The Kid from Hong Kong
W: Sam Locke & Milton Pascal. GS:
Phil Chambers, Teresa Jaw. Mike becomes the foster father of a little girl
in Hong Kong.

Alice and the Professor
W: Bob Mosher & Charles Stewart.
GS: Leonid Kinskey. Alice's harp
teacher asks her to marry him.

The Moon Rocks
W: Dick Bensfield & Perry Grant.
Sam gets his friend at NASA to bring
the moon rock to Mayberry so Howard can have a private showing.

Howard the Dream Spinner
W: Bob Mosher. Howard becomes the host of a local literary TV program and becomes attached to an anonymous girl named Melissa whom Goober and Emmett created.

The World Traveler
W: Dick Bensfield & Perry Grant. Emmett plans a cheap tour of Europe for his wife.

Emmett's Invention
W: John McGreevey. A large company wants to buy the rights to Emmett's old invention.

Goober the Hero
W: Bob Mosher. Goober gets lost in a cave.

Howard the Swinger
W: Dick Bensfield & Perry Grant. Howard moves into a swinging singles apartment.

Mike's Car
W: Dick Bensfield & Perry Grant. Sam lets Mike buy Goober's old car.

The City Planner
W: Bob Mosher & Charles Stewart. GS: Ruta Lee. The female city planner makes a play for Sam.

McHALE'S NAVY

On the air 10/11/62, off 8/30/66. ABC. B&W Film. 30 min. 138 episodes. Broadcast: Oct 1962-Sept 1963 Thu 9:30-10; Sept 1963-Aug 1966 Tue 8:30-9. Producer: Edward J. Montagne. Prod Co/Synd: Universal TV.

CAST: Lt. Cdr. Quinton McHale (played by Ernest Borgnine), Capt. Wallace Binghamton (Joe Flynn), Ensign Charles Parker (Tim Conway), Lester Gruber (Carl Ballantine), Christy (Gary Vinson), Harrison "Tinker" Bell (Billy Sands), Happy Holmes (Gavin McLeod), Fuji Kobiaji (Yoshio Yoda), Lt. Elroy Carpenter (Bob Hastings), Nurse Molly Turner (Jane Dulo), Mayor Mario Lugatto (Jay Novello).

WRITERS: Ralph Goodman, Walter Kempley, Elroy Schwartz, Frank Gill, George Carlton, Marty Roth, Michael Morris, Sam Locke, Joel Rapp, Larry Marks, William Raynor, Miles Wilder, Tom & Frank Walman, John Fenton Murray. DIRECTORS: Edward J. Montagne, Sidney Lanfield, Earl Bellamy, Oscar Rudolph, Charles Barton, Jean Yarbrough, Sidney Miller, John Newland, Hollingsworth Morse.

Set in the South Pacific on the island of Taratupa during World War II, the series deals with the bickering relationship between Lt. Cdr. Quinton McHale and Captain Wallace B. Binghamton, who feels his life is plagued by McHale and his crew of thieves who have turned Taratupa into a gambling den. Capt. Binghamton plans to expose McHale and his men, hoping at least to get McHale transferred if not court-martialed. Later in the series, McHale and his crew move from their island to Voltafiore, Italy, where they are still pursued by Capt. Binghamton. *McHale's Navy* is sometimes seen on local stations, but World War II comedy series are not very popular these days.

An Ensign for McHale [Pilot]
W: Unknown. D: Sidney Lanfield. Captain Binghamton assigns Charles Parker to McHale's PT boat crew as executive officer, hoping the new ensign can shape up the shoddy outfit.

Movies Are Your Best Diversion
W: Larry Markes & Michael Morris. D: Edward J. Montague. GS: Mako. McHale and his crew are assigned the task of saving the United States convoy. They use movie soundtracks to

In McHale's Navy are, from top, Joe Flynn, Ernest Borgnine, and Tim Conway.

divert attention and complete their mission.

A Purple Heart for Gruber
W: Danny Arnold. D: Sidney Lanfield. GS: Dale Ishimoto. During a Japanese attack, Gruber scratches his finger and puts in for a Purple Heart.

PT 73 Where Are You?
W: Joe Heller. D: Edward J. Montague. McHale and his crew lose their ship on a mission in New Caledonia, but end up with two different ones.

Three Girls on an Island
W: Si Rose & Fred Finkelhoffe. D: Sidney Lanfield. Captain Binghamton

plans an intimate dinner for three USO girls, but McHale and crew have their own plans for a luau for them the same night.

Beauty and the Beast
W: Tom & Frank Waldman. D: Sidney Lanfield. Binghamton tells McHale whichever PT boat passes inspection will have the honor of escorting a lady correspondent on a pacific tour.

The Ensign Gets a Zero
W: Walter Kempky. D: Sidney Lanfield. Binghamton wagers his ship's clock that Parker can outshoot another ensign, and when he loses plans a trip for him to the Aleutian Islands.

McHale's Paradise Hotel
W: Walter Kempky. D: Sidney Lanfield. GS: Jane Dulo. McHale opens a profitable resort hotel for tired naval personnel, then Binghamton shows up.

Operation Wedding Party
W: Marty Roth. D: Edward J. Montagne. GS: Don Matheson, Jane Dulo, Cindy Robbins. McHale tries to arrange a wedding for Christy and Lt. Winters without Binghamton knowing about it.

McHale and His Seven Cupids
W: Larry Markes & Michael Morris. D: Sidney Lanfield. McHale tries his hand at matchmaking with Parker and Navy nurse Brown as his victims.

The Captain's Mission
W: Jerry Davis & Danny Simon. D: Sidney Lanfield. GS: Mako, Walter Brooke. Tired of being tied to a desk, Binghamton borrows McHale's PT boat and crew and sails in search of the enemy.

Send Us a Hero
W: Larry Markes & Michael Morris. D: Sidney Lanfield. A Congresswoman looking for a hero to spearhead a war bond tour in the United States picks McHale.

The Day They Captured Santa Claus
W: Larry Markes & Michael Morris. D: Sidney Lanfield. McHale and his crew run into a Japanese ambush on Christmas Day while playing Santa Claus to a group of native children.

The Mothers of PT 73
W: Larry Markes & Michael Morris. D: Sidney Lanfield. GS: Naomi Stevens, Dan Frazer. McHale's crew holds a gambling event on the same day Binghamton is bringing over the mothers of three of McHale's men.

The Battle of McHale's Island
W: Marty Roth. D: Sidney Lanfield. Binghamton decides to throw McHale and his men off Taratupa to make room for an officers' club.

Who Do the Voodoo?
W: Gene L. Coon. D: Edward J. Montagne. GS: Jacques Aubuchon. When Binghamton refuses to reimburse witch doctor Urulu for the loss of his coconut orchard, he puts a powerful curse on him.

Six Pounds from Paradise
W: Marty Roth & Sidney Lanfield. Binghamton embarks upon a campaign to fatten up McHale so that he will be so overweight he'll be shipped out.

The Captain Steals a Cook
W: Frank Gill & George Carlton Brown. D: Oscar Rudolph. GS: Frank Ferguson, Paul Smith. Binghamton, wanting to impress a visiting admiral, decides to round up the best cook in the Pacific who happens to be McHale.

The Big Raffle
W: Marty Roth. D: Sidney Lanfield. GS: Marcel Hillaire, Claudine Longet. To raise money for a party to celebrate the birth of Quartermaster Christy's child, McHale's crew raffles off a date with a French beauty.

One of Our Engines Is Missing
W: Frank Gill & George Carlton

Brown. D: Oscar Rudolph. McHale's boat breaks down, giving Binghamton an excuse for asking headquarters to transfer the skipper and crew of PT 73 to another command.

Nippon Nancy Calling
W: Danny Arnold. D: Sidney Lanfield. Binghamton believes McHale is the source of an information leak and sends Parker out to spy on him.

Uncle Admiral
W: Frank Gill & George Carlton Brown. D: Sidney Lanfield. GS: Harry Von Zell. When Binghamton learns Parker is related to an admiral, he has the young officer reassigned as his aide.

The Confidence Game
W: Frank Gill & George Carlton Brown. D: Sidney Lanfield. Parker feels the crew of PT 73 has no respect for him, so McHale sets out to give him an opportunity to prove himself a worthy leader.

Parents Anonymous
W: Marty Roth. D: Sidney Lanfield. When a hospital ship sails from Mc-Hale's Island, leaving a little girl behind, McHale and his crew decide to adopt the child.

The Natives Get Restless
W: Bob Marcus. D: Norman Abbott. Binghamton upsets a native chieftain when he puts his village off limits to US Naval personnel at the same time a native relations officer visits.

One Enchanted Weekend
W: Frank Gill & George Carlton Brown. D: Edward J. Montagne. GS: Marcel Hillaire, Mako. Binghamton turns down Parker's request to spend a leave on the plantation of a pretty young French girl, so McHale decides to help out.

Washing Machine Charlie
W: William Raynor & Myles Wilder. D: Oscar Rudolph. GS: Mike Farrell. Binghamton cancels the leave to New Caledonia planned by McHale and his crew, refusing to let them go until they get rid of a Japanese plane harrassing the base.

Instant Democracy
W: Howard Leeds. D: Oscar Rudolph. GS: Olan Soule. Binghamton is forced to enlist McHale's aid in commandeering Chief Urulu's tribe to work on enlarging the Taratupa air strip.

A Wreath for McHale
W: Marty Roth. D: Sidney Lanfield. GS: Allan Melvin. Binghamton conducts memorial services for McHale and the crew of PT 73 presumed killed in action on the island of Kalakai.

H.M.S. 73
W: William Raynor & Myles Wilder. D: Sidney Lanfield. Binghamton plans to transfer McHale to permanent duty as a liaison officer to the British Navy, sending Parker to the rescue.

The Monster of McHale's Island
W: William Raynor & Myles Wilder. D: Sidney Lanfield. The ten-year-old son of an admiral is keeping tabs on McHale and his crew and plans to inform his father of their illegal actions.

Portrait of a Peerless Leader
W: Frank Gill & George Carlton Brown. GS: Herb Vigran. Binghamton sees a chance to get McHale out of his command by having him transferred to the States to teach a PT boat school.

Camera, Action, Panic
W: Marty Roth. D: Sidney Lanfield. GS: Arte Johnson. When a photographer is assigned to McHale's PT boat to take combat pictures, Gruber uses his camera to photograph some native girls.

The Hillbillies of PT 73
W: Frank Gill & George Carlton Brown. McHale and crew stage a Tennessee hoedown to cheer up Willy who has received a Dear John letter.

Alias Captain Binghamton
W: Robert Fisher & Arthur Marx. D: Sidney Lanfield. When a lookalike for Binghamton is assigned to McHale's crew, McHale's men are convinced he is a spy for the captain.

McHale's Millions
W: William Raynor & Myles Wilder. D: Sidney Canfield. McHale and crew find four million dollars they presume to be counterfeit, but Binghamton discovers the money is real.

Have Kimono, Will Travel
W: William Raynor & Myles Wilder. D: Sidney Lanfield. GS: Mako, Robert Kino. When PT 73 runs out of gas, McHale and his crew pull in at an island densely populated by Japanese troops.

A Letter for Fuji
W: Bill Persky & Sam Denoff. D: Sidney Lanfield. GS: John Zaremba. Fuji writes a letter to his girlfriend in Tokyo and McHale and his men set out to mail it from a Japanese-held island.

McHale and His Schweinhunds
W: Frank Gill & George Carlton Brown. D: Sidney Lanfield. GS: Mako. Parker, acting as skipper of PT 73, blows the end off a valuable island with torpedoes intended for a German U-boat.

To Binghamton with Love
W: Marty Roth & Danny Simon. D: Sidney Lanfield. GS: Bill Quinn. Hoping to impress Admiral Benson, Binghamton orders McHale and his men to give him a testimonial dinner.

My Ensign the Lawyer
W: William Raynor & Myles Wilder. D: Sidney Lanfield. GS: Roy Roberts. Tinkerbell is accused of stealing Binghamton's cherished printing press and is sentenced for court-martial with Parker as his attorney.

The Binghamton Murder Plot
W: Robert Fisher & Arthur Marx. D: Sidney Lanfield. When McHale and his men are acting even more sneaky than usual, Binghamton thinks they are out to do him in.

The Day the War Stood Still
W: William Raynor & Myles Wilder. D: Sidney Lanfield. GS: Roy Roberts. When Binghamton finds Fuji and imprisons him, McHale and his crew try to convince Binghamton the war is over.

The Happy Sleepwalker
W: Frank Gill & George Carlton Brown. D: Sidney Lanfield. Happy's baldness leads to frustration, women-wise, which leads to sleepwalking causing Binghamton to decide to ship him out.

Is There a Doctor in the Hut?
W: William Raynor & Myles Wilder. D: Sidney Lanfield. McHale and crew scheme to insure that a visiting movie star spends some unanticipated time on McHale's Island.

Today I Am a Man!
W: Unknown. D: Sidney Lanfield. GS: Joyce Bulifant. Girl-shy Parker is assigned to train five beautiful nurses in judo and self-defense.

Jolly Wally
W: Robert Fisher & Arthur Marx. D: Sidney Lanfield. GS: Peter Leeds. To impress a war correspondent, Binghamton keeps on giggling no matter what setbacks, humiliations or disasters beset him.

The August Teahouse of Quint McHale
W: Ralph Goodman & Stan Dreben. D: Sidney Lanfield. Binghamton catches McHale apparently trading rifles to the Japanese for coconuts and draws up treason charges.

The Balloon Goes Up
W: Barry Blitzer & Ray Brenner. D: Sidney Lanfield. GS: Mako. Binghamton enlists McHale's aid to locate a $140,000 shortage in the base inventory.

Scuttlebutt

W: Arnold Horwitt. D: Sidney Lanfield. McHale's men try to help Tinker impress his girlfriend by pretending that a routine PT 73 mission is extremely dangerous.

Creature from McHale's Island

W: William Raynor & Myles Wilder. D: Sidney Lanfield. Parker takes over a salvaged two-man Japanese submarine and, disguised as a sea monster, tries to scare a nosy Binghamton off McHale's Island.

French Leave for McHale

W: Ralph Goodman & Stan Dreben. D: Sidney Lanfield. GS: George Kennedy, Benny Rubin. McHale meets up with Big Frenchy, an old buddy, who ends up having McHale and his men thrown in jail while he makes off with their boat.

Who'll Buy My Sarongs?

W: William Raynor & Myles Wilder. D: Sidney Lanfield. McHale's men are split into two strongly opposing camps while competing for the distinction of making the most fetching sarongs for the nurses' bazaar.

Orange Blossoms for McHale

W: Arnold Horwitt. D: Sidney Lanfield. GS: Joyce Jameson. When Binghamton learns that married men with two years of overseas duty are to be sent home, he arranges a marriage for McHale.

A Medal for Parker

W: Ralph Goodman & Stan Dreben. D: Sidney Lanfield. A chapter of Parker's war novel, in which he takes over the command of PT 73 and sinks a Japanese battleship, appears in his hometown paper, sending a dignitary out to meet him.

Babette Go Home

W: Ralph Goodman & Stan Dreben. D: Sidney Lanfield. GS: Susan Silo. Babette, pretty daughter of a French planter, stows away on PT 73 and is discovered by Binghamton who accuses McHale of kidnapping.

Stars Over Taratupa

W: Sam Locke & Joel Rapp. D: Sidney Lanfield. GS: Robert F. Simon. A Hollywood director, impressed by the everyday activities of McHale's men, selects them as the cast for his PT boat documentary film.

Urulu's Paradise West

W: Barry Blitzer & Ray Brenner. D: Sidney Lanfield. Bimghamton arrests Gruber and Chief Urulu for selling lots on Navy-held Taratupa Island, only to discover he has been ordered to buy an island Urulu owns.

The Great Impersonation

W: William Raynor & Myles Wilder. D: Sidney Lanfield. GS: Henry Corden. Parker, disguised as a British general famed for his heroism, embarks on a dangerous decoy mission to help McHale.

Evil-Eye Parker

W: Unknown. D: Sidney Lanfield. McHale and crew stage a charity show against Binghamton's wishes and are about to be arrested when Parker discovers he can hypnotize the pesty Captain.

Comrades of PT 73

W: Arnold Horwitt. D: Sidney Lanfield. GS: Cliff Norton, Sue Ane Langdon. McHale's men are delighted when a Russian officer assigned to study PT boat operations turns out to be a beautiful woman.

Dear Diary

W: William Raynor & Myles Wilder. D: Sidney Lanfield. Binghamton handcuffs himself to Parker and sets out for fleet headquarters where Parker is to testify against McHale and crew.

Alias PT 73

W: Sam Locke & Joel Rapp. D: Sidney Lanfield. Binghamton discovers that McHale and his men were on a neighboring island enjoying a luau during an air raid on Taratupa.

Carpenter in Command
W: Barry Blitzer & Ray Brenner. D: Hollingsworth Morse. Carpenter becomes acting commander of the base when the Captain sprains his ankle, and promptly turns into a worse tyrant than Binghamton.

Ensign Parker E.S.P.
W: Frank Gill & George Carlton Brown. D: Sidney Lanfield. Parker's dreams tell McHale and his crew they can find buried treasure ten feet under the Captain's office.

The Novocain Mutiny
W: William Raynor & Myles Wilder. D: Sidney Lanfield. When Fuji has a toothache, McHale has to figure out a way to get his Japanese friend to a dentist.

The McHale Mob
W: William Raynor & Myles Wilder. D: Hollingsworth Morse. GS: Hoke Howell, Nestor Paiva. Chief Urulu exercises his legal right and orders McHale and his men off his island.

Big Frenchy
W: Ralph Goodman & Stan Dreben. D: Sidney Lanfield. GS: George Kennedy. Big Frenchy tries to swindle the captain out of a boatload of valuable supplies.

Marryin' Chuck
W: Marty Roth. D: Sidney Lanfield. GS: John Zaremba, Eleanor Audley. Trying to retrieve some stolen art treasures, Parker becomes involved with the admiral's daughter.

The Rage of Taratupa
W: Robert Fisher & Arthur Marx. D: Sidney Lanfield. A singing sensation is assigned to McHale's squadron and soon discovers he'll never fit in as he is itching to come to grips with the enemy.

A Da-Da for Christy
W: Burt Styler & Albert E. Lewin. D: Frank MacDonald. McHale and his men attempt to talk to Christy's year-old son via shortwave radio, but are interrupted by the captain.

The Dart Gun Wedding
W: William Raynor & Myles Wilder. D: Norman Abbott. GS: George Furth. Ensign Roger Whitfield, son of Binghamton's boss, arrives on the island and the Captain becomes his servant.

Laugh, Captain, Laugh
W: William Raynor & Myles Wilder. D: Earl Bellamy. McHale's men charge Binghamton up with laughing gas to prevent him from court-martialing Parker.

McHale's Floating Harem
W & D: Unknown. When he learns of the impending arrival of a visiting sultan and his three beautiful daughters, the Captain attempts to get rid of McHale by sending him off on a mission.

The Ghosts of 73
W: William Raynor & Myles Wilder. D: Earl Bellamy. Binghamton's latest plan for getting rid of McHale and his crew is to scare them off the island.

The Missing Link
W: William Raynor & Myles Wilder. D: Hollingsworth Morse. Binghamton assigns Parker as a one-man lookout on an island used by enemy ships for target practice.

Lester the Skipper
W & D: Unknown. Gruber gets in hot water with the Captain and his girlfriend when he falsely claims to be a lieutenant commander.

Senator Parker, Suh!
W: Tom & Frank Waldman. D: Edward Andrews. Mistaking Binghamton for a dummy, Parker hits him giving the Captain every reason to court-martial Parker.

McHale, the Desk Commando
W: Tom & Frank Waldman. D: Edward Andrews. When a sneak inspection approaches, Binghamton not wanting to take the blame for the poor condition of the base puts McHale in charge.

Fountain of Youth
W & D: Unknown. Binghamton, attempting to impress an admiral, takes McHale out on a mission which results in the destruction of McHale's liquor still, which Binghamton mistakes for the Fountain of Youth.

It's A Mad, Mad, Mad War
W: William Raynor & Myles Wilder. D: Charles T. Barton. Parker loses the base payroll, sending McHale to the rescue.

Will the Alligator Take the Stand
W: Ralph Goodman & Stan Dreben. D: Earl Bellamy. GS: Walter Brooke. Parker is put on trial for stealing Binghamton's wallet, unaware that it was actually eaten by an alligator.

The British Also Have Ensigns
W: Sam Locke & Joel Rapp. D: Earl Bellamy. A bumbling British sub-lieutenant is assigned to McHale's unit.

McHale and His Jet Set
W: John Fenton Murray. D: Hollingsworth Morse. GS: Lee Bergere. McHale helps the Captain expose a real estate swindler.

The Late Captain Binghamton
W: Barry E. Blitzer. D: Charles T. Barton. The Captain believes that he has only 48 hours to live when one of McHale's men touches up his X-rays.

The Great Eclipse
W: Ralph Goodman & Stan Dreben. D: Frank MacDonald. GS: Stanley Adams, Ned Romero. McHale and his crew try to get a tribe of headhunters to sign a peace treaty.

The Truth Hurts
W: Henry Garson. D: Hollingsworth Morse. Binghamton orders truth serum shots for McHale and his crew in the hopes of obtaining information he can use to finally get rid of them.

Christy Goes Traveling
W: Stan Dreben & Ralph Goodman. D: Charles T. Barton. GS: Leonard Stone. McHale puts Christy in a sack and mails him to San Diego so he can see his baby daughter.

Fuji's Big Romance
W: Barry E. Blitzer. D: Charles T. Carton. Fuji falls in love with a native chief's daughter, but must fight her jealous boyfriend for her.

The Stool Parrot
W: Sam Locke & Joel Rapp. W: Hollingsworth Morse. McHale's pet parrot is telling their secret plans to the Captain.

Rumble on Taratupa
W: Stan Dreben & Ralph Goodman. D: Earl Bellamy. The Captain needs McHale's help to save him from a mob of gangsters.

McHale's Floating Laundromat
W: Allan Manings. D: Hollingsworth Morse. Binghamton assigns Carpenter to spy on McHale.

The PT 73 Follies
W: Sam Locke & Joel Rapp. D: Sidney Miller. Binghamton and Parker are sent to a deserted island for a survival test.

Pumpkin Takes Over
W: Ray Brenner & Barry E. Blitzer. D: Jean Yarbrough. GS: Yvonne Craig. Binghamton's wife comes for a visit at the same time as he is producing a show starring an exotic dancer.

All Chiefs and No Indians
W: Ralph Goodman & Stan Dreben. D: Jean Yarbrough. GS: John Zaremba. Binghamton tries to get all of McHale's men to become CPOs when he learns that all Chief Petty Officers are being shipped home.

All Ahead Empty
W: John Wright & Bill C. Jackson. D: Hollingsworth Morse.   GS: Marvin Kaplan.   An electronics genius takes over the PT 73.

Send This Ensign to Camp
W: Sam Locke & Joel Rapp. W: Hollingsworth Morse. After getting hit on the head, Parker thinks he is ten years old and back at summer camp.

The Seven Faces of Ensign Parker
W: William Raynor & Myles Wilder. D: Charles T. Barton.   GS: Gary Owens, Jimmy Cross.   McHale rescues Parker from the brig when Binghamton accuses him of grand larceny.

The Great Necklace Caper
W: Ray Brenner & Barry E. Blitzer. D: Sidney Miller.   A chimp steals the valuable necklace Binghamton bought for his wife.

By the Numbers, Paint
W: Sam Locke & Joel Rapp. W: Hollingsworth Morse.   McHale's men sell the Captain a phony painting.

Will the Real Admiral Please Stand Up?
W: William Raynor & Myles Wilder. D: Hollingsworth Morse.   GS: Stanley Adams, Redd Foxx.   The Shah of Durani refuses to sign an oil agreement unless his friend Parker is made an admiral.

Chuckie Cottontail
W: Sam Locke & Joel Rapp. W: Hollingsworth Morse.   When the Japanese see Parker in an Easter Bunny costume, they think he is an evil demon.

Hello, McHale? — Colonna!
W: William Raynor & Myles Wilder. D: Sidney Miller.   GS: Jerry Colonna. McHale's men remove the obstacle keeping Jerry Colonna from putting on a show on the island.

The Vampire of Taratupa
W: William Raynor & Myles Wilder.

D: Hollingsworth Morse.   Parker impersonates all sorts of horrible creatures to escape from Binghamton's quarters where he is imprisoned.

A Star Falls on Taratupa
W: Ray Brenner & Barry E. Blitzer. D: Hollingsworth Morse.   GS: Gary Owens, Jean Hale.   A movie star plans to get marooned with McHale and his men on an island to increase publicity.

Birth of a Salesman
W: Sam Locke & Joel Rapp. D: Jean Yarbrough.   GS: Steve Franken.   Binghamton gets McHale and his men to take out insurance policies in order to impress an insurance tycoon.

Make Room for Orvie
W: John Fenton Murray. D: Jean Yarbrough.   A chimp steals the PT 73 and goes off to fight the enemy.

War Italian Style
W: Frank Gill & George Carlton Brown. D: Hollingsworth Morse.   Now stationed in Italy, Binghamton assigns McHale and his men to a dismal camp outside of a village, unaware that they are next door to a wine cellar.

The Bathtub Thief
W: John Fenton Murray. D: Hollingsworth Morse.   McHale's men disguise themselves as an Italian family to fool a German patrol.

A Nip in Time
W: Sam Locke & Joel Rapp. D: Hollingsworth Morse.   Fuji disguises himself as a Japanese admiral in order to save McHale from the Germans.

Giuseppe McHale
W: Hugh Wedlock & Allan Manings. D: Hollingsworth Morse.   Parker gets McHale's lookalike cousin to take his place when McHale leaves the base illegally.

A Wine Cellar Is Not a Home
W: William Raynor & Myles Wilder. D: Hollingsworth Morse.   McHale and his

men fake an air raid to protect their wine cellar from being discovered by the Captain.

Piazza Binghamtoni
W: William Raynor & Myles Wilder. D: Hollingsworth Morse. GS: Ralph Manza. McHale hires a sculptor to help Parker who is in the brig for spilling spaghetti on the Captain.

Marriage McHale Style
W: Ralph Goodman & Bruce Howard. D: Hollingsworth Morse. McHale performs a wedding ceremony aboard the PT 73.

The Bald-Headed Contessa
W: John Fenton Murray. D: Hollingsworth Morse. Binghamton discovers McHale and his men at a party when they should have been on a 25-mile hike.

Blitzkrieg at McHale's Beach
W: John Fenton Murray. D: Hollingsworth Morse. GS: Rachel Roman. Col. Harrington takes over McHale's beach quarters for his own personal playground.

Vino! Vino! Vino! Who's Got the Vino?
W: Elroy Schwartz. D: Hollingsworth Morse. Binghamton recovers the wine McHale boobytrapped for the Germans.

Voltafiore Fish-Fry
W: Ralph Goodman & Bruce Howard. D: Hollingsworth Morse. Binghamton tries to get McHale arrested on charges of profiteering at the same time he captures an enemy submarine.

The Good-Luck Fountain
W: Henry Garson. D: Hollingsworth Morse. McHale tries to convince the Captain he is the victim of a curse after he shuts down the mayor's good-luck fountain.

The McHale Opera Company
W: Ralph Goodman & Bruce Howard.

D: Hollingsworth Morse. Binghamton's operatic debut is interrupted by an air raid.

The Fugitive Ensign
W: William Raynor & Myles Wilder. D: Hollingsworth Morse. Parker joins a band of gypsies when he thinks he killed the Captain with a machine gun.

Reunion for PT 73
W: Sam Locke & Joel Rapp. D: Hollingsworth Morse. McHale tries to convince the Captain that the war is over so they can recover the taped recorded evidence he has against him.

The Return of Giuseppe
W: Ralph Goodman & Bruce Howard. D: Hollingsworth Morse. Binghamton suspects McHale is dealing in the black market when he spots him in town against orders visiting his look-alike cousin.

The Boy Scouts of 73
W: Hugh Wedlock & Allan Manings. D: Hollingsworth Morse. McHale and his men are arrested and accused of stealing Binghamton's clock.

Secret Chimp 007
W: Elroy Schwartz. D: Hollingsworth Morse. Binghamton sees Parker with a chimp carrying stolen top secret orders and assumes he has cracked a spy ring.

Fire in the Liquor Locker
W: William Raynor & Myles Wilder. D: Hollingsworth Morse. Binghamton organizes a volunteer fire department and then takes the fire truck McHale was using as a still.

La Dolce 73
W: Sam Locke & Joel Rapp. D: Hollingsworth Morse. Binghamton plans to film McHale and his men at a wild party in order to get the evidence he needs to finally get rid of them.

The Wacky WAC
W: Bruce Howard & Brad Radnitz. D: Hollingsworth Morse. GS: Janice Car-

roll.   McHale tries to bring a WAC and her boyfriend back together.

Little Red Riding Doctor
W: John Fenton Murray. D: Hollingsworth Morse.   Binghamton is psychoanalyzed after he fails to win the King of Voltafiore award, an honor now bestowed upon McHale.

McHale's Country Club Caper
W: Ralph Goodman. D: Hollingsworth Morse. GS: Pat Harrington. The Captain unknowingly deals with a con man when he spends $1000 to have a golf course built at the base.

36-24-73
W: Sam Locke & Joel Rapp. D: Hollingsworth Morse. McHale and his men get into big trouble over a beauty contest.

Who Was That German I Seen You With?
John Fenton Murray. D: Hollingsworth Morse. Binghamton and Parker are captured by the Germans.

My Son the Keeper
W: Bruce Howard & Brad Radnitz. D: Hollingsworth Morse.   Binghamton puts Parker in charge of McHale's men when he is away.

Wally for Congress
W: Elroy Schwartz. D: Hollingsworth Morse. GS: Stanley Adams. Binghamton's moment of heroism to impress a visiting politician is ruined by a GI patrol.

The McHale Grand Prix
W: Ralph Goodman.   D: Hollingsworth Morse.   McHale stages a road race through the town, just as the Captain plans to enforce strict traffic control laws.

An Ensign's Best Friend
W: John Fenton Murray. D: Hollingsworth Morse.   Binghamton is constantly being chased by a pack of dogs.

Binghamton, at 20 Paces
W: Robert J. Hillard & Mickey Freeman. D: Hollingsworth Morse. Binghamton tries to catch Parker having an illegal duel with an Italian count.

McKEEVER AND THE COLONEL

On the air 9/23/62, off 6/16/63. NBC. B&W Film. 30 min. 26 episodes. Broadcast: Sept 1962-Jun 1963 Sun 6:30-7. Producer: Tom McKnight. Prod Co/Synd: Four Star International.
CAST: Cadet Gary McKeever (played by Scott Lane), Col. Harvey Blackwall (Allyn Joslyn), Sgt. Barnes (Jackie Coogan), Mrs. Warner (Elizabeth Fraser), Tubby (Keith Taylor), Monk (Johnny Eimen).
The misadventures of Gary McKeever, a mischievous cadet enrolled at the Westfield Military Academy for boys.   Episodes depict the trouble the youth gets into and the attempts of Col. Blackwell, the school's commander, to discipline him. Although syndicated, the series is dormant.

General McKeever
GS: Peter Hansen, Shirley Mitchell, Jim Houghton.   McKeever wants to join his father in Paris, so he tries to get himself thrown out of school.

The Army Mule
GS: Howard Smith, Henry Kulky.

Colonel Blackwell's former commanding officer leaves an Army mule in his care.

TV or Not TV
McKeever and his friends sell bars of soap in order to win a TV set.

Straight and Narrow
GS: Stanley Adams. McKeever tries to win a good conduct medal in order to impress his father.

The Mascot
GS: Elisabeth Fraser. The kids want to keep an escaped baby elephant as a mascot.

The Cookie Crumbles
GS: El Brendel, Benny Baker, Doris Singleton. The kids plan to bake and sell cookies so they can raise enough money to keep Tubby in school.

The Bugle Sounds
GS: Joe Flynn, Richard Deacon, Howard Caine. McKeever gets a job working on the school yearbook.

Blackwell's Stand
GS: Charles Lane, Phil Phillips. It's the town's 50th anniversary and the Colonel gives McKeever the job of producing the celebration pageant.

McKeever and the Celestial Bells
GS: Carolyn Kearney. The kids have been ordered to take a class in ballroom dancing.

Hand in Glove
A school trustee is coming for a surprise inspection.

Hair Today Gone Tomorrow
The kids buy a toupee for Barnes.

Happy Birthday Colonel
The kids plan a surprise party for Colonel Blackwell.

For Dear Old Westfield
GS: George Neise, Kevin Brodie. The Colonel enrolls an athlete at the school.

Too Many Sergeants
GS: Ann B. Davis, Mike Mazurki. Blackwell hires a tough female ser-geant to enforce the rules.

McKeever's Astronaut
A space chimp visits the school.

The Neighbor
GS: Jim Backus. An eccentric millionaire moves next door to the school.

Love Comes to Westfield
GS: Susan Gordon. The Colonel's niece has a crush on McKeever.

The Big Charade
GS: Charles Ruggles, Walter Coy. Barnes's visiting father thinks his son runs the school.

The Old Grad
GS: Soupy Sales, Chick Hearn. An old prankster returns to the school to get an award.

All Quiet on the Westfield Front
Vandals deface a statue while McKeever is on guard duty.

Feat of Clay
The kids make a bust of the Colonel.

Make Room for Mother
GS: Ellen Corby, J. Pat O'Malley. The Colonel's mother turns the school into a nursery.

Project: Walkie-Talkie
GS: David White, William Schallert. The Colonel thinks he is going to be fired.

Blackwell, the Retread
GS: Robert Emhardt, Phil Coolidge. The Colonel thinks McKeever would be better off in industrial work.

McKeever Meets Munroe
GS: Guy Marks, James Flavin. McKeever cures a K-9 dog from chasing cats.

By the Book
No available story.

MR. ED

On the air 10/1/61, off 9/8/65. CBS. B&W Film. 143 episodes. Broadcast: Oct 1961-Sept 1962 Sun 6:30-7; Sept 1962-Mar 1963 Thu 7:30-8; Mar 1963-Oct 1964 Sun 6:30-7; Dec 1964-Sept 1965 Wed 7:30-8. Producer & Director: Arthur Lubin. Prod Co/Synd: Filmways.

CAST: Wilbur Post (played by Alan Young), Carol Post (Connie Hines), Roger Addison (Larry Keating), Kay Addison (Edna Skinner), Gordon Kirkwood (Leon Ames), Winnie Kirkwood (Florence MacMichael), Voice of Mr. Ed (Alan "Rocky" Lane).

The adventures of Wilbur Post, architect, and his talking horse Mr. Ed. Stories depict the trouble Wilbur has as he attempts to conceal the fact he owns a talking horse from his wife and their neighbors. Other stories deal with the trouble Wilbur gets into as a result of Ed's zany escapades. *Mr. Ed* is still popular today even though the horse and the actor who play the horse's voice have long since died and no reunion is planned. Because of the comedic talents of Alan Young and the witty writing of Larry Rhine, Ben Starr and Lou Derman (who later went on to *All in the Family*), *Mr. Ed* remains a classic comedy of our time.

The First Meeting [Pilot]
Wilbur and Carol buy a new house and meet Mr. Ed.

The Ventriloquist
Wilbur has designs for a new clubhouse.

Stable for Three
Wilbur and Roger are banished to the barn.

Busy Wife
Carol joins a women's club and has no time for Wilbur.

The Kiddy Park
Mr. Ed wants to go on a fishing trip, but Wilbur says no.

Sorority House
Mr. Ed is kidnapped when Wilbur tries to enter a girls' sorority.

Ed the Lover
Mr. Ed is chosen to star in a western film.

The Pageant
Wilbur removes Ed's phone from the stable.

The Aunt
Mr. Ed is upset when a parrot takes over his stable.

The Missing Statue
Mr. Ed is upset when Carol buys a statue and Wilbur returns it.

Ed the Witness
In Mexico, Wilbur finds himself locked in jail.

Ed's Mother
Mr. Ed finds his lost mother and wants Wilbur to buy her.

The Little Boy
Carol brings an unhappy child home and it takes Mr. Ed to help get him friends.

Ed the Tout
Mr. Ed knows how to pick winners at the racetrack.

Ed the Songwriter
Kay's brother needs a new hit song, so Mr. Ed writes one.

Ed the Stoolpigeon
Mr. Ed is jealous when Wilbur puts a poodle in his barn.

Psychoanalyst Show
GS: Richard Deacon. Mr. Ed is frightened of high places.

Alan Young with the horse of the title, Mr. Ed.

A Man for Velma
Mr. Ed proposes to the cook Wilbur brings home.

Ed Agrees to Talk
Carol hitches Ed to a surrey and drives him around town.

Ed's New Shoes
A handyman destroys Wilbur's house.

The Mustache
Wilbur doesn't want to shave off his new mustache.

The Contest
Wilbur wins a contest and Ed thinks he's going to Europe.

The Other Woman
Mr. Ed wants Wilbur to buy a horse named Bernadine for him.

Wilbur Sells Ed
Mr. Ed wants to be sold to Wilbur's neighbor.

Ed Cries Wolf
While celebrating Carol's birthday, Mr. Ed drives Wilbur crazy.

Pine Lake Lodge
GS: William Bendix. While vacationing at a lodge, Wilbur is caught cutting down a tree.

My Son My Son
Mr. Ed fears old age and wants Wilbur to buy him a pony.

The Horsetranaut
Mr. Ed volunteers to be the first horse in space.

Ed the Jumper
Wilbur's old friend challenges him to a steeplechase.

Ed and the Redecorator
Mr. Ed wants his stall redone in Hawaiian modern.

Ed's Ancestors
Mr. Ed runs away after hearing bad rumors about his relatives.

Ed the Hero
Mr. Ed rescues a little girl on a runaway horse.

Ed the Voter
Mr. Ed wants to vote in the coming election.

Ed the Hunter
Mr. Ed wants Wilbur to take him along on the duck hunt.

Mr. Ed's Blues
Mr. Ed is lovesick and writes a new song about it.

Ed and the Elephant
Wilbur brings home an elephant and puts him in Ed's stall.

Ed the Salesman
Carol takes up dance lessons to earn some extra money.

Ed the Pilgrim
The story of Thanksgiving according to Mr. Ed.

Zsa Zsa
GS: Zsa Zsa Gabor. An actress in need of a horse.

Ed the Beneficiary
Wilbur makes his will out to Mr. Ed.

Ed the Horse Doctor
Mr. Ed analyzes a racehorse named Lady Linda because she can't win a race.

George Burns Meets Ed
GS: George Burns. George Burns pays a visit to Mr. Ed.

Wilbur the Masher
Mr. Ed's new girlfriend Flossie causes Wilbur some trouble.

Ed's New Neighbors
Mr. Ed befriends the new neighbors.

Bald Horse
Mr. Ed wants to be left at the Briarcliff Stables.

No Horses Allowed
A neighbor is sending around an anti-horse petition.

Ed the Matchmaker
Mr. Ed plays cupid for two lovers.

Clint Eastwood Meets Mr. Ed
GS: Clint Eastwood. Clint Eastwood pays a visit to the Posts.

Ed and the Secret Service
The girls organize a hunt club after seeing a newspaper photo of the First Lady on horseback.

Lie Detector
Wilbur puts Mr. Ed under a lie detector.

Ed the Beachcomber
Mr. Ed hits the beach with a bunch of Beatniks.

Ed Gets Amensia
Mr. Ed gets amnesia after a bucket of carrots hits him on the head.

Wilbur the Good Samaritan
Mr. Ed complains about the new delivery boy.

The Wrestler
Wilbur and Roger become the manager of a wrestler.

Wilbur's Father
Wilbur's father is thinking of remarrying.

Ed's Christmas Story
Mr. Ed is upset when Wilbur refuses to buy presents for his friends.

Wilbur in the Lion's Den
GS: Charles Lane. Wilbur won't be able to work with bothersome Ed around the office.

The Bashful Clipper
A shy hairstylist is the latest investment of Roger and Wilbur.

Ed's Word of Honor
Mr. Ed is accused of eating Roger's fish.

Wilbur and Ed in Show Biz
Wilbur and Mr. Ed perform in a variety show. After a basket of apples is found near Ed's stall, Wilbur is accused of stealing them.

Horse Wash
Mr. Ed has a new girlfriend named Chicquetta.

Ed and the Allergy
Roger doesn't want his mother to visit, but she does.

Horse Sense
Mr. Ed's bridle path is to be closed.

Ed and Paul Revere
Mr. Ed becomes the model for a statue.

Horse Party
Today is Mr. Ed's birthday and he is determined to have a party.

The Disappearing Horse
Wilbur and Mr. Ed perform a magic trick.

Ed and the Bicycle
Wilbur removes the TV from Ed's barn after he refuses to apologize, and then he buys a bicycle.

Horse of a Different Color
Mr. Ed wants Wilbur to take him to the circus.

The Blessed Event
Mr. Ed's new friend is a horse named Domino, who is expecting a colt.

Ole Rockin' Chair
Wilbur makes a repulsive rocking chair out of horseshoes.

Unemployment Show
Wilbur wants Ed to get a job.

Big Pine Lodge
Wilbur and Roger are taken in by card sharks.

Horse Talk
A race attendant is accused of doping a horse.

Wilbur Post Honorary Horse
Wilbur interviews Mr. Ed for a book of horses.

Patter of Little Hooves
Wilbur has to complete a jigsaw puzzle contest by midnight.

Leo Durocher Meets Mr. Ed
Mr. Ed gives the L.A. Dodgers some tips on baseball.

Ed's Bed
Mr. Ed is not eating and Wilbur's got a hard choice: stay and nurse Ed or go to the ballet with Carol.

Working Wives
Mr. Ed tries to hypnotize Wilbur into spending more time with him.

Ed the Emancipator
Mr. Ed frees a lot of imprisoned animals in Roger's house.

Ed Discovers America
Mr. Ed wants a horse put up in front of a museum.

The Price of Apples
Wilbur has to pay a higher price for apples because Ed eats too much.

Doctor Ed
Mr. Ed gets mad when Roger borrows his TV set.

Ed and the Zebra
Wilbur wants Ed to put on a silly suit for a photography contest.

Taller Than She
Mr. Ed feels insecure because his girlfriend is taller than he.

Be Kind to Humans Week
Mr. Ed invites three hoboes to stay in Wilbur's barn, but Wilbur's father is coming.

Don't Laugh at Horses
Wilbur and Paul put on a horse suit that offends Mr. Ed.

Getting Ed's Goat
Mr. Ed brings home an old goat and then is banished to an animal shelter.

Ed the Musician
Ed's new hobby is playing the harmonica.

Oh, Those Hats!
GS: Spring Byington. Mr. Ed puts on a campaign to save the zoo.

Ed the Shishkebob
Wilbur performs another variety act at Ed's expense.

Ed the Desert Rat
Mr. Ed doesn't want a swimming pool put in his yard.

Home Sweet Trailer
Colonel Kirkwood visits the Posts and then takes over Wilbur's house.

Love Thy New Neighbor
Gordon buys the house next door.

Moko
The Posts are visited by an alien from outer space.

Ed in the Peace Corps
Mr. Ed volunteers for the Peace Corps after Wilbur ignores him.

Ed Gets the Mumps
Mr. Ed wants Wilbur to spend more time with him so he fakes a case of the mumps.

Ed's Dentist
Gordon sees Wilbur playing chess with Ed and thinks he is crazy.

Ed Visits a Gypsy
A gypsy reads Ed's hoof and Ed believes what the gypsy tells him.

Ed the Chauffeur
Mr. Ed tells Wilbur he can drive and proves it in a milk truck.

Old Swayback
Mr. Ed befriends an old carnival horse.

Ed the Donkey
Mr. Ed thinks he is the descendant of the mule family.

Mae West Meets Mr. Ed.
GS: Mae West. Mae West pays a visit to Mr. Ed.

Saddles and Gowns
Mr. Ed wants a new expensive saddle.

The Prowler
Wilbur helps the police track down a burglar.

Ed the Pool Player
Mr. Ed plays billiards.

Ed Writes Dear Abby
GS: Abigail van Buren. Mr. Ed writes a letter to Dear Abby and everyone thinks Wilbur wrote it.

Hi Fi Horse
Mr. Ed wants to use Wilbur's new stereo.

Like Father Like Horse
Mr. Ed thinks that he and Wilbur are related.

Ed's Tunnel to Freedom
Wilbur locks Mr. Ed in the barn and he digs his way out and into Wilbur's living room.

What Kind of Foal Am I?
Mr. Ed is jealous of a baby.

Ed the Racehorse
Wilbur wants Ed to win a race and Ed doesn't want to run.

Jon Provost Meets Mr. Ed
Mr. Ed gets to meet Lassie.

My Horse the Ranger
Wilbur decides to go hiking without Mr. Ed.

The Heavy Rider
Mr. Ed gives a 300-pound bankrobber the slip.

Ed the Pilot
Mr. Ed takes up flying and then parachutes out of a plane.

Stowaway Horse
Wilbur goes on a cruise and Mr. Ed stows away in the bathroom.

Animal Jury
Aunt Martha returns with her troublesome parrot.

Anybody Got a Zebra?
Mr. Ed wants to meet his long-lost father.

The Dragon Horse
Mr. Ed becomes superstitious and Wilbur has to put up with it.

Ed's Juice Stand
Mr. Ed's new business is a drink with a special ingredient: hay.

Never Ride Horses
Mr. Ed begins a campaign to end horseback riding.

Ed the Sentry
Carol is allergic to Mr. Ed and Wilbur may have to sell him.

Ed's Diction Teacher
Mr. Ed doesn't want to be left alone with Gordon.

Ed the Godfather
Mr. Ed brings home a horse that is about to give birth.

Ed's Contact Lenses
After a man laughs at Ed for wearing glasses, he decides to get contact lenses.

Ed's Cold Tail
Mr. Ed wants a new heating system in his barn to combat the cold weather.

The Bank Robbery
Mr. Ed helps capture a bank robber by the use of a photograph.

Robin Hood Ed
Wilbur puts on a Robin Hood outfit and is arrested.

Whiskers and Tails
GS: Sebastian Cabot. A new neighbor of the Posts does not like horses.

Ed the Artist
Wilbur's new headache is Ed's new hobby: painting.

My Horse the Mailman
Mr. Ed tries to revive the Pony Express singlehanded.

Ed the Counterspy
Mr. Ed and Wilbur investigate three spies.

Ed a Go-Go
The new neighbors' loud music is keeping everyone awake.

Coldfinger
Wilbur and Mr. Ed are threatened by a hood who likes duck chow mein.

Love and the Single Horse
Mr. Ed is writing his autobiography.

Ed Breaks the Hip Code
Someone has been stealing valuable government information, so Ed investigates.

TV or Not TV
Mr. Ed says he sees color and wants a new color TV set.

The Horse and the Pussycat
Mr. Ed is upset when a Siamese cat receives more attention than he does.

Ed the Bridegroom
Mr. Ed falls for a horse named Rosita.

Don't Skin That Bear
The gift that Carol's father bought her offends Mr. Ed.

My Horse the Motorcycle Hater
Mr. Ed decides it is time to try motorcycle riding.

Cherokee Ed
Mr. Ed learns that he may have Indian ancestry.

Mr. Ed Goes to College
Mr. Ed wants to be a horse doctor.

MR. ROBERTS

On the air 9/17/65, off 9/2/66. NBC. Color Film. 30 min. 30 episodes. Broadcast: Sept 1965-Sept 1966 Fri 9:30-10. Producer: Unknown. Prod Co/Synd: Warner Bros. TV.

CAST: Lt. Douglas Roberts (played by Roger Smith), Ensign Frank Pulver (Steve Harmon), Captain John Morton (Richard X. Slattery), Doc (George Ives).

Set in the South Pacific during World War II, this is the story of Lt. Douglas Roberts, a cargo officer aboard the USS Reluctant. Mr. Roberts, feeling he is on the wrong ship and desperately wishing to serve aboard a fighting vessel, requests a transfer only to be constantly refused by the Captain. Captain Morton feels that Roberts is too great an inspiration to his men to grant him a transfer. Week after week, Mr. Roberts tries to come up with some excuse that will win his freedom from the Reluctant. This series is based on the movie of the same name. It is not currently seen on any station, although still available.

Bookser's Honeymoon
GS: Timothy Rooney, Charles Doherty. Someone has crushed a cigar in Captain Morton's beloved potted plant. Morton wants revenge, so he cancels shore leave, destroying Seaman Bookser's hopes of seeing his new bride.

Liberty
GS: Henry Gibson. The Captain thinks he has just sunk a Japanese submarine, when in reality he sunk a washtub which Pulver had planted in an attempt to arrange liberty for the men.

Physician Heal Thyself
GS: Henry Gibson. Roberts arranges for Doc to perform an operation on Pulver in order to bring Doc out of his depression.

The Conspiracy
GS: Tsu Kobayashi, Albert Morin.

Roberts is shocked to find that part of the cargo he is supposed to load on board is a beautiful woman.

Old Rustysides
GS: Woodrow Parfrey, Lou Wills. A congressman plans to visit the ship after he reads Pulver's letter about the heroic exploits of the crew.

Lover Come Forward
GS: Lisa Gaye, Dennis Robertson. The crew discovers that the Captain is in love.

Captain's Party
Pulver passes off his girlfriend as French royalty in order to explain her presence on the ship.

Happy Birthday to Who?
The crew ask Roberts to get the musical film hidden in the Captain's cabin after seeing the same monster film for the sixth time.

Love at 78 R.P.M.
Roberts takes his anger out on the crew when his transfer request is denied.

Don't Look Now, But Isn't That the War?
Roberts orders new parts for the ship which will allow it to join a convoy headed for a combat area.

Which Way Did the War Go?
A Japanese pilot assists the crew to make necessary repairs on the ship, when they are stuck in the middle of the ocean with no help in sight.

Getting There Is Half the Fun
GS: George Takei, Bill Quinn. The Captain asks Roberts to help him create a cover-up story to explain the fact that the ship fouled up its mission.

Dear Mom
Pulver asks his influential mother to get Roberts transferred to a ship in combat, but he gets transferred instead.

Reluctant Mutiny
The Captain plans to block Roberts's transfer which has finally come through.

Rockabye Reluctant
GS: Naomi Stevens. The ship leaves port with an expectant mother in the sickbay.

Carry Me Back to Cococe Island
GS: Joy Harmon. Pulver kills the Captain's plant by feeding it chipped beef.

The Replacement
GS: Shelley Berman. Roberts's replacement is a bumbler, which prevents Roberts from leaving when his transfer comes through.

Black and Blue Market
GS: Tiger Joe Marsh. Pulver gives away medical supplies to a pretty lieutenant without authorization.

World's Greatest Lover
GS: Linda Gaye Scott, Reginald Denny. Pulver can't bring himself to talk to the girl he is in love with.

Eight in Every Port
GS: Alan Mowbray, Pamela Wodman. Roberts tries to patch up their relations with the local natives, after the Captain orders them off the ship.

The Super Chief
The new chief warrant officer gets anything he wants from the Captain, including permission to search Roberts and Pulver's cabin.

Doctor's Dilemma
Doc must get a woman named Beulah Cronk to allow the Navy to place an observation post on her island.

Reluctant Draggin
GS: Lyle Talbot, Edd Byrnes. Roberts wants a new crewman to fight a crewman of another ship in a boxing match where the loser will pay for the damage to a saloon.

#*@% (Damn) the Torpedoes
GS: Mimsy Farmer, Yvonne Craig, Kelly Peters. The ship has been ordered to transfer three USO girls. The Captain, however, orders them to stay below decks in order to keep them away from the men.

A Turn for the Nurse
GS: Vince Howard, Barbara Stuart. The Captain refuses to allow Doc to remove his appendix as it will mean he will have to give up command of the ship.

Son of Eight in Every Port
GS: Keely Smith. The crew return to the island of Namu, this time to take a survival test.

Unwelcome Aboard
Doc thinks Roberts is seeing things when he tells him he saw a girl aboard the ship.

Undercover Cook
GS: Wally Cox, Robert Ito. The new cook causes nothing but trouble.

In Love and War
GS: Mamie Van Doren. Roberts and Pulver try to win a role in a movie star's new film.

Captain, My Captain
GS: Darlene Patterson, Jeanne Riley. A German spy who is a lookalike for the Captain has been planted aboard the ship.

MR. TERRIFIC

On the air 1/4/67, off 8/28/67. CBS. Color Film. 30 min. 15 episodes. Broadcast: Jan 1967-Aug 1967 Mon 8-8:30. Producer: Jack Arnold. Prod Co: Universal. Not syndicated.

CAST: Stanley Beamish (Mr. Terrific) (played by Stephen Strimpell), Barton J. Reed (John McGiver), Hal Walters (Dick Gautier), Harley Trent (Paul Smith).

WRITER: David P. Harmon.

A clone of *Captain Nice* set in Washington, D.C., Stanley Beamish, proprietor of a gas station, turns from weakling to superhero with the aid of a secret government power pill. Stories involve Stanley's investigation of enemy agents, his struggle to adjust to a secret identity, and the problems that occur when the pill (which can only last for one hour) wears off. *Mr. Terrific* is not in syndication because it involves PILLS, a subject considered harmful to child viewers.

Matchless
GS: Harold J. Stone, Iggie Wolfington. Mr. Terrific has to find a defecting scientist who has invented a power paralyzer.

Mr. Big Curtsies Out
GS: Kathie Browne. Mr. Terrific meets Mr. Big, a lady crime boss. There is only one problem, Stanley has forgotten to bring his power pills.

I Can't Fly
Mr. Terrific's power pills fail to work just as a crippled airplane is about to crash.

The Formula Is Stolen
GS: Lee Bergere, Joan Huntington. Spies steal the formula for the power pills and they have also sent a lady spy to capture Stanley.

Stanley the Safecracker
GS: Barbara Stuart, Robert Strauss. Stanley impersonates a lookalike safecracker to catch a gang of crooks.

Stanley, the Fighter
GS: Leo Gordon, Charles Dierkop. Stanley tries to break up a gang of crooks who are using a gym as a hideout.

Stephen Strimpell as Mr. Terrific.

My Partner, the Jailbreaker
GS: Richard X. Slattery. Stanley poses as a criminal to help another crook break out of jail, hoping he will lead him to his hidden loot.

Fly, Ballerina, Fly
GS: Barrie Chase, Cynthia Lynn. Mr. Terrific goes to the aid of a defecting Russian ballerina.

Harley and the Killer
GS: Henry Brandon. Stanley tries to protect Harley from an escaped killer.

Stanley and the Mountaineers
Stanley tries to find a moonshine still

and Harley is headed for a shotgun wedding.

Has Mr. Terrific Sold Out?
GS: Arnold Moss, Ned Glass. Stanley demonstrates his powers for a group of visiting dignitaries, one of whom is an imposter.

Stanley the Track Star
GS: Chris Dark, Ziva Rodann, Don Marshall. Stanley tries to rescue an athlete who was kidnapped at a track meet.

Stanley Goes to the Dentist
GS: John Hoyt. Stanley goes to a spy

dentist who plants a transmitter in his mouth in the hopes of overhearing government secrets.

The Sultan Has Five Wives
GS: John Vivyan, Ulla Stromsteat. Stanley is supposed to plant phony missile plans on an enemy agent,

except he hands over the real plans instead.

Stanley Joins the Circus
Stanley has to fight a strongman, a gorilla, and a team of high-wire aerialists when he tries to recover a missing code book at the circus.

MRS. G. GOES TO COLLEGE/THE GERTRUDE BERG SHOW

On the air 10/4/61, off 4/5/62. CBS. B&W Film. 26 episodes. Broadcast: Oct 1961-Jan 1962 Wed 9:30-10; Jan 1962-Apr 1962 Thu 9:30-10. Producer: Gertrude Berg. Synd: Four Star International.
CAST: Sarah Green (played by Gertrude Berg), Prof. Crayton (Sir Cedric Hardwicke), Maxfield (Mary Wickes), Joe Caldwell (Skip Ward), Susan Green (Marion Ross), Jerry Green (Leo Penn), George Howell (Paul Smith), Irma Howell (Aneta Corseaut), Carol (Karyn Kupcinet).
The former star of *The Goldbergs*, Gertrude Berg returned to television to appear in a short-lived series about an older woman who returns to college. This was the only TV series in which Sir Cedric Hardwicke has a featured role as he died less than two years after the series was cancelled. The series was originally called *Mrs. G. Goes to College*, but it was changed to the *Gertrude Berg Show* in mid-season. It hasn't turned up on a station since it went off in 1962.

The First Day
GS: Aneta Corsaut, Marion Ross, Paul Smith. Sarah meets Professor Green who happens to hate all Freshmen.

First Test
GS: Peter Lorre, Skip Ward. Sarah and Joe Caldwell are having difficulty with science.

Sam's Car
GS: Marion Ross, Herbie Faye, George Petrie. Sarah tries to sell her old car.

Lonely Sunday
GS: Stuart Margolin, Carol Oileany. Sarah prepares a big dinner, but all of her friends are going away for the weekend.

Mrs. G. Meets Dr. Hennesey
GS: Jackie Cooper, Mary Wickes. Joe Caldwell decides to join the Navy when he gets a low grade. [This is a crossover episode from the "Hennesey" series.]

The Baby Affair
GS: Marion Ross, Leo Penn, Mae Questal. Sarah helps her daughter with her little girl.

Crayton on TV
GS: Parley Baer, Tom Browne Henry. Professor Crayton gives a book report on a TV program.

Red, Red Rose
GS: Isobel Elson. Professor Crayton is giving a reception for a British poetess.

Romance for Maxie
GS: Karyn Kupcinet, Charles Watts. Maxfield has a new boyfriend, which makes everyone want to meet him.

The Trouble with Crayton
GS: Peter Lorre, Robert Emhardt, Phillip Coolidge. Sarah and Dr. Barber want Professor Crayton to take a rest, so they hide the results of his physical exam.

The Teacher
GS: Steven Geray, Lili Valenty, Jack Petruzzi. Sarah holds classes in the back of a tailor shop.

Mrs. G. Meets the Faculty
GS: Parley Baer, Lou Krugman, Tom Brown Henry. Sarah is the only one looking forward to the faculty reception for the Freshman class.

Mrs. G.'s Private Telephone
GS: Leo Penn, Yvonne Craig. Sarah has a phone installed in her room.

Maxie's Silent Partner
Sarah invests in the campus boarding house. She then tries to get Professor Crayton to get along with the other boarders.

Mrs. G. vs. the Kingston Trio
GS: The Kingston Trio, Phillip Coolidge. Sarah gets upset when she learns the Kingston Trio is appearing on the same night as the Faculty String Quartet.

Sunday Dinner
GS: Brian Davies, Susan Hope. Sarah sells home-cooked dinners to the tenants to raise money.

The Mother Affair
GS: Arlene Francis, Alan Reed. A coed with an overprotective mother moves into the boarding house.

Peace Corps
GS: Fabian, Will Kuluva. Sarah helps out when a student wants to join the Peace Corps, but his father won't let him.

Goodbye, Mr. Howell
GS: William Windom, Doris Singleton, Ken Berry. George's poor old classmate is now a very rich man.

How Now, Brown Cow?
GS: Phillip Coolidge, Doug Lambert, Dani Lynn. Sarah is chosen to take part in a class debate.

High Finance
GS: Stuart Margolin, Bob Hastings. Sarah helps Charlie Hughes when his money problems may force him to leave school.

One of Our Books Is Missing
GS: Vaughn Taylor, Kip King. The library claims Sarah did not return a book but she is sure that she did return it.

Curfew Shall Not Ring Tonight
Joe and Carol are upset; they feel they are too old for the faculty-imposed curfew.

Gentleman Caller
GS: Robert F. Simon, Mae Questal. Sarah's matchmaking sister Dora is sending a man over for her to meet.

Dad's Day
GS: Alan Reed, Sr., Alan Reed, Jr., Stafford Repp, Cliff Norton. Sarah finds room for Amy and Susan's fathers on Dad's Day at the school.

The Bird
GS: Frank Aletter, John Astin. Sarah finds a bird's nest in the atom smashing cyclotron.

THE MONKEES

On the air 9/12/66, off 8/19/68. NBC. Color Film. 30 min. 58 episodes. Broadcast: Sept 1966-Aug 1968 Mon 7:30-8. Producer: Robert Raffelson, Bert Schneider. Prod Co/Synd: Columbia Pictures TV.

CAST: The cast portrayed themselves: Davy Jones, Peter Tork, Mickey Dolenz, Mike Nesmith.

WRITERS: Gerald Gardner, Dave Evans, Bernie Orenstein, Peter Meyerson, Coslough Johnson, Jack Winter, David Panich, Stanley Ralph Ross, Paul Mazursky, Dee Caruso, George Gardner, Larry Tucker. DIRECTORS: James Frawley, Robert Rafelson, Bruce Kessler, Sidney Miller, Russ Mayberry, Alex Singer, Peter Tork, Mickey Dolenz.

The misadventures of The Monkees, a rock and roll group traveling the U.S. Typical episodes involve one or more of the group getting into trouble, sending the others to the rescue. Although most episodes are silly, *The Monkees* remains the first running television series to feature a famous singing group. *The Monkees* enjoys a cult status today and this show is one of the most frequently requested series.

The Monkees [Pilot]
W: Paul Mazursky & Larry Tucker. D: Mike Elliot. The Monkees get their first break when they play at the sweet sixteen party held by a country club owner.

Royal Flush
W: Peter Meyerson & Robert Schlitt. D: James Frawley. GS: Vincent Beck. Davy uncovers a plot to kill a beautiful princess, sending him to the rescue.

Monkey See, Monkey Die
W: Treva Silverman. D: James Frawley. GS: Henry Corden, Stacey Maxwell. After visiting a mansion, the Monkees enter a seance to help solve a murder.

Monkee vs. Machine
W: David Panish. D: Robert Rafelson. GS: Severn Darden, Stan Freeberg. Peter tries to help an old toymaker keep from losing his job to a computer.

Your Friendly Neighborhood Kidnappers
W: Dave Evans. D: James Frawley. GS: Vic Tayback. The Monkees compete in a recording contest in which they are ultimately kidnapped.

The Spy Who Came in from the Cool
W: Dee Caruso & George Gardner. D: Robert Rafelson. GS: Booth Coleman, Billy Curtis, Jacques Aubuchon, Arlene Martel. Davy buys a pair of maracas with secret microfilm hidden in them, causing a wild chase for the possession of the maracas to begin.

Success Story
W: Dee Caruso & George Gardner. D: James Frawley. Davy must convince his visiting grandfather that he has become a wealthy superstar.

Monkees in a Ghost Town
W: Peter Meyerson & Robert Schlitt. D: James Frawley. GS: Lon Chaney, Rose Marie. The Monkees are captured in a ghost town by two hoods and find themselves locked in the local jail.

Gift Horse
W: Dave Evan. D: Robert Rafelson. GS: Jerry Colonna. The boys become reluctant owners of a pet horse and must find a way to hide it from their landlord.

The Chaperone
W: Dee Caruso & George Gardner. D: Bruce Kessler. GS: Arch Johnson, Sherry Alberoni. Davy falls in love with a retired general's daughter who can only attend chaperoned parties.

Monkees a la Carte
W: Bernie Orenstein, Dee Caruso & George Gardner. D: James Frawley. GS: Harvey Lembeck. The Monkees attempt to win back Pop's Restaurant from the "mob" by becoming waiters, cooks and hatcheck girls in the restaurant.

I've Got a Little Song Here
W: Treva Silverman. D: Bruce Kessler. GS: Phil Leeds. Mike is swindled out of $100 by a phony music publishing firm.

One Man Shy
W: Treva Silverman, Dee Caruso & George Gardner. D: James Frawley.

GS: George Furth, Lisa James. Peter is caught in a love triangle between a girl he loves and her jealous boyfriend.

Dance Monkee Dance
W: Bernie Orenstein. D: James Frawley. GS: Hal March. Peter wins free dance lessons and then is duped into signing a lifetime contract.

Too Many Girls
W: Dave Evans, Dee Caruso & George Gardner. D: James Frawley. GS: Reta Shaw. A con artist tries to convince Davy that he should help her daughter succeed in show business.

Son of a Gypsy
W: Treva Silverman, Dee Caruso & George Gardner. D: James Frawley. GS: Vic Tayback, Vincent Beck. After being threatened with torture, the Monkees steal a priceless statuette for a band of spies.

Case of the Missing Monkee
W: Dee Caruso & George Gardner. D: Robert Rafelson. GS: Vito Scotti, Vincent Gardenia. While trying to foil a kidnapping of a nuclear scientist, the Monkees almost lose Peter.

I Was a Teenage Monster
W: Dave Evans, Dee Caruso & George Gardner. D: Sidney Miller. GS: John Hoyt, Richard Kiel. A mad scientist transplants the Monkees' musical talent into the body of a monster.

Find the Monkees
W: Dee Caruso & George Gardner. D: Richard Nonis. GS: Bobo Lewis, Carl Ballentine. A TV producer searches for the Monkees, unaware they are searching for him at the same time.

Monkees in the Ring
W: Dee Caruso & George Gardner. D: James Frawley. GS: Ned Glass, Robert Lyons. A crooked fight promoter convinces Davy he can be a world champ.

The Prince and the Pauper
W: Peter Meyerson. D: James Komack.

GS: Oscar Beregi. Davy disguises himself as a prince to save his throne and kingdom.

Monkees at the Circus
W: David Panich. D: Bruce Kessler. GS: Richard Devon. The Monkees pose as aerialists to save a small circus from bankruptcy.

Captain Crocodile
W: Gerald Gardner & Dee Caruso. D: James Frawley. GS: Joey Foreman. After appearing on a children's TV show, Captain Crocodile, the star, feels the Monkees are trying to take over his job.

Monkees a la Mode
W: Gerald Gardner & Dee Caruso. D: Alex Singer. GS: Patrice Wymore. The Monkees receive an award for grace and gentility from the editors of a fashion magazine.

Alias Mickey Dolenz
W: Gerald Gardner & Dee Caruso. D: James Frawley. GS: Robert Strauss. Mickey's resemblance to a killer finds the Monkees being chased once more by the mob.

Monkee Chow Mein
W: Gerald Gardner & Dee Caruso. D: James Frawley. GS: Joey Foreman, Dave Barry. The Monkees meet up with a Red Chinese spy ring when Peter takes the wrong fortune cookie with a secret message hidden in it.

Monkee Mother
W: Peter Meyerson & Bob Schlitt. D: James Frawley. GS: Rose Marie, William Bramley. When the Monkees fall behind in their rent, the landlord moves in another tenant who takes over the pad and the Monkees.

Monkees Get Out More Dirt
W: Gerald Gardner & Dee Caruso. D: James Frawley. GS: Julie Newmar. The Monkees' friendship is threatened when they all fall for the same girl.

Monkees on the Line
W: Coslough Johnson, Gerald Gardner
& Dee Caruso.   D: James Frawley.
GS: Milton Frome.   The Monkees
get everyone's wires crossed when they
take over an answering service.

Monkees in Manhattan
W: Gerald Gardner & Dee Caruso. D:
Russell Mayberry.   GS: Phil Ober,
Olan Soule, Doodles Weaver.   While
trying to get a job in a Broadway musical, the Monkees end up caring for
some bunny rabbits.

Monkees in the Movies
W: Gerald Gardner & Dee Caruso. D:
Russell Mayberry.   GS: Bobby Sherman, Jerry Lester. A Hollywood producer puts the Monkees in one of his
films, causing sparks to fly between
the main star of the film and Davy.

Monkees on Tour
W & D: Robert Rafelson.   While the
Monkees are on tour, they must find
ways of avoiding thousands of screaming fans.

It's a Nice Place to Visit
W: Treva Silverman.   D: James Frawley.   GS: Peter Whitney. Davy falls in
love with a bandit's girl and they must
fight their way out of a seedy Mexican village.

The Picture Frame
W: Jack Winter.   D: James Frawley.
GS: Cliff Norton, Henry Beckman.
Fooled into believing they are making
a movie, the Monkees help a gang rob
a bank.

Everywhere a Sheik, Sheik
W: Jack Winter.   D: Alex Singer. GS:
Arnold Moss.   To avoid a man she de-
spises, a beautiful princess wants to
marry Davy.

Monkee Mayor
W: Jack Winter.   D: Alex Singer. GS:
Peter Brocco, Irwin Charone.   Mike
runs for mayor to stop crooked politicians from turning the city into
parking lots.

Art for Monkees' Sake
W: Coslough Johnson. D: Alex Singer.
GS: Monte Landis, Vic Tayback. The
Monkees stop the theft of an art mas-
terpiece from a museum.

Ninety-Nine Pound Weakling
W: Unknown. D: Alex Singer. Mickey, upset over his physical condition,
takes a course in bodybuilding to impress a beautiful girl.

Hillbilly Honeymoon
W: Peter Meyerson. D: James Frawley.
GS: Lou Antonio, Melody Patterson.
The Monkees become involved in set-
tling a dispute between two feuding
families in Swineville, USA.

Monkees Marooned
W: Stanley Ralph Ross.   D: James
Frawley. GS: Monte Landis, Burt Mustin.   After Peter buys a phony pirate
map, the Monkees go on a buried treasure expedition.

The Card-Carrying Red Shoes
W: Lee Sanford.   D: James Frawley.
GS: Vincent Beck, Leon Askin.   The
Monkees play for a ballet company
that in reality is an international spy
ring.

Wild Monkees
W: Stanley Ralph Ross & Corey Upton.
D: Jon G. Anderson.   GS: Henry Corden, Norman Grabowski.   The Monkees are mixed up with a motorcycle
gang and their four beautiful girlfriends.

A Coffin Too Frequent
W: Stella Linden.   D: David Winters.
GS: George Furth, Ruth Buzzi.   At a
seance, the Monkees keep an old lady
from being swindled.

Hitting the High Seas
W: Jack Winter.   D: James Frawley.
GS: Ted De Corsia, Noam Pitlik, Chips
Rafferty.   The Monkees sign on as sea-
men and find their captain plans to
hijack the Queen Elizabeth.

Monkees in Texas
W: Jack Winter. D: James Frawley. GS: Barton MacLane, Jacqueline De Witt. Out West, the Monkees outwit a notorious gang to save Mike's aunt's ranch.

Monkees on the Wheel
W: Coslough Johnson. D: Jerry Shepard. GS: Rip Taylor, David Astor. The Monkees break the bank in Las Vegas and find themselves pursued by the mob.

Christmas Show
W: Unknown. D: Jon G. Anderson. GS: Larry Gelman, Butch Patrick. The Monkees try to show the real meaning of Christmas to a cynical little boy.

Fairy Tale
W: Peter Meyerson. D: James Frawley. In a trip through Fairy Tale Land, Peter rescues a damsel in distress.

Monkees Watch Their Feet
W: Coslough Johnson. D: Alex Singer. GS: Pat Paulsen, Nita Talbot. The Monkees foil an invasion from the planet Spritz.

Monstrous Monkee Mash
W: Neil Burstyn & David Panich. D: James Frawley. GS: Ron Masak, Arlene Martel, David Pearl. In an old castle, the Monkees meet the Wolfman, the Mummy, and Frankenstein.

The Monkees' Paw
W: Unknown. D: James Frawley. GS: Hans Conreid. An actual monkey's paw brings bad luck to all the Monkees including dealing with Mendrek, a broken-down magician.

Devil and Peter Tork
W: Robert Kaufman. D: James Frawley. GS: Monte Landis. At a pawn shop, Peter sells his soul for a golden harp and then must pay his debt to the devil.

Monkees Race Again
W: Dave Evans & Elias Davis. D: James Frawley. GS: Stubby Kaye, David Hurst. Davy enters the Monkeymobile in an auto race when the British entry is put out of action by a villainous gang.

Monkees in Paris
W & D: Robert Rafelson. While vacationing in Paris, the Monkees are pursued by four screaming girls.

Monkees Mind Their Manor
W: Coslough Johnson. D: Peter H. Thorkelson (Peter Tork). GS: Laurie Main, Bernard Fox. In order to inherit an English castle, Davy must win a duel with lances.

Some Like It Lukewarm
W: Joel Kane & Stanley Z. Cherry. D: James Frawley. GS: Deana Martin. To win a contest, Davy poses as a girl and falls in love with Daphne, a girl posing as a boy.

Monkees Blow Their Minds
W: Peter Meyerson. D: David Winters. GS: Milton Frome, Monte Landis, Burgess Meredith. The Monkees meet up with an evil hypnotist who puts them under his spell, or so he thinks.

Mijacged
W: Jon G. Anderson & Mickey Dolenz. D: Mickey Dolenz. GS: Rip Taylor. The Monkees encounter a pulsing eye that freezes people to their TV sets.

MORK & MINDY

On the air 9/14/78, off 9/82. ABC. Color Film. 91 episodes. Broadcast: Sept 1978-Aug 1979 Thu 8-8:30; Aug 1979-Dec 1979 Sun 8-8:30; Jan 1980-

Pam Dawber, Mindy, and Robin Williams, Mork.

Jan 1980-Sept 1982 Thu 8-8:30.   Producer: Garry Marshall.   Prod Co/Synd:
Paramount TV.
   CAST: Mork (Played by Robin Williams), Mindy McConnell (Pam Dawber),
Fred McConnell (Conrad Janis), Cora Hudson (Elizabeth Kerr), Eugene (Jeffrey
Jacquet), Orson (voice) (Ralph James), Mr. Bickley (Tom Poston), Exidor (Rob-
ert Donner), Mearth (Jonathan Winters).
   A spinoff of *Happy Days*. An alien from another planet comes to Earth and
moves in with a single girl in order to learn about Earth customs. Popular on
network. It entered syndication in September 1983 and immediately died.

Mork Moves In [Pilot]   Henry Winkler, Dick Yarmy. Mork is
GS: Penny Marshall, Cindy Williams,   sent to study primitive human society.

To Tell the Truth
Fred wants to know if Mork is going to be a permanent houseguest.

Mork Runs Away
GS: Jeff Jacquet.   Mork feels he is cramping Mindy, so he runs away.

Mork in Love
Mork doesn't understand love, so he sets out to experience it.

Mork Runs Down
GS: Susan Elliot. Mork gets sick when he forgets to take his usual dose of gleek.

Mork's Seduction
GS: Morgan Fairchild.   Mindy is jealous when a girlfriend of hers makes a date with Mork.

Mork Goes Public
A reporter looking for a scoop suspects Mindy of hiding an Alien.

A Mommy for Mork
GS: Barry Van Dyke, Susan Lawrence. Mork decides to try life as a baby at the most inopportune moment.

Gullible Mork
GS: Dan Barrows. Mork is taken in by a prisoner's sob story, so he springs the man with the understanding that he will turn himself in later.

Young Love
GS: Barry Van Dyke. Mindy begins to think about marrying her former boyfriend.

Mork's Greatest Hits
GS: Brian James. Mork's dedication to nonviolence is tested when a neighborhood bully challenges him to a fight.

Mork and the Immigrant
GS: Tim Thomerson. Mork befriends a Russian immigrant, an alien he is sure is from outer space.

Christmas Show
GS: Dave Ketchum. Mork sets out to find the perfect gifts for his human friends.

Mork the Tolerant
Mork teaches Bickley the meaning of tolerance to calm his nasty disposition.

Old Fears
The death of her card partner makes Cora feel very old.

Snowflakes Falling
Mork and Mindy journey to Exidor's private mountain resort.

Mork Goes Erk
Mork is being transferred to another planet.

Mork's Mixed Emotions
GS: George Pentecost. Mork forsakes Orkan training and lets go of his emotions for the first time.

Yes Sir That's My Baby
Eugene decides it is time to leave home and go some place where there is no more spinach.

In Mork We Trust
GS: Sandi Newton, David Wall. Mork and Mindy suspect one of their friends of being a thief.

Mork's Night Out
GS: Ruta Lee, Robin Eisenmann. Mork and Bickley go to a singles' bar when Mindy goes away.

Mork's Best Friend
Mork persuades Mindy to let him keep a caterpillar named Bob as a pet.

It's a Wonderful Mork
An Orkan essence reverser shows Mork what life would have been like if he had never arrived.

Invasion of the Mork Snatchers
GS: Robert Hogan, Alan McRae, David Haskall. Mork uncovers a nuclear accident that is being covered up by the military.

Clerical Error
Mork receives notice from the Immigration authorities to register as an alien or be deported.

Hold That Mork
GS: Linda Henning, Melanie Vincz, Lorrie Mahafrey. Cheerleaders from the Denver pony express encourage Mork to try out for the squad, but the management disagrees.

Mork vs. Mindy
GS: Jay Thomas, Gina Hect. Mork picks a fight with Mindy and she throws him out.

Mork Gets Mindy-itis
GS: Jim Stahl. Mork finds that he is allergic to Mindy.

Dr. Morkenstein
GS: Robby the Robot and the voice of Roddy McDowall. Mork tampers with a robot and turns him into an emotional being.

Mork in Wonderland [Part 1]
GS: John Haymer, Ronnie Schell. As a result of a cold medicine, Mork shrinks into a parallel universe.

Mork in Wonderland [Part 2]
Mork tries to find a way back to Mindy.

Mork Learns to See
GS: Tom Sullivan. Mork is homesick and is singing the blues until he meets Bickley's blind son.

Mork's Baby Blues
GS: Diana Manoff, Carl Gottlieb. A golddigger makes life miserable for Mork when she leaves him with a child.

A Morkville Horror
Mindy's old house is up for sale and is believed to be haunted.

Mork's Health Hints
GS: Vernon Wendle, Wayne Morton. Mork's apprehension over Mindy's tonsillectomy turns to horror when a hospital error schedules her for brain surgery.

Exidor Affair
GS: Georgia Engel. Exidor falls for a meter maid.

Exidor's Wedding
GS: Anita Dangler. News of Exidor's wedding brings out his long-lost and equally strange mom.

Mork Syndrome
GS: Ed Peck. Nelson sends Mork to obtain the endorsement of the Committee to Clean Up Boulder, unaware that the organization wants to rid the city of minorities.

Raided Mind-Skis
GS: Jack Dodson. Mork goes on an Orkan holiday swapping minds with beings on faraway planets, leaving Mindy to contend with strangers in Mork's clothing.

Dial N for Nelson
GS: Jim Stahl. Mindy's Cousin Nelson is thinking about a political career until he gets an anonymous threat.

Mork vs. the Necrotrons [Part 1]
GS: Raquel Welch, Vicki Frederick, Debra Jo Fondren. An intergalactic war between the planets Ork and Necrotron reaches Earth when Mork becomes the target of an enemy agent.

Mork vs. the Necrotrons [Part 2]
GS: Raquel Welch. Mork tries to defeat the enemy agent sent to destroy him.

Stark Raving Mork
GS: Gary Goodrow, Paul Wilson. Intrigued by a priest's good deeds, Mork decides to become a man of the cloth.

Mork's Vacation
Looking for rest, Mork and Mindy travel to Exidor's private retreat.

A Mommy for Mindy
Mindy is outraged by the antics of her chauvinistic cousin, an aspiring politician who believes women are no good.

A Genie Loves Mork
GS: Gina Hect. Jeannie writes to the lonely hearts club column, unaware that Mindy is the editor.

The Way Mork Were
Mork and Mindy reminisce via flashbacks to previous episodes.

Little Orphan Morkie
Mork and Mindy produce and perform in a children's TV show that also serves to plug Nelson's political career.

Loonie Tunes and Morkie Melodies
Mork falls prey to the inane ad campaign slogans and jingles.

Putting the Ork Back in Mork
Mork seems to have assimilated into American culture so well that he forgets his Orkan training.

Mork in Never Never Land
GS: David Spielberg. Mork tries to lift Mindy's spirits by bringing home a friend, a man who thinks he's Peter Pan.

Dueling Skates
GS: Reid Smith. Mork challenges the owner of a roller rink to a skating contest—across the Rocky Mountains.

Mork the Prankster
Mork's sudden interest in practical jokes lacks one thing—good judgment.

Mork's the Monkey's Uncle
Mork goes to the zoo to visit a friend— a chimp that he ends up taking home when he finds its mother is missing.

Gunfight at the O.K. Corral
GS: Corey Feldman. Mork preaches nonviolence to a boy at the daycare center, who then challenges Mork to a shootout at a nearby ghost town.

Mork's New Look
Fred begins to worry about looking too old, which inspires Mork to try to change his own appearance—with plastic surgery.

Alas, Poor Mork, We Knew Him Well
GS: Will Porter. Mork begins to fear everything after an insurance agent quotes him some high accident statistics.

Mork and the Bum Rap
GS: Ross Martin. Mork tries to help Mindy solicit donations for a children's hospital with help from a bum.

Mindy Gets Her Job
GS: Foster Brooks. Despite her total lack of experience, Mindy is hired by a TV station to do the news on her very first night.

Twelve Angry Appliances
GS: Richard Libertini. In the interest of consumerism, Mork confronts the owner of a repair shop who did a lousy job of fixing.

Mork and the Family Reunion
GS: Lyle Waggoner. Mork is thrilled when his idol from Ork arrives at the apartment—until learning he has come as his replacement.

Mork Meets Robin Williams
Mork accompanies Mindy on an interview with a famous comedian—Robin Williams.

Mindy, Mindy, Mindy
GS: Vidal I. Peterson. When Mindy leaves town on an assignment, Mork is so lonely he decides to build a temporary replacement.

Mork the Swinging Single
GS: Bill Kirchenbauer, Crissy Wilzak. Mindy creates a monster when she suggests to Mork that he meet other single women.

Mork and Mindy Meet Rick and Ruby
GS: Joshua Brady, Brian Seff, Monica Ganas.   Remo fires a music group because the singer is seven months' pregnant, prompting Mork and Mindy to picket his restaurant.

There's a New Mork in Town
GS: Jonathan Winters. Mindy's pompous uncle is so wrapped up in himself that Mork decides it's time to redirect his attentions.

Old Muggable Mork
When Cora is mugged during her visit, Mork uses his powers to show the muggers just what it's like to be old.

I Heard It Through the Morkvine
Mindy becomes the TV station's gossip reporter and Mork gets carried away supplying her with juicy tidbits.

Mindy and Mork
Mork becomes the lady of the house when Mindy's job begins to take up all of her time.

Bickley's Birthday
At Bickley's 50th birthday party, the guests reveal their life's regrets while Mindy regrets having no place to hide when it is her turn.

Limited Engagement
GS: Pat Cranshaw. Mork pops the question to a dazed Mindy who decides she will marry the alien Mork.

The Wedding
Mork defies Orson's orders not to marry Mindy, prompting Orson to unleash his wrath by slowly turning Mork into a sheepdog at the altar.

The Honeymoon
GS: Ronald Welch, Donald Welch. Mork and Mindy honeymoon on Ork where the main tourist attraction turns out to be Mindy.

Three the Hard Way
Mork returns from his honeymoon on Ork and discovers that he is pregnant.

[Jonathan Winters joins the cast as baby Mearth.]

Mama Work, Papa Mindy
Mork becomes a mother and Mindy is the father in this strange household where newborn Mearth is learning about life.

My Dad Can't Beat Up Anyone
Mearth hero-worships Superman, so insecure Mork claims that he is a superhero too.

Long Before We Met
GS: Robin Strand. Meeting Mindy's handsome and successful high school boyfriend sends Mork back ten years to see how he would fare in a competition for her attention.

Rich Mork, Poor Mork
Mork sinks all of his savings into Exidor's sure-fire moneymaker—a boutique featuring nothing but Exidor originals.

Alienation
GS: John Larroquette.   Mearth runs away when he learns he is half Orkan and will never be like other children.

P.S. 2001
GS: Harvey Lembeck, Maureen Arthur. Mearth starts school on Ork—and comes home crying after being called an "Earth-head" by his fellow students.

Pajama Game II
GS: Maureen Arthur. Mork and Mindy permit Mearth to have a friend sleep over and the friend he chooses is the beautiful Zelka.

Present Tense
GS: Hamilton Camp, Ray Girarden. With Mearth away for a few days, Mork and Mindy are just like many other couples—they have nothing to talk about.

Title Unknown
A short circuit switches Mork's mind

with Mearth's on the night Mindy's new boss wants to meet his employees' families.

Drive, She Said
GS: Max Maven, Bill Kirchenbauer. Mork becomes a road hazard when Mindy decides it's time he learned how to drive.

I Don't Remember Mama
GS: Martin Ferrero. Orson doesn't think Mork can handle both a job and a family, so he eliminates the family from Mork's memory.

Midas Mork
The voice of John Houseman gives life to MLT, a super computer built by Mearth that's slowly taking over the house. Cameo by William Shatner.

Cheerleaders in Chains
GS: Barbara Billingsley. Mindy's jailed for contempt of court when she refuses to reveal a news source.

The Mork Report
Mork's Orkan promotion depends on how well Orson receives his report on married life.

Gotta Run [Part 1]
GS: Joseph Regalbuto. Mork strikes up a friendship with what he hopes is a kindred spirit, a Neptunian with an Earth wife.

Gotta Run [Part 2]
Mork decides to tell the world that he is an alien, hoping it will stop Kalnik the Neptunian's attacks.

Gotta Run [Part 3]
GS: Joseph Regalbuto, Stephen Stucker. Suddenly notorious, Mork must fight off fans, marketing executives, television producers, and Kalnik the Neptunian.

THE MOTHERS-IN-LAW

On the air 9/10/67, off 9/7/69. NBC. Color Film. 30 min. 56 episodes. Broadcast: Sept 1967-Sept 1969 Sun 8:30-9. Producer: Desi Arnaz. Prod Co/ Synd: United Artists TV.
CAST: Eve Hubbard (played by Eve Arden), Kaye Buell (Kaye Ballard), Roger Buell (Roger C. Carmel, 1967-68; Richard Deacon, 1968-69), Herb Hubbard (Herbert Rudley), Jerry Buell (Jerry Fogel), Susie Hubbard Buell (Deborah Walley).
The struggles of the Hubbards and the Buells, two families who are constantly at war with each other. Typical episodes depict the troubles Jerry and Susie encounter when their mothers (who want only the best for their children) manage to foul up their lives. Once popular in syndication, the program is now reduced to appearing on rural UHF stations.

[Every episode was written by Madelyn Davis & Bob Carroll, Jr. (except where noted) and every episode was directed by Desi Arnaz (except where noted).]

On Again, Off Again, Lohengrin
A fight breaks out between the Hubbards and the Buells about their children's wedding plans.

Everybody Goes on a Honeymoon
GS: Carl Reindel, Bart Greene. The newlyweds' honeymoon is over when the Hubbards and the Buells show up at their resort hotel.

All Fall Down
W: Hugh Wedlock, Jr. & Allan Manings. Problems arise when both Kaye and Eve break their legs skiing.

Kaye Ballard (left) and Eve Arden, in The Mothers-in-Law.

A Night to Forget
D: Maury Thompson. GS: Desi Arnaz, Lou Krugman. Kaye and Eve are locked inside a store for the night.

The Newlyweds Move In
GS: Judy Franklin, Larry Bishop. Kaye and Eve promise not to interfere in their kids' lives when the kids move into their apartment above the Hubbards's garage.

The Career Girls
W: Fred S. Fox & Seamon Jacobs. GS: Rob Reiner. Kaye and Eve audition for parts in a play.

Who's Afraid of Elizabeth Taylor?
Kaye and Eve throw their husbands out after they both admit they would like to have an affair with Elizabeth Taylor.

My Son, the Actor
The Hubbards and the Buells help

Jerry win a part in the school play.

How Do You Moonlight a Meatball?
W: Fred S. Fox & Seamon Jacobs. GS: Percy Helton. Eve helps Kay sell her famous spaghetti and meatballs on the college campus to help pay off Suzie's ring.

I Thought He'd Never Leave
W: Sydney Zelinka & Ronald Axe. D: Elliot Lewis. GS: Larry Storch. A fugitive bankrobber hides out at the Hubbard's home.

The Great Bicycle Race
D: Elliot Lewis. The Hubbards and the Buells join a cycling club.

Through the Lurking Glass
W: Howard Ostroff. GS: Jay Novello, Stafford Repp, Alan Reed, Sr. When Roger gets arrested, the whole family arrives in costumes to rescue him.

Divorce-Mother-in-Law Style
W: Bill Idelson & Harvey Miller. D: Elliot Lewis. The kids create a fake divorce to teach their mothers a lesson.

The Not Cold Enough War
W: William O'Hallaren. GS: Herb Edelman, Bobs Watson. Eve gives her old refrigerator to Kaye when she gets a new one, but when it breaks down, Kaye gets mad.

You Challenge Me to a What?
Roger and Herb have a fight, which leads to Roger challenging Herb to a duel.

Everybody Wants to Be a Writer
W: William O'Hallaren.   D: Elliot Lewis & Desi Arnaz. GS: Peter Whitney. Eve and Kaye try to write a TV script but it turns out they stole it from another writer.

The Kids Move Out
D: Elliot Lewis. The kids decide to move out when their mothers' interference in their lives becomes too much for them to endure any longer.

The Hombre Who Came to Dinner [Part 1]
D: Elliot Lewis & Desi Arnaz. GS: Desi Arnaz, Miguel Landa. The Hubbards get an unexpected visit from their friend Raphael Del Gado, the bullfighter, who plans to stay for a while.

The Hombre Who Came to Dinner [Part 2]
D: Desi Arnaz & Elliot Lewis. GS: Desi Arnaz & Desi Arnaz, Jr. The Hubbards and the Buells go to Mexico to appear on a variety show hosted by their friend the bullfighter.

Don't Give Up the Sloop
W: Bill Idelson & Harvey Miller. D: Elliot Lewis. The Hubbards and the Buells fight over who owns the boat they won on a game show.

I'd Tell You I Love You But We're Not Speaking
W: Robert Daniel & Mark Howard. GS: Brooks West. The kids use a group therapy session to get their parents to speak to each other again.

Herb's Little Helpers
D: Elliot Lewis. GS: Jerome Cowan, Herb Vigran. Eve becomes Herb's secretary when his regular calls in sick.

Bye, Bye Blackmailer
D: Elliot Lewis. Eve uses Herb's reserve money to pay back the loan he gave to Roger, without telling Herb he is being repaid with his own money.

The Wig Story
W: Michael Morris. Kaye thinks that Roger is in love with the blonde wig she borrowed from Eve and not her.

It's Only Money
W: Sidney Zelinka. D: Elliot Lewis. GS: Benny Rubin, Romo Vincent. Herb plans to get even with Roger when he makes him pay half the bill at a restaurant despite the fact that Roger and Kaye ordered the more expensive dinners.

I Haven't Got a Secret
W: Peggy Chandler Dick. Roger tells Kaye not to tell anyone that his scripts are being considered for a TV series, but Kaye doesn't know how to keep a secret.

Jerry's Night Out with the Boys
D: Elliot Lewis & Desi Arnaz. GS: Jim Begg. When Jerry wants to go play poker and Suzie won't let him, their parents start taking sides in the fight.

The Long, Long Weekend
D: Elliot Lewis. GS: Paul Napier. The Hubbards and the Buells become trapped in their mountain cabin when a snowstorm hits.

Jealousy Makes the Heart Grow Fonder
D: Elliot Lewis. GS: Beverly Garland.

Eve becomes jealous when one of Herb's old girlfriends comes for a visit.

How Not to Manage a Rock Group
W: Don Nelson. GS: Joe Besser, John Myhers, The Seeds. The Hubbards and the Buells invest in a new rock group called the Warts.

Here Comes the Bride, Again
GS: William Lanteau, Jeanette Nolan. The kids agree to hold a second wedding ceremony for Kaye's mother who is visiting from Italy.

The Match Game
D: Elliot Lewis. GS: Paul Lynde. The Hubbards and the Buells plan to help Jerry keep his job at a computer dating service.

A Little Pregnancy Goes a Long Way
D: Elliot Lewis. GS: Shirley Mitchell, Harry Hickox. Kaye and Eve think Roger and Herb are going to take them on a cruise to Hawaii.

Love Thy Neighbor—If You Can't Get Him to Move
W: Fred S. Fox & Seamon Jacobs. D: Elliot Lewis. Flashbacks show how the Hubbards first met the Buells when they bought the house next door.

I Didn't Raise Myself to Be a Grandmother
D: Elliot Lewis. GS: Bruce Kirby. Eve and Kaye decide that they haven't done very much with their lives and set out to improve themselves.

Even Mothers-in-Law Have Mothers-in-Law
W: Fred S. Fox & Seamon Jacobs. D: Elliot Lewis. GS: Doris Packer, Barbara Morrison. Herb and Roger's mothers pay a visit.

The Matador Makes a Movie
GS: Desi Arnaz, Desi Arnaz, Jr., John Myhers, Joseph Mell. The Hubbards and the Buells try to get parts in a film being made by their friend Raphael Del Gado, the bullfighter.

It's a Dog's Life
W: Robert Fisher & Arthur Marx. D: Elliot Lewis. GS: John Byner. Kaye and Eve both give the kids a puppy as a present.

The First Anniversary Is the Hardest
GS: Joe Besser, Stafford Repp. Suzie gives away Jerry's jacket, unaware that their parents hid money in it as a surprise gift for them.

The Birth of Everything but the Blues
W: Elaine Di Bello Bradish. D: Elliot Lewis. GS: Herb Voland, Del Moore, Frank Inn, and Mel Blanc as the voice of the mynah bird. Suzie becomes an animal babysitter to earn some extra money.

Nome, Schnome, I'd Rather Have It At Home
W: Henry Garson. Jerry and Suzie announce they are moving to Alaska.

Hail, Hail, the Gang's Still Here
D: Elliot Lewis. GS: Shirley Mitchell, Harry Hickox. Eve and Herb hide under the bed so they won't be bothered by Kaye and Roger.

Didn't You Used to Be Ossie Snick?
W: Fred S. Fox & Seamon Jacobs. GS: Ozzie Nelson. Kaye's former boyfriend bandleader comes for a visit.

Make Room for Baby
D: Elliot Lewis. The Hubbards and the Buells decide to add another room to the kids' apartment and to save money by doing it themselves.

Haven't You Had That Baby Yet?
D: Elliot Lewis. GS: Herb Voland, Vonda Barra. Kaye and Eve lose Suzie on the way to the hospital.

And Baby Makes Four
D: Elliot Lewis. GS: Alice Ghostley, Avery Schreiber. Suzie gives birth to twins, causing fights between the families about what they will be named.

Nanny Go Home
W: Elaine Di Bello Bradish. D: Elliot

Lewis.   GS: Jeanette Nolan, Jerry Hausner. Eve and Kaye try to get rid of the nanny hired to watch the babies when she refuses to let them visit when they want to.

Double Trouble in the Nursery
W: Bruce Howard. D: Elliot Lewis. Eve and Kaye volunteer to watch the babies while Jerry and Suzie go away for the weekend.

Void Where Prohibited by In-Laws
W: Skip Webster. D: Elliot Lewis. GS: Benny Rubin, Flip Mark. The girls try to win a cereal contest in order to win money to send the babies to college.

Guess Who's Coming Forever
W: Arthur Marx and Robert Fisher. D: Elliot Lewis. GS: Scoey Mitchlll. Eve and Kaye rent the kids' apartment to a black man when the kids decide to move out.

Every In-Law Wants to Get into the Act
W: Bruce Howard. D: Elliot Lewis. GS: Jimmy Durante, Herbie Fay, Del Moore. The Hubbards and the Buells decide to take Jerry's place performing at a nightclub when he comes

down with the flu.

Two on the Aisle
W: Sidney Zelinka. D: Elliot Lewis. GS: Joe Besser, Terry Carr. The Hubbards and the Buells fight over who will use the two theater tickets they got in the mail.

Take Her, He's Mine
D: Elliot Lewis.   GS: Joi Lansing. Kaye becomes jealous of Roger's new secretary.

Show Business Is No Business
W: Arthur Marx & Robert Fisher. D: Elliot Lewis. GS: Don Rickles. Kaye and Eve both try to be Don Rickles's partner for the lodge benefit show.

The Charge of the Wife Brigade
W: Arthur Marx & Robert Fisher. D: Elliot Lewis. GS: Roy Stuart. Kaye and Eve try to find jobs to pay off their bills at the department store.

The Not-So-Grand Opera
W: Elaine Di Bello Brandish. D: Elliot Lewis. GS: Marni Nixon, Mary Jane Croft.   Eve and Kaye try to get the leading role in their club opera production.

THE MUNSTERS

On the air 9/24/64, off 9/1/66. CBS. B&W Film. 70 episodes. Broadcast: Sept 1964-Sept 1966 Thu 7:30-8. Producer: Joe Connelly & Bob Mosher. Prod Co/Synd: Universal/MCA.
CAST: Herman (played by Fred Gwynne), Lily (Yvonne DeCarlo), Grandpa (Al Lewis), Eddie (Butch Patrick), Marilyn (Beverly Owen, 1964; Pat Priest 1964-66).
WRITERS: James Allardice, Tom Adair, Bob Mosher, Joe Connelly, Dick Conway, Ted Bergman, Doug Tibbles, George Tibbles, Richard Baer, Dennis Whitcomb. DIRECTORS: Ezra Stone, Charles Rondeau, Donald Richardson, Gene Reynolds, Joseph Pevney, Lawrence Dobkin, Earl Bellamy, Norman Abbott.
The Munsters was a series about a family of famous Hollywood monsters, but played for laughs. The head of the family, Herman Munster, was in reality the Frankenstein monster. His wife Lily was a female vampire. Lily's father, also known as Grandpa, was Count Dracula. Herman and Lily's son Eddie was a werewolf. The only human in the family was Marilyn, Lily's niece. The thing that made this series unique was that the entire family never once thought of themselves as anything but an average American family. The series spawned a feature film in 1966 entitled "Munster Go Home." [It was originally made as

A Munster family reunion as three original cast members reprise their roles in the 1981 NBC "Munster's Revenge" movie. Here shown are (front) K.C. Martel, and Yvonne DeCarlo (left), Fred Gwynne, Bob Hastings, Jo McDonnell, and Al Lewis.

a TV movie but was diverted to the theaters at the last moment.] This was also the only time the series was seen in full color. In 1981 a TV movie reunion was filmed entitled *The Munsters' Revenge*, which reunited the three major cast members (Gwynne, Lewis and DeCarlo) for the first time since the series ended in 1966. The series is still very popular today especially with children.

Pike's Pique
GS: Richard Deacon, Pat Harrington, Jane Withers. The gas company breaks into the Munsters' dungeon while trying to lay a pipeline.

Munster Masquerade
GS: Linden Chiles, Mabel Albertson. Herman, Lily and Grandpa attend a costume party given by the parents of Marilyn's latest boyfriend.

A Walk on the Mild Side
GS: Cliff Norton, Roy Roberts. Herman is mistaken for a monster who is attacking women in the city park.

Low-Cal Munster
GS: Paul Lynde. Herman goes on a diet so he can wear his old uniform to his Army reunion.

The Munsters [Pilot]
GS: John Fiedler, Claire Carleton, Edward Mallory. Grandpa's love potion causes trouble for Herman and Lily.

Autumn Croakus
GS: Neil Hamilton. Grandpa's mail order bride is the Black Widow, who marries then murders her husbands for their money.

Tin Can Man
GS: Arch Johnson, Richard Simmons. Eddie's robot for the school science fair is sabotaged.

Knock Wood, Here Comes Charlie
GS: Mike Mazurki. Herman's twin brother, a notorious con man, comes for a visit.

Rock-a-Bye Munster
GS: Paul Lynde, Sid Melton, Peter Robbins. Herman believes Lily is going to have a baby.

Family Portrait
GS: Harvey Korman, Fred Beir, William Daniels, Roy Roberts. A magazine chooses the Munsters as the average American family.

Herman the Great
GS: John Hubbard, Johnny Silver, Jimmy Lennon, Tiger Joe Marsh. Herman becomes a professional wrestler in order to win money for Eddie's education.

The Midnight Ride of Herman Munster
GS: Lennie Weinrib, Slapsie Maxie Rosenbloom, Val Avery. Herman is mistaken for a bank robber by a gang of crooks.

The Sleeping Cutie
GS: Grant Williams, Walter Woolf King, John Hoyt, Gavin MacLeod. Grandpa gives Marilyn a sleeping potion and invents a gasoline pill which changes water into gasoline.

Grandpa Leaves Home
GS: Robert Strauss, Iris Adrian. Grandpa leaves home when he feels nobody needs him.

Dance with Me, Herman
GS: Don Rickles, Joyce Jameson. Herman unknowingly takes dancing lessons from a crooked dance school.

Grandpa's Call of the Wild
GS: Mike Ragan, Bing Russell, Don Haggerty, Ed Peck. While on a camping trip Grandpa turns himself into a wolf, but forgets how to turn himself back.

Herman's Rival
GS: Lee Bergere, Chet Stratten, Tommy Farrell, Irwin Charone. Lily gets a job when she thinks they are broke, unaware that Herman lent their money to her brother Lester, the Wolfman.

All-Star Munster
GS: Pat Buttram, Robert Easton, Frank Maxwell. While trying to straighten out Marilyn's tuition problems at school, Herman unknowingly signs up to play on the school basketball team.

Bats of a Feather
GS: Barbara Babcock, Alvy Moore, Alan Hunt, Gilbert Green. Grandpa turns into a bat so Eddie can take him to the school pet fair, but Eddie trades him for a squirrel.

Eddie's Nickname
GS: Paul Lynde, Alice Backes. Instead of Grandpa's magic milkshake making Eddie grow taller, it grows a beard.

Don't Bank on Herman
GS: Pitt Herbert, Jack Bernardi, Mousey Garner. Herman and Grandpa are mistaken for bank robbers when they try to make a withdrawal at the bank.

Love Locked Out
GS: Elliot Reid, Bryan O'Byrne. After staying out too late at an office party, Lily throws Herman out of the house.

Follow That Munster
GS: Ken Lynch, Doris Singleton. Herman becomes a mail-order detective and Lily thinks he is fooling around.

Far Out Munsters
GS: The Standells, Zalman King. The Munsters move to a hotel when they rent their house to a rock group but return to find a wild party in progress.

Movie Star Munster
GS: Jesse White, Walter Burke. A pair of con artists posing as movie producers plan to kill Herman in order to collect the insurance money.

Munsters on the Move
Herman sells their house when he learns his new promotion will mean moving to another city.

Come Back Little Googie
GS: Billy Mumy, Russ Conway. Grandpa thinks he turned Eddie's friend into a monkey.

Herman the Rookie
GS: Leo Durocher, Elroy Hirsch. Herman signs up as a baseball player for the L.A. Dodgers.

Country Club Munsters
GS: Woodrow Parfrey, J. Edward McKinley, Dan Tobin, Johnny Jacobs, Al Checco. Herman wins a family membership in a country club.

Herman's Raise
GS: John Carradine, Benny Rubin. Herman demands a raise and is fired. He tries to find another job, with terrible results.

Love Comes to Mockingbird Heights
Uncle Gilbert, the Creature from the Black Lagoon, sends the Munsters a crate of money to deposit for him. But a golddigger thinks the money belongs to Marilyn, so he plans to marry her and take her money.

Lily Munster, Girl Model
GS: Roger C. Carmel, Kimberly Beck. Lily feels she is not needed around the house, so she takes a job as a fashion model.

Munster the Magnificent
GS: Dave Ketchum, Eddie Ryder. Eddie volunteers no-talent Herman to entertain at the school talent show, claiming he is a great magician.

Mummy Munster
GS: Pat Harrington. Herman is mistaken for an Egyptian mummy when he falls asleep in a museum sarcophagus.

Herman's Happy Valley
GS: John Hoyt, Richard Reeves, Bartlett Robinson. Herman buys a worthless ghost town from two con men. When the property becomes valuable, the con men try to scare the Munsters into selling the land back to them.

Hot Rod Herman
GS: Henry Beckman, Brian Corcoran. Herman bets the family car in a drag car race and loses.

Yes, Galen, There Is a Herman
GS: Brian Naish, Harvey Korman, Walter Brooke, Marge Redmond. Herman saves a young boy and no one will believe him.

Herman, the Master Spy
GS: Val Avery, Bella Bruck, John Zaremba. While Scuba diving, Herman is caught by a Russian fishing trawler whose crew thinks he is a missing link.

Bronco-Bustin' Munster
GS: Don "Red" Barry, William Phipps. Eddie enters cowardly Herman in a rodeo bronco-riding contest.

Operation Herman
GS: Dayton Allen, Don Keefer, Bill Quinn. Herman is mistaken for an accident victim when he visits Eddie in the hospital.

Will Success Spoil Herman Munster?
GS: Gary Owens, Frank Evans, Penny Kunard. Herman becomes a mystery folk singer, causing Lily to worry when success goes to his head.

Herman, Coach of the Year
GS: Emmaline Henry, Henry Beckman. Herman tries to coach Eddie for the tryouts of the school track team.

Lily's Star Boarder
GS: Charles Bateman, Buddy Lewis, Chet Stratten. Herman becomes jealous of the boarder who moved into

their spare room.

Herman Munster, Shutterbug
GS: Herbie Faye, Joe De Santis. Herman accidentally photographs two bankrobbers, now the robbers and the cops are after him.

Herman, the Tire Kicker
GS: Frank Gorshin, Johnny Silver, Jack Perkins. Herman buys a used car from a fast-talking con man.

Herman's Child Psychology
GS: Michael Petit, Bill Quinn, Janos Prohaska. Herman tries psychology when Eddie threatens to run away from home.

The Man for Marilyn
GS: Roger Perry, Dick Wilson, Jackie Coogan, Jr., Dave Willock. Grandpa tries to turn a frog into a boyfriend for Marilyn.

Happy 100th Anniversary
GS: Foster Brooks, Vinton Hayworth, William O'Connell, Robert Cornthwaite, Jack Grinnage, Noam Pitlik. Herman and Lily take part-time jobs to buy each other anniversary presents.

Herman's Driving Test
GS: Charlie Ruggles. Herman tries to renew his driver's license so he can drive the hearse for the parlor.

John-Doe Munster
GS: Frank Maxwell, Olan Soule, Willis Bouchey. Herman loses his memory when he gets hit on the head with a 300-pound safe.

The Most Beautiful Ghoul in the World
GS: Elvia Allman, Charles Lane. The Munsters split a $10,000 inheritance; Herman and Grandpa spend their share on a new invention, Lily and Marilyn open a beauty parlor.

Herman's Peace Offering
GS: Chet Stratten, Jack Minty, Bryan O'Byrne. Herman and Eddie are bullied by a couple of bullies.

Herman Picks a Winner
GS: Charlie Callas, Barton MacLane, Joyce Jameson. Herman tries to teach Eddie a lesson by betting on the races.

The Treasure of Mockingbird Heights
Herman and Grandpa hunt for a pirate's treasure in their backyard.

Underground Munster
GS: J. Edward McKinley, Hoke Howell, Buck Kartalian. Herman insults Spot, so he runs away from home and into the city sewer system.

Grandpa's Lost Wife
GS: Jane Withers, Douglas Evans. A rich woman claims Grandpa is her long-lost husband.

Just Another Pretty Face
GS: Dom DeLuise, Jackie Joseph. Herman is turned into a normal human when he is hit by a bolt of lightning.

Heap Big Herman
GS: Ned Romero, Len Lesser, Felix Loucher. While on vacation, Herman is mistaken for the spirit Wanitoba by a tribe of Indians.

Cyrano De Munster
GS: Chet Stratten, Joan Staley. Herman ghost writes love letters for a fellow employee, which makes Lily think he is fooling around with another woman.

The Fregosi Emerald
GS: Paul Reed, Joan Swift. Herman is in trouble when he gets a ring stuck on his finger and the ring has a curse on it.

Eddie's Brother
GS: Rory Stevens, Wendy Cutler. Grandpa builds a robot playmate named Boris for Eddie.

Zombo
GS: Louis Nye, Digby Wolfe, Jack Minty. Herman is jealous of Eddie's hero Zombo, the host of a monster TV show.

The Musician
GS: John Carradine. Grandpa makes a potion which will turn Eddie into a great musician in order to impress Herman's boss, Mr. Gateman.

Herman's Sorority Caper
GS: Bonnie Franklin, David Macklin, Ken Osmond, Frank Garder. After Grandpa puts Herman into a trance to cure his hiccups, he awakens to find himself inside a girls' sorority house.

A House Divided
Herman divides the house in half when he has a fight with Grandpa over Eddie's birthday present.

A Visit from Johann
GS: John Abbott, Jeff County. Dr. Frankenstein's great grandson and Johann, one of the Doctor's rejects who

is a lookalike for Herman, visit the Munsters.

Herman's Lawsuit
GS: Jerome Cowan, Than Wyenn, Dorothy Green. When Herman gets hit by a car, he thinks the driver wants to sue him for wrecking the car.

A Visit from the Teacher
GS: Pat Woodell, Willis Bouchey. Eddie's teacher comes for a visit when he writes an unusual composition about his family.

If a Martian Answers, Hang Up
Herman thinks he contacted the planet Mars with his ham radio set.

Prehistoric Munster
GS: Harvey Korman. Herman is mistaken for the missing link by a college professor.

MY FAVORITE MARTIAN

On the air 9/29/63, off 9/4/66.   CBS.   Film.   107 episodes (32 in color). Broadcast: Sept 1963-Sept 1966 Sun 7:30-8. Producer: Jack Chertok. Prod Co: Metromedia Producer's Corp. Synd: Telepictures.

CAST: Uncle Martin, the Martian (played by Ray Walston), Tim O'Hara (Bill Bixby), Mrs. Brown (Pamela Britton), Det. Brennan (Alan Hewitt).

Tim O'Hara, a newspaper reporter, investigates the crash landing of a spaceship and discovers a middle-aged Martian. Tim adopts the stranded Martian who now goes by the name of Martin O'Hara, Tim's uncle. Episodes show the struggle of the Martian trying to adjust to Earth culture while in the process of attempting to repair his spaceship. This is a show of true class which is, unfortunately, rarely seen, another old series forgotten by the passage of time. A cartoon spinoff of the series was created for Saturday morning entitled *My Favorite Martians* in 1973, starring Jonathan Harris as the voice of the Martian.

My Favorite Martian [Pilot]
W: John L. Greene. D: Shelton Leonard. GS: Simon Oakland, J. Pat O'Malley. Tim O'Hara sees a spacecraft crash in the woods, where he finds a 450-year-old Martian.

The Matchmakers
W: John L. Greene & Paul David. D: Sidney Miller. GS: Ann Marshall. Tim watches his editor's dog, only to find

that the dog is in love with the dog next door owned by her man-hating mistress.

The Man on the Couch
W: William Blinn & Michael Gleason. D: Sidney Miller. GS: Henry Beckman. Martin is mistaken for a man attempting suicide when he climbs to the top of a tall building to escape Earth's rich oxygen atmosphere.

Ray Walston (left, The Martian) and Bill Bixby, in My Favorite Martian.

Man or Amoeba
W: Jerry Seelen & Leo Rifkin. D: Alan Rafkin. GS: John Fiedler. Martin and Tim are involved in a fight with a space scientist regarding the existence of life on Mars.

A Nose for News
W: William Blinn & Michael Gleason. D: Alan Rafkin. GS: David White. Martin writes a successful story for Tim's newspaper and is offered a job as a reporter.

There Is No Cure for the Common Martian
W: James Komack. D: Sidney Miller. GS: Willard Waterman, Sharon Farrell. Martin has a cold which causes him to disappear and reappear at every sneeze he makes.

How to Be a Hero Without Really Trying
W: Ed James & Seamon Jacobs. D: Sidney Miller. GS: Butch Patrick. On a picnic, Martin goes searching for

Glink, a material needed to repair his ship, while Tim climbs a mountain to rescue a trapped boy.

Russians "R" in Season
W: James Komack. D: Alan Rafkin. GS: Richard Deacon, Frank Aletter. Martin is suspected of being a Russian spy.

Raffles No. 2
W: Austin Kalish & Elroy Schwartz. D: Oscar Rudolph. GS: Howard Morton, Madge Blake. Martin applies for a driver's license but doesn't have any fingerprints, so he unknowingly uses the prints of a jewel thief.

That Little Old Matchmaker, Martin
W: Terry Ryan. D: Oscar Rudolph. GS: Robert Colbert, Nancy Rennick. When Tim's advances on a woman reporter fail, he seeks out advice from Martin.

The Awful Truth
W: Arnold & Lois Peyser. D: Oscar

Rudolph. GS: J. Pat O'Malley, Alan Reed, Jr. Martin gives Tim the power to read minds for 24 hours.

Rocket to Mars
W: Elroy Schwartz & Austin Kalish. D: Leslie Goodwins. GS: Cliff Norton, Vito Scotti, Tom Kennedy. Martin repairs his spaceship but Mrs. Brown sells it to a junk dealer who then sells it to an amusement park.

The Atom Misers
W: James Menzies. D: Leslie Goodwins. GS: Jerome Cowan, Jean Hale, Emil Sitka. Martin enlists the aid of a 13-year-old genius and a college's cyclotron to try and repair his damaged spaceship.

Rx for a Martian
W & D: James Komack. GS: Yale Summers. Martin is about to return to Mars, but he takes a bad fall which lands him in the hospital.

Poor Little Rich Cat
W & D: James Komack. GS: Bernie Kopell, Dub Taylor. Martin is disturbed to find out that a cat has been left $650,000 and sets out to convince the cat's trustee to donate the money to charity.

Uncle Martin's Wisdom Tooth
W: James Komack. D: Oscar Rudolph. GS: Francine York, Lennie Weinrib. Martin has a toothache which causes him to see everything in the wrong direction.

Blood Is Thicker Than the Martian
W: Al Martin & Bill Kelsey. D: Oscar Rudolph. GS: Paul Smith. When Tim's Cousin Harvey pays a visit, Martin has to remain invisible until he leaves.

Going, Going, Gone
W: Elroy Schwartz & Austin Kalish. D: Oscar Rudolph. GS: Robert Lieb. A heavy flareup of sun spots causes Martin to disappear.

Who Am I?
W: Ben Starr. D: Leslie Goodwins.

GS: Michael Fox, Sally Carter. When Martin gets amnesia, Tim has to convince him that he is a 450-year-old Martian.

Now You See It, Now You Don't
W: Ben Gershman & Bill Freedman. D: Leslie Goodwins. In an attempt to elevate Tim culturally, Martin removes a famous work of art from a museum.

My Nephew, the Artist
W: Ben Starr. D: Oscar Rudolph. GS: Richard Deacon, J. Pat O'Malley. Martin turns to selling paintings to raise some expense money.

Uncle Martin's Broadcast
W: James Komack. D: Oscar Rudolph. GS: Don Haggerty, Dick Wilson. After listening to private police calls on Martin's antenna, Tim is arrested.

Hitchhike to Mars
W: Bill Freedman & Ben Gershman. D: Oscar Rudolph. GS: Vito Scotti, Herb Rudley. Martin plans to hop a ride to Mars on an instrument- bearing rocket.

Super-Duper Snooper
W: Al Martin & Bill Kelsey. D: Leslie Goodwins. GS: Cliff Norton. Mrs. Brown takes a private eye correspondence course and picks Martin as her practice subject.

An Old, Old Friend of the Family
W: John L. Greene. D: Leslie Goodwins. GS: Henry Corden. Tim tries to get an interview with the president of a newly created East Indian country.

Martin and the Eternal Triangle
W: Ben Gershman & Bill Freedman. D: Oscar Rudolph. GS: Albert Cartier. Both Martin and a Frenchman make a play for Mrs. Brown.

The Sinkable Mrs. Brown
W: Al Martin & Bill Kelsey. D: Oscar Rudolph. GS: Allan Melvin. A real

estate agent tries to talk Mrs. Brown into selling her home.

Unidentified Flying Uncle Martin
W: James Komack. D: Leslie Goodwins. GS: James Callahan. Martin takes his ship out for a short ride and is sighted as a UFO.

Danger! High Voltage!
W: Ben Gershman & Bill Freedman. D: Leslie Goodwins. GS: Milton Frome, Henry Gibson. Martin turns on all the radios and television sets in town after he absorbs too much electricity in an experiment.

If You Can't Lick 'Em
W: Blanche Hanalis. D: Oscar Rudolph. GS: Hal Smith, Dennis Rush. After a little boy sees Martin's raised antennae, he puts on his own pair which sparks a toy manufacturer to distribute antennae all over the country.

How You Gonna Keep Them Down on the Pharmacy
W: James Komack. D: Leslie Goodwins. GS: Herbie Faye. Martin has a vitamin deficiency that causes anyone who looks him in the eyes to fall asleep.

Miss Jekyll and Hyde
W: Al Martin & Bill Kelsey. D: Oscar Rudolph. GS: Marlo Thomas. Martin tries to stop Tim from marrying a girl who plans to reveal his identity.

Who's Got the Power?
W: James Komack. D: Leslie Goodwins. GS: Justin Smith. An electrical storm grounds Martin while he is sleeping. It causes him to appear and disappear uncontrollably.

Oh, My Aching Antenna
W: Ted Sheredeman & Jane Klove. D: Oscar Rudolph. GS: Jay Sheffield. Martin's extended stay on Earth has depleted his resistance to gravity causing him to constantly float to the ceiling.

The Disastro-Nauts
W: Bill Freedman & Ben Gershman. D: Leslie Goodwins. Martin plans to return to Mars in an inventor's experimental missile.

Shake Well and Don't Use
W: Al Martin & Bill Kelsey. D: Oscar Rudolph. GS: Kip King. Martin helps Tim get a promotion by inviting his boss over for Martian stew.

Dreaming Can Make It So
W: Ben Gershman & Bill Freedman. D: Oscar Rudolph. Martin's dreams come to life, causing Tim to see the strangest things including a sausage tree.

The Memory Pill
W: Benedict Freedman. D: Oscar Rudolph. GS: David White. Martin stores Tim's memory on a pill in order to help him keep track of his girlfriends.

Never Trust a Naked Martian
W: James Komack. D: Leslie Goodwins. GS: Bobby Jellison. When Tim accidentally touches Martin's antennae, he vanishes into thin air.

Three to Make Ready
W: Bruce Howard & Bud Nye. D: Leslie Goodwins. GS: Jan Arvan. Martin splits himself into three persons to try and decide if he should return to Mars.

Nothing But the Truth
W: Blanche Hanalis. D: Oscar Rudolph. GS: Don Keefer, Rory Stevens. Mrs. Brown's seven-year-old nephew sees Martin fly his spaceship into the garage but no one will believe him.

Dial M for Martin
W: Fred S. Fox & Iz Elinson. D: Oscar Rudolph. GS: Lee Kreiger. While fixing the TV antenna, a phone line falls on Martin turning him into a walking telephone.

Has Anybody Seen My Electro-Magnetic Neutron Converting Gravitator?
W: Albert E. Lewin & Burt Styler. D:

Leslie Goodwins. GS: Herb Ellis. A little boy takes a joyride in Martin's spaceship and runs off with his gravity device.

Extra! Extra! Sensory Perception!
W: James Komack. D: Leslie Goodwins. GS: Leonid Kinskey. In order to avoid suspicion, Martin shifts his extra-sensory perception powers to Mrs. Brown.

The Great Brain Robbery
W: Rik Vollaerts. D: Oscar Rudolph. GS: Keith Taylor, Frank Marth. Martin tutors a boy with silver braces, causing him to lose most of his intelligence to the child because Martians are allergic to silver.

My Uncle the Folk Singer
W: Lee Karson. D: Oscar Rudolph. GS: Pat Priest. A malfunction in his brain recorder causes Martin to become a popular singer at a coffee house.

Don't Rain on My Parade
W: James Komack. D: Leslie Goodwins. GS: Joey Walsh, Jan Arvan. During a dry hot spell, Martin accidentally causes it to rain without stopping.

Double Trouble
W: Ben Gershman & Bill Freedman. D: Leslie Goodwins. GS: Irene Tsu. Martin's duplicating machine accidentally creates a double of Mrs. Brown.

Night Life of Uncle Martin
W: Albert E. Lewin & Burt Styler. D: Oscar Rudolph. GS: Joyce Jameson, Dick Wilson. While Martin sleeps, his subconscious is out on the town having a good time.

Martian Report #1
W: Blanche Hanalis. D: Oscar Rudolph. GS: Olan Soule, Katie Sweet. After examining an Earth child, Martin believes that all human adults should be transformed back into children.

To Make a Rabbit Stew—First Catch a Martian
W: Al Martin & Bill Kelsey. D: Leslie Goodwins. GS: Pamela Goodwins. A rabbit eats one of Martin's vitamin pills and becomes a giant.

Won't You Come Home, Uncle Martin, Won't You Come Home?
W: Al Martin & Bill Kelsey. D: Leslie Goodwins. GS: Dodie Marshall. One of Martin's devices causes Tim to become a man everyone loves to hate.

Gesundheit, Uncle Martin
W: Ben Gershman & Bill Freedman. D: Leslie Goodwins. Martin has come down with Sneezaphobia, which causes temporary lapses of memory.

The Case of the Missing Sleuth
W: Bill Freedman & Ben Gershman. D: Oscar Rudolph. GS: Michael Constantine. Brennan is reduced to individual molecules by Martin's latest invention.

How're Things in Glocca Martin?
W: Albert E. Lewin & Burt Styler. D: Byron Paul. GS: Sean McClory. Tim's Uncle Seamus arrives from Ireland and accuses the levitating Martin of being a leprechaun.

Uncle Martin and the Identified Flying Objects
W: Marty Roth. D: Byron Paul. GS: Vaughn Taylor. Martin's levitation finger goes out of control when it is over-exposed to the sun's cosmic rays.

Gone but Not Forgotten
W: Benedict Freeman. D: Byron Paul. GS: Hedley Mattingly, Dick Winslow. Martin adjusts his invisibility mechanism causing everything he touches to disappear.

Humbug, Mrs. Brown
W: Al Martin & Bill Kelsey. D: Oscar Rudolph. GS: Harry Lauter. Martin tries to protect Mrs. Brown from giving away too much of her time and money to charity, by turning her into Scrooge.

A Martian Fiddles Around
W: Albert E. Lewin & Burt Styler. D: Oscar Rudolph. GS: Michael Pataki. Mrs. Brown's fiddle playing short circuits Martin's nervous system, making him transparent.

Crash Diet
W: Robert & Phyllis White. D: Byron Paul. GS: Cliff Norton, Sue Randall. Martin tries to lose weight so he can fit into his spacesuit.

Stop or I'll Steam
W: Burt Styler & Albert E. Lewin. D: Oscar Rudolph. GS: Harry Lauter. Martin releases clouds of steam from his ears to relieve the pressure from being bothered by Detective Brennan.

A Martian's Sonata in Mrs. B's Flat
W: Ron Friedman. D: Oscar Rudolph. GS: Leon Belasco, Mona Bruns. Martin invents a device which turns music into liquid. Tim thinks he can make a fortune with it.

The Magnetic Personality and Who Needs It
W: Bill Freedman & Ben Gershman. D: Oscar Rudolph. GS: Herbie Faye. Martin accidentally transfers his power of magnetism to an ex-con.

We Love You, Miss Pringle
W: Blanche Hanalis. D: James V. Kern. GS: Doris Packer, Randy Kirby. Tim tries to convince the students of one of his old teachers to vote her the Teacher of the Year.

Once Upon a Martian's Mother's Day
W: Bill Kelsey. D: James V. Kern. GS: Madge Blake, James Millhollin. Martin becomes depressed because he won't be able to visit his mother on Mother's Day, but he cheers up when he meets a little old lady who looks like his mother's twin.

Uncle Baby
W: Marty Roth. D: James V. Kern. GS: Jackie Russell, Natalie Masters. Tim accidentally causes Martin to be transformed into a baby.

006¾
W: Blanche Hanalis. D: Oscar Rudolph. GS: Les Tremayne. Tim accidentally uncovers a secret enemy organization known as CRUSH.

Uncle Martin's Bedtime Story
W: Burt Styler & Albert E. Lewin. D: Oscar Rudolph. Mrs. Brown's new electric bed enables her to read Martin's mind.

The Martian's Fair Hobo
W: Marty Roth. D: James V. Kern. GS: Guy Marks. Martin misunderstands a message from Mars and takes in a hobo named Shorty, thinking messages will follow but they don't.

Martin's Favorite Martian
W: Phyllis & Robert White. D: James V. Kern. GS: Olan Soule, Linda Evans. A businessman's family mistakes Tim for a Martian when they see him wearing Martin's spacesuit.

The Green-Eyed Martian
W: Phyllis & Robert White. D: Oscar Rudolph. GS: Henry Corden. Mrs. Brown becomes irresistible to men when she gets some of Martin's spaceship fuel spilled on her.

El Senor from Mars
W: Ben Gershman & Bill Freedman. D: Oscar Rudolph. GS: Dan Seymour, Bernie Kopell. Martin's antennae become stuck in the upright position just as he is about to go on an important trip to South America.

Time Out for Martian
W: Marty Roth. D: James V. Kern. GS: Anne Wakefield. Tim and Martin meet King John when they are transported via a time machine back to the year 1215.

Portrait in Brown
W: Phyllis & Robert White. D: James V. Kern. GS: Harvey Lembeck. One of Martin's machines robs Mrs. Brown

of her third dimension, causing her to be mistaken for a painting.

Go West, Young Martian [Part 1]
W: Marty Roth. D: David Alexander. GS: Jeff De Benning. Brennan accidentally starts Martin's time machine, sending Martin and Tim back to St. Louis in 1849 where they meet Brennan's great grandfather.

Go West, Young Martian [Part 2]
W: Marty Roth. D: David Alexander. While trying to get back home, Tim and Martin are assaulted by riverboat thieves.

Avenue "C" Mob
W: Blanche Hanalis. D: John Erman. GS: John Crawford, Jamie Farr. Martin turns himself into an old man so he can make a first-hand study of old age on Earth.

Martin of the Movies
W: Albert E. Lewin & Burt Styler. D: John Erman.   GS: Yvonne Craig, Noam Pitlik, Don Diamond.   Martin uses his futuroid camera to take a picture of Tim.   It shows him getting married within 24 hours to an unidentified girl.

I'd Rather Fight Than Switch
W: Phillip Rapp. D: David Alexander. Martin's molecular reassembler accidentally switches his personality with Mrs. Brown's personality.

Tim, the Mastermind
W: Burt Styler & Albert E. Lewin. D: David Alexander. GS: Lee Bergere. Martin develops an allergy to his memory pills, so he turns Tim into a genius to help him cure himself.

Martin Goldfinger
W: Burt Styler & Albert E. Lewin. D: Wesley Kenney. GS: Stan Ross. Martin, suffering from gold starvation, causes everything he touches to turn into gold.

Bottled Martin
W: Albert E. Lewin & Burt Styler. D:

Wesley Kenney.   GS: Howard Caine, Linda Scott. Martin reduces himself in size and gets trapped inside a wine bottle which is shipped to Baghdad by Mrs. Brown.

Hate Me a Little
W: Gene L. Coon.   D: Mel Ferber. GS: Norman Alden. Martin fills Brennan with brotherly love, which has disastrous effects on his job.

Girl in the Flying Machine
W: Blanche Hanalis. D: Mel Ferber. GS: Jill Ireland, Bernie Kopell. Martin accidentally pulls a foreign spaceship and its female pilot to Earth and must figure out a way to send her back.

That Time Machine Is Waking Up That Old Gang of Mine
W: James Allardice & Tom Adair. D: Jean Yarbrough.   A malfunction in Martin's time machine causes Jesse and Frank James to be transported into Tim's kitchen.

Tim and Tim Again
W: Bill Kelsey. D: John Erman. Martin's duplicating machine makes a copy of Tim who causes trouble for the real Tim.

Loralie Brown vs. Everybody
W: Bill Kelsey. D: Jean Yarbrough. GS: Victor French. Honorary police officer Mrs. Brown becomes a supercop when she eats one of Martin's pills.

Who's Got a Secret?
W: Marty Roth. D: John Erman. GS: Gavin MacLeod, Larry D. Mann. Mrs. Brown's brother Alvin's comments convince a general that he and Martin are working on a secret spaceship.

The O'Hara Caper
W: Albert E. Lewin & Burt Styler. D: John Erman.   GS: Howard Morton. Tim uses Martin's time machine to go back to the moment of a great robbery to get a valuable news story.

Heir Today, Gone Tomorrow
W: Ben Starr. D: Jean Yarbrough.
GS: Allan Melvin, Jonathan Hole. Tim will lose an inheritance unless he can prove Martin is a real member of the O'Hara family.

Martin's Revoltin' Development
W: Leigh Chapman. D: Jean Yarbrough. GS: Michael Conrad, Harry Russo. Martin inadvertently causes a photographer to be fired after he appears invisible on an important photograph.

TV or Not TV
W: Michael Stein & Jack Gross, Jr. D: John Erman. GS: Conrad Janis. Martin becomes a television station transmitting pictures of a famous movie star in a most embarrassing situation.

Man from Uncle Martin
W: James Allardice & Tom Adair. D: John Erman. GS: Gavin MacLeod. Martin tries to locate the con man who sold a worthless toy robot to Mrs. Brown's brother.

Martin the Mannequin
W: Marty Roth. D: David Alexander. GS: Woodrow Parfrey. While visiting a department store, Martin is mistaken for a store mannequin when he smells a cologne which causes him to become frozen.

Butterball
W: Blanche Hanalis. D: David Alexander. GS: Larry D. Mann. CRUSH kidnaps Tim thinking he holds secret information, and Martin sets out to rescue him.

When a Martian Makes His Violin Cry
W: Austin & Irma Kalish. D: John Erman. GS: John Considine, Len Lesser. A gypsy puts a curse on Mrs. Brown, sending Martin to the rescue.

Doggone Martin
W: Albert E. Lewin & Burt Styler. D: John Erman. GS: James Frawley, Sarah Marshall. Martin becomes a talking dog when he reduces himself to liquid in order to send himself to Mars, but a stray dog licks him up.

Our Notorious Landlady
W: Gene Thompson. D: David Alexander. GS: Peter Brocco. One of Martin's devices turns Mrs. Brown into a jewel thief.

Virus M for Martin
W: Bill Kelsey. D: David Alexander. GS: Jamie Farr, Gilbert Green. Tim contracts a strange Martian disease that causes him to develop red stripes on his face.

Horse and Buggy Martin
W: Albert E. Lewin. D: David Alexander. GS: Janis Hansen, Bern Hoffman. After a mosquito bites Martin and a racehorse, Martin feels everything the horse does.

Stop the Presses I Want to Get Off
W: Austin & Irma Kalish. D: Jean Yarbrough. GS: Roy Engel. Martin loses his sixth sense to Mrs. Brown.

Martin Meets His Match
W: Gene Thompson. D: David Alexander. GS: Michael Constantine, Joe Higgins. Martin uses his time machine to bring his old friend Leonardo da Vinci into the present to help him with a problem on his spaceship.

When You Get Back Home to Mars, Are You Going to Get It
W: Marty Roth. D: Jean Yarbrough. GS: Wayne Stam. Martin's 11-year-old nephew crash lands and decides to stay with him, causing problems for Tim who must explain the boy's presence to Brennan.

Pay the Man the $24
W: Burt Styler. D: John Erman. GS: Shelley Morrison, Michael Carr. Martin discovers that Tim's visit to New Netherland in 1629 has somehow ruined the sale of Manhattan Island to Peter Minuit.

My Nut Cup Runneth Over
W: Bill Kelsey & Gene Thompson. D: John Erman. GS: Hal England. Martin turns a harmless squirrel into a very nervous human being.

A Loaf of Bread, a Jug of Wine and Peaches
W: Earl Barret. D: Alan Rafkin. GS: Kathie Browne, Noam Pitlik. Martin sets out to experience the Earth emotion of love and winds up dating a showgirl.

MY HERO

On the air 11/8/52, off 8/1/53. NBC. B&W Film. 30 min. 33 episodes. Broadcast: Nov 1952-Apr 1953 Sat 7:30-8; Apr 1953-Aug 1953 Sat 8-8:30. Producer: Mort Green. Prod Co: Fusco Entertainment. Synd: Unknown.
CAST: Robert S. Beanblossom (played by Robert Cummings), Julie Marshall (Julie Bishop), Willis Thackery (John Litel).
The story of Robert S. Beanblossom, salesman for the Thackery Realty Co. in Los Angeles. Beanblossom, a sort of mild-mannered real estate agent, is always thwarted in his efforts to land a really big sale, something he badly wants. *My Hero* is in syndication, but is currently unaired in the United States.

Cinderella's Revenge
Peggy's father seeks investment advice from Beanblossom, who knows nothing about the stock market.

The Hesse Story
Beanblossom mistakenly asks one of the most expensive photographers in Hollywood to photograph a piece of real estate.

The Fishing Story
Bob goes along to carry Mr. Thackery's equipment during the big real estate board fishing contest.

Africa Calling
Beanblossom decides that Mrs. Trevor, a famous woman explorer, would be an ideal wife for Mr. Thackery.

Bum for a Day
Beanblossom impersonates a skid row bum to find the office porter, a former hobo, who disappeared with $18,-000 from the office safe.

Sky High
Mr. Thackery gets mad when an efficiency expert tricks Beanblossom into refusing to sell a house.

The Boat
Beanblossom discovers that the men he sold a $17,500 cabin cruiser to are actually crooks.

Surprise Party
Beanblossom and Julie encounter a few problems when they plan on giving a surprise party for Mr. Thackery.

The Tiger
Beanblossom decides to show Mr. Thackery that he is actually a tiger and not a mouse by evicting people who have not paid their rent.

Jailbreak
Beanblossom hires a former porter as the new salesman for the Thackery Real Estate Company.

Wheel of Fortune
Mr. Thackery's old maid aunt, who happens to be his financial backer, thinks he has not been running the business properly.

Very South Pacific
When Beanblossom sells a piece of land that Mr. Thackery has already sold, he loses his job, his girl and finds himself on a South Pacific island fight-

ing off an attack of cannibals.

The Big Crush
A little girl develops a mad crush on Beanblossom, who wants no part of it.

The Bicycle
When an old man's bicycle crashes, Beanblossom helps him to repair it and in return offers him a job. The man just so happens to be the president of a bank.

Odd Man In
When some of his important real estate papers disappear, Beanblossom asks a strange woman to help him catch the thief.

Movie Star
In order to gain a new client, Beanblossom shows up on the golf course wearing a weird 1920s costume and does his best to play badly.

Jimmy Valentine
The town's leading bank president asks Beanblossom to break into the courthouse and fix his birth certificate so he won't have to retire.

Arabian Nights
Mr. Thackery and Beanblossom try to join the Ancient and Exalted Order of Araby.

Saltwater Daffy
Mr. Thackery must rent a 25-room beach house within one day, as a school of 23 seals shows up on the beach.

Top Secret
Beanblossom is sent to survey a desert area for a secret test site.

Lady Mortician
Beanblossom becomes involved with the vampirish daughter of Mr. Thackery's client.

El Toro
Beanblossom's attempts at capturing a crook are seen in a flashback.

Lady Editor
A lady photographer tricks Beanblossom into pretending they are married for a publicity stunt.

Oil Land
Beanblossom sells a piece of land but, unfortunately, he sells the wrong piece.

Catered
Beanblossom is working as a French caterer and in the office at the same time.

Viva Beanblossom
Mr. Thackery and Beanblossom are kidnapped by two prospective customers. They disguise themselves as Mexican peasants in order to escape.

Beauty and the Beast
The jealous fiance of a film star breaks off the engagement because of Beanblossom's "strictly business" relations with the girl.

Cupid
An office boy humiliates Beanblossom, and Beanblossom is now planning to get even with him.

Hillbilly
Beanblossom finds himself in the middle of a Kentucky feud when one of the hillbillies proposes to him.

Beauty Queen
Mr. Thackery enters his secretary in a beauty contest, unaware that Beanblossom hired a no-talent blonde bombshell to take her place.

Duel
Beanblossom arranges for a sculptress who is also a potential real estate buyer to sculpt Mr. Thackery.

Horse Trial
Beanblossom trades an old shack for a horse that is destroying the office.

Income Tax Investment
Beanblossom is investigated by the IRS for tax fraud.

MY LITTLE MARGIE

On the air 6/16/52, off 8/24/55. CBS, NBC. B&W Film. 126 episodes. Broadcast: Jun 1952-Sept 1952 CBS Mon 9-9:30; Oct 1952-Nov 1952 NBC Sat 7:30-8; Jan 1953-July 1953 CBS Thu 10-10:30; Sept 1953-Aug 1955 NBC Wed 8:30-9. Producer: Hal Roach, Jr. Synd: Weiss Global Prod.

CAST: Margie (played by Gale Storm), Vernon (Charles Farrell), Roberta (Hillary Brooke), Freddie (Don Hayden), Mr. Honeywell (Clarence Kolb), Mrs. Odetts (Gertrude Hoffman), Charlie (Willie Best).

Margie, a 21-year-old girl, lived with her widower father in a Fifth Avenue apartment. Her father considered himself a swinger, while she tried to get him to become more conservative. She always managed to get her father into some sort of trouble. This series is hardly ever run because it is really outdated.

The Do-Gooder
Margie tries to help a honeymoon couple who are separated when the groom has to go away on secret business.

The Convention Story
Margie goes with Vern to Miami to attend a business convention.

Make Up Your Mind
Margie and her friend try to convince one of Vern's clients to take a trip to Hawaii so they could come along.

Too Many Ghosts
Margie tries to find a castle that comes complete with a ghost for Vern's company to sell.

The Hawaii Story
Vern and Margie pretend to be a father and his 12-year-old daughter when they visit a client in Hawaii who prefers younger men.

The Las Vegas Story/The Beauty Contest
Vern takes Margie to Las Vegas but warns her not to gamble.

Vern's Flying Saucer
Margie finds herself in the middle of a science fiction program when she joins Vern at a TV studio where he is shooting a commercial for a client.

Vern's Son
Margie plays Vern's son in order to make a client happy.

Margie's Manproof Lipstick
Margie ruins a demonstration of a permanent lipstick.

Vern's Two Daughters
Vern sends Margie out of town and has Roberta portray Margie so she won't ruin another one of his business deals.

Margie's Phantom Lover
Vern and Mr. Honeywell invent a secret admirer to keep Margie from entering an auto race.

Comedy of Terrors
Margie tries to protect Vern when a gangster vows revenge on him when he was the foreman of the jury who convicted him.

Margie's Baby
Margie takes care of a friend's baby for a while, but she tells everyone it is her baby.

Meet Mr. Murphy
Margie earns some extra money by babysitting with a monkey named Mr. Murphy.

Radioactive Margie
Margie tricks Vern into hiring Freddie by writing a fake letter which states that there is uranium under the property Freddie just inherited.

That's the Spirit
Margie holds a seance where she gets the spirits to tell Vern he should become more aggressive.

Father's Little Helper
Margie helps Vern and Mr. Honeywell land a deal with two rich Texans.

A Present for Dad
Margie tries to raise enough money to have a portrait painted of Vern for his birthday present.

Campus Homecoming
Margie goes to Vern's college homecoming week to help him get some investment business from the dean.

Vern's Secret Fishing Place
Mr. Honeywell asks Margie to help him win the annual fishing contest.

What's Cooking?
Margie lets Freddie do the cooking when Mr. Honeywell and client come to dinner.

Chubby Little Margie
Margie inflates herself to look like she weighs 300 pounds in order to get out of a date with one of Vern's clients.

A Light Misunderstanding
Margie and her neighbor Dick plan to make his wife jealous, but it turns out with everyone thinking that they are having an affair.

The San Francisco Story
Margie interferes in the lives of Vern's prospective client, Mr. Tung and his family.

The Shipboard Story
Margie pretends she is going to elope in order to get Vern to agree to take her on his business trip to England on a cruise ship.

A Job for Freddie
Margie tries to get Freddie a job as a headwaiter in a restaurant.

The Switzerland Story
Margie convinces Vern to take a trip to Switzerland to find an heir to an estate.

Big Chief Vern
Margie and Vern search for a goldmine in the Indian country of Oklahoma.

Vern's Winter Vacation
Margie wants to go with Vern on his trip to Bermuda.

Operation Rescue
Margie and Mrs. Odetts try to help Vern scare away his fiancee by pretending that everyone in the family is nuts.

The Star of Khyber
Margie hires a private detective to search for a missing jewel.

Real George
A man named George mistakes Mrs. Odetts for Margie and proceeds to send her flowers.

The All-American
Margie wants to go along with Vern on a trip for his old school.

Margie's New Boyfriend
Vern tells Margie to find an athlete for a boyfriend and not weak Freddie.

Corpus Delicti
Margie and Freddie try to find the murderer when she reads a confession by a movie producer in an old diary.

Mr. Uranium
Margie and Vern try to get a man to sign a contract. The problem is that ever since he discovered uranium, he thinks everyone is after it.

The Big Telecast
Margie has some circus performers staying at the house when Vern is supposed to be the subject of a live in-home interview TV show.

Margie's Recipe
Margie tries to impress a client by singing opera while she cooks dinner.

Papa and Mambo
Vern takes mambo lessons to impress

a Spanish client.

Matinee Idol
Margie tries to prove to Vern that she fulfills the Ideal Woman standards a famous movie star expects to find in the woman he marries.

Countess Margie
Vern and Mr. Honeywell are worried that Margie will ruin a deal with a visiting countess.

Margie and the Bagpipes
Margie accidentally breaks the bagpipes of the owner of the lodge of which Mr. Honeywell was planning to become a member.

Dutch Treat
Margie pretends to be a 12-year-old Dutch girl in order to help Mr. Todd prove to his wife that he was not fooling around.

Kangaroo Story
Freddie babysits for a kangaroo at the same time Roberta's father comes for a visit.

Parrot Gold
Margie helps Vern search for the missing fortune of an eccentric millionaire.

Vern's Guilty Feeling
Vern tries to become closer to Margie when he feels that he has been neglecting her.

Careless Margie
Vern tries to teach Margie how to manage money.

Mrs. Margie Calkins
Margie poses as her neighbor's wife in order to scare off his old girlfriend.

Vern's New Girlfriend
Margie tries to stop a golddigger who is after her father.

Delinquent Margie
Margie helps Mrs. Odetts buy a sports car.

A Mother for Vern
Margie dresses up as Vern's mother in order to get a client for him.

Freddie's Formula
Freddie invents a quick-drying permanent hair dye.

Double Trouble
Margie uses a set of twins to trick Vern into taking her along on his trip to South America.

My Little Clementine
Vern thinks Margie's lookalike cousin is really Margie in disguise.

Vern Gets the Bird
Margie becomes a bird lover in order to impress a client of Vern's.

Motorcycle Cop
Margie falls for the cop who gave her a speeding ticket.

New Neighbors
Margie and Vern learn that their new neighbor is one of Vern's clients.

Hillbilly Margie
Margie and Vern attempt to buy some land from a family of hillbillies.

The Hypochondriac
Margie pretends to be a hypochondriac in order to impress a real one who is one of Vern's clients.

Cry, Wolfe
Margie hires a press agent to prove to Vern that she will become wolfbait for every single man in town if he goes on a trip to Mexico without her.

The Trapped Freddie
Vern promises to take Margie to London if she doesn't see Freddie for a week.

Homely Margie
Vern tries to get Margie to get rid of her current boyfriend by telling her she is too homely. She plans to prove he is wrong.

The Failure
Margie tries to boost Vern's ego after he returns from his college reunion thinking he is a failure.

Buried
Margie runs into gangsters when she goes hunting for buried treasure at a desert resort.

The Subconscious Approach
Margie plans to use subconscious teaching to plant an idea in Vern's head.

The New Neighbor
Margie takes a job with her inventor neighbor in order to earn enough money to pay for the mink coat she just bought.

Miss Whoozis
Margie plans to get even with the photographer who insulted her while she modeled some designer clothes.

The Unexpected Guest
Margie and Vern return home from a trip to find that Mr. Honeywell has lent their apartment to one of his clients.

Mardi Gras
Vern and Margie help a client in New Orleans get rid of a permanent house guest.

Vern's Mother-in-Law
Vern tells Margie about her grandmother who tried to prove if he was the right kind of husband for her daughter.

Margie Saves Money
Margie rents out the apartment to a couple of wrestlers when she thinks her father has gone broke.

Margie's Sister Sally
Margie dresses up as a little girl when she goes on a date with a client's son.

Margie's Mink
A mink coat gets sent to Margie by mistake.

Efficiency Expert
Vern tries to get Margie to date an efficiency expert.

The Hooded Vern
Margie gets into trouble with the FBI.

Vern's Chums
Margie gives a dinner party on Labor Day to help her father win an account.

Margie Sings Opera
Margie gets an opera singer to perform for one of Vern's clients.

Daughter-in-Law
Margie takes offense when Vern still treats her like a child.

Margie's Client
Vern and Mr. Honeywell try to get rid of a client so they can sign up his competitor.

Margie the Writer
Margie visits the police station for a story when she takes up writing.

The Health Farm
Margie befriends one of Vern's rich clients and almost wrecks his business with her.

Conservative Margie
Margie finds that she is expected to marry the grandson of one of Vern's clients.

Margie's Career
Margie becomes a singer at a nightclub.

Vern Needs a Rest
Margie tries to convince Vern to take a vacation to Florida.

The Blonde Margie
Margie makes herself into a blond in order to make Freddie jealous.

The Missing Link
Margie becomes the promoter of a has-been wrestler.

Who's Married?
Margie poses as Freddie's wife so he

can get a job from a man who hires only married people.

Hollywood Trip
Margie and Mrs. Odetts plan to break into the movie business when they go with Vern on a trip to Hollywood.

Vern Retires
Margie tries to get Vern to retire.

Day and Night
Margie tries to make sure that Vern does not back out of his promise to send her to Sun Valley.

Mexican Standoff
Vern takes Margie and Mrs. Odetts to Mexico to help impress a client.

Margie Baby Sits
Margie captures the Old Lady Robber while babysitting.

Case of the Helping Hand
Margie tries to help Vern when she thinks he is going to be replaced by a man who reads murder mysteries.

Sleep Walking
Margie pretends to sleepwalk in order to convince Vern that they should move into a street-level apartment.

A Proposal for Papa
Margie tries to get rid of a client's daughter who wants to marry Vern.

Insurance
Margie tries to help her father out when she thinks he is broke.

A Day at the Beach
Margie tries to get her father to take the day off and join her at the beach.

Margie Plays Detective
Vern promises to take Margie with him to Havana providing she is careful about how she conducts herself.

The Indians
Margie interferes in her father's business when a Swedish client's arrival prevents them from going to Bermuda.

Costume Party
Margie and Mr. Honeywell try to trick Vern into going to a costume ball in order to meet a big client.

The Truck Driver
Margie has a date with a truck driver but her father refuses to let her go.

My Little Bookie
Vern tells Margie that he is going broke so she will save money and not spend his bonus on a new car.

The New Freddie
Vern gets Freddie to act like a caveman so Margie will finally get rid of him.

Margie's Millionth Number
Margie is notified that her "son" Vern has been named the one millionth member of the Stratosphere Scouts.

Tugboat Margie
Margie stows away on a tugboat to join her father and Freddie who have been recalled to active duty by the Navy.

En Garde
Vern neglects Roberta while he takes fencing lessons, causing her to teach him a lesson.

Honeyboy Honeywell
Margie tries to soften up Mr. Honeywell by trying to get him married off.

Vern on the Lam
Vern and Margie go to Central America to visit a client, but Vern has to make a run for it when he can't find his entry visa.

Margie and the Shah
Margie plans to meet Vern's fraternity brother, the Shah of Zena, despite Vern's objections.

Stock Control
Margie finds that she has the control-

ling stock in a big company.

They Also Serve
Margie and Vern become servants at a resort when they can't get rooms.

The Golf Game
Freddie uses a trick dog to retrieve his golf balls.

To Health with Yoga
Margie tries to get friendly with the author of a book about yoga.

The Newlyweds
Margie gets into trouble when she tries to befriend a newlywed couple.

Young Vern
Margie tries to boost Vern's spirit when he becomes depressed because he thinks he is getting old.

A Horse for Vern
Margie may lose her job as a reporter when a horse disappears.

Girl Against the World
Margie tries to sell Freddie's rotten play.

The Two Lieutenants
Margie finds that she is going to have a date with one of the servicemen that Mrs. Odetts has been writing to, be-

cause she sent him a picture of Margie instead of herself.

A Friend for Roberta
Margie tries to get Roberta a date with a famous TV star so she will leave Vern alone for a while.

Margie's Baseball Player
Margie tries to help Vern get the owner of a baseball club to sign a contract.

Vern's Butterflies
Margie convinces Vern that his butter-fly-collecting client is visiting the resort she wants to go to.

Margie's Elopement
Vern thinks Margie has eloped with a sailor.

Margie's Helping Hand
Margie asks Vern to help her pay a charity pledge.

The Contract
Vern finds that he has two dates for the same night, so he asks Margie to help him solve his problem.

Go North Young Girl
Vern promises Margie that he will take her to Hawaii if she survives a week of hunting with him in Canada.

MY MOTHER THE CAR

On the air 9/14/65, off 9/6/66. NBC. Color Film. 30 min. 39 episodes. Broadcast: Sept 1965-Sept 1966 Tue 7:30-8. Producer: Rod Amateau. Prod Co/Synd: United Artists TV

CAST: Dave Crabtree (played by Jerry Van Dyke), His Mother's Voice (Ann Sothern), Barbara Crabtree (Maggie Pierce), Cindy Crabtree (Cindy Eilbacher), Randy Crabtree (Randy Whipple), Captain Mancini (Avery Schreiber).

The misadventures of Dave Crabtree, a Los Angeles lawyer, who buys a 1928 Porter which turns out to be a reincarnation of his late mother Abigail Crabtree. Episodes depict the struggles Dave has in concealing the fact that the car is his mother and thwarting the diabolical attempts of Captain Mancini, an antique car collector, to steal the Porter. *My Mother the Car* is one of the strangest comedy series and, although not seen these days, is often referred to in comedy reviews and retrospectives.

Come Honk Your Horn [Pilot]
W: Allan Burns & Chris Hayward. D: Rod Amateau. GS: George Neise. Dave Crabtree buys a rundown 1928 Porter that turns out to be his mother's reincarnation.

The Defenders
W: Allan Burns & Chris Hayward. D: Rod Amateau. GS: Bill Daily. Dave sleeps in the garage in order to protect his mother from the car strippers working in the neighborhood.

What Makes Auntie Freeze?
W: Allan Burns & Chris Hayward. D: Sidney Miller. GS: Alvy Moore, Joyce Taylor. While on his way to a wedding, Dave is arrested when it appears he is a drunk driver, when in reality his mother is drunk on anti-freeze.

Lassie . . . I Mean, Mother, Come Home
W: Phil Davis. D: David Davis. GS: Jose Gonzalez. Dave accidentally forgets to set the parking brake, sending his mother on a wild ride into Mexico.

Burned at the Steak
W: Jim Parker & Arnold Margolin. D: David Davis. GS: Charles Grodin. Dave and Barbara try to show an inexperienced couple how to get along when the wife is a bad cook.

I'm Through Being a Nice Guy
W: George Kirgo. D: David Davis. GS: Barbara Bain. Captain Manzini wants to buy the car; when Dave refuses, he enlists the aid of three crooks to steal her.

Lights, Camera, Mother
W: Frank Fox. D: Sidney Miller. GS: Stanley Adams, Peter Leeds. The car is going to star in a TV commercial for brakes, but the director changes everything in the commercial from the drapes to the furniture.

The Captain Manzini Grand Prix
W: Allan Burns & Chris Hayward. D: Tom Montgomery. GS: Joe Ryan. Captain Manzini challenges Dave to a race. The winner will get to keep "mother." Manzini plans to win even if he has to cheat.

TV or Not TV
W: Allan Burns & Chris Hayward. D: James Sheldon. GS: Harold Peary, Ed Deemer. Dave gets his mother a TV for the garage, where she wins 5,000 gallons of gas on a quiz show and must appear in person to collect it.

My Son the Ventriloquist
W: Phil Davis. D: Sidney Miller. GS: Harold Peary, The Spats. Dave wants to impress a client in order to buy air conditioners for Barbara and his mother. The only problem is how to win over the client.

My Son the Judge
W: Lila Garrett, Bernie Kahn & Phil Davis. D: Sidney Miller. GS: Dave Willock, Florida Friebus. Dave has been offered a judgeship and Barbara and the family will do anything to see that he gets it.

And Leave the Drive-In to Us
W: Lou Breslow & Alan Woods. D: David Davis. GS: Herbie Faye, Leo De Lyon. Dave takes mother to a drive-in for her birthday.

For Whom the Horn Honks
W: George Kirgo. D: Rod Amateau. GS: Del Close, Jack Raine. Manzini pretends that he is dying in the hope that Dave will soften and give up the car.

Hey Lady, Your Slip Isn't Showing
W: Tom Koch. D: Tom Montgomery. Manzini tries to get mother by having Barbara sign over the registration papers to him, but no one can find them.

Many Happy No-Returns
W: Phil Davis. D: Tom Montgomery. GS: Dave Willock, Chris Noel. For Christmas, Dave and Barbara each paint a picture for a charity auction.

They know no one will bid on them so they each hire a phony bidder financed by their own Christmas funds.

Shine On Shine On Honeymoon
W: Allan Burns & Chris Hayward. D: Rod Amateau. GS: Alvy Moore, Stuart Nesbit. After 8 years of marriage, the Crabtree family finally take their honeymoon despite a warning from Barbara's mother, an astrology nut.

I Remember Mama, Why Can't You Remember Me?
W: Jim Parker & Arnold Margolin. D: Rod Amateau. GS: Harry Holcombe. Mother gets amnesia from a bump on the bumper. The only way to cure her is to give her an even harder bump.

Goldporter
W: Phil Davis. D: David Davis. GS: Milton Frome. Manzini injects Dave with a mind suggestion drug, forcing him to consent to sell mother to him. However, the drug wears off in time.

The Incredible Shrinking Car
W: Allan Burns & Chris Hayward. D: Rod Amateau. GS: Bill Glover, Gertrude Astor. Manzini, using a special device, shrinks mother down to miniature size. Mother manages to switch the machine into reverse.

I'd Rather Do It Myself, Mother
W: Phil Davis. D: David Davis. GS: Anita Gordon. Dave hires an overly efficient maid to help Barbara with the housework.

You Can't Get There from Here
W: Jim Parker & Arnold Margolin. D: Tom Montgomery. GS: Del Close. Dave is arrested for driving with an expired driver's license while on his second honeymoon.

Riddler on the Roof
W: Phil Davis. D: Rod Amateau. GS: Richard Kiel, Frank Delfino. Mother uncovers a plot to kill a foreign president, sending Dave and her off to prevent the murder.

My Son, the Criminal
W: Phil Davis. D: Rod Amateau. GS: Byron Foulger, Don Haggerty. The mailman overhears Dave talking to mother and thinks he has killed her and buried her under the garage, so he calls the police.

An Unreasonable Facsimile
W: Jim Parker & Arnold Margolin. D: David Davis. Manzini hires a lookalike for Dave then gets the real Dave out of town. He tries to get the imposter to convince Barbara to sign the registration over to him.

Over the Hill and to the Junkyard
W: Phil Davis. D: Rod Amateau. GS: Dick Wilson, Charlie Brill. When Barbara wins a car, Dave can't afford to keep two cars. He must now decide which car to get rid of: the new one or mother.

It Might as Well Be Spring as Not
W: James L. Brooks. D: Rod Amateau. GS: Lois Roberts, George Washburn. Dave's business dealings with a housing developer lead to the loss of his secretary and his mother, the car.

Absorba the Greek
W: Phil Davis. D: David Davis. GS: John Holland, Dan Seymour. One of Dave's clients is a landlord who wants to break his lease with a nightclub on the grounds that the floor show is obscene. So Dave takes Barbara to the show to judge for themselves, where they run into the landlord.

The Blabbermouth
W: Mitch Persons & James L. Brooks. D: Rod Amateau. GS: Patty Regan, Marianne Kanter. Barbara and the kids find out mother can talk, thereby setting off a chain of neighbors who want to hear her talk.

When You Wish Upon a Car
W: John Barbour & Whitney Mitchell. D: Rod Amateau. GS: Kelley Van Dyke, Joel Davison. When mother helps fulfill a little child's wishes, the neighborhood children all want

mother to fulfill their wishes . . . at 5 cents a wish.

Desperate Minutes
W: Phil Davis. D: David Davis. GS: Barbara Bain, Dave Willock. Two armed men hold the Crabtrees captive in their home. Their neighbor Phil tries to help but is also captured. It is up to mother to save the day.

MY SISTER EILEEN

On the air 10/5/60, off 4/12/61. CBS. B&W Film. 26 episodes. Broadcast: Oct 1960-Apr 1961 Wed 9-9:30. Producer: Al Simon. Prod/Synd: Filmways.

CAST: Ruth Sherwood (played by Elaine Stritch), Eileen Sherwood (Shirley Bonne), Mr. Appopolous (Leon Belasco), Chick (Jack Weston), Bertha (Rose Marie), Mr. Beaumont (Raymond Bailey), Marty Scott (Stubby Kaye).

The story of two sisters who move to New York to further their careers in show business. Ruth was a writer and Eileen was an actress. The show has not been run since the early sixties.

The Photography Mixup
GS: Jack Weston, Rose Marie, Raymond Bailey. Ruth is all for a magazine story about her until she sees the magazine.

Super—Ruth Saves Eileen
GS: Rose Marie, Peter Adams, Mark Tuttle. Ruth saves Eileen in her dreams when she sees her being interviewed by a girl-crazy producer.

Ruth Becomes a Waitress
GS: Raymond Bailey, John Banner, Lyle Talbot. Ruth substitutes for Eileen when she gets a part in a play.

The Lease Breakers
GS: Joe Besser, Jo Morrow. The Sherwood sisters throw a wild party; among the guests are two bongo-playing beatniks and a fireman with a siren.

Ruth Sells a Story
GS: Richard Deacon. Ruth writes a story and buys a few dresses, then she sees the editor about revisions and ends up in a fierce fight.

Eileen's Big Chance
GS: Bert Convy, John Shay. Playwright Doug Cartwright hears Eileen read and gives her a part in his new play. Ruth tries to persuade him to rewrite Eileen's part for her.

Ruth Welcomes a Hometown Friend
GS: William Hudson. Ruth is alarmed when her old school friend named Fatso plans to visit her, but finds that Fatso has changed.

The Perfect Male
GS: John Stephenson, Susan Dorn. Roger Purcell wants to remake Eileen into the perfect female before he marries her.

Three's a Crowd
GS: Rose Marie, Lennie Bremen, Pat McCaffrie. The Sherwood girls decide to get a roommate to share the rent.

Ebenezer Scrooge Appopolous
GS: Rose Marie, Mary Grace Canfield, George Kennedy. The girls forget to invite Mr. Appopolous to their Christmas party which makes him very mad.

Eileen and the Intern
GS: Edward Mallory, Billy Greene, Leon Belasco. Eileen and Ruth decide to make a pilot film for prospective sponsors.

Eileen Becomes a Star
GS: Peter Leeds, Robert Casper. An

old boyfriend is coming to marry her, so Eileen tries to discourage him by showing how show biz will interfere.

The Perfect Secretary
GS: Hayden Rorke, Marla Craig, Joanna Lee.   Marty wants Ruth to replace a TV producer's secretary so Eileen can get into TV.

Ruth's Double Life
GS: Stubby Kaye. Ruth is writing for a true confession magazine.

Barefoot and Unashamed
GS: Peter Whitney, Jonathan Hole. Ruth must entertain author Malcolm Talbot for her boss.

Ruth Becomes a Success
GS: Frankie Avalon.   Ruth meets Frankie Avalon when her company is handling his first TV drama script.

Ruth the Starmaker
GS: William Schallert, Linden Chiles, Wally Cassel. Eileen decides to go home when she feels she has had it with the theater.

About Clark Carter
GS: Linden Chiles, Joanna Barnes. Eileen's boyfriend Clark is the target of a golddigger.

Aunt Harriet's Way
GS: Agnes Moorehead, Richard Webb. Aunt Harriet comes for a visit and

recommends the helpless female act, so Eileen gets Ruth a date with a friend who wants a strong-willed girl.

Ruth's Fella
GS: Richard Webb, Allen Jung. Ruth tries to keep Eileen away from her boyfriend.

Separate Ways
Ruth gets Eileen to move into her own apartment but later regrets it.

Ruth the Reformer
GS: Gordon Gebert. A teenager shows up at their door with stolen hubcaps and a cop right behind him.

The Protectors
GS: Agnes Moorehead, Roy Roberts. A stranger asks visiting Aunt Harriet to invest ten thousand dollars for him.

Marty's Best Friend
GS: Bill Williams, Lloyd Kino. Marty's friend Frank Mitchell invites the girls to dinner where he boasts about himself and puts Marty down.

Ruth's Holiday
GS: Kurt Kreuger, George Eldridge. Ruth plans to go skiing but doesn't want to leave Eileen alone for the weekend.

Monkey Shines
No available story.

MY THREE SONS

On the air 9/29/60, off 8/24/72. ABC, CBS. B&W Color (only color episodes syndicated). 160 episodes syndicated. 369 filmed. Broadcast. Sept. 1960-Sept 1963 ABC Thu 9-9:30; Sept 1963-Sept 1965 ABC Thu 8:30-9; Sept 1965-Aug 1967 CBS Thu 8:30-9; Sept 1967-Sept 1971 CBS Sat 8:30-9; Sept 1971-Dec 1971 CBS Mon 10-10:30; Jan 1972-Aug 1972 Thu 8:30-9. Producer: Don Fedderson. Synd: Viacom.
CAST: Steve Douglas (played by Fred MacMurray), Robbie Douglas (Don Grady), Chip Douglas (Stanley Livingston), Charley O'Casey (William Demarest), Ernie Douglas (Barry Livingston), Katie Miller Douglas (Tina Cole), Barbara Harper Douglas (Beverly Garland), Dodie Harper Douglas (Dawn Lyn), Polly Williams Douglas (Ronne Troup).

Fred MacMurray, Dawn Lyn, and Beverly Garland, in My Three Sons.

The trials and tribulations of the Douglas family, a typical middle-class suburban family living in Southern California. The main family consists of Steve, a widower and aeronautical engineer, and his three sons and their Uncle Charley. (Their grandfather, Bub, only appears in the nonsyndicated episodes.) *My Three Sons* is in syndication, but for unknown reasons only 160 color episodes are available. The B&W and the final color season are not syndicated.

[Every episode is directed by James V. Kern.]

The First Marriage
W: George Tibbles. GS: Vera Miles. When his son Mike gets married, Steve begins to think he is getting old.

Red Tape Romance
W: George Tibbles. GS: Virginia Gregg, Vera Miles. Steve plans to adopt Ernie, but Uncle Charley objects.

Brother Ernie
W: George Tibbles. GS: John Gallaudet, Vera Miles. Ernie can't be adopted unless there is a woman in the Douglas house.

Robbie and the Chorus Girl
W: Gail Ingram Clement. GS: Pam Austin. Charley and Steve worry about the chorus girl Robbie's been dating.

There's a What in the Attic?
W: James Allardice & Tom Adair. GS: Jon Silo, Quentin Sondergaard. Ernie thinks he saw a lion in the house.

My Son the Ballerina
W: John McGreevey. GS: Sharon Farrell, Jeanette Nolan. Robbie joins the ballet class to help him make the track team.

Office Mother
W: Danny Simon. GS: Joan Blondell, John Howard, Barry Brooks. Steve hires a grandmother as his new secre-

tary who turns his office into a kitchen.

Monsters and Junk Like That
W: Stan Davis & Frank Crow. GS: Wayne Heffley. Steve gets stuck inside a robot costume.

Robbie's Double Life
W: Doug Tibbles. GS: Lori Martin. Robbie tries to date two girls at the same time.

Mary Lou
W: John McGreevey. GS: Patty Gerrity. Chip dates an older woman.

Charley and the Dancing Lesson
W: Joseph Hoffman. GS: Joanna Moore, Mike Monahan. Charley signs up for a lifetime membership in a dance club.

The Ernie Report
W: Dorothy Foote. GS: Jimmy Garrett, Patty MacDonald. Ernie feels left out when the rest of the family doesn't have any time to spend with him.

The Hong Kong Story
W: George Tibbles. GS: Frances Fong, George Takei, Harold Fong. The family goes to Hong Kong where Charley searches for his old girlfriend.

Marriage and Stuff
W: George Tibbles. GS: Chris Noel, Dana Dillaway. The family is convinced that Steve is planning a secret marriage for himself.

Douglas a Go-Go
W: Austin & Irma Kalish. GS: Ilana Dowding. Chip decides to give a party, complete with girls, at the house.

Charley the Pigeon
W: Joseph Hoffman & Ray Brenner. GS: Quinn O'Hara, Mary Mitchell, Booth Coleman. When Robbie is taken by two female pool sharks, Charley comes to the rescue.

What About Harry?
W: Cynthia Lindsay. GS: Lee Meriwether, Gil Lamb. A big shaggy dog follows Steve home.

From Maggie with Love
W: Bill O'Hallaren. GS: Dana Wynter, Lou Krugman. A rich woman tries to get Steve to marry her by giving his family expensive presents.

Robbie and the Slave Girl
W: John McGreevey. GS: Benson Fong, Irene Tsu, Beulah Quo. Robbie saves the life of a Chinese girl who claims that she is his slave.

Steve and the Huntress
W: Dorothy Foote. GS: Terry Moore. A lady hunter asks Steve to join her on a safari to Africa.

Robbie the College Man
W: Joseph Hoffman. GS: Suzanne Benoit, Barbara Pepper. Robbie gets a job so he can afford to rent an apartment near the college.

Whatever Happened to Baby Chip?
W: Doug Tibbles. GS: Jay North, Pitt Herbert, Charles Herbert. Steve becomes concerned when Chip lets his hair grow to his shoulders.

Robbie and the Little Stranger
W: James Allardice & Tom Adair. GS: Tina Cole. Robbie has a fight with his girlfriend while he babysits for some friends, causing him to take the baby home with him.

London Memories
W: Doug Tibbles. GS: Anna Lee, Nora Marlowe, Richard Peel, Ben Wright. Steve finds himself in love with a widow while in London.

Call Her Man
W: James Allardice & Tom Adair. GS: Kipp Hamilton. Steve has to put up with a lady engineer at the same time Chip has a run-in with a female hockey player.

Kid Brother Blues
W: John McGreevey. GS: Donald Losby. Chip and his friend break up Robbie's date with his new girl.

Our Boy in Washington
W: Austin & Irma Kalish. GS: Susan Silo, Tol Avery, Maurice Marsac. The French government invites the family to Washington when Ernie writes a letter thanking them for the Statue of Liberty.

Ernie and That Woman
W: John McGreevey. GS: Vicki Cos. Ernie dates an older woman.

The State vs. Chip Douglas
W: Leo & Pauline Townsend. GS: Charles Herbert, Flip Mark. Chip wants to hold a trial to prove he did not take a valuable coin from Ernie's collection.

The Wrong Robbie
W: George Tibbles. GS: Fred Wayne, Melinda Plowman. Robbie is mistaken for an exact lookalike who almost gets Robbie into serious trouble.

A Hunk of Hardware
W: Gail Clement. GS: Dallas Mitchell. Ernie plans to run away from home when he doesn't win a trophy.

The Wheels
W: John McGreevey. GS: Sherry Jackson. Robbie is not allowed to use the car when his girlfriend gets a ticket while she was driving it.

Stag at Bay
W: Elroy Schwartz. GS: Leslie Parrish, Paul Sorenson. The family invites a lady dancer to move in when she is evicted from her apartment.

Fly Away Home
W: James Allardice & Tom Adair. GS: Virginia Grey, Eddie Rosson, Dave Willock. Steve is disappointed when he returns to his hometown and meets his old girlfriend.

Arrivederci Robbie
W: John McGreevey. GS: Jay Novello, Judy Cannon. Robbie is shocked when he learns that the Italian girl he took for a walk in the park tells him that he must now marry her.

Forget Me Not
W: Joseph Hoffman. GS: Joan Caulfield. Steve thinks his old girlfriend wants to marry him.

Good Guys Finish Last
W: Henry Garson & Edmund Beloin. GS: Benson Fong, Jay North. Steve and his friends take part in a father versus son quiz show.

If at First . . .
W: Edmund Beloin & Henry Garson. GS: Yvonne Craig, Chet Stratton. Steve gets a parking ticket from Robbie's meter maid girlfriend.

Robbie's Underground Movie
W: John McGreevey. GS: Linda Foster, Jerry Rannow, Paul Sorenson. Robbie and his girlfriend make a film for his college film class.

Fiddler Under the Roof
W: Austin & Irma Kalish. GS: Leon Belasco, Jerry Hausner. Charley tries to teach no-talent Ernie how to play the violin.

Happy Birthday World
W: John McGreevey. GS: Brenda Benet, Ralph Hart, Richard Bull. Robbie opens a birthday cake business at home to earn extra money.

The Awkward Age
W: Joseph Hoffman. GS: Susan Oliver, Oliver McGowan. Steve and Robbie are involved with the same girl.

A Real Nice Time
W: Elroy Schwartz. GS: Tommy Noonan, Sherry Alberoni. Chip is chosen for a date with a movie star.

My Dad, the Athlete
W: Ray Singer. GS: Herb Anderson,

Jack Minty, Bill Zuckert. Steve joins a cross-country race when Ernie brags about how good an athlete he really is.

Tramp or Ernie
W: Gail Clement.   GS: Bill Quinn. Ernie is allergic to their dog Tramp.

Grandma's Girl
W: Dorothy Foote. GS: Jeanette Nolan.   Chip rents a horse and buggy to impress his girlfriend's grandmother.

Falling Star
W: Dorothy Foote & Joseph Hoffman. GS: Jaye P. Morgan.   Steve tries to help a singer's career by getting her to sing with Rob's band.

You Saw What?
W: Eugene Thompson. GS: Del Moore, Rory Stevens, Alan Baxter.   Ernie is ordered to keep quiet when he reports a UFO sighting to the Air Force.

Both Your Houses
W: John McGreevey.   GS: Elvia Allman, Kevin Corcoran.   Robbie and the girl next door try to stop a fight from starting between their families.

My Pal Dad
W: Phil Leslie. GS: Aki Hara.   Chip and Robbie volunteer Ernie to go with Steve on a fishing trip.

TV or Not TV
W: John McGreevey. GS: Jenny Maxwell.   When the family fights over the TV, Charley declares that there will be no more television for a week.

The Good Earth
W: Tom Adair & John Elliotte.   GS: Doodles Weaver.   Charley is the victim of a con man who tricked him into buying some worthless land.

My Son, the Bullfighter
W: Elroy Schwartz.   GS: Alejandro Rey, Heather North.   Robbie takes up bullfighting to impress his girlfriend who has fallen for a bullfighter.

The Best Man
W: Edmund Beloin & Henry Garson. GS: Marianna Hill.   Robbie is asked to be the best man at the wedding of his old girlfriend.

Now, in My Day
W: Doug Tibbles & Gail Clement. GS: Susan Gordon.   Chip is dating two girls at the same time.

The Sky Is Falling
W: Danny Simon. GS: Steve Franken. Robbie makes a small fortune selling real estate.

Melinda
W: Joseph Hoffman. GS: Suzanne Cupito.   Chip is asked to date the daughter of Steve's new girlfriend.

Charley o' the Seven Seas
W: Joseph Hoffman. GS: Jan Clayton, Lillian Bronson.   Ernie's teacher wants to run away with Charley to Pago-Pago.

Help, the Gypsies Are Coming
W: Cynthia Lindsay.   GS: Kurt Kasznar.   Ernie is adopted by a band of gypsies.

Ernie's Folly
W: Austin & Irma Kalish.   GS: Teddy Eccles, Ila Briton.   Steve refuses to help Ernie with his science fair project.

Ernie's Crowd
W: Cynthia Lindsay.   GS: Julie Parrish.   Ernie wants to go along with his brothers on their dates.

Ernie and the O'Grady
W: Dorothy Foote.   GS: Eddie Foy, Jr., Bobby Jellison.   Ernie brings a bum home with him.

So Long Charley Hello
W: Henry Garson & Edmund Beloin. GS: James Gregory.   Charley decides to leave and take a job on a fishing boat.

Weekend in Paradise
W: George Tibbles & Edmund Hartmann.   GS: Susan Seaforth, Richard Loo.   The family gets into trouble when they take a trip to Hawaii.

[Every episode is now directed by Fred De Cordova.]

Moving Day
W: George Tibbles.   GS: Kathleen Freeman.   The family moves to California where they get the cold shoulder treatment from their neighbors.

Robbie Loves Katie
W: George Tibbles.   Robbie proposes to Katie.

Inspection of the Groom
W: George Tibbles.   GS: Kay Cole, Joan Tompkins.   Katie's family and her friends give him the once-over to see if he checks out.

Countdown to Marriage
W: George Tibbles.   GS: Oliver McGowan, Jane Zachary.   Robbie and Katie have a fight and cancel the wedding.

Wedding Bells
W: Lois Hire.   GS: Kathryn Givney. Robbie and Katie are married.

The Homecoming
W: Lois Hire.   Katie and Robbie move into his old room.

My Wife the Waitress
W: Henry Garson & Edmund Beloin. GS: Dick Wilson, Lou Krugman. Katie gets a job as a cigarette girl.

The Computer Picnic
W: Doug Tibbles.   GS: Ed Begley, Jr., Buck Young.   A computer chooses who will take whom to a school picnic.

The Chameleon
W: Douglas Tibbles.   GS: Paul Picerni, Gina Picerni.   Ernie is reluctant to befriend a girl.

Designing Woman
W: Paul West.   GS: Anne Baxter. Steve is taken in by an attractive woman.

Ernie, the Bluebeard
W: Douglas Tibbles.   GS: Claire Wilcox.   Ernie gets two dates for the same night.

Heartbeat
W: Bernard Rothman.   GS: Olan Soule. Katie thinks the strange noise she is hearing in the house is a giant heart beating.

The Aunt Who Came to Dinner
W: William Raynor & Myles Wilder. GS: Marsha Hunt.   Katie's aunt moves in and takes over the house.

Liverpool Saga
W: Freddy Rhea.   GS: Jeremy Clyde. Chip adds a British musician to his rock band.

Leaving the Nest
W: Peggy Elliot.   Robbie and Katie decide to move into an apartment.

You're Driving Me Crazy
W: George Tibbles.   GS: George Neise. Katie and Robbie are the prime suspects when a big scratch is found on the family car.

The Chaperones
W: Paul West.   Robbie and Katie chaperone Chip and his friends at a cabin in the mountains.

Green-Eyed Robbie
W: Lois Hire.   GS: Mark Sturges, Shirley Mitchell.   Robbie becomes jealous when Katie tutors one of her old boyfriends.

Charley's Tea
W: Paul West.   GS: Colleen Peters, Janis Oliver.   Katie fights back when Charley makes her feel useless.

Ernie, the Jinx
W: Austin & Irma Kalish. GS: Bella Bruck, John Craig. The family has to convince Ernie that he is not a jinx.

Ernie and Zsa Zsa
W: William Kelsay. GS: Zsa Zsa Gabor. Ernie and Tramp spend the day at a movie studio with Zsa Zsa Gabor.

A Horse for Uncle Charley
W: Edmund Beloin & Henry Garson. GS: James Westerfield. Charley buys a trotting horse.

Dear Enemy
W: George Tibbles. GS: Kenneth Washington, Bobby Crawford. While trying to visit Robbie in the Army reserve, the whole family is captured during a war game.

Uncle Charley's Aunt
W: George Tibbles. GS: Rolfe Sedan, Gil Lamb, Frank Scannell. Charley gets arrested while he is dressed as a chorus girl.

The Standing-Still Tour
W: George Tibbles. GS: Douglas V. Fowley. Charley and Ernie are left home alone when the rest of the family goes out on a date.

Honorable Guest
W: Austin & Irma Kalish. GS: Benson Fong, Beulah Quo, Philip Ahn. The Douglas family meet their Chinese friends from their old neighborhood when they go on a camping trip.

The Perfect Separation
W: Jim Brooks. GS: Lynn Loring, Robert Dunlap. Robbie and Katie almost break up their friends' marriage when they invite them over for dinner.

Gossip, Inc.
W: Lois Hire. GS: Abby Dalton, Gail Fisher, Marvin Kaplan. The people at Steve's new office think he is a bigamist.

The Masculine Mystique
W: George Tibbles. GS: Joel Davison, Dirk Browne. Ernie has a fight with his best friend.

The Tire Thief
W: Doug Tibbles. GS: Sheldon Collins, Kevin Tate. Ernie and his friends are wanted by the police.

The Great Pregnancy
W: George Tibbles. GS: Kathryn Givney. Katie announces that she is pregnant.

Dr. Osborne, M.D.
W: George Tibbles. GS: Leon Ames. A fight starts over the choices for Katie's new doctor.

Life Begins in Katie
W: George Tibbles. GS: Butch Patrick. Robbie tries to become a more responsible person when he realizes that he will be a father.

The Grandfathers
W: Lois Hire. GS: Arthur O'Connell. Steve is nervous about being a grandfather.

The Baby Nurse
W: George Tibbles. Charley takes up babysitting to prepare himself for when the baby is born.

Big Ol' Katie
W: George Tibbles. GS: Leon Ames. Katie learns that she is going to have more than one baby.

My Three Grandsons
W: George Tibbles. GS: Charles Robinson, Leon Ames. Katie gives birth to triplets.

Tea for Three
W: George Tibbles. Robbie learns that caring for the triplets is more than he expected.

Back to Earth
W: George Tibbles. GS: Vince Howard, Ricky Allen. Robbie decides to

quit school and go to work.

First Night Out
W: Roccina Chatfield. GS: Rose Marie. The family becomes nervous when a baby sitter and Ernie take care of the triplets.

Casanova O'Casey
W: Ramey Idriss. GS: Horace McMahon, Johnny Silver. Charley goes looking and finds several new girlfriends.

Expendable Katie
W: Lois Hire. GS: Leon Ames. When Katie leaves for the day, the rest of the family find they can't keep the house neat without her around.

The New Room
W: George Tibbles. GS: Gary Clarke, Ed Begley. Katie is the only one who can get along with the contractor who is adding the new room to the house.

The Fountain of Youth
W: George Tibbles. GS: Wanda Hendrix. Steve meets a widow who first comes on to him and then rejects him.

Three's a Crowd
W: George Tibbles. GS: Butch Patrick. The babies get mixed up and they have to be returned to the hospital in order to be identified.

Chip and Debbie
W: Diana Johnson & Aljean Harmetz. GS: Angela Cartwright. Chip becomes engaged to his new girlfriend.

What Did You Do Today, Grandpa?
W: Henry Garson. GS: Anne Jeffreys, Johnny Haymer, Mike Mazurki. The family is unaware that Steve has been asked to help capture some enemy agents.

Chip on Wheels
W: Lois Hire. GS: Jeff Burton. Steve gives Chip a used car for his birthday.

Honorable Expectant Grandfather
W: George Tibbles. GS: Benson Fong, Brian Fong. Steve's Chinese friend comes to him for advice when his daughter marries a hippie.

Other Woman
W: Douglas Whitcomb. Chip and Ernie think Robbie is fooling around with another woman.

Goodbye Forever
W: Doug Tibbles. GS: Butch Patrick. Ernie's best friend moves away.

The O'Casey Scandal
W: Lois Hire. GS: Claire Wilcox. Ernie and his girlfriend are shocked when Charley and her grandmother act like swingers and not like old people.

Ernie's Pen Pal
W: Doug Tibbles. GS: Gil Rogers, Silvia Marion, Valentin de Vargas. Ernie's pen pal from Latin America comes for a visit.

Ernie the Transmitter
W: Dorothy Foote. GS: Booth Coleman. Ernie thinks he has ESP and predicts danger for Robbie and Katie.

The Matchmakers
W: Doug Tibbles. GS: Don DeFore. Steve and his business partner find that their kids hate each other.

Ernie Is Smitten
W: Doug Tibbles. GS: Julia Benjamin. Ernie falls for a girl who doesn't seem to like him.

Two O'Clock Feeding
W: Doug Tibbles. Steve tries to keep a young couple's marriage from falling apart.

Teacher's Pet
W: Freddy Rhea. GS: Sylvia Sydney. Ernie is put in a special English class with a very strict teacher.

The First Meeting
W: George Tibbles. GS: Beverly Garland. Steve meets an attractive widow (who is to be his wife) at the high school.

Instant Co-Worker
W: George Tibbles. GS: Eleanor Audley, Naomi Stevens. Robbie gets a job at his father's company.

Is It Love?
W: George Tibbles. The whole family tries to convince Steve that he should continue to date his girlfriend Barbara.

A Ring for Barbara
W: George Tibbles. Steve asks Barbara to marry him.

The Littlest Rebel
W: George Tibbles. Barbara tries to get Steve's family to accept her.

Two Weeks to Go
W: George Tibbles. Steve and Barbara disagree over the type of wedding ceremony they should have.

One Week to Go
W: George Tibbles. GS: Maurice Manson. Steve and Barbara have a fight and decide to cancel the wedding.

Came the Day
W: George Tibbles. GS: Brenda Benet. Steve and Barbara get married.

Mexican Honeymoon
W: George Tibbles. GS: Paul Peterson. Steve and Barbara spend their honeymoon in Mexico.

After You, Alfonse
W: Lois Hire. Katie tries to give Charley some lessons in manners.

Rough on Dodie
W: Doug Tibbles. Dodie thinks she doesn't fit with the rest of the family.

It's a Woman's World
W: Si Rose. Steve is conned into playing a tree in Dodie's school play.

Silver Threads
W: Doug Tibbles. Katie becomes upset when she finds a few gray hairs on her head.

Table for Eight
W: Bob Touchstone. GS: John Gallaudet. Barbara has to prepare dinner for Steve's business friends.

Double Jealousy
W: Roccina Chatfield. GS: Brenda Benet. Barbara and Katie become jealous of the new secretary who is assisting Robbie and Steve.

You Can't Go Home
W: George Tibbles. GS: Burt Mustin, Olan Soule. Robbie visits his old neighborhood and finds that it has all changed.

Dodie's Tonsils
W: Doug Tibbles. GS: Jane Dulo, Roy Roberts. Dodie wants Steve to stay with her overnight when she has her tonsils out.

Who Is Sylvia?
W: George Tibbles. GS: Jane Wyman. Barbara becomes jealous when Steve's old girlfriend, who is now a rich divorcee, comes for a visit.

Guest in the House
W: Lois Hire. Barbara has to visit one of Chip's teachers when Steve goes out of town.

Charley's Cello
W: Ramez Idriss. Barbara invites three lady musicians to join Charley when he plays his cello.

The Honeymoon Is Over
W: George Tibbles. Barbara and Katie visit Steve and Robbie when they have to stay very late at the office.

Baubles, Bangles and Beatrice
W: Doug Tibbles. GS: Victoria Meyerink. Dodie's little friend has a crush on Ernie.

Mister X
W: Lois Hire. GS: Lew Ayres, Charles Bateman. A mysterious bearded man is watching the Douglas house.

Dodie's Dilemma
W: Lois Hire. GS: Erin Moran. Dodie asks her brothers to defend her against a bully.

Love They Neighbor
W: Gwen Bagni & Paul Dubov. GS: Jerry Mathers. Robbie and Katie have a fight with their new neighbors.

J.P. Douglas
W: B.W. Sandefur. GS: Pitt Herbert. Chip decides to make a lot of money all at once.

The First Anniversary
W: George Tibbles. GS: Norman Alden. Dodie makes a surprise party for Steve and Barbara on their anniversary.

The Once-Over
W: George Tibbles. Chip's girlfriend asks him to elope with her.

The Return of Albert
W: George Tibbles. GS: Craig Stevens. Barbara's old boyfriend comes for a visit.

The Non-Proposal
W: George Tibbles. Polly, Chip's girl, thinks they are engaged.

Polly Wants a Douglas
W: George Tibbles. Chip and Polly have a fight when he refuses to elope with her.

The Cat Burglars
W: George Tibbles. Steve is arrested when he is mistaken for a cat burglar.

The Elopement
W: George Tibbles. Chip and Polly ask their parents' permission to elope.

The Honeymoon
W: George Tibbles. GS: Natividad Vacio, Veronica Cartwright. Chip and Polly elope to Las Vegas.

One by One They Go
W: George Tibbles. Polly's father refuses to talk to her again.

My Four Women
W: Bob Touchstone. Steve agrees to be a model at a fashion show but then backs out.

The Bride Went Home
W: George Tibbles. Polly leaves Chip after he gets sick from eating her cooking.

The Power of Suggestion
W: Doug Tibbles. Ernie uses the family as the subject for his psychology project.

NANNY AND THE PROFESSOR

On the air 1/21/70, off 12/27/71. ABC. Color Film. 30 min. 54 episodes. Broadcast: Jan 1970-Aug 1970 Wed 7:30-8; Sept 1970-Sept 1971 Fri 8-8:30; Sept 1971-Dec 1971 Mon 8-8:30. Producer: David Gerber. Prod Co/Synd: 20th Century Fox TV.

CAST: Phoebe Figalilly (Nanny) (played by Juliet Mills), Prof. Harold Everett (Richard Long), Hal Everett (David Doremus), Butch Everett (Trent Lehman), Prudence Everett (Kim Richards), Aunt Henrietta (Elsa Lanchester).

Phoebe Figalilly, better known as Nanny, a British psychic comes to live in the Everett home as their housekeeper and nanny. Her employer, Prof. Harold Everett, a young widower with three children, is always perplexed by her uncanny ability to foresee the future. Her uniqueness is a source of mystery for the

David Doremus (left), Kim Richards (child), Juliet Mills, Richard Long, Trent Lehman, in Nanny and the Professor.

Professor and joy for the children. The series is seen frequently on small rural stations (mainly UHF) but rarely in large cities.

Nanny Will Do [Pilot]
W: A.J. Carothers. D: Peter Tewksbury. GS: Robert Ito, Leonard Stone, Patty Regan, Fred Holiday, Edith Atwater. A mysterious Nanny comes to take care of a professor and his three children.

The New Butch
W: George Tibbles. D: David Alexander. GS: Lauren Gilbert, Michael Barbera, Don Beddoe. The professor tries to prove to Butch that he is still important to the family.

The Wiblet Will Get You If You Don't Watch Out
W: A.J. Carothers. D: Russ Mayberry.

GS: Joanna Moore. Nanny tries to cure Prudence of the monster in her nightmares.

The Scientific Approach
W: John McGreevey. D: Norman Abbott. GS: Joanna Barnes, Jodie Foster, Lola Cannon. A child psychologist believes Butch and Prudence are ill-adjusted because they believe in Nanny's strange abilities.

The Philosopher's Stone
W: Joanna Lee. D: Jerry Bernstein. GS: Kathleen Richards, Sean Kelly. Nanny gives Hal a stone which will give the owner three wishes.

The Astronomers
W: Joseph Bonaduce. D: Norman Abbott. GS: Sam Jaffe, Larry Gelman. Butch accidentally sights a comet, taking the credit away from a noted scientist.

Spring, Sweet Spring
W: A.J. Carothers. D: Russ Mayberry. GS: William Bramley, Patsy Garrett. Nanny tries to get the family together for a spring picnic.

Nanny on Wheels
W: Austin & Irma Kalish. D: Gary Nelson. GS: Charles Lane, Bill Zuckert, Art Metrano. Nanny buys an old car but she doesn't have a driving license.

The Tyrannosaurus Tibia
W: Earl Hamner. D: Richard Kinon. GS: Jim Backus, Diana Cheshney. Waldo finds and buries a dinosaur bone causing problems for Nanny's garden.

Strictly for the Birds
W: John McGreevey. D: Gary Nelson. GS: Edward Everett Horton, J. Pat O'Malley. Nanny tries to save three homeless ducklings and help a lonely old professor.

The Games Families Play
W: Rick Mittleman. D: Richard Kinon. GS: Hal Buckley, Bob Maloney, Felton Perry, Melissa Newman. The professor upsets the family when he tells them he is thinking about moving in order to take a new job.

I Think I Shall Never See a Tree
W: Joanna Lee. D: Jay Sandrich. GS: Henry Jones, Ron Masak, Ellen Corby. The city plans to tear down the tree with the children's tree house in order to widen the street.

An Element of Risk
W: John McGreevey. D: Gary Nelson. GS: Lee Meriwether. The professor is afraid to see his old girlfriend and Prudence is afraid to blow up a balloon.

A Fowl Episode
W: Earl Hamner. D: Richard Kinon. GS: Roger Perry, Jerry Hausner, Steve Dunne. Prudence's pet rooster is waking up the whole neighborhood.

Nanny and the Smoke-Filled Room
W: Lila Garrett. D: Bernie Kahn. D: William Wiard. GS: Roger Bowen, Virginia Christine. Butch runs for homeroom president with Nanny's help.

From Butch, with Love
W: Bob Mosher. D: Ralph Senensky. GS: Eddie Mayehoff, Joe Mell, Helena Hatcher. Butch tries to earn money to buy an old phonograph.

The Human Element
W: Arthur Alsberg & Don Nelson. D: David Alexander. The professor conducts a race between two old cars using a computer.

Star Bright
W: Joseph Hoffman. D: David Alexander. GS: Arthur O'Connell, Jan Shutan, Lee Delano, Brenda Kelly. Prudence wishes for a different part in a school play and the professor must decide whether or not to hire an old professor or a young one.

A Diller, a Dollar
W: Jean Holloway. D: Gary Nelson. GS: Katherine Justice, Herbert Anderson, Eric Olson. Prudence and her teacher start their first day at school.

The Haunted House
W: Earl Hamner. D: Gary Nelson. GS: Jack Albertson, Joey Foreman. Nanny and the children explore a haunted house inhabited by an old actor.

The India Queen
W: Paul West. D: Ralph Senensky. GS: Paul Bryar, Ted Grossman, Tom Moses. The boys build a raft.

Back to Nature
W: John McGreevey. D: Ralph Senen-

sky. GS: Roger Perry. Nanny and the family go camping.

E.S. Putt
W: Robert Fisher & Arthur Marx. D: Ralph Senensky. GS: Joe Cypher, Patrick O'Moore. Butch breaks the professor's lucky putter right before the big tournament.

The Great Broadcast of 1936
W: Arthur Alsberg & Don Nelson. D: Jay Sandrich. GS: Bridget Hanley, Burt Mustin, Mike Sims. Nanny's old radio broadcasts only programs from the 1930s.

A Letter for Nanny
W: Gene Thompson. D: Jay Sandrich. GS: Don Beddoe. The children try to cheer up Nanny who is unhappy after receiving a letter.

Kid Stuff
W: John McGreevey. D: Gary Nelson. GS: Eddie Foy, Jr., James Millhollin, Eileen Baral. Nanny and the children put on a show to raise money to restore a park fountain.

The Masculine-Feminine Mystique
W: Joanna Lee. D: Gary Nelson. GS: Abby Dalton, Roger Perry. The professor's new assistant is a militant feminist.

The Visitor
W: Earl Hamner. D: Gary Nelson. GS: Lee Casey, Van Williams, Carolyn Conwell. Butch's pen-pal, a runaway Canadian orphan, comes for a visit.

The Humanization of Herbert T. Peabody
W: John McGreevey. D: Ralph Senensky. GS: Paul Winchell, Vincent Van Patten, Dabney Coleman. Nanny and the children help an old puppeteer.

My Son, the Sitter
W: Arthur Alsberg & Don Nelson. D: Bruce Bilson. GS: Aneta Corsaut, Pat Morita. Hal believes he is old enough to babysit Butch and Prudence.

The Prodigy
W: Gene Thompson. D: Bruce Bilson. GS: Todd Baron, Dave Willock, George Barrows. A 12-year-old genius visits, causing resident genius Hal to be jealous.

The Art of Relationships
W: A.J. Carothers. D: Bruce Bilson. GS: Bert Convy, Noam Pitlik, Ryan MacDonald, Cindy Williams. Nanny falls for her night-school professor.

The Communication Gap
W: Micharl Morris. D: Russ Mayberry. GS: Tommy Tune, Elizabeth Baur. The professor gets a love note from one of his students.

How Many Candles?
W: Juliet Mills. D: David Alexander. GS: Ruth McDevitt, Percy Helton, Steven Perry. Butch finds Nanny's passport which says she is 107 years old.

The Man Who Came to Pasta
W: Joanna Lee. D: Jack Arnold. GS: Cesar Romero, Shep Sanders, Alfred Dennis. An Italian director comes to dinner but can't leave when he is besieged by the gout.

The Unknown Factor
W: John McGreevey. D: Gary Nelson. Butch tries to pay for Nanny's present by entering a fishing contest.

Separate Rooms
W: Arthur Alsberg & Don Nelson. D: Gary Nelson. GS: Van Johnson. The boys have a fight, causing them to demand separate bedrooms.

The Balloon Ladies
W: A.J. Carothers. D: Richard Kinon. GS: Ida Lupino, Marjorie Bennett, Don Beddoe. Nanny's two aunts arrive for a visit by balloon.

The Human Fly
W: A.J. Carothers. D: Richard Kinon. GS: John Mills, Tommy Tune, Eric Shea. Nanny's Uncle Alfred, a human fly, comes for a visit.

Oh, What a Tangled Web
W: Joanna Lee. D: Bruce Bilson. GS: Annette Ferra, Barry Hamilton, Harry Moses. Hal lies about his age in order to get a date.

Aunt Henrietta's Premonition
W: A.J. Carothers. D: Richard L. Bare. GS: Elsa Lanchester, Bob Hastings, Bruce Morgan, Anthony Caruso. Nanny's psychic aunt predicts she will be menaced by a man with a mustache.

Aunt Henrietta and the Jinx
W: Gene Thompson. D: Norman Abbott. GS: Elsa Lanchester. Butch gets a good luck charm from Nanny's aunt when he thinks he is jinxed.

Whatever Happened to Felicity?
W: Austin & Irma Kalish. D: Bruce Bilson. GS: Don Beddoe, Walter Baldwin, Edith Evanson. Prudence becomes attached to Nanny's old doll when she is ignored by her brothers.

The Flower Children
W: Bob Mosher. D: Richard L. Bare. GS: Alvy Moore, Larraine Stephens. Prudence tries to get her seeds to grow faster, and the professor upsets his girlfriend when he doesn't try to save a dying tree.

Sunday's Hero
W: Arthur Alsberg & Don Nelson. D: Bruce Bilson. GS: Howard Cosell, Ryan MacDonald, Ric Carrott, Dick Wilson, Roger Perry, Jim Murray. The professor tries to get out of playing football with his friends.

South Sea Island Sweetheart
W: A.J. Carothers. D: Richard Kinon. GS: Ray Bolger, Naomi Stevens, Martin Speer. Nanny's Uncle Horace arrives from the South Seas to perform a rain dance in order to cure a drought.

Aunt Henrietta and the Poltergeist
W: A.J. Carothers. D: Richard Kinon.

GS: Elsa Lanchester. When the furniture is disarranged every night, Nanny's aunt thinks there is a ghost in the house.

Cholmondeley Featherstonehaugh
W: Jean Holloway. D: Richard Kinon. GS: Brian Bedford. Nanny's old boyfriend from England visits and tries to get her to marry him.

The Conversion of Brother Ben
W: Arthur Alsberg & Don Nelson. D: Hollingsworth Morse. GS: Robert Sterling, Roger Perry, Ryan MacDonald. The professor's rich brother donates two million dollars to the college.

Goodbye Arabella Hello
W: Arthur Alsberg & Don Nelson. D: Bruce Bilson. GS: Bob Kramer, Eddie Ryder, Bella Bruck, Jack Burns. Nanny's old car is traded for a new car.

Nanny and Her Witch's Brew
W: Albert E. Lewin. D: Richard Kinon. GS: Frank Aletter, Eileen Baral. Nanny is accused of being a witch.

Professor Pygmalion Plays Golf
W: John McGreevey. D: Ralph Senensky. GS: William Bakewell, Noam Pitlik. Hal enters a golf tournament with strange clubs given to him by Nanny.

The Great Debate
W: Michael Morris. D: Hollingsworth Morse. GS: Chick Hearn, Ed Begley, Jr., Frank Campanella, John Larch. Nanny and Hal help the professor keep a basketball player from failing math.

One for the Road
W: Arthur Alsberg & Don Nelson. D: Bruce Bilson. GS: Pat Harrington, Charles Lane, Brian Tochi, Clint Howard. Hal tries to visit his uncle, but doesn't quite make it.

NO TIME FOR SERGEANTS

On the air 9/14/64, off 9/6/65. ABC. B&W Film 34 episodes. Broadcast: Sept 1964-Sept 1965 Mon 8:30-9. Producer: William T. Orr. Prod Co/Synd: Warner Bros. TV.

CAST: Will Stockdale (played by Sammy Jackson), Sgt. King (Harry Hickox), Ben Whitledge (Kevin O'Neal), Capt. Martin (Paul Smith), Grandpa Anderson (Andy Clyde), Col. Farnsworth (Hayden Rorke), Capt. Krupnick (George Murdock).

The story of Private Will Stockdale, a reluctant Georgia farm boy who is drafted into the Air Force. Episodes relate his attempts to adjust to military life and the trouble he causes his superior officers. This series is based on the movie of the same name. It is not currently shown on any station.

WRITERS: Norman Paul, John L. Greene, Elon Packard, William Burns. DIRECTOR: Richard Crenna.

No Time for Sergeants [Pilot]
Will is inducted into the Air Force and Sgt. King assigns him to KP.

Blue's Wild Yonder
GS: Bill Zuckert. Will gets a package from home: his bloodhound Blue.

Bloodhounds Are Thicker Than Water
GS: George Murdock. In order to keep his dog, Will joins the Air Force police and plans to turn Blue into a sentry dog.

Grandpa's Airlift
GS: John Qualen, Pedro Gonzales-Gonzales. When Ben comes down with the measles, Will and his friends are quarantined on Grandpa Anderson's farm.

Two Aces in a Hole
GS: Alan Hewitt, Jerry Rannow. Will and his friend Jack Langdon are hypnotized into thinking they're high-ranking officers in WW II and take off in a plane with the intention of bombing Germany.

The Spirit of Seventy-Five
GS: Eddie Quillan, Richard X. Slattery. Will tries to keep Grandpa out of the house so a surprise birthday party can be set up.

Will Gets a Right-Hand Man
GS: Paul Smith. Will and Grandpa are accidentally handcuffed together.

Have No Uniform Will Travel
GS: Beulah Quo, John Harmon, Frank Wilcox, John McCook. Will is entrusted to have Captain Martin's dress uniform cleaned and pressed before an officer's ball that evening.

The Farmer in the Deal
The Air Force wants to buy Grandpa's land, but he wants too much money.

Will Goes to Washington
Captain Martin tries to impress his girl by saying he is working on a top secret project. Will accidentally mails the phony telegram he wrote to back up his story.

O Krupnik, My Krupnick
GS: Terry Becker. Captain Martin plans to transfer Will, in order to improve his chances of getting a promotion, instead of Krupnik.

Stockdale's Island
GS: Robert Casper, Joey Tata, Victoria Shaw. Will volunteers to take a survival test on an island.

Stockdale's Millions
GS: Ken Berry. Will accidentally gets a large paycheck, so he uses the money to turn the barracks into a resort.

Two for the Show
GS: Ken Berry, Ron Stokes. Will is put in charge of getting volunteers for the base's annual talent show.

The Living End
GS: Nicolas Coster, Penny O'Donnell. Will and Sgt. King believe that Captain Martin is dying.

Stockdale, General Nuisance
Captain Martin and Sgt. King are planning to transfer Stockdale to another base.

Too Many Stockdales
GS: Stacey Maxwell, Frank Ferguson. Will's father and sister pay a visit to the base.

A Hatful of Muscles
GS: George Ives, Margret Mason. Will and Ben take part in physical exercises to see if the Air Force should toughen up its standards.

It Shouldn't Happen to a Sergeant
GS: Eileen O'Neil, Amzie Strickland. Will has been allowed to become the base's new telephone switchboard operator.

How Now Brown Cow?
The Air Force jets are upsetting Grandpa's cows, so much that they won't give milk.

The Case of the Revolving Witness
GS: Terry Becker, George Murdock, Karen Jenson, Burt Mustin. Will is a witness to a traffic accident involving Captain Martin and Krupnick.

The Sergeants Kimino
GS: Bill Zuckert, Joey Tata, Freddy Cannon. Sgt. King is assigned to watch Will around the clock because the Inspector General is due at any moment.

Stockdale of the Stockade
GS: Terry Becker, Mousie Garner, Joan Mitchum. Will accidentally hits Captain Martin, so he reports to the stockade.

Will's Misfortune Cookie
GS: Woodrow Chambliss, Hope Summers, Tommy Lee, John Kellogg. Will believes his friends are in danger when he reads a fortune cookie.

The Day Blue Blew
GS: Alan Hewitt, Donald May. Captain Martin and Sgt. King bet on Will in a sharpshooting match.

Whortleberry Roots for Everybody
GS: Woodrow Parfrey, Richard Bakalyan. Will volunteers to take a serum which will cure all tropical diseases.

Andy Meets His Match
GS: Mabel Albertson. Colonel Farnsworth's mother visits and has a fight with Grandpa.

Target Stockdale
GS: Del Moore, Grace Lee Whitney. Will scores high on an IQ test and Intelligence wants Will for their own.

The Velvet Wiggle
GS: Sue Ane Langdon, Phillip Pine, Donald Barry. Will is picked to star in an Air Force recruiting film with a Hollywood actress.

[The following episodes have no available stories.]

Bully for Ben
Do Me a Favor and Don't Do Me Any
My Fair Andy
The $100,000 Canteen
Where There's a Way, There's a Will Stockdale

THE ODD COUPLE

On the air 9/24/70, off 7/4/75. ABC. Color Film. 114 episodes. Broadcast: Sept 1970-Jan 1971 Thu 9:30-10; Jan 1971-Jan 1973 Fri 9:30-10; Jan 1973-Jan

The Odd Couple: Tony Randall (left) and Jack Klugman.

1974 Fri 8:30-9; Jan 1974-Sept 1974 Fri 9:30-10; Sept 1974-Jan 1975 Thu 8-8:30; Jan 1975-Jul 1975 Fri 9:30-10. Producer: Garry Marshall. Prod Co/Synd: Paramount TV.

CAST: Oscar Madison (played by Jack Klugman), Felix Unger (Tony Randall), Murray (Al Molinaro), Speed (Garry Walberg), Vinnie (Larry Gelman), Roy (Ryan McDonald), Miriam (Elinor Donahue), Myrna (Penny Marshall), Nancy (Joan Hotchkis), Gloria (Janis Hansen), Gwendolyn Pigeon (Carol Shelly), Cecily Pigeon (Monica Evans).

The misadventures of two divorced men sharing an apartment, one a slob and the other a neat freak. Adapted from the play by Neil Simon, *The Odd Couple* is one of the most well-written and hilarious comedies of all time. The series did fairly well on the network but is a big hit in syndication.

The Flight of the Felix
W: Peggy Elliott & Ed Scarlach. D: Bruce Bilson. GS: Richard X. Slattery, Ann Elder. Felix is challenged to a fight by a hockey player who thinks Felix is flirting with his girlfriend.

Oscar's Ulcer
W: Bob Rodgers. D: Bruce Bilson. Oscar develops an ulcer and blames Felix for causing it.

The Laundry Orgy
W: Jerry Belson & Garry Marshall. D: Bruce Bilson. Oscar and Felix conspire to break up a poker game so they can go out with the Pigeon sisters.

It's All Over Now, Baby Bird
W: Dale McRaven. D: Jerry Paris.

GS: James Millhollin. Felix's pet parrot dies, leaving him and Oscar with the trouble of disposing of the dead bird.

The Jury Story
W: Lloyd Turner & Gordon Mitchell. GS: Barney Martin. Felix tells the story of how he and Oscar first met while on jury duty.

Felix Gets Sick
W: Albert E. Lewin. D: Hal Cooper. GS: Bridget Hanley. When Felix gets sick, he ruins Oscar's plans for a romantic evening with a stewardess.

The Big Brothers
W: Peggy Grant & Bruce Mansfield. D: Bruce Bilson. GS: Clint Howard.

Felix volunteers Oscar to be a big brother to a fatherless boy.

I Do, I Don't
W: Carl Kleinschmidtt. D: Bruce Bilson. GS: George Furth, Joyce Van Patten. Felix settles a dispute between a young couple who don't realize how much they really love each other.

The Break Up
W: Ruth Brooks Flippen. D: Charles Rondeau. GS: Alice Ghostley. Oscar throws Felix out, sending him off in an adventure to find new living quarters.

The Blackout
W: Bill Idelson & Harvey Miller. D: Charles Rondeau. GS: Cynthia Lynn. Felix suspects Oscar has stolen $50 from their weekly poker game.

Oscar the Model
W: Jerry Belson & Garry Marshall. D: George Tyne. GS: Albert Brooks, Peter Brocco. Felix asks Oscar to pose for a layout advertising a new men's cologne, but soon realizes that Oscar has no talent.

Felix Is Missing
W: Albert E. Lewin. D: George Tyne. GS: Lloyd Gough, Albert Brooks. While Felix is away on a photo assignment, Oscar thinks he has been killed.

Scrooge Gets an Oscar
W: Ron Friedman. D: George Tyne. After turning down the role of Scrooge in a Christmas play, Oscar dreams his own version of "A Christmas Carol."

The Hideaway
W: Harry Winkler. D: Dick Michaels. GS: Reni Santoni, Dub Taylor. Oscar prevents an Alaskan college football player from being corrupted by professional football.

They Use Horse Radish, Don't They?
W: Garry Marshall & Jerry Belson. D: Garry Marshall. GS: Marlyn Mason, Francine York. A woman uses Oscar to get Felix's gravy recipe for use in a cooking contest.

Bunny Is Missing
W & D: Unknown. GS: E.J. Peaker, Lisa Gerritsen, Pamelyn Ferdin. A disastrous rainy weekend in a mountain cabin ends with Oscar playing mother to three little girls while Felix pouts over his ex-wife.

Engrave Trouble
W: Peggy Elliott. D: Alan Rafkin. GS: Michael Constantine, Herb Vigran. Felix tries to make up with Gloria by having a watch re-engraved for their anniversary, but the watch is stolen.

Lovers Don't Make House Calls
W: Ron Friedman. D: Bruce Bilson. When Felix gets sick, Oscar develops a crush on the pretty woman doctor who makes the house call.

You've Come a Long Way Baby
W: Albert E. Lewin. D: Garry Marshall. Felix brings home an abandoned Chinese baby on the eve of an important sports award dinner.

Oscar's New Life
W: Jack Winter. D: Alan Rafkin. GS: John Astin, Ed Platt. Oscar is fired from his job as a sportswriter and gets a new job as a writer for "Harem," a girlie magazine. [This is the only episode of the series that does not have a laugh track.]

A Taste of Money
W: Lloyd Turner & Gordon Mitchell. D: Alan Rafkin. GS: Chris Shea, William O'Connell, Peter Brocco. Felix and Oscar turn detective to find out where Phillip, the kid next door, got hold of two thousand dollars.

What Makes Felix Run
W: Bill Manoff. D: Jerry Paris. GS: Johnny Scott Lee. Felix tries to reform after his finicky ways ruin his evening with Gloria; through flashbacks we get a look at his childhood.

What Does a Naked Lady Say to You?
W: Peggy Elliott & Ed Scarlach. D: Hal Cooper. GS: Marj Dusay, Johnny Silver. Felix doesn't know that his girlfriend is an actress in a nude play.

Trapped
W: Alan Mandel & Charles Shyer. D: Jerry Belson. GS: Dave Ketchum. Felix, Oscar and Nancy find themselves locked in a basement, unable to attend a costume ball.

Hospital Mates
W: Garry Marshall. D: Jerry Paris. Felix and Oscar both check into the hospital for minor operations.

Felix's Wife's Boyfriend
W: Ron Friedman. D: Jerry Paris. GS: Fred Beir. Nancy's visiting brother Ray drives Felix insane with jealousy when he begins dating Gloria.

Surprise! Surprise!
W: Jim Fritzell & Everett Greenbaum. D: Jerry Paris. GS: Hal Smith. Oscar upsets Felix's plans for his daughter Edna's birthday party when he plans a poker party for the same day.

Natural Childbirth
W: Bill Idelson & Harvey Miller. D: Hal Cooper. GS: Hilarie Thompson. Oscar's pregnant niece arrives at the apartment and proclaims that she wants to have her baby by natural childbirth. Felix agrees but Oscar doesn't.

A Grave for Felix
W: Richard Bensfield & Perry Grant. D: Hal Cooper. GS: Dan Tobin, Ivor Francis. Felix selects a gravesite and entrusts Oscar with the money, only to find that he gambled it away on a horse.

Sleepwalker
W: Mickey Rose. D: Jack Donahue. Oscar becomes a sleepwalker bent on braining Felix every night while he sleeps.

Felix the Calypso Singer
W: Perry Bryant & Richard Bensfield. D: Jack Donahue. GS: Vito Scotti, Jack Perkins. Oscar, Felix, and Nancy all spend their vacation together in Jacaloma, a Caribbean tourist trap.

Security Arms
W: Jerry Belson. D: George Tyne. GS: John Fiedler. After their apartment is robbed, Felix talks Oscar into moving to a high security building.

The Fat Farm
W: Albert E. Lewin. D: Mel Ferber. GS: Walter Janowitz, Dave Ketchum. Oscar discovers he is in poor physical condition and reluctantly goes along with Felix for a two-week visit to a health farm.

Murray the Fink
W: Perry Grant & Richard Bensfield. D: Jay Sandrich. GS: Curt Conway. After being taunted by Oscar for being soft, Murray arrests his poker pals for gambling.

Win One for Felix
W: Arthur Julian. D: Jack Donahue. GS: William Aames. Hoping to get closer to his son, Felix becomes the coach of the boys' football team.

And Leave the Greyhound to Us
W: Arthur Cohen. D: Hal Cooper. GS: Phil Leeds, Buddy Lester, Herbie Faye. In a poker game, Oscar wins a greyhound racing dog that Felix wants to pamper, but Oscar wants to race.

Does Your Mother Know You're Out, Rigoletto?
W: Ron Friedman. D: Jack Donahue. GS: Richard Fredricks. Felix's amateur opera company needs a "Rigoletto" for its yearly production. So, Oscar gets opera star Richard Fredricks for Felix.

The Odd Couple Meet Their Host
W: Bill Idelson & Harvey Miller. D: Hal Cooper. GS: David Steinberg.

Oscar and Felix both appear on a popular talk show hosted by David Steinberg.

Being Divorced Is Never Having to Say, I Do
W: Rick Mittleman. D: Bruce Bilson. GS: Billy Sands. When Blanche, Oscar's ex-wife, is about to remarry, Felix interjects and breaks up the marriage.

Speak for Yourself
W: Peggy Elliot & Ed Scarlach. D: Hal Cooper.   GS: Rhonda Copland.   In flashbacks, Oscar tells the story of how Felix first met Gloria.

Good, Bad Boy
W: Richard Bensfield & Perry Grant. D: Hal Cooper. GS: Jimmy Van Patten, Pamelyn Ferdin. Felix talks Oscar into being a big brother to a young hoodlum who takes a fancy to Edna, Felix's daughter.

Oscar's Promotion
W: Martin Cohan. D: Jack Donahue. GS: Jack Soo, Bobby Baum. Oscar hires Felix to photograph an international wrestling match, but Felix advises the Chinese wrestler to retire.

You Saved My Life
W: Bob Rodgers. D: Jack Donahue. Oscar saves Felix's life, then pays the penalty as Felix shows that too much gratitude can be very annoying.

Where's Grandpa?
W: Albert E. Lewin. D: Jack Donahue.   GS: Madge Kennedy.   Felix's grandfather, tossed out by his wife because of his insane jealousy, takes up residence with Oscar.

Partner's Investment
W: Bill Idelson & Harvey Miller. D: George Tyne. GS: Pat Morita. Felix invests in a Japanese restaurant, but finds himself in trouble when he ends up doing all the cooking.

Psychic, Shmycic
W: Ron Friedman. D: Mel Ferber.

GS: Bernie Kopell.   Felix may have psychic ability when he tells Oscar he is going to be the victim of a strangler when he attends an award dinner in his honor.

A Night to Dismember
W: Rick Mittleman. D: George Marshall. GS: Joan Van Ark. At a get-together, Felix, Oscar and Blanche recount different stories of what led to Oscar's divorce on New Year's Eve.

The Princess
W: Bill Idelson. D: Jerry Paris. GS: Jean Simmons. Oscar falls in love with a princess.

Felix's First Commercial
W: Albert E. Lewin. D: Jerry Paris. GS: Deacon Jones. Felix directs his first television commercial which almost ends in disaster.

The Murray Who Came to Dinner
W: Ron Friedman.   D: Jerry Paris. GS: Jane Dulo, Patty Regan. When Murray's wife throws him out, he moves in with Felix and Oscar and eventually drives them crazy.

Big Mouth
W: Ben Joelson & Art Baer. D: Jerry Paris. GS: Howard Cosell. Oscar starts a fight with Howard Cosell whom Felix is photographing for an ad.

Gloria, Hallelujah
W: Rick Mittleman. D: Garry Marshall.   When Oscar's computer date turns out to be Gloria, Felix sets out to prove that he is a superior man devoid of jealousy.

The Odd Monks
W: Garry Marshall. D: Jerry Belson. GS: Richard Stahl, Ed Peck, Jack Collins, Charles Lampkin. Oscar and Felix visit a monastery to escape the pressure of their lives.

Don't Believe in Roomers
W: Peggy Elliott & Ed Scharlach. D: Jack Donahue. GS: Marlyn Mason. Oscar and Felix befriend a girl named

Lisa, a loner, only to discover she leaves them as quickly as she found them.

I'm Dying of Unger
W: Joe Glauberg. D: Mel Ferber. Oscar and Felix decide to spend the weekend in a mountain cabin so Oscar can have peace and quiet in order for him to finish the book he is writing.

The Pen Is Mightier Than the Pencil
W: Jack Winter. D: Bob Birnbaum. GS: Elliott Reid, Wally Cox, Phil Leeds. Felix invests in a writing course and Oscar is out to prove he has been swindled by a dishonest professor.

Sometimes a Great Ocean
W: Dennis Klein. D: Hal Cooper. GS: John Qualen, Karl Swenson. When Oscar's ulcer begins to act up, Felix books them on an ocean voyage complete with senior citizens and bland food.

The Odd Couples
W: Harvey Miller. D: Hal Cooper. GS: Jane Dulo. When Oscar's mother visits, he tries to hide his divorce by moving Felix out and Blanche in.

The Odd Father
W: Steve Zacharias & Michael Leeson. D: Jack Donahue. GS: Frank & Sadie Delfino, Doney Oatman. Felix can't communicate with his daughter whose latest interest is baseball umpiring, so he asks Oscar for help.

Oscar's Birthday
W: Albert E. Lewin. D: George Marshall. GS: Hal Smith, Andy Rubin. Felix plans a surprise party for Oscar, only that is the last thing Oscar wants.

The First Baby
W: Garry Marshall & Bob Brunner. D: Alex March. Oscar tells Myrna the story of why Felix has been banned from the hospital ever since his daughter's birth.

Password
W: Frank Buxton. D: Alex March. GS: Allen Ludden, Betty White, Rhonda Copland. Oscar and Felix both appear on the game show Password, but Felix has strange ideas of how to win.

I Gotta Be Me
W: Susan Harris, David Duclon & Joe Glauberg. D: Mel Ferber. GS: Barbara Rhoades. Felix and Oscar reverse roles to try to get along better but it turns out they end up fighting even more.

The Ides of April
W: Mark Rothman & Lowell Ganz. D: Bob Birnbaum. GS: Vivian Bonnell. Felix is a nervous wreck wondering why the IRS is investigating his tax return.

Myrna's Debut
W: Perry Grant & Richard Bensfield. D: Jerry Paris. GS: Bob Hastings, Bella Bruck. Felix persuades Myrna to pursue her lifelong ambition of tap dancing, leaving Oscar without a secretary.

The Hustler
W: Mark Rothman & Lowell Ganz. D: Jerry Paris. GS: Stanley Adams, Louis Guss. Felix arranges for a Monte Carlo night in order to raise funds for his amateur opera club which ends up losing money. So, to get even, Oscar challenges a pool hustler to an all or nothing game.

My Strife in Court
W: Mark Rothman. D: Jerry Paris. GS: Curt Conway. Felix is arrested for ticket scalping and in court proves one should never "assume" a man is guilty.

Let's Make a Deal
W: David Duclon & Joe Glauberg. D: Frank Buxton. GS: Monty Hall. Felix and Oscar wear a horse suit to appear on Monty Hall's "Let's Make a Deal."

The Oddyssey Couple
W: Dennis Kahn & Bob Brunner. D: Jerry Paris. GS: Titos Vandis, Elvia Allman. Oscar's mother is back, and this time she wants to meet Oscar's girlfriend, so Felix fixes him up with a Greek girl.

Take My Furniture, Please
W: Harvey Miller. D: Jack Winter. GS: Bubba Smith, Charles Lane, Bella Bruck. Oscar and Felix fight over how to redecorate their apartment.

Gloria Moves In
W: Mark Rothman & Lowell Ganz. D: Garry Marshall. Felix puts Oscar out when he invites Gloria to spend the weekend in their apartment. Unfortunately, Felix ruins Oscar's poker game.

Last Tango in Newark
W: Ron Friedman. D: Jay Sandrich. GS: Edward Villella. At an amateur production of Swan Lake, Felix persuades Edward Villella to let him perform.

The Odd Decathlon
W: Jack Winter. D: Jay Sandrich. GS: Cliff Norton. Felix and Oscar decide to hold their own decathlon to determine who is in better physical shape.

That Was No Lady
W: Lee Kalcheim. D: Jerry Belson. GS: Alex Karras, Patricia Harty. Felix's latest girlfriend turns out to be the wife of a very large and jealous football player.

The New Car
W: Mark Rothman & Lowell Ganz. D: Garry Marshall. GS: Dick Clark, John Byner, Bella Bruck. Felix and Oscar win a new car and then find out that keeping a car in New York City is too much trouble.

The Odd Holiday
W: Philip Miskin. D: Mel Ferber. GS: Victor Brandt. Felix reveals how he destroyed his own marriage by trying

to save Oscar's while on vacation in the Caribbean.

This Is the Army, Mrs. Madison
W: Garry Marshall & Bob Brunner. D: Mel Ferber. GS: Richard Stahl. In flashbacks, Felix reveals the hectic events leading up to Oscar's marriage when both he and Oscar were in the Army reserve.

A Barnacle Adventure
W: Mark Rothman & Lowell Ganz. D: Bob Birnbaum. GS: Val Avery, Malcolm Atterbury, John Myhers. Oscar and Felix invest in barnacle glue invented by Oscar's dentist.

Felix Directs
W: Harvey Miller. D: Jerry Paris. GS: David White, Louis Guss. Felix directs a movie around Oscar's life and gets mixed up with an X-rated film producer.

The Songwriter
W: Buzz Cohan & Bill Angelos. D: Mel Ferber. GS: Wolfman Jack, Jaye P. Morgan. Felix is inspired by Oscar's new girlfriend, Jaye P. Morgan, to write an original song for her act.

Maid for Each Other
W: Marlene Barr. D: Norm Gray. GS: Reta Shaw. Felix tries to find a perfect maid to take care of Oscar while he is recuperating from an ulcer attack.

The Pig Who Came to Dinner
W: Mickey Ross. D: Jack Donahue. GS: Bobby Riggs, Billie Jean King. Oscar loses everything to hustler Bobby Riggs, including Felix.

The Exorcists
W: Frank Buxton & Michael Leeson. D: Jack Donahue. GS: Victor Buono. Felix is convinced there is a ghost in the airconditioner and hires an exorcist to get rid of it.

Moonlighter
W: Philip Miskin & Mickey Rose. D: Frank Buxton. GS: Phyllis Davis, Karl

Lucas. Felix finds Oscar moonlighting as a cook after Oscar gambles away the money Felix gave him to buy season tickets for his client.

The Flying Felix
W: Mark Rothman & Lowell Ganz. D: Jack Donahue. GS: George Furth. Oscar tries to cure Felix of his fear of flying so he can cover a photo assignment in Houston.

Cleanliness Is Next to Impossible
W: Mark Rothman. D: Frank Buxton. GS: Janice Lynde, Allan Arbus. Oscar tries hypnotism to reform his sloppy ways to please his latest girlfriend.

Vocal Girl Makes Good
W: Buzz Cohan & Bill Angelos. D: Dan Dailey. GS: Marilyn Horne, Janice Lynde. A shy singer is discovered by Felix, but she will not sing without Oscar around.

Shuffling Off to Buffalo
W: Mark Rothman & Lowell Ganz. D: Frank Buxton. GS: William Redfield. Felix moves out to take a job in Buffalo in his brother's bubble gum factory, only to discover that he is unhappy in his new life.

The Insomniacs
W: Mickey Rose. D: Jack Donahue. Felix develops a severe case of insomnia and Oscar tries to help his roommate when Felix prevents him from getting any sleep too.

A Different Drummer
W: Frank Buxton & Michael Leeson. D: Mel Ferber. GS: Monty Hall. Felix hopes to get his band booked on a new television show hosted by Monty Hall.

New York's Oddest
W: Ben Joelson & Art Baer. D: Harvey Miller. GS: Billy Sands, Michael Lerner. Felix becomes involved in the Police reserves and drives every tenant on his floor crazy with his security measures.

One for the Bunny
W: John Rappaport. D: Jerry Paris. GS: Hugh Hefner. Oscar tells Murray a story recalling a time when Felix worked for Playboy magazine and photographed Gloria for a centerfold.

Felix the Horse Player
W: Jack Winter. D: Jerry Paris. GS: Fritz Feld, Jerry Maren, Don Diamond, Johnny Silver. Oscar's years of gambling begin to pay off when he gets racing tips from a midget.

Two on the Aisle
W: Unknown. D: Jay Sandrich. GS: John Simon, John Barbour, Neil Simon. Oscar has Felix help him write reviews for Broadway plays, then panics when he is asked to appear in person on a television program featuring famous critics.

To Bowl or Not to Bowl
W: Mickey Rose. D: Jay Sandrich. GS: Noam Pitlik. Oscar gets mad when Felix suddenly gets a severe backache right before their bowling championship game.

The Big Broadcast
W & D: Frank Buxton. GS: Stanley Adams, Tina Andrews, Graham Jarvis. Oscar takes a job as a sports radio talk show host and tries to keep it a secret from radio crazy Felix.

Old Flames Never Die
W: Buzz Cohan & Bill Angelos. D: Frank Buxton. GS: Leonard Barr, Jean Gillespie. When he learns that his high school sweetheart, Mildred Fleener, is a grandmother, Felix believes he is getting old.

The Frog
W: Richard Bensfield & Perry Grant. D: Mel Ferber. GS: Richard Stahl. Oscar loses Felix's son's prize jumping frog the day before a big contest, leading them on a search to find a replacement.

The Hollywood Story
W: Al Gordon. D: Hal Goldman. GS:

George Montgomery, Bob Hope, Leonard Barr, Allan Arbus. Oscar gets a chance to appear in a Hollywood movie, and Felix messes things up by acting as his self-appointed agent.

The Rain in Spain
W: Rick Mittleman. D: Harvey Miller. GS: Rob Reiner, Garo Yepremian. Felix tries to help Myrna win back her boyfriend Sheldn by convincing her to change her image and personality.

The Odd Candidate
W: Mark Rothman & Lowell Ganz. D: Garry Marshall. GS: Howard K. Smith, Peter Hobbs, Guy Marks. Felix is determined to see to it Oscar wins the city councilman election.

The Dog Story
W: Ben Joelson & Art Baer. D: Frank Buxton. GS: John Fiedler. Felix kidnaps a famous dog from its owner, who he believes is mistreating it.

Our Fathers
W: Martin Donovan. D: Harvey Miller. GS: Giorgio Tozzi, Elisha Cook, Barbara Rhoades, Louis Guss. Felix recounts a story of how his father and Oscar's knew each other during the 1920s.

Strike Up the Band . . . or Else
W: Rick Mittleman. D: Jay Sandrich. GS: Pernell Roberts. Oscar loses money in a poker game and when he can't pay off, donates Felix's band as payment instead.

The Subway Story
W: Mark Rothman & Lowell Ganz. D: Norm Gray. GS: Billy Sands, Garry Marshall, Barney Martin, Scatman Crothers, Ben Frommer. Felix tries to prove to Oscar that New Yorkers are really kind and concerned, but it seems Oscar is right when they get stuck in a stalled subway train.

The Bigger They Are
W: David Duclon. D: Harvey Miller. GS: John Byner, Peter Hobbs, Cliff

Emmich. Felix photographs Oscar in a phony fat suit for a new diet pill and then refuses to accept the award he wins dishonestly.

The Rent Strike
W: Martin Ragaway. D: Norm Gray. GS: Victor Buono, Rodney Allen Rippy, Peter Hobbs. Felix leads his angry tenants on a rent strike when the new landlord refuses to keep up the maintenance on their building.

The Paul Williams Show
W: Rick Mittleman. D: Harvey Miller. GS: Paul Williams, Doney Oatman. Edna has a crush on Paul Williams and runs away to follow him.

The Roy Clark Show
W: Howard Albrecht & Sol Weinstein. D: Frank Buxton. GS: Roy Clark, Albert Paulsen. Oscar's practical joke playing friend comes for a visit, only to prove he is a talented musician.

Oscar in Love
W: Carl Gottlieb. D: Mel Ferber. GS: Dina Merrill. Oscar falls in love with a woman with two children and finds out the hard way he is not quite ready to get married again.

Two Men on a Hoarse
W: Martin Donovan. D: Chuck Shyer. GS: Phil Foster, Dick Cavett. Oscar has a throat operation and Felix loses his voice at the same time as their apartment is being robbed.

Laugh, Clown, Laugh
W: Fred Bernard. D: Norm Gray. GS: Richard Dawson, Mark Wilson. Oscar co-hosts a TV show with Richard Dawson, but Felix gets upset because in the Army Dawson upstaged an act they once had.

Your Mother Wears Army Boots
W: John Rappaport. D: Frank Buxton. GS: Howard Cosell, Jack Carter, Martina Arroyo, Roone Arledge. Howard Cosell returns, willing to give Oscar a shot at sportscasting in ex-

change for a performance by Felix's opera singer friend, Martina Arroyo.

Felix Remarries
W: Sidney Reznick & Larry Rhine. D: Jack Donahue. In the final episode of the series, Felix mends his fussy ways enough to convince Gloria to remarry him. Oscar is so delighted he vows to turn neat.

ONE DAY AT A TIME

On the air 12/16/75, off: still continuing. CBS. Color Videotape. 113 episodes (currently being syndicated). Broadcast: Dec 1975-Jul 1976 Tue 9:30-10; Sept 1976-Jan 1978 Tue 9:30-10; Jan 1978-Jan 1979 Mon 9:30-10; Jan 1979-Mar 1979 Wed 9-9:30; Mar 1979-Sept 1982 Sun 8:30-9; Sept 1982-Present Sun 9-9:30. Producer: Norman Lear. Prod Co/ Synd: Embassy Pictures.

CAST: Ann Romano (played by Bonnie Franklin), Julie (Mackenzie Phillips), Barbara (Valerie Bertinelli), Schneider (Pat Harrington), David Kane (Richard Masur), Ginny (Mary Louise Wilson), Max (Michael Lembeck), Grandma Romano (Nanette Fabray), Nick Handris (Ron Rifkin), Alex Handris (Glenn Scarpelli, Ed (Joseph Campanella).

The story of Ann Romano, a divorcee, who is trying to raise her two daughters by herself as well as be a career woman. The series is very popular on the network.

Ann's Decision [Pilot]
Ann makes her first big parental decision since her divorce when she refuses to allow Julie to go on a coed backpacking trip.

How to Succeed Without Trying
Ann rejects her family's suggestion that she play up to her prospective employer in order to get the job.

Jealousy
Ann becomes jealous of her daughters' relationship with their father's new girlfriend.

Chicago Rendezvous
Ann has to find a way to tell her daughters that she is planning to have an affair with an airline pilot.

David Loves Ann
David tries to pressure Ann into marrying him.

Julie's Best Friend
Ann objects when David offers to loan her the money so Julie can attend a private school with her new rich friend.

Super Blues
Schneider feels rejected when Ann throws a party for the people in her building but doesn't invite him.

All the Way
Julie tries to decide whether to sleep with her boyfriend or wait till she is older.

Fighting City Hall
The Secret Service pays a visit to Ann when she sends a threatening letter to the President.

David Plus Two
Ann becomes jealous when she catches David with another woman.

Julie's Job
Ann becomes worried when Julie takes a job as a waitress in a rundown cafe.

The College Man
Julie accuses Ann of trying to steal her date away when she dates an older college man.

Father David
David becomes the chaperone at Barbara's first party.

Dad Comes Back [Part 1]
When Ed comes to tell Ann and the girls that he is getting married again, Barbara tries to get Ann and her father back together.

Dad Comes Back [Part 2]
Ann and Ed have to explain to the girls that they are not getting married to each other again.

The Runaways [Part 1]
Julie and her boyfriend run away in a van.

The Runaways [Part 2]
The continuation of the above story.

The Runaways [Part 3]
Julie and her boyfriend pick up a hippie couple in their van.

The Runaways [Part 4]
Julie decides to return home.

David's New Job [Part 1]
David is offered a job in California and asks Ann to marry him.

David's New Job [Part 2]
Ann and David call off their wedding and David moves to California by himself.

Barbara's Emergence
Barbara accuses Julie of stealing her boyfriend.

The Upholstery Ripoff
Ann finds that the company that is reupholstering her furniture is trying to rip her off.

Schneider's Pride and Joy
GS: Mark Hamill. Schneider's visiting nephew turns out to be a thief.

A Visit from Dad
Ann's father tries to get her to return with him to her old hometown.

The New Car
Ann gets upset when Ed decides to buy a car for the girls.

J.C. and Julie [Part 1]
Julie joins a religious cult and becomes a Jesus fanatic.

J.C. and Julie [Part 2]
Julie brings home a drunken bum in order to save him from booze.

The Maestro
Ann falls in love with a symphony conductor.

Happy New Year
The cast puts on a musical show at a retirement hotel.

Schneider Loves Ginny
Schneider becomes depressed when Ginny rejects his marriage proposal.

Ginny's Child
The family is shocked to learn that Ginny has a child.

Julie's Operation
Ann doesn't trust the doctor who is going to perform Julie's appendectomy.

The Butterfields
Ann plays marriage counselor for a fighting married couple.

Barbara Plus Two
Barbara finds that she has two dates for the Spring Dance.

The Singles Bar
Ann pays a visit to a singles bar.

The College Question
Julie and Ann decide whether or not she should attend college in the fall.

The Girls Alone
Ann bcomes worried when she has to leave the girls alone while she goes away on a business trip.

The Traveling Salesperson
No available story.

The Older Man [Part 1]
GS: Jim Hutton (all four parts). Julie falls in love with her new boss, a middle-aged veterinarian.

The Older Man [Part 2]
Ann becomes upset when she catches Julie and her doctor boyfriend kissing.

The Older Man [Part 3]
The doctor proposes to Julie and she accepts.

The Older Man [Part 4]
Julie begins to realize that she has very little in common with the doctor and calls off the wedding.

Barbara's Friend [Part 1]
Barbara's new girlfriend threatens to kill herself when she believes Barbara is trying to steal her boyfriend away from her.

Barbara's Friend [Part 2]
When her friend winds up in the hospital, after she tried to kill herself, Barbara is held responsible by the girls' parents.

Bob Loves Barbara
Bob tries to gain some sexual experience in the hopes that Barbara will become interested in him.

Ann's Out-of-Town Client
Ann finds that she has to fix her visiting client up with a girl for the night in order to get him to sign a contract, causing her to become upset.

The Ghost Writer
Barbara borrows some of Julie's old poems and submits them as her own for a writing assignment.

The Second Mrs. Cooper
The girls try to break up their father's marriage so they can have him for themselves.

Ann's Crisis
On her 36th birthday, Ann begins to feel that she is getting old.

Schneider's Kid
Schneider's son comes for a visit.

The Race Driver [Part 1]
The girls try to bring their mother and the racing car driver who just moved into the building together.

The Race Driver [Part 2]
Ann tries to break off her relationship with her racer boyfriend.

Ann's Secretary
Julie's epileptic girlfriend gets a job as Ann's secretary.

Barbara's Rebellion
Barbara and Bob decide to run off to a motel for the weekend so she can lose her good and trustworthy image.

The New Owner
Schneider decides to romance the new female owner of the apartment building in order to keep his job.

Ann's Competitor
Ann takes on an assistant in order to help her with an account, when she becomes ill, only to have her assistant steal her ideas and her job.

The Dress Designer
Julie decides to enter a dress designing contest.

Take the Money
Julie finds that there is an extra $125 in her bankbook and plans to keep it.

Barbara the Fink
Barbara witnesses the vandalization of an office at school but refuses to tattle on her guilty friend.

Julie's Big Move [Part 1]
Julie decides to move out of the house and share an apartment with her friend.

Julie's Big Move [Part 2]
Ann becomes upset when she learns that Julie's roommate dates for a living.

Ann the Father
Bob has a fight with his father and moves in with Ann and the girls.. . . . .

Father Dear Father [Part 1]
Ed asks Ann to help him out when he admits he is going broke.

Father Dear Father [Part 2]
Ann tries to get Ed to tell his wife Vicki about his financial problems.

Ann's Friends
Ann has to keep her married girlfriend from leaving her husband, because she thinks that being a divorcee is more fun than being a housewife.

Schneider's Helper
Barbara convinces Schneider to hire a mentally retarded boy to help him take care of the building while he recovers from his back injury.

Bob's New Girl
Barbara becomes upset when Bob dates another girl.

The Dating Game
Ann tries to find a way to date one of her clients without appearing too aggressive.

Yes Sir, That's My Baby
Barbara learns that her boyfriend is the father of her girlfriend's illegitimate baby.

Jealousy [Part 1]
GS: Greg Evigan. Barbara falls in love with a rock musician.

Jealousy [Part 2]
GS: Greg Evigan.   Barbara becomes jealous when Julie steals her musician boyfriend away from her.

The Arab Connection
Julie protests against an Arab businessman who is one of Ann's biggest clients.

Peabody's War
An old man holds Schneider hostage in Ann's apartment in order to protest his eviction when he can't afford to pay the rent increase.

The Married Man [Part 1]
Schneider tells Ann that the man she is in love with is married.

The Married Man [Part 2]
Ann tries to break off her relationship with her married boyfriend

The Married Man [Part 3]
Ann learns that her boyfriend is going to get a divorce, but he still breaks off their relationship.

Hold the Mustard
Barbara talks Bob into getting her a job at the hamburger joint where he works.

Girl Talk
Ann and the girls spend Christmas in Schneider's mountain cabin.

Francine Strikes Again
Ann finds that her former assistant, who is now working in her office, is trying to steal away her account.

Going Nowhere
Julie becomes depressed when she feels her life is over and that she has no future.

Schneider Gets Fired
When Schneider gets fired, Ann helps him open a dance studio.

The Broken Nose
Barbara becomes upset when Schneider accidentally breaks Barbara's nose right before she is to present an award at the school banquet.

The Piano Teacher
An insecure piano teacher moves into the building.

The Graduation
Barbara finds her plans for graduation night ruined when both her grandmothers appear with their own plans.

The Dental Hygienist
Schneider falls in love with Ann's visiting friend.

Mad for Each Other
Julie clashes with an independent film maker who is doing a film about the free clinic where Julie works.

Fear of Success
Ann is offered a new job and finds herself unable to make the decision to take the job or not.

Back to School
Ann goes to college and finds that she is in the same class as Barbara.

Pressure
Barbara is pressured by her boyfriend to go to bed with him.

Julie's Wedding [Part 1]
Julie finds that she is in love with the best man at her wedding.

Julie's Wedding [Part 2]
Julie decides to marry Max instead of the man she intended to marry.

Between Mother and Daughter
Ann and her mother express their inner feelings for each other while having lunch in a restaurant.

Home Again, Home Again
Max and Julie move in with Ann when his airline goes on strike.

Small Wonder
Barbara dates the 12-year-old genius who is tutoring her.

Et Tu Ann
Ann finds that she is chasing after her male secretary.

A Little Larceny
Schneider gets arrested when Barbara involves him in her illegal football pool activities.

The Heart Attack
Ann suffers a heart attack.

Schneider the Model
Schneider is offered a job as a male model, but he becomes depressed when he learns the role he is going to portray.

Male Jealousy
Max and Schneider fight over the attention of Ann and the girls.

Happy New Year II
Ann and the family once again put on a show at a senior citizen hotel.

The Laughing Academy
Barbara gets upset when Ann begins to date a comic.

So Long, Mom
Max and Julie prepare to leave and Barbara wants to get her own apartment.

Triple Play
Ann gets a visit from a distant cousin.

Old Horizons
Ann's parents move to Indianapolis, which causes her to be bothered constantly by her mother's good intentions.

Grecian Yearn
Ann falls in love with an archeology professor who asks her to live with him in Greece.

Endless Elliot
Barbara finds that one of her classmates has a crush on her.

Girl with a Past
Barbara has to decide whether or not to tell her old friend Bob that his girl-

friend has a reputation as a loose woman.

Pen Pals
An escaped convict comes to Schneider for a job.

The Spirit Is Willing
Schneider becomes upset when the girl he was making love to has a heart attack.

Connors' Crisis
Schneider fixes up Ann's boss, Mr. Connors, with another woman when

his wife leaves him.

Retrospective [Part 1]
Schneider and the girls learn that their building is being turned into a condominium and that they are going to have to move out. Flashbacks show some of the various events that have happened to them while they lived in their apartment.

Retrospective [Part 2]
The flashbacks continue, until Schneider learns that the building is not becoming a condominium and that they won't have to move.

OUR MISS BROOKS

On the air 10/3/52, off 9/21/56. CBS. B&W Film. 127 episodes. Broadcast: Oct 1952-Jun 1953 Fri 9:30-10; Oct 1953-Jun 1955 Fri 9:30-10; Oct 1955-Sept 1956 Fri 8:30-9. Producer: Andrew/Mitchell. Prod Co: Desilu/Paramount. Synd: Viacom.

CAST: Connie Brooks (played by Eve Arden), Osgood Conklin (Gale Gordon), Philip Boynton (Robert Rockwell), Walter Denton (Richard Crenna), Margaret (Jane Morgan), Harriet Conklin (Gloria McMillan), Oliver Munsey (Bob Sweeney), Mrs. Nestor (Nana Bryant; Isabel Randolph, 1956), Gene Talbot (Gene Barry), Benny Romero (Ricky Vera).

The story of a single high school English teacher and the trouble she caused her principal and her friends. Very popular during its run on the network, but hasn't done much in reruns. It is rarely if ever shown in the U.S.

Trying to Pick a Fight [Pilot]
Connie takes Walter's advice and starts a fight with Philip so she can kiss and make up with him later.

Birthday Bag
Connie's friends borrow all of her money so they can surprise her with a new pocketbook for her birthday.

Embezzled Dress
Connie's landlady unknowingly spends the school funds on a new dress for Connie.

Boynton Playacts
Connie asks Philip to pretend that they are married so that she can get a job at a college where the staff has to be married.

The Loaded Custodian
Connie tries to help the alcoholic custodian replace a broken window.

Madison Country Club
Mr. Conklin tries to get a rich widow to donate money to the school.

Living Statues
Connie and Philip paint the school office with a paint developed by Walter which glues all of them to the walls.

Mr. Whipple
Connie and her friends try to help a poor man who has not eaten for ten days, unaware that he is a very rich man on a self-imposed diet.

Blue Goldfish
The staff tries to get Mr. Conklin to turn on the heat at the school because everyone is turning blue from the cold, including the goldfish.

Aunt Hattie Boynton
Connie and a rival teacher try to be as industrious as Philip's Aunt Hattie was, hoping this will attract his attention.

Stolen Aerial
Connie takes the staff's television aerials to be fixed, causing Conklin to think Connie is the aerial thief who has been operating in the neighborhood.

The Big Game
Connie has to help an ex-football hero pass an English exam so he can coach the team in the big game.

Hobby Show
Everybody thinks Connie needs a hobby so she spends an exhausting day indulging herself in everyone else's hobbies.

Hurricane
While Conklin is away, Connie closes the school when she hears that a hurricane is on the way.

Christmas Show
On the day before Christmas, everyone is exchanging gifts at the local department store.

The Pet Shop
Connie arranges to meet Philip outside the pet shop for a date. When he stands her up, she plans to get even.

Cure That Habit
Walter requests information from Alcoholics Anonymous using Mr. Conklin's name. When the material arrives at the school, Conklin is suspected of drinking.

Old Marblehead
Mr. Conklin, with Connie's help, tries

to take up a collection to erect a bust of himself to put in his office.

Model Teacher
Connie enters the Model Teacher of the Year contest and the beautiful girl reporter sent to cover the story falls for Philip.

The Cafeteria Strike
Connie, Mr. Conklin and Walter try to pass Philip off as the school chef so he can prepare his special dish in order to impress the editor of a newspaper.

Mr. Casey
Everyone is invited to the reading of Mr. Casey's will. Only Connie knows that Mr. Casey was a cat.

Wake-Up Plan
Connie accidentally takes sleeping pills instead of aspirin, causing her to oversleep. She then has to explain to Mr. Conklin why she is late.

Conklin's Love Nest
Connie tries to get Philip to share the cost of an apartment, but he gets the wrong idea.

Honest Burglar
Connie gets a burglar a job in the school cafeteria, only to find that several items begin to disappear.

Fisher's Pawn Shop
Connie pawns her landlady's vacuum cleaner to buy a new dress.

Lulu, the Pin-Up Boat
Connie finds that one of her students is playing a prank on Mr. Conklin by decorating his office with pin-up pictures.

Yodar Kritch Award
Connie tries to help a student improve his English grades so that she can attend the party that the student is throwing.

Madame DuBarry
Philip and Connie are forced to spend

the night in the car when it runs out of gas.

Marinated Hearing
Mr. Conklin's speech to the school board is mixed up with a report on baboons.

The Festival
Connie and Philip save their money to buy a costume which will win the prize for the most unique costume at the ball.

Suzy Prentiss
Connie borrows some evening clothes so that a student can take his girlfriend to a formal banquet.

Conklin Plays Detective
Connie and Mr. Conklin set a trap for the thief who stole Conklin's typewriter and made a long-distance call from his office.

Public Property on Parade
Connie tries to write a speech for Mr. Conklin on the use of public property.

Davis Reads Tea Leaves
Mrs. Davis predicts that Connie and Philip will get married and have children.

The Stolen Wardrobe
Two crooks who have just robbed a department store run out of gas and have to hide the stuff at the school.

June Bride
Connie becomes the stand-in for Mr. Le Blanche's fiancee who is still in France.

Capistrano's Revenge
When Connie's bird disappears, her friends each get her another one.

Bones, Son of Cyrano
Philip helps Walter write a love poem to Harriet Conklin.

Spare That Rod
Mr. Conklin changes his ways when he finds a letter from the school board telling him to stop being a tyrant, unaware that the letter was an old one meant for the previous principal.

Trial by Jury
Connie tries to hide her traffic ticket from Mr. Conklin who is promoting a Safe Driving campaign.

Clay City Chaperone
Connie and Miss Enright fight it out so that one of them can become the chaperone to the football team when it goes out of town, especially since Philip will be going along.

The Little Visitor
Connie overhears a conversation and jumps to the conclusion that Mrs. Conklin is expecting a baby. Actually, Mr. Conklin is expecting a baby monkey which he is adding to his menagerie.

Faculty Band
Connie tries to join the school band because Philip is the conductor, even though she doesn't have any musical talent.

Phonebook Follies
Connie and Mr. Conklin accuse each other of stealing their phonebooks.

Thanksgiving Show
Connie tries to find another place to eat her Thanksgiving dinner when she finds that her landlady won't have enough food for her to eat.

Vitamin E4
Connie, Philip and Mr. Conklin each answer an ad for a job without knowing that the others will be there.

Swap Week
Walter sells shares in his car to several people who each want to use the car at the same time to go to several different places.

Golden Slippers
Connie receives a beautiful gown, a

bouquet of flowers and a pair of golden slippers to wear to the school ball from an unknown admirer.

Christmas Show
Connie spends Christmas alone with her cat Minerva; she dreams about a magic tree which will grant her every request.

Hospital Capers
Connie visits Philip in the hospital where he is recovering from a fall he took on Mr. Conklin's property.

Postage Due
Connie and Philip try to find Mr. Bagley, her mailman, who has suddenly disappeared.

The Jockey
Connie agrees to allow Philip's jockey friend and his horse to stay at her house.

Bobbsey Twins in Stir
Connie unknowingly helps Mrs. Davis sell phony tickets to the policemen's ball and winds up in jail.

Do It Yourself
Connie helps Mr. Conklin build a new garage.

Brooks's New Car
Connie buys a new car and then has an accident with Mr. Conklin's car.

Hobo Jungle
Connie tries to help a student find a suitable place to live. He had been living under a bridge with his hobo father and his friends.

Wild Goose
Walter plays a practical joke on Mr. Conklin. He makes him think he won a TV set on a radio giveaway show.

Hello Mr. Chips
Connie tries to make Philip think he is getting old so he will want to get married before it is too late.

Parlor Game
Mr. Conklin asks Connie to break up the romance between his daughter Harriet and Walter.

A Dry Scalp Is Better Than None
Connie and her friends are taken in by a student who claims she is dying just so she can get attention.

The English Test
Connie plans on going to a nightclub with Philip, but she has to coach three students for their English exams.

Second-Hand First Aid
Connie is assigned to take over the first-aid course when Miss Enright leaves the school.

The Egg
Mr. Conklin plans to take photos of the actual hatching of a chicken egg, unaware that Walter has substituted an egg-shaped stone for the real egg.

The Bakery
Connie tries to locate Philip's former girlfriend Rosalie.

The Miserable Caballero
A ten-year-old boy wants to enroll at the high school.

The Hawkins Travel Agency
Connie tries to get Mr. Conklin and Philip to join her on a trip to Switzerland.

Old Age Plan
Connie tries to earn extra money by selling her friends memberships in an old age plan.

The Jewel Robbery
Connie and her friends plead guilty to robbing the jewelry store. Each one thinks one of the others did it and they are trying to cover for them.

The Bicycle Thief
Connie helps a poor boy who stole Mr. Conklin's bicycle.

Angela's Wedding
When Connie makes a play for the new school coach, Philip becomes jealous.

Blood, Sweat and Laughs
Connie and Mr. Conklin hide out in a steam room in order to avoid a visiting state education official.

Life Can Be Bones
Connie gets Mr. Conklin to hire a replacement teacher to help Philip who has taken over the work of another teacher who has resigned. Unfortunately for Connie, the replacement is a beautiful girl who also wants Philip.

Two-Way Stretch Snodgrass
The school athlete moves in with his aunt, thus putting him in the district of Madison's rival school. Now both schools fight to have him on their team.

Van Gogh, Man, Gogh
Mr. Conklin tries to win the special award being offered by an art dealer.

Space, Who Needs It?
Mr. Conklin claims he has discovered a new planet with his homemade telescope.

The Novelist
A former student of Connie's has written a book about his school days. Included in the book are the comments she made about Mr. Conklin which she doesn't want printed.

Four-Leaf Clover
Bad things begin to happen after Connie finds a four-leaf clover.

Buddy
Mr. Conklin and Philip both think the threatening note was meant for them.

The Citizens' League
Connie and Mr. Conklin unknowingly prevent the church organist from playing at the governor's wedding.

Noodnick, Daughter of Medic
Mr. Conklin thinks Connie is going to

replace him as school principal.

The Stuffed Gopher
Mr. Conklin wants to punish the school athlete for tearing the school apart. It seems he was trying to catch a gopher.

Safari O'Toole
Connie and the others plan a surprise birthday party for Mrs. Davis.

Public Speaker's Nightmare
Connie helps Mr. Conklin prepare to give a speech to guests from the education department.

The Weighing Machine
Connie fights to get her money back from the company that owns the weighing machine she lost her money in.

The Auction
Connie arranges an auction to raise money for a new playground.

The Mambo
Mr. Conklin decides that the reason that many students come to school unprepared is that they spend too much time dancing at the malt shop.

The Dream
Connie dreams about marriage, babies and anniversaries

Return of Red Smith
Connie helps Mrs. Davis look like a rich lady when her blueblooded ex-suitor comes for a visit.

Le Chien Chaud et Le Mouton Noir
Connie needs extra money so she answers an ad which has her working for Mr. Conklin in a hotdog stand.

Kritch Cave
Connie and Walter persuade Mr. Conklin to sell the land near Kritch Cave. Conklin unknowingly sells the deed to the school instead.

Blind Date
Walter and Harriet arrange a blind date

between Connie and Philip.

Fargo's Whiskers
Connie tries to attract Philip's attention by wearing different wigs, but Philip and Mr. Conklin think she has flipped her wig.

Baseball Slide
Connie buys five percent in Madison High's star baseball player.

Turnabout Day
Walter tricks Mr. Conklin into creating Turnabout Day. This makes Walter the principal and the teachers become the students.

Here Is Your Past
Connie is being followed by a strange man. Every time he follows her, something disappears and she is getting blamed for it.

The Madison Mascot
Connie is given the task of getting Madison High a mascot.

The Big Jump
Nobody wants to jump off the roof of the school into a net as a Civil Defense demonstration, so it is up to Connie.

Home Cooked Meal
Connie accidentally locks Mr. Conklin in the school's lunchroom freezer.

Transition Show
When Madison High is closed down to make way for a freeway, Connie and Mr. Conklin get jobs at Mrs. Nestor's private elementary school.

Who's Who?
Connie is required by the school to move to a place nearer the school.

Picnic Basket
Mrs. Nestor, Mr. Munsey and Connie pack a picnic lunch for the school. She puts the food in what she thinks is the refrigerator, but is in reality the incinerator.

Big Ears
Angela predicts that Connie will meet a stranger with large ears. It turns out that she meets dozens of rabbits.

Will Travel
Connie and Angela try to get Mrs. Davis to move in with them and take care of the house.

Protest Meeting
Connie and Mr. Munsey plan to hold a protest meeting to complain about Mr. Conklin's strict faculty rules.

King and Brooks
GS: Desi Arnaz, Ricky Vera, Carlos Vera. One of Connie's students is the son of an Indian king who offers her wealth if she will return to his palace in India.

Mad Munsey
Mr. Conklin installs an intercom system throughout the school so he can listen in on the teachers' conversations.

Connie and Bonnie
Connie is arrested in a gambling joint and must convince Mr. Conklin that it was her twin sister Bonnie, a burlesque queen, that was arrested and not she.

Music Review
The school puts on its version of "A Christmas Carol."

Gym Instructor
Connie gets to choose the new gym instructor. She hires the least qualified but the handsomest man who applies for the job.

Skeleton in the Closet
Connie is blackmailed by an old acquaintance from her school days.

Amalgamation
Connie tries to prevent Mrs. Nestor from merging her school with a nearby progressive school.

Reunion
Connie wants to leave and take a job where she will meet more men; the staff plan to find a way to make her stay.

Twins at School
Connie revives her imaginary twin sister Bonnie so she can get another job to help pay for a new car.

Nestor's Boyfriend
Mrs. Nestor wants no social fraternization between the teachers, so Connie plots to find Mrs. Nestor a boyfriend to soften her up.

Acting Director
Connie and the staff prepare to audition for a visiting casting director who is coming to the school to find undiscovered talent.

Boynton's Return
Connie's old boyfriend Philip comes for a visit. She wants to go out with him but she has a date with Gene who also happens to be an old friend of Philip's.

White Lies
Connie takes Mrs. Davis's place when her old boyfriend of 35 years ago returns to court her.

Land Purchase
Connie and Mrs. Davis try to buy Angela's house for as little as possible; Mr. Conklin tries to sell his old house for a fortune.

Raffle Ticket
Connie wins $1000 in a raffle. However, Mr. Conklin reminds her that gambling at the school can get her fired.

Library Quiz
Connie and Mr. Conklin face two chil-

dren in a quiz where the winner will win a complete library for his school.

Mother for Benny
Benny Romero wants Connie to marry his widowed father so she can be his stepmother.

Connie and Frankie
Philip returns to join the staff of the school and he convinces the school to hire his friend, a beautiful blonde, as the athletic director.

White Tie, Top Hat and Bindle
Connie plays cupid to get Benny's father and a little girl's mother married.

Twenty-Four Hours
Connie makes a bet that if she can show Philip only happily married couples in 24 hours, he will ask her to marry him.

Geraldine
Connie accidentally buys an old milk-wagon horse for the school instead of a horse for the riding academy.

$350,000 Question
Connie, thinking she has won dozens of expensive prizes on a television game show, tells off Mr. Conklin.

Principal for a Day
The school is up for sale. Mr. Romero and a group of his friends say they will buy the school, but he insists on making Connie the new principal.

Travel Crazy
GS: Jack Albertson. Connie and the other teachers pool their money so that one of them can go on a super vacation. The winner will be selected by a spelling contest.

THE PARTRIDGE FAMILY

On the air 9/25/70, off 8/31/74. ABC. Color Film. 96 episodes. Broadcast: Sept 1970-Jun 1973 Fri 8:30-9; Jun 1973-Aug 1974 Sat 8-8:30. Producer: Bob Claver/Paul Junger Witt. Prod Co/Synd: Columbia Pictures TV/Screen Gems.

CAST: Shirley (played by Shirley Jones), Keith (David Cassidy), Laurie (Susan Dey), Danny (Danny Bonaduce), Chris (Jeremy Gelbwaks, 1970-71; Brian Foster, 1971-74), Tracy (Suzanne Crough), Reuben Kincaid (Dave Madden).

WRITERS: Bernard Slade, Richard Deroy, Ron Friedman, Dale McRaven, William S. Bickley, Susan Harris, Steve Zacharias, Michael Leeson, Lloyd Turner, Gordon Mitchell, Dick Bensfield, Perry Grant. DIRECTORS: Jerry Paris, Bob Claver, Peter Baldwin, Ralph Senensky, Richard Kinon, Lou Antonio, Jerry London, Bruce Bilson, E.W. Swackhamer.

The adventures of the Partridge family, a singing group made up of a mother and her five kids. The episodes depict the home and show biz lives of an ordinary family trying to cope with fame and fortune and at the same time remain unaffected. The series is seen on many stations across the nation.

What? And Get Out of Show Business? [Pilot]
W: Bernard Slade.   D: Jerry Paris. Five musical children and their mother graduate from playing in their garage to Caesar's Palace in Las Vegas.

The Sound of Money
W: Martin Ragaway.   D: Peter Baldwin.   GS: Harry Morgan.   The Partridges manage to convince an outraged motorist who wants to sue them for whiplash to drop his case.

Whatever Happened to the Old Songs?
W: Bernard Slade.   D: Jerry Bernstein. GS: Ray Bolger, Rosemary De Camp. Shirley's elderly mod father proves that songs of his day are still relevant to the new generation.

See Here, Private Partridge
W: Lloyd Turner & Gordon Mitchell. D: Claudio Guzman.   GS: Jonathan Daly, Jared Martin.   Danny is almost inducted into the Army but is finally rejected because of his height.

When Mother Gets Married
W: Bernard Slade.   D: Ralph Senensky.   The Partridge kids start to worry when they think their mother is planning to get married.

Love at First Slight
W: Steve Pritzker.   D: Bob Claver. Keith is pursuing one girl while being chased by another.

Danny and the Mob
W: Ron Friedman.   D: Jerry Bernstein. GS: Pat Harrington, Barbara Rhoades. In Las Vegas, Danny goes out of his way to give a pretty girl advice while the mob pursues him.

But the Memory Lingers On
W: Bernard Slade.   D: E.W. Swackhamer.   GS: Gino Conforti.   After a skunk leaves his scent on their bus, the Partridges fear their bad odor will spoil their next performance.

Did You Hear the One About Danny Partridge?
W: Ron Friedman.   D: Paul Junger Witt.   GS: Morey Amsterdam.   Danny tries to become a comedian, but everyone knows he doesn't have the talent except Danny.

Go Directly to Jail
W: Dale McRaven.   D: Claudio Guzman.   GS: Stuart Margolin.   The Partridges spend a night in prison while performing for the convicts at a Federal Penitentiary.

This Is My Song
When Keith seems to have run out of new songs, Danny tries his luck at composing.

Partridge Family: left to right, top, Suzanne Crough, Susan Dey, Dave Madden, bottom, Brian Foster, Danny Bonaduce, and David Cassidy.

My Son, the Feminist
W: Richard DeRoy. D: Peter Baldwin. GS: Jane Actman, Leonard Stone. Keith's new girlfriend is involved with women's liberation.

Star Quality
W: Bernard Slade. D: Harry Falk. GS: Dick Clark, Mitzi Hoag. A complimentary newspaper article gives Danny a big head until he learns that it's lonely being a star.

The Red Woodlow Story
W: Coslough Johnson. D: Peter Baldwin. GS: William Schallert. A famous folk singer disappears when the moment arrives for him to give a long-anticipated performance.

Mom Drops Out
W: Peter Meyerson. D: Harry Falk. GS: Gino Conforti. The kids are worried that a European promoter has convinced Shirley to drop out of the group.

Old Scrapmouth
W: James Henerson. D: Herbert Kenwith. GS: Mark Hamill, Alan Oppenheimer. Laurie tries to keep her new braces a secret from her boyfriend.

Why Did the Music Stop?
W: Bernard Slade. D: Alan Rafkin. GS: Richard Mulligan. The kids think Shirley's new boyfriend will force her to quit the group.

Soul Club
W: Harry Winkler & Harry Dolan. D: Paul Junger Witt. GS: Richard Pryor. When Reuben makes a mistake, the Partridges spend a weekend performing in an old firehouse in a Detroit ghetto.

To Play or Not to Play
W: Stan Cutler & Martin Donovan. D: Ralph Senensky. GS: Harvey & Michael Lembeck. At a nightclub, Danny becomes a labor negotiator for striking workers.

They Shoot Managers, Don't They?
W: Lloyd Turner & Gordon Mitchell.
D: Peter Baldwin.   Shirley's matchmaking attempts almost lose their
manager.

Partridge Up a Pear Tree
W: Lloyd Turner & Gordon Mitchell.
D: Ralph Senensky. GS: Carl Ballantine, Annette O'Toole. Keith learns
the value of money when he buys his
first car.

Road Song.
W: Dale McRaven. D: Alan Rafkin.
GS: Laurie Prange, Ian Wolfe. The
Partridge family becomes involved
with a young runaway girl.

Not with My Sister, You Don't
W: Dale McRaven. D: Mel Swope.
GS: Michael Ontkean.   Laurie finds
out the hard way that the rumors
about a new boy in school are true.

A Partridge by Any Other Name
W: Ron Friedman. D: Harry Falk.
GS: Bernard Fox, Ned Glass. Danny
is convinced that he is an adopted
child and sets out to find his real
parents. [This episode is not run by
some stations due to the objection-
able material of its story.]

A Knight in Shining Armor
W: Bernard Slade. D: Earl Bellamy.
GS: Bobby Sherman, Wes Stern. The
Partridges meet a young songwriter
in their garage and help team him up
with a lyricist.   [This was the pilot
for the short-lived series "Getting Together."]

Dora, Dora, Dora
W: Lloyd Turner & Gordon Mitchell.
D: Ralph Senensky. Keith is in love
with a girl who can't sing a note and
wants the Partridges to back her up in
a performance.

In 25 Words or Less
W: Martin Ragaway. D: Richard Kinon. GS: Kay Medford, Gerald Hiken.
Reuben stages a contest and the winner is granted a week with the Partridges. It turns out the winner is a 60-
year-old Jewish mother who tries to
take over the family.

A Man Called Snake
W: Chuck Shyer & Alan Mandel. D:
Richard Kinon. GS: Rob Reiner. A
motorcycle rider named Snake takes
a fancy to Laurie.

The Undergraduate
W: Susan Silver. D: Ralph Senensky.
GS: Norman Fell, Michael Burns.
Shirley goes back to college and soon
has a freshman student chasing her.

Anatomy of a Tonsil
W: Coslough Johnson. D: Lou Antonio.   GS: Marshall Thompson. When
Danny has his tonsils out, he thinks he
has lost his singing voice.

Whatever Happened to Moby Dick?
W: Peggy Chandler Dick. D: E.W.
Swackhamer.   GS: Howard Cosell,
Bert Convy. The Partridge family be-
come involved in the fight to save the
whales from extinction.

Dr. Jekyll and Mr. Partridge
W: William S. Bickley. D: Mel Swope.
Keith tries to prove he is the man of
the family and gets more responsibility
than he can handle.

Days of Acne and Roses
W: Dale McRaven. D: Richard Kinon.
A young awkward 16-year-old has
flipped over Laurie, prompting Danny
to get him a date with her.

Tale of Two Hamsters
W: Lloyd Turner & Gordon Mitchell.
D: Roger Duchowny. Danny tries another money-making venture, this
time he is breeding hamsters.

Forty Year Itch
W: Steve Pritzker. D: Ralph Senensky. GS: Ray Bolger, Rosemary De
Camp. The Partridges try to straighten
out a domestic problem between Shirley's parents.

I Can Get It for You Retail
W: Bernard Slade. D: Russ Mayberry.
Danny begins selling Keith's possessions to earn enough money to buy a
mink coat for his mother.

Guess Who's Coming to Drive
W: Bob Rodgers. D: Ralph Senensky.
GS: Milt Kamen, Vic Tayback. The
Partridges hire a driver who turns out
to be a parolee from prison.

*Don't Bring Your Guns to Town,
Santa*
W: Susan Silver. D: Richard Kinon.
GS: Dean Jagger. During Christmas,
the Partridge family's bus breaks down
in a ghost town.

Where Do Mermaids Go?
W: Peggy Chandler Dick. D: Lou Antonio. GS: Meredith Baxter. A
wealthy girl gives the Partridges one
million dollars, a gift that turns out to
be more trouble than they expected.

Home Is Where the Heart Was
W: Richard Bensfield & Perry Grant.
D: Jerry London. After being scolded,
Chris and Tracy run away to Reuben's
apartment.

Fellini, Bergman and Partridge
W: Martin Cohan. D: Jerome Courtland. GS: Richard Stahl. Keith takes
a fling at movie making and almost
makes a success of it.

Waiting for Bolero
W: Martin Cohan. D: Jerry London.
Bachelor Keith gets his own apartment
but finds living alone is not as much
fun as he thought.

I Am Curious Partridge
W: Bob Rodgers. D: Lou Antonio.
GS: Mitzi Hoag. Danny gets Keith and
Shirley in trouble with revealing arti-
cles he has written for the local paper.

My Heart Belongs to a Two-Car Garage
W: William S. Bickley. D: Jerry London. GS: Arte Johnson. A painting
of a nude lady on the garage door

causes trouble for the family with the
local community.

Hel-l-l-l-p
W: Dale McRaven. D: Paton Price.
When Shirley and Laurie decide to go
camping, Keith, Danny and Reuben
decide they'll need protection, until
the girls come to their rescue.

*Promise Her Anything but Give Her a
Punch*
W: Dale McRaven. D: Bob Claver.
Danny falls in love for the first time
with a girl who loves another.

The Partridge Papers
W: William S. Bickley. D: Jerry London. Laurie is upset when her diary
falls into the hands of the school editor who threatens to publish it in the
school paper.

All's War in Love and Fairs
W: John Wilder. D: Mel Swope. GS:
Harry Morgan. The Partridge family
use their vacation time to help the
plight of the American Indian.

*Who Is Max Ledbetter and Why Is He
Saying All Those Terrible Things?*
W: Bernie Kahn & Christopher Mor-
gan. GS: John Banner. Keith and
Danny get involved with a psychic
whose powers are limited.

*This Male Chauvinist Piggy Went to
Market*
W: Dale McRaven. D: Richard Kinon.
Keith's case of male chauvinism is tem-
pered when Laurie beats up Goose, the
school bully.

M Is for the Many Things
W: William S. Bickley. D: Lou Antonio. GS: Rick Hurst, Mitzi Hoag. Mother of the Year Shirley ends up in
court to fight a speeding ticket on the
way to receive the award.

Princess and the Partridge
W: William S. Bickley. D: Richard Kinon. GS: Season Hubley. Keith almost causes an international incident

when he escorts a young princess who is visiting the U.S.

Each Dawn I Diet
W: Lloyd Turner & Gordon Mitchell. D: Richard Kinon. Reuben and Danny try life without smoking or eating fattening foods.

A Penny for His Thoughts
W: Dale McRaven. D: Bob Claver. GS: Stuart Margolin, Judie Stein. The Partridges are hosts to a dejected biker whose marriage proposal has been turned down by his girlfriend.

You're Only Young Twice
W: Susan Silver. D: Lee Phillips. GS: Charlotte Rae. Danny finds out that being an adult is not as much fun as he imagined.

The Mod Father
W: Susan Harris. D: E.W. Swackhamer. GS: Ray Bolger, Rosemary De Camp. Grandma and Grandpa try using an encounter group to patch their marriage back together.

A Likely Candidate
W: Martin Cohan. D: Herb Wallerstein. GS: Bert Convy. Keith becomes jealous of a politician for whom he is campaigning when the man starts taking an interest in his mother.

Swiss Family Partridge
W: Martin Cohan. D: Lou Antonio. The Partridges find themselves secluded in an isolated mountain cabin during a record-breaking rainstorm.

Ain't Loveth Grand
W: William S. Bickley. D: Herb Wallerstein. GS: Anthony Geary. Laurie's latest romance is a minister who wants to lead her to the altar.

Whatever Happened to Keith Partridge?
W: Susan Harris. D: Bruce Bilson. Keith is chosen to play an important role in a Hollywood movie and lets success go to his head.

Nag, Nag, Nag
W: Steve Pritzker. D: E.W. Swackhamer. GS: Slim Pickens. Danny acquires a racehorse that has insomnia.

For Sale by Owner
W: Charlotte Brown. D: Russ Mayberry. GS: Bert Freed, Lurene Tuttle. The Partridges decide to move to a larger house and are faced with the trouble of selling their old house.

Aspirin at 7, Dinner at 8
W: Susan Harris. D: Bob Claver. GS: Nancy Walker, Gerald Hiken. Shirley accepts a date from an old admirer and later has to figure out how to get rid of both him and his mother.

For Whom the Bell Tolls . . . and Tolls . . . and Tolls
W: Dale McRaven. D: E.W. Swackhamer. GS: Arte Johnson. An escaped convict holds the Partridge family and Reuben hostage.

Trial of Partridge One
W: Steve Zacharias & Michael Leeson. D: Jerry London. Covering up for a friend, Laurie is accused of stealing a math test.

I Left My Heart in Cincinnati
W: Dale McRaven. D: Bob Claver. GS: Johnny Bench, Mary Ann Mobley. Keith falls in love with an older woman, only to have Danny show him the error of his ways.

The 11-year Itch
W: William S. Bickley. D: Richard Kinon. GS: Jodie Foster, Bert Convy. Danny is annoyed by the affections of an 11-year-old girl, until he realizes he really likes her.

Bedknobs and Drumsticks
W: Lloyd Turner & Gordon Mitchell. D: Herb Wallerstein. GS: William Windom. The Partridges put on chicken suits to make a commercial for a take-out chicken restaurant.

Everything You Wanted to Know About Sex . . . but Couldn't Pronounce
W: Dale McRaven. D: Bob Claver. GS: Ramon Bieri. Keith is humiliated when he finds out he is failing sex education at school.

Forgive Us Our Debts
W: Skip Webster. D: Bruce Bilson. GS: Alan Oppenheimer, Vic Tayback. A computer error plays havoc with Shirley's credit rating at a department store, causing her great anguish.

The Partridge Connection
W: Steve Zacharias & Michael Leeson. D: E.W. Swackhamer.   GS: Henry Jones. Danny is caught shoplifting after his friend Punky challenges him to prove he is not a coward.

Selling of the Partridges
W: Steve Zacharias & Michael Leeson. D: Lee Phillips. Keith has to overcome some very stiff competition in order to win the election for the school presidency.

Diary of a Mad Millionaire
W: Steve Zacharias & Michael Leeson. D: Lou Antonio. GS: John Astin. The Partridges bring a lonely millionaire out of his self-imposed seclusion of many years.

Me and My Shadow
W: Dale McRaven. D: Jerry London. GS: Richard Stahl. A bet for the Partridges to hide from a mystery writer in order to win $25,000 for charity leads to a wild chase around town.

Hate Thy Neighbor
W: George Tibbles & William S. Bickley. D: Richard Kinon. GS: Ricky Segall, Nita Talbot. The Partridges' new neighbor hates show business, especially musicians.

None but the Lonely
W: Dale McRaven. D: Charles Rondeau. Keith's scheme to meet a cute newcomer through his sister's newspaper column backfires.

Beethoven, Brahms and Partridge
W: Dale McRaven. D: Charles Rondeau. A lover of classical music menaces the Partridges.

The Strike-Out King
W: William S. Bickley. D: E.W. Swackhamer. GS: Herb Edelman. Danny becomes a little league hero but his family finds his new attitude impossible.

Reuben Kincaid Lives
W: Steve Zacharias & Michael Leeson. D: E.W. Swackhamer. GS: Margaret Hamilton. Reuben feels he is not long for this world when the Partridges start giving him special attention.

Double Trouble
W: Richard Bensfield & Perry Grant. D: Herb Wallerstein.   GS: Cheryl Ladd. Keith has two dates for Saturday night and tries to scheme his way out of trouble.

The Last of Howard
W: Dale McRaven. D: Richard Kinon. Keith and Danny are convinced that Laurie's new boyfriend is an international jewel thief.

The Diplomat
W: Paul Lichtman.   D: Herb Wallerstein. GS: Richard Mulligan, Pat Harrington, Florida Friebus. Shirley is being pursued by a presidential ambassador and she turns him down.

Heartbreak Keith
W: Bill Manhoff. D: Charles Rondeau. GS: Brooke Bundy. Keith falls for an older college student and then discovers she is married.

A Day of Honesty
W: Lloyd Turner & Gordon Mitchell. D: Ross Bowman. GS: Joseph Perry. When Danny gets caught trying to sneak into a movie theater without a ticket, the whole family tries an experiment in honesty.

Al in the Family
W: William S. Bickley.   D: Charles

Rondeau. Reuben's nephew is a total failure at everything he tries, but he longs to be a comedian.

Made in San Pueblo

W: William J. Keenan. D: Charles Rondeau. GS: Jackie Coogan, Rosemary De Camp. Shirley's parents are battling again and this time Grandma decides to go to work as the Partridges' maid.

Art for Mom's Sake

W: Michael Leeson. D: Ross Bowman. GS: Alan Oppenheimer. Shirley's art teacher thinks her paintings are masterpieces, but the family thinks they are disasters.

Two for the Show

W: William S. Bickley. D: Charles Rondeau. GS: Andy and David Williams. Andy and David, 14-year-old singing twins, both develop a crush on Laurie that threatens to break up their act.

Danny Drops Out

W: Richard Bensfield & Perry Grant. D: Roger Duchowny. GS: James Gregory. Deciding that he knows everything he'll ever need, Danny drops out of school.

Queen for a Minute

W: Lloyd Turner & Gordon Mitchell. D: Ernest Losso. GS: Tracy Brooks Swope. When Laurie's girlfriend tries out for the basketball team and is discriminated against because of her sex, the girls plot their revenge.

Danny Converts

W: Richard Bensfield & Perry Grant. D: Richard Kinon. GS: Noam Pitlik, Larry Gelb. Danny weaves a tangled web when he is smitten with a rabbi's daughter and tells her he is Jewish.

Miss Partridge, Teacher

W: Art Baer & Ben Joelson. D: Roger Duchowny. Danny's English class is taken over by Laurie, the new student teacher.

Keith and Lauriebelle

W: Richard Bensfield & Perry Grant. D: Roger Duchowny. GS: Sherry Miles. Keith has Laurie pose as his date, a Southern belle, in order to make a girl jealous.

Morning Becomes Electric

W: Lloyd Turner & Gordon Mitchell. D: Richard Kinon. GS: Jack Collins. The Partridge's home is being used in an effort to show the public how easy it is to cut down on electricity.

Pin It on Danny

W: Art Baer & Ben Joelson. D: Richard Kinon. Danny finds and gives his mother an expensive brooch for her birthday, only to discover a newspaper ad offering a reward for its return.

. . . — — . . . (S.O.S.)

W: Richard Bensfield & Perry Grant. D: Bob Claver. GS: George Chakiris. Danny and Keith follow their mother when she goes out on a date with her high school sweetheart, now a handsome Navy captain.

THE PATTY DUKE SHOW

On the air 9/18/63, off 8/31/66. ABC. B&W Film. 104 episodes. Broadcast: Sept 1963-Aug 1966 Wed 8-8:30. Producer: Crislaw. Prod Co/Synd: United Artists TV.

CAST: Patty/Cathy Lane (played by Patty Duke), Martin Lane (William Schallert), Natalie (Jean Byron), Ross (Paul O'Keefe), Richard (Eddie Applegate).

WRITERS: Sidney Sheldon, Ed Jurist, Sam Locke, Joel Rapp, Arnold Horwitt. DIRECTORS: Rod Amateau, Claudio Guzman, Don Weis, James Sheldon,

Gary Nelson, Bruce Bilson.

The tale of the Lane family: Martin, the editor of a newspaper, his wife and their two children. Plus a visiting cousin who is an exact lookalike for their daughter Patty. Typical episodes depict the amusing situations that occur when Patty and Cathy are mistaken for each other. *The Patty Duke Show* is in syndication, but possibly only airing on one or two stations in the entire country.

The French Teacher
GS: Jean Pierre Aumont. When Patty falls in love with her French teacher, her grades suddenly improve.

The Genius
GS: Paul Lynde. An IQ-testing computer accidentally rates Patty a genius.

The Elopement
Patty schemes to arrange a weekend for her parents at the same fishing lodge where they spent their honeymoon.

The House Guest
GS: Ilka Chase. Spinster Aunt Pauline arrives and immediately takes over running the house and feeding the family.

The Birds and the Bees Bit
GS: Susan Melvin. Invited to a dance by a young girl, Patty and Cathy try to teach Ross all he has to know about women in two days.

Slumber Party
At the girls' slumber party, Ross secretly tape records their private conversations and suddenly becomes king of the house.

Baby Sitters
When Mr. Lane refuses to pay for an evening gown for Patty, she decides to go into the babysitting business.

The Conquering Hero
The school basketball star is moving to Michigan during the height of the school's most successful season, so Patty suggests he live with her until the end of the basketball season.

The President
Patty and Cathy are competing against each other for the presidency of the senior class.

Double Date
When Cathy suddenly becomes ill on the eve of a party, Patty takes her place and goes out with her date.

The Actress
The school is putting on a lavish version of "Anthony and Cleopatra"; Cathy tries out for the lead but Patty unexpectedly gets it.

How to Be Popular
Jealous that her Cousin Patty is more popular than she, Cathy tries out some new ways of winning friends with disastrous results.

The Songwriters
Richard and Patty have an argument, so Patty writes a love poem which in reality has been stolen out of a collection in the family library.

The Princess Cathy
Cathy falls in love with a foreign exchange student at the high school, but things get too serious when he proposes marriage.

The Christmas Present
Christmas is a day away and Cathy anxiously awaits a visit from her father, only to learn he is a prisoner in a foreign country.

Auld Lang Syne
Martin's brother Kenneth sets out to write his autobiography but discovers writing a book is more difficult than he imagined.

Horoscope
To earn money to buy her mother a birthday gift, Patty becomes an astrolgist.

The Tycoons
After making a dress that turns out to be a masterpiece, Cathy decides to start manufacturing dresses without considering the risks.

Author! Author!
Patty writes a novel presenting the viewpoint of the American teenager and immediately gets a publishing contract.

The Continental
After Patty's father tells the family they will have to move to Paris for a year, they begin to realize how much they appreciate their home.

Let 'em Eat Cake
GS: Margaret Hamilton, George S. Irving. Patty's mother bakes a cake for a contest that Patty and Cathy eat; their solution, bake another cake.

Going Steady
Patty and Richard decide to go steady setting their parents off to break up the amorous pair.

Are Mothers People?
Natalie Lane begins to feel unwanted and devises a plan to get even with her family for the uncaring way they have been acting.

The Con Artist
After a smooth-talking salesman talks Cathy into buying a vacuum cleaner for Natalie's birthday, she discovers the cost is too much for her to handle.

The Perfect Teenager
Patty concludes that she is a flop after she flunks a psychology exam for teenagers. To overcome her deficiencies, she decides to enroll in a modeling school.

Chip off the Old Block
To increase the circulation of the school paper, Patty uses scandalous stories which infuriate the school principal.

The Wedding Anniversary Caper
Ross enters Patty's photo in a teenage beauty contest to earn enough money to get his parents a wedding anniversary gift.

Pen Pals
After receiving many poetic pen pal letters, Patty begins to lose interest in Richard.

A Slight Case of Disaster
Patty buys an expensive dress she can't afford in order to compete with her arch rival Sue-Ellen and finds she can't return it after Cathy stains it.

The Friendship Bit
Patty seems to be allergic to Cathy and is forced to stay far away from her cousin.

Patty, the Foster Mother
Patty is put in charge of a campaign to adopt a Korean war orphan and must explain to her parents that the boy is her son.

Drop Out
Richard has decided to drop out of school and look for a job.

Leave It to Patty
Patty is a candidate for chairwoman of the class prom and can insure her victory by supplying a celebrity guest, which is exactly what she intends to do.

The Little Dictator
Cathy is appointed student principal for a week and sends in a bad report on Patty who declares war on her cousin.

The Working Girl
Patty's latest moneymaking venture is as a waitress in the local ice cream parlor.

The Cousins
Flashbacks reveal the events that led up to how Cathy came to live with the Lane Family.

The Green-Eyed Monster
W: Sidney Sheldon.   D: S. Prager.
Richard vies for Patty's attention against a handsome cousin of Patty's in town for a visit.

Practice Makes Perfect
W: Sidney Sheldon.   D: S. Prager.
Patty decides to take up the tuba and almost drives her family crazy with her constant practicing.

Simon Says
W: Sidney Sheldon.   D: S. Prager.
Patty's advice column has taken a turn for the worse, all her advice backfires sending angry students out looking for her.

The Organizer
W: Sidney Sheldon.   D: Rod Amateau.
Patty, Cathy and Ross revolt against their parents and go on strike until they receive additional privileges.

Patty the Pioneer
W: Sidney Sheldon.   D: Rod Amateau.
Patty decides to live the life of a pioneer for a week and discovers there is more to life than TV, hair dryers and hot water.

The Boy Next Door
W: Sidney Sheldon.   D: Rod Amateau.
Patty and Cathy vie for the affection of the young man who has just moved in next door.

Patty, the People's Voice
W: Arnold Horwitt.   D: Claudio Guzman.   Patty and Cathy join the political campaign of a friend, only to decide his opponent is a better choice.

The Greatest Psychologist in the World
W: Sidney Sheldon.   D: Dave Butler.
Patty decides to use applied psychology on her friends, family and boyfriend.

Patty and the Peace Corps
W: Sidney Sheldon.   D: Claudio Guzman.   Patty prepares for the Peace Corps by studying Swahili and learn-ing all about African customs, while trying to figure out a way of telling her folks about her upcoming trip.

How to Succeed in Romance
W: Arnold Horwitt.   D: Claudio Guzman.   Cathy falls in love with the new student, Christopher, and seeks advice from Patty while Chris seeks out help from Richard.

Block That Statue
W: Austin & Irma Kalish.   D: Claudio Guzman.   GS: Daniel Travanti.   A football hero falls in love with Cathy who is not the least bit interested.

That Little Patty Went to Market
W: Austin & Irma Kalish.   D: Claudio Guzman.   Patty sells stock in her new apricot jam business and discovers that big business has too many pitfalls for her to handle.

Best Date in Town
W: Sidney Sheldon.   D: S. Prager.
Patty's upset that her father cancels out of attending the Father-Daughter dance and decides to make things miserable for her dear old dad.

Can Do Patty
Patty's father suggests Patty concentrate on her schoolwork and chores, only to find Patty has involved the whole family in her school projects.

Hi, Society
W: Arnold Horwitt.   D: Claudio Guzman.   Patty and Sue Ellen clash in a head-on battle trying to impress the newest handsome member of their class.

Patty, the Witness
W: Sidney Sheldon.   D: Claudio Guzman.   Patty witnesses an accident and mistakes a man taking his pregnant wife to the hospital for a gangster.

Every Girl Should Be Married
W: Sidney Sheldon.   D: Don Weis.
GS: Frank Sinatra, Jr.   Patty mistakenly believes her parents are trying to

marry her off when they invite a young professor to dinner.

Patty Meets a Celebrity
W: Sidney Sheldon.   D: Don Weis. GS: Sal Mineo. Sal Mineo in a return visit to Brooklyn Heights High, meets, befriends and completely overwhelms Patty.

The Perfect Hostess
W: Sidney Sheldon.   D: S. Prager. When Patty's distant lookalike cousin comes for a visit, she captivates all the eligible young men.

The Raffle
W: Sidney Sheldon. D: Claudio Guzman.   GS: Jean Stapleton, Marcia Strassman. Patty plans to raise money for a church bazaar by raffling off her boyfriend Richard.

Patty and the Newspaper Game
W: Sidney Sheldon.   D: Don Weis. GS: Bobby Vinton.   Patty's father thinks a new reporter has been hired to replace him on the paper, but in reality he is only there to make it possible for him to go on a much-needed vacation.

Little Brother Is Watching You
W: Ed Jurist. D: D. Davis. The Lanes decide Ross is too old for another surprise birthday party and plan to take him to a movie, unaware that Ross expected the party and invited all his friends over.

Patty Pits Wits; Two Brits Hits
W: Arnold Horwitt. D: S. Colleran. GS: Chad and Jeremy. After hearing a great singing team on the school radio, Patty sets out to make them success ful.

It Takes a Heap of Livin'
W: Arnold Horwitt. D: Don Weis. The Lanes discover that their house is a historical landmark and may have to move out of their beloved home.

Will the Real Sammy Davis Please Hang Up
W: Arnold Horwitt. D: Richard Kinon. GS: Sammy Davis, Jr., Peter Lawford, Susan Anspach. Patty sets out to get a great entertainer for the junior prom and almost blows her chances when she mistakenly refuses to accept a call from Sammy Davis, Jr.

Don't Monkey with Mendel
W: G. Abrams.   D: Richard Kinon. Patty decides to find a husband with a perfect family background.

Patty the Practical Joker
W: Arnold Horwitt.   D: Don Weis. After Ross puts a frog in Patty's bed, she and Ross compete in a never-ending series of practical jokes.

Patty the Master Builder
W: Sidney Sheldon. D: Dave Butler. Patty tries to help her brother build a homemade racing car.

Patty and the Cut-Rate Casanova
W: Arnold Horwitt. D: Howard Morris. Patty drops her boyfriend Richard for Carlos, a terrific dancer, whose father owns a dance studio. Richard vows to win Patty back.

The Daughter Bit
W: Arnold Horwitt. D: S. Colleran. Patty's father is upset because Patty is spending too much time away from home.

Cathy the Rebel
W: Sidney Sheldon. D: James Sheldon. Cathy writes a letter to the editor strongly disagreeing with one of their editorials, only to learn that Patty's father wrote the offending piece.

Patty the Folk Singer
W: Sidney Sheldon. D: Don Weis. GS: Arnold Soboloff. Patty gets a job as a folksinger at the local coffee shop and discovers she cleans floors, then sings songs.

What's Cooking, Cousin?
W: Sidney Sheldon. D: James Sheldon. Patty tries to improve her cooking skills to win over Richard who has acquired a taste for fine French food.

Take Me Out to the Ball Game
W: Sidney Sheldon. D: James Sheldon. Ross tries out for Little League and is surprised when his parents aren't the least bit interested, so Patty tries to cheer up her depressed brother.

My Cousin the Heroine
W: Sidney Sheldon. D: Don Weis. Cathy rescues a drowning boy and becomes an instant hero, much to Patty's dismay.

Patty the Chatterbox
W: Sidney Sheldon. D: Don Weis. Patty bets her father she can go three days without saying a word.

A Foggy Day in Brooklyn Heights
W: Roswell Rogers. D: Bruce Bilson. GS: Frankie Avalon. When Frankie Avalon's car breaks down, he rings Patty's doorbell to use the phone but Patty's not about to let her idol get away so soon.

Operation Tonsils
W: Ted & Mathilde Fero. D: Bruce Bilson. GS: Troy Donahue. Patty falls in love with the doctor who plans to remove her tonsils.

Partying Is Such Sweet Sorrow
W: Ed Jurist. D: Bruce Bilson. GS: The Shindogs. Upset over not being invited to a party, Patty schemes revenge by holding a private party of her own using a popular singing group.

The Guest
W: Sid Morse. D: Bruce Bilson. When Richard becomes a houseguest for a week he drives Patty and her family crazy with his daily activities.

Our Daughter the Artist
W: Arnold Horwitt. D: Gary Nelson. Patty takes up painting and doesn't have much talent, but no one wants to hurt her feelings by telling her the awful truth about her paintings.

Patty's Private Pygmalion
W: Arnold Horwitt. D: Gary Nelson. Patty decides to help a shy girl develop self-confidence, but her plan backfires when the girl runs against her for class president.

The Girl from Nephew
W: Sam Locke & Joel Rapp. D: Gary Nelson. Patty thinks an international spy ring is out to capture a government agent who stops for a visit at her house.

I'll Be Suing You
W: Mort Green. D: Richard Kinon. Richard borrows his father's car and has his first accident and is promptly handed a $10,000 lawsuit he believes to be the work of a swindler.

Patty and the Eternal Triangle
W: Ben Gershman & Bill Freedman. D: Gary Nelson. Patty, acting as Cathy, tests Richard to see how he will react to interest from another girl and to her surprise invites the imitation Cathy out for a date.

Sick in Bed
W: Ed Jurist. D: Bruce Bilson. Patty is sick and becomes a terrible burden to her family with her constant requests for everything from water to television.

Ross, the Peacemaker
W: Ed Jurist. D: Bruce Bilson. Ross acts as peacemaker when Patty has a fight with Richard.

Patty, the Candy Striper
W: William Raynor & Myles Wilder. D: Bruce Bilson. GS: Ronnie Schell, Milton Parsons. Patty becomes a nurse's aide at the same time her father is admitted to the hospital for a weekend of total rest.

Patty Meets the Great Outdoors
W: Ben Gershman & Bill Freedman.
D: Bruce Bilson. GS: James Brolin,
Kim Carnes. Patty becomes interested
in camping after the handsome painter
next door tells her he is a forestry student.

Cathy Leaves Home—But Not Really
W: Sid Morse & Roy Kammerman. D:
Richard Kinon. GS: Don Diamond.
To prove to herself the Lanes will not
let her leave home, Cathy applies for
an exchange student scholarship, but
the plan backfires when the family is
in favor of the idea.

The History Paper Caper
W: Joseph Hoffman. D: Richard Kinon. Patty maneuvers a history whiz
to write a term report for her and lets
her conscience pay the price.

A Very Phone-y Situation
W: Sam Locke & Joel Rapp. D: Gary
Nelson. Martin Lane has had it with
the phone situation at home and re-
stricts everyone to 15-minute calls,
but the family feels this is unfair.

Ross Runs Away—But Not Far
W: William Raynor & Myles Wilder.
D: Gary Nelson. While Patty is in
charge when her parents are away,
Ross feels she is being too strict with
him and decides to run away.

Poppo's Birthday
W: Ed Jurist & Sam Locke. D: Gary
Nelson. The family mistakenly believes Mr. Lane wants an expensive
rifle for his birthday and set out to
earn the sum of $99.50 to buy it for
him.

Anywhere I Hang My Horn Is Home
W: Arnold Horwitt. D: Gary Nelson.
GS: Dick Gautier. When Patty invites
an out of work musician over for a
meal, he decides to make the Lane
home his permanent residence.

*The Greatest Speaker in the Whole
Wide World*
W: Sidney Sheldon. D: Gary Nelson.
Mr. Lane plans to teach Patty a lesson
when she commits him to speak before her class without checking with
him first.

Big Sister Is Watching
W: Sidney Sheldon. D: Bruce Bilson.
GS: Les Brown, Jr. Ross gets into a
fight with a bully. When Patty goes to
straighten things out, she falls for the
boy's handsome brother.

Patty Leads a Dog's Life
W: Arnold Horwitt. D: Bruce Bilson.
To earn extra money, Patty takes up
dog sitting. She ends up feeding the
animals steak and giving them bubble
baths.

Too Young and Foolish to Go Steady
W: Arnold Horwitt. D: Bruce Bilson.
Patty makes a mistake and drops Richard who is suddenly a free man pursued by all of Patty's girlfriends.

Patty the Diplomat
W: Sidney Sheldon. D: Richard Kinon. Patty writes a letter to the Russian Ambassador, causing confusion
between her family, school and the
United States government.

Do You Trust Your Daughter?
W: Ed Jurist. D: Gary Nelson. Patty
is dating an older man and her parents
don't approve and ground her for two
weeks, sending Patty into a rage.

A Visit from Uncle Jed
W: Arnold Horwitt. D: Gary Nelson.
Patty's banjo playing Uncle Jed pays
a visit, disrupting Patty's plans for a
formal dinner party.

Patty the Psychic
W: Sidney Sheldon. D: Gary Nelson.
Patty believes she has ESP and surprises her family by actually foresee-
ing events in the lives of her friends
and family.

Don't Bank on It
W: Phil Sharp.   D: Harry Falk, Jr.
Patty loses the money her father in-
structed her to deposit in the bank
and learns a lesson in responsibility.

The Three Little Kittens
W: Ed Jurist.   D: Harry Falk, Jr. GS:
Clint Howard.   Patty and Ross buy
three kittens and are faced with the
task of reselling the kittens before
they grow up to be full-grown cats.

Fiancee for a Day
W: Ed Jurist. D: Harry Falk, Jr. GS:

Judy Carne. Richard and Patty decide
they will marry right after graduation,
but they don't tell their parents.

The Invisible Boy
W: Clifford Goldsmith. D: Gary Nelson. Patty and her friend Chuck plan
a quiet evening together but are constantly interrupted by Ross.

Do a Brother a Favor
W: Sidney Sheldon. D: Gary Nelson.
GS: Aron Kincaid.   Patty agrees to
help Ross become a Tiger Club member by dating the president.

THE PAUL LYNDE SHOW

On the air 9/13/72, off 9/8/73. ABC. Color Film. 26 episodes. Broadcast:
Sept 1972-May 1973 Wed 8-8:30; Jun 1973-Sept 1973 Sat 8:30-9. Producer:
Harry Ackerman. Prod Co/Synd: Columbia Pictures TV.
   CAST: Paul Simms (played by Paul Lynde), Martha (Elizabeth Allen), Sally
(Pamelyn Ferdin), Barbara (Jane Actman), Howie (John Calvin), Barney (Jerry
Stiller), Grace (Anne Meara), T.J. McNish (Herb Voland), T.R. Scott (James
Gregory), Alice (Allison McKay).
   The story of Paul Simms, attorney, who lives with his family which drives him
crazy. The series did not fare very well in the ratings and was dropped in 1973
and hasn't turned up since.

Howie Comes Home to Roost
W: Ron Clark & Sam Bobrick. D: William Asher. Paul's daughter Barbara
returns home from college with her
jobless husband Howie, for whom
Paul tries to find a job.

Whiz Kid Sizzles as Quiz Fizzles
W: Ed Jurist. D: William Asher. GS:
Jonathan Daly, Roy Rowan, Anson
Williams. Paul's plan to get Barbara
and Howie out of the house backfires
when Howie refuses to take the $3000
he won on a game show.

The Landlord
W: S.A. Long. D: William Asher. GS:
Jerry Stiller, Anne Meara. Howie and
Barbara move into Paul's basement
and Howie's parents come for a visit.

No Nudes Is Good Nudes
W: Bob Fisher & Arthur Marx. D: Wil-

liam Asher. GS: Arthur O'Connell,
Allison McKay, Herb Voland, Allen
Jenkins. Howie gets a part in an all-
nude play. Paul tries to prevent it
from opening.

To Commune or Not to Commune
W: Bob Fisher & Arthur Marx.   D:
Bruce Bilson. GS: Jack Bender, Jodie
Foster, Anne Wyndham, Kenneth
Washington. Howie and Barbara join
a commune after Paul throws them
out of the house.

How to Be Unhappy Though Poor
W: Phil Sharp. D: George Tyne. GS:
Herb Voland, Cliff Norton, Holly Irving. Paul's plan to get the kids out of
the house by faking unemployment
backfires.

Pollution Solution
W: Bob Fisher & Arthur Marx.   D:

Jack Donohue. GS: Edward Andrews, Jerry Fogel. Paul must defend the oil company that Howie and Barbara are demonstrating against.

To Wed or Not to Wed
W: Bud Grossman. D: Ernest Losso. GS: Jerry Stiller, Anne Meara, Chuck McCann. Howie and Barbara learn their marriage is invalid, so Paul tries to convince them to remarry.

Unsteady Going
W: Bob Fisher & Arthur Marx. D: Jack Donohue. GS: Alan Oppenheimer, Stuart Getz. Paul hates Sally's new boyfriend, so she runs away from home.

Whose Lib?
W: Bob Fisher & Arthur Marx. D: Ernest Losso. GS: Barbara Rhoades, Herb Voland. Paul hires Howie as his temporary secretary.

Meet Aunt Charlotte
W: Ed Jurist & Stan Dreben. D: George Tyne. GS: Charlotte Rae, Ray Walston. Paul's eccentric sister visits, while Paul is entertaining a Japanese businessman.

An Affair to Forget
W: Bob Fisher & Arthur Marx. D: George Tyne. GS: Jo Anne Worley, Roger Perry, Dick Wilson. Paul and Martha take sides when their friends separate.

Martha's Last Hurrah
W: William Raynor & Myles Wilder. D: George Tyne. GS: Charlotte Rae. Paul's sister returns to cause trouble for Paul. She is siding with the candidate who is opposing the mayor's son whom Paul is helping.

Paul's Desperate Hour
W: Ben Starr. D: Bruce Bilson. GS: James A. Watson, Jr., Paul Smith, Carol Speed. Howie invites the black man who mugged his wife to dinner, who then proceeds to rob the house.

No More Mr. Nice Guy
W: Bernie Kahn. D: George Tyne. GS: Marcia Strassman, Eugene Troobnick. Paul has to be nice to Howie, after he learns he has high blood pressure.

The Bare Facts
W: Bob Fisher & Arthur Marx. D: George Tyne. GS: Henry Jones, Dick Wilson, Richard X. Slattery, Byron Morrow. Paul loses the nomination for the Bar Association presidency when Howie's nude portrait of Barbara is printed in the local newspaper.

Howie's Inheritance
W: Laurence Marks. D: Jerry London. GS: Jerry Stiller, Anne Meara, Milt Kamen. Howie inherits $10,000 but refuses to accept it.

P.S. I Loathe You
W: Bob Carroll, Jr. & Madelyn Davis. D: Jack Donohue. Paul writes a nasty letter to his boss, which is accidentally mailed.

The Congressman's Son
W: Leo Rifkin. D: George Tyne. GS: Tom Bosley, Stephen Nathan, Gordon Jump, Paul Sorenson. Paul loses a big job when Howie changes a congressman's son into a hippie.

Out of Bounds
W: William Raynor & Myles Wilder. D: Oscar Rudolph. GS: Bernie Kopell, Liam Dunn, Barney Phillips. Paul's fence extends one foot onto his neighbor's property. He must either buy the land or move the fence.

Is This Trip Necessary?
W: Bob Fisher & Arthur Marx. D: George Tyne. GS: Mabel Albertson. Paul's mother-in-law comes for a visit. In order to get rid of her, Paul arranges for her to win a free trip.

Everything You Wanted to Know About Your Mother-in-Law ***** But Were Afraid to Ask
W: Bob Fisher & Arthur Marx. D:

Coby Ruskin. GS: Mabel Albertson, Alan Hale, Richard X. Slattery, Dick Wilson. Paul's mother-in-law sprains her leg and moves in for a very long visit.

Back Talk
W: Phil Sharp. D: Oscar Rudolph. GS: Dick Van Patten, Herbert Anderson, Victor Sen Yung. Paul hurts his back, but is cured when he learns Howie's friend agrees to help him with acupuncture.

Barbara Goes Home to Mother
W: Sumner A. Long. D: Jerry London. GS: Jerry Stiller, Anne Mears, Doney Oatman. Barbara and Howie have a fight about not fighting enough, so she moves into her parents' room, causing Paul to move in with Howie.

Togetherness
W: Barry E. Blitzer. D: Ernest Losso. Paul is afraid the family unit is breaking up, so he begins family day but everyone tries to end the fun.

Springtime for Paul
W: Sumner A. Long. D: Ernest Losso. GS: Roger C. Carmel, Christopher Norris, Frank Welker. Martha is jealous when their 18-year-old neighbor is impressed with Paul's legal abilities.

THE PEOPLE'S CHOICE

On the air 10/6/55, off 9/25/58. NBC. B&W Film. 104 episodes. Broadcast: Oct 1955-Dec 1955 Thu 8:30-9; Jan 1956-Sept 1958 Thu 9-9:30. Producer: E.J. Rosenberg. Synd: Worldvision.

CAST: Socrates "Sock" Miller (played by Jackie Cooper), Mandy (Pat Breslin), Aunt Gus (Margaret Irving), Mayor Peoples (Paul Maxey), Cleo's Voice (Mary Jane Croft), Roger Crutcher (John Stephenson), Hex "Rollo" Hexley (Dick Wesson).

The story of Socrates Miller, a Bureau of Fish and Wildlife ornithologist, who is elected city councilman and the head of Barkerville, a California Housing development. In the series, Sock secretly marries his girl Mandy and tries to hide their marriage from her father, the mayor. A twist in the series has Cleo, Sock's basset hound, able to talk and comment on her master's actions. The series is never aired anymore.

Pilot
Socrates Miller, a Bureau of Wildlife ornithologist, finds himself living in New York in a trailer and has been picked by write-in votes as the people's choice.

An Adventure of Sock
Sock buys his girlfriend a puppy named Cleopatra. When Barbara and Cleo do not get along together, Sock is forced to go between them.

How Sock Met Mandy
A flat tire, a frightened bird, and a booby trap shower lead to embarrassing moments for Sock.

The Unseating of Councilman Sock
Sock's eligibility for the office of city councilman is questioned on the basis of insufficient residency in New York City.

Sock Plays Cupid
A French mind-reading act is fired when the star, Yvette, loses her memory.

Sock vs. Crutcher
A legal hassle centers over Sock's dog Cleo who is accused of having bitten Sock's rival Roger Crutcher.

Sock's New Secretary
Sock's new secretary is the wealthy

and charming daughter of a friend of Mayor Peoples. Her only drawback is she can't even take shorthand.

Nature Study
Sock goes on a camping trip with a beautiful schoolteacher and her three spoiled children.

Sock Hires Mandy
Sock's girlfriend Mandy applies for a job as his secretary.

The Parting of Sock and Mandy
When Sock and Mandy decide to stop seeing each other for a while, they arrange to furnish each other with blind dates.

Sock and the Beauty Contest
Sock is selected to judge a beauty contest.

Sock's Teenage Trouble
Sock finds himself the unwilling object of a pretty girl's affection. He tries to get help from the local football hero, but the results are not good.

The Christmas Story
Mandy breaks her traditional date for Christmas Day to spend the holiday with Sock, but Sock has plans for bird-watching.

Sock and Pierre's Job
Sock tries to convince Mayor Peoples to give his artist friend Pierre a job painting a mural for one of the city's schools.

Aunt Gus Leaves Sock
When it seems Sock has persuaded Aunt Gus to leave town for a vacation, Mandy sees an opportunity to get him in the mood for marriage.

Sock and Augie
Sock's efforts to raise money for a boys' club hits a snag when one youngster resorts to stealing cars.

Sock, the Marriage Broker
Attempting to rid himself of his boss,

Miss Larson, Sock turns cupid and promotes a wedding between her and a Mr. Baxter, the man she has been seeing for eight years.

Sock, the Dedicated Councilman
Councilman Miller gets his picture in a national magazine when he is seen climbing a tree to watch a bird.

Sock Proposes to Mandy
Sock finds himself in hot water with Mandy when, on a TV panel, he says he is still a bachelor because he hasn't found the perfect girl.

Sock, the Businessman
Sock goes into the laundry business, but plans revenge when he learns that Mandy tricked him into it.

The Domestic Relations
Sock advises his married friend Ernie on how to handle women.

Sock, the City Father
Sock champions the establishment of a city-operated day nursery.

Sock Strikes It Rich
Sock buys some uranium stock and finds out what it feels like to be rich. Everyone wants to get into the deal and even Mayor Peoples decides that Sock would be a fine son-in-law.

Sock and the Mayor's Romance
Sock's girlfriend Mandy is progressing in her attempts to get her father, the Mayor, romantically interested in Sock's Aunt Gus.

Sock and the Syrene
Sock invites a Marine Corps sergeant to his house. The sergeant turns out to be a woman who wants to use Sock to make her boyfriend jealous.

Sock and the Movie Offer
A famous film director sees Sock, Mandy and Cleo on television.

Sock vs. Stone Kenyon
Sock has a severe attack of jealousy

when a western movie star moves in on Mandy.

Wedding Bells
Mandy and Aunt Gus create a story that Gus has at last found the man of her dreams.

Sock and Captain Turner
A lonely boy is heartbroken when he discovers that his father, whom he thought was a Navy hero, is in reality the captain of a Staten Island ferry boat.

Sock and the Proxy Marriage
Sock agrees to stand in as bridegroom for a Marine buddy in a proxy marriage ceremony, but he has a lot of explaining to do when the bride's grandfather shows up with a shotgun.

Sock, the Budget Balancer
GS: Lola Albright.   Sock rescues a pretty dancer who gets her heels caught in a loose grating. She claims her twisted ankle can ruin her plans for stardom and the Mayor claims she arranged the whole thing in order to bilk him.

Sock, the Fund Raiser
Mandy takes over Sock's duties as chairman of the Mayor's annual boxing bouts, while Sock becomes the victim of an accomplished thief.

Sock and the Lonely Hearts
Aunt Gus decides to get even with Sock and Mandy for their efforts to marry her off to the Mayor. She decides to arrive at the Mayor's home in a glamorous get-up that has a bad effect on a visiting congressman.

Sock and Mandy's Career
Sock advises Mandy to take a job but regrets it when the job she takes will be in San Francisco working for a handsome young man.

Sock and the Mayor's Election
Mandy tries to convince her friend that Sock should be the Mayor's assistant.

Sock and the Peoples' Pageant
GS: Ellen Corby. Sock wants to get his city on the map by staging a centennial pageant to honor an ancestor of a prominent congressman.

Sock Loses a Bet
Sock returns from his fishing trip with a beard, but Mandy has a job lined up for him as manager of a new television station and the station owner will object to the beard.

The Mayor Proposes
The mayor turns down a marriage proposal.

The Wedding Plans
Sock wants his Aunt Gus and the mayor to have a wedding with all the trimmings, so he invests in a restaurant which turns out to be a cover for a bookie joint.

The Bachelor Party
The mayor overhears Sock ordering champagne and caviar and is convinced he is a freeloader and talks him into signing up for an Arctic expedition.

Sock Gives Gus Away
Both Sock and the mayor are suffering pre-marital jitters.   Sock is preparing to give Aunt Gus away during the ceremony as well as advise the mayor about some bees in a vent at City Hall.

Sock, the Acting Mayor
While the mayor is on his honeymoon, Sock takes over as acting mayor and is faced with a blackmail suit. A mysterious woman claims she had an encounter with the mayor in a nightclub.

Sock Takes a Boarder
Mandy tries to convince Sock he should take in a boarder.

Sock and the Law
Mandy is wondering how a long blonde hair was found on Sock's suit.

Sock Takes the Plunge
Sock and Mandy decide to get married in a small town in Nevada, but neither

thought they would spend the night in jail.

Mandy's Male Animal
Mandy presents Sock to her former school friends as her husband.

Sock, the Greek God
In an interview, Mandy tells a reporter that Sock wants a new playground for a crowded section of town. Mayor Peoples tells Sock he must get the playground free or resign.

Sock and the Hex
GS: Dick Wessel. The mayor tells Sock he can't see Mandy anymore until he passes his bar exam, and then Sock finds out his old friend Hex has moved in with him.

How Sock Met Rollo
Cleo, Sock's bassett hound, tells the story of how Sock met Rollo while they were Marines.

Sock's Secret Honeymoon
Sock attempts to have a secret honeymoon with Mandy by getting the mayor out of town and Sock's roommate away.

Sock's Bivouac
Sock is called up for his annual two weeks' training in the Marine reserves.

Sock's Master Plan
Sock and Mandy plan to spend a weekend together at Palm Springs.

Sock Gets the Works
Sock is upset when Mandy accepts a date with another man.

Aunt Gus Tells All
Aunt Gus promises to keep the secret that Sock and Mandy are married, but she has a habit of talking in her sleep.

Sock's Tight Squeeze
Sock and Mandy's plans for a secret honeymoon cruise to Hawaii are ruined when the mayor tells Sock he has to work.

Almost a Father
Mandy accompanies her cousin's wife to an obstetrician and Sock mistakenly believes he is soon to be a father.

The Patsy
Mandy's former college roommate borrows Sock for her own selfish reasons.

The Domestics
Sock and Mandy attempt to spend their honeymoon at a friend's cabin at Big Bear Lake, but are mistaken for the servants.

Sock's Out-of-Town Job
Sock decides it is time to look for a new job, but just how far must he look—too far for anyone's convenience.

One-Ring Circus
Sock and Mandy officially announce their engagement even though they have been secretly married for four months.

Sock Goes for Dough
Sock does his best to resist when a quiz show offers him $5000 if he can date a gorgeous girl for one week without getting romantic.

The Ink Blots
Mandy's well-meaning father asks a visiting psychologist friend to determine whether Sock is the right man to marry his daughter.

Sock and Mandy, Paperhangers
While Mayor Peoples is out of town, Sock takes over for him at City Hall, but he botches things up by giving a painting contractor the go-ahead to decorate the mayor's home.

The Late Husband
Cleo is in love with a handsome French poodle owned by an actress.

The Queen and Me
Secretly married, Sock resents Mandy's request that he stop going out with the boys.

Boomerang
Sock has to think fast when a salesman arrives in town to sue the mayor.

The Hot Certificate
Mandy and Sock are frantic when they learn the mayor is looking for their marriage license, so they hide it under Cleo's sweater.

The Sophisticates
GS: Joi Lansing. The mayor seems on the verge of finding out that Mandy and Sock are married so they stage a fake breakup to stop his suspicions, but the mayor goes further and arranges a date for Sock.

Sock, the Matchmaker
Sock decides to play cupid when he sees the perfect match between Rollo and the daughter of a very wealthy family.

The Nickel Pickle
Sock takes on a job for the district attorney in an effort to trap a thief who has been robbing the city's parking meters.

The Giveaway
When Sock passes his bar exam, he and Mandy decide to reveal to her father that they have been secretly married for nearly a year, but before they tell him the mayor unveils his plans to give them a huge formal wedding.

The Caveman
Sock gets hit on the head and dreams he is in the Stone Age, complete with father-in-law trouble.

The Retiring Mayor
A female reporter gets an erroneous story from Rollo to the effect that the mayor is retiring.

The Reluctant House Guest
It seems imminent that Sock and Mandy are about to move out of her father's house.

The Legal Eagle
Newly admitted to the bar, Sock finds

himself in a precarious position before he has brought his first case to court.

Barkerville
The Millers and Cleo move into a new neighborhood. Sock accepts the position as the head of a new housing development.

The Model House
Mandy persuades Sock to buy new furniture which gets mixed up with the new development's furniture.

Movies Are Badder Than Ever
A cheap movie company descends on Barkerville to make a movie about a typical American community, but Mandy is upset over the whole idea.

The Runaway Dog
An influential home buyer who is thinking of moving to the Barkerville housing development reveals his hatred for dogs. Sock finds out and decides to hide Cleo.

The Helpmate
Mandy's meringue cake converts a reluctant prospect for a house into an enthusiastic buyer, but Sock resents Mandy's interference in his business and tells her to be more retiring.

Sock's Old Flame
Sock receives a phone call from an old girlfriend of his and prepares to meet her without telling Mandy.

The Cookie Jar
Mandy has put her hard-earned savings into a cookie jar and now has $100. She resists the temptation to spend it and so does Sock—until Mandy's uncle visits, that is.

The Wrong Indians
GS: Howard McNear, Rodd Redwing. Sock's boss warns him that he is not selling houses fast enough, so he thinks of a way that will enable him to sell a whole block of houses.

The Sheriff
A prospector makes a grand entrance

into Barkerville with Calamity, his trusted mule. The only trouble is that the man is in the wrong town.

The Salted Cellar
Through Mandy's prompting, Sock decides to hire Rollo as a real estate salesman and tells him he must sell at least one house.

Sleeping Beauty
Sock starts suffering from a bad case of insomnia due to his inability to sell houses, so he tries phonograph recordings guaranteed to induce sleep.

Distaff Stuff
Mandy decides to apply for a job as county tax agent, but Sock thinks a woman should not have to support herself.

The Male Ego
Sock becomes depressed when he loses the sale of a home to a prospective buyer.

The Family Way
Before leaving for a vacation, the family doctor tells Sock he is about to become a father. He and Mandy then plan a celebration.

The Veteran
Sock is about to become a father, but the mayor feels Mandy's doctor is too far away from their home.

Cleo, Secret Dog
Mayor Peoples learns that he is about to become a grandfather and decides Cleo's barking will annoy the baby when it arrives home.

The Practical Joker
GS: Alan Reed, Jr. Sock plans for linking his housing development with the main highway. All he has to do is buy a piece of land belonging to a big practical joker.

The Tycoon
An old boyfriend of Mandy's drops in for a visit and Sock gets jealous.

Little White Lie
Sock feels sorry for a young man who is trying to enlist members for a club of junior chemists to win a prize. They need only one more member, so Sock volunteers.

Sock's Lifesaver
Sock agrees to spend a week babysitting for the teenage daughter of his former Marine Corps commander.

Sock's Uncle
The mayor insists on paying all the expenses toward the birth of his grandchild, but Sock and Mandy refuse his offer when they receive a large sum of money from Uncle Willie.

Ladies' Aide
Sock enlists the aid of three teenage girls to help him raise funds for a local boys' club.

Rollo Makes Good/Ore Rush
Rollo suddenly gets a bad case of spring fever. He wants to get married, but Sock is apprehensive of the girl Rollo is dating.

The First Anniversary
Sock is invited to go on a fishing trip with an old buddy from the Marine Corps on the day of his wedding anniversary.

Rollo's Wedding
Rollo announces he and Geraldine are going to elope, but Sock thinks he should ask her father for permission to marry his daughter.

Missing Moolah
A middle-aged couple asks Sock to marry them. When he learns they don't have a license, the couple moves in with him until it arrives.

Daisies Won't Tell
Sock's boss J.P. Barker comes for a visit and seems very interested in Aunt Hattie.

PETE & GLADYS

On the air 9/19/60, off 9/10/62. CBS. B&W Film. 72 episodes. Broadcast: Sept 1960-Sept 1962 Mon 8-8:30. Producer: Parke Levy/Devery Freeman. Synd: Viacom.

CAST: Pete Porter (played by Harry Morgan), Gladys Porter (Cara Williams), Hilda (Verna Felton), George (Peter Leeds), Janet (Shirley Mitchell), Uncle Paul (Gale Gordon), Alice (Barbara Stuart).

A spinoff of *December Bride*. The misadventures of Pete and dopey wife Gladys. Popular when first aired, but now has disappeared from every station.

For Pete's Sake
Hilda meets Pete's much maligned but never seen wife.

Crime of Passion
GS: Cesar Romero. A dance instructor wants Pete to join in Gladys's dancing lessons.

The Bavarian Wedding Chest
Pete brings home a huge Bavarian wedding chest.

The Handyman
GS: Peter Leeds. Pete decides to prove that he is a match for anyone as a handyman.

Movie Bug
GS: Jack Albertson, Joey Faye. Unknown to Peter, Gladys lets a movie company use the Porter residence for some exterior shots then asks for a part.

OO-La-La
Pete persuades a French girl to do a charity number at a benefit.

The Goat Story
GS: Ronny Howard. A man from the animal pound is after Tommy's pet goat, so Gladys and Hilda help out.

Pete's Personality Change
GS: Willis Bouchey, Whitney Blake. Pete loses a big sale, so his boss calls in a psychologist to put some life back into his salesmanship.

Camping Out
Pete and Howie want to go on a camp-

ing trip, but they have to prove to their wives that they are tough enough to rough it.

Bowling Brawl
GS: Gale Gordon. Pete thinks it is time Gladys and her Uncle Paul end their long feud, but Gladys decides she has got to prove she is a good sport.

Pete Takes Up Golf
GS: Milton Frome. Pete wants to join the country club to play golf, but Gladys won't join him for social reasons.

Christmas Shopping
No available story

Gladys and the Piggy Bank
It is the Colton's anniversary and Pete and Gladys decide to buy them a cheap gift in return for the one they got for them.

No Man Is Japan
GS: Phillip Ahn. Pete may become manager of a Tokyo branch, so he arranges for a Japanese exchange student to move in and teach him Japanese customs.

Misplaced Weekend
GS: David Lewis. Pete and Gladys want to get away from it all and spend a few days in Palm Springs, so Gladys uses a scheme on Pete's boss to get him out of work only to find his boss at Palm Springs.

Gladys Rents the House
GS: Morey Amsterdam, Stanley

Adams. Gladys wants a Hawaiian vacation, so she rents a room to a couple of Pete's friends in town for a convention.

Gladys's Political Campaign
Gladys campaigns for the presidency of the women's civic league.

Cousin Violet
GS: Tommy Farrell, Alvy Moore. Gladys's Cousin Violet, a fat girl, has sent Gladys's photo to her Navy pen pal implying it is a picture of herself.

The House Next Door
GS: Alvy Moore, Christine Nelson. The house next door is empty but Gladys does a good turn by renting it for a friend.

The Insurance Faker
Gladys uncovers evidence which seems to show that an insurance company is bilking its policyholders.

Skin Deep/The Great Stone Face
GS: Barbara Stuart. Pete gets a raise and a reduction in his workload. He just tells Gladys about the reduction and she thinks less work means less money so she decides to get a job.

The Six Musketeers
Pete and Gladys have planned a weekend in the mountains, but they have to share the cabin with two other couples.

Panhandler
Gladys attends a dress rehearsal of a community play. After the rehearsal, Gladys goes home but without any money.

Gladys Opens Pete's Mail
To keep Gladys from opening his mail, Pete writes a phony letter to himself claiming he is in deep trouble.

The Garage Story
GS: Ernest Truex. Gladys forces Pete to take her father to work with him and then suggests he get Pop a job.

The Orchid Story
Pete learns Pop has been sending off complaint letters to the city government so Pop decides it is time for a change, to start growing orchids instead of writing letters.

Secretary for a Day
GS: Willard Waterman. Gladys wants to run off a batch of resumes for her job-hunting father, but Pete won't allow her to use his duplicating machine.

The Fur Coat Story
GS: John Fiedler. It's Pete and Gladys's anniversary and Gladys wants a fur coat, but Pete wants a motorboat.

Peaceful in the Country
Pete and Gladys are going to spend the weekend at his boss's cabin in the mountains so that Pete can show the place to a couple of prospective buyers.

Junior
GS: Jonathan Hole. Gladys convinces Pete that they should care for his friend's seven-year-old child, but Junior turns out to be a chimp.

Gladys Cooks Pete's Goose
GS: Peter Brocco, Tom Brown. Gladys always garbles Pete's business messages and she is determined to make up for it.

A Study in Gray
Pete's painter cancels out on him, so Gladys decides Pop should paint his den.

Pop's Girlfriend
GS: Fifi D'Orsay. Pop inherits an estate and decides to move into an apartment of his own. Gladys doesn't want Pop to get lonely so she tries to get him a roommate.

Ring-a-Ding-Ding
At a party, Gladys loses an expensive ring in one of the hors d'oeuvres.

The Mannequin Story
GS: Alan Hewitt, Donna Douglas. Invited to a party, Gladys has her eye on a dress she can't afford, so Pop, who has taken a job, thinks he can help.

The Projectionist
GS: Sterling Holloway. Gladys's Cousin Violet returns, still trying to trap a man, so Gladys begins a program designed to reduce her fat relative.

Gladys Goes to College
Gladys goes to school to learn Spanish. Pete, thinking Gladys speaks it well, invites some friends to dinner in a Mexican restaurant, but Gladys doesn't speak Spanish very well.

Crossed Wires
GS: Gene Barry. Gladys picks up the phone to call the movie theater and instead overhears a conversation with a man she thinks is Gene Barry.

Fasten Your Seat Belts
While trying to exchange a cheap piece of luggage, a gift from Pete's boss, Gladys runs into Pete's boss's wife.

The Hoarder and the Boarder
Gladys is unhappy about removing junk from the garage, so she moves it to the spare bedroom. Then Pete tells her he is taking in a boarder.

Second Car
GS: Bob Hopkins. Peggy and Gladys decide to buy a new car with their husbands' money.

Uncle Paul's New Wife
GS: Gale Gordon, Reta Shaw. Uncle Paul and his new bride show up and Gladys must convince them she is not a kook.

Money, Money, Who's Got the Money?
After Pete gets rid of one freeloading boarder, Gladys's nephew Bruce shows up.

Uncle Paul's Insurance
GS: Gale Gordon, Alvy Moore. Pete can't bring himself to sell insurance to Uncle Paul, so he tries hypnotism.

Down with Togetherness
The neighbors are planning to turn a weekend at the lake into a surprise anniversary party for Pete and Gladys, but Gladys gets into a fight with Janet.

Eyewitness
GS: Jerome Cowan, Majel Barrett. Gladys saw an accident and decides to offer her services as a witness.

Three Loves of Gladys
Bruce is blackballed by a college fraternity and Aunt Gladys launches a one-woman investigation to find out who is responsible and why.

Sick, Sick, Sick
Gladys is a contestant on a television giveaway show and wins the big prize with a story about her husband's serious illness, but Pete's boss sees the show and sends him to the hospital.

The Live-In Couple
A bank will award a prize to the person opening the 5000th account and Gladys is determined to win, no matter how long it takes, including sleeping in the bank.

Lover Go Away
GS: Lee Patrick, Byron Foulger, Bob Hastings. In order to stop Aunt Kitty from visiting, Pete and Gladys decide to rent an apartment without a guest room.

Hero in the House
GS: Henry Kulky. When Pete and Gladys go to the theater, a man insults Gladys but Pete decides he is too big to fight with.

Continental Dinner
Gladys suspects Horton, their gardener, has developed a crush on her when he gives her gifts, but is unsure when his girlfriend shows up.

Pete's Hobby
GS: Jesse White, Herb Vigran. After Gladys sells an old car she learns is valuable, she tries to retrieve it only to learn it has been turned into a hot rod.

Who Was That Man?
GS: Byron Foulger, Reva Rose. Gladys's ex-boyfriend is in town and she manages to make a fool of herself by spilling coffee all over herself.

Garden Wedding
GS: Bob Hastings, Will Wright. Pete and Gladys celebrate their tenth anniversary by visiting the place where they were married and the justice of the peace who married them.

Follow That Skeleton
GS: Howard McNear. Gladys is dying to know what is in the trunk of Uncle Paul's car, but she regrets it when she finds a skeleton.

Will the Real Michele Tabour Please Stand Up?
GS: Leonid Kinsky. Gladys's double, a French dancer, disappears before an important press conference and Gladys volunteers to take her place.

The Prize
GS: Tol Avery, Richard Deacon, Barbara Perry. Gladys wins a jingle contest, but she doesn't know what the prize is.

Yak, Yak, Yak
GS: Marjorie Bennett. Uncle Paul's afraid Gladys's talkative nature will spoil a deal he has going with an antique buyer.

Never Forget a Friend
GS: Cliff Norton. Gladys's old friend comes to town and suggests everyone get together for dinner to reconcile an old misunderstanding.

Office Way
GS: Frank Nelson, Nancy Kulp. An efficiency expert has turned Pete's office upside down and Pete becomes upset, sending Gladys to the rescue as his secretary.

The Chocolate Cake Caper
GS: Strother Martin. Uncle Paul believes a thief is after his expensive jade buddha.

Sleepytime Wife
Pete invites a big insurance executive to dinner hoping he might offer Pete a vice presidency, but Gladys has been acting strangely lately.

Maternity House
The Porters are packing for a vacation in the mountains. They promised Cousin Helen and her husband they can use their home while they are away.

Pete's Party Dress
Gladys wants to open a box addressed to Pete's uncle, but it is nailed tight.

The Top Banana
GS: Mickey Rooney. Peter suggests Gladys ask Mickey Rooney to perform at her club's annual benefit show.

Go Help Friends
GS: Cliff Norton. After Pete and Gladys tell a neighbor to watch their house while they are away, they decide not to leave and are faced with the problem of telling their hypersensitive neighbor he is not needed.

The Expectant Gardener
GS: Don Diamond. While rushing to the hairdresser, Gladys locks bumpers with an old truck. She manages to free the car, but not before she hires the other driver as a gardener.

The Lame Excuse
GS: Frank Wilcox. Gladys tells Pete's boss that he is sick, so they can attend a costume party rather than go to dinner with him.

Step on Me
GS: Tom Browne Henry. Gladys wants to buy some new furniture, but Pete is happy with the old furniture.

The Case of the Gossipy Maid
GS: Patsy Kelly. Pete decides it is time to hire a maid, but not for long.

The Arrival
Gladys reminisces about some humorous events from past episodes.

PETER LOVES MARY

On the air 10/12/60, off 5/31/61. NBC. B&W Film. 32 episodes. Broadcast: Oct 1960-May 1961 Wed 10-10:30. Producer: Dan Simon. Synd: Four Star Entertainment.

CAST: Peter Lindsey (played by Peter Lind Hayes), Mary Lindsey (Mary Healy), Wilma (Bea Benaderet), Charlie (Arch Johnson), Happy Richman (Alan Reed, Jr.)

The story of Connecticut dwellers Peter and Mary Lindsey, a show business couple, and their children Leslie and Steve. Typical segments relate Peter and Mary's attempts to divide their time between a career on Broadway and a home life in the country. This series is not airing on any station.

The Suburbanites
GS: Glenn Langan. As the Lindseys settle into their new home, a new TV opening beckons. Peter likes the idea, but Mary doesn't.

High Society
GS: Paul Hartman, Linda Watkin. The big social event of the year is the Haggermeyers' party, so Mary tries to get an invitation.

Wilma
The Lindseys think Wilma, their housekeeper, is acting strangely. They haven't found out yet that she broke a valuable vase.

Make a Million
GS: Allyn Joslyn, Marianne Stewart. Peter thinks he can make a million dollars if he invests in some land offered by fast-talking Jack Crawford.

Life with Father-in-Law
GS: Howard Smith, Harriet MacGibbon. Mary's parents, the Gibneys, have come for a visit. Mrs. Gibney believes Peter and Mary are broke.

The Classic Car
GS: Ronny Graham. The Lindseys plan to spend a week at Lake Placid with Barry and Gloria Watkins. So

Peter and Barry go shopping for a boat but return with an old car.

A Star Is Born
GS: Leo Fuchs, Barbara Heller, Susan Crane. Peter directs Leslie's school play. He finds he has to cut her part because she can't act.

Peter Joins a Committee
GS: Herb Ellis, Marty Ingels. Peter is a failure at trying to raise money for the new school, so he decides to leave town.

The Best Man
GS: Sarah Marshall, Joan Tompkins, David Lewis. Mary and her friends are running for president of their garden club.

Wilma's Phantom Lover
GS: John Astin, Gil Smith. Wilma has a fight with her boyfriend Charlie, so she looks for a new boyfriend in the personal ads.

Peter Gets the Business
GS: Howard Smith, Harriet MacGibbon. Mr. Gibney tries to talk Peter into leaving show business and going into the plastics business.

Tin Pan Ali
GS: Herb Ellis, Donald Buka, Joseph Ruskin. The Lindseys meet the Prince of Taos who is also a composer.

Operation Red Dress
GS: Alvy Moore, Harry Holecombe, Alan Dexter, Barney Phillips. On the way to his Army reunion, Peter is mistaken for an Air Force courier and is sent to a secret missile test site.

The Movie Star
GS: Ralph Bell, Werner Klemperer, Fredd Wayne. Peter tries to talk Mary into joining him in movies.

Horace Gets Into the Act
GS: Terry Huntington. Mr. Gibney talks Mary into leaving the act. He later regrets it when he sees Peter's new partner.

Wilma's Apple Butter
GS: David Lewis. Wilma claims store-bought apple butter is her own. The Lindseys like it so much they plan to sell it.

The Last Train from Oakdell
GS: John McGiver, John Anderson, Claude Stroud, Henry Hunter. Peter joins a committee to replace the old train with a super freeway.

That Certain Age
GS: Yvonne Craig, Richard Gaines, Bill Tennant, James Ragan. While directing the high school play, a student gets a crush on Peter.

The Perfect Father
GS: John Emery, Bob Hastings, John Zaremba. Peter wants to get a TV father role, so he tries to convince the sponsor he is a good father.

Peter Writes a Book
GS: Jack Weston, Wally Vernon. Peter hires a ghost writer to write his autobiography.

Doctor's Dilemma
GS: Stu Erwin, J. Pat O'Malley. Peter gets the town to hold a retirement party for old Doc Bailey.

Getting Peter's Putter
GS: David Lewis, John Fiedler, Arte Johnson. Peter and Bill Rogers race to collect trading stamps to see who can win a set of golf clubs.

Peter Takes Stock
GS: Howard Smith, Ned Glass, Peter Leeds. Peter invests in a failing nightclub.

The Aptitude Test
GS: Elliott Reed, Charles Irving, Frank Behrens. Peter takes an intelligence test and is declared a genius.

Wilma's Uncle Charlie
GS: Wallace Ford. Wilma's uncle visits, which causes Peter to feel left out.

Witness for the Persecution
GS: Lee Krieger, Connie Sanger. Peter witnesses Mr. Gibney's traffic accident but refuses to testify in court.

Peter's Protege
GS: Lennie Weinrib, Herb Ellis. Peter volunteers to help Jerry Arden get into show business.

New Deal for Wilma
GS: Byron Morrow, Betty Garde. Wilma wants a new contract when the Lindseys start taking advantage of her.

Mr. Santini Writes a Letter
GS: Renzo Cesana. The flower shop owner is writing love letters to Mary.

The Bridey Lindsey Story
GS: Reginald Owen, Jack Albertson. Peter falls under the spell of a hypnotist.

No, My Darling Daughter
GS: Bob Crawford, Jr., Bern Hoffman. Peter learns that Leslie has a grade school admirer who plays the stock market.

Birth of a Salesman
GS: Dick Patterson. Nephew Wally becomes a clothing salesman.

PETTICOAT JUNCTION

On the air 9/24/63, off 9/12/70. CBS. Color Film. 148 episodes (currently being syndicated). Sept 1963-Sept 1964 Tue 9-9:30; Sept 1964-Aug 1967 Tue 9:30-10; Sept 1967-Sept 1970 Sat 9:30-10. Producer: Paul Henning. Prod. Co: Filmways. Synd: Viacom.

CAST: Kate Bradley (played by Bea Benaderet), Joe Carson (Edgar Buchanan), Billie Jo (Jeannine Riley, 1963-65; Gunilla Hutton, 1965-66; Meredith MacRae, 1966-70), Bobbie Jo (Pat Woodell, 1963-65; Lori Saunders, 1965-70), Betty Jo (Linda Kaye Henning), Dr. Janet Craig (June Lockhart), Steve Elliot (Mike Minor), Selma Plout (Elvia Allman), Homer Bedlow (Charles Lane), Sam Drucker (Frank Cady).

A depiction of life in Hooterville, a small farm valley. The main characters are Kate Bradley, owner of the Shady Rest Hotel, her three beautiful daughters, and their Uncle Joe Carson, the self-proclaimed manager of the hotel. Later in the series, Dr. Janet Craig replaced Kate and Betty Jo married Steve Elliot, a pilot. A typical story depicts the struggles of the three girls to secure their lives, and the endless attempts of Joe to invest in moneymaking schemes. Cast members from *Green Acres* and *The Beverly Hillbillies* frequently made crossover appearances on this show. The series is still very popular in rural areas. Its first two seasons are not in syndication because they were filmed in black and white.

Dear Minerva
Kate anonymously writes an advice to the lovelorn column for the local paper.

The Baffling Raffle
GS: Eddie Albert, Eva Gabor. Uncle Joe has to get his winning raffle ticket from Kate, who is on jury duty.

The Dog Turns Playboy
GS: Eddie Albert, William Lanteau. The Bradley's dog inherits two hundred dollars.

The Good Luck Ring
GS: Eddie Albert, Eva Gabor, Byron Foulger. Bobbie loses her good luck ring right before a spelling contest.

Joe Carson, General Contractor
GS: Eva Gabor, Eddie Albert. Uncle Joe pretends to be a contractor so he can make some extra money renovating the Douglas's farmhouse.

Bobbie Jo's Sorority
GS: Bobby Pickett. Bobbie Jo finds that she must perform the impossible in order to become a member of the Hooterville High School sorority.

A Doctor in the House
GS: Alan Reed, Jr., Eddie Albert,

Frank Ferguson. Kate objects when the hotel gets its own doctor.

Hooterville a Go-Go
GS: Eddie Albert, Eva Gabor, Milton Frome. Kate's daughters want her to hire a rock and roll singer to perform at a benefit show.

Hooterville Hurricane
GS: Michael Ross, Marjorie Bennett. Uncle Joe becomes a fight promoter with a young muscular plumber as his fighter.

Betty Jo Goes to New York
GS: Eddie Albert, Eva Gabor, Garry Goodrich. After spending a week in New York, Betty Jo returns with a change in her appearance and her personality.

Bedloe's Successor
GS: Donald Curtis. Homer Bedloe returns to Hooterville broken and poor.

The Crowded Wedding Ring
GS: Whit Bissell, Hope Summers. Kate's old boyfriend returns in the hope that she will marry him.

Uncle Joe Plays Post Office
GS: Charlotte Knight, Damian O'Flynn. Uncle Joe moves the post

Meredith MacRae (left), Lori Saunders, and Linda Kaye Henning, in Petticoat Junction.

office to the hotel when he becomes the new postmaster.

What a Trajectory?
GS: Arthur O'Connell. Uncle Joe thinks the mysterious guest at the hotel is a bank robber.

The Butler Did It
GS: Maurice Dallimore. Bobbie Jo wins an English butler in a contest.

Better Never Than Late
GS: Herbert Anderson, Vinton Hayworth, Vaughn Taylor. Kate tries to retrieve a nasty letter she didn't want mailed before it is delivered.

Betty Jo Catches the Bouquet
Betty Jo goes looking for a husband.

Billie Jo's Independence Day
GS: Minerva Urecal. Billie Jo moves away from the hotel and her mother.

Yogurt, Anyone?
Betty Jo poses as a college girl to attract the attentions of a college boy.

Only Boy in the Class
GS: Bobby Pickett. Bobbie Jo asks Kate to help the only boy in the home economics class pass the course.

The County Fair
GS: Pat Buttram. The Bradleys expect to be the big winners at the county fair.

Jury at the Shady Rest
GS: Emory Parnell, Parley Baer. The jury staying at the hotel refuse to decide on a verdict because they like Kate's cooking so much they don't want to leave.

The Invisible Mr. Dobble
GS: Frank Aletter, Russ Conway. Kate thinks she has gone nuts when she learns one of her guests is invisible.

It's Not the Principle, It's the Money
GS: Don Keefer. Joe plans to wreck the hotel in order to pay less taxes.

War of the Hotels
GS: J. Pat O'Malley. Kate holds a hotel war with the owner of the Pixley Hotel.

The Windfall
GS: Hank Patterson, Tom Fadden. While in Pixley, Joe finds a fortune in buried money.

Second Honeymoon
GS: Emmaline Henry, Steve Dunne. A couple celebrating their tenth anniversary comes to the hotel for a second honeymoon.

Kate Sells the Hotel
GS: Hank Patterson, Richard St. John. Kate tries to sell the hotel when she thinks her daughters would rather live in New York.

Kate Bradley, Peacemaker
GS: Eddie Albert. Kate tries to end a fight between Floyd and Charlie.

What Ever Happened to Betty Jo?
Kate thinks Betty Jo ran away to get married when she is late getting home from school.

The Young Matchmakers
GS: Jack Collins. Kate's daughters start a lonely hearts club to find her a husband.

Every Bachelor Should Have a Family
GS: Hugh Beaumont. Kate tries to impress a bachelor who is considering marriage.

Hooterville Valley Project
GS: John Hoyt. Homer Bedloe plans to build a dam which will flood the hotel.

Betty Jo's Bike
Betty Jo starts a babysitting service in order to earn enough money to buy a bike.

Young Love
GS: Tom Lester, Ernest Truex, Richard Hale, Janet Waldo. Joe starts a free wedding and honeymoon contest to get more business for the hotel.

Birdman of Shady Rest
GS: George Chandler. Kate's daughters have a crush on the cropdusting pilot who crashed near the hotel. [This is the first appearance of the character of Steve Elliot who would later marry Betty Jo.]

Hooterville, You're All Heart
GS: Jesse White, Lloyd Corrigan. Steve will lose his plane unless he can get the money to make a payment on it.

The All-Night Party
GS: Tom Lester, Melinda Plowman. Kate refuses to let Bobbie Jo go on an all-night outing with her friends.

Cannonball, Inc.
The town residents take over the operation of the Cannonball, but their constant demands for changes causes the crew to quit.

He Loves Us, He Loves Us Not
The Bradley girls all want to marry Steve.

Kate Grounds Selma Plout
Kate prevents Selma from trying to get Steve to marry her daughter.

Shoplifter at the Shady Rest
The hotel becomes a temporary jail when the sheriff goes on vacation.

The Almost Annual Charity Show
Kate becomes upset when she loses the job as the producer of the annual charity show to Selma.

How Bugged Was My Valley
Joe tries to create some business for Steve.

Twenty-Five Years Too Late
GS: Dennis O'Keefe. Mr. Drucker tells Kate that he is in love with her.

The Runt Strikes Back
Betty surprises her sisters when she dates two men.

Is There a Doctor in the Valley?
GS: Richard Tyler. Homer Bedloe tries to stop the railroad when he learns that its schedule was changed for medical reasons.

The Santa Claus Special
GS: Roy Roberts. Homer Bedloe refuses to allow Kate to hold a Christmas party on the train.

My Daughter the Secretary
Selma plans to cheat Billie Jo out of a weekend in New York.

The Rise and Fall of a Tycoon
Uncle Joe becomes the general manager of the railroad.

Girls! Girls! Girls!
GS: Jack Bannon. The girls invite each other's boyfriends to the Turnabout Dance.

His Highness the Dog
Uncle Joe tries to make some extra money as a dog sitter.

Temperance, Temperance
GS: John Hoyt, Buddy Foster. Kate tries to teach a temperance lecturer that he has been neglecting his son.

A Star Is Born
GS: Walker Edmiston. A talent contest is held in town.

Don't Call Us
GS: Frank Nelson, Jan Arvan. Billie Jo gets a one-night stand as a singer at the Springdale Hotel.

That's Max . . . ?
Billie is shocked when Steve appears to be planning to marry his old girlfriend.

Hey Look Me Over
Billie Jo becomes jealous when Steve dates Betty Jo.

The Fishing Derby
Joe and Sam Drucker hold a fishing contest to boost the hotel's business.

Kate's Big Deal
Kate plans to sell the hotel.

Author! Author!
Bobbie Jo wins a poetry award and begins hanging out with some beatniks.

Kate's Cousin Mae
GS: Shirley Mitchell. Kate's cousin comes for a visit.

That Was the Night That Was
GS: Frank DeVol. Everyone thinks the new guest at the hotel is from outer space.

The Eternal Rectangle
Bobbie Jo and Betty Jo fight over Billie Jo's boyfriend Steve.

Steve's Ol' Buddy
Steve's old Air Force friend comes for a visit.

A House Divided
The election of a new county supervisor divides the house over the question of who should get the job.

Go Away, Fat
Cousin Mae turns the hotel into a fat farm.

Is This My Daughter?
GS: David Watson. Betty Jo returns from her European trip a changed woman.

It's Not Easy to Be a Mother
GS: Herb Vigran, Herbie Faye. Kate becomes suspicious of her daughter's actions.

One Dozen Roses
Betty Jo has a secret admirer.

Pop Goes the Question
Uncle Joe tells everyone that Steve is going to marry Betty Jo.

*You Know I Can't Hear You When
the Thunder Is Clapping*
Kate begins to worry when she realizes
that her youngest daughter is going to
get married and leave her.

A Cottage for Two
Betty Jo and Steve fight over their
new house.

Mind If We Join Your Wedding?
Floyd tries to convince Steve that they
should have a double wedding when
he announces that he is also getting
married.

Meet the In-Laws
GS: Hugh Beaumont, Ann Doran.
Steve's parents come to meet Betty Jo
and her family.

With This Gown I Thee Wed
GS: Richard Hale. Betty Jo has to decide from four gowns the one she
wants to wear at her wedding.

Kate's Birthday
Kate believes that Betty Jo and Steve
forgot about her birthday when they
left on their honeymoon.

The Honeymoon Is Over
Betty Jo and Steve have their first
fight.

A Horse on You, Mr. Bedloe
Homer Bedloe finds another way to
get rid of the train.

Kate's Day in Court
GS: Ralph Manza, Parley Baer, Jack
Bannon. Kate tries to fight a jaywalk-
ing ticket.

Uncle Joe and the Master Plan
GS: Reginald Gardiner. Joe tries to
impress a representative of a hotel
association.

All That Buzzes Ain't Bees
Uncle Joe becomes a bee keeper, but
finds that his bees are bothering Betty
Jo and Steve.

All Sales Final
GS: William O'Connell. Steve and
Betty Jo both buy new furniture with-
out telling each other.

The Power of the Press
GS: Geoff Edwards, Burt Mustin.
Bobbie Jo and her boyfriend take over
the town newspaper.

Steve, the Apple Polisher
GS: Frank Wilcox, Joi Lansing. Betty
Jo tells Steve to become an apple pol-
isher to win a big cropdusting contract.

The Barbershop Quartet
Joe is thrown off the barbershop quartet right before a local talent contest.

Higgins Come Home
A fight starts over the family dog.

Girl of Our Dreams
GS: Paul Hartman. Joe and Sam
Drucker find that the girl they once
dated no longer recognizes them.

Uncle Joe Runs the Hotel
Joe takes over the hotel and is shunned
when he is accused of throwing an old
man out of the hotel when he didn't
pay his rent.

Billie Jo's First Record
GS: Del Moore, J. Pat O'Malley. A
record promoter makes up a phony
publicity story in order to sell Billie
Jo's first record.

Mae's Helping Hand
GS: Rosemary De Camp, Shirley
Mitchell. Aunt Helen comes to help
run the hotel when Mae almost wrecks
it.

Bad Day at Shady Rest
GS: Paul Hartman, Geoff Edwards,
Alan Reed, Jr. Joe captures a bank
robber.

Cannonball for Sale
Homer Bedloe plans to sell the railroad.

Ring-a-Ding-Dong
GS: Dabbs Greer. Betty Jo loses her wedding ring down the kitchen sink drain.

Kate's Homecoming
Kate comes home and finds everything as crazy as she left it.

Birthplace of a Future President
GS: Regis Toomey. Steve decides to take Betty Jo to a hospital in Baltimore to have her baby.

The Singing Sweethearts
GS: Dave Ketchum, Sid Melton. Betty Jo appears on a TV show as a member of the Singing Sweethearts.

Only a Husband
Steve goes fishing with Joe when he feels that Betty Jo is getting all the attention.

The Valley Has a Baby
GS: Eddie Albert, Eva Gabor. Betty Jo finds that she has to operate the railroad herself in order to get to the hospital in time to have the baby.

Granny, the Baby Expert
GS: Irene Ryan. Granny goes to Hooterville to care for the new baby, but she loses her glasses and mistakes the family dog for the baby.

Wings
GS: Richard Arlen, Buddy Rogers. The town holds a premiere for a 40-year-old movie.

The Lady Doctor
The town becomes upset when they learn that the doctor's new associate is a woman. [This episode introduces the character of Dr. Janet Craig.]

The Sneaky Ways of a Woman Who Is Both Beautiful and Smart
Dr. Craig tries to win over the men of the town.

The Strange Case of Joseph P. Carson
Joe fakes an illness to get rid of Dr. Craig.

Bye, Bye Doctor
GS: Dennis Morgan. Dr. Craig falls in love and may leave the valley.

First Night Out
Betty Jo and Steve go out for the evening. When they return, they find that the baby and the babysitter are in jail.

A Cake for Granny
GS: Irene Ryan, Nancy Kulp. Homer Bedloe returns to sabotage the railroad.

The Feminine Mistake
Bobbie Jo decides to leave Hooterville.

The Ballad of the Everyday Housewife
GS: Benny Rubin, Eva Gabor. Bobbie Jo steps in when it appears Steve has taken Betty Jo for granted.

The Christening
Betty Jo finds that she has five volunteers to be the godfather of little Kathy Jo.

Billie Jo and the Big Big Star
GS: Rich Little. A comedian makes fun of the people of Hooterville.

Steve's New Job
Steve must decide whether or not to take a job offer in New York.

The Cannonball Bookmobile
GS: Betty White. A beautiful librarian causes rivalry among the men of Hooterville.

A Man Called Cyrus Plout
A fight almost wrecks the plans for the annual Hooterville Founder's Day celebration.

Joe Saves the Post Office
Joe goes to Washington to save Sam's post office.

I'm Allergic to Daddy
Kathy Jo is allergic to her father Steve.

Uncle Joe Retires
Joe announces his retirement.

The Organ Fund
The townspeople try to raise enough money to buy a new organ for the church.

The Great Race
GS: Hal Smith, Jonathan Hole. The future of the hotel will be determined by the winner of a race between the Cannonball and an overland taxi.

Tune in Next Year
The townspeople try to prevent Dr. Craig from leaving to work for a famous doctor.

By the Book
GS: Kenneth Washington. Steve performs a cropdusting job without knowing he underbid for the assignment by $1800.

Make Room for Baby
The dog feels neglected when Steve, Betty Jo and the baby move into the hotel.

The Game Warden
GS: Jonathan Daly. Joe is threatened with a jail sentence when he is caught by the game warden for catching too many fish.

The Other Woman
GS: Marvin Kaplan, Pat Buttram. Betty Jo and Steve's home is disturbed by intruders.

One of Our Chickens Is Missing
GS: Dean Stanton, Jack Bannon, Jonathan Daly. The game warden is afraid to arrest two motorcyclists who he suspects are poachers.

The Three Queens
GS: Hal Peary. Dr. Craig and the three Bradley girls are all contestants in a beauty contest.

The Glen Tinker Caper
GS: Glenn Ash, Sharann Hisamoto. A singer tries to smuggle a Vietnamese orphan into the country by taking her to Hooterville.

The Tenant
GS: Frank Aletter, Leslie Parrish. Billie Jo tries to get rid of a beautiful authoress.

A Most Momentous Occasion
GS: Pat Buttram. Joe installs a bathroom at the hotel to keep Steve and Betty Jo from moving out.

Sorry Doctor, I Ain't Taking No Shots
Dr. Craig tries to convince a hillbilly family to let her give them flu shots.

The Camping Tree
Bobbie Jo's boyfriend Orrin saves Uncle Joe from a hungry bear.

Kathy Jo's First Birthday
GS: Buck Buchanan, Herbie Faye. Uncle Joe and the baby go to jail, causing her to almost miss her birthday party.

The Golden Spike Ceremony
GS: Frank Wilcox, Harry Hickox. Joe strikes oil when he drives in the golden spike, connecting Hooterville to Pixley.

Goodbye Mr. Chimp
GS: Herb Vigran. Joe tries to get rid of the pet chimp who is wrecking the hotel.

But I've Never Been in Erie, Pa.
GS: Rudy Vallee. An industrialist offers Joe a chance to make a fortune.

How to Arrange a Marriage
GS: Greg Mullavey. Bobbie Jo tries to soften up Billie Jo's boyfriend for marriage.

Selma Plout's Plot
GS: Jack Sheldon. Selma's plan to get her daughter married almost wrecks Steve's business.

With This Ring . . .
GS: Merlin Olsen.   Everyone thinks
Orrin is going to propose to Bobbie Jo
when he buys a ring.

The Valley's New Owner
Orrin finds an old deed which makes
him the legal owner of the entire valley.

Steve's Uncle George
GS: Don Ameche.   Steve's trouble-
making uncle comes for a visit.

Susan B. Anthony, I Love You
Billie Jo tries to get a women's liberation movement started in the valley.

Spare That Cottage
GS: Robert Rockwell.   Steve and
Betty Jo's cottage is in the way of the
new highway.

Whiplash, Whiplash
GS: Buddy Lester.   Selma tries to sue

Joe for whiplash after she falls from
his hammock.

Last Train to Pixley
GS: Percy Helton, Parley Baer.   The
railway company decides to sell the
Cannonball for a tax write-off.

Love Rears Its Ugly Head
GS: Roy Roberts.   Billie Jo tries to
spread love through sensitivity training.

No, No, You Can't Take Her Away
GS: Keith Andes.   The Bradleys believe that the handsome doctor coming
to visit Dr. Craig will take her away
with him.

Betty Jo's Business
GS: Dodo Denney, Nancy Marlowe.
Betty Jo starts a day nursery to earn
extra money.

THE PHIL SILVERS SHOW

On the air 9/20/55, off 9/11/59. CBS. B&W Film. 138 episodes. Broadcast:
Sept 1955-Oct 1955 Tue 8:30-9; Nov 1955-Feb 1958 Tue 8-8:30; Feb 1958-
Sept 1959 Fri 9-9:30. Producer: Nat Hiken. Synd: Viacom.
CAST: Sgt. Ernie Bilko (played by Phil Silvers), Col. John Hall (Paul Ford),
Duane Doberman (Maurice Gosfield), Sgt. Ritzik (Joe E. Ross), Henshaw (Allan
Melvin), Rocco (Harvey Lembeck), Paparelli (Billy Sands), Joan (Elisabeth
Fraser).
The saga of Master Sergeant Ernie Bilko stationed in Roseville, Kansas. Bilko,
a master con artist, is totally dedicated to acquiring money.   Typical segments
show Bilko swindling fellow soldiers or running illegal gambling operations.   The
series is seen on a few scattered intelligent stations.   The show is also called *Bilko*
and *You'll Never Get Rich.*

New Recruits
Bilko tries to get money from the new
recruits so he can win back his losses
in a poker game.

Empty Store
GS: Michael Dreyfuss.   Bilko rents an
empty store and refuses to explain
why he bought it.

The Horse
GS: John Alexander.   Bilko and his
men buy a sick racehorse and hope to
cure him and make a fortune when he
races.

Eating Contest
GS: Bern Hoffman, Janet Ward, Fred
Gwynne.   Bilko enters one of his men
in the camp eating contest.

Kids in Trailers
Bilko babysits in a trailer so one of his men can go away with his wife for a few days.

Reunion
GS: John Anderson, Henry Beckman. Bilko discovers that living in the Army is not as bad as he used to think.

The Hoodlum
GS: Paul Porter. One of Bilko's men tries to get thrown out of the Army.

A.W.O.L.
GS: Pat Hingle. Bilko attends a wedding when he goes to Chicago to pick up a soldier who is AWOL.

Singing Contest
Bilko enters his men in a singing contest so he can win a free trip to Miami.

WAC
GS: Barbara Barrie, Jane Dulo. Bilko and a WAC sergeant fight over who will have their own personal jeep.

War Games
GS: Don Keefer. Bilko finds himself in the middle between a wedding and Army war games.

The Twitch
GS: Charlotte Rae, John Stephen. Bilko and his men are ordered to attend a lecture on Beethoven by a captain's wife.

The Centennial
GS: Al Checco. The colonel orders that all gambling be stopped in the camp.

Bivouac
Bilko fakes a disease so he won't have to go on bivouac.

Rich Kid
GS: Mark Rydell, Dodie Goodman. Bilko plans to use a rich kid's money to buy a saloon.

Investigation
GS: Ralph Dunn, Howard Freeman. Bilko turns the camp into a slum in order to get money from Congress to fix up the camp.

Hollywood
GS: Jule Styne, Howard Smith, David Sheiner. Bilko goes to Hollywood to act as a technical director on a war film.

Hair
GS: Elisabeth Fraser. Bilko gets a toupee to impress a girl.

Revolutionary War
GS: Ford Rainey, Charles McClelland. Bilko learns that his ancestor served with George Washington.

Boxer
GS: Bill Hellinger. Bilko learns that one of his men is an ex-fighter, so he decides to use him to win some money.

Mardi Gras
GS: Constance Ford. Bilko plans to teach a society girl a lesson when she refuses to be the queen of the motor pool mardi gras.

Transfer
GS: Bob Hastings. Bilko asks to be transferred when he disagrees with the colonel.

The Rest Cure
GS: David White. Bilko gets the whole camp to act like they have all gone crazy in the hopes they will be sent to a rest camp.

Dinner at Sowicis
Bilko tries to show his girlfriend Joan how married couples really live, in order to discourage her from proposing to him.

Army Memoirs
Bilko is courtmartialed and reduced to a private.

Miss America
GS: Judith Lowry. Bilko is convinced that a potential beauty queen lives right near the camp.

Furlough in New York
Bilko tries to avoid Joan while on a furlough to New York.

The Court-Martial
GS: Zippy, the chimp. Bilko is blamed when a chimp is inducted into the Army.

The Big Uranium Strike
Bilko discovers uranium beneath the colonel's living room.

The Con Men
GS: Danny Dayton, Grant Richards. Bilko tries to teach Doberman to beware of card sharks.

Bilko and the Beast
GS: George Matthews. The colonel sends for a tough sergeant to put Bilko and his men in their places.

The Physical Check-Up
Bilko goes on a 20-mile hike to prove he is in perfect shape.

Recruiting Sergeant
GS: King Calder. Bilko gets a tip on a horse but can't leave the base to place the bet.

Bilko in Wall Street
GS: Morton Stevens, Jack Sheehan. Bilko helps an old friend get ahead in the banking business.

Platoon in the Movies
Bilko produces a musical Army training film.

It's for the Birds
GS: Fred Gwynne, Joe Verdi. One of Bilko's men would be great on a quiz show, but he hits his head and forgets everything he knows.

Bilko Goes to College
GS: Robert Strauss, Harry Holcombe, Bobby Morse. Bilko teaches motor pool techniques at a local college.

Bilko's War Against Culture
GS: Dina Merrill. A beautiful officer is assigned to take the men's interests away from gambling.

Bilko's Engagement
GS: Terry Carter. Bilko finds that he has become engaged to Joan because of a mixup at a jewelry store.

The Face on the Recruiting Poster
GS: Tom Poston. Doberman gets picked to become the new face on the recruiting posters.

The Girl from Italy
GS: Anna Rosselli. Bilko helps a friend find romance.

The Song of the Motor Pool
GS: David White. Bilko finds that the Signal Corps has stolen the tune he was going to use for the new motor pool song.

A Mess Sergeant Can't Win
Bilko tries to lose a bet to help his friend but finds that he can't ever lose.

Doberman's Sister
Bilko tries to find a date for Doberman's visiting sister. They all think she is a real beauty, when she really is a lookalike for her brother.

Where There's a Will
GS: Bruce Kirby. Bilko tries to help a friend to collect his inheritance.

Bilko's Tax Trouble
GS: Alan Hewitt, Dan Frazer. Bilko's tax return is being investigated by mistake.

Mink, Incorporated
Bilko opens a mink farm at the camp in order to pay back the money he borrowed for the men.

Sgt. Bilko Presents Ed Sullivan
GS: Ed Sullivan, Ray Bloch.   Bilko

goes to New York to appear on the Ed Sullivan show.

Bilko Gets Some Sleep
GS: Robert Webber. The camp psychiatrist helps Bilko reform his ways, or so everyone thinks.

Love That Guardhouse
GS: Tom Poston. The colonel tries to keep Bilko from getting hold of Ritzik's money.

The Blue Blood of Bilko
Bilko gets some society people to allow an Army father to attend his son's wedding to their daughter.

Sgt. Bilko Presents Bing Crosby
GS: Bing Crosby, Everett Crosby. Bing Crosby entertains at Fort Baxter.

Bilko Goes to Monte Carlo
Bilko takes the platoon's money to Monte Carlo where he plans to test his new gambling system.

Bilko Enters Politics
Bilko backs Doberman as a candidate for the office of mayor of Roseville.

Bilko's Television Idea
GS: Danny Dayton, Dagmar. A TV comic comes to the fort to look for some new material.

The Son of Bilko
GS: Joe Silver. Bilko acts like a father to a practical-joking orphaned draftee.

Rock 'n' Roll Rookie
GS: Tom Gilson. A rock singer named Elvin Pelvin is assigned to Bilko in order to keep him away from his fans.

Bilko's Black Magic
GS: Gerald Hiken. Bilko goes after the back pay of a soldier who was marooned on an island since 1942.

Bilko Goes South
Bilko and his men volunteer for a special project so they can spend the winter in Florida.

Bilko Goes 'Round the World
GS: Mike Todd. This episode is a satire on the film "Around the World in Eighty Days."

The Mess Hall Mess
Bilko steals a recipe from a French chef to enter a cooking contest.

The Secret Life of Sergeant Bilko
GS: Phillip Coolidge. Bilko tries to teach a reporter a lesson when he tries to prove that GIs are stealing important Army secrets.

Radio Station B-I-L-K-O
Bilko opens a radio station on the base to make some fast money.

Bilko the Marriage Broker
GS: Biff McGuire. Bilko and his men try to get a tough officer married off.

The Big Scandal
GS: Julie Newmar. Bilko gets the colonel's wife involved in a big scandal.

Bilko Acres
Bilko buys the swampland next to the camp when he hears that the camp is going to be abandoned.

Bilko's Perfect Day
GS: Bob Hastings, Danny Dayton. Bilko finally has a day of good fortune.

The Colonel Breaks Par
GS: Sam Snead. The colonel finally plays a good game of golf with the help of Sam Snead.

Show Segments
GS: Ed Sullivan. Scenes of past shows that didn't make it on the air because they ran too long.

His Highness, Doberman
GS: Bruce Kirby. Doberman is thrown out of his girlfriend's house by her filthy rich parents.

The Big Man Hunt
GS: Bert Freed, Bob Gist. Bilko plans to become the part owner of a diamond mine.

Bilko's Boys' Town
GS: Sandy Kenyon.   Bilko opens a boys' camp at the fort to earn some extra money.

Bilko F.O.B. Detroit
Bilko goes to Detroit to pick up a shipment of trucks.

Bilko's Valentine
Bilko tries to get an assignment to a fort in South Carolina so he can get his girlfriend to rejoin the Army.

Bilko's Double Life
In New York, Bilko is mistaken for a lookalike millionaire.

Papa Bilko
Bilko tries to explain why the girl he met in France calls him papa.

Bilko Buys a Club
Bilko plans to open a nightclub near the fort.

Hillbilly Whiz
GS: Yogi Berra, Whitey Ford, Red Barber, Dick Van Dyke, Phil Rizzuto. Bilko finds that one of his men could be a great baseball player.

Sgt. Bilko Presents
Bilko tries to find someone to back his new play.

Cherokee Ernie
Ernie finds a clause in a treaty which would give Oklahoma back to the Indians.

Bilko Talks in His Sleep
Bilko gives away his gambling secrets when he talks in his sleep.

Bilko and the Flying Saucers
Bilko claims he sees a flying saucer so he can go to Washington to keep a date with a singer.

Lieutenant Bilko
Bilko finds that the Army has failed to cancel his battlefield commission.

Bilko's Cousin
GS: Dick Van Dyke. Bilko's country cousin comes to visit the fort.

Bilko at Bay
Bilko tries to get some money so he can go on a furlough to New York.

Bilko's Pigeons
Bilko is told to get rid of the fort's carrier pigeons.

Bilko and the Colonel's Secretary
Bilko gets to choose the colonel's new secretary.

Doberman the Crooner
Bilko becomes Doberman's manager when he learns that he is a great singer.

Cyrano De Bilko
GS: Lee Meriwether, Kay Medford. Bilko proposes to a woman he doesn't love.

The Colonel's Reunion
Bilko fights back when the colonel tries to stop him from gambling.

Bilko Saves Ritzik's Marriage
Bilko brings Ritzik and his wife back together.

Bilko, the Art Lover
GS: Alan Alda. Bilko tries to help a father and son get back together over a fight about the boy's future as an artist.

Bilko the Genius
GS: Mason Adams, David Sheiner, Graham Jarvis, Phil Foster.   Bilko introduces the Army intellectuals to gambling.

Bilko, Male Model
GS: David White. Bilko becomes the high-fashion model with the friendly face.

The Colonel's Inheritance
Bilko invests the colonel's $5000 inheritance in the stock market.

Bilko's Honeymoon
GS: Gretchen Wyler.   Bilko dresses one of his men as a woman so he can get an all-expense paid trip.

Bilko's Chinese Restaurant
GS: John Lee.   Bilko opens a Chinese restaurant but then learns that he and his men are being transferred to an island.

Bilko's TV Pilot
GS: Alexander Scourby, Jane Dulo. Bilko produces a pilot film for a TV western starring Doberman.

Operation Love
GS: Peggy Cass.   The WACs have themselves transferred because their boyfriends spend more time gambling with Bilko than with them.

Bilko Retires from Gambling
Colonel Hall hires a card expert to teach Bilko a lesson about gambling.

Bilko's Vacation
Bilko tries to get the whole platoon to vacation at a lodge so he can get a free vacation.

Bilko's Insurance Company
GS: Orson Bean.   Bilko tries to open an insurance company but is wiped out when he has to pay out his first benefit.

Bilko's Prize Poodle
GS: Barnard Hughes.   Bilko tries to win a dog show prize with the dog he found.

Bilko's School Days
GS: Frank Marth.   Bilko learns that the Army is opening up a school for recruits nearby, which means more money for Bilko to win gambling.

Joan's Big Romance
GS: Richard Derr, Jane Dulo.   Joan decides to teach Ernie a lesson by making him jealous.

Gold Fever
Bilko gets the whole camp moved out west in order to prospect for gold.

Bilko's DeLuxe Tours
Bilko invests the platoon's money in the bus tour business.

Bilko vs. Covington
GS: Keefe Brasselle, Iggy Wolfington. Bilko meets a sergeant who is better at gambling than he is.

Bilko's Big Woman Hunt
GS: Hildy Parks, Elliott Reed, Horace McMahon, Paul Lynde.   Bilko falls for a cute dancing teacher.

Bilko's Vampire
GS: Paul Reed.   Bilko tries to cure Ritzik who, after watching too many horror films, thinks he is turning into a vampire.

Bilko, the Potato Sack King
GS: Herb Voland, Richard Keith. Bilko becomes the sales manager for a burlap bag company.

Bilko's Allergy
Bilko becomes allergic to playing cards.

Bilko Joins the Navy
Bilko finds himself on an aircraft carrier headed for Alaska when he dresses up as a sailor in order to join a Navy crap game.

Bilko's Giveaway
GS: Morey Amsterdam, Frank Albertson.   Bilko wins a prize on a quiz show, but now finds that he must get rid of it because he can't pay the tax on it.

Bilko and the Chaplain
GS: Harold Huber, Donald Barry.   Bilko and the chaplain find themselves in jail, thanks to Ernie.

Bilko's Secret Mission
GS: Al Hodge. Bilko goes on a secret mission to Yucca Flats, but first makes a side trip to Las Vegas.

Bilko and the Medium
GS: Charlotte Rae. Bilko holds a phony seance to fleece Ritzik out of his money.

Bilko's Bopster
GS: Ronny Graham, Larry Storch. Bilko tries to form an Army jazz band when a drummer is assigned to his platoon.

Bilko's Hollywood Romance
GS: Leon Belasco, Frank Maxwell. Bilko is picked by a publicity agent to become the boyfriend of a movie star.

Bilko's Grand Hotel
GS: Irwin Corey, Jane Dulo. Bilko opens a hotel, only to have two soldiers burn it down.

Bilko's Credit Card
GS: Marcel Hillaire. Bilko creates a diner's club card for GIs only.

Viva Bilko
GS: Harold Huber, Leon Belasco, Carlos Montalban, Arny Freeman. While in Mexico, Bilko and his friends have a run-in with some bank robbers.

The Colonel's Promotion
Bilko tries to get the colonel promoted by getting him to join the President when he plays golf.

Bilko's Sharpshooter
GS: Peggy Cass. Bilko tries to turn a sharpshooter into a famous personality.

Bilko's Formula 7
GS: Natalie Schafer. Bilko creates a wrinkle cream made from applejack and crankcase oil.

Warrant Officer Paparelli
Bilko gets one of his men promoted to warrant officer.

Bilko's Ape Man
Bilko dresses up Doberman in an ape suit in the hopes of breaking into the movies.

Bilko's Godson
Bilko tries to enroll his godson in college 20 years ahead of time.

Guinea Pig Bilko
GS: Dan Frazer, Jim Boles. Bilko stops gambling after he takes a tranquilizer.

Bilko the Butler
Bilko plans to meet a wealthy family but finds himself as the butler at a dinner party.

Ritzik Goes Civilian
Ritzik leaves the Army to get away from Bilko.

Bilko's Small Car
Bilko turns a jeep into a small foreign car in order to go into the auto business.

Doberman, Missing Heir
GS: Ronald Long, Jason Evers, Jane Kean. Doberman becomes a millionaire, but refuses to give any money to Bilko.

Bilko's Casino
GS: Murray Matheson. Bilko finds one place in California where gambling is legal.

The Colonel's Second Honeymoon
Bilko vacations at the same resort as Colonel Hall and his wife.

Bilko in Outer Space
GS: Paul Lynde. Bilko and two men play poker in what seems to be a dummy space chamber.

The Bilko Boycott
GS: Jane Kean, Jane Dulo. Bilko sets out to gamble with the women when the men no longer want to gamble with him.

Weekend Colonel
GS: Jane Dulo. Bilko gets a look-alike for the colonel who turns the officers' club into a casino.

PLEASE DON'T EAT THE DAISIES

On the air 9/14/65, off 9/2/67. NBC. Color Film. 58 episodes. Broadcast: Sept 1965-Aug 1966 Tue 8-8:30; Sept 1966-Sept 1967 Sat 8-8:30. Producer: Paul West. Prod Co/Synd: MGM TV.

CAST: Joan Nash (played by Patricia Crowley), Jim Nash (Mark Miller), Kyle Nash (Kim Tyler), Joel Nash (Brian Nash), Tracy Nash (Joe Fithian), Trevor Nash (Jeff Fithian), Herb Thornton (King Donovan), Marge Thornton (Shirley Mitchell).

The story of a Ridgemont, N.Y. family headed by James Nash, an English professor, whose wife Joan is a freelance magazine writer. Typical episodes deal with the pressures the parents feel in raising their four young sons and in trying to stimulate their own careers. The series is sometimes seen on small independent stations.

My Eldest Child
GS: Ned Glass. Joan's column is a hit with everyone except Jim.

How About Two Gorillas?
Jim and Joan try to collaborate on an act for the school show.

Who's Kicking That Gong Around?
GS: Robert Nichols. Joan tries to write her column if the kids will let her.

Dinner on the Rocks
A problem in the kitchen occurs when Joan tries to fix a meal for Jim's faculty friend.

We're Bigger Than They Are But . . .
GS: Alan Hewitt. No one at home or school can tell the twins apart.

Two Seats on the Moon Shot
GS: Steve Franken. While in a restaurant, a man offers Joan an expense-paid trip to New York.

Somewhere George Is Calling
GS: Reginald Denny. In order to raise money to buy gifts, Kyle and Joel conduct tours through their house.

Shape Up or Ship Out
Joan puts Joel in charge of the twins.

Don't Fool Around with the Man Upstairs
GS: Glenn Kessler, Bill Zuckert. Joel feels guilty when he goes to a carnival instead of going to Sunday school.

Of Hitches and Stitches and Big Round Dogs
Joan tries to make her sister-in-law's wedding a success.

Very Very Huckleberry
GS: Bonnie Franklin, Oliver McGowan. Joan panics when the boys plan to go to sea and end up on a rickety raft.

It's Lad By a Nose
GS: Janet Waldo. Joel finds that he is allergic to Lad, the family dog.

Big Brass Blonde
GS: Audrey Meadows. Jim and Joan await a movie star's appraisal of their play.

The Big Train
GS: Dub Taylor. A strange thunderstorm occurs every ten years, causing someone to disappear.

Swing That Indian Club
GS: Clint Howard. Joan plays hostess to Kyle's Indican club, unaware that he wants to quit.

The Pied Piper of Ridgemont
GS: J. Pat O'Malley. Joan's father pays a visit after seven years in Africa.

Say U.N.C.L.E.
GS: Robert Vaughn, David McCallum. The twins are convinced that their father is a secret agent.

Nobody's Perfect
GS: Paul Newlan, Jonathan Hole. Joan forgets to pay a parking ticket, so Jim goes to jail.

My Good Friend What's His Name
GS: Ed Asner. Jim tries to recall the name of his former classmate he invited to dinner.

Monster in the Basement
GS: Leon Ames. The Nashes try to fix their old furnace before a visiting VIP arrives.

Wring Out the Welcome Mat
GS: Pat Carroll, Gene Blakely. A leaky roof convinces the Nashes that their house is a lemon.

Move Over Mozart
GS: Alice Ghostley. Joan tries to guide Joel's musical career after she learns he has an unusual aptitude for music.

Who's Walking Under the Bed?
GS: Enid Markey, Melinda Plowman. Jim's request for a raise finally makes it to the dean.

How Now Hausfrau
GS: Jesse White, Robert Emhardt. A newspaper columnist with a reputation-destroying newspaper wants to interview Joan.

Big Man on Campus
GS: Laurie Sibbald, Ned Glass, Bonnie Franklin. Joan tries to keep Jim from reading her unfinished play.

The Magnificent Muldoon
GS: Frank Wilcox, Burgess Meredith. The twins invite a hobo to dinner on the same night Jim entertains his boss.

The Leaning Tower of Ridgemont
GS: Judi Merideth, Dub Taylor. The Nashes face eviction when a building inspector condemns their house.

Mine Is the Luck of the Irish
GS: J. Pat O'Malley. Joan's father tries to get the Nashes to invest in a uranium mine.

Night of Knights
GS: Doodles Weaver, Bonnie Franklin. Jim's drama class tries to make his birthday a memorable one.

The Purple Avenger
GS: Dom DeLuise. The twins learn that Joan once dated their favorite TV hero.

My Mother's Name Is Fred
GS: Louis Quinn, George Ives. Joan sells an article to a girlie magazine under another name.

A Hunting We Will Go
GS: David Brian, Maxine Stuart. Jim has to entertain a visiting sportsman.

At Home with the Faculty
GS: Hans Conreid, Peter Hebla. The Nashes prepare for an appearance on a TV show.

The Holdouts
The boys try to get a share of the money Joan got for an article about their antics.

Trouble Right Here in Ridgemont City
Joan and Marge both claim ownership to a winning raffle ticket.

Black Is the Color of My Love's Eye
GS: Arch Johnson, Cindy Eileher. A neighborhood boy has been giving Joel black eyes.

My Son the Genius
Joel gets a high IQ score leading everyone to think he is a genius.

The End of the Trailer
GS: Bill Quinn. Jim tries to talk the dean out of buying his old trailer.

My Son the Actor
Joan wonders if the kids have any acting ability.

Of Haunted Houses, Little Boys and a Ghost Named Malcolm
GS: Harry Townes. A drifter secretly moves into the Nashes' house.

And What Does Your Husband Do?
GS: George Fenneman. Jim is jealous when Joan is named Woman of the Year.

Just for Laughs
GS: Charlie Ruggles. At an auction, Joan tries to retrieve the family tax return which is glued to the twins' painting.

The Guardian
Joan gets her arm stuck in the garbage disposal.

Look Who's Talking
GS: Harry Hilcox. The boys spread a false rumor that Joan is expecting a baby.

Peace, It's Wonderful
Joan and Jim have a fight when they try to help Herb settle an argument.

The Silent Butler Spoke
GS: Whit Bissell. The Nashes hire a former thief to work in their home.

The Officer of the Court
Herb is representing Jim and Joan in two different cases, which is causing him to become confused.

The Cupid Machine
GS: Donald Harrom. Joan signs up with a computer dating service in order to write an article.

The Play's the Thing
GS: John Fiedler. Jim's reputation as a drama coach is at stake when Joan's play is entered in a drama competition.

None So Righteous
GS: The Righteous Brothers. The Righteous Brothers perform in a PTA musical.

Remember Lake Serene
GS: Stephanie Powers. Joan and Marge plan to marry off her bachelor friend.

Pest in the House
GS: Harry Hilcox, Kathleen Freeman. House guest Herb forgets to do his share of the chores.

Help Desperately Wanted
GS: Ellen Corby. The Nashes' new maid is extremely slow moving.

Just While You're Resting
GS: Ellen Corby. Joan's new maid is all heart but little help.

When I Was a Young Man
Jim and Joan remember the early days when they were first married.

Professor Please
GS: Rory Martin. A wealthy woman comes between Jim and Joan's marriage.

A Matter of Concentration
GS: Ed Perry. Jim's pride is hurt when Joan buys gifts for everyone and he doesn't.

The Day the Play Got Away
GS: Bobs Watson. Jim begins his sabbatical full of doubts. It seems he can't concentrate on his writing.

PRIDE OF THE FAMILY

On the air 10/2/53, off 9/24/54. ABC. B&W Film. 40 episodes. Broadcast: Oct 1953-Sept 1954 ABC Fri 9-9:30. Producer: Unknown. Prod Co: Revue Studios. Synd: Universal/MCA.

CAST: Albie Morrison (played by Paul Hartman), Catherine Morrison (Fay Wray), Ann Morrison (Natalie Wood), Junior Morrison (Bobby Hyatt).

The story of the Morrison family, Albie, the advertising head of a small-town newspaper, his wife Catherine, and their two kids. Episodes depict the struggles of a local businessman to raise his family and at the same time deal with the pressures of the advertising world. This series is unaired in the U.S.

Pride of the Family [Pilot]
Albie tries to prove to his family that he really does like the finer things in life.

Albie and New Catherine
Catherine decides to spend less time on her household chores and more time with her children.

Albie Babysits
Junior takes a job as a babysitter, but it isn't long before the whole family is asked to help him.

Albie Buys a Sports Coat
At the annual Board of Directors meeting, Albie is supposed to deliver a very conservative financial speech. He plans to give it while wearing a very loud sports coat.

Albie Feels His Age
Albie has become convinced that he has become old before his time.

Bringing Back Romance
Albie tries to stage a surprise birthday party for his wife.

Albie Sells a House
Albie is looking to sell his house because there is only one bathroom and everyone wants to use it at the same time.

Albie the Clown
Albie gets a chance to play a clown for the hospitalized orphans.

Albie's Comfort Campaign
Albie tries to perform a good deed for his family and winds up giving them a good scare.

Albie's Discipline Campaign
Albie decides to be more strict with the children.

Albie's Dishwasher
Albie decides to spend a quiet afternoon at home, but his plans are upset when his wife decides to clean up the house.

Albie's Economy Wave
Albie uses psychology to get his family to save money.

Albie's Health Diet
Albie goes on a special diet of sauerkraut and watercress.

Albie's Homework
Albie tries to help Junior with his arithmetic and gets in trouble with both Junior and his teacher.

Albie's New Chair
Albie has a favorite chair, but Catherine thinks it looks awful so she replaces it with a scientific health chair.

Albie's Old Flame
GS: Barbara Billingsley, Doug Kennedy.   When Albie's old girlfriend comes for a visit, Catherine becomes jealous.

Albie's Rebellion
Albie decides to fight a battle against the institution of marriage.

Albie's Train Trip
Albie decides to take the family with him on a business trip to Cleveland.

Anniversary Story
Albie and Catherine make plans for a second honeymoon to celebrate their anniversary, only someone interrupts their plans.

Ann's Boyfriends
GS: Hal Baylor. Ann's boyfriend is a bragging football player.

Ann's Stage Struck Phase
Albie helps to get his daughter a job as an actress.

The Antique Watch
Albie finds his boss's antique watch in Junior's bedroom.

Arts and Crafts Story
Junior will only eat his dinner in front of the TV set.

Barbecue Story
Albie decides to build a backyard barbecue but his neighbor, Frank, won't let him work on it.

Big Boss's Son
Albie tries to help the Boss's son, but soon learns that it is impossible.

Albie Helps the Lovelorn
Albie invites a fighting couple over to see how a good marriage works.

Catherine's Old Friend
Catherine's old boyfriend, who is now a successful businessman, comes for a visit.

The Chicken Farm
Albie visits his uncle's chicken farm and finds himself in the middle of a feud.

The Dance Story
Albie tries to get his daughter and her boyfriend back together so he can take her to the prom.

A Dueling Story
Albie gets quite a shock when an industrial tycoon returns to town.

Honest Albie
Albie judges a flower show and the winning flowers turn out to be those of his wife.

Income Tax Story
Albie tries to evade the tax collector.

Portrait Story
Albie models for a portrait of a caveman.

Radioactive Story
Albie believes that he is the victum of a deadly radioactive solution.

The Shaggy Dog Story
Junior gets a dog as a gift, the only problem is the dog hates Albie.

Thanksgiving Story
Albie uses his life insurance policy as collateral for a loan to allow Ann to take a graduation trip. The rest of the family think he is planning to kill himself so they can have the insurance money.

Uncle Harry's Visit
Uncle Harry arrives and decides to take over the household.

The Women Haters
Junior falls in love with a girl just after he joins a woman haters club.

Christmas Story
Albie is asked to play Santa Claus in the PTA school pageant.

QUARK

On the air 2/24/78, off 4/14/78. NBC. Color Videotape. 8 episodes. Broadcast: Feb 1978-April 1978 Fri 8-8:30. Producer: David Gerber/Buck Henry. Prod Co/Synd: Columbia Pictures TV.

CAST: Adam Quark (played by Richard Benjamin), Gene/Jean (Tim Thomerson), The Head (Alan Caillou), Otto Palindrome (Conrad Janis), Ficus (Richard

Richard Benjamin, as Quark.

Kelton), Andy the Robot (Bobby Porter), Betty 1 & 2 (Tricia and Cyb Barnstable).

The travels of Commander Quark, an outerspace garbage collector. Quark's crew consists of a half plant-half man, a cowardly robot, a male-female mutant, and two beautiful twins. Each episode has Quark facing a deadly enemy while quietly trying to collect rubbish. *Quark* is a cult show currently not being shown.

Pilot Episode
W: Buck Henry. D: Peter Hunt. A garbage collecting spaceship run by an assorted crew of strange characters unknowingly saves the galaxy from an all-devouring enzyme cloud.

May the Source Be with You [One Hour]
W: Steven Zacharias. D: Hy Averback. GS: Hans Conreid, Henry Silva, Chris Capen. Quark and his crew, along with the all-powerful orb called The Source, save the galaxy from an attack by the evil Gorgons and their Doomsday Machine.

The Old and the Beautiful
W: Bruce Kane. D: Bruce Bilson. GS: Barbara Rhoades, Dana House. Quark contracts an aging disease on route to signing a peace treaty with Princess Carna of Kamamor.

The Good, the Bad and the Ficus
W: Stuart Gillard. D: Hy Averback.
GS: Geoffrey Lewis, Sean Fallon Walsh. Quark and his crew split into two exact duplicates: one good and the other evil, after passing through a black hole.

Goodbye Polumbus
W: Bruce Kane. D: Hy Averback. GS: Denny Miller, Mindi Miller. Quark investigates the planet Polumbus from which several expeditions have never returned. There they encounter a machine which makes their fantasies come true.

All the Emperor's Quasi-Norms [Part 1]
W: Jonathan Kaufer. D: Bruce Bilson.

GS: Ross Martin, Joan Van Ark. Quark is captured by Zorgon the Malevolent and is forced to reveal the location of "IT."

All the Emperor's Quasi-Norms [Part 2]
W: Jonathan Kaufer. D: Bruce Bilson. GS: Ross Martin, Joan Van Ark. Quark is saved from death by the forest people and returns with "IT" to destroy Zorgon.

Vanessa 38-24-36
W: Robert A. Keats. D: Hy Averback. Quark's ship is chosen to test an experimental computer which attempts to take over the ship.

RANGO

On the air 1/13/67, off 9/1/67. ABC. Color Film. 17 episodes. Broadcast: Jan 1967-Sept 1967 Fri 9-9:30. Producer: Aaron Spelling. Synd: William Morris Agency.
CAST: Rango (played by Tim Conway), Pink Cloud (Guy Marks), Capt. Horton (Norman Alden).
"Rango" by Earle Hagen, sung by Frankie Laine.
The misadventures of Rango, a bumbling Texas Ranger. Episodes depict his struggles to successfully carry out his assignments and glorify the dignity of the Texas Rangers. Rango is assisted by Pink Cloud, a wild Indian. *Rango* is not in syndication but is considered one of the funniest spoofs ever produced.

Rango the Outlaw [Pilot]
GS: Ned Romero, Ted De Corsia. The rangers plan to trap a gang of outlaws but they must get Rango out of the way first.

The Daring Holdup of the Deadwood Stage
GS: Parley Baer, Leo Gordon. Rango plays a wild hunch while he tracks down a gang of bank robbers.

The Town Tamer
GS: Paul Richards. Rango believes he has tamed an outlaw, unaware that his gang is waiting to steal a gold shipment.

Gunfight at the K.O. Saloon
GS: Joan Staley, Howard Caine. Rango impersonates a classy thief in order to find his hidden loot.

The Spy Who Was Out Cold
GS: Paul Mantee. Rango tries his hand at being a detective and he just so happens to find two prime suspects from a gun-running gang.

What's a Nice Girl Like You Doing Holding Up a Place Like This?
GS: Carolyn Jones. Rango mistakes a lady bank robber for the governor's daughter, so he helps her case the bank.

Requiem for a Ranger
GS: Billy DeWolfe. Rango plays dead in order to find the thieves who stole a gold shipment.

Diamonds Look Better Around Your Neck Than a Rope
GS: Mike Mazurki. Rango tries to solve a jewel robbery and a murder.

My Teepee Runneth Over
GS: Jesse White. Rango disguises himself as a pots and pans salesman in order to rescue Pink Cloud who has been captured by unfriendly Indians.

The Not So Great Train Robbery
GS: Myrna Fahey, William Mimms. Rango mistakes a disguised Captain Horton as a gang member of the lady prisoner he is transporting.

Viva Rango
GS: Vito Scotti. Rango is ordered to guard his girlfriend's jewels.

It Ain't the Principle, It's the Money
GS: Robert Wilke. Rango and Pink Cloud pretend to be an infamous outlaw and his sidekick so they can break up a gang of crooks.

Shootout at Mesa Flats
GS: Lane Bradford. Rango helps a wounded Captain Horton guard an outlaw.

In a Little Mexican Town
Rango and Pink Cloud go to Mexico to capture a bandit.

If You Can't Take It with You, Don't Go
GS: Tom Stern. The two prisoners Rango captured are tunneling from their jail cell into the safe next door.

You Can't Scalp a Bald Indian
GS: Anthony Caruso. Rango dresses up as an Indian in order to capture Chief Angry Bear. Rango finds that it won't be as easy as he thought, because the Chief's daughter wants to marry him.

The Rustlers
Rango tries to prove a family of sheepherders are really a gang of rustlers.

THE RAY MILLAND SHOW

On the air 9/17/53, off 9/30/55. CBS. B&W Film. 30 min. 76 episodes. Broadcast: Sept 1953-Jun 1955 Thu 8-8:30; Jul 1955-Sept 1955 Fri 9:30-10. Producer: Unknown. Prod Co/Synd: Universal TV.
CAST: Prof. Ray McNutley/McNutly (played by Ray Milland), Peggy McNutley/McNutly (Phyllis Avery), Dean Josephine Bradley (Minerva Urecal), Pete Thompson (Gordon Jones).
The story of Prof. Ray McNutley, English professor at Lynnhaven, an all-female college. In the second season his name was changed to McNutly and he became a drama instructor at Comstock University. Episodes depict the struggle the professor has in dealing with the problems of his fellow students and faculty members. During the first season the series was called *Meet Mr. McNutley*. The show is no longer seen in the U.S.

Adult Education
Professor McNutley teaches a course in the adult education division of the college and finds that he has all of the female students after him.

Babes in the Wood
Ray discovers a baby boy in his car and tries to leave the child at an orphanage.

Back in Uniform
Ray has an argument with Miss Bradley over whether or not he is joining the Army.

Birthday Present
Ray gets himself into trouble when he gives a birthday present to a laundress. It gets her wrestler boyfriend after him.

The Camping Trip
Peggy has to pretend to be a boy in order to join Ray and Pete on a camping trip.

The Checking Account
Everyone in town is complaining; it seems that the checks Ray has been writing all bounced.

The Christmas Story
The professor and his wife share their Christmas with a French student who cannot afford to go home to Canada for the holidays.

Civic Improvement
Peggy and the other faculty wives set out to fight the telephone company when they string up some unsightly wires throughout their neighborhood.

Dancing Lesson
Peggy signs Ray up for dancing lessons with a 68-year-old instructor.

Dean for a Day
While appointed acting Dean, Ray encounters Sorority rush week and finds that some of the college property disappears.

The Egg and Ray
When his parakeet lays an egg, Ray tries to build an incubator when the bird neglects the egg.

The Faculty Dance
The professor decides to leave Lynnhaven so a farewell party is held in his honor.

Fashion Model
Peggy is asked to be a model for a fashion show, but Ray objects when he sees just what she has to model.

The Fishing Trip
Ray tries to relax by taking up deep-sea fishing.

Happy Anniversary
On their 8th wedding anniversary, Ray and Peggy return to the place where they first met.

Parlor Game
Ray and Peggy invite a young student couple over for dinner to show them how a happily married couple lives.

Helpful Hand
Ray helps his neighbor who has lost her key enter her house through the back window.

Hobbies
Ray becomes upset when Peggy takes up art and begins to use male models.

House Guest
GS: Jill Jarmyn. A home economics major is assigned to the McNutley home. Ray thinks it is a wonderful idea, but Peggy doesn't.

House Party
The professor holds a party for his students in order to prove he's not unsympathetic towards them.

A Man Around the House
Ray tries to prove that he is the man of the house and the boss of his family.

Masquerade Ball
When the college holds its annual masquerade ball, Ray swears he won't wear a costume.

The Most Glamorous Professor
Peggy sends Ray's picture to a movie company's contest.

The New Car
Ray and Peggy find a baby in their car and don't know what to do with it.

New Dress
Ray is commissioned by the school to buy a dress for a prize-winning student, but he makes the mistake of putting it where his wife will find it.

The New Job
A friend sends Ray a fake telegram offering him a job at Yale.

Peggy's Night Out
Ray and Peggy celebrate their first date together.

Peggy's Old Flame
Ray tries to remain calm when Peggy's old boyfriend comes for a visit.

The Perfect Marriage
The Dean feels that Ray and Peggy are a model married couple and convinces them to help another faculty couple settle their marital differences.

Ray Plays Cupid
Ray fixes up Miss Harrison with his extroverted friend Pete.

Ray's Nephew
Ray discovers a girlie magazine in the room of his visiting 17-year-old nephew.

Ray's Promotion
Ray is informed by the college board of directors that he has been chosen to replace Dean Bradley.

School Girl Crush
One of Ray's students falls in love with him.

Shabby Gentility
An old classmate of Ray's shows up dressed as a hobo.

Skylark
Ray starts receiving unsigned poetry in the mail.

Swimming Problem
Ray becomes the acting athletic director, and a young swimming instructor comes to his assistance.

The Tree
Ray plants a tree in an area that has some strict property restrictions.

Vacation Days
Peggy meets Ray's assistant who is an attractive young Ph.D. from Wellesley.

The Arrival
Ray and Peggy are nervous about meeting the new faculty of Comstock University.

Battle of the Sexes
Ray and Peggy are each backing a different candidate for the school election.

Be Bop
GS: Ross Bagdasarian, Milton Frome. Peggy helps a pop singer write two new songs.

Call Me Dad
Ray and Peggy hire a clumsy lovesick college girl as a part-time maid.

Chinese Luck
Peggy attends an auction where she unknowingly buys a Chinese god statue.

Christmas Story
Ray and Peggy try to restore a little girl's belief in Christmas.

Doll's House
Ray rehearses the play "A Doll's House," while Peggy wants a new fur coat.

Faculty Wife
Ray helps a female student get even with the dean when she was unjustly punished.

Family Tree
A student claims that her parents are famous Shakespearean actors, but now she has to prove it.

Field Trip
Ray is accidentally involved in the love life of a French movie star.

Green Thumb
GS: Jack Haley, Jim Fish. Ray discovers a former actor is now working as the school gardener. He decides to use him in the school play, but academic red tape interferes.

Hangout
Ray's informal discussions with the students in his home turn it into a campus and Peggy into a short order cook.

Hollywood Story
GS: Biff Elliot, Bill Barnes. A famous movie director asks Ray to become the dramatic coach to a singing star who wants to become a dramatic actor.

International Accident
Two foreign students are miscast in the play "Romeo and Juliet," causing complaints from everyone.

Jury Duty
Ray and Peggy are both called for jury duty on the case of a husband who is seeking alimony from his wife.

Mr. Sargent and the Lady
Ray and Peggy try to break up a romance between the son of a rich alumnus and a bubble dancer.

Molehouse Collection
A returning female professor's diary causes trouble for many of the male members of the college faculty.

Now, Coach
An Irishman and a Scotsman, rivals in the same business, ask Ray to give them lessons in private speaking.

Happy Home
Attempting to fix his fireplace, Ray only succeeds in springing leaks in the roof.

Poet and Peggy
GS: John Sutton. A poet visits the

college for a lecture but finds he has fallen for Peggy.

Prodigy
Ray meets his match when Peggy's pre-teen genius cousin enrolls in the college.

The Professor Meets Author
Ray becomes involved with a rich alumnus who writes a bad play.

Professor Writes a Play
Peggy challenges Ray to write a play of his own.

Ray's Other Life
Peggy suspects that an actress visiting the college has really come to visit Ray.

Retirement Deferred
Ray tries to prevent the mandatory retirement of one of the school's favorite professors.

Reunion in Comstock
Peggy tries to help Ray produce a musical revue and welcome alumni for their reunion.

The Robbery
Ray finds himself the prime suspect in a series of robberies.

Sabrina Comes to Town
Ray convinces a famous actress that she should visit Comstock instead of the State University, but this threatens the future of a new football stadium.

Silver Cord
Ray notices that a student's work falls off every time his mother visits the campus.

Soap Opera
Ray promises to buy Peggy anything she wants if she can show him one person who has the same qualities as the character on a soap opera.

Stagestruck
Ray finds himself in the middle of a

family argument. The mother of a stagestruck coed wants to let her go on the stage, but her father doesn't.

A Star Is Born
Peggy joins Ray's class in order to get a role in the school play.

Stratford on the Ozarks
Ray conducts a search for future playwrights by holding a national contest.

Strike It Rich
Two students find uranium during a field trip so Ray and his friends start a corporation.

The TV Story
A TV producer offers Ray a chance to bring his lectures to TV.

Try Out
One of Ray's students sends a play to a Broadway playwright, causing the dramatist to come to the college to meet her.

A Week with Cinderella
Ray makes sure that he reaches the theater on time by leaving the house several hours ahead of time.

THE REAL McCOYS

On the air 10/3/57, off 9/22/63. ABC, CBS. B&W Film. 224 episodes. Broadcast: Oct 1957-Sept 1962 ABC Thu 8:30-9; Sept 1962-Sept 1963 CBS Sun 9-9:30. Producer: Danny Thomas/Irving Pincus. Prod Co: Bob Neece. Synd: National Telefilm.

CAST: Grampa Amos McCoy (played by Walter Brennan), Luke McCoy (Richard Crenna), Kate McCoy (Kathleen Nolan), Hassie (Lydia Reed), Little Luke (Michael Winkleman), Pepino (Tony Martinez), George MacMichael (Andy Clyde), Flora MacMichael (Madge Blake).

The adventures of the McCoys, a poor farming family living in California. Grampa Amos, a widower, is the head of the family and it is his decisions that guide his grandson Luke and his wife Kate. *The Real McCoys* ran for six years yet today it is hardly ever seen.

Californy, Here We Come [Pilot]
The McCoys move from West Virginia to a ranch in California.

Luke Gets His Freedom
Luke tries to prove to Grampa that he is not hen-pecked.

Grampa's Date
Luke and Kate try to get Grampa to invite Flora MacMichael to a dance.

Kate's Dress
The men want to buy a gun with the money in the cookie jar, while the women want to buy a new dress for Kate.

The Egg War
The McCoys start a war with their neighbor when they open up a roadside egg stand.

You Can't Cheat an Honest Man
Luke and Kate believe Grampa was swindled out of some valuable farm land.

Grampa Sells His Gun
Grampa decides to sell his great grandfather's gun to raise $150 to pay the mortgage.

A Question of Discipline
Grampa takes over the disciplining of Hassie and Little Luke when they get bad grades in school.

It's a Woman's World
Grampa tries to prove that women have no place in politics.

Little Luke's Education
Grampa comes to the rescue when Little Luke is called a dumb hillbilly by his classmates.

You're Never Too Old
Luke and Kate try to get Grampa to join a senior citizen's club.

The Matchmaker
Grampa arranges a date between Flora MacMichael and a man's son in return for the man's hunting dog.

The Lady's Man
Luke becomes jealous of the photographer who comes to take Kate's picture when she is chosen as a model by a magazine.

The Fishing Contest
Grampa and George MacMichael compete against each other in a fishing contest.

Time to Retire
Grampa feels he isn't needed when the family tries to convince him to retire and take it easy.

Gambling Is a Sin
Grampa gives permission to let a sign advertising a gambling casino be painted on his barn roof, at the same time as a minister comes to visit.

The Goodys Come to Town
Kate becomes jealous when Frank Goody's daughter makes a play for Luke.

The Bigger They Are
Grampa wrecks Flora's apple tree when he thinks she is seeing another man.

It Pays to Be Poor
A rich couple spend a few days at the ranch and try to convince the McCoys that money is the most important thing in life.

New Doctor in Town
Grampa refuses to see the new doctor in town when he comes down with a cold. He would rather use his old home remedies instead.

Let's Be Buddies
Grampa is invited to join a lodge, only to learn that his friend George's admission to the lodge was rejected.

Grampa and the Driver's License
Grampa is told he needs glasses in order to pass the eye test for his driver's license.

Luke's Mother-in-Law
Kate's mother comes for a visit.

The Honeymoon
Grampa plans to send Kate and Luke on the honeymoon they never had.

Grampa's Proposal
Grampa proposes to Flora but she turns him down.

Grampa's Birthday
Grampa thinks the family has forgotten his birthday, unaware that they have planned a surprise party for him.

Once There Was a Traveling Saleswoman
Kate and Grampa help Luke cancel the contract he signed for a new swimming pool forced on him by a saleswoman.

My Favorite Uncle
Kate's Uncle Dave visits and tells them some tall stories about his business deals.

Volunteer Fire Department
Grampa tries to become a volunteer fireman but is turned down because of his age.

For Love of Money
Pepino goes to work for George when the McCoy's can't afford to give him a raise.

Kate's Career
Kate is being paid to make alterations for friends which causes Grampa to

get upset and demand that she quit.

When a Fellow Needs a Friend
Grampa tries to find a character witness to help him testify in court.

The Life of the Party
Grampa doesn't realize that he is intruding when Kate and Luke invite some young people to a party at their house.

Three Is a Crowd
Grampa tries to break up George's romance with a widow.

The New Look
Luke and Kate try to get Grampa to use new farming methods.

You Can't Always Be a Hero
Grampa is happy that Little Luke does everything that he does, until he copies his bad habits too.

The Homely Boy
Hassie is stuck with the homely boy in her class as her date to the class dance.

The Corn Eating Contest
Grampa bets that Little Luke will win the corn eating contest.

Her Flaming Youth
Grampa is turned off by a photo of Flora wearing scanty attire taken when she was much younger.

Do You Kiss Your Wife?
Luke and Kate have a fight over the idea of kissing in public.

Grampa Learns About Teenagers
Grampa becomes upset when Hassie learns to dance rock and roll and wears makeup to attract a boy in her class.

The Dancin' Fool
Kate gets Luke to take dancing lessons.

The New Car
Luke and Kate trade in Grampa's old car to buy a new one.

The New Dog
Grampa and George try to teach two con men a lesson after they try to sell him a dog.

Blow the House Down
Little Luke drives everyone crazy when he practices the trumpet in order to win a spot in the school band.

Sing for Your Supper
Luke enters a radio station singing contest.

The New Hired Hand
Pepino thinks the new hired hand will cause him to lose his job.

The New Well
Grampa uses his divining rod to locate water for a new well.

Leave It to the Girls
Grampa teaches Luke and Hassie's boyfriend how to handle a woman.

The Perfect Swine
Grampa tries to compete against George in the county fair by having the better pig.

The Gift
Grampa gives Kate an ancient vacuum cleaner as a gift.

The New Neighbors
Kate and Luke think their new neighbors are snobs.

The McCoys Visit Hollywood
Kate takes the family to Hollywood to meet her old school friend who is now a movie star.

Luke Gets a Job
Luke gets a nighttime and Saturday job.

The Bank Loan
Grampa almost ruins the family's chances of getting a bank loan.

The Great Discovery
Grampa and Luke decide to sell the dinosaur bone on their property.

Sweet Fifteen
Hassie feels neglected when her request for a birthday party is refused. She is unaware that the others have planned a surprise party for her.

Son of the Mystic Nile
Luke is scheduled to receive an honor award at the lodge.

Kate Learns to Drive
Luke teaches Kate to drive despite objections from Grampa.

Grampa's Private War
Grampa makes up stories about his adventures during several wars.

The Rainmaker
Grampa hires an Indian to perform a rain dance to end a drought.

The Perfect Houseguest
George becomes a houseguest of the McCoys.

The Wedding
Grampa, Luke and Kate are worried that the man Kate's mother wants to marry is after her money.

Kate's Diet
Kate tries to lose some weight so she can fit into her party dress.

What's a Family For?
Hassie has a fight with her boyfriend, causing her to feel depressed.

Grampa Takes the Primrose Path
Grampa thinks a young widow has fallen in love with him.

Batter Up!
Grampa tries to convince Luke to coach the little league team.

Go Fight City Hall
Grampa fights the county road commissioner when he plans to fix a hole in the road by himself.

Two's Company
Kate tries to show Luke that he has been neglecting her.

The Mrs. Homemaker Contest
Luke and Grampa convince Kate to enter the Mrs. Homemaker contest.

The Tax Man Cometh
Grampa hides the furniture when the tax man comes to appraise the ranch so it will look like they are very poor.

The Insurance Policy
Luke and Kate take out an insurance policy. Grampa tries to save them money by not paying his premium.

How to Paint a House
The McCoys are taken in by a con man who gets them to sign a contract to have their house painted.

The Great Woodsman
Grampa agrees to go on a camping trip with Little Luke and his friends.

The Big Skeet Shoot
Luke competes against Grampa in a skeet shooting contest.

Grampa's New Job
Grampa helps the lodge answer its mail, even though he can't read.

The Actor
An actor hurts his back on the McCoy's property, so he moves in till he recovers. However, Grampa tries to prove he is faking.

Fire When Ready, Grampa
Grampa rescues Little Luke from the clutches of a crook who stole the ticket money from the church social.

The Farmer Took a Wife
Kate's old boyfriend and his wife come for a visit.

The Game Warden
George becomes the new game warden which causes problems for his friendship with Grampa.

The Screen Test
Hassie receives a letter from a con man to take a screen test.

Work No More, My Lady
The family decides Kate needs a rest so they hire a housekeeper.

The Garden Club
Kate tries to impress the ladies of the garden club so they will consider her for membership.

The Weaker Sex?
Grampa is surprised to learn that his new neighbor is a he-man type female.

The Fighter and the Lady
A fighter and his manager try to con Luke into taking part in a boxing match.

The Gas Station
George opens a gas station, causing Grampa to insist on being the attendant.

Grampa Fights the Air Force
Grampa goes to the air base in order to get the Air Force to change the flight pattern of its jets.

The Girls at Mom's Place
Grampa helps a poor widow and her daughter run a diner.

The Politician
A visiting political office seeker comes to town looking for votes.

Pepino Takes a Bride
Pepino asks the McCoys to help him impress his fiancee's visiting uncle who is coming to see the man who wants to marry his niece.

Hot Rod
Grampa becomes involved with racing cars and a dragstrip when he gets run off the road by a hot rod.

The Ghostbreakers
Little Luke is required to visit a haunted house at midnight as part of an initiation ceremony.

The Marriage Broker
Grampa tries to find a wife for a for-eigner who is being deported for over-staying his visa.

How to Build a Boat
Grampa and Luke decide to build a boat but have difficulty reading the blueprints.

The Artist
Grampa makes fun of George's hobby of painting, until he sells one of his paintings.

The Perfume Salesman
Luke decides to sell barnyard deod-orants to earn some extra money.

The Television Set
Grampa is the only one who doesn't want to buy a television set.

The Lawsuit
George threatens to sue Grampa for negligence when he wrecks his car in Grampa's ditch.

The Town Councilman
Grampa and Luke help George run for Town Councilman.

Cousin Naomi
Grampa tries to get rid of George's visiting cousin who has become a house guest of the McCoys.

The Bowling Champ
Kate gets jealous when Luke tutors a beautiful member of his bowling team.

The Talk of the Town
Little Luke chooses Grampa as the subject of his school composition.

Once There Was a Man
Grampa and Luke are shocked to learn that their visiting cousin is a henpecked husband.

Weekend in Los Angeles
Grampa, Kate and Luke attend a lodge convention in Los Angeles.

First Date
Little Luke finds that he has to take

the tallest girl in his class to the school dance.

How to Discover Oil
Grampa and George decide to swap property, but each one tries to call the deal off when they think they have discovered oil on the land that they are trading.

A House Divided
Grampa thinks Luke and Kate are too strict with Hassie and Little Luke, so he decides to handle their discipline.

Foreman of the Jury
Grampa learns that George will be on the jury when he sues the phone company for the loss of his bull, so he tries to butter him up with gifts.

One for the Money
Little Luke becomes selfish when he decides to spend his paper route money on himself instead of sharing it with the family.

That Was No Lady
Luke and Grampa are shocked to learn that Kate is wearing a strapless dress for the Grange dance.

The Tycoon
Grampa tries to undersell the other farmers who try to form a co-op to get higher prices for their eggs.

Where There's a Will
Grampa inherits some old furniture which he sells for $25, unaware that they are antiques.

The Jinx
Grampa tries to get rid of the visiting family jinx.

The Delegates
Grampa and George compete with each other to see which of them will be chosen as the delegate to their lodge's convention.

The Gigolo
Grampa tries to get the spinster who owns the mortgage on their farm to marry him so he can prevent her from foreclosing.

Teenage Wedding
Grampa encourages Hassie after she decides to get married, despite protests from the boy's grandfather.

McCoys, Ahoy
Grampa leads a protest march to a Navy base when he hears the U.S.S. West Virginia is going to be scrapped.

Beware a Smart Woman
Grampa gets worried when Kate enrolls in night school.

Executive Wife
Kate is asked by a canning company to sell her prize-winning piccalilly on the commercial market.

Pepino McCoy
Pepino entertains at a nightclub to help earn extra money for the family.

Father and Son Day
Little Luke believes that Luke will be his partner in the games at the Grange picnic.

Farmer or Scientist
Grampa visits Little Luke's teacher when he decides to become a scientist and not a farmer like him.

The New Librarian
Grampa tries to break up George's romance with the new librarian.

Smothered in Love
Kate and Luke decide to cater to Grampa when they think he is working too hard.

Baldy
Luke becomes worried when he learns that all of the men in his family have gone bald before they were 50.

The Hermit
Grampa learns that a local hermit had been stealing their food and leaving coyote skins in their place.

The Legacy
Luke tries to get George to disinherit Kate and himself from his will and leave it all to Grampa.

A Bundle from Japan
Grampa and Luke decide to hire a young Japanese girl to help Kate with the housework.

The Horse Expert
Luke and Kate choose a palomino, instead of the work horse Grampa wanted, as payment of a debt.

The City Boy
The McCoys take a city boy into the home for the summer.

The Investors
Grampa and his friends invest in his cousin's phony oil well.

If You Can't Lick 'Em
Grampa tries to cut out the middleman and sell his produce himself.

The Rival
Luke becomes jealous of the neighbor Kate described to him from a letter she wrote at her mother's house in Bakersfield.

The Good Neighbor Policy
Grampa wrecks the family car. He learns that his insurance only covers his passenger, George, so they set out to collect the insurance money.

You Can't Beat the Army
Gramp tries to reclaim the cow that the Army took away from them.

The Bazaar
Luke and Grampa get arrested after they are accused of opening gambling booths at a bazaar.

The Swedish Girl
The McCoys hire a beautiful Swedish girl to help look after them while Kate is away.

The New Sunday School Teacher
Grampa becomes the new Sunday school teacher as payment for a $25 pledge to the church.

Baseball vs. Love
Grampa learns that Little Luke is in love, which has a bad effect on his baseball playing.

Theatre in the Barn
GS: Fay Wray. Grampa becomes jealous when George gets the lead role in the Grange play opposite Fay Wray.

George Retires
Grampa tries to discourage George from selling his farm and taking a world cruise with his sister Flora.

Pepino's Wedding
Grampa agrees to pay for Pepino's wedding reception.

Sorority Girl
Hassie tries to win an election to a high school sorority.

Kate Comes Home
Hassie helps Kate with the housework until she makes full recovery.

Money in the Bank
The family decides to open a bank account instead of keeping their money in the cookie jar.

A Man of Influence
Grampa is asked to join the members of the Civic Improvement Committee in a real estate deal, only because he is friends with a big land developer.

Back to West Virginny
The family goes back to their home in West Virginia to help Grandma McCoy celebrate her 100th birthday.

Fly Away Home
Grampa upsets a deal to expand a paper box factory where many of his relatives work.

September Song
Grampa visits with his old childhood sweetheart and tries to remember what he was like when he was much younger.

Kate's Competition
Kate becomes jealous of Luke's attention to their talented new female neighbor.

Lost and Found
Grampa finds $200 when it floats down out of the sky.

First Love
The family teaches Little Luke a lesson in manners when he gets a swelled head from all of the attention he is getting from the girls in his class.

Hassie's European Tour
A wealthy neighbor offers to send Hassie to Europe as a traveling companion for his granddaughter.

How to Win Friends
Grampa tries to teach Luke to have self-confidence.

The Matador
Pepino's cousin, a famous matador, comes for a visit and offers to teach his cousin how to be a bullfighter.

George's Housekeeper
Grampa tries to get George to hire a housekeeper to look after him while his sister is away.

Excess Baggage
Grampa takes a job as salesman in a hardware store.

The Trailer Camp
Luke doesn't know what to do when a family asks him if they can park their trailer at the ranch for a week.

Luke Leaves Home
Luke and Grampa have a fight over what will grow on their farm.

The New Piano
Hassie decides that she wants piano lessons.

The Handsome Salesman
Luke becomes upset when Kate is pressured into buying a lot of expensive beauty aids from a fast-talking salesman.

Honesty Is the Best Policy
Grampa rents the farm's fruit and vegetable stand to a man from town.

Cyrano McCoy
Grampa teaches George how to court a girl.

The Diamond Ring
Grampa regrets giving Luke the money from the cookie jar so he can buy an expensive Christmas present for Kate when she gets very sick.

The Berry Crisis
Grampa decides to let Luke make all the decisions on the farm.

The Rich Boy
Grampa becomes worried when Hassie befriends the son of their new rich neighbor.

The Gamblers
Grampa becomes upset when Luke and Kate try their hands at the stock market.

The Marriage Counselor
Grampa thinks Kate and Luke are breaking up when he learns that Kate has been seeing a marriage counselor.

The Washing Machine
Kate turns the house into the women's community clubhouse to spite Grampa because he won't give her money to buy a washing machine.

Pepino McCoy, Citizen
The family helps Pepino prepare to take his citizenship test.

Meeting Hassie's Friends
Hassie's new friends are a group of rock and roll boys and girls who make fun of Grampa.

The Law and Mr. McCoy
Grampa goes to jail when he refuses to pay the fine he got for burning his trash.

George's Nephew
Grampa and George try to teach George's visiting nephew a lesson.

Double Date
Grampa finds that he has two dates for the church social.

Made in Italy
The family hires an Italian girl to help Kate with her canning.

Who's Margie?
Kate tries to find out who the girl is whose name Luke mentioned in his sleep.

You're as Young as You Feel
Grampa is surprised to learn that he is really 61 and not 68 as he thought.

In Grampa We Trust
Grampa becomes resentful when Luke is asked to sell Geroge's apple crop and not he.

Never a Lender Be
Grampa and George have a fight over who owns a tree sprayer.

Allergies Anonymous
Grampa learns that George is allergic to the checkerboard they play on.

Pepino's Fortune
Grampa uses the money Pepino gave him to hold to pay off some of his own bills.

Pepino's Vacation
Pepino thinks he is being replaced when Grampa sends him on a vacation and hires a temporary farmhand.

Bubble, Bubble, Toil and Trouble
Grampa insults Pepino's voodoo adviser who, in return, puts a curse on him.

Don't Judge a Book
Grampa thinks his cousin Sarah is being abused by her husband.

The Raffle Ticket
Grampa and George win a piglet in a contest. They decide to have it for a barbecue, but Luke and Kate want to keep it for a pet.

Grampa Pygmalion
GS: Tina Louise. Grampa arranges for a girl from their home town to become their new housekeeper. She later falls in love with Luke.

Army Reunion
Grampa ruins George's election as the commander of the VFW post.

The Good Will Tour
Grampa gets a visit from a foreign nation's farm tour.

Three Strikes and Out
Grampa uses three women to do his housekeeping for him.

The New Housekeeper
GS: Una Merkel. The new housekeeper tries to fix her daughter up with Luke.

Actress in the House
GS: Taina Elg. Luke falls for the young actress who is staying at the farm.

Money From Heaven
Grampa plans to get a lot of money out of the Army when a paratrooper lands on top of his chicken coop, causing it to crumble.

The Roofing Salesman
Grampa helps Luke who has been taken by a saleswoman with a roof painting swindle.

Luke the Reporter
GS: Pat Buttram. Luke sells gossip stories to a newspaper for extra money.

The Girl Veterinarian
Luke pretends that a female veterinarian is his girlfriend so she can treat their cow without Grampa complaining about women doctors.

Pepino's Inheritance
Grampa finds that Pepino is not getting any work done since he inherited a valuable Arizona estate.

Uncle Rightly and the Musical Milker
GS: Jack Oakie. Uncle Rightly dates Flora in the hopes that she will finance his musical milking machine.

The Love Bug Bites Pepino
Pepino and Pedro find that they are dating the same girl.

The Health Addict
Luke becomes the athletic director at a health spa.

Up to Their Ears in Corn
GS: Jack Oakie. Uncle Rightly promotes a corn-growing contest and volunteers a prize of $500 to be donated by Luke and Grampa.

The Farmer and Adele
Luke is tricked into signing a 20-year contract for dancing lessons.

The Crop Duster
Luke and a cropduster fight over the same rich girl.

Sir Fergus McCoy
The head of the Scottish branch of the McCoy family comes for a visit and takes over as the head of the clan. Grampa tries to get rid of him.

How're You Gonna Keep 'Em Down on the Farm?
Luke and Louise don't believe the story Greg tells them about the convicts that were captured at their home by the police.

Cupid Wore a Tail
Luke falls for the owner of the cow that trampled their cornfield.

Skeleton in the Closet
GS: Jack Oakie. Luke tries to get rid of Uncle Rightly before Louise and her aunt come over to visit.

The Other Side of the Fence
Grampa finds that he has to pick Louise's tomato crop himself when he tries to get Luke to help her harvest the crop.

The Little Boy Blew
Greg runs away from home when he feels his mother doesn't love him any more.

Pals
Greg becomes jealous when Luke makes out with his mother.

Luke in the Ivy League
Luke is hired by an advertising company to make slogans.

The Peacemaker
Luke and Louise try to bring a fighting couple back together.

Aunt Win Arrives
GS: Joan Blondell. Louise's Aunt Win becomes Grampa's campaign manager when he decides to run for the presidency of the Grange.

Aunt Win Steps In
GS: Joan Blondell. Aunt Win tries to get Luke to marry Louise by fixing her up with another man in the hopes of making him jealous.

Aunt Win's Conquest.
GS: Joan Blondell. Aunt Win dates George so she can help Luke win an important loan.

Grampa's Apron Strings
Grampa tries to break up Luke's romance with Louise when he believes that Luke might marry her and leave the farm.

Luke the Dog Catcher
Luke becomes the local dog catcher. He finds that he hasn't the heart to get rid of the dogs he collected, so he takes them home with him.

The McCoy Hex
Grampa threatens to put a curse on George because he voted against him in the lodge election.

The Incorruptibles
Grampa, Luke and George are chosen as the judges of the local homemaker's contest.

Don't Be Nosey
George has a fight with Flora and moves in with the McCoys.

The McCoy Sound
Luke rents a room to some traveling jazz musicians.

Pepino's Mama
Luke decides to back Pepino's mother's frijole business.

Luke Grows a Beard
Luke grows a beard which causes a change in his personality.

The Auction
Luke buys some paintings at an auction.

The Partners
Luke and Pat decide to share the cost of a new boat.

RHODA

On the air 9/9/74, off 12/9/78. CBS. Color videotape. 109 episodes. Broadcast: Sept 1974-Sept 1975 Mon 9:30-10; Sept 1975-Jan 1977 Mon 8-8:30; Jan 1977-Sept 1978 Sun 8-8:30; Sept 1978-Dec 1978 Sat 8-8:30. Producer: James L. Brooks. Prod Co: MTM. Synd: Jim Victory Television.

CAST: Rhoda Morganstern (played by Valerie Harper), Brenda (Julie Kavner), Joe (David Groh), Ida (Nancy Walker), Martin (Harold Gould), Carlton (voice) (Lorenzo Music), Myrna (Barbara Sharma), Benny (Ray Buktenica), Jack (Ken McMillan), Gary (Ron Silver).

A spinoff of the *Mary Tyler Moore Show*. Rhoda goes back to New York and gets married. The average episodes tell about Rhoda's relationships with her family and her friends. This series has done very poorly in syndication.

Joe [Pilot]
GS: Mary Tyler Moore, Bill Zuckert. Rhoda meets Joe while on a trip to New York.

You Can Go Home Again
GS: Wes Stern, James Hong, Henry Winkler. Rhoda moves in with her parents when she can't find an apartment.

I'll Be Loving You, Sometimes
GS: Howard Hesseman. Rhoda decides that she and Joe should date other people.

Parents' Day
GS: Norman Bartold, Robert Alda, Paula Victor. Rhoda and Joe visit each other's parents.

The Lady in Red
GS: Louise Latham, James Burrows. Rhoda delivers the eulogy at the funeral of an x-rated author.

Pop Goes the Question
GS: Tom Atkins, Mary Tyler Moore. Joe asks Rhoda to live with him.

The Shower
GS: Beverly Sanders, Barbara Sharma. Brenda throws a surprise bridal shower for Rhoda.

Rhoda's Wedding [Part 1]
GS: Georgia Engel, Cloris Leachman, Mary Tyler Moore, Gavin McLeod. Ida plans a big wedding for Rhoda against her wishes.

Rhoda's Wedding [Part 2]
GS: Mary Tyler Moore, Cloris Leachman.   Rhoda has to take the subway to her wedding when Phyllis forgets to pick her up.

Honeymoon
GS: Charles Lane, Marjorie Bennett, Richard Masur. Rhoda and Joe spend their honeymoon on board a ship of senior citizens.

9-E Is Available
GS: Wes Stern, Pamela Bellwood, Richard Romanus.   Rhoda tries to convince Joe into taking a new apartment.

Anything Wrong?
GS: Robert Alda. Joe and Rhoda have difficulty speaking to each other.

I'm a Little Late, Folks
GS: Cara Williams, Beverly Sanders. Rhoda thinks she is pregnant.

'S Wonderful
GS: Barry Brown, Pat Sturges. Rhoda tries to prove that Brenda's new boyfriend is a married man.

Good-Bye Charlie
GS: Candy Azzars, Richard Schaal. Rhoda finds she hates Joe's best friend.

Guess What I Got You for the Holidays
GS: Joe Sirola, Cara Williams. Joe's business may be going bankrupt.

Whattaya Think It's There For?
GS: Scoey Mitchlll, Cara Williams. Rhoda gets Joe to ask her father for some money to save his business.

Not Made for Each Other
GS: Wes Stern, Barbara Sharma, Richard Schaal.   Rhoda's friend Myrna dates Joe's best friend Charlie.

Strained Interlude
GS: Candy Azzars, Allen Garfield. Joe becomes jealous when one of her old boyfriends asks her out to dinner.

Everything I Have Is Yours, Almost
GS: Scoey Mitchlll.   Rhoda worries when she finds out that Joe has been going to see a doctor.

Chest Pains
GS: Norman Fell, Julie Mannix. Ida is frightened to go to a doctor's appointment.

Windows by Rhoda
GS: Will MacKenzie, Louis Guss. Rhoda opens her own office.

A Nice Warm Rut
Brenda decides to move to San Francisco.

Ida, the Elf
GS: Frank Campanella. Ida becomes a hospital volunteer.

Along Comes Mary
GS: Mary Tyler Moore.   Mary comes for a visit, ruining Joe and Rhoda's plans for the weekend.

Kiss Your Epaulets Goodbye
GS: Ruth Gordon.   Rhoda blames Carlton for their apartment being robbed.

The Party
GS: Paul Lichtman, Stuart Margolin, Denise Nicholas. A psychiatrist holds a group encounter session at her party.

Rhoda Meets the Ex-Wife
GS: Joan Van Ark, Ned Wilson. Rhoda meets Joe's ex-wife whom she finds to be very beautiful.

Ida's Doctor
GS: Norman Fell. Ida considers having an affair with her doctor.

Mucho, Mucho
GS: Ron Silver. Rhoda and Joe have a fight while celebrating their first anniversary.

Call Me Grandma
GS: Shane Sinutko, Billy Braver. Ida fixes Brenda up with a date.

Somebody Down There Likes Him
GS: Rita Taggart, Denise Galik. Brenda looks for a roommate to share the expense of the apartment.

With Friends Like These
GS: Melanie Mayron, James Kiernan. Rhoda and Brenda get mad when their friends take advantage of them.

Brenda's Unemployment
GS: Sid Melton. Brenda quits her job at the bank but can't find another.

Myrna's Story
GS: Michael Lerner. Rhoda tries to stop Myrna from dating the customers.

Love Song of J. Nicholas Lobo
GS: Louis Guss. Brenda convinces Joe to hire Nick Lobo as a wrecker.

Friends and Mothers
GS: Vivian Vance, David White. A motherly woman moves in next door to Rhoda.

Rhoda's Sellout
GS: Dick O'Neill, Dennis Kort. Rhoda has to dress the window of a tuxedo store the way the owner wants it or lose the account.

A Night with the Girls
GS: Beverly Sanders. Rhoda tries to prove to her friends that they can have a good time without men.

Bump in the Night
GS: Robert Rothwell. Rhoda is the only one who can identify a burglar and she thinks he will come after her.

If You Don't Tell Her, I Will
GS: Sherry Hursey. Brenda and Rhoda have some uninvited guests moving in with them.

Attack on Mr. Right
GS: John Ritter. Rhoda teaches Brenda how to catch a man.

If You Want to Shoot the Rapids You Have to Get Wet
GS: David Ogden Stiers, Mike Henry.

Rhoda plays marriage counselor to her married friends.

The Return of Billy Glass
GS: Jack Gilford, Florida Friebus. Martin's best friend and formerly Ida's boyfriend comes for a visit.

A Federal Case
GS: Tim Matheson. Brenda falls for a security agent who uses her apartment to spy on the apartment building across the street.

The Marty Morgan Story
GS: Marion Scherer. Ida thinks Martin is fooling around.

It's Not My Fault . . . Is It?
GS: Eileen Heckart, Jack Bernardi. Lenny becomes depressed when Brenda turns down his proposal.

Don't Give Up the Office
GS: Liam Dunn, Robert Moore. Rhoda is going broke, causing her to give up her office and her business.

The Separation
GS: Phoebe Dorin. Rhoda and Joe agree to have a separation.

Together Again for the First Time
GS: Wendy Schaal, Terry Kiser. Rhoda and Joe go out on their first date since their separation.

No Big Deal
GS: Ron Silver. A swinger tries to get a date with Rhoda.

I Won't Dance
GS: Anne Meara. Rhoda and Brenda go away on a singles weekend.

H-e-e-e-r-e-'-s Johnny
GS: Anne Meara, Michael Delano. Rhoda goes on a blind date with an egotistical singer.

Two Little Words: Marriage Counselor
GS: Rene Auberjonois. Rhoda and Joe go to a marriage counselor.

An Elephant Never Forgets
GS: Joyce Jameson. Rhoda puts on weight while Brenda loses some weight.

Rhoda Questions Life and Flies to Paris
GS: Anne Meara. Rhoda goes to Paris to prove to Joe she is not a dull person.

Meet the Levys
GS: Doris Roberts, Norman Burton, Nedra Volz. Gary takes Rhoda to see his parents, where she pretends to be his future wife in order to impress his parents.

Man of the Year
GS: Richard Schaal. Joe's old friend Charlie returns for a visit.

You Deserve a Break Today
GS: Harold Oblong, Erica Yohn, Jeremy Stevens. Brenda dates a man who owns three McDonalds franchises.

Touch of Classy
GS: Jerry Stiller. Sally's ex-husband returns to ask her to take a reduction in alimony and announces he is getting married again.

Guess Who I Saw Today
GS: Tim Reid, Charles Murphy. Rhoda becomes jealous when she sees Joe with another woman.

What Are You Doing New Year's Eve?
GS: Queenie Smith. Rhoda throws a Halloween party on New Year's Eve.

Love for Sale
Brenda and Rhoda help Gary save his business by helping him run a giant sale.

A Night in the Emergency Room
GS: Chip Fields, Andre Pavon, Paul Cavonis. Nick accidentally breaks Rhoda's toe.

Somebody Has to Say They're Sorry
GS: Valerie Curtin, Robert Walden.

Rhoda is mistaken for a prostitute and is arrested.

The Ultimatum
GS: Rene Auberjonois. Rhoda tells Joe to come back or she will start dating other men.

Rhoda's Mystery Man
GS: Michael Delano, Larry Gelman. Rhoda receives anonymous gifts from that egotistical singer Johnny Venture.

Nick Lobo Superstar
Nick must decide to either continue as a musician or help his father with his garbage collecting business.

The Second Time Around
GS: Frank Converse. Rhoda dates Brenda's boss.

Nose Job
GS: David Ogden Stiers. Brenda decides to have a nose job.

Pajama Party Bingo
During a pajama party Brenda and Rhoda learn that each one is jealous of the other.

To Vegas with Love
GS: Michael Delano. Rhoda goes to Las Vegas to meet with Johnny Venture.

The Return of Ida
GS: Michael Delano. Ida returns from traveling around the country for a year.

The Job
GS: Kenneth McMillan, Rafael Campos. Rhoda gets a job at a costume rental company.

Lady's Choice
Gary and Benny both plan to date Brenda on the same night.

One Is a Number
GS: Anne Jackson. Rhoda has two theater tickets and can't find anyone to go with her.

Ida Works Out
Ida takes a part-time job at the Doyle Costume Company.

Rhoda Likes Mike
GS: Judd Hirsch, Howard Witt. Rhoda falls for a restaurant owner.

The Weekend
GS: Judd Hirsch. Rhoda decides to spend the weekend with her new boyfriend Mike without telling Ida.

Home Movies
Rhoda and Brenda spend the night with their parents watching home movies.

Johnny's Solo Flight
GS: Michael Delano, Sharon Redd. Rhoda tries to cheer up Johnny after his nightclub debut is a bomb.

Who's Shy?
GS: K Callan. Brenda joins a shyness clinic for help.

Blind Date
GS: David Landsberg. Ida fixes Rhoda up with a blind date.

All Work and No Play
GS: George Pentecost. Rhoda is so busy that she can't attend Brenda's birthday party.

Happy Anniversary
GS: Jack Bernardi. Rhoda and Brenda are trapped in an elevator while going to celebrate their parents' 40th wedding anniversary.

The Jack Story
GS: Howard Witt, Candy Azzars. Rhoda goes on a date with Jack so she can help him impress some of his friends.

Ida Alone
GS: Vanda Barra, Erica Yohn. Ida becomes depressed when she realizes all of her old friends are dead.

Rhoda Cheats
GS: Peter Hobbs, Elizabeth Kerr.

Rhoda is accused of cheating on her night school final exam.

Gary and Ida
Gary turns to Ida when his own mother moves to Florida.

As Time Goes By
Rhoda gets Jack to throw a party to bring in new costumers.

Two's Company
GS: Jon Lormer. Benny invests his life savings in Gary's jeans store.

Brenda the Bank Girl
GS: Kit McDonough. Brenda doesn't want to enter the Miss Security Bank Girl contest.

So Long, Lucky
GS: Carmine Caridi. Rhoda thinks she is a jinx.

Jack's Back
Jack hurts his back and moves in with Rhoda till it gets better.

Five for the Road [Part 1]
Rhoda, Ida, Brenda, Jack and Benny plan to have dinner at one of Jack's favorite restaurants.

Five for the Road [Part 2]
GS: John Evans. Rhoda and her friends must spend the night at a deserted restaurant.

Martin Doesn't Live Here Anymore
GS: Wil Albert. Rhoda and Brenda are shocked when they learn that their parents are separated.

In Search of Martin
GS: Jane Rose. Rhoda, Brenda and Benny go to Florida to find Martin.

Rhoda vs. Ida
GS: Charles Siebert. Rhoda doesn't like the idea that her mother is dating a younger man.

Brenda Gets Engaged
GS: Fredd Wayne. Benny asks Brenda

to marry him, but Ida refuses to accept him as part of the family.

Meet the Goodwins
GS: Howard Honig, Peggy Pope, George Wyner. Brenda asks Rhoda to join her when she meets Benny's parents.

Ida's Roommate
GS: Phillip Sterling. Ida asks a couple to share her house.

Jack's New Image
GS: Barbara Rhoades. Ronda convinces Jack that he needs some new clothes.

The Date in the Iron Mask
Rhoda's date gets his head stuck in an iron mask right before an awards dinner.

Martin Comes Home
Martin returns home to make up with Ida.

Martin Swallows His Heart
Martin accidentally swallows a heart-shaped charm he was going to give to Ida.

Earl's Helping Hand
GS: George Wyner. Benny's brother lends Jack $5000 to help keep his company going.

Brenda Runs Away
GS: Florida Friebus, Joseph Perry. Brenda runs away when everyone is running her life for her.

The Total Brenda
GS: Michael Alldredge. Brenda tries to cheer up Benny when he gets depressed.

ROOM FOR ONE MORE

On the air 1/27/62, off 9/22/62. ABC. B&W Film. 26 episodes. Broadcast: Jan 1962-Sept 1962 Sat 8-8:30. Producer: Ed Jurist. Prod Co/Synd: Warner Bros. TV.

CAST: George Rose (played by Andrew Duggan), Anna Rose (Peggy McCay), Flip Rose (Ronnie Dapo), Laurie Rose (Carol Nicholson), Jeff Rose (Tim Rooney), Walter Burton (Jack Albertson).

The story of the Rose Family: George, an engineer, and his wife Anna and their children Laurie and Flip as well as their adopted children Jeff and Mary. Episodes depict Anna's fond love of children and her attempts to help the misplaced and lonely. This series is syndicated but does not air on U.S. TV.

The Anniversary
GS: Jimmy Baird, Howard McNear. The dog befriends an orphan boy who is robbing the house.

Greeks Bearing Gifts
GS: Peter Mamakos, Dick Wessel, Dan Tobin. When he misses his turn to use the shower, George decides to buy a bigger house.

Seated One Day at the Organ
GS: Henry Corden, Cheerio Meredith. Anna buys an old pump organ whose

notes are breaking all the glass in the house.

Girl from Sweden
GS: Sue Ane Langdon, Paul Comi, Madge Blake. The new Swedish maid doesn't know how to do anything.

Angel in the Attic
GS: Jimmy Gaines, Frank Jenks. Two surprises arrive at the house: Sam, a five-year-old boy and a pile of monthly bills.

A Trip to the Beach
GS: Tommy Farrell, John Hiestand. George and Anna plan to spend the weekend at the beach alone, but wind up taking the kids.

This Gun for Hire
GS: Jack Albertson, Maxine Stuart. Anna hides her friend's rifle at the house, but George thinks it is a present for him.

Speaker of the House
GS: Tommy Farrell, Blossom Rock, Byron Morrow. Anna is paid to speak on the subject of foster children.

Strength Through Money
GS: Tommy Farrell, John Hiestand. Anna asks George how to invest $6,000, but he can't figure out where she got the money.

I Retake This Woman
GS: Pitt Herbert, Debbie Morgan. George and Anna can't find their marriage license.

Love Thy Neighbor
GS: Anna Lisa, Dan Tobin. Anna is jealous of George's attention to the new divorcee who's moved into the house next door.

The Real George
GS: Doris Packer. Someone has offered to give the kids a horse.

Too Many Parents
GS: Jack Davis. George and Anna both find a couple who want to take care of a nine-year-old orphan.

Our Men in Brazil
George is asked to handle an assignment in South America, but he doesn't want to leave his family.

Flip's Loyalty Test
GS: Craig Marshall, George Cisar. Jeff and Arthur borrow a lantern from a work site, causing Anna to drive into fresh tar.

What Is It?
GS: Sandra Gould, Walter Baldwin. Jeff is hurt because George and Anna gave away a gift he made for them.

King of the Little People
GS: Don McArt, Dorothy Ford. Flip finds a leprechaun in the attic.

Danger: Man at Work
GS: Richard Tyler, Diane Hall. A health nut turns the house into a gym.

The Right Wrong Number
GS: Robert Q. Lewis, Patty Sanborn. George thinks a reporter wants to do a story about his getting a hole-in-one while playing golf.

Little School House in the Red
GS: Benny Baker, Hazel Shermes. Anna and her friend Else plan to open a nursery school to earn extra money.

A New Twist
GS: Dan Tobin, William Woodson. George doesn't want to go to the charity dance, so he suddenly gets a sprained ankle.

Out at Home
GS: Jack Albertson, Maudie Prickett. Anna delivers an ultimatum: Jeff must pass his history test or he can't pitch in the little league championship game.

Happiness Is Just a State of Mind
GS: Robert Rockwell, Dorothea Lord, Louise Beavers. Anna tries to convince her traveling friends to settle down.

Bonjour, Rose Family
GS: Michael Petit, Craig Marshall. A French boy's good manners make George and Anna feel inferior.

Ribbin's and Beaus
GS: Jenny Maxwell, Buzz Martin. Mary invents a new boyfriend to make Marcia jealous.

Son of a Boss
GS: Amzie Strickland, Rickie Sorensen, Parley Baer. The boss's son is staying with George and Anna while his parents are out of town.

ROOM 222

On the air 9/17/69, off 1/11/74. ABC. Color Film. 112 episodes. Broadcast: Sept 1969-Jan 1971 Wed 8:30-9; Jan 1971-Sept 1971 Wed 8-8:30; Sept 1971-Jan 1974 Fri 9-9:30. Producer: Gene Reynolds & William D'Angelo. Prod Co/Synd: 20th Century Fox TV.
CAST: Pete Dixon (played by Lloyd Haynes), Liz McIntyre (Denise Nicholas), Seymour Kaufman (Michael Constantine), Alice Johnson (Karen Valentine), Helen Loomis (Judy Strangis), Jason Allen (Heshimu), Bernie (David Jolliffe), Pam (Ta-Tanisha), Larry (Eric Laneuville), Richie Lane (Howard Rice).
This semi-comical series featured the continuing problems and mishaps which occurred at Walt Whitman High School (located somewhere in California). It featured Lloyd Haynes as a dedicated black history teacher and Denise Nicholas as his girlfriend and school counselor. This series was one of the first to feature a black actor and actress as the leading characters and in a realistic way. The series won many awards from different educational and civil rights groups because of the way it handled many serious problems faced by the youths of the early seventies. Although some of the stories might contain subject matter which could be considered dated by today's standards, it should not prevent the series from being shown today. However, for some unknown reason, the series is rarely seen any more, despite the fact that it is available if any station would like to buy it.

Richie's Story [Pilot]
W: James L. Brooks. D: Gene Reynolds. GS: Ron Stuart, Jan Shutan, Howard Rice. The teachers try to help a student remain at the school even though he lives outside of the school district.

Flu
W: Allan Burns. D: Leo Penn. GS: John Rubinstein, Yvonne Wilder. Pete tries to teach several classes when most of the teachers come down with the flu.

Arizona State Loves You
W: James L. Brooks. D: Leo Penn. GS: Paul Winfield, Beah Richards, Larry Linville, Roy Pettie. Pete and Mr. Kaufman help a football player choose a college.

First We'll Eat, Then We'll Strike
W: Treva Silverman. D: Gene Reynolds. GS: Ivor Francis, Robert Casper, Gino Conforti, Helen Kleeb, Bill Zuckert. Pete is chosen to lead a teacher's strike.

Teacher's Dropping Out
W: Peggy Elliot. D: Gene Reynolds. GS: Frank Campanella, Morris Erby, Jan Burrell. Pete is offered a job with a corporation helping high school dropouts.

Naked Came We into the World
W: George Kirgo. D: Alan Rafkin. GS: Teri Garr, Sidney Clute. The students plan to end their school show by taking off all of their clothes.

Funny Boy
W: Allan Burns. D: Gene Reynolds. GS: Liam Dunn, Richard Bull, Jan Arvan, William Elliot. Pete tries to help a fat boy put his sense of humor to good use.

The Coat

W: Michael Zagor. D: Gene Reynolds. GS: Mary Robin Redd, Joseph Carey, Ivor Francis. Liz tries to help Jason put his artistic talents to good use, in return, Jason steals a coat from a department store to give her as a present.

El Genio

W: Doug Tibbles & Ron Rubin. D: William Wiard. GS: Tom Nardini, Willard Sage, Natividad Vacio. Alice tries to get a bright Mexican student to continue his education by going on to college.

Our Teacher Is Obsolete

W: Ron Rubin. D: William Wiard. GS: Helen Kleeb. The students try to get an elderly teacher to resign because they think she is too old.

Triple Date

W: Jeanne Taylor. D: Gerald Meyer. GS: Lynn Hamilton, Allison Arngrim, Sid McCoy, Brenda Sykes. Jason becomes upset when the snobby parents of his latest girlfriend think he isn't right for their daughter.

Fathers and Sons

W: John Whedon & Ron Rubin. D: Terry Becker. GS: William Schallert, Ann Morgan Guilbert, Richard X. Slattery, Bob Balaban. The father of a student blames Pete for the problems he has been having with his son.

Clothes Make the Boy

W: Allan Burns. D: Lee Phillips. GS: Bud Cort, Kenneth Mars, Ramon Bieri. Pete tries to change the now-outdated school dress code.

Alice in Blunderland

W: Steve Pritzker. D: Lee Phillips. GS: Marjorie Bennett, Ed Begley, Jr. With a student teacher supervisor coming to judge her work, Alice suddenly finds teaching a class is more than she can handle.

Seventeen, Going on Twenty-Eight

W: Allan Burns. D: Terry Becker. GS: Diane Young. A conniving student tries to take Pete away from Liz and keep him for herself.

The Exchange Teacher

W: Treva Silverman. D: William Wiard. GS: Charmion King, Cindy Williams, Hilly Hicks. A liberal British exchange teacher comes to work at the school.

Ralph

W: Steve Pritzker. D: Leo Penn. GS: Ron Rifkin, Bruce Kirby. Liz gets upset when one of Pete's students constantly tags along with him even on their dates.

The New Boy

W: Ron Rubin. D: Robert Mintz. GS: Rick Kelman, Jamie Farr, Jerry Hausner. Pete tries to help a student who is constantly playing hookey from school.

Once Upon a Time, There Was Air You Couldn't See

W: John D.F. Black. D: Lee Phillips. GS: Byron Chung, Walter Brooke, Liam Dunn. Richie and Jason stage a TV campaign against smog.

Operation Sandpile

W: George Kirgo. D: Richard Kinon. GS: Meg Wyllie. Mr. Kaufman tries to help a student who feels her education will not help her become a housewife, while another student brings her baby sister to school when she can't get a babysitter on the day of a big test.

Play It Loose

W: Steve Pritzker, Peggy Elliot & Ed Scarlach. D: Norman Abbott. GS: Nancy Wilson, Woodrow Parfrey, Yvonne Wilder. Liz gets upset when a former student who is now a big singing star pays a visit to the school and makes a play for Pete.

Goodbye Mr. Hip

W: Dale McRaven. D: Terry Becker. GS: Bernie Kopell. A swinging teacher tells his class that he smokes marijuana but then has second thoughts when a student leaves what appears to be a marijuana cigarette on his desk.

I Love You, Charlie—I Love You, Abbie
W: John D.F. Black. D: John Erman. GS: Brad David, Kathy Gackle, Cindy Williams. Two students plan to elope to Mexico and invite Pete and Liz along as the best man and maid of honor.

Funny Money
W: Steve Pritzker. D: Terry Becker. GS: Rob Reiner, Alan Vint. Pete tries to find a way to help students who have difficulty reading.

The Whole World Can Hear You
W: E. Arthur Kean. D: Malcolm Black. GS: Bruce Kirby, Lillian Bronson, Priscilla Morrill, Ethelinn Block. Liz tries to help a student attend beauty school against her father's wishes for her to attend college instead.

Only a Rose
W: Ron Rubin. D: Gene Reynolds. GS: Naomi Stevens, Lieux Dressler, Lillian Randolph. A lonely old woman wanders into the school and proceeds to make it her second home.

The Laughing Majority
W: Richard DeRoy. D: Gene Reynolds. GS: Andrew Parks, Jane Actman, Elliot Street. The school "class Clown" decides to run for student council president.

Write On, Brother
W: John D.F. Black. D: Terry Becker. GS: Wes Stern, Ramon Bieri. Pete helps the students put out an underground school newspaper.

Choose One: And They Lived [Happily/Unhappily] Ever After
W: John D.F. Black. D: Richard Kinon. GS: Ramon Bieri, Dabney Coleman, John David Carson, Gary Tigerman, Michael Lembeck, Anthony Geary. Pete is chosen to train for the job of school vice principal.

The Lincoln Story
W: Bud Freeman & Lewis Paine. D: Charles Dubin. GS: Dana Elcar, Irene Tedrow, Holly Near. A heated debate about Lincoln costs Pete the Teacher of the Year award.

Adam's Lib
W: William Wood. D: William Wiard. GS: William Bramley, Terri Messina, Denice Stradling. Women's Lib moves into the school when a girl tries to join the varsity basketball team.

Captain of the Team
W: Bud Freeman. D: Charles Dubin. GS: Arthur Batanides, Rick Kelman, Dennis Redfield. A hippie student goes head to head with a clean-cut, snobby student over their different viewpoints on everything.

The Fuzz That Grooved
W: John D.F. Black. D: Gene Reynolds. GS: John Schuck, Joe Brown, Ramon Bieri. The friendly cop on the beat is replaced by a tough no-nonsense one who causes nothing but tension at the school.

Half Way
W: Richard DeRoy. D: Ivan Dixon. GS: Noam Pitlik, Bonnie Jones. A prejudiced father tries to transfer his daughter to a private school in order to keep her away from the black students at the school.

What Would We Do Without Bobbie?
W: William Wood. D: William Wiard. GS: Nicole Jaffe, Andrew Parks. While Bobbie spends all of her time planning the school prom, Richie decides to help her out by getting her a date for the prom.

The Valediction
W: Richard DeRoy. D: John Erman. GS: Richard Dreyfuss, Danny Goldman, Dick Patterson. A liberal-minded student is given the chance to write a valedictorian speech for the school graduation.

Dreams of Glory
W: Anthony Lawrence. D: Robert Sweeney. GS: Chuck Norris, Mike Stone, Eric Laneuville, Glynn Turman, Angela Satterwhite. Pete tries to get a shy boy interested in karate in order to impress the girl he loves.

Cheating
W: Bud Freeman. D: Richard Kinon. GS: George Ives, Elizabeth Baur, Chris Beaumont. Pete tries to help a student who was mistakenly accused of cheating by a tough teacher.

Mel Wertz and the Nickel-Plated Toothpick
W: Bob Rodgers. D: Richard Kinon. GS: Jack Bender, Jerry Hausner, Craig Hundley, Connie Sawyer. Pete tries to help a student decide between becoming a teacher or a musician.

How About That Cherry Tree
W: Albert Rubin. D: Hy Averback. GS: Ivor Francis, Bill Zuckert, Edwina Gough. A black student is accused of forging a teacher's signature on a scholarship application form.

The Long Honeymoon
W: William Wood. D: Terry Becker. GS: Tim Matheson, Eve McVeagh, Eric Laneuville. Mr. Kaufman tries to help a student whose mother ran off with a man and left her son alone to fend for himself.

Laura Fay, You're Okay!
W: Joanna Lee. D: Terry Becker. GS: Linda Haynes, Cindy Williams. Alice and Liz try to help a beautiful girl cope with all of the attention she is getting from the boys at the school.

Mr. Bomberg
W: Nicholas E. Baehr. D: William Wiard. GS: Sorrell Booke, Phillip Pine. An overly demanding and severe teacher upsets the students at the school.

The Last Full Moon
W: Robert Sabaroff & Bud Freeman.

D: William Wiard. GS: Brad David, Kathy Lloyd, Joe Perry, Clark Gordon. Pete and Liz try to get a pair of secretly married students to tell their parents about their marriage.

Opportunity Room
W: Bel Kaufman. D: Gene Reynolds. GS: Dennis Redfield, Sandy Brown Wyeth, George Ives. Liz tries an experiment in which problem students teach each other.

Hip Hip Hooray
W: Albert Ruben. D: Richard Kinon. GS: Paul Lambert, Richard Young, David Huddleston. Pete tries to avert a riot between his school and a rival school over the upcoming football game.

You Can't Take a Boy Out of the Country But . . .
W: Dale McRaven. D: Richard Kinon. GS: William Bramley, Jay Ripley, Todd Sussman, Michael Lembeck. Pete asks Jason to show a new student from the country the ways of city life.

Paul Revere Rides Again
W: Anthony Lawrence. D: William Wiard. GS: Kurt Russell, Milton Selzer, Ken Sansom, Barry Cahill. A student who dresses up like Paul Revere in order to alert people about pollution disrupts the entire school.

A Sort of Loving
W: John D.F. Black. D: Charles Dubin. GS: Christopher Cain, James McCallion. Pete creates a student-teacher rap group in order to avert drug problems at the school.

If It's Not Here, Where Is It?
W: Don Balluck. D: Ivan Dixon. GS: Martin Golar, Murray MacLeod. A Vietnam veteran returns to the school so he can finish his education.

I Hate You, Silas Marner
W: Steve Kandel. D: Michael Gordon. GS: Todd Susman, Dwan Smith, Hillary Thompson, Ivor Francis, June

Dayton. Alice allows the students to read "Catch 22" instead of the book assigned by the head of the English department "Silas Marner."

K-W-W-H

W: Douglas Day Stewart. D: Seymour Robbie. GS: Burgess Meredith, Carol Green, Jane Dulo. A city councilman arranges for a radio station to be built in the school, but regrets it when the students air programs which he believes are meant to make him look bad.

The Stutterer

W: Bernie Kahn. D: Richard Kinon. GS: Jim Wakefield, Diane Sherry. Pete tries to help a student who stutters.

America's Guest

W: Tom & Helen August. D: Seymour Robbie. GS: Jane Dulo, Todd Crespi. Pete tries to help a student who has been using his charming personality to get through school instead of using his brains.

Welcome Back, Miss Brown

W: Joanna Lee. D: James Sheldon. GS: Gail Fisher, Len Ross. Pete tries to help a teacher who, while going through a divorce, is taking out her anger on the boys in her class.

Hi, Dad

W: Anthony Lawrence. D: Charles Rondeau. GS: Stanley Clay, Stack Pierce, Frieda Rentie, Robert Casper. One of Pete's students, who was adopted, believes Pete is his real father.

Suitable for Framing

W: Bud Freeman & Gene Reynolds. D: Lee Phillips. GS: Bruce Kirby, Sr., Bruce Kirby, Jr., Tani Phelps Guthrie, Lloyd Kino. A fast-talking student is using the school and the students to further his own profit-making schemes.

They Love Me, They Love Me Not

W: Albert Ruben. D: Charles Rondeau. GS: Paulene Myers, Mwako Cumbuka, Karen Ann Williams. Alice and Pete try to teach some deprived youngsters living in a slum area.

Who Is Benedict Arnold?

W: Phyllis & Robert White. D: Lee Phillips. GS: Jack Dodson, Herb Bress, Jerry Houser, Carol Green. The students play detective in order to determine which one of them is working as an informant for Mr. Kaufman.

Hail and Farewell

W: Bill Manhoff. D: Ivan Dixon. GS: Virginia Vincent, Jay Robinson, Ed McCready, June Dayton, Gary Barton. Plagued by numerous problems, Mr. Kaufman decides to take a sabbatical, much to the dismay of everyone, especially when they learn that his replacement is known to be a tyrant.

Stay Awhile, Mr. Dream-Chaser

W: Elise Mayberry & Douglas Day Stewart. D: William Wiard. GS: Ben Cooper, Larry Wilcox. Pete tries to help a substitute teacher who hides his fear of teaching behind his talent for impersonations of famous people out of history

Dixon's Raiders

W: Jerry Mayer. D: William Wiard. GS: Ivor Francis, June Dayton, Greg Mabrey, Gary Morgan, Maidie Norman. While investigating the allocation of school funds for Pete's class project, a student uncovers a scandal in the cafeteria.

The Sins of the Fathers

W: Roland Wolpert. D: Allen Baron. GS: DeForest Kelley, Mark Lambert, Oscar DeGruy, Tanis Montgomery. Pete tries to help a boy whose father is involved in a political scandal.

What Is a Man?

W: Don Balluck. D: Seymour Robbie. GS: Frederick Herrick, Bobby Griffin, Ric Carrott, Bart Burns. Trouble starts when the students harrass a boy they assume to be gay.

The Fading of the Elegant Beast
W: Richard Bluel, Sherli Evans & Erwin Goldman. D: Ivan Dixon. GS: Arthur O'Connell, Rafael Lopez, Dick Patterson. Pete tries to help the school Latin teacher who is being replaced with a teaching computer.

Where Is It Written?
W: Joanna Lee. D: Charles Rondeau. GS: Aretha Franklin, Richard Kelton, John David Carson, Joy Bang. Liz tries to help a student who wants to become a minister by taking him to a religious nightclub.

House Made of Dark Mist
W: William S. Bickley, Ivy Ruckman & the students of Class 108 of Skyline High School in Salt Lake City, Utah. D: James Sheldon. GS: Joe Renteria, Michael Shea. The students try to help a boy who resents his Indian heritage.

Suing Means Saying You're Sorry
W: Milt Rosen. D: Richard Kinon. GS: Richard X. Slattery, Jan Burrell, Michael McGreevey, Michael Shea. Pete accidentally injures a boy after breaking up a fight, which causes the boy's parents to sue him.

And in This Corner
W: Richard Bluel. D: Charles Rondeau. GS: Georg Stanford Brown, Vince Howard, Setsuko Eejima, Sandy Champion. Pete tries to discourage a student who wants to quit school to become a professional boxer.

We Hold These Truths
W: Joyce Perry & Stephen Kandel. D: Leslie H. Martinson. GS: Fritz Weaver, Harry Holcombe, Mike DeAnda, Sacha Berger. A man attending night school citizenship classes destroys the political artwork of one of Alice's students because he felt it degraded the U.S.

There's No Fool Like
W: Warren S. Murray. D: Charles Rondeau. GS: Ivor Francis, George Neise, Dee Carroll, Dennis Renfield. Pete tries to help a teacher and a student to quit smoking.

The Witch of Whitman High
W: Joanna Lee & Susan Silver. D: Sid McCoy. GS: Candy Clark, Lew Brown. The students believe that the new girl in school is a witch.

I Gave My Love
W: Joanna Lee. D: Charles Rondeau. GS: Ruth McDevitt, Walker Edmiston, Tol Avery. An elderly teacher could lose her job when she teaches the students about VD without their parents' permission.

The Quitter
W: Douglas Day Stewart. D: Charles Rondeau. GS: Gerald S. O'Laughlin, Richard Hatch, John Alderman, Byron Kane. A student swimming champion decides to quit swimming in order to pursue acting, despite protests from his father.

A Little Flyer on the Market
W: John McGreevey. D: Charles Rondeau. GS: Linda Morrow, Jim Poyner. Pete and his class enter the stock market in order to earn money for a new school intercom.

Just Call Me Mr. Shigematsu
W: Stephan Kandel. D: Oscar Rudolph. GS: Mako, John Kirk, Lou Cutell, Tina Andrews, Bob Hastings, Jesse Dizon. Pete tries to help a Japanese student who bought a defective motorcycle from a crooked dealer who refuses to replace it.

And He's Not Even Lovable
W: Bernie Kahn. D: Allen Baron. GS: Ty Henderson, Tina Andrews, Patsy Garrett, Kitty Carl. Jason is assigned to work on a school project with a boy whose parents are bigots.

Hands Across the Sea
W: Gene Thompson. D: Sid McCoy. GS: John Hamilton, Kitty Carl. Jason finds himself resenting a polished and

well-mannered black student from England.

Walt Whitman Goes Bananas
W: Martin Donovan. D: James Sheldon. GS: Bruce Kirby, Jr., Carol Worthington. A student holds a banana-eating contest in order to attract summer job offers for the other students.

Lift, Thrust and Drag
W: Lloyd Haynes, Leonard & Arlene Stadd. D: Dick Michaels. GS: Paul Picerni, James Sikking, Mwako Cumbuka, Rory Stevens, John Hawker. Pete tries to interest some bored students in learning how to fly a plane.

You Don't Know Me, He Said
W: Douglas Day Stewart. D: Seymour Robbie. GS: Chip Hand, Art Riddle, Charles Martin Smith, Phillip Horn. Pete learns that one of his students is dying of leukemia.

The Impostor
W: Richard Bluel & Arnold Somkin. D: Herman Hoffman. GS: Joe Santos, Alan Abelew. Pete tries to help a teacher who has been teaching without a degree or a license.

Bleep
W: John McGreevey. D: James Sheldon. GS: Jane Actman, Angela Greene. The students become upset when a school faculty advisor begins to censor their stories for the school newspaper.

Shoestring Catch
W: Bud Freeman. D: Sid McCoy. GS: Mark Savage, Betty Cole, Jeanne Bates, Jerilyn Polk, James Johnson. Alice tries to help a boy with a learning disability.

The Nichols Girl
W: Martin Donovan. D: Charles Rondeau. GS: Angela Cartwright, Ed Begley, Jr., Alice Backes, Holly Irving. The mother of a student becomes upset when her son falls for a girl who doesn't wear a bra.

Elizabeth Brown Is Failing
W: Jerry Rannow & Greg Strangis. D: Bill Bixby. GS: Ruth McDevitt, Virginia Vincent, Tina Andrews. Mr. Kaufman tries to help an elderly English teacher who is becoming senile.

Pardon Me—Your Apathy Is Showing
W: John McGreevey. D: Charles Rondeau. GS: Barry Livingston, Frank Maxwell, Mimi Saffian. Mr. Kaufman reluctantly allows a student to form a Marxist-Lenin club at the school in order to save the school speaker's fund.

Mr. Wrong
W: Martin Donovan. D: Leslie H. Martinson. GS: Bernie Kopell, James Daughton. The new teacher who came to the school to teach a course in poise and personality develops a crush on Alice.

The Noon Goon
W: Arnold & Lois Peyser. D: Bill Bixby. GS: Craig Gardner. The students learn about responsibility when they become members of the campus patrol.

Rights of Others
W: Jerry Rannow & Greg Strangis. D: Harry Falk. GS: Dabney Coleman, Wendell Burton. An unwed student father learns he has no rights to his unborn child.

Man, If You're So Smart...
W: Martin Donovan. D: Allen Baron. A probationary student proves too much for everyone to handle, especially when he brings a loaded gun to school.

The Hand That Feeds
W: Richard Bluel. D: James Sheldon. GS: Paul Comi, Chris Beaumont, Ivor Francis. Pete tries to advise a student who doesn't believe in any form of competition.

Fifteen Years and What Do You Get?
W: Leonard & Arlene Stadd. D: Charles Rondeau. GS: Brendon Burns.

The teachers prepare a surprise party for Mr. Kaufman who is celebrating his fifteenth year as school principal.

Someone Special
W: Jerry Rannow & Greg Strangis. D: Leslie H. Martinson. A 12-year-old genius enrolls at the school and soon finds himself falling for Helen.

A Hairy Escape
W: Martin Donovan. D: Charles Rondeau. GS: Stanley Livingston, Paul Micale. When a student comes into a lot of money, the other students find themselves thinking of ways to spend it.

To Go with the Bubbles
W: Leonard & Arlene Stadd. D: Herman Hoffman. An Olympics champion returns to the school to continue her education but finds it is more difficult than she thought when she is constantly hounded with offers to enter show business.

I've Got the Hammer, If You've Got the Thumb
W: Stephen Kandel. D & GS: Unknown. A boy educated in the mountains enrolls at the school and finds it is not what he expected city life to be like.

Of Smoke-Filled Rooms
W: Richard Bluel. D & GS: Unknown. One of the students decides to run for a seat on the board of education.

Can Nun Be One Too Many?
W: Martin Donovan. D & GS: Unknown. Mr. Kaufman falls for a teacher who was once a nun.

Jason and Big Mo
W: Richard Bluel. D & GS: Unknown. A student suddenly gets a swelled head when he is offered a contract to play professional baseball.

No Island Is an Island
W: Leonard & Arlene Stadd. D & GS: Unknown. Liz and Pete try to help a Mexican boy who is too proud to ask for some needed help.

I Didn't Raise My Girl to Be a Soldier
W: Tony Palmerio, Leonard & Arlene Stadd. D & GS: Unknown. Problems arise when a girl decides to join the Army ROTC in order to become a doctor against the wishes of her father.

Twenty-Five Words or Less
W: Leonard & Arlene Stadd. D & GS: Unknown. Liz is offered a job in Washington, and a student's love of contests is driving everyone crazy.

Pete's Protege
W: Martin Donovan. D & GS: Unknown. A student teacher decides to quit after he is allowed to teach a class of his own for the first time.

Love Is a Many-Splintered Thing
W: Martin Donovan. D & GS: Unknown. Alice falls for the widowed father of one of her students.

MPG
W: Leonard & Arlene Stadd. D & GS: Unknown. Pete tries to teach the students about cooperation when they enter a miles per gallon competition in auto shop class.

Pi in the Sky
W: Leonard & Arlene Stadd. D & GS: Unknown. A math genius reprograms the school's computer in order to get needed school supplies.

Here's to the Boy Most Likely
W: Jerry Rannow & Greg Strangis. D: Unknown. GS: Mark Hamill. A student turns to alcohol in order to escape from the building pressures at home and at school.

Mismatch Maker
W: Leonard & Arlene Stadd. D & GS: Unknown. Alice finds herself in the middle when she encourages a student to become a poet despite his father's wish that he enter his real estate business.

El Greco to Jason
W: Martin Donovan. D & GS: Unknown. Jason falls in love and decides to quit school in order to get married.

Cry, Uncle
W: Martin Donovan. D & GS: Unknown. Mr. Kaufman's nephew neglects his education in order to pursue a career as a comedian.

RUN, BUDDY, RUN

On the air 9/12/66, off 1/2/67. CBS. Color Film. 16 episodes. Broadcast: Sept 1966-Jan 1967. Producer: Leonard Stern. Prod Co: Talent Artists. Not syndicated.

CAST: Buddy Overstreet (played by Jack Sheldon), Devere (Bruce Gordon), Junior (Jim Connell), Wendell (Nick Georgiade), Harry (Gregg Palmer).

The adventures of Buddy Overstreet, a mild-mannered accountant, who is constantly being chased by Mr. Devere, an underworld leader. Devere believes Buddy will finger him for a murder he plans to commit, and hires the underworld's best assassins to eliminate him. Each week finds Buddy in a different city, hiding from Devere, while his men search the town for a clue to his location. This series is not syndicated, but is a most unusual comedy patterned after *The Fugitive.*

Did You Ever Have One of Those Days? [Pilot]
W: Mel Tolkin & Ernest Chambers. D: Leonard Stern. GS: Bernie Kopell, Henry Beckman. In a steamroom, Buddy overhears syndicate killers planning a murder. They chase Buddy all over town but lose him temporarily in a supermarket.

[The Director credit for the remaining episodes is unavailable.]

Buddy, the Life Saver
W: Jack Elinson & Norman Paul. GS: Signe Hasso. In San Diego, Buddy accidentally saves a woman from drowning.

Win, Place, Die
W: Jack Elinson & Norman Paul. GS: J. Pat O'Malley. Buddy gets a job as a groomer for a thoroughbred race horse; however, the horse has a reputation of throwing everyone who rides it.

Death of Buddy Overstreet
W: William Raynor. GS: Jack Albertson, Don Briggs. Buddy sees his old friend Norman Klute who suggests that he fake his death to get Devere's men from chasing him.

Killer Cassidy
W: Myles Wilder. GS: Gladys Cooper, Jill Andre. Devere hires a professional killer to get rid of Buddy who is now working in a health spa.

The Bank Holdup
W: Seamon Jacobs & Ed James. GS: Sid Melton, Robert Strauss. Buddy steals a car in order to get away from Devere's men, only to discover the crooks in the back seat are friends of Devere.

Wild Wild Wake
W: Ray Singer. GS: Dave Willock, Vaughn Taylor. Buddy is in a new town and, seeking refuge, asks the local sheriff to lock him up for protection. But the sheriff refuses because he hasn't done anything wrong.

Down on the Farm
W: Jack Winter. GS: Julie Sommars. Buddy is hiding out on a farm with a tomboy named Betsy who can outfight anyone.

I Want a Piece of That Boy
W: Budd Grossman. GS: Bernie Hamilton, Allan Melvin. Buddy's new job is as a sparring partner to a promising boxer, the only problem is that the boxer is owned by Devere.

My Son, the Killer
W: Budd Grossman. GS: Lou Levy, Ray Brown, Jack Marshall. Buddy is spotted by Junior Devere as a waiter in a nightclub. He wants to make his father proud of him so he decides to get him by himself.

Grand Hotel
W: Al Gordon & Hal Goodman. GS: Henry Calvin, Judy March. Buddy is in Mexico working in a rundown hotel. He soon turns it into a thriving tourist lodge. He gets a big surprise when Devere checks into the hotel.

Death with Father [Part 1]
W: Ben Gershman & Bill Freedman. GS: Ann Elder, Ken Lynch. Buddy is in the hospital with amnesia, sending Devere to come and take care of him. What Devere doesn't know is that a rival gang, known as "W," is also interested in Buddy.

Death with Father [Part 2]
W: Ben Gershman & Bill Freedman. GS: Ken Lynch, Ann Elder. Mr. "W" kidnaps Buddy and wants to know why he is so valuable to Devere, but Buddy can't remember his own name.

Runaway Kid
W: Izzy Elinson. GS: Keith Nakata. Buddy finds a runaway kid on the road and decides the boy should return home.

Buddy Overstreet, Forgive Me
W: Budd Grossman. GS: Ken Lynch, Bob Kaliban. A doctor tells Devere that he has only three months to live. Devere decides to stop chasing Buddy and offers him a job instead.

Dying Is My Life
W: Myles Wilder. GS: Gregg Palmer, Dave Ketchum, Jackie Joseph. Tired of running, Buddy decides to talk to Devere in the hopes he can work things out with him, but Devere has other plans.

SANFORD & SON

On the air 1/14/72, off 9/2/77. NBC. Color Videotape. 136 episodes. Broadcast: Jan 1972-Mar 1976 Fri 8-8:30; Apr 1976-Aug 1976 Wed 9-9:30; Sept 1976-Sept 1977 Fri 8-8:30. Producer: Bud Yorkin. Prod Co/Synd: Tandem.

CAST: Fred Sanford (played by Redd Foxx), Lamont (Demond Wilson), Bubba (Don Bexley), Grady (Whitman Mayo), Aunt Esther (LaWanda Page), Julio (Gregory Sierra), Hoppy (Howard Witt), Smitty (Hal Williams).

A very popular series about an old junk dealer and his son, both trying to make a buck any way they can. The series did extremely well on the network. It did fine for a while in syndication, but it now seems to be dying out.

Crossed Swords [Pilot]
Fred and Lamont try to sell a valuable porcelain figure at an auction.

Happy Birthday, Pop
Lamont takes Fred for a night on the town when Fred celebrates his 65th birthday.

Here Comes the Bride, There Goes the Bride
Fred tries to talk Lamont out of getting married.

The Copper Caper
GS: Leonard Stone. Lamont buys some used copper pipes at a cheap

price, unaware that the man he bought them from stole them from Lamont's own house.

A Matter of Life and Breath
Lamont convinces Fred to take a test for tuberculosis. When the tests come back, Lamont discovers that he has the disease and not his father.

We Were Robbed
Fred breaks Lamont's porcelain and glass collection and tries to blame it on a gang of robbers.

A Pad for Lamont
Lamont moves out of the house to prevent Fred from interrupting his dates.

The Great Sanford Siege
GS: Dick van Patten. Fred fakes an accident to keep bill collectors from repossessing his furniture.

Coffins for Sale
Lamont buys two coffins and plans to sell them for a higher profit, but superstitious Fred doesn't want them in the house.

The Barracuda
Lamont objects to Fred's plan to marry his girlfriend Donna Harris.

TV or Not TV
Fred fakes amnesia to con Lamont into buying him a color TV.

The Suitcase Case
Lamont finds a suitcase full of money, unaware that the crook who stole it is coming back to get it.

The Return of the Barracuda
Lamont once again tries to break up Fred's wedding to Donna by threatening to get married himself.

The Piano Movers
Lamont and Fred attempt to deliver a piano to a rich collector.

The Light Housekeeper
GS: Mary Wickes, Beah Richards.

When Fred hurts himself, Lamont hires him a maid.

Blood Is Thicker Than Junk
Lamont goes to work for another junk man.

By the Numbers
Lamont refuses to let Fred play the numbers.

The Card Sharps
GS: Thalmus Rasulala, David Moses, Ron Glass. Fred tries to prove to Lamont that his friends are trying to cheat him out of his money.

Whiplash
When Fred has an accident, he plans to sue the driver for whiplash.

Have Gun, Will Sell
Fred tries to sell a gun left behind by a burglar.

The Dowry
GS: Albert Reed, Marguerite Ray. Fred tries to get Lamont to marry a relative's daughter in order to collect a $10,000 dowry.

Jealousy
GS: Roscoe Lee Browne. Donna brings one of her patients to dinner at Fred's house where he becomes jealous of her attentions to this other man.

Tooth or Consequences
Fred goes to the free clinic to cure his toothache where he demands that a white dentist and not a black one treat him.

The Shootout
GS: Leo Fuchs. Fred thinks he killed his next door neighbor with an antique gun.

The Puerto Ricans Are Coming!
Fred objects when a Puerto Rican named Julio opens a junk business next door to his place.

A Visit from Lena Horne
GS: Lena Horne. Fred tricks Lena Horne into coming to his house so he can collect money from his friends to see her.

Sanford and Son and Sister Makes Three
GS: Ja'net DuBois, Emily Yancy. Fred's old girlfriend arrives with a girl who turns out to be his daughter.

Fred & Carol & Fred & Donna
Fred is dating two girls at the same time and Lamont doesn't think it is fair to either of them so he tries to break up the relationship by having the two girls meet each other.

A Guest in the Yard
GS: Liam Dunn. Fred tries to prove that the bum who claims he hurt himself in their yard is faking.

The Big Party
GS: Gabe Dell, Danny Black. Fred decides to make extra money by holding a neighborhood party and charge admission.

Lamont Goes African
GS: Paula Kelly. Lamont acts like an African in order to impress a visiting Nigerian woman who is more impressed by Fred.

Watts Side Story
Fred tries to stop Lamont from dating Julio's sister.

Pops 'n' Pals
Fred tries to make Lamont feel guilty for not spending enough time with him as he would like him to spend.

The Infernal Triangle
Fred intends to marry one of Lamont's old girlfriends.

Home Sweet Home for the Aged
Fred goes to a retirement home when Lamont plans to travel around the world on a tramp steamer.

Pot Luck
GS: Jonathan Harris, Herb Voland. Lamont is the victim of a con game when he buys an antique commode.

The Kid
GS: Lincoln Kilpatrick, Jr. Fred befriends a nine-year-old runaway.

Rated X
Lamont, Rollo and Fred unknowingly agree to perform in a porno film.

Lamont Is That You?
Bubba tells Fred that he thinks Lamont has turned gay when he sees him go to a gay bar with Rollo.

Lamont as Othello
GS: Maureen Arthur. Lamont decides to take up acting.

This Little TV Went to Market
Fred unknowingly buys the TV set which was stolen from his friend Grady.

Presenting the Three Degrees
GS: The Three Degrees. Fred and his friends enter a singing contest.

Libra Rising All Over Lamont
When Lamont starts acting nice to Fred, he thinks he is dying.

Fred, the Reluctant Fingerman
Fred witnesses a burglary at Julio's place but refuses to testify.

Fuentes, Fuentes, Sanford and Chico
Lamont and Julio start a used car parts business.

A House Is Not a Poolroom
Lamont buys Fred a pool table for his birthday, which turns his house into a pool hall when all of Fred's friends show up to use it.

The Blind Mellow Jelly Collection
Fred donates his jazz record collection but tries to get them back when he finds out just how valuable they really are.

Superflyer
Lamont tries to convince Fred that it is safe to fly in a plane.

The Members of the Wedding/The Engagement
When Fred announces his upcoming marriage to Donna, Lamont calls his aunts to break up the marriage before it starts.

Grady, the Star Boarder
Fred tries to make extra money by taking in Grady as a paying boarder.

Mama's Baby, Papa's Maybe
Fred has been told that he may not be Lamont's real father.

Wine, Women and Aunt Esther
After a funeral, Fred plans a cheer-up party.

Fred Sanford, Legal Eagle
Fred becomes Lamont's lawyer when he plans to fight a traffic ticket.

This Land Is Whose Land
Fred hires a surveyor to determine where the boundary line between his property and Julio's is.

Fred's Cheating Heart
Lamont sends Fred to the hospital to see why he has so many heart attacks.

The Party Crasher
Fred tries to join Lamont and Rollo on their dates.

Lamont Goes Karate
Lamont takes up karate to defend himself against a bully.

Will the Real Fred Sanford Please Do Something
Grady is mistaken for Fred by a woman who claims that Fred promised to marry her.

Tyranny, They Name Is Grady
Grady tries to keep Esther's bible meetings and Lamont's "orgies" out of the house when Fred is out of town.

Aunt Esther and Uncle Woodrow Pffttt . . .
Esther throws Woodrow out and he moves in with Lamont and Grady.

The Way to Lamont's Heart
Lamont's girlfriend tries to make him jealous by making a play for Grady, who takes her seriously.

Hello, Cousin Emma . . . Goodbye, Cousin Emma
Grady's cousin moves in and they can't get rid of her.

Fred's Treasure Garden
Grady makes a salad from the vegetables in Fred's garden, including marijuana which he thinks is wild parsley.

Once a Thief
GS: Ron Glass. Grady tries to protect the house when Lamont invites his ex-convict friend to stay over.

A Little Extra Security
Grady accidentally gets a couple of extra social security checks and plans to go to Las Vegas to spend them.

There'll Be Some Changes Made
Fred refuses to allow a sensitivity group to meet at the house.

Going Out of Business
Fred goes to help Lamont who has taken a job in a clothing store.

Ol' Brown Eyes
Fred thinks that the ring Lamont gave him was stolen from Frank Sinatra.

Matchmaker, Matchmaker
Fred tries to get Lamont a wife so he can claim his uncle's inheritance.

Grady and His Lady
Fred tries to break up Grady's upcoming marriage.

The Surprise Party
Fred ruins the surprise party that Lamont and Grady had arranged for him.

My Kingdom for a Horse
Fred unknowingly buys a gelded race-horse and plans to use him as a breeder.

Home Sweet Home
Fred tries to get as much money as he can from a Japanese company which plans to buy his property.

Sanford & Niece
GS: Tina Andrews. Fred begins to take over the life of his visiting niece who looks just like his deceased wife, Elizabeth.

Strange Bedfellows
GS: Margaret Avery. Lamont plans to run for the office of state assembly-man.

Julio and Sister and Nephew
Fred helps Julio's nephew who is refused admission to school because he can't speak English.

The Merger
Lamont plans to merge his business with Julio's business.

Tower Power
GS: Janee Michelle. Fred makes a tower of junk in his back yard.

My Brother-in-Law's Keeper
GS: Allen Drake. Fred is shocked when he finds that his sister married a white man.

The Masquerade Party
Fred, Grady and Bubba try to win prizes on a TV game show where you have to come to the show dressed in a costume.

Golden Boy
Fred buys half ownership in a professional fighter.

The Stand-In
GS: Scatman Crothers, Al Williams, Billy Eckstine. Fred and Lamont substitute for their friends at a nightclub when one of them hurts his back.

The Headache
GS: Darrell Zwerling, Robert DoQui. A psychiatrist tells Lamont that his headaches are caused by Fred.

The Older Woman
Fred tries to break up Lamont's relationship with an older woman.

The Stung
GS: Richard Ward. Fred gets a professional gambler to teach Lamont and his friends a lesson about gambling.

The Family Man
GS: Carole Cole, Joe Morton. Grady moves in with his daughter and her family. [This is the pilot to the spin-off series "Grady."]

The Over-the-Hill Gang
GS: Lena Horne. Lamont and Rollo arrange a date with Lena Horne for Fred when they think he is dying.

The Oddfather
Fred witnesses a murder and now the killer is after him.

Donna Pops the Question
Donna tells Fred that she has another marriage proposal. He must either marry her now or lose her to the other man.

The Olympics
Fred joins the senior olympics to impress Donna.

Divorce, Sanford Style
Fred tries to get Esther back together with Woodrow and to move out of his house.

Bank on This
Fred is taken hostage by a gang of bank robbers.

The TV Addict
Lamont has Fred hypnotized so he won't watch so much television.

The Sanford Arms
Fred and Lamont buy an apartment

house then try to get tenants to fill it.

Earthquake II
Fred plans to sell his house and move to Las Vegas when he hears that a giant earthquake is about to strike.

Brother, Can You Spare an Act
Fred helps his brother-in-law out of the house by helping him keep his job at a local theater.

Steinberg and Son
GS: Lou Jacobi, Robert Guillaume. Fred tries to sue the network which is producing the Jewish version of their lives as a television series.

My Fair Esther
Fred tries to turn Esther into a lady in order to collect $500 from her husband.

Greatest Show in Watts
Fred stages a circus in order to keep him from being sued for keeping an elephant at his house.

Della, Della, Della
GS: Della Reese. Fred lets Della Reese use his house as a campaign headquarters for a political candidate.

Can You Chop This
GS: Danny Wells, Cesare Danova. Fred interrupts a television show to sell a load of Whopper Choppers which he bought with Lamont's money.

Sanford and Rising Son
Fred turns his house into a Japanese restaurant when he discovers that his Japanese friend can cook.

Fred Sanford Has a Baby
Fred rents Lamont's room to a pregnant lady.

Ebenezer Sanford
Fred dreams that he is Scrooge and that his friends are the members of the Christmas Carol story come to life.

Lamont in Love
Fred plays detective to find out all he can about Lamont's new girlfriend.

The Escorts
Fred and his friends start an escort service.

The Engagement Man Always Rings Twice
Fred is upset when Lamont tells him that when he gets married he is moving out.

A Pain in the Neck
Fred is about to receive an award but he is afraid his back problem will get in the way, so Lamont convinces him that acupuncture is the only cure.

Camping Trip
Fred and Lamont recall past episodes as they find themselves stranded in the woods when their truck breaks down.

The Director
GS: George Foreman. Fred and Lamont put on a play for the community.

Sergeant Gork
GS: Wolfman Jack. Fred rehearses the story he will tell his grandchildren: How he was a great war hero.

Fred's Extra Job
GS: Milton Frome. Fred gets an extra job in a restaurant to pay back a loan he borrowed to give to Lamont as a gift.

I Dream of Choo Choo Rabinowitz
GS: Leonard Stone. Fred tries to get into the Guinness Book of World Records by staying awake for several days.

The Winning Ticket
Fred starts a winning number contest to drum up business in the junkyard.

The Hawaiian Connection [Part 1]
GS: Sheldon Leonard, Greg Morris, Barbara Rhoades, David Huddleston.

A gang of jewel thieves send Fred and Lamont a free trip to the junkman's convention in Hawaii in order to use them to smuggle some diamonds off the islands for them.

The Hawaiian Connection [Part 2]
GS: Sheldon Leonard, Greg Morris, Barbara Rhoades. Fred and Lamont arrive at the convention in Hawaii, unaware that he has been given the case containing the stolen diamonds. [The first two parts of this episode were originally aired as a one-hour show.]

The Hawaiian Connection [Part 3]
GS: Don Ho. When Fred accidentally finds the diamonds, the thieves try to get them back chasing Fred and Lamont all over Hawaii.

The Stakeout
Fred falls for a man who is disguised as a woman in order to escape from the police.

California Crude
GS: Ross Martin.   An Arab believes that there is an oil supply under Fred's property.

Committee Man
GS: Edward Andrews, Ronnie Schell. Fred is chosen to represent the Watts businessmen on the Community Relations Committee.

Aunt Esther Has a Baby
Fred takes Woodrow's place when he gets drunk and threatens their chances of adopting a child.

Aunt Esther Meets Her Son
Aunt Esther throws her adopted son out of the house when she finds out that he doesn't believe in God.

Sanford and Gong
Fred, Bubba and Lamont appear on the "Gong Show."

Fred Meets Redd
GS: Jack Carter, Benny Rubin. Fred enters a Redd Foxx lookalike contest.

Carol
A friend from Fred's past pays him a visit but he doesn't remember just who the friend is.

Here Today, Gone Today
Fred thinks he was robbed when he finds all of his furniture missing.

Chinese Torture/The Defiant One
Fred handcuffs Esther and himself together but can't figure out how to get them out of it.

A Matter of Silence
Fred decides to play deaf in order to gain sympathy from his girlfriend.

When John Comes Marching Home
Janet's ex-husband returns, causing her to have second thoughts about marrying Lamont.

The Reverend Sanford
GS: R.G. Brown. Fred becomes a mail order minister to avoid paying taxes.

The Will
Fred thinks he is dying when Esther hits him on the head with her purse and knocks him out.

Fred the Activist
Fred joins a gang of old people to protest a store which refuses to grant credit to people over 65 years old.

The Lucky Streak
Fred hopes to win enough money in Las Vegas to buy the Sanford Arms.

Funny, You Don't Look It
GS: Milton Selzer.   Fred traces his roots and finds that he might be Jewish.

Fred Sings the Blues
GS: B.B. King. Fred thinks that B.B. King is out to kill him because he took Elizabeth away from him many years ago.

School Daze
Everyone thinks Fred is fooling around with a white school teacher.

THE TAB HUNTER SHOW

On the air 9/18/60, off 9/19/61. NBC. B&W Film. 32 episodes. Broadcast: Sept 1960-Sept 1961 Sun 8:30-9. Producer: Norman Tokar. Prod Co: Shunto Prod/Famous Artists. Synd: National Telefilm.

CAST: Paul Morgan (played by Tab Hunter), Peter Fairfield III (Richard Erdman), John Larson (Jerome Cowan), Thelma (Reta Shaw).

The romantic adventures of Paul Morgan, playboy and creator/artist of the comic strip "Bachelor at Large." Episodes relate the saga of Paul's attempts to live the life of luxury while at the same time remain faithful to his work. The series is not currently running in the U.S.

One Blonde Too Many
GS: Mary Murphy, Joan Staley. Paul meets a girl who has everything, including a flair for cooking.

For Money or Love
GS: Elizabeth Montgomery, Charles Fredericks. Paul is going to date Peter's cousin who is very rich but very cheap.

My Brother, the Hero
GS: John McGiver, Pat Close, Charles Saari. Paul's brother brags about his military wartime heroics.

Be My Guest
GS: Nita Talbot, Reta Shaw, Kaye Elhardt. A girl wants to marry Paul because he likes her dog.

Operation Iceberg
GS: Pat Crowley, Reta Shaw, Autumn Russell. Paul tries to warm up a cold female editor.

The Matchmaker
GS: Spring Byington, Howard McNear, Jody Warner. An elderly lady wins a week with Paul in Hollywood.

I Love a Marine
GS: Nancy Walker, Jackie Coogan, Doodles Weaver, Reta Shaw. Paul gets a visit from a Marine nurse who once saved his life.

Double Trouble
GS: Gena Rowlands, Beverly Englander, Marilyn Molloy. Paul makes a date with a girl but her twin sister arrives for the date.

The Doll in the Bathing Suit
GS: Tuesday Weld, Elaine Browne, Harry Jackson. A starlet tries to drown herself in front of Paul's house.

Hot and Cold
GS: Sarah Marshall, Joe Flynn. Paul goes to a health farm for a rest.

My Darling Teacher
GS: Pat Close, Jack Albertson, Lori Nelson. Chris studies for a math test at Paul's house.

One Night in Paris
GS: Luciana Paluzzi, Sandra Dale. Paul meets a pretty author in France.

Devil to Pay
Pete is ordered home for a wedding by his grandmother; he thinks it's his wedding.

How to Lose a Girl
GS: Chris White, Olan Soule. Paul misses his deadline so Larsen hires a female cartoonist to give him competition. [Tab performs a dual role in this episode.]

Happily Unmarried
GS: Dean Miller, Carol Byron. Larsen sends a beautiful messenger to tell Paul to get back to work.

Portia Go Home
GS: Joanna Barnes, Vickie Trickett. Paul is sued when a lady claims the heroine in his comic strip is based on her.

Turnabout
GS: Ruta Lee, Byron Morrow. Paul and Peter change houses so Paul can rest.

Weekend on Ice
GS: Suzanne Pleshette, Jack Albertson. Paul and Peter vacation at a winter resort.

Girl Overboard
GS: Liliane Montevecchi, Raymond Bailey. Paul is on an ocean liner headed for Europe, where he meets a beautiful girl.

The Art Patron
GS: Stanley Adams, Roxane Berard. Paul and Peter go girl hunting in Paris.

The Golden Arrow
GS: Diana Millay, Richard Peel, Ben Wright, Maurice Dallimore. Paul falls for a British girl of nobility on a boat train to London.

Galatea
GS: Antoinette Bower, Barbara Bricker. Paul runs an "Ideal Girl" contest in London.

Me and My Shadow
GS: Norman Fell, Jack Albertson. Paul has an assistant cartoonist who is dirving him crazy.

A Star Is Born
GS: Leo Fuchs, Suzanne Lloyd. Peter lets a movie company use Paul's house for a movie.

Sultan for a Day
GS: Allen Jenkins, Lori Nelson. Paul and Peter win a fortune in Las Vegas.

Holiday in Spain
GS: Linda Crystal, Lawrence Dobkin. Paul meets a famous female matador while in Spain.

Italian Riviera
GS: Chana Eden, Benny Rubin, Annalena Lund. Paul's new girl appears to be a mermaid.

Crazy Over Horses
GS: Audrey Dalton, Tommy Cook, Jack Albertson. Paul tries to get a date with a British girl who is only interested in horses.

Dream Boy
GS: Joanna Barnes, Sig Ruman. Peter dreams he is a dashing prince.

Personal Appearance
GS: Peter Leeds, Yuki Shimoda. A TV interview show comes to Paul's house which causes Peter to feel left out.

Those Happy College Days
GS: Mabel Albertson, Jody Warner, Susie Carnell. Paul is asked to lecture at a women's college.

The Invitation
GS: Ziva Rodann, Ellen Corby, Anita Sands. Larsen tries to get rid of Paul and Peter so he can use the house to entertain an Indian Maharani.

TAXI

On the air 9/12/78, off 8/83. ABC, NBC. Color videotape. 46 episodes (up to 1980). Broadcast: Sept 1978-Oct 1980 Tue 9:30-10; Nov 1980-Jan 1981 Wed 9-9:30; Feb 1981-Sept 1982 Thu 9:30-10; Sept 1982-Aug 1983 NBC Thu 9:30-10. Producer: James L. Brooks. Prod Co/Synd: Paramount.

CAST: Alex Rieger (played by Judd Hirsch), Louie DePalma (Danny DeVito), Elaine Nardo (Marilu Henner), Bobby Wheeler (Jeff Conaway), Tony Banta (Tony Danza), Latka Gravas (Andy Kaufman), Jim Ignatowski (Christopher Lloyd), Simka Gravas (Carol Kane), John Burns (Randall Carver).

Taxi: left to right, top, Andy Kaufman, Randall Carver, Marilu Henner, and Danny De Vito; bottom, Jeff Conaway, Judd Hirsch, and Tony Danza.

The adventures of a group of New York taxi drivers and their never-ending pursuit to meet their goals in life. A very popular show that was rescued in 1982 by NBC when the series was cancelled by ABC. However, NBC then cancelled the series after only one season.

Taxi [Pilot]
GS: Talia Balsam. Alex Rieger is re-united with his daughter whom he hasn't seen in 15 years.

Blind Date
Alex finds himself attracted to an overweight and abrasive blind date.

The Great Line
GS: Ellen Regan, Dolph Sweet. Incurably meek John gets enough courage to pick up a girl in a bar and then marries her the next morning.

Come as You Are
Elaine asks Alex to come to a party, but he must lie about his career to make a good impression.

One Punch Banta
GS: Carlos Palomino. Tony brings the boxing champ to his knees with a knockout punch.

Bobby's Acting Career
GS: Taurean Blacque. Bobby prays he'll land an acting job he has been waiting three years for.

High School Reunion
GS: Joanna Cassidy. Louie's insecurity makes him reluctant to attend his 20-year high school reunion.

Paper Marriage
GS: Rick Taggart, Christopher Lloyd. Latka's visa has expired and the only way he can avoid deportation is to marry an American girl.

Money Troubles
John and his new bride are in serious financial trouble and only Alex has the resources to help them.

A Full House for Christmas
GS: Richard Foronry. Louie's brother makes a surprise visit to sour the Christmas spirit.

Sugar Momma
GS: Gail Edwards. Tony can't break free from his possessive girlfriend.

Men Are Such Beasts
GS: Ruth Gordon. A free-spirited widow named Dee Wilcox rides in Alex's cab and finds his company delightful.

Elaine and the Lame Duck
GS: Jeffrey Tambor. Elaine dates a congressman in need of self-esteem and confidence.

Bobby's Big Break
Bobby leaves the cab company after landing a job in a soap opera.

Friends
Tony mourns the passing of his beloved goldfish which he left in Bobby's care.

Louie Sees the Light
Louie makes a vow to change his nasty ways if the Lord will let him live through his operation.

Substitute Father
GS: Mike Hersheul. The cabbies become substitute fathers when they babysit Elaine's son and go to a spelling bee.

Mama Gravis
GS: Susan Kellerman. Latka's mother comes for a visit.

Alex Tastes Death
GS: James Stacy. After being grazed by a mugger's bullet, Alex decides to give up driving a cab.

Hollywood Calling
GS: Martin Mull. A Hollywood producer decides to make a movie about the life of cabbies.

Cab 804 [Part 1]
GS: Tom Selleck. The cabbies exchange stories about their experiences in cab 804, the garage's mascot cab, which was just wrecked.

Cab 804 [Part 2]
The cabbies continue their stories about cab 804.

Honor Thy Father
GS: Richard Beauchamp, Ian Wolfe, Jack Gilford. Alex's father has a near-fatal heart attack.

Reluctant Fighter
GS: Armando Muniz. Tony has mixed emotions over his upcoming bout with a former champ who has decided to

dedicate his life to a young cripple.

Louie and the Nice Girl
GS: Rhea Pehlman. The cabbie Louie is dating has a bad reputation.

Bobby Wherefore Art Thou?
GS: Mike Horton. Bobby is sure his acting career is starcrossed when an acquaintance just passing through town lands him an off-Broadway role as Romeo.

Reverend Jim
The cabbies try to make something out of a 1960s hippie who hasn't quite recovered.

Nardo Loses Marbles
GS: Tom Ewell. Elaine is working too hard and the pressures begin to mount up.

Woman Between Friends
GS: Constance Forslund. Bobby and Tony jeopardize their friendship by competing for the same woman.

Alex's Affair
GS: Dee Wallace. Alex starts out to console an out of work actress and winds up romancing her.

The Great Race
GS: James Hong, Jean Owens Hayworth, Fred Stuthman. The cabbies bet on Alex in a contest with Louie to see who can bring in the most money.

The Apartment
Latka finds an apartment that suits his taste but it also costs $3000 a month to rent.

Elaine's Secret Admirer
Elaine's new admirer is sending her unsigned love notes.

Angela's Lighter Side
An old friend of Alex's has dropped 100 pounds and wants to start a romance.

Latka Revolting
GS: Lenny Baker. Latka decides to return to his homeland to fight a revolution.

Louie Meets the Folks
GS: Rhea Pehlman, John Becher. Louie is unnerved by having to meet his girlfriend's parents, so he hires Alex to come along.

Tony and Brian
GS: Marc Danza. Tony hopes to adopt a nine-year-old boy but finds himself competing with a wealthy couple whom the boy would rather have.

Jim Gets a Pet
Jim wins a bundle at the racetrack so he invests in a horse and wants to set it free in New York.

What Price Bobby?
GS: Susan Sullivan. An agent agrees to represent Bobby in exchange for sexual favors.

Guess Who's Coming for Brefnish
GS: Carol Kane. Latka falls in love with a woman from his own country but from a socially inferior class.

Shut It Down [Part 1]
The cabbies go on strike.

Shut It Down [Part 2]
Elaine resolves the cabbies' strike by agreeing to date management's negotiator: Louie.

Fantasy Borough [Part 1]
GS: Eric Sevareid. Herve Villechaize leaves some publicity photos in Tony's cab, which prompt the cabbies to indulge in their own fantasies.

Fantasy Borough [Part 2]
GS: Herve Villechaize. Herve comes to reclaim his photos as the cabbies continue their fantasies.

Artwork
The cabbies pool their money to invest in a painting they hope to buy at an auction.

Alex Jumps Out of an Airplane
Alex survives a ski jump and finds the exhilaration addictive.

THAT GIRL

On the air 9/8/66, off 9/10/71. ABC. Color Film. 136 episodes. Broadcast: Sept 1966-Apr 1967 Thu 9:30-10; Apr 1967-Jan 1969 Thu 9-9:30; Feb 1969-Sept 1970 Thu 8-8:30; Sept 1970-Sept 1971 Fri 9-9:30. Producer: Danny Thomas. Prod Co: Daisy Prod. Synd: Metromedia Producers Corp.

CAST: Ann Marie (played by Marlo Thomas), Don (Ted Bessell), Lou Marie (Lew Parker), Helen Marie (Rosemary DeCamp), Jerry (Bernie Kopell).

The adventures of an aspiring actress and her magazine executive boyfriend. This series featured Marlo Thomas as a clumsy, well-meaning actress who always manages to get herself into trouble. It was very popular on the network and was popular for a while in reruns, but has recently disappeared from many stations.

Break a Leg [Pilot]
An accident-prone Broadway star is suspicious of Ann, her understudy.

I'll Be Suing You
Ann argues her case against a pedestrian who Ann says hit her car.

Never Change a Diaper on Opening Night
Ann tries to impress a hot-tempered acting teacher at an audition.

Anatomy of a Blunder
Ann plans to introduce Don to her parents on a nice relaxing picnic.

Don't Just Do Something, Stand There
Ann gets an offer to do a TV commercial.

Goodbye, Hello, Goodbye
Ann and her father learn a lesson about independenc.

Rich Little Rich Girl
GS: Sam Melville. A rich playboy tries to repay Ann's kindness with expensive favors.

Little Auction Annie
Ann gets a tempting offer for a box of junk she bought at an auction.

Help Wanted
Unemployed Ann presses Don to hire her as a secretary.

Beware of Actors Bearing Gifts
Ann tries to keep a modern day Robin Hood out of jail.

What's in a Name
Ann's agent wants her to change her name but her father objects.

Time for Arrest
Ann tries to explain why she's in jail clad only in a leotard skin.

Soap Gets in Your Eyes
GS: Kurt Kasznar. Don's mother believes the character that Ann portrays on a soap opera is for real.

All About Ann
Ann tries to find out why Don is seeing another woman.

Phantom of the Horse Opera
Ann and Don try to find work for an old silent movie accompanist.

Among My Souvenirs
Ann plans a sentimental reunion with her high school boyfriend.

Ted Bessell and Marlo Thomas in That Girl.

These Boots Weren't Made for Walking
Don covers a big UN event wearing the shoddy shoes Ann sold him.

Christmas and the Hard Luck Kid
Ann cares for a poor child during the holiday season.

Gone with the Breeze
Ann misplaced Don's unpublished novel somewhere in Manhattan.

Kimono My House
GS: Caroline Kipo. Don's Japanese maid plans to stay in America by marrying a citizen.

Rain, Snow and Rice
GS: Arlene Golonka. An out-of-town wedding creates problems for Ann and Don.

Paper Hats and Everything
A surprise party for Ann lacks just one thing, Ann.

What Are Your Intentions?
Ann's father mentions marriage and a pleasant dinner party turns into a trial.

A Tenor's Loving Care
Don tries to interview a playboy singer who will talk only to Ann.

Leaving the Nest Is for the Birds
Ann tries to stop a man from taking a plunge from her window ledge.

You Have to Know Someone to Be Unknown
Ann pulls a string of crazy stunts to attract a producer's attention.

The Honeymoon Apartment
Ann's tightwad cousin and his bride come to stay at Ann's apartment.

This Little Piggy Had a Ball
Ann gets her toe stuck in a bowling ball.

Author, Author
The jokes Don wrote for Ann aren't funny.

The Mating Game
Ann goes on a TV dating show, unaware that Don is one of her choices for a date.

Black, White and Read All Over
GS: Ruth Buzzi. Ann's play gets bad reviews, including one from Don.

The Good Skate
Ann and Don team up to get parts in a TV commercial.

Thanksgiving Comes But Once a Year, Hopefully
GS: Mabel Albertson. Ann has to make last-minute preparations for a dinner which becomes a disaster.

The Philadelphia Story
Don has to convince Ann's father that his racy novel is not about Ann.

To Each Her Own
Ann and Don try computer match-making.

Pass the Potatoes, Ethel Merman
GS: Ethel Merman. A Broadway star cooks dinner in Ann's apartment.

65 on the Aisle
Ann's parents and 63 friends come to see her in a play in which her part was just cut out.

The Apartment
When Ann gets evicted, she moves into Don's apartment.

Mod Mod World [Part 1]
An out-of-town modeling job causes problems for Ann and Don.

Mod Mod World [Part 2]
Don imagines a romance between Ann and her photographer.

The Collaborators
Ann and Don get into some sticky scenes while working together on a play.

There's Nothing to Be Afraid of But Freud Himself
Don tries his hand at psychiatry and the results are totally unexpected.

When in Rome
Ann gets a movie role which calls for a nude scene.

A Friend in Need
Ann sprains her ankle, so all of her friends drive her crazy trying to help.

The Mailman Cometh Out
GS: Dick Shawn. Ann must share a publicity date with a comic.

'Twas the Night Before Christmas, You Are Under Arrest
Ann and Don are afraid that Jerry's apartment will be robbed on Christmas Eve, so they remove all the valuables only to be caught by the police.

Fur All We Know
Ann borrows a chinchilla to wear to a jet set party.

The Rivals
Ann is the only witness to a car accident involving Don and her father.

Call of the Wild
GS: Jesse White. Ann is worried that she has no sex appeal.

The Other Woman
GS: Ethel Merman. A gossip column links Ethel Merman and Ann's father.

He, She and He
Don is upset. British photographer Gary Marshall has proposed to Ann and she is considering his offer.

Odpdypahimcaifss
GS: Mabel Albertson. Ann becomes tongue-tied while trying to impress Don's fussy mother.

Great Guy
GS: Ruth Buzzi. Ann considers interfering in the romance of her girlfriend Pete.

The Detective Story
A handsome detective spends the night in Ann's apartment to catch a crank telephone caller.

If You Were Almost the Only Man in the World
Ann goes to a doctor who looks ex-

actly like Don.

Just Spell the Name Right
Ann's cheap press agent links her with a divorce scandal.

The Beard
Ann tries to get used to Don's new beard while trying to get him to get rid of it.

The Drunkard
GS: Sid Caesar.   A pompous and drunk comedian sobers up in Ann's apartment.

Old Man's Darling
GS: Cecil Kellaway.   An old millionaire is in love with Ann.

Sock It to Me
GS: Barry Sullivan, Pat Sullivan, Milton Selzer.   Ann may lose her job when she is required to slap an actor.

The Hijack and the Mighty
GS: Arlene Golonka, Valentin De Vargas.   Ann is working as a stewardess on a flight to Miami where she spots a potential hijacker.

Decision Before Dawn
GS: Dave Ketchum, Stuart Margolin, Hope Summers.   Ann is the only juror who voted not guilty and the other jurors don't like it.

7¼ [Part 1]
GS: Buddy Lester.   Ann goes with Don on a three-week trip to Hollywood, but first she has to convince her father that they will have separate rooms.

7¼ [Part 2]
GS: Jesse White.   Ann is chosen as the star of a TV commercial which requires her to perform crazy stunts.

The Secret Ballot
GS: Rosemary De Camp.   A family get together on Halloween Eve becomes a political fight over who Ann is going to vote for in the coming election.

The Face in the Shower Door
GS: Cesare Danova.   Don is jealous of a restaurateur who moved into Ann's building.   It seems she got stuck in the shower and he rescued her.

Dark Goes Well on Everything
Don dresses up as a woman to research a story on a police unit trapping muggers in Central Park.

Donald and Me and Jerry Makes Three
GS: Bernie Kopell.   Ann and Don are constantly being pestered by recently separated Jerry.

Ann vs. Secretary
Don's new secretary is keeping him away from Ann.

My Part Belongs to Daddy
GS: Larry Storch.   Ann gets a residual check and everyone is telling her how to spend it.

New Year's Eve
Ann's quiet New Year's Eve dinner for Don turns into a large party when everybody comes.

The Home Breaker and the Window Washer
GS: Bobo Lewis, Jules Munshin.   A window washer's wife thinks Ann is fooling around with her husband.

Eye of the Beholder
Ann spends the night at her parents' house and goes through all her old stuff.

The Earrings
Don gives Ann a pair of diamond earrings, then she loses one of them.

Many Happy Returns
GS: Jack Mullaney.   The IRS is investigating Ann.   They claim she owes $2500 and she keeps terrible records.

My Sister's Keeper
GS: Danny Thomas, Terre Thomas, Tony Thomas, McLean Stevenson. Ann tries to boost a young singer's career.

There Is Time for Ann the Pieman
GS: Jesse White. Ann loses her pride when she plays an elegant lady who gets hit in the face with a pie.

Subject Was Rabies
GS: Stuart Margolin, Ed Peck. Ann's father was bitten by a stray dog which might have rabies.

The Defiant One
GS: Terry Carter. Ann helps a lost black boy.

Fly Me to the Moon
GS: Robert Colbert. Ann takes a job as Miss Air Force.

Nice to Have a Mouse Around the House
GS: William Bramley. Ann and Don switch apartments because there is a mouse in hers.

Bad Day at Marvin Gardens
While playing Monopoly, Ann, Don and her parents have a fight.

Sue Me and What Will You Do to Me?
GS: Alan Oppenheimer, Ned Glass. Ann's father falls in Don's office and he plans to sue for damages.

Seventh Time Around
GS: Benay Venuta. Ann is jealous of Don's friendship with a society matron who wants Don to be her seventh husband.

Never Do Business with Friends
Ann's friends insult an abstract statue given to her by Don

Mission Improbable [Part 1]
GS: Lou Jacobi. Ann is chosen to spy on a sleepwear company in the garment district.

Mission Improbable [Part 2]
GS: Lou Jacobi. Ann continues her adventure as a spy in the garment industry.

Minnie the Moocher
GS: Dave Ketchum. Ann directs a show at her father's country club.

Nobody Here Knows Chickens
GS: Slim Pickens. A fried chicken king wants Ann to be Miss Chicken Big.

At the Drop of a Bucket
GS: Monty Hall. Ann puts herself on a budget one day then goes on a spending spree the next day.

Fix My Screen and Bug Out
Don spends the day as nursemaid to Ann and her head cold.

All's Well That Ends [Part 1]
Ann, Don and her parents are stranded at the airport when a blizzard strikes.

Write Is Wrong [Part 2]
Don writes a script about the day that they were stranded at the airport by the blizzard.

Shake Hands and Come Out Acting
GS: Scoey Mitchlll. Ann tries to promote the acting ambitions of a professional fighter.

Hearing Today Gone Tomorrow
Ann is tricked into becoming the chairman of her apartment building's grievance committee.

Kiss That Girl Goodbye
Ann is depressed when Don considers taking a job in Paris.

I Don't Have the Vegas Notion [Part 1]
GS: Jack Cassidy, Morty Gunty. Ann gets a job in a Las Vegas show.

I Don't Have the Vegas Notion [Part 2]
GS: Jack Cassidy, Morty Gunty. Ann and Don fly to Vegas despite the rumors of the resort's wild wild ways.

I Am Curious Lemon
Ann babysits with a little girl with a lemon tree which needs tending.

10% of Nothing Is Nothing
GS: Morty Gunty. Ann plays the straight woman in a standup comedy act.

Opening Night
GS: Patty Regan. Ann gets her finger stuck in a water faucet on the eve of her opening in a Broadway play.

That Meter Maid
GS: Dennis Weaver. A flashback episode to when Ann was a meter maid in a small town where she fought City Hall.

Fly by Night [Part 1]
GS: Russell Johnson. A flashback to previous episodes as Ann is on board an airplane.

Ugh Wilderness [Part 2]
GS: Russell Johnson. Ann and Don face a survival test after their plane crashes.

Stocks and the Single Girl or the Wolf of Wall Street
GS: Harry Townes. Ann tries her hand at the stock market after she gets a tip.

The Night They Raided Daddy's
GS: Bill Quinn. Ann plans to remodernize her father's restaurant.

Reunion
GS: Iggy Wolfington. Ann goes to her high school reunion with Don.

Gone-a-Courtin'
GS: Frank Maxwell. Ann helps producer William Samuels fight a lawsuit in court.

They Shoot Pictures Don't They?
Ann and Don accidentally film a close friend's wife kissing another man.

Easy Faller
GS: Warren Berlinger. Ann is Don's nursemaid when he gets a sprained back.

Chef's Night Out
GS: Tom D'Andrea, Jane Connell. Ann tries to promote brotherly love in the apartment building.

Soot Yourself (Air Today Gone Tomorrow)
Ann fights pollution by picketing Don's office building.

I Ain't Got Nobody
A nude centerfold has Ann in lots of trouble.

Super Reporter
Don is forced to wear an outlandish costume to a meeting with a city official.

That's Daddy's Girl
Ann babysits on her birthday with a kid who might have the mumps.

Counter Proposal
Don proposes marriage to Ann and complications set in.

Rattle of a Single Girl
GS: Alan Oppenheimer. Ann and Don pay a premarital visit to a marriage counselor.

Don and Sandi and Harry and Snoopy (But Would You Want One to Marry Your Sister)
GS: Cloris Leachman. Don's sister is about to get married.

That Cake
Ann accidentally bakes her engagement ring inside a cheese cake.

That Girl's Daddy
Ann's father is acting like a swinging young bachelor.

Stop the Presses I Want to Get Off
Ann's sudden success in writing for a magazine has little to do with talent.

That Senorita
GS: Rodolfo Hoyos. Ann's latest problem is an ethnic role that could be a hit or offend lots of people.

An Uncle Herbert for all Seasons
GS: Joe Flynn. Ann's eccentric Uncle Herbert pays a visit.

That Script
GS: William Windom. Ann badgers an evasive novelist.

There Are a Bunch of Carts in St. Louis [Part 1]
GS: Mabel Albertson, Frank Faylen. Ann is nervous meeting her future inlaws for the first time.

There Are a Bunch of Cards in St. Louis [Part 2]
Ann's trying to impress her future inlaws leads her into trouble.

The Russians Are Staying
GS: Bob Dishy. A Russian seeks political asylum in Ann's apartment.

A Limited Engagement
As the wedding date approaches, Don gets cold feet.

Two for the Money
Ann loses her friend's winning ticket on the daily double.

Those Friars
GS: Milton Berle, Danny Thomas. Berle and Thomas are besieging Ann for her vaudeville mementos.

Stag Party
GS: George Furth. Don's frightened fantasies of married life are visualized in this episode.

That Shoplifter
GS: Jerry Hausner. Ann is accused of shoplifting.

That King
GS: Brook Fuller. Ann's dinner with an obnoxious young king almost causes a political crisis.

That Elevated Woman
Ann recalls in flashbacks her stifled existence as a female.

THIS IS ALICE

Syndicated: 1958. B&W Film. 36 episodes. Prod: Desilu. Synd: National Telefilm.

CAST: Alice Holliday (played by Patty Ann Gerrity), Mr. Holliday (Tommy Farrell), Mrs. Holliday (Phyllis Coates). Also, Stephen Woolton.

Very little is known about this series except that it is the adventures of a nine-year-old girl. It has never been seen since it first appeared in 1958, but it is still available if any station wants it.

Alice Plays Cupid
Alice decides to help along the romance between her teacher and a janitor.

Alice Plays Detective
Alice becomes a private eye to earn money with which to buy a pony.

American Beauty
Alice tries to direct the course of true love at a beauty pageant.

Big Louis Comes Through
Alice meets Big Louie, a bookie. Soon

the two of them are selling real estate.

Callahan
Alice decides to help a young man earn money as a boxer.

Christmas Story
Alice is busy selling trees so that she can buy a gift.

Circus Time
Alice tries to help a runaway child and becomes involved in the lives of the circus people.

Class Reunion
Alice is given the opportunity to put a young romance aright.

Dandy Donovan
Alice and her friends take to horse racing.

The Elephant
Alice brings an elephant home as a pet. Her parents insist she get rid of it; instead, Alice runs away.

The Fortune Teller
Alice turns fortune teller for a bazaar and she is a suspect in a swindle scheme.

Guest in the House
Mr. Holliday invites a distinguished lecturer to the house.

Help Wanted
Alice helps out a romance between a maid and a wealthy man.

The Letter
Alice invades an advertising agency to do something about a couple's 50th anniversary.

Mail Order
Alice, busy with her club activities, meets a scientist and accidentally helps him discover a new chemical solution.

Man's Best Friend
Alice plays Pygmalion when a butcher falls in love with a socialite.

Mr. USA
Mr. Holliday saves money to take his wife on a second honeymoon to Niagara Falls.

No Place Like Home
The Holliday family spends a vacation full of mishaps.

One in a Million
Alice brings a tramp home for a meal unaware that he is an eccentric Wall Street tycoon.

Paper Drive
While searching for paper for a paper drive, Alice finds a paper that could change a man's life.

Pie in the Sky
Alice enlists the aid of a retired head of a bakery.

Pig in a Poke
Alice buys a pig from a tramp to enter in her club's county fair.

The Princess
While trying to help her friend's mother keep her dressmaking business, Alice goes to a former actress for aid.

Problem Child
Alice brings home a bad report card.

The Prophet
A mystic comes to town and has all of the women charmed.

Rags to Riches
Alice looks to perform a service for a millionaire.

Rock 'n' Roll
Alice's house guest is in love with a rock 'n' roll singer.

Rodeo
Alice rides a Brahma bull in Times Square, which touches off a strange series of events.

Song for Sale
Alice decides to save her Sunday school teacher's job.

Too Many Fathers
Alice thinks she is an adopted child.

Trial Balloon
Alice and Soapy launch a passenger-carrying balloon.

Two Yanks in Georgia
Alice meets two homeless boys and their grandfather.

The Weightlifter
Alice turns diplomat when a visiting aunt has the family on a diet.

When the Bow Breaks
Alice helps a yacht captain win the love of a beautiful heiress.

[The following episodes have no available story.]

Alice Goes to Washington
Freedom of the Press
House Beautiful
The Hypnotist
The Quiz Show

THE THREE STOOGES

The Three Stooges were a collection of 190 two-reel shorts syndicated to local stations. The Stooges were and still are a cult classic. Produced and syndicated by Columbia Pictures. The Stooges played themselves: Moe Howard, Larry Fine, Curly Howard, Shemp Howard, Joe Besser. Their comedies contain a lot of violence and are usually edited for current television showings.

[All of the following are with Curly until noted otherwise.]

Woman Haters
The Stooges join a woman haters club but problems arise when Larry gets married. [The dialogue for this episode is spoken in rhyme.]

Punch Drunks
Curly goes crazy every time he hears "Pop Goes the Weasel," causing Moe and Larry to turn him into a professional fighter.

Men in Black
The Stooges make a mess of a hospital when they become doctors.

Three Little Pigskins
The Stooges are mistaken for famous football players.

Horse Collars
The Stooges are detectives who help a girl who is being blackmailed by a villain in a western town. Also, Curly goes crazy every time he sees a mouse, and the only way to stop him is to feed him cheese.

Restless Knights
The Stooges return to their homeland to protect their queen.

Pop Goes the Easel
The Stooges invade an art studio while trying to hide from a cop.

Uncivil Warriors
The Stooges are Union soldiers who try to spy on the Confederate army.

Pardon My Scotch
The Stooges dress up as Scotsmen in order to sell their homemade Scotch.

Hoi Polloi
A professor bets his friend that he can turn the Stooges into gentlemen.

Three Little Bears
While trying to deliver a shipment of beer, the Stooges wreck a golf course.

Ants in the Pantry
The Stooges infest a house with insects and mice so they can exterminate it.

Movie Maniacs
The Stooges are mistaken for movie studio executives and proceed to destroy the studio.

Half-Shot Shooters
The Stooges accidentally rejoin the army and find that they are assigned to their old adversary, their sergeant.

Disorder in the Court
The Stooges play musicians who are the main witnesses in a murder case.

The Three Stooges: Larry Fine (left), Curly Howard, and Moe Howard, in "Three Little Sew and Sews."

A Pain in the Pullman
The Stooges wreak havoc on a train full of entertainers.

False Alarms
The Stooges are firemen who try to sneak out of the station to attend a birthday party.

Whoops, I'm an Indian
The Stooges disguise themselves as Indians in order to evade the man they tried to swindle.

Slippery Silks
The Stooges wreck a valuable Chinese cabinet and then inherit a dress shop.

Grips, Grunts and Groans
Curly takes the place of a wrestler they accidentally knocked out. Curly goes crazy when he smells wild hyacinth perfume.

Dizzy Doctors
The Stooges try to sell a miracle medicine called Brighto in a hospital.

Three Dumb Clucks
The Stooges try to prevent their father (a lookalike for Curly) from marrying a golddigger.

Back to the Woods
The Stooges are banished from England and are sent to fight wild Indians in Colonial America.

Goofs and Saddles
The Stooges try to capture a band of cattle rustlers.

Cash and Carry
The Stooges try to help a crippled boy and his sister by finding buried treasure so the boy can have an operation.

Playing the Ponies
The boys trade their restaurant for a race horse.

The Sitter Downers
The Stooges go on strike until their girlfriends' father gives them permission to marry his daughters.

Termites of 1938
The Stooges play exterminators who are mistaken for professional escorts.

Wee Wee Monsieur
The Stooges wind up in trouble when they join the French Army.

Tassels in the Air
The Stooges are mistaken for famous interior decorators. Also, Curly goes crazy when he sees a tassel.

Flat Foot Stooges
The Stooges play firemen who try to put out a fire at their own station.

Healthy, Wealthy and Dumb
Curly wins a fortune in a radio contest and three golddigging females try to con them out of it.

Violent Is the Word for Curly
The Stooges are mistaken for college professors at a women's college where they sing "Swinging the Alphabet."

Three Missing Links
Moe and Larry appear as cavemen while Curly plays a gorilla in a movie.

Mutts to You
The Stooges run a dog wash and find what they think is an abandoned baby, which they take home with them.

Three Little Sew and Sews
The Stooges capture a spy who is trying to steal a submarine when they dress up as Navy officers to attend a party.

We Want Our Mummy
The Stooges go to Egypt to find a missing archaeologist who was searching for the mummy of King Rutentuton.

A Ducking They Did Go
The Stooges unknowingly go to work for two con men by selling memberships to a phony duck-hunting club.

Yes, We Have No Bonanza
The boys go hunting for gold and get mixed up with some bandits.

Saved by the Belle
The Stooges try to sell winter clothing in a hot country, but then decide to sell pillows as earthquake shock absorbers.

Calling All Curs
The Stooges operate a pet hospital. They find that two crooks stole a valuable dog from them and now have to get it back before the owner finds out.

Oily to Bed, Oily to Rise
The Stooges try to help an old lady and her three daughters who have been swindled by some con men out of their property. She was unaware that there was an oil well on the property.

Three Sappy People
The Stooges are mistaken for famous psychiatrists and are asked to cure a man's crazy wife.

You Natzy Spy
The Stooges do a take-off on Hitler when they become the dictators of Moronica.

Rockin' Through the Rockies
The Stooges play entertainers who are traveling across the country with a group of women when they are attacked by Indians.

A Plumbing We Will Go
The Stooges are mistaken for plumbers and proceed to destroy a mansion while trying to fix their plumbing.

Nutty But Nice
The Stooges try to find the father of a sick little girl who was captured by a gang of crooks.

How High Is Up?
The Stooges become construction workers and proceed to wreck a new building.

From Nurse to Worse
Moe tries to convince a doctor that Curly thinks he is a dog in order to collect on an insurance policy.

No Census, No Feeling
The Stooges become census takers and join a bridge party in order to take the census, then try to interview some football players in the middle of a game.

Cuckoo Cavaliers
The Stooges unknowingly buy a beauty salon in Mexico.

Boobs in Arms
The Stooges unknowingly join the Army and are captured by the enemy where, with the aid of laughing gas, they make fools of the enemy and escape on a mortar shell.

So Long Mr. Chumps
The Stooges go to jail to find an honest man.

Dutiful But Dumb
The Stooges visit the country of Vulgaria to photograph a new weapon.

All the World's a Stooge
A man gets the Stooges to pretend to be refugee children so he can pass them off to his socially active wife.

I'll Never Heil Again
A sequel to "You Natzy Spy." The former King of Moronica tries to get rid of the dictators, the Stooges.

An Ache in Every Stake
The Stooges play icemen who have to deliver a block of ice to a house on the top of a hill.

In the Sweet Pie and Pie
The Stooges are saved from hanging by three society girls who now find that they are stuck with them.

Some More of Samoa
The Stooges seek a rare persimmon tree on the island of Rhum Boogie.

Loco Boy Makes Good
The Stooges help save a widow's hotel.

Cactus Makes Perfect
Curly invents a device which sniffs out gold, which leads them to a lost gold mine and some bandits.

What's the Matador?
The Stooges go to Mexico where they perform a comic bullfighting routine and get mixed up with a jealous husband.

Matri-Phony
The Stooges try to save a beautiful girl from a lecherous emperor.

Three Smart Saps
The Stooges go to jail to rescue their future father-in-law.

Even as I.O.U.
The Stooges are conned into buying a "talking" racehorse.

Sock-a-Bye Baby
The Stooges are accused of kidnapping when they take in an abandoned baby.

They Stooge to Conga
The Stooges get mixed up with Nazi spies when they try to fix a doorbell.

Dizzy Detectives
The Stooges play cops who are trying to capture a gorilla who steals jewelry.

Spook Louder
The Stooges become caretakers at the home of a mad inventor.

Back From the Front
The Stooges unknowingly find themselves aboard a Nazi ship where they succeed in capturing the entire crew.

Three Little Twirps
The Stooges go to work at a circus in order to pay for the damage they caused.

Higher Than a Kite
The Stooges wind up in Germany

when they hide out in a bomb dropped in enemy territory.

I Can Hardly Wait
Moe tries to cure Curly's toothache.

Dizzy Pilots
The Stooges try to invent a new plane.

Phony Express
The Stooges are mistaken for detectives by a gang of bank robbers.

A Gem of a Jam
The Stooges are mistaken for doctors by some gangsters who want them to remove a bullet from their leader.

Crash Goes the Hash
The Stooges pose as servants in order to snap a picture of a visiting nobleman.

Busy Buddies
Moe enters Curly in a cow milking contest.

The Yoke's on Me
The Stooges' farm is invaded by Japanese soldiers.

Idle Roomers
The Stooges play bellboys who find a wolfman loose in their hotel.

Gents Without Cents
The Stooges do a benefit show at a shipyard where they perform the Niagara Falls routine.

No Dough Boys
The Stooges pretend to be Japanese soldiers so they can capture a house full of German spies.

Three Pests in a Mess
The Stooges think they accidentally killed a man so they try and get rid of the body at a pet cemetery.

Booby Dupes
The Stooges decide to catch their own fish to sell.

Idiots Deluxe
The Stooges go on a camping trip so Moe can rest his shattered nerves.

If a Body Meets a Body
The Stooges go to a haunted mansion so Curly can collect an inheritance.

Micro-Phonies
Curly, dressed as a woman, is mistaken for a famous Spanish singer.

Beer Barrel Polecats
The Stooges decide to make their own beer, which lands them in jail.

A Bird in the Head
The Stooges are captured by a mad scientist who wants to put Curly's brain inside the head of a gorilla.

Uncivil Warbirds
The Stooges disguise themselves as black minstrels in order to escape from the Confederate Army during the Civil War.

Three Troubledoers
The Stooges become lawmen in the old west.

Monkey Businessmen
The Stooges visit a sanitarium run by a crook.

Three Loan Wolves
The Stooges run a pawn shop and find themselves mixed up with a gangster and an abandoned child.

G.I. Wanna Go Home
The Stooges try to find some place to live when they decide to get married.

Rhythm and Weep
The Stooges are hired by a crazy man who thinks he is a millionaire to put on a show.

Three Little Pirates
The Stooges disguise themselves as a visiting Maharajah in order to fool the Governor of Dead Man's Island.

Half Wits Holiday

A professor tries to turn the Stooges into gentlemen, but his efforts succeed in starting a giant pie fight.

[Every episode is now with Shemp until further notice.]

Fright Night

The Stooges become boxing managers and run into trouble with some gangsters.

Out West

The Stooges try to stop a notorious outlaw in the old West.

Hold That Lion

The Stooges get mixed up with a crooked lawyer and a lion on a train. Curly makes a cameo appearance.

Brideless Groom

Shemp has to find a wife within 24 hours so he can collect $500,000.

Sing a Song of Six Pants

The Stooges run a tailor shop and find themselves in trouble with a gangster.

All Gummed Up

The Stooges, working in a drugstore, invent a youth serum.

Shivering Sherlocks

The Stooges join a beautiful girl and spend the night in the haunted house she has inherited.

Parton My Clutch

The Stooges plan to go on a vacation to cure Shemp's nervous condition.

Squareheads of the Round Table

The Stooges help a blacksmith fight an evil Black Prince.

Fiddlers Three

The Stooges help Old King Cole find his kidnapped daughter.

Heavenly Daze

Shemp dreams he has died and is ordered to return to Earth to reform Moe and Larry of their crooked ways.

Hot Scots

The Stooges go to Scotland to find out who has been taking a rich Earl's valuables.

I'm a Monkey's Uncle

The Stooges play cavemen who are trying to romance three cave girls.

Mummy's Dummies

The Stooges play used chariot dealers in old Egypt who sell a broken down chariot to a nobleman.

Crime on Their Hands

Shemp swallows a valuable diamond and finds that he now has a gang of thieves and a gorilla after him.

The Ghost Talks

The Stooges play moving men who encounter the ghost of Peeping Tom in a haunted castle.

Who Done It?

The Stooges play detectives assigned to protect a millionaire from a gang of crooks.

Hocus Pocus

A magician hypnotizes the Stooges and turns them into flagpole sitters.

Fuelin' Around

Shemp is mistaken for a famous scientist and, along with Moe and Larry, is taken to a foreign country where they try to force him to make his secret rocket fuel.

Malice in the Palace

The Stooges dress up as Santa Claus in order to try and recover a famous stolen diamond.

Vagabond Loafers

The Stooges get mixed up with some crooks while they are trying to fix the plumbing in a mansion.

Dunked in the Deep

The Stooges find themselves as stowaways when they try to prevent a spy from sneaking some important microfilm out of the country in some watermelons.

Punchy Cowpunchers
The Stooges are hired by the Cavalry to capture some border thieves.

Hugs and Mugs
The Stooges learn that some valuable pearls were hidden in one of the chairs in their upholstery shop.

Dopey Dicks
A mad scientist wants to put one of the Stooges' brains inside his robot.

Love at First Bite
The Stooges prepare for a visit from their wartime girlfriends from France.

Self-Made Maids
The Stooges play dual roles as artists and their models who fall in love with each other.

Three Hams on Rye
The Stooges make a mess of a theater when they are finally given a chance to act on stage.

Studio Stoops
The Stooges, who are now working for a movie studio as PR men, fake a kidnapping of a famous star to get publicity but find that the kidnapping is real.

Slap Happy Sleuths
The Stooges are hired by an oil company to find out why their oil is disappearing.

A Snitch in Time
The Stooges get mixed up with some gangsters when they deliver some furniture.

Three Arabian Nuts
The Stooges find a magic lamp and then some evil Arabs are after them.

Baby Sitter Jitters
The baby the Stooges are sitting for disappears.

Don't Throw That Knife
The Stooges get into trouble with a jealous husband when they try to take census from the wife of a circus knife thrower.

Scrambled Brains
Shemp finds himself suffering from hallucinations when he falls in love.

Merry Mavericks
The stooges are mistaken for lawmen by a band of outlaws.

The Tooth Will Out
The Stooges become dentists.

Hula La La
The Stooges go to a tropical island to teach the natives how to dance.

The Pest Man Wins
The Stooges infest a house with bugs in order to exterminate it.

A Missed Fortune
When Shemp wins a fortune in a contest, three golddiggers try to take it from him.

Listen, Judge
The Stooges get into trouble with a judge when they are accused of stealing chickens.

Corny Casanovas
The Stooges unknowingly date the same golddigging girl.

He Cooked His Goose
Larry is dating Moe's wife and Shemp's girlfriend at the same time.

Gents in a Jam
The Stooges find that they have to charm three beautiful girls in order to collect their legacy.

Three Dark Horses
The Stooges become involved in politics and run into some crooked politicians.

Cuckoo on a Choo Choo
The Stooges get into trouble while living in an abandoned train car.

Up in Daisy's Penthouse
The Stooges try to prevent their father (who is a lookalike for Shemp) from marrying a golddigger.

Booty and the Beast
The Stooges unknowingly help a robber, then try to find him on a train.

Loose Loot
The Stooges try to collect their inheritance from a crooked lawyer who is hiding out at a theater.

Tricky Dicks
The Stooges try to get arrested so they can find a jailed murderer.

Spooks
The Stooges try to rescue a girl from a mad scientist in a haunted house. [Filmed in 3-D.]

Pardon My Clutch
Running a garage, the Stooges meet some gangsters. [Filmed in 3-D.]

Rip Sew and Stitch
The Stooges, who run a tailor shop, try to capture a crook who is loose in their store for the reward money.

Bubble Trouble
Working in a drugstore, the Stooges turn their landlord into a gorilla.

Goof on a Roof
The Stooges put up a roof antenna.

Income Tax Sappy
The Stooges try to find a way to cheat on their income tax.

Musty Musketeers
The Stooges try to rescue a princess.

Pals and Gals
The Stooges go out west to rescue a girl from the clutches of an evil villain.

Knutzy Knights
The Stooges try to rescue their king in medieval days.

Shot in the Frontier
In the old west, the Stooges fall for some bad guys' girlfriends.

Scotched in Scotland
The Stooges go to Scotland to help discover who is robbing a haunted castle.

Fling in the Ring
The Stooges become boxing managers and become mixed up with gangsters.

Of Cash and Hash
The Stooges get mixed up with gangsters while trying to run a restaurant.

Gypped in the Penthouse
The Stooges all fall for a golddigger and plan to get revenge.

Bedlam in Paradise
Shemp dreams that he dies and is denied admission to heaven unless he reforms Moe and Larry.

Stone Age Romeos
The Stooges portray cavemen who go looking for wives.

Wham Bam Slam
The Stooges and their families go on a camping trip.

Hot Ice
The Stooges try to recover a stolen diamond from a lady crook and a gorilla.

Husbands, Beware
Moe and Larry try to get Shemp married off so he will become as henpecked as they are.

Creeps
The Stooges tell their lookalike children a ghost story about the time when they were moving men who had to work in a haunted castle.

Flagpole Jitters
The Stooges are hypnotized and turned into flagpole sitters.

For Crimin' Out Loud
The Stooges try to rescue a kidnapped politician.

Rumpus in the Harem
The Stooges try to rescue three girls from becoming slaves to a Sultan.

Hot Stuff
The Stooges try to protect a scientist and his daughter from being kidnapped by foreign powers.

Scheming Schemers
The Stooges get mixed up with thieves while fixing the plumbing in a giant mansion.

Commotion on the Ocean
The Stooges try to recover some microfile for a spy aboard an ocean liner.

[The following episodes are with Joe Besser.]

Hoofs and Goofs
Joe believes that his sister has been reincarnated as a horse.

Muscle Up a Little Closer
The Stooges confuse everyone when they portray identical triplets.

Space Ship Sappy
The Stooges visit the planey Sunev where they meet vampire women and giant lizards.

Guns a-Poppin
The Stooges go to a mountain cabin so Moe can rest his nerves.

Horsing Around
A sequel to "Hoofs and Goofs." The Stooges try to save their sister-horse's husband from the glue factory.

Rusty Romeos
The Stooges find that they are dating the same girl.

Outer Space Jitters
The Stooges visit another planet where they meet evil aliens and a prehistoric caveman called the Goon.

Quiz Whiz
A gang of crooks tries to swindle Joe out of the money he won on a quiz show.

Fifi Blows Her Top
Joe finds that his old girlfriend is now living across the hall with her jealous husband.

Pies and Guys
A professor tries to turn the Stooges into gentlemen.

Sweet and Hot
Moe plays a psychiatrist who tries to help Joe's sister overcome her fear of singing in public.

Flying Saucer Daffy
Joe tries to take a picture of a flying saucer in order to win a contest.

Oil's Well That Ends Well
The Stooges try to help a widow who was swindled by some con men get back her land when they discover oil on her property.

Triple Crossed
Larry dates Moe and Joe's girlfriend at the same time.

Sappy Bullfighters
The Stooges get mixed up when they perform a comedy bullfight act in Mexico.

THREE'S COMPANY

On the air 3/15/77, off: Still continuing. ABC. Color/Videotape. 140 episodes (currently syndicated). Broadcast: Mar 1977-Apr 1977 Thu 9:30-10; Aug

1977-Sept 1977 Thu 9:30-10; Sept 1977-present Tue 9-9:30. Producer: D.L. Taftner. Prod Co/Synd: D.L. Taftner.

CAST: Jack Tripper (played by John Ritter), Janet Wood (Joyce DeWitt), Chrissy Snow (Suzanne Somers), Helen Roper (Audra Lindley), Stanley Roper (Norman Fell), Larry (Richard Kline), Ralph Furley (Don Knotts), Cindy Snow (Jenilee Harrison), Terri Alden (Priscilla Barnes), Lana Shields (Ann Wedgeworth).

This is the continuing adventures of two single girls, Janet (who works in a flower shop) and Chrissy (a scatterbrained typist), who ask Jack (studying to be a chef) to move in with them in order to share the cost of renting an apartment. In order for him to move in without upsetting their landlords, the Ropers, they tell them that Jack is gay. The Ropers later spun off into their own short-lived series (entitled *The Ropers*) and were replaced by a bumbling middle-aged swinger played by Don Knotts. Due to contract problems, Suzanne Somers was dropped from the show and replaced by Jenilee Harrison as Chrissy's clumsy cousin, and later by Priscilla Barnes who is a nurse. The series is still continuing on the network and entered syndication in September 1982. It has since become a very big hit in reruns, and will probably continue to be a hit for many years to come. This series was based on a British sitcom entitled *Man About the House.*

A Man About the House
W: Don Nicholl, Michael Ross & Bernie West. D: Bill Hobin. GS: Kit McDonough. Janet and Chrissy try to convince Mr. Roper that their new roommate Jack is gay so he won't think they are fooling around.

And Mother Makes Four
W: Don Nicholl, Michael Ross & Bernie West. D: Bill Hobin. GS: Priscilla Morrill. Chrissy's visiting mother decides to spend the night at the apartment, unaware Jack is living there.

Roper's Niece
W: Paul Wayne & George Burditt. D: Bill Hobin. GS: Christina Hart. Mr. Roper, believing Jack is gay, is convinced that he is the perfect date for his visiting niece.

No Children, No Dogs
W: Paul Wayne & George Burditt. D: Bill Hobin. Jack and the girls try to hide the puppy Larry gave them from dog-hating landlord Mr. Roper.

Jack the Giant Killer
W: Dennis Koenig & Larry Balmagia. D: Bill Hobin. GS: Peter Palmer, Peter Schuck. Jack believes himself a coward when a muscleman makes a play for Chrissy and he is too scared to help her get rid of him.

It's Only Money
W: Paul Wayne & George Burditt. D: Bill Hobin. GS: William Pierson, Joey Foreman. Jack and the girls believe their apartment was robbed when Mr. Roper takes their rent money from the apartment and fails to leave a receipt.

Ground Rules
W: Richard Orloff. D: Bill Hobin. GS: Jenifer Shaw, Gary Cooksen. Jack creates a privacy rule when he and Chrissy accidentally intrude on Janet and her date.

Jack Looks for a Job
W: Don Nicholl, Michael Ross & Bernie West. D: Bill Hobin. GS: Bill Fiore, John Fiedler, Sally Kirkland. Jack gets a part-time job as a male model, unaware that he is expected to pose in the nude.

Janet's Promotion
W: Alan J. Levitt, Paul Wayne & George Burditt. D: Bill Hobin. GS: Sandra deBruin, J.J. Barry, Margaret Wheeler. Jack and Chrissy convince Janet to apply for the manager's job at the flower shop where she works.

Strange Bedfellows
W: Paul Wayne, George Burditt & Alan J. Levitt. D: Bill Hobin. GS: Karen

Smith-Bercovici, Alan Koss. While the girls are away, Jack throws a wild party that ends up with Jack waking up to find himself in bed with Mr. Roper.

Chrissy's Date
W: Don Nicholl, Michael Ross & Bernie West. D: Bill Hobin. GS: Dick Sargent, Joyce Bulifant. Jack and Janet try to convince Chrissy that she is dating a married man.

Alone Together
W: Bryan Joseph. D: Bill Hobin & Michael Ross. GS: Sondra Currie, Stuart Nisbet, W.G. McMillian. While Mr. Roper is away, Janet moves in with Mrs. Roper in order to keep her company, but then she becomes worried about leaving Jack and Chrissy alone by themselves.

Roper's Car
W: Alan J. Levitt. D: Bill Hobin. GS: Tom Lacy. Mr. Roper regrets selling his old car to Jack and the girls when he learns that it could be a valuable classic.

Cyrano De Tripper
W: Paul Wayne & George Burditt. D: Bill Hobin & Michael Ross. GS: Jess Nadelman, Sarah Smith. Chrissy tries to impress her new gourmet boyfriend by claiming she is a great cook. She then tries to get Jack to cook dinner for them so she can take the credit.

Chrissy's Night Out
W: Phil Hahn & Stuart Gillard. D: Bill Hobin & Michael Ross. GS: James Cromwell. Jack comes to Chrissy's aid when he defends her honor from a man she met at the pub, unaware that the man is a cop.

Stanley Casanova
W: Gary Belkin. D: Bill Hobin & Michael Ross. GS: Alba Francesca, Ivana Moore. Chrissy, Janet and Mrs. Roper believe that Mr. Roper is fooling around with another woman.

Janet's High School Sweetheart
W: Dixie Brown Grossman. D: Bill Hobin. GS: John Elerick. Janet's high school boyfriend comes for a visit and proceeds to chase Janet all over the apartment.

Jack's Uncle
W: Paul Wayne, George Burditt & Mike Marmer. D: Bill Hobin. GS: Don Porter, Shirley Mitchell. Jack's fast-talking uncle comes for a visit. Not only does he pay Jack's rent with a bad check, but he then tries to con Mr. Roper out of some money.

Helen's Job
W: Paul Wayne & George Burditt. D: Bill Hobin. Mrs. Roper gets a job at a cafeteria in order to teach her husband a lesson.

Three's Christmas
W: Don Nicholl, Michael Ross & Bernie West. D: Bill Hobin. Jack and the girls try to get out of spending Christmas Eve with the Ropers so they can attend a big party.

The Gift
W: Paul Wayne & George Burditt. D: Bill Hobin. GS: William Pierson. Jack buys a coat for Mr. Roper to give to his wife, but Chrissy mistakenly believes that it is her birthday present.

The Rivals
W: Chuck Stewart & Bernie Hahn. D: Bill Hobin. GS: Jack Fink. Jack gets caught in the middle when Janet accuses Chrissy of stealing away her new boyfriend.

The Baby Sitter
W: Don Nicholl, Michael Ross & Bernie West. D: Sam Gary. GS: Archie Hahn, Lee Bryant, Gary Hollis, Sheila Rogers, Brian Kend. Janet gets Jack and Chrissy to take her place babysitting while she goes out on a date.

Home Movies
W: Don Nicholl, Michael Ross & Ber-

nie West. D: Bill Hobin. GS: Stuart Gillard. Chrissy takes up filmmaking in order to impress her new film buff boyfriend. Woody Woodpecker makes a cameo appearance.

Jack in the Flower Shop
W: Ziggy Steinberg, Paul Wayne & George Burditt. D: Bill Hobin. GS: Natalie Schafer, J.J. Barry, Mickey Deems. Janet becomes Jack's boss when he takes a job at the flower shop.

Jack's Navy Pal
W: Paul Wayne, George Burditt & Alan J. Levitt. D: Bill Hobin. GS: David Dukes. Jack's old Navy friend arrives just in time to ruin the dinner he planned for the Ropers.

Will the Real Jack Tripper
W: Don Nicholl, Michael Ross & Bernie West. D: Bill Hobin & Michael Ross. GS: Anne Schedeen, Susan Blu, Ted Gehring. The girls are shocked when a pregnant girl arrives at the apartment naming Jack as the father of her baby.

Days of Beer and Weeds
W: Don Nicholl, Michael Ross & Bernie West. D: Bill Hobin. GS: David Tress, Ludi Claire. Jack and the girls discover some pretty weeds while cleaning up the Roper's garden. They later give the weeds to Mrs. Roper so that she can use them in her flower arranging class, unaware that the weeds are really marijuana plants.

Chrissy Come Home
W: Joyce & George Burditt. D: Bill Hobin. GS: Peter Mark Richman. Chrissy's minister father arrives for a visit, unaware that Jack is now living in the apartment.

Bird Song
W: Don Nicholl, Michael Ross & Bernie West. D: Bill Hobin. Jack and Chrissy babysit for Mr. Roper's parakeet.

Coffee, Tea or Jack?
W: Kathy Donnell & Madeline DiMaggio Wagner. D: Bill Hobin. GS: Loni Anderson, Bruce Bauer. Jack's old stewardess girlfriend arrives just as the girls are planning to give him a surprise birthday party.

Double Date
W: Bob Baublitz. D: Dave Powers. GS: Anne Schedeen, Rebecca Clemmons. Jack pretends that he is sick so he can break his date with his girlfriend and go out with another girl.

Good Old Reliable Janet
W: Roger Shulman & John Baskin. D: Dave Powers. GS: Ellen Sherman, Nadia Caillou. Janet and Chrissy plan to attend a demonstration at a nude beach.

Love Diary
W: Gary Belkin & Deborah Hwang. D: Dave Powers. GS: Paul Barselou. Mr. Roper believes that Chrissy is in love with him after reading the x-rated diary that she has been typing.

The Fast
W: Thomas E. Szollosi & Richard Christian Matheson. D: Dave Powers. GS: Angel Tompkins. Jack bets that he can give up women longer than Chrissy can give up food.

Helen's Rendezvous
W: Jim Rogers. D: Dave Powers. GS: Art Kassul. Jack and the girls believe that Mrs. Roper is having an affair with her husband's best friend.

My Sister's Keeper
W: Franelle Silver, Paul Wayne & George Burditt. D: Dave Powers. GS: Devon Ericson. Janet jumps to the wrong conclusion when she finds Jack in bed with her sister.

Chrissy and the Guru
W: Vicki King, Paul Wayne & George Burditt. D: Dave Powers. GS: Michael Bell, Regie Baff, Diane Sommer-

field. Jack and Janet try to save Chrissy who has fallen under the spell of a guru who has convinced her to join a commune.

Larry's Bride
W: Martin Roth. D: Dave Powers. GS: Cecilia Hart, John Lawrence. Larry's golddigging fiancee falls for Jack.

Chrissy's New Boss
W: Al Gordon & Jack Mendelsohn. D: Dave Powers. GS: Emmaline Henry, Richard McKenzie. Jack and Janet become upset when they learn that Chrissy is planning to take an overnight trip with her new boss.

The Crush
W: Al Gordon & Jack Mendelsohn. D: Dave Powers. GS: Lauri Hendler, Lois Areno, Steve Shaw. The Ropers' teenage houseguest tries to get rid of the girls so she can have Jack all for herself.

The Kleptomaniac
W: Don Nicholl, Michael Ross, Bernie West, Paul Wayne & George Burditt. D: Dave Powers. Jack and Janet believe that Chrissy is a kleptomaniac.

The Party's Over
W: Don Nicholl, Michael Ross & Bernie West. D: Dave Powers. GS: Diane Herbert. On the night of Jack and the girls' big party, Mr. Roper plays a trick on them which causes Mrs. Roper to walk out on him.

Eleanor's Return
W: Roger Shulman & John Baskin. D: Dave Powers. GS: Marianne Black. When Eleanor, the girls' former roommate, returns for a visit, Jack believes the girls are planning to throw him out so she can move back in.

The Older Woman
W: Paul Wayne & George Burditt. D: Dave Powers. GS: Claudette Nevins, Irene Tedrow. Janet and Chrissy mistakenly believe Jack's girlfriend's mother is the older woman he said he was dating.

Stanley's Hotline
W: Sam Greenbaum. D: Dave Powers. GS: Anne Schedeen. Mr. Roper accidentally overhears a conversation which leads him to believe that Chrissy is pregnant.

The Catered Affair
W: Al Gordon & Jack Mendelsohn. D: Dave Powers. GS: Emmaline Henry, Bibi Osterwald, Macon McCalman. Jack comes to the rescue when Chrissy is on the receiving end of a pass from her firm's president.

The Best Laid Plans
W: Roger Shulman & John Baskin. D: Dave Powers. GS: Jenny Sherman. Janet moves into Jack's room when she discovers a mouse in her bedroom.

The Harder They Fall
W: Susan Sisko, Al Gordon & Jack Mendelsohn. D: Dave Powers. GS: Rod McCary. Janet and her boyfriend discover Jack and Chrissy in bed together.

The Bake-Off
W: Paul Wayne, George Burditt & Jerry Kenion. D: Dave Powers. GS: Leon Askin, William Pierson. Chrissy unknowingly eats the pie Jack was going to enter in a baking contest.

Jack Moves Out
W: Paul Wayne & George Burditt. D. Dave Powers. GS: Cynthia Harris, Jordan Charney, Paul Kent. Jack moves out of the apartment and becomes the live-in cook for Larry's boss.

An Anniversary Surprise
W: Roger Shulman & John Baskin. D: Dave Powers. GS: Ruta Lee. Mrs. Roper mistakenly believes that Mr. Roper is having an affair, unaware that the woman she caught him with is the real estate agent who is helping him sell the apartment house.

Moving On
W: Johnnie Mortimer & Brian Cooke. D: Dave Powers. GS: Jeffrey Tambor, Patricia McCormack, Evan Cohen. The Ropers move into a new town-house and find they have a very snob-by neighbor. [This was the pilot for the short-lived spinoff series "The Ropers."]

Triangle Troubles
W: Al Gordon & Jack Mendelsohn. D: Dave Powers. GS: Peter Mark Rich-man, Barrie Youngfellow, Terence Goodman, Robert Machray. The girls try to help Jack convince his new girl-friend that he lives alone.

Stanley, the Ladies Man
W: George Burditt. D: Jack Shea. GS: Jeffrey Tambor, Patricia McCor-mack, Evan Cohen. Mr. Roper invites Jack and the girls over to his house for a surprise disco party being held in his wife's honor.

Jack on the Lam
W: Neil Lebowitz. D: Dave Powers. GS: Dick O'Neill, James Staley, Ru-dolph Willrich. Jack dresses up as a woman and pretends to be Chrissy in order to avoid a pair of FBI agents.

Love Thy Neighbor
W: Mark Tuttle. D: Dave Powers. GS: Damian London. Jack takes Larry's place as a male escort in order to earn some extra money. Ann Wedgeworth joins the cast as next-door neighbor Lana Shields.

The New Landlord
W: Kim Weiskopf & Michael S. Baser. D: Dave Powers. Jack and the girls un-knowingly sell all of the new landlord's furniture, thinking it belonged to the Ropers. Don Knotts joins the cast as the new landlord, Ralph Furley.

Snow Job
W: Rowby Goren. D: Dave Powers. GS: Paul Avery, John Miranda, Taafe O'Connell, Melanie Vincz. Chrissy gets a job selling cosmetics door-to-door.

Jack the Ripper
W: Bill Richmond & Gene Perret. D: Dave Powers. Jack takes assertiveness training and turns into a pushy loud-mouth.

The Lifesaver
W: George Atkins. D: Dave Powers. GS: Phil Leeds. Jack and the girls get evicted from the apartment and plan to move into a plush penthouse.

Old Folks at Home
W: Kim Weiskopf & Michael S. Baser. D: Dave Powers. GS: J.Pat O'Malley, Simone Griffeth, Jeanne Bates, Joseph-ine Livingston. Chrissy invites an old man to stay with them while he looks for a new apartment.

A Camping We Will Go
W: Kim Weiskopf & Michael S. Baser. D: Dave Powers. GS: Louise Williams. Jack plans to spend the weekend in a mountain cabin, unaware that just about everyone else in the apartment building is going to tag along for the ride.

Chrissy's Hospitality
W: Mark Tuttle. D: Dave Powers. GS: Keene Curtis, Ruth Manning, Hope Clarke. Chrissy is taken to the hospital when she falls in the bathtub.

The Loan Shark
W: Mark Tuttle. D: Dave Powers. GS: Harold J. Stone, Livia Genise, Mickey Morton. Jack finds himself giving cooking lessons to a gangster's wife in order to pay back the interest on a loan.

The Love Barge
W: Bill Richmond & Gene Perret. D: Dave Powers. GS: Bob Hastings. Jack gets a job as an assistant chef on a cruise ship.

Ralph's Rival
W: George Atkins. D: Dave Powers. GS: Reb Brown. Ralph tries to im-press his old boyhood friend by try-ing to pass Chrissy off as his wife.

A Black Letter Day
W: Mark Chambers. D: Dave Powers. After they both read a lovelorn column in the newspaper, Janet and Chrissy are both convinced that Jack is having an affair with the other.

The Reverend Steps Out
W: Kim Weiskopf & Michael S. Baser. D: Dave Powers. GS: Peter Mark Richman, Ric Carrott, Patricia Barry. Chrissy believes that her minister father is having an affair with another woman.

Larry Loves Janet
W: John Boni. D: Dave Powers. Jack and Chrissy try to help Janet discourage Larry who finds that he has a crush on her.

Mighty Mouth
W: Howard Gewirtz & Ian Praiser. D: Dave Powers. GS: Steve Sandor, Tori Lysdahl. Jack finds himself in big trouble when he dates a beautiful gym instructor with an overprotective big brother.

The Love Lesson
W: Mark Tuttle. D: Dave Powers. GS: Joanna Kerns. Jack accidentally lets Mr. Furley know that he isn't gay.

Handcuffed
W: Len Richmond, Kim Weiskopf & Michael S. Baser. D: Dave Powers. GS: Alan Manson, Daniel Trent, Cameron Young, Heather Lowe. Jack and Chrissy accidentally lock themselves together with a pair of handcuffs.

And Baby Makes Two
W: Ellen Guylas. D: Dave Powers. GS: Phillip Charles MacKenzie, Robert Quigley, Mark Siegel. Jack and Chrissy believe that Janet placed an ad in the newspaper for a man to father her baby.

Jack's Bad Boy
W: Mark Tuttle. D: Dave Powers. GS: Shane Sinutko, Joe George. A lonely rich kid moves in with Jack and the girls.

Lee Ain't Heavy, He's My Brother
W: Kim Weiskopf & Michael S. Baser. D: Dave Powers. GS: John Getz, Albert Carrier. Jack becomes jealous when his older brother comes for a visit and begins to make a play for Chrissy.

The Root of All Evil
W: Howard Albrecht & Sol Weinstein. D: Dave Powers. GS: Joel Brooks. A fight breaks out when Chrissy wins a lot of money on the races and then decides to split her winnings with her roommates.

Secret Admirer
W: Joyce Gittlin, Steve Clements & Mark Tuttle. D: Dave Powers. GS: Barry Gordon, Stephen Johnson, David Hines, Indy Shriner. Chrissy tries to find out who has been sending her secret love notes.

The Goodbye Guy
W: Howard Albrecht & Sol Weinstein. D: Dave Powers. GS: Gloria LeRoy. Jack and the girls throw a party for Mr. Furley in order to help him win the affections of a beautiful blonde.

Jack's Graduation
W: Kim Weiskopf & Michael S. Baser. D: Dave Powers. GS: William Pierson, Steve Vinovich, Lynda Beattie. Jack has to prove to the Dean of his cooking school that another student exchanged dishes during the final exam, in order to graduate.

Upstairs, Downstairs, Downstairs
W: Martin Rips & Joseph Staretski. D: Dave Powers. GS: Lee Crawford, Marie Laurin. Jack finds himself preparing three gourmet dinners in three different apartments at the same time.

. . . And Justice for Jack
W: George Burditt. D: Dave Powers. GS: Jan Sterling, Ellen Travolta, Steven Anderson, Pamela McMyler. Jack gets a job at a diner but finds that his new female boss has the hots for him.

A Hundred Dollars a What?
W: George Burditt. D: Dave Powers. GS: Elaine Giftos, Mickey Deems. Chrissy is unaware that her old high school friend is now a call girl.

Downhill Chaser
W: Martin Rips & Joseph Staretski. D: Dave Powers. GS: Laurette Spang, Kate Murtaugh, John Gibson. Jack tries to impress his new girlfriend by claiming that he is an expert skier.

A Crowded Romance
W: Mark Tuttle. D: Dave Powers. GS: Vernon Weddle, Rebecca Holden, Fay DeWitt. Janet tries to keep Larry and Jack from finding out that they are both dating the same woman.

Room at the Bottom
W: Martin Rips & Joseph Staretski. D: Dave Powers. GS: Michael Lombard, Jennifer Gay, Edmund Stoiber, Frank O'Brien. Jack gets a job at a French restaurant as a busboy, but his friends believe he is the new head chef.

Chrissy's Cousin
GS: Barbara Stuart, Shauna Sullivan, Jordan Clarke, Karen Austin. While Chrissy is home taking care of her sick mother, her beautiful but clumsy Cousin Cindy moves in with Jack and Janet. Jenilee Harrison joins the cast as Cindy.

Jack to the Rescue
W: George Burditt. D: Dave Powers. GS: Rod Colbin, Ruth Manning, Nancy Andrews, Amy Nachbar. Jack accidentally gets Cindy fired from her job when he convinces her that her boss is taking advantage of her.

The Not So Great Impostor
W: Michael S. Baser & Kim Weiskopf. D: Dave Powers. GS: Hank Garrett, Gino Conforti, Jillian Kesner, Britt Leach. Jack gets himself into trouble when he poses as an infamous chef in order to get a job at Angelino's restaurant. Jordon Charney joins the cast as Mr. Angelino.

Jack's Other Mother
W: Mark Tuttle. D: Dave Powers. GS: Amzie Strickland, Lois Areno, Bob Sherman, Geroge Dickerson, Maida Severn. An elderly neighbor adopts Jack as her substitute son and begins to drive him crazy by smothering him with love.

Make Room for Daddy
W: Martin Rips & Joseph Staretski. D: Dave Powers. GS: Keene Curtis, Janice Kent, Joe George. Jack teaches his girlfriend's widower father how to get girls.

Janet's Secret
W: Michael S. Baser & Kim Weiskopf. D: Dave Powers. GS: Macon McCalman, Paula Shaw, Sondra Currie. Janet tells her visiting parents that she is married to Jack.

Father of the Bride
W: Tom Dunsmuir. D: Dave Powers. GS: Jeffrey Tambor, Sarah Marshall, Mickey Deems. Jack and Janet try to help Cindy get rid of a rich man who plans to make her his bride.

Furley vs. Furley
W: Michael S. Baser & Kim Weiskopf. D: Dave Powers. GS: Hamilton Camp. Mr. Furley moves in with Jack and the girls after his brother Bart, the owner of the apartment building, fires him as manager.

In Like Larry
W: Martin Rips & Joseph Staretski. D: Dave Powers. Jack and Larry switch apartments after Jack has a fight with the girls.

Teacher's Pet
W: Mark Tuttle. D: Dave Powers. GS: William Pierson, Dorian Lopinto. Jack finds himself in trouble when he gets a job teaching at his old cooking school, because the dean's beautiful niece offers herself in exchange for a good grade.

And Baby Makes Four
W: Martin Rips & Joseph Staretski. D: Dave Powers. GS: John McCook, Frances Lee McCain. Jack and Janet mistakenly believe that Cindy is pregnant.

The Night of the Ropers
W: George Burditt. D: Dave Powers. Jack and the girls try to bring the fighting Ropers back together.

Double Trouble
W: Martin Rips, Joseph Staretski & Mark Fink. D: Dave Powers. GS: Robin G. Eisenmann. Jack poses as his own twin brother, Austin, in order to be able to date Mr. Furley's visiting niece.

Dying to Meet You
W: Budd Grossman. D: Dave Powers. GS: Terry Kiser, Pamela Brull, Brad Blaisdell. Jack finds himself in a tight situation when the jealous boyfriend of the girl who has a crush on him threatens to kill him.

The Case of the Missing Blonde
W: Michael S. Baser & Kim Weiskopf. D: Dave Powers. GS: Alan Manson, Toni Berrell. When Cindy disappears, Jack and Janet believe she was murdered.

Honest Jack Tripper
W: Mark Tuttle. D: Dave Powers. GS: Anne Schedeen, Shell Kepler. Jack decides that he will always tell the truth no matter what the situation.

Jack Bares All [Part 1]
W: Martin Rips & Joseph Staretski. D: Dave Powers. GS: Gino Conforti. When Cindy moves away to college, Jack and Janet start to look for a new roommate. Priscilla Barnes joins the cast as Terri Alden.

Jack Bares All [Part 2]
W: Martin Rips & Joseph Staretski. D: Dave Powers. GS: Shell Kepler. Jack tries to get rid of Terri.

Terri Makes Her Move
W: Ellen Guylas. D: Dave Powers. GS: Hugh Gillin, Mina Kolb, Jennifer Walker. Janet mistakenly believes that Terri has fallen for Jack.

Professor Jack
W: Laura Levine. D: Dave Powers. GS: Paul Kent, Sally Kemp, Frank Aletter. Terri believes Jack is fooling around with a married woman and then plans to move out.

Some of That Jazz
W: Martin Rips & Joseph Staretski. D: Dave Powers. GS: Michael Bell, Deborah Bartlett. Terri and Jack mistakenly believe that the only way Janet will make it as a dancer is by sleeping with her dance teacher.

Lies My Roommate Told Me
W: George Burditt. D: Dave Powers. GS: Teresa Ganzel. Larry tries to get Jack to fix him up with Terri.

Two Flew Over the Cuckoo's Nest
W: Shelley Zellman. D: Dave Powers. GS: Jeffrey Tambor, Murray Matheson. Jack and Janet mistake Terri's psychiatrist friend for an escaped mental patient.

Eyewitness Blues
W: Michael S. Baser & Kim Weiskopf. D: Dave Powers. GS: Alan McRae, Donald Petrie, Edmund Gilbert, Dennis Robertson. Jack fears his life is in danger after he witnesses an armed robbery at the flower shop.

Boy Meets Dummy
W: Ellen Guylas. D: Dave Powers. GS: Gino Conforti, Christina Hart. Jack tries to convince Mr. Angelino's daughter that he is married in order to get her to leave him alone.

Dates of Wrath
W: Ellen Guylas. D: Dave Powers. GS: Brad Maule, Connie Hill. Janet accidentally fixes Terri up with the man she wanted as her own date.

Macho Man
W: John Boni. D: Dave Powers. GS: Kenneth White, Rod Gist, Sheldon Feldner, George McDaniel. Jack unknowingly attacks a cop whom he mistakes for a mugger.

Strangers in the Night
W: Shelley Zellman. D: Dave Powers. GS: Pamela Dunlap, Gwen Humble, Jacque Lynn Colton. Jack tries to win back his southern girlfriend he accidentally insulted.

The Matchbreakers
W: Bryan Joseph. D: Dave Powers. GS: Ruta Lee. Larry tries to prove that Mr. Furley's new girlfriend is a golddigger.

Oh, Nun
W: Calvin Kelly. D: Dave Powers. GS: Susan Plumb, Britt Leach, John Brandon. Jack believes that Terri's nun friend is planning to leave the convent to marry him.

Maid to Order
W: Laura Levine. D: Dave Powers. GS: Peter Isacksen, Jenifer Shaw, Charlie Stavola. Cindy volunteers to clean for her former roommates. The trouble starts when she finds a lot of money while cleaning up Jack's room.

Hearts and Flowers
W: Ellen Guylas. D: Dave Powers. GS: Laurie Schaefer, Rod Colbin, Jane Dulo. Janet quits her job when her boss hires an efficiency expert.

Urban Plowboy
W: Martin Rips & Joseph Staretski. D: Dave Powers. GS: Sue Ane Langdon, Herman Poppe. Jack joins the girls for the weekend at Cindy's aunt's farm.

A Friend in Need
W: James Ritz. D: Dave Powers. GS: Gino Conforti, Terry Kiser. Jack becomes the temporary chef at Angelino's restaurant where he cooks a dinner for a visiting mobster.

Jack's 10
W: Ken Hecht & Bob Brunner. D: Dave Powers. GS: Karen Austin, Melanie Vincz. Jack falls under the spell of a pushy girl who convinces him to marry her.

Doctor in the House
W: John Boni. D: Dave Powers. GS: Edward Andrews, Keith Lawrence, Toni Lamond. Jack pretends to be a doctor in order to impress his visiting grandfather.

Critic's Choice
W: Shelley Zellman. D: Dave Powers. GS: Jay Garner, Louise Williams. Jack challenges a food critic and then invites him to dinner in order to get a good review.

Paradise Lost
W: Shelley Zellman. D: Dave Powers. GS: Sheila Rogers, Alvah Stanley, Faith McSwain. Larry and Mr. Furley try to convince Jack and the girls not to move into a beach house.

And Now, Here's Jack
W: Martin Rips, Joseph Staretski & Hank Bradford. D: Dave Powers. GS: Frank O'Brien, Marty Brill. Jack appears on a TV talk show promoting Angelino's restaurant, but ruins the cooking demonstration he was to perform.

Janet Wigs Out
W: Budd Grossman. D: Dave Powers. Janet buys a blonde wig but soon finds that she has fallen in love with her new image so much that she is turning off all of her friends.

Up in the Air
W: Shelley Zellman. D: Dave Powers. GS: Barry Williams, Lauree Berger, Gertrude Flynn, Paul Marin. Jack agrees to be Janet's date at a fancy party, but he ruins everything when he gets drunk and starts acting like a wild man.

Mate for Each Other
W: Ellen Guylas. D: Dave Powers.
GS: Brian Byers, Judy Kain, Mickey
Deems. Jack signs up for computer
dating but winds up with Janet as his
date.

The Best of Three's Company [Part 1]
W: Michael Ross, Bernie West &
George Burditt. Lucille Ball is the
host of a two-part special featuring
clips from past shows. This episode
recalls the day when Jack first moved

into the apartment and how the roommates first got along with each other.
[This episode was originally a one-
hour special.]

The Best of Three's Company [Part 1]
W: Michael Ross, Bernie West &
George Burditt. Lucille Ball is the
host of a two-part special featuring
clips from past shows. This episode
features clips of the Ropers, Larry and
Mr. Furley.

THE TOM EWELL SHOW

On the air 9/27/60, off 7/18/61. CBS. B&W Film. 32 episodes. Broadcast:
Sept 1960-Jul 1961 Tue 9-9:30. Producer: Unknown. Prod Co/Synd: Four Star.
CAST: Tom Potter (played by Tom Ewell), Fran Potter (Marilyn Erskine),
Irene Brady (Mabel Albertson), Carol Potter (Cindy Robbins), Debbie Potter
(Sherry Alberoni), Sissie Potter (Eileen Chesis).
The story of the Potter family. Tom, a real estate salesman, his wife Fran and
their three daughters, and Tom's mother-in-law Irene. Segments relate Tom's
struggle to raise his children and earn a respectable living. The show is available
but not run.

Advice to the Lovelorn
GS: Whit Bissell, Ray Strickland.
Carol and her boyfriend are all set to
get married but their parents are dead
set against it.

Big Brother
GS: Eddie Ryder, Damian O'Flynn,
Pat Close. Tom takes in an orphan
during Big Brother week.

The Chutney Caper
GS: Alice Ghostley. Tom's eccentric
sister thinks Tom will suffer every
pain she gets.

Debbie Takes up the Tuba
Tom thinks it's okay for Debbie to
join the school band, until she brings
home a tuba.

A Fellow Needs a Friend
GS: Alan Reed, Jr., Robert and Jean
Carson. Nobody is interested in going
to the football game with Tom, who

has 50-yard-line seats, so he gets Carol's
visiting friend to go with him.

The Friendly Man
GS: Mildred Dunnock, Ernest Truex.
Tom sells a home insurance policy to a
family whose home begins to crumble
right before his eyes.

The Handwriting on the Wall
GS: David Lewis. Tom's new hobby
is handwriting analysis, but then he
analyzes the handwriting of a pompous banker he plans to do business
with.

Handyman
GS: Dave Willock, Herbie Faye. Tom
decides to lay the new floor himself,
when Harvey the Handyman asks too
much.

I Don't See It
GS: Alice Ghostley, Robert Emhardt.
Tom helps spinster Lavinia Barrington
sell her paintings.

The Middle Child
Debbie's teacher thinks Tom has been neglecting her so he gives all of his attention to her and ignores Carol and Cissie.

Mr. Memory
GS: Don Beddoe, Ralph Bell. Tom hires a memory expert to help him pass the real estate board exam.

Mr. Shrewd
GS: Stanley Adams, John Dehner, Herbie Faye. Tom tries to teach his family how to save money.

Mrs. Dynamite
GS: Dorothy Konrad. Tom hires Mrs. Rafferty to clean up his office.

Never Do Business with Relatives
GS: Dick Bernie, Cully Richards. Tom sells his old car to Grandma, then the car dies.

No Fun in the Sun
GS: Bob Hastings. Tom and Fran plan to spend their vacation at Lake Tahoe without the children.

The Old Magic
GS: John Emery. Tom's wealthy college roommate invites them to a big party with Hollywood stars.

Our Vacation
GS: Byron Morrow, Stafford Repp, Constance Sawyer. Everyone wants to go to different places on their vacation.

Out at Left Field
GS: Larry Sherry, Stan Williams, Hub Lewis. A baseball flies into Tom's yard, prompting him into selling some land to members of the L.A. Dodgers.

Passenger Pending
GS: George Petrie, David Alpert. Tom falls asleep and misses his plane to Canada.

The Prying Eye
GS: George Fenneman, Allyn Joslyn.

Tom will be on a hidden camera show only by believing the show's a fake.

Put It On—Take It Off
GS: Eleanor Audley, Jane Dulo, Bartlett Robinson. Tom is putting in a lot of work at the office because he needs a new coat.

The Safety Lesson
Tom, tired of playing chauffeur to his family, teaches them how to drive.

Salesmanship Lesson
GS: John Wilder. Tom gives a young man advice on how to get along as a real estate salesman.

The Second Phone
Tom tries to get a second phone when his daughters keep using the phone.

Site Unseen
GS: Dick Powell. Tom tries to get Dick Powell to use some city-owned property for location shots. This he hopes will bring the city a lot of money and help him become a city councilman.

The Spelling Bee
Tom tries to help the girls win a spelling contest.

Storm Over Shangri-La
Tom is commissioned to buy an old apartment house which stands in the way of a new shopping center, the only problem is that there are three old ladies still living in it and they refuse to leave.

Tom Cuts Off the Credit
GS: Raymond Bailey, Ray Kellogg. Tom gets mad when the girls overdo it with the credit cards, so he takes them away.

Tom Puts the Girls to Work
Tom thinks it is a great idea that the girls get part-time jobs, but Fran and Irene find without the girls around they have to do more of the housework.

Tom Takes Over
Tom takes over the housework when Fran gets appendicitis and has to go to the hospital.

The Trouble with Mother
GS: Mabel Albertson, Gage Clarke. Grandma Brady complains that her current boyfriend is dull.

Try It on for Size
The girls try to tell Tom what to wear, but he won't listen. He goes shopping by himself, buys a suit he hates, and now insists on wearing it.

TOPPER

On the air 10/9/53, off 9/55. CBS. B&W Film. 78 episodes. Broadcast: Oct 1953-Sept 1955 Fri 8:30-9. Producer: Jay W. Loveton and Bernard L. Schubert. Synd: Lorimer.

CAST: Cosmo Topper (played by Leo G. Carroll), George Kirby (Robert Sterling), Marion Kirby (Anne Jeffreys), Henrietta Topper (Lee Patrick), Mr. Schuyler (Thurston Hall), Katie (Kathleen Freeman), Maggie (Edna Skinner).

The story of a banker who moves into a house which is haunted by the ghosts of the former owners. The ghosts proceed to get Topper into all sorts of trouble. Popular for two seasons. Although in syndication, it has not been seen for a few years.

Pilot
The Kirbys are killed in an avalanche, but return as ghosts. They are only visible to the new owner of their old house, Cosmo Topper.

The Movers
The Kirbys try to prevent Cosmo and wife from moving into their house.

Hiring the Maid
Topper begins a search for a new maid; George's candidate is a burlesque queen.

Hypnotist
A hypnotist, an old friend of Henrietta's, comes to visit the Toppers.

Bank Securities
Cosmo misplaces several thousand dollars' worth of securities which he is supposed to deliver to the richest woman in town.

Reducing
Cosmo goes on a reducing campaign without reckoning on the Kirbys.

The Socialite
Henrietta invites some people to dinner whom she hopes to interest in publishing her poetry.

Spinster
Henrietta's friend Thelma is looking for a husband. She brings a new beau to dinner at the Topper home.

Surprise Party
While Henrietta is in the hospital, the Kirbys decide to throw a party to celebrate Marion's birthday.

The Kid
Topper brings home an annoying spoiled little boy.

Burglar Episode
George Kirby decides to play private eye.

Trip to Lisbon
When Topper is sent on a highly secret trip to Lisbon by the bank president, the Kirbys decide to go along.

Car Story
The Kirbys want Cosmo to get a sports car for Henrietta's birthday so they can use it.

Christmas Carol
Topper is assigned to foreclose a mortgage on Christmas Eve.

Uncle Jonathan
George's Uncle Jonathan comes for a visit.

Second Honeymoon
The Toppers plan to spend their 25th wedding anniversary at the same inn where they first spent their honeymoon.

Decorating Episode
An interior decorator convinces Henrietta that she should do over her living room to match her personality.

The Proposal
Angry with George because he hasn't noticed her new hat, Marion declares that they are no longer married.

Economy
While making out his income tax report, Topper decides that entirely too much money is being spent on household expenses.

Katie's Nephew
With Henrietta away for the weekend, Katie, the maid, brings in her baby nephew to stay at the house.

Astrology
The astrological charts indicate that Cosmo will be ruined financially.

Masquerade
New Year's Eve leads to a costume party which leads Topper to jail.

George's Old Flame
George's old girlfriend comes for a visit.

Henrietta Sells the House
The Kirbys are distraught when Henrietta decides it's time to sell the house and move away.

Painting Episode
Henrietta takes up painting with a dubious but expensive art teacher.

Theatricals
Henrietta's club women are at the Topper home planning their annual play. The Kirbys stuff the ballot boxes so Henrietta gets the lead in the play.

Preparations for Europe
Henrietta wins a magazine contest prize which turns out to be a trip to Europe.

College Reunion
Cosmo makes a donation to the alumni fund.

Diamond Ring
Cosmo has to prove that the Kirbys are not alive.

Topper Runs for Mayor
Topper reluctantly accepts the nomination for mayor and starts an all-out campaign to win.

Legacy
Grandpa Augustus Kirby dies, leaving George and Marion a million dollars.

Topper Goes to Las Vegas
Topper is sent to Las Vegas to make a bid for a client who wishes to purchase a hotel.

Topper Goes to Court
Topper goes to New Mexico on business to inspect a cattle ranch.

Sweepstakes
The Kirbys fool Topper into believing he has won the Irish Sweepstakes.

The Package
The Kirbys receive a package by mail but are unable to keep it.

Neil Disappears
Neil, the Kirbys' St. Bernard, walks off with a State Department official's diplomatic pouch.

The Picnic
Topper's Cousin Willie, a health fanatic, pays Topper a visit.

Wedding
Henrietta plans for her niece's modest home wedding.

The Boat
As the Toppers prepare to sail for home, the Kirbys sneak into another cabin and sneak out with someone else's gifts.

Topper Tells All
Topper relates the history of the Topper house and its inhabitants, both spiritual and physical, including the origin of the Kirbys' ghostly antics.

Topper's Ransom
When robbers are foiled by Topper in their plan to rob the bank, they get even by kidnapping him.

County Fair
Topper's boss puts him in charge of his favorite prize chicken.

Seance
Henrietta goes away on a visit and the Kirbys set out to bring a little color into Topper's life.

Topper Strikes Gold
Topper is sent to Goldrush Alaska to close a gold mine for an estate.

Chess Player
For some time Cosmo has been beaten at chess by telegram by his opponent, J. Francis Prescott.

Topper Goes to Washington
Topper flies to Washington, D.C. to convince the government it needs to adopt a seven cent dime.

Jury Duty
Topper has jury duty and it interferes with his plans to attend a bankers' convention.

Topper Lives Again
The Kirbys start instructing Topper in the art of ghosting.

Army Game
Cosmo receives an unanticipated draft notice.

Topper's Accident
Topper had an accident and the Kirbys will see to it that he stays in bed.

Topper's Quiet Christmas
Topper plans a traditional Christmas, including a tree, presents and turkey, but things don't quite turn out that way thanks to the Kirbys.

Topper's Happy New Year
The Kirbys need a new supply of ectoplasm in order to materialize during the new year.

Topper's Reception
Topper and his wife act as a cook and a butler.

Topper's Guest
Topper arranges for the arrival of a Senor Lopez from South America who is in this country for the reading of a will.

Topper's Rejuvenation
A client informs Mr. Schuyler that the bank is in need of young blood.

Topper in Mexico
A meek bank cashier takes off for Mexico with a half million dollars in bonds.

Topper Hits the Road
Topper is assigned by the bank to find a wealthy but anonymous depositor.

Topper at the Races
Topper is assigned by the bank to accompany a new client to the races and make bets for him.

Topper's Racket
George's former bookie moves into Topper's neighborhood.

Topper's Amnesia
Topper hits his head on a potted plant and can't remember who he is.

Topper's Arabian Nights
Topper's bank sends him to Arabia.

House Wreckers
The city doesn't have a heart and they have decided to move Topper's house so they can build on his land.

Topper Makes a Movie
Topper and his friends the Kirbys all make a movie.

King Cosmo the First
Topper impersonates a king for Mr. Schuyler.

Topper's Double Life
George enters a contest to win some pigeons and signs Topper's name to the entry.

Topper Fights a Duel
A visiting Frenchman challenges Topper to a duel.

Topper's Egyptian Deal
Topper finances an archeologist's expedition in Egypt.

Topper's Uranium Pile
While George is playing golf in Topper's back yard, he discovers uranium.

Topper's Spring Cleaning
Topper invents a vacuum cleaner that also mixes martinis.

Topper Goes to School
Henrietta persuades Topper to try and get a loan from Mr. Schuyler when she learns her college is in need of funds.

The Blood Brother
A letter from an old pal of George's arrives in the Topper home; the fact that it is from Alcatraz doesn't help either.

Topper's Highland Fling
Topper takes a drastic step after getting news of his inheritance from a great uncle in Scotland.

Topper's Desert Island
The Toppers accompany Mr. Schuyler on a flight to Bali on a business trip.

The Neighbors
Cosmo's cook falls in love with the neighbors' butler.

Topper's Counterfeiters
The bank discovers that phony ten dollar bills are being distributed and Topper gets caught in the middle when he is asked to assist a federal investigator.

Topper's Insurance Scandal
Certain that Topper can acquire a great sum of money, the Kirbys insist Topper remain in bed when the claims adjuster arrives.

Topper's Other Job
Topper is facing the problem of finding new employment.

Topper's Vacation
Mr. Schuyler suggests Topper take a vacation and then goes along with him to his lake lodge.

TO ROME WITH LOVE

On the air 9/28/69, off 9/21/71. CBS. Color Film. 48 episodes. Broadcast: Sept 1969-Sept 1970 Sun 7:30-8; Sept 1970-Jan 1971 Tue 9:30-10; Jan 1971-Sept 1971 Wed 8:30-9. Producer: Don Fedderson. Synd: Universal/MCA.
CAST: Michael Endicott (played by John Forsythe), Aunt Harriet (Kay Medford), Grandpa Pruitt (Walter Brennan), Alison Endicott (Joyce Menges), Penny

Endicott (Susan Nehor), Pokey (Melanie Fullerton), Gino (Vito Scotti), Nico (Gerald Michenaud).

Set in Rome, Italy, a professor and his three daughters take up residence at Mama Vitale's boarding house. Episodes depict the struggle of an American family to adjust to a new country. The series is syndicated, but due to the small number of episodes produced it remains unshown.

To Rome with Love [Pilot]
GS: Vito Scotti. The Endicotts move from the United States to an apartment in Rome.

Hello, Aunt Harriet
Aunt Harriet arrives from Iowa expecting to find her brother and his three daughters leading a swinger's life.

The Roman from Iowa
GS: Joan Freeman, Reva Rose. Endicott poses as an Italian rather than embarrass the American woman who mistook him for one.

Goodbye Aunt Harriet
Aunt Harriet decides to go home after some bad experiences in the communal bathroom.

The Telephone
GS: Romo Vincent. The Endicotts finally get a phone but find that everyone else in the building wants to use it.

We Want to Go Home
Aunt Harriet gets the girls convinced that they want to go back to Iowa.

A Palazzo Is Not a Home
A beautiful decorator remodels the bathroom and then Endicott's daughters.

The Long Road Home
Endicott gets upset when he feels the vagabond girl he gave a room to will stir up his daughters.

The Secret Day
GS: Geraldine Brooks. Endicott remembers an Italian girl he loved while he was stationed in Rome during WW II.

And One More Spring
GS: John Myler. Aunt Harriet falls in love, while Pokey comes down with the mumps.

Affair of Honor
GS: John Roper. The Endicotts are surprised when a young man sells everything he owns to get enough money to take Alison out to a fancy restaurant.

Anything Can Happen in Rome
GS: Anna Maria Alberghetti. Endicott is visited by a beautiful ballerina.

A Gown for Alison
Alison tries to save her money so she can buy a gown for her date with a young Count.

One Coin in the Fountain
Pokey unknowingly tosses a rare coin into a fountain.

To Go Home Again
GS: Diane McBain. Alison plans to elope, against Endicott's wishes.

The Pied Piper of Rome
Endicott's vision of Alison is shattered when she falls in love. He realizes that she is no longer a child.

My Daughter Penny
Endicott and Alison try to turn tomboy Penny into a lady.

The Beautiful People
GS: Heather Menzies, Nina Foch. When a student develops a crush on him, Endicott has an interesting visit with the girl's mother.

Birds, Bees, and Bushes
When Pokey is told that babies are found under bushes, she goes out to find one.

Pretty Little Girl
GS: Vitina Marcus. Endicott is flattered when a young woman falls in love with him.

Father's Choice
Endicott finds that he has to watch Penny's dance recital on the same night he is supposed to take Alison to a dance.

A Friend for Penny
The Endicotts befriend the daughter of an Italian tycoon.

Spring Vacation
GS: Francine York. Endicott's daughters plan to get their father away for a vacation in the Alps with a beautiful model.

Our Friend, Gino
GS: Patricia Medina. The Endicotts help Gino impress his former girlfriend who is now a rich society woman.

We Remember Mama
GS: Nancy Malone. The girls remember their mother when the professor dates a woman who is in love with him, but the professor doesn't realize it.

Here Comes Andy
The professor's father-in-law comes to live with them in Rome.

A Day in the Country
GS: Michael Blodgett, Frank Puglia. Grandpa objects to Alison going with her hippie boyfriend on a trip to the country.

Baby of the Family
GS: Mary Ann Mobley. Pokey feels she is left out of all the fun, because she is too young, when a movie star comes for a visit.

Roman Affair
GS: Sebastian Cabot, Johnnie Whittaker, Anissa Jones. Penny, acting as a tourist guide, brings the Endicotts

face to face with Buffy and Jody of "Family Affair," while Mr. French has been arrested for theft at the airport.

A Boy to Remember
GS: Jonathan Lippe. Penny is determined to provide a home for a runaway waif.

Rome Is Where You Find It
GS: William Demarest, Don Grady, Tina Cole, Argentina Brunetti. Some of the cast of "My Three Sons" visit Rome as the Endicotts try to reunite Uncle Charley with a young lady he met during WW I.

Line from Heaven
GS: Barbara McNair. An owner of a nightclub sends a bunch of gifts to the Endicotts with the explanation "One Who Remembers."

Fly Away Home
GS: Lilyan Chauvin. The Endicotts say goodbye to Alison who is going to study art in Paris, and to an injured baby dove.

Grandpa in Charge
Grandpa is put in charge of the girls while the professor is away in Venice.

The Catnip Club
GS: Craig Stevens. An old friend of the professor's talks him into moonlighting as the manager of the Catnip Club—a Roman club with kitten-clad waitresses.

The Rose Garden
GS: Dana Wynter. A noblewoman has a fight with Grandpa over the poor condition of her garden.

The Boy Next Door
GS: Josephine Hutchinson, Richard Bull, Rick Kelman. Alison falls in love with her old boyfriend who is visiting from Iowa.

The Runaways
GS: Linda Foster. Penny and Pokey run away from home in order to allow their father to marry a stewardess.

Doctor Andy
The Endicotts meet a mother-to-be and a student whose wife is about to give birth at a hospital.

Making the Scene
GS: Geoffrey Deuel. Alison gets involved with some hippie filmmakers when she appears in an improvisational movie.

Bonsai
GS: Page Forsythe. The daughter of a Japanese couple tries to adopt American life styles by copying Alison.

Beauty and the Judge
Endicott is chosen to be the judge of a local beauty contest, the only problem is that Alison is one of the contestants.

The Age of Love
GS: Margaret Field. Grandpa falls for a woman half his age, while Penny falls for an older man.

Mike and the Countess
GS: Victoria Shaw. Alison falls for a young count. However, his mother wants him to marry a rich girl.

The Stray Cat
GS: Beth Ann Rees. The Endicotts try to help a down and out American girl who just lost her job as an exotic dancer.

The Yankee Trader
Grandpa tries to find out who owns their apartment building when the unknown landlord tries to evict everyone out of the building.

Boy Meets Penny
GS: Randy Whipple. The mother of a lonely rich boy pays Penny to play with him.

West of Rome
Story unavailable.

THE UGLIEST GIRL IN TOWN

On the air 9/26/68, off 1/30/69. ABC. Color Film. 20 episodes. Broadcast: Sept 1968-Jan 1969 Thu 7:30-8. Producer: Robert Kaufman, Jerry Bernstein, and Jerry Davis. Prod Co/Synd: Columbia Pictures TV.
CAST: Timmy (played by Peter Kastner), Julie (Patricia Brake), Gene (Garry Marshall), Sondra (Jenny Till), David Courtney (Nicholas Parsons).
A young man dresses up as a woman and becomes a top fashion model in London. This strange show went off the air almost as soon as it came on and it hasn't been seen since.

Pilot Episode
W: Robert Kaufman. D: James Frawley. GS: William Bramley, Richard Steele, Michael Balfour. Timothy Blair poses as a hippie girl to be with his girlfriend in London.

Visitors from a Strange Planet
W: Robert Kaufman. D: George McCowan. GS: Larry Cross, Milton Reid, Andy Ho, Evelyn Keyes. Gene tells their parents that Tim is working for the S.I.A. when they find him posing as a girl.

A Pain in Timmy's Tummy
W: Stan Cutler & Martin Donovan. D: George McCowan. GS: Maria Charles, Eric Chitty, Joy Stewart. Rushed to the hospital with an inflamed appendix, Timmy causes vast confusion.

The Cover-Up Girl
W: Lila Garnett & Bernie Kahn. D: George McCowan. GS: Dick Bentley, Totti Truman Taylor, Maurice Browning. Tim Blair panics when Timmy is to do a bathtub scene in a movie.

One of Our Models Is Missing
W: Martin Ragaway. D: Peter Duffell. GS: Eric Baker, Norman Chappell, Charles Leno. In order to get out of his double life, Tim reports that Timmy has been kidnapped.

Up the Thames without a Paddle
W: Stan Cutler & Martin Donovan. D: Lindsey Shonteff. GS: Victor Maddern, The Spectrum, Danny Green. Tim quits posing as Timmy until his brother runs up another gambling debt.

The Perfect Young Lady
W: Bernard Rothman. D: E.W. Swackhamer. GS: Doris Rogers, Alec Bregonzi. A columnist insists on moving in with Timmy for a story about an old-fashioned girl.

The Lookalikes
W: Arthur Julian. D: Peter Duffell. GS: Murray Kash, Dick Emery, Cal McCord, Bill Hutchinson. A Timmy lookalike contest winner takes over while Tim serves with his National Guard unit.

Timmy the Mother
W: Arthur Julian. D: E.W. Swackhamer. GS: Louis Mansi, Dennis Coffey, Keith Smith. Timmy becomes a weekend mother for a hippie's baby.

Popped Star
W: Robin Hawdon. D: John Robins. GS: Lulu, Sydney Rafler, Clive Dunn. A pop producer tries to make a singing star out of Timmy.

The Paris Incident
W: Brad Ashton. D: E.W. Swackhamer. GS: Roddy-Maude-Roxby, Ewen Solon, John Serret. Timmy and Julie are caught up in the mad world of fashion.

The Jewel Robbery
W: Robert Kaufman. D: Jerry Bernstein. GS: Geoffrey Sumner, Wendy Craig, Julian Orchard, Maggie Kimberley. Timmy faces exposure in the course of a jewel robbery.

My Sister the Genius
W: Robert Kaufman. D: Ray Austin. GS: Trudi Van Doorn, Leon Thau, Penny Service. Julie's brilliant young sister discovers that Tim and Timmy are the same person.

The Ugliest Boy in Town
W: Joel Rapp & Sam Locke. D: Jerry David. GS: Arthur Howard, Clayton Green, Karl Held. Gene arranges for Timmy to make a parachute jump for charity and publicity.

The Trouble with England
W: Lila Garnett & Bernie Kahn. D: Jerry Davis. GS: Robert McBain, Edwin Brown, Fred Emney. Both Tim and Timmy are nominated for the same political office.

A Little Advice Goes a Long Way
W: Lila Garnett & Bernie Kahn. D: Jerry Davis. GS: Patsy Rowlands, William Rushton. Tim needs advice when he substitutes for Miss Beatrice, an advice to the lovelorn columnist.

Match Mates
W: Robert Kaufman. D: John Robins. GS: Bob Hornery, Anita West, Paul Ferris. Courtney gets Timmy a boyfriend through a computer matchmaker for a publicity stunt.

He Lost His Girlish Laughter
W: Howard Leeds. D: Jerry Bernstein. GS: Michael Gover, Deryck Guyler. Tim fakes a drowning to end Timmy's career as a model.

Tubby Timmy
W: Ronald Wolff & Ronald Chesney. D: Peter Duffell. GS: Clive Morton, Nicholas Smith. Timmy must lose 20 pounds in two weeks for an advertising campaign.

The Track Star
W: Stanley Price & Brad Ashton. D: Peter Duffell. GS: Bill Maynarn, Tanya Vigay, Anthony Bailey. A Russian athlete falls for Timmy and defects to the West.

WELCOME BACK, KOTTER

On the air 9/9/75, off 8/10/79. ABC. Color Videotape. 95 episodes. Broadcast: Sept 1975-Jan 1976 Tue 8:30-9; Jan 1976-Aug 1978 Thu 8-8:30; Sept 1978-Oct 1978 Mon 8-8:30; Oct 1978-Jan 1979 Sat 8-8:30; Feb 1979-Mar 1979 Sat 8:30-9; May 1979-Aug 1979 Fri 8:30-9. Producer: James Komack. Prod Co/Synd: Warner Bros. TV.

CAST: Gabe Kotter (played by Gabe Kaplan), Julie Kotter (Marcia Strassman), Mr. Woodman (John Sylvester White), Barbarino (John Travolta), Horshack (Ron Palillo), Epstein (Robert Hegyes), Washington (Lawrence Hilton-Jacobs), Beau (Stephen Shortridge), Hotsy Totsy (Debralee Scott).

The story of Gabe Kotter who returns to the high school he graduated from ten years earlier to teach a class of juvenile delinquents. Typical episodes depict the struggles of Mr. Kotter to solve his students' problems without having them lose their faith in him. The show is seen frequently all over the country.

Welcome Back, Kotter [Pilot]
W: Peter Meyerson. D: James Komack. Gabe Kotter is assigned to teach the Sweathogs.

The Election
W: Eric Cohen & Tiffany York. D: Bob LaHendro. Barbarino plans to run for student body president.

Basket Case
W: Jerry Ross. D: Bob LaHendro. Gabe has to find a way to keep Washington from quitting school to play basketball.

Whodunnit?
W: Jerry Rannow & Jewel Jaffe Rannow. D: Bob LaHendro. Gabe is determined to find out who got Hotsy Totsy pregnant.

The Great Debate
W: Rick Mittleman. D: Bob LaHendro. Gabe challenges the debating team to a debate when their teacher insults the Sweathogs.

No More Mr. Nice Guy
W: George Yanok. D: Bob LaHendro. Mr. Woodman becomes a nice guy when he starts teaching again.

One of Our Sweathogs Is Missing
W: Marilyn Miller. D: Bob LaHendro. Epstein loses a fight and is so ashamed he disappears from sight.

Classroom Marriage
W: Bill Raynor and Myles Wilder. D: Bob LaHendro. Gabe creates a classroom marriage for Washington and Vernajean to show them that they are not ready to get married.

Mr. Kotter, Teacher
W: Jerry Rannow & Jewel Jaffe Rannow. D: Bob LaHendro. Gabe refuses to obey Mr. Woodman so he is suspended.

Barbarino's Girl
W: Eric Cohen. D: Bob LaHendro. Gabe convinces Barbarino to get a tutor to help him raise his grades.

The Reunion
W: George Yanok. D: Bob LaHendro. Gabe's old friend Lyle Flanagan comes for a visit.

California Dreamin'
W: Mike Weinberger. D: Bob LaHendro. A new female student from California has a crush on Gabe.

Arrivederci, Arnold
W: Jerry & Jewel Jaffe Rannow. D: Bob LaHendro. Horshack is promoted to the next grade but wants to stay with his friends and Mr. Kotter.

The Sit-In
W: William Bickley & Mike Warren. D: Bob LaHendro. The Sweathogs

John Sylvester White (left) and Gabe Kaplan, in Welcome Back, Kotter.

hold a sit-in to protest the liver served in the school cafeteria.

The Longest Weekend
W: Carl Kleinschmitt. D: Bob LaHendro. Gabe gets lonesome when Julie goes away for the weekend on a skiing trip.

Doctor Epstein, I Presume . . .?
W: George Yanok. D: Bob LaHendro. Epstein gives all his pets to Gabe when the school guidance counselor tells him that he isn't smart enough to become a veterinarian.

Follow the Leader [Part 1]
W: Jerry & Jewel Jaffe Rannow. D: Bob LaHendro. The Sweathogs hold an election and Barbarino is thrown out as their leader.

Follow the Leader [Part 2]
W: Jerry & Jewel Jaffe Rannow. D: Bob LaHendro. When dejected Barbarino moves in with Gabe, Julie moves into a hotel.

One Flu Over the Cuckoo's Nest
W: Eric Cohen. D: Bob LaHendro. When the flu hits the school some of the smarter students are put in with the Sweathogs, causing problems for Gabe.

The Telethon
W: Pat Proft & Bo Kaprall. D: Bob LaHendro. Gabe and the Sweathogs hold a telethon to raise money for their class.

Kotter Makes Good
W: Eric Cohen & George Yanok. D: Bob LaHendro. During finals week, Woodman tells Gabe that he never took his finals when he graduated.

Father Vinnie
W: Eric Cohen. D: Bob LaHendro. Barbarino plans on becoming a priest when his dying grandmother makes it her last request.

Sweatside Story
W: Eric Cohen. D: Bill Persky. Gabe

tries to stop the Sweathogs from fighting another gang.

A Love Story
W: Jerry & Jewel Jaffe Rannow. D: James Komack & Gary Shimokawa. Epstein gets upset when his sister Carmen becomes a Sweathog and dates Barbarino.

Gabe Under Pressure
W: George Yanok. D: Bob LaHendro. Gabe is ordered to take a physical examination.

The Museum
W: Bob Shayne. D: Bill Davis. GS: John Astin. Gabe and the Sweathogs get locked in a mummy's tomb in the museum overnight.

Career Day
W: Eric Cohen. D: Bill Hobin. GS: Pat Morita. A Japanese inventor offers Gabe a good job in Chicago.

Inherit the Halibut
W: George Tricker & Neil Rosen. D: Bill Hobin. Washington, the class treasurer, is accused when the class fund is missing.

Sweathog Clinic for the Cure of Smoking
W: Eric Cohen & Steve Hayden. D: Bob LaHendro. Gabe and the Sweathogs try to help Epstein to stop smoking.

Chicken a la Kotter
W: Raymond Siller. D: Bob LaHendro. Gabe gets an extra job working as a chicken in a fast-food restaurant.

The Fight
W: Jerry & Jewel Jaffe Rannow. D: Bob LaHendro. After a fight, the Sweathogs refuse to speak to each other.

Sweathog, Nebraska Style
W: George Yanok. D: Bob LaHendro. Julie's sister from Nebraska becomes a Sweathog and begins to date Epstein.

Sadie Hawkins Day
W: Eric Cohen. D: Bob LaHendro. Barbarino is the only one without a date for the school dance.

Hello Ms. Chips
W: Royce B. Applegate & Ira Miller. D: Bob LaHendro. A new student teacher finds that teaching the Sweathogs is not what she expected.

Whatever Happened to Arnold [Part 1]
W: Jerry & Jewel Jaffe Rannow. D: James Komack & Bob LaHendro. Arnold quits the school play and disappears.

Whatever Happened to Arnold [Part 2]
W: Jerry & Jewel Jaffe Rannow. D: James Komack & Bob LaHendro. When Arnold's fifth father dies, he plans to take over as the head of the house. [This episode was a spinoff pilot for a series about the Horshack family, which didn't sell.]

Horshack vs. Carvelli
W: Gary Shandling. D: Bob LaHendro. Horshack volunteers to fight Carvelli.

Hark, the Sweatkings
W: Peter Meyerson & Nick Arnold. D: Bob LaHendro. The Sweathogs befriend a bum who appears every Christmas.

Sweatgate Scandal
W: Eric Cohen. D: Bob LaHendro. The Sweathogs join the school newspaper and uncover a scandal in the school cafeteria.

Caruso's Way
W: Eric Cohen. D: Bob LaHendro. GS: Scott Brady. The gym teacher hits Barbarino in front of the girls' gym class.

Kotter & Son
W: Peter Meyerson & Nick Arnold. D: Bob LaHendro. GS: Harold J. Stone. Gabe's father comes for a visit.

The Littlest Sweathog
W: Eric Cohen. D: Bob LaHendro.
Julie tells Gabe that she is pregnant.

I'm Having Their Baby
W: George Tricker & Neil Rosen. D:
Bob LaHendro. While Gabe is out of
town, the Sweathogs try to cheer Julie
up.

Radio Free Freddie
W: Nick Arnold, Peter Meyerson &
George Yanok. D: Bob LaHendro.
GS: George Carlin. Freddie can't man-
age success when he becomes a hit disc
jockey on the school radio station.

I Wonder Who's Kissing Gabe Now
W: Peter Meyerson & Nick Arnold. D:
Bob LaHendro. The Sweathogs think
that Gabe is having an affair with the
school art teacher who has a crush on
him.

Buddy Can You Spare a Million?
W: Peter Meyerson & Nick Arnold.
D: Bob Claver. Gabe and Barbarino
fight over who owns a lottery ticket.

And Baby Makes Four [Part 1]
W: Eric Cohen. D: Bob Claver. Julie
is about to give birth and the Sweathogs are promoted to the 11th grade.

And Baby Makes Four [Part 2]
W: Eric Cohen. D: Bob Claver. Julie
gives birth to twins.

And Baby Makes Four [Part 3]
W: Gabe Kaplan. D: Bob Claver.
When Gabe and Julie bring the babies
home they never have a peaceful moment.

Just Testing
W: George Bloom & Beverly Bloomberg. D: Bob Claver. Gabe has to decide between helping Barbarino pass
his test or spending time with Julie
and the twins.

*The De-Programming of Arnold Hor-
shack*
W: Mike Barrie & Jim Mulholland. D:

Bob Claver. Arnold joins a religious
cult.

What a Move!
W: Peter Meyerson & Nick Arnold. D:
Bob Claver. GS: Herb Edelman. Epstein helps Gabe move to a new building.

A Novel Idea
W: George Bloom & Beverly Bloomberg. D: Bob Claver. Mr. Woodman
writes a novel and includes everyone
in it.

Barbarino in Love [Part 1]
W: Peter Meyerson & Nick Arnold. D:
Bob Claver. The Sweathogs are in the
state finals of the school talent contest and Barbarino is in love with one
of their competition.

Barbarino in Love [Part 2]
W: Peter Meyerson & Nick Arnold. D:
Bob Claver. Barbarino must choose
between his girl or winning the contest.

Kotter for Vice-Principal
W: Steve Clements & Joyce Gittlin.
D: Bob Claver. Gabe is considered for
the job of Vice Principal.

Swine & Punishment
W: Nick Rossner & Bob Silberg. D:
Bob Claver. Woodman accuses Wash-
ington of cheating on a test.

Epstein's Madonna
W: Eric Cohen. D: Bob Claver. Epstein paints a naked lady on the school
wall.

Angie
W: George Bloom & Beverly Bloomberg. D: Bob Claver. Woodman
wants to expel the Sweathogs because
the new girl in school wants to join
them.

Sweatwork
W: Eric Cohen. D: Bob Claver. A
takeoff on the film "Network," when
Arnold is about to be taken off the
school radio station for bad ratings.

Meet Your New Teacher: Batteries Not Included
W: Judy Skelton & Tony Schurer. D: Bob Claver. Gabe is replaced by a computer teacher.

Epstein's Term Paper
W: Eric Cohen. D: Bob Claver. Epstein buys Gabe's old term paper.

There's No Business . . . [Part 1]
W: Gabe Kaplan. D: Bob Claver. Gabe auditions at a local club and an agent wants to turn him into a full-time comedian.

There's No Business . . . [Part 2]
W: Gabe Kaplan. D: Bob Claver. Gabe becomes a comedian and leaves Julie and the Sweathogs behind.

What Goes Up
W: Nick Arnold. D: Jeff Bleckner. Washington gets hooked on pills and the Sweathogs try to help him quit.

Goodbye Mr. Kripps
W: Garry Ferrier & Audrey Tadman. D: Bob Claver. GS: Jack Fletcher. Barbarino turns himself in for murder when Mr. Kripps dies after yelling at him.

Horshack & Madame X
W: Peter Meyerson. D: Al Schwartz. Horshack falls in love with Julie.

The Kiss
W: Peter Meyerson & Max Goldenson. D: Bob Claver. Gabe gives artificial respiration to a girl and he is accused of kissing her.

Class Encounters of the Carvelli Kind
W: George Bloom & Beverly Bloomberg. D: Bob Hegyes. Carvelli sees a UFO and Woodman has been chosen to go with Carvelli when the UFO returns to pick him up.

The Return of Hotsy Totsy
W: Gabe Kaplan. D: Bob Claver. GS: Debralee Scott. Hotsy Totsy is discovered to be a mother and a stripper.

Sweathog Christmas Special
W: Eric Cohen & Mel Stewart. B: Bob Claver. The Sweathogs celebrate Christmas with Gabe and Julie.

Sweathog Back-to-School Special
W: Peter Meyerson & Nick Arnold. D: Bob Claver. The Sweathogs and Gabe recall events from previous episodes as they prepare to start a new semester.

Frog Day Afternoon
W: George Bloom & Earl Barret. D: Nick Arnold. Horshack refuses to kill a frog for biology class.

Beau's Jest
W & D: Unavailable. The new Sweathog, Beau, plays a practical joke on Epstein.

The Sweatmobile
W: Rich Hawkins. D: Norman Abbott. The Sweathogs buy a car.

Don't Come Up and See Me Sometime
W: Liz Sage & Rich Hawkins. D: Nick Arnold. Barbarino gets his own apartment but won't let the Sweathogs visit.

The Drop-Ins [Part 1]
W & D: Unavailable. Woodman is promoted to Principal, Gabe becomes the Vice Principal and the Sweathogs quit school to get jobs.

The Drop-Ins [Part 2]
W & D: Unavailable. The Sweathogs realize that they do not have the education or the experience needed to get a job. [This episode was originally a one-hour episode.]

Once Upon a Ledge
W: Rich Hawkins & Liz Sage. D: Nick Arnold. Arnold saves the life of a confused girl who was going to jump off the ledge of the school building.

Barbarino's Boo Boo
W & D: Unavailable. Barbarino loses Mr. Woodman some place in the hospital.

Washington Clone
W & D: Unavailable. A straight "A" student wants to be a Sweathog just like Washington.

X-Rated Education
W & D: Unavailable. Epstein unknowingly switches an x-rated film for a sex education film.

The Barbarino Blues
W & D: Unavailable. Barbarino believes he has lost his touch with women.

A Little Fright Music
W & D: Unavailable. Freddie wants to write a new school song.

Bride and Gloom
W & D: Unavailable. Barbarino plans to get married.

The Goodbye Guy
W & D: Unavailable. Epstein and Mr. Woodman's niece plan to live together.

A Winter's Coat Tale
W & D: Unavailable. Barbarino buys a new winter coat, but it is stolen before he has a chance to use it.

Barbarino's Baby
W & D: Unavailable. Barbarino delivers a baby while stuck in an elevator.

The Sweat Smell of Success
W & D: Unavailable. Epstein turns the school newspaper into a gossip magazine.

I'm Okay, But You're Not
W & D: Unavailable. Beau is accused of talking about the Sweathogs to Woodman behind their backs.

The Gang Show
W & D: Unavailable. Washington and Epstein try to win the school talent contest.

Come Back, Little Arnold
W & D: Unavailable. Arnold wants to impress his girlfriend so he starts drinking to gain confidence.

Oo-Oo I Do [Part 1]
W & D: Unavailable. Arnold finds he might be transferred just as he and his girlfriend are becoming very close.

Oo-Oo I Do [Part 2]
W & D: Unavailable. The Sweathogs plan to give Arnold a bachelor party when he announces that he is going to marry his girlfriend Mary.

The Bread Winners
W & D: Unavailable. Juan goes on an interview for a job only to find that Washington took it right out from under him.

WENDY & ME

On the air 9/14/64, off 9/6/65. ABC. B&W Film. 34 episodes. Broadcast: Sept 1964-Sept 1965 Mon 9-9:30. Producer: George Burns. Prod Co: Natwill Prods. Synd: Worldvision.

CAST: George Burns (played by himself), Wendy Conway (Connie Stevens), Jeff Conway (Ron Harper), Danny Adams (James Callahan), Mr. Bundy (J. Pat O'Malley).

The adventures of the Conways: Jeff, an airline pilot, and his beautiful but dim-witted wife Wendy. During the show, the two are visited by their landlord George Burns who speaks to the audience and further complicates what Wendy has accomplished. The show is a direct descendant of *The Burns and Allen Show*. *Wendy & Me* is syndicated but never aired.

Wendy and Me [Pilot]
GS: Diane McBain, John Hubbard. Jeff and Wendy want to be sure Danny passes his annual airline physical, so they take away his little black book to help keep his blood pressure down.

Wendy's Anniversary Fun?
On their first wedding anniversary, Wendy wants to re-enact the time Jeff proposed to her.

Belle of the Malt Shop
GS: Donald Losby, Iland Dowling. Wendy's house guest is the teenage daughter of Jeff's boss; she is stricken with puppy love.

A Bouquet for Mr. Bundy
GS: Dabbs Greer. Bundy catches a wedding bouquet and Wendy immediately announces she will have to find him a bride.

Call Me or I'll Call You
GS: Robert Hogan, Bill Idelson. Jeff promises to call Wendy when he gets to Seattle, but then the phone goes dead.

Danny, the Married Bachelor
GS: Med Flory, Bonnie Jones. Danny's old girlfriend is coming to town with her burly brother, so Danny asks Wendy if she will pretend to be his wife.

Danny's Double Life
GS: Herb Vigran. Wendy learns that Danny rented an apartment in another building but she doesn't know it is for another pilot and his family.

East Is East and West Is Wendy
Wendy poses as a harem girl in order to meet a visiting Shah.

Five Minutes to Show Time
GS: Jackie Gayle. Jeff is producing the airline's annual show and Wendy is sent to ask George Burns to emcee.

Four of a Kind
GS: Shary Marshall. Danny thinks he

wants to date Wendy's new house guest whom he doesn't know is a sheep dog.

George Burns While Rome Fiddles
When Jeff is assigned to pilot a plane to Rome, Wendy wears a black wig and goes along as a stewardess to spy on him.

Happiness Is a Thing Called Misery
GS: Charles Lane, Russ Conway. Wendy is certain her marriage is in trouble because she and Jeff never fight.

How Not to Succeed in Stealing
GS: Brenda Benet, Laurie Main. A stewardess gives Wendy a string of pearls, unaware that she substituted a strand worth $200,000 for her inexpensive gift.

It Takes Two to Tangle
GS: Sue Randall, George Ives. Wendy takes care of a little girl whose mother is getting a divorce.

Jeff Takes a Turn for the Nurse
GS: Virginia Gregg, Jon Lormer. Jeff thinks Wendy is sick when she volunteers at the hospital.

Jeff, the Senior Citizen
GS: Howard Wendell, Harry Harvey, Sr. Jeff asks Wendy to invite some of his old college classmates to a reunion dinner, but she invites his father's classmates by mistake.

Let's Go Where the Wild Geisha Goes
GS: Yuki Shimoda, Fuji, Pat Li. Wendy invites Mr. Bundy along when Jeff pilots a plane to Japan.

Room at the Bottom
GS: Coleen O'Sullivan. Jeff invites the president of the airlines home for dinner, not knowing that Wendy lent the apartment to Mr. Bundy who wants to impress a visiting niece.

Swing Low, Aunt Harriet
GS: Sheila Bromley. Wendy invites

some Japanese stewardesses to spend the weekend at the same time that Aunt Harriet is coming for a visit.

Tacos, Enchiladas and Wendy
GS: Vito Scotti, Pitt Herbert. Wendy talks her friends into going to what turns out to be a sleazy tropical resort.

Tea Leaves for Two
GS: Ron Harper, James Callahan, J. Pat O'Malley. A tearoom fortune teller forecasts a tall, handsome man in Wendy's life, and she doesn't mean Jeff.

Wendy Gives Uncle the Brush
GS: Walter Sande, Rachel Romen. Wendy accidentally spills paint all over her visiting Uncle Benson's portrait.

Wendy Is Stranger Than Fiction
GS: Woodrow Parfrey. Wendy learns that a famous novelist in the building needs help with his book.

Wendy Lends a Helping Voice
GS: Earl Twins, Sid Clute. Wendy takes in the singing Earl twins as boarders.

The Wendy Mob
No available story.

Wendy Sails in the Sunset
GS: Raquel Welch, Harry Lauter. Jeff planned on spending his second honeymoon aboard Mr. Norton's boat all alone, but Wendy invites some additional passengers.

Wendy the Waitress
GS: Nancy Rennick, John Hubbard. Wendy substitutes for a waitress who wanted to attend her sister's wedding.

Wendy, the Woman in the Gray Flannel Suit
Wendy tries to take over an airline.

Wendy's Five Thousand Dollar Chair
GS: Herb Ellis, Jean Carson, Robert Lieb. Wendy sits in an expensive chair and it collapses, now she has to pay for it.

Wendy's Instant Intellect
GS: Darlene Patterson, Doris Packer. Wendy crams in order to join an exclusive literary club.

Wendy's Private Eye
GS: Stanley Adams, Eileen O'Neil. Wendy hires a detective to trail Jeff after she finds lipstick in his jacket.

Wendy's Secret Weapon
GS: Jonathan Hole, Ken Berry. Wendy holds a secret wedding for her stewardess friend Laura.

Who's in the Guest Room Tonight?
GS: Robyn Grace, Sandra Warmer. Wendy invites Norton's daughter to stay in the guest room while her parents are out of town.

You Can't Fight City Hall
GS: Frank Ferguson, Melodie Patterson, Richard X. Slattery. Danny knows a judge who will fix Wendy's parking ticket.

WHAT'S HAPPENING!

On the air 8/5/76, off 4/28/79. ABC. Color Videotape. 65 episodes. Broadcast: Aug 1976 Thu 8:30-9; Nov 1976-Dec 1976 Sat 8-8:30; Dec 1976-Jan 1978 Thu 8:30-9; Jan 1978-Apr 1978 Sat 8-8:30; Apr 1978-Jan 1979 Thu 8:30-9; Feb 1979-Mar 1979 Fri 8:30-9; Mar 1979-Apr 1979 Sat 8-8:30. Producer: Bud Yorkin. Prod Co: TOY Prod. Synd: Columbia Pictures TV.
CAST: Roger Thomas [Raj] (played by Ernest Thomas), Rerun [Fred Stubbs] (Fred Berry), Dwayne Nelson (Haywood Nelson), Mabel Thomas (Mabel

King), Dee Thomas (Danielle Spencer), Shirley (Shirley Hemphill), Bill Thomas (Thalmus Rasulala), Marvin (Bryan O'Dell), Big Earl (John Welsh), Little Earl (David Hollander).

The urban adventures of three young black youths who always end up in trouble. The boys could be found hanging out at Rob's Soda Shop where all their problems begin. It didn't do very well on the network, but it is doing rather well in syndication.

The Runaway
W: Alan Eisenstock & Larry Mintz. D: Dennis Steinmetz. GS: Helen Martin, Ted Wilson. Raj hires a babysitter so he can go to a party and returns home to find Dee missing.

The Birthday Present
W: Saul Turtletaub & Bernie Orenstein. D: Bud Yorkin. GS: Helen Martin. Raj is accused of shoplifting when he tries to buy his mother a present for her birthday.

When Daddy Comes Marching Home
W: Dawn Aldrege & Marion Freeman. D: Jack Shea. Raj's father returns to ask his ex-wife for some money.

My Three Tons
W: Jim Mulligan. D: Alan Rafkin. GS: Stu Gilliam, Wolfman Jack. Rerun is hired to join a dance group because he is fat.

Saturday's Hero
W: Alan Eisenstock & Larry Mintz. D: Mark Warren. GS: Benny Baker. Rerun is a football star, but he is threatened with suspension unless his grades improve.

The Burger Queen
W: Saul Turtletaub & Bernie Orenstein. D: Dick Harwood. GS: Dick Van Patten, David White. Rerun auditions for a TV hamburger ad, but Dee gets the job with Shirley posing as her mother.

Speak for Yourself, Dwayne
W: Fred Fox & Seamon Jacobs. D: Hal Alexander. Dwayne asks Raj to get him a date with a girl, but he falls for her himself.

Shirley's Date
W: Robert Illes & James Stein. D: Tony Chickey. GS: Cinque Atuks. Shirley won't come to Roger's party, so he tries to get her a date.

The Sunday Father
W: Robert Illes & James Stein. D: Mark Warren. GS: Fritzi Burr. Bill realizes that being a full-time father to his kids is more than he expected.

Christmas Show
W: Saul Turtletaub & Bernie Orenstein. D: Hal Alexander. Roger and Dee arrange to spend Christmas with their father when they think their mother will be working.

The Maid Did It
W: Marty Farrell. D: Mark Warren. GS: Alice Ghostley, Frank Aletter. Mabel is accused of stealing her employer's diamond ring, unaware that her husband lost it gambling.

The Incomplete Shakespeare
W: Mort Scharfman. D: Dick Harwood. GS: Warren Berlinger. Raj accuses the producer of a TV series of stealing his script.

The Hospital Stay
W: Alan Eisenstock & Larry Mintz. D: Mark Warren. GS: Mel Stewart. Dee tries to bring a retired baseball player and his estranged daughter back together.

The Firing Squad
W: Rick Mittleman. D: Mark Warren. Shirley is fired for meddling in Rob's business, but he soon finds that he has no business without her.

The Boarder
W: Alan Eisenstock & Larry Mintz. D:

Mark Warren. Bill becomes a boarder at his ex-wife's house.

Dwayne's Dilemma
W: Jerry Ross. D: Dick Harwood. GS: Ren Wood. Dwayne is threatened by his blind date's ex-boyfriend.

The Tickets
W: Richard Baer. D: Mark Warren. Raj is arrested for ticket scalping when he tries to exchange his tickets to a concert.

What's Wrong with Raj?
W: Gene Farmer. D: Mark Warren. Raj fakes an illness in order to teach his sister a lesson about snooping.

Nice Guys Finish Last
W: Carol Gray. D: Mark Warren. GS: Vernee Watson, Harold Sylvester. Dee's prison pen pal escapes from jail and hides out at her house.

From Here to Maternity
W: Rick Mittleman. D: Mark Warren. GS: Chip Fields. Shirley's unwed, pregnant sister comes for a visit.

Puppy Love
W: Bill Richmond & Gene Perret. D: Mark Warren. Mabel makes a big mistake when she thinks Roger got a girl pregnant, when actually he was talking about a dog.

Rerun Gets Married
W: Bruce Howard. D: Mark Warren. GS: Irene Cara. An illegal alien asks Rerun to marry her so she can stay in the country.

It's All in Your Head
W: Alan Eisenstock & Larry Mintz. D: Mark Warren. GS: Tim Reid. Dee asks the school psychologist about a girlfriend's problem, which he thinks are Dee's problems.

Trial and Error
W: Rick Mittleman. D: Lee Bernhardi. Roger goes to court to sue the man who hit him with his car.

Raj Goes to Press
W: David Pollock. D: Mark Warren. GS: Davis Roberts, Fritzi Burr. Raj starts an underground newspaper after his editorials for the school paper are censored.

Nothing Personal
W: Alan Eisenstock & Larry Mintz. D: Mark Warren. GS: Ellen Travolta. Shirley gets a job at a balloon company because she is black.

If I'm Elected
W: Winston Moss. D: Lee Bernhardi. GS: Greg Morris. Dwayne's father is running for the city council, but Dwayne is confused when his father fires a close family friend during the election.

The Play's the Big Thing
W: Saul Turtletaub & Bernie Orenstein. D: Ron Richards. GS: Debbie Morgan. Rerun ruins Raj's chance to make it big when a famous producer comes to see Roger's play.

Give Me Odds
W: Alan Eisenstock & Larry Mintz. D: Mark Warren. Rerun's brother-in-law wants to know Dwayne's system for betting on football games.

Bill Gets Married
W: Carol Gray. D: Dick Harwood. GS: Lee Chamberlin, Bill Walker. Bill announces he is getting married.

Mama the School Girl
W: D. Berkowitz. D: Mark Warren. GS: Percy Rodriguez. Mabel goes to night school where she falls for a young man.

One Strike and You're Out
W: Rick Mittleman. D: Mark Warren. GS: Neil Schwartz, Thomas Carter. Roger threatens to get the staff of the supermarket where he works to go on strike if his demands are not met.

The Testimonial
W: Nick De Marco. D: Mark Warren.

Roger and his friends play a practical joke on their teacher but regret it later.

Black and White Blues
W: William Bickley & Michael Warren. D: Mark Warren. Raj and Rerun borrow the church raffle prize color TV, and then accidentally break it.

Going Going Gong
W: Alan Eisenstock & Larry Mintz. D: Mark Warren. GS: Chuck Barris, Wolfman Jack, Barbara Rhoades, Kene Holliday. Rerun appears on the "Gong Show."

Dee's First Date
W: Joe Neustein. D: Mark Warren. After Dee's first date, her escort decides to run away from home to stay with her.

Doobie or Doobie Not [Part 1]
W: Sally Wade. D: Mark Warren. GS: The Doobie Brothers, Theodore Wilson. Rerun is offered free concert tickets in exchange for illegally tape recording the Doobie Brothers Concert.

Doobie or Doobie Not [Part 2]
W: Sally Wade. D: Mark Warren. After taping the show, Rerun and the Doobies plot to capture the man who hired Rerun to tape the concert.

Rerun Sees the Light
W: Thad Mumford. D: Mark Warren. GS: Jonelle Allen. Rerun falls for an attractive cult member who turns out to be a con artist.

Raj and the Older Woman
W: Sally Wade. D: Mark Warren. Roger lies about his age in order to date a model.

Diplomatic Immunity
W: Ted Bergman. D: Mark Warren. GS: Jeff Corey, Malachi Throne. Rerun gets into an auto accident with the son of an Arabian diplomat.

Shirley's a Mother
W: Saul Turtletaub & Bernie Orenstein. Shirley watches Raj and Dee while their mother is away.

The Apartment
W: Thad Mumford. D: Mark Warren. Raj and Rerun move into their own apartment.

Disco Dollar Disaster
W: Deborah Pastoria. D: Mark Warren. Rerun sells stock in himself to raise a dance contest entry fee.

Shirley's Boyfriend
W: Tom Moore & Jeremy Stevens. D: Mark Warren. Raj unknowingly fixes Shirley up with a married man.

Basketball Brain
W: Ted Bergman. D: Mark Warren. GS: Sorrell Booke, Leland Smith. Roger tutors a basketball hero who has to pass his English exam to stay on the team.

Creep Detective
W: Ted Bergman. D: Mark Warren. Rerun and Raj are arrested for possessing stolen merchandise.

Shirley's Cookies
W: Ken Hecht. D: Mark Warren. Shirley decides to sell her homemade cookies, but is almost taken in by a con man out to make a fast buck off of her.

The Landlady
W: Gerald Gardner & Dee Caruso. D: Mark Warren. Raj develops a crush on his landlady.

Charge
W: Eric Bowers. D: Mark Warren. Rerun gets a credit card and buys everything in sight, until he remembers that he doesn't have the money to pay for it.

Raj Moves Out
W: Marty Brill & Barry Meadow. D: Mark Warren. Raj makes plans to move in with a female student who, unknown to Raj, is really using him to make her boyfriend/roommate jealous

so he will move back in.

No Clothes Make the Man
W: Sally Wade. D: Mark Warren. Rerun and Dwayne steal Raj's clothes when he gets a part-time job posing in the nude.

Positive Identification
W: Bill Box & Richard Westerschulte. D: Bill Foster. GS: Stu Gilliam. Raj and Rerun have to identify the man who robbed their apartment.

Making Out
W: Joanne Pagliaro. D: Mark Warren. Raj and Rerun agree to swap dates.

Dee, the Cheerleader
W: Sally Wade. D: Mark Warren. GS: Davis Roberts, Lauren Adams. Dee is thrown off the cheerleading team and replaced with a white girl.

A Present for Dee
W: Sally Wade. D: Lee Bernhardi. GS: Richard Deacon. Little Earl unknowingly gives Dee a stolen piece of jewelry for her birthday.

Dwayne's Dream
W: Joanne Pagliaro. D: Mark Warren. Dwayne dreams about dropping out of school.

Shirley's Fired
W: Levi Taylor & David Tyree. D: Danny Simon. Shirley thinks the beautiful waitress that replaced her is a thief.

Food Poisoning
W: Jeremy Stevens & Tom Moore. D: Mark Warren. Rerun is hospitalized for possible food poisoning after eating at Rob's place. Now a shyster lawyer is trying to get him to sue Rob.

The Eviction
W: Joanne Pagliaro. D: Mark Warren. GS: Hal Williams. Roger and Rerun are evicted after they complain about the defects in the apartment.

The Thomas Treasure
W: Bill Box & Dick Westerschulte. D: Joe Scanlon. Roger finds an old newspaper which leads him to think that there is a fortune hidden in the house.

The Last Page
W: Sally Wade. D: Mary Hardwick. Rerun decides to become an actor after he gets tired of being an ABC page.

First Class Coach
W: Jeremy Stevens & Tom Moore. D: Lee Bernhardi. GS: Sparky Marcus. Little Earl becomes upset when his basketball team wants to replace his father with Dwayne as coach.

Dwayne's Debate
W: Sally Wade. D: Mark Warren. GS: Greg Morris. Dwayne runs for student council president to impress his friends.

The Benefit Show
W: Joanne Pagliaro. D: Mark Warren. Rerun promises to get Sammy Davis, Jr. to appear at the school benefit show.

WHEN THINGS WERE ROTTEN

On the air 9/10/75, off 12/24/75. ABC. Color Film. 12 episodes. Broadcast: Sept 1975-Dec 1975 Wed 8-8:30. Producer: Mel Brooks. Synd: Paramount TV.

CAST: Robin Hood (played by Dick Gautier), Friar Tuck (Dick Van Patten), Alan-a-Dale (Bernie Kopell), The Sheriff (Henry Polic II), Prince John (Ron Rifkin), Maid Marian (Misty Rowe), Renaldo/Bertram (Richard Dimitri), Little John (David Sabin).

Dick Gautier and Misty Rowe, in When Things Were Rotten.

The comical adventures of Robin Hood and his Merry Men. Each week Robin tries to outwit the evil sheriff and win back the throne for King Richard. This series was created by Mel Brooks. It is one of the most different and appealing comedies ever produced and, although not in syndication, is a series worthy of mentioning.

The French Disconnection
GS: Sid Caesar. Robin and his men try to prevent a French ambassador from signing a peace treaty with Prince John.

There Goes the Neighborhood
While Robin and his men are on vacation, the sheriff's men dress up as the Merry Men and terrorize the countryside.

Wedding Blue Blue
GS: Dudley Moore. Prince John offers Marion as part of a deal with a rich sheik who deals in olive oil.

A Ransom for Richard
Prince John plans to get rid of Robin and King Richard when he learns that the King has been kidnapped.

The Ultimate Weapon
GS: John Byner. A professor sells Prince John a weapon which is capable of destroying all of Sherwood Forest.

Ding Dong, the Bell Is Dead
GS: Thalmus Rasulala. The Merry Men plan to take back the Nottingham Abbey bell which the sheriff stole to give to an Ethiopian prince.

The House Band
GS: Paul Williams. The sheriff plans to build a housing development called Sherwood Meadows on what is now Sherwood Forest.

Birthday Blues
Renaldo is captured by the sheriff on his way to the castle with a gift for his evil twin brother Bertram.

Quarantine
Robin and his Merry Men, along with the sheriff and the prince, are quarantined together in the castle when an outbreak of plague occurs.

The Spy [Part 1]
GS: Lainie Kazan.   One of Robin's

men is an informer.

The Spy [Part 2]
Robin tries to discover the identity of the informer by setting a trap for him.

This Lance for Hire
GS: Ron Glass.   The sheriff hires the Black Knight to get rid of Robin.

WKRP IN CINCINNATI

On the air 9/18/78, off 9/82. CBS. Color Videotape. 65 episodes (up till 1980). Producer: Hugh Wilson. Prod Co: MTM. Synd: Jim Victory Television.

CAST: Andy Travis (played by Gary Sandy), Mr. Carlson (Gordon Jump), Jennifer Marlowe (Loni Anderson), Les Nessman (Richard Sanders), Herb Tarlek (Frank Bonner), Venus Flytrap [Gordon Sims] (Tim Reid), Johnny Fever [Caravella] (Howard Hesseman), Bailey Quarters (Jan Smithers).

The adventures of the staff of a small radio station in Ohio. Each week the nutty staff would find itself in all sorts of different situations and then they would help each other solve their problems. The series has done well in syndication.

Pilot [Part 1]
W: Hugh Wilson. D: Jay Sandrich. GS: Sylvia Sydney. Andy becomes the new program director and changes the station's format to rock music, much to the disapproval of Mama Carlson.

Pilot [Part 2]
W: Hugh Wilson. D: Michael Zinberg. GS: Richard Stahl, Nedra Volz. Andy tries to boost advertising sales lost when he changed formats, by turning a demonstration into a publicity stunt.

Les on a Ledge
W: Hugh Wilson. D: Asaad Kelada. Les is accused of being gay, so he climbs out on the window ledge to jump.

Hoodlum Rock
W: Hugh Wilson. D: Michael Zinberg. GS: Ned Wertimer, Peter Elbling, Michael Des Barres, Jim Henderson, music by "Detective." An English Punk Rock group called "Scum of the Earth" comes to Cincinnati for a concert.

Hold-Up
W: Tom Chehak. D: Asaad Kelada. GS: Hamilton Camp, Bill Dial. Herb's idea to broadcast live from a stereo store backfires when a man with a gun demands to use the microphone.

Bailey's Show
W: Joyce Armor & Judie Neer. D: Asaad Kelada. GS: Woodrow Parfrey, Kathryn Ish. Bailey produces an interview show which attracts all kinds of weirdos.

Turkeys Away
W: Bill Dial. D: Michael Zinberg. Carlson plans a secret promotion by throwing live turkeys out of a helicopter over a shopping mall.

Love Returns
W: Bill Dial. D: Asaad Kelada. GS: Barrie Youngfellow, Hugh Gillin, Mickey McMeel. A contest at the station with Venus and Johnny as the prizes, and Andy's old girlfriend comes between him and the station.

Richard Sanders (left), Loni Anderson, Tim Reid, Jan Smithers, Gordon Jump, and Frank Bonner, in WKRP in Cincinnati.

Momma's Review
W: Hugh Wilson. D: Asaad Kelada.
GS: Carol Bruce. Flashbacks show how the station coped within the four months since the station changed its format.

A Date with Jennifer
W: Richard Sanders & Michael Fairman. D: Asaad Kelada. Jennifer agrees to go to an award banquet as Les's date.

The Contest That Nobody Could Win
W: Hugh Wilson. D: Asaad Kelada. GS: Vincent Schiavelle, Tracey Walter. While on the air, Johnny inadvertently changes the amount of a contest prize from $50 to $5000.

Tornado
W: Blake Hunter. D: Will Mackenzie. GS: Rene Enriquez, Bill Saito, David Chow. Andy is knocked unconscious when he is hit by a window, broken by a tornado, but Jennifer comes to the rescue. Also, a group of Japanese radio executives visit the station.

Goodbye Johnny [Part 1]
W: Blake Hunter. D: Asaad Kelada. GS: Bobby Ramsen, Edie McClurg. Johnny is offered a better job and decides to leave, but Mr. Carlson has other plans.

Johnny Comes Back [Part 2]
W: Blake Hunter. D: Asaad Kelada. GS: Jeff Altman, Phillip Charles Mackenzie. Fired from his new job, Johnny returns, only to find he has been replaced.

Never Leave Me Lucille
W: Bill Dial. D: Asaad Kelada. GS: Edie McClurg. Herb separates from his wife. He now plans to lead a swinging bachelor's life much to the displeasure of his friends at the station.

I Want to Keep My Baby
W: Hugh Wilson. D: Asaad Kelada. GS: Mary Betten, Michael Flanagan. Johnny receives a gift from an admirer: a baby in a basket.

A Commercial Break
W: Richard Sanders & Michael Fair-

man. D: Rod Daniel. GS: Fred Stuthman. An undertaker offers the station
a lot of money to play his funeral
ads on the station.

Who Is Gordon Sims?
W: Tom Chehak. D: Rod Daniel. GS:
Nicholas Worth. Venus refuses to
allow his picture to be printed in a
newspaper because he is an Army de-
serter.

I Do, I Do . . . for Now
W: Tom Chehak. D: Will Mackenzie.
GS: Hoyt Axton. Jennifer's childhood
sweetheart shows up determined to
marry her as they first vowed.

Young Master Carlson
W: Hugh Wilson. D: Will Mackenzie.
GS: Carol Bruce, Sparky Marcus. Mr.
Carlson's 11-year-old son causes havoc
at the station.

Fish Story
W: Hugh Wilson. D: Asaad Kelada.
GS: Lee Bergere, M.G. Kelly, Jack
O'Leary, Jerry Hardin. Herb, Bailey
and Les are in jail, Johnny and Venus
are drunk, and there is a man in a pig
suit in the lobby.

The Preacher
W: Bill Dial. D: Michael Zinberg. GS:
Michael Keenan. The staff must deal
with a former wrestler turned preacher
whose show is getting the station in
trouble.

For the Love of Money [Part 1]
W: Mary Maguire. D: Will Mackenzie.
GS: Julie Payne. Johnny's old girlfriend returns to sue him for half of
all he earned when they lived together.

For the Love of Money [Part 2]
W: Mary Maguire. D: Will Mackenzie.
GS: Julie Payne. Johnny's girlfriend
pretends to poison him.

Baseball
W & D: Hugh Wilson. GS: Bill Dial,
Wyatt Johnson, Ross Bickell. Les ac-
cepts a challenge to the WKRP staff

from rival station WPIG to a baseball
game, even though he has never played
baseball in his life.

Bad Risk
W: Gene Fournier & Tom Joachim.
D: Will Mackenzie. GS: William Glover, Helena Carroll. Herb decides to
sell insurance on the side. He regrets it
when his first client, Les, has a strange
accident.

Jennifer Falls in Love
W: Paul Hunter. D: Will Mackenzie.
GS: Thomas Calloway. Jennifer's
new boyfriend is only interested in
her money. Also, Les wants a raise.

Carlson for President
W: Jim Paddock. D: Will Mackenzie.
GS: Howard Witt, Lillian Garrett-
Bonner, Howard Morton, Dick Mc-
Garuin. Mr. Carlson becomes a candi-
date for the city council, then regrets
it.

Mike Fright
W: Dan Guntzelman. D: Will Mackenzie. GS: Christian Seaborn, Tim Cul-
bertson. Johnny's on-the-air joke succeeds in getting his listeners to dump
garbage on the city hall's steps; realizing the power he has, gives him mike
fright.

The Patter of Little Feet
W: Blake Hunter. D: Will Mackenzie.
GS: Carol Bruce, Allyn Ann McLerie.
Mr. Carlson's wife is pregnant, but
Momma Carlson feels she is too old
and should have an abortion.

Baby, If You Ever Wondered
W: Bill Dial. D: Rod Daniel. Even
though the ratings have gone up, Andy
feels he could raise them even more if
he had the guts to fire the staff.

Bailey's Big Break
W: Steve Marshall. D: Will Mackenzie.
Bailey is promoted to newscaster,
much to the distress of Les.

Jennifer's Home for Christmas

W: Dan Guntzelman & Steve Marshall. D: Rod Daniel. GS: George Gaynes, Don Diamond, Steve Marshall. The staff changes their plans to spend Christmas with Jennifer, who they think is spending the holiday all alone, but she has other plans.

Sparky

W: Peter Torokvei & Steven Kampann. D: Rod Daniel. GS: Sparky Anderson, Hugh Gillin, Andrew Bloch. Carlson hires baseball manager Sparky Anderson to host a sports talk show.

God Talks to Johnny

W: Hugh Wilson. D: Will Mackenzie. Johnny claims he talked to God, making the staff think he should see a doctor.

Family Affair

W: Tim Reid. D: Rod Daniel. Andy faces his own hidden bigotry when his sister dates Venus.

Herb's Dad

W: Peter Torokvei & Steven Kampmann. D: Rod Daniel. GS: Bert Parks. Herb's father leaves the rest home to visit his son, only to cause trouble at the station.

Put Up or Shut Up

W: Blake Hunter, Steve Mitchell & Steven Kampmann. D: Will Mackenzie. Jennifer, tired of Herb constantly asking for a date, takes drastic action by turning the tables on him.

The Americanization of Ivan

W: Dan Guntzelman & Steve Mitchell. D: Hugh Wilson. GS: Michael Pataki, Alex Rodine, Sam Anderson. Bailey returns from a press conference with a defecting Russian hog expert.

Les's Groupie

W: Steve Mitchell. D: Rod Daniel. GS: Kristine Callahan, Alice Nunn. Les's first groupie moves into his house and refuses to leave.

In Concert

W: Steven Kampmann. D: Linda Day. The staff publicizes a rock concert, then later reflects back after 11 youngsters are killed in a crowd trying to get seats. [Based on a real event.]

The Doctor's Daughter

W: Lissa Levin. D: Frank Bonner. GS: Petrie Allen, Derrel Maury. Johnny is challenged by his parental responsibilities when his 19-year-old daughter and her live-in boyfriend visit.

Filthy Pictures

W: Steve Mitchell & Dan Guntzelman. D: Rod Daniel. GS: George Wyner. A photographer takes nudes of Jennifer; the staff tries to recover them. [Originally one hour, now shown in two parts.]

Venus Rising

W: Steve Mitchell & Dan Guntzelman. D: Nicholas Stamos. GS: Terry Kiser, Brenda Elder. Venus is offered a better job at a rival station; Herb tries a trade deal which fails.

Most Improved Station

W: Michael Fairman & Richard Sanders. D: Rod Daniel. GS: Colleen Kelly. Johnny wins a broadcasting award which makes the rest of the staff jealous.

The Airplane Show

W: Richard Sanders & Michael Fairman. D: Rod Daniel. GS: Michael Fairman. Les nearly loses his life when he does his newscasting from an old bi-plane.

Jennifer Moves

W: Hugh Wilson. D: Linda Day. GS: Judith-Marie Bergan, Terry Wills, Ken Kimmins, Dan Barrows. The staff helps Jennifer settle into an old mansion she bought, but she is not prepared for the problems yet to come.

Real Families

W: Peter Torokvei. D: Rod Daniel.

GS: Edie McClurg, Peter Marshall, Daphne Maxwell, Stacy Heather Tolkin. Herb and his family make fools of themselves on a TV show.

The Baby
W: Blake Hunter. D: Rod Daniel. GS: Allyn Ann McLerie, Richard Venture, Edward Marshall, Jacque Lynn Colton, Dolores Albin. The staff invades the hospital when Carlson's baby is born.

Hotel Oceanview
W: Steven Kampmann. D: Rod Daniel. GS: Linda Carlson, Larry Hawkins, Dr. Joyce Brothers. While on a business trip, Mr. Carlson is suspected of being the Dayton poisoner by an undercover cop.

A Mile in My Shoes
W: Dan Guntzelman. D: Rod Daniel. GS: Noble Willingham, Walter Janowitz. Herb is called for jury duty so Andy takes over sales and Venus becomes program manager.

Bah, Humbug
W: Lissa Levin. D: Rod Daniel. GS: Parley Baer, Don Diamond. Johnny's "special" brownies cause Mr. Carlson to experience his own version of Dickens's Christmas Carol.

Baby, It's Cold Inside
W: Blake Hunter. D: Rod Daniel. GS: Carol Bruce. The furnace goes out at the station, but Johnny has a bottle of brandy which he shares with everyone including Momma Carlson.

The Painting
W: Steven Kampmann. D: Rod Daniel. Herb buys a painting at Carlson's church bazaar; he sells it to Bailey only to learn it might be valuable.

Daydreams
W: Peter Torokvei. D: Rod Daniel. Mr. Carlson puts everyone to sleep with his speeches, giving them all daydreams.

Frog Story
W: Bob Dolman. D: Rod Daniel. GS: Kenneth Tigar, Stacy Heather Tolkin. Herb accidentally spraypaints his daughter's frog pink; the staff all try to help the frog while Les plays doctor to the staff.

Venus and the Man
W: Hugh Wilson. D: Rod Daniel. GS: Keny Long, Veronica Redd. Venus takes on the challenge of teaching a dropout the story of the atom.

Dr. Fever and Mr. Tide
W: Steve Mitchell. D: Rod Daniel. GS: Mary Frann. Johnny turns into the repulsive Rip Tide who plays top hits and threatens to take over his old show's time slot.

Ask Jennifer
W: Joyce Armor & Judie Neer. D: Linda Day. GS: Eileen Barnett, Mickey Cherney. Jennifer takes over as a last-minute host of an advice talk show which becomes a big hit, much to the regret of Mr. Carlson.

I Am Woman
W: Lissa Levin. D: Linda Day. The station must move out of its building when it is condemned, causing Bailey to campaign to save the building.

The Secrets of Dayton Heights
W: Dan Guntzelman. D: Frank Bonner. GS: Sam Anderson, Bill McLean. Les traces his roots when the Secret Service informs him his father is a communist.

Out to Lunch
W: Peter Torokvei. D: Nicholas Stamos. GS: Craig T. Nelson, Michael Sherman. Herb's drinking is affecting his work, causing Andy to get mad.

A Simple Little Wedding
W: Blake Hunter. D: Nicholas Stamos. GS: Carol Bruce, Allyn Ann McLerie. Mr. Carlson's plan for a simple second wedding to celebrate his 25th anniversary are spoiled by Herb who throws a

stag party and by Momma Carlson who wants to make it a high society affair.

Nothing to Fear But . . . .
W: Dan Guntzelman. D: Asaad Kelada. The station is burglarized, causing the staff to become paranoid.

Till Debt Do Us Part
W: Howard Hesseman & Steven Kampmann. D: Frank Bonner. GS: Ruth Silveira, John Matuszak. Johnny gets a call from his ex-wife, causing him to believe she is getting married and freeing him from paying alimony.

ANIMATED SERIES

THE ALVIN SHOW

On the air 10/4/61, off 9/5/62. CBS. Color Film. Broadcast: Oct 1961-Sept 1962 Wed 7:30-8. Prod & Prod Co: Ross Bagdasarian. Synd: Viacom.

VOICES: Dave Seville and the Chipmunks (performed by Ross Bagdasarian), Clyde Crashcup (Shep Menken).

The animated adventures of Dave Seville and his singing chipmunks, Alvin, Simon and Theodore, plus the adventures of inventor Clyde Crashcup and his assistant Leonardo. The series usually turns up on Saturday mornings.

[The episodes of this series do not have any titles. They were made up of individual cartoons. The following are presented in the original order of the 1961-1962 season.]

The Chipmunks lend a helping hand to an eagle who doesn't know how to fly. Alvin sings "I Wish I Could Speak French." David Seville and the Chipmunks sing "Oh Gondalero." Clyde Crashcup, the man who invented the horse, sets out to invent soap. He invents swimming and the bathtub along the way.

Dave hires Sam Valiant, Private Nose, to find a missing tape recording. Alvin and the Chipmunks sing "August Dear." And a take-off on "Ach Du Lieber Augustin."

Dave and the Chipmunks are shopping for a foreign car. They find one that an ostrich has mistaken for its egg and is desperately trying to hatch. The Chipmunks visit the bullfights and sing "The Brave Chipmunks." Clyde Crashcup is trying to invent the lark, but he ends up with the stork and is deluged with babies.

Dave and the Chipmunks find that a neighbor who works nights is quite upset by their daytime rehearsals. The Chipmunks sing "Little Doggies." Clyde Crashcup decides to invent electricity. Dave and the Chipmunks sing "Old MacDonald Had a Farm."

Dave and the Chipmunks visit the seashore and later sing "Japanese Banana." Clyde Crashcup is proud of his new invention, the trombone, but he forgets to invent music first.

Alvin thinks that Dave is working him too hard and he plans to run away. The Chipmunks sing "The Pidgin-English Hula." Clyde Crashcup having just invented the horse decides to invent the West. Lastly: "Chipmunk Fun."

Detective Sam Valiant goes into the real estate business. Dave and the Chipmunks sing "Stuck in Arabia."

Dave and the Chipmunks venture into the great outdoors and later sing "I Wish I Had a Horse" and "The Good Morning Song." Clyde Crashcup invents the joke.

Alvin runs away from home. The Chipmunks sing "The Chipmunk Song" and the "Witch Doctor" song. Clyde Crashcup invents flight.

Sam Valiant becomes a song writer. The Chipmunks sing "Home on the Range." Alvin runs for President. Clyde Crashcup invents first aid.

Alvin falls in love. Dave and the Chipmunks visit Italy and later sing "When Johnny Comes Marching Home." Clyde Crashcup invents electricity.

Alvin leaves home. The Chipmunks visit a bullfight. Clyde Crashcup invents the bathtub. The Chipmunks sing "Old MacDonald Had a Farm."

Dave and the Chipmunks visit the jungle. The Chipmunks sing "Row, Row, Row Your Boat." Clyde Crashcup invents Egypt.

Alvin decides to show wealthy Bentley Van Rolls that he can't have everything his own way. Dave and the Chipmunks visit Scotland and later sing "Swing Low Sweet Chariot." Clyde Crashcup invents self-preservation.

Sam Valiant tries to sell part of an Indian reservation to Dave and the Chipmunks. Clyde Crashcup invents the joke. The Chipmunks sing "Japanese Banana."

The Chipmunks think Dave is going to get married. The Chipmunks visit Spain and later sing "Pop Goes the Weasel." Clyde Crashcup invents the bed.

On an ocean cruise, Seville and the Chipmunks are just beginning to enjoy the ocean breezes when the recreation director asks them to join in the calisthenics. Clyde Crashcup invents the telephone. The Chipmunks sing "Alvin's Harmonica" and "If You Love Me."

Alvin and his brother Chipmunks try to interfere with Cupid. Clyde Crashcup invents the time machine. The Chipmunks sing "Comin' Round the Mountain" and "Three Blind Mice."

[The remaining episodes were made up of a combination of previously aired segments with new segments included. Only the new segments are listed below.]

Clyde Crashcup invents baseball.

Dave and the Chipmunks meet Sam Valiant at a dude ranch. Clyde Crashcup invents the stove.

Mrs. Frumptington wants to rid the world of rock and roll music. Clyde Crashcup invents the wife.

Stanley the eagle falls in love. Clyde Crashcup invents Do-It-Yourself. The Chipmunks sing "Clementine" and "Dancing Lesson."

Mrs. Frumpington tries to teach the Chipmunks good manners. Clyde Crashcup invents physical fitness. The Chipmunks sing "Bicycle Built for Two" and "Ragtime Cowboy Joe."

Dave inherits a haunted house. Clyde Crashcup invents glass. The Chipmunks sing "Whistle While You Work" and "My Wild Irish Rose."

Dave has an argument with the Chipmunks. Clyde Crashcup appears on This Is Your Life. The Chipmunks sing "I Dream of Jeannie With the Light Brown Hair" and "The Band Played On."

The Chipmunks try to keep a neighbor's dog from destroying Dave's garden. Clyde Crashcup invents the ship. Songs: "The Alvin Twist" and "The Man on the Flying Trapeze."

Alvin makes a dragon appear. Clyde Crashcup invents Crashcupland. Songs: "Get Along Little Doggies" and "Down in the Valley."

Alvin tries to get Dave's new record played on the radio. Clyde Crashcup invents the birthday party. Songs:

"Funiculi Funicula" and "Polly Wolly Doodle."

"On Top of Old Smokey" and "America the Beautiful."

Alvin teaches Stanley the eagle to play the cymbals. Clyde Crashcup invents the art of self-defense. Songs:

Clyde Crashcup invents music.

Clyde Crashcup invents the wife.

BULLWINKLE

On the air 9/24/61, off 9/16/62. NBC. Color. 30 minutes animated. Broadcast: Sept 1961-Sept 1962 Sun 7-7:30. Producer: Jay Ward. Prod Co: Jay Ward/Bill Scott. Synd: Television Programs Dist.

CAST: Voices only: Rocky (June Foray), Bullwinkle (Bill Scott), Boris Badenov (Paul Frees), Natasha Fataly (June Foray). Additional voices: Hans Conreid, Walter Tetley, Charles Ruggles, Edward Everett Horton, Bill Conrad.

Residing in Frostbite Falls, Minnesota, Bullwinkle J. Moose and Rocket J. Squirrel are constantly pursued by enemy agents Boris Badenov and Natasha Fataly. Bullwinkle, who is not too bright, causes more trouble than Rocky can handle, and each segment ends with the two heroes about to be done in by their evil adversaries. *Bullwinkle* is the most sophisticated television cartoon ever produced. Filled with biting satire, the dialogue goes over the heads of most children who are perplexed, while adults are surprisingly amused. *Bullwinkle* is as popular today as ever, but new episodes have never been produced because of network interference with producer Jay Ward. Although *Bullwinkle* only ran in prime time for one year, it continued for a few more years in afternoon and Saturday morning schedules on ABC. It is actually a spinoff of the *Rocky and His Friends* series which began on ABC in 1959, whose episodes are syndicated as part of the *Bullwinkle* show.

[The following is a list of adventures of Rocky and Bullwinkle.]

Jet Formula
Box Top Robbery
Upsidaisium
Metal Munching Mice
Greenprint Oogle
Rue Britannia
Buried Treasure
Last Angry Moose
Wailing Whale
Three Mooseketeers
Lazy Jay Ranch
Missouri Mish Mash
Topsy Turvy World

Painting Theft
Guns of Abalone
Treasure of Mote Zoom
Goof Gas Attack
Banana Formula
Bumbling Brothers Circus
Mucho Loma
Pottsylvania Creeper
Moosylvania
Ruby Yacht
Bull's Testimonial Dinner
The Weather Lady
Louse on 92nd Street
Wassamotto U
Moosylvania Saved

CALVIN AND THE COLONEL

On the air 10/3/61, off 9/22/62. ABC. Color Film. 26 episodes. Broadcast: Oct 1961-Nov 1961 Tue 8:30-9; Jan 1962-Sept 1962 Sat 7:30-8. Producer: Joe Connelly & Bob Mosher. Prod Co: Kayro-Vue TV. Synd: MCA/Universal.

VOICES: The Colonel (Freeman Gosden), Calvin (Charles Correll), Maggie Belle (Virginia Gregg), Sister Sue (Beatrice Kay), Oliver Wendell Clutch (Paul Frees).

The animated adventures of Amos and Andy, only disguised as a fox and a bear so as not to offend anyone. The series ran for one season and disappeared from television since it was cancelled in 1962.

Back to Nashville
The Colonel tries to take Calvin with him to pay the expenses on the way to visit his uncle in Tennessee.

Calvin Gets Psychoanalyzed
Calvin visits a psychiatrist after Georgianna marries another man.

Calvin's Glamour Girl
Calvin must prove he is rich in order to marry an heiress.

Calvin's Tax Problem
The Colonel gives Calvin illegal tips on filing his taxes.

The Car Nappers
The Colonel didn't pay his bills, so the gas, electricity and the telephone are shut off.

Cloakroom
The Colonel inherits money from his Uncle Beauregard. Maggie wants him to invest it but he has other plans.

Colonel Outfoxes Himself
Belle and Sister Sue leave town, leaving the Colonel with paying the rent.

The Colonel Traps a Thief
Calvin and the Colonel plan to capture the thief in the Colonel's building.

The Colonel's Old Flame
Boo Boo Winters, the Colonel's old girlfriend, shows up to marry him.

The Costume Ball
No available story.

Jealousy
The Colonel thinks Maggie is seeing another man.

Jim Dandy Cleaners
Maggie is in charge of cleaning the office typewriters.

Magazine Romance
The Colonel takes Maggie to a nightclub.

Money in the Closet
No available story.

Nephew Newton's Fortune
Newton shows up with a locked suitcase he never opens.

The Polka Dot Bandit
The Colonel thinks Sister Sue is the woman who robbed several jewelry stores.

The Ring Reward
Calvin buys a ring which turns out to be stolen.

Sister Sue and the Police Captain
Sue is engaged to the Police Captain.

Sister Sue's Sweetheart
Sue's boyfriend asks her to marry him.

Sycamore Lodge
The Colonel rents a mountain cabin without seeing it first.

TV Job
Maggie Belle and Sister Sue force the Colonel to take a job delivering TV sets.

Thanksgiving Dinner
The Colonel invites a few dozen relatives to dinner, but forgets to buy the food.

Wheeling and Dealing
The Colonel's nephew wants his car back, but after the Colonel finished using it, it's ready for the junkyard.

The Winning Number
The Colonel finds out that Calvin has the winning number in a contest, only he doesn't know it yet.

Woman's Club Picnic
Maggie is planning a picnic, so she gives the Colonel the money to make the plans.

The Wrecking Crew
The Colonel takes a job on a construction crew and collects the insurance money when he has an accident.

THE FAMOUS ADVENTURES OF MR. MAGOO

On the air 9/19/64, off 8/7/65. NBC. Color Film. Broadcast: Sept 1964-Dec 1964 Sat 8-8:30; Jan 1965-Aug 1965 Sat 8:30-9. Producer: Henry G. Saperstein. Prod Co/Synd: UPA.

VOICES: Mr. Magoo (Jim Backus). Other voices: Marvin Miller, Howard Morris, Paul Frees, Everett Sloane.

The animated Mr. Magoo hosted and starred in famous literary stories presented in animated form. The series was constantly seen on Saturday mornings, when it went into reruns. Still very popular.

[The following titles need no explanation as to their content.]

The Three Musketeers [Two Parts]
Robin Hood [Four Parts]
Snow White [Two Parts]
Treasure Island [Two Parts]
Cyrano
King Arthur
The Count of Monte Cristo
William Tell
Don Quixote [Two Parts]
Dick Tracy
Dr. Frankenstein
Rip Van Winkle
Noah's Ark
Captain Kidd
Moby Dick
Paul Revere
Midsummer Night's Dream
Gunga Din
Sherlock Holmes

THE FLINTSTONES

On the air 9/30/60, off 9/2/66. ABC. Color Film. 166 episodes. Broadcast: Sept 1960-Sept 1963 Fri 8:30-9; Sept 1963-Dec 1964 Thu 7:30-8; Dec 1964-Sept 1966 Fri 7:30-8. Producer: Hanna-Barbera. Prod Co: Screen Gems. Synd: DFS Program Exchange.

VOICES: Fred Flintstone (Alan Reed, Jr.), Wilma Flintstone (Jean Vander Pyl), Barney Rubble (Mel Blanc), Betty Rubble (Bea Benaderet; Gerry Johnson, 1964-1966), Dino (Mel Blanc), Pebbles (Jean Vander Pyl), Bamm Bamm (Don Messick), Mr. Slate (John Stephenson), Hoppy (Don Messick), The Great Gazoo (Harvey Korman), Mrs. Flaghoople [Wilma's mother] (Verna Felton), Arnold (Don Messick).

Fred, a gravel pit worker, and his wife Wilma, along with their friends the Rubbles, struggle to survive in prehistoric times. This was the first prime-time cartoon series. It is still a big hit over twenty years since it was first created, as it can never become dated. This cartoon series was based on "The Honeymooners."

Flintstone Flyer
Fred and Barney scheme to go bowling instead of going to the opera with their wives.

Hot Lips Hannigan
After believing his magic trick made Wilma and Betty disappear, Fred and Barney go to a dancehall.

The Swimming Pool
Fred and Barney share the costs and the problems of building a backyard swimming pool.

No Help Wanted
Fred gets Barney a job repossessing furniture, including Fred's TV set.

The Split Personality
After Fred accidentally hits himself on the head, he assumes a new personality, that of a sophisticated gentleman.

Monster from the Tar Pits
Fred, Wilma and Betty become involved in Gary Granite's new movie.

The Baby Sitters
Fred and Barney babysit for Wilma's friend's baby Egbert on the night of the big fight.

At the Races
Fred bets his paycheck on a horse in order to win enough money to buy a pool hall.

The Engagement Ring
Barney buys a ring for Betty and gives it to Fred for safe keeping, only Wilma thinks it's for her.

Hollyrock Here I Come
The Flintstones and the Rubbles go to Hollyrock and appear in a TV show called The Frog Mouth.

The Golf Champion
Club President Barney refuses to give Fred his golf trophy until he pays his dues.

The Sweepstakes Ticket
Trouble begins when Fred and Barney and Wilma and Betty buy sweepstakes tickets.

The Drive-In
Fred and Barney plan to get rich by buying a drive-in restaurant.

The Prowler
Betty and Wilma take judo lessons when a prowler invades Bedrock.

The Girls' Night Out
Fred and Barney take the girls to an amusement park where Fred winds up a music idol.

Arthur Quarry's Dance Class
Fred and Barney secretly take dancing lessons so they can be a hit at the charity ball.

The Big Bank Robbery
Bank robbers hide their loot in Barney's back yard. When Fred and Barney try to return it, they are mistaken for the robbers.

The Snorkasaurus Story
The Flintstones and the Rubbles go camping and encounter a troublesome dinosaur. [The dinosaur would later become their pet Dino.]

The Hot Piano
Fred unknowingly buys a stolen piano and then is mistaken for the thief.

The Hypnotist
Fred practices hypnotism on Barney and turns him into a dog.

Love Letters on the Rocks
Fred finds a love letter addressed to Wilma and hires private eye Perry Gunite to find the identity of the writer.

The Big Tycoon [Pilot]
Fred changes places with rich lookalike J.L. Gotrocks, causing confusion for everyone.

The Astra-Nuts
Fred and Barney unknowingly sign up for the Army and wind up as astronauts.

The Long, Long Weekend
The Flintstones and the Rubbles vacation at a friend's seaside resort but wind up as the staff when the regular staff quits.

In the Dough
Fred and Barney impersonate their wives in a baking contest when their wives contract the measles.

The Good Scout
Fred becomes the leader of a boy scout troop, then everything goes wrong.

Rooms for Rent
Betty and Wilma rent rooms to a couple of musicians working their way through college.

Fred Flintstone—Before & After
Fred appears in a weight-reducing commercial.

The Hit Song Writers
GS: Hoagy Carmichael. Fred and Barney plan to stike it rich by writing only hit songs.

Droop-a-Long Flintstone
While ranch sitting for Cousin Tumbleweed, Fred gets mixed up with a movie company shooting a western.

The Missing Bus
Fred quits his job at the Rock Quarry to drive a school bus.

Alfred Brickrock Presents
Fred thinks his strange neighbor murdered his wife and sets out to prove it.

Fred Flintstone Woos Again
Fred and Wilma go on a second honeymoon along with the Rubbles.

The Rock Quarry Story
Fred brings home movie star Rock Quarry to dinner, but big fan Wilma fails to recognize him.

The Soft Touchables
GS: Dagmar. Fred and Barney become part-time detectives but wind up helping bank robbers.

Flintstone of Prinstone
Fred attends night school and winds up as the quarterback of the school football team.

The Little White Lie
Fred lies about the money he won in a poker game to Wilma, who thought he was with a sick friend.

Social Climbers
Fred and Barney attend charm school in order to fit in at the ambassador's reception.

The Beauty Contest
Fred and Barney become judges at the Water Buffaloes Beauty Contest.

The Masquerade Ball
Fred plans to butter up his boss when he learns what costume he will wear at the masquerade ball.

The Picnic
Fred abandons Barney for Joe Rochead as his partner for the field day events at the lodge picnic.

The House Guest
While their house is being repaired, the Rubbles move in with the Flintstones.

The X-Ray Story
Dino's X-ray is mistaken for Fred's, so everyone thinks Fred has a Dinopeptic germ which is fatal in humans.

The Gambler
Fred loses his furniture to Arnold in a wager.

A Star Is Almost Born
Wilma is discovered by a TV producer. Fred quits his job to handle her career.

The Entertainer
While Wilma is away, Fred entertains a lady buyer for his boss but Wilma returns and jumps to the wrong conclusion.

Wilma's Vanishing Money
Fred finds the money Wilma was hiding for his birthday present and spends it on a bowling ball.

Feudin' and Fussin'
Fred insults Barney but refuses to apologize, causing a feud to start between the two of them.

Impractical Joker
Barney tries to cure Fred of his habit of playing practical jokes.

Operation Barney
Fred and Barney call in sick so they can attend a baseball game.

The Happy Household
Wilma becomes the star of a TV show called the Happy Housewife, which makes Fred anything but happy.

Fred Strikes Out
Fred plans to play in the bowling league playoff and take Wilma to a movie at the same time.

This Is Your Lifesaver
GS: Walker Edmiston. Fred rescues J. Montague Gypsum from killing himself, then regrets it when he moves into his home and won't leave.

Trouble-in-Law
GS: Verna Felton. Fred's mother-in-law moves in and Fred fixes her up with a rich Texan, hoping she will get married and leave.

The Mailman Cometh
Fred writes a nasty letter to his boss when he doesn't get his raise.

The Rock Vegas Story
The Flintstones and the Rubbles go to Rock Vegas where Fred plans to win a fortune.

Divided, We Sail
Fred and Barney share a houseboat they won on a game show, but each one wants to be the Captain.

Kleptomaniac Caper
Fred thinks Wilma is a kleptomaniac when he finds his closet ransacked.

Latin Lover
Wilma tries to turn Fred into a dashing playboy.

Take Me Out to the Ball Game
Fred is discovered by a big league scout while umpiring a little league game.

Dino Goes Hollyrock
GS: Herschel Bernardi. Dino auditions for a part on his favorite TV show—The Adventures of Sassie.

Fred's New Boss
Fred gets Barney a job at the quarry but he winds up as Fred's boss.

Barney the Invisible
Fred invents a new soft drink which causes Barney to become invisible.

The Bowling Ballet
Fred takes ballet lessons to improve his bowling form.

The Twitch
Fred tries to get a rock star, Rock Roll, to appear at Wilma's auxiliary's benefit show.

Here's Snow in Your Eyes
Fred and Barney attend a lodge convention at a ski resort, complete with diamond thieves and a beauty contest.

The Buffalo Convention
Fred gives a talking Dodo bird to Wilma as a birthday present, but regrets it when it tells her of his plans to attend a lodge convention in Frantic City.

The Little Stranger
GS: Verna Felton. Fred calls for his mother-in-law when he thinks Wilma is expecting.

Baby Barney
Fred tries to pass Barney off as a baby to impress his rich uncle.

Hawaiian Escapade
Wilma and Betty enter a contest where the winner gets to appear on the Hawaiian Spy TV series.

Ladies Day
Fred dresses Barney up as a woman in order to get into the ballpark for free.

Nothing But the Tooth
Fred tries to save money by pulling Barney's tooth himself.

High School Fred
Fred will be fired unless he gets his high school diploma.

Dial S for Suspicion
Fred thinks Wilma wants to kill him and collect the money when she asks him to take out health insurance.

Flashgun Freddie
Fred invests in a polarock camera and with Barney goes into business.

The Kissing Burglar
Wilma upsets Fred when she tells him he has nothing valuable a burlgar would want to steal.

Wilma, the Maid
When the Flintstones' maid Lollobrickida quits, Wilma masquerades as a maid in order to help Betty impress her guests.

The Hero
Barney rescues a baby, but Fred takes all the credit.

The Surprise
Fred and Barney have a fight over Barney's baby nephew Marblehead.

Mother-in-Law's Visit
Wilma is expecting, so Fred promises to get along with her mother.

Foxy Grandma
Fred's new housekeeper turns out to be a bank robber, Grandma Dynamite.

Fred's New Job
Fred asks for a raise to help pay for the baby's added expenses.

Dress Rehearsal
Fred practices taking Wilma to the hospital, with Barney in her place. [Pebbles is born in this episode.]

Carry On, Nurse Fred
Fred's nerves are on edge; the baby nurses are driving him crazy.

Ventriloquist Barney
Barney uses ventriloquism to trick Fred into believing that Pebbles can talk.

The Big Move
Fred moves his family to a high-class neighborhood in order to get Pebbles away from the uncultured Rubbles.

Swedish Visitors
Wilma secretly spends their vacation money just when Fred decides they should travel.

Groom Gloom
Fred dreams that Pebbles and Arnold the newsboy have eloped.

Little Bamm Bamm
Barney discovers Bamm Bamm on his doorstep and tries to adopt him.

Dino Disappears
Dino runs away from home when Fred forgets his anniversary of when he joined the family.

Fred's Monkeyshines
When Fred puts on the wrong pair of glasses, he mistakes a monkey for Pebbles.

The Flintstone Canaries
Fred plans to win a contest on the Hum Along With Herman TV show by forming a barber shop quartet.

Glue for Two
Fred accidentally glues himself and Barney to a bowling ball.

Big League Freddie
Fred is accidentally signed to a baseball team when he is mistaken for his game substitute.

Old Lady Betty
Betty dresses up as an old lady to get a part-time job, only her boss is a counterfeiter.

Sleep On, Sweet Fred
Betty and Wilma practice sleep teaching in order to get what they want.

Kleptomaniac Pebbles
Fred thinks Pebbles is a kleptomaniac when he discovers her with a valuable bracelet planted on her by a jewel thief.

Daddy's Little Beauty
Fred enters Pebbles in a beauty contest against Wilma's objections.

Daddies Anonymous
Fred and Barney join a club in order to avoid doing their chores.

The Birthday Party
Wilma plans a surprise birthday party for Fred, but when the party starts, Fred can't be found.

Ann Margrock Presents
GS: Ann Margret. Singer Ann Margrock babysits for Pebbles while Fred and Barney audition for a TV show.

Peek a Boo Camera
Fred and Barney carry on at a stag party unaware that it is being filmed for television.

Once Upon a Coward
Fred tries to prove he is not a coward by tracking down a robber.

Ten Little Flintstones
A flying saucer unleashes ten Fred Flintstone robots on Bedrock.

Fred El Terrifico
Jewel thieves plant a million dollars worth of diamonds on Fred while in Rockapulco.

The Bedrock Hillbillies
Fred inherits a rundown shack and a 100-year-old feud with the hillbilly Hatrocks.

Flintstone and the Lion
Fred makes a pet out of a baby lion, but problems arise when he begins to grow.

Cave Scout Jamboree
Fred and Barney take their families camping, unaware that the spot they chose is the site of a Boy Scout jamboree.

Room for Two
Barney helps Fred add an extra room onto the house.

Ladies Night at the Lodge
Betty and Wilma disguise themselves as men in order to sneak into the boys' lodge.

Reel Trouble
Fred bores everyone with home movies of Pebbles.

Son of Rockzilla
Fred wears a monster suit to publicize a horror movie.

Bachelor Daze
The Flintstones and the Rubbles reminisce about how the girls first met the boys.

Operation Switchover
Fred and Wilma exchange jobs to see how hard each other's job is.

Hop Happy
The Rubbles's pet Hopperoo causes trouble for Fred.

Monster Fred
A mad scientist, Dr. Frankenstone, switches Fred's personality with Dino's.

Itty Bitty Fred
Fred's new reducing formula causes him to shrink. Fred and Barney plan an appearance on the Ed Sullystone Show as a ventriloquist and his dummy.

Pebbles' Birthday Party
Fred is in trouble when he arranges Pebbles' party at the same time as his lodge's party.

Bedrock Rodeo Roundup
Fred is jealous of a rodeo star who happens to be Wilma's old boyfriend.

Cinderallastone
Fred's fairy godmother appears when Fred does not get an invitation to his boss's party.

A Haunted House Is Not a Home
Fred must spend a night in a haunted house in order for him to inherit the estate of his uncle, J. Giggles Flintstone.

Dr. Sinister
Fred and Barney encounter spies: Madame Yes and Dr. Sinister in this take-off on the James Bond films.

The Gruesomes
The spooky Gruesome family moves into the house next door to the Flintstones.

The Most Beautiful Baby in Bedrock
Fred and Barney each try to get the best of each other when Pebbles is entered against Bamm Bamm in a beautiful baby contest.

Dino and Juliet
Fred and his new neighbor Mr. Loudmouth are at each other's throats until their dogs bring them together.

King for a Night
Fred substitutes for the king of Stonesylvania when the real king runs away.

Indianrockolois 500
Fred enters a car race as Goggles Pisanno in order to win money to send Pebbles to college.

Adobe Dick
While on a lodge fishing trip, Fred and Barney meet up with Adobe Dick, the giant whaleasaurus.

Christmas Flintstone
Fred takes a job as a department store Santa Claus and winds up substituting for the real Santa when he gets sick.

Fred's Flying Lesson
Fred takes flying lessons so he can become an airline pilot.

Fred's Second Car
Fred buys a car at a police auction, unaware there are stolen jewels hidden in it.

Time Machine
The Flintstones and the Rubbles travel into the future when they enter a time machine at the world's fair.

The Hatrocks and the Gruesomes
Fred tries to scare away the visiting Hatrocks with the help of the Gruesome family.

Moonlight and Maintenance
Fred moves his family into a modern apartment house where he becomes the janitor so he can live rent free.

Sheriff for a Day
Fred becomes the sheriff of a western town and then must fight a band of dangerous outlaws.

Deep in the Heart of Texarock
Fred and Barney help rich Uncle Tex fight off cowasaurus rustler Billy the Kidder.

Superstone
Fred substitutes for TV hero Superstone and then must capture the crooks who framed him.

The Rolls Rock Caper
Fred and Barney help the millionaire policeman Aaron Boulder solve a murder case.

Fred Meets Hercurock
Fred is cast as the star of the film Hercurock and the Maidens, but lives to regret it when the work gets too dangerous.

Surfin' Fred
GS: James Darren.   Fred teaches a group of surfers how to surf while Jimmy Darrock sings.

No Biz Like Show Biz
Fred dreams that Pebbles and Bamm Bamm become singing idols.

House That Fred Built
Fred buys an old shack and plans to fix it up himself when he learns Wilma's mother is coming to live with them.

Return of Stoney Curtis
GS: Tony Curtis. Stoney Curtis comes to Bedrock to make a movie and Fred is cast as his stuntman.

Disorder in the Court
Fred and Barney serve on a jury. The Mangler vows revenge when Fred as Foreman declares him guilty.

Circus Business
Fred buys a carnival, but regrets it when all of the acts quit when they don't get paid.

Samantha
GS: Elizabeth Montgomery, Dick York.   Wilma and Betty go camping with new neighbor Samantha, the witch. [This was a crossover episode from "Bewitched."]

The Great Gazoo
GS: Harvey Korman.   Fred and Barney rescue the Great Gazoo, an alien exiled to Earth; in return, he is required to serve them.

Rip Van Flintstone
Fred falls asleep at the company picnic and dreams he slept for 20 years.

The Gravelberry Pie King
Fred goes into business selling Wilma's pies to a supermarket.

The Stonefinger Caper
Barney is mistaken for a scientist by arch criminal Stonefinger.

Masquerade Party
Fred is mistaken for a spaceman when a rock group called the Wayouts invade Bedrock.

Shinrock a Go Go
Fred appears on a TV show to demonstrate a new dance called the Frantic.

Royal Rubble
Barney is mistaken for the lost prince Barbaruba of Rockarabia.

Seeing Double
In order to bowl in the playoffs and take their wives to dinner, Fred and Barney order Gazoo to create duplicates of themselves.

How to Pick a Fight with your Wife without Really Trying
The Flintstones and the Rubbles play a game in order to bring togetherness into their home, but it only starts a fight.

Fred Goes Ape
Fred takes the wrong pills for his allergy and turns into an ape.

The Long, Long Weekend
Fred dreams with Gazoo's help of life in the 21st century.

Two Men on a Dinosaur
Gazoo helps Fred and Barney win at the dinosaur races, but their bookies don't like it.

The Treasure of the Sierre Madrock
Fred and Barney are tricked into buying a phony gold claim.

Curtain Call at Bedrock
Fred and Barney appear in the PTA show, Romeorock and Julietstone, with the aid of the Great Gazoo.

Boss for a Day
Gazoo puts Fred in charge of the Quarry in order to experience what it is like to be boss.

Fred's Island
Fred spends the day on Mr. Slate's boat, which later drifts onto an island Fred claims for his own.

Jealousy
Fred is jealous of Wilbur Terwilligerock, a former classmate of Wilma's, so Gazoo helps Fred make her jealous.

Dripper
Barney is kidnapped by accident and it's trained seal Dripper to the rescue.

My Fair Freddy
Fred is mistaken for royalty and is enrolled in a country club where he teaches the rich folks about rock 'n' roll.

The Story of Rocky's Raiders
Fred reads the diary of World War I hero Grandpa Flintstone.

HUCKLEBERRY HOUND

On the air 9/58, off: unknown.   Syndicated.   Color Film.   Broadcast: Sept 1958.   Producer: Hanna-Barbera.   Prod Co: Kelloggs Inc.   Synd: Columbia Pictures TV.

VOICE: Huckleberry Hound (Daws Butler).

The adventures of Huckleberry Hound, a slow-thinking dog who takes on odd jobs in an attempt to find the true meaning of life. Most episodes deal with Huckleberry being chased by bulldogs, cows, thieves, and other various characters. The character roughly resembles Andy Taylor of the *Andy Griffith* show. Once a popular series, it is rarely seen anymore. The series was syndicated to local stations with various other cartoons contained in each half-hour segment, but there were only a little over 50 Huckleberry cartoons made.

Huckleberry Meets Wee Willie
Lion Hearted Huck
Tricky Trapped
Sir Huckleberry Hound
Sheriff Huckleberry
Rustler-Hustler-Huck
Freeway Patrol
Cock-a-Doodle Huck
Two Corny Crows
Fireman Huck
Dragon Slayer Huck
Hookey Daze
Skeeter Trouble
Sheep Shape Sheepherders
Barbeque Hound
Hokum Smokum
Bird House Blues
Postman Panic

Ski Champ Chump
Lion Tamer Huck
Little Red Riding Huck
Tough Little Termite
Ten Pin Alley
Grim Pilgrim
Jolly Roger & Out
Somebody's Lion
A Bully Dog
Nottingham and Yeggs
Huck, the Giant Killer
Cop and Saucer
Pony Boy Huck
Pet Vet
Picadilly Dilly
Wiki Waki Huck
Huck's Hack
Spud Dud

Legion Bound Hound
Science Fiction
Knight School
Nuts Over Mutts
Huck Hound's Table
Unmasked Avenger
Fast Gun Huck
Hillbilly Huck
Lawman Huck
Huck and Ladder
Astro-Nut Huck

Cluck and Dagger
Caveman Huck
Huck of the Irish
Jungle Bungle
Ben Huck
Huck De Parree
Bullfighter Huck
Two for Tee Vee
Bars and Stripes
Scrubby Brush Man

THE JETSONS

On the air 9/23/62, off 9/8/63. ABC. Color film. 24 episodes. Broadcast: Sept 1962-Sept 1963 Sun 7:30-8. Producer: Hanna-Barbera. Synd: DFS Program Exchange.

VOICES: George (George O'Hanlon), Jane (Penny Singleton), Judy (Janet Waldo), Elroy (Daws Butler), Astro (Don Messick), Mr. Spacely (Mel Blanc).

The animated adventures of a futuristic family. The series is still constantly running on local stations and on the network Saturday morning lineups despite it having so few episodes.

A Date with Jet Screamer
Judy enters a contest to win a date with singing star Jet Screamer.

Rosie the Robot
The Jetsons hire a robot maid who almost costs George his job.

Jetsons' Night Out
George and Mr. Spacely attend a football game where he wins a mink coat.

The Space Car
George and Jane go shopping for a new car and get mixed up with gangsters.

The Coming of Astro
Elroy finds Astro in the park and brings him home. Now he has to hide Astro from his father who doesn't want a dog in the house.

The Good Little Scouts
George takes Elroy's scout troop on a camping trip.

Elroy's TV Show
Elroy and Astro become stars of their own TV show.

The Flying Suit
George accidentally picks up the wrong suit from the cleaners, which causes him to believe that Elroy's new flying pill really works.

Rosie's Boyfriend
Rosie falls in love with the janitor's new robot assistant.

Uniblab
Mr. Spacely hires a robot named Uniblab to manage the office for him.

Astro's Top Secret
No available story.

A Visit from Grandpa
George's swinging grandfather pays a visit.

Las Venus
George and Jane go on a second honeymoon to Las Venus.

Elroy's Pal
Elroy wins a visit from his TV hero, The Great Nimbus.

Test Pilot
George, thinking he is dying, volunteers to be the test pilot for a new indestructible suit.

Millionaire Astro
A millionaire claims that Astro is his dog and tries to reclaim him.

The Little Man
George accidentally falls into Spacely's new shrinking machine and then finds that he can't change back to his normal size when the machine breaks down.

Jane's Driving Lesson
Jane gets mixed up with a gangster when she decides to take driving lessons.

GI Jetson
George is drafted into the Army.

Miss Solar System
George becomes the judge at a beauty pageant, unaware that Jane is one of the contestants.

Private Property
George finds that the building owned by competitor Cogswell was built six inches onto Mr. Spacely's property.

Dude Planet
George takes the family on a vacation to a dude planet.

TV or Not TV
The family fights over the TV set.

Elroy's Mob
Elroy accidentally gets mixed up with a gangster and his mob.

QUICK DRAW McGRAW

On the air 9/59, off 9/63. Syndicated. Color Film. Producer: Hanna Barbera. Prod Co/Synd: Columbia Pictures TV.

VOICE: Quick Draw McGraw (Daws Butler), Baba Looey (Daws Butler).

The adventures of Quick Draw McGraw, a U.S. Marshal in the territory of New Mexico. McGraw, a dim-witted horse assisted by trusty burro Baba Looey, struggles to maintain law and order in the West. Episodes sometimes feature Quick Draw dressed as El Kabong, a guitar-carrying hero in the likes of Zorro. The series is sometimes shown on small stations. The half-hour segments are composed of other cartoons as well.

Scarey Prairie
Bad Guys Disguise
Scat, Scout Scat
Choo-Choo Chumps
Masking for Trouble
Lamb Chopped
Double Barrel Double
Riverboat Shuffled
Dizzy Desperado
Sagebrush Brush
Bow Wow Bandit
Six Gun Spook

City Slicker
Cattle Battle Rattled
Doggone Prairie Dog
El Kabong
Gun Gone Goons
El Kabong Strikes Again
Treasure of El Kabong
Locomotive Loco
Bronco Bustin Boobs
The Lyin' Lion
Chopping Spree
Elephant Boy Oh Boy

Bull Leave Me	*Scooter Rabbit*
Kabong Kabongs Kabong	*Talky Hawky*
El Kabong Meets El Kazong	*Extra Special Extra*
Bullet Proof Galoot	*El Kabong, Jr.*
Two, Too Much	*El Kabong Was Wrong*
Twin Troubles	*Dynamite Fright*
Ali Baba Looey	*Baba Bait*
Shooting Room Only	*Big Town El Kabong*
Yippee Coyote	*Mine Your Manners*
Gun-Shy Girl	*The Mark of El Kabong*
Who Is El Kabong?	

TOP CAT

On the air 9/27/61, off 9/26/62. ABC. Color Film. 30 episodes. Broadcast: Sept 1961-Sept 1962 Wed 8:30-9. Producer Hanna-Barbera. Synd: DFS Program Exchange.

VOICES: Top Cat (Arnold Stang), Benny (Maurice Gosfield), Choo Choo (Marvin Kaplan), Spook & The Brain (Leo DeLyon), Fancy-Fancy (John Stephenson), Officer Dibble (Allen Jenkins).

The animated version of Sgt. Bilko, only played by a group of alley cats. Top Cat was the leader and boss who frequently outwitted his nemesis, Officer Dibble. Extremely popular with cartoon fans but it has now disappeared from every station.

The $1,000,000 Derby
Top Cat has big plans for the gang but they desert him for a disgraceful activity: work.

Hawaii—Here We Come
When Benny the Ball wins a ticket to the Islands, Benny boards the ship Aloha Hooey and T.C. and the gang go along with him.

Top Cat Falls in Love
Benny the Ball is in the hospital and all his buddies are paying him regular visits.

The Violin Player
Benny the Ball is discovered when a famous impresario named Gutenhad hears him play the violin. That is, Gutenhad thinks he hears Benny play; actually the music comes from a nearby record shop.

The Missing Heir
The missing heir was the pet cat of a wealthy eccentric who left a fortune to his favorite feline. Top Cat notes that Benny the Ball fits the description of the missing mouser and decides to pass him off as the proper puss.

The Unscratchables
A couple of hoods steal a valuable diamond from Stiffany's jewelry store, but Officer Dibble arrives before they can get away.

All That Jazz
Known to his friends as A.T. is a new cat in the neighborhood who is out to usurp T.C.'s leadership. A.T. is making great progress and T.C. announces that he is getting out.

Choo Choo's Romance
Choo Choo has developed a crush on Goldie, a new cat in the neighborhood. T.C. says he will arrange a date for him.

A Visit from Mother
Benny the Ball is worried about his mother's impending visit—she thinks he is the mayor of New York.

Sergeant Top Cat
The police captain is coming for an inspection and Dibble tells T.C. and the gang that they will have to get their alley cleaned up.

Naked Town
A television series called Naked Town is going to use Officer Dibble's beat as background.

The Maharajah of Pookajee
The Maharajah of Pookajee is coming to town and T.C. and the gang would like to call on the potentate and some of his fabulous wealth. The boys just have to figure out a way to get past His Highness's bodyguard: Officer Dibble.

The Long Hot Winter
The alley looks like it's going to be a pretty cold place during the winter, so the gang tricks Dibble into arresting them and taking them to a nice warm jail cell.

The Tycoon
The tycoon is a philanthropist named Vanderfeller. When he sees Top Cat and his boys in rags out peddling raffle tickets, he gives them a check for one million dollars.

The Grand Tour
T.C., who thinks the neighborhood needs a little more class, puts the gang to work creating Historic Landmarks. Soon, their alley becomes the one where Paul Revere fed his horse.

Space Monkey
Top Cat and the gang are faced with a desperate crisis—Officer Dibble has threatened to jail them for vagrancy unless one of them gets a job.

T.C. Minds the Baby
Out looking for food, the gang comes across a picnic basket in the park. But instead of a meal, there is a squeal from an abandoned baby tucked inside.

The Golden Fleecing
Benny the Ball receives a large insurance dividend and T.C. and the gang intend to help him celebrate the occasion at the Pink Palm night club.

The Case of the Missing Anteater
Benny encounters a very strange-looking animal and brings it home with him, only to be reminded by T.C. that the gang has a firm policy against pets.

Farewell, Mr. Dibble
Fresh out of the police academy, Officer Prowler decides to waste no time in reforming the city. He gets his uncle, the sergeant in charge, to assign him to Dibble's beat.

The Late T.C.
Top Cat and the gang pay a visit to Yankee Stadium for a look at the Bronx Bombers in action. Sure enough, Mickey Mantle steps up to the plate and belts a long one which lands right on Top Cat's head.

Choo Choo Goes Ga Ga
Choo Choo is depressed and decides to end it all by jumping into the Central Park lake. He asks one last favor of his pal T.C., to deliver a farewell note to movie star Lola Glamore.

Dibble Breaks the Record
Officer Dibble is about to set a new record for uninterrupted service and win a paid vacation as a reward. All he has to do is put in one more day on the beat.

The Con Men
T.C. and the gang hear some shocking news: the source of their free meals, Tony the hot dog man, is retiring from business.

Dibble's Birthday
Dibble's birthday is coming and Choo Choo proposes that the gang hold a surprise party for him.

Dibble Sings Again
T.C. is in need of some cash to pay

a debt but he is broke. Then he and the gang come up with the idea of a wishing well.

Griswald
T.C. doesn't know it yet, but Dibble has a new partner named Griswald, a trained police dog.

Dibble's Double
Officer Dibble is trying to stop T.C. from booking bets on turtle races.

King for a Day
T.C. and the gang make Dibble fall for another of their con games. Before he realizes it, he's wearing his own handcuffs.

Rafeefleas
Benny the Ball, who has been napping in the museum, returns with an old-looking jade scarab. It doesn't look like much to T.C., so he turns it over to Fancy-Fancy to impress the girls.

WAIT TILL YOUR FATHER GETS HOME

Syndicated: 9/72-9/74. Color Film. 48 episodes. Producer: Hanna Barbera, Synd: Worldvision.

VOICES: Harry Boyle (Tom Bosley), Irma Boyle (Joan Gerber), Alice Boyle (Kristina Holland), Chet Boyle (David Hayward), Jamie Boyle (Jackie Haley), Ralph (Jack Burns).

The animated saga of Harry Boyle, president of the Boyle restaurant supply company, as he, an old-fashioned father, tries to close the generation gap that exists between him and his children. Episodes depict the trouble his liberal daughter causes in the community, forcing Harry to bail her out. This is the last animated prime-time series to appear on the networks. This series has been rarely seen since it left the air in 1974. The pilot aired as a segment of *Love, American Style*.

[There are no available stories for this series, only the titles.]

The Fling
Alice's Dress
The Hippie
Help Wanted
The Victim
Love Story
The Beach Vacation
Chet's Job
Chet's Fiancee
The Mouse
Expectant Papa
The New Car
Duty Calls
The New House
The Prowler
Papa the Patient
Mama's Identity
The Swimming Pool
The Commune
Sweet Sixteen
The Music Tycoon
The Neighbors

Papa in New York
Accidents Will Happen
Bringing Up Jamie
The Lady Detective
   GS: Phyllis Diller.
Car 54
Permissive Papa
The Boyles on TV
Marriage Counselor
My Wife the Secretary
Papa, the Housewife
Jamie's Project
Don for the Defense
   GS: Don Adams.
Alice's Diet
Mama Loves Monty
   GS: Monty Hall.
Alice's Crush
Rich Little, Supersleuth
   GS: Rich Little.
Papa's Big Check
Mama's Charity
Chet's Pad
Papa, the Coach

Maude Loves Papa
   GS: Jonathan Winters
Don Knotts, the Beekeeper
   GS: Don Knotts

Alice's Freedom
Back to Nature
Birdman Chet

YOGI BEAR

Syndicated 1958. Color Film. Producer: Hanna-Barbera. Synd: Columbia
Pictures TV.
   VOICES: Yogi Bear (Daws Butler), Boo Boo (Don Messick), Ranger John
Smith (Don Messick).
   The misadventures of Yogi Bear, a resident of Jellystone Park, who, despite
warnings from the park ranger, schemes to acquire picnic baskets from the tour-
ists who come to the park. Yogi is still shown on many stations.

The Brave Little Brave
Yogi becomes the target for a little Indian boy and his bow and arrow.

Stout Trout
Yogi goes fishing for trout.

Buzzin' Bear
Yogi borrows a helicopter but finds
that he can't turn it off.

Runaway Bear
Yogi is the target for a famous hunter
who wants to add him to his collection.

Be My Guest Pest
Yogi visits a little man in the city
where he is mistaken for a bear rug by
the man's wife.

Duck in Luck
Yogi tries to protect a little duck from
a hunter and his dog.

Bear on a Picnic
Yogi tries to keep a little baby from
getting into trouble.

Prize Fight Fright
Yogi becomes the sparring partner for
a boxing champion.

Brainy Bear
Yogi and Boo Boo are captured by a
mad scientist who wants to transfer
their brains.

Robin Hood Yogi
Yogi and his friend play Robin Hood
in order to steal food from the tourists.

Daffy Daddy
Yogi tries to help a spoiled kid.

Scooter Looter
Yogi steals a motor scooter and finds
that he can't turn it off.

Hide and Go Peek
Yogi tries to hide an elephant which
has escaped from the circus.

Show Biz Bear
Yogi gets a part in a movie which is
being filmed at the park.

Lullabye-Bye Bear
Yogi refuses to hibernate.

Bare Face Bear
Yogi believes that a bandit in a bear
suit is a real bear.

Papa Yogi
Yogi and Boo Boo disguise themselves
as a father and son so they can steal
the food from the father and son
picnic.

Stranger Ranger
Yogi believes that a gorilla wearing a
ranger uniform is a substitute for the
vacationing Ranger Smith.

Rah Rah Bear
Yogi joins the park football team.

Bear for Punishment
A magician turns Yogi and Boo Boo invisible.

Nowhere Bear
Yogi hypnotizes Boo Boo into thinking he is a bird.

Wound-Up Bear
Yogi has Boo Boo pretend to be a windup bear so he can get their attention while Yogi steals their food.

Be-Witched Bear
Yogi steals a witch's broom to help him steal picnic baskets.

Hoodwinked Bear
Yogi tries to get Little Red Riding Hood to give him her picnic basket.

Snow White Bear
Yogi and Boo Boo's winter sleep is interrupted by Snow White and the Seven Dwarfs.

Space Bear
A spaceman dresses up like Yogi, which causes Yogi to get into a lot of trouble.

Oinks and Boinks
Yogi and Boo Boo meet the three little pigs.

Booby Trapped Bear
The ranger booby traps some picnic baskets to teach Yogi a lesson.

Gleesome Threesome
Yogi and Boo Boo vacation with Ranger Smith in Miami.

A Bear Pear
Yogi and Boo Boo win a trip to Paris.

Spy Out
The Ranger plants hidden TV cameras and microphones in the park in order to catch Yogi stealing picnic baskets.

Do or Diet
The ranger tries to trick Yogi into believing that he is sick.

Bears and Bees
Yogi sells honey in the park.

Biggest Show on Earth
Yogi gets a visit from a bad-tempered circus bear.

Genial Genie
Yogi finds a magic teapot complete with a genie.

Cub Scout Boo Boo
Yogi and Boo Boo dress up as scouts in order to join the scout's picnic.

Home Sweet Jellystone
Yogi plans to live it up when Ranger Smith leaves to take over his uncle's mansion.

Love Bugged Bear
Yogi falls in love with another bear.

Bear Faced Disguise
Ranger Smith dresses up as a polar bear in order to catch Yogi breaking park rules.

Slaphappy Birthday
Yogi plans a surprise party for Ranger Smith's birthday.

A Bear Living
Yogi builds a wishing well so he can use the money to buy the food he used to steal.

Disguise and Gals
Yogi catches two bandits disguised as grandmothers.

Touch and Go-Go-Go
Yogi's fairy godmother gives Yogi the power to turn anything he touches into picnic baskets.

Acrobatty Yogi
Yogi joins the circus to visit his old girlfriend Cindy Bear.

Picnic Basket
The ranger tries to trap Yogi with a ring-a-ding picnic basket.

Iron Hands Jones
A tough ranger takes over when Ranger Smith goes on vacation.

Yogi's Pest Guest
Yogi gets a visit from a Japanese bear.

Missile Bound Yogi
Yogi and Boo Boo find themselves in the middle of war games when they enter a restricted area.

Locomotive Yogi
Yogi steals the park kiddie train and finds that he can't stop it.

Missile Bound Bear
Yogi gets trapped on a rocket bound for outerspace.

A Wooin' Bruin
Yogi and Bruno bear fight over Cindy bear's affections.

Yogi in the City
Yogi hides in a house trailer and finds himself in the big city.

Queen Bee for a Day
Yogi dresses Boo Boo up as a queen bee in order to get the bees away from their hive so he can steal their honey.

Batty Bear
Yogi dresses up in a Bat Guy costume to steal picnic baskets.

Droop-a-Long Yogi
Yogi and Boo Boo are chosen to be shipped to the Cincinnati zoo.

Ice Box Raider
Yogi tries to break into Ranger Smith's refrigerator.

Bear Foot Soldiers
Ranger Smith thinks the park bears are revolting when the Army dresses up as bears and invades the park on war games.

Yogi Bear Birthday Party
A 30-minute special with all of Yogi's cartoon friends coming to his birthday party.

INDEX

E

L

M

N

T

U

V

Y

Z